AAI-8610

P9-CCZ-551

Please remember that this is a library book, and that it belongs only temporarily to each person who uses it. Be considerate. Do not write in this, or any, library book.

WITHDRAWN

ABORTION, MEDICINE, AND THE LAW

Third Edition, Completely Revised

Edited By
J. DOUGLAS BUTLER
and DAVID F. WALBERT

ABORTION, MEDICINE, AND THE LAW

Third Edition, Completely Revised

Edited By
J. DOUGLAS BUTLER
and DAVID F. WALBERT

Facts On File Publications
New York, New York ● Oxford, England

Copyright © 1986 by J. Douglas Butler and David F. Walbert

All rights reserved. No part of this book may be reproduced or utilized in any form or by any means, electronic or mechanical, including photocopying, recording or by any information storage and retrieval systems, without permission in writing from the Publisher.

All opinions expressed are those of the authors and do not necessarily reflect those of the editors or the Publisher.

Library of Congress Cataloging-in-Publication Data
Main entry under title:

Abortion, medicine, and the law.

  Rev. ed. of: Abortion, society, and the law. 1973.
  Includes bibliographies and index.
  1. Abortion—United States—Addresses, essays,
lectures. I. Butler, J. Douglas (John Douglas),
1942-   . II. Walbert, David F. III. Abortion,
society, and the law. [DNLM: 1. Abortion, Induced.
2. Ethics, Medical. 3. Forensic Medicine.
HQ 767.5.U5 A1536]
HQ767.5.U5A265 1985   363.4'6   85-16137
ISBN 0-8160-1198-2

Printed in the United States of America
10 9 8 7 6 5 4 3 2

We dedicate this book to the memory of Alan F. Guttmacher.

ACKNOWLEDGMENTS

We would like to express our gratitude to Sharon Butler, Vickie Stroh, Eleanor Wenner, and Charlotte Walbert for their time and their interest in this book.

Contents

Introduction

In 1966, the editors of the *Case Western Reserve Law Review* (then the *Western Reserve Law Review*) commissioned a series of essays on the subject of abortion. Those essays appeared in a special issue of the *Law Review*, and because of the extreme interest in the essays, they were subsequently published by the Case Western Reserve University in 1967 under the title *Abortion and the Law*. That volume was the first major book on abortion that contained legal reviews of the issues.

In 1972, because of the interest in the earlier volume, and with the rapidly changing legal, ethical, medical, and political aspects of the subject, another volume was undertaken at the Case Western Reserve University. These efforts culminated in the publication of the *Case Western University Law Review* of several articles pertaining to abortion, and in the publication of *Abortion, Society, and the Law* in 1973. The editors of this edition were David F. Walbert (then editor-in-chief of the *Case Western Reserve Law Review*) and J. Douglas Butler, who also graduated from the Law School in 1972.

The 1973 volume became the authoritative treatise for lawyers, legislators, doctors, students, and others. It was a comprehensive resource that examined the legal, ethical, religious, psychological, and medical aspects of the subject. The book was very well received, but has been out of print for years.

The 1973 edition contained an exceptionally comprehensive overview of the evolving law of abortion and the status of abortion laws in every state in the nation by Professor B. J. George, Jr.; an article by Dr. Alan F. Guttmacher, whom many consider to be the nestor of the abortion movement, relating his personal involvement in the issues since the 1920s; discussions of ethical and religious issues by Daniel Callahan, Rabbi Immanuel Jakobovits, and then-Congressman Robert F. Drinan, S.J.; psychiatrists Richard A. Schwartz and Stephen Fleck wrote on the role of psychiatrists in the field of abortion, both from a historical and a current perspective; Dr. Kenneth R. Niswander reviewed abortion practices in the United States from a medical viewpoint; M. Neil Macintyre reviewed the genetic and prenatal diagnosis considerations that are inherent in liberalized abortion choices; Harriet F. Pilpel and Ruth J. Zuckerman wrote on the specific rights of minors in the area of abortion; and Gerald A. Messerman wrote the seminal article on abortion counseling.

The present volume draws only slightly on the previous edition. The same editors are involved, of course, but the selections are almost all new. Because we have had a continuous demand for the previous edition, we have undertaken the new effort in hopes that we can provide a book that responds to the current needs of scholars, students, legislators, practitioners in many fields, and the public at large. With our previous edition, we were always pleased to receive comments from people who found, in one volume, a comprehensive, in-depth, and objective treatment of the topic. Our aim is to do the same for the subject in the new volume, with a realization that the area is even broader today than it was 10 years ago.

Daniel Callahan's article from the last volume has been maintained intact because it remains one of the most concise discussions of the ethical issues relating to abortion. The late Dr. Alan F. Guttmacher's article has also been preserved because of his exceptional role in the abortion movement in the United States and around the world. However, it has been updated for the new volume by Dr. Irwin H. Kaiser.

These two articles account for a small proportion of the new book. Because of the complete revolution in both constitutional and statutory law that affects the abortion area, because of the great changes in medical practice and the abundant sociological data available, and because of the significant changes in the field of genetic analysis and prenatal diagnosis, the remainder of the book is entirely new. Legal articles focus on what has happened since 1973, and what may happen in the future. Professor B. J. George has again written an extraordinary comprehensive review of the laws in all the states as they affect all abortion-related issues. Stephen M. Krason and William B. Hollberg have explored an important, but often-neglected side of the debate. They provide what we feel is the best published criticism of the Supreme Court's decisions from the conservative point of view. Janet Benshoof and Harriet F. Pilpel have written "Minors' Rights to Confidential Abortions: The Evolving Legal Scene." This topic has been the subject of significant litigation in the United States Supreme Court recently, and their article is both timely and informative.

One cannot adequately address the abortion revolution of the past decade without devoting significant attention to the ongoing counterrevolution. Therefore, we include an article by Senator Bob Packwood describing the efforts of the anti-abortion members of Congress to overturn the Supreme Court's 1973 decision by statute and constitutional amendment. We have included an article by Professor Albert M. Pearson and Paul M. Kurtz of the University of Georgia, who write from a more scholarly and less personal view, about the legislative and constitutional efforts as a mixture of law and politics.

A wealth of extraordinary material was developed during the Senate hearings that arose in conjunction with the conservatives' efforts to overturn legislatively the *Roe v. Wade* and *Doe v. Bolton* decisions. Senator Orrin Hatch, a critical actor in the legislative drama (as chairman of the Judiciary subcommittee that specifically reported on the proposals), switched his vote in light of the testimony that was submitted to his subcommittee, contributing to the demise of the conservatives' efforts. We have reviewed all the presentations to the Senate, as well as all the Senate reports of recent years concerning the abortion proposals introduced, and we have chosen certain portions that we think are of particular value. We have taken the materials that include the most well-developed, well-reasoned, and scholarly commentary on the issues that were before the Senate.

Mark Tushnet has given us a detailed study of the relevant Supreme Court cases on abortion. This list of cases continues to grow as the Court defines the meaning of the *Roe* decision.

The concluding legal article is from Don C. Smith, Jr. who writes on what is now only an emerging topic among practicing lawyers and law professors: the legal implications for "wrongful birth" and "wrongful life" issues that arise uniquely in the context of abortion and genetic evaluations.

Dr. M. Neil Macintyre and his coauthors have again provided us with what we believe will be the authoritative review of prenatal diagnosis and selective abortion.

We felt especially fortunate to have Dr. Christopher Tietze agree to write for us because of his stature, knowledge, and experience in the issue of abortion throughout the world. His article, published posthumously, will provide the reader with a concise discussion and summary of the actual practice of abortion since the Supreme Court's liberalizing decisions in 1973. His information should be of profound value to sociologists, legislators, and students of this topic.

Dr. Kenneth R. Niswander and Manuel Porto describe the medical practices associated with abortion, past and present. Dr. Willard Cates, Jr., who is with the Centers for Disease Control, provides a short article that includes a provocative discussion of what, from a medical viewpoint, would likely occur in the event that the law should change and the nation return to a conservative position on abortions. Finally, Dr. Irwin Kaiser, from the Albert Einstein College of Medicine, completes the review of the medical and sociological aspects of abortion as it exists today.

Dr. Richard A. Schwartz addresses the psychiatric implications of abortion, providing new and current material.

Finally, two important spokesmen of the Right-to-Life movement, Ronald Reagan and John T. Noonan, Jr. through powerfully expressed writings, present the conservative view.

These articles represent what we believe is the best available in-depth coverage of a vast area. In terms of the overall percentage of the book, the ethical and religious dimensions comprise a less significant portion than in the past volume because those topics have changed little and discussions of them are adequately available in print elsewhere. As to the legal and historical aspects of abortion, we have selected those topics that are of the most compelling scholarly and political interest today and those that will remain so in the future. While we well recognize that the Senate material is extensive, we feel it is very important. Most readers have no practical access to these materials, and even knowledgeable students and researchers could get them only with great effort. These materials fully round out the legal and historical material in the book.

The medical and sociological articles will provide the most comprehensive and up-to-date information available in any one source, and will be of tremendous value to a wide potential readership.

J. Douglas Butler, D.P.M., J.D.
David F. Walbert, M.S., J.D.

Contributors

Janet Benshoof, J.D.
   American Civil Liberties Union, New York, New York
Daniel Callahan
   Director of Hastings Center, New York, New York
Willard Cates, M.D., M.P.H.
   Centers for Disease Control, Atlanta, Georgia
B. J. George, Jr., J.D.
   Professor of Law, New York Law School, New York, New York
Alan F. Guttmacher, M.D.
   Past President of Planned Parenthood—World Population (deceased), New York, New York
William B. Hollberg, J.D.
   Attorney, Atlanta, Georgia
Irwin H. Kaiser, M.D.
   Professor of Obstetrics and Gynecology, Albert Einstein College of Medicine, New York, New York
Llew Keltner, M.D., Ph.D.
   Department of Biometry, Case Western Reserve University School of Medicine, Cleveland, Ohio
Dorothy A. Kovacevich, Ph.D.
   Assistant Professor of Special Education, Kent State University, Kent, Ohio
Stephen M. Krason, Ph.D., J.D.
   Eastern Director of Intercollegiate Studies Institute, Bryn Mawr, Pennsylvania

Paul M. Kurtz, J.D.
  Professor of Law, University of Georgia School of Law, Athens, Georgia
M. Neil Macintyre, Ph.D.
  Professor Emeritus of Developmental Genetics, Medicine and Pediatrics,
  Case Western Reserve University School of Medicine, Cleveland, Ohio
Kenneth R. Niswander, M.D.
  Professor of Obstetrics and Gynecology and Chairman of the Department at
  the School of Medicine, University of California, Davis, Sacramento,
  California
John T. Noonan, Jr., J.D.
  Professor of Law, University of California, Berkeley, California
Bob Packwood
  U.S. Senator from Oregon, Washington, D.C.
Albert M. Pearson, J.D.
  Professor of Law, University of Georgia School of Law, Athens, Georgia
Harriet F. Pilpel, J.D.
  Attorney, New York, New York
Manuel Porto, M.D.
  Assistant Professor of Obstetrics and Gynecology, School of Medicine at the
  University of California, Davis, Sacramento, California
Ronald Reagan
  40th President of the United States, Washington, D.C.
Richard A. Schwartz, M.D.
  Euclid Clinic Foundation, Chief of Department of Psychiatry and Psychol-
  ogy, Senior Clinical Instructor, Department of Psychiatry, Case Western
  Reserve University School of Medicine, Cleveland, Ohio
Don C. Smith, J.D.
  Attorney, Denver, Colorado
Christopher Tietze, M.D.
  Senior Consultant, The Population Council, New York, New York
Mark Tushnet, J.D.
  Professor of Law, Georgetown University Law Center, Washington, D.C.

1 · LAW

Senator Packwood presents a 10-year history of abortion in Congress. As early as 1973, some 18 constitutional amendments on the topic had been proposed, but often there was disagreement among the many groups proposing the amendments. The amendments took several focuses: states' rights to decide the legality of abortion, life begins at conception, the unborn are persons within the meaning of the Fifth and Fourteenth Amendments. The article also discusses the issues of fetal research, abortion funding, and the ''Baby Doe'' legislation. Senator Packwood, the junior senator from Oregon, has long been a champion of reproductive freedom and equal rights for women. He is Chairman of the Senate Finance Committee.

1 · The Rise and Fall of the Right-To-Life Movement in Congress: Response to the Roe Decision, 1973–83*

*Senator Bob Packwood***

It has been 10 years since the historic *Roe*[1] decision, 10 years of legislative and judicial skirmishes to guarantee a woman's right to reproductive freedom. During this decade, the right-to-life movement has grown into a singularly effective single-issue grass roots organization. But not effective enough. The right-to-lifers have tried repeatedly during the past 10 years to reverse *Roe*. They have tried to pass constitutional amendments; they have tried to enact laws; they have tried to limit the availability of abortions by restricting funding; they have tried to change the philosophical orientation of the Senate by promoting the election of candidates whose primary platform is an opposition to abortion rights; and they have tried to get courts to reverse or qualify *Roe*. In a few of these efforts they have succeeded. But they lost the big ones in 1983.

June 1983 may come to be viewed as a pivotal month in the battle to guarantee a woman's right to choose. In two weeks' time, the right-to-life movement suffered as many major defeats. The first was the Supreme Court's decision in *Akron v. Akron Center for Reproductive Health*,[2] a strong reaffirmation of *Roe*. Thirteen days later, the Republican-controlled Senate overwhelmingly rejected a proposed constitutional amendment that stated: "A right to abortion is not secured by this Constitution."[3] This 49–50 defeat is particularly significant for several reasons: First, in addition to falling far short of the two-thirds vote (67 votes) required to approve a constitutional amendment, the

*This article was completed for publication in December, 1983.

**I am grateful for assistance in preparing this chapter from two of my legislative assistants, Jill Beimdiek and Eleanor Wenner, and from my administrative assistant, Sana F. Shtasel.

right-to-life movement failed to convince even a simple majority of the Senate. The margin of defeat was greater than anyone on either side of the issue had imagined. Second, this vote was taken in the Republican-controlled Senate. In light of the jubilance of the right-to-life movement following the 1980 elections in which the Republicans gained a Senate majority, this is particularly noteworthy since the right-to-life movement had targeted a number of pro-choice senators and claimed responsibility for the Republican gains. Finally, the simple text of the defeated amendment, "A right to abortion is not secured by this Constitution," was a watered-down proposal, one that was deemed the most likely to pass of all the proposed constitutional amendments. The right-to-life movement's best hope for victory was in the 97th Congress (1981–82) and in the first session of the 98th Congress (1983), and that victory was soundly denied.

A discussion of the right-to-life movement logically begins in 1973 with the *Roe* decision. A few brief comments about the years preceding that decision, however, are necessary. The right-to-life movement originated in the Catholic church in the early 1960s, when several states began to consider liberalizing restrictive anti-abortion laws. Tentative reform of abortion laws began when the American Law Institute (ALI) proposed a Model Penal Code in 1959. State-level opposition intensified in the late 1960s and early 1970s when many states adopted more liberal abortion laws, 13 of which were based on the ALI Model Code.[4] However, a nationwide right-to-life effort did not coalesce until after *Roe*.[5]

Congressional consideration of the abortion issue also began before *Roe*. The question of federal funding was addressed in the Family Planning Services and Population Research Act of 1970:

> *Section: 1008. Prohibition of Abortion.*
> *None of the funds appropriated under this title shall be used in programs where abortion is a method of family planning.*[6]

This was watershed legislation, because restricting the use of federal funds in specified programs was to become one of the right-to-life movement's chief activities and, to date, its only successful one.

I, too, attempted pre-*Roe* statutory involvement by introducing legislation in the 91st (1969–70) and 92nd (1971–72) Congresses to *legalize* abortions both in the District of Columbia and in the entire United States.[7] No action was taken on these bills; the right to reproductive freedom was not yet a controversial question on the national level.

It was soon to become one. On January 22, 1973, the U.S. Supreme Court handed down its landmark decisions in *Roe v. Wade*[8] and *Doe v. Bolton*.[9] In *Wade,* the Court held that the decision of a woman to terminate her pregnancy is protected by the right to privacy. The Court said a woman's right to choose is a "fundamental right," guaranteed by the privacy component of the due process clause. In *Doe,* the Court bolstered *Roe* by ruling that a state may not unduly burden the exercise of that fundamental right by regulations that prohibit or substantially limit access to abortions.

Congressional reaction to the *Roe* decision was swift. The right-to-life movement, led primarily by the Catholic church, pushed Congress to consider proposed constitutional amendments that would effectively overturn *Roe*. No fewer than 18 proposed constitutional amendments were introduced before the end of September 1973. The right-to-lifers knew then, as they know now, that the only way to overturn the *Roe* decision was by enacting a constitutional amendment, but they did not limit their legislative initiatives accordingly. There were also attempts to reverse *Roe* by a simple statute and to limit federal involvement in and funding of abortions. By the end of the year, nearly 10 percent of the membership of the House of Representatives had co-sponsored some form of anti-abortion legislation.

It is important to note both that the involvement of religious groups in the abortion rights issue predates the *Roe* decision and that there has never been consensus on the issue among them. No fewer than 27 religious groups endorsed the pro-choice position before the 1973 Supreme Court decisions. A 1972 statement by the United Methodist Church is representative:

> *Our belief in the sanctity of unborn human life makes us reluctant to approve abortion. But we are equally bound to respect the sacredness of the life and well-being of the mother, for whom devastating damage may result from an unacceptable pregnancy.*
>
> *In continuity with past Christian teaching, we recognize tragic conflicts of life with life that may justify abortion. . . . We support removal of abortion from the criminal code, placing it instead under laws relating to other procedures of medical practice. A decision concerning abortion should be made after thorough and thoughtful consideration by the parties involved, with medical and pastoral counsel.*[10]

In 1973, three distinct types of constitutional amendments were introduced in Congress. The first was the "right-to-life" amendment. H.J. Res. 261,[11] for example, sponsored by Congressman Lawrence Hogan (R-Maryland),[12] sought to ensure that due process and equal protection under the Fourteenth Amendment be extended to all individuals "from the moment of conception."[13]

The second type of amendment was a "states' rights" amendment, such as H.J. Res. 468, sponsored by Congressman William Whitehurst (R-Virginia).[14] This amendment stated that nothing in the Constitution shall bar any state "from allowing, regulating or prohibiting the practice of abortions." Such amendments sought to allow each of the 50 states to regulate abortion one way or another, as they had before the *Roe* decision.

The third type of constitutional amendment is typified by the one proposed by Senator James Buckley (Conservative–New York), S.J. Res. 119.[15] This amendment sought to extend the definition of the word "person" within the meaning of the Fifth and Fourteenth Amendments to "all human beings, including their unborn offspring at every stage of biological development." This "personhood" amendment displeased many purists in the right-to-life movement because it included an exception for women whose lives would be threatened by continued pregnancy. These purists argued that they must remain consistent and seek to protect the absolute right to life of the unborn with no exceptions allowed.[16]

Many in the right-to-life movement contended that Congress should correct the Court's decision in *Roe* through enactment of a simple statute, holding that the Court erred in its *Roe* decision, and a number of bills to accomplish this were introduced. Congressman Frank Denholm (D-South Dakota) introduced H.R. 7752, which defined the word "person" to include the fetus or "viable human cells."[17] Congressman Harold Froehlich (R-Wisconsin) introduced a bill, H.R. 8682, which extended power to the states to regulate abortion under the Fourteenth Amendment (this bill included the exception for danger to the life of the woman).[18]

Congressman Froelich also offered an amendment to the 1973 Legal Services Corporation Bill that would have prohibited Legal Services lawyers from assisting women to obtain nontherapeutic abortions or from forcing medical facilities or personnel to participate in abortions.[19] This amendment was approved by a vote of 316–52, but the bill stalled in the Senate and was not enacted until 1974.

The issue of compelling a medical facility or its personnel to perform abortions or sterilizations as a condition to receive federal aid was also addressed in the Health Programs Extension Act.[20] A so-called conscience clause that prohibited coercion was included in the act. Many similarly restrictive provisions were attached to other bills, including some not directly related to health programs. The Foreign Assistance Act of 1973, for example, provided that:

> *None of the funds made available to carry out this part shall be used to pay for the performance of abortions as a method of family planning or to motivate or coerce any person to practice abortions.*[21]

The abundance of proposals introduced in 1973 on the abortion issue clearly shows a growing interest in the right-to-life movement, but, with the exceptions noted above, little congressional activity occurred. This inactivity prompted Congressmen Froelich, William Keating (R-Ohio), and Angelo Roncallo (R-New York) to introduce H. Res. 585, which would have created a special congressional committee to address the abortion issue and to hold hearings on it.[22] No action was taken on this proposal, however.

In the 1973 legislative attempts to restrict abortion rights, we can see the beginnings of the initiatives introduced in 1983—the proposed constitutional amendments and bills to overturn *Roe* are still around 10 years later, although in different forms. Although funding restrictions were spotty in 1973, this was to become an increasingly important focus of the right-to-life movement in the late 1970s and the 1980s.

January 24, 1974 was the beginning of some new traditions on Capitol Hill. The right-to-life movement held what was to become an annual March for Life, in which participants delivered red roses to each congressional office. This practice grew from the original 6000 marchers to a reported 26,000 in 1983. The pro-choice movement also made its presence felt, however. Pro-choice speeches were made in the House and the Senate and pro-choice activists demonstrated their support for reproductive freedom around Capitol Hill. In my remarks to the Senate, I listed more than 60 religious, medical, and miscellaneous groups including the American Bar Association and the YWCA that had publicly declared pro-choice positions.[23] Support for reproductive freedom seemed to be the position of the majority of Americans, but the efforts of the right-to-life movement continued unabated.

The pro-life movement in 1974 extended its fight to protect the unborn by seeking to prohibit fetal research particularly in connection with abortion. *In utero* research on fetuses and testing with fetal tissue have provided many advances in the areas of maternal and child health and much of the medical information on fetal development and pregnancy. In the early 1970s, however, concern had grown over human experimentation in general, especially on live subjects in prisons and mental institutions, as well as on aborted fetuses.

The right-to-life movement made fetal research one of its primary battle-grounds, and they won several victories. The National Science Foundation Authorization Act of 1974 prohibited the use of federal funds for fetal research.[24] The National Research Service Award Act of 1974 authorized the National Commission for the Protection of Human Subjects of Biomedical and Behavioral Research and placed a moratorium on fetal research.[25]

In 1974 and 1975, the Department of Health, Education and Welfare (HEW) issued regulations on research on pregnant women and fetuses, and the commission completed its study on fetal research, resulting in the lifting of the moratorium.[26] Since then, it has been generally acknowledged that there has been little, if any, abuse of the 1974 regulations, and that any further restrictions could endanger research projects from improved maternal and child health.[27]

The fiscal year 1975 budget for the Departments of Labor and HEW[28] was the next major battle site. Attempts to restrict the use of any Labor-HEW funds to pay for abortions were made in both the House and the Senate. Congressman Roncallo offered the amendment in the House, which rejected it by a vote of 123–247. Congressman David Obey (D-Wisc.), a Catholic who personally opposed abortion, was among those speaking against the Roncallo amendment:

> *I will be damned if I, a male legislator, will vote to prohibit a woman from having a therapeutic abortion necessary to save her life by any action I take tonight. I am going to vote against this and you should too.*[29]

Senator Dewey Bartlett (R-Oklahoma) offered in the Senate language similar to that rejected by the House. The debate was impassioned, and a motion to table the Bartlett amendment was offered by Senator William Hathaway (D-Maine), who said:

> *As Members of Congress, we do not have the right to deny constitutional rights to people because they are poor, and that is what we would be doing with this amendment. Constitutional rights should be equally available to all, and until the Constitution itself is changed in this regard, this right should not be available to some, but not to others.*[30]

Senator Hathaway's words and those of other pro-choice senators failed to persuade a majority in the Senate; the tabling motion was defeated and the Bartlett amendment was then accepted by a voice vote.

A House-Senate conference committee, formed to work out the differences between the two versions of the Labor-HEW bill, deleted the Bartlett amendment. The conference report included a specific comment on the funding questions:

> *Nevertheless [the conferees] are persuaded that an annual appropriations bill is an improper vehicle for such a controversial and far-reaching legislative provision whose implications and ramifications are not clear, whose constitutionality has been challenged and on which no hearings have been held.*[31]

The right-to-life movement ignored this comment about the appropriateness of using annual appropriations bills as vehicles to block federal funding of abortions. The battle on the Labor-HEW bill became an annual protracted one.

Hearings on the abortion issue were held intermittently during 1974, but no further action was taken on any of the bills or proposed constitutional amendments.

However, in 1975, the Senate Judiciary Subcommittee on Constitutional Amendments, chaired by Senator Birch Bayh (D-Indiana), held extensive hearings on the various proposed amendments. All sides of the issue—pro-choice, right-to-life religious groups, the medical profession, constitutional lawyers— were represented. In my March 10 testimony before Senator Bayh's committee, I maintained that the Supreme Court's decision in *Roe* was precisely correct:

> *The abortion issue is highly complex and emotional, and one on which there is no consensus among theologians and others who deal with values in our society. The Supreme Court importantly recognized this fact, and the broad range of values in our pluralistic society, and wisely placed the state in a neutral stand on the theological questions. At the same time, the Court acted appropriately to protect the health and welfare of our citizens, their right to privacy, and the right of physicians to make medical decisions according to their best judgments.*[32]

I included in my testimony a statement made by the American Lutheran Church (ALC). The ALC asserts that its pro-choice position is a "pro-life" one, but that in some cases it is preferable to choose to obtain an abortion. The statement concludes:

> *We have no need to itemize a list of circumstances under which abortion is acceptable or is forbidden. We have the responsibility to make the best possible decision we are capable of making in light of the information available to us and our sense of accountability to God, neighbor and self.*[33]

Senator Bayh summed up the beliefs of many who opposed the constitutional amendments considered by his subcommittee:

The question of whether we, as elected representatives, feel that amending the Constitution to impose one conception of life on all our citizens is indeed the most responsible course of action. I have concluded it is not. . . . Each of us must make that important choice for himself or herself.[34]

Six months later the subcommittee voted not to report a number of the proposed constitutional amendments to the full Judiciary Committee for its consideration. The subcommittee session was not open to the public, but it is reported that one of the states' rights amendments failed by a 4–4 tie vote.

The House Judiciary Subcommittee on Constitutional Rights also held hearings on proposed constitutional amendments to limit reproductive freedom. Subcommittee Chairman Don Edwards (D-California) held seven days of hearings in 1976, but no further action was taken.[35]

No additional hearings were held on proposed constitutional amendments on the abortion issue until 1981. Senator Jesse Helms (R-North Carolina), however, insisted in 1976 that the full Senate consider his resolution, S.J. Res. 178,[36] a proposed amendment that would grant personhood to every human being from the moment of fertilization. On April 28, 1976, he called for consideration of his resolution even though identical language in another of his resolutions, S.J. Res. 6, had earlier been rejected by the Constitutional Amendments Subcommittee by a 5–2 vote.[37] Senator Bayh moved to table Senator Helms's motion to proceed[38] to his resolution, and the tabling motion was agreed to by a 47–40 vote. This was the last formal consideration of constitutional amendments to overturn the *Roe* decision until 1983.

When the right-to-life movement realized that they could muster neither the votes in subcommittees nor those in the full Senate to approve a constitutional amendment, they changed their focus. Proposed amendments were still introduced in each Congress, but no particular effort was made to move them. The new focus was funding: The goal was to eliminate all federal funding for the performance of abortions, counseling about abortions, even a study about abortions by the Civil Rights Commission.

In 1975, both the Senate and the House defeated amendments barring the use of Medicaid funds for abortions under the FY76 Labor-HEW appropriations bill.[39] In the House, an amendment offered by Congressman Robert Bauman (R-Maryland) was defeated by voice vote. In the Senate a similar amendment offered by Senator Bartlett was tabled by a vote of 77–14 after a heated floor debate.

The annual battle on the Labor-HEW appropriations was even more prolonged on the FY77 bill[40]—the House and Senate engaged in an 11-week stare-down over the disputed abortion funding language. The House version included a prohibition against all funding for abortions with no exceptions. The Senate deleted that language and neither body budged. The eventual compromise language has come to be known as the Hyde Amendment after Congressman Henry J. Hyde (R-Illinois) even though the actual compromise language was offered by Congressman Silvio O. Conte (R-Massachusetts):

None of the funds contained in this Act shall be used to perform abortions except where the life of the mother would be endangered if the fetus were carried to term.[41]

Lawsuits against the abortion funding language were filed immediately after it was enacted, and a federal judge in New York held that the language was unconstitutional. The issue was finally decided by the Supreme Court on June 20, 1977. In *Maher v. Roe*[42] and *Beal v. Doe*,[43] the Court ruled that the states, and by implication the federal government, are not required to fund nontherapeutic abortions.[44] The injunction against the Hyde Amendment was lifted on August 20, 1977, and the language in the Labor-HEW appropriations was put into effect. To this date, we have not been able to rid ourselves of it, although it has been liberalized from time to time.

By the time the Hyde language went into effect, however, we were back in battle on the FY78 Labor-HEW appropriations.[45] After a five-month struggle, the pro-choice forces gained a significant victory: The House retreated and voted 181–167 to agree to the Senate language that allowed abortion funding in cases of rape and incest, where continuing the pregnancy would result in "severe and long-lasting physical damage" to the woman as determined by two physicians, for the termination of an ectopic pregnancy, and where carrying the pregnancy to term would threaten the life of the woman.

Although the right-to-life movement had been dealt a setback, they were not dismayed. William Cox, executive director of the National Committee for a Human Life Amendment, remarked in 1977 after the enactment of the 1978 Labor-HEW appropriations:

> *The most important aspect of this entire thing is that the pro-life movement established itself as a major political force in this Congress. We'll come back much wiser and better prepared to get a narrower provision in 1978.*[46]

The right-to-life movement did flex its growing muscle in the political arena in 1978, claiming victory in and responsibility for defeating two pro-choice senators, Dick Clark (D-Iowa) and Thomas J. McIntyre (D-New Hampshire). Losing Clark and McIntyre was a blow to pro-choice efforts in the Senate, but the biggest strategic loss was the defeat of Edward Brooke of Massachusetts, a pro-choice Republican. While we did not lose a pro-choice vote, we did lose a senator who held a key position. Brooke had been a ranking minority member of the Senate Appropriations Subcommittee on Labor-HEW, and in that role he was fundamental in ensuring liberal Senate language on abortion funding.

Some important victories ensued in 1978 in restricting federal funding of abortions outside the Labor-HEW programs. Funding restrictions were successfully attached to the FY79 Department of Defense appropriations,[47] which affected military personnel and their dependents, and the foreign assistance appropriations,[48] which affected members of the Peace Corps. The exceptions in both of these bills, as well as in the FY79 Labor-HEW appropriations,[49] included the same exceptions as in the FY78 Labor-HEW bill. The inclusion of restrictive language in the defense and foreign assistance bills was a first, however.

A nonfunding victory by the right-to-life movement was achieved in the 1978 bill to extend the Civil Rights Commission.[50] The House accepted an amendment by Congressmen David Treen (R-Mississippi) and Tom Hagedorn (R-Minnesota) to bar the commission from studying or recommending any action on abortion or federal laws, policies, or other government authorities affecting it. The commission had only addressed the abortion issue once during its 21-year history, a study entitled "Constitutional Aspects of the Right to Limit Childbearing," and there had been no accusations that the commission had exceeded its jurisdiction in this study. Congressman Treen maintained that this amendment was necessary because abortion was not, in his view, a civil rights issue. This is an ironic position in light of the *Roe* decision, in which the Supreme Court declared that the right to abortion was encompassed in the constitutionally protected right to privacy.

The absence of Senator Brooke and his pro-choice influence from the Senate Appropriations Committee was evident during the committee's consideration of the FY80 Labor-HEW bill.[51] Members could not agree among themselves about abortion funding language, so they decided to incorporate the House-approved, more restrictive language in the Senate bill. Brooke had consistently argued for the "medically necessary" exception in Senate appropriations language; it was not included in the FY80 bill. As appropriated under a continuing resolution, the Labor-HEW funding allowed exceptions for the life of the woman, rape and incest victims, and termination of ectopic pregnancies. The growing influence of the right-to-life movement can be seen in the Senate's reluctance to insist on the more liberal language it had previously approved. While the end result may not have differed, the Senate would at least have had a bargaining point with the House conferees.

Other funding battles won by the right-to-life movement during 1979 included the FY80 Department of Defense[52] and District of Columbia appropriations,[53] which included language essentially the same as that in the Labor-HEW bill. A new twist on the "conscience clause" was enacted in the 1979 Nurse Training Amendments.[54] The prohibition against coercing a health professional to participate in or perform abortions or to discriminate against students because of their religious or moral convictions concerning abortions or sterilizations was broadened to include all programs or institutions that received federal grants, loans, or other subsidies under the Health Programs Extension Act of 1973.[55]

If June 1983 is viewed as a pivotal month for the pro-choice forces, November 1980 may be seen as the apex for the right-to-life movement. The Republican Party regained control of the Senate after 25 years of Democratic control. With that change in control came a change in emphasis, a move away from developing social programs toward more controversial social issues such as allowing prayer in schools and restricting abortion rights. Leaders of the right-to-life movement were quick to claim a large share of credit for the GOP gains. Nine senators had been targeted by the right-to-life organizations in 1980; pro-choice senators Frank Church (D-Idaho), John Culver (D-Iowa), Birch Bayh (D-Indiana), Gaylord Nelson (D-Wisconsin), Jacob Javits (R-New York), and George McGovern (D-South Dakota) were all defeated by candidates whose platforms included opposition to abortion rights. I was among the three targeted senators who were reelected in 1980; the others were Alan Cranston (D-California) and Patrick Leahy (D-Vermont). In addition, four other candidates who were strongly opposed to abortion rights won Senate seats: Don Nickles (R-Oklahoma), Jeremiah Denton (R-Alabama), John East (R-North Carolina), and Paula Hawkins (R-Florida).[56]

In 1981, prospects for a big right-to-life victory in the Senate looked very promising indeed. Opponents of reproductive freedom chaired key committees and subcommittees. The new freshman class was eager to make good on their campaign promises to abolish abortion. But what the right-to-life movement did not anticipate was the divisiveness within its ranks. Put simply, the various players in the movement could not agree on how to proceed. Some held out for a "perfect" constitutional amendment, an absolute prohibition on abortions. Others offered amendments that included exceptions for the life of the woman. Still others argued that ratification of a constitutional amendment was too far in the future and that a simple statute declaring the beginning of life and the establishment of personhood for fetuses was the logical—and necessary—first step.

The first hearings on abortion legislation in this changed environment were held in the Senate Judiciary Subcommittee on the Separation of Powers, chaired by Senator John East (R-North Carolina), on S. 158, Senator Jesse Helms's Human Life Bill.[57] The bill would have "provided that human life shall be deemed to exist from conception" and held that "the Congress finds that present day scientific evidence indicates a significant likelihood that actual human life exists from conception." Senator East had planned to hold brief hearings only on the narrow medical issue of when life begins, but vociferous protests from pro-choice groups and the subcommittee's ranking Democrat, Senator Max Baucus of Montana, forced him to broaden the scope of the hearings.

During the hearings Senator Baucus introduced into the record numerous letters he had received from constitutional and medical scholars.[58] Baucus also received a letter from six former attorneys general which he inserted into the *Congressional Record*.[59] The disagreement among the attorneys general on the abortion issue was admitted—some were pro-choice, some anti-abortion; some agreed with the Supreme Court's decision in *Roe,* some believed the Court was in error. But there was unanimous agreement that S. 158 was unconstitutional.

I never believed that S. 158 was simply a declaration of the beginning of life. It was really an attempt to ban abortions in the United States until a constitutional amendment could be passed by the Congress and ratified by the states. This was the focus of my testimony before the Separation of Powers Subcommittee on May 21.[60] I also tried to establish historical precedent for *not* restricting abortions. Our founders had wisely chosen not to extend the Fifth and Fourteenth Amendment protection to fetuses. English common law, on which we patterned our Constitution, did not hold abortion to be a crime. I argued against making it a crime in the 1980s.

The Separation of Powers Subcommittee held a total of eight days of hearings on S. 158 and then voted favorably to send it to the full Judiciary Committee for consideration. The 3–2 vote was strictly along party lines, but the unanimous Republican vote was not reflective of unanimous support for the bill among the leaders of the right-to-life movement. An agreement was reached in an attempt to bring the factions of the right-to-life movement together: before the full Judiciary Committee would consider S. 158, the Constitution Subcommittee would hold hearings on proposed constitutional amendments.

The Constitution Subcommittee did not begin its hearings on the abortion issue until fall. Senator Hatch's proposed amendment, S.J. Res. 110, a compromise among anti-abortion amendments, was the focus of attention:

A right to abortion is not secured by this Constitution. The Congress and the several States shall have the concurrent power to restrict and prohibit abortions: Provided, *That a law of a State which is more restrictive than a law of Congress shall govern.*[61]

I testified on October 5 against the proposed amendment, arguing again that abortion had been around when our founders drafted our Constitution, and they had wisely chosen not to address it in the document.[62] I firmly believe that our Constitution was written to protect liberties, not to restrain them. I believe that an amendment which imposes a single moral view on abortion—or any issue—has no place in our Constitution.

Nine days of hearings were held on S.J. Res. 110, and diverse opinions were expressed by many interested groups and individuals. The National Conference of Catholic Bishops, a group that had previously supported only absolute bans of abortions, endorsed the Hatch amendment in November, claiming it was the only proposal with a realistic chance of passing. Some of the major right-to-life groups, however, withheld their support. For some, the only legislation worth supporting was that which would ban all abortions without exception. This fragmentation among right-to-life groups was a major contributing factor to their inability to move any legislation to the Senate floor.

The Constitution Subcommittee voted on S.J. Res. 110 only one hour after the hearings concluded on December 16. The vote was 4–0, but pro-choice Senator Leahy withheld his vote, asserting that the vote was taken too soon, that the intent of hearings was to present views which would be carefully considered before a vote was taken.

The right-to-life movement may have been successful in obtaining a constitutional amendment approved by a subcommittee, but they couldn't move it to the floor for full Senate consideration. In 1982, the focus of the right-to-life movement, therefore, shifted to two bills that sought to overturn *Roe* by means of a simple statute.

S. 2148,[63] introduced in March by Senator Helms, was an expanded version of his Human Life Bill, S. 158.[64] Like S. 158, the new bill declared that life begins at conception, and it extended "personhood" and protection under the Fourteenth Amendment to fetuses. The bill also contained a provision that would have *permanently* prohibited almost all federal funding of abortions, allowing exceptions only when the life of the woman was jeopardized. The congressional procedure regarding abortion funding at that time—which has not been changed—was an annual review; restrictions on funding were enacted on departmental appropriations bills each year. Senator Helms's bill would have also restricted abortion coverage under federal employees' health insurance policies, referrals for abortion, and training in abortion techniques.

Senator Mark Hatfield (R-Oregon) introduced S. 2372 in April.[65] While it was similar to the Helms bill in its funding restrictions, it differed in its findings of "personhood." S. 2372 found, "Unborn children who are subjected to abortion are living members of the human species." The Hatfield bill stopped short of conferring "personhood" to fetuses; instead, it encouraged states to enact legislation more restrictive than that allowed by *Roe,* based on the finding quoted above.

Both the Hatfield and Helms bills would also have provided a direct appeal to the Supreme Court if restrictive abortion language were enacted by a state and subsequently invalidated by a lower court. The intent of the expedited appeal process was to bombard the Supreme Court with new anti-choice cases and try to force the Court to reconsider its *Roe* decision. No action was taken on either bill.

Action did occur, however, in 1982—big action. I filibustered the abortion amendment that Senator Helms sought to attach to the resolution to extend the debt ceiling, H.J. Res. 520.[66] Senator Helms had been dangling the possibility of attaching amendments on abortion and other controversial social issues to the "must pass" debt ceiling extension, legislation that had to be passed if the government were to continue to borrow money.[67] Twelve senators joined me in writing to our Senate colleagues, announcing our intention to filibuster if any abortion amendment were offered.[68] We believed it was inappropriate—as well as unconstitutional—to try to overturn a Supreme Court decision by a simple statute.

Let me explain a bit about filibusters and why we threatened one. The Senate basically operates on the principle of unfettered debate. There are few restrictions on germaneness of amendments,[69] and it is a common practice to offer amendments unrelated to the bill under consideration in order to circumvent standing procedures. For example, a senator can offer as an amendment the substance of a bill that is held up in committee. Since there was no way to prevent Senator Helms from offering his amendment, we announced in advance our intention to filibuster, which would inevitably delay progress on the "must pass" debt ceiling extension. We hoped either that Senator Helms would choose to withhold his amendment or that Senate leadership would convince him that the full Senate would address the substance of his amendment, essentially the same as S. 2148[70] except that "personhood" and Fourteenth Amendment protection was not extended to the fetus in the amendment, at another time. If Senator Helms proceeded to offer his amendment, we planned to tie up the Senate proceedings by filibustering for as long as necessary.

Senator Helms offered his amendment on August 16.[71] We began our filibuster shortly thereafter. Once a filibuster begins, it can only be cut off if the senator loses his or her right to the floor or if cloture is invoked. Invoking cloture requires 60 votes, and once invoked, limits are placed on the debate: each senator is entitled to one hour of debate, a germaneness requirement is imposed on amendments, and an overall 100-hour cap is placed on the consideration of the clotured provision. It is important to remember that cloture can be invoked on a single amendment as well as on a bill or resolution.

In preparation for the filibuster, pro-choice senators coordinated a strategy, each assuming responsibility for a particular argument. Extensive materials were accumulated which could be read as part of the debate. My staff prepared more than 700 amendments to offer if we needed to stall further. I gained recognition by the presiding officer and made some initial remarks. Then I began to read from *Abortion in America,* a history of abortion by University of Maryland professor James C. Mohr.[72] Our filibuster was under way.

The filibuster continued for almost a month. Several unsuccessful attempts to invoke cloture were made, and on September 13 Majority Leader Howard Baker (R-Tennessee) announced his intention to bring S.J. Res. 110,[73] Senator Hatch's proposed constitutional amendment, to the floor for consideration by the full Senate on the following day. Senator Hatch was absent the next day, so Senator Baker chose not to bring up S.J. Res. 110. Debate continued on the debt ceiling extension amendments.

On September 15, Senator Hatch withdrew S.J. Res. 110 from consideration. He believed its chances for passage were nearly nonexistent. Senator Baker agreed to bring up a constitutional amendment early in 1983. That afternoon the third attempt to invoke cloture was voted on and rejected. Senator S. I. Hayakawa (R-California) then moved to table the Helms abortion amendment. The tabling motion was approved by a one-vote margin, 47–46. Our filibuster was more successful than anticipated: in addition to blocking Senator Helms's abortion amendment on the debt ceiling extension, we had laid the constitutional amendment to rest until 1983.

Additional action on abortion during 1982 was confined to sporadic attempts to restrict abortion funding. Several of these attempts were successful, but the enacted language was no more restrictive than what had been approved in prior appropriations bills.

With the beginning of the 98th Congress in January 1983, both pro-choice and right-to-life forces knew the agenda: the full Senate debate of Senator Hatch's constitutional amendment, numbered S.J. Res. 3 in the new Congress.[74] No one could have anticipated the defeats the right-to-life movement would experience.

Two days of hearings were held on S.J. Res. 3. Senator Hatch had reintroduced language identical to his proposal in the 97th Congress, S.J. Res. 110.[75] In the Constitution Subcommittee hearings, which were chaired by Senator Hatch, an amendment was offered by Senator Thomas Eagleton (D-Missouri) to delete all the language except for the first 10 words: "A right to abortion is not secured by this Constitution." This amendment was approved, after Senator Eagleton pointed out that this was the only form of constitutional amendment that had any chance of passing. Ten years had passed since *Roe,* and Senator Eagleton was convinced that a simple 10-word amendment was the only hope for the right-to-life movement. The subcommittee approved S.J. Res. 3 as amended, and the full Judiciary Committee reported it to the Senate without recommendation after a tie 9–9 vote was taken on the proposal.[76]

The rest of the story on S.J. Res. 3 is well-known: on June 28, after two days of debate in the Senate, the measure was defeated soundly, 49–50, failing even to get a majority of the votes cast. The right-to-life movement had had its "day in court"—and the jury had come in against it. This was the first time abortion legislation had been debated on its merits by either the House or the Senate and a vote had been cast on substance, not procedure.[77]

But two weeks earlier, on June 15, the Supreme Court had also spoken, handing down decisions in *Akron v. Akron Center for Reproductive Health,*[78] *Planned Parenthood Association of Kansas City v. Ashcroft,*[79] and *Simopoulos v. Virginia*[80]. These decisions strongly reaffirmed and strengthened the *Roe* decision by ruling that government may not interfere with a woman's fundamental right to choose abortion unless it is clearly justified by accepted medical practice and by striking state statutes that sought to impede. The Court ruled that state/ abortion requirements for second trimester hospitalization, 24-hour waiting periods, and "informed" consent place significant obstacles in the path of women seeking abortions.

The right-to-life movement was stunned by the two defeats it suffered, but its attempts to restrict abortion funding have only intensified since June 1983.

During its consideration of the FY84 Labor–Health and Human Services (HHS) appropriations bill in the fall of 1983, the House approved an outright ban on abortion funding.[81] The Senate insisted on an exception for cases in which the life of the woman would be threatened, and that language was included in the signed appropriation.[82]

The right-to-life movement did win a new one, however: a restriction on abortion funding under the Federal Employees Health Benefits Program, the umbrella program of more than 120 health insurance plans available to federal workers as an employee benefit, was enacted.[83] This restriction is known as the Ashbrook amendment, after the late Congressman John M. Ashbrook (R-Ohio), who had tried repeatedly until his death in 1982 to enact such restrictive provisions. The House had approved the Ashbrook amendment as part of the FY81 and FY82 Treasury, Postal Service, and general government appropriations bills, but the language was never enacted.[84] The Ashbrook language was approved in a continuing resolution in 1982 that expired on December 17.[85] The further continuing resolution approved that December did not include the Ashbrook language.[86]

During Senate consideration of the continuing resolution in December 1982, the Ashbrook language was deleted by the Senate from the House-passed bill by a one-vote margin, 49–48. In November 1983, we were not so lucky: the Senate approved the Ashbrook language by a 44–43 vote as part of the continuing resolution.[87] These one-vote margins reflect the continuing vitality of the abortion funding fight—and the strength of the commitment on both sides.

No sooner had the Ashbrook language been approved than we faced another abortion amendment, this time a resurrected form of Senator Helms's Human Life Bill. Senator Roger Jepsen (R-Iowa) offered an amendment[88] to the Civil Rights Commission Reauthorization Bill[89] that was similar to the amendment Senator Helms offered on the debt ceiling extension in 1982.[90] The Jepsen amendment was essentially the same as his Respect Human Life Bill, S. 467,[91] which would declare that life begins at conception, impose a permanent ban on most abortion funding, and allow expedited review to the Supreme Court for restrictive state language on abortion that is overturned by a lower court. The Jepsen bill also addresses one of the peripheral issues that has been adopted by the right-to-life movement, the "Baby Doe" issue.

The Baby Doe issue arose during the spring of 1982 when a Bloomington, Indiana, couple refused to allow an operation and medical intervention on their newborn baby who was born with Down's syndrome and several other serious medical problems. The infant died when nutritional sustenance was not provided, and an Indiana court upheld the parents' right to decide how their child should be treated. In response to this decision, HHS issued regulations on March 7, 1983.[92]

The regulations have not been finalized yet because of numerous legal conflicts.[93] The right-to-life movement has also seized "Baby Doe" as one of its issues.

Senator Jepsen's Respect Human Life Bill addresses the Baby Doe issue by denying federal financial assistance to any institution that withholds nutritional sustenance or medical or surgical treatment to handicapped infants. This provision was also included in the amendment he offered to the Civil Rights Commission Reauthorization Bill.

We got off easy on the Jepsen amendment this time: The Civil Rights Commission Bill was a carefully designed compromise among the Congress, the White House, and civil rights groups. The Jepsen amendment was simply too controversial, and its inclusion in the bill would have resulted in unacceptable delays. When Senator Jepsen offered his amendment, I threatened to filibuster for six weeks until Christmas. The amendment was subsequently tabled, the last of the abortion skirmishes in the first session of the 98th Congress.

The right-to-life movement has been dealt a couple of big defeats in the *Akron* decision and the Senate's defeat of Senator Hatch's proposed constitutional amendment, but they are far from ready to send white roses instead of red. The Jepsen amendment will certainly resurface on other legislation; Baby Doe provisions are included in several bills that are awaiting consideration by the full House and Senate.[94] Comprehensive funding restrictions have been approved by a Senate committee as part of a bill to provide health insurance for unemployed Americans.[95]

Clearly, battles with the right-to-life movement remain to be fought. And I will fight. I am convinced that victories in the funding area are the only ones the right-to-life movement can even hope to attain; someday we will win those too. The constitutionally protected right to reproductive freedom has been unquestionably upheld. The right-to-life movement's chiseling efforts reflect their knowledge that they simply cannot overturn *Roe*. In that sense, they have been defeated.

NOTES

1. Roe v. Wade, 410 U.S. 113 (1973).
2. 462 U.S., 416 (1983).
3. S.J. Res. 3, 98th Cong., 1st Sess. (1983).
4. Ark. Stat. Ann. § 41–304 to 41–310 (Supp. 1971); Cal. Health & Safety Code § 25950 to 25955.5 (Supp. 1972); Colo. Rev. Stat. Ann. § 40–2–50 to 40–2–53 (Cum. Supp. 1967); Del. Code. Ann. tit. 24, § 1790–1793 (Supp. 1972); Fla. Law of April 13, 1972, C. 72–196; Ga. Code § 26–1201 to 1203; Kan. Stat. Ann. § 21–3407 (Supp. 1971); Md. Ann. Code art. 43 § 137–139 (1971); N.M. Stat. § 40A–5–1 to 40A–5–3 (1972); N.C. Gen. Stat. § 14045.1 (Supp. 1971); Ore. Rev. Stat. § 435.405 to 435.495 (1971); S.C. Code Ann. § 16–82 to 16–89 (1962 and Supp. 1971); Va. Code Ann. § 18.1–62 to 18.1–62.3 (Supp. 1972).
5. A. A. Merton, Enemies of Choice: The Right-to-Life Movement and Its Threat to Abortion at 7 (1981).
6. Pub. L. No. 91–572 § 1008, 84 Stat. 1504 (1970).

7. S. 3501, 91st Cong., 2d Sess. (1970); S. 3746, 91st Cong., 2d Sess. (1970); S. 1750, 92d Cong., 1st Sess. (1971); S. 1751, 92d Cong., 1st Sess. (1971).

8. 410 U.S. 113 (1973).

9. 410 U.S. 170 (1973).

10. B. Packwood, *The Wisdom of the Supreme Court Decision on Abortion,* 121 Cong. Rec. 6085 (March 11, 1975).

11. 93d Cong., 1st Sess. (1973).

12. "R" designates a member of the Republican Party and "D" designates a member of the Democratic Party.

13. On July 10, 1973, Congressman Hogan filed a "discharge petition," a device used as an alternative to regular legislative procedures in the House. When a specific bill or resolution is delayed in a committee and a member of the House wishes to bring it before the full House immediately, he or she may file a discharge petition. If more than half the House members sign the petition, the committee to which the legislation has been referred can be discharged from consideration of the measure and the measure can be brought before the full House. Hogan failed to obtain the necessary signatures on his discharge petition and the resolution was never considered by the full House.

14. 93d Cong., 1st Sess. (1973).

15. *Id.*

16. A. Schardt, *Saving Abortion,* American Civil Liberties Union (1973).

17. 93d Cong., 1st Sess. (1973).

18. *Id.*

19. Pub. L. No. 93–335 § 1007, 88 Stat. 378 (1973).

20. Pub. L. No. 93–45 § 401, 87 Stat. 91 (1973).

21. Pub. L. No. 93–189 § 2, 87 Stat. 714 (1973).

22. 93d Cong., 1st Sess. (1973).

23. B. Packwood, *Supreme Court Abortion Decision and Freedom of Conscience,* 120 Cong. Rec. 214–15 (January 22, 1974).

24. Pub. L. No. 93–96 § 10, 87 Stat. 315 (1973).

25. Pub. L. No. 93–348 § 213, 88 Stat. 342 (1973).

26. 45 C.F.R. § 46, subpart B.

27. In 1982 and 1983, there have been attempts to ban fetal research under legislation to reauthorize the National Institutes of Health (NIH). In 1982, I prevented final passage of the FY83 NIH bill because of restrictive language proposed by Representative William Dannemeyer (R-California) and passed by the House.

28. Pub. L. No. 93–517, 88 Stat. 1634 (1974).

29. D. Obey, 120 Cong. Rec. 21693 (June 27, 1974).

30. W. Hathaway, 120 Cong. Rec. 31456 (September 17, 1974).

31. Making appropriations for the Departments of Labor, Health, Education and Welfare and Related Agencies, Conf. Rep. 93–89 to accompany H.R. 15580, 93d Cong., 2d Sess. at 20 (1974).

32. *Hearings Before the Senate Judiciary Committee on S.J. Res. 6, S.J. Res. 10 and 11, and S.J. Res. 91,* 94th Cong., 1st Sess., Part 4 at 7 (1975).

33. *Id.* at 13.

34. B. Bayh, *Constitutional Amendments Relating to Abortion,* 121 Cong. Rec. 29058 (September 17, 1975).

35. *Hearings Before the House Judiciary Committee on Proposed Constitutional Amendments on Abortion,* 94th Cong., 2d Sess., Sev. 46 (1976).
36. 94th Cong., 2d Sess. (1976).
37. S.J. Res. 6, 94th Cong., 1st Sess. (1975).
38. A motion to proceed is a parliamentary procedure than can be used to compel the Senate to consider a particular measure. The majority leader, in conjunction with the committee chairmen and the minority leader, sets the schedule for bringing legislation before the Senate; a motion to proceed is used when the measure desired to be considered is not on the schedule.
39. Pub. L. No. 94–206, 90 Stat. 3 (1975).
40. Pub. L. No. 94–439 § 209, 90 Stat. 1418 (1976).
41. *Id.*
42. 432 U.S. 464 (1977).
43. 432 U.S. 438 (1977).
44. In Harris v. McRae, 448 U.S. 297 (1980), and William v. Zbaraz, 448 U.S. 358 (1980), the Supreme Court upheld both federal—the Hyde Amendment—and state laws prohibiting governmental funding of therapeutic abortions.
45. H.R. 7555, 95th Cong., 1st Sess. (1977). Regular Labor-HEW/HHS appropriations bills were not enacted from fiscal years 1978 through 1983. During these years, funding for these agencies was included under continuing appropriations bills (continuing resolutions). All departmental appropriations that have not been enacted by the beginning of the new fiscal year are funded under a single appropriations, known as a continuing resolution. Many continuing resolutions have specific expiration dates. If the designated date is reached and a departmental appropriations bill still has not been enacted, an additional continuing resolution known as a further continuing resolution is enacted. Labor-HEW appropriations for FY78 were included in Pub. L. No. 95–205 § 101, 91 Stat. 1460 (1977).
46. Congressional Quarterly Almanac, 1977, at 296.
47. Pub. L. No. 95–457 § 863, 92 Stat. 1254 (1978).
48. Pub. L. No. 95–481, tit. 111, 92 Stat. 1597–1599, (1978).
49. H.R. 12929, 95th Cong, 2d Sess. (1978). Funding appropriated under Pub. L. No. 95–480 § 210, 92 Stat. 1586 (1978). *See* note 45 *supra.*
50. Pub. L. No. 95–444 § 3 (a), 92 Stat. 1067 (1978).
51. H.R. 4389, 96th Cong., 1st Sess. (1979). Funding appropriated under Pub. L. No. 96–123, Sec. 109, Stat. 126 (1979). The Department of Health, Education, and Welfare (HEW) was redesignated the Department of Health and Human Services (HHS) when a separate Department of Education was created in 1979. Pub. L. No. 96–88, 93 Stat. 668 (1979).
52. Pub. L. No. 96–154 § 762, 93 Stat. 1162 (1979).
53. Pub. L. No. 96–93 § 220, 93 Stat. 719 (1979).
54. Pub. L. No. 96–76 § 208, 93 Stat. 583–584 (1979).
55. Pub. L. No. 93–45 § 401, 87 Stat. 91 (1973).
56. A strong opponent of abortion rights was elected to the presidency in 1980. Candidate Ronald Reagan voiced strong opposition to reproductive freedom throughout his campaign. He has reiterated that position throughout his presidency.
57. 97th Cong., 1st Sess. (1981).

58. *Hearings Before the Senate Judiciary Committee on S. 158, a Bill to Provide That Human Life Shall Be Deemed to Exist From Conception,* 97th Cong., 1st Sess. § J–97–16 at 260–962 (1981).
59. M. Baucus, 128 Cong. Rec. 10579 (August 16, 1982). This letter, dated May 1, 1981, stated that S. 158 and its House companion bill, H.R. 900, were unconstitutional. Former attorneys general signing the letter were Herbert Brownell, Jr. (1953–57), Nicholas Katzenbach (1965–66), Ramsey Clark (1967–68), Elliott L. Richardson (1973), WIlliam B. Saxbe (1973–74), and Benjamin R. Civiletti (1979–81).
60. *Hearings on S. 158, supra* note 58, at 155.
61. 97th Cong., 1st Sess. (1981).
62. *Hearings Before the Senate Judiciary Committee on S.J. Res. 17, S.J. Res. 18, S.J. Res. 19, and S.J. Res. 110, Bills Proposing a Constitutional Amendment with Respect to Abortion,* 97th Cong., 1st Sess. § J–97–62 at 24 (1981).
63. 97th Cong., 2d Sess. (1982).
64. 97th Cong., 1st Sess. (1981).
65. 97th Cong., 2d Sess. (1982).
66. Pub. L. No. 97–270, 96 Stat. 1156 (1982).
67. The government is prohibited from exceeding the debt limit as established by law. When the public debt approaches the limit, Congress must approve and the president must sign legislation to raise the limit.
68. Senators Max Baucus (D-Montana), Alan Cranston (D-California), Gary Hart (D-Colorado), Nancy Landon Kassebaum (R-Kansas), Edward Kennedy (D-Massachusetts), Patrick Leahy (D-Vermont), Howard Metzenbaum (D-Ohio), George Mitchell (D-Maine), Daniel Patrick Moynihan (D-New York), Arlen Specter (R-Pennsylvania), Paul Tsongas (D-Massachusetts), and Lowell Weicker (R-Connecticut) signed the letter.
69. Germaneness restrictions can only be imposed in very limited circumstances, including by unanimous consent, during consideration of budget resolutions, and when cloture is invoked.
70. 97th Cong., 2d Sess. (1982).
71. This was an unprinted, unnumbered amendment. For the text of this amendment, *see* 128 Cong. Rec. 10736 (August 18, 1982).
72. J. Mohr, Abortion in America: The Origins and Evolution of National Policy (1978).
73. 97th Cong., 1st Sess. (1981).
74. 98th Cong., 1st Sess. (1983).
75. 97th Cong., 1st Sess. (1981).
76. On April 19, 1983 the Judiciary Committee debated a motion to favorably report S.J. Res. 3 to the Senate. After the 9–9 tie vote, there was a motion to report S.J. Res. 3 *without* recommendation. This subsequent motion was approved by voice vote without objection.
77. Previous votes on the abortion issue had been taken when the issue was linked (or when attempts were made to link the issue) to other legislation (e.g., appropriations bills, foreign aid). S.J. Res. 3 was the first abortion measure to be considered in either the House or Senate on the merits of abortion per se. The previous votes were not votes solely on abortion; for

example, when attempts were made to add abortion amendments to appropriations bills, some senators who support restrictions on abortion funding voted against those amendments because they believed the vehicle (the appropriations bill) was an inappropriate one to carry the abortion amendment. This is an example of a procedural, not substantive, vote.

78. 462 U.S. 416 (1983).
79. 103 S. Ct. 2517 (1983). 462 U.S. 476 (1983).
80. 462 U.S. 506 (1983).
81. H.R. 3913, 98th Cong., 1st Sess. (1983).
82. Pub. L. No. 98–139 § 204, 97 Stat. 871 (1983).
83. Pub. L. No. 98–151 § 101(f), 97 Stat. 964 (1983).
84. H.R. 7584, 96th Cong., 2d Sess. (1980); H.R. 4121, 97th Cong., 1st Sess. (1981).
85. Pub. L. No. 97–276 § 101(a) (1), 96 Stat. 1186 (1982).
86. Pub. L. No. 97–377, 97 Stat. 1830 (1982).
87. Pub. L. No. 98–151 § 101(f), 97 Stat. 964 (1983).
88. Senate Amendment Nos. 2607 and 2608, 98th Cong., 1st Session. (1983).
89. Pub. L. No. 98–183, 97 Stat. 1301 (1983).
90. Pub. L. No. 97–270, 96 Stat. 1156 (1982).
91. 98th Cong., 1st Sess. (1983).
92. 48 Fed. Reg. 9630 (March 7, 1983).
93. In American Academy of Pediatrics v. Heckler, 561 F. Supp. 395 (D.D.C. 1983), the D.C. District Court struck down these regulations on the procedural grounds that they failed to follow the requirements of the Administrative Procedures Act (APA) concerning notice and comment. This decision is presently being appealed. On July 5, 1983, HHS issued proposed rules (48 Fed. Reg. 30846) that are very similar to the March rules, although they followed relevant APA procedure. In fall 1984 Congress created a new grant requirement for states to qualify for Federal grants on child abuse programs (48 Fed. Reg. 1340, 1985 Federal Register 14878–14893).
94. Sections dealing with the Baby Doe issue were added to both the House and Senate bills concerning the reauthorization of the Child Abuse Prevention and Treatment Act. Both bills, H.R. 1904 and S. 1003, 98th Cong., 1st Sess., were reported out of their respective committees on May 16, 1983.
95. S. 242, 98th Cong., 1st Sess. (1983).

Professor George presents a complete analysis of state abortion laws before 1967, between 1968 and 1973, and after 1973. After he carefully examines each state law, along with the definitions of terms contained in those laws, he makes a comparison between present state laws and the Constitution. Finally, the state legislative responses to the *Roe* and *Doe* decisions are presented, further indicating the continuing legislative activity on the abortion issue after 1973. The detailed footnotes that accompany the article give added material to classify state abortion laws.

2 · State Legislatures Versus The Supreme Court: Abortion Legislation In The 1980s _____

B. J. George, Jr., J.D.

Abortion regulation was a matter exclusively for state legislatures until 1973, when the United States Supreme Court brought medically indicated abortions within the protection of the Fourteenth Amendment in *Roe v. Wade*[1] and *Doe v. Bolton*.[2] As will be surveyed in Parts I and II of this chapter, some liberalization in the scope of lawful abortions was evident in several legislatures before 1973, but few statutes approached the breadth of the privacy right decreed by the Court in *Roe* and *Doe*. Since 1973, a majority of legislatures have tried to impose functional limitations on the availability of abortions both before and after viability. Many of these efforts have been invalidated by subsequent decisions by the Court, but in many instances the legislatures have left their statutes unrevised. That in turn places the onus on courts to squelch efforts (if they occur) to invoke laws of either clear or probable unconstitutionality against pregnant women and their physicians. It is apparent that in many states a majority of legislators are hostile to freely available abortions,[3] while in others they appear to be cowed by threats of reprisals at the polls from the so-called right-to-life movement if constitutional legislation is enacted to replace unconstitutional statutes.

A pragmatic understanding of the causes of unsatisfactory legislative coverage of abortion law does not change the fact, however, that state statutes in all too many jurisdictions provide no guidance to and protection for pregnant women and their medical advisers. That in turn creates a legislative limbo in which either of two phenomena likely will appear. One is that medical abortion becomes an out-of-view dimension of hospital administration governed by local or state public health regulations. That may prove a practical accommodation acceptable to both legislators and physicians: Legislators are not called on to take action visible to

23

their constituents that the latter will view as approving abortions, while the medical profession can treat abortion like any other dimension of medical practice. A second, however, is official disapproval of therapeutic abortions that force pregnant women, their physicians, and the administrators of clinics where abortions can be performed safely and inexpensively to turn to the judiciary for redress. Whether this state of affairs will change within the next decade or so is debatable. If it does, however, it will be because state legislatures accept as immutable the constitutional doctrines espoused by the Supreme Court; the Court has not retreated from its basic interpretation of the Constitution, as evidenced by its reaffirmation of *Roe v. Wade* principles in its 1983 decision in *Akron v. Akron Center for Reproductive Health*.[4]

In the pages that follow, we will survey the state of the law of abortion to 1973, consider the basic constitutional principles set forth by the Court in 1973 and since, survey the coverage of state legislation in 1984, and evaluate the compatibility of this state legislation with the federal Constitution. First, however, it may be helpful to review briefly the conflicting interests recognized in or affected by abortion legislation.

I. Conflicting Interests Affected by Abortion Legislation

Discussions of the desirability or illicitness of abortion necessarily revolve about four focal points: the fetus, the pregnant woman, the family into which a child will be born if a pregnancy goes to term, and the surrounding community.

As to the first, there clearly is a semantic issue, in that a choice from among an array of terms—conceptus, zygote, embryo, fertilized ovum, fetus, or prenatal infant—advertises the thinking of the speaker and not a scientifically impeccable choice of terms.[5] Whatever the term selected, concern about fetuses typically reflects two contradictory schools of thought. According to one of these schools, inviolate life comes into being from the time an ovum is fertilized. The strongest adherence to this view, of course, has been found within the Roman Catholic faith, which has condemned abortion under all circumstances,[6] but there is strong Protestant support for the idea.[7] The second view is that the possible fate of a fetus, should it go to term, should be taken into account. If a child would be born deformed, mentally defective, or otherwise incapable of living a normal life, or born into a highly detrimental environment that could not be compensated for adequately,[8] it is preferable to nip its incipient life in the bud. This premise is likely to be an argument incident to advocacy of liberalized abortion based on social necessity.[9] Adoption of the first view of fetal life impels rejection of all abortion, or any abortion unnecessary to save the life of the mother;[10] to adopt the second usually is to favor abortion in a relatively wider array of instances.

The second focus is pregnant women.[11] Most of those concerned with their legal position favor a free choice on their part; that, indeed, is a strong dimension of the Supreme Court's constitutional analysis.[12] The only exception is the contention that intercourse producing pregnancy is licit only if done within marriage and for procreation,[13] and that an unwanted pregnancy is not only unfortunate, but the fulfillment of divine mandate as well. Hence, a woman must carry a fetus to term, whatever the consequences. This school of thought aside, most statements of policy are sympathetic toward pregnant women, although not all of them favor a completely free choice in the matter of abortion;[14] health concerns are paramount.

A third focus can be the family unit of which a pregnant woman is a part and into which a new baby will be born. Some stress concern for the freedom of sexual partners to decide whether and when they will have children.[15] Others emphasize the economic well-being of the whole family, which may be affected adversely if limited resources must be stretched to care for another member, or the emotional deprivation experienced by living siblings if parental care is diluted by yet another addition to the family unit.[16] Concentration on factors like these almost always leads to support of liberal abortion.

A final focus is on the needs of the community. Any of the concerns already listed, of course, can be restated in terms of social interests (*e.g.*, protection of life of fetus or pregnant woman, protection of maternal health, or protection of the health of a viable family unit). But within the community dimension there are at least two additional concerns. One is the factor of population control. Abortion clearly can be a means of birth control, albeit a much less satisfactory form than mechanical or chemical contraceptive methods.[17] The population control use of abortion has been evident in some cultures in recent times,[18] but as programs promoting contraception have become increasingly effective, reliance on abortion for that purpose has become less necessary, at least in certain educational and economic strata.

Some writers have suggested that legalized abortion as a means of population control manifests an impermissible exercise of state power,[19] or have expressed fears that it will result in too stark a decline in population levels to permit the state to survive.[20] In reality, however, abortion produces only incidental population control consequences,[21] and so poses no serious threat either to population levels or to citizens' liberties.[22] A second social factor repeatedly advanced in support of freer abortion has been the freedom of the medical profession to approach termination of pregnancies on the same basis as other medical problems, free from arbitrary controls. This, too, has found strong support in the United States Supreme Court's constitutional jurisprudence.[23]

These concerns, then, although not necessarily comprehensive, demonstrate the principal policy interests implicated by abortion legislation and constitutional precedents governing it. In most American jurisdictions to 1967, abortions were allowed only to save the lives of pregnant women;[24] to activists within the self-proclaimed right-to-life movement, the United States Constitution should be amended today to prohibit all abortions, or at a minimum all that are unnecessary to save maternal life. The Supreme Court's constitutional analysis, in contrast, recognizes freedom of choice early in pregnancy for any woman who, in consultation with a physician willing as a professional to perform it, chooses abortion; as pregnancy advances, medical considerations become more significant but can never be eclipsed by a desire solely to preserve fetal life. Accordingly, the tension in the 1980s is between abortion as a dimension of medical practice and prohibition of abortion as unwarranted termination of human fetal life. Abortion for purposes of population control, eugenics, or preservation of family strength and harmony is not within the ambit of the Supreme Court's constitutional concerns, and finds no home in today's legislative chambers. For now, concerns of this nature are the stuff of moral, ethical, and theological debate, not litigation or the legislative process.

II. Legal Regulation of Abortion Before 1967[25]

A. Criminal Statutes

1. STATUTES PENALIZING ABORTION   Criminal statutes outlawing abortion were of relatively recent vintage;[26] common law precedent was so scant that it played no significant role in evaluating the legality of abortions.[27] Statutes were roughly classifiable into those that prohibited all abortions and those that allowed some abortions under carefully limited circumstances. The laws of four states[28] provided no exceptions to a general prohibition against abortion, although judicial interpretations softened the harsh impact of the legislation.[29] In the remaining states and the District of Columbia, abortions were permissible to preserve maternal life.

Even during that era, a few states went beyond saving the lives of pregnant women. Seven permitted abortions to preserve the life of an unborn child,[30] a qualification with little or no other effect than to exempt induced labor at or near term from the scope of abortion law.[31] Two states allowed abortions necessary to forestall serious and permanent bodily injury,[32] while two other jurisdictions recognized any maternal health considerations.[33]

A number of difficult legal problems arose in administering restrictive legislation. One had to do with classes of persons authorized to perform abortions in instances of exigency. Twenty-four states appeared to allow anyone to perform an abortion,[34] while the rest required that abortions be done by physicians or surgeons. A second legal problem turned on whether necessity was to be determined on an objective or strict liability basis, or whether a good faith belief in the existence of justifying medical grounds would suffice. Many statutes seemingly defined necessity as an objective element of the crime,[35] although some courts interpreted them to embrace a good faith professional belief that necessity existed, despite the rather plain statutory language to the contrary.[36] The harshness of the usual language was ameliorated to some extent if the burden of proving want of medical necessity was placed on the prosecution.[37] Legislation in three states[33] and the District of Columbia were specific that belief or motivation, and not objective necessity, governed the statutory exception from coverage.

The common-law requirement that a fetus be quick before there could be a criminal abortion[39] had disappeared from statute law, which in 29 states[40] referred only to pregnancy; three other states used the phrase, "whether quick or not."[41] Duration of pregnancy had begun to reemerge as a legal element of abortion in a handful of states that had begun to expand the scope of noncriminal abortion; therapeutic abortions were limited in three states to the period of nonviability,[42] while six others set forth a limited time in terms of weeks or months.[43]

Another array of legal problems arose when, despite efforts to abort a woman, no miscarriage occurred. This might have resulted from an interrupted or incompetently performed abortion or from the fact the woman was not pregnant. Some 32 states[44] and the District of Columbia eliminated the first problem by penalizing the administration of drugs, use of instrument, or any other means intended to produce an abortion. If a woman was not pregnant, however, it might have been argued under common law concepts that the crime was "impossible" to attempt.[45] Such a defense was unavailable under abortion statutes that prohibited abortion activity affecting "any woman,"[46] a woman "whether pregnant or not,"[47] or a woman believed by a defendant to be pregnant.[48] Several courts relied on such language to affirm convictions for abortion even though the affected women were not pregnant.[49]

2. STATUTES PROHIBITING KILLING UNBORN QUICK CHILDREN   Six states made it a separate offense willfully to kill an unborn quick child under circumstances in which, had the mother and not the fetus been killed, the crime would have been murder.[50] The aim of these generally quite elderly statutes was not entirely evident from either language or interpreting precedent, but their target probably was those who intended to cause pregnant women to miscarry without their consent and who used physical violence against them for the purpose.[51]

3. STATUTES PENALIZING DEATH OF PREGNANT WOMEN RESULTING FROM ABORTION   Under classical theory, should a pregnant woman die as a result of a criminal abortion, the abortionist should be guilty of either second-degree murder, based on felony murder in the setting of a felony not enumerated under traditional first-degree murder statutes, the intentional infliction of grave bodily injury, or the reckless performance of activity with known dangerous consequences, or manslaughter based on criminal negligence.[52] Several states, however, confronted such cases directly by providing for augmented punishment for abortion should a woman die as a result,[53] or by characterizing the death as either murder[54] or manslaughter.[55]

4. STATUTES PENALIZING WOMEN WHO SEEK ABORTIONS   In default of specific legislation, women who sought or submitted to abortions were generally not viewed as accomplices to the crime.[56] Rhode Island and Vermont preserved that doctrine by statute.[57] In several states, however, legislatures decreed that women who solicited or submitted to abortions were criminals.[58] These statutes had two significant legal consequences and one practical result as well.

One was that accompanying statutes sometimes required corroboration of a woman's testimony,[59] or were interpreted in that way.[60] A second was that, as putative criminal defendants, women who underwent abortions could claim privilege against self-incrimination when summoned to testify for the prosecution against an abortionist.[61] Because, however, that testimony frequently is critical to establishing guilt, some legislatures either purported to abolish privilege in such cases[62] or conferred immunity on women who testified against prosecution for complicity in abortion.[63] That brought the matter around full circle to where it would have been had participating women not been denominated criminals in the first place.[64] However, legislation penalizing women abortion patients may have conferred a practical advantage on prosecutors by allowing them to threaten prosecution if women did not cooperate and to promise immunity from prosecution if they did.

5. STATUTES PENALIZING ACTIVITY FACILITATING PERFORMANCE OF ABORTIONS   Physicians performing abortions use instruments that are part of the ordinary equipment of gynecologists and obstetricians.[65] It is unrealistic for law enforcement officials to try to control traffic in such instruments; in any event, the very nature of physician and hospital supply channels makes it unlikely that laypersons can procure them. In the decades before Roe v. Wade, however,

self-induced abortions were a major public health problem,[66] and the devices and chemical substances used were clearly identifiable and devoid of legitimate modern uses. Therefore, they were controllable without adverse impact on legitimate medical practice, and legislatures consistently tried to control their availability.

Advertising abortifacients was penalized in 23 states. In 19 of them, a special statute covered abortifacients either alone or in the context of medicines preventing conception, curing venereal disease, and the like,[67] while in others the prohibition appeared in the context of obscenity regulation.[68] The unconstitutionality of this form of legislation was recognized only recently.[69] State legislatures also sought to regulate commerce in abortifacients by prohibiting their manufacture,[70] distribution,[71] furnishing,[72] sale or keeping or exposing for sale,[73] giving away,[74] or lending.[75] Two states required all sales to be under registerable prescriptions.[76] Oregon penalized those who furnished premises knowing that nontherapeutic abortions would be performed there. Most of this legislation, too, is incompatible with modern First Amendment notions.[77]

III. Accelerating Trends Toward Legalized Therapeutic Abortion: 1968–73

A. Coverage of Revised Abortion Legislation

1. GROUNDS FOR THERAPEUTIC ABORTIONS   The Model Penal Code,[78] promulgated by the American Law Institute in 1962, asserted a strong and perhaps paramount influence on a legislative expansion of the grounds for legal abortion during the period 1968–73. The code posited the lawfulness of abortions necessary to safeguard the physical and mental health of pregnant women; 13 states had recognized that ground by 1973.[79] A second ground for abortion, accepted in 12 states, allowed pregnancies to be terminated on eugenic grounds, *i.e.*, because a fetus if born would be seriously handicapped mentally or physically.[80] A third, based on humanitarian considerations, permitted victims of rape[81] or incest[82] to have their pregnancies terminated. Three states, however, went far beyond the Model Penal Code pattern to eliminate all restrictions on medically indicated abortions.[83] Consequently, only those jurisdictions were relatively free of impact from the 1973 Supreme Court decisions in *Roe* and *Doe,* as far as grounds for justifiable abortion were concerned.

2. LENGTH OF PREGNANCY   As mentioned earlier,[84] length of pregnancy often bore on the lawfulness of therapeutic abortions. Even the three most liberal states before 1973, therefore, found this dimension of their statutes invalidated.

3. RESIDENCY REQUIREMENTS   As some legislatures expanded the permissible scope of therapeutic abortions, they manifested a fear that their states would become abortion havens for residents of other jurisdictions with restrictive laws. Therefore, a number required periods of residency before an otherwise lawful abortion could be performed.[85] Such legislation usually placed the burden on pregnant women to assert residency, not on physicians to ascertain the truth of claims of residency; only the Georgia and Virginia statutes attached perjury consequences to declarations of residency. These statutes fell under *Doe v. Bolton.*[86]

4. PRELIMINARY APPROVAL BY MEDICAL PEERS   Even before the abortion law revision movement, a number of states required[87] or permitted, as an

alternative to an operating physician's professional judgment,[88] the advice of other independent physicians. Later legislation generally mandated preliminary consultation with or approval by medical colleagues before abortions could be performed. Approval could be gained through certification by medical practitioners other than a physician wishing to terminate a pregnancy,[89] approval by a hospital review committee,[90] or both.[91] Because peer concurrence took time, several states legislated an emergency exception if a woman's life was in jeopardy unless an abortion were performed immediately; a ratification of medical necessity had to be obtained swiftly after an abortion.[92] The degree to which such requirements have survived the Court's 1973 abortion decisions will be discussed below.[93]

5. SPECIAL APPROVAL IN RAPE AND INCEST CASES   Statutes that allowed abortion in rape and incest cases on humanitarian grounds[94] generally required some form of substantiation of a woman's claim of violation, because purely medical grounds did not necessarily justify abortion in all instances of sexual assaults. Sometimes some form of complaint or affidavit by a victim sufficed,[95] but more commonly approval or certification by prosecuting authorities was needed.[96]

6. PERSONS AUTHORIZED TO PERFORM ABORTIONS   Revised statutes before 1973 all required terminations of pregnancy to be performed by physicians licensed in the jurisdiction.[97] The statutes did not touch on the legal status of those such as nurses and medical paraprofessionals who performed or participated in lawful therapeutic abortions, but one may assume that prosecuting authorities were unenthusiastic about prosecuting persons acting in such a capacity; no precedent on the matter emerged, at any rate.

7. PLACE OF PERFORMANCE OF ABORTIONS   Statutes that restricted the grounds for lawful abortion to health, eugenic, or humanitarian concerns almost always required abortions to be performed in accredited hospitals.[98] Two states, however, allowed abortions to be performed in approved clinics away from full-service hospitals.[99] The unconstitutionality of some situs restrictions is discussed below.[100]

8. REQUIRED RECORDS AND REPORTS   As legislatures began to recognize the licitness of medically indicated abortions, they also instituted recordkeeping and reporting requirements. Sometimes, applications or certificates needed only to be retained in medical office or hospital patient files,[101] but periodic reports to state agencies came increasingly to be mandated.[102] Requirements usually were imposed that the identity of abortion patients be kept confidential. The constitutionality of much broader contemporary reporting legislation is commented on below.[103]

9. FREEDOM OF CONSCIENCE EXEMPTIONS   Many doctors, nurses, and hospitals employees have strong religious or moral scruples against abortion, and many private, particularly church-affiliated, hospitals will not tolerate the performance of abortions on their premises. As therapeutic abortion came increasingly to be recognized, the question arose whether individuals or hospitals could refrain legally from participation. Many states had legislated to allow a freedom of conscience exemption;[104] the number of such statutes has markedly increased since *Roe* and *Doe* were decided.[105]

B. Resort to Litigation: The New Frontier

The wave or, perhaps more accurately, ripple of legislative reform probably had peaked by 1973. In any event, advocacy increased rapidly for constitutional invalidation of legislative restrictions on therapeutic abortion.[106] The principal grounds advanced were vagueness and indefiniteness in abortion legislation denying due process of law;[107] infringement of equal protection, through either an arbitrary legislative classification of eligibility and ineligibility for abortion[108] or financial discrimination against indigents;[109] or invasion of a constitutionally protected right of privacy.[110] What might have evolved from a long process of constitutional litigation is unknowable, because the Supreme Court in 1973 asserted its primacy in the constitutional regulation of abortion legislation.

IV. Basic Constitutional Doctrine

As matters eventuated, the Court built its doctrinal framework on the constitutional right to privacy, which it thought "broad enough to encompass a woman's decision whether or not to terminate her pregnancy."[111] It has adhered to that analysis in cases since,[112] most recently in 1983 in *Akron v. Akron Center for Reproductive Health*.[113] In selecting that rationale, it specifically repudiated the claim that fetuses are "persons" within the meaning of the Fourteenth Amendment: "[T]he unborn have never been recognized as persons in the whole sense."[114] Thus, a human being entitled to direct constitutional protection emerges at live birth, not conception;[115] that premise, too, the Court since has reaffirmed.[116]

The Court's basic constitutional premise is also attested by the Court's rulings on standing to attack abortion legislation. A woman who is pregnant at the time legal action commences[117] has standing because her right of privacy is directly affected by legal prohibitions against abortion,[118] but married women (with their husbands) who assert they might become pregnant in the future and require termination of pregnancy for health reasons do not.[119] Doctors who may be prosecuted or otherwise interfered with in their practice also are directly affected[120] (for reasons expanded on immediately below), as are clinics and facilities providing abortion services.[121]

Having recognized that women's claims to abortion find support in a constitutional right to privacy, the Court nevertheless rejected the contention that such a right is absolute, allowing a woman "to terminate her pregnancy at whatever time, in whatever way, and for whatever reason she alone chooses."[122] A "pregnant woman cannot be isolated in her privacy," for she "carries an embryo and, later, a fetus."[123] Accordingly, abortion is never completely free from state regulation, although the scope of state powers grows slowly with a pregnancy and has ceiling limitations far lower than those recognized in state legislation before 1973.

Thus, during approximately the first trimester of pregnancy[124] "the abortion decision and its effectuation must be left to the medical judgment of the pregnant woman's attending physician, without interference from the State."[125] "The participation by the attending physician in the abortion decision, and his responsibility in that decision"[126] underlie the standing accorded to physicians to litigate abortion decisions.[127] During early pregnancy, minor regulations can be imposed if they further "important health-related State concerns," but only if they do not "interfere with the physician-patient consultation or with the woman's choice between abortion and childbirth."[128]

After the first stage, states may choose to impose reasonable restrictions reasonably relating to the preservation and protection of maternal health,[129] but state regulation cannot "depart from accepted medical practice" or increase the costs and limit the availability of abortions "without promoting important health benefits."[130] After viability,[131] a state "may regulate an abortion to protect the life of the fetus and even may proscribe abortion except where it is necessary, in appropriate medical judgment, for the preservation of the life or health of the mother."[132]

These, then, are the basics of the Court's regulation of abortion, the constitutional structure for most of its decisions on specific aspects of abortion law. That does not mean, however, that no other constitutional rationales will be invoked. For example, the Court has relied on the vagueness and indefiniteness concept under the due process clause[133] to strike down penal statutes invoked against physicians.[134] Equal protection, in contrast, has not had significant impact on abortion law.[135] Against this constitutional background, an evaluation of the coverage and constitutionality of current state abortion legislation is in order, the matter to which we turn now.

V. Scope and Constitutionality of Current Abortion Legislation[136]

A. Legislative Responses to the 1973 Decisions

The initial impact of *Roe* and *Doe* was manifested by state high court decisions invalidating traditional abortion legislation.[137] On occasion, legislatures apparently decided to do nothing. The recent New Jersey criminal code contains no abortion provisions,[138] while the text of the Texas provisions no longer appears, having been replaced by a notation of "unconstitutional."[139] Most legislatures, however, revamped their statutes in response to or anticipation of judicial invalidation of pre-1973 legislation.

A handful of states retained[140] or adopted[141] a policy of leaving regulation of therapeutic abortion exclusively or for the most part to administrative agencies. Most, however, accomplished substantial revisions with the Supreme Court's constitutional principles as their guide.[142] Several legislatures, however, voiced their restiveness or outright opposition to the Court's doctrine. Some stated a preference for normal childbirth over abortion,[143] and others affirmed the state's obligation to protect human life whether unborn or not.[144] Nebraska objected to Supreme Court "intrusion" and "deplored" the destruction of unborn human lives which would result,[145] while Montana announced its intent to restrict abortions to the extent it could do so constitutionally.[146] Illinois[147] and Kentucky[148] declared their intent to prohibit abortions should the Supreme Court reverse its constitutional stance or should the Constitution be amended to permit them to do so. Idaho has gone the furthest in that regard. It has standby provisions[149] to come into force through gubernatorial proclamation should the constitutional picture change.[150] Obviously, legislative resonations of that sort, while therapeutic for anti-abortion legislators and their constituents, have no legal force and must be ignored by state judges.

States vary in the placement of therapeutic abortion provisions within the body of statutes. Some have continued the tradition of penal code regulation supported by ancillary provisions elsewhere, but a great many have chosen the context of laws governing the healing professions with residual or ancillary criminal provisions. The statutory analysis that follows looks first at civil or civil-oriented legislation, then at criminal law provisions, and finally at restrictions affecting publicly funded abortion services.

B. Noncriminal Regulation of Therapeutic Abortion

1.   DEFINITIONS   *(a)* "Abortion"   The new focus on abortion as a medical technique has brought about modernized legal definitions, usually of the term "abortion," but sometimes of "miscarriage"[151] or "feticide."[152] A few statutes content themselves with defining abortion as termination of (human) pregnancy,[153] while others specify methods in a comprehensive way.[154] Abortion implies intent or purpose, but statutes frequently spell it out anyway, either generally[155] or in terms of intent to produce fetal death.[156] More frequently, the intent element is stated inversely, *i.e.*, a purpose other than to induce live birth[157] or to remove a dead fetus.[158] Only rarely does a definition of abortion include references to viability[159] or period of gestation;[160] such matters usually are dealt with in substantive provisions.

(b) "Conception"   A definition of conception probably is functionally unnecessary to delineate the scope of therapeutic abortion. Nevertheless, some states have specially provided one in neutral terms like "fecundation of the ovum by the spermatozoa."[161] Sometimes the definition relates to some other term like "pregnancy," but at others it ties to definitions of "fetus" or "unborn child," which themselves are of doubtful constitutionality if invoked to limit therapeutic abortions.[162]

(c) "Pregnancy"   The term "pregnancy" is defined variously as implantation of an embryo in the uterus,[163] or as the condition of a woman carrying a fetus or embryo within her body as a result of conception.[164] The first is another legislative means of exempting contraceptive techniques which prevent implantation (morning-after pills) from the coverage of abortion statutes,[165] but the second usually is tied to legislative descriptions of fetuses or unborn children.

(d) "Fetus" and related definitions   Those state legislatures that have defined "fetus" have not been motivated by a desire to assure medical personnel that medical terminology is recognized in the law. Instead, they seem to have used such definitions as another way of sniping at the Supreme Court.[166] Thus, Illinois states that "fetus" and "unborn child" each means a human being from fertilization until birth,[167] and Kentucky defines "fetus" the same way.[168] Other states use the term "unborn child" to the same effect.[169] To the extent provisions like this serve simply to vent legislative steam and soothe right-to-life constituents, no harm is done. If, however, they are intended to limit the availability of medically indicated abortions, they are a nullity under the Supreme Court's constitutional doctrine.

(e) "Trimester"   A few statutes contain definitions of trimesters, perhaps because that is significant under *Roe v. Wade*.[170] Idaho defines the first trimester as the first 13 weeks of pregnancy,[171] the second trimester as the portion of gestation between the 14th week and viability,[172] and the third as the segment after

viability.[173] Pennsylvania uses the period of 12 weeks.[174] Illinois delineates the first trimester as 12 weeks from ovulation rather than computed on the basis of menstrual cycle,[175] while South Carolina computes it from conception.[176] Indiana divides each pregnancy into three equal parts of three months each.[177]

It should be noted that in 1983 the Supreme Court selected the beginning of the last menstrual period experienced by a woman impregnated thereafter,[178] and adhered to a trimester analysis as "a reasonable legal framework for limiting a State's authority to regulate abortions."[179] To the extent that state legislatures uses a variant definition to limit the availability of abortions which the federal Constitution guarantees, they invite invalidation of the offending provisions.[180]

(f) "Viability"   The point of viability is important under the Supreme Court's delineation of constitutionally protected abortion;[181] it defined viability as the point in a pregnancy at which "the fetus is 'potentially able to live outside the mother's womb, albeit with artificial aid,' and presumably capable of 'meaningful life outside the mother's womb,' [which] 'is usually placed' at about seven months or 28 weeks, but may occur earlier."[182] Quite a number of states have picked up that language or a near variant of it.[183] That is obviously the only safe course, because the Court is clear that viability cannot be determined arbitrarily in terms of time, but must rest on each woman's pregnancy.[184]

(g) "Live born"   Four statutes contain definitions of live birth and live born.[185] These do not impact directly on abortion, but are relevant in connection with legal responsibility to safeguard the lives of viable fetuses born alive during or as a consequence of an abortion.[186]

2.   PERSONS PERFORMING ABORTIONS   Roe v. Wade was explicit that abortion is a medical matter and that licit abortions must be performed by professionally qualified persons.[187] Accordingly, therapeutic abortion laws are uniform in restricting the performance of abortions to licensed physicians.[188] The converse of this is that persons other than physicians who perform abortions can be punished.[189] Perhaps the only potential area of litigation lurks in the question of whether nurses or medical paraprofessionals who perform abortions during the first trimester under the direction and supervision of a licensed physician, following accepted medical techniques, can be prosecuted because they are not licensed physicians. One may assume that if a restriction of lawful abortion to licensed physicians is not consonant with accepted medical practice, and a consequence is to impede pregnant women in their quest for lawful abortions, the restriction is constitutionally unacceptable.[190]

3.   PHYSICIAN-PATIENT CONSULTATION   The Supreme Court has spoken of abortion as something based on physician-patient consultation;[191] consent by the patient is a condition to lawful abortion.[192] Counseling is reflected in different ways in legislation. It may be sanctioned for minors,[193] or posited as an appropriate subject of administrative regulation.[194] As a form of consumer protection law, institutions announcing the availability of counseling services must have qualified staff members to provide it.[195] Illinois and Pennsylvania specifically require it as a condition for a determination that an abortion is necessary.[196] Some legislation,[197] however, clearly is ancillary to more elaborate statutory requirements concerning information that must be communicated to pregnant women before they can consent to abortion. If the informational process

functions to deter or impede decisions to have abortions, it is unconstitutional,[198] and associated counseling requirements will fall with it.

4.   INFORMATION TO PATIENT   An informed consent is a prerequisite to a lawful therapeutic abortion.[199] Therefore, a patient must be given information about "just what would be done and . . . its consequences,"[200] and state legislation may ensure that her decision is made "in the light of all attendant circumstances—psychological and emotional as well as physical—that might be relevant to the well-being of the patient."[201] In the case of immature minors, state concerns to protect pregnant girls and to promote family integrity justify special measures to ensure that "the abortion decision is made with understanding and after careful deliberation."[202] A sizable number of states have picked up on this dimension of the Court's jurisprudence, in some instances to implement its intent but at times with an obvious purpose of scaring patients away from decisions to seek abortions. The latter form of legislation has produced a new level of constitutional intervention by the Court.[203]

Statutes call for communicating information that, in a physician's best professional judgment, a woman is pregnant[204] and the length of the pregnancy to the time of consultation.[205] They require information about the abortion procedure to be used[206] and the effects[207] and risks[208] associated with abortion. Three states call for patients to be provided with the name of the physician who will perform the abortion.[209] Several authorize communication of any other information a counselor believes significant to an informed consent.[210] With the possible exception of certain language in the Missouri, Nevada, and North Dakota statutes bearing on the consequences of abortion, which may or may not be supportable by current medical knowledge,[211] the information required to be given is compatible with the Supreme Court's expectations.[212] That probably cannot be said, however, of requirements that pregnant women be told about the use of anesthesia or analgesics to prevent fetal pain[213] or informed that abortion is a major surgical technique.[214]

A very common legislative requirement is that a pregnant woman be told about alternatives to abortion,[215] including the availability of services and financial aid,[216] adoption,[217] and counseling.[218] In several states, public agencies are available to help women if they request.[219] One state provides for advice that a woman cannot be denied public assistance if she refuses to consent to an abortion.[220] With some hesitancy, one can assume that these requirements, standing alone, may be imposed constitutionally. The Court noted that "a State is not always foreclosed from asserting an interest in whether pregnancies end in abortion or childbirth,"[221] and information about alternatives and support services appears to be as necessary for an informed selection among alternatives as information about the medical dimensions of abortion and childbirth.

The same cannot be said, however, of statutory requirements that patients be told the specifics of fetal development and characteristics. Utah has gone the furthest in that regard,[222] but several other states require similar information.[223] The Supreme Court voided language typical of these statutes because it "would involve at best speculation by the physician."[224] Therefore, one may doubt that a physician or counselor constitutionally could be prosecuted for a failure to comply with legislative requirements that seem on their face to be intended to discourage free choice of abortion, and not to provide neutral information relevant to a woman's decision.

In sum, although some of the specific information required under several state laws cannot constitutionally be required of physicians, most of the individual requirements are probably valid. Nevertheless, if one stands apart and surveys the totality of information mandated in some jurisdictions, particularly Illinois, Kentucky, Missouri, Nevada, North Dakota, Pennsylvania, Tennessee, and Utah, the legislative purpose seems clear to discourage consents to abortion, a governmental motive that the Supreme Court has declared unconstitutional.[225]

There is one other dimension of unconstitutionality in many information statutes. Some do not specify who must impart the information,[226] or allow for alternative sources to physicians personally.[227] A number of states, however, require physicians, often on threat of criminal penalties, to communicate the information personally.[228] The Supreme Court invalidated that approach in *Akron v. Akron Center for Reproductive Health,*[229] although it confirmed that a physician cannot abdicate his or her ultimate responsibility for the medical aspects of abortion. Therefore, states can require physicians to verify that adequate counseling has been provided and that a patient's consent is informed, and to ensure that counseling is provided by qualified persons.

One may also note in passing that two states require information to be given to spouses,[230] and in one state to parents or guardians.[231] The legitimacy of these mandates turns on the constitutionality of requiring spousal or parental consent, a matter covered below.[232]

5. CONSENT *(a) General requirements* As noted, medically indicated abortions must be consented to.[233] That means a free choice on a woman's part, free from any coercion.[234] It is common to encyst the requirement of consent in legislation,[235] quite frequently with the additional mandate that a consent be in writing[236] or certified.[237] Consent may be dispensed with only in cases of emergency threatening a woman's life[238] or health.[239] Otherwise, criminal[240] or civil[241] sanctions may be visited on those who perform abortions.

(b) Consent by minor A minor pregnant female must consent to an abortion in the same way as her elders. This is noted specifically in some statutes,[242] subject to an emergency exception.[243] The bulk of litigation, however, has been generated by requirements of consent by parents or legal guardians.[244]

(c) Consent by parent or guardian It has been common to require consent by both parents,[245] one parent,[246] or a guardian[247] before an unmarried, unemancipated minor can have the abortion she wants. A guardian may be given the exclusive power to decide whether someone judically determined to be mentally incompetent will have an abortion.[248]

The constitutionality of these provisions has been the object of considerable decisional law. During the first trimester of pregnancy, a state cannot impose a blanket requirement that every pregnant minor obtain the consent of a parent or guardian;[249] a minor pregnant woman's consent controls if she is capable of giving it.[250] If a minor is unmarried and unemancipated, and there is doubt whether the minor can make an informed consent to an abortion, the Court has indicated that either parental[251] or judicial[252] consent may be required. To the extent that state statutes recognize complete discretion on the part of emancipated (or married) minors to select abortion as the mode of terminating their pregnancies, and provide expeditious judicial proceedings to determine whether unemancipated minors are capable of choice, they are constitutional. Many states, however, have not revised their legislation to reflect the refinements expected by the Supreme Court.

(d) Spousal consent   The Supreme Court invalidated all requirements of spousal consent,[253] which has shifted legislative attention in most jurisdictions to spousal notification as a condition to abortion.[254] Nevertheless, a few states continue to retain in their codes a requirement of spousal consent;[255] this probably reflects a disinclination to recognize Supreme Court doctrine, but serves only to impel judicial nullification. If statutes refer to spousal consent for minor married women and mental incompetents,[256] issues of constitutionality should be resolved on the basis of parental consent in such instances.[257]

(e) Judicial approval for abortions   As noted, the Court has required that if a minor is not emancipated, a state may require either parental consent or a judicial determination in lieu of it.[258] If there is no specific legislation, a parental consent requirement will be ruled unconstitutional.[259] Several states have provided for such a judicial avenue.[260] If the procedures are clear and expeditious, such legislation will be sustained as a legitimate alternative to parental consent for minors incapable of giving it.[261] However, if a court concludes that a minor is competent to give an informed consent, it can only certify that fact, allowing the minor to exercise her *Roe v. Wade* rights; it cannot forbid an abortion because it believes she ought not have one. The latter determination is to be made only if the minor is not capable of consenting; denial of an abortion then must rest on a showing that abortion is inimical to her best interests.[262]

6.   NOTICE TO PARENTS AND SPOUSES   When most legislation requiring parental or spousal consent to abortion fell before the Court's constitutional axe, a number of states substituted requirements that parents[263] or spouses[264] be given notice[265] before an abortion is performed[266] of that fact; sometimes, the same litany of information required to be given a patient[267] must be given along with the basic notice.[268]

The Supreme Court has not yet ruled directly in a majority opinion on the constitutionality of such notice statutes. If statutes require that information be given to parents or spouses which, if required to be communicated to pregnant women, would place an obstacle in the way of a free choice, they are probably unconstitutional, because they are designed to increase pressures from family members against abortions. If notice is restricted to the fact of abortion, but goes to one whose consent cannot be required constitutionally, one may ask what function it is to play. Language in some of the opinions in *H.L. v. Matheson*[269] suggests that if a pregnant minor is not emancipated, but still a part of a family unit, a parental notice requirement promotes familial harmony and an ability on the part of parents to help a daughter make an informed choice. If, however, a minor is emancipated or alienated from her parent, a requirement of parental notice would appear to impose a burden on the minor's free choice and thus to be unconstitutional; at least one court has so ruled.[270] If a spousal consent requirement is unconstitutional, and notice is a preliminary to exercise of a power to consent, one may doubt the constitutionality of a duty to inform imposed on physicians. If, however, some other interest, for example, the maintenance of interspousal harmony, is promoted by a notice requirement, not outweighed by its impact on a woman's free exercise of discretion under *Roe v. Wade*, there is at least an arguable basis for sustaining a spousal notice requirement.[271]

7. GROUNDS FOR ABORTION   *(a) Incest*   Several states have continued their pre-*Roe* coverage of incest as a humanitarian basis for abortion[272] in current statutes.[273] Laws of this nature should be unconstitutional if they are invoked to prevent abortions otherwise medically justified under *Roe v. Wade,*[274] but if they legitimate abortions not based strictly on medical considerations (assuming pregnancies from such causes do not cause sufficient emotional trauma to constitute a medical ground), they probably are constitutional.[275]

(b) Rape   Rape as a humanitarian ground for abortion, recognized before 1973,[276] continues to be acknowledged in some legislation,[277] in some instances subject to rape or confirmation requirements.[278] The constitutionality of such provisions turns on the same considerations mentioned in the context of incest as a ground for abortion.[279]

(c) Physical or mental defect in child if born alive   Abortion based on eugenic considerations was acknowledged in some states before *Roe v. Wade,*[280] and continues to be today in a few jurisdictions.[281] The constitutionality of this form of legislation turns on whether, in an obverse application of *Roe v. Wade* principles,[282] the potentiality of human life in a fetus precludes abortions on this basis if not otherwise medically indicated from the standpoint of maternal life or health.

(d) Maternal life   As discussed earlier, for many years in almost every jurisdiction, abortions could be performed only to save the life of a pregnant woman.[283] Some states have continued this as the sole basis for lawful abortions,[284] in some instances only in later stages of gestation.[285] There may be no constitutional barrier to recognizing this as an exception to an aggravating factor under penal statutes when abortions are performed other than by licensed physicians in later stages of pregnancies[286] (even granted the rarity of cases in which laypersons properly could manage abortions), or in limiting availability of public funds for abortions unless danger to maternal life is involved.[287] But limiting legislation of this sort is unconstitutional if invoked to prevent a woman and her physician from reaching an abortion decision within the parameters of *Roe v. Wade*. Perpetuation of such statutes can be attributed only to legislative inertia or reluctance to acknowledge Supreme Court doctrine.[288]

(e) Maternal life or health   Several states have continued a requirement that all abortions be based on considerations of maternal life or health,[289] frequently qualified by a requirement like "gravely impair."[290] This form of legislation, however, is unconstitutional under *Roe v. Wade,*[291] which makes "medical judgment" the criterion during the first trimester of pregnancy, and regulation of abortion procedures "reasonably related to maternal health" the standard during the period before viability. Only after viability does the criterion of "preservation of life or health of the mother" become valid.[292] Many states, therefore, have legislated the "life or health" standard only for abortions following viability[293] or after a stated number of weeks of gestation.[294]

The difficulty with the latter standard, however, is that, although there may have been a basis in *Roe v. Wade* for use of a time standard as an alternative to viability, the Supreme Court has rejected it in the setting of the place of performance of abortions; viability is the sole acceptable criterion in that context.[295] Hence, application of the "life or health" standard before actual viability in each pregnancy risks a declaration of unconstitutionality if physicians are prosecuted, sued, or disciplined for performing medically indicated abortions in the period between the beginning of the statutorily prescribed period and viability.

(f) General medical grounds   Roe v. Wade, as noted, legitimates the constitutional claim of pregnant women to abortions before viability if medically indicated.[296] Some states acknowledge the constitutional norm only indirectly by legislating specific standards following viability.[297] Several others, however, have enacted the Supreme Court standard or an equivalent.[298] Such legislation has no observable constitutional defect, but is probably superfluous.

8.   RESIDENCY REQUIREMENTS   A small residue of states[299] retains a residency requirement[300] limiting the availability of abortions. These statutes are unconstitutional;[301] their continued presence in statute books reflects legislative inertia or unwillingness to acknowledge constitutional doctrine.

9.   PLACE OF PERFORMANCE   A few states retain requirements that all abortions be performed in hospitals licensed by the state,[302] accredited by outside agencies,[303] or both.[304] Invoked as a limitation on performance of first-trimester abortions, such restrictions violate the constitutional rights of pregnant women and their physicians.[305] Language in Doe v. Bolton was taken, however, to approve a prohibition against abortions after the first trimester elsewhere than a hospital. Accordingly, a lengthy roster of states has legislated an in-hospital requirement.[306] In hindsight, reliance on Supreme Court dicta proved unfortunate, because in 1983 the Court invalidated all statutes requiring performance of abortions in general hospitals between the beginning of the second trimester of pregnancy and viability.[307] A state must allow abortions during that time to be performed in clinics and outpatient facilities as well as hospitals; statutes so providing are constitutional.[308] Several states have had such legislation in place for some years.[309]

A few states have provided specifically for the licensing and regulation of abortion clinics.[310] Although the limited authority is not unanimous, licensing is constitutional as long as its attendant requirements promote maternal health and do not impose unacceptable barriers against women's free exercise of the right to choose abortion.[311] Requirements that designated personnel be in attendance, not mandated by medical needs,[312] that equipment be provided not dictated by good medical practice,[313] or that clinic physicians maintain a hospital affiliation[314] have been declared unconstitutional. One may assume like vulnerability in statutes prohibiting fees or compensation for abortion referrals[315] or abortion referrals for profit.[316] Administrative search provisions may also infringe patients' rights to privacy.[317] However, if regulations otherwise are constitutional, there should be no infirmity in legislation allowing nuisance abatement procedures against places where abortions are performed in violation of law.[318]

10.   PEER APPROVAL   A few states have preserved statutes requiring that all abortions be concurred in by other physicians,[319] hospital review committees,[320] or both.[321] The Supreme Court invalidated both requirements, at least as far as first-trimester abortions are concerned.[322] Accordingly, legislation was approved in some jurisdictions requiring such approval in the third trimester[323] or after viability.[324] Mandates of this sort are probably constitutional if applied after

viability, since the Court in result approved a requirement that a second physician be in attendance at the time of an abortion after viability.[325] Between the beginning of the second trimester and viability, however, limitations of this sort are likely to be viewed as barriers to women's free choice, unless similar requirements govern other medical and surgical techniques of approximately the same seriousness. There should be no impediment to requirements that, if a consulting physician refers the case to another physician for performance of an abortion, full medical details be transmitted.[326]

11. WAITING PERIODS A technique for delaying abortions has been to impose waiting periods between receipt of information required to be imparted to a woman,[327] her spouse,[328] or parent,[329] and performance of an abortion,[330] perhaps subject to an emergency exception if an abortion must be performed to protect maternal life or, in some instances, health.[331] Such requirements at times have been augmented by an ensuing waiting period between a woman's submission of a signed consent form and performance of an abortion,[332] again subject to an emergency exception.[333]

The Supreme Court has invalidated the latter form of waiting period[334] as an arbitrary, inflexible limitation without a medical basis, and a costly imposition that could require two separate trips to an abortion facility.[335] Although the Court did not have before it a mandated waiting period between receipt of information and submission of a consent, its rationale in *Akron* seems germane, particularly in light of the Court's invalidation of several items of information intended to discourage decisions to undergo an abortion.[336] Legislatures are best advised to eliminate all time-delay requirements in light of the Court's flexible, medically oriented approach to counseling and consent.[337]

12. ABORTION TECHNIQUES *(a) General standard of care* The Supreme Court's constitutional focus is on maternal health as the sole concern after the first trimester of pregnancy,[338] based on contemporary medical standards.[339] Hence, no legislative statement is required to establish positive medical standards for abortions; general licensure requirements suffice. Nevertheless, there is no constitutional defect in reaffirming in the setting of therapeutic abortion legislation the applicability of usual standards of professional care.[340] Constitutional problems arise only when statutes purport to restrict accepted medical practice.

(b) Precluded techniques At least two states continue to forbid the use of saline amniocentesis as an abortion technique after the first trimester of pregnancy, absent a special justification;[341] the objective is to impel use of other techniques that increase the possibility that a viable fetus might be born alive. The Supreme Court, however, has invalidated such prohibitions as not reasonably related to maternal health; they proscribe techniques which pose less of a risk to maternal health than those which would have to be used as an alternative.[342] Continuation of these statutes can only be attributed to a legislative unwillingness to bow to Supreme Court mandate; they are dead letters as to enforceability.

There appears no constitutional objection to a legislative restatement of the Court's doctrine in the form of a requirement that medical personnel use all reasonable medical procedures to enhance the live birth of a viable fetus if that is consistent with maternal health.[343] Only if maternal health were relegated to a subordinate status would there be a constitutional problem.[344]

(c) Testing requirements Two states require blood typing and Rh_o-testing

before an abortion may be performed.[345] To the extent such a requirement applies to second-trimester abortions before viability (and perhaps the stage of viability) when survival after live birth is medically impossible, it is probably unconstitutional under the Supreme Court's doctrine that all limitations on abortion be supported by current medical practice standards and paramount concerns for maternal health. If, in contrast, such legislation is interpreted to govern only those stages of pregnancy when live fetal birth is a medical possibility, there is probably no impermissible barrier to an unfettered abortion decision and its effectuation.

(d) *Attending physician*   Statutes occasionally require a second physician to be present when a viable fetus is aborted.[346] In result, the Supreme Court sustained such a legislative condition to abortion.[347] Its rationale, as far as can be gleaned from the judgmental majority's opinions, was that such a requirement reasonably relates to preservation of the life or health of a live-born fetus, without detrimental consequences to maternal health.

13.   STATUS OF INFANTS, FETUSES AND FETAL TISSUE   (a) *Live-born infants* There is no need for special statutes confirming that viable fetuses born alive are persons entitled to the full protection of civil and criminal law. Those who terminate human life, whether neonate or of greater duration, intentionally, recklessly, or with criminal negligence may be prosecuted for murder or manslaughter, and incur wrongful death liability as well if they act intentionally or negligently. Nevertheless, some statutes confirm in the setting of abortion legislation long-established general legal principles, by providing a definition of human life[348] or confirming a duty, usually enforced by criminal penalties,[349] to care for fetuses born alive.[350] Other provisions, perhaps reflecting difficult proof problems in establishing beyond a reasonable doubt the independent human existence of a fetus/child, legislate a special obligation to safeguard fetal life during abortion processes.[351] These are seemingly constitutional as long as, expressly or through judicial interpretation, the protection of maternal life or health takes priority over the preservation of fetal life.[352]

(b) *Experimentation involving fetuses*   Quite a number of states have prohibited experimentation with and research on embryos and fetuses before[353] and after[354] abortions and on stillborn[355] and live-born[356] infants. Exceptions, however, are provided to cover acts done to advance fetal[357] or maternal[358] health, and pathological examinations.[359] Traffic in fetal or neonate tissue for such purposes may also be penalized.[360] Limited authority sustains the constitutionality of such provisions.[361]

(c) *Tissue analysis*   Several states require that pathological examinations be performed on dead fetuses and on removed fetal tissue,[362] or at least contemplate that such examinations properly may be conducted.[363] The Supreme Court has sustained the constitutionality of such a requirement,[364] apparently because tissue examinations are an incident to surgical techniques generally and do not impose a special economic hardship on women desiring abortions.

(d) *Disposition of fetal remains*   Some states have legislated with reference to the disposition of fetal remains, sometimes through specific criminal legislation[365] and sometimes by recognizing the need for administrative regulations on the matter.[366] The Supreme Court invalidated a criminal statute requiring physicians to ensure that fetal remains be "disposed of in a humane and sanitary manner" on vagueness and indefiniteness grounds.[367] Arguably, a purely administrative law approach is not vulnerable as long as residual criminal penalties are not provided.

14. RECORDS AND REPORTS As noted earlier,[368] with the recognition of therapeutic abortions came a concern for documentation of the fact of and medical grounds for abortion. Since 1973, such requirements have become the norm. Physician and hospital records may have to reflect consents[369] and information given to patients,[370] as well as data of purely medical significance.[371] In addition, physicians and institutions are expected to submit statistical information,[372] more or less detailed information about each abortion,[373] or both. The contents of reports may be left for determination through administrative regulation or provision of state reporting forms.[374] Most legislation reflects the Supreme Court's concern[375] over patient privacy by requiring the names of patients[376] and at times physicians[377] to be kept confidential, subject perhaps to a possibility of disclosure through court order.[378] Hospitals also may be required to report to authorities cases of complications apparently flowing from abortions.[379]

Reporting and record-maintenance requirements are constitutional as long as they are not abused or overdone to the point they accomplish an unacceptable burden on exercise of the constitutional right to abortion.[380] For the most part, state laws appear to respect that qualification. A few, however, for example, Illinois, Nevada, Oklahoma, Pennsylvania, and Utah, decree such detailed requirements or tie report contents to matters of consent and information (some of which are unconstitutional in isolation), that one may doubt they are consonant with the Supreme Court's concerns.

15. SANCTIONS Many of the details of therapeutic abortion practice are found outside criminal codes. Nevertheless, supplementary criminal penalties may well be provided,[381] in addition to criminal penalties attached to nontherapeutic abortions.[382] In general, the former are directed at medical personnel who fail to conform to statutory requirements, while the latter have laypersons as their targets. Moreover, participation in criminal abortions is usually a basis for professional discipline.[383] Wrongful death liability also may be confirmed specifically in abortion legislation.[384]

16. CONSCIENCE EXCEPTION The legalization of medically indicated abortions, which had begun to emerge before 1973 in some states, necessitated protective legislation for institutions and medical professionals whose religious, ethical, or moral beliefs foreclosed their participation in abortion practice.[385] These statutes today are nearly universal. A number of states allow all hospitals,[386] including publicly operated facilities,[387] to refuse to allow abortions or admit patients for the purpose of abortion. There is no constitutional infirmity in granting a conscience exception to public facilities.[388] A few states, however, limit the conscience exemption to private or religious institutions.[389] Hospitals cannot be held civilly liable[390] or denied public subsidies[391] because of refusals to allow abortions, although they may be required to notify patients beforehand of their policies.[392]

The private right of conscience is usually delineated in terms of religious, moral, ethical, or professional scruples,[393] but may be left unrestricted.[394] Most frequently, conscientious objectors are required to file a written statement of objection,[395] but in some jurisdictions that burden is not specifically imposed.[396] Laws may be drafted simply to allow the exception to any person,[397] or may designate physicians,[398] nurses,[399] or other hospital, clinic, or medical office personnel.[400] Those who invoke their personal conscience rights cannot be held criminally[401] or civilly[402] liable, or subjected to administrative penalties,[403] or to disciplinary[404] or recriminatory[405] action. Statutes also proscribe discrimination against those relying on their statutory rights,[406] particularly in connection with employment[407] or educational[408] opportunities.

On occasion sanctions are supplied for violations of the conscience exception, in the form of criminal penalties[409] and civil injunctive[410] and damage[411] remedies.

C. Criminal Statutory Provisions Affecting Abortions

1. GENERAL PRINCIPLES   In the immediate aftermath to *Roe v. Wade,* a few states voided their abortion legislation entirely, eliminating criminality for nonphysician abortionists as well as medical practitioners performing therapeutic abortions.[412] That was judicial overkill, because in *Connecticut v. Menillo,*[413] the Court confirmed that its 1973 decisions were not intended to provide a constitutional exemption from criminal law coverage for nonphysician abortionists.[414] State decisions now are uniform in recognizing the state's power to prosecute nonphysician abortionists;[415] that power extends as well to physicians who violate constitutionally acceptable regulations of therapeutic abortions.[416]

When prosecutions of the latter sort are initiated, however, federal constitutional principles require that the underlying legislation be sufficiently precise to give warning of prohibited and acceptable activities. If it is vague and indefinite, it will be invalidated.[417] Beyond that, consistent with the Court's general approach to strict liability legislation,[418] abortion statutes imposing felony or serious misdemeanor penalties must include a scienter (intent or knowledge) component, or they will be invalidated.[419]

There is no constitutional barrier to a statutory requirement that proof of a medical justification be advanced by a physician defendant as an affirmative defense.[420]

2. PERSONS COVERED   As noted above, criminal statutes can be invoked constitutionally only against nonphysicians or physicians who depart from acceptable medical practice.[421] This is express in some statutes;[422] if not, courts must so construe the general term, "any person," if constitutional problems are to be avoided.[423]

3. ACTUS REUS   The objective acts embodied in traditional abortion legislation, still in force in some jurisdictions, are administering drugs or substances[424] or using instruments or other means[425] to terminate pregnancy. A majority of states, particularly those which have modernized their criminal legislation, require that the woman be pregnant,[426] while a minority do not include that specific requirement.[427] If pregnancy is required but the particular woman in fact was not pregnant, general attempt provisions in contemporary codes will cover the activity because traditional doctrines of impossibility have been abrogated.[428] However, statutes based on activities with intent to produce a miscarriage function as a crystallized application of attempt law;[429] at times, attempted abortion is covered specifically.[430]

Some statutes continue to embody distinctions based on the stage of a pregnancy, in terms of time[431] or viability.[432] These cannot be invoked against physicians practicing within the constitutional bounds established by the Supreme Court. They are, however, appropriately applied to laypersons as a means of grading punishments; the further into pregnancies illicit abortions are performed, the greater the danger to maternal life and health and the greater the justification for augmented penalties. If, however, they restrict the coverage of criminal abortion legislation as applied to nonphysicians, they are unwise, because there should be no lawful scope for such abortions.[433]

4. SCIENTER   Traditional statutes are clear that abortional acts must be done with intent to produce an abortion or miscarriage. Thus, they create no constitutional infirmities as far as scienter requirements are concerned. That seems to be a problem exclusively generated by recent therapeutic abortion statutes supported by residual criminal penalty provisions.[434]

5. WEIGHT   The overwhelming majority of abortion statutes carry felony-level punishments,[435] but a few offenses are punished as misdemeanors.[436] It is possible that this field of penal law will prove susceptible to restriction under the Eighth Amendment prohibition against disproportionate punishments.[437]

6. CRIMINALITY BASED ON NEONATAL DEATH   Statutory provisions governing care of neonates and fetuses during abortion and birth processes have been noted.[438] Specific criminal penalties usually are set forth governing what in usual instances is a form of medical malpractice.[439] The chief deficiencies observable in some of these statutes are lack of a clear scienter requirement, vagueness problems in statement of the standard of duty,[440] and disproportionality of punishments.

7. CRIMINALITY BASED ON MATERNAL DEATH   There is no need for special legislation governing the death of a woman in the course of an unlawful abortion or manifesting criminal negligence in the setting of a therapeutic abortion.[441] Nevertheless, several states specially address that form of homicide.[442]

8. LIABILITY FOR SEEKING CRIMINAL ABORTION   Some jurisdictions penalized women before 1973 for seeking abortions;[443] some continue such penal law coverage as far as nontherapeutic abortions are concerned.[444] Perpetuation of that form of criminality, however, is as unwise today as it was before 1973 because of the difficulties it creates in criminal justice administration.[445]

9. ADVERTISING ABORTIFACIENTS   Criminal statutes penalizing the advertising of abortions and abortifacients have been evident for generations.[446] A number of such provisions continue to exist in unmodified form.[447] They are, however, unconstitutional in that form because they do not exempt dissemination of information about lawful therapeutic abortions; that constitutes a First-Amendment–protected form of commercial speech.[448] Therefore, several statutes have been amended to conform with *Bigelow* concepts;[449] the residual coverage would seem to be constitutional.[450]

10. SOLICITING ABORTIONS   Some traditional statutes have penalized the act of soliciting women for abortions.[451] To the extent they fall within the advertising cases discussed immediately above, they are subject to equivalent constitutional attack. However, even if they apply only to personal contacts, they seem clearly unconstitutional under *Roe v. Wade* because they impede access by women to lawful therapeutic abortions. Recent legislation occasionally reflects such concerns.[452]

11. TRAFFICKING IN ABORTIFACIENTS   Criminal regulation of abortifacients, like restrictions on advertising and solicitation, came onto statute books in the 19th century.[453] Many such laws have been continued in force without change.[454] However, to the extent they burden the availability of lawful therapeutic abortions, they are unconstitutional.[455] Consequently, most contemporary statutes either exempt therapeutic abortions[456] or limit their coverage to unlawful abortions.[457]

12. SPECIAL EVIDENTIARY PROVISIONS   A few statutes require that a woman's testimony concerning a criminal abortion be corroborated.[458] Vermont allows a woman's statements in evidence as a dying declaration if she dies following an abortion.[459] Two jurisdictions immunize a woman's testimony against incriminating use so that she may be called as a prosecution witness.[460] Legislation of this sort is probably residual from earlier times and deserves repeal.

Rhode Island states that it is unnecessary for the prosecution to prove that an abortion was not legally justified.[461] Current constitutional doctrine legitimates placement of a burden of going forward with evidence on the defendant, but is not clear about imposition on the defense of a burden of persuasion.[462] The volatile and controversial context of abortion is probably not the most appropriate one to test such issues, however.

D. Economic Aspects of Therapeutic Abortions

1. PUBLIC FUNDING OF ABORTIONS   A logical corollary of the Supreme Court's holding in *Roe v. Wade* seemingly would have been that states and the federal government should be required to provide the same financial support for therapeutic abortions as they offer for other medical services to financially unable citizens. Otherwise, government would burden the free exercise of women's rights to have abortions and create invidious distinctions among classes of patients based on financial considerations. However, logic lost as the issue came before the Supreme Court.

In *Maher v. Roe,*[463] welfare recipients attacked a state exclusion of Medicaid payments to patients receiving therapeutic abortions; a federal district court found the preclusion to deny equal protection. The Supreme Court disagreed. Although it did not depart from its *Roe v. Wade* principle that the Constitution protects women from unduly burdensome interference with the freedom to terminate pregnancies, it thought there is no constitutional barrier to a state's making "a value judgment favoring childbirth over abortion" and "implement[ing] that judgment by the allocation of public funds."[464] Financially unable patients not wishing to take advantage of state-supported childbirth must depend on private sources: "The State may have made childbirth a more attractive alternative, thereby influencing the woman's decision, but it has imposed no restriction on access to abortions that was not already there. The indigency that may make it difficult—and in some cases, perhaps impossible—for women to have abortions is neither created nor in any way affected by the [state's] regulation."[465] In short, it perceived a "basic difference between direct state interference with a protected activity and state encouragement of an alternative activity consonant with legislative policy. Constitutional concerns are greatest when the State attempts to impose its will by force of law; the State's power to encourage actions deemed to be in the public interest is necessarily far broader."[466]

Two other decisions the same term documented the Court's theme. In *Beal v. Doe*,[467] the Court applied an identical analysis to title XIX of the Social Security Act,[468] which it construed not to require state funding of nontherapeutic abortions, but not to preclude contrary legislation either.[469] In *Poelker v. Doe*,[470] it ruled that publicly owned and operated hospitals did not have to offer hospital abortion services even though they provided free childbirth facilities. The rationale was that of *Maher v. Roe*.

While *Beal v. Doe* was awaiting final resolution, Congress had begun enacting an annual prohibition[471] which in varying forms banned the use of federal Medicaid funding for nontherapeutic abortions or therapeutic abortions other than for certain restricted reasons.[472] Constitutional attacks on it were launched immediately, since *Beal v. Doe* had dealt only with construction of Medicaid provisions not bearing the Hyde Amendment limitation. In *Harris v. McRae*,[473] the Court reiterated its *Maher v. Roe* premise that legislative bodies, including Congress, can refuse to underwrite therapeutic abortions and, "by means of unequal subsidization of abortion and other medical services, encourage alternative activity deemed in the public interest."[474] Moreover, it rejected a contention that the Hyde Amendment, by embodying Roman Catholic and other religious theology rejecting abortion, violated the "establishment" dimension of the First Amendment,[475] as well as a claim that the legislation constituted an "invidious discrimination" violating the equivalent to Fourteenth Amendment equal protection incorporated in the Fifth Amendment. Congress could authorize federal reimbursement for medically necessary services generally, but not for medically indicated abortions: "Abortion is inherently different from other medical procedures, because no other procedure involves the purposeful termination of a potential life."[476]

The Court's 1977 and 1980 rulings have served to legitimate legislation in about one-quarter of American jurisdictions limiting the use of state,[477] local,[478] and on occasion federal pass-through[479] funding for purposes of abortion. Similar restrictions may govern public employee or other health insurance plans,[480] family planning services,[481] and miscellaneous benefits.[482] Exceptions may be indicated, however, to cover abortions necessary to preserve maternal life,[483] or used to terminate pregnancies resulting from rape[484] or incest.[485] Moreover, a few state appellate courts have invalidated or limited the impact of restrictive legislation on state legal grounds.[486]

2.   PROTECTING WOMEN ELECTING ABORTIONS   It would be a clear violation of *Roe v. Wade* standards for state officials in any way to coerce women to have or to decline abortions; a few states specifically prohibit the former.[487] Beyond that, legislation may bar discrimination or loss of privileges[488] or denial of public benefits[489] to women who refuse to have abortions[490] or, on occasion, consent.[491] The latter, of course, is a preferably neutral statement, but neutrality is not an evident objective of most such legislation.

VI. Conclusions and Recommendation:
A Sunset Law Analogy for Abortion Legislation?

Unless, someday, a right-to-life amendment to the United States Constitution is ratified, the right of women to elect medically indicated abortions is protected, as the Court's 1983 decisions attest. On the other hand, it is unlikely the Court will depart from its position in *Harris v. McRae* that the Constitution does not require that therapeutic abortions be underwritten for financially unable women, probably because of the ripple effect a contrary interpretation would have on allocation of public funds on other sensitive areas.[492] The want of public funding may in time impel resort by women to clandestine abortionists and thus re-create a public health problem manifest before 1973,[493] but that does not yet appear to be the case.

State legislatures hostile to the Court's doctrines no doubt will stand pat with their present legislation,[494] because they are unwilling to reopen the volatile issue of abortion reform. If other legislatures in good faith track the details of each Supreme Court decision, they may well find themselves out of step with the next sequence of constitutional precedent, with defective or inadequate legislation productive of new litigation. Legislating the details of rights to privacy is as futile and unproductive as endeavoring to duplicate through statute the myriad of refined points of doctrine adjudicated under the fourth amendment.

Therefore, as we move into the late 1980s, one may wonder whether abortion legislation of any sort is any longer needed. Civil, administrative, and disciplinary proceedings can be brought against medical providers who reach professionally unsound decisions to abort, and hospitals and clinics can be required to provide appropriate personnel and equipment to safeguard maternal and fetal health and life. Laypersons who offer medically unsupervised abortion services can be proceeded against for unlawful practice of medicine, just as if they had purported to offer any other form of surgical or pharmaceutical treatment. Abortion regulation adds nothing not already achievable through existing general legislation and administrative regulations.

Nor is there a need for special criminal abortion statutes aimed at clandestine or nonmedically indicated abortions, even though they are constitutional.[495] If a pregnant woman dies as a result of a criminally negligent abortion or bungled aftercare, or if a viable fetus born alive dies for similar reasons, the coverage of manslaughter or criminally negligent homicide statutes is clear. If a neonate's life is snuffed out intentionally, murder or manslaughter provisions are fully available.

If an unqualified person performs an abortion, or a medically qualified person departs the bounds of proper abortion techniques without causing maternal or neonatal death, criminality is clear under modern assault statutes. Administering a substance other than for lawful medical or therapeutic purpose can be made a form of assault,[496] and the use of instruments almost certainly causes physical injury[497] or serious physical injury.[498] If an abortion is unlawful, a woman's consent to it is legally irrelevant to the criminality of the abortionist, since it does not tend to raise a reasonable doubt about the existence of the actus reus element of physical injury or serious physical injury.[499] If there is an unclear area, it is the criminality of negligent or intentional activity which snuffs out fetal life during birth processes; if that is a problem, curative legislation should be addressed directly at the basic problem without regard to whether birth processes result from abortion of a viable fetus, induced labor, or spontaneous premature or near-term miscarriage.

Accordingly, just as some states have legislated the demise of a great many regulatory provisions affecting professions, occupations, businesses, industries, and enterprises, which have no affirmative justification for perpetuation,[500] so legislatures should recognize that abortion legislation is currently unnecessary and unproductive, and terminate all special legislation relating to abortions, whether lawful or unlawful.

STATUTORY APPENDIX

Ala.Code §§ 13A–13–7, 34–24–25 (Supp. 1985).

Alaska Stat. §§ 08.64.105, 08.64.330, 08.64.380 (1982); 18.16.010 (1981).

Ariz. Rev. Stat. Ann. §§ 13–3603 to 13–3605, 15–1630, 32–1401, 35–196.02, 36–2151, 36–2152, 36–2271, 36–2301 to 36–2303 (Supp. 1984).

Ark. Stat. Ann. §§ 41–2551 to 41–2560, 72–613, 82–516 (Supp. 1985).

Cal. Bus. & Prof. Code §§ 601, 2660, 2746.6, 2761, 2878, 4520, 4520 (Supp. 1985); Gov't Code § 27491 (Supp. 1985); Health & Safety Code §§ 429.50, 25950–25957 (Supp. 1985); Penal Code §§ 274–276, 3405, 3406, 4028 (Supp. 1985); Welf. & Inst. Code §§ 220, 1773, 16145 (Supp. 1984).

Colo. Rev. Stat. §§ 12–36–117, 18–3–402, 18–6–101 to 18–6–105, 18–6–302 (Supp. 1984).

Conn. Gen. Stat. §§ 53–29 to 53–33, 20–45 (Supp. 1984–85).

Del. Code Ann. tit. 11, §§ 222, 651–654 (Supp. 1982); tit. 24, §§ 1766, 1790–1795 (Supp. 1982).

D.C. Code Ann. §§ 2–1301, 2–1326, 22–201 (Supp. 1982).

Fla. Stat. Ann. §§ 390.001–390.021, 406.11, 458.331, 459.015, 462.14, 743.066, 782.09, 797.02, 934.07 (West Supp. 1984).

Ga. Code Ann. §§ 26–1201 to 26–1204, 40–3302, 84–916 (West Supp. 1984); 88–2902 (West 1981); 88–1719 (West Supp. 1984).

Haw. Rev. Stat. §§ 442–9, 445–119, 453–8, 455–6, 460–11, 460–12 (Supp. 1982).

Idaho Code §§ 18–603 to 18–615, 19–2115, 54–1814 (Supp. 1984).

Ill. Ann. Stat. ch. 23, §§ 5–5, 5–6, 5–9, 6–1 (Smith-Hurd Supp. 1984–85); 6–1.1 (Smith-Hurd 1967); 7–1 (Smith-Hurd Supp. 1984–85); ch. 38, §§ 81–21 to 81–32, 81–54 (Smith-Hurd Supp. 1984–85); ch. 70, § 3–2.2 (Smith-Hurd Supp. 1983–84); ch. 111 1/2, §§ 87–9, 157–8.2 to 157–8.4, 157–86 (Smith-Hurd 1976); 157–8.6–1, 5201 (Smith-Hurd Supp. 1984–85); ch. 127, § 526 (Smith-Hurd Supp. 1984–85).

Ind. Code §§ 16–10–1–7, 16–10–1.5–8, 16–10–3–2 to 16–10–3–4 (1974); 35–1–58.5–1 to 35–1–58.5–7 (Supp. 1984).

Iowa Code Ann. §§ 146.1, 146.2, 147.55, 205.1, 702.20, 707.7–707.10 (West Supp. 1983–84).

Kan. Stat. Ann. §§ 21–3407 (Vernon 1982); 65–443 to 65–445, 65–1120, 65–2836, 65–2837, 65–2912 (Vernon Supp. 1982).

Ky. Rev. Stat. §§ 205.560, 213.055 (1982); 311.710, 311.715, 311.720, 311.723, 311.726, 311.729, 311.730, 311.732, 322.735, 311.750, 311.760, 311.770, 311.780, 311.790, 311.800, 311.990 (1983); 436.026 (Supp. 1984).

La. Rev. Stat. Ann. §§ 14:87 (West Supp. 1984); 14:87.4 (West 1978); 14:87.5, 14:88, 37:1285 (West Supp. 1984).

Me. Rev. Stat. Ann. tit. 22, §§ 1591–1596 (1964); 1597–1599 (Supp. 1984–85); tit. 32, § 3282 (Supp. 1984–85).

Md. Health-General Code Ann. §§ 20–103, 20–203, 20–205, 20–208 to 20–211, 20–214; Health Occ. Code Ann. 14–504 (Supp. 1982).

Mass. Gen. Laws Ann. ch. 38, § 6 (West Supp. 1983–84); ch. 112, §§ 12F–12S (West 1983); ch. 272, §§ 19–21B (West Supp. 1983–84).

Mich. Comp. Laws Ann. §§ 333.2687, 333.2689, 333.2835, 750.14, 750.15, 750.34, 750.322, 750.323 (1975); Mich. Stat. Ann. §§ 14.15(2687), 14.15(2689), 14.15(2835), 28.204, 28.205, 28.223, 28.554, 28.555 (Callaghan Supp. 1983–84).

Minn. Stat. Ann. §§ 144.343, 145.411–145.424, 145.925, 147.021, 147.101, 62D.20 (West Supp. 1984); 256B.011, 246B.40 (West 1982); 261.28, 393.07 (West Supp. 1984).

Miss. Code Ann. §§ 41–61–9, 73–25–29, 97–3–3, 97–3–5, 97–3–37 (Supp. 1983).

Mo. Ann. Stat. §§ 188.010–188.015 (Vernon 1983); 188.020–188.025 (Vernon Supp. 1984); 188.027 (Vernon 1983); 188.028, 188.030 (Vernon Supp. 1984); 188.035–188.045 (Vernon 1983); 188.047 (Vernon Supp. 1984); 188.050 (Vernon 1983); 188.052–188.085, 197.032, 208.152 (Vernon 1983).

Mont. Code Ann. §§ 41–1–103, 41–1–401, 41–1–402, 50–101 to 50–112 (1983); 66–1036 to 66–1038, 66–4003 (Supp. 1977).

Neb. Rev. Stat §§ 28–325 (1979), 28–326 to 28–328 (Supp. 1984); 28–329 to 28–332 (1979); 28–333 to 28–334 (Supp. 1984); 28–335 to 28–342 (1979); 28–343 (Supp. 1984); 28–344 to 28–346 (1979), 28–347 (Supp. 1982); 71–148 (1984).

Nev. Rev. Stat. §§ 175.301 (1981), 200.210, 200.220 (1984); 201.120, 201.130 (1979); 442.240, 442.250–442.253 (1983); 442.254–442.257, 442.257, 442.260, 442.265, 442.270 (1981); 630A.030, 632.320 (1983); 632.475 (1979); 633A.100 (1981), 634.010 (1983).

N.H. Rev. Stat. Ann. §§ 329:17 (Supp. 1981); 585:12–585:14, 630:1 (1974).

N.J. Stat. Ann. §§ 2A:65A–1 to 2A:65A–3 (West Supp. 1983–84); 2C:2–10, 2C:12–1 (West 1982); 30:4D–6.1 (West 1981); 45:9–16, 45:10–9, 45:10–10 (West 1978); 45:1–21, 45:9–16 (West Supp. 1983–84).

N.M. Stat. Ann. §§ 30–5–1, 30–5–3, 61–6–14, 61–10A–5, 30–5–1 to 30–5–3, 24–14–18 (1984).

N.Y. Civ. Rights Law § 79i (McKinney Supp. 1982–83); Exec. Law § 291 (McKinney Supp. 1982–83); Penal Law §§ 10.00, 110.10, 120.00, 120.10, 125.05, 125.40–125.60 (McKinney Supp. 1982–83); Pub. Health Law § 4164 (McKinney Supp. 1982–83).

N.C. Gen. Stat. §§ 14–44 to 14–45.1 (Interim Supp. 1981); 90–13, 90–14 (Supp. 1981).

N.D. Cent. Code §§ 14–02.1–01 to 14–02.1–09, 14–02.3–01 (1981); 14–02.3–02 to 14–02.3–04 (1983); 23–16–14 (1978); 43–17–31 (Supp. 1981).

Ohio Rev. Code Ann. §§ 3701.341 (Page 1980); 4731.22, 4731.91 (Page Supp. 1982).

Okla. Stat. Ann. tit. 21, §§ 713, 714, 861, 862 (West 1983); tit. 59, §§ 509, 1648 (West Supp. 1984); tit. 63, §§ 1–730 to 1–741, 938, 2602 (West Supp. 1984).

Or. Rev. Stat. §§ 435.405–435.995, 465.110, 677.190, 685.110 (1981).

Pa. Code tit. 16, §§ 51.1 (1978); 51.2, 51.31–51.33, 51.41 (1980); 51.42–51.44, 51.51, 51.52, 51.61 (1978); tit. 18, §§ 3201–3220 (1983); tit. 55, §§ 1141.57, 1221.57 (1982); tit. 62, § 453 (Supp. 1983–84); tit. 63, § 421.3 (Supp. 1983–84).

P.R. Laws Ann. tit. 10, § 315 (1976); tit. 11, § 203 (Supp. 1982); tit. 20, § 52 (Supp. 1981); tit. 24, §§ 231–234 (1979); 235 (Supp. 1982); tit. 33, § 4020 (Supp. 1981).

R.I. Gen. Laws §§ 11–9–18, 11–23–5, 23–4.7–1 to 23–4.7–8, 23–17–11 (Supp. 1984); 36–12–2.1 (1976).

S.C. Code Ann. §§ 1–13–30 (Law. Co-op Supp. 1982); 44–41–10 (Law. Co-op 1976); 44–41–20, 44–41–30 (Law. Co-op Supp. 1982); 44–41–40, 44–41–50 (Law. Co-op 1976); 44–41–60 (Law. Co-op Supp. 1982); 44–41–70, 44–41–80, 61–12–1 to 61–12–7 (Law. Co-op 1976); Health & Environment Control Dep't R. 61–12, § 201.

S.D. Codified Laws Ann. §§ 22–17–5 (1979); 34–23A–1 to 34–23A–21 (1977).

Tenn. Code Ann. §§ 39–4–201 to 39–4–208 (1982); 53–474, 63–6–214, 63–9–111 (Supp. 1982).

Tex. Fam. Code Ann. §§ 12.05, 15.022 (Vernon Supp. 1984); Rev. Civ. Stat. Ann. arts 4512.5, 4512.7, 4495b, § 3.08 (Vernon Supp. 1984); Penal Code §§ 22.01, 22.02, 22.05, 22.06 (Vernon 1974), 4512.1–4512.4, 4512.6 (Vernon 1972).

Utah Code Ann. §§ 26–2–23, 26–18–4, 26–18–5, 26–18–10 (1976); 58–12–7 (Supp. 1981), 58–12–31 (1974); 58–12–36 (1981); 76–7–301 to 76–7–314, 76–7–321 to 76–7–324 (Supp. 1981); 78–11–24, 78–11–25 (Supp. 1983).

Vt. Stat. Ann. tit. 13, §§ 101–103 (1974); 104 (Supp. 1984); tit. 26, § 1354 (1975).

V.I. Code Ann. tit. 14, §§ 151–156 (Supp. 1984); tit. 19, §§ 291–293 (1976).

Va. Code §§ 18.2–71 to 18.2–76.1 (1982); 19.2–8, 32.1–92.1, 32.1–92.2, 32.1–264 (1983); 54–317 (1982).

Wash. Rev. Code Ann. §§ 9.02.010–9.02.090 (Supp. 1983–84); 9.68.030 (1977); 9A.32.060 (Supp. 1983–84); 18.36.140, 18.36.150 (1978); 18.50.100, 18.57.170, 18.72.030 (Supp. 1983–84).

W. Va. Code §§ 16–2B–1 to 16–2B–4 (1984); 62–2–8 (1977).

Wis. Stat. Ann. §§ 20.927, 59.07, 66.04, 140.42, 143.075, 146.80, 441.06 (West Supp. 1982–83); 441.06 (West 1974); 441.07 (West Supp. 1982–83); 448.06, 448.065 (West Supp. 1982–83); 448.18 (West 1974); 940.04 (West 1982).

Wyo. Stat. §§ 35–6–101 to 35–6–115 (1977); 35–6–116 (Supp. 1983).

NOTES

1. 410 U.S. 113 (1973).
2. 410 U.S. 179 (1973).
3. *See* text accompanying notes 137–50 *infra.*
4. 462 U.S. 616 (1983).
5. On other semantic aspects of the abortion debate, *see* Fromer, *Abortion Ethics,* 30 Nursing Outlook 234, 234–35 (April 1982); Hardin, *Semantic Aspects of Abortion,* 24 Etc.: A Review of General Semantics 263 (1967). *See also* Chemerinsky, *Rationalizing the Abortion Debate: Legal Rhetoric and the Abortion Controversy,* 31 Buffalo L. Rev. 107 (1982).
6. Canon 1398 (1983): "A person who actually procures an abortion incurs a *latae sententiae* [automatic] excommunication." On the corresponding predecessor provision, canon 2350 § 1, *see* 8 C. Bachofen, Commentary on Canon Law 397–402 (1931); 3 T. Bouscaren, Canon Law Digest 669–70

(1954); 2 S. Woywood, *Practical Commentary on the Code of Canon Law* 625 (C. Smith rev. 1962).

In support of the Roman Catholic position, *see, e.g.,* Brown, *Recent Statutes and the Crime of Abortion,* 16 Loy. L. Rev. 275 (1970); Decker & Decker, *The Credibility Gap That Kills,* 131 America 47 (August 10, 1974); Granfield, *Law and Morals,* Criminologica (February 1967) at 11; Noonan, *Abortion: From "An Almost Absolute Value in History",* in Moral Problems in Medicine 290 (S. Gorovitz et al. eds. 1976); Trinkaus, *The Abortion Decision: Two Years Later: Dred Scott Revisited,* 101 Commonweal 384 (February 14, 1975); Editorial, *Abortion Ten Years Later,* 110 Commonweal 35 (January 28, 1983). Not all writers from a Roman Catholic background adhere unconditionally to that position. *See, e.g.,* Decker, *The Abortion Decision: Two Years Later: More Christian Than Its Critics,* 101 Commonweal 384 (February 14, 1975); Giannella, *The Difficult Quest for a Truly Humane Abortion Law,* 13 Vill. L. Rev. 257 (1967–68); Editorial, *Abortion, Religion and Political Life,* 106 Commonweal 35 (February 2, 1979).

7. *See, e.g.,* D. Bonhoeffer, Ethics 130–31 (N. Smith transl. 1955); H. Thielicke, Ethics of Sex 226–47 (J. Doberstein transl. 1964); Baum, *Abortion: An Ecumenical Dilemma,* 99 Commonweal 231 (November 30, 1973); Brown, *An Evangelical Looks at the Abortion Phenomenon,* 135 America 161 (September 25, 1976); Eller, *Let's Get Honest About Abortion,* 92 Christian Century 16 (January 1–8, 1975); Ramsey, *Ethics of a Cottage Industry in an Age of Community and Research Medicine,* 284 N.E. J. of Med. 700, 701–03 (1971); Note, *Abortion Laws, Religious Beliefs and the First Amendment,* 14 Val. U. L. Rev. 487 (1980).

    Mainline Protestant denominations generally take a contrary view.

    Traditional Jewish law views abortion as tort, not crime, although some contemporary rabbinic sources speak of it in terms of homicide. *See* Sinclair, *Legal Basis for the Prohibition of Abortion,* 15 Israel L. Rev. 109 (1980).

8. Dahlberg, *Abortion,* in Sexual Behavior and the Law 379, 389 (R. Slovenko, ed. 1965); Krimmel & Foley, *An Inspection Into the Nature of Human Life and Potential Consequences of Legalizing Its Destruction,* 46 U. Cin. L. Rev. 725, 780–89 (1977).

9. *See* Samuels, *Termination of Pregnancy: A Lawyer Considers the Arguments,* 7 Medicine, Sci. & L. 10, 12–13 (1967); Hardin, *Abortion—Or Compulsory Pregnancy?,* 30 J. Marr. & the Fam. 246, 247 (1968).

10. *See* H. Thielicke, *supra* note 7, *but see* Giannella, *supra* note 6, at 301–02.

11. *See* Jones, *Abortion and the Consideration of Fundamental Irreconcilable Interests,* 33 Syracuse L. Rev. 565, 612–13 (1980); Thomson, *Defense of Abortion,* 1 Philosophy & Pub. Affairs 47 (1971); *cf.* Note, *Isolating the Male Bias Against Reform of Abortion Legislation,* 10 Santa Clara L. Rev. 301 (1970).

    Maternal life and health are increasingly recognized as grounds for lawful therapeutic abortions in other countries through legislation. For a survey of national laws, *see* Dourlen-Rollier, *Legal Problems Related to Abortion and Menstrual Regulation,* 7 Colum. Human Rights L. Rev. 120, 126–32 (1975); Thomas, Ryniker & Kaplan, *Indian Abortion Law Revision and Population Policy: An Overview,* 16 Indian L. Inst. J. 514, 520–28 (1974).

    The English Abortion Act, 1967, has had influence in other Commonwealth nations. *See* Dickens & Cook, *Development of Commonwealth Abortion Laws,* 28 Int'l & Comp. L.Q. 424, 442–56 (1979); Menon, *Law of Abortion With Special Reference to Commonwealth Caribbean,* 5 Anglo-Am. L. Rev. 311, 327–35 (1976); Veitch & Tracey, *Abortion in the Common Law World,* 22 Am. J. Comp. L. 652 (1974). On New Zealand law, *see* Kember, *Abortion and the Crimes Amendment Act 1977,* 1978 N.Z.L.J. 109.

The Canadian Criminal Code § 251(4) allows licensed medical practitioners to terminate pregnancies in licensed hospitals if necessary to preserve a woman's life or health. *See generally* Dickens, *Eugenic Recognition in Canadian Law,* 13 Osgoode Hall L. Rev. 547, 562–65 (1975); Micallef, *Meaning and Interpretation of "Unlawful" in Canada's Abortion Law,* 23 C. de D. 1029 (1982); Somerville, *Reflections on Canadian Abortion Law: Evacuation and Destruction—Two Separate Issues,* 31 U. Toronto L.J. 1 (1981); Note, *Abortion Law in Canada: A Need for Reform,* 42 Sask. L. Rev. 221, 229–32 (1977) (legislative history). The Supreme Court of Canada rejected *Wade*-like contentions and sustained a conviction for criminal abortions and conspiracy to commit criminal abortions against a licensed physician who operated a clinic for open performance of first-trimester abortions. Morgentaler v. Regina, (1975) 53 D.L.R.(3d) 161. *See* Dickens, *The Morgentaler Case: Criminal Process and Abortion Law,* 14 Osgoode Hall L.J. 229 (1976); Leigh, *Necessity and the Case of Dr. Morgentaler,* 1978 Crim. L. Rev. 151.

Therapeutic abortion is asserted to be contrary to the Eire Constitution. Mathews, *Quantitative Interference with the Right to Life: Abortion and Irish Law,* 22 Catholic Law. 344, 356–58 (1976). On a "right to life" amendment to that constitution, *see Recent Developments: This Amendment Could Kill Women,* 7 Harv. Women's L.J. 287 (1984)

In India, the Medical Termination of Pregnancy Act, 1971 (MTPA) replaced § 312 of the Indian Penal Code, which had allowed abortions only to save maternal life. MTPA § 3(2) allows termination of pregnancy by an individual medical practitioner during the first trimester, and from the 13th through the 20th week on the good faith medical opinion of two practitioners, that continuation of pregnancy would risk the life of a pregnant woman or threaten grave injury to her physical or mental health, or that there is a substantial risk that the child, if born, will suffer from physical or mental abnormalities which will seriously handicap it. Grave injury to mental health is presumed in instances of rape and contraceptive failure, and a woman's "actual or reasonably foreseeable environment" may be taken into account in determining the risk to maternal health. Abortions can be performed only by registered practitioners in a governmentally approved facility, and must be consented to by the patient or her guardian if she is younger than 18. After the 20th week of pregnancy, abortions are allowed only if necessary to preserve a woman's life; life-threatening emergencies also justify performance of abortions without the concurrence of a second practitioner in other than licensed facilities. *See generally* Bose, *Abortion in India: A Legal Study,* 16 Indian L. Inst. J. 535 (1974); Menon, *Population Policy, Law Enforcement and the Liberalization of Abortion: A Socio-Legal Inquiry Into the Implementation of the Abortion Law in India,* 16 Indian L. Inst. J. 626 (1974); Pande, *Some Inhibiting Factors in the Implementation of the*

Medical Termination of Pregnancy Act, 1971—A Study of Acceptability, 16 Indian L. Inst. J. 660 (1974).

In Israel, the Criminal Law Amendment (Abortion) Law, 1977, allows consensual abortion for women under 17 or over 14; women pregnant because of illegal, consanguinous, or nonmarital relations; women whose fetuses are likely to be born with physical or mental handicaps; or women whose pregnancies might cause grievous harm to them or their other children because of difficult family or social conditions experienced by them or their families. *See* Falk, *The New Abortion Law of Israel,* 13 Israel L. Rev. 103 (1978) (containing English translation of text, *id.* at 109–10); Seater, Weiner, & Davis, *Illegal Abortion in Israel,* 13 Israel L. Rev. 422 (1978).

In Christian League of South Africa v. Rall, [1981] 2 S.A. 820, the court denied the petitioning organization's claim to be appointed curator ad litem for the unborn child of an unmarried woman, pregnant as the result of rape, who had obtained a judicial certification for an abortion. *See* Bedil, *Can a Fetus Be Protected From Its Mother?,* 98 S. Afr. L.J. 362 (1981).

The West German therapeutic abortion statute, Law of June 18, 1974, [1974] BGB1. I, § 1297 (*see* legislative history in Horton, *Abortion Law Reform in the German Federal Republic,* 28 Int'l & Comp. L.Q. 288 [1979]), was declared unconstitutional by the Federal Constitutional Court, Jt. of Feb. 25, 1975, 39 BVerfGl, 1975 Juristenzeitung 206, on the basis that it conflicted with the Grundgesetz (Basic Law), art. 2(2), which guarantees everyone "the right to life and to inviolability of his person"; the term "Jeder" (everyone) was construed to embrace fetal life. *See* Gerstein & Lowry, *Abortion, Abstract Norms, and Social Control: The Decision of the West German Federal Constitutional Court,* 25 Emory L.J. 849 (1976); Kommers, *Abortion and Constitution: United States and West Germany,* 25 Am. J. Comp. L. 255 (1977). On subsequent unsuccessful efforts by pro-choice proponents to invoke art. 8(1) of the European Convention before the European Commission on Human Rights, see Note, *Abortion Law Reform in Europe: The European Commission on Human Rights Upholds German Restrictions on Abortion (Bruggemann and Scheuten v. Federal Republic of Germany),* 15 Tex. Int'l L.J. 162 (1980) (also surveying contemporary legislative developments in Austria, France and Italy).

On efforts addressed to the European Commission on Human Rights to forestall therapeutic abortions as improper termination of human life, *see* X v. United Kingdom (Application No. 8416–79), European Commission of Human Rights, 19 Decisions & Reports 244 (1980), *noted,* Andrews, *The Unborn Child and the Right to Life,* 6 European L. Rev. 420 (1981) (husband was not allowed to contest therapeutic abortion obtained by wife because a fetus is not within art. 2[1] of the European Convention: "Everyone's right to life shall be protected by law"); Mathews, *supra,* at 354–55.

12. *See* Roe v. Wade, 410 U.S. 113, 152–54 (1973).

13. For an interpretation of Saint Augustine's view of sexual relations not too removed from this, *see* D. Bromley, Catholics and Birth Control 9–15 (1965).

14. *See, e.g.,* Comment, *The Right to Privacy: Does It Allow a Woman the Right to Determine Whether to Bear Children?,* 20 Am. U. L. Rev. 136 (1970). Roe

v. Wade, 410 U.S. at 154, rejected constitutional protection for abortions of choice not based on medical considerations.

15. *See* J. Fletcher, Morals and Medicine 92–99 (Beacon Press ed. 1960); Thompson, *A Defense of Abortion,* 1 Philosophy & Pub. Affairs 47 (1971).

16. *See* Krimmel & Foley, supra note 8, at 791–96. Only Japan appears to embody this specifically in its statute. Eugenic Protection Law (*Yūseighogohō*) (Law No. 156 of 1948, as amended), art. 3(5) permits abortion "if there are several children and the mother's health will be seriously impaired if she again delivers." Art. 14 permits a doctor authorized by a district medical association to terminate a pregnancy in his or her discretion, with consent of both husband and wife, for several reasons, including the likelihood of substantial injury to the mother's health for either physical or economic reasons if the pregnancy continues to term (author's translation and paraphrase). Some Scandinavian legislation extends about as broadly. Clemmesen, *State of Legal Abortion in Denmark,* 112 Am. J. Psych. 662 (1956); Klintskog, *Survey of Legislation on Legal Abortion in Europe and North America,* 21 Medico-Legal J. 79 (1953).

   The English Abortion Act, 1967, c. 87, § 1(2), permits medical practitioners to take account of "the pregnant woman's actual or reasonably foreseeable environment" in deciding whether, under § 1(1)(a), there is risk of "injury to the physical or mental health of the pregnant woman or any existing children of her family, greater than if the pregnancy were terminated." *See,* G. Williams, Textbook of Criminal Law 256 (1978); Simms, *Abortion Law Reform: How the Controversy Changed,* 1970 Crim. L. Rev. 567, 568–71. India's Medical Termination of Pregnancy Act, 1971, § 3(2) embodies similar considerations. *See* note 11 *supra.*

17. The dividing line between abortion, on the one hand, and contraceptive devices or pharmaceuticals preventing the implantation on the uterine wall of a fertilized ovum, is not intrinsically clear. *See* Roe v. Wade, 410 U.S. at 160–61; Brahams, *Postcoital Pill and Intrauterine Device: Contraceptive or Abortifacient?,* 1 Lancet 1039 (May 7, 1983); Tunkel, *Modern Anti-Pregnancy Techniques and the Criminal Law,* 1974 Crim. L. Rev. 461. On amniocentesis and other sex-determining and sex-selecting techniques, *see* Warren, *Law of Human Reproduction: An Overview,* 3 J. Legal Med. 1, 49–51 (1982); Nolan-Haley, *Amniocentesis and the Apotheosis of Human Quality Control,* 2 J. Legal Med. 347 (1981); Note, *Genetic Screening, Eugenic Abortion, and Roe v. Wade: How Viable Is Roe's Viability Standard?,* 50 Brooklyn L. Rev. 113, 125–30 (1983); Note, *Sex-Selection Abortion: A Constitutional Analysis of the Abortion Liberty and a Person's Right to Know,* 56 Ind. L.J. 281, 284–86 (1981).

   On other socioeconomic concerns, *see* Menon, *supra* note 11, at 317–18.

18. *See* Roemer, *Abortion Law Reform and Repeal: Legislative and Judicial Developments,* 61 Am. J. Pub. Health 500, 505–06 (1971), describing such a reliance on abortion in several Pacific Basin nations. India's Medical Termination of Pregnancy Act, 1971 seems strongly aimed at population control. *See* Kelkar, *Impact of the Medical Termination of Pregnancy Act, 1971: A Case Study,* 16 Indian L. Inst. J 693, 603 (1974); Thomas, Ryniker, & Kaplan, *supra* note 11, at 529.

Traditional Japanese attitudes viewed the use of contraceptives as improper, even by married couples, *see* R. Beardsley, J. Hall & R. Ward, Village Japan 335–36 (1959), but that view has weakened substantially, particulary in urban areas where nuclear families have replaced the extended family units typical of rural Japan. *See* R. Dore, City Life in Japan 205 n. 196 (1958). Kelkar, *supra,* at 619 records advice by former Premier Sato to Indian authorities not to rely heavily on abortion as a means of population control, based on Japanese experience.

19. H. Thielicke, *supra* note 7, at 215–25; Krimmel & Foley, *supra* note 8, at 796–97. *Cf.* Planned Parenthood Association of Kansas City v. Ashcroft, 655 F.2d 848, 868–69 (8th Cir. 1981), *aff'd on other grounds,* 462 U.S. 476 (1983), (requirement that woman be told approximate length of pregnancy unconstitutional because it would eliminate use of menstrual extraction and similar techniques, which under the state law would be an abortion); Margaret S. v. Edwards, 488 F. Supp. 181, 190–91 (E.D. La. 1980) (definition of abortion was not impermissibly vague even though it might have included IUDs and morning-after pills [two forms of birth control], since no other statutory formulation would be more precise, and abortion does not include contraceptive measures). N.M. Stat. Ann. § 30–5–1(A) (1984) defines pregnancy as implantation of an embryo in the uterus, which excludes morning-after pills from the scope of abortion provisions. Okla. tit. 63, § 1–730(8) (West 1984) excludes from the definition of abortion birth control devices or medications. 18 Pa. Code § 3203 (1983) excludes from the statutory definition of abortion the use of IUDs or birth control pills "to inhibit or prevent ovulation, fertilization or the implantation of a fertilized ovum within the uterus. W. Va. Code § 16–2B–2 (1979) states that abortion is not considered an approved method of family planning and is excluded from state-supported family planning programs, and Wis. Stat. Ann. § 146.80(1) (West Supp. 1983–84) prohibits family planning services from promoting, encouraging, or performing voluntary terminations of pregnancy.

On contraception as a desirable alternative to abortion, *see* Sneideman, *Abortion: A Public Health and Social Policy Perspective,* 7 N.Y.U. Rev. L. & Soc. Change 187, 206–12 (1978).

The matter of *in vitro* fertilization is also addressed in some legislation, *e.g.,* Ill. Ann. Stat., ch. 38, § 81–26(7) (Smith-Hurd Supp. 1984–85) (person causing fertilization of human ovum outside body of a living human female is deemed to have care and custody of child for purposes of neglect statute, but does not apply to lawful participation in pregnancy termination); Minn. Stat. Ann. § 145.422(3) (West Supp. 1984) (felony to buy or sell living human conceptus); 18 Pa. Code § 3213(e) (1983) (various data to be reported, including "number of fertilized eggs destroyed or discarded"). *See* Dickens, *supra* note 11, at 573–74; Warren, *supra* note 17, at 5.

20. That may have underlain the rescission in 1956 of the USSR law allowing easy abortion. *See* G. Williams, The Sanctity of Life and the Criminal Law 219–20 (1957). That rescission in turn, however, is reported to have been modified. P. Gebhard, W. Pomeroy, C. Martin & C. Christenson, Pregnancy, Birth and Abortion 208–11 (1958). So was a similar change in Bulgarian law. Roemer, *supra* note 18, at 504.

21. Sulloway, *Legal and Political Aspects of Population Control in the United States,* 25 Law & Contemp. Prob. 593, 596–98 (1960); Tietze, *Current Status of Fertility Control,* 25 Law & Contemp. Prob. 426, 442–44 (1960). Abortion as a means of population control seems to be significant in the People's Republic of China. Luk, *Abortion in Chinese Law,* 25 Am. J. Comp. L. 372, 389 (1977).

22. Indeed, Dr. Thielicke's concerns find no home in American constitutional jurisprudence, which stresses the right of married and unmarried persons to have information about contraception and access to contraceptives. *See* Bolger v. Youngs Drug Products Corp., 463 U.S. 60 (1983); Carey v. Population Services International, 431 U.S. 678 (1977); Eisenstadt v. Baird, 405 U.S. 438 (1972); Griswold v. Connecticut, 381 U.S. 479 (1965).

23. *See* Roe v. Wade, 410 U.S. 113, 156; text accompanying notes 111–32 *infra.*

24. *See* text accompanying notes 28–33 *infra.*

25. In Parts II and III of this chapter, only the names of the states and not specific statutory citations appear. This is because almost all the legislation in force through 1973 has been replaced; current statutes are cited fully in the statutory appendix to the chapter. Persons wishing then-contemporary citations may find them in George, *Evolving Law of Abortion,* 23 Case W. Res. L. Rev. 708 (1972) (*passim*).

26. *See* G. Williams, *supra* note 20, at 152–56; Quay, *Justifiable Abortion— Medical and Legal Foundations,* 49 Geo. L.J. 173, 231–38 (1960).

27. Most common law cases covered only conduct that caused miscarriages after fetuses had quickened. *See* R. Perkins & R. Boyce, Criminal Law 186–88 (3d ed. 1982).

    On the historical antecedents and development of the law of abortion, *see* Dellapena, *History of Abortion: Technology, Morality, and Law,* 40 U. Pitt. L. Rev. 359, 365–407 (1979); Destro, *Abortion and the Constitutions: The Need for a Life-Protective Amendment,* 63 Calif. L. Rev. 1250, 1267–82 (1976); Dickens & Cook, *supra* note 11, at 425–41; Means, *Law of New York Concerning Abortion and the Status of the Foetus, 1664–1968: A Case of Cessation of Constitutionality,* 14 N.Y.L.F. 411 (1968); Means, *The Phoenix of Abortional Freedom: Is a Penumbral or Ninth-Amendment Right About to Arise From the Nineteenth-Century Legislative Ashes of a Fourteenth-Century Common-Law Liberty?,* 17 N.Y.L.F. 335 (1971); Menon, *supra* note 11, at 323–26; Special Project: *Survey of Abortion Law,* 1980 Ariz. St. L.J. 67, 73–100.

28. Louisiana, Massachusetts, New Jersey, and Pennsylvania. In New Hampshire, the attempted abortion statute allowed no exceptions, while a companion provision penalizing completed abortions justified acts necessary to save maternal life.

29. Commonwealth v. Brunelle, 341 Mass. 675, 677, 171 N.E.2d 850, 852 (1961) (physicians who acted in an honest belief that abortions were necessary to avoid great peril to maternal life or health did not violate the statute, if their judgments corresponded with the average judgment of doctors in the communities where they practiced); State v. Brandenburg, 137 N.J.L. 124, 58 A.2d 709 (1948) (abortions necessary to save life, but not health).

30. Connecticut, Minnesota, Missouri, Nevada, New York (before the 1967 Penal Law), South Carolina, and Washington.
31. This is dealt with today in statutory definitions of abortion. *See* text accompanying notes 151–60 *infra*.
32. Colorado and New Mexico.
33. Alabama and the District of Columbia. Occasionally, broad judicial interpretations achieved the same result. Walsingham v. State, 250 So. 2d 857 (Fla. 1971) (physical and mental health); Commonwealth v. Brunelle, 341 Mass. 675, 171 N.E.2d 850 (1961).
34. Alabama, Arizona, Connecticut, Idaho, Indiana, Iowa, Kentucky, Maine, Michigan, Minnesota, Montana, Nebraska, Nevada, North Dakota, Ohio, Oklahoma, Rhode Island, South Dakota, Tennessee, Texas, Utah, Vermont, West Virginia, and Wyoming. Missouri legislation of the era appeared to favor unlicensed abortionists: Abortion was proscribed unless necessary to preserve the life of a woman or her unborn child, but if the person performing an abortion was not a licensed physician, it was a defense that the performance had been advised by a duly licensed physician to be necessary for the purpose. Thus, a licensed physician was held to a standard of objective necessity while an unlicensed person could rely on medical advice whether or not the abortion was objectively necessary. The statute probably was intended to protect registered nurses and other hospital and medical staff personnel, but was not so limited.
35. Alabama, Arizona, Connecticut, Idaho, Illinois, Indiana, Iowa, Kentucky, Maine (good faith belief no defense: State v. Rudman, 126 Me. 177, 136 A. 817 [1927]), Michigan, Minnesota, Missouri, Montana, Nevada, North Dakota (good faith belief no defense: State v. Shortridge, 54 N.D. 779, 211 N.W. 336 [1926]), Oklahoma, Rhode Island, South Dakota, Utah, Vermont, and Wyoming.
36. Steed v. State, 27 Ala. App. 263, 170 So. 489, *aff'd,* 233 Ala. 159, 170 So. 490 (1936) (*semble*: a woman who consented to an abortion was an accomplice unless acting under an honest belief that an abortion was necessary to save her life); Honnard v. People, 77 Ill. 481 (1875); State v. Dunklebarger, 206 Iowa 971, 221 N.W. 592 (1928).
37. *Compare* the Supreme Court interpretation of the District of Columbia Code to that effect, in United States v. Vuitch, 402 U.S. 62 (1971).
38. Tennessee, Texas, and West Virginia. Several statutes enacted after 1967 in Arkansas, Florida, Georgia, New York, North Carolina, Oregon, and South Carolina set a standard of "reasonable belief." That was a compromise position between strict liability and criminality turning on exclusively subjective considerations, but it achieved criminality based on criminal negligence. That standard of culpability seems inappropriate in the context of abortion, although perhaps recognizable in manslaughter prosecutions if a woman dies from the effects of a bungled abortion.
39. *See generally* G. Williams, *supra* note 16, at 252–53; Note, *Abortion Reform: History, Status, and Prognosis,* 21 Case W. Res. L. Rev. 521, 526–27 (1970).
40. Alabama, Arizona, Colorado, Delaware, Florida, Georgia, Idaho, Illinois, Indiana, Kansas, Kentucky, Louisiana, Michigan, Mississippi, Montana, Nebraska, Nevada, New Jersey, New Mexico, North Carolina, North

Dakota, Oklahoma, South Carolina, South Dakota, Tennessee, Texas, Utah, and Wyoming.

41. Arkansas, Kentucky, Maine, and Tennessee. Statutes punishing attempted abortion also reduced the practical significance of pregnancy as an element of the crime of abortion. *See* text accompanying notes 44–49 *infra*.

42. Alaska, Hawaii, and Washington. Under several older statutes in California, Colorado, Delaware, New York, Oregon, and Washington, the fact of quickening or the passage of a specified part of the gestation period governed severity of punishment.

43. California, Colorado, Delaware, New York, Oregon, and Washington.

44. Alabama, Arizona, Arkansas, California, Connecticut, Delaware, Georgia, Idaho, Illinois, Indiana, Iowa, Kentucky, Louisiana, Maine, Massachusetts, Michigan, Missouri, Montana, Nebraska, Nevada, New Hampshire, New Jersey, New York, North Carolina, North Dakota, Ohio, South Carolina, South Dakota, Tennessee, Utah, Virginia, and Washington. Texas had a special attempt provision which achieved the same result.

45. *See* W. LaFave & A. Scott, Criminal Law 438–46 (1972); R. Perkins & R. Boyce, Criminal Law 627–35 (3d ed. 1983). The doctrine of impossibility is repudiated in ALI Model Penal Code § 5.01(1)(a) (Permanent ed. with revised commentary, 1985); *see also, e.g.,* N.Y Penal Law § 110.10 (McKinney 1975).

46. California, District of Columbia, Iowa, Louisiana, Massachusetts, Ohio, Pennsylvania, Virginia, Washington, and West Virginia.

47. Illinois, Missouri, and New York.

48. Indiana, Kentucky, Rhode Island, Vermont, and Wyoming.

49. People v. Kuts, 187 Cal. App. 2d 431, 435, 9 Cal. Rptr. 626, 629 (1960); Urga v. State, 155 So. 2d 719, 723 (Fla. App. 1963), *cert. denied,* 379 U.S. 829 (1964); People v. Marra, 27 Mich. App. 1, 5, 183 N.W.2d 418 (1971); Wyatt v. State, 77 Nev. 490, 503, 367 P.2d 104, 111 (1961); *cf.* Williams v. State, 218 Tenn. 359, 363–66, 403 S.W.2d 319, 322–23 (1966) (no defense that substances and instruments could not cause miscarriage). The Kentucky and Maine statutes, however, varied punishment levels according to whether a miscarriage actually resulted.

50. Arkansas, Florida, Michigan, Mississippi, North Dakota, and Oklahoma.

51. Such statutes clearly accorded independent personality to fetuses because the crime was called manslaughter and usually placed with other homicide offenses (where abortion legislation did not usually appear).

52. *See* G. Williams, *supra* note 16, at 244–45; Wechsler & Michael, *Rationale of the Law of Homicide,* 37 Colum. L. Rev. 701, 702–23 (1937). The English authorities are canvassed and applied in Regina v. Creamer, [1965] 3 All E.R. 257, [1965] 3 W.L.R. 583 (Crim. App.); Regina v. Buck, 44 Crim. App. 213 (N.E. Cir. 1960).

53. Colorado, Florida, Massachusetts, New Jersey, New Mexico, Rhode Island, South Carolina, and Vermont.

54. District of Columbia, New Hampshire, Texas, and West Virginia.

55. Michigan, Missouri, New York, and North Dakota.

56. *See, e.g.,* Heath v. State, 249 Ark. 217, 219, 459 S.W.2d 420, 422 (1970), *cert. denied,* 404 U.S. 910 (1971) (no corroboration of woman's testimony required); Commonwealth v. Follenbee, 155 Mass. 274, 277, 29 N.E. 471

(1892); *In re* Vickers, 371 Mich. 114, 118–19, 123 N.W.2d 253, 254–55 (1963) (woman could not claim privilege against self-incrimination); *In re* Vince, 2 N.J. 443, 450, 67 A.2d 141, 144 (1949) (no self-incrimination unless fetus had quickened, in which case the offense was against the fetus and not the woman); State v. Shaft, 166 N.C. 407, 409, 81 S.E. 932, 933 (1914); Smartt v. State, 112 Tenn. 539, 553, 80 S.W. 586, 589 (1904); Willingham v. State, 33 Tex. Crim. 98, 99, 25 S.W. 424 (1894); *contra,* Steed v. State, 27 Ala. App. 263, 170 So. 489, *aff'd* 233 Ala. 159, 170 So. 490 (1936); State v. McCoy, 52 Ohio St. 157, 160, 39 N.E. 316 (1894). *Compare* State v. Clifford, 133 Iowa 478, 480, 110 N.W. 921, 922 (1907) (victim could not be charged because she had died as a result of the abortion, but court characterized her as a conspirator so that her statements were admissible against the abortionist as a declaration promoting the common criminal enterprise), *with* Snyder Appeal (Commonwealth v. Fisher), 398 Pa. 237, 246, 157 A.2d 207, 212 (1960) (woman is a victim and cannot be a conspirator).

On the English law, *see* 11 Halsbury's Laws of England ¶¶ 1191–92 (4th ed. 1976); G. Williams, *supra* note 16, at 253.

57. Reviser's comments to the Louisiana statute indicated an intent to preserve earlier case law to the same effect.

58. Arizona, California, Connecticut, Idaho, Indiana, Minnesota, New York, North Dakota, Oklahoma, South Carolina, South Dakota, Utah, Washington, Wisconsin and Wyoming. State courts did not always apply the literal language of these statutes outside their specific coverage, and thus held that women were not accomplices under the primary abortion statutes. *See* State v. Burlingame, 47 S.D. 332, 198 N.W. 824 (1924); State v. Cragun, 85 Utah 149, 38 P.2d 1071 (1934).

59. California, Idaho, Montana, North Dakota, and South Carolina.

60. People v. Peyser, 380 Ill. 404, 44 N.E.2d 58 (1942); State v. McCoy, 52 Ohio St. 157, 39 N.E. 316 (1894).

61. *See* Snyder Appeal (Commonwealth v. Fisher), 398 Pa. 237, 157 A.2d 207 (1960).

62. Minnesota and Washington. Such statutes were unconstitutional under Murphy v. Waterfront Commission, 378 U.S. 52 (1964); Malloy v. Hogan, 378 U.S. 1 (1964).

63. Nevada, New Jersey, Ohio, and South Carolina.

64. *See, e.g., In re* Vickers, 371 Mich. 114, 123 N.W.2d 253 (1963); *In re* Vince, 2 N.J. 443, 67 A.2d 141 (1949).

65. J. Bates & E. Zawadski, Criminal Abortion 38–39 (1964).

66. *Id.* at 85–91.

67. Arizona, California, Connecticut, Delaware, Florida, Idaho, Illinois, Indiana, Louisiana, Massachusetts, Michigan, Missouri, Pennsylvania, Rhode Island, South Dakota, Vermont, Virginia, Wisconsin, and Wyoming. Like statutes were repealed in 1967 and 1968 in Maine and Maryland.

68. *E.g.,* Colorado and Mississippi.

69. *See* text accompanying note 448 *infra.*

70. Massachusetts (subsequently declared unconstitutional in Eisenstadt v. Baird, 405 U.S. 438 [1972], in its application to contraceptives), Minnesota, Nevada, New York, and Washington.

71. Colorado, Illinois, Louisiana, and Maryland.
72. Texas (invalidated in Roe v. Wade, 314 F. Supp. 1217 [N.D. Tex. 1970], *aff'd on other grounds,* 410 U.S. 113 [1973]).
73. Colorado, Delaware, Illinois, Iowa, Maryland, Massachusetts, Michigan, Minnesota, Mississippi, Missouri, Nevada, Rhode Island, Vermont, and Washington.
74. Colorado, Delaware, Iowa, Massachusetts, Minnesota, Mississippi, Missouri, Nevada, Vermont, and Washington.
75. Colorado, Massachusetts, and Mississippi.
76. Colorado and Michigan.
77. *See* text accompanying note 455 *infra.* On the English law, *see* 11 Halsbury's Laws of England ¶ 1193 (4th ed. 1976); G. Williams, Criminal Law, *supra* note 16, at 264–65.
78. ALI Model Penal Code § 230.3 (1980).
79. Arkansas, California, Colorado, Delaware, Florida, Georgia, Kansas, Maryland, New Mexico, North Carolina, Oregon, South Carolina, and Virginia. English legislation adopted the same position. Abortion Act, 1967, c. 86, § 1 (1)(a). *See* G. Williams, *supra* note 16, at 257–60.
80. Arkansas, Colorado, Delaware, Florida, Georgia, Kansas, Maryland, New Mexico, North Carolina, Oregon, South Carolina, and Virginia. The English Abortion Act, 1967, contains similar coverage. § 1.(1)(b) ("substantial risk" of "such physical abnormalities as to be seriously handicapped"). *See* G. Williams, *supra* note 16, at 256–57. Similar legislation is found in Singapore, Singapore Abortion Act, 1969, and South Australia. *See* Roemer, *supra* note 18.
81. Arkansas, California, Colorado, Delaware, Florida, Georgia, Kansas, Maryland, Mississippi, New Mexico, North Carolina, Oregon, South Carolina, and Virginia. Whether statutory as well as forcible rape was included had to be determined in each state in light of statutory cross-references.
    Parliament declined to recognize rape as an independent basis for abortion. *See* G. Williams, *supra* note 16, at 260–61.
82. Arkansas, California, Colorado, Delaware, Florida, Kansas, New Mexico, North Carolina, Oregon, South Carolina, and Virginia.
83. Alaska, Hawaii, and Washington. The English Abortion Act, 1967, § 1(1)(a). (2), reaches about the same result by permitting medical practitioners to consider the actual or reasonably foreseeable environment of pregnant women in deciding whether their physical or mental health may be injured by pregnancy, as well as the risk to siblings if an additional child is born. *See also* note 16 *supra.*
84. *See* text accompanying notes 39–43 *supra.*
85. Alaska, Arkansas, Delaware, Georgia, Hawaii, North Carolina, Oregon, South Carolina, Virginia, and Washington.
86. *See* text accompanying notes 299–301 *infra.*
87. Louisiana and Mississippi.
88. Florida (repealed 1972), Nebraska, New Hampshire, Ohio, and Wisconsin. Missouri provided for advice by one duly licensed physician if an abortion was performed by one who was not a duly licensed physician. On this anomaly, *see* note 34 *supra.*

89. Arkansas, Delaware, Georgia, Kansas, North Carolina, Oregon, and South Carolina. Concurring physicians generally could not be relatives of or associated in medical practice with a doctor who wished to perform an abortion. The English Abortion Act, 1967, § 1(1), requires the good faith opinion of two medical practitioners, as does India's Medical Termination of Pregnancy Act, 1971, § 3(2).
90. California, Colorado, Delaware, Georgia, Maryland, New Mexico, and Virginia. Alaska left the matter to administrative regulation. On the counterpart requirement under the Canadian Criminal Code, § 251(4). *see* Harris & Tupper, *Study of Therapeutic Abortion Committees in British Columbia*, 11 U.B.C. L. Rev. 81 (1977) (in comparison with the English Abortion Act, 1967).
91. Delaware and Georgia.
92. Arkansas, Kansas, North Carolina, Oregon, South Carolina, and Washington. The English Abortion Act, 1967, § 1(4), creates an emergency exception if abortion is necessary to save the life or prevent grave permanent injury to a pregnant woman's physical or mental health.
93. *See* text accompanying notes 319–26 *infra*.
94. *See* text accompanying notes 81–82 *supra*.
95. Arkansas, Georgia, New Mexico, North Carolina, South Carolina, and Virginia.
96. California, Colorado, Delaware, Georgia, Maryland, Oregon, South Carolina.
97. Arkansas, California, Colorado, Delaware, Florida, Georgia, Hawaii, Kansas, Maryland, New Mexico, New York, North Carolina, Oregon, South Carolina, Virginia, and Washington. English Abortion Act, 1967, §§ 1(1), 2(1)(b), contain a like requirement.
98. Arkansas, California, Colorado, Delaware, Florida, Georgia, Hawaii, Kansas, Maryland, New Mexico, North Carolina, Oregon, South Carolina, Virginia, Washington, and Wisconsin.
99. Alaska and Washington. English Abortion Act, 1967, § 1(3), allows abortions to be performed in a hospital or place approved by the Minister of Health or Secretary of State, subject to an emergency exception in § 1(4).
100. *See* text accompanying notes 302–09 *infra*.
101. Arkansas, Colorado, and New Mexico. Sometimes this form of recordkeeping was imposed in addition to reporting requirements, as in Georgia, Maryland, and Oregon.
102. Delaware, Florida, Maryland, and South Carolina. Oregon left the matter to administrative regulation, which also is the stance of the English Abortion Act, 1967, § 2.
103. *See* text accompanying notes 368–80 *infra*.
104. Alaska, Arkansas, Colorado, Delaware, Florida, Georgia, Hawaii, Maryland, New Mexico, Oregon, South Carolina, Virginia, and Washington. A similar exemption for medical practitioners is provided in England's Abortion Act, 1967, § 4(1), but the burden of proof is on a practitioner who refuses an abortion on that basis. For a criticism of India's Medical Termination of Pregnancy Act, 1971 based on a failure to include similar language, *see*

Minattur, *Medical Termination of Pregnancy and Conscientious Objection,* 16 Indian L. Inst. J. 704 (1974).
105. *See* text accompanying notes 385–411 *infra.*
106. *See generally* Baude, *Constitutional Reflections on Abortion Reform,* 4 J. Law Reform 1 (1970); Lucas, *Federal Constitutional Limitations on the Enforcement and Administration of State Abortion Statutes,* 46 N.C.L. Rev. 730 (1968); Comment, *Abortion Laws: A Constitutional Right to Abortion,* 49 N.C. L. Rev. 487 (1971), indicating the thinking of the time.
　　For a retrospective view *see* Moore, *Moral Sentiment in Judicial Opinions on Abortion,* 15 Santa Clara Law. 591 (1975).
107. *See generally* Kolender v. Lawson, 461 U.S. 352 (1983); Smith v. Goguen, 415 U.S. 566 (1974); Papachristou v. Jacksonville, 405 U.S. 156 (1972).
108. *See, e.g.,* Craig v. Boren, 429 U.S. 190 (1976) (invalidating legislation penalizing sale of alcoholic beverages to males at a greater age than females).
109. *See, e.g.,* Harris v. McRae, 448 U.S. 297, 321–25 (1980); Mayer v. Chicago, 404 U.S. 189 (1972).
110. *See* the contraceptives cases cited in note 22 *supra*; Stanley v. Georgia, 394 U.S. 557 (1969) (private possession of pornography).
111. Roe v. Wade, 410 U.S. 113, 153. *See generally,* among the voluminous literature bearing on the Court's doctrine, Chemerinsky, *supra* note 5; Krimmel & Foley, *supra* note 8; Jones, *supra* note 11, at 605–12; King, *Juridical Status of the Fetus: A Proposal for the Legal Protection of the Unborn,* 77 Mich. L. Rev. 1647, 1650–57 (1979); Moore, *Moral Sentiment in Judicial Opinions on Abortion,* 15 Santa Clara Law. 591, 625–34 (1975); Morgan, *Roe v. Wade and the Lesson of the Pre-Roe Case Law,* 77 Mich. L. Rev. 1724 (1979); Parness & Pritchard, *To Be or Not To Be: Protecting the Unborn's Potentiality of Life,* 51 U. Cin. L. Rev. 257 (1982); Regan, *Rewriting Roe v. Wade,* 77 Mich. L. Rev. 1569 (1979); Wardle, *The Gap Between Law and Moral Order: An Examination of the Legitimacy of the Supreme Court Abortion Decisions,* 1980 B.Y.U. L. Rev. 811; Note, *Technological Advances and Roe v. Wade: The Need to Rethink Abortion Law,* 29 U.C.L.A. L. Rev. 1194 (1982).
112. Colautti v. Franklin, 439 U.S. 379, 386 (1979); Planned Parenthood of Central Missouri v. Danforth, 428 U.S. 52, 60 (1976).
113. 426 U.S. 416, 419–20 (1983) (*Roe* is entitled to *stare decisis* recognition).
114. Roe v. Wade, 410 U.S. at 162.
115. *Id.* at 161–62.
116. Akron v. Akron Center for Reproductive Health, 462 U.S. 416, 444 (1983): "[The ordinance] requires the physician to inform his patient that 'the unborn child is a human life from the moment of conception,' a requirement inconsistent with the Court's holding in *Roe* v. *Wade* that a State may not adopt one theory of when life begins to justify its regulation of abortions."
　　That this is the crux of the Court's abortion rationale is reflected in efforts to persuade Congress to adopt for presentation to the states for ratification a right-to-life amendment or to enact a human life statute on the strength of section 5 of the Fourteenth Amendment ("The Congress shall have the power to enforce, by appropriate legislation, the provisions of this article"). On the constitutionality of the latter approach, *see* Emerson, *The Power of*

Congress to Change Constitutional Decisions of the Supreme Court: The Human Life Bill, 77 Nw. U.L. Rev. 129 (1982) (questioning constitutionality); Estreicher, *Congressional Power and Constitutional Rights: Reflections on Proposed "Human Life" Legislation,* 68 Va. L. Rev. 333 (1982) (questioning constitutionality); Gordon, *Nature and Uses of Congressional Power Under Section 5 of the Fourteenth Amendment to Overcome Decisions of the Supreme Court,* 72 Nw. U.L. Rev. 656, 689–94 (1976) (questioning constitutionality); Hyde, *The Human Life Bill: Some Issues and Answers,* 27 N.Y.L. Sch. L. Rev. 1077 (1982); Isaacs, *Law of Fertility Regulation in the United States: A 1980 Review,* 19 J. Fam. L. 65, 70–71 (1980); Pilpel, *Hyde and Go Seek: A Response to Representative Hyde,* 27 N.Y.L. Sch. L. Rev. 1101 (1982); Uddo, *The Human Life Bill: Protecting the Unborn Through Congressional Enforcement of the Fourteenth Amendment,* 27 Loy. L. Rev. 1079 (1981) (supporting constitutionality); Note, *Constitutionality of the Human Life Bill,* 61 Wash. U.L.Q. 219 (1983) (suggesting constitutionality). The implications of such a bill for certain forms of contraception are discussed in Note, *Personhood and the Contraceptive Right,* 57 Ind. L.J. 579 (1982).

On the constitutional amendment, *see* Destro, *supra* note 27, at 1319–51. A survey of constitutional provisions in other nations may be found in Mukerjee, *World Constitutions and Population: A Preliminary Survey of World Constitutions,* 16 Indian L. Inst. J. 675, 679–87 (1974).

117. In Roe v. Wade, 410 U.S. at 113–14, the Court rejected the appellee's contention that the case had been mooted because Roe's pregnancy long since had been terminated by birth or abortion. Pregnancies will come to term before usual appellate processes can be completed, but "[p]regnancy often comes more than once to the same woman, and in the general population, if man is to survive, it will always be with us." Therefore, pregnancy truly "could be 'capable of repetition, yet evading review' " (quoting Southern Pacific Terminal Co. v. ICC, 219 U.S. 498, 515 [1911]).

118. *Id.* at 113.

119. *Id.* at 127–29.

120. Doe v. Bolton, 410 U.S. 179, 188–89 (1973); *see also* Colautti v. Franklin, 439 U.S. 379 (1979). In Roe v. Wade, 410 U.S. at 124–27, a medical doctor, a defendant in a pending criminal prosecution, was not allowed to appeal. This was not because of a want of standing, but because the Court's doctrine of preclusion, set forth in, *e.g.,* Samuels v. Mackell, 401 U.S. 66 (1971), and Younger v. Harris, 401 U.S. 37 (1971), prohibits federal courts from intervening in matters pending in state courts; potential prosecutions are not within the doctrine. In Doe v. Bolton, 410 U.S. at 189, the Court thought it unnecessary to decide whether nurses, clergy, social workers, and counseling services had standing because it resolved all the issues affecting them in connection with the physicians' attack on the state statute.

In Harris v. McRae, 448 U.S. 297, 318 n. 21 (1980), discussed in text accompanying notes 471–76 *infra,* the Court found that the constitutional entitlement of a physician advising financially unable Medicaid recipients was no greater than the entitlement of the patient; he or she had no greater due process protections, therefore.

121. Abortion clinics were allowed to litigate constitutional issues in Planned Parenthood of Central Missouri v. Danforth, 428 U.S. 52 (1976), and Akron v. Akron Center for Reproductive Health, 462 U.S. 416, 103 S. Ct. 2481 (1983). *See also* Deerfield Medical Center v. Deerfield Beach, 661 F.2d 328 (5th Cir., Unit B 1981) (abortion clinic had standing to assert privacy rights of women who might be unable to obtain abortions if municipality denied occupational license to clinic on basis of zoning ordinance).

122. Roe v. Wade, 410 U.S. at 153.

123. *Id.* at 159.

124. The Court's definition of "trimester" is discussed in text accompanying notes 177–79 *infra*.

125. Planned Parenthood of Central Missouri v. Danforth, 428 U.S. at 61 (quoting Roe v. Wade, 410 U.S. at 164).

126. *Id.*

127. *See* text accompanying note 120 *supra*.

128. Akron v. Akron Center for Reproductive Health, 462 U.S. at 431.

129. Roe v. Wade, 410 U.S. at 163.

130. Akron v. Akron Center for Reproductive Health, 462 U.S. at 431. On the minimal risk of medically administered abortion, *see* Sneideman, *supra* note 19, at 194–97.

131. "[A] point purposefully left flexible for professional determination, and dependent upon developing medical skill and technical ability." Planned Parenthood of Central Missouri v. Danforth, 428 U.S. at 61. *See also* text accompanying notes 180–83 *infra*.

132. Planned Parenthood of Central Missouri v. Danforth, 428 U.S. at 61 (paraphrasing Roe v. Wade, 410 U.S. at 164–65).

133. *See* cases cited in note 107 *supra*.

134. Akron v. Akron Center for Reproductive Health, 462 U.S. at 451–52 (ordinance making it a misdemeanor not to dispose of remains of unborn children in "a humane and sanitary manner," held vague and indefinite); Colautti v. Franklin, 439 U.S. at 390–401 (viability determination and standard of care provisions in felony statute voided for vagueness).

135. *See* text accompanying notes 463–66, 475–76 *infra*. Efforts to claim a right to abortion based on free exercise of religion under the first amendment likewise have been rejected. Harris v. McRae, 448 U.S. 297, 318–21 (1980); Women's Services v. Thone, 636 F.2d 206, 209 (8th Cir. 1980).

136. From this point forward, in the interests of economy of space, only the name of a state and section citations of pertinent legislation will appear. A full reference to statutory sources, including years of main volume and supplement publication, appears in a statutory appendix.

137. *E.g.,* People v. Norton, 181 Colo. 147, 507 P.2d 862 (1973); State v. Sulman, 165 Conn. 556, 339 A.2d 62 (1973), disapproved in its application to nonphysicians in State v. Menillo, 171 Conn. 141, 368 A.2d 136 (1976) (on remand from Connecticut v. Mcnillo, 423 U.S. 9 [1975]); State v. Mirmelli, 54 Ill, 2d 25, 294 N.E.2d 267 (1973); State v. Hultgren, 295 Minn. 299, 204 N.W.2d 197 (1973) (nonphysician); State v. Hodgson, 295 Minn, 294, 204 N.W.2d 199 (1973) (physician); Spears v. State, 278 So. 2d 443 (Miss. 1973); Commonwealth v. Jackson, 454 Pa. 429, 312 A.2d 13 (1973) (nonphysician);

State v. Lawrence, 261 S.C. 18, 198 S.E.2d 253 (1973); State v. Munson, 87 S.D. 245, 206 N.W.2d 434 (1973); Doe v. Burk, 513 P.2d 643 (Wyo. 1973).

138. The matter was left to a legislative study commission. New Jersey Criminal Law Revision Commission Final Report, Commentary 259 (1971). A comprehensive abortion regulation statute was approved by the New Jersey Legislature, Assembly Bill No. 1285, but was vetoed by Governor Brendan Byrne on January 3, 1980.

Illegal abortions can be prosecuted under assault provisions, N.J. Stat. Ann. § 2C:12–1(a)(1) (West 1982), since consent to acts causing more than trifling inconvenience is legally irrelevant to criminality. *Id.* § 2C:2–10(b); ALI Model Penal Code § 2.11(2)(Permanent ed. with revised commentary, 1985).

139. Tex. Penal Code §§ 4512.1–4512.4, 4512.6 (Vernon 1972). Criminal abortions could be prosecuted as assault under *id.* §§ 22.01(a)(1), 22.02(a)(1), however, and consent is valid only if a victim knows the injury to be a risk of "recognized medical treatment." *Id.* § 22.06(2)(B).

140. Alaska § 08.64.105. *See* Cleveland v. Anchorage, 631 P.2d 1073 (Alaska 1981). The state had taken this approach to the problem before 1973. *See* note 83 *supra.*

141. *E.g.,* Nev. § 442.260(1) (although § 442.250 tracks the *Roe* grounds for lawful abortion); Ohio § 3701.341(A) (although the provision lists only some matters for regulation without an *ejusdem generis* clause). Failure to comply with procedures in an administrative procedure act governing promulgation of regulations can invalidate regulations. *See, e.g.,* McKee v. Likins, 261 N.W.2d 566 (Minn. 1977) (regulation restricting use of public funds for therapeutic abortion invalidated for failure to comply with APA notice requirements).

142. *Cf.* Mo. § 188.010 ("It is the intention of the [legislature] to reasonably regulate abortion in conformance with the decisions of the supreme court of the United States"); Pa. tit. 18 § 3202(c) ("In every relevant civil or criminal proceeding in which it is possible to do so without violating the Federal Constitution, the common and statutory law of Pennsylvania shall be construed so as to extend to the unborn the equal protection of the laws and to further the public policy of this Commonwealth encouraging childbirth over abortion").

Articles on current abortion legislation from the standpoint of theology and ethics include Fletcher, *Abortion and the True Believer,* 91 Christian Century 1126 (November 27, 1974); Fromer, *supra* note 5, at 239–40; Orloski, *Abortion: Legal Questions and Legislative Alternatives,* 131 America 50 (Aug. 10, 1974).

143. *E.g.,* Ind. § 16–10–3–4; Minn. § 256B.011; N.D. § 14–02.3–01.

The Supreme Court indicated that states are not prevented from making such a value judgment and implementing it by allocation of public funds. Maher v. Roe, 432 U.S. 464, 474, (1977); *see also* Harris v. McRae, 448 U.S. 297, 314–15 (1980) (utilizing *Maher v. Roe* principles in the context of the Hyde Amendment prohibiting the use of Medicaid funds for abortions; *see* text accompanying notes 471–76 *infra*).

144. *E.g.,* Ill. ch. 38, § 81–21 ("the unborn child is a human being from the time of conception and is, therefore, a legal person for purposes of the unborn

child's right to life and is entitled to the right to life from conception under the laws and Constitution of this State"); Ky. § 311.710(5) ("declared policy . . . to recognize and to protect the lives of all human beings regardless of their degree of biological development"); Mont. § 50–20–102 ("tradition of the state of Montana to protect every human life, whether unborn or aged, healthy or sick"; "intent to extend the protection of the laws of Montana in favor of all human life"); Neb. § 28–325(4) ("this state is prevented from providing adequate legal remedies to protect . . . unborn human life"); N.D. § 14–02.1–01 ("purpose . . . to protect unborn human life"; "reaffirms tradition of the state of North Dakota to protect every human life whether unborn or aged, healthy or sick").

145. Neb. § 28–325.
146. Mont. § 94–5–623.
147. Ill. ch. 38, § 81–21.
148. Ky. § 311.710(5).
149. Idaho §§ 18–614 to 18–615.
150. *Id.* at § 18–613.
151. Maine tit. 22, § 1596(1)(B).
152. Iowa § 707.7. This may well reflect a legislative bias against abortion. *See* text accompanying notes 5, 143–50 *supra*.
153. *E.g.,* La. § 37:1285(8)–(9); Md. § 20–208(a); Va. § 18.2–72; Wash. § 9.02.070.
154. *E.g.,* Ill. ch. 38, § 81–22(6) (criminal code context); Me. tit. 22, §§ 1596(1)(A), 1598(2)(A); Pa. tit. 18, § 3203; Utah § 76–7–301(1) (including all procedures undertaken to kill a live unborn child and to produce miscarriage). *See generally* Warren, *supra* note 17, at 27; Note, *Criminal Liability of Physician: An Encroachment on the Abortion Right?*, 18 Am. Crim. L. Rev. 581, 592–93 (1981).
155. *E.g.,* Idaho § 18–604(1) (intentional); Iowa § 707.7 (intentional); Kan. § 21–3407 (purposeful); Maine tit. 22, §§ 1596(1)(A), 1598(2)(A) (intentional); Mass. ch. 112, § 12K (knowing destruction or intentional expulsion or removal); Mich. § 333.2835(1) (purposeful); Mo. § 188.015(1) (intentional); Neb. § 28–326(1) (intent); N.Y. Penal Law § 125.05(2) (intent); Okla. tit. 63, § 1–730(1) (purposeful); R.I. § 23–4.7–1 (intent); Va. § 18.2–72 (intent) (criminal code); Wyo. § 35–6–101(a)(i) (intent).
156. *E.g.,* Ill. ch. 38, § 81–22(6); Ky. § 311.720(1); Tenn. § 39–5–201(a)(1); Wyo. § 35–6–101(a)(i).
157. *E.g.,* Fla. § 390.011(2); Idaho § 18–604(1) (viable birth); Ind. § 35–1–58.5–1(B); Iowa § 702.02 (in conscience exception provision); Kan. § 21–3407 (other than by live birth); Maine tit. 22, §§ 1596(1)(A), 1598(2)(A); Mass. ch. 112, § 12K; Mo. 188.015(1) (to increase probability of live birth); Mont. § 50–20–104(4); Neb. § 28–326(1) (if "unborn child's viability is threatened by continuation of the pregnancy, early delivery after viability shall not be construed as an abortion"); Nev. § 442.240; N.D. § 14–02.1–02(1); Okla. tit. 63, § 1–730(1); Or. § 435.455(1); R.I. § 23–4.7–1 (*semble*: not including completion of incomplete spontaneous miscarriage); S.C. § 44–41–10(a) (delivery of viable birth); S.D. § 34–23A–a(1); Utah § 76–7–301(1); V.I. tit. 14, § 151(a); Wyo. § 35–6–101(a)(i) (except when

viability is threatened by continuation of pregnancy and early delivery is induced after viability by commonly accepted obstetrical practices).

158. *E.g.,* Fla. § 390.011(2); Ind. § 35–1–58.5–1(b); Iowa § 702.02 (in conscience exception provision); Maine tit. 22, §§ 1596(1)(A), 1598(2)(A); Mass. ch. 112, § 12K; Mo. § 188.015(1) (dead or dying unborn child); Nev. § 442.240; N.D. § 14–02.1–02(1); Okla. tit. 63, § 1–730(1); S.C. § 44–41–10(a); S.D. § 34–23A–1(1); Utah § 76–7–301(1); V.I. tit. 14, § 151(a).

159. Alaska § 18.16.010 (nonviable fetus). On the unconstitutionality of prohibitions against all abortions after viability, *see* text accompanying notes 131–32 *supra,* notes 181–84 *infra.*

160. *E.g.,* Iowa § 707.7 (after end of second trimester); Maine tit. 22, § 1596(1)(B) (miscarriage defined as interruption of pregnancy of less than 20 weeks duration).

161. *E.g.,* Okla. tit. 63, § 1–730(4) ("sperm of a male individual"); S.C. § 44–41–10(g); Wyo. § 35–6–101(iii).

162. *See* text accompanying notes 221–23 *infra.*

163. N.M. § 30–5–1(A).

164. *E.g.,* Mass. ch. 112, § 12K; Pa. tit. 18, § 3203; S.C. § 44–41–10(f); Wyo. § 35–6–101(a)(vi).

165. *See* note 19 *supra.*

166. *See* text accompanying notes 143–50 *supra.*

167. Ill. ch. 38, § 81–22(9).

168. Ky. § 311.720(5).

169. *E.g.,* Mass. ch. 112, § 12K; Mo. 188.015(5) ("human offspring from conception until birth at every stage of biological development"); Okla. tit. 63, § 1–730(2) ("from the moment of conception, through pregnancy, and until live birth including the human conceptus, zygote, morula, blastocyst, embryo and fetus").

On Canadian doctrine, *see* Weiler & Catton, *The Unborn Child in Canadian Law,* 14 Osgoode Hall L. Rev. 643, 645–47 (1976); Note, *Abortion Law in Canada: A Need for Reform,* 42 Sask. L. Rev. 221, 232–38 (1977).

170. *See* text accompanying notes 124–32 *supra.*

171. Idaho § 18–604(4).

172. *Id.* at § 18–604(5); the provision sets out a conclusive, unrebuttable presumption in favor of licensed physicians that the second trimester does not end before the beginning of the 25th week of pregnancy.

173. *Id.* at § 18–604(6).

174. Pa. tit. 18, § 3203.

175. Ill. ch. 38, § 81–22(1). "Viability" is the only other term defined. *Id.* at § 81–22(2).

176. S.C. § 44–41–10(i) (through 12th week); conception is defined *id.* at § 44–41–10(g). The second trimester extends from the 13th through the 24th week, *id.* at § 44–41–10(j), and the third trimester from the 25th week through termination of pregnancy. *Id.* at § 44–41–10(k).

177. Ind. § 35–1–58.5–1(a).

178. Akron v. Akron Center for Reproductive Health, 462 U.S. at 431.

179. *Id.* at 429 n.11. *See also* Comment, *The Trimester Approach: How Long Can the Legal Fiction Last?,* 35 Mercer L. Rev. 891, 909–13 (1984).

180. A declaration of unconstitutionality is even more likely if criminal penalties turn on ascertaining the stage of pregnancy. Ind. § 35–1–58.5–3 requires a physician to determine and certify which trimester of pregnancy the patient is in, as well as viability, and § 35–1–58.5–4 makes noncompliance a class C felony. If such a standard functions as an impediment to free implementation of a pregnant woman's constitutional claim to a therapeutic abortion, it will be struck down. *See* Akron v. Akron Center for Reproductive Health, 462 U.S. at 430.

181. *See* text accompanying notes 131–32 *supra. See also* Griffin, *Viability and Fetal Life in State Criminal Abortion Laws,* 72 J. Crim. L. & Criminology 324 (1981); Special Project, *supra* note 27, at 128–46; Note, *Criminal Liability of Physicians: An Encroachment on the Abortion Right?,* 18 Am. Crim. L. Rev. 591, 600–01 (1981); Note, *Current Technology Affecting Supreme Court Abortion Jurisprudence,* 27 N.Y.L. Sch. L. Rev. 1221, 1239–42 (1982); Note, *Viability and Fetal Life in State Criminal Abortion Laws,* 72 J. Crim. L. & Criminology 324 (1981); Comment, *Fetal Viability and Individual Autonomy: Resolving Medical and Legal Standards for Abortion,* 27 U.C.L.A. L. Rev. 1340, 1356–64 (1980); Comment, *Technological Advances and Roe v. Wade: The Need to Rethink Abortion Law,* 29 U.C.L.A. L. Rev. 1194, 1202–14 (1982).

182. Planned Parenthood of Central Missouri v. Danforth, 428 U.S. at 63 (quoting Roe v. Wade, 410 U.S. at 160, 163). *See also* Colautti v. Franklin, 439 U.S. at 386.

183. *E.g.,* Idaho § 18–604(7); Ill. ch. 38, § 81–22(2) (reasonable likelihood of more than momentary survival of fetus outside womb, with or without artificial support); Ind. § 35–1–58.5–1(e); Iowa § 702.2 ("indefinitely outside womb"; "the time . . . may vary with each pregnancy, and the determination of whether a particular fetus is viable is a matter of responsible medical judgment"); Ky. § 311.720(8); La. § 14:87.5 (indefinitely outside womb); Minn. § 145.411(2); Mo. § 188.015(6); Neb. § 28–326(6); N.D. § 14–2.1–02(7); Okla. tit. 63, § 1–730(3); Pa. tit. 18, § 3203 (stage of fetal development, when in physician's judgment "in light of most advanced medical technology and information available" there is a reasonable likelihood of sustained survival of the unborn child outside the body of the mother, with or without artificial support); S.C. § 44–41–10(*1*); Tenn. § 39–4–202(b)(3) (*semble:* in providing information for pregnant women, physician must describe viability in equivalent terms); Wyo. § 35–6–101(a)(vii).

184. Planned Parenthood of Central Missouri v. Danforth, 428 U.S. at 64–65. There is latent difficulty in, *e.g.,* Minn. § 145.411(2) ("during the second half of its gestation period a fetus shall be considered potentially 'viable' "), if that is intended to extend the limitations on post-viability abortions to women whose fetuses are not yet viable. South Carolina establishes a presumption of viability no sooner than the 24th week of pregnancy, § 44–41–10(*1*); this is acceptable if a woman with a viable fetus can obtain an abortion based on medical considerations not related to her life and health (assuming that does not infringe the constitutional status of the fetus, an implication of its *Roe v. Wade* analysis the Court has not yet explored), but

unacceptable if invoked to deny an otherwise proper abortion to a woman who has not experienced fetal life by the 24th week of pregnancy.

    See also Fromer, *supra* note 5, at 237–39.

185. *E.g.,* Ill. ch. 38, § 81–26(2) (*semble*: human born alive is an individual under criminal code); Maine tit. 22, § 1595; N.D. § 1402.1–02(4); Pa. tit. 18, § 3203 ("human being was completely expelled or extracted from his or her mother and after such separation breathed or showed evidence of any of the following: beating of the heart, pulsation of the umbilical cord, definite movement of voluntary muscles or any brain-wave activity").

186. *See* text accompanying notes 348–52, 438–40 *infra*. In Constitutional Right to Life Committee v. Cannon, 117 R.I. 52, 363 A.2d 215 (1976), the court held that states are bound by Supreme Court definitions of "life" and "trimester," despite a tender of expert data that the Court's premises were not scientifically valid.

187. 410 U.S. at 165.

188. *E.g.,* Alaska § 18.16.010; Cal. Health & Safety Code § 25951; Colo. § 18–6–101(1); Conn. § 53–3a(c); Del. tit. 24, § 1790(a); Fla. § 390.001(1)(a), (3); Ga. § 26–1202(a); Idaho §§ 18–604(2), 18–608, 18–609, *and see* § 18–606(2) (hospital, nurse, or other health care personnel do not commit a crime if in good faith they provide abortion-related services in reliance on the directions of a physician or pursuant to a hospital admission authorized by a physician); Ill. ch. 38, §§ 81–22(3), 81–23.1; Ind. §§ 35–1–58.5–1(d), 35–1–58.5–2(a); Iowa § 707.7; Kan. § 21–3407(2); Ky. §§ 311.720(7), 311.750; La. 37:1285(8.1), (9) (unless physician lacks training and experience to perform the procedure); Maine tit. 22, § 1598(1), (3)(A); Md. §§ 20–207, 20–208(a); Mass. ch. 112, §§ 12L, 13M; Minn. § 145.412(1)(1) (or physician in training under supervision of licensed physician); Mo. § 188.020; Mont. § 50–20–109(1)(a); Neb. §§ 28–326(3), 28–335 (abortion by other than a licensed physician a felony); Nev. § 442.250(1)(a) (including physician in employ of United States); N.M. § 30–5–1(C); N.Y. Penal Law § 125.05(3) (abortion by duly licensed physician is justifiable); N.C. § 14.45.1(a), (b); N.D. § 14.02.1–04(1); Okla. tit. 63, § 1–731(A); Or. § 435.415(3); R.I. §§ 23–4.7–1, 23–4.7–7 (*semble*: unprofessional conduct defined as performance of abortion by physician without obtaining requisite consent); Pa. tit. 18, § 3204(a); S.C. § 44–41–20; S.D. §§ 34–23A–1(2), 34–23A–3, 34–23A–4 (including physician in employ of United States); Tenn. § 39–4–201(c); Utah §§ 76–6–301(2), 76–7–302(1) (including qualified physician in federal employment); Va. §§ 18.2–72 to 18.2–74; Wash. § 9.02.070; Wyo. §§ 35–6–102, 35–6–103, 35–6–111 (*semble*: statutory references are to physicians performing abortions, and abortion by other than a physician is punishable as a felony).

    V.I. tit. 14, § 151(b)(1) refers to licensed physicians during the first 12 weeks of pregnancy, but subsections (2) and (3) limit abortions thereafter to those performed by licensed surgeons or gynecologists. If there is no supportable medical basis for that limitation, and it serves to make otherwise lawful abortions less readily available than otherwise would be the case, the latter limitation is unconstitutional under Akron v. Akron Center for Reproductive Health, 462 U.S. at 461–66.

    If a state legislature does not legitimate therapeutic abortions performed by licensed physicians, a court must read in that exemption from penal law coverage. *See, e.g.,* People v. Bricker, 389 Mich. 524, 208 N.W.2d 172 (1973).

189. Connecticut v. Menillo, 423 U.S. 9 (1975); *see* text accompanying notes 413–16 *infra*.

190. *See* Akron v. Akron Center for Reproductive Health, 462 U.S. at 461–66.

191. *See id.* at 430–31.

192. Planned Parenthood of Central Missouri v. Danforth, 428 U.S. at 65–67; *see* text accompanying notes 233–51 *infra*.

193. *E.g.,* V.I. tit. 18, § 291(a) (public or private hospitals, institutions and personnel may counsel minors concerning pregnancy, including abortion).

194. *E.g.,* Ill. ch. 38, § 81–23.1(B)(1) (with legislatively mandated content); Ky. § 311.723(b)(2)(a) (but with legislative objectives specified); Ohio § 3701.34.1(A)(5).

195. Mo. § 188.063; Okla. tit. 63, § 1–738; S.C. Health & Environment Control Dep't R. 61–12, § 203(C).

196. *E.g.,* Ill. ch. 38, § 81–23.1(B)(1)(a) (administrative regulations must provide for this); Pa. tit. 18, § 3204(b).

197. Md. § 20–209(c); Okla. tit. 63, § 1–738; S.D. § 34–23A–10 (physicians must make available to patients at request information about professional social service and counseling service agencies in the state providing a full spectrum of alternative solutions for problem pregnancies).

198. *See* text accompanying note 224 *infra*.

199. Planned Parenthood of Central Missouri v. Danforth, 428 U.S. at 67, 85; *see also* Akron v. Akron Center for Reproductive Health, 462 U.S. at 442–44.

200. Planned Parenthood of Central Missouri v. Danforth, 428 U.S. at 67.

201. Colautti v. Franklin, 439 U.S. at 394.

202. Akron v. Akron Center for Reproductive Health, 462 U.S. at 443.

203. *See* text accompanying notes 221–23 *infra*.

204. *E.g.,* Me. tit. 22, § 1599; Mo. § 188.039(2); Nev. § 442.253 (with copy of pregnancy test results if available); N.D. § 14–02.1–02(5)(a); R.I. § 23–4.7–3; Tenn. § 39–4–202(b)(l).

205. *E.g.,* Ill. ch. 38, § 81–23.2(1)(iii) (gestational age of fetus at time abortion will be performed); Ky. § 311.762(2) (same); Me. tit. 22, § 1599 (number of weeks from probable time of conception); Mo. § 188.039(2) (same); Nev. § 442.253 (same); N.D. § 14–02.1–02(5)(b) (based on information provided by patient or medical and laboratory evaluations); Pa. tit. 18, § 3205(a)(1)(iv) (probable gestational age of unborn child at time abortion is to be performed); R.I. § 23–4.7–3 (gestational age of fetus at time of disclosure); Tenn. § 39–4–202(b)(2) (number of weeks elapsed from conception based on last menstrual period or after physical examination or laboratory tests).

206. *E.g.,* Del. tit. 24, § 1794(a)(1); Fla. § 390.025(2); Ind. § 35–1–58.5–1(f); Me. tit. 22, § 1599; Mass. ch. 112, § 12S; Minn. § 145.412(1)(4); Mont. § 50–20–104(3)(a); Neb. § 28–326(8); Okla. tit. 63, § 1–738 (*semble*: such information must be given before a hospital can advertise that it offers counseling services); R.I. § 23–4.7–3; S.C. Health & Environment Control Dep't R. 61–12, § 201(C); Utah § 76–7–305(1); Va. § 18.2–76.

207. *E.g.,* Del. tit. 24, § 1794(a)(2) (probable effects of procedure on woman,

including effects on childbearing ability and possible future pregnancies);
Fla. § 390.025(2); Idaho § 18–609 (possible emotional or psychological
consequences); Minn. § 145.412(1)(4); Mo. § 188.039(2); Mont. §
50–20–104(3)(b) (physical and psychological effect); Nev. § 442.253 (any
known immediate and long-term physical or psychological dangers); Pa. tit.
18, § 3205(a)(1)(ii) ("the fact that there may be detrimental physical and
psychological facts which are not accurately foreseeable"); S.C. Health &
Environment Control Dep't R. 61–12, § 201(C).

208. *E.g.,* Del. tit. 24, § 1794(4); Idaho § 18–609 (likelihood of woman becoming
pregnant again); Ill. ch. 38, § 81–23.2(1)(ii) (particular medical risks associated with particular abortion procedure to be employed); Ky. § 311.726(2)
(same); Me. tit. 22, § 1599 (same); Mass. ch. 112, § 12S (possible complications associated with use of procedure and performance of abortion itself);
Mo. § 188.039(2) (immediate and long-term physical dangers of abortion and
psychological trauma resulting from abortion and any increased incidence of
premature births, tubal pregnancies and stillbirths following abortion); Neb.
§ 28–326(8) (reasonably possible medical and mental consequences resulting
from abortion, pregnancy, and childbirth); Nev. § 442.253 (similar language
to Missouri); N.D. § 14–02.1–02(5)(d) (same); Pa. tit. 18, § 3205(a)(1)(iii)
("the particular medical risks associated with the particular abortion procedure to be employed including, when medically accurate, the risks of
infection, hemorrhage, danger to subsequent pregnancies and infertility"),
(v) (medical risks associated with carrying child to term); R.I. § 23–4.7–3 (but
information need not be communicated if there is a medical basis, certified in
writing in patient's record, for nondisclosure); Tenn. § 39–4–202(b)(6)
(numerous benefits and risks are attendant on either continued pregnancy
and childbirth or to abortion depending on patient's circumstances; physician to explain benefits and risks to best of ability and knowledge of
circumstances), (7) (particular risks associated with pregnancy and childbirth and abortion or child delivery technique to be employed, including at
least a general description of medical instructions to be followed after
abortion or childbirth to ensure safe recovery); Utah § 76–7–305(2); Va. §
18.2–76 (risks if any in her particular case to her health).

209. *E.g.,* Ill. ch. 38, § 81–23.2(1)(i); Ky. § 311.726(2); Pa. tit. 18, § 3205(a)(1)(i).

210. *E.g.,* Ill. ch. 38, § 81–23.2(3) (physician or persons associated with them can
express personal views concerning the validity or importance of information
required to be communicated); Ky. § 311.726(4) (same); Mo. § 188.039(2);
Nev. § 442.253; N.D. § 14–02.1–02(5) (any other explanation of information
which in the exercise of the physician's best medical judgment is reasonably
necessary to allow the woman to give an informed consent with full
knowledge of the nature and consequences of abortion); R.I. § 23–4.7–3
(same); Utah § 76–7–305(2) (other factors deemed necessary to a voluntary
and informed consent).

At least four states, Ill. ch. 38, § 81–26(6); Nev. § 442.253(*1*); Pa. tit. 18, §
3208(a); R.I. § 23–4.7–5(c), require women to receive printed information in
a language they can understand, with a notation whether an interpreter has
been used during counseling. Statutes in R.I. § 23–4.7–5(d) and S.D. §
34–23A–10.1 allow for a copy to the patient at her request.

211. To the extent there is no significantly greater risk of premature births, tubal pregnancies and stillbirths following induced abortion in comparison to spontaneous miscarriages and normal childbirth, based on current medical experience, the statutory language probably provides the "parade of horribles" which leads to constitutional invalidation. *See* Akron v. Akron Center for Reproductive Health, 462 U.S at 445; text accompanying notes 221–23 *infra*.

212. This pattern of legislation is constitutional, from indications in Akron v. Akron Center for Reproductive Health, 462 U.S. at 446–47, sustaining ordinance language not dissimilar to most of the cited statutes.

213. Ill. ch. 38, § 81–26(6) (class B misdemeanor to fail to inform). This seems unconstitutional in light of Supreme Court comments in Akron v. Akron Center for Reproductive Health, 462 U.S. at 444.

214. Tenn. § 39–4–202(b)(4) (abortion in a considerable number of cases constitutes a major surgical procedure). Such a warning was invalidated in Akron v. Akron Center for Reproductive Health, 462 U.S. at 444, ("a dubious statement"; trial court expert evidence supported a conclusion that it is a minor surgical procedure, *id.* at n. 35).

215. *E.g.,* Del. tit. 24, § 1794(a)(5); Fla. § 390.025(1); Ky. § 311.729(1); Me. tit. 22, § 1599; Mass. ch. 112, § 12S; Mo. § 188.039(2); Mont. § 50–20–104(3)(c); Neb. § 28–326(8); Nev. § 442.253; N.D. § 14–02,1–02(5)(f); Pa. tit. 18, § 3203(b)(1); R.I. § 23–4.7–3; S.C. Health & Environment Control Dep't R. 61–12, § 201(C); Tenn. § 39–4–202(b)(5). The Massachusetts statute was held constitutional in Planned Parenthood League of Massachusetts v. Bellotti, 641 F.2d 1006, 1020–21 (1st Cir. 1981).

216. *E.g.,* Ill. ch. 38, § 81–23.5(1); Ky. § 311.729(1); Me. tit. 22, § 1599; Md. § 20–209; Pa. tit. 18, § 3205(a)(2)(i) (medical assistance benefits may be available for prenatal care, childbirth and neonatal care), (ii) (father is liable to assist in support of child, even if father has offered to pay for abortion).

217. *E.g.,* Md. § 20–209; R.I. § 23–4.7–3; Utah § 76–7–305(2).

218. S.D. § 34–23A–10.

219. *E.g.,* Ill. ch. 38, § 81.23.5; Ky. § 3111.729(1); Mass. ch. 112, § 12S; Pa. tit. 18, § 3205(a)(2)(iii); R.I. § 23–4.7–5(a); Utah § 76–7–305.5(1)(a).

220. Mass. ch. 112, § 12S. The statute was sustained as constitutional in Planned Parenthood League of Massachusetts v. Bellotti, 641 F.2d 1006, 1020–21 (1st Cir. 1981). *See also* text accompanying notes 487–91 *infra*.

221. Akron v. Akron Center for Reproductive Health, 462 U.S. at 443.

222. Utah § 76–7–305.5(1)(b) requires the state department of health to provide descriptions of physical characteristics of normal unborn children at two-week intervals, beginning with the fourth week and ending with the 24th week, accompanied by scientifically verified photographs of an unborn child at each stage of development, including information about physiological and anatomical characteristics, brain and heart function, and presence of external members and internal organs during applicable stages of gestation.

223. *E.g.,* Del. tit. 24, § 1794(a)(3) (facts of fetal development to time proposed abortion is to be performed); Idaho § 18–609 (similar); Ill. ch. 38, § 81–23.5(2) (probable anatomical and physiological characteristics of fetus at various gestational ages at which abortion might be performed, including relevant

information concerning possibility of fetal survival); Ky. § 311.729(3) (same); Mass. ch. 112, § 12S (information about stage of development of unborn child); Mo. § 188.039(2) (like Delaware); Mont. § 50–20–104(3)(a) (similar); N.D. § 14–02.1–02(5)(c) (similar); Pa. tit. 18, § 3202(b)(i).

224. Akron v. Akron Center for Reproductive Health, 462 U.S. at 444. *See also* Planned Parenthood Association of Kansas City v. Ashcroft, 462 U.S. at 476, *aff'd on other grounds,* 462 U.S. at 476 (woman's decision was burdened insofar as anxiety and tension involved in such a decision are increased without medical justification); Planned Parenthood League of Massachusetts v. Bellotti, 641 F.2d 1006, 1021–22 (1st Cir. 1981) (information was not directly related to any medically relevant fact, would cause many women "emotional distress, anxiety, guilt, and in some cases increased physical pain," and provided nothing the essence of which most if not all women do not understand before receiving it).

225. Akron v. Akron Center for Reproductive Health, 462 U.S. at 445: "By insisting upon recitation of a lengthy and inflexible list of information, Akron has placed 'obstacles in the path of the doctor upon whom [a woman is] entitled to rely for advice in connection with her decision' " (quoting Whalen v. Roe, 429 U.S. 589, 604 n.33 [1977]).

226. *E.g.,* Del. tit. 24, § 1794(a); Ind. § 35–1–58.5–1(f); Md. § 20–209; Minn. § 145.412(1)(4); Neb. § 28–326(8) (*semble*: physician certifies that patient has been advised); Pa. tit. 18, § 3205(a)(3) (woman to certify in a writing that she has received the information required), (4) (physician must receive copy of woman's certification before performing abortion).

227. *E.g.,* Ill. ch. 38, § 81–23.5(3); Ky. § 311.729(4); Pa. tit. 18, § 3205(a)(3) (woman certifies that physician or agent has given required information); and R.I. § 23–4.7–3 designate a physician or associated personnel or authorized agents. Fla. § 390.025(2) covers only abortion counseling or referral agencies. S.C. Health & Environment Control Dep't R. 61–12, § 201(C), refers to properly qualified personnel. S.D. § 34–23A–10 is triggered only by a patient's request for information about counseling service agencies.

228. *E.g.,* Idaho § 18–609; Me. tit. 22, § 1599; Mo. § 188.039(2); Mont. § 50–20–106(2), (5); Nev. § 442.253; N.D. § 14–02.1–02(5); Tenn. § 39–4–202(b) (patient must sign form indicating physician has orally informed her); Utah § 76–7–305(2); Va. § 18.2–76.

229. 462 U.S. at 446–49.

230. Idaho § 18–609; Ill. ch. 38, § 81–23.4.

231. The Illinois provision, Ill. ch. 38, 18–233 (A), was repealed in 1984. A similar Missouri provision was held invalid in Planned Parenthood Association of Kansas City v. Ashcroft, 462 U.S. at 476, *aff'd on other grounds.*

232. *See* text accompanying notes 253–57 *infra* (spousal consent), notes 245–52 *infra* (parental).

233. Planned Parenthood of Central Missouri v. Danforth, 428 U.S. at 65–67; *cf.* Guste v. Jackson, 429 U.S. 399 (1977) (court should not have invalidated state consent statute as far as women generally were concerned); *see also* Smith v. Bentley, 493 F. Supp. 916, 928 (E.D. Ark. 1980).

234. That norm appears occasionally in legislation. *See, e.g.,* Iowa § 707.8(3)

(procuring consent through force or intimidation a felony); Pa. tit. 18, § 3206(g) (minor or mental incompetent); Tenn. § 39–4–201(b)(3) (obtain or procure abortion); Utah § 76–7–312 (coercion to obtain abortion). *Query,* does the coverage only of a decision to have an abortion, and not of one to forego abortion, constitute an unreasonable legislative classification denying equal protection? *See* text accompanying notes 487–91 *infra.*

Cf. Sanchez v. Sirmons, 121 Misc. 2d 249, 467 N.Y.S.2d 757 (Sup. Ct. 1983) (arbitration clause in a medical consent form was not binding in malpractice suit based on bungled abortion unless defendant physician established that the woman knew she was waiving the right to a jury trial; the circumstances of an abortion decision made such awareness unlikely).

A refusal to undergo an abortion cannot be asserted as a defense in a "wrongful birth" action (*see* note 384 *infra*), based on a claim that a plaintiff had brought about the damages through her own choice. Morris v. Frudenfeld, 135 Cal. App. 3d 23, 185 Cal. Rptr. 76 (1982); Rivera v. State, 94 Misc. 2d 157, 163, 404 N.Y.S.2d 950, 954 (Ct. Claims 1978) (any interpretation of traditional doctrine which would require an abortion would be "an invasion of privacy of the grossest and most pernicious kind").

A constitutional issue is inherent in statutory provisions, *e.g.,* Ill. ch. 38, §§ 81–27 to 28 (*semble*: physician and hospital must notify juvenile court that infant has been born and juvenile court must determine whether it has been abandoned); Ind. § 35–1–58.5–7(c); Mo. § 188.040; Mont. § 50–20–108(2); N.D. § 14–02.1–08; S.D. § 34–23A–18 (*semble*: all facts and circumstances involving birth and abortion are relevant and material evidence in parental rights termination, dependency or neglect proceedings; state department of social services may commence proceedings); Tenn. § 39–4–207; Tex. Civ. Code § 15.022 (*semble*: action to terminate parental rights may be based on abortion other than to save woman's life), that after a consent has been filed and a live birth results, the child is deemed abandoned and a ward of the state unless the consent is retracted before birth occurs.

The constitutionality of such provisions appears suspect. *Cf.* Freiman v. Ashcroft, 584 F.2d 247 (8th Cir. 1978), *aff'd,* 440 U.S. 941 (1979) (court invalidated statutory requirement that physician inform patient of that consequence). The Supreme Court in Planned Parenthood of Central Missouri v. Danforth, 428 U.S. at 62 n. 2, found that the physician plaintiffs lacked standing to attack this portion of the Missouri statute. *See also* Parness & Pritchard, *supra* note 111, at 293–95.

One should consider, however, in instances of termination of the rights of a mother, Lassiter v. Department of Social Services, 452 U.S. 18, 27 (1981), in which the Court acknowledged that "a parent's desire for and right to 'the companionship, care, custody, and management of his or her children' is an important interest that 'undeniably warrants deference and, absent a powerful countervailing interest, protection' " (quoting Stanley v. Illinois, 405 U.S. 645, 651 [1972]). Hence, a state which terminates that interest "will have worked a unique kind of deprivation," *id.*; "a parent's interest in the accuracy and justice of the decision to terminate his or her parental interest is, therefore a commanding one." *Id.* Consequently, a hearing meeting the administrative due process requirements established in Mathews v.

Eldridge, 424 U.S. 319 (1976), is a prerequisite to termination of parental rights. An automatic termination by statute, or based on presumptions of neglect resting on consents to lawful post-viability abortions, does not meet that constitutional standard. *Cf. also* Smith v. Organization of Foster Families, 431 U.S. 816, 847–56 (1977) (foster parents had a limited liberty interest in termination of custodial status, but state procedures amply recognized *Mathews v. Eldridge* concerns). A husband presumably would have equivalent claims.

As to putative fathers (fathers of children born outside marriage), the Court has indicated they must be given an opportunity to develop a relationship with their children. Lehr v. Robinson, 463 U.S. 248, 262–63 (1983). Only if they do not avail themselves of an opportunity can their claims to parental status be terminated summarily through adoption proceedings. *Id.*; Quilloin v. Walcott, 434 U.S. 246 (1978). Otherwise, they have procedural protections, Stanley v. Illinois, 405 U.S. 645 (1972), which as a matter of equal protection must be equal to those an illegitimate child's mother enjoys. Caban v. Mohammed, 441 U.S. 380 (1979). These holdings, too, seem to preclude invocation of the above state statutes against fathers of illegitimate children.

235. *E.g.,* Colo. § 18–6–101(1) (at woman's request); Idaho § 18–609, *and see* § 18–610 (refusal to consent is binding irrespective of nonage or incompetency); Ill. ch. 38, § 81–23.2(A)(1)(1); Iowa § 707.8(2); Ky. § 311.726; Minn. § 145.412(1)(4); N.M. § 30–5–1(C); N.Y. Penal Law § 125.05(3) (abortion not justified without consent); N.D. § 14–02.1–03(1); Wash. § 9.02.070(a).

Pa. tit. 18, § 3216(f) forbids any court, judge, executive officer, or administrative agency to issue orders, other than in instances of a medical emergency, to require abortions without express, voluntary consent, and Wis. § 66.04(1)(m) prohibits payment of incentive funds for abortions.

236. *E.g.,* Del. tit. 24, § 1794(a); Fla. § 390.001(4); Md. § 20–214(c)(1) (*semble*: refusal to consent cannot be penalized); Mass. ch. 112, § 12S, *and see* § 12Q (must be delivered to physician performing abortion [presumably, in referral cases]); Mo. § 188.027; Mont. §§ 50–20–104(3), 50–20–106(2); Neb. §§ 28–326(8), 28–327; Nev. § 442.252; Okla. tit. 63, § 1–738(2) (*semble*: physician's report must indicate who signed consent form); Or. § 435.435(1); Pa. tit. 18, § 3205(3) (*semble*: informed consent requires certification by woman that required information has been given her); R.I. § 23–4.7–2; S.C. § 44–41–10(h) (form must be witnessed); S.D. § 34–23A–7; Tenn. § 39–4–202(a); Utah § 76–7–305(1); V.I. tit. 14, § 151(b); Va. § 18.2–76.

237. Women may be required to certify they have been given the information required by statute (*see* text accompanying notes 199–225 *supra*), *e.g.,* Me. tit. 22, § 1598(1); Md. § 20–211(d); Pa. tit. 18, § 3205(3), or a physician may be required to certify the same thing as a condition to receiving a valid consent. *See, e.g.,* Mo. § 188.045; Mont. § 50–20–106(2).

238. *E.g.,* Del. tit. 24, § 1794(b); Fla. § 390.001(4)(c); Ind. § 35–1–58.5–2; Minn. § 145.41(1)(2) (unlawful to perform abortion on unconscious woman unless unconscious for purpose of abortion or necessary to save woman's life); Mont. § 50–20–106(3); Neb. § 28–327; Or. § 435.445(a); S.C. § 44–41–10(h) (and unless woman has been adjudicated mentally incompetent).

239. *E.g.,* Fla § 390.001(4)(c) (medical emergency); Idaho § 18–609 (grounds recognized in law); Ill. ch. 38, § 38–23.2(B)(2) (medical emergency); Iowa § 707.8(2) (life or health of pregnant woman or fetus); Nev. § 129.030(2) (medical emergency posing serious and immediate threat to minor's health).

240. *E.g.,* Ill. ch. 38, § 81–23.2(C); Pa. tit. 18, § 3205(c); S.D. § 34–23A–10.2 (and matter reported to professional disciplinary authority); Utah § 76–7–314(2).

241. *E.g.,* Ill. ch. 38, § 81–23.3(C); Pa. tit. 18, § 3205(d) (physician who complies with consent provisions is not civilly liable).

242. *E.g.,* Mo. § 188.027(2) (emancipated minor), (3) (minor must consent like adult); Neb. § 28.030(2); N.M. § 30–5–1(C) (at request of minor and parent or guardian); Okla. tit. 63, § 2602(A)(3) (general consent law); Pa. tit. 18, § 3206(a) (pregnant minor and a parent). Occasionally, a general consent law allowing minors capable of doing so to consent to medical techniques contains a specific exception in cases of abortion. *See, e.g.,* Ga. § 88–2902. That might suggest an equal protection violation, unless there is a medical basis to support the exclusion—a medical basis difficult to document in light of, *e.g., Roe v. Wade* and *Akron v. Akron Center for Reproductive Health.*

243. *E.g.,* Mo. § 188.028(3); Nev. § 129.030(2); Okla. tit. 63, § 2602(A)(3).

244. *See* text accompanying notes 245–52 *infra. Cf.* State v. Norflett, 67 N.J. 268, 287–89, 337 A.2d, 609, 619–20 (1975) (in prosecution against lay abortionist for contributing to delinquency of minor, a minor can manifest delinquency by consenting to abortion).

245. *E.g.,* Alaska § 18.16.101; Ariz. § 36–2271 (surgical consent law); Ark. § 41–2555; Colo. § 18–6–101(1); Fla. § 390.001(4)(a); Ill. ch. 38, §§ 81.51–81.54; Ky. § 311.732(1); Mass. ch. 112, § 12S; Minn. § 144.343(4)(b) (*semble:* if parent or guardian authorizes abortion in writing, doctor need not comply with parental notice provision); N.D. § 14–02.1–03.1(1)(1); Okla. tit. 63, § 1–738(2) (*semble:* reporting form must indicate who signed consent, including parents); S.C. § 44–41–30(b); S.D. § 34–23A–7.

246. *E.g.,* Del. tit. 24, § 1790(b)(3) (if minor not residing in household with either of parents or guardian); Ill. ch. 38, § 81–54(3) (remaining parent if one parent has died, deserted his or her family or is unavailable); Mass. ch. 112, § 12S (surviving parent or divorced parent with custody); Mo. § 188.028; N.M. § 30–5–1(C); N.D. §§ 14–02.1–03(2)(b) (for abortion after viability, a parent if living), 14–02.1–03.1(1)(a) (for abortion after viability, surviving parent or custodial parent if separation or divorce); Or. § 435.435(1)(a) (parent with custody); Pa. tit. 18, § 3206(a) (one parent); R.I. § 23–4.7–6 (one parent); S.C. § 44–41–30(b), (c) (unmarried minor judicially adjudicated mentally incompetent); Va. § 18.2–76 (parent of woman adjudicated mentally incompetent).

247. *E.g.,* Alaska § 18.16.010; Del. tit. 24, § 1790(b)(3); Ill. ch. 38, § 81–54(3); Ky. § 311.732(2) (or person *in loco parentis* if no parent or guardian); Mass. ch. 112, § 12S; Minn. § 144.343(4)(b) (*semble:* if guardian authorizes abortion in advance, physician need not comply with parental notice requirement); Mo. § 188.028; N.M. § 30–5–1(C); N.D. §§ 14–01.1–03.1(1)(b), 14–02.1–03.1(1)(a); Okla. tit. 63, § 1–738(2) (*semble:* reporting form must indicate whether guardian signed consent); Or. § 435.435(1)(a); R.I. § 23–4.7–6; S.C. § 44–41–30(b); Wash. § 9.02.070(a).

248. *E.g.,* Ark. § 41–2555; Del. tit. 24, § 1790(b)(3); Fla. § 390.001(4); Ill. ch. 38, § 81–54 (consultation and notice); Ky. § 311.732(1); Or. § 435.435(1)(b); Pa. tit. 18, § 3206(a); S.C. § 44–41–30(c); Va. § 18.2–76.

249. Planned Parenthood of Central Missouri v. Danforth, 428 U.S. at 72–75; *see also* Bellotti v. Baird (*Bellotti II*), 443 U.S. 622 (1979) (in result, Court invalidated Massachusetts statute requiring parental consultation and consent; no majority opinion).

250. *See* Planned Parenthood of Central Missouri v. Danforth, 428 U.S. at 75. *See generally* Buchanan, *The Constitution and the Anomaly of the Pregnant Teenager,* 24 Ariz. L. Rev. 553 (1982).

    Danforth suggests the legal legitimacy of requiring parental consents to abortions (or denials of consent) for minor mental incompetents. Analogies for resolving the constitutionality and lawfulness of a guardian's or parent's decision concerning abortion probably must be drawn from the jurisprudence relating to sterilization of mental retardates. *See, e.g.,* Buck v. Bell, 274 U.S. 200 (1927) (Court sustained constitutionality of sterilization statute invokable against "feeble-minded" persons); Matter of C.D.M., 627 P.2d 607 (Alaska 1981) (court approved use of same conditions as the New Jersey Supreme Court established in *In re* Grady, *infra*); Guardianship of Tulley, 83 Cal. App. 3d 698, 146 Cal. Rptr. 266 (1978), *cert. denied sub nom.* Tulley v. Tulley, 440 U.S. 967 (1979) (no statutory authority for sterilization order requested by father concerning mentally retarded daughter); Matter of A.W., 637 P.2d 366 (Colo. 1981) (general parental consent statute did not allow parents to approve sterilization of a mentally retarded child); P.S. by Harbin v. W. S., 452 N.E.2d 969 (Ind. 1983) (juvenile court had power to order sterilization of mentally retarded son with parental consent); Wentzel v. Montgomery General Hospital, 293 Md. 685, 447 A.2d 1244 (1982), *cert. denied,* 459 U.S. 1147 (1983) (court has inherent *parens patriae* authority to entertain parental application for sterilization of incompetent minor; guardian *ad litem* must be appointed; court must determine by clear and convincing proof that the individual is incompetent to decide about sterilization, the incompetency is unlikely to change in the foreseeable future, there is no reasonable alternative to sterilization, and sterilization is in the incompetent's best interests; legislature invited to enact comprehensive legislation on matter); Interest of M.K.R., 515 S.W.2d 467 (Mo. 1974) (no statutory or other authority for juvenile court order for sterilization of minor female at parents' request); *In re* Grady, 85 N.J. 235, 426 A.2d 467 (1981) (court has inherent *parens patriae* jurisdiction to allow sterilization of noninstitutionalized female, at parental request, but must find that minor cannot understand nature and significance of sterilization, incompetency is probably permanent, incompetent person is fertile and capable of procreation; an attorney must be appointed as guardian *ad litem* for the minor and represent the minor during proceedings; applicants must demonstrate good faith and a primary concern for the best interests of the incompetent and not their own or the public's convenience); *In re* Moore, 289 N.C. 95, 221 S.E.2d 307 (1976) (court approved sterilization order for mental retardate at parents' request); Matter of Guardianship of Hayes, 93 Wash. 2d 228, 608 P.2d 635 (1980) (court has inherent power to order sterilization of mentally incompetent person at parental request, but should not do so unless substantial medical evidence has been adduced establishing that sterilization is in the best interests of the retardate; court established a presumption against sterilization which proponents must overcome by clear, cogent and convincing evidence); Matter of Guardianship of Eberhardy, 102 Wis. 2d 539, 307 N.W.2d 881 (1981) (judiciary should not establish public policy to allow sterilization of 22-year-old woman, incapable of consent, at instance of parents; should be a matter for legislation).

On sterilization in relation to abortion, *see, e.g.,* Dickens, *supra* note 11, at 556–72; Green, *The Law, Sex and the Population Explosion,* 19 Malaya L. Rev. 81 (1977); Isaacs, *supra* note 116, at 80–86; Isaacs, *Reproductive Rights 1983: An International Survey,* 14 Colum. Human Rights L. Rev. 311, 328–39 (1982); Parness & Pritchard, *supra* note 111, at 288–91; Warren, *supra* note 17, at 14–20.

251. Akron V. Akron Center for Reproductive Health, 442 U.S. at 439–42 (explaining the Court's ruling in *Bellotti II*); *see also* Planned Parenthood League of Massachusetts v. Bellotti, 641 F.2d 106, 1011–13 (1st Cir. 1981) (court rejected due process and equal protection attack on Massachusetts statute that required either parental consent or judicial determination that minor was competent to consent). The Supreme Court has explained its decision in H.L. v. Matheson, 450 U.S. 398 (1981), as turning on an unmarried, unemancipated pregnant minor's lack of standing to attack the potential application of a parental consent provision to emancipated or married minors. Akron v. Akron Center for Reproductive Health, 462 U.S. at 440. There was no majority opinion in *H.L. v. Matheson.*

252. *See* text accompanying notes 258–62 *infra.*

253. Planned Parenthood of Central Missouri v. Danforth, 428 U.S. at 67–72; *cf.* Hagerstown Reproductive Health Services v. Fritz, 295 Md. 268, 454 A.2d 846, *cert. denied,* 463 U.S. 1208 (1983) (court vacated as moot an appeal against a lower court injunction, issued at a husband's request, against performance of an abortion until he consented; an abortion already had been performed); Coleman v. Coleman, 57 Md. App. 755, 471 A.2d 1115 (1984) (husband cannot enjoin medically indicated abortion for wife). English case law adopts a similar position, although not, of course, on constitutional grounds. *See* Paton v. Trustees of British Pregnancy Advisory Service, [1978] 2 All E.R. 987, [1978] 3 W.L.R. 687.

A corollary is that the father of a child cannot defeat his duty to provide financial support for his child on the basis that he had not been given an opportunity to decide whether a fetus should be aborted, or that he had offered to pay for a first-trimester abortion. *See* People in the Interest of S.P.B., 651 P.2d 1213 (Colo. 1982) (citing authorities); Note, *Child Support: Implications of Abortion on the Relative Parental Duties,* 28 U. Fla. L. Rev. 988 (1976).

254. *See* text accompanying notes 264–71 *infra.*

255. *E.g.,* Colo. § 18–6–101(1) (*semble*: abortion must be at request of woman and husband); Fla. § 390.001(b) (written spousal consent to indicate notice and opportunity to consult; predecessor provision held unconstitutional in Poe v. Gerstein, 517 F.2d 787 [5th Cir. 1975], *aff'd,* 428 U.S. 901 [1976]); Idaho § 18–609 (if husband has not abandoned wife); N.D. § 14–02.1–03(2)(a) (unless voluntarily separated); Or. § 435.435(1)(c) (if spouses have been living together); Wash. § 9.02.070(a) (same).

256. *E.g.*, Ark. § 41–2555; S.C. § 44–41–30(c).
257. *See* text accompanying notes 249–52 *supra*.
258. *See* note 251 *supra*.
259. Akron v. Akron Center for Reproductive Health, 462 U.S. at 441–42; *see also* Planned Parenthood of Kansas City v. Ashcroft, 462 U.S. at 490–93 (plurality opinion).
260. *E.g.*, Ariz. § 36–2152(2); Fla. § 390.001(4)(a); Idaho § 18–609; Ill. ch. 38, § 81–54(3); Ind. § 35–1–58.5–2.5; Ky. § 311.732(3)–(6); Mass. ch. 112, § 12S; Minn. § 144.343(6); Mo. § 188.028(2); Neb. § 28–347(2); N.D. § 14–02.1–03.1(2); Pa. tit. 18, § 3206(c)–(f), (h); R.I. § 23–4.7–6.
261. *See generally* Scheinberg v. Smith, 659 F.2d 476, 480–82 (5th Cir. Unit B, 1981); Zbaraz v. Hartigan, 584 F. Supp. 1452, 1460–62 (N.D. Ill. 1984).
262. *See* Akron v. Akron Center for Reproductive Health, 462 U.S. at 439–42; on a requirement of good cause, *see* Planned Parenthood of Kansas City v. Ashcroft, 462 U.S. at 493 (plurality opinion).
263. *E.g.*, Ariz. § 36–2152(A); Fla. § 391.021(2)–(3); Ill. ch. 38, § 18–23.3(A); Me. tit. 22, § 1597; Md. § 20–103 (not required if minor does not live with parent or guardian or if notice may lead to physical or emotional abuse of minor; physician is not civilly or criminally liable for decision not to give notice on latter basis); Minn. § 144.343 (not required if minor declares she is a victim of sexual abuse as defined in § 636.556); Mont. § 50–20–107(1)(b); Neb. § 18–347; Nev. § 442.255 (if possible to notify); Tenn. § 39–4–202(f) (if parents cannot be located, then to agency or other individual to whom the minor's custody has been transferred); Utah § 76–7–304(2) (if possible); V.I. tit. 19, § 292(c) (if reason to know whereabouts).
264. *E.g.*, Ill. ch. 38, § 81–23.4(A); Ky. § 311.735 (within 30 days after abortion if reasonably possible; failure to notify is prima facie evidence of interference with family relations, in appropriate civil actions, allowing punitive damages or damages for emotional distress even if unaccompanied by physical complications, and with no prejudice to husband's common law rights); Mont. § 50–20–107(1)(a) (unless husband is voluntarily separated); Nev. § 442.254 (unless woman is legally separated from husband or has obtained a judicial declaration of paternity stating that a man other than the husband is father of the unborn child); R.I. §§ 23–4.8–2 (if woman consents and notice is reasonably possible), 23–4.8–3 (unnecessary if woman furnishes written statement that she has given notice to her husband, that the fetus was not fathered by the husband, or that she has filed for divorce; or husband gives physician written notice that he has been notified); Utah § 76–7–304(2) (if possible).

    See Note, *Spousal Notification: An Unconstitutional Limitation on a Woman's Right to Privacy in the Abortion Decision*, 12 Hofstra L. Rev. 531 (1984).
265. Some statutes provide for notice by certified or registered mail if notice is not communicated orally. *See, e.g.*, Me. tit. 22, § 1597 (if cannot notify orally or by mail, must notify state department of human services in writing of inability to give notice and of intention to perform abortion); Md. § 20–103 (proof of mailing is conclusive evidence of notice); Neb. § 18–347; N.D. § 14–02.1–03(1).

A medical or life-threatening emergency may justify a failure to give notice to parents, *e.g.,* Ariz. § 36–2152(B)(1) (immediate and grave threat to woman's life); Me. tit. 22, § 1596 (life or health of minor will be endangered unless an abortion is performed immediately; notice to be given within 24 hours thereafter); Minn. § 144.343 (emergency which may cause death); Neb. § 18–347(3) (physician must certify by affidavit that continuation of pregnancy provides immediate threat and grave risk to life or health of pregnant woman), or spouse. *See, e.g.,* R.I. § 23–4.8–3(d) (emergency requiring immediate action; physician must certify medical basis for opinion in patient's medical record).

266. Notice statutes frequently require a 24- or 48-hour waiting period after notice before an abortion can be performed. The constitutionality of waiting periods generally is discussed in text accompanying notes 327–37 *infra.*

267. *See* text accompanying notes 204–24 *supra.*

268. *E.g.,* Ill. ch. 38, § 81–23.3(A)(1); N.D. § 14–02.1–03(1).

269. 450 U.S. 398 (1981).

270. Planned Parenthood Association of Kansas City v. Ashcroft, 655 F.2d 848, 858–49 (8th Cir. 1981), *aff'd on other grounds,* 462 U.S. 476 (1983) (plurality opinion).

271. *See* Scheinberg v. Smith, 659 F.2d 476, 482–87 (5th Cir. Unit B, 1981) (remanding for a district court determination whether a husband's concern for, *e.g.,* a more than de minimis decrease in his wife's procreative potential following an abortion, outweighed the influence of a spousal notice requirement on the wife's abortion decision). *Cf.* Hagerstown Reproductive Health Services v. Fritz, 295 Md. 268, 454 A.2d 846, *cert. denied,* 463 U.S. 1208 (1983) (court vacated as moot an appeal against a lower court's issuance of an injunction against an abortion, at a husband's request, because abortion had been performed).

272. *See* text accompanying note 81 *supra.*

273. *E.g.,* Ark. § 41–2554 (criminal statute); Cal. Health & Safety Code § 25952(c)(2), Penal Code § 274 (exempts such abortions); Colo. § 18–6–101(b) (within first 16 weeks of pregnancy; limitation held unconstitutional in People v. Norton, 181 Colo. 47, 507 P.2d 862 [1973]); Del. tit. 24, § 1790(a)(3)(a); Idaho § 18–608(1) (limited to first trimester); Kan. § 21–3407(2); N.M. § 30–5–1(C)(4); Or. § 434.415(1)(c) (felonious intercourse, as defined in § 435.405[1]).

In some states, concern for such pregnancies is evidenced in provisions allowing public funding for abortions based on incest. *See, e.g.,* Minn. § 265B.02(13)(c); Pa. tit. 55, §§ 1141(a)(2), 1221.57(a)(2); R.I. 36–12–2.1 (public employee health plans may include abortions resulting from incest); Va. § 18.2–92.1; text accompanying note 485 *infra.*

274. For example, because they are not reported, *see, e.g.,* Ark § 41–2554 (must be reported within seven days), or are not within time limitations. *See, e.g.,* Colo. § 18–6–101(b) (within first 16 weeks of pregnancy); Idaho § 18–608(1) (first trimester).

275. This would require a consideration of whether the Court's concern in Roe v. Wade, 410 U.S. at 164, over the "potentiality of human life" translates into a restriction on abortions based other than on medical necessity. In context, however, the Court's language is a limitation on a state's power to regulate

abortions following viability. *Cf.* the Court's language in Harris v. McRae, 448 U.S. 297, 325 (1980), *quoted* in text accompanying note 476 *infra.*

276. *See* text accompanying note 81 *supra.*

277. *E.g.*, Ark. § 4–254; Cal. Health & Safety Code § 25951(c)(2), Penal Code § 274 (exempting such cases); Colo. 18–6–101(b) (only in first 16 weeks of pregnancy); Del. tit. 24, § 1790(a)(3)(b); Idaho § 18–608(1) (first trimester only; in cases of rape or felonious intercourse; all illicit intercourse with female under 16 deemed felonious intercourse); Kan. § 21–3407(2); Md. § 20–208(a)(4); Miss. § 97–3–3(1)(b); N.M. § 30–5–1(C)(3); Or. § 435.415(1)(c); Wyo. § 35–6–102 (after viability, when imminent peril that pregnancy will substantially endanger women's life or health, in physician's best medical judgment).

Recognition in some states is in the form of recognition of rape as a ground for publicly funded abortion. *See, e.g.*, Minn. § 256B.02(13)(b); Pa. tit. 55, §§ 1141.57(a)(2), 1221.57(a)(2); R.I. § 36–12–2.1 (public employee health insurance plans may include as a basis); Va. § 18.2–92.1; text accompanying note 484 *infra.*

278. *E.g.*, Ark. § 4–2554 (must be reported within seven days); Del. tit. 24, § 1790(a)(3)(b) (certification by attorney general after 48 hours following rape); Md. § 20–208(a)(4) (if state's attorney for county informs hospital abortion review authority in signed writing that probable cause exists to believe alleged rape occurred); N.M. § 30–5–1(C)(3) (woman must submit to special hospital board an affidavit that she has been raped and that rape has been or will be reported to appropriate law enforcement officials); Or. § 435.425(2) (hospital administrator must send copy of certificate by two physicians that pregnancy resulted from felonious intercourse to district attorney of county where hospital located); Va. § 18.2–92.1 (public funding allowed only if rape was reported to law enforcement or public health agency).

279. *See* text accompanying notes 274–75 *supra.*

280. *See* text accompanying note 80 *supra.*

281. *E.g.*, Ark. § 41–2554 (grave defect); Del. tit. 24, § 1790(a)(2) (substantial risk of grave and permanent physical deformity or mental retardation); Idaho § 18–608(1) (physical or mental health, first trimester only); Iowa § 707.7 (life or health of fetus, final trimester coverage); Kan. § 21–3407(2) (child born with physical or mental defect); Md. § 20–208(a)(3) (substantial risk of grave and permanent physical deformity or mental retardation); N.M. § 30–5–1(C)(2) (child probably will have grave physical or mental defect); Or. § 435.415(1)(b) (serious physical or mental defect). Public funds are available for abortion on this ground in Virginia, § 18.2–92.2 (if qualified physician certifies in writing after appropriate tests a belief that fetus will be born with gross and totally incapacitating physical deformity or mental deficiency).

282. *See* note 275 *supra. Cf.* the matter of whether others may intervene to contest a parental-physician decision not to use life support systems to preserve an infant born with serious birth defects. Weber v. Stony Brook Hospital, 60 N.Y.2d 208, 456 N.E.2d 1186, 469 N.Y.S.2d 63 (1983) (lawyer with no disclosed relationship to infant or her family could not obtain judicial authorization for surgery, overriding parental and physicians' decision not to provide extraordinary medical treatment for infant born with spina bifida

and other serious complications). *See also* Maguire, *Can Technology Solve the Abortion Dilemma?*, 93 Christian Century 918 (October 27, 1976); Smith, *Life and Death Decisions in the Nursery: Standards and Procedures for Withholding Lifesaving Treatment From Infants*, 27 N.Y.L. Sch. L. Rev. 1125 (1982).

283. *See* text accompanying note 29 *supra.*

284. *E.g.,* Ariz. § 13–3603; Mich. § 750.14; Miss. § 97–3–3(1); N.H. § 585:13 (certified by two physicians to be necessary, or objectively so justified); Vt. tit. 13, § 101; W. Va. § 61–2–8 (good faith belief in necessity); Wis. § 940.04(5)(b).

The Supreme Court found nothing vague and indefinite in the term. Harris v. McRae, 448 U.S. 297, 311 n.17 (1980).

285. *E.g.,* Idaho § 18–604(3) (third trimester, defined in § 18–604[6]); N.H. § 585:13 (quick child); Or. § 435.425(1) (following 150th day of pregnancy); R.I. § 11–23–5 (quick child).

286. *E.g.,* R.I. § 11–23–5; Wash. § 9.02.010. A similar restriction may be imposed through judicial interpretation. *See, e.g.,* People v. Bricker, 389 Mich. 524, 208 N.W.2d 172 (1973).

287. *E.g.,* Minn. § 256B.02(13)(b); Pa. tit. 55, §§ 1141.57(a)(1), 1221.57(a)(1); R.I. § 36–12–2.1; S.C. § 1–13–30(*1*) (public employee health insurance plans may include abortions in which woman's life would be endangered by carrying pregnancy to term). Constitutional aspects of withholding public funding are discussed in text accompanying notes 436–76 *infra.*

288. *See* text accompanying notes 137–50 *supra.*

289. *See, e.g.,* Ala § 13A–13–7 (criminal code); D.C. § 22–201 (*and see* United States v. Vuitch, 402 U.S. 62 [1971]); Kan. § 21–3407(2); P.R. tit. 33, § 4010; Tenn. § 39–4–201(c)(3); V.I. tit. 14, § 151(b). Nev. § 442.250(1)(c) requires that there be "reasonable cause to believe" there is necessity.

290. *E.g.,* Ark. § 41–2554; Cal. Health & Safety Code § 25951(c)(1); Colo. § 18–65–101 (serious permanent impairment); Del. tit. 24, § 1790(a)(4) (substantial risk of permanent injury); Md. § 20–208(a)(1)–(2); N.M. § 30–5–1(C)(1); Or. § 435.415(1)(a) (greatly impair); Va. § 18.2–74 (substantial or irremediable impairment). The pattern for the "gravely impair" qualifier is the Uniform Abortion Act § 1(b)(2) (1972); *see* Roe v. Wade, 410 U.S. at 146 n. 40.

291. 410 U.S. at 164.

292. *Id.* at 165.

293. *E.g.,* Ill. ch. 38, § 81–25(2); Ind. § 35–1–58.5–2(C)(2); Ky. § 311.780; La. § 38:1285(8) (third trimester or after viability); Me. tit. 22, § 1598(4); Mo. § 188.030(1); Mont. § 50–20–109(1)(c); Neb. § 28–329; Okla. tit. 63, § 1–732(A); Pa. tit. 18, § 3210(a); Utah § 76–7–302(3) (*semble:* if child is sufficiently developed to have any reasonable possibility of survival outside womb).

294. *E.g.,* Fla. § 390.001(2) (third trimester); Iowa § 707.7; Mass. ch. 112, § 12M (24 weeks or later); Minn. § 145.412(3) (*semble:* potentially viable); Nev. § 442.250(1)(c) (after 24th week); N.Y. Penal Law § 125.05(3) (after 24 weeks); N.C. § 14–45:1(b) (after 20th week); N.D. § 14–02.1–04(3) (*semble:* after point at which fetus may reasonably be expected to have reached viability);

S.C. § 44–41–30(c) (third trimester); S.D. § 34–23A–5 (after 24th week of pregnancy).

295. Akron v. Akron Center for Reproductive Health, 462 U.S. at 432–35.
296. *See* Roe v. Wade, 410 U.S. at 165–66. The medical determination may be reached in light of all attendant circumstances. Colautti v. Franklin, 439 U.S. at 387–89; Doe v. Bolton, 410 U.S. at 190–91.

On the relative safety of abortion in comparison to childbirth, *see* Cates, Smith, Rochat & Grimes, *Mortality From Abortion and Childbirth: Are the Statistics Biased?*, 248 J.A.M.A. 192 (1982); LeBoll, Grimes & Cates, *Mortality From Abortion and Childbirth: Are the Populations Comparable?*, 248 J.A.M.A. 188 (1982); Sneideman, *supra* note 19, at 194–97.

297. *E.g.*, Florida, Maine, New York, and North Carolina.
298. *E.g.*, Ga. § 26–1202(a) (best clinical judgment that abortion is necessary); Idaho § 18–608(1) (appropriate in medical judgment based on factors including but not limited to physical, emotional, psychological, or familial); Ill. ch. 38, § 81–23.1(A) (best medical judgment; first trimester only); La. § 38:1285(8.1), (9) (unprofessional conduct to terminate pregnancy if contrary to or unnecessary in best medical judgment of physician); Mass. ch. 112, § 12L (best medical judgment under all attendant circumstances); Nev. § 442.250(1)(b) (same); S.C. §§ 44–41–20(a), (b) (pursuant to professional medical judgment); S.D. § 34–23A–3, 34–23A–4 (medically indicated); Tenn. § 39–4–201(c)(1)–(2) (medical judgment of attending physician); Utah §§ 76–7–303 (concurrence of attending physician based on best medical judgment), 76–7–304(1) (best medical judgment; must consider all facts relevant to woman's well-being including but not limited to physical, emotional and psychological health and safety, age and familial situation); *cf.* Wyo. § 35–6–112 (a felony to use other than accepted medical procedures to abort).
299. *E.g.*, Alaska § 18.16.010 (30 days); Ark. § 41–2556 (four months unless life-threatening emergency); Del. tit. 24, § 1799(a)–(b) (120 days; inapplicable if woman or spouse is employed in state, if woman is a patient of a Delaware physician, or if there is a life-threatening emergency); Tenn. § 39–4–201(d) (woman must prove bona fide residency; hospital records must retain supporting documentation); Wash. § 9.02.070(b) (90 days).
300. *See* text accompanying notes 85–86 *supra*.
301. Doe v. Bolton, 410 U.S. at 200; Smith v. Bentley, 493 F. Supp. 916, 929 (E.D. Ark. 1980). Residency requirements affecting access to nonemergency hospitalization or medical care at public expense constitute an invidious classification violating equal protection and the constitutional right of interstate travel. Memorial Hospital v. Maricopa County, 415 U.S. 250 (1974).
302. *See, e.g.*, Alaska § 18.16.010 (or hospital operated by federal government or agency); Colo. § 18–6–101 (held unconstitutional in People v. Norton, 181 Colo. 47, 507 P.2d 862 [1973]); Conn. § 53–31a(c); Or. § 435.415(3); Wis. § 940.04(4)(c) (unless emergency prevents).
303. *E.g.*, Cal. Health & Safety Code § 25951(a) (accredited by Joint Commission on Accreditation of Hospitals [JCAH]); Del. tit. 24, § 1790(a) (accredited by nationally recognized medical or hospital accreditation authority); N.M. § 30–5–1(C) (accredited hospital).

304. *E.g.,* Ark. § 14–2557 (licensed by state and accredited by JCAH); Kan. § 21–3407(2)(a) (*semble*: certificate of necessity for abortion to be filed in hospital licensed by state and accredited by JCAH); Md. § 20–208(a) (state licensed and JCAH-accredited).

305. Doe v. Bolton, 410 U.S. at 193–95; Roe v. Wade, 410 U.S. at 163.

306. *E.g.,* Fla. § 696.03(3) (third trimester); Idaho § 18–608(2)–(3) (second and third trimesters); Ill. ch. 38, § 81–24 (hospital inpatient after first trimester); Ky. § 311.760(2) (after first trimester, unless emergency to protect woman's life or health); La. § 37:1285(8.1) (after first trimester; unprofessional conduct); Mass. ch. 112, § 12Q (24th week or after); Mo. § 188.025 (after first 12 weeks of pregnancy); Mont. § 50–20–109(1)(b) (after first three months of pregnancy); N.Y. Pub. Health Law § 4164(1) (after 12th week, on hospital inpatient basis); N.C. § 14–45.1(b) (after 20th week); N.D. § 14–02.1–04(2)–(3) (after first 12 weeks of pregnancy); Okla. tit. 63, § 1–731(B) (subsequent to first trimester); Pa. tit. 18, § 3209 (after first trimester); S.C. § 44–41–20(c) (third trimester); Tenn. § 39–4–201(c)(2)–(3) (after three months); V.I. tit. 14, § 151(b)(2)–(3) (after first trimester).

   On abortion services for women prisoners, *see* Cal. Welf. & Inst. Code §§ 220 (pregnant females in local juvenile facility may obtain lawful abortions), 1773 (same for females in Youth Authority custody; notice of right to abortion to be posted in at lease one conspicuous place to which residents have access); Cal. Penal Code §§ 3405 (abortion rights of adult female prisoners, with requirement of posted notice), 3406 (right to services of private physician to determine whether pregnant or not, and during pregnancy), 4028 (rights for local detention facility inmates). *See also* Note, *Inmate Abortion—The Right to Government Funding Behind the Prison Gates,* 48 Fordham L. Rev. 550 (1980).

307. Planned Parenthod Association of Kansas City v. Ashcroft, 462 U.S. at 481–82; Akron v. Akron Center for Reproductive Health, 462 U.S. at 432–39. The requirement imposed a significant burden on women wishing abortions, in terms of costs and restricted availability of abortion services in full-service general hospitals. Medical data recognized by the Court also established that abortions can be performed safely in clinics or outpatient facilities during the second trimester to the time of viability.

308. In Simopoulos v. Virginia, 462 U.S. 506, 517–19 (1983), the Court sustained the constitutionality of a state requirement that second-trimester abortions be performed in a hospital, defined to include clinics and outpatient facilities; the legislation comported with good medical practice. Simopoulos had used the saline injection system in his office and allowed the pregnant minor to go to a motel where she aborted; his criminal conviction was held valid.

309. *E.g.,* Fla. § 696.03(a)(1) (in licensed hospital, abortion clinic or physician's office), (3) (in hospital during third trimester); Ga. § 26–1202(b) (after first trimester); Idaho § 18–608(1) (during first trimester only); Ind. § 35–1–58.5–2(b)(2), (c)(1); Minn. § 145.412 (after first trimester to point of "potential viability"); Nev. § 442.250(2); N.C. § 14–45.1 (within first 20 weeks; in hospital thereafter); S.C. § 44–41–20(b)–(c) (second trimester; in certified hospitals during third trimester); S.D. § 34–23A–4 (*semble*: between 12th and 24th week, if hospital facilities unavailable); Utah §§ 76–7–301(3),

76–7–302(2); Va. §§ 18.2–73, 18.2–74 (validated in Simopoulos v. Virginia, 462 U.S. 506 [1983]); Wash. § 9.02.070(c) (may terminate elsewhere if medical emergency makes abortion immediately necessary).

Licensed abortion clinics are protected by criminal trespass laws, and right-to-life protesters who invade and occupy such premises cannot invoke the "choice of evils" or "balance of harms" defense, (see, e.g., ALI Model Penal Code § 3.02[1] [Permanent ed. with revised commentary, 1985]; N.Y. Penal Law § 35.05[2] [McKinney 1975]), based on a claim of necessity to preserve the lives of unborn fetuses. See, e.g., Cleveland v. Anchorage, 631 P.2d 1073 (Alaska 1981); Gaetano v. United States, 406 A.2d 1291 (D.C. 1979); People v. Stiso, 93 Ill. App. 3d 101, 416 N.E.2d 1209 (1981); Sigma Reproductive Health Center v. State, 297 Md. 660, 467 A.2d 483 (1983).

310. E.g., Fla. § 390.014; Ill. ch. 111 1/2, §§ 157–8.1 to 157–8.16; Md. § 20–203 (semble: abortion referral services); Pa. tit. 18, § 3207; S.C. § 44–41–70, and see Health & Environment Control Dep't R. 61–12.

311. Baird v. Massachusetts Public Health Dep't, 599 F.2d 1098 (1st Cir. 1979); Florida Women's Medical Clinic v. Smith, 536 F. Supp. 1048, 1057–58 (S.D. Fla. 1982), appeal dismissed, 706 F.2d 1172 (11th Cir. 1983); Westchester Women's Health Organization v. Whalen, 475 F. Supp. 734 (S.D.N.Y. 1979); Fox Valley Reproductive Health Care Center v. Arft, 446 F. Supp. 1072 (E.D. Wis. 1978); Oak Lawn v. Marcowitz, 86 Ill. 2d 406, 427 N.E.2d 36 (1981); Indiana Hospital Licensing Council v. Women's Pavilion of South Bend, Inc., 420 N.E.2d 1301 (Ind. App. 1981); contra, Word v. Poelker, 495 F.2d 1349 (8th Cir. 1974) (facilities for first-trimester abortions); Margaret S. v. Edwards, 488 F. Supp. 181, 223–24 (E.D. La. 1980) (facilities for first-trimester abortions); Mahoning Women's Center v. Hunter, 444 F. Supp. 12 (N.D. Ohio 1977), aff'd, 610 F.2d 456 (6th Cir. 1979), vacated on other grounds and remanded, 447 U.S. 918 (1980) (ordinance covering only abortion clinics denied equal protection because other surgery with equivalent medical risks could be performed in unlicensed facilities); Wright v. State, 351 So. 2d 708 (Fla. 1977) (term "approved placed" unconstitutional in relation to first-trimester abortions, although it might be valid thereafter); People v. Dobbs Ferry Medical Pavillion, 33 N.Y.2d 584, 301 N.E.2d 435, 347 N.Y.S.2d 452 (1973) (terms "facility" and "clinic" in medical care facility licensing statute were overinclusive and thus unconstitutional).

Efforts to use zoning regulations targeted at abortion clinics alone constitute an impediment to exercise of Roe v. Wade rights. Deerfield Medical Center v. Deerfield Beach, 661 F.2d 328 (5th Cir., Unit B 1981); Framingham Clinic v. Southborough Board of Selectment, 373 Mass. 279, 367 N.E.2d 606 (1977).

A statutory prohibition against performance of abortions at an educational facility other than to save life, Ariz. § 15–1630, was sustained as constitutional in Roe v. Arizona Board of Regents, 113 Ariz. 178, 549 P.2d 150 (1976), in part because of the availability of abortion facilities elsewhere.

312. Birth Control Centers, Inc. v. Reizen, 743 F.2d 352, 364–65 (6th Cir. 1984); Florida Women's Medical Clinic v. Smith, 536 F. Supp. 1048, 1057 (S.D. Fla. 1982).

313. Florida Women's Medical Clinic v. Smith, 536 F. Supp. 1048, 1056 (S.D. Fla. 1982).

314. Women's Medical Center of Providence v. Cannon, 463 F. Supp. 531 (D.R.I. 1978) (invalidating requirement that physician performing first-trimester abortions had to have unsupervised privileges at an accessible hospital).

315. *E.g.*, Ky. § 311.820 (although some of the terms like "kickbacks" are probably not objectionable as long as the practice is condemned in every context; if only abortion is singled out, there is an equal protection problem); Pa. tit. 18, § 3213(b) (at least unless all other physicians and clinics are under a similar disability).

316. *E.g.*, Md. § 20–204.

317. Margaret S. v. Edwards, 488 F. Supp. 181, 214–17 (E.D. La. 1980). Basic administrative search doctrine is delineated, *e.g.*, in Donovan v. Dewey, 452 U.S. 594 (1981); Michigan v. Tyler, 436 U.S. 499 (1978); Marshall v. Barlow's, Inc., 436 U.S. 307 (1978); United States v. Biswell, 406 U.S. 311 (1972); See v. Seattle, 387 U.S. 541 (1967); Camara v. Municipal Court, 387 U.S. 523 (1967).

318. *See* Or. § 465.110.

319. *E.g.*, Ark. § 41–2558 (three physicians); Kan. § 233407(2)(a) (three physicians); Miss. § 97–3–3(2) (two reputable licensed physicians); Or. § 435.425(1) (two physicians); Wis. § 940.04(5)(b) (two physicians).

320. *E.g.*, Cal. Health & Safety Code § 25951(b) (unanimous approval if no more than three licensed physicians on staff committee); Colo. § 18–6–101(1), (4) (ruled unconstitutional in People v. Norton, 181 Colo. 47, 507 P.2d 862 [1973]); Md. § 20–208(b)(2); N.M. § 30–5–1(C)–(D).

321. *E.g.*, Del. tit. 24, § 1790(a) (abortion review committee plus two licensed physicians certifying necessity).

322. Doe v. Bolton, 410 U.S. at 195–200; *see also* Smith v. Bentley, 439 F. Supp. 929 (E.D. Ark. 1980).

323. *E.g.*, Fla. § 390.001(2)(a)–(b) (two physicians); Ga. § 26–1202(c); Idaho § 18–609(3) (one physician; otherwise, no consultation is necessary, § 18–611); S.C. § 44–41–20(c) (one other physician); Va. § 18.2–74(b) (two consulting physicians).

324. *E.g.*, Mont. § 50–20–109(2)(b) (two physicians); N.D. § 14–02.1–04(3) (two physicians).

325. This was the result in Planned Parenthood Association of Kansas City v. Ashcroft, 462 U.S. 476, 505, although there was no majority opinion. The provision related to protection of live-born fetuses. *See* text accompanying notes 348–52, 438–40 *infra*.

326. *E.g.*, Ky. § 311.723(1)(b); Mass. ch. 113, § 12R.

327. *See* text accompanying notes 204–29 *supra*.

328. *See* text accompanying note 230 *supra*.

329. *See* text accompanying note 231 *supra*.

330. Statutes triggered by information to pregnant women include Ind. § 35–1–58.5–2(d) (24-hour period between receipt of consent form and submission of signed form to physician); Me. tit. 22, § 1599(1) (48 hours); Mo. § 188.039(1) (48 hours); Pa. tit. 18, § 3205(a)(2) (24 hours); S.D. § 34–23A–10.1 (24 hours); Tenn. § 39–4–202(d) (two-day minimum excluding day on which information was given); Utah § 76–7–305.5(2) (24 hours if possible).

    Spousal information laws imposing a waiting period include Ill. ch. 38, § 81–23.4(A)(1), (2)(b) (24 hours; 72 hours if mail notice); Ky. § 311.735 (before or, if not possible, within 30 days after); Nev. § 442.254 (24 hours if possible).

Waiting periods based on notice to parents or guardians of minor pregnant females are found in *e.g.,* Ill. ch. 38, § 81–23 (24 hours; 72 hours if mail notice); Me. tit. 22, § 1597 (24 hours; 48 hours if mail notice); Minn. § 244.343(2) (48 hours); Neb. § 28–347(1) (24 hours; 48 hours if mail notice); Nev. § 442.255 (24 hours); N.C. § 14–02.1–03(1) (24 hours; 48 hours if mail notice); Tenn. § 39–4–202(f) (two days minimum).

331. *E.g.,* Ill. ch. 38, §§ 81–23.3(B)(2), 81–23.4(B)(2); Ky. § 311.735; Me. tit. 22, §§ 1597, 1599(1); Neb. § 28–347(3); Tenn. § 39–4–202(f).

332. *E.g.,* Del. tit. 24, § 1794(b) (24 hours); Ill. ch. 38, § 81–23.2(A)(1)(a) (24 hours); Ky. § 311.726 (two hours); Mass. ch. 112, § 12S (24 hours); Neb. § 28–327 (48 hours); Nev. § 442.252 (24 hour minimum, 30-day maximum validity of consent); N.C. § 14–02.1–03(1) (same).

333. *E.g.,* Del. tit. 24, § 1794(b); Ill. ch. 38, § 81–23.2(B)(1); S.D. § 34–23A–10.1.

334. Akron v. Akron Center for Reproductive Health, 462 U.S. at 449–51.

335. The Kentucky imposition of a two-hour period might or might not fall afoul of such criteria. The Nevada and North Carolina fixing of a 30-day maximum period during which consents are effective should prove valid, at least in the absence of an indication that other medical consent forms are not subject to equivalent time limitations. If only abortion consent forms are so limited, there would appear to be an invidious classification violative of equal protection.

336. *See* text accompanying notes 222–25 *supra*.

337. Akron v. Akron Center for Reproductive Health, 462 U.S. at 450–51: "In accordance with the ethical standards of the profession, a physician will advise the patient to defer the abortion when he thinks this will be beneficial to her. But if a woman, after appropriate counseling, is prepared to give her written informed consent and proceed with the abortion, a State may not demand that she delay the effectuation of her decision."

338. Roe v. Wade, 410 U.S. at 163: "It follows that, from and after [the end of the first trimester], a State may regulate the abortion procedure to the extent that the regulation reasonably relates to the preservation and protection of maternal health."

339. Akron v. Akron Center for Reproductive Health, 462 U.S. at 434–39. The Court concluded that the dilatation and evacuation technique for abortion could be safely performed away from a general service hospital, at least until viability, rendering a a city ordinance requirement that all abortions after the first trimester be performed at a hospital an unreasonable burden on women's free choice, not justified on medical grounds.

340. *See, e.g.,* Colo. § 18–6–101(1) (licensed physician using accepted medical procedures); Neb. § 28–335 (abortion other than according to accepted medical procedure a felony); Wyo. § 35–6–112 (same); Dellapena, *supra* note 27, at 361–65, 411–14. To the extent, however, that more severe penalties are visited on those, otherwise allowed to perform abortions, who use substandard abortion techniques than on other erring medical practitioners, there may be an equal protection problem or a manifestation of disproportionality

of punishment to offense, violative of the Eighth Amendment. On the latter, *see* Solem v. Helm, 463 U.S. 277 (1983).

341. Ill. ch. 38, § 81–29, *and see* § 81–26(6) (if there is a reasonable medical certainty that an abortion technique will cause pain to fetus which use of anesthetic or an analgesic will prevent or alleviate, physician must inform woman of the technique that will forestall pain); Ky. § 311.770; *cf.* Wyo. § 35–6–103 (physician is not intentionally to terminate viability of infant prior to, during or following abortion).

342. Planned Parenthood Association of Central Missouri v. Danforth, 428 U.S. at 78–79: "Moreover, as a practical matter, [the proscription] forces a woman and her physician to terminate her pregnancy by methods more dangerous to her health than the method outlawed." *See also* Note, *Criminal Liability of Physicians: An Encroachment on the Abortion Right,* 18 Am. Crim. L. Rev. 591, 604–05 (1981).

343. *E.g.,* Fla. § 390.001(5); Idaho § 18–608(3); Ill. ch. 38, § 81–26(3)–(5); Mass. ch. 112, § 120 (unless technique would create greater risk of death or serious bodily harm to mother at time of abortion or subsequently during future pregnancy; *query,* are the qualifiers constitutional under *Danforth,* 428 U.S. at 81–84?); Mo. § 188.030; Neb. § 28–330; Okla. tit. 63, § 1–734(B); Pa. tit. 18, § 3210(b); Utah § 76–7–307.

344. On required protection of live-born fetuses in the context of abortion, *see* text accompanying notes 348–52, 438–40 *infra.*

345. Mass. ch. 112, § 12R; S.D. § 34–23A–6.

346. *E.g.,* Mo. § 188.030(3); N.Y. Pub. Health Law § 4164(1) (after 20th week of pregnancy); N.D. § 14–02.1–05; Okla. tit. 63, § 1–732(E); Pa. tit. 18, § 3210(c).

347. Planned Parenthood Association of Kansas City v. Ashcroft, 462 U.S. 476, 482–86, 505 (five Justices concurring in separate opinions).

348. *See* text accompanying notes 185–86 *supra.* Tex. Family Code § 12.05(b) provides alternative medical standards by which live birth is to be determined.

349. *See* text accompanying notes 438–40 *infra.*

350. *E.g.,* Cal. Health & Safety Code § 25955.9; Del. tit. 24, § 1795(a); Ga. § 26–1202(c) ("if capable of meaningful or sustained life"); Ind. § 35–1–58.5–7(b); Iowa § 707.10; La. § 14:87.5, *and see* § 37:1285(28) (taking life of viable fetus aborted alive is a basis for license revocation); Me. tit. 22, § 1594; Mass. ch. 112, § 12P; Minn. § 145.415; Mont. § 50–20–108(1); Neb. §§ 28–325(3), 28–330; Nev. § 442.270(2); N.Y. Exec. Law § 291(3), Pub. Health Law § 4164(2); N.D. § 14.02.1–08; Okla. tit. 63, § 1–734(A), (C); Pa. tit. 18, §§ 3202(b)(3), 3212(b); R.I. § 11–9–18; S.D. § 34–23A–16.1; Tenn. § 39–4–206(a); Tex. Family Code § 12.05(a) (*semble:* "A living human child born alive after abortion or premature birth is entitled to the same rights, powers and privileges as are granted by the laws of this state to any other child born alive after the normal gestation period"); Wyo. § 35–6–104.

The Georgia statutory exception seemingly is based on eugenic grounds. *See* text accompanying notes 8–9, 80 *supra.*

Two states, Ind. § 35–1–58.5–7(b); Ky. § 311.790, provide for issuance of a birth certificate for a live-born fetus.

351. *E.g.,* Idaho § 18–608(3); Ill. ch. 38, §§ 81–24 (measures for life support for fetus must be available and utilized if there is clearly visible evidence of viability), 81–26(3); Iowa § 707.7; Ky. § 311.780; La. § 14:87.1; Mass. ch. 112, § 12P (*semble*: must have life-support equipment, as defined by state department of public health, in room where abortion is performed); Neb. § 28–325(3); Okla. tit. 63, § 1–734(C) (all reasonable measures to preserve life of child alive when partially or totally removed from uterus as long as such measures do not create a significant danger to woman's life or health); Pa. tit. 18, §§ 3202(b)(4), 3210(b); Tenn. § 39–4–206(a) (however, extraneous life support measures need not be attempted if it can be determined through amniocentesis or medical observation that a fetus is severely malformed); Tex. Penal Code § 4512.5 (during parturition, destroying vitality or life if child would have been born alive); Utah § 76–6–308; Va. § 18.2–74(c); Wyo. § 35–6–103.

The Tennessee exception is obviously based on eugenic considerations. *See* text accompanying notes 8–9, 80 *supra*.

See also the discussion of requirements that attending physicians be present during abortions during viability, text accompanying notes 346–47 *supra*.

352. *See* text accompanying notes 338–44 *supra*.

353. *E.g.,* Ariz. § 36–2302; Fla. § 390.001(6); Ill. ch. 38, § 81–26(3); La. § 14:87.2; Me. tit. 22, § 1593; Okla. tit. 63, § 1–735(B); Pa. tit. 18, § 3216(a); Utah § 76–7–310; Wyo. § 35–6–115 (*semble*: persons consenting to, aiding or abetting traffic in viable aborted children commit a felony).

354. *E.g.,* Arizona; Florida; Cal. Health & Safety Code § 25956 (exempting public or private educational institutions); Ill. ch. 38, § 81–32; Ind. § 35–1–58.5–65; Maine; Mass. ch. 112, § 12J(a); Mich. § 333.2688(1); Minn. § 145.422; Neb. § 28–346; N.D. § 14–02.2–01; Oklahoma; Pennsylvania; S.D. § 34–23A–17; Tenn. § 39–5–208(a) (including photography); Wyoming. Under the Massachusetts, Michigan, North Dakota, South Dakota, and Tennessee statutes, a mother can consent to and therefore legalize fetal experimentation.

355. *E.g.,* N.D.; Pa. tit. 18, § 3216(b).

356. *E.g.,* Ill. (written consent from one parent in instances of stillbirth or fetal death not resulting from abortion), Kentucky, Louisiana, Minnesota, Missouri, Montana, Nebraska, and N.D. § 14–02.2–01.

357. *E.g.,* Florida (life or health); Illinois (protection of life or health); La. (life and health of live-born child; preserve life or improve health of embryo or fetus); Minnesota (protect life or health); Missouri (same); Montana (same); Nebraska (diagnostic or remedial procedures to preserve life or health); Oklahoma (unless therapeutic to child or unborn child); Pa. tit. 18, § 3216(a) (life or health); Utah (allowed when, in a physician's best medical judgment, a technique should be used to test for genetic defects).

358. *E.g.,* Arizona (strictly necessary to diagnose disease or condition in mother, if abortion was performed because of that disease or condition); Nebraska.

359. *E.g.,* Massachusetts, Michigan, North Dakota, and Oklahoma. *See* note 442 *infra*.

360. *E.g.,* Ill. ch. 38, § 81–26(3); Indiana (transporting fetus out of state);

Kentucky; Maine, Neb. § 28–342; N.D. § 14–02.2–02; Oklahoma; Utah § 76–7–311; and Wyoming.

361. Margaret S. v. Edwards, 488 F. Supp. 181, 219–21 (E.D. La. 1980). *See also* Destro, *supra* note 27, at 1315–16; Note, *Ethical Standards for Fetal Experimentation,* 43 Fordham L. Rev. 547 (1975).

362. *E.g.,* Ill. ch. 38, § 83–32; Mo. § 188.047; Pa. tit. 18, § 3214(c); S.D. § 34–23A–19(3) (if facility is equipped to complete pathology reports); Utah §§ 76–7–309, 76–7–313.

363. *E.g.,* Ind. § 35–1–58.5–5(8) (physician's report to include results of pathological examination, if performed); Ohio § 3701.343(3) (public health council to adopt rules concerning pathological reports following abortions).

364. Planned Parenthood Association of Kansas City v. Ashcroft, 462 U.S. at 486–90, 505. There was no majority opinion.

365. *E.g.,* N.D. § 14–02.1–09 (physician performing abortion).

366. *E.g.,* Cal. Health & Safety Code § 25957(a); Fla. §§ 390.001(7), 390.012(e); Ill. ch. 38, § 81–32 (*semble:* no exploitation of aborted fetus or tissue); Minn. § 145.423(3) (child born alive and dying after birth to be disposed of according to general statutes governing human burials); N.Y. Pub. Health Law § 4164(4) (similar); Ohio § 3701.34.1(4) (public health council to adopt rules relating to humane disposition of products of human conception); Wyo. § 35–6–109 (state board of health to prescribe rules and regulations for disposal of bodies, tissues, organs and parts of unborn child, human fetus or aborted human embryo).

367. Akron v. Akron Center for Reproductive Health, 462 U.S. at 451–52. *Cf.* Feminist Women's Health Center, Inc. v. Philibosian, 157 Cal. App. 3d 1076, 203 Cal. Rptr. 918 (1984).

368. *See* text accompanying notes 101–03 *supra.*

369. *E.g.,* Idaho § 18–611 (discretionary); Ind. § 35–1–58.5–2(d); Nev. § 442.252 (as well as marital status and age); Or. § 435.435(2); R.I. §§ 23–4.7–5, 23–4.8–3(d); Utah § 76–7–313.

370. *E.g.,* Indiana; Nevada; R.I. § 23–4.7–5.

371. *E.g.,* Ill. ch. 38, §§ 81–25(3), 81–29; Ind. §§ 35–1–58.5–2(c)(2), 35–1–58.5–3; Mo. § 188.052; Nev. § 442.250(3); N.Y. Pub. Health Law § 4164(3) (life-sustaining efforts for viable fetus born alive); North Dakota; Okla. tit. 63, § 1–732(B)–(D); Or. § 435.425(1); R.I. § 23–4.7–4 (medical emergency requiring immediate abortion).

Some statutes require medical records to be retained for a specified time. *See, e.g.,* Mo. § 188.060 (seven years); Nev. § 442.256 (consents and information documentation retained at least five years); N.D. § 14–02.1–07 (seven years); Okla. tit. 63, § 1–739 (seven years). Courts disagree as to whether these are unreasonable requirements burdening therapeutic abortion decisions. *Compare* Planned Parenthood League of Massachusetts v. Bellotti, 641 F.2d 1006, 1018 (1st Cir. 1981) (constitutional), *with* Margaret S. v. Edwards, 488 F. Supp. 181, 213–14 (E.D. La. 1980) (burdensome requirement attached only to abortion case records).

372. *E.g.,* Ark. § 82–516; Del. tit. 24, § 1790(c); Ga. § 16–1202(d); Kan. § 65–445; Ky. § 213.055; Md. § 20–208(c); N.M. § 24–14–18; N.Y. Pub. Health Law §

4164(3); N.C. § 14–45.1(c); N.D. § 14–02.1–07; Pa. tit. 18, § 3124(e)–(f); Tenn. § 53–474(a); Utah § 26–2–23(3); Va. § 32.1–264.

373. *E.g.,* Cal. Health and Safety Code §§ 429.50(3), 25955.5; Ill. ch. 38, § 81–30; Ind. § 35–1–58.5–5; Mass. ch. 112, § 12R; Mich. § 333.2835; Mo. § 188.052; Neb. § 28–343; Pa. tit. 18, § 3214(a); P.R. tit. 24, § 232; S.D. § 34–23A–19; Tenn. § 39–4–201(c)(3); Utah § 76–7–313.

374. *E.g.,* Cal. Health & Safety Code § 25955.5; Ky. § 211.027; Me. tit. 22, § 1596(2); Minn. § 145.413; Mont. § 50–20–106(2); Nev. § 442.260(2); Ohio § 3701.341(2) (public health council to adopt rules relating to abortion reporting forms); Okla. tit. 63, § 1–738; Or. § 435.495(1); P.R. tit. 24, § 234; S.C. § 44–41–60; Wyo. § 35–6–107.

375. Planned Parenthood of Central Missouri v. Danforth, 428 U.S. at 80: reporting and recordkeeping requirements are constitutional as long as they "properly respect a patient's confidentiality and privacy." Despite the latter reservation, some courts have held that the names of patients and physicians reported to government offices become public records accessible under freedom of information laws. *See, e.g.,* State *ex rel.* Stephan v. Harder, 230 Kan. 573, 641 P.2d 366 (1982); Minnesota Medical Association v. State, 274 N.W.2d 84 (Minn. 1978); *cf.* Schulman v. New York City Health & Hospitals Corp., 38 N.Y.2d 234, 342 N.E.2d 501, 379 N.Y.S.2d 702 (1975) (reporting requirement sustained in absence of indications that identification information was leaked or made available to other governmental agencies for illegitimate purposes). If harassing use is made of information obtained by members of the public, release would seem to infringe through public action the privacy rights of patients and their physicians in the exercise of federal constitutional rights.

376. *E.g.,* Arkansas; Cal. Health & Safety Code § 25955.5; Delaware; Georgia; Kansas; Ky. § 213.055; Maine; Maryland; Michigan; Minnesota; Mo. §§ 188.055, 188.070; Neb. § 28–343; New Mexico; North Carolina; North Dakota; Or. § 435.495(2); Pa. tit. 18, § 3214(a) (patient identification); P.R. tit. 24, § 233; South Carolina; South Dakota; Tenn. § 53–474(b) (but some means of identification must be used in case further information is needed); Utah § 76–7–313; Wyo. § 35–6–108.

377. *E.g.,* Neb. § 28–343; New Mexico; Pa. tit. 18, 3214(e)(2) (unique identifying number to be substituted for physician's name). *See, however,* the decisions cited in note 375 *supra.*

378. *E.g.,* Georgia; Ill. ch. 38, § 81–30; Ky. § 213.055; Neb. § 28–343; P.R. tit. 24, § 233 (except as furnished to judges, prosecutors or police or peace officers for proper action).

379. *E.g.,* Ill. ch. 38, § 81–30.1; Minnesota; Nev. § 422.265; Pa. tit. 18, § 3214(g)–(h).

380. Planned Parenthood of Central Missouri v. Danforth, 428 U.S. at 79–81.

381. *E.g.,* Alaska § 18.16.010; Ill. ch. 38, § 81–31a; Me. tit. 22, § 1598(4); Md. § 20–210; Mass. ch. 112, § 12N; Minn. § 145.412(4); Nev. § 442.257; N.D. § 14–02.1–04(4); Or. § 435.455(1); S.D. § 22–17–5; Tenn. § 39–4–201(b)(1); Utah § 76–7–314; Wash. § 9.02.070; Wyo. § 35–6–110.

382. *See* text accompanying notes 412–19 *infra.*

383. *E.g.,* Alaska § 08.64.830(3)(A); Ariz. § 32–1401(10)(a); Ill. ch. 38, § 81–31;

Kan. §§ 65–2837(b)(5) (healing arts), 65–2912(f) (physical therapist); La. §
37:1285(8)–(9); Me. tit. 32, § 3282(5)(A); Md. § 14–504(24); Minn. §§
147.021(h), 147.101; Miss. § 75–25–29(5); Mo. § 188.065; Mont. § 66–1037(2);
Neb. § 71–148; Nev. §§ 630.030(1)(i) (physician), 632.320(6)(b) (nurse);
633A.100(1)(i) (naturopath); 634.020(3)(b) (chiropractic); N.J. §§ 45:9–16
(medicine, surgery, or chiropractic), 45:10–9 (midwifery); N.M. §§
61–10A–5(A) (osteopathic physician's assistant), 61–6–14(B)(1) (medicine
and surgery); N.C. § 90–14(2); N.D. § 43–17–31(3); Okla. tit. 59, § 509(1); Or.
§§ 677.190(2) (medicine), 685.110(4) (naturopathy); Pa. tit. 18, § 3219; R.I. §
23–4.7–7 (failure to obtain consents is unprofessional conduct), 23–4.8–4
(failure to notify spouse is unprofessional conduct); S.D. § 36–4–30(1); Tenn.
§§ 63–6–214(6) (medicine and surgery), 63–9–111(6) (osteopathic physicians);
Tex. Civ. Code art. 4495b, § 3.08(14); Utah §§ 58–12–36(1) (medicine),
58–12–7(1) (osteopathy); Va. § 54–317(1); Wash. §§ 18.36.150(1) (drugless
healer), 18.50.100 (midwifery), 18.57.170(1) (osteopathy), 18.72.030(2) (physician); Wis. § 448.18(1)(a).

If abortion is not specified, convicted abortionists can be disciplined on
the basis of their criminal record. *See, e.g.,* Mich. § 333.16221(v); N.H. §
329:17(VI)(d), (j); P.R. tit. 20, § 42(b); Vt. tit. 26, § 1354(3). On constitutional
requirements of administrative due process governing professional discipline, *see* Withrow v. Larkin, 421 U.S. 35 (1975).

384. This usually is aimed at failure to preserve the lives of live-born fetuses. *See,
e.g.,* Ill. ch. 70, ¶ 3, § 2.2; Ind. § 35–1–58.5–7(b); Me. tit. 22, § 1595; Nev. §
442.270(2); Tenn. § 39–4–206(c); Utah § 78–11–24.

On the traditional refusal to consider a fetus a human being with a
consonant right to sue for prenatal injuries persevering after live birth, *see*
Roe v. Wade, 410 U.S. at 161–62; *cf.* Mont. § 41–1–103 ("a child conceived
but not yet born is to be deemed an existing person, so far as may be
necessary for its interests in the event of its subsequent birth"). Precedent
conflicts as to whether a wrongful death action may be maintained for
injuries after viability which result in a stillbirth, although a majority of
jurisdictions appear to allow such litigation. *See, e.g.,* Shirley v. Bacon, 154
Ga. App. 203, 267 S.E.2d 809 (1980); Chrisafogeorgis v. Brandenberg, 55 Ill.
2d 368, 304 N.E.2d 88 (1973); O'Neil v. Morse, 385 Mich. 130, 188 N.W.2d
785 (1971); Ryan v. Beth Israel Hospital, 96 Misc. 2d 816, 409 N.Y.S.2d 681
(Sup. Ct. 1978) (guardian *ad litem* not allowed to maintain action which was
an effort to attack a lawful abortion); Libbee v. Permanente Clinic, 268 Or.
258, 518 P.2d 636 (1974) (summarizing authorities to date of opinion). If the
fetus is not viable, such an action seems not to be allowed. *See, e.g.,* Toth
v. Goree, 65 Mich. App. 296, 237 N.W.2d 297 (1975). If a viable fetus is born
alive and expires after even a short existence, a wrongful death action will be
allowed. *See, e.g.,* Group Health Association v. Blumenthal, 295 Md. 104,
453 A.2d 1198 (1983); Weiler & Catton, *supra* note 169, at 651–55; Special
Project, *supra* note 27, at 152–55.

A now-repealed statute allowing the parents of a fetus aborted in noncompliance with abortion statutes to maintain a wrongful death action against a
physician who performed the abortion was held unconstitutional as an

unacceptable burden on the woman's and physician's abortion decision. Doe v. Rampton, 366 F. Supp. 189, 193 (D. Utah 1973) (three-judge court).

Courts generally rule out homicide criminality based on acts causing stillbirths. *See, e.g.,* People v. Greer, 79 Ill. 2d 103, 402 N.E.2d 203 (1980); Hollis v. Commonwealth, 652 S.W.2d 61 (Ky. 1983); State v. Brown, 378 So. 2d 916 (La. 1979); People v. Guthrie, 97 Mich. App. 226, 293 N.W.2d 775 (1980), *appeal denied,* 417 Mich. 1006, 334 N.W.2d 616 (1983); State v. Amaro, 448 A.2d 1257 (R.I. 1982). If a fetus is born alive and then dies, however, a contrary conclusion is appropriate. *See, e.g.,* People v. Bolar, 109 Ill. App. 3d 384, 440 N.E.2d 639 (1982) (defendant properly convicted of reckless homicide as drunken driver of car which struck car in which pregnant woman was riding, necessitating a cesarean section).

Because of the legitimacy of contraception and abortion, some parents have sued because bungled techniques have resulted in birth of defective children. *See, e.g.,* Robak v. Robak, 658 F.2d 471 (7th Cir. 1981) (rejecting argument that, because case facts arose in 1972 before *Roe v. Wade,* an abortion would have been unavailable to a mother suffering rubella and the government should not be liable under the Federal Tort Claims Act); Morris v. Frudenfeld, 135 Cal. App. 3d 23, 185 Cal. Rptr. 76 (1982); Fulton-Dekalb Hospital Authority v. Graves, 252 Ga. 441, 314 S.E.2d 653 (1984); Schroeder v. Perkel, 87 N.J. 53, 432 A.2d 834 (1981); Speck v. Finegold, 497 Pa. 77, 439 A.2d 110 (1981); Certification *re* Harbeson v. Harbeson, 98 Wash. 2d 460, 656 P.2d 483 (1983). *See generally* Parness & Pritchard, *supra* note 111, at 257, 270–75; Stoutamire, *Effect of Legalized Abortion on Wrongful Life Actions,* 9 Fla. St. L. Rev. 137 (1981); Warren, *supra* note 17, at 51–55; Weiler & Catton, *supra* note 169, at 651–55; Note, *Genetic Screening, Eugenic Abortion, and Roe v. Wade: How Viable Is Roe's Viability Standard?,* 50 Brooklyn L. Rev. 113, 137–41 (1983); Note, *Wrongful Birth in the Abortion Context—A Critique of Existing Case Law and a Proposal for Future Actions,* 53 Denver L.J. 501 (1976); Comment, *Wrongful Life: Birth Control Spawns a Tort,* 13 J. Mar. L. Rev. 401 (1980).

Utah § 78–11–25 states that a failure or refusal to prevent a live birth is not a defense in any action and is not to be considered in awarding damages or child support, or in imposing a penalty in any action. Speck v. Finegold, *supra,* disallowed a so-called wrongful life action, but there is contrary authority. *See, e.g.,* Rivera v. State, 94 Misc. 2d 157, 404 N.Y.S.2d 950 (Ct. Claims 1978); Certification *re* Harbeson v. Harbeson, *supra* (citing authorities). *See generally* Parness & Pritchard, *supra* note 111, at 275–81; Warren, *supra* note 17, at 55–57.

Precedent allowing wrongful death actions based on the deaths of women resulting from improperly performed abortions, observable before 1973, *see, e.g.,* Wolcott v. Gaines, 225 Ga. 373, 169 S.E.2d 165 (1969); Martin v. Hardesty, 91 Ind. App. 239, 163 N.E. 610 (1928); True v. Older, 227 Minn. 154, 34 N.W.2d 700 (1948); Milliken v. Heddesheimer, 110 Ohio St. 381, 144 N.E. 264 (1924); Andrews v. Coulter, 163 Wash. 429, 1 P.2d 320 (1931) (only for negligent aftercare, not an abortion itself), clearly remains valid today, although the availability of therapeutic abortions and the low risk rate for previability abortions has caused such litigation to drop from sight.

On malpractice liability in abortion cases before *Roe v. Wade, see* Richey v. Darling, 183 Kan. 642, 331 P.2d 281 (1958); Lembo v. Donnell, 117 Me. 143, 103 A. 11 (1918); Henrie v. Griffith, 395 P.2d 809 (Okla. 1964). After 1973, there has been no basis to treat abortion-related medical malpractice actions differently from all other such actions, at least if the abortion was lawful. *See, e.g.,* Salinetro v. Nystrom, 341 So. 2d 1059 (Fla. Dist. Ct. App. 1977) (*semble*: no negligence in X-raying pregnant accident victim who did not know she was pregnant; pathologist report after abortion showed fetus already dead); Byrne v. Pilgrim Medical Group, 187 N.J. Super. 386, 454 A.2d 920 (1982) (husband allowed wages lost in caring for wife, to amount which would have been necessary to pay professional attendant); S.R. v. City of Fairmont, 280 S.E.2d 712 (W. Va. 1981) (*semble*: state long-arm statute gave plaintiff ability to sue Pennsylvania facility for failure to provide proper care following lawful abortion there). *Compare* Reno v. D'Javid, 55 A.D.2d 876, 390 N.Y.S.2d 421, *aff'd,* 42 N.Y.2d 1040, 369 N.E.2d 766, 399 N.Y.S.2d 210 (1977) (no malpractice action is allowed arising from unlawful abortion which woman solicited, on principle that she could not profit from an illegal act in which she had participated).

385. *See* text accompanying notes 104–05 *supra*; Isaacs, *supra* note 116, at 77–78: Warren, *supra* note 17, at 34–38. On the recognition of the conscience exception under the English Abortion Act, 1967, § 4, *see* Royal College of Nursing v. Department of Health & Social Security, [1981] A.C. 800 (H.L.).

386. *E.g.,* Alaska § 18.16.010; Ariz. § 36–2151; Ark. § 41–2560(b); Colo. § 18–6–104; Del. tit. 24, § 1791(b); Fla. § 390.001(8); Ga. § 16–1202(e); Idaho § 18–612; Ill. ch. 111 1/2, § 87–9, ¶ 5201; Ind. § 16–10–1.5–8; Kan. § 65–444; Me. tit. 22, § 1591; Md. § 20214(b); Mass. ch. 112, § 12*I*, ch. 272, § 21B (private hospitals and facilities); Minn. §§ 145.414, 62D.20 (health maintenance organizations); Neb. § 28–337; N.J. § 2A:65A–2; N.M. § 30–5–2; N.C. § 14–45.1(f); N.D. § 23–16–14; Tenn. §§ 39–4–204, 39–4–205; Va. § 18.2–75; Wash. § 9.02.080; Wis. § 140.42(1).

387. *E.g.,* Ky. § 311.800(1) (public), (3) (private); Mo. § 197.032 (public or private); Ohio § 4731.91 (public or private).

388. Poelker v. Doe, 342 U.S. 519 (1977) (public hospitals may refuse to allow therapeutic abortions even though they subsidize childbirths).

389. *E.g.,* Cal. Health & Safety Code § 25955(c) (religious or nonprofit); Mont. § 50–20–111(1) (private hospital or health care facility); Okla. tit. 63, § 1–741(A); Pa. tit. 16, § 51.31(a) (public hospitals or health care facilities cannot utilize exemption), (b)–(d), tit. 18, §§ 3202(d), 3213(d); S.C. § 44–41–40 (private or nongovernmental hospital or clinic); S.D. §§ 34–23A–14, 34–23A–15 (public hospitals cannot adopt policy excluding or denying admissions for abortions); Tex. Civil Code art. 4512.7, § 2 (private hospitals); Utah § 76–7–306(2) (private or denominational hospital not required to admit patients for abortions); Wyo. § 35–6–105 (private institutions).

Doe v. Bridgeton Hospital Association, 71 N.J. 478, 366 A.2d 641 (1976), *cert. denied,* 433 U.S. 914 (1977), interpreted state law to prohibit private, nonprofit, nonsectarian hospitals from closing their facilities to first-trimester abortions. *See also* the case on remand, 160 N.J. Super. 266, 389

A.2d 526 (1978) (state decision unaffected by United States Supreme Court decisions in *Maher, Beal,* and *Poelker* [discussed in text accompanying notes 463–70 *infra*]).

The European Court of Justice has recognized that medical facilities in one member state can refuse abortions for visiting workers, authorized by another member state, if abortion is prohibited in the competent institution's own nation. Bestuur van het Algemeen Ziekenfonds Drenthe-Platteland v. G. Pierik (Case 182/78), [1979] E.C.R. 1977, 1990.

390. *E.g.,* Alaska, Arkansas, California, Colorado, Delaware, Georgia, Idaho, Illinois, Kansas, Ky. § 311.800(5), Maine, Maryland, Mass. ch. 112, § 12*I,* Minn. § 145.414, Missouri, Montana, Nebraska, N.J. § 2A:65A–3, New York, Ohio, Oklahoma, Pa. tit. 18, § 3213(d), Rhode Island, South Carolina, S.D. § 34–23A–14, Utah, Virgin Islands, Virginia, Wisconsin, and Wyoming.

Several jurisdictions reject invocation of the hospital conscience exemption in cases of emergency. *See, e.g.,* Cal. Health & Safety Code § 25955(d) (or in instances of spontaneous abortion); Fla. § 390.001(9) (inapplicable to induced labor); South Carolina (emergency admittance); Virgin Islands (except in case of emergency).

391. *E.g.,* Montana, Pennsylvania, and Virgin Islands.

392. *E.g.,* Ill. ch. 38, § 81–33; Nebraska, Oregon; (physician to advise patient), Pa. tit. 16, §§ 51.31(e), 51.32 (conspicuously posted for public inspection), Wyoming.

393. *E.g.,* Ariz. § 36–2151; Cal. Health & Safety Code § 25955(a); Colo. § 18–6–104; Ga. § 26–1202(e); Fla. § 390.001(8); Idaho § 18–612; Ind. § 16–10–3–2; Ky. § 311.800(4); Mass. ch. 112, § 12*I*; Mo. § 197.032; Mont. § 50–20–111(2) ("religious beliefs and moral convictions"); Nev. § 632.475(1); N.M. § 30–5–2; N.Y. Civ. Rights Law § 79–i; N.C. § 14–45.1(e); R.I. § 23–17–11; Utah § 76–7–306(1); Va. § 18.2–75; Wis. § 140.42(1).

394. *E.g.,* Alaska § 18.16.010; Ark. § 41–2560(a); Ill. ch. 38, § 81–33 ("conscience"); Kan. § 65–443; Me. tit. 11, § 1591; Md. § 20–214(a); Minn. § 145.42; Neb. § 28–338; N.J. § 2A:65A–1; N.D. § 23–16–14; Ohio § 4731.91; Okla. tit. 63, § 1–741(B); Or. § 435.485(1); S.C. § 44–41–50(a); S.D. § 34–23A–13; Tenn. § 39–4–204; Tex. Civ. Code art. 4512.7, § 1; V.I. tit. 14, § 154; Wash. § 9.02.080; Wyo. § 35–6–106. Pa. tit. 16, §§ 51.41(a), 51.42(a), specify religious or moral grounds, but tit. 18, §§ 3202(d), 3213(d), denote only "conscience." Although the latter is stated to be supplementary to the former, presumably the specific abortion statute governs the more general law.

The conscience exemption may not be invoked in emergency situations. *See. e.g.,* Florida (induced labor), Iowa, Nev. § 632.475(3), and Oklahoma.

395. *E.g.,* Arizona, California, Colorado, Georgia, Idaho, Illinois, Kentucky, Massachusetts, Montana, Nevada, New York, Pennyslvania, South Carolina, Virginia, and Wisconsin.

396. *E.g.,* Florida, Indiana, Iowa, Minnesota, New Mexico, North Dakota, Oregon, and Utah.

397. *E.g.,* Arkansas, Colorado, Delaware, Florida, Georgia, Iowa, Kansas, Maryland, Minnesota, Montana, Nebraska, New Jersey, New York, Oklahoma, Virginia, and Wyoming.

398. *E.g.,* Arizona, Arkansas, California, Florida, Idaho, Illinois, Indiana, Kentucky, Maine, Massachusetts, Minnesota, Missouri, North Carolina, North Dakota, Oregon, Pennsylvania, Rhode Island, South Carolina, South Dakota, Tennessee, Texas, Utah, Virgin Islands, Washington, and Wisconsin.

399. *E.g.,* California, Idaho, Illinois, Kentucky, Maine, Minnesota, Missouri, Nevada, North Carolina, North Dakota, Pennsylvania, South Carolina, South Dakota, Texas, Virgin Islands, Washington, and Wisconsin. *See* Durham, Wood & Condie, *Accommodation of Conscientious Objection to Abortion: A Case Study of the Nursing Profession,* 1982 B.Y.U. L. Rev. 253.

400. *E.g.,* Arizonia, California, Florida, Idaho, Indiana, Kentucky, Maine, Massachusetts, Minnesota, Nevada, New Mexico, North Dakota, Oregon, Pennsylvania, Rhode Island, South Carolina, South Dakota, Texas, Utah, Virgin Islands, Washington, and Wisconsin.

401. *E.g.,* N.J. § 2A.65A–3; Pa. tit. 18, § 3213(d); V.I.

402. *E.g.,* Alaska, Arkansas, California, Colorado, Delaware, Florida, Georgia, Idaho, Ill. ch. 111 1/2 ¶ 5201(a), Kansas, Ky. § 311.800(5), Maine, Maryland, Massachusetts, Minnesota, Missouri, Montana, Nebraska, New Jersey, N.Y. Civ. Rights Law § 79–i(2), North Carolina, Ohio, Oklahoma, Pennsylvania, Rhode Island, South Carolina, South Dakota, Utah, Virgin Islands, Virginia, Wis. § 140.42(2), and Wyoming.

403. *E.g.,* Ill. ch. 38, § 81–33; Pa. tit. 18, § 3213(d).

404. *E.g.,* Arkansas, Colorado, Delaware, Florida, Georgia, Illinois, Indiana, Maine, Maryland, Minnesota, Montana, New Jersey, New Mexico, North Carolina, Ohio, Oklahoma, Pennsylvania, Rhode Island, Utah, Virginia, and Wisconsin.

405. *E.g.,* Arkansas, Colorado, Delaware, Florida, Georgia, Idaho, Maine, Maryland, Massachusetts, Montana, New Mexico, North Carolina, Oklahoma, Rhode Island, Utah, Virginia, and Wisconsin. Minn. § 145.414 proscribes coercion to allow abortions.

406. *E.g.,* New Jersey, New York, North Dakota, and Ohio.

407. *E.g.,* California (but medical employer can inquire into conscience reservation before hiring), Illinois, Indiana, Iowa, Kansas, Kentucky, Maine, Massachusetts, Minnesota, Missouri, Montana, Nebraska, Nev. § 632.475(2), Pennsylvania, South Carolina, South Dakota, Texas, Utah (including employment with other discrimination), Virginia, Washington, Wisconsin, and Wyoming.

408. *E.g.,* Cal. Health & Safety Code § 25955(b), Indiana, Ky. § 311.800(5), Massachusetts, Pennsylvania, and Texas.

409. *E.g.,* Neb. § 28–339 (class II misdemeanor); Nev. § 632.475(4) (misdemeanor); N.Y. Civ. Rights Law § 79–i(1) (misdemeanor); Wyo. § 35–6–113 ($10,000 fine).

410. *E.g.,* Mont. § 94–5–620(3); Neb. § 28–341; Tex. Civ. Code art. 4512.7, § 4; Wyo. § 35–6–114.

411. *E.g.,* Ill. ch. 111 1/2, ¶ 5201(c) (treble damages with minimum $2,000 recovery); Ind. (reinstatement of employment also available); Mo. § 197.032(3); Neb. § 28–340; Ohio; Pa. tit. 18, § 3213(d); S.C. § 44–41–50(c); Wyoming (for employment discrimination).

412. *E.g.,* State v. Hodgson, 295 Minn. 294, 204 N.W.2d 199 (1973); Commonwealth v. Jackson, 454 Pa. 429, 312 A.2d 13 (1973).

413. 423 U.S. 9 (1975).

414. The Court noted that it was concerned with maternal health, and had legitimated only "abortion . . . performed by medically competent personnel under conditions insuring maximum safety for the woman." *Id.* at 9. Hence, prosecutions of nonphysicians for first-trimester abortion infringe "no realm of personal privacy secured by the Constitution against state interference"; thereafter, "the ever-increasing state interest in maternal health provides additional justification for such prosecutions." *Id.*

415. *See, e.g.,* State v. Menillo, 171 Conn. 141, 368 A.2d 136 (1976) (on remand from *Connecticut v. Menillo*); State v. Orsini, 187 Conn. 264, 445 A.2d 887, *cert. denied,* 459 U.S. 861 (1982) (*semble*: persistent felony offender claimed record of earlier conviction for aiding in criminal abortion was silent as to whether the principal was a physician; the court thought indications in the record that the abortion was performed in a motel room using a "shoehorn device" was a sufficient indication the abortion was criminal); Rhim v. State, 264 Ind. 682, 348 N.E.2d 620 (1976); Spears v. State, 278 So. 2d 443 (Miss. 1973) (before *Menillo*); State v. Norflett, 67 N.J. 268, 337 A.2d 604 (1975) (before *Menillo*; cites precedent in accord); *see also* Smith v. Bentley, 493 F. Supp. 916, 924–27 (E.D. Ark. 1980).

416. Simopoulos v. Virginia, 462 U.S. 506.

417. Akron v. Akron Center for Reproductive Health, 462 U.S. at 451–52 (invalidating criminal statute requiring disposal of fetal remains "in a humane and sanitary manner"); Colautti v. Franklin, 439 U.S. 379 (1979) (statutes turning on viability and requiring care of fetus); Planned Parenthood of Central Missouri v. Danforth, 428 U.S. at 81–84 (statute imposing criminal penalties for failure to exercise degree of professional skill, care and diligence necessary to preserve life and health of fetus).

418. United States v. United States Gypsum Co., 438 U.S. 422, 434–46 (1978); Morrissette v. United States, 342 U.S. 246 (1952).

419. Colautti v. Franklin, 439 U.S. at 390, 394–397.

420. Simopoulos v. Virginia, 462 U.S. at 510 (placing burden of going forward with evidence on an affirmative defense generally is permissible).

421. *See also* text accompanying notes 187–90 *supra.*

422. *See, e.g.,* Alaska § 18.16.010; Ark. § 41–2551; Colo. § 28–6–101; Del. tit. 11, § 651; D.C. § 22–201; Fla. § 390.001(3); Ga. § 26–1201(a); Idaho §§ 18–606(2), 18–608; Ill. ch. 38, § 38–23.1(A) (defined in § 81–22[3]); Ind. §§ 35–1–58.5–2, 35–1–58.5–4; Iowa § 707.7, ¶ 3; Kan. § 21–3407(2); Ky. §§ 311.750, 311.760(2), *cf.* 311.760(1) (woman herself is not criminal for producing abortion during first trimester on advice of licensed physician); La. § 37:1285(8)(9) (*semble*: therapeutic abortions are dealt with under medical licensing statutes; this would seem to qualify § 14:87); Me. tit. 22, § 1598(3)(A); Md. § 20–210(a)(3); Mass. ch. 112, §§ 12L, 12M; Minn. § 145.412; Mo. § 188.020; Mont. § 50–20–109(1)(a); Neb. § 28–335; Nev. § 442.250(1)(a); N.M. § 30–5–1(C); N.Y. Penal Law § 125.05(3); N.C. §§ 14–45.1(a)(b), 14–44, 14–45; N.D. § 14.02.1–04(5); Okla. tit. 63, 1–731(A); Or. § 435.415(3); P.R. tit. 33, § 4010; S.C. § 44–41–20 (defined in § 44–41–10[b]); S.D.

§ 34–23A–3 to 34–23A–5; Tenn. § 29–4–201(c); Utah § 76–7–302(1) (defined in § 76–7–301[2]); V.I. tit. 14, §§ 151(b), 156; Va. § 18.2–72 to 18.2–74; Wash. § 9.02.070; Wis. § 940.04(5)(a); Wyo. § 35–6–111.

423. *See, e.g.,* People v. Bricker, 389 Mich. 524, 208, N.W.2d 172 (1973); Beecham v. Leahy, 130 Vt. 164, 287 A.2d 836 (1972).

424. *E.g.,* Ala. § 12A–13–7; Ariz. § 13–3603; Ark. §§ 41–2551, 41–2553; Cal. Penal Code § 274; Conn. §§ 53–29, 53–31a(a); Del. tit. 11, § 654; D.C. § 22–201; Ga. § 26–1201; Idaho § 18–605; Ill. ch. 38, § 81–22(6); La. § 14:87(1); Me. tit. 22, § 1598(2)(A); Mass. ch. 272, § 18; Mich. § 750.14; Miss. § 97–3–3(1); Nev. § 200.20; N.Y. § 585:13; N.M. § 30–5–3; N.Y. Penal Law § 125.05(2); N.C. §§ 14–44, 14–45; Okla. tit. 21, § 861; P.R. tit. 33, § 4010; R.I. § 11–23–5; S.C. § 44–41–80(a); Tenn. § 39–4–201(A)(1), (2); Vt. tit. 13, § 101; Va. § 18.2–71; Wash. § 9.02.010(1); W. Va. § 61–2–8.

425. The statutes cited in note 424 contain this alternative with the following exceptions and additions. Colo. § 18–6–101(1); Del. tit. 11, §§ 651, 654; Ky. § 311.720(1); Nev. § 201.120(2); Wash. § 9.02.020(2).

426. *E.g.,* Ala. § 12A–13–7; Ariz. § 13–3603; Ark. § 41–2551; Colo. § 18–6–101(1) (terminating pregnancy); Del. tit. 11, § 651; Idaho § 18–6505; Ill. ch. 38, § 81–22(6) (woman known to be pregnant; *see,* however, §§ 81–31[f], 81–31.1[II], making it a class 2 felony to perform abortions on women who are not pregnant); Ind. § 35–1–58.5–1(b) (termination of human pregnancy); Iowa §§ 707.7, 707.8(2) (termination of pregnancy); Kan. § 21–3407(1); Ky. § 31.720(1) (woman known to be pregnant); Me. tit. 11, § 1598 (interruption of pregnancy); Me. § 20–208 (terminating human pregnancy); Mass. ch. 112, § 12K; Mich. § 750.14; Minn. § 145.411(5) (must result in termination of pregnancy); Miss. § 97–3–3(1) (pregnant with child); Mo. § 188.015(1) (termination of pregnancy); Neb. § 28–326(1) (woman known to be pregnant); N.H. §§ 585:12 (pregnant woman), 585:13 (pregnant with quick child); N.M. § 30–5–3 (pregnant woman); N.C. §§ 14–44 (pregnant or quick with child), 14–45 (pregnant woman); N.D. § 14–02.1–02(1) (definition of abortion as termination of human pregnancy); Or. § 435.455(1) (terminate pregnancy); P.R. tit. 33, § 4010 (pregnant woman; R.I. § 11–23–5 (unborn quick child); S.C. § 44–41–10(a) (abortion defined as termination of human pregnancy); S.D. § 34–23A–1(1) (same); Tenn. § 39–5–201(a)(1) (pregnant, whether quick or not); Utah § 76–7–301(a) (termination of pregnancy); V.I. tit. 14, § 151(b) (pregnant female); Va. §§ 18.2–71 (intent to destroy unborn child, producing abortion or miscarriage and thus destroying child); W.Va. § 61–2–8 (producing abortion or miscarriage); Wis. § 940.04 (destruction of life of unborn child); Wyo. § 35–6–102 (after viability).

427. *E.g.,* Cal. Penal Code § 274; Conn. §§ 53–29, 53–31a(a); D.C. § 22–201; Ga. § 26–1201(a); Idaho § 18–605; La. § 14:87; Mont. § 50–20–104(4); Nev. § 201.120(1) (whether pregnant or not); N.Y. Penal Code § 125.02 (same); Okla. tit. 21, § 861; Vt. tit. 13, § 101 (pregnant or supposed to be pregnant); Va. § 18.2–71; Wash. § 9.02.010(2) (whether pregnant or not).

428. *See* authorities cited in note 45 *supra.*

429. *E.g.,* Ark. § 41–2551; Cal. Penal Code § 274; Colo. § 18–6–103 (pretending to end real or apparent pregnancy); Conn. § 53–29; Del. tit. 11, § 654; Ga. § 26–1201; Idaho § 18–605; Ill. ch. 38, §§ 81–31.1, 81–31.2; La. § 14:87; Mass.

ch. 272, § 19; Mont. § 50–20–104(4); Nev. § 201.120(1); N.H. § 585:12; Okla. tit. 21, § 861; Vt. tit. 13, § 101; Va. § 18.2–71.

430. *E.g.,* D.C. § 22–201; Md. § 20–208(a); N.M. § 30–5–3; Tenn. § 39–4–102(a)(2); Utah § 76–7–301(1).

431. *E.g.,* Del. § 24, § 1790(b)(1); Iowa § 707.7; Md. § 10–108(b)(1); Minn. § 145.412; Nev. § 442.250(c); N.Y. Penal Law § 125.45; Or. § 435.425(1); Wash. § 9.02.070.

432. *E.g.,* Alaska § 18.16.010; Ark. § 41–2551; Me. tit. 22, § 1598; Mich. §§ 750.14, 750.15; Neb. § 28–329; N.H. § 585:13; N.C. § 14–44; R.I. § 11–23–5; Wis. § 940.04.

433. *See* Connecticut v. Menillo, *quoted* in note 414 *supra.* Illustrations of legislation apparently so limited include Iowa § 707.7; Wyo. § 35–6–102.

434. *See* text accompanying notes 418–19 *supra. See also* Harris v. McRae, 448 U.S. 297, 311 n.17 (1980) (Hyde Amendment criminal sanctions were valid because they contained "a clear scienter requirement under which good-faith errors are not penalized").

435. *See* statutes cited in notes 424–32 *supra,* all of which, except as listed in note 436 *infra,* carry felony penalties.

436. *E.g.,* Ala, § 13A–13–7; Ill. ch. 38, § 81–31(a) (remaining provisions are punishable as felonies); N.H. § 585:12 (pregnant woman not quick with child); N.D. § 14–02.1–04(4) (class A misdemeanor if physician violates regulations); Wash. § 9.02.070 (gross misdemeanor, if physician); Me. tit. 11, § 1598 uses a hierarchy of "crimes"; abortion by a physician after viability is a class D crime, all other abortions are class C crimes.

437. *See* Solem v. Helm, 463 U.S. 277 (1983).

438. *See* text accompanying notes 348–52 *supra.*

439. *E.g.,* Del. tit. 24, § 1795(a) (knowing and reckless conduct detrimental to life or health of live-born infant after abortion a class A misdemeanor); Fla. § 782.09 (killing unborn child by injury to mother deemed manslaughter); Ill. ch. 38, §§ 81–24, 81–26(a) (class 2 felonies); Ind. § 35–1–58.5–7(a) (subject to homicide and manslaughter criminality); Iowa §§ 707.9 (intentional killing of live-born fetus a class B felony), 707.10 (failure to preserve life and health of viable fetus a serious misdemeanor); La. §§ 14:87.1 (killing child during delivery punishable by life imprisonment), 14:87.5 (intentional failure to sustain life and health of live-born viable infant punishable by up to 21 years' imprisonment); Mass. ch. 112, § 12T (failure to take reasonable steps to protect life and health of live-born child a misdemeanor, together with any other criminal liability); Mich. §§ 750.322 (willful killing of unborn quick child by injury to mother is manslaughter), 750.323 (successful efforts to kill unborn quick child is manslaughter); Mont. § 50–20–108(1) (criminal homicide purposely, knowingly or negligently to cause death of premature viable infant born alive); Neb. § 28–331 (class IV felony to fail to take reasonable steps to preserve life of live-born infant); Nev. § 442.270(2) (failure to preserve life and health of live-born person subjects person to general criminal statutes); N.D. §§ 14–02.1–05, 14–02.1–08 (class C felony to fail to preserve life and health of unborn child); Okla. tit. 63, § 1–734(D) (persons killing neonate or failing to take reasonable measures to preserve life of infant are guilty of homicide); Pa. tit. 18, § 3210(b) (third-degree felony to fail

to protect life of unborn viable child); R.I. § 11–9–18 (manslaughter knowingly and intentionally to fail to provide reasonable medical care and treatment, causing death of live-born infant); S.D. § 22–17–6 (intentional killing of human fetus by causing injury to mother, other than during therapeutic abortion, a class 4 felony); Tenn. § 39–4–206(b) (felony to fail to use good medical skill to preserve life and health of live-born infant); Tex. Civil Code § 4512.5 (destroying life during parturition if child would have been born alive is a felony punishable by a minimum five years' imprisonment to life); Utah § 76–7–314(2) (third-degree felony to fail to use medical skills to preserve life of unborn child); Wash. § 9A.32.060(b) (intentionally killing unborn quick child by injuring mother is first-degree manslaughter; Wyo. § 35–6–110 (felony intentionally to terminate viability of unborn infant or to fail to use accepted means of preserving live-born fetus).

See State v. Lewis, 429 N.D.2d 1110 (Ind. 1981), cert. denied sub nom. Lewis v. Indiana, 457 U.S. 1118 (1982) (doctor could be retried for unlawful post-viability abortion performed at clinic rather than hospital; viability demonstrated by fact fetus had been born alive and had survived two hours).

440. See materials cited in note 417 supra. See also Commonwealth v. Edelin, 371 Mass. 497, 359 N.E.2d 4 (1976) (insufficient evidence that physician's conduct was negligent or reckless, so that verdict of acquittal should have been directed; court divided equally as to whether death of fetus could be manslaughter); Special Project, supra note 27, at 156–59; Note, Criminal Liability of Physicians: An Encroachment on the Abortion Right?, 18 Am. Crim. L. Rev. 591, 609–15 (1981); Note, Current Technology Affecting Supreme Court Abortion Jurisprudence, 27 N.Y.L. Sch. L. Rev. 1221, 1249–55 (1982).

441. See text accompanying notes 52–55 supra.

442. E.g., Colo. § 16–6–102(2) (class 2 felony); D.C. § 22–201 (second-degree murder); Mass. ch. 272, § 19 (felony punishable by five to 20 years' imprisonment); Miss. § 97–3–3(1) (murder); N.H. § 585:14 (second-degree murder); N.M. § 30–5–3 (second-degree felony); N.Y. Penal Law § 125.15(2) (second-degree manslaughter); Vt. tit. 13, § 101 (felony punishable by five to 20 years' imprisonment); Wis. 940.04(2) (felony punishable by not more than 15 years' imprisonment).

Several statutes require coroners or medical examiners to inquire into deaths apparently resulting from criminal abortions. See, e.g., Fla. § 406.11(1)(a)(9); La. § 33:1561; Mass. ch. 38, § 6; Miss. § 41–61–9; P.R. tit. 20, § 52.

On wrongful death civil liability, see text accompanying note 384 supra.

443. See text accompanying notes 56–64 supra.

444. E.g., Ariz. § 13–3604; Cal. Penal Code § 274 (exempting therapeutic abortions); Conn. §§ 53–30, 53–31a(a); Del. tit. 11, §§ 652 (self-abortion), 654 (submitting to other than therapeutic abortion); Idaho §§ 18–606(2) (soliciting, submitting to, or self-inducing), 18–609 (except for lawful abortion); Ky. §§ 311.750 (self-abortion), 311.760(1) (except on advice of licensed physician); Mont. § 50–20–104(4) (abortion defined to include "submission to act or operation"); Nev. §§ 200.220 (submission to abortion after 24th week of gestation except as authorized under therapeutic abortion statute),

201.120(2) (self-abortion except as a therapeutic abortion on advice of licensed physician); N.Y. Penal Law §§ 125.05(3) (woman's act is justifiable if she believes it is done by physician performing lawful abortion), 125.50 (second-degree self-abortion through 24th week of pregnancy; class B misdemeanor), 125.55 (first-degree self-abortion if more than 24 weeks pregnant; class A misdemeanor); Okla. tit. 21, § 862 (soliciting, taking substance or using means to procure miscarriage; misdemeanor), tit. 63, § 1–733 (no woman to perform or induce abortion on self except under supervision of licensed physician); P.R. tit. 33, § 4011; S.C. § 44–41–80(b) (misdemeanor to solicit abortion unless justified); V.I. tit. 14, §§ 152 (woman lawfully may submit when physician lawfully may perform abortion), 156 (violation a felony); Wash. § 9.02.020 (submitting to abortion a felony unless justified).

    Some states, *e.g.*, Pa. tit. 18, § 3218; Vt. tit. 13, § 101, specifically preclude a woman's criminality.

445. *See* text accompanying notes 59–64 *supra*.

446. *See* text accompanying notes 67–69 *supra*.

447. *E.g.*, Ariz. § 13–3605; Ark. § 41–2552; Fla. § 797.02; Haw. § 445–119 (outdoor advertising); La. §§ 37:87.4, 37:88(1); Mass. ch. 272, § 20; Mich. §§ 750.15, 750.34; Miss. § 97–3–5; Mont. § 50–20–109(4); Nev. § 442.270(1); N.D. § 14–02.1–06; P.R. tit. 10, § 315 (public display or advertising), tit. 33, § 4012; Vt. tit. 13, § 104; V.I. tit. 14, § 153 (*semble*: not to create organization or society to solicit candidates for abortion); Wash. § 9.68.030; Wyo. § 35–6–116.

448. *See* Bolger v. Youngs Drug Products Corp., 463 U.S. 60 (1983) (contraceptives and contraceptive information); Carey v. Population Services International, 431 U.S. 678, 700–02 (1977) (same); Bigelow v. Virginia, 421 U.S. 809 (1975) (advertisement of lawful therapeutic abortion services).

449. Bigelow v. Virginia, 421 U.S. 809 (1975) *See, e.g.*, Conn. §§ 53–31, 53–31a(b); Idaho §§ 18–604 (physicians and licensed health care providers), 18–607 (except to physicians or druggists or distributors to others, or in trade or professional channels unlikely to reach the general public); Md. § 20–210(a)(2) (other than by physicians in licensed and accredited hospitals [probably too limited an exception to meet *Bigelow* requirements]); Va. § 18.2–76.1 (amended after *Bigelow*); Wis. § 450.11(2).

450. *Cf.* Baird v. La Follette, 72 Wis. 2d 1, 239 N.W.2d 536 (1976) (statute construed not to cover educational and informational exhibits in the context of free public lectures; could not ban even in a commercial setting good faith educational presentation of general information regarding contraception). *See generally* Warren, *supra* note 17, at 45–47.

451. *E.g.*, Conn. §§ 53–29, 53–31a(a); Idaho § 18–606(1); Mass. ch. 272, § 20; Mont. § 50–20–109(4) (by physician, hospital, or other person or agency); Nev. § 422.270(1) (person or organization not to advertise directly or indirectly abortion costs or conditions); N.D. § 14–02.1–06; P.R. tit. 33, § 4010; V.I. tit. 14, § 153 (no public or private organization or society is to be created for purpose of soliciting candidates for abortion).

452. *E.g.*, Cal. Penal Code § 276; Del. tit. 24, § 1792(2).

453. *See* text accompanying notes 70–76 *supra*.

454. *E.g.,* La. § 14:88(1); Miss. § 97–3–5; Nev. § 201.130; Vt. tit. 13, § 104.

455. *See* Carey v. Population Services International, 431 U.S. 678, 688 (1977): The "same test must be applied to state regulations that burden an individual's right to . . . terminate pregnancy by substantially limiting access to the means of effectuating that decision as is applied to state statutes that prohibit the decision entirely. Both types of regulation 'may be justified only by a "compelling state interest" . . . and . . . must be narrowly drawn to express only the legitimate state interests at stake.' "

456. *E.g.,* Cal. Penal Code § 274; Colo. § 18–6–105 (other than to licensed physician); Conn. § 53–31a(b) (exempts licensed physician or hospital); Del. tit. 11, § 653, tit. 24, § 1792(1) (exempting for purposes of lawful abortion under § 1791); Idaho § 18–607 (except to physician or druggist or distributor, or on prescription or order of physician, or possession with intent to supply to lawful recipient); Ill. ch. 38, § 81–31(d) (without prescription); Iowa §§ 205.1 (exempting supplying on prescription), 205.2 (exempts those supplying physicians, *etc.,* for use in the practice of their profession); Md. § 20–210(a)(1) (other than by licensed physicians in licensed hospitals [probably too narrow under *Carey*]); Mich. § 750.15 (except on prescription [probably too narrow under *Carey*]); S.C. § 44–41–80(a) (except in connection with therapeutic abortions; women on whom abortions performed are not within criminal provisions); Wis. § 450.11(2) (except to licensed physicians or medical services).

457. *E.g.,* Mass. ch. 272, § 21; N.Y. Penal Law § 125.60; Wash. § 9.02.030.

458. *E.g.,* Idaho § 19–2115; Nev. § 175.301 (unless the person on whom the offense was committed was at the time a police officer or deputy sheriff [legitimating use of policewomen decoys]); P.R. Crim. Proc. R. 154. *See also* text accompanying notes 59–60 *supra.*

459. Tit. 13, § 102.

460. Nev. § 201.140 (abortion, attempted abortion, or selling abortifacients); Wash. § 9.020.040 (no person can claim self-incrimination in prosecutions for abortion, attempted abortion or selling drugs, but is immunized under § 10.52.090). *See also* text accompanying notes 61–64 *supra.*

461. Section 11–23–5 (unnecessary to save woman's life [the basic provision is unconstitutional under *Roe v. Wade* if applied to physicians, and superfluous in actuality in instances of criminal abortion]).

462. *See* Simopoulos v. Virginia, 462 U.S. at 510. Whether the burden of persuasion may be placed on the defendant requires a harmonization of language in Engle v. Isaac, 456 U.S. 107 (1982); Patterson v. New York, 432 U.S. 197 (1977); and Mullaney v. Wilbur, 421 U.S. 684 (1975), an important issue which, nevertheless, need not be elaborated upon here.

463. 432 U.S. 464 (1977). *See generally* Appleton, *Beyond the Limits of Reproductive Choice: The Contribution of the Abortion-Funding Cases to Fundamental-Rights Analysis and to the Welfare-Rights Thesis,* 81 Colum. L. Rev. 721, 724–31 (1980); Canby, *Government Funding, Abortions, and the Public Forum,* 1979 Ariz. St. L.J. 11; Horan & Marzen, *The Moral Interests of the State in Abortion Funding: A Comment on Beal, Maher & Poelker,* 22 St. Louis U.L.J. 566 (1978); *Jones, supra* note 11, at 594–600; Petersen, *The*

Public Funding of Abortion Services: Comparative Developments in the United States and Australia, 33 Int'l & Comp. L.Q. 158 (1984).

464. *Id.* at 474.
465. *Id.*
466. *Id.* at 475–76.
467. 432 U.S. 438 (1977).
468. 42 U.S.C. §§ 1396a(a)(13)(B), (17), 1396d(a)(1)–(5) (1976).
469. Maher v. Roe, 432 U.S. at 438.
470. 432 U.S. 519 (1977). *Poelker* was distinguished, however, when the only hospital in the community, publicly owned, refused to allow staff physicians to perform lawful abortions for paying patients. Nyberg v. City of Virginia, 667 F.2d 754 (8th Cir. 1982), *appeal dismissed,* 462 U.S. 1125.
471. Called the Hyde Amendment after its original congressional sponsor. *See* Harris v. McRae, 448 U.S. 297, 302–03 (1980); Vinovskis, *Politics of Abortion in the House of Representatives in 1976,* 77 Mich. L. Rev. 1790 (1979).
472. The 1977 version acknowledged only danger to maternal life, while the 1979 language recognized "severe and long-lasting physical health damage"; the 1980 version included rape or incest if reported promptly to a law enforcement agency or public health service. *See id.* The FY84 version covers only instances "where the life of the mother would be endangered if the fetus were carried to term." Departments of Labor, Health and Human Services, and Education Appropriations Act. Pub. L. 98–139 § 204, 97 Stat. 871, 887 (1983).
473. 448 U.S. 297 (1980). Later the same term, in Williams v. Zbaraz, 448 U.S. 358 (1980), the Court held that a state participating in the Medicaid program is not obligated to underwrite medically indicated abortions for which federal reimbursement is unavailable under the Hyde Amendment; the Court confirmed that state funding restrictions patterned on the Hyde Amendment do not violate Fourteenth Amendment equal protection. *See generally* Appleton, *supra* note 464; Isaacs, *supra* note 11, at 171–75; Jones, *supra* note 11, at 600–05; Yarbrough, *The Abortion-Funding Issue: A Study in Mixed Constitutional Cues,* 59 N.C.L. Rev. 611 (1981).
474. Harris v. McRae, 448 U.S. at 315.
475. *Id.* at 318–20; it found the plaintiffs to lack standing to litigate whether the Hyde Amendment interfered with their "free exercise" rights under the First Amendment. *See also* Note, *Abortion Laws, Religious Beliefs and the First Amendment,* 14 Val. U. L. Rev. 487 (1980); Comment, *The Establishment Clause and Religious Influences on Legislation,* 75 Nw. U. L. Rev. 944 (1980).
      On the religious dimension of the Hyde Amendment and similar legislative efforts to limit the impact of *Roe v. Wade, see, e.g.,* Symonds, *The Denial of Medi-Cal Funds for Abortion: An Establishment of Religion,* 9 Golden Gate U. L. Rev. 421 (1978–1979); Pilpel, *The Fetus as Person: Possible Legal Consequences of the Hogan-Helms Amendment,* 6 Fam. Plann. Perspect. 6 (Winter 1974); Editorial, *Do Catholics Have Constitutional Rights?,* 105 Commonweal 771 (December 8, 1978).
476. Harris v. McRae, 448 U.S. at 325.

477. *See, e.g.,* Ariz. § 35–196.02; Ill. ch. 23, §§ 5–5, 6–1; Ind. § 16–10–3.3; Ky. §§ 205.560(1), 311.715; Minn. §§ 145.935(2), 256B.40; N.J. § 30:4D–6.1 (*but see* Right to Choose v. Byrne, note 486 *infra*); N.D. §§ 14–02.3–01, 14–02.3–05 (violation a class B misdemeanor); Pa. tit. 18, § 3215(a), tit. 55, §§ 1141.57, 1221.57(a), tit. 62, § 483; Utah §§ 26–18–4(3)–(4), 26–18–10(6); W. Va. § 16–2B–2 (*semble*: state funds not to be used for abortion as a means of family planning); Wis. § 20.927(1).

478. *E.g.,* Arizona; Indiana; Kentucky; Minn. §§ 261.28, 393.07(11); New Jersey; North Dakota; Pennsylvania; Utah; West Virginia; and Wisconsin.

479. *E.g.,* North Dakota (invalidated in Valley Family Planning v. North Dakota, 661 F.2d 99 [7th Cir. 1981], under the supremacy clause because it conflicted with 42 U.S.C. §§ 300 *et seq.* [1976]); Pa. tit. 62, § 453; Wisconsin.

480. Ill. ch. 127, § 526 (noncontributory health insurance payments to state employees); N.D. § 14.02.3–03 (all health insurance policies, except as optional rider with extra premium); Pa. tit. 18, § 3215(d) (funded for employees out of public monies); R.I. § 36–12–2.1 (state or local health insurance plans); S.C. § 1–13–30(*l*) (sex discrimination statute does not require employer to pay health benefits for abortion, but employer may agree to do so through collective bargaining).

481. N.D. § 14–02.3–02; Utah §§ 76–7–322, 76–7–323; W. Va. § 16–2B–2.

482. Including prohibitions against providing hospital or nursing care services, *e.g.,* Ill. ch. 23, § 7.1; N.D. § 14–02.3–04; Pa. tit. 18, § 3215(a), (b) (except for treatment of post-abortion complications or when no other facility performing abortions is available within a radius of 20 miles), disability benefits, *e.g.,* Illinois, or burial benefits. *Id.*

483. *E.g.,* Arizona; Illinois; Indiana; Ky. §§ 205.560(6), 311.715; Minn. §§ 256B.02(13), 256B.40; New Jersey; North Dakota, Pennsylvania, Utah, Wis. § 20.927(2)(a). Ill. ch. 23, §§ 6–1, 7–1, exempt in addition abortions necessary to the health of either mother or unborn viable child, while Wis. § 29.927(2)(b) exempts cases in which a preexisting condition will cause grave, long-lasting physical health damage to a woman if she is not given an abortion. The health of an unborn viable child may be recognized under Ill. ch. 23, §§ 6–1, 7–1, and Va. § 32.1–92.2 recognizes the eugenic ground of a physician's certification that a fetus will be born with a gross and totally incapacitating physical deformity or mental deficiency.

484. *E.g.,* Minnesota; Pa. tit. 18, § 3215(c); Virginia; Wis. § 20.927(2)(a).

485. Minnesota; Pennsylvania; Virginia; and Wisconsin.

486. *E.g.,* Committee to Defend Reproductive Rights v. Unruh, 29 Cal. 3d 252, 625 P.2d 779, 172 Cal. Rptr. 866 (1981) (budget act excluding funds to underwrite therapeutic abortions was declared in violation of the state constitution); Kindley v. Governor, 289 Md. 620, 426 A.2d 908 (1981) (court construed state legislation to cover all abortions determined by physicians to be medically necessary, but noted the lack of a legal obligation to fund abortions); Bayne v. Secretary of State, 283 Md. 560, 392 A.2d 67 (1978) (budget appropriation for public funding of abortions was not subject to state constitutional provision for popular referendum, which specifically excluded budgetary legislation); McKee v. Likens, 261 N.W.2d 566 (Minn. 1977) (restrictive regulations invalidated for failure to comply with state APA

notice requirements); Right to Choose v. Byrne, 91 N.J. 287, 450 A.2d 925 (1982) (state constitution required invalidation of state legislation tracking Hyde Amendment; public funding must extend to all abortions necessary to maternal health).

In Reina & Reina v. Landeskreditbank Baden-Württemberg (Case 65/81), [1982] E.C.R. 33, 40, the European Court of Justice held that special interest-free loans to residents upon childbirth were a "social advantage" which could not be denied workers from another member state under art. 7(1) of the EEC Treaty and art. 7(2) of Regulation (EEC) No. 1612/68 of the Council. The court rejected a justification advanced by Baden-Württemberg that childbirth loans were intended to help prevent voluntary abortions by residents; demographic objectives of countering falling birth rates among a member state's nationals cannot be pursued in a way which discriminates against nationals of other member states.

487. *E.g.,* Minn. § 145.925(8) (misdemeanor); Mont. § 50–20–106(4); § N.D. § 14–02.1–03(3); Pa. tit. 18, § 3215(f).

488. *E.g.,* Ark. § 41–2560(c); Cal. Health & Safety Code § 25955.3; Del. tit. 24, § 1791(c); Ky. § 311.810; Minn. § 145.414; Mo. § 197.032(3); Or. § 435.435(3).

489. *E.g.,* Arkansas; California; Delaware; Kentucky; Me. tit. 22, § 1591(c); Md. § 20–214(c); Mass. ch. 112, § 12S (*semble*: patients are to be informed that refusal to undergo abortion is not a ground for denial of public assistance); Missouri; Or. § 435.435(3); Pa. tit. 18, § 3215(g).

490. *E.g.,* Arkansas, California, Delaware, Kentucky, Maine, Maryland, Massachusetts, Minnesota, Missouri, Oregon, and Pennsylvania.

491. *E.g.,* Kentucky, Maine, and Maryland.

492. "Although the liberty protected by the Due Process Clause affords protection against unwarranted government interference with freedom of choice in the context of certain personal decisions, it does not confer an entitlement to such funds as may be necessary to realize all the advantages of that freedom. To hold otherwise would mark a drastic change in our understanding of the Constitution. It cannot be that because government may not prohibit the use of contraceptives, . . . or prevent parents from sending their child to a private school, . . . government, therefore, has an affirmative constitutional duty to ensure that all persons have the financial resources to obtain contraceptives or send their children to private schools. To translate the limitation on governmental power implicit in the Due Process Clause into an affirmative funding obligation would require Congress to subsidize the medically necessary abortion of an indigent woman even if Congress had not enacted a Medicaid program to subsidize other medically necessary services. Nothing in the Due Process Clause supports such an extraordinary result." Harris v. McRae, 448 U.S. at 317–18.

493. Clandestine abortion was viewed as a public health problem before 1973, *see, e.g.,* Calderone, *Illegal Abortion as a Public Health Problem,* 50 Am. J. Pub. Health 948 (1960), and has that potential today if the availability of lawful therapeutic abortion is restricted. Sneideman, *supra* note 19, at 192–94.

494. *See* text accompanying notes 140–50 *supra.*

495. *See* text accompanying notes 413–16 *supra.*

496. *See, e.g.* N.Y. Penal Law § 120.05(5) (McKinney 1975); 30 Halsbury's Laws of England ¶ 43 (4th ed. 1980); II–1 ALI Model Penal Code 187–90, comment to § 211.1 (1980).

497. *See* N.Y. Penal Law §§ 10.00(9) (McKinney 1975) (impairment of physical condition or substantial pain), § 120.00(1), (2).

498. *See id.* §§ 10.00(10) (physical injury which creates a substantial risk of death, or which causes death or serious and protracted disfigurement, protracted impairment of health or protracted loss or impairment of the function of any bodily organ), 120.05(1), (2), (4), 120.10(1), (3). The crime of reckless endangerment also may be available in abortion cases not producing death or injury but substantially risking either. *See, e.g.,* ALI Model Penal Code § 211.1 (1980); N.Y. Penal Law §§ 120.20, 120.25; Tex. Penal Code § 22.05(a) (Vernon 1974).

499. *See, e.g.,* ALI Model Penal Code § 2.11(1), (2)(a); State v. Brown, 143 N.J. Super. 571, 364 A.2d 27 (Super. Ct., Law Div. 1976), *aff'd,* 154 N.J. Super. 511, 381 A.2d 1231 (1977); Green, *supra* note 250, at 99–100; Comment, *Mayhem: Consent of Maimed Party as a Defense,* 47 Iowa L. Rev. 1122 (1961–62).

500. *See, e.g.,* Ala. Code §§ 41–20–1–16 (1982), Opinion of Justices, 381 So. 2d 183 (Ala. 1980); Fla. Stat. Ann. § 11.61 (West Supp. 1984), Sellars v. Florida Real Estate Communication, 380 So. 2d 1052 (Fla. Dist. Ct. App. 1980); N.H. Rev. Stat. Ann. §§ 17–G:1–G.10 (Supp. 1983), Opinion of Justices, 118 N.H. 582, 392 A.2d 125 (1978); W. Va. Code §§ 4–10–1–14 (Supp. 1984) (Sunset Law).

For a model abortion law consistent with the Supreme Court's doctrines, see Comment, *A Decade of Cementing the Mosaic of* Roe v. Wade: *Is the Composite a Message to Leave Abortion Alone?*, 15 U. Tol. L. Rev. 681, 749–53 (1984). Other legislative proposals appear in Walker & Puzder, *State Protection of the Unborn After* Roe v. Wade: *A Legislative Proposal*, 13 Stetson L. Rev. 237 (1984).

This article examines the abortion controversy and the political reaction that followed. The discussion is done in light of the many cases that have followed the *Roe* decision before the Supreme Court. The authors give specific references to the Human Life Bill (part of which is in the Appendix) and the issue of subject matter restrictions on lower federal court jurisdiction (which was presented by Stephen H. Galebach in his prepared testimony).

3 · The Abortion Controversy: A Study in Law and Politics_____

Albert M. Pearson, J.D. and Paul M. Kurtz, J.D.

I. Introduction

The Supreme Court's 1973 decision of *Roe v. Wade*,[1] which held that women have a federal constitutional right to an abortion, has generated considerable controversy. The abortion issue became politically significant in the 1960s, when, emboldened by the Supreme Court's recognition of a constitutionally based right of privacy, activists initiated a series of legal challenges to the validity of state abortion laws. Their efforts finally succeeded in 1973 when the Supreme Court in *Roe* and *Doe v. Bolton*[2] struck down as unconstitutional the Texas and Georgia abortion laws. These decisions sparked an intense reaction. For those who objected to the result in *Roe*, however, the occasion was not necessarily one of final defeat. Though *Roe* was a decisive victory for the pro-abortion forces, it was only the first battle in what was to become a fierce struggle over fundamental principle.

The purpose of this article is not to explore the evolution of Supreme Court doctrine concerning abortion. Rather, the purpose is to look at the abortion controversy in terms of the political reaction that it engendered. This study concentrates on two aspects of what since 1973 can be described as the ongoing guerrilla war against *Roe*. The first concerns the post-*Roe* legislation at both the state and federal levels purporting to regulate abortion through time, place and manner restrictions. Much of this legislation was an attempt to circumvent *Roe* or at the least to minimize its consequences.

The second aspect of the study concerns the various proposals designed not merely to mitigate the effects of *Roe*, but to overrule it. The bulk of this discussion deals with the rather surprising variety of constitutional amendments put forward in Congress. A significant part, however, focuses on legislative substitutes for a constitutional amendment. These include proposed jurisdictional restrictions on the Supreme Court and lower federal courts and proposed substantive legislation based on section 5 of the Fourteenth Amendment, which defines "life" for constitutional purposes. While it is true that limiting the jurisdiction of the federal courts to hear abortion cases would not explicitly overrule *Roe* because of the doctrine of stare decisis, it would effect a shift of power to the state courts which alone would have the ability to grant remedies in abortion cases. In practice, the force of *Roe* would be greatly reduced.

The opponents of *Roe,* however, have not been able to unite on an approach for overruling it because some believe that the primary problem with the decision is a moral one, namely its approbation of abortion, while others object to it because of its implications for federalism and the policy-making role of the judiciary. This split in the anti-abortion ranks, which we shall call the "moralist"–"federalist" split, has hindered the opponents of *Roe,* rendering it unlikely that Congress will pass a measure designed to overrule *Roe* in the near future. Given the current political climate, the most serious and immediate threat to *Roe* is the possibility of a change in the composition of the Supreme Court.

II. Roe v. Wade and the Strategy of Subversion

A. Abortion Regulation in Transition: Theory and Practice

Until the *Roe* decision in 1973, abortion in this country was almost universally classified as criminal; many states sought to deter abortions by establishing severe penalties.[3] Anti-abortion laws were often difficult to enforce, however. Those who knew of the offense normally had no incentive to report it to the law enforcement authorities. The involved male very often supported the woman's decision to have an abortion. The woman's parents and friends, if they knew of the abortion at all, rarely wanted to see her condemned as a criminal. Finally, the absence of a fetus which had no identity was not noticed by the community at large.

Of course, no legal sanction, criminal or civil, deters with complete effectiveness. The abortion laws, however, were particularly difficult to enforce because violations were underreported. If the states had difficulty enforcing abortion laws prior to *Roe,* how could they expect to prevent a rise in the abortion rate after *Roe*? This dilemma highlights the situation facing legislatures seeking to enforce abortion standards without appearing to be terribly obvious about it.

Despite these enforcement difficulties, many states gave constitutional ground most grudgingly and enacted legislation in response to *Roe* anyway. This strategy, which will be referred to as "massive resistance," served at least three key objectives of the states. The first was to circumvent *Roe* by achieving indirectly what the *Roe* decision prohibited them from doing directly. The second objective was to impress the Supreme Court with the intensity of public hostility to *Roe* and thereby to persuade the Court to limit *Roe* significantly or perhaps even to reconsider it. The third objective was to create a political climate receptive to a constitutional amendment (or a congressional substitute) overruling *Roe*. These objectives have proven to be most elusive.

B. A Comment on the Strategy of Massive Resistance

The strategy of local massive resistance to federal policy works best when the state has been ordered to alter its ways, because it can then be dilatory in implementing the required changes. For example, recalcitrant local officials have been able to blunt the Supreme Court decisions involving school desegregation, school prayer, prison conditions, and police practices by using tactics of delay, minimal compliance, and outright subversion of judicial orders. The difficulties associated with monitoring institutional change are such that the offending state practices or policies may persist for years after they have been ruled unconstitutional. School prayer is perhaps the best example of this.[4]

Massive resistance is less effective in those situations where the activity at issue is not performed by the state but by individuals. As the state is not the primary actor, it has much less control over the activity. The right to abortion can be exercised fully and effectively without the involvement of the state. To resist the federal policy on abortion, the state must act affirmatively by passing and enforcing legislation to restrict the individual's activity. This is a greater burden for the state to carry. Whenever the state tries to restrict a constitutionally protected activity, such as freedom of speech or abortion, it faces the double hurdle of identifying those who violate time, place, and manner restrictions and of prosecuting cases without appearing to flout constitutional standards. Given these enforcement problems, one can understand why massive resistance as a response to *Roe* has been a failure. As will be seen in the remainder of Part II, the premise that an unyielding attitude toward *Roe* would wear down judicial resolve to enforce the *Roe* standards has proven to be faulty.

C. Indirect Regulation of Abortion

Before considering legislation enacted in the aftermath of *Roe,* a brief review of the *Roe* decision itself is in order. Under Texas law, it was a felony to administer any drug or to utilize any means to procure an abortion.[5] The statute applied to all stages of pregnancy and was subject only to the exception of an abortion performed to save the life of the mother. In striking down this statute, the Court substantially discounted the fundamental premise of abortion regulation, namely the primacy of the state's interest in protecting prenatal life. Indeed, the Court so reduced the importance of that interest that it may not count seriously in constitutional analysis until the last trimester of pregnancy, though it then becomes compelling. Until that point, a state cannot make abortions illegal. After the first trimester, however, the state may regulate abortions "to the extent that the regulation reasonably relates to the preservation and protection of maternal health."[6]

Once the new constitutional order was established, the logic that followed from *Roe* was clear. As pregnancy progresses through its trimesters, the state's interest in regulating abortion increases. Prior to fetal viability, which the Court in *Roe* held is reached 24 to 28 weeks after conception or approximately at the beginning of the final trimester of pregnancy,[7] the state cannot interfere with the woman's decision to have an abortion. Even during the final trimester, the state cannot impose an absolute ban on abortion; *Roe* recognizes an exception whenever an abortion is "necessary to preserve the life or health of the mother."[8]

The critical question after *Roe* was how far the Supreme Court would pursue the doctrinal implications of its decision.

Many state legislatures, perhaps guided more by moral outrage than astute legal judgment, implemented strategies for the indirect regulation of abortion to test the Court's resolve to stand firm on *Roe*. None of these strategies represented a direct challenge to the Supreme Court's authority. Yet beneath the facade of official resignation or acceptance lay defiance. Indirect abortion regulations were in many instances instruments of that defiance; their value lay in their potential to evade *Roe* and to erode the Supreme Court's authority. The statutes have come in two general forms. One involves "power investiture," the delegation to a third party of the power to prevent an abortion. The other involves "burden creation," the enhancement of the costs or risks associated with abortion, reducing its appeal to pregnant women.

1.   POWER INVESTITURE   Denied the option of direct criminalization of abortion, some legislatures tried an ingenious method to circumvent *Roe*. They delegated the power to prevent abortions to people who had family ties to the woman and who, by virtue of those ties, could be said to have an interest in the decison about whether to terminate a pregnancy. Under this type of scheme, the third party (either a parent or husband) could effectively veto the abortion decision by withholding consent.[9]

This technique seemed to offer several advantages to the opponents of *Roe*. First, and perhaps unexpectedly, it had the potential of discouraging abortions even more effectively than criminal prohibitions, because the pregnant woman's parents or husband might be more willing to inform the authorities in order to prevent the abortion once there was no fear of criminal liability attaching to the woman. Furthermore, the existence of an unused veto power might itself have a deterrent effect on abortions. The very prospect of an encounter with members of one's immediate family over abortion might influence a pregnant woman's thinking far more than the prospect of an unlikely encounter with the law.

A second advantage of the power investiture scheme was that it appeared to vindicate constitutionally protectible interests of the parents and the husband. The husband of a woman seeking an abortion could claim a vital interest in protecting a fetus partly his own; he could argue that abortion was an intrusion on his constitutionally protected right to parenthood.[10] In a similar vein, the parents of a minor female seeking an abortion could claim a constitutionally protected right to direct her upbringing even to the point of deciding whether to permit her to have an abortion.[11]

The power investiture strategy failed to win Supreme Court approval, however. In *Planned Parenthood of Central Missouri v. Danforth*,[12] the Court rather summarily rejected the requirement of written spousal consent for a first-term abortion. The Court thought little of the state's explanation that this regulation furthered a tradition that major family decisions ought to be made unanimously. It saw the scheme as a subterfuge and reasoned that since the legislature had no power to prevent first-term abortions under *Roe*, it could not create an equivalent power in the husband. While the majority did not respond to the dissent's argument that spousal consent was premised on an independent right of parenthood in the husband, it implicitly held that the woman's right to abort outweighed any constitutionally rooted interests that the father might possess.[13]

Parental consent schemes have had a more complicated history[14]; the Court has nonetheless held that states may not invest parents generally with the power to prevent abortions by their unmarried minor female children.[15] In *Bellotti v. Baird,*[16] the Court ruled that minor females who possess some maturity of judgment have a constitutional right to decide for themselves whether to have an abortion. They do not need parental permission to pursue that course and may even have an abortion in the face of parental opposition. In fact, even immature minors may secure an abortion against their parent's wishes, although in such cases the state can require approval by a state official.[17]

However much the spousal and parental consent provisions might have appealed to some, the state could not hide the fact that it was trying to assert interests superior to those of the pregnant woman to justify denying the prerogatives recognized in *Roe.* The fact that a private citizen, rather than the prosecutor, would initiate legal action against the woman only superficially distinguished consent provisions from the criminal statute struck down in *Roe.* Ultimately, the coercive power of the law could be brought to bear to enforce the veto.

2.   THE BURDEN CREATION STRATEGY   Unlike power investiture, the burden creation strategy did not authorize either the state or an individual to prevent a woman from carrying out her abortion decision. Instead, it operated to make the decision to abort less attractive or more difficult for her to implement. Four types of abortion statutes fell within this category. They were statutes that: (1) increased the risks associated with undergoing or performing an abortion; (2) reduced accessibility to private medical facilities which performed abortions; (3) increased the costs of abortions; and (4) established pre-abortion procedures which might undermine a pregnant woman's willingness to proceed with the decision to have an abortion.

As a whole, the Supreme Court has been less hostile to the burden creation strategy than to power investiture schemes. In large measure, this results from the fact that the plaintiff must prove that a law indirectly regulating abortion unduly burdens the exercise of her constitutional right. This is a light burden when state law gives someone the power to prevent an abortion altogether; it is a harder burden when the state ostensibly asserts interests only in how an abortion is performed. To establish a constitutional violation under *Roe,* the challenger must show that the enforcement of a law makes it substantially more difficult to secure an abortion than would be the case if the law had never been enacted or if some alternative version of the law had been enacted instead. Then the challenger must show that the state cannot adequately justify the interference with her right to an abortion.[18] On this issue, the challenger will have two options. She can either question the importance of the asserted interests underlying the law or she can question the strength of the relationship between those interests and the law enacted to promote them. The challenger must overcome every hurdle to win.

The Supreme Court has sustained several arguably burdensome schemes for two principal reasons: either they appeared to further legitimate state goals, or they did not intrude on the right to abortion at all. While these schemes have been more acceptable to the Supreme Court, they have not been as attractive to abortion opponents, however, since they do not discourage abortions nearly as effectively as direct regulation. In fact, the more effective a law is in burdening the right to abortion, the greater the likelihood that it will arouse judicial opposition. So it should not be surprising that even as some of these schemes have received Supreme Court approval, the rate of abortions in this country has not been slowed.[19]

(a) Increasing the risks   One method of influencing the decision to have an abortion is to increase the health or legal risks associated with abortion. In theory, either type of disincentive should reduce the abortion rate. The Supreme Court has rejected two statutory schemes of this variety.

Collautti v. Franklin[20] involved a Pennsylvania statute that imposed a special duty of care on physicians to preserve fetal life whenever they had "sufficient reason to believe that the fetus may be viable."[21] A breach of this duty of care rendered the physician liable under the criminal homicide statutes as if "the fetus [had] been a child who was intended to be born and not aborted."[22] By exposing physicians to potential criminal liability, the state created a risk of prosecution for an erroneous judgment about viability. Pointing to the ambiguity in the wording of the statute, the Supreme Court struck it down. The Court reasoned that, whether intended or not, this ambiguity "could have a profound chilling effect on the willingness of physicians to perform abortions near the point of viability in the manner indicated by their best medical judgment."[23] To the extent that physicians were unwilling to perform abortions near viability, the right to elect abortion would be constricted correspondingly.

In *Planned Parenthood of Central Missouri v. Danforth,*[24] the validity of a Missouri statute forbidding saline amniocentesis after the first term of pregnancy was at issue. In drafting the statute, the state apparently relied on the *Roe* holding that abortion laws applicable during the second trimester of pregnancy would be sustained if reasonably related to the preservation of maternal health. The legislature therefore made a finding that the saline amniocentesis method of abortion was "deleterious to maternal health."[25] The Court, however, struck down this statute as well. It cited several reasons for its decision, perhaps the most important of which was that the statute, while forbidding saline amniocentesis, permitted more dangerous methods of abortion to be used. The Court found that by forbidding a relatively safe abortion technique, the state, far from vindicating its interest in maternal health, was actually increasing health risks to the mother.[26]

(b) Restricting the availability of abortion facilities   Instead of increasing the hazards faced by abortion participants, some laws had the effect of making abortion-performing facilities scarcer, thereby rendering it more difficult to obtain an abortion. Courts addressing the constitutionality of such laws have balanced the magnitude of the burden the law imposes on women seeking an abortion against the asserted state interest. If there is a significant intrusion on the decision to abort, there must be a significant state interest justifying this intrusion. By contrast, a slight intrusion requires only a slight justification.

Thus, in a recent case, the city of Akron required all post-first term abortions to be performed in hospitals (ostensibly to protect maternal health), thereby eliminating the abortion clinic as an option, and reducing the opportunities available to the abortion-seeking woman.[27] Such a law would be especially significant in rural areas where few (or no) hospitals might be willing to perform abortions, making the right to abort after the first term largely meaningless. A related burden is that the cost of an abortion performed in a hospital is generally greater than the cost of one performed in an abortion clinic.[28] It should be noted that Akron, in enacting this ordinance, was relying on specific language in *Roe* which appeared to authorize a post-first term hospitalization requirement to protect maternal health. The *Roe* Court, in identifying possible health regulations, wrote that "[e]xamples of permissible state regulation in this area are requirements as to . . . the facility in which the procedure is to be performed, that is, whether it must be a hospital or may be a clinic or some other place of less-than-hospital status."[29]

Consistent with its constant reliance on the medical model of analysis, the Supreme Court struck down the ordinance as overbroad. The Court considered the present state of the medical arts and found that early in the second trimester of pregnancy some abortions could be performed as safely outside hospitals as in them.[30] This fact reduced the weight of the maternal health interest to the point that it was outweighed by the burden placed on women. In other words, banning abortion clinics would not protect maternal health interests sufficiently to justify this burden on the right of abortion. Thus, the Court rejected the resource-constricting ordinance.

An analytically similar resource-constricting action was the use of the zoning power to reduce the number of abortion clinics in a particular locale. In *Deerfield Medical Center v. Deerfield Beach*,[31] the city made virtually no attempt to maintain even the appearance of acting pursuant to the traditional police power concerns normally effectuated through the zoning power. In this Fifth Circuit case, the city commissioners denied an occupational license for the operation of an abortion clinic in an area zoned for business operations. After a hearing highlighted by the testimony of many witnesses opposed to abortion, the commission unanimously denied the license. The court found that there was a significant burden on the decision to abort which was not outweighed by any legitimate concerns of the city. The court implied that the purpose of the ordinance was the burdening of a constitutional right. It noted that none of the justifications offered by the city were contained in the zoning code and that none reflected traditional zoning concerns such as reduction of traffic, reduction of noise and provision of adequate municipal services.[32]

(c) Statutes increasing the costs of abortion Some statutes increase the monetary costs associated with the performance of abortions, thus imposing a further burden on some women. The Supreme Court has balanced the extent of the burden on the abortion right against the weight of the state interests vindicated by such statutes. In its 1983 decision of *Planned Parenthood Association of Kansas City v. Ashcroft*,[33] the Supreme Court upheld the constitutionality of two such provisions.

The Missouri statute at issue in *Planned Parenthood Association of Kansas City* contained two separate cost-increasing provisions. One required the presence of two physicians at all post-viability abortions. Under this scheme, the first physician had the primary responsibility for taking care of the mother, while the second was to take all reasonable steps to preserve fetal life and health. By requiring the presence of a second physician, the state added to the cost of an abortion. The Court nevertheless upheld the provision on the theory that it vindicated the state's post-viability interest in the potentiality of fetal life[34]; this interest in fetal life outweighed the costs of a second physician.

A second part of the *Ashcroft* statute mandated that a qualified pathologist make a tissue sample analysis in all abortions.[35] The pathologist had to send a copy of his report to the abortion facility, where it was to become part of the patient's record. The state justified this as a protection of maternal health, while the plaintiffs argued that it was too burdensome and did not sufficiently further any cognizable health interests. A divided Supreme Court upheld the requirement, finding that it served a legitimate state interest and added a relatively insubstantial cost to abortions.[36] The four dissenters argued that the cost of this examination might deter some women from having an abortion. Of course, the same could be said with respect to any increase in the cost of abortion, regardless of how small such an increase might be. Implicit in the Court's decision is the conclusion that the legitimacy of any burden must be determined from the perspective of the entire class of women desiring abortions and not from the point of view of an individual indigent woman.

The *Ashcroft* holding is a narrow one. First, while the actual motivation of the legislators who enacted the statute might have been to reduce the number of abortions performed, the Court perceived the statute's provisions as intruding upon the right of abortion less than other "burden strategy" type legislation. That is, there is a qualitative difference between significantly increasing health and medical risks and merely making abortion more expensive. The legislation in *Ashcroft* only increased cost; it did not ban abortions, tacitly encourage the use of a dangerous method, delegate a veto power to a third party, or diminish the resources available to women seeking abortions. Second, regardless of the actual motivations of individual legislators, the state actions could be explained plausibly as involving the pursuit of previously recognized state interests in maternal health and the potentiality of fetal life. This is not true of all cost-increasing measures. Finally, it should be stressed that the additional cost of having an abortion was not large. Whether such a scheme which did add a significant cost to abortion would be successful would depend on the strength of the state interest.

(d) Other abortion laws with potentially coercive effects   This final category consists of state laws that confront a woman with administrative or procedural steps that could discourage her from proceeding with an abortion. As all can be rationalized as effectuating a legitimate state purpose, the plaintiff is put to a difficult burden of proof with regard to the motivation behind a law. The Court has upheld several statutes falling into this category, despite being skeptical about the state's true motives.

In *H.L. v. Matheson,*[37] a six-member majority upheld a Utah provision requiring parental notification of the fact that a minor was seeking an abortion. Earlier cases had rejected state attempts to establish a parental consent requirement. The *Matheson* Court recognized that, like the rejected consent requirement, a notification statute has the potential of deterring a minor from procuring an abortion. Nevertheless, the majority upheld the statute, emphasizing the state interests in preserving parental authority within the family, in preserving parental opportunity to consult with the minor concerning this important and stressful decision, and in preserving an opportunity to supply important health-related information to the physician.[38] Both the majority and the dissent emphasized the narrowness of the *Matheson* holding.[39] The minor involved was unemancipated, lived with her parents and did not allege that the notification of her parents would interfere with her best interests. The Court left open the issue of whether the statute could constitutionally be applied in other situations, implying that some- times the state interest might not outweigh the burden.

A lower court decision after *Matheson* concerned a spousal notification statute. In *Scheinberg v. Smith*,[40] the court held that there was no evidence that a properly conducted abortion posed more than a de minimis threat to the procreational potentiality of a marriage. Since the state argued that the protection of this procreational potential justified requiring spousal notification, the court struck down the statute as not vindicating a legitimate state interest. While the state in *Scheinberg* explained its attempt to give the husband a voice in the abortion decision in terms of protecting his potential to father children in the future, a more persuasive justification might be the vindication of the father's interest in the present fetus. Though the spousal consent cases had found that the husband's interest in the present fetus did not justify such a broad intrusion as a veto, it is not at all clear that such an interest could not be perceived as justifying a spousal voice in the decision about abortion.

While the parental and spousal notification statutes gave an opportunity to interested third parties to have a voice in the abortion decision, another type of potentially burdensome statute actually required that some third party speak to the woman about her decision. In *Danforth*, the statute required that the physician obtain written informed consent from the pregnant woman. The plaintiffs argued that this provision imposed an "extra layer and burden of regulation" on the abortion decision, which would deter some women from electing abortion.[41] The *Danforth* Court, however, rejected the attack and upheld the statutory provision. While the Court did not detail its reasoning, it did recognize that the abortion decision is an "important, and often a stressful one, and it is desirable and imperative that it be made with full knowledge of its nature and consequences."[42] This is a recognition that the state has a legitimate interest in assuring itself that a woman seeking an abortion has given the matter rational consideration. Alternatively, the Court may have determined that the intrusion on the right to elect abortion was relatively minimal.

The decision in *Akron v. Akron Center for Reproductive Health*,[43] however, showed that there are limits on the state's ability to regulate abortions even if the purpose is to provide information to pregnant women. The Akron ordinance at issue had a much more detailed informed consent requirement than the general one imposed by the *Danforth* statute. It required the attending physician to tell the patient that "life begins at conception," to give her a detailed description of the "anatomical and physiological characteristics of the particular unborn child at the particular gestational point of development . . . including . . . appearance, mo- bility, tactile sensitivity, including pain, perception or response, brain and heart function, the presence of internal organs and the presence of external members" and to inform her that abortion is a major surgical procedure which can result in serious physical and emotional complications.[44]

The Court summarily rejected this portion of the ordinance, concluding that the actual statutory purpose was to dissuade women from having abortions.[45] The information was to be conveyed to them in a one-on-one relationship by their physicians, imposing power figures garbed in an aura of authority and medical certainty. The Court, however, did not explicitly condemn as impermissible the state's adoption of a preference for childbirth. It merely held that this particular method of expressing that preference was too intrusive. By contrast, in the funding context, where the state's preference for childbirth was expressed to the citizenry at large through the denial of public funds, the Court upheld the state's action on the basis that such a preference was constitutionally permissible under appropriate circumstances.[46] In other portions of the *Akron* case, the Court struck down a provision which made the attending physician the only person capable of obtaining the required consent and a provision mandating a 24-hour waiting period between the signing of the informed consent and the abortion. The Court held that neither of these two provisions furthered the state interest in provision of information to the abortion-seeking woman and, therefore, did not outweigh the intrusion on the abortion right.[47]

A final legislative provision respecting abortion was the requirement at issue in *Danforth* which mandated detailed recordkeeping of abortions.[48] A governmental unit was to collect the information for the purpose of protecting maternal health. The data would be used to further research and to monitor individual abortions to assure that they had been performed properly. The plaintiffs argued that this requirement burdened the right of abortion by creating a risk of disclosure that a particular woman had had an abortion. While the statute purported to assure confidentiality, the plaintiffs noted that once a document existed with all the pertinent information concerning a particular woman's abortion, there was a risk that unauthorized individuals would eventually gain access to it. To the extent that a woman feared this risk, she would be deterred from seeking an abortion. The Court nonetheless upheld the statute, acknowledging the privacy interests and the risk of disclosure, but concluding that the health interests asserted by the state outweighed them.[49]

The Court has been much more hospitable toward this group of indirect restrictions on abortion than toward others. It should be obvious, however, that these statutes have a minimal deterrent effect on the number of abortions performed. A woman determined to have an abortion can easily overcome the "hurdles" of a third party "voice," informed consent and recordkeeping. These restrictions do not grant anyone the power to alter her decision, they add very little extra expense to an abortion and effect no contraction of available resources.

D. Public Assistance for Pregnancy and Abortion

By 1977, it was still an open question whether the states were constitutionally obligated to provide assistance to indigent women who wished to have abortions. There was a significant difference between compelling the states to allow a woman to have an abortion and compelling them to subsidize abortions for those women who could not afford them. Such a requirement, if judicially imposed, would add insult to the injury inflicted upon abortion opponents by the Supreme Court's decision in *Roe*. Not surprisingly, a number of states resisted the claim that they had any obligation, statutory or constitutional, to subsidize or support abortions. In their view, a woman who desired an abortion had no more than a right to secure one as best she could; she did not have a claim on state resources.

The argument that *Roe* required the states to assume an affirmative duty of subsidization had major political and constitutional ramifications. The public funding question suddenly placed the abortion plaintiff in an unfamiliar and perhaps uneasy position. Rather than asking that the state be further removed from the abortion process, she now demanded that the state become more deeply involved, namely to the extent of paying the bills for indigent women and providing facilities for abortions in public hospitals.

In *Maher v. Roe*,[50] the Supreme Court ruled that the state of Connecticut did not violate either the due process or equal protection rights of indigent women desiring nontherapeutic abortions by withholding Medicaid assistance from them. With only a brief discussion, the Court pointed out that the case did not involve a suspect classification and thus there was no basis for heightened equal protection scrutiny. It noted that the government has no general obligation to overcome all disadvantages to an individual because of financial need.[51] The Court then turned to the due process contention and declared that the statute did not burden the indigent woman's right to an abortion.[52] It placed "no obstacles—absolute or otherwise—in the pregnant woman's path to an abortion."[53] The Court went on to add that "[t]he State may have made childbirth a more attractive alternative, thereby influencing the woman's decision, but it has imposed no restriction on access to abortions that was not already there."[54] In the absence of an officially imposed burden, therefore, Connecticut did not have to demonstrate a compelling interest to sustain its attempt at encouraging women to pursue an alternative to abortion. It merely had to demonstrate that the statutory scheme bore a rational relationship to the state's interest in encouraging childbirth.[55] In closing its discussion, the Court acknowledged the plight of indigent women, but deferred to legislative judgment in resolving the problem.[56]

Maher involved only a nontherapeutic abortion and left open the question whether a state, in the interest of promoting childbirth, could deny financial assistance to an indigent woman even when her need for an abortion was for medical rather than nontherapeutic reasons. The Supreme Court decided in the affirmative in *Harris v. McRae*,[57] a 1980 decision upholding the constitutionality of a federal Medicaid abortion funding restriction known as the "Hyde Amendment." Though its terms varied from year to year, it prohibited the use of federal Medicaid funds to reimburse the costs of abortions except in strictly limited circumstances. In 1980, for example, Medicaid funding for abortions was available *only* when the life of the mother would be endangered if the fetus was carried to term or when the woman had been the victim of rape or incest.[58]

The Court closely tracked its reasoning in *Maher v. Roe* and rejected due process and equal protection challenges to the Hyde Amendment. Focusing first on the due process claim, the Court emphasized that the Hyde Amendment placed no governmental obstacles in the path of a woman who wanted to terminate her pregnancy.[59] There was, in the Court's view, a fundamental difference between state-coerced childbirth and state-created incentives to persuade women to carry pregnancy to full term. The plaintiffs argued that the Hyde Amendment put the health of the indigent woman in jeopardy and thus affected an interest which lay at the core of the constitutional freedom recognized in *Roe*. By degree, it was far harsher in its consequences to the indigent woman than denial of funding for elective abortions.[60]

The Court, however, was unmoved by this argument. It held fast to the theme central to its conclusion in *Maher*. Rights require governmental forebearance and limit government's range of action; they do not, at least under the due process clause, entail an affirmative duty for the government to subsidize the exercise of rights, including those arising under *Roe*.[61] The plaintiff's equal protection argument fared no better.[62] Indeed, the Court found the Hyde Amendment to be indistinguishable from the statute upheld in *Maher*. The fact that its impact was felt only by indigent women could not be constitutionally decisive. The only remaining issue was whether the Hyde Amendment satisfied the rational basis test and the Court had no difficulty in deciding, as it had in *Maher,* that subsidizing childbirth was rationally related to the valid governmental objective of protecting potential life.

On one level, *Maher* and *Harris* represented the first important Supreme Court successes for abortion opponents. They did not exactly reverse a trend, but they did slow it and, in so doing, managed to establish two crucial points. One was that by withholding public funds for abortions, the state could disassociate itself entirely from the abortion decision. The second was that the state did not have a constitutional obligation to remain neutral between abortion and childbirth. Indeed, the state could act on its preference by subsidizing childbirth without triggering an obligation to give equivalent financial support to women seeking abortions. Nevertheless, as important as these developments were, they could not obscure an ironic aspect of the *Maher* and *Harris* opinions. Rather than arousing hope that a turning point might lie ahead, they tended to highlight the impotence of efforts to make significant inroads upon the *Roe* decision.[63]

III. The Direct Assault on *Roe v. Wade*

A. The Constitutional Amendment Movement

As noted above, legislative efforts to undermine *Roe* indirectly have generally proven ineffective. With a surprising firmness, the Supreme Court has refused to retreat from the basic principle of *Roe*. This experience has taught abortion opponents that their political strategy may have been wrong. Rather than trying to slip constitutionally questionable abortion laws past the federal courts, they might have made better use of their energies by attacking the constitutional premise on which *Roe* rested. Although constitutional amendment movements are rarely successful, the chances of passing an amendment overruling *Roe* have perhaps been better than usual in the political climate prevailing since 1973. Literally hundreds of such amendments have been introduced in Congress during that period. Thus far, however, not one has been able to secure the necessary two-thirds approval of either the House or the Senate. Indeed, only one proposed constitutional amendment on abortion has ever been reported out of committee and put to a vote of either body.[64] The discussion in this section explores reasons why the strategy of constitutional amendment has met with failure. The cumbersome nature and likely futility of the ratification process offer only a partial explanation.

A significant, but largely unexplored, reason for the failure of the constitutional amendment process has been the division among the opponents of the *Roe* decision over the most appropriate means of achieving constitutional change. The division is a result of the different perspectives, moral or federalist, from which objections to *Roe* originate. Those who view abortion primarily from a moral perspective have as their paramount objective the ending of abortions and thus they support proposed constitutional amendments banning abortion outright even at the cost of a possible loss of state and local control over the subject. Some who hold this approach favor legislation limiting the jurisdiction of the Supreme Court and the lower federal courts, despite serious institutional costs to the judiciary. By contrast, those who view abortion primarily from a legal perspective are most concerned with the issues of federalism and judicial lawmaking. They would find acceptable proposed constitutional amendments that simply reestablish state and local authority over abortion, even though some jurisdictions, in the exercise of their authority, might not choose to make abortions illegal. To these individuals, the values of diversity and federalism override a personal preference for moral uniformity concerning abortion.[65] Similarly, they would probably be hesitant to support jurisdiction limiting experiments out of a concern for preserving the separation of powers among the branches of government.

1.   EXTENDING CONSTITUTIONAL PROTECTION TO THE UNBORN   One of the most controversial passages in Justice Blackmun's opinion in *Roe* states that "the word 'person,' as used in the Fourteenth Amendment, does not include the unborn."[66] That this premise was central to the Court's reasoning is evidenced by Justice Blackmun's candid admission that if the fetus were a person, its "right to life would then be guaranteed specifically" by the Constitution.[67] It is therefore not surprising that some proponents of a constitutional amendment believe that *Roe* could be overruled either by a clarification of the term "person" as used in the due process and equal protection clauses of the Constitution or by a declaration of the moment when life begins. Within the last 10 years, many such constitutional amendments have been proposed in Congress.

In 1973, two versions of this kind of amendment were put forward. One such amendment, S.J. Res. 119, provided:

> *SECTION 1. With respect to the right to life, the word "person," as used in this article and in the fifth and fourteenth articles of amendment to the Constitution of the United States, applies to all human beings, including their unborn offspring at every stage of their biological development, irrespective of age, health, function, or condition of dependency.*
> *SECTION 2. This article shall not apply in an emergency when a reasonable medical certainty exists that continuation of the pregnancy will cause the death of the mother.*[68]

A second amendment, S.J. Res. 130, was framed in different language but its objective was the same:

> *SECTION 1. Neither the United States nor any State shall deprive any human being, from the moment of conception, of life without due process of law; nor deny to any human being, from the moment of conception, within its jurisdiction, the equal protection of the laws.*

> *SECTION 2. Neither the United States nor any State shall deprive*
> *any human being of life on account of illness, age, or incapacity.*[69]

The precise effects of enacting either S.J. Res. 119 or S.J. Res. 130 require close examination. Each would appear to reestablish legislative primacy over the question of abortion standards. Some jurisdictions would undoubtedly take immediate advantage of this opportunity and enact legislation restoring pre-*Roe* standards. Other jurisdictions might not want to pass any anti-abortion legislation at all.

There is room for doubt whether S.J. Res. 119 and S.J. Res. 130 would completely overrule *Roe*. The underlying premise of these proposed amendments was that if a fetus is a "person" or "human being," then it may not have its life taken without due process of law. Presumably, both amendments were calculated to deny the Supreme Court the authority to balance the state's interest in protecting prenatal life against the woman's interest in terminating an unwanted pregnancy. This rationale has initial plausibility, but on reflection one must ask whether either proposed amendment would really compel the Supreme Court to abandon its holding in *Roe*. The fact that life is at risk does not mean that the Constitution affords it absolute protection. Interests other than life can be taken into account.[70]

Thus, it is conceivable, that even if a fetus were a "person" in the constitutional sense, the fact that it is unborn might still matter. Fetal life, at least prior to viability, might not *always* be important enough to override a woman's interest in terminating an unwanted pregnancy. S.J. Res. 119 itself recognizes the inevitability of having to weigh the value of one life against another, for it would permit an abortion when the death of the mother might result from continuation of the pregnancy. Thus, even if the Supreme Court were to interpret S.J. Res. 119 or S.J. Res. 130 as overruling *Roe,* such a holding would not foreclose the development of constitutionally grounded exceptions to abortion laws.[71]

2.   DIRECT CONSTITUTIONAL PROHIBITION OF ABORTION   The prospect of accommodation on abortion standards has prompted a few amendment proposals that go beyond S.J. Res. 119 or S.J. Res. 130. Rather than giving the states discretion to set substantive abortion rules, they would require the states to enact a general ban on the performance of abortions. In form, these prohibitions resemble criminal statutes. The most striking example is section 2 of S.J. Res. 17, proposed in 1981, which provided that:

> *No unborn person shall be deprived of life by any person: Provided,*
> *however, that nothing in this article shall prohibit a law permitting*
> *only those medical procedures required to prevent the death of the*
> *mother.*[72]

This direct constitutional prohibition of abortion appeared in conjunction with a redefinition of the term "person." As indicated in the preceding section, a redefinition of "person" would open the way for local, state, or federal restrictions on abortion. Nothing in a constitutional amendment redefining "person" would require such action. An explicit constitutional ban on the performance of abortions, however, arguably would mandate legal protection for all prenatal life.

Therein lies its appeal, as well as its inherent weakness. To some opponents of abortion, it is unacceptable merely to overrule *Roe* and leave abortion controls to legislative determination; the arduous process of constitutional amendment is not worth undertaking unless it would outlaw abortion completely.

The ramifications of enacting a constitutional amendment in the language of S.J. Res. 17 are obviously a matter of speculation. Still, the possibilities are worth considering. First, S.J. Res. 17 might be construed as obligating the state to enforce on behalf of the unborn all existing laws, criminal or otherwise, protecting "persons," such as the law of homicide or wrongful death. A failure by the state to heed this affirmative duty might lead to civil rights liability under 42 U.S.C. 1983.[73] Second, S.J. Res. 17 might be read to require the state to enact legislation specifically protecting the unborn. Enforcement of this affirmative duty to legislate would present truly unprecedented issues.[74] Finally, S.J. Res. 17 might be read as authorizing a private cause of action on behalf of the unborn against any person who aborted or otherwise injured it.

However attractive S.J. Res. 17 may have been to some initially, it had serious difficulties. In light of its comprehensiveness, such an amendment appealed primarily to those opponents of *Roe* who were motivated by moral concerns. The federalist opponents found S.J. Res. 17 considerably less palatable because it would limit state authority to set abortion standards. Furthermore, while it is frequently difficult to regulate *governmental* action through a constitutional amendment, it is even more difficult to regulate *private* conduct by that means. Attainment of the latter objective is dependent on the goodwill and assistance of the legislative and executive branches of government, especially at the state and local levels. It is unclear whether the proponents of S.J. Res. 17 appreciated this fact. The Eighteenth Amendment, which ushered in Prohibition, provides an example of a constitutional amendment whose aim was to change private rather than government behavior.[75] Prohibition was a failure in no small measure because the underlying political will to enforce it was lacking. The success of S.J. Res. 17 would hinge on the same factor. If future generations did not share the values underlying S.J. Res. 17, its moral injunction would go unheeded.

3. "DECONSTITUTIONALIZING" THE RIGHT TO ABORTION   In 1983, Senator Orrin Hatch introduced into the Senate S.J. Res. 3, the Human Life Federalism Amendment ("the Hatch Amendment"). The amendment read in its entirety that "A right to abortion is not secured by this Constitution."[76] It would directly overrule the holding of *Roe* that abortion is protected by a constitutionally based right of privacy, and offer the states the opportunity to enact legislation prohibiting abortion; however, it would not forbid them from recognizing a right to abortion or from declining to address the issue legislatively. As a result, the federalist opponents of *Roe* have rallied behind the Hatch Amendment, but the moralist opponents have condemned it. Senator Jesse Helms, the author of the Human Life Bill discussed below, voted against the Hatch Amendment because "[it] does not advance the principle that human life is inviolable. Instead, it surrenders forever this principle in exchange for the illusory hope that some lives may be saved."[77]

Furthermore, the Hatch Amendment would not end all judicial review of abortion legislation. Despite that fact that no specific constitutional right would exist, courts would retain the authority to test anti-abortion legislation against a rational basis standard under the due process and equal protection clauses. All governmental action is subject to at least this requirement. The possibility therefore would clearly exist that an abortion ban could prove to be too harsh. For example, if a state were to enact an absolute prohibition on abortion, a court applying the rational basis standard might conclude that the ban could not be applied in a case where the life of the mother were threatened. It requires little imagination to see that a court might take a similar stance when pregnancy resulted from rape or incest.

The Hatch Amendment, the only proposed abortion amendment yet to reach the floor of Congress, was rejected by the Senate on June 28, 1983 after receiving only 49 favorable votes. On balance, if it had been made part of the Constitution, it probably would have accomplished as much as any of the many constitutional amendments proposed since 1973. It would not have eliminated abortion in this country. It would simply have made it possible for the states and the federal government to regulate abortion. Judgment about the form such regulations should take would be left to the political process except in extreme situations. It is perhaps true that if the Hatch Amendment were in force today, many jurisdictions would act swiftly to revive tight restrictions on abortion. There is nothing in the Amendment, however, that would prevent future legislative bodies from changing their minds. To the abortion opponent who sees the issue in moral terms, the Hatch Amendment did not go far enough. But to the abortion opponent who believes that abortion raises important questions of federalism in addition to moral questions, it would suffice that the Hatch Amendment returned the abortion question to the political arena where majoritarian values prevail.

4.   FEDERALISM AND ABORTION: A NOTE ON WHO GETS THE FINAL WORD
Any constitutional amendment enacted to overrule *Roe* would enlarge the role of state legislatures or Congress in setting abortion standards, while reducing significantly that of the judicial branch. A related question of considerable importance is whether the states or Congress would have primary responsibility for setting abortion standards. Virtually all abortion amendments proposed over the last decade have contained a section authorizing the enactment of enforcement legislation. The model for this type of provision has been section 5 of the Fourteenth Amendment.

These provisions have come in two basic variations, which reflect yet another dilemma for abortion opponents seeking to overrule *Roe*. If, as has been suggested earlier, the most that can reasonably be expected of a constitutional amendment is to return the abortion issue to the political arena, the question is which arena. Should Congress and the states have plenary authority to enact abortion statutes within their respective spheres of power? Or should Congress have the ultimate authority to establish a uniform national standard on abortion and thereby preempt all state legislation to the contrary?

(a)   Non-concurrent enforcement power   One kind of enforcement provision would grant Congress and the states the power to pass legislation in their separate spheres. The most common form of this provision is, "Congress and the several States shall have power to enforce this article by appropriate legislation within their respective jurisdiction."[78] Under this language, abortion would once again be subject to the general police powers of the states and could be regulated

on a federal level only by a law passed pursuant to one of the enumerated legislative powers of Congress in Article 1. This enforcement provision reflects a belief in the virtues of democratic pluralism. Its greatest appeal would be to those whose opposition to *Roe* stems primarily from federalism concerns.

(b) Concurrent enforcement power Several proposed abortion amendments have authorized Congress and the states to exercise *concurrent* legislative power over abortion. One version provides that "Congress and the several States shall have concurrent power to enforce this article by appropriate legislation."[79] Another version says that "The Congress and the several States shall have power to enforce this [article] by appropriate legislation."[80] This language suggests that federal and state legislation could apply simultaneously to the same conduct or activity, as is true of much criminal law today. A troublesome question is whether Congress under this provision could preempt state law in the area of abortion. Initially, the option of federalizing abortion law might seem attractive to abortion opponents, particularly those who desire a uniform rule banning abortion in virtually all circumstances. However, many of *Roe's* critics objected to the decision precisely because it effected *both* the federalization and constitutionalization of abortion law. A preemptive national ban on abortion has significant long-term risks. It might backfire on the moralists if Congress ever took a more liberal attitude toward abortion than the state legislatures. It would be supremely ironic if an enforcement provision of the type now under discussion enabled future supporters of abortion to restore the principle of *Roe* through nationally binding federal legislation. On balance, then, overruling *Roe* and decentralizing the power to regulate abortion is the safest strategy for abortion foes.

The original Hatch Amendment, S.J. Res. 110, attempted to address the federal preemption issue:

> *A right to abortion is not secured by this Constitution. The Congress and the several States shall have the concurrent power to restrict and prohibit abortions: Provided: That a law of a State which is more restrictive than a law of Congress shall govern.*[81]

The object of this provision was not only to nullify *Roe,* but to insure that Congress could preempt only in the direction of more restrictive laws. Abortion opponents could then seek federal legislation that would supersede the abortion laws in states whose restrictions were not sufficient.[82] S.J. Res. 110, however, met with considerable opposition because its prospect of a uniform ban on abortion ran counter to the more compelling tradition of political diversity. It was replaced by S.J. Res. 3, which dropped the concurrent-power language and retained only the first sentence: "A right to abortion is not secured by this Constitution."[83] Silence on the question of enforcement effectively remits the regulation of abortion to the states under their reserved police powers. Thus, S.J. Res. 3 truly would have granted the states the power to restore the law to its pre-*Roe* status.

B. Legislative Substitutes for An Abortion Amendment

Roe v. Wade is just one of a number of Supreme Court decisions over the last quarter century to trigger an intensely hostile public reaction. The obvious, but rarely implemented, solution to such objectionable decisions is a constitutional amendment. The difficulty of generating an overriding national consensus on social issues such as school busing, school prayer, and abortion, however, has led opponents of Supreme Court decisions in these areas to look for alternatives to constitutional amendment. Some have recommended devising legislation that might achieve the same result as a constitutional amendment. The most commonly proposed "substitute" for a constitutional amendment has been legislation that would restrict the jurisdiction of the Supreme Court or the lower federal courts to hear abortion cases. The purpose of this section is to describe those proposals and the Human Life Bill, a most unusual amendment "substitute" which is based on section 5 of the Fourteenth Amendment.

1.   SUBJECT MATTER RESTRICTIONS ON LOWER FEDERAL COURT JURISDIC-TION   This type of legislation represents a second best approach to constitutional amendment. Its guiding force is the sentiment that if it is not practicable to overturn *Roe,* then Congress can render it ineffective by denying abortion rights claimants access to the federal judicial system that has provided a generally friendly environment for the litigation of abortion issues. The most extreme of these restrictions would take away federal district court authority to hear any case concerning state or local abortion laws. An illustration is H.R. 867, which was introduced in the 97th Congress. After eliminating the Supreme Court's certiorari and appellate jurisdiction in abortion cases laws, H.R. 867 went on to withdraw lower federal district court jurisdiction in abortion cases as well.[84] Under this provision, therefore, a federal district court could not entertain a damages action under Section 1983, enter an order granting declaratory or injunctive relief or even consider a habeas corpus petition from a person convicted under a state or local abortion law. The blanket withdrawal of federal jurisdiction based on the subject matter of the claim involved is generally regarded as presenting the most serious constitutional issue.[85]

Less extreme forms of jurisdiction limiting legislation would not foreclose all access to lower federal courts by abortion rights claimants, but would restrict the availability of remedies. For example, there have been several legislative proposals similar to H.R. 73, which was introduced during the 97th Congress. H.R. 73 provided:

> [Sec. 1] Notwithstanding any other provision of law, a court of the United States may not issue any restraining order or temporary or permanent injunction in any case—
>
> (a) involving or arising out of any Federal or State law or municipal ordinance that prohibits, limits, or regulates abortion (including any such law or ordinance that regulates abortion clinics or persons that provide abortions);
>
> (b) involving or arising out of any Federal or State law or municipal ordinance that prohibits, limits, or regulates the provision at public expense of funds, facilities, personnel, or other assistance for the performance of abortions.
>
> [Sec. 2] As used in this Act, the terms "court of the United States" means any court established by or under Article III of the Constitution of the United States other than the Supreme Court.[86]

H.R. 73's jurisdictional limitations are aimed at eliminating prospective relief, the most effective remedy against unconstitutional abortion laws. If enacted, H.R. 73 would prevent a federal district court from enjoining the enforcement of abortion legislation by state and local officials. Prospective relief would be available to the abortion right claimant only in the state courts. For all practical purposes, federal review of state abortion laws would be confined to direct appeal to the Supreme Court.

The benefits of this type of legislation are chiefly tactical and symbolic. Abortion opponents fully understand that such legislation does not overrule *Roe* or later Supreme Court decisions interpreting *Roe;* however, they must recognize that it can assist states to evade *Roe*. Legislation restricting or eliminating federal court jurisdiction in abortion cases makes sense only if it would reduce the level of state and local compliance with *Roe*.

The mere availability of direct Supreme Court review of state court decisions would do very little to halt state evasion of *Roe*. The Supreme Court can give plenary consideration to only a small number of cases each term. If state court decisions which ignore or narrowly interpret *Roe* become too numerous, the Court simply will not be able to review them all. Abortion opponents are certainly aware of this. Indeed, it is plausible to suppose that abortion opponents intend to take full advantage of the Supreme Court's institutional limitations. Legislation restricting lower federal court jurisdiction in abortion cases would amount to an open invitation to state courts to decline to follow binding Supreme Court precedent.

Those who oppose abortion in the strongest moral terms might be willing to contemplate even measures of doubtful constitutionality in order to reduce the availability of abortions in this country. However, those who object to *Roe* primarily for reasons rooted in federalism (and the separation of powers) are much less likely to support jurisdiction-limiting legislation. To them, the independence and integrity of the judiciary are not to be interfered with lightly. Nevertheless, there are some who wish to do more than relieve federal district judges of the responsibility of monitoring state and local compliance with *Roe*. They would like to eliminate the jurisdiction of the United States Supreme Court as well.

2. SUBJECT MATTER RESTRICTIONS ON THE SUPREME COURT'S APPELLATE JURISDICTION Over the past 25 years, many bills have been proposed in Congress that would eliminate Supreme Court appellate jurisdiction in certain classes of cases, though none have become law.[87] Generally, the subject matter restrictions contained in the bills concerning the jurisdiction of the Supreme Court to review decisions involving abortions are the same as those in legislative proposals to curb the jurisdiction of the lower federal courts. In fact, it is not unusual to find proposed restrictions on both the Supreme Court and the lower federal courts in the same bill. H.R. 867 is an example of the two-pronged approach:

> *Notwithstanding the provisions of sections 1253, 1254 and 1257 of [chapter 81 of title 28] the Supreme Court shall not have jurisdiction to review, by appeal, writ of certiorari, or otherwise, any case arising out of any State statute, ordinance, rule, regulation or any*

> *part thereof, or arising out of any Act interpreting, applying, or*
> *enforcing a State statute ordinance, rule, or regulation, which*
> *relates to abortion.*[88]

In a subsequent provision, H.R. 867 removes all lower federal court jurisdiction over abortion as well.

The debate over the constitutionality of subject matter restrictions on the Supreme Court's appellate jurisdiction is a longstanding one. Since Professor Hart's famous 1953 article,[89] the issue has been the topic of much scholarly writing. Professional opinion is split over whether Congress has the authority to remove classes of cases from the Supreme Court's appellate jurisdiction. Throughout the nation's history, certain classes of cases have not been subject to appellate review by the Supreme Court despite falling within the judicial power of Article III.[90] Indeed, in *Ex parte McCardle,*[91] the Supreme Court upheld a congressional statute repealing a grant of appellate jurisdiction over certain federal habeas corpus cases. Balanced against this history and precedent is the concern that if Congress can freely regulate the Supreme Court's appellate jurisdiction, the role of the Court in the constitutional scheme will change dramatically and perhaps irreversibly.

The enfeeblement of the Supreme Court is probably what some opponents of abortion desire. Supreme Court precedent on abortion would be the law of the land in theory, but there would be no mechanism to vindicate it. Abortion opponents have every reason to expect state courts and state legislatures to take full advantage of such a situation and to restore, at least in large degree, the pre-1973 abortion laws. Thus far, Congress has shown no inclination to impinge on the institutional integrity of the Supreme Court.

3.   THE HUMAN LIFE BILL   In 1981, Senator Helms introduced S. 158, the Human Life Bill, which took a moralist approach to the problem of how to overrule or neutralize *Roe,* as opposed to the federalist approach championed by Senator Hatch. It contained two major provisions. One restricted the jurisdiction of lower federal courts in cases involving state and local abortion legislation. This technique has been discussed above. The second provision, predicated upon the congressional enforcement power under section 5 of the Fourteenth Amendment, defined ''person'' for purposes of Fourteenth Amendment due process analysis in a way that was calculated to neutralize the Supreme Court's reasoning in *Roe.* The bill provided as follows:

> *SECTION 1. The Congress finds that present day scientific evidence*
> *indicates a significant likelihood that actual human life exists from*
> *conception.*
>
> *The Congress further finds that the fourteenth amendment to*
> *the Constitution of the United States was intended to protect all*
> *human beings.*
>
> *Upon the basis of these findings, and in the exercise of the*
> *powers of the Congress, including its power under section 5 of the*
> *fourteenth amendment to the Constitution of the United States, the*
> *Congress hereby declares that for the purpose of enforcing the*

*obligation of the States under the fourteenth amendment not to
deprive persons of life without due process of law, human life shall
be deemed to exist from conception, without regard to race, sex,
age, health, defect, or condition of dependence; and for this
purpose 'person' shall include all human life as defined herein.*[92]

This bill sought to accomplish by legislation what S.J. Res. 119 and S.J. Res. 130
attempted to do by constitutional amendment. It stirred a great controversy.

Many critics of *Roe,* including some personally opposed to abortion, have
argued that section 5 of the Fourteenth Amendment cannot sustain the Human
Life Bill. They are deeply troubled by the bill's implication for the Supreme
Court's power of judicial review. If Congress under section 5 can actually impose
an interpretive gloss on the due process and equal protection clauses, the
Supreme Court's role as the final authority on matters of constitutional law would
be seriously diminished. One can scarcely imagine a more dramatic shift in the
respective roles of Congress and the Supreme Court.

Many see the amendment process, despite its difficulties, as a more suitable
method of bringing about fundamental constitutional change than a political
assault on the interpretive authority of the Supreme Court. On the other hand,
constitutional amendment is the better method only if one believes that the
judicial system that produced *Roe* is worth preserving in its present form. The
persistence of institutional concerns, whether for the integrity of the Supreme
Court or for the autonomy of the states, illuminates once again the dilemma of
those who would like to see *Roe* overruled. The choice is either the hard and
uncertain road of constitutional amendment or some form of constitutional
subversion. Clearly, for some opponents of *Roe,* the greater evil would lie in
further tolerating a decision that to them lacks any moral or legal foundation.

Several Supreme Court decisions since 1966 provide insight into the validity
of the Human Life Bill. All of these decisions involve the Voting Rights Act of
1965 and its extensions. Under that act, the states are subject to a number of direct
regulations which apply without regard to whether the underlying conduct of state
or local officials independently violates the Fourteenth or Fifteenth Amendments.
Thus far, the Supreme Court has sustained the Voting Rights Act against every
constitutional challenge except one on the theory that congressional regulation of
state and local electoral practices is "remedial" legislation.[93] In other words, that
act is "appropriate" enforcement legislation under section 5 of the Fourteenth
Amendment because it seeks to eliminate electoral practices which have been
employed in the past either to deny racial minorities the vote or to deter them from
voting in significant numbers.

In *Oregon v. Mitchell,*[94] the one case in which Congress was found to have
exceeded its authority under section 5, the Supreme Court struck down a
provision of the 1970 amendments to the Voting Rights Act extending the right to
vote in state elections to all citizens eighteen years of age or older. Though there
was no majority opinion, the theme underlying the plurality opinions in *Oregon v.
Mitchell* is that congressional power under section 5 of the Fourteenth Amendment is not plenary and that Congress cannot ignore Supreme Court precedent

and constitutional language in framing appropriate enforcement legislation. The minimum voting age provisions, unlike other provisions of the Voting Rights Act, were not conceived to eliminate the effects of a form of discrimination (age) to which the Fourteenth Amendment has any special relevance. Thus, by imposing a discrimination standard theretofore unrecognized by the Supreme Court, Congress had created a new right instead of vindicating a preexisting one. This is roughly the boundary line between substantive and remedial legislation under section 5 of the Fourteenth Amendment.

As a proposed exercise of power under section 5, the Human Life Bill does not lend itself to ready classification under this substantive/remedial dichotomy. From one vantage point, the bill was clearly substantive. It was written to expand state authority to restrict the rights of pregnant women as recognized by the Supreme Court. Its primary effect would have been to strip away the protections established in *Roe* and subsequent cases.

Those who argued that the Human Life Bill was merely remedial contended that it would simply have expanded the universe of rights claimants under the due process clause. Under this view, Justice Blackmun's declaration in *Roe* that the protection of the Fourteenth Amendment does not extend to the unborn would not be an authoritative statement of the constitutional limits of the term "person." It may make sense to regard "person" as excluding the unborn when it is used in the Constitution in conjunction with extradition, qualifications for the presidency, citizenship, or the return of fugitive slaves, but not in conjunction with due process. One could argue that during the debate over the ratification of the Fourteenth Amendment, no one anticipated the question whether the term "person" included the unborn. The text of the Fourteenth Amendment due process clause surely does not foreclose such an interpretation. Given this textual gap, clarification of the meaning of the term "person" is an instance where congressional exercise of power under section 5 of the Fourteenth Amendment may not only be appropriate, but necessary. So viewed, the Human Life Bill might be understood as conferring standing upon prenatal life and thus as having a remedial dimension.

The fallacy in this argument becomes readily apparent when it is recognized that the rights of the woman and the fetus are mutually exclusive in the setting of an abortion. The vindication of the right to life of the fetus necessarily requires the sacrifice of the woman's right to reproductive choice and vice versa. Hence, to call the Human Life Bill remedial legislation because of its superficial resemblance to a standing measure is quite misleading. The clear purpose and probable effect of the bill would have been to undercut *Roe* drastically and possibly lead to its overruling.

In any event, however one chooses to characterize the Human Life Bill, its enactment would probably make it more tempting for some future Congress to pass unquestionably "substantive" legislation under section 5 of the Fourteenth Amendment. Thus, the "substantive" versus "remedial" legislation distinction turns out to be another more doctrinal way of debating the fundamental policy questions about the role of the Supreme Court. So far, the abortion opponents most concerned with the moral aspects of *Roe* have been unable to persuade the federalist opponents to undertake what might be a costly experiment in constitutional brinksmanship.

V. Conclusion

The Supreme Court may possess the power to declare the law of the land, but this power is less definitive in practice than in theory. Supreme Court pronouncements in many instances are both the culmination of one debate and the beginning of a new one. That has certainly been the case in the abortion context. As the Court extended the themes of privacy and personal autonomy to the conclusion reached in *Roe,* it simultaneously ignited a debate over the meaning of "life." Committed and formidable opposition to *Roe* sprang forth almost immediately. The lesson from this experience is that the study of constitutional law is not solely the study of doctrinal development. It can, and perhaps should, include a study of the shifting equilibrium of values within which legal doctrine evolves. It is primarily through this latter inquiry that scholars, lawyers, judges, and elected officials form opinions about possible lines of future development and, indeed, how they shape those developments.

This study has shown how, through the interaction of law and politics, abortion doctrine has reached its present status. The strategy of massive resistance failed to produce a significant erosion in the rights recognized in *Roe.* The opponents of *Roe* then embraced the alternative of constitutional amendment. Thus far, neither approach has proven successful and this suggests that the division within the ranks of *Roe* opponents is fundamental. Until the tension between the moralist and federalist or institutional perspectives can be reconciled, abortion opponents have no realistic hope of forcing the abandonment of *Roe.* In the meantime, as mentioned earlier, many opponents of abortion believe that their best short term hope is a change in the composition of the Supreme Court.[95] Ironically, acceptance of that fact implies a grudging tribute to the flexibility and responsiveness of an institution whose efforts they are often so quick to decry.

NOTES

1. 410 U.S. 113 (1973).
2. 410 U.S. 179 (1973).
3. Roe v. Wade, 410 U.S. at 118 n.2 (1973).
4. The Supreme Court decisions on prayer and religious observance in public schools were decided more than 20 years ago. Abington School District v. Schempp, 374 U.S. 203 (1963); Engel v. Vitale, 370 U.S. 421 (1962). Yet, in some areas of the country, prayer and religious observance continue in public schools as though the Court's rulings did not exist.
5. The Texas Penal Code § 1191 provided:

   If any person shall designedly administer to a pregnant woman or knowingly procure to be administered with her consent any drug or medicine, or shall use towards her any violence or means whatever externally or internally applied, and thereby procure an abortion, he shall be confined in the penitentiary not less than two nor more than five years; if it be done without her consent, the punishment shall be doubled. By 'abortion' is meant that the life of the fetus or embryo shall be destroyed in the woman's womb or that a premature birth thereof be caused. *See* Roe, 410 U.S. at 117 n.1.

6. Roe. 410 U.S. at 163.

7. *Id*. at 160.

8. *Id*. at 164.

9. The*Wade* Court had expressly refrained from deciding the constitutionality of such a provision. *See Id*. at 165 n.67.

10. Stanley v. Illinois, 405 U.S. 645 (1972) (due process clause of the Fourteenth Amendment guarantees an unwed father the right to a hearing on his fitness as a parent before the state can take his children from him in a dependency proceeding).

11. *See, e.g.,* Pierce v. Society of Sisters, 268 U.S. 510 (1925); Meyer v. Nebraska, 262 U.S. 390 (1923).

12. 428 U.S. 52 (1976).

13. *See id*. at 69–71.

14. *See* Bellotti v. Baird, 443 U.S. 622 (1979); Bellotti v. Baird, 428 U.S. 132 (1976); Planned Parenthood of Central Missouri v. Danforth, 428 U.S. 52 (1976).

15. Planned Parenthood of Central Missouri v. Danforth, 428 U.S. 52 (1976).

16. Bellotti v. Baird, 443 U.S. 622 (1979).

17. The Massachusetts statute provided that the state official be a trial court judge. In his plurality opinion, Justice Powell suggested that a juvenile court judge or an administrative agency be able to approve an abortion: "Indeed, much can be said for employing procedures and a forum less formal than those associated with a court of general jurisdiction." *Id*. at 643 n.22.

18. *See* 410 U.S. at 155.

19. In 1976, there were 1,179,300 abortions in the United States or 24.2 per thousand women; in 1980, there were 1,553,900 abortions or 29.3 per thousand women. The ratio of abortions per 1,000 live births rose in the same period from 361 to 428. (Bureau of the Census, U.S. Dep't of Commerce, Statistical Abstract of the United States 71 [1984]).

20. 439 U.S. 379 (1979).

21. Pennsylvania Abortion Control Act, 1974 Pa. Laws, Act No. 209, Pa. Stat. Ann., Title 35, § 6605(a) (Purdon 1977).

22. Collautti, 439 U.S. at 396.

23. *Id*. at 396.

24. 428 U.S. 52 (1976).

25. H.C.S., House bill No. 1211, § 9 (appr'd June 14, 1974), *quoted in* 428 U.S. at 76, 86–88.

26. *Id*. at 78.

27. "No person shall perform or induce an abortion on a pregnant woman subsequent to the end of the first trimester of her pregnancy, unless such abortion is performed in a hospital." Akron v. Akron Center for Reproductive Health, 103 S.Ct. 2481, 2488 n.3 (1983) (quoting *Akron Codified Ordinances* § 1870.03).

28. *See Akron,* 103 S.Ct. at 2495.

29. 410 U.S. at 163.

30. The *Akron* court explicitly refused to redefine the point at which the state

interest in maternal health becomes compelling, reasserting that this point is reached at the end of the first trimester of pregnancy. The Court conceded that there was medical evidence that the point at which abortion is as safe or safer than childbirth may have extended into the second term, but found that the retention of the end of the first term as the bright line was "prudent." 103 S.Ct. at 2492 n.11.

31. 661 F.2d 328 (5th Cir. 1981). *See also* Mahoning Women's Center v. Hunter, 610 F.2d 456 (6th Cir. 1979). *vacated and remanded on other grounds,* 447 U.S. 918 (1980); Planned Parenthood v. Citizens for Community Action, 558 F.2d 861 (8th Cir. 1977); Westside Women's Services v. Cleveland, 450 F. Supp. 796 (N.D. Ohio 1978), *remanded,* 582 F.2d 1281 (6th Cir. 1978), *cert. denied,* 439 U.S. 983 (1979).

32. *Deerfield,* 661 F.2d at 336, 337.

33. 103 S.Ct. 2517 (1983).

34. 103 S.Ct. at 2522.

35. Mo. Rev. Statutes § 188.047 (1979) provides:
    A representative sample of tissue removed at the time of abortion shall be submitted to a board eligible or certified pathologist, who shall file a copy of the tissue report with the state division of health, and who shall provide a copy of the report to the abortion facility or hospital in which the abortion was performed or induced and the pathologist's report shall be made a part of the patient's permanent record.

36. 103 S.Ct. at 2524 (estimated cost of compliance was $19.40 per abortion).

37. 450 U.S. 398 (1981).

38. *See id.* at 409–11.

39. *See id.* at 413 n.25 (majority opinion of Burger, C.J.); *id.* at 425 n.1 (dissenting opinion of Marshall, J.).

40. 550 F. Supp. 1112 (S.D. Fla. 1982). *See also* Planned Parenthood v. Bd. of Medical Review, 598 F. Supp. 625 (D.R.I. 1984) (holding that Rhode Island's spousal notification law burdens the fundamental right of abortion and is not supported by any compelling state interest).

41. 428 U.S. at 65–66.

42. *Id.* at 67.

43. 103 S.Ct. 2481 (1983).

44. Akron Codified Ordinances ch. 1870.05, cited by the Court, 103 S.Ct. at 2489.

45. 103 S.Ct. at 2489.

46. *See* discussion below in Section D.

47. 103 S.Ct. at 2502–03.

48. Section 10. 1.
    Every health facility and physician shall be supplied with forms promulgated by the division of health, the purpose and function of which shall be the preservation of maternal health and life by adding to the sum of medical knowledge through the compilation of relevant maternal health and life data and to monitor all abortions performed to assure that they are done only under and in accordance with the provisions of the law.

Mo. Ann. Stat. § 188.055(l) (Vernon 1974), quoted in *Danforth,* 428 U.S. at 87 app.
49. *Danforth,* 428 U.S. at 80.
50. 432 U.S. 464 (1977).
51. *Id.* at 469.
52. *Id.* at 471. Note that Justice Powell does not acknowledge this analysis as coming under the due process clause. Instead, he places it under the fundamental rights strand of equal protection. Nevertheless, in this section of the *Maher* opinion, he discusses only substantive due process cases. *Id.* at 471–75.
53. *Id.* at 474.
54. *Id.* at 474.
55. The holding that there is a valid governmental interest in childbirth throughout pregnancy is not inconsistent with the *Roe* analysis. *Roe* held that the interest in potential life did not become compelling until the point of viability. It did not hold that the interest arose only at that point.
56. "Indeed, when an issue involves policy choices as sensitive as those implicated by public funding of non-therapeutic abortions, the appropriate forum for their resolution in a democracy is the legislature." *Id.* at 479.
57. 448 U.S. 297 (1980).
58. Pub. L. No. 96–123, § 109, 93 Stat. 926 (1980).
59. 448 U.S. at 315.
60. Denial of access to therapeutic abortions threatens the health or life of the patient. *Roe* recognized a right to a therapeutic abortion throughout pregnancy. *See* 410 U.S. at 165.
61. 448 U.S. at 318.
62. *Id.* at 323.
63. A related issue involved the denial of public funding assistance to pregnancy counseling organizations. There have been two circuit court decisions concerning state statutes which provided grants to all family planning organizations except those which offered as one of their services abortion counseling or referral. *See* Planned Parenthood v. Kempiners, 700 F.2d 1115 (7th. Cir. 1983); Planned Parenthood v. Arizona, 718 F.2d 938 (9th Cir. 1983).
64. This proposal was the Human Life Federalism Amendment, S.J. Res. 3, 98th Cong., 1st Sess. (1983). On June 28, 1983, S.J. Res. 3 was defeated in the Senate, securing only 49 votes when it needed a two-thirds majority for passage.
65. This discussion is not intended to imply that opponents of *Roe* are necessarily opposed to abortion as a personal matter. It is likely that some who oppose *Roe* because they believe that the legality of abortion should be decided by the majoritarian political process nonetheless believe that abortion should be legal.
66. 410 U.S. 113, 158.
67. *Id.* at 156–57.
68. S.J. Res. 119, 93rd Cong., 1st Sess. (1973).
69. S.J. Res. 130, 93rd Cong., 1st Sess. (1973).
70. For example, the death penalty is constitutionally acceptable in this country because in certain circumstances societal interests in deterrence and retribu-

tion outrank a convicted defendant's right to life. For a discussion of this theme in still another context, see Fletcher, *The Right to Life,* 12 Ga. L. Rev. 1371 (1979); Regan, *Rewriting Roe v. Wade,* 77 Mich. L. Rev. 1569, 1639–46 (1979).

71. The two most obvious exceptions would be for pregnancies resulting from rape or incest. The Supreme Court might well be persuaded that the interest in protecting prenatal life is simply not enough to justify inflicting additional anguish on a woman who has become pregnant as a result of criminal conduct.

72. S.J. Res. 17, 97th Cong., 1st Sess. (1981). A proposal of similar import was H.J. Res. 133. 95th Cong., 1st Sess. (1977), which provided: No human fetus shall be aborted after its heart begins to beat, except when the life of the mother is endangered unless that abortion takes place.

73. The distinction between culpable acts and omissions can present difficult factual issues. *See, e.g.,* Bowers v. DeVito, 686 F.2d 616, 618 (7th Cir. 1982). Nevertheless, if the state fails to act in the face of a clear constitutional duty, it will bear liability under 42 U.S.C. § 1983. *See, e.g.,* Hays v. Jefferson City, 668 F.2d 869, 874 (6th Cir. 1982); Wade v. Haynes, 663 F.2d 778, 780, 781 (8th Cir. 1981).

74. It is one thing to establish a federal remedy, such as damages or injunctive relief, to deal with a situation in which the actions or policies of the state violate the Constitution. But it is quite another to assert that the states must enact ameliorative legislation. One of the premises of Reconstruction era civil rights legislation was that since the southern states refused to protect the federal rights of blacks, Congress had to take the initiative. It did not attempt to force the southern states to enact protective legislation. Rather, it passed the Civil Rights Act of 1866, the Anti-Peonage Act of 1867, the Enforcement Act of 1870, the Force Act of 1871, the Ku Klux Klan Act of 1871 and the Civil Rights Act of 1875. These acts created federal protection against violation of federal rights.

75. The Thirteenth Amendment is another major example. It was enacted to eliminate slavery as a legally sanctioned institution in this country, but it also prohibited involuntary servitude which did not originate with the state. Enforcement legislation was considered necessary to make the Thirteenth Amendment effective, however. Accordingly, Congress passed the Civil Rights Act of 1866, which now survives as 42 U.S.C. §§ 1981 and 1982, and the Anti-Peonage Act of 1867, which today is codified as 18 U.S.C. §§ 1581–84.

76. S.J. Res. 3, 98th Cong., 1st Sess. (1983).

77. *Court, Senate Rebuff Anti-Abortion Efforts,* 1983 Congressional Quarterly Almanac 309 (1983).

78. *See e.g.,* S.J. Res. 17, 97th Cong., 1st Sess. (1981); H.J. Res. 17, 96th Cong., 1st Sess. (1979).

79. H.J. Res. 115, 95th Cong., 1st Sess. (1977).

80. This is probably the most common enforcement clause wording in the many abortion amendments proposed since 1973. *See, e.g.,* S.J. Res. 130, 93rd Cong., 1st Sess. (1973); S.J. Res. 18, 97th Cong., 1st Sess. (1981).

81. S.J. Res. 110, 97th Cong., 1st Sess. (1981).

82. Professor Wardle of Brigham Young Law School discussed this aspect of S.J.

Res. 110 on November 12, 1981, in a prepared statement before the Subcommittee on the Constitution of the Senate Committee on the Judiciary. Wardle suggested that two interpretations of the S.J. Res. 110 enforcement clause were possible: (1) the states and Congress are separate, but co-equal sovereigns and therefore their laws cannot conflict; and (2) both the states and Congress have the power to regulate abortion, but in the event of a conflict, the stricter law prevails. While Wardle concluded that the first interpretation (dual sovereignty) was intended by the sponsors of S.J. Res. 110, he thought that the second interpretation was "plausible." *Constitutional Amendments Relating to Abortion: Hearing on S.J. Res. 17, S.J. Res. 18, S.J. Res. 19 and S.J. Res. 110 Before the Subcommittee on the Constitution of the Senate Committee on the Judiciary,* 97th Cong., 1st Sess. 646, 660–64 (1981). One can validly question Wardle's description of the second interpretation as being merely "plausible." The argument for minimum federal standards on abortion would have strong textual support under S.J. Res. 110.

83. S.J. Res. 3, 98th Cong., 1st Sess. (1983).
84. H.R. 867, 97th Cong., 1st Sess. (1981).
85. C. Wright, *Federal Courts 35* (4th ed. 1983).
86. H.R. 73, 97th Cong., 1st Sess. (1981).
87. In the 1950s, Senator Jenner sponsored two proposals of this type. *See* S. 2646, 85th Cong., 1st Sess. (1957) (would have eliminated Supreme Court appellate jurisdiction in cases involving the federal employee security program and state bar admissions); and S. 3386, 85th Cong., 2d Sess. (1958) (would have eliminated appellate jurisdiction in cases involving state bar admissions). In the aftermath of the Supreme Court's decisions in the reapportionment and custodial interrogation cases in the 1960s, other proposals surfaced. *See, e.g.,* H.R. 11926, 88th Cong., 2d Sess. (1964) (would have withdrawn Supreme Court and lower federal court jurisdiction to hear reapportionment cases); and S. 917, 90th Cong., 2d Sess. (1968) (would have withdrawn Supreme Court and lower federal court jurisdiction in state cases involving the admissibility of confessions). More recently, a monograph of the New York City Bar Association stated that in 1981 there were at least 25 bills pending before Congress to restrict the jurisdiction of either the Supreme Court, the lower federal courts of both. The Association Of The Bar Of The City Of New York, Jurisdiction Stripping Proposals In Congress: The Threat To Judicial Constitutional Review 2 (1981).
88. H.R. 867, 97th Cong., 1st Sess. (1981).
89. Hart, *The Power of Congress to Limit the Jurisdiction of Federal Courts: An Exercise in Dialectic,* 66 Harv. L. Rev. 1362 (1953).
90. The most notable example is appellate jurisdiction in criminal cases. Prior to 1891, no federal criminal cases were appealable to the Supreme Court. United States v. More, 7 U.S. (3 Cranch) 159, 172 (1805). This changed with the Evarts Act of March 3, 1891, 26 Stat. 826.
91. 74 U.S. (7 Wall.) 506 (1868).
92. S. 158, 97th Cong., 1st Sess. (1981).
93. For a relatively recent discussion of the distinction between "remedial" and "substantive" legislation under Section 5 of the Fourteenth Amendment, *see* Rome v. United States, 446 U.S. 156 (1980).

94. 400 U.S. 112 (1970).
95. It should be noted that three justices of the Court already have expressed extreme hostility toward the *Roe* doctrine. In the *Akron* case, supra, the two *Roe* dissenters (White and Rehnquist) joined the dissenting opinion of Justice O'Connor, the newest member of the Court. The opinion, while not explicitly calling for the overruling of *Roe,* described the trimester approach of the earlier decision as "completely unworkable." 103 S. Ct. at 2505. The approach was also described as violating "the fundamental aspiration of judical decision making through the application of neutral principles 'sufficiently absolute to give them roots throughout the community and continuity over significant periods of time. . . .' " *Id.* at 2507. The addition of only two justices to the anti-*Roe* delegation on the Court might result in a sea change concerning the constitutional law of abortion.

This article discusses minors' rights to abortion. Presented here are the complicating factors that evolve when the patient is a minor. Various questions arise: whether the minor is mature, immature, or emancipated; whether there is parental or spousal consent; whether there are state interests, constitutional rights, informed consent, parental notice, or alternative judicial or administrative procedures. Janet Benshoof and Harriet Pilpel present the case law that helps define and solve the problems of minors and abortion.

4 · Minors' Rights to Confidential Abortions: The Evolving Legal Scene

Janet Benshoof, J.D.
and Harriet F. Pilpel, J.D.

I. Current Status of Minors' Rights

A minor's right to choose abortion, and particularly the right to effectuate that decision without parental knowledge or consent, has emerged as one of the most hotly debated and frequently litigated constitutional privacy issues of 1980s. Sixteen states currently have laws requiring either notification of parents or their consent prior to a minor's abortion.[1] It is a major legislative issue in nearly every state.[2] Although the Supreme Court since 1976 has decided six cases involving parental consent or notification statutes, there are still critical unanswered constitutional questions regarding minors' rights to abortion.[3] However, the Supreme Court opinions in these cases delineate an important body of constitutional law that prevails over the varying state laws, case laws, and administrative rulings that had governed minors' access to abortion prior to 1976.[4] Although minors have a fundamental privacy right to choose abortions, it is not coextensive with the constitutional right of adult women. The majority opinions of the Supreme Court recognize:

1. "Mature" minors, who are capable of understanding the consequences of pregnancy and abortion, have a constitutional right to obtain confidential abortion services without parental involvement.
2. "Immature" minors have a constitutional right to abortion services if this would be in their best interests, and a right to abortion without parental

Copyright © 1986 by Harriet F. Pilpel and Janet Benshoof

involvement if such involvement would be detrimental to their best interests.

3. In order to protect "immature" minors from improvident decisionmaking, states may require parental notification or consent prior to a minor's abortion, but such laws covering all minors must contain an administrative or judicial bypass mechanism whereby mature or immature "best interests" minors can be exempted from the mandated parental involvement.

4. When state laws that interfere with minors' rights to abortion are challenged, courts will examine them under a "significant state interests" test as opposed to the "compelling state interests" test required for laws that interfere with the abortion rights of adult women.

Despite these rather loosely defined principles, the dimensions of minors' constitutional right to choose abortion are less clear that those of adult women. An examination of the Supreme Court opinions in the minors' area reveals that there is no clear majority of justices that follow one legal doctrine, and future cases will, no doubt, reveal yet different lineups. Furthermore, the Supreme Court has never examined any of the state parental consent or notification laws once they have been implemented, so it has not been faced with weighing the degree of burden these laws actually place on teenagers against the importance of the state interests at stake and the degree to which the state accomplishes its purposes.[5] In order to understand the constitutional questions involved, and the extent to which future legislation impinging on minors' access to abortion may be upheld, it is important to review the current status of adult women's right to choose abortion, and to contrast that with the rights thus far accorded minors.

A. Adult Women's Rights

In 1973, in the two companion cases, *Roe v. Wade*[6] and *Doe v. Bolton*,[7] the Supreme Court held by a 7–2 majority that a Texas abortion law and a Georgia abortion law were unconstitutional on the ground they violated a woman's constitutional right to privacy guaranteed by the Fourteenth Amendment to the Constitution. The Court also established a judicial standard of review for courts to use when adjudicating the constitutionality of any future abortion regulations. Because the right to choose abortion was deemed part of the "fundamental" constitutional right to privacy, state regulations that interfere with that right will be strictly scrutinized by the courts and will be upheld only if they are narrowly tailored to further certain compelling state interests. Furthermore, the Supreme Court carefully limited those interests that the state could assert in support of laws interfering with abortion. During the first trimester there are no compelling state interests. The state must leave the abortion decision and its effectuation to a woman and her doctor.[8] During the second trimester, because of the increasing medical risks of abortion, the state may regulate if such regulations are narrowly tailored to further only the interest in women's health and medical standards.[9] During the third trimester of pregnancy, or after viability, the state may regulate or proscribe abortion to protect fetal life, but even then such laws must contain exceptions that permit abortion when a woman's life or health is at stake.[10]

In 1983, in *Akron v. Akron Center for Reproductive Health*,[11] the Supreme Court reaffirmed this rigorous standard of judicial review and reiterated that there exist only two compelling state interests (women's health after the first trimester and fetal life after viability) that can justify state interference when the right of adult women to seek abortion is at issue.[12]

B. Minors' Rights

Although the 1973 decisions firmly established that the right to choose abortion is protected by the Constitution, it was not until 1976 that the Supreme Court addressed the question of minors' rights. In *Planned Parenthood of Central Missouri v. Danforth*,[13] the Court struck down portions of a Missouri statute enacted in 1974, including a requirement that unmarried minors obtain at least one parent's consent prior to any abortion,[14] recognizing that minors have a constitutional right to privacy, including the right to choose abortion. The majority opinion in *Danforth*, written by Justice Blackmun, joined by Justices Brennan, Stewart, Marshall, and Powell, held that the state may not impose a blanket provision requiring the consent of a parent as a condition of an abortion of an unmarried minor during the first 12 weeks of her pregnancy.[15]

Justice Blackmun stressed that constitutional rights do not mature and come into being "magically only when one attains the state-defined age of majority."[16] And he explained, "Just as with the requirement of consent from the spouse, so here, the State does not have the constitutional authority to give a third party an absolute, and possibly arbitrary, veto over the decision of the physician and his patient to terminate the patient's pregnancy, regardless of the reason for withholding the consent."[17] The opinion in *Danforth*, however, acknowledged that states do have broader authority to regulate the activities of children to a greater degree than those of adults, and that where minors are concerned the state could pass laws in furtherance of interests other than fetal viability or maternal health.

In examining the state interests presented in *Danforth*,[18] the Court held that neither safeguarding the family unit nor safeguarding parental authority were sufficient state interests to sustain a law that would occasion a veto of a minor's decision. The state interest viewed most convincing by Justices Stewart and Powell in their concurring opinion was the interest the state has in helping a minor who may be ill-equipped to make the abortion decision. "There can be little doubt that the State furthers a constitutionally permissible end by encouraging an unmarried pregnant minor to seek the help and advice of her parents in making the very important decision whether or not to bear a child."[19]

In 1976, in *Bellotti v. Baird*,[20] the Supreme Court considered a Massachusetts statute requiring parental consent. Although this particular statute provided that if one or both parents refused their consent the minor could try to obtain consent from a state court judge, the Supreme Court abstained from deciding whether this was constitutional and sent it back for an interpretation by the Massachusetts Supreme Court.[21] Subsequently, the Massachusetts state court interpreted the statute to require every minor to go initially to her parents.[22] This case then went back to federal court, on the federal constitutional issues,[23] and was appealed again to the United States Supreme Court which, in an 8–1 decision, ruled the statute, as interpreted by the state court, unconstitutional.[24] This decision is the most definitive Supreme Court decision to date on minors' rights to abortion. It establishes that minors' constitutional right to choose abortion cannot be arbitrarily abrogated through mandatory parental involvement statutes, holding: (1)

that mature minors have a right to make their own decisions about abortion without parental involvement; (2) that mature and immature minors must, as a matter of constitutional law, have the opportunity, through an alternative judicial or administrative procedure, to obtain an abortion without parental consent or consultation; and (3) that with respect to immature minors, the sole test must be their own best interests.

Although eight of the justices agreed that the Massachusetts statute was unconstitutional, they disagreed as to how far the state can legislate in this area and filed two separate opinions. One opinion, written by Justice Powell joined by Chief Justice Burger and Justices Stewart and Rehnquist, states that they believe a more carefully designed parental consent statute may be constitutional. The opinion of Justice Stevens, joined by Justices Brennan, Marshall, and Blackmun, strongly implies that any parental or judicial consent statute is per se, an undue burden on the abortion right and unconstitutional under *Planned Parenthood of Central Missouri v. Danforth* and *Roe v. Wade*.[25] Because these two opinions together make up the most comprehensive discussion of minors' rights in this area, it is important to examine them both.

The opinion by Justice Powell stresses that, where important decisions are involved, the state may protect youths from their own immaturity by requiring parental involvement. States may also defer to parents because parents have the right and "duty" to prepare children for their place in society, including the "inculcation of moral standards, religious beliefs, and elements of good citizenship."[26] And he concluded with a finding that the American tradition of parental authority is "one of the basic presuppositions" of individual liberty.[27] But even though there are important state interests, the statute may not "unduly burden" the minors' right to seek an abortion.[28]

Attempting to balance the minors' right to an abortion with the constitutionally permissible state interest in encouraging parental involvement in the minor's decision, the opinion concludes:

> *[I]f the State decides to require a pregnant minor to obtain one or both parents' consent to an abortion, it also must provide an alternative procedure whereby authorization for the abortion can be obtained.*[29]

A pregnant minor is entitled in such a proceeding to show either: (1) that she is mature enough and well enough informed to make her abortion decision, in consultation with her physician, independently of her parents' wishes; or (2) that even if she is "immature" and not able to make this decision independently, the desired abortion would be in her best interests.

> *The proceeding in which this showing is made must assure that a resolution of the issue, and any appeals that may follow, will be completed with anonymity and sufficient expedition to provide an effective opportunity for an abortion to be obtained. In sum, the procedure must ensure that the provision requiring parental consent does not* in fact *amount to the "absolute, and possibly arbitrary, veto" that was found impermissible in* Danforth [emphasis added].[30]

The Powell opinion found that the Massachusetts statute violated these constitutional standards because: (1) Massachusetts required a minor always to go to her parents *before* going to Court, and parents were to be notified of the court proceeding; and (2) the judge in Massachusetts could withhold authorization even if the minor was mature.[31]

The opinion by Justice Stevens is more limited in scope and accords more rights to minors. It states that because the Massachusetts statute in effect sets up a system permitting a third-party veto, it is unconstitutional under *Danforth*. This opinion recognizes that in reality any special judicial or administrative requirement imposed on minors probably would be burdensome and unconstitutional:

> *As a practical matter, I would suppose that the need to commence judicial proceedings in order to obtain a legal abortion would impose a burden at least as great as, and probably greater than, that imposed on the minor child by the need to obtain the consent of a parent.*[32]

This decision in *Bellotti v. Baird* rendered unconstitutional, under the privacy protections of the Fourteenth Amendment due process clause,[33] all state statutes that required parental consent or notification, but did not contain the full procedural guarantees enabling ''mature'' or ''best interests'' minors to bypass their parents.

In 1981, in *H.L. v. Matheson*,[34] the Supreme Court had the opportunity to examine a Utah state statute requiring the doctor to notify the parents prior to any abortion on an unemancipated minor under age 18. Although this particular parental notification statute, which contained no judicial bypass procedure, was upheld, the decision was a very narrow one since, in the opinion of the Court, it was constitutional *only* as to the very small class of minors represented by the one named plaintiff.

Therefore, the narrow legal issue decided by the majority was that the Utah statute requiring notice to parents was constitutional only ''(a) when the girl is living with and dependent upon her parents, (b) when she is *not* emancipated by marriage or otherwise, and (c) when she has made *no* claim or showing as to her maturity or as to her relation with her parents [emphasis added].''[35] In fact, five justices indicated that, if the same Utah statute were challenged again by a mature minor or by a minor with a good reason why her parents should not be told (''best interests''), they would hold it unconstitutional because it does not include a judicial or administrative bypass route for such minors.[36]

The Burger opinion stresses that the Utah statute, because it involves notification, not consent, does *not* give parents or judges a veto power over the minor's abortion decision, even that of an immature or unemancipated minor.[37] The opinion finds that the statute, ''as applied to immature and dependent minors . . . serves the important considerations of family integrity and protecting adolescents''[38] and ''a significant state interest by providing an opportunity for parents to supply essential medical and other information to a physician.''[39]

Justice Marshall wrote a dissenting opinion in *H.L. v. Matheson*, joined by Justices Brennan and Blackmun.[40] Justice Marshall finds that the parental notice requirement imposes a burden on the fundamental, personal right of some minors, because "involving the minor's parents against her wishes effectively cancels her right to avoid disclosure of her personal choice."[41] Besides the burden on the right to make a "confidential decision," the Marshall opinion also finds that the parental notice requirement "may limit 'access to the means of effectuating that decision,' " because "[m]any minor women will encounter interference from their parents after the state-imposed notification."[42]

Justice Marshall holds that the state must justify the burdens imposed by the statute by a "significant state interest,"[43] and that the statute fails to do this.[44]

C. Minors' Rights in 1983

In 1983, the Supreme Court decided three abortion cases,[45] two of which contained provisions requiring parental consent.[46] In *Akron v. Akron Center for Reproductive Health,*[47] in a 6–3 decision, the Supreme Court affirmed the Sixth Circuit Court of Appeals decision holding unconstitutional a city of Akron criminal ordinance prohibiting physicians from performing abortions on a minor under the age of 15 unless the physician obtains the consent of one parent or "an order from a court." The majority opinion, written by Justice Powell, held that the statute was unconstitutional because it did not contain the constitutionally mandated alternative procedure required as set forth in *Bellotti v. Baird.*[48]

This opinion supports the argument that the Supreme Court will not read in procedural guarantees for minors in this type of statute, but will require that guarantees of anonymity, speed, and appointed counsel are written into the statutes.[49] The dissent in *Akron,* written by Justice O'Connor joined by Justices White and Rehnquist, would have abstained from deciding the minors section of the Akron ordinance pending an interpretation by the Ohio state courts.[50]

In a companion case, *Planned Parenthood Association of Kansas City v. Ashcroft,*[51] the Supreme Court by a 5–4 vote upheld the facial validity of a Missouri statute requiring parental consent prior to a minor's abortion with a provision for a judicial bypass. The Court's opinion, written by Justice Powell, joined by Chief Justice Burger, in which Justice O'Connor concurred in an opinion joined by Justices White and Rehnquist, reiterated that "a State's interest in protecting immature minors will sustain a requirement of a consent substitute, either parental or judicial."[52] They found that the Missouri statute provided for a judicial alternative consistent with the legal standards outlined in *Bellotti v. Baird.*[53] Justice Blackmun wrote a dissent to this holding, joined by Justices Stevens, Brennan, and Marshall, finding that the need to commence a judicial proceeding imposes as great a burden on the minor as having to obtain parental consent, making it fundamentally at odds with the basic privacy interest afforded her constitutional decision.[54]

Therefore, as of 1983, the Supreme Court has recognized that minors have a fundamental constitutional right to make and effectuate the decision to choose abortion. Although the state may legislate to interject parents in order to protect immature minors and perhaps for other "family integrity" reasons, any such consent or notification statute must contain a mechanism whereby "mature" or "best interests" minors are exempted from parental involvement.

However, as the effects of these statutes begin to be realized, future court challenges may take a variety of forms. These include attacking the statutes as overbroad and therefore unconstitutional,[55] since preliminary evidence from the two states that have these statutes indicates that over 95 percent of the unemancipated minors forced to go through the judicial bypass procedure are adjudged mature or "best interests" minors, and since there is a substantial and demonstrable burden and chilling effect caused by the statutes.[56]

Other approaches might be to rely on state constitutional grounds, including state equal protection clauses, state guarantees of rights to privacy,[57] and state equal rights amendments.[58]

The challenge most likely to succeed, however, would be one based on existing Supreme Court standards, providing the court with proof that these statutes as applied in various states in effect unduly burden minors, are not narrowly drawn, and fail actually to further significant state interests.

II. The Effect of Parental Consent or Notification Laws On Minors: An Unsettled Constitutional Question

Although 16 states[59] currently have laws requiring either parental notification or consent prior to a minor's abortion,[60] many of these are facially unconstitutional under the standards set forth in *Bellotti v. Baird* and have never gone into effect.[61] Parental notification statutes have been implemented in Utah, Minnesota, Arizona, Maryland, Montana, West Virginia, and Idaho; parental consent statutes in Indiana, Louisiana, Massachusetts, Missouri, North Dakota, and Rhode Island.[62] The most critical constitutional question remaining to be addressed by the Supreme Court is whether a minor's right to choose abortion is constitutionally protected from laws that, when implemented, do not, in fact, further the asserted state interests and which, in practice, severely burden the minor's right to privacy.[63]

The Supreme Court has proffered several state interests to justify parental notification and consent laws: family integrity or parental authority,[64] aiding the decisionmaking of immature minors,[65] providing the parents with an opportunity to provide medical information,[66] and protecting potential life.[67] Although it has been suggested that parents have an independent constitutional right to be told about any abortion request,[68] even those members of the Supreme Court who would uphold parental consent laws have never suggested that they would do so because of this ground.[69] The only circuit court of appeals to address this argument in the context of minors obtaining contraceptives flatly rejected it.[70] Even though a majority of the Court has indicated that, where minors are concerned, they will require the state to show "significant state interests" as opposed to the compelling ones needed to uphold laws restricting adult women's access to abortion, the burden is still on the state to show that the laws actually promote these interests, and that the laws are carefully drawn to interfere with privacy to the least degree possible.[71]

Do these laws actually achieve these purposes in the most narrowly tailored way? Statutes in Louisiana, Minnesota, Massachusetts, and Missouri have been upheld, at least preliminarily, as facially constitutional and are currently being challenged as unconstitutional as applied.[72] Both Massachusetts and Minnesota have had parental notification (Minnesota) and consent (Massachusetts) laws with a judicial bypass system in effect for over two years. In analyzing the constitutionality of these state statutes as applied, it is very important to keep in mind the dimensions of the problems of teenage pregnancy and childbirth. There is no question that these factors are considered constitutionally relevant by the Supreme Court in assessing the degree of "burden" imposed on the constitutional right to choose abortion.[73]

Teenage pregnancy and teenage childbirth present enormous health problems in this country.[74] Pregnancy rates among U.S. teenagers are increasing, and U.S. teenage birth rates are among the highest in the world.[75] There are over 11 million sexually active teenagers in this country, and four out of 10 girls will become pregnant while still in their teens.[76]

The economic, mental, psychological, educational, and physical consequences of early teenage childbearing are well documented. Teenagers who continue pregnancy suffer a much higher mortality and morbidity risk than do older women, and up to 10 times the mortality risk of an early abortion.[77] Teenagers who have children are much more likely to have additional children while they are still teenagers, to go on welfare, and to remain on welfare, forfeiting educational opportunities and opportunities for independence and self-advancement.[78] Furthermore, approximately one-fourth of female minors who attempt suicide do so because they are, or believe they are, pregnant.[79] And the children born to these children face greatly increased risks of death in infancy, as well as a host of serious childhood diseases, birth injuries, and neurological defects, including retardation.[80]

Although abortion has also been identified as one of the harms of teenage pregnancy,[81] the Supreme Court has repeatedly recognized that early abortion is safer than childbirth,[82] and that abortion regulations that restrict access can have severe effects on women's health.[83] Regulations that limit access to abortions and increase the time and expense of obtaining them may mean that women suffer additional health and life risks from delays,[84] do not get abortions at all, or that they will seek illegal abortions.[85]

Although the Supreme Court has considered the detrimental effects of such regulations as 24-hour waiting periods and in-hospital rules, it has yet to consider the degree of actual burden created by parental consent or notification statutes.[86] Actual experience, as well as studies, show the strong deterrent effect on minors of parental notification and consent statutes.[87] Furthermore, in comparing the deterrent effect of the Minnesota statute with that of the Massachusetts statute, it is clear that, as a practical matter, notification is as great a deterrent as consent.[88]

In Minnesota, for example, the two-parent[89] notification requirement implemented on August 1, 1981, has added burdens on teenagers who already had problems with access. Minnesota is a largely rural state, with abortion providers located only in the Minneapolis-St. Paul and Duluth areas. Therefore, teenagers routinely travel large distances to reach an abortion provider.[90] Prior to the mandatory parental notification law, a study showed that 75 percent of minors had not told both parents, but 45 percent had told one.[91] The younger the teenager, the more likely that at least one parent was involved with the abortion decision.[92] Subsequent to the implementation of this statute, there has been a decrease of about one-third of the number of abortions obtained by minors, documenting the deterrent effect of the statute.[93] In Minnesota, there has been no noticeable increase in the number of Minnesota teenagers going to neighboring states for abortions,[94] although in Massachusetts, statistics indicate that about one-third of the teenagers seeking abortions go out of state.[95] The difference between the states is probably due to the fact Massachusetts residents have shorter distances to travel to reach out-of-state abortion providers.[96] Although the Minnesota statute contains many facial procedural guarantees for the court bypass alternative, such as requiring that courts will be open 24 hours a day, seven days a week, in fact, the statute does not assure that mature or best interests minors have their right to a confidential abortion protected.

Courts are open in only three of the 87 counties, many judges will not hear these cases, and virtually all of the petitions are heard by three judges who now limit their hearings for minors to certain days a week and certain hours.[97] No judges hear these cases evenings or on weekends, when it is easiest for teenagers who otherwise have to miss school.[98] Preliminary data from Minnesota show a "survival of the fittest" situation. Older, white, more sophisticated and more affluent teenagers are the only ones who can "work" the judicial system.[99] Nearly all the teenagers are adjudged "mature," the remaining "best interests." Those teenagers who go to court and who obtain abortions, routinely suffer health-endangering delays and personal trauma.[100] When one parent goes to court with the teenager in order that the other parent (who may never have seen the child, or has been adjudged "unfit" for custody or visitation) not be notified prior to the abortion, there is no question of the levels of outrage and affront of the invasion, not only on teenagers' privacy, but of putting strain on and undermining the family unit.[101]

Thus, the experience in one state has shown that the court bypass procedure is inflicting severe harm on minors seeking abortions by denying their privacy rights. Has the statute helped the decisionmaking of immature minors?[102] There is no evidence how many, if any, minors are in this category,[103] nor that the statute has promoted increased parental involvement that has helped them reach a decision in their best interests, or strengthened the family unit. State court judges in Minnesota seeing the minors do not believe the state accomplishes these purposes.[104] Certainly, it is acknowledged that some parents oppose abortion for anyone, would never allow their daughters to have one, and would not consider only what would be in their daughters' "best interests."[105] Furthermore, the Minnesota law cannot be considered "narrower with its tailored" two-parent requirement irregardless of who has legal custody.

In addition, the failure of states to appropriate any money for more judges, counselors, or additional court hours to implement the court bypass system, and facilitate minors' access to that system is one proof that the statutes are not, in fact, designed for their stated purposes, but rather for the purpose of deterring as many abortions as possible. A statute that is designed to deter abortions and in effect does just that might be found antithetical to the privacy rights protected by *Roe v. Wade*[106] and to our system of constitutionally protected individual rights.

Minors have a protected constitutional right to choose abortion, and have greatly benefited from implementation of those constitutional guarantees.[107] Because the scope of judicial scrutiny of laws restricting minors' access to abortion by mandating parental notification or consent is less defined, teenagers in certain states are suffering a cutback in their ability to obtain abortions. How the Supreme Court will view these burdens on teenagers, and how state legislatures will react to this situation, is not known. However, there is no question of the irreversible impact of denial of a teenager's choice of abortion, or of the lifelong consequences brought on by teenage childbearing. In the scheme of constitutional rights, protection of privacy rights are most critical to a young woman's future.

NOTES

1. Ariz. Rev. Stat. Ann. § 36–2152 (1982); Idaho Code § 18–609, subd. 6 (Supp. 1982–83). Ill. Ann. Stat. ch. 38, § 81–21–23.3 (Smith-Hurd Supp. 1983–84), is currently under court injunction. Charles v. Carey, 79 C 4551 (N.D. Ill. November 16, 1979). However, Illinois just passed a new parental notification law scheduled to be effective some time between November 1, 1983, and January 1, 1984. Ill. Rev. Stat. ch. 38, § 81–53–68.1(Supp. 1984). La. Rev. Stat. Ann. § 40:1299–35.5 (West Supp. 1983); Md. Health Gen. Code Ann. §§ 20–102, 103 (1982); Mass. Laws Ann. ch. 112, § 12S (Michie Law Coop. Supp. 1983). In Minnesota, a two-part parental notification statute was passed in 1981. One part, requiring parental notification with no judicial bypass (Minn. Stat. Ann. § 144.343 subd. 2 [Supp. 1983]), has been enjoined, Hodgson v. Minnesota, 3–81 Civ. 538 (D. Minn. March 22, 1982); the second section of the statute, which came into effect once the first was enjoined, is a parental notification requirement with a judicial bypass. Minn. Stat. Ann. § 144.343 subd. 6 (Supp. 1983). Mo. Rev. Stat. § 188.028 (1983); Mont. Code Ann. § 50–20–107 (1981). 1985 Nev. Stat. ch. 681 § 8, currently under court injunction, Glick v. McKay, CV–R–85–331–BCR CV Nev. July 17, 1985. N.D. Cent. Code § 14–02.1–03.1 (1981); 18 Pa. Cons. Stat. Ann. § 3206 (Purdon Supp. 1983–84); R.I. Gen. Laws § 23–4.7–6 (Supp. 1982); Utah Code Ann. § 76–7–304 (1978); W.Va. Code § 16–2F–3(a) (1984).
2. Benshoof, *Reproductive Rights* in *Lobbying for Freedom in the 1980s* 93 (K.P. Norwick, ed. 1983).
3. Bellotti v. Baird (Bellotti I), 428 U.S. 132 (1976); Planned Parenthood of Central Missouri v. Danforth, 428 U.S. 52 (1976); Bellotti v. Baird (Bellotti II), 443 U.S. 622 (1979); H.L. v. Matheson, 450 U.S. 398 (1981); Akron v. Akron Center for Reproductive Health, 103 S. Ct. 2481 (1983); Planned Parenthood Association of Kansas City v. Ashcroft, 103 S. Ct. 2517 (1983).
4. See Pilpel & Zuckerman, *Abortion and the Rights of Minors.* 23 Case W. Res. 779 (1972); Pilpel & Paul, *Teenagers and Pregnancy: The Law in 1979,* 11 Fam. Plann. Perspect. 297 (September/October 1979).
5. In *H.L. v. Matheson,* 450 U.S. 398 (1981), the Supreme Court had before it a Utah parental notification statute that was in effect. However, there was no trial record on its effect, burden on minors, or whether it was fully implemented. The only plaintiff was an immature minor who alleged no particular burden imposed by the notification, and the Court's opinion was limited to those circumstances.
6. 410 U.S 113 (1973).
7. 410 U.S. 179 (1973).
8. Roe v. Wade, 410 U.S. at 153.
9. *Id.* at 154; Akron v. Akron Center for Reproductive Health, 103 S. Ct. at 2492–95.

10. Roe v. Wade, 410 U.S. at 163–64.
11. 103 S. Ct. 2481.
12. *Id.* at 2491, 2492.
13. 428 U.S. at 52.
14. 428 U.S. at 75.
15. This decision provides constitutional protection not only to those minors whose parents would withhold consent, but also to those minors who want to exercise their "fundamental right to give birth," but whose parents try to force abortions. *See,* Matter of Mary P., 444 N.Y.S.2d 545, 547 (N.Y. Fam. Ct. 1981).
16. 428 U.S. at 74.
17. *Id.*
18. Although the Court in *Danforth* failed to articulate the standard of review it was applying to the parental consent requirements, in contrast to the "compelling state interest test" carefully laid out for adult women in *Roe v. Wade,* the Court's analysis reveals that it applied an intermediate level of review. Rather than requiring a compelling state interest, the Court looked to see whether there was "any *significant* state interest in conditioning an abortion on the consent of a parent" and whether the statute in fact furthered that interest. 428 U.S. at 75. Intermediate level review is generally triggered if "important, though not necessarily 'fundamental or preferred interests are at stake . . . or if sensitive, although not necessarily suspect criteria of classification are employed." L. Tribe, American Constitutional Law (1978), at 1089, 1091. Such scrutiny has been applied in cases involving sex discrimination and commercial speech.
19. 428 U.S. at 91. In *Danforth,* four justices (White, Burger, Rehnquist, and Stevens) dissented. In a dissent written by Justice White, and joined by Burger, and Rehnquist, the three justices would have upheld the parental consent requirement on the ground that it would protect the minor's best interests and protect children from improvident decisionmaking. *Id.* at 95. Justice Stevens's additional dissent focused on the fact that the young pregnant woman would need help in the decisionmaking, and that the legislative determination that her choice would be made more wisely with advice of a parent was not irrational. *Id.* at 103. Therefore, he would have sustained the requirement on the basis of the state's interest in the welfare of young citizens.
20. Bellotti v. Baird, 428 U.S. 132 (1976).
21. *Id.* at 151–52.
22. Baird v. Attorney General, 371 Mass. 741, 360 N.E.2d 288 (1977).
23. Baird v. Bellotti, 450 F. Supp. 997 (D. Mass. 1978).
24. Bellotti v. Baird, 443 U.S. 622 (1979).
25. *Id.* at 654–56. Justice Stevens's concurring opinion in *Bellotti* marked a significant shift of opinion from *Danforth.* In *Danforth,* Justice Stevens would have upheld outright a parental consent requirement. Such a requirement, he argued, was consistent with *Roe* and justified by the state's interest in protecting the welfare of its young citizens. 428 U.S. at 102–05. In *Bellotti,* Justice Stevens argued that the Massachusetts statute should be judged only

on its face and that under *Roe* and *Danforth* it was unconstitutional. 443 U.S.
at 652–656.

26. 443 U.S. at 637, 638, quoting Wisconsin v. Yoder, 406 U.S. at 205, 233
(1972).

27. 443 U.S. at 638.

28. *Id.* at 640, citing Planned Parenthood of Central Missouri v. Danforth, 428
U.S. at 147. The Court in *Bellotti* did not articulate any standard of review
for minors' cases. However, in 1977, in Carey v. Population Services
International, 431 U.S. at 678 (1977), it struck down a New York statute
restricting contraceptive sales to minors under 16 on the grounds such
restrictions violated minors' privacy rights. The plurality opinion of Justice
Brennan articulates that the significant state interest test he was utilizing "is
apparently less rigorous than the 'compelling state interest' test applied to
restrictions on the privacy rights of adults." *Id.* at 693 n. 15. However, it is
significant that the Powell opinion in *Bellotti* distinguishes the abortion
choice from other critical decisions made by teenagers in language that
supports the argument that courts must review state statutes in this area with
the degree of judicial scrutiny usually reserved for the strictest constitutional
test, *i.e.* the compelling state interest test. "The abortion decision differs in
important ways from other decisions that may be made during minority. The
need to preserve the constitutional right and the unique nature of the
abortion decision, especially when made by a minor, require a State to act
with particular sensitivity when it legislates to foster parental involvement in
this matter." 443 U.S. at 642.

29. *Id.* at 643.

30. *Id.* at 643, 644.

31. *Id.* at 645–48.

32. *Id.* at 655.

33. In *Bellotti II,* the Court did not address the equal protection problems raised
by treating minors seeking abortions differently from minors seeking to
continue their pregnancies or seeking other medical care. 443 U.S. 650 n. 30.
However, in *Bellotti I,* the question was raised as to whether it was
permissible to distinguish consent required for minors in the abortion
context from consent prequired for other medical procedures. The Court
held, "not all distinction between abortion and other procedures is forbidden," (citing *Danforth,* 428 U.S. at 80–81), and that "[t]he constitutionality
of such distinction will depend upon its degree and the justification for it."
Id. at 428 U.S. 149, 150.

34. 450 U.S. 398 (1981).

35. *Id.* at 407.

36. *Id.* at 420 (Powell, J., joined by Stewart, J., concurring; 450 U.S. at 454
(Marshall, J., joined by Brennan, Blackmun, J.J., dissenting). The Utah
statute is currently being challenged in federal court, L.R. v. Wilkinson, Civ.
No. C–80–0078J (D. Utah, filed February 4, 1980). Thus far, the trial court
has only enjoined the statute as to individual named plaintiffs who have
intervened and asserted their status as mature or "best interests" minors.

37. Chief Justice Burger distinguishes the legal burden imposed by parental
notification as opposed to parental consent, 450 U.S. at 408–11, as does

Justice Stevens in a separate concurring opinion where he states he would uphold a blanket parental notification requirement as to all minors, mature or immature. *Id.* at 421–25 (Stevens, J., concurring). Justice Stevens holds that Planned Parenthood of Central Missouri v. Danforth, 428 U.S. 52 (1976), is not controlling because this statute involves notification, not consent, and the issues are different. 450 U.S. at 421. He holds that the state interest is "fundamental and substantial," *id.*, and is an interest in "protecting a young woman from the consequences of an incorrect [abortion] decision." *Id.* at 425, quoting Planned Parenthood of Central Missouri v. Danforth, 428 U.S. at 102–03. Justice Stevens concludes by reiterating his conclusion in this case and *Danforth* "that a state legislature may rationally decide that most parents will, when informed of their daughter's pregnancy, act with her welfare in mind" 450 U.S. at 423, n. 1.

38. *Id.* at 411.

39. *Id.* The decision finds that notification furthers these interests because "the Utah statute is reasonably calculated to protect minors in appellant's class by enhancing the potential for parental consultation concerning a decision that has potentially traumatic and permanent consequences." *Id.* at 412.

40. 450 U.S. at 425–54 (Marshall, J., dissenting).

41. *Id.* at 437 (footnote omitted).

42. *Id.* at 438 (footnote omitted), quoting Carey v. Population Services International, 431 U.S. 678, 688 (1977).

43. 450 U.S. at 441 quoting Planned Parenthood of Central Missouri v. Danforth, 428 U.S. 52, 75 (1976). Justice Marshall, in his dissent in *Matheson,* argues that the "compelling state interest" test should be the standard of review used in cases involving restrictions on minors' access to abortion, even though the state interest need only be "significant" and not the "compelling" ones recognized as legitimate in the case of adult women. 450 U.S. at 441 n. 32.

44. First, the statute fails to ensure that the parents will give medical information helpful to the physician, since it does not require, or even encourage, an active conversation between the physician and the parents; notice can be given moments before the abortion. *Id.* at 443–46. Second, the Marshall opinion finds that the notice requirement does not give parents the opportunity to contribute to the minor woman's abortion decision, since it does not require notice to be timely, nor is such mandatory consultation legitimate "where the minor's pregnancy resulted from incest, where a hostile or abusive parental response is assured, or where the minor's fears of such a response deter her from the abortion she desires." *Id.* at 446. Finally, Marshall finds that this statute does not protect or advance "parental authority" because the statute "reaches beyond the legal limit of those [parental] rights." *Id.* at 450. Marshall concludes by stating:

> I have no doubt that the challenged statute infringes upon the constitutional right to privacy attached to a minor woman's decision to complete or terminate her pregnancy. None of the reasons offered by the State justifies this intrusion, for the statute is not tailored to serve them. Rather than serving to enhance the physician's judgment, in cases such as the appellant's, the statute prevents imple-

mentation of the physician's medical recommendation. Rather than promoting the transfer of information held by the parents to the minor's physician, the statute neglects to require anything more than a communication from the physician moments before the abortion. Rather than respecting the private realm of family life, the statute invokes the criminal machinery of the State in an attempt to influence the interactions within the family. Accordingly, I would reverse the judgment of the Supreme Court of Utah insofar as it upheld the statute against constitutional attack.

Id. at 454.

45. Akron v. Akron Center for Reproductive Health, 103 S. Ct. 2481 (1983); Planned Parenthood Association of Kansas City v. Ashcroft, 103 S. Ct. 2517 (1983); Simopoulos v. Virginia, 103 S. Ct. 2532 (1983).

46. 103 S. Ct. 2481 (1983); 103 S. Ct. 2517 (1983).

47. 103 S. Ct. 2481 (1983).

48. 443 U.S. 622 (1979). The Supreme Court found that the state juvenile court in Ohio has no procedure for finding minors "mature," or for an adjudication that a confidential abortion would be in a minor's "best interests." Furthermore, the Court noted that Ohio state law requires routine parental notification whenever any minor files a petition in juvenile court. 103 S. Ct. at 2497–99.

49. In *Akron,* the Court, citing Bellotti v. Baird, 443 U.S. at 643 n. 23, stated, "[W]e do not think that the Akron ordinance, as applied in Ohio juvenile proceedings, is reasonably susceptible of being construed to create an 'opportunity for case-by-case evaluations of the maturity of pregnant minors.' " 103 S. Ct. at 2498–99. Following the Court's decision in *Akron,* the Seventh Circuit, in Indiana Planned Parenthood v. Pearson, 716 F.2d 1127 (7th Cir. 1983), refused to abstain from ruling on a parental notification statute to allow the state courts to have the opportunity to construe the statute's procedural aspects, and held it unconstitutional. Like the ordinance in Akron, the Indiana statute was silent about many of the judicial procedures required by *Bellotti II,* and, in addition, the court was concerned that many minors would be deterred from seeking waiver of the parental notification requirement pending state interpretation. 716 F.2d at 1133.

50. Since Justice O'Connor would have abstained from deciding the parental consent provision, there is no explicit statement concerning whether or not she would uphold such a provision. It is likely, however, that parental consent and notification provisions would survive under the standard of scrutiny put forth in her dissent. Justice White would uphold parental consent provisions even without a bypass, Bellotti v. Baird, 443 U.S. 622 (1979) (White dissenting). Justice Rehnquist has indicated he would uphold consent provisions with a judicial bypass. *Id*. at 651–52 (Rehnquist, concurring).

51. 103 S. Ct. 2517, 2525, 2526.

52. *Id*. at 2525.

53. 443 U.S. 622; 103 S. Ct. at 2525.

54. 103 S. Ct. at 2531, 2532.

55. Overbreadth has generally been used only in First Amendment–free speech

cases, but at least one justice, Justice Marshall, has suggested that it would be an appropriate basis for challenging parental consent or notification statutes. *See* H.L. v. Matheson, 450 U.S. 398 (J. Marshall, dissenting). The theory behind the overbreadth doctrine is one of deterrence, specifically that certain regulations will have a chilling effect on the exercise of protected rights by placing too great a burden on their exercise and that they further deter a potential litigant from challenging the regulation because she might be reluctant to risk criminal prosecution or private reprisals. *See generally,* Tribe, American Constitutional Law, 1st ed. (1978), at 710–14. Here, laws designed to protect immature minors actually act in nearly every instance to burden "mature" minors who are entitled to full-blown privacy protection. The doctrine has two elements: first, that the protected activity is a significant part of the law's target, and, secondly, that there is no satisfactory way of severing the constitutional from the unconstitutional applications. In these situations, the normal judicial approach of gradually chipping away the constitutional aspects of the statute by invalidating improper applications on a case-by-case basis (*i.e.,* using the as-applied method) is not sufficient. *Id.* at 711.

56. Out of the total of 1478 petitions filed in Minnesota through August 1983, only five were reported to have been denied. Donovan, P., *Judging Teenagers: How Minors Fare When They Seek Court Authorized Abortions,* 15 Fam. Plann. Perspect. 259 (November/December 1983). In this first comprehensive article on the effect of parental consent and notification statutes, the author concludes that "while the judicial bypass laws and procedures . . . may appear reasonable and workable on paper, in practice they constitute a serious, and in some cases insurmountable, barrier confronting minors who wish to obtain abortions." At 259.

57. Parental notification or consent statutes may be unconstitutional under state constitutions or common law. Several state supreme courts have recently ruled that their respective constitutions afford a greater degree of protection to the abortion rights than does the federal Constitution, as outlined in Harris v. McRae, 448 U.S. 297 (1980), and that, as a result, those states must reimburse all medically necessary abortions under their Medicaid plans, so long as they reimburse for pregnancy and childbirth, and so long as they reimburse for all medical services for poor men. *See* Committee to Defend Reproductive Rights v. Myers, 29 Cal. 3d 252, 625 P.2d 779 (1981). Moe v. Secretary of Administration and Finance, 382 Mass. 629, 417 N.E. 2d 387 (1982); Right to Choose v. Byrne, 91 N.J. 287, 450 A.2d 925 (1982). *See also* Fisher v. Department of Public Welfare, 66 Pa. Commw. 70, 444 A.2d 774 (1982); Doe v. Maher, No. 196874 (Conn. Super. Ct., Jud. Dist. of New Haven, August 21, 1981). State constitutions may impose greater constitutional protections on abortion decisions in a variety of ways. For example, the State Supreme Court of California was rigorous in scrutinizing the actual state interest behind the California funding cutoff, finding that, "as far as the interest in encouraging childbirth is concerned, the California legislature has not embraced a general policy of encouraging *unwanted* children." Committee to Defend Reproductive Rights v. Myers, 29 Cal. 3d at 278, 625 P.2d at 795. If this degree of scrutiny were used in minors' cases, a court might find

that the intent was to deter minors' abortions, not to help immature minors, and that such deterrence is at odds with the protected privacy right.

58. Sixteen states now have state equal rights amendments, and these may also provide state constitutional grounds upon which to challenge the parental notice and consent requirements. Since such requirements affect only women, they could be found to constitute unconstitutional sex discrimination, particularly if the statutes are shown to deter teenagers who would otherwise choose abortions and who accordingly suffer the physical, economic, and social consequences of continuous pregnancy and childbirth. Young men are left unencumbered in their reproductive decisions while young women are not, and restrictions on reproductive freedom have been the historical means by which all women have been kept from full and equal participation in the society. *See,* Law, S., *Rethinking Sex and the Constitution,* Penn. L. Rev., (June 1984). Furthermore, state ERAs may encourage courts to examine more carefully all asserted state interests, since the standard of review would be one of strict scrutiny. *See* Petition of New Bedford Child and Family Services, 385 Mass. 482, 432 N.E.2d 103 (1982); Page v. Welfare Commissioner, 170 Conn. 258, 365 A.2d 1118 (1976); R. McG. v. J.W., 200 Colo. 345, 615 P.2d 666 (1980). *See also,* Fischer v. Department of Public Welfare, No. 283 C.D. 1981 (Pa. Commw. Ct. March 9, 1984), wherein the Pennsylvania Commonwealth Court held that the state's restrictions on Medicaid funding for abortion violate the ERA guarantees of the state constitution by unlawfully discriminating against women with respect to a physical condition unique to women.

59. *See* note 1 *supra.*

60. In addition to state and local legislation requiring notice or consent, many abortion providers voluntarily impose such requirements. According to a survey of abortion providers, 38 percent of hospitals and 19 percent of clinics have parental consent or notification requirements for minors under 18; and 48 percent and 38 percent of hospitals and clinics respectively have such requirements for those under 15. Torres, J.D. Forrest & S. Eisman, *Telling Parents: Clinic Policies and Adolescents' Use of Family Planning and Abortion Services,* 12 Fam. Plann. Perspect. 284 (November/December 1980).

61. Ariz. Rev. Stat. Ann. § 36–2152 (1982) is in facial conflict with the Court's decisions in *Akron, Ashcroft,* and *Bellotti,* since it does not provide any explicit procedural guarantees such as expeditious adjudication of the petition, or anonymity of the minor in the court proceedings. Idaho Code § 18–609, subd. 6 (Supp. 1982–83) does not contain a judicial bypass and should be declared unconstitutional under *Akron* and *Bellotti.* Illinois's Parental Notification of Abortion Act of 1983, SB5211, contains a judicial bypass, and the act has been challenged on the grounds that it fails to assure expedited resolution of an appeal from the denial of a petition, fails to adequately guarantee that the proceedings will be completed with anonymity, and fails to provide an effective opportunity for a minor to seek judicial waiver. The law has been permanently enjoined, Zbaraz v. Hartigan, 584 F. Supp. 1452 (N.D. Ill. 1984); *vacated in part and remanded,* 763 F.2d 1532 (7th Cir. 1532 (1985); *appeal pending* nos. 84–1958, 84–1959). It is unclear

whether this judicial bypass complies with the requirements of *Bellotti*. Ky. Rev. Stat. § 311.732 (Bobbs-Merrill 1983), has been permanently enjoined and Eubanks v. Brown, 604 F. Supp. 141 (W.D. Ky. 1984) contained a judicial bypass which contained a statutory presumption that the court first consult the parents of a minor before adjudicating the petition under a "best interests" test, and thus conflicted with *Bellotti*. Me. Rev. Stat. Ann. tit. 22, § 1597 (1980), has been permanently enjoined, Women's Community Health Center v. Cohen, No. 79–162P CD. Me. Sept. 13, 1983, does not have a judicial bypass and is thus unconstitutional under *Bellotti*. Mont. Code Ann. § 50–20–107 (1981) contains no judicial bypass and is clearly unconstitutional under *Bellotti*. Neb. Rev. Stat. § 28–347 (Supp. 1981), was recently struck down by a federal court, Orr v. Knowles, No. CV 81–0–301 (D. Neb. September 19, 1983). The court held the law's 24-hour notice requirement an unconstitutional interference with the abortion right under *Akron* and held that the judicial bypass did not contain sufficient procedural guarantees, *i.e.,* it failed to assume a speedy, nonburdensome substitute and did not provide for appointment of counsel to minors. 1985 Nev. Stat. ch. 681, currently under court injunction, § 8, Glick v. McKay, CV–R–85–331–BCR CD Nev. July 17, 1985. The Abortion Control Act passed in Pennsylvania, 18 Pa. Cons. Stat. Ann. § 3206 (Purdon Supp. 1983–84), requires parental consent but allows for a judicial bypass. This law has been challenged on the grounds that it contains fewer procedural guarantees than is required by *Ashcroft*. American College of Obstetricians and Gynecologists v. Thorndurgh, 699 F.2d 644 (1983), *review granted*, 53 U.S.L.W. 3726 (U.S. 4/16/85 No. 84–495). The Utah parental notification statute, Utah Code Ann. § 76–7–304 (1978), does not contain any judicial bypass. This notice was upheld by the Supreme Court in H.L. v. Matheson, 450 U.S. 398 (1981), but only as to the class of minors represented by the sole plaintiff, immature minors living at home who had no reasons why their parents should not be notified.

62. For statute cites, *see* note 1 *supra*. Although the Supreme Court upheld the facial constitutionality of the Missouri statute challenged in *Ashcroft,* the statute was subsequently enjoined as unconstitutional since no appellate procedures were implemented. *T.L.J. v. Ashcroft,* No. 83–4398–CV–C–5 (W.D. Mo., November 4, 1983).

63. Four Justices of the Supreme Court have already stated that they believe that the burden of initiating a judicial proceeding is such an obstacle for a minor that when parental consent statutes are at issue, even with a judicial bypass, they violate minors' privacy rights. Planned Parenthood of Central Missouri v. Ashcroft, 103 S. Ct. at 2531. (Blackmun, Brennan, Marshall, and Stevens, JJ., dissenting).

64. H.L. v. Matheson, 450 U.S. at 411; Bellotti v. Baird, 443 U.S. at 637–39.

65. Planned Parenthood of Central Missouri v. Ashcroft, 103 S. Ct. at 2525; H.L. v. Matheson, 450 U.S. at 41; Bellotti v. Baird, 443 U.S. at 634–37.

66. 450 U.S. at 411.

67. *Id.,* citing Harris v. McRae, 448 U.S. 297, 325 (1980).

68. In his dissenting opinion from a three-judge court decision holding a Massachusetts parental consent requirement unconstitutional, Senior District Judge Julian found that the statute would protect "the rights of parents

to the liberties guaranteed them by the Fifth and Fourteenth Amendments."
Baird v. Bellotti, 393 F. Supp. 847, 862 (D. Mass. 1975). Judge Julian found
that the statute furthered the state's "compelling interest in protecting the
parental rights and duties against unauthorized intrusion by third persons."
Id. at 861; Baird v. Bellotti, 450 F. Supp. 997, 1019 (D. Mass. 1973) (Judge
Julian, dissenting).

69. The dissenting opinions of those justices in the Court's decisions invalidating
parental consent statutes have not articulated this as a ground for upholding
the constitutionality of the statutes. In Danforth, 428 U.S. 52 (1976), and
Bellotti II, 443 U.S. 622 (1979), the dissenting opinions by Justice White,
joined by Chief Justice Burger and Justice Rehnquist in *Danforth*, would
have upheld the statutes in question on the basis that the State is entitled to
"protect" minors in making the abortion decision by requiring parental
consent. Bellotti II, 443 U.S. at 656–57; Danforth, 428 U.S. at 94–95. *See
also*, Danforth, 428 U.S. at 101–05 (Stevens, J., concurring in part and
dissenting in part).

70. In Doe v. Irwin, 615 F.2d 1162 (6th Cir.), *cert. denied*, 449 U.S. 829 (1980),
a case brought by parents against a publicly operated family planning center
and county officials alleging that the center's distribution of contraceptives
to unemancipated minors without the consent or knowledge of their parents,
violated parents' constitutional rights, the Sixth Circuit found no unconstitutional interference with plaintiffs' rights as parents. The court distinguished this case from the established line of cases recognizing the right of
parents to the care, custody, and nurture of their children (Meyer v.
Nebraska, 262 U.S. 390 [1923]; Pierce v. Society of Sisters, 268 U.S. 510
[1925]; Wisconsin v. Yoder, 406 U.S. 205 [1972]) in that those cases involved
state requirements or prohibitions of some activities, whereas in the *Irwin*
case, the state did not impose any compulsory requirements or prohibitions
which would affect the rights of parents.

71. The state must have a "significant state interest" for the minors' abortion
regulation, Danforth, 428 U.S. 52; Carey v. Population Services International, 431 U.S. 678, 693 n. 15 (plurality opinion); Akron, 103 S. Ct. at 2491,
n. 10, rather than a compelling interest, Roe v. Wade, 410 U.S. at 162–65, or
merely any interest at all. The state must also prove that the regulations
actually further the asserted interest, Carey, 431 U.S. at 696 (plurality
opinion) (*see* also Justice White concurring at 703); Danforth, 428 U.S. 75.
And the laws must be carefully drawn to interfere with privacy to the least
degree possible. See H.L. v. Matheson, 450 U.S. at 413, articulating though
not, in fact, applying, the test that statutes affecting minors' rights to
abortion must serve important state interests, be narrowly drawn to protect
only those interests, and must not violate any guarantees of the Constitution;
see also, Wynn v. Carey, 582 F.2d 1375 (7th Cir., 1978), interpreting *Roe,
Carey,* and *Danforth* to require that statutes interfering with minors'
fundamental rights must be narrowly drawn to express only the legitimate
interests of the state.

72. Planned Parenthood League of Massachusetts v. Bellotti, *aff'd in relevant
part,* 641 F.2d 1006 (1st Cir. 1981) (interlocutory appeal); Margaret S. v.
Edwards, No. 78–2765 Sec. C (E.D. La. November 27, 1981); Hodgson v.

Minnesota, 3–81 Civ. 538 (D. Minn. March 22, 1982); T.L.J. v. Ashcroft No. 83–4398–CV–C–5 (W.D. Mo., November 4, 1983).

73. Like the psychological harms of segregation considered in Brown v. Board of Education, 347 U.S. 483, 493–95 (1953), the psychological, sociological, and physical effects of pregnancy and abortion have taken on constitutional dimensions in Supreme Court decisions. For example, in Roe v. Wade, 410 U.S. at 153, the Court cited the harms resulting from pregnancy in support of the determination that the right to privacy is broad enough to encompass a woman's decision whether or not to terminate her pregnancy. The Court stated: "The detriment that the state would impose upon the pregnant woman by denying this choice altogether is apparent. Specific and direct harm medically diagnosable even in early pregnancy may be involved. Maternity, or additional offspring, may force upon the woman a distressful life and future. Psychological harm may be imminent. Mental and physical health may be taxed by child care. There is also the distress, for all concerned, associated with the unwanted child, and there is the problem of bringing a child into a family already unable, psychologically and otherwise, to care for it. In other cases . . . the additional difficulties and continuing stigma of unwed motherhood may be involved." The irreparable effects of teenage pregnancy were recognized by the Court in Michael M. v. Superior Court of Sonoma County. 450 U.S. 464 (1981) and Bellotti v. Baird, 443 U.S. 662. In *Bellotti,* Justice Powell observed, "[T]he potentially severe detriment facing a pregnant woman (citing *Roe* at 153) is not mitigated by her minority. Indeed considering her probable education, employment skills, financial resources and emotional maturity, unwanted motherhood may be exceptionally burdensome for a minor," 443 U.S. at 642. Justice Rehnquist, in *Michael M.,* made a similar observation, stating: "[T]eenage pregnancies, which have increased dramatically over the last two decades, have significant social, medical, and economic consequences for both the minor and her child, and the State." 450 U.S. at 470.

74. Teenage Pregnancy: The Problem That Hasn't Gone Away, Alan Guttmacher Institute, 1981.

75. *Id.* at 5.

76. *Id.* at 17, 21.

77. The risk of maternal death for minors under age 15 is two and a half times the rate for mothers aged 20 to 24, and nonfatal complications are also higher for teens than for others. Statistics between 1975 and 1978 reveal that teenage mothers were 15 percent more likely to suffer from toxemia, 92 percent more likely to have anemia, and 23 percent more likely to suffer from complications attendant upon a premature birth than were mothers who gave birth between the ages of 20 and 24. *Id.* at 29.

78. *See* Michael M. v. Superior Court of Sonoma County, 450 U.S. at 470 n. 4, (Stewart, J., concurring).

79. Teicher, *A Solution to the Chronic Problem of Living: Adolescent Attempted Suicide,* in Current Issues in Adolescent Psychiatry 129, 136 (J. Schoolar, ed. 1973).

80. *Teenage Pregnancy, supra* note 74, at 29.

81. Michael M. v. Superior Court of Sonoma County, 450 U.S. at 471.

82. Roe v. Wade, 410 U.S. at 149, 163; Akron v. Akron Center for Reproductive Health, 103 S. Ct. at 2492, n. 11.

83. In *Akron,* the Court struck down a variety of "abortion-inhibiting" regulations (103 S. Ct. at 2487, n. 1) which, rather than furthering women's health, actually threatened it. For example, the Court struck down a regulation which required that all second-trimester abortions be performed in a hospital, stating, "It requires no great familiarity with the cost and limited availability of such hospitals to appreciate that the effect of [upholding this regulation] would be to drive the performance of many abortions back underground free of effective regulation and often without the attendance of a physician." *Id.* This regulation would result "in both financial expense and additional health risk." *Id* at 2495. The Court also struck down a 24-hour waiting period requirement which had no medical basis, increased the cost of obtaining an abortion, and which plaintiffs contended would cause health-threatening delay. *Id.* at 2503. *See* Cates et al., *Sounding Board: Regulation of Abortion Services—For Better or Worse?* 301 N.E. J. of Med. 720–23, (1979). And in *Danforth,* the Court struck down a statute prohibiting the use of saline amniocentesis in part because this prohibition would force women to use more dangerous techniques. 428 U.S. at 78.

84. The risk of death and major complications from abortion rises with every week the procedure is delayed after the eighth week. Delays are particularly serious for minors, because they generally delay seeking abortions in the first place until the later, riskier weeks of gestation. *Teenage Pregnancy, supra* note 74, at 55. And the increased expense and time means added emotional stress and disruption of home and work life.

85. A study of 17 illegal abortion deaths from 1975 to 1979 revealed that one-third of the women sought illegal abortions because legal abortions were either too expensive or not readily available in their areas. Binkin, Gold & Cates, Jr., *Illegal Abortion Deaths in the United States: Why Are They Still Occurring?* 14 Fam. Plann. Perspect. 163 (May/June 1982). Suicide is also the result of such regulations. *See, e.g.,* the case of a pregnant 17-year-old in Ohio who attempted suicide by shooting herself in the abdomen because she did not have the $600 cash needed to pay for an abortion in a Cleveland hospital. "Suicide Attempt Failure for Teen but Fetus Dies," *The Plain Dealer,* July 28, 1979, at 5a, col. 1.

86. Justice Marshall, in his dissent on *Matheson,* did posit that these statutes would have an impact on the actions of pregnant teenagers: "[T]he threat of notice may cause minor women to delay past the first trimester of pregnancy, after which the health risks increase significantly. Other pregnant minors may attempt to self-abort or to obtain an illegal abortion rather than risk parental notification. Still others may forsake an abortion and bear an unwanted child . . ." 450 U.S. at 439, 440. He also noted, "Besides revealing a confidential decision, the parental notice requirement may limit access to the means of effectuating that decision." *Id.* at 438, quoting Carey v. Population Services International, 431 U.S. 678, 688. Many minor women will encounter interference from their parents after state-imposed notification. In addition to parental disappointment and disapproval, the minor may confront physical or emotional abuse, withdrawal of financial support, or

actual obstruction of the abortion decision. H.L. v. Matheson, 450 U.S. at 438, 439.

87. Both studies and actual experience show that mandatory parental involvement statutes deter and delay teenagers from seeking medical help. In a study of unmarried teenage abortion patients, approximately one-quarter of those surveyed said that they would not come to an abortion clinic if parental notification were required. The responses indicated that "a sizable proportion of teenagers believe that the notification of their parents would put them in a desperate situation and that they would be forced to resort to desperate measures to deal with it." Torres, Forrest & Eisman, *Telling Parents: Clinic Policies and Adolescents' Use of Family Planning and Abortion Services,* 12 Fam. Plann. Perspect. 284, (November/December 1980) 288. The experience in Minnesota and Massachusetts has shown a marked decrease in the number of abortions performed on minors after the laws went into effect. In Minnesota, the number of minors' abortions decreased by nearly 33 percent between 1980, the last full year without the notification law, and 1982. In Massachusetts, there was a decrease of 34 percent between 1980, the last full year without the consent requirement, and 1981, the year the law went into effect. Donovan, *Judging Teenagers: How Minors Fare When They Seek Court-Authorized Abortions,* 15 Fam. Plann. Perspect. 259, 266 (November/December 1983). Parental consent and notification provisions for contraceptive services similarly deter minors. *See* State of N.Y. v. Schweiker, 557 F. Supp. 354 (S.D.N.Y. 1983), *aff'd,* Nos. 1318, 1531, (2d Cir. 1983); Planned Parenthood Federation of America, Inc. v. Schweiker, 559 F. Supp. 658 (D.D.C. 1983), *aff'd sub nom.* Planned Parenthood Federation of America v. Heckler, 712 F.2d 650 (D.C. Cir. 1983). Chamie et al. *Factors Affecting Adolescents' Use of Family Planning Clinics,* 14 Fam. Plann. Perspect. 126 (May/June 1982); A. Torres, *Does Your Mother Know. . .?* 10 Fam. Plann. Perspect. 280 (September/October 1978).

88. *Id.*

89. This statute requires notification of both parents of unemancipated minors, even if the parents are living apart, divorced, have never married, or if custody has been granted one, etc. Minn. Stat. § 144.343, subds. 2–4.

90. In 1980, 39 percent of teenagers obtaining abortions in Minnesota traveled 50 miles or more to reach an abortion provider, and 15.9 percent of the teenagers traveled over 200 miles. See, Affidavit of Jane Hodgson, M.D., dated July 27, 1981, Exh. B, Hodgson v. Minnesota, 3–81 Civ. 538 (D. Minn. filed July 30, 1981).

91. See, Findings of Fact, Conclusions of Law and Order, at 5, Hodgson v. Minnesota 3–81 Civ. 538 (D. Minn. March 22, 1982).

92. Sixty-seven percent of those aged 15 or younger had told one parent, while only 40 percent of those aged 16 or 17 had done so. Affidavit of Ronald Anderson, Ph.D., dated July 28, 1981 at 4, Hodgson v. Minnesota, No. 3–81 Civ. 538 (D. Minn. filed July 30, 1981).

93. Between 1980, the last full year without the notification law, and 1982, the number of abortions performed on minors in the state dropped from 2327 to 1567, a decrease of nearly 33 percent. Similarly, the number of abortions performed minors in Massachusetts dropped by 34 percent between 1980 and

1981, the year that state's parental consent law went into effect. Donovan, *supra* note 87, at 30.

94. Cartoof, *Parental Consent for Abortion: A Case Study of the Consequences of Massachusetts' Law* (1984) (submitted for publication).

95. *See* Donovan, *supra* note 87, at 261–62.

96. Telephone survey conducted by Myra Needleman, summer 1983 law intern to American Civil Liberties Union Foundation Reproductive Freedom Project, July 1983. The results of the survey showed that, overall, there has been no trend of minors leaving Minnesota for abortions.

97. See Donovan, *supra* note 87, at 264; Hudgins, "Abortion Law Creates Delays, Irritates Judges," *The Minneapolis Star,* October 30, 1981, at 1, col. 1. Over 97 percent of the petitions filed in Minnesota through August 1983 were heard in one of three counties (Hennepin, Ramsey, and St. Louis). Donovan, *supra,* at 264.

98. The loss of privacy surrounding the abortion decision for minor and adult women subjects them to the possibility of harrassment. *See, e.g.,* the Chicago anti-abortion group which hired a private detective to track down a mother who wanted to obtain an abortion for her pregnant 11-year-old daughter. The group went to the family's home to persuade the girl not to have the abortion and picketed the hospital where they expected her to have the abortion. "Agent Hired in Fight to Prevent Abortion of 11-Year-Old Girl," *New York Times,* June 10, 1982.

99. Those involved with the minors' petitions in Minnesota have noted that it is mostly white, middle-class and upper middle-class teenagers who are utilizing the judicial alternative system. See Donovan, *supra* note 87, at 262, at 11–12; Parry, "Teen Abortion Rate in State Drops by 28%," *Minneapolis Star and Tribune,* Oct. 20, 1983, at 1A, col 1.

100. Those involved in the administration of parental notification and consent provisions have observed that what these laws do accomplish is to erect a barrier to obtaining an abortion and to put minors who go to court through an emotionally difficult and sometimes traumatic experience. Donovan, *supra* note 87, at 260.

101. Donovan notes that a "substantial number of minors in Massachusetts and Minnesota go to court even though one parent is aware of their pregnancy and supports their decision to have an abortion." *Id.* at 262.

102. The interests proffered by the state in support of the notification law are "to protect the interest of the minor woman in making the [abortion] decision and to encourage and foster her relationships with her parents." State Defendants Memorandum of Points and Authorities in Opposition to Motion for Preliminary Injunction, *Hodgson v. Minnesota,* No. 3–81 Civ. 538 (D. Minn. filed August 28, 1981).

103. The Supreme Court decisions involving minors' rights to abortion do not define the term "immaturity". It should be noted that, even without a mandatory notification requirement, physicians, as a matter of course, will not perform abortions on minors who are too immature to give informed consent without the involvement of a parent, other adult family member, social worker, etc.

104. Interviews with Judge George O. Peterson, Ramsey County Juvenile Court,

and Judge Allen Oleisky, District Court of Minnesota, Fourth Judicial District, Juvenile Court Division, in Minneapolis, August 1, 1983).

105. As the Honorable Nanette Dembitz of Family Court of the State of New York observed, parents "who have opposed their unmarried daughters' efforts to secure abortions variously have expressed a vengeful desire to punish the daughter for her sexual activity by making her suffer the unwanted child, a fervor to impose a religious conviction the mother has failed to instill in her daughter, a hope of caring for her daughter's baby as her own because of an inability or unwillingness to bear another child herself, a defensive or resentful attitude because [the mother of the pregnant minor] bore illegitimate children without seeking or being able to secure an abortion, or a general distaste for abortion. None of these parental reasons for objecting relates to the daughter's well-being—only to that of the mother." Dembitz, *The Supreme Court and a Minor's Abortion Decision*, 80 Colum. L. Rev. 1251, 1255 (1980). Cases in which a parent has opposed an abortion despite the circumstances surrounding the minor's pregnancy and the welfare of the minor are not unknown in the courts. One example involves a court action where the mother of a 12-year-old girl who was raped by three teenagers and became pregnant and contracted VD as a result sought to prevent the daughter from having an abortion because of the mother's religious beliefs. The district court of Oklahoma issued an order finding that the life of the minor was endangered as a result of the pregnancy and ordering that the girl be made a ward of the court as deprived and that the state be authorized to consent to the abortion and any other necessary medical treatment. The mother pursued her opposition to the abortion to the state supreme court, which affirmed the lower court's order. *In re D.C.*, JF–81–1555 (Okla. Dist. Ct. Okla. Ct. Okla. Cty., September 23, 1981), *aff'd*, No. 57,472 (Okla. Sup. Ct. September 28, 1981).

106. As Justice Powell stated in Bellotti v. Baird, 443 U.S. at 638, "[A]ffirmative sponsorship of particular ethical, religious, or political beliefs is something we expect the state *not* to attempt in a society constitutionally committed to the ideal of individual liberty and freedom of choice."

107. *See Safe and Legal: 10 Years' Experience With Legal Abortion in New York State*, The Alan Guttmacher Institute (1980). The report concludes that legal abortions help reduce high teen birthrates and their adverse economic and social consequences. *See also*, Cates, *Legal Abortion: The Public Health Record*, 215 Science 1586 (1982).

Some authorities on constitutional law claim that the *Roe* decision is one that will go down in history as one of the weaker reasoned cases of the Supreme Court. Mark Tushnet discusses both the strengths and weaknesses of the *Roe* decision along with other cases which may have added to the confusion on the abortion issue.

5 · The Supreme Court on Abortion: A Survey _____

Mark Tushnet, J.D.

Since 1973, when the Supreme Court held in *Roe v. Wade*[1] that the Constitution limited the states' power to restrict the availability of abortions, it has decided a number of cases that establish the contours of the right to an abortion. These decisions remain controversial not only because of deep social division over the issue but also because of disquiet about the constitutional premises of *Roe v. Wade* and about the coherence of the post-*Roe v. Wade* doctrine the Court has developed. This article first surveys the Supreme Court's abortion decisions, and then describes the controversy over the fundamental propriety of *Roe v. Wade* as a matter of constitutional theory. Finally, it examines difficulties found in the present doctrinal structure of the constitutional law of abortion.

I. The Supreme Court Cases

In *Roe v. Wade,* the Court found a constitutional right on the part of a pregnant woman, in conjunction with her physician, to decide to have an abortion. That right, the Court held, had to be balanced against two state interests: preserving the health of the woman in the actual performance of the abortion, and protecting the potentiality of human life. As the Court has gone about the job of striking the balance, it has evolved a general approach to the abortion issue in constitutional law.

    Roe v. Wade divided the period of pregnancy into three stages. In roughly the first trimester, "the abortion decision . . . must be left to the medical judgment of the pregnant woman [and her] attending physician,"[2] but the state may adopt regulations "that have no significant impact on the woman's exercise of her right [if they are] justified by important state health objectives."[3] During the second trimester, or—what the Court has regarded as equivalent—until the fetus becomes viable, the state may adopt regulations reasonably related to the health of the woman. After viability, the state may prohibit all abortions, except those necessary to preserve the woman's life or health. Despite the apparent differences in the tests at each stage, the Court has defined the terms it uses to create a unified approach: It has prohibited regulations that unduly burden the decision to have or to refrain from having an abortion. The "undue burden" approach has been applied in three groups of cases. The first, of which *Roe v. Wade* is an example, involves regulations of the abortion process itself. These regulations have a relatively direct effect on the woman's decision in the name of preserving her health or protecting potential life. The second group involves regulations designed to promote the interests of persons other than the woman and the potential infant. The third involves regulation of the financing of abortion.

A. Direct Regulation of the Abortion Decision

Roe v. Wade recognized that states had interests in protecting maternal health and potential life. Probably most state regulation of the abortion decision is intended to advance the state's interest in potential life. Yet because abortion today means both the removal of the fetus from its carrier's womb and its destruction, there is no obvious way simultaneously to permit abortions and advance the interest in potential life. Thus, most of the accommodations between the woman's "privacy" interests and state interests deal with the woman's health.

The final stage of pregnancy under *Roe v. Wade* occurs after the fetus becomes viable.[4] After viability, the state could regulate or prohibit abortions unless they were "necessary, in appropriate medical judgment," to preserve the life or health of the woman. This standard must be read, however, in light of the Court's decision the same day in *Doe v. Bolton,* that clinical judgment "may be exercised in light of all factors—physical, emotional, psychological, familial, and the woman's age—relevant to the well-being of the patient."[5] Thus, the Court nominally allowed the state to prohibit post-viability abortions except in apparently limited cases, but it actually defined the limitation in a way that bars a state from prohibiting such abortions if physicians are willing to perform them.

In a later case the Court sustained a statute defining viability as the stage when the fetus's life "may be continued outside the womb by the natural or artificial life-supportive systems."[6] This definition allows the state to regulate the decision to have an abortion, a decision made while the fetus is in the womb, on the basis of what must at that time be a prediction about what will happen after the fetus is removed from the womb. The uncertainty of this prediction might lead physicians to refrain from performing abortions if, as *Roe* seemed to suggest, states could readily prohibit post-viability abortions. The Court thus stressed that viability was essentially a medical judgment, and invalidated a law making physicians criminally liable for performing abortions when the fetus "is viable" or when there is "sufficient reason to believe that the fetus may be viable."[7] The threat of criminal liability in the face of the uncertainty associated with viability determinations unacceptably burdened the abortion decision.

In the same case the Court held unconstitutionally vague a provision requiring that the physician use the abortion technique making fetal survival most likely, so long as no other technique was necessary to protect the woman's health or life. These decisions severely restrict what the state may do to protect the potential life of the fetus even after viability, when *Roe v. Wade* holds that the state's interest in protecting potential life is compelling. However, the Court has upheld a requirement that two physicians attend a post-viability abortion, one to care for the woman and the other to care for the fetus.[8] Even though the two-physician requirement increases the cost of an abortion and even though most abortion techniques now inevitably lead to the destruction of the fetus, the state's interest in protecting potential life outweighed the cost impact on the woman's decision to have an abortion.

Some regulations are designed to serve both women's health and potential life interests. *Doe v. Bolton* invalidated requirements that a hospital committee approve abortions and that two physicians other than the woman's agree that an abortion was appropriate.[9] Where post-viability abortions are involved, such requirements might inform the attending physician's judgment about whether the stage of viability had been reached and about the proper abortion technique to use. While the Court did not discuss whether these requirements could be applied only to post-viability abortions, presumably the regulations also impose too substantial a burden on the abortion decision at that stage.

The Court has upheld requirements that special records be kept when abortions are performed,[10] and that pathology examinations be done on tissues removed during abortions.[11] These requirements provide the basis for medical studies of abortion practices and for diagnoses of conditions associated with pregnancy. According to the Court, these regulations did not impose an undue burden on the abortion decision even though they increased the costs of abortion by $20 to $40, or roughly 10 percent to 20 percent of the cost of a first-trimester abortion.

Roe v. Wade allows states to regulate second-trimester abortions in ways "reasonably related to maternal health."[12] The Court has been rather severe in its application of the "reasonableness" standard. For example, Missouri's legislature apparently believed that a relatively novel second-trimester abortion technique was safer for women than the widely available saline amniocentesis technique. The Court held that because Missouri's preferred technique was essentially unavailable in Missouri, its prohibition of saline amniocentesis was unreasonable.[13]

In *Roe v. Wade,* the Court suggested that the interest in the woman's health would justify a requirement that second-trimester abortions be performed in a hospital.[14] More recently, relying on a newly adopted position by medical organizations that clinics were no less safe for their patients than hospitals, the Court invalidated a requirement that second-trimester abortions be performed in hospitals.[15] Outpatient abortions could be performed safely by techniques available in clinics, and the risks of complications requiring the services of a full hospital were not so great as to justify a ban on such relatively inexpensive and accessible abortion.

Abortions are medical techniques and, as such, are subject to the common requirement that patients give informed consent to the procedures used.[16] But the Court has not been receptive to claims that abortion is so stressful a procedure that special safeguards are needed to ensure that the consent is truly informed. It invalidated a requirement that the procedure could not occur until 24 hours after the consent form had been signed.[17] This increased the cost by requiring two separate trips and complicating the scheduling of abortions, and did not enhance the quality of the woman's consent as derived from her physician's advice. In the same case the Court insisted that the physician, not the state, determine what information must be provided for the consent to be truly informed. It invalidated an ordinance requiring the attending physician personally to inform the woman of the stage of the fetus's development, its date of possible viability, the physical and emotional complications of abortion, and the availability of agencies to assist in adoption and childbirth.[18] The Court was skeptical about the claim that this information was designed to improve the quality of consent. Some of the required information was a "parade of horribles," and another item was that the fetus was "a human life from the moment of conception"; these requirements were intended not to inform consent but "to persuade [the woman] to withhold it altogether."[19] In addition, the Court believed that requiring the physician to recite a "litany of information" interfered with the physician's discretion to decide what information was appropriate in individual cases.[20]

In sum, the Court has substantially restricted the kinds of regulations a state may adopt to protect potential life by requiring that abortions be allowed where necessary to protect the woman's life or health and then by giving "health" a broad definition. Similarly, it has restricted the regulations a state may adopt to protect the woman's health by insisting that those regulations conform to standard medical judgments. Direct regulation of the abortion decision is therefore quite difficult.

B. Regulation to Promote "Third-Party" Interests

The fetus, the physician, and the woman are not the only ones affected by an abortion, though they may be more affected than the putative father or the woman's parents. The Court has concluded that these others have interests in the abortion decision but that the woman's interest is primary and that regulations must be justified by reasons of health. Applying these tenets, the Court has not allowed states to advance the interests of these "third parties" very effectively.

Third-party interests might be advanced by requiring that they consent to an abortion or that they be notified prior to an abortion so that they might attempt to influence the woman's decision. Third-party consent statutes, giving spouses or parents a right to veto the woman's decision, have been rejected as unduly burdensome.[21] However, the Court has been concerned that some minors might not be mature enough to give a truly informed consent to abortion. Parental consent or notification might have been seen as an effort to improve the quality of the minor's consent. But the Court has held that the state must offer an alternative to parental consent by allowing the minor to establish to a court's satisfaction either that she is "mature and well-informed enough to make intelligently the abortion decision on her own," or that an abortion would be in her best interest.[22] H.L. v. Matheson[23] upheld a narrowly construed notification requirement applicable to minors who did not claim to be either mature or at odds with their parents, and who were living with or dependent on their parents. These limitations are likely to give the approval of the notification requirements little practical significance.

C. Financing Abortions

In a society where most goods are available only to those who can pay the going price, we usually do not think that the government imposes a burden on a person's decision to consume something when it simply allows the market to operate. Thus it would seem obvious that the principles of *Roe v. Wade* would not be violated if the government did nothing with respect to the financing of abortions but instead let women purchase abortions if they could afford to pay for them. Faced with the question of whether it violated the Constitution to refuse to subsidize abortions through the Medicaid system, the Court divided 5–4 in upholding that refusal.[24]

The Hyde Amendment prohibited federal funding for almost all abortions.[25] Those who challenged it raised a number of arguments. They began by noting that the government had made a decision that the medical needs of poor people would not be subject to the usual forces of the marketplace. When the government refused to pay for abortions, it placed a burden on the woman's decision because its actions had created an expectation that all medical services for poor women would be subsidized, and because by funding childbirth but not abortion, the government made it more difficult for a poor woman to choose to have an abortion.[26] The Court rejected these arguments, saying that the government could not "place obstacles in the path of a woman's exercise of her freedom of choice, [but] it need not remove those not of its own creation."[27] The inability to pay a market price for an abortion was not created by the government; thus poor women were no worse off under the Hyde Amendment than they had been when all medical services had to be purchased on the market. Because the denial of funding did not burden the right to choose an abortion, funding childbirth but not abortion was constitutional if Congress had some reason to believe that the distinction served permissible governmental goals. The Court acknowledged that abortions were less costly than childbirth, but found the distinction justified by the permissible goal of protecting potential life.

Despite this decision, a number of state courts have found that denial of funds for abortions violates state constitutions, and some legislatures have chosen to provide funds for abortions.[28] The Supreme Court's decision on financing abortions appears to have affected primarily poor women in less populous states who find it difficult to travel to other states soon enough to be eligible for public financing of their abortions.

II. The Criticisms of *Roe v. Wade*

Most academic commentators probably believe that, as a matter of sound public policy, access to abortions should be relatively unrestricted. But none has been able to provide conclusive arguments that the Supreme Court correctly found that policy in the Constitution. Criticisms of *Roe v. Wade* fall into two categories. The first focuses on the logic of the decision itself. The second asserts that the decision cannot be reconciled with any general theoretical approach to constitutional adjudication.

A. The Logic of *Roe v. Wade*

As we will see, much of the controversy over *Roe v. Wade* questions its fundamental premise, that a woman has a constitutionally protected right to have an abortion. Once that right is established, it seems sensible to balance it against state interests. Yet the Court's threefold classification may have the balance backwards, and in any event is subject to increasing instability as technology develops to allow fetuses to develop outside the womb.

The Court recognized a state interest in protecting potential life. It concluded that the strength of that interest increased as the fetus approached viability, and might outweigh the woman's interest after viability, and that the state could prohibit post-viability abortions except to preserve the woman's life or health. If viability means ability to survive outside the womb, the Court's rule is quite odd. A fetus removed from the womb after viability can by definition survive on its own (or aided by mechanical devices). The state's interest in protecting potential life is not advanced by prohibiting a post-viability removal of the fetus from the womb. Conversely, its interest in protecting potential life is greatest at the early stages of pregnancy, when the potentiality of life cannot be realized unless the pregnancy continues.

The Court's confusion on this issue probably resulted from its failure to distinguish between two aspects of an abortion. An abortion removes the fetus from the womb and, under present conditions, destroys the fetus. If all abortions are destructive removals, the Court's position on post-viability destructive removals makes more sense. After viability the alternative to a destructive removal is a nondestructive one: instead of an abortion, a premature delivery. The state's interest in potential life is properly regarded as greater where nondestructive removals result in live births.

The distinction between removal and destruction also makes the Court's threefold classification unstable as medical specialists develop the technology for nondestructive removal and for sustaining fetuses in artifical environments until they are able to survive on their own. These developments will create anomalies in the second trimester. Suppose that after a nondestructive removal, the abortus can be sustained until "viability." This possibility itself would make the fetus viable, and the nondestructive removal could therefore be prohibited, in which case the difficulty noted above, the state's lack of interest in such a prohibition, would arise. Alternatively, the fetus would not be viable, and only regulations aimed at the woman's health would be permitted under the Court's approach. Yet if the nondestructive technique were widely available and posed no greater threats to the woman's health than destructive techniques, it is difficult to understand why the state could not require that the nondestructive technique be used even though that requirement promotes only the interest in potential life, which is assumed to be less than compelling in the second trimester.[29]

Technological developments will also make the date of viability occur earlier in pregnancy. At some point the Court's second stage will disappear, and then there will be a square conflict between its toleration of prohibitions on post-viability abortions and its insistence that at the early stages of pregnancy the state may not impose significant burdens on the woman's decision.

B. Constitutional Theory

As mentioned above, the primary challenge to *Roe v. Wade* comes from those who cannot reconcile it with general theories of constitutional adjudication. For convenience, those theories can be collected into three groups: those concerned with constitutional text and judicial precedent, those concerned with morality, and those concerned with the processes of democratic decisionmaking.

1.   TEXT AND PRECEDENT   One way to decide constitutional cases is to rely on the text of the Constitution and its history. *Roe v. Wade* paid little attention to the text as a source of the woman's right. Instead it devoted a surprising amount of space to the question of whether fetuses were "persons" within the meaning of the Constitution.[30] The Court stated that the case against restrictions on abortion would "collapse" if fetuses were persons, but this seems wrong. Many constitutional cases are resolved by balancing competing constitutional interests, and if the fetus were a person, the issue would still remain of what accommodation the Constitution requires between the fetus's right to life and the woman's right to privacy. Nor, of course, does the conclusion that the fetus is not a person within the meaning of the Constitution establish that the woman's right necessarily prevails. States may choose to protect the interests of beings that are nonhuman, as in prohibitions on cruelty to animals. When it protects interests not grounded in the Constitution, the state may nonetheless inhibit constitutionally protected interests. For example, the state may prohibit embezzlement and it may restrict speech that creates an imminent danger that embezzlement will occur.[31] Thus, the Court's inquiry into fetal "personhood" was misguided, because the Court had to engage in the same balancing process no matter how it resolved that inquiry.[32]

The central issue in *Roe v. Wade* was not the constitutional status of the fetus but the constitutional basis for the woman's right. Justice Rehnquist's dissent argued that that right could have no basis in the Constitution because in 1868, when the Fourteenth Amendment was adopted, 36 state or territorial legislatures had enacted laws limiting abortions. Thus, he said, the only possible conclusion was that "the drafters did not intend to have the Fourteenth Amendment withdraw" state power to enact limitations on abortions.[33] This argument relies on a particular and controversial theory of constitutional interpretation. It holds that the framers could not have meant the general terms they inserted in the Constitution to invalidate widespread practices at the time, unless there is strong reason to believe that they did so intend.

This theory of interpretation is questioned by those who treat the general constitutional terms as political compromises designed to avoid confrontations over particularly contentious issues. As compromises, the terms license courts in the future to act in a manner consistent with the broad purposes of the provisions, notwithstanding the coexistence at the time of the framing of the broad provisions and specific statutes presently under attack.[34] Further, it is indisputable that the framers of the original Constitution and those of the Fourteenth Amendment were influenced by general ideas of natural justice, which many of them thought would make some statutes unconstitutional. Many of the framers also thought that courts would properly find statutes invalid because they were inconsistent with natural justice.[35]

Legal commentators are sharply divided on the theory of interpretation offered by Justice Rehnquist. Those who reject it for the reasons sketched here end up relying on the theories discussed in the next section of this article. For them, the absence of specific textual or historical support for the woman's right to choose is less important than the broader commitment they find in the Constitution to the idea that principles of natural justice exist and may be enforced by the courts.

Another dimension of history is judicial precedent. The Court's opinion in *Roe v. Wade* relied exclusively on precedent to establish the woman's right. The crucial passage listed a series of cases protecting the privacy of the home through the free speech and search and seizure clauses, and other cases specifically protected some dimensions of marriage, procreation, contraception, and child-rearing. The Court concluded that these cases established a "right to privacy" that was "broad enough to encompass a woman's decision whether or not to terminate her pregnancy."[36] This conclusion rests on a theory of precedent nearly as controversial as Justice Rehnquist's theory of interpretation.

Critics of *Roe v. Wade* properly point out that none of the cases cited involved the abortion decision. For example, one invalidated an anti-miscegenation statute;[37] others invalidated state laws prohibiting private schools and instruction in German in such schools.[38] These cases need not be understood as invoking a general principle of privacy, let alone a principle broad enough to cover the question in *Roe v. Wade*. Indeed, the language in some almost compels that they should be understood as relying on far more discrete principles regarding precise problems of free speech, race discrimination, and the like.

Yet the Court's approach in *Roe v. Wade* is not indefensible. Some of the cases it cited, such as the German language case, explicitly invoke the natural law tradition. Further, courts frequently look back at a series of cases, each decided independently and invoking discrete grounds, and conclude that the prior courts were groping toward reliance on a single underlying principle that they incompletely discerned. The right to privacy might be such a principle. However, even if it is, the Court has to establish the dimensions of the underlying principle to see what issues other than those addressed in the prior cases are covered by the principle. The Court's rather cavalier statement that the privacy right was broad enough to cover *Roe v. Wade* is widely regarded as unsatisfactory even within the theory of precedent on which the Court implicitly relied.

Justice Douglas's concurring opinion is more satisfactory in this regard. As he analyzed the prior cases, they established three principles: "autonomous control over the development of one's intellect, interests, tastes, and personality[;] freedom of choice in the basic decisions of one's life respecting marriage, divorce, [and] procreation [;] freedom to care for one's health and person, [and] freedom of bodily restraint or compulsion."[39] If the prior cases are characterized in that way, as seems permissible, *Roe v. Wade* is not a striking departure from precedent insofar as it establishes a right to privacy encompassing the abortion decision.

Roe v. Wade can be defended in the face of the theory of interpretation offered by Justice Rehnquist, but only by offering an alternative theory relying in some way on notions of natural justice. Precisely what those notions are is itself highly controversial.

2. CONVENTIONAL AND SYSTEMATIC MORAL PHILOSOPHY   Early defenders of *Roe v. Wade* argued that it rested on moral notions widely shared among the American people. For example, one version of the defense contends that Americans generally believe that government may not coerce intimate acts.[40] Given such a principle, restrictions on abortions are quite suspect. However, this

defense is effective only so long as the principle of conventional morality is stated at a relatively high level of generality.[41] There are no obvious reasons for doing so. Rather, one might take enacted statutes to exemplify the precise contours of what Americans conventionally believe is correct. By looking at responses to particular problems, we arguably acquire a better understanding of what conventional morality requires and permits than we do by looking at relatively abstract principles.

A slightly stronger version of the defense based on conventional morality relies not on general principles or on enacted statutes but on polling data. These indicate that the public generally supports the outcome of *Roe v. Wade*.[42] This conclusion must be qualified in two ways. First, the data are apparently quite sensitive to the way in which the question is asked: People do not approve of "abortion on demand" but they support a "woman's right to choose," which amounts to the same thing. Second, because the Supreme Court is a respected institution, the very fact that it decided *Roe v. Wade* as it did may have led some people to support the result. Still, the polling data are consistent with the pre–*Roe v. Wade* trend in legislation and law enforcement toward greater tolerance of abortions,[42] and such tolerance may now be part of our conventional morality. There remains a problem of constitutional theory: The usual method by which conventional morality becomes part of the law is through legislation. By definition, moral views so broadly shared as to be conventional have support by more than a majority of the people. Those views could be enacted into law by ordinary legislative processes. Yet *Roe v. Wade* overrode legislative decisions. It would seem, therefore, that defenders of *Roe v. Wade* would have to argue that for some reason adherents of conventional morality were unfairly unable to get legislatures to act. The next section of this article discusses some reasons for this inability. For the present, it only bears emphasizing that legislative revision of abortion laws was well under way by 1973. It is not obvious that the claim of inability to secure legislation can be supported by strong empirical evidence. If it cannot, the defense of *Roe v. Wade* as implementing conventional morality will remain rather weak.

Roe v. Wade has also been defended on the ground that its view of the morality of abortion is correct in light of systematic moral philosophy. One early defense argued that state laws restricting the availability of abortions rested on the theological premises of Roman Catholicism.[43] Such laws would violate the constitutional requirement that church and state be separated. In the funding cases, the Court expressly rejected that line of argument. Restrictive abortion laws are consistent with Catholic moral preaching, but they are consistent as well with ethical positions taken by other religious groups. Perhaps more important for the church-state argument, restrictive abortion laws can be justified by entirely secular moral arguments. These considerations led its initial proponent eventually to reject the church-state defense of *Roe v. Wade*.[44]

Secular defenses of restrictive abortion laws rest on two premises.[45] First, a fetus has at least the potentiality of developing into a full-fledged human being if normal processes are not interfered with. Second, it is prima facie wrong to take an innocent potential human life, and the wrong can be excused or justified only in limited circumstances. Only if the woman acts in something analogous to self-defense is abortion morally justified. Those who defend *Roe v. Wade* tend to challenge the proposition that a potential human being is so similar to a "true" human being that similarly stringent restrictions on taking its life—on cutting short its development before its full potential is reached—are appropriate. They argue that we feel little regret in crushing an acorn though we would strive to preserve the noble oak tree into which it could have grown.

Philosophers have challenged restrictive abortion laws in two ways. The first treats the fetus as part of the woman's body, lacking any morally significant potential for development once separated from her body. In this regard, the fetus is just like a woman's finger or spleen, and just as she has the right to cut off her finger or pay a doctor to remove her spleen for whatever reasons she has, so she has a right to have the fetus removed from her body. In political debates the argument based on the woman's right to control her body is probably the most potent, but its moral status is problematic. The finger or spleen would never in the normal course of events develop into something with moral significance. The fetus would, and as the "potentiality" argument suggests, that difference seems to be morally significant. Further, supporters of the result in *Roe v. Wade* usually treat abortions as regrettably necessary, and the woman's choice to have an abortion as an understandable choice between unpleasant alternatives, whereas the choice to cut off a finger would seem a curious personality quirk with no real moral significance one way or the other.

Judith Jarvis Thomson, in a widely admired article, defends the proposition that restrictions on abortion are morally improper in a different way.[46] She begins by imagining that someone has been kidnapped in the night and attached to a world-famous violinist whose life can be sustained only if the kidnapped person remains connected for nine months. Thomson argues that no sensible moral theory would find it wrong for the kidnapped person simply to disconnect the attachment and walk away, knowing that this act would inevitably lead to the violinist's death. In this story, the violinist is the fetus and the kidnapped person the woman to whom the fetus is attached.

Although Thomson's argument is persuasive on its own terms, it gains much of its force from the coercion implied by the kidnapping that creates the woman's problem. Many opponents of abortion accept it in cases where pregnancy arises from rape, a situation to which Thomson's argument speaks directly. But where the coercion is less obvious, as in most instances of intercourse, it is unclear that Thomson's argument is relevant. Thomson does address the situation in which a woman takes reasonable precautions to avoid pregnancy, arguing that denying access to abortion where those precautions fail is as coercive as the initial kidnapping example. Critics would respond that almost all pregnancies terminating in abortions result from failures to take reasonable precautions and that Thomson therefore establishes that abortion is permissible in only a small proportion of real cases. In this aspect of the argument, much turns on the meaning of "reasonable precautions." If access to contraceptives and sex education is widely available, failure to use contraceptives might be unreasonable; if access to and knowledge about contraceptives is limited, taking precautions short of abstinence might be regarded as reasonable.

Thomson's argument can be strengthened by invoking a more limited concept of privacy than the Court used in *Roe v. Wade*. Thomson establishes that abortion is not wrong when it terminates pregnancies resulting from coercion or failures to use reasonable contraceptive measures. One dimension of privacy is informational: We are privileged to withhold from others information about intimate matters. Determining whether a woman used reasonable contraceptive measures would require an inquiry into matters protected by this right of informational privacy.

One curiosity of Thomson's argument is that it fails to rely on what plainly animates those who support the woman's right to choose abortion—the fact that restrictive abortion laws directly affect women but not men. Donald Regan has drawn on Thomson's work to make an argument grounded in notions of equal treatment that does rely on the gender aspects of the abortion issue.[47] Regan puts aside the difficulties inherent in the notions of coercion and reasonable precautions by arguing that women unable to obtain abortions are placed in an extraordinary relationship under our usual concepts of appropriate action, even for people who are not coerced and do not take reasonable precautions. Regan says that such women should be treated as "Good Samaritans," that is, as people who undertake severe burdens in order to assist or to preserve the life of others. In general, American law does not require anyone to become a Good Samaritan, nor does it penalize those who begin to undertake the Good Samaritan role and then withdraw without worsening the prospects of those they began to aid. Restricting access to abortions, in Regan's view, treats women differently from men in ways not justified by the sorts of reasons usually required for differential treatment. Regan's argument is quite powerful, but it may not be strong enough to overcome the objection that the relationship between the woman and the fetus is different from all other Good Samaritan relationships in that the fetus is created in part by the woman and is under no threat until the woman decides to have an abortion.

In short, philosophers have provided some strong secular arguments against restrictions on abortions, but even the strongest seem open to question.

3. DISCRIMINATION AGAINST WOMEN   Regan's argument treats restrictive abortion laws as one form of gender-based discrimination. A popular approach to problems of discrimination regards judicial invalidation of discriminatory laws as appropriate where the processes of democratic representation are insufficient to protect those discriminated against.[48] That approach can be quite subtle, but for present purposes we can consider a simplified version.

Ordinarily, people advance their interests by participating in legislative politics. They seek to influence legislators by giving and withholding support based on the positions legislators and candidates for office take on issues the people care about. When every interest is represented, there usually is little reason to think that legislation advancing one group's concerns at the expense of another's ought to be treated as questionable. However, some groups are at a systematic disadvantage in the political process. Numerical underrepresentation is often taken as a good measure of systematic disadvantage. When underrepresentation occurs, the majority's representatives may rely on stereotypes about the underrepresented groups and may therefore adopt statutes that burden the group on the basis of inaccurate stereotypes. Thus, the statutes should be examined carefully to assure that they do not rest on such stereotypes. Most commentators believe that women are an underrepresented group in the relevant sense, especially with respect to stereotypes about homemakers and workers in the standard labor force. They conclude that legislation differentially affecting women should be strictly scrutinized.

Although this argument has some force, it is vulnerable in several ways. First, it is not clear that abortion laws are discriminatory in a way addressed by the argument. Usually we question discriminatory laws because they aid the "overrepresented" group at the expense of the underrepresented group. Perhaps one could argue that restrictive abortion laws benefit men by perpetuating a stereotype of women as essentially mothers, but that argument has not been widely adopted. It is difficult to discern any other advantage to men from restrictive abortion laws. Further, it seems clear that the primary beneficiaries of such laws are male and female fetuses. It is not obvious that even a predominantly male legislature would be overvaluing their interests at the expense of women's in adopting restrictive abortion laws.

Second, perhaps women are not at a systematic disadvantage in the legislative process anyway. They are certainly allowed to vote, and the fact that more men than women are elected does not establish a lack of sufficient political influence. Women can bargain and lobby, insisting on support for their program as a condition for their support for other programs. Indeed, as noted earlier, legislatures were in the process of easing restrictions on the availability of abortions by 1973, under the combined pressure of women's and physicians' groups.

As with the philosophical arguments, the discrimination arguments have some force to them. But they do not quite establish that restrictive abortion laws are discriminatory in the sense used by those who find the source of discrimination in underrepresentation.

III. Criticisms of the Post–*Roe v. Wade* Doctrine

Most discussion since *Roe v. Wade* has focused on that decision alone, with an exception for the financing cases. Nonetheless, some questions should be raised about the general outlines of abortion doctrine after *Roe v. Wade*.

First, the Court's application of its articulated approach seems disingenuous. Few restrictions pass the Court's tests, and those that do are likely to have almost no impact on the number of abortions performed. Thus, although Chief Justice Burger's concurring opinion in *Roe v. Wade* insisted that the decision did not require states to allow "abortion on demand,"[49] that is the true result of the doctrine it has developed. It is not obvious what the Court gains by cloaking a rule requiring essentially unrestricted access to abortions in an articulated doctrine that appears to offer the states opportunities to restrict access. The Court thereby creates a structure in which recalcitrant legislators who oppose *Roe v. Wade* itself can continue their efforts to evade its implications. Second, the Court's approach requires that statutes aimed at promoting third-party interests be defended as promoting health interests. Because that approach is rather obviously ill-suited to the underlying problem, the Court's analyses do not grapple with the validity of the real purposes of the statutes.

Third, the financing decisions have received heavy criticism, primarily on the ground that they are inconsistent with the premises of *Roe v. Wade*.[50] The arguments take a variety of specific forms, but they can be summarized as claiming that, for poor women who must use their limited private resources for other necessities of life, denial of public financing for abortions places a severe burden on their decision to have an abortion or bear a child. Such arguments open up fundamental issues of constitutional law. The immediate response is the Court's: "Burdens," in the relevant sense, simply do not arise when the government leaves the allocation of a good or service to the ordinary operation of the market. Poor people must choose how to allocate their limited resources among a variety of unsubsidized goods and services, and their choices are not burdened by leaving one particular good in that variety. Further, it deserves mention that jurisdictions in which most of the nation's abortions are performed have continued to use local resources to subsidize abortions.[51] On this view, the Court's decision to leave the financing issue to local legislative and judicial processes appears to be sound.

However, the defense of the financing decisions assumes that the basic rule is that goods are allocated by market processes. If the government allocates most or many goods, relegating some particular good to the market isolates that good from the rest, presumably because the government wishes to see less consumption of the good that would occur if it were subsidized. Yet actions designed to discourage consumption place burdens on the decision to consume in any reasonable sense. Critics of the financing decisions argue that in our society the government does indeed allocate most of the goods that poor people consume. Their shelter is subsidized in public housing, their consumption of food is subsidized by food stamps, their use of most medical services is subsidized by Medicaid, and they have few remaining resources to devote to purchases of unsubsidized goods. Thus, they are in precisely the situation described, where a decision not to subsidize constitutes a burden.

There is no satisfactory analytic solution to this dispute. Its resolution turns on whether one regards our society as basically market-oriented with a few deviations to serve particular goals, or as basically a welfare state with a few areas in which market processes operate with less-than-normal supervision. The choice between those views is fundamentally political.

IV. Conclusion

In its 1985–86 term, the Supreme Court had another opportunity to examine the constitutionality of regulations of abortion. It had before it decisions holding unconstitutional a number of provisions of abortion statutes in Pennsylvania and Illinois. The lower court in the Pennsylvania case had held it unconstitutional to: prohibit osteopaths from performing abortions; require that the woman be given information regarding the psychological and physical effects of abortion and the availability of financial support before and after delivery of a live baby; require that the abortion technique most likely to result in a live birth be used, even if that technique increases the medical risk to the woman; and require a detailed report on such aspects of the procedure as the basis for the conclusion that the fetus was not viable and the method of payment for the abortion. The Illinois case held unconstitutional provisions defining the standard of care to be used when performing an abortion on a fetus known to be viable, and requiring physicians to inform patients that they have administered a drug that will terminate pregnancy.

No matter how these cases are resolved, the law of abortion is unlikely to change substantially in the near future.

The present Court seems satisfied with the confused and in many ways indefensible statutes of the law of abortion. It seems unlikely that that law will be developed in novel ways. But in part because politically influential segments of the society do not accept *Roe v. Wade,* changes in the composition of the Court may lead to a reversion to the pre–*Roe v. Wade* law. That would remove the issue from the domain of constitutional discussion and transfer it completely to the legislative process. Given the development of broad public support for less restrictive abortion laws, perhaps even so drastic a reversion would not significantly alter the number of abortions performed in the United States.

NOTES

1. 410 U.S. 113 (1973).
2. *Id*. at 164.
3. Akron v. Akron Center for Reproductive Health, 103 S. Ct. 2481, 2492–93 (1983), 462 U.S. 416, 430 (1983).
4. 410 U.S. at 163–64.
5. 410 U.S. 179 (1973).
6. Planned Parenthood of Central Missouri v. Danforth, 428 U.S. 52, 63–65 (1976).
7. Colautti v. Franklin, 439 U.S. 379 (1979).
8. Planned Parenthood Association of Kansas City v. Ashcroft, 103 S. Ct. 2517, 2521–22 (1983), 462 U.S. 476, 482–86 (1983).
9. 410 U.S. at 195–200.
10. Planned Parenthood of Central Missouri v. Danforth, 428 U.S. at 79–81.
11. Planned Parenthood Association of Kansas City v. Ashcroft, 103 S. Ct. at 2522–25, 462 U.S. at 486–90.
12. 410 U.S. at 164.
13. Planned Parenthood of Central Missouri v. Danforth, 428 U.S. at 75–79.
14. 410 U.S. at 163.
15. Akron v. Akron Center for Reproductive Health, 103 S. Ct. at 2493–96, 462 U.S. at 431–39.
16. *Danforth* upheld a requirement that physicians obtain and keep written records, not required for other medical procedures, of the patient's informed consent to an abortion. 428 U.S. at 65–67. Even as applied to first-trimester abortions, this requirement did not significantly affect the decision to have an abortion.
17. Akron v. Akron Center for Reproductive Health, 103 S. Ct. at 2503, 462 U.S. at 449–51.
18. *Id*. at 442–45.
19. *Id*. at 444–45.
20. *Id*. The Court also held that the physician had to be allowed to delegate this informing function to another qualified individual, although the state could establish minimum qualifications for such counselors.
21. Planned Parenthood of Central Missouri v. Danforth, 428 U.S. at 67–75.

22. Bellotti v. Baird, 443 U.S. 622, 643–44 (1979) (opinion of Powell, J.).
23. 450 U.S. 398 (1981).
24. Harris v. McRae, 448 U.S. 297 (1980).
25. The Hyde Amendment was adopted in various forms from 1976 to 1980, when the Court upheld it. The most restrictive version prohibited funding for abortions except where the woman's life would be endangered; less restrictive ones included exceptions for pregnancies resulting from rape or incest reported promptly to the police, and where severe and long-lasting physical and health damage to the mother would occur. *See* G. Gunther, Constitutional Law, 10th ed. 622 n. 13 (1980).
26. The challengers also argued that the Hyde Amendment violated the establishment clause of the First Amendment because it was motivated by a specific religious idea regarding the time when human life begins. The Court rejected that challenge because although the amendment coincided with one tenet of the Roman Catholic church, it also rested on the secular view that childbirth was more deserving of subsidy than was abortion.
27. 448 U.S. at 316.
28. *See* Cates, *The Hyde Amendment in Action,* 246 J.A.M.A. 1109 (1981).
29. Some residual problems, relating primarily to the psychological dimensions of the issue, remain. They are discussed in Tushnet, *An Essay on Rights,* 62 Tex. L. Rev. 1363 (1984).
30. 410 U.S. at 156–59.
31. *See* Brandenburg v. Ohio, 395 U.S. 444 (1969).
32. Of course, it might have struck the balance differently had it concluded that states were required by the Constitution to protect the fetus's life, instead of concluding that the states could do so if they chose.
33. 410 U.S. at 174–77 (Rehnquist, J., dissenting).
34. The general argument here is presented in more detail in Tushnet, *Following the Rules Laid Down: A Critique of Interpretivism and Neutral Principles,* 96 Harv. L. Rev. 781 (1983).
35. *See generally* Grey, *Origins of the Unwritten Constitution,* 30 Stan. L. Rev. 843 (1978); J. Ely, Democracy and Distrust 48–50 (1980).
36. 410 U.S. at 153.
37. Loving v. Virginia, 388 U.S. 1 (1967).
38. Pierce v. Society of Sisters, 268 U.S. 510 (1925); Meyer v. Nebraska, 262 U.S. 390 (1923).
39. 410 U.S. at 211–13 (Douglas, J., concurring).
40. P. Bobbitt, Constitutional Fate, 159ff. (1982). *See also* Perry, *Abortion, the Public Morals and the Police Power,* 23 U.C.L.A. L. Rev. 689 (1976); Wellington, *Common Law Rules and Constitutional Double Standards,* 83 Yale L.J. 221 (1973).
41. *See* L. Tribe, American Constitutional Law 944–46 (1978).
42. *See* K. Luker, Abortion and the Politics of Motherhood (1983).
43. Tribe, *Foreword: Toward a Model of Roles in the Due Process of Life and Law,* 87 Harv. L. Rev. 1 (1973).
44. Tribe, *supra* note 41, at 928.
45. A good collection of articles on the philosophical dimensions of the abortion

issue is The Rights and Wrongs of Abortion (M. Cohen, T. Nagel, & T. Scanlon, eds. 1977.)

46. Thomson, *A Defense of Abortion,* 1 Phil. & Pub. Affairs 47 (1971).
47. Regan, *Rewriting Roe v. Wade,* 77 Mich. L. Rev. 1569 (1979).
48. The most influential presentation of this theory is J. Ely, *supra* note 35.
49. 410 U.S. at 208 (Burger, C.J., concurring).
50. *See, e.g.,* Perry, *Why the Supreme Court Was Plainly Wrong in the Hyde Amendment Case,* 32 Stan. L. Rev. 1113 (1980); Simson, *Abortion, Poverty and the Equal Protection of the Laws,* 14 Ga. L. Rev. 505 (1979).
51. *See* Cates, *supra* note 28.

In 1967, the issue of wrongful birth (*Gleitman v. Cosgrove*) was not recognized; however, with the *Roe* decision in 1973 emerged the cause of action termed wrongful birth and wrongful life (*Park v. Chessin* and *Turpin v. Sortini*). This, of course, now places an additional burden on the physician or genetic counselor to inform the patient of potential fetal health problems. Special note is made by Don Smith of the state legislative activity now occurring in these areas.

6 · Wrongful Birth, Wrongful Life: Emerging Theories of Liability_____

Don C. Smith, Jr., J.D.

I. Introduction

A. Generally

Until recently, the potential legal liability of a physician or genetic counselor who misadvised prospective parents about the health of an unborn child had never been addressed by an American court. It was generally assumed that the birth of a child, regardless of the child's health at birth, was a blessing.[1] However, two recent developments have led to judicial consideration of this novel question of legal liability. First, recent advances in medical technology and genetic study now permit physicians and genetic counselors, in some instances, to predict whether an infant may be born in a severely unhealthy condition.[2] Moreover, the United States Supreme Court has held that a woman has a constitutionally protected right to obtain an abortion during the first trimester of pregnancy, free of state interference.[3]

My aim here is to address the rights of a newly born unhealthy child, and the child's parents, to recover damages against a physician or genetic counselor who fails to detect a genetic, hereditary, or physical disorder in time to avoid the birth of the child. Specifically, this article will consider these questions: Does the birth of a severely unhealthy infant, under some circumstances, represent a legally cognizable injury? If so, may the infant and the infant's parents maintain actions against the physician or genetic counselor? And if actions may be maintained, what elements of damages are recoverable?

Initially, the article will define and discuss the types of issues involved and the descriptive legal terms used for the respective actions. Next, it will discuss the medical considerations involved. Then it will explore the two novel causes of action: wrongful birth and wrongful life, and the background, development, and status of both actions. Recent legislative activity that may have a significant impact on the development of the actions will also be noted.

In considering the issues arising in the contexts of wrongful birth and wrongful life cases, it is important to note that the infant involved in these cases is a severely deformed or unhealthy child. The infant has suffered, and will continue to suffer, personal injury because of the physical or hereditary defect that could have been diagnosed before conception or during pregnancy. The infant is not a child who is afflicted with a minor or nonserious ailment.

B. Definitions

A clear delineation of certain definitional distinctions is essential to understand birth-related causes of action. The action brought by, or in the name of, the unhealthy infant is known as a wrongful life action. This action alleges that the infant would not have been born but for the physician's or genetic counselor's negligence in failing adequately to inform the infant's parents that the infant would be born in a defective or diseased condition.[4] The basis of the action is that the parents were denied the opportunity to make an informed decision about whether to continue the pregnancy.[5] Moreover, the action alleges that the infant will be subjected to a life of misery, lack of accomplishment, and pain.[6] The infant seeks to be recompensed for the costs associated with the extraordinary expenses for medical care during the infant's life, and for pain and suffering.[7]

By contrast, the action brought by the parents is referred to as a wrongful birth action. The wrongful birth action alleges that, as a proximate cause of the physician's or genetic counselor's negligence, the parents were deprived of the opportunity to terminate the pregnancy or to avoid conceiving the child.[8] The parents seek compensation for their injuries arising from the emotional distress associated with giving birth to a severely unhealthy child, and for the continuing costs and expenses they will incur in providing for the unhealthy infant.[9]

It is important to note that the parents' action for wrongful birth is separate and distinct from the infant's action for wrongful life.[10] Moreover, wrongful life and wrongful birth actions should be distinguished from two other similar, but different, actions: wrongful conception and wrongful pregnancy. The latter two actions involve the birth of an unplanned, but usually healthy infant due to a contraceptive failure.[11] Wrongful conception and wrongful pregnancy actions are brought by the parents, and these actions seek recovery for the parents' expenses associated with the birth and rearing of the unplanned infant.[12]

Wrongful birth and wrongful life actions are also to be distinguished from actions involving malpractice where a plaintiff asserts that a defendant's deviation from sound medical practices increased the probability that the infant would be born with defects.[13] Nor are these actions concerned with situations in which an individual's negligence during gestation caused what otherwise would have been a normal and healthy infant to come into existence in an impaired condition.[14]

II. Medical Considerations

Only in the last few years have modern medicine and science begun to consider and research, in a comprehensive manner, the possibility of determining the potential health of an unconceived or conceived-but-unborn infant. For many years it was generally assumed that the medical practitioner's only patient was the mother. Therefore, relatively little consideration was given to predicting the eventual health of an infant. This occurred primarily because of the lack of diagnostic techniques on which to base such a prediction. The medical approach to pregnancy was that the mother and fetus were inseparable and the sanctum of the mother's womb was not to be disturbed.[15] Moreover, the understanding of hereditary maladies was not particularly sophisticated.[16] Recent development in these areas, however, have now made it possible for the early detection of some genetic, physical, and hereditary defects.

For example, biochemical tests have been recently developed which allow for a more thorough detection of preconception genetic health risks.[17] Thus, there now exists a greatly improved ability to predict the occurrence and recurrence of genetic disorders.[18] Two congenital defects that are transmitted genetically, and which now may be predicted in some instances, are Down's syndrome[19] and Tay-Sachs disease.[20]

Moreover, recently developed medical technology now makes it possible for physicians to test pregnant women for a variety of fetal health risks, caused both genetically and environmentally, that may be discovered in the prenatal stage of development. Approximately 60 to 90 prenatal health problems may be diagnosed with present medical testing procedures.[21]

The most common type of diagnostic procedure now used is amniocentesis,[22] a procedure which is no longer deemed scientifically experimental.[23] In fact, at least one court has recognized that amniocentesis is an effective method of predicting the presence of prenatal chromosomal defects.[24] Other frequently used diagnostic techniques include ultrasonography[25] and chorionic villus biopsy.[26]

In addition, there is a growing medical understanding of the relationship between some types of high-risk prospective mothers and the possibility that these women will give birth to severely unhealthy infants. For instance, there is a significant correlation between the age of the mother at the time of the pregnancy and the possibility that the infant may be afflicted with Down's syndrome. The older the expectant mother, the greater the chance that the infant may be born with Down's syndrome.[27]

Thus, no longer are all preconception or prenatal health maladies or defects unpredictable. Rather, in some instances, physicians and genetic counselors have the necessary diagnostic techniques to perform sophisticated and accurate tests in order to predict the eventual health of an unconceived or unborn infant. The legal issue that arises from this current medical understanding is this: May liability flow from the negligent failure to perform, or the inaccurate performance of, these tests and procedures where subsequently a severely unhealthy infant is born?

III. Wrongful Birth

A. Background

The concept of wrongful birth was first considered in 1967 in *Gleitman v. Cosgrove*.[28] In *Gleitman,* the mother of a child born in a severely unhealthy condition had contracted rubella[29] during pregnancy. The mother claimed that she informed her physician of this fact, but that the physician did not warn her of the dangers of prenatal exposure to the disease. The Gleitmans also alleged that it was a well-known medical fact that prenatal exposure to rubella could result in serious defects in an unborn infant. The *Gleitman* court refused to recognize the wrongful birth action for two reasons. First, the court believed that the measurement of damages would be impossible. It observed:

> *In order to determine their [the parents'] compensatory damages a court would have to evaluate the denial to them of the intangible, unmeasurable, and complex human benefits of motherhood and fatherhood and weigh these against the alleged emotional and money injuries . . . When the parents say their child should not have been born, they make it impossible for a court to measure their damages in being the mother and father of a defective child.*[30]

Moreover, the court thought that substantial public policy objections reflected in the then existing prohibition against abortion precluded judicial allowance of tort damages for the denial of the opportunity to undergo an abortion.

However, even in this initial rejection of the wrongful birth action there was support for recognition of the action. In a dissenting opinion, Justice Jacobs stated:

> *While the law cannot remove the heartache or undo the harm, it can afford some reasonable measure of compensation towards alleviating financial burdens. In declining to do so, it permits a wrong with serious consequential injury to go wholly unredressed . . . . Surely a judicial system engaged daily in evaluating such matters as pain and suffering, which admittedly have "no known dimensions, mathematical or financial" should be able to evaluate the harm which proximately resulted from the breach of duty.*[31]

The *Gleitman* decision was the first and only wrongful birth decision before the *Roe v. Wade*[32] decision. Therefore, although the *Gleitman* decision refused to recognize the wrongful birth action, its judicial persuasiveness became in large measure invalid before the next wrongful birth case was considered by an appellate court.

B. Wrongful Birth Action Recognized

1. GENERALLY   Following the *Gleitman* decision, no other court accepted the *Gleitman* rationale regarding wrongful birth. By contrast, every court that has considered the issue since *Gleitman* has chosen to recognize the wrongful birth action.[33] In the course of considering the action, courts addressed and resolved a number of primary issues: Do tort principles allow for such an action? If so, does public policy prevent recognition of the action? And finally, how does the concept of an action for wrongful birth interact with the right to obtain an abortion?

It is now generally recognized that a wrongful birth action conforms to the structure of tort principles, and that recognition of wrongful birth claims is a logical and necessary development in tort law.[34] The basis for this rationale is that an action for wrongful birth is not a new and distinct cause of action, but rather is an action that can be addressed through conventional tort principles.[35] For example, in *Phillips v. United States*,[36] the court said that the increasing importance of medical procedures such as amniocentesis and their entry into the mainstream of accepted medical practices, as well as the sensitivity of the interests and issues involved, dictate that the parents' rights be afforded some protection, and that the most appropriate mechanism for this protection is the constantly evolving doctrine of negligence.

Moreover, it is not necessarily true that public policy considerations should always dictate the rejection of the action. It has been said that it is impossible to justify a public policy that would deprive parents of information on the basis of which they could elect to terminate a pregnancy likely to produce an infant with serious health problems and then would deny the parents recovery of the costs of treating and caring for the defects of the infant.[37]

The third primary issue that had to be resolved centers on the relationship between the action and the right to an abortion. At the time *Gleitman* was decided, 1967, a constitutional right to have an abortion performed did not exist. However, that changed with the *Roe v. Wade* decision. Now the right to an abortion is perhaps the single most important reason for the recognition of a wrongful birth action. The proposition that a woman should not be impermissibly denied a meaningful opportunity to make an informed decision about whether to undergo an abortion, especially when there is a significant chance that a severely unhealthy infant will be born if the pregnancy goes to term, has constitutional protection by virtue of *Roe*.[38] Thus, a physician whose negligence has deprived a mother of the opportunity to make an informed decision on abortion should be required to make amends for the damages which proximately result.[39]

Wrongful birth actions have been recognized in a variety of factual settings. For example, a wrongful birth action has been recognized where a physician negligently failed to advise the prospective parents regarding the risks of pregnancy and the possible birth of a deformed child to an older woman.[40] Wrongful birth actions have also been recognized in the following contexts: A prospective parent was not informed of the availability of amniocentesis;[41] an amniocentesis was negligently performed;[42] genetic counseling was negligently performed;[43] there was a failure to diagnose and/or warn of an inheritable disease;[44] there was a failure to diagnose or advise a woman regarding the danger of prenatal exposure to rubella;[45] there was a negligent failure to diagnose a hereditary ailment in an earlier-born infant that led to the conception and birth of a second severely unhealthy infant.[46]

2.   ELEMENTS OF PRIMA FACIE CASE   The elements of a prima facie case in a cause of action for wrongful birth are the same as in other medical malpractice actions. The plaintiff must plead and prove duty, breach of duty, injury, and proximate cause.[47]

It is now generally agreed that a physician or genetic counselor has a duty to advise the prospective parents regarding the possibility of the birth of a severely unhealthy child where appropriate medical tests indicate such a possibility. This duty has been described as correlative to the parents' right to prevent the birth of a defective child.[48] Thus, where a woman's physician failed to inform her that prenatal exposure to an anticonvulsant drug would harm her future offspring, and two severely unhealthy children were then born to the mother, the physician failed to fulfill the duty to provide material information as to the likelihood of future children being born defective. This information would have enabled the potential parents to decide whether to avoid the conception and birth of such infants.[49] Moreover, where a woman after having contracted rubella saw a physician, it was held that the physician had a duty to inquire whether the woman was pregnant. This duty was imposed on the physician because of the harmful effects of rubella on a fetus, and the possibility that the parents would have chosen to abort the fetus.[50] And where parents underwent genetic testing, the laboratory conducting the tests owed a duty of reasonable care in the handling of the blood withdrawn for the tests. This duty necessarily encompasses the obligation to provide the parents with reasonably accurate information concerning the condition of their unborn child so that the parents can make an informed decision about a possible abortion.[51]

The finding of breach of the physician's or genetic counselor's duty of care is based on the failure to act in accordance with the appropriate professional standard. Breach of duty in a wrongful birth action has been found in a number of factual settings. For example, breach of the physician's duty of care has been held to exist where a physician's services did not conform to the appropriate standard of care, skill, and learning because the physician did not conduct a literature search about the potential prenatal impact of a drug being ingested by the mother.[52] And the duty to use due care in genetic laboratory tests was breached where it was concluded that a laboratory mislabeled the prospective father's blood, thus leading to the dissemination of inaccurate advice to the prospective parents, who then gave birth to a severely unhealthy child.[53]

The third element of the prima facie case, the existence of an injury, is now commonly recognized in wrongful birth actions. It has been stated that an inevitable consequence of recognizing the parents' right to avoid the birth of a defective child is to recognize that the birth of such a child is an actionable injury.[54] Thus, a direct injury to the parents occurs when they are deprived of the opportunity to decide whether to accept or reject the birth of a severely unhealthy child.[55]

The final element of a prima facie case in a wrongful birth action involves a determination of whether there is a proximate cause relationship between the negligence of the defendant and the resulting injury. It has been argued that no such relationship exists because irrevocable injury has already occurred before the negligent act is committed. However, it would appear that this contention misstates the nature of the test for proximate cause at least in some states. Negligent conduct need not be the sole cause of the injury complained of in order to be a proximate cause of that injury. The conduct need only be a proximate cause of that injury.[56] Thus, where a clinical staff breached a duty to inform an expectant mother of the potential ill health of her unborn infant and thus denied the mother the right to consider having an abortion, it was held that the defendant's negligence was a proximate cause of the parents' injuries.[57]

3. RECOVERABLE DAMAGES   The next logical question is to determine what elements of damages may be recovered. In fact, this question has been the most litigated issue in recent wrongful birth cases as courts have sought to define the parameters of damage recovery.[58] The specific elements of damages have generally included recovery for pecuniary losses and emotional distress.

Recovery for pecuniary losses has been based on the parents' expenditures for the care and education of the unhealthy child. Thus, parents have been allowed the pecuniary losses arising from the extraordinary expenses attributable to the defective condition of the infant.[59] These expenses are generally limited to those which the parents have reasonably and necessarily suffered, and will to a reasonable medical certainty suffer in the future.[60] However, the expenses that are generally recoverable are limited to those costs encountered in excess of the costs for the birth and rearing of a normal child.[61]

The parents' recovery for emotional distress has been based on the rationale of compensating the parents for the suffering attributable to their emotional anguish upon the realization that they have a severely unhealthy child. The monetary equivalent of this distress has been deemed an appropriate measure of the harm suffered by the parents.[62] A number of courts that have granted recovery for this element of damages have said that any emotional benefits to the parents resulting from the birth of the child should be considered in setting the amount of emotional damages.[63] However, not all courts have accepted the recoverability of this element of damages. They have stated that recovery for emotional distress would lead to artificial and arbitrary boundaries.[64]

IV. Wrongful Life

A. Background

The term "wrongful life" first appeared in a 1963 decision, *Zepeda v. Zepeda.*[65] In *Zepeda,* an illegitimate child brought an action against his putative father for damages associated with the child's status. The infant alleged that his father had injured him by causing him to be born as a bastard. The court rejected the action, which it referred to as one for wrongful life, reasoning that an illegitimate birth is not the type of injury that is actionable at law. A later decision, based on similar facts, also referred to an action by an illegitimate child as one for wrongful life.[66] These cases, although often referred to as the first wrongful life cases, are now more properly denominated as dissatisfied life actions.[67]

The first of the modern wrongful life actions was *Gleitman v. Cosgrove.*[68] The infant's cause of action for wrongful life was rejected in *Gleitman* based on the court's belief that an ascertainment of damages in a wrongful life action was impossible. The court noted that the primary purpose of the tort law is to compensate persons for injuries they have suffered wrongfully at the hands of others. As such, damages are ordinarily computed by comparing the plaintiff's impaired condition with the condition the plaintiff would have been in had the defendant not been negligent. In the case of a claim predicated on wrongful life, such a computation would require the trier of fact to measure the difference in value between life in an impaired condition and the void of nonexistence. Such a measurement is literally impossible to make, the court concluded.[69] Moreover, Chief Justice Weintraub wrote:

> *Ultimately, the infant's complaint is that he would be better off not to have been born. Man, who knows nothing of death or nothingness, cannot possibly know whether that is so . . . . To recognize a*

right not to be born is to enter an area in which no one could find his way.[70]

Following the *Gleitman* decision, it was 15 years before a state supreme court recognized a wrongful life action.[71]

B. Wrongful Life Action Recognized

1. GENERALLY   After the *Gleitman* decision, the initial trend of the cases indicated a judicial reluctance to recognize the action.[72] Rejection of the action was based primarily on the difficulty of ascertaining damages,[73] considerations of public policy,[74] and a refusal to hold that the infant had suffered a legally cognizable injury by being born.[75] It appeared that the proposed action might not receive any judicial acceptance.

However, in 1977 an appellate court ended this pattern of rejection. In *Park v. Chessin*,[76] a cause of action for wrongful life was recognized. The court said:

> *[C]ases are not decided in a vacuum; rather decisional law must keep pace with expanding technological, economic and social change . . . The breach of this right [to have an abortion performed] may also be said to be tortious to the fundamental right of a child to be born as a whole, functional human being. Thus . . . the cause, asserted on behalf of the child [states] a cause of action.*[77]

Although the *Park* court's recognition of the wrongful life cause of action was later reversed,[78] the holding was significant since it interrupted, if only briefly, the steadfast rejection of the action.

There was another middle-level appellate court decision in 1980 recognizing the action,[79] but the most significant decisions were handed down from 1982 to 1984. These decisions were significant because they represented rulings by state supreme courts, and they are among the most recent supreme court decisions on the issue.

In 1982, the California Supreme Court heard *Turpin v. Sortini*.[80] In *Turpin*, the parents of an unhealthy infant had taken a child born earlier, Hope, to a physician to check on Hope's hearing problems. During the physician's care of Hope, the physician failed to diagnose her problem as stemming from an hereditary hearing defect. In reliance on the physician's diagnosis that her hearing problem was not hereditary, the parents conceived another child. During the last stages of the mother's pregnancy, the physician determined that, in fact, Hope's hearing problems were genetic and would probably be transmitted to the parents' next child. However, it was too late in the pregnancy for the mother to undergo an abortion. The later-born child, Joy, was afflicted with the hearing defect. Joy's wrongful life suit alleged that had her parents known that the hearing defect would be transmitted to Joy, they would have sought an abortion. The court rejected the argument that public policy necessarily requires the rejection of the action and said:

> *[W]hile our society and our legal system unquestionably place the highest value on all human life, we do not think that it is accurate to*

> *suggest that this state's public policy establishes—as a matter of*
> *law—that under all circumstances "impaired life" is "preferable"*
> *to "nonlife."*[81]

Shortly after the *Turpin* decision another state supreme court recognized the action. In *Harbeson v. Parke-Davis,*[82] the Washington Supreme Court reasoned that the action simply places the burden and costs of maintaining the unhealthy infant on the party whose negligence proximately caused the infant's continuing need for special care. The court reasoned that it would be illogical to permit only the parents (in a wrongful birth action), and not the child to recover for the cost of the child's medical care. Subsequently, the supreme courts in New Jersey[83] and North Carolina[84] have recognized the action.

Thus, when a physician or other medical provider negligently fails to diagnose a hereditary or physical ailment, the parents are deprived of the opportunity to make an informed and meaningful decision whether to conceive and bear a handicapped child. When this happens, the physician or medical provider harms the potential child as well as the parents by depriving the parents of information that may be necessary for them to determine whether it is in the child's own interest to be born with defects or not be born at all.[85]

2.   ELEMENTS OF PRIMA FACIE CASE   In a wrongful life action, the infant must plead and prove the four traditional negligence elements: duty, breach of duty, injury, and proximate cause.[86]

The first potential difficulty with a wrongful life action is establishing that a duty toward the unborn infant was owed by the physician or genetic counselor. The difficulty arises because in every wrongful life action the alleged negligent act occurs before the birth of the infant, and in some cases before the infant is even conceived. However, those courts sustaining the action have held that a duty may extend to persons not yet conceived or born at the time of the negligent act or omission.[87] Such a duty is limited, nonetheless, by the element of foreseeability.[88] The duty, in a wrongful life case, may consist of adequately informing the unborn infant's parents that the infant may be born in a severely unhealthy condition,[89] or it may consist of a general duty to observe an appropriate standard of care in prenatal care.[90]

Although the cases that have recognized the action for wrongful life have not discussed in detail the issues of breach of duty and injury to the infant, it would appear that these elements of the prima facie case may be established under appropriate circumstances.[91]

Finally, the causation element in a wrongful life case requires asking whether, but for the physician's or genetic counselor's negligence, the parents would have avoided conception, or aborted the pregnancy, and the child would not have been born.[92] In one of the cases that recognized the action, it was expressly held that a physician's negligence could be the proximate cause of an infant's injuries where the infant would not have been born had the parents known of the infant's severely unhealthy condition.[93]

3.   RECOVERABLE DAMAGES   The primary purpose of tort law is to compensate persons for the injuries thay have suffered wrongfully at the hands of others. As such, damages are ordinarily computed by comparing the condition the plaintiff would have been in, had the defendant not breached his or her duty, with

the plaintiff's impaired condition. In the case of a claim based on wrongful life, such a computation was originally cited as one of the reasons to reject the action in view of the difficulty of computing damages.[94] However, there is precedent for the recovery of some damages.

Although the courts that have allowed recovery in wrongful life actions have continued to require that damages be ascertainable and certain, they have defined some damages as being measurable enough so as not to violate this requirement. Consequently, the only recoverable damages in wrongful life actions have been those relating to the extraordinary expenses resulting from the infant's unhealthy condition. The primary reason for this stems from the belief that extraordinary expenses for medical care and special training are measurable and can be established with reasonable certainty.[95]

Damages for general pain and suffering endured by the infant have been refused because of the difficulty in measuring these damages. There is a difference between the difficulties faced by a jury in assessing these damages in a normal personal injury or wrongful death action and the task before a jury in a wrongful life action, it has been suggested.[96] However, applying the general rule of damages in tort that an injured party may recover for all detriment caused whether it could have been anticipated or not, it would seem that a stronger argument could be made that the infant should be able to recover damages for pain and suffering. This argument is based on accepting the right of the infant to recover damages for the pain and suffering to be endured during the life span available to the infant and a rejection of the notion that a wrongful life cause of action involves an attempt to evaluate a right not to be born. Infants are presumed to experience pain and suffering when injury has been established. Admittedly, the terms "pain" and "suffering" refer to subjective states, and the infant may be unable to testify and describe the pain and suffering. But the detriment, nonetheless, is genuine and should be compensated.

C. Wrongful Life Action Rejected

1. GENERALLY   The majority of cases that have considered the wrongful life action have rejected it for one of three reasons. First, a number of courts have held that the difficulty in measuring damages makes it unwise to recognize the action.[97] In addition, other courts have held that public policy prevents recognition of the action.[98] And finally, it has been held that the infant in a wrongful life action has suffered no injury, thus preventing the establishment of a prima facie case.[99]

2. DIFFICULTY IN ASCERTAINING DAMAGES   The primary reason courts have refused to recognize wrongful life actions has centered on the difficulty in ascertaining damages. The remedy afforded in a negligence action is intended to place the injured party in the position he or she would have been in but for the negligence of the defendant. However, it has been suggested that a cause of action brought on behalf of an infant seeking recovery for wrongful life demands a calculation of damages between life in an impaired state and nonexistence, and this represents a calculation the law is not equipped to make. Moreover, to allow the recovery of damages for wrongful life would lead to speculative damage awards, it has been said.[100]

3. PUBLIC POLICY CONSIDERATIONS   Some decisions that have rejected the

wrongful life action have cited public policy as the basis of the rejection. Among these arguments is that life, no matter how defective or unsatisfactory, is preferable to nonexistence.[101] It has also been suggested that the entire question is inscrutable and enigmatic and, consequenly, is beyond the realm of human understanding or ability to solve. And some courts have stated that a substantial increase in litigation and the possibility of fraudulent claims require the rejection of the action.[102]

4.   NO INJURY SUFFERED BY INFANT   The belief that the infant bringing a wrongful life action has suffered no legally cognizable injury has also been the basis for rejecting the action. For instance, one court feared the staggering implications of the proposition. Would claims be honored for less than a perfect birth? the court asked.[103] Moreover, it has been held that the unhealthy infant, by virtue of birth, will be able to love and be loved and to experience happiness and pleasure, emotions that are the essence of life and that more than compensate for any suffering he or she may endure.[104]

V. Legislative Activity

In addition to judicial consideration of wrongful birth and wrongful life actions, a number of state legislatures have addressed the issues involved in these actions. In fact, one court has stated that, at least in the context of the wrongful life action, recognition of so novel a cause of action is best reserved for legislative attention.[105]

Thus far, the statutes that have been enacted have severely limited, and perhaps proscribed, bringing these actions. For example, a statute enacted by the South Dakota Legislature provides in part:

> *There shall be no cause of action or award of damages based on the claim of that person that, but for the conduct of another, he would not have been conceived or, once conceived, would not have been permitted to have been born alive.*[106]

Similar statutes were enacted in Minnesota in 1982 and in Utah in 1983.[107]

Legislation similar in intent to the South Dakota, Minnesota and Utah statutes has been introduced in several states.[108] In Kansas, the legislation was supported in a committee hearing by only one group, the Kansas Right to Life organization.[109] Thus it appears that anti-abortion groups may be the primary supporters of this type of legislation.

Although there have been no cases interpreting the South Dakota, Minnesota, or Utah statutes, it appears clear that the intent of these statutes is to reject legislatively the wrongful birth and wrongful life causes of action. Whether such legislative action is constitutional remains to be considered in future court cases, but a case may be made that the statutes are unconstitutional. The basis for the argument would be that parents have a fundamental right to seek an abortion where there is a significant chance that they would give birth to a severely unhealthy child. It could then be argued that tort laws cannot be designed specifically to impair the exercise of a constitutionally protected right. In sum, where a fundamental right has been violated, the law must provide a remedy.[110]

VI. Conclusion

With the advent of new and more sophisticated techniques for determining the eventual health of an unborn child, and with the *Roe v. Wade* decision, it is certain athat the issues regarding wrongful birth and wrongful life actions will continue to arise throughout the remainder of this decade.

It is difficult to determine precisely where American jurisprudence is headed as it considers these actions because of the great divergence in the relevant court decisions. However, the law must keep pace with expanding medical, economic, and social changes. The lag between cultural and social mores and medical advancements, although perhaps justifiably relied on in the early cases to reject the wrongful life action and to limit recovery in the wrongful birth action, should now be more closely examined.

The reality of wrongful birth and wrongful life is that an unhealthy child is born and suffers due to the negligence of a physician or genetic counselor. And today the certainty of prenatal and preconception genetic or physical impairment is no longer a mystery.

Fundamental in American jurisprudence is the principle that for every wrong there is a remedy, and that every injured party, with rare exceptions, should be compensated for all damages proximately caused by the wrongdoer. Thus, in wrongful birth actions the parents should be entitled to recover for all the costs associated with the child, including the costs of raising and educating the child. Moreover, the parents should also be entitled to recover for their emotional distress since it is only natural that, under these circumstances, the parents would experience anguish and emotional suffering. In wrongful life actions the child should be able to recover for all injuries suffered, including recovery for general pain and suffering that will be experienced by the child during his or her lifetime. Certainly, the child's pain and suffering may be difficult to measure. However, the harm the child has suffered is real, and the issue of pain and suffering damages should be resolved by impartial jurors who may be expected to act in harmony with the evidence.

Moreover, it is worth noting when considering these new causes of action that for many years there was no cause of action recognized for even prenatal injuries on behalf of the infant since, at the time of the injury, the fetus was considered to have no separate legal existence.[111] However, after the first decision holding that such a cause of action was proper,[112] there was what has been called perhaps the most rapid reversal of a common law tradition ever witnessed as every court considering the issue subsequently held that such a cause of action was indeed proper.[113]

In light of the historical, social, medical, and legal aspects of wrongful birth and wrongful life actions, a strong case emerges for the recognition of these actions and for the recovery of all damages suffered as the result of a physician's or genetic counselor's malpractice.

NOTES

1. Smith, ed., Handling Pregnancy and Birth Cases (Shepard's/McGraw-Hill, 1983).
2. *See* notes 15–27 *infra* and accompanying text.
3. *Roe v. Wade*, 410 U.S. 113 (1973).
4. Peters & Peters, *Wrongful Life: Recognizing the Defective Child's Right to*

a Cause of Action, 18 Duquesne L. Rev. 857 (1980). Generally, wrongful life actions are brought against physicians for negligent conduct with regard to genetic counseling or testing. However, the issue of whether a wrongful life action might be successfully brought against the unhealthy child's parents has received some consideration. In Curlender v. Bio-Science Laboratories, 106 Ca. App. 3d 811, 165 Cal. Rptr. 477 (1980), the court in dictum suggested that in an appropriate case, parents of a seriously unhealthy child, who with full knowledge of the child's likely condition, made a conscious choice to proceed with the pregnancy involving the child could be held liable for the pain, suffering, and misery experienced by the child. In evident response to this suggestion of possible parental liability for deciding to conceive or failing to abort a potentially defective child, the California legislature enacted Cal. Civ. Code § 43.6 effective Jan. 1, 1982. The statute relieves parents of any liability in this situation and also provides that the parent's decision shall neither be a defense in a wrongful life action against a third party nor be considered in awarding damages in any such action. No other court or legislature has addressed this particular issue.

5. *See, e.g., Blake v. Cruz,* 10 Family Law Reporter 1660 (Idaho 1984); Procanik v. Cillo, 97 N.J. 339, 478 A.2d 755 (1984).
6. Petition in Phillips v. United States, 508 F. Supp. 537 (D.S.C. 1980).
7. *See, e.g.,* Turpin v. Sortini, 31 Cal. 3d 220, 182 Cal. Rptr. 337, 643 P.2d 954 (1982).
8. Peters & Peters, *supra* note 4.
9. *See, e.g., Phillips v. United States,* 508 supp. 544 (D.S.C. 1980) *later proceeding,* 575 F. Supp. 1309 (D.S.C. 1983) (South Carolina law); Blake v. Cruz, 10 Family Law Reporter 1660 (Idaho 1984).
10. Peters & Peters, *supra* note 4.
11. Holt, *Wrongful Pregnancy,* 33 S.C. L. Rev 759 (1982). Some of the types of contraceptive failures have included: tubal ligations (*see, e.g.,* Clevenger v. Haling, 379 Mass. 154, 394 N.E.2d 1119 [1979]); laproscopic cauterizations (*see, e.g.,* Hartke v. McKelway, 526 F. Supp. 97 [D.D.C. 1981] *aff'd,* 707 F.2d 1544 [D.C. Cir. 1983], *cert. denied,* 104 S. Ct. 425 [1983]); vasectomies (*see, e.g.,* Sherlock v. Stillwater Clinic, 260 N.W.2d 169 [Minn. 1977]); and failure properly to dispense oral contraceptives (see Troppi v. Scarf, 31 Mich. App. 240, 187 N.W.2d 511, *leave denied,* 385 Mich. 753 [1971]). For a more complete discussion of wrongful conception and wrongful pregnancy actions, *see* Handling Pregnancy and Birth Cases, *supra* note 1. It should be noted that there are wrongful conception and wrongful pregnancy cases in which the infant was born in a severely unhealthy condition. *See, e.g.,* Elliott v. Brown, 361 So. 2d 546 (Ala. 1978); Speck v. Finegold, 497 Pa. 77, 439 A.2d 110 (1981).
12. Some of the expenses that have been held to be recoverable include hospital costs (*see, e.g.,* Ochs v. Borrelli, 187 Conn. 253, 445 A.2d 883 [1982]); medical costs (*see, e.g.,* Hartke v. McKelway, 526 F. Supp. 97 [D.D.C. 1981] *aff'd,* 707 F.2d 1544 [D.C. Cir. 1983], *cert. denied,* 104 S. Ct. 425 [1983] [District of Columbia law]); and pain and suffering costs (*see, e.g.,* McKernan v. Aasheim, 102 Wash. 2d 411, 687 P.2d 850 (1984).
13. *See, e.g.,* Sylvia v. Gobeille, 101 R.I. 76, 220 A.2d 222 (1966).

14. *See, e.g.,* Smith v. Brennan, 31 N.J. 353, 157 A.2d 497 (1960); Prosser, Law of Torts § 55 (4th ed. 1971).
15. Pritchard & MacDonald, Williams Obstetrics, 16th ed. (1980) (chapter 14: Techniques to Evaluate Fetal Health).
16. Textbook of Obstetrics and Gynecology, 2nd ed. (Danforth, ed. 1971) (chapter 2: Genetic Considerations).
17. For a discussion of the concepts and terminology involved in preconception genetic counseling, *see* Pritchard & MacDonald, *supra* note 15.
18. Fraser, *Survey of Counseling Practices,* Ethical Issues in Human Genetics 7 (1973).
19. Down's syndrome is a syndrome of congenital defects especially noted by mental retardation; at one time was referred to as mongolism. Blakiston, Gould Medical Dictionary, 4th ed. (1979).
20. Tay-Sachs disease begins during the first three to six months of age and is characterized by an abnormal startle reaction which leads to spasticity and death at three to five years of age. *Id.*
21. Milunsky, *Prenatal Diagnosis of Genetic Disorders,* 48 Obstet. and Gynec. 497 (1976).
22. In amniocentesis, amniotic fluid is removed from the fetal sac and analyzed to predict the unborn infant's health status. Blakiston, Gould Medical Dictionary, 4th ed. (1979).
23. Milunsky and Reilly, *The "New" Genetics: Emerging Medicolegal Issues in the Prenatal Diagnosis of Hereditary Disorders,* 1 Am. J. of L. and Med. 71 (1975).
24. Berman v. Allan, 80 N.J. 421, 404 A.2d 8 (1979).
25. Ultrasonography is a diagnostic technique used to identify the location of anatomic structures; can be used to detect such fetal anomalies as polycystic kidney disease and limb defects; performed by use of intermittent high frequency sound waves. *See* Pritchard & MacDonald, *supra* note 15.
26. Chorionic villus biopsy is a technique which involves the sampling of fetal tissue as early as the 8th to 10th week of pregnancy; the tissue is subjected to biochemical and chromosomal analyses. Diagnostic Techniques for Genetic Diseases, Human Gene Therapy–A Background Paper (1984).
27. Rogers, *Wrongful Life and Wrongful Birth: Medical Malpractice in Genetic Counseling and Prenatal Testing,* 33 S.C. L. Rev. 713 (1982). For other sources considering prenatal testing procedures see Goodner, *Prenatal Diagnosis: Present and Future,* 19 Clin. Obstet. and Gynec. 965 (1976); Hirchborn, *Prenatal Diagnosis of Genetic Disease in Developmental Genetics* 87 (Fenoglio, Goodman, & King editors 1976); Kass & Shaw, *The Risk of Birth Defects: Jacobs v. Theimer and the Parents' Right to Know,* 2 Am. J of L. and Med. 213 (1977); Diagnostic Technologies for Genetic Diseases, Human Gene Therapy–A Background Paper (1984).
28. 49 N.J. 22, 227 A.2d 689 (1967).
29. Rubella is associated with fetal abnormalities when maternal infection occurs early in pregnancy. Blakiston, *Gould Medical Dictionary,* 4th ed. (1979).
30. 49 N.J. at 29, 227 A.2d at 693.
31. *Id.* 49 N.J. at 49, 227 A.2d at 703.

32. 410 U.S. 113 (1973).
33. See Robak v. United States, 658 F.2d 471 (7th Cir. 1981) (Alabama law); Gildiner v. Thomas Jefferson University Hospital, 451 F. Supp. 692 (E.D. Pa. 1978) (Pennsylvania law); Phillips v. United States, 508 F. Supp. 544 (D.S.C. 1980), *later proceeding,* 575 F. Supp. 1309 (D.S.C. 1980) (South Carolina law); Turpin v. Sortini, 174 Cal. Rptr. 128, 119 Cal. App. 3d 690 (1981), *rev'd on other grounds,* 31 Cal. App. 3d 220, 182 Cal. Rptr. 337, 643 P.2d 954 (1982); Call v. Kezirian, 135 Cal. App. 3d 189, 185 Cal. Rptr. 103 (1982); Moores v. Lucas, 405 So. 2d 1022 (Fla. 1981); Blake v. Cruz, 10 Family Law Reporter 1660 (Idaho 1984); Goldberg v. Ruskin, 128 Ill. App. 3d 1029, 84 Ill. Dec. 1, 471 N.E. 2d 530 (1984); Eisbrenner v. Stanley, 106 Mich. App. 351, 308 N.W.2d 209 (1981); Schroeder v. Perkel, 87 N.J. 53, 432 A.2d 834 (1981); Berman v. Allan, 80 N.J. 421, 404 A.2d 8 (1979); Becker v. Schwartz, 46 N.Y.2d 401, 413 N.Y.S.2d 895, 386 N.E.2d 807 (1978); Azzolino v. Dingfelder, 71 N.C. App. 289, 322 S.E.2d 567 (1984); Nelson v. Krusen, 678 S.W.2d 918 (Tex 1984) reh. ovrld.; Jacobs v. Theimer, 519 S.W.2d 846 (Tex. 1975); Naccash v. Burger, 290 S.E.2d 825 (Va. 1982); Harbeson v. Parke-Davis, 98 Wa. 2d 460, 656 P.2d 483 (1983); Dumer v. St. Michael's Hospital, 69 Wisc. 2d 766, 233 N.W.2d 372; (1975).
34. Harbeson v. Parke-Davis, 98 Wa.2d 460, 656 P.2d 483 (1983).
35. Phillips v. United States, 508 F. Supp. 544 (D.S.C. 1980), *later proceeding,* 575 F. Supp. 1309 (D.S.C. 1983) (South Carolina law).
36. *Id.*
37. Jacobs v. Theimer, 519 S.W.2d 846 (Tex. 1975).
38. Berman v. Allan, 80 N.J. 421, 404 A.2d 8 (1979).
39. *Id.*
40. Becker v. Schwartz, 46 N.Y.2d 401, 413 N.Y.S.2d 895, 386 N.E.2d 807 (1978).
41. Berman v. Allan, 80 N.J. 421, 404 A.2d 8 (1979).
42. Gildiner v. Thomas Jefferson University Hospital, 451 F. Supp. 692 (E.D. Pa. 1978).
43. Phillips v. United States, 508 F. Supp. 544 (D.S.C. 1980); *later proceeding,* 575 F. Supp. 1309 (D.S.C. 1983) (South Carolina law).
44. Moores v. Lucas, 405 So. 2d 1022 (Fla. 1981).
45. Robak v. United States, 658 F.2d 471 (7th Cir. 1981) (Alabama law); Jacobs v. Theimer, 519 S.W.2d 846 (Tex. 1975); Dumer v. St. Michael's Hospital, 69 Wisc. 2d 766, 233 N.W.2d 372 (1975).
46. Schroeder v. Perkel, 87 N.J. 421, 432 A.2d 834 (1981).
47. Harbeson v. Parke-Davis, 98 Wa. 2d 460, 656 P.2d 483 (1983).
48. Azzolino v. Dingfelder, 71 N.C. App. 289, 322 S.E.2d 567 (1984); Harbeson v. Parke-Davis, 98 Wa.2d 460, 656 P.2d 483 (1983).
49. *Id.* Harbeson case only; not Azzolino.
50. Dumer v. St. Michael's Hospital, 69 Wisc. 2d 766, 233 N.W.2d 372 (1975).
51. Naccash v. Burger, 290 S.E.2d 825 (Va. 1982). For a discussion of duty in wrongful birth actions *see also* Schroeder v. Perkel, 87 N.J. 53, 432 A.2d 834 (1981); Becker v. Schwartz, 46 N.Y.2d 401, 413 N.Y.S.2d 895, 386 N.E.2d 807 (1978).
52. Harbeson v. Parke-Davis, 98 Wa. 2d 460, 656 P.2d 483 (1983).

53. Naccash v. Burger, 290 S.E.2d 825 (Va. 1982).
54. *Id.*; Harbeson v. Parke-Davis, 98 Wa. 2d 460, 656 P.2d 483 (1983).
55. Naccash v. Burger, 290 S.E.2d 825 (Va. 1982).
56. Robak v. United States, 658 F.2d 471 (7th Cir 1981) (Alabama law).
57. *Id.*
58. See notes 61–66 *infra* and accompanying text.
59. Goldberg v. Ruskin, 128 Ill. App. 3d 1029, 84 Ill. Dec. 1, 471 N.E.2d 530 (1984); Harbeson v. Parke-Davis, 98 Wa. 2d 460, 656 P.2d 483 (1983).
60. Dumer v. St. Michael's Hospital, 69 Wisc. 2d 766, 233 N.W. 2d 372 (1975).
61. *Id.* However, one court has recognized that the parents may recover not only for the extraordinary costs of raising an unhealthy child, but also the ordinary costs parents would incur in raising a normal, healthy child. The rationale for this position is that had it not been for the defendant's negligence, the plaintiffs would not have had the child. Robak v. United States, 658 F.2d 471 (7th Cir 1981). [Alabama law].
62. Berman v. Allan, 80 N.J. 421, 404 A.2d 8 (1979).
63. Blake v. Cruz, 10 Family Law Reporter 1660 (Idaho 1984); Eisbrenner v. Stanley, 106 Mich. App 351, 308 N.W.2d 209 (1981); Naccash v. Burger, 290 S.E.2d 825 (Va. 1982); Harbeson v. Parke-Davis, 98 Wa. 2d 460, 656 P.2d 483 (1983).
64. Becker v. Schwartz, 46 N.Y.2d 401, 413 N.Y.S.2d 895, 386 N.E.2d 807 (1978).
65. 41 Ill. App. 2d 240, 190 N.E.2d 839 (1963), *cert. denied,* 379 U.S. 945 (1964).
66. Williams v. State, 18 N.Y.2d 481, 276 N.Y.S.2d 885, 223 N.E.2d 343 (1966).
67. Handling Pregnancy and Birth Cases, *supra* note 1.
68. *See* text accompanying note 28 *supra* for facts of the case.
69. Gleitman v. Cosgrove, 49 N.J. 22, 227 A.2d 689 (1967).
70. *Id.* at 63. 227 A.2d at 711.
71. Turpin v. Sortini, 31 Cal. 3d 220, 182 Cal. Rptr. 337, 643 P.2d 954 (1982).
72. See, e.g., Berman v. Allan, 80 N.J. 421, 404 A.2d 8 (1979); Becker v. Schwartz, 46 N.Y.2d 401, 413 N.Y.S.2d 895, 386 N.E.2d 807 (1978); Dumer v. St. Michael's Hospital, 69 Wisc. 2d 766, 233 N.W.2d 372 (1975).
73. See note 97 *infra* and accompanying text.
74. See note 98 *infra* and accompanying text.
75. See note 99 *infra* and accompanying text.
76. 60 N.Y. App. Div. 2d 80, 400 N.Y.S.2d 110 (1977).
77. *Id.* 60 N.Y. App. Div. 2d at 88; 400 N.Y.S.2d at 114.
78. Becker v. Schwartz, 46 N.Y.2d 401, 413 N.Y.S.2d 895, 386 N.E.2d 807 (1978).
79. Curlender v. Bio-Science Laboratories, 106 Cal. App. 3d 811, 165 Cal. Rptr. 477 (1980).
80. 31 Cal. 3d 220, 182 Cal. Rptr. 337, 643 P.2d 954 (1982).
81. 31 Cal. 3d at 233; 182 Cal. Rptr. at 345; 643 P.2d at 962.
82. 98 Wa.2d 460, 656 P.2d 483 (1983).
83. Procanik v. Cillo, 97 N.J. 339, 478 A. 2d 755 (1984).
84. Azzolino v. Dingfelder, 71 N.C. App. 289, 322 S.E. 2d 567 (1984).
85. Turpin v. Sortini, 31 Cal. 3d 220, 182 Cal. Rptr. 337, 643 P.2d 954 (1982).
86. Harbeson v. Parke-Davis, 98 Wa. 2d 460, 656 P.2d 483 (1983).

87. *Id.* For a discussion of preconception torts in general *see* Handling Birth and Pregnancy Cases, *supra* note 1.
88. *Id.*
89. Turpin v. Sortini, 31 Cal. 3d 220, 182 Cal Rptr. 337, 643 P.2d 954 (1982).
90. Azzolino v. Dingfelder, 71 N.C. App. 289, 322 S.E.2d 567 (1984); Harbeson v. Parke-Davis, 98 Wa. 2d 460, 656 P.2d 483 (1983).
91. *Id.*
92. Comment, *Wrongful Life: The Right Not To Be Born,* 54 Tulane L. Rev. 480 (1980).
93. Harbeson v. Parke-Davis, 98 Wa. 2d 460, 656 P.2d 483 (1983).
94. See note 100 *infra* and accompanying text.
95. Turpin v. Sortini, 31 Cal. 3d 220, 182 Cal. Rptr. 337, 643 P.2d 954 (1982).
96. *Id.*
97. See note 100 *infra* and accompanying text.
98. See notes 101–102 *infra* and accompanying text.
99. See notes 103–104 *infra* and accompanying text.
100. Goldberg v. Ruskin, 128 Ill. App. 3d 1029, 84 Ill. Dec. 1, 471 N.E.2d 530 (1984); Eisbrenner v. Stanley, 106 Mich. App. 351, 308 N.W.2d 209 (1981). *See also* Strohmaier v. Associates in Obstetrics & Gynecology, 122 Mich. App. 116, 332 N.W.2d 432 (1982); Dorlin v. Providence Hospital, 118 Mich. App. 831, 325 N.W.2d 600 (1982).
101. Nelson v. Krusen, 635 S.W.2d 582 (Tex. 1982).
102. Phillips v. United States, 508 F. Supp. 537 (D.S.C. 1980) (South Carolina law).
103. Becker v. Schwartz, 46 N.Y.2d 401, 413 N.Y.S.2d 895, 386 N.E.2d 807 (1978).
104. Berman v. Allan, 80 N.J. 421, 404 A.2d 8 (1979).
105. Becker v. Schwartz, 46 N.Y.2d 401, 413 N.Y.S.2d 895, 386 N.E.2d 807 (1978).
106. S.D. Cod. L. Ann. §§ 21–55 (1981).
107. Minn. Stat. § 145.424; Utah Code Ann §§ 78–11–24, 78–11–25.
108. Alabama, Indiana, Kansas, New Jersey, and Oklahoma.
109. Minutes from Kansas State Senate Judiciary Committee, February 25, 1983.
110. See, e.g., Ochs v. Borrelli, 187 Conn 253, 445 A.2d 883 (1982); Rivera v. State, 94 Misc. 2d 157, 404 N.Y.S.2d 950 (1978); Speck v. Finegold, 497 Pa. 77, 439 A.2d 110 (1981). However, it should be noted that all of these cases are wrongful conception or wrongful pregnancy cases. Nonetheless, because of the similarities between wrongful birth, wrongful life, wrongful conception, and wrongful pregnancy cases, an argument could be made that the reasoning should also apply to wrongful birth and wrongful life cases.
111. Dietrich v. North Hampton, 138 Mass. 14 (1884).
112. Bonbrest v. Kotz, 65 F. Supp. 138 (D.D.C. 1946) (District of Columbia law).
113. Renslow v. Mennonite Hospital, 67 Ill. 2d 348, 367 N.E.2d 1250 (1977), quoting Prosser, Law of Torts (4th ed. 1971).

This article has as its basis an examination of the common law foundations of the abortion decisions—particularly the *Roe* case. Because of the complexity of the task, the authors must scrutinize law, history, philosophy and other disciplines. However, it should be noted that with some of the points raised in the article, further research may reveal a contrary view.

7 · The Law and History of Abortion: The Supreme Court Refuted*_____

Stephen M. Krason, Ph.D., J.D.
and Willam B. Hollberg, J.D.

We undertake here to examine critically the conceptual framework of the United States Supreme Court in its abortion opinions, particularly *Roe v. Wade*.[1] In doing this, we shall review the history of abortion at common law; its status in 19th-century American law and the purpose of the criminal statutes enacted against abortion at that time; the way the unborn child has been treated in other areas of the law; and the probable intent embodied in the Constitution and the Fourteenth Amendment regarding the unborn child. We shall also make some observations about the Court's interpretation and application of the right of privacy, and we shall demonstrate that the Court has seriously deviated from legal history and applicable precedents in opinions that are more expressions of personal, social, and political theories than they are of sound legal judgment.

I. The Court's Understanding of Ancient History and the Hippocratic Oath

A. Ancient Political Societies

The part of the *Roe* opinion dealing with ancient attitudes about abortion is not intended to provide a rationale for the Court's decision. The Court simply uses it as part of its historical analysis to show that "restrictive criminal abortion laws . . . are of relatively recent vintage."[2]

The amount of documented material about abortion in the pre-Christian era is scanty, partly because it was then a dangerous procedure and also because

---

*This article by Stephen M. Krason is revised from his book, *Abortion: Politics, Morality and the Constitution,* published by University Press of America in 1984.

196

infanticide was so widely practiced as to make it unnecessary.[3] The Court, citing Arturo Castiglioni's mammoth volume on the history of medicine,[4] correctly states that abortion was condemned by the ancient Persians. The Persians, however, were not the only ancient people who opposed and punished abortion, nor were they the first.

The earliest known laws on abortion were contained in the Code of Hammurabi in Babylon, which was promulgated in 1728 or 1727 B.C.[5] These laws apparently dealt only with one person's unintentionally but culpably causing a woman to miscarry. They imposed a financial penalty on the perpetrator, but if a woman who was a noblewoman also died, the perpetrator's daughter would have to be put to death.[6]

The next known ancient laws on abortion were those of the Assyrian King Tiglath-Pileser I, who in the 12th century B.C. codified laws that had accumulated from the 15th to the 12th century B.C.[7] Unlike the Code of Hammurabi, that of Tiglath-Pileser imposed a punishment of death for the woman who caused herself to miscarry. Penalties were also prescribed for accessories to her act, but the part of the surviving text of the code relating to this is defective.[8]

Another ancient civilization that proscribed abortion was that of the Hittites, even though, as Eugene Quay puts it, "[t]heir sexual morality was notoriously low."[9] Their laws of the second century B.C. condoned some sexual deviations, but the prohibition against abortion applied to all persons, means used, and circumstances. They prescribed financial penalties.[10]

There have been no codes of law discovered from the ancient Egyptian civilization. An indication of its view of abortion, however, can be seen in a 14th-century B.C. religious hymn to the Sun-god Aton, which is thought to have been composed by the pharaoh, Amenhotep IV. They hymn talks of Aton "[g]iving life to the son in the body of his mother" and of his being "[n]ursed (even) in the womb."[11] Also, a prominent historian of embryology has written that there is no evidence that the Egyptians of this period believed the unborn child not to be alive until birth.[12] This suggests that the ancient Egyptians, at least in the period indicated, exhibited a respect for unborn life that would seem incompatible with abortion.

The ancient condemnation of abortion was not limited to Near Eastern civilizations. Quay writes that abortion was opposed in ancient Indian religious writings, such as the Vedas and the Vinayas of the Buddhists. This condemnation was repeated in one of the ancient Indian legal codes that has been discovered, the Code of Manu. This dates from A.D. 100, but the laws it brings together go back hundreds of years before that.[13]

Another ancient people who opposed abortion were the Jews. There were two traditions regarding abortion among the Jews of the pre-Christian and early Christian periods. The first was based on the Hebrew text of that part of the Book of Exodus called the book of the covenant (the Palestinian tradition); the other was based on the Septuagint version of the same text. The Exodus text mentions explicitly only abortion caused by a third party; it says nothing about abortion caused by the mother herself. The Palestinian tradition, which was the earlier of the two, did not consider the unborn child a human being in the complete sense until birth. Nonetheless, abortion or dismemberment of the unborn child was permitted *only* when necessary to save the mother's life. The fact that the child was considered part of the mother until birth was primarily applied to settle questions of property ownership, and, since this understanding of the status of the unborn was applied also on the subhuman level, to determine the ownership of an embryo carried by a newly purchased female animal.[14]

John Connery, S.J., explains that ancient Jews could not have accepted easily available abortions because the Jews viewed barrenness as a curse, fertility as a blessing, and hoped for the coming of the Messiah.[15]

The later of the ancient Jewish traditions, based on the Septuagint version of Exodus, seemed to consider the unborn child a complete human being from the time he was formed, that is, his body parts were well shaped, not from birth. Anyone who caused a woman to have a miscarriage of a formed unborn child was to experience the death penalty. Causing abortions before formation led to a less severe penalty to be decided by the woman's husband.[16]

This survey of attitudes about abortion in the civilizations mentioned suggests two points of disagreement with the Court's interpretation: first, at least outside of the Greco-Roman world, ancient peoples did not accept abortion as a moral good that was to go without rebuke, and some legislated against it; and, second, ancient religions cannot be said to have uniformly refused to condemn abortion.

With that, let us now move on to consider what the Court says about Greek and Roman abortion practices. The Court cites a number of sources as saying that abortion was practiced in these civilizations,[17] another who says "it was resorted to without scruple,"[18] and another who disputes this latter claim.[19] It thus seems to leave the point unresolved. The evidence is that abortion was *not* practiced without scruple. Some of the most eminent physicians, philosophers, and moral spokesmen of Greece and Rome opposed abortion. The law was also not silent about it.

Soranus spoke out against abortion; he opposed it except when necessary to save the mother's life, and said, "[I]t is the task of medicine to maintain and save what nature has engendered."[20]

Seneca, while defending infanticide, indicates that he has a sense of the wrongfulness of abortion by writing in praise of his mother for not having had an abortion, like so many others.[21]

The poet Ovid viewed abortion as unnatural and impious. He wrote that " 'the first one who thought of detaching from her womb the fetus forming in it deserved to die by her own weapons.' "[22]

The first-century Stoic Musonius Rufus referred to abortion as a "danger to the commonwealth" and expressed approval of the laws against it, despite the fact that the Stoics generally believed that life did not begin until birth.[23]

The Court indicates that Plato and Aristotle were among the Greek thinkers (a majority, according to the Court) who "commended abortion."[24] A closer look at the works of these two great philosophers that were cited by the Court indicates that its conclusion is quite problematical. In the *Republic,* Plato writes of an ideal polity. The Court cites Plato's *Republic,* Book V, 461C, where Socrates is speaking to Glaucon about how the relations between the sexes must be ordered so as to ensure that the best men and women will be the guardians, or highest caste, in the best city. The best men must be brought together with the best women in order to produce the best children (*i.e.,* those most capable of being guardians). He says that only those who are within certain age limits will bear children for the city. In the following passage, Socrates speaks of the free sexual practices of men and women who are beyond these age limits:

> *However, with all this allowance, we must warn them to be as careful as possible not to bring any of these conceptions into the light, not even one; but if a child is born, if one forces its way through, they must dispose of it on the understanding that there is no food or nurture for such a one.*[25]

The Court's understanding of Plato is deficient both with regard to: (1) its interpretation of this particular passage; and (2) the position of Plato as determined from *The Republic* generally.

Regarding the Court's interpretation, the passage can be read as an endorsement of the regulation of childrearing generally, and possibly of infanticide, but perhaps not specifically abortion. Moreover, it is possible that Socrates may be referring to neither abortion nor infanticide in this passage. He talks of bringing "such conceptions into the light." Just before this passage, in 461A–B, he speaks of a child being placed among the population of the city after having been born of parents who were past their prime for childbearing. Since this will weaken the stock of people in the city, the child will be excluded from receiving holy rites and being prayed over like other children. Socrates says that such a child "was begotten in darkness with incontinence to the common danger."[26] In 461C, then, Socrates may simply be instructing that the child born in the circumstance described should experience the same "darkness," denial of being brought into the "light" of social acceptability, as the one in the circumstance in 461A–B. We can only be confident that Socrates refers to the attitudes that others should have toward such a child, not to whether he should be permitted to live.

To put the quoted section in context, we must consider another statement in which Socrates says that any children of couples within the childbearing limits "who may be born defective, they [nurses who take charge of children after they are born] will put away as is proper in some mysterious, unknown place."[27] Socrates says that defective children will be hidden from the city; he does not say that they will be killed or exposed. If he is not proposing infanticide for defective children, which was a common practice in the ancient Greek world, he is unlikely to do so for normal, healthy children just because their parents are outside the permitted age limits for childbearing.

There are also problems with the Court's interpretation beyond the particular passage cited. First, the Court errs in believing that Socrates is automatically a mouthpiece for Plato and that *everything* he says, without considering the manner and context in which it is stated and its relationship to the larger work, is to be taken at face value. Plato's thought is not so transparent. Through this dialogic mode, we can say that this or that is probably his view *only* after close examination of the work, gaining an understanding of the general point the speaker addresses and the overall argument of the work, and a consideration of the circumstances in which the speaker speaks, his likely purpose in saying what he does, and the statements made by the other characters.

Secondly, we can see that Socrates' view, when taken in the context of the overall point he is discussing with Glaucon and the entire work, appears in a quite different light than it would otherwise. We must realize that what Socrates prescribes for his city in *The Republic* cannot be taken as a guide or recommendation for conducting one's life or establishing laws or moral norms for a real political regime. He describes a " 'city in speech.' " He never suggests that it be a guide for a program of political action.[28] Moreover, as John T. Noonan, Jr. emphasizes, even if he *were* advocating abortion or infanticide, it would not be for the sake of bestowing a new liberty or right on parents. Rather, it would be to bring about a desired objective of the city.[29]

Regarding the advocacy of community of women and children and free sexual "cavorting," Allen Bloom says that "[g]iven that there will be many erotic improprieties in this city . . . it seems that Socrates' approach to the matter is quite light-hearted."[30] Socrates is not making his suggestions as serious political proposals. Instead, the city that he constructs is symbolic, a true example of what we commonly know today as a "Platonic ideal."

The other place in Plato's works that some point to as indicating an endorsement of abortion is Book V of *The Laws*. The passage in question is the following:

> *There are many ways of regulating numbers; for they in whom generation is affluent may be made to refrain,[31] and, on the other hand, special care may be taken to increase the number of births by reward and stigmas, or we may meet the evil by the elder men giving advice and administering rebuke to the younger—in this way the object may be attained. And if after all there be very great difficulty . . . and we are at our wits' end, there is still the old device . . . of sending out a colony . . .[32]*

Abortion as an alternative for controlling population is not mentioned in this passage and, in fact, as a last resort solution, Plato proposes *not* abortion but colonization.

The section of Aristotle to which Plato refers opposes abortion as a means of controlling population, which is the subject of Plato's attention in the passage from *The Laws*. It is a part of this section (*Politics,* Book VII, 1335.25) that the Court cites supposedly to establish that Aristotle also "commended abortion."[33]

Yet we see that Aristotle makes the following points: (1) abortion is considered only as an alternative to infanticide to regulate population; (2) abortion is condoned only for the purpose of aiding what Aristotle believes to be an important objective of the state (it is not seen as a liberty to be exercised as the mother wishes); (3) abortion is approved only up to the point when sensation in the unborn child begins and life exists (40 days for the male and 90 days for the female, based on the biology of his day; as sex could not be predetermined the unborn child was assumed to be male); and (4) by the phrase "if children are conceived in excess of the limit so fixed," he seems to indicate the preferred means of keeping the population down is not abortion, but preventing conception in some way. Aristotle thus can hardly be said to be advocating easily available abortion, but rather, as Noonan observes, he offers a tool for achieving important public objectives "with remarkable caution."[34]

The Court is also not correct in its view that the ancient Greeks and Romans generally did not believe that abortion should be addressed by their laws. Sparta did not permit abortion.[35] Lycurgus, the ancient Spartan lawgiver, and his eminent Athenian contemporary, Solon, both prohibited abortion.[36] In making its assertions about the supposed legality and moral acceptability of abortion in Greece and Rome, the Court dismissed a contrary view attributed to the late historian of medicine, Arturo Castiglioni. Castiglioni states that Roman law actually did punish abortion, at least from the time of Augustus (31 B.C.–A.D. 13):

> *The law against abortion was . . . strict. Thus the* Lex Cornelia *prescribed that whoever gave an aphrodisiac beverage or caused an abortion should be punished with deportation and the loss of his goods. If the patient should die as a result of these practices, the guilty party was condemned to death.*[37]

The later pagan emperors, Septimius Severus (A.D. 193–211) and Antonius Caracalla (A.D. 211–217) both punished abortion with banishment.[38]

The Castiglioni passage makes it clear that abortion in ancient Rome was worthy of punishment not only because of harm to the mother, but apparently for the father's benefit, and in order to restrain the "bad example" of giving magical potions (abortifacients) that *could* cause death to the recipient.[39] Harold O. J. Brown says the rationale of the Roman laws may have gone beyond this. Even though infanticide was so common, the Greeks and Romans may have shared the view, possibly reflected in the other ancient laws, that abortion is undesirable because interfering with the course of nature (as occurs when pregnancy is interrupted) is wrong.[40]

The only objective conclusion that can be fairly drawn is that the extent to which abortion was prohibited and punished in the ancient world is uncertain, and the reasons for the legislation that existed against it are unclear. The Court is simply incorrect in suggesting in its summary fashion that abortion was not morally reproved or the subject of legislation.

B. The Hippocratic Oath

The other aspect of ancient attitudes addressed by the Court concerned the Hippocratic Oath. The Oath, which bears the name of the eminent ancient Greek physician Hippocrates of the fifth and fourth centuries B.C., contains a strong condemnation of abortion. The pertinent passage is as follows:

> *I will neither give a deadly drug to anyone if asked for it, nor will I make a suggestion to this effect. Similarly I will not give to a woman an abortive remedy.*[41]

In its discussion of the Oath, the Court relied primarily on the conclusions of the late Ludwig Edelstein in his 1943 monograph *The Hippocratic Oath*. The Court says that the Oath was unable to stop the practice of abortion in Hippocrates' time because it "was not uncontested" even then and actually reflected the "dogma" of the Pythagorean school of philosophers to which Hippocrates belonged, who believed that life begins at the moment of conception.

The Oath thus represented "only a small segment of Greek opinion" and "was not accepted by all ancient physicians,"[42] but took hold finally because of the rise of Christianity, which agreed with the Pythagorean ethic.[43]

Harold O. J. Brown, however, has criticized the Court's interpretation of Edelstein. Brown states that Edelstein does not seek to question the validity of the Oath as merely reflecting the ethic of a minority, but rather to show how an ethic that came to enjoy universal acceptance originated.[44] Further, Brown states the Court is incorrect in suggesting that Edelstein believed that it does not represent universally valid and unchanging principles merely because it was originally espoused by only a small minority, the Pythagoreans.[45] This interpretation by the Court is perhaps a reflection of its underlying philosophical position in these decisions that universal truths are essentially unknowable.

II. The Court's Understanding of Abortion at Common Law

Let us now consider the Court's view of abortion at common law. The Court stated that abortion, whether before or after quickening, was never a crime at common law, in apparent reliance on the work of Cyril Means.

Means relies on three early English cases to establish his position that abortion was a liberty at common law. The first is a 1327 case which he denominates *The Twinslayer's Case*. The full text is as follows:

> *Writ issued to the sheriff of Gloucestershire to apprehend one D. who, according to the testimony of Sir G[eoffrey] Scrop[e] [the Chief Justice of the King's bench], is supposed to have beaten a woman in an advanced stage of pregnancy who was carrying twins, where-upon directly afterwards one twin died and she was delivered of the other, who was baptized John by name, and two days afterwards, through the injury he had sustained, the child died: and the indictment was returned before Sir G. Scrop[e], and D. came and pled Not Guilty, and for the reason that the Justices were unwilling to adjudge this thing a felony the accused was released to mainpernors, and the argument was adjourned sine die. [T]hus the writ issued, as before stated, and Sir G. Scrop[e] rehearsed the entire case and how he [D.] came and pled.*
>
> *Herle: to the sheriff: Produce the body, etc. And the sheriff returned the writ to the bailiff of the franchise of such place, who said, that the same fellow was taken by the Mayor of Bristol, but of the cause of this arrest we are wholly ignorant.*[46]

One critic of Means's pro-abortion interpretation of this case, Robert A. Destro, writes in summary of this case that the writ to bring D. into court was postponed, the argument was adjourned, and later, D. could not respond to Herle's demand because D. was under arrest in Bristol on another charge. Destro concludes:

> *Since another of the original uses of the writ of mainprise upon which D. had been released was to procure release prior to trial*

when there was some doubt as to whether or not the killing was felonious, D.'s recall to answer the charges lends support to the proposition that the judges had indeed characterized D.'s actions as a crime.[47]

Another critic of Means, Robert M. Byrn, supports this conclusion. He says of this case:

It is authority for nothing except the unwillingness of the court to let the abortionist go unpunished and the justices' puzzlement over how properly to deal with him. Subsequent history would suggest that the justices' dilemma was rooted in problems of proof. Had the abortionist's act really been the cause of the stillbirth? Had the two-day-old twin died from the abortion or some other cause?[48]

The next case that Means relies on is one he calls *The Abortionist's Case* (1348). Its text is as follows:

One was indicted for killing a child in the womb of its mother, and the opinion was that he shall not be arrested on this indictment since no baptismal name was in the indictment, and also it is difficult to know whether he killed the child or not, etc.[49]

Byrn says that the court did not dismiss the indictment in this case because abortion was not a crime at common law, as Means says. If that were the case, there either would have been no indictment in the first place or else the indictment would have been dismissed expressly on that ground. Rather, Byrn infers that abortion was indeed a criminal offense, but the indictment had to be dismissed for a defect in pleading because there was no baptismal name and an impossibility of proof as to the cause of the child's death.[50]

Before discussing the third case, let us review the views of the early common law commentators regarding abortion. The Court refers to the writings of the following commentators: Bracton, Fleta, Coke, and Blackstone. As the Court acknowledges, Bracton, writing in the 13th century before either of the two cases above was decided, regarded abortion as homicide "if the fetus is already formed or quickened, especially if it is quickened."[51] Fleta, writing a century later (apparently also before the cases), concurs, including liability of the woman herself.[52]

In the 17th century, Edward Coke wrote the following famous passage in his *Third Institute*:

If a woman be quick with childe, and by a Potion or otherwise killeth it in her wombe; or if a man beat her, whereby the childe dieth in her body, and she is delivered of a dead childe, this is a great misprision, and no murder: but if the childe be born alive, and dieth of the Potion, battery, or other cause, this is murder: for in the Law it is accounted a reasonable creature; in rerum natura, *when it is born alive. And the Book in IE. 3 [the Twinslayer's Case] was never*

> *holden for law. And 3 Ass. p. 2* [The Abortionist's Case] *is but a*
> *repetition of that case. And so horrible an offense should not go*
> *unpunished.*[53]

The important term in this passage is "misprision." Contemporary commentators have translated this to mean "misdemeanor." The *Oxford English Dictionary* translates it as it applies to law as follows: "a wrong action or omission, specifically a misdemeanour or failure of duty on the part of a public official."[54] The *OED* refers to Blackstone's *Commentaries IV* in 1759 as defining misprisions as "generally understood to be all such high offenses as are under the degree of capital, but nearly bordering thereon."[55] The impression we are left with, particularly in light of the fact that Coke emphasized that abortion was a *great* misprision, is that the translation of "misdemeanor" in its current sense hardly expresses the gravity of the offense in Coke's mind. It was possibly an offense that could be equated with some felonies today that are not punished with death.

Blackstone accepted Coke's understanding of the common law of abortion in his *Commentaries*. He treats abortion in Book I of his *Commentaries,* which is entitled "On the Rights of Persons." Including it in this book suggests that Blackstone regarded abortion as an offense against the unborn child; thus, his concern was at least partly with the protection of the child and not just the mother. The context of the passage in which he writes about the crime of abortion indicates, more specifically, that he believed the unborn child to be endowed with a legally protected right to life that is included within a broader right of personal security.[56]

James Fitzjames Stephen's account of the history of English criminal law reports that even before the time of Bracton, indeed, before the Norman Conquest, abortion was a crime. Before the Conquest, it was apparently regarded as an ecclesiastical offense only,[57] but given the role of ecclesiastical courts at that time, and the fact that both ecclesiastical and secular courts derived their authority from the Crown,[58] this fact does not make it any less of a crime in the law of the realm.

What we must conclude from these commentators and from glancing at early English legal history is that abortion was not a common law liberty and appears to have long been regarded as a punishable offense, for the most part less than homicide, under English criminal law. Both the Court and Means mention the earliest commentator, Bracton, and the Court mentions Fleta. Neither seems to regard what they say as important, even though each is seeking an answer to the question of whether there was a common law liberty of abortion. Neither discusses what Blackstone says about the unborn child's right to life or right of personal security. The Court seems to accept completely Means's rationale for dismissing Coke's views. This neglect shall be the focus of the discussion of the third of the important cases that Means believes shapes the common law of abortion.

The third case, *Sims's Case,* was decided in 1601, and is as follows:

> *Trespasse and assault was brought against one Sims by the Hus-*
> *band and Wife for beating of the woman, Cook, the case is such, as*
> *appears by examination. A man beats a woman which is great with*

*child, and after the child is born living, but hath signes, and bruises
in his body, received by the said batterie, and after dyed thereof, I
say that this is murder. Fenner & Popham, absentibus caeteris,
clearly of the same opinion, and the difference is where the child is
born dead, and where it is born living, for if it be dead born it is no
murder, for non constat, whether the child were living at the time of
the batterie or not, or if the batterie was the cause of the death, but
when it is born living, and the wounds appear in his body, and then
he dye, the Batteror shall be arraigned of murder, for now it may be
proved whether these wounds were the cause of the death or not,
and for that if it be found, he shall be condemned.*[59]

This case is consistent with what has been said about the two previous cases
and the conclusions stated about the status of abortion at common law. The court
states that the killing of the child in the womb is not to be treated as murder (this
is not a case of voluntary abortion) and the difficulty-of-proof problem is again
pivotal. The court is unable to indict, specifically for murder; nothing is said about
not permitting indictment for a lesser offense, unless the child is born alive with
wounds and later dies.

Means sees other significance in the case. He says, "It is difficult to ascertain
whether this was a decision or not . . ."[60] since Coke was the attorney general at
the time of this case, and it may be Coke and not the Queen's Bench who is
speaking. Means, and following him, the Supreme Court in *Roe,* accuse Coke of
inventing a crime of abortion in defiance of the two earlier cases.[61] Actually, Coke
followed Bracton and Fleta in considering abortion a criminal offense. As Byrn
emphasizes, Coke deviated from them not in assigning criminality to abortion for
the first time, but in treating it as a lesser offense than they did.[62]

Further evidence of the fact that abortion was not a common law liberty is
provided by Dennis J. Horan and Thomas J. Marzen. They point out that prior to
the 19th century, it was midwives and not physicians who for the most part aided
women in reproductive and birth matters. From very early in American history
the laws that governed midwifery prohibited abortion. Horan and Marzen point to
the example of an ordinance passed by the Common Council of New York City in
1716, which required licensing of midwives and expressly forbade their aiding
women to procure abortions.[63] This fact directly refutes Means's assertion that
prior to 1830 only the common law regulated abortion in New York State.[64]
Moreover, there was no reference to quickening in the ordinance,[65] suggesting
that abortion was prohibited at all stages of pregnancy. Horan and Marzen thus
argue that "on its face, the law was clearly directed toward protection of prenatal
life, not preservation of maternal health."[66] They also state that the law was based
on English midwife licensing legislation, which similarly forbade abortion. The
English legislation differed from the American, however, in that it was administered by ecclesiastical, instead of civil, authorities.[67]

Means states that "only if in 1791 elective abortion was a common law
liberty, can it be a ninth-amendment right today."[68] The Court gave itself a bit
more leeway than this, asserting that the right of privacy which includes the right
to abortion is found *either* in the Ninth Amendment or in the liberty clause of the
Fourteenth Amendment. We shall consider whether the Fourteenth Amendment

can validly be considered the basis for such a liberty shortly. The claim that it is based on the Ninth Amendment fails as demonstrated. However, a few additional observations are in order.

A number of commentators on the Ninth Amendment have contended that one of the unenumerated rights which it protects is that of privacy.[69] No commentator, however, in the years before the pro-abortion movement gained momentum, suggested that this right might include the right to abortion.

Knowlton H. Kelsey makes some insightful observations about the Ninth Amendment and our constitutional liberties generally. He states:

> *The Colonists had argued, petitioned and contended, and finally waged war, not for philosophical perfection of any utilitarian doctrine of rights, but for the rights of Englishmen. These rights were best expressed by and most familiar to the colonists in Blackstone's Commentaries . . .*[70]

What were these fundamental rights of Englishmen? Blackstone classifies them under three basic headings: (1) personal security, (2) personal liberty, and (3) private property.[71] He also states that among certain subordinate rights under the heading of "Personal Security" is the right to life and this, for Blackstone, extended to the unborn child.

If Blackstone's notions of rights were indeed the basis for our Ninth Amendment, not only does this amendment *not* include a right to abortion, but it specifically includes the right to life of the unborn child. There could thus be no basis at all under the Ninth Amendment for the Court to come to the conclusion it did in *Roe*.

Kelsey's reference to a "utilitarian doctrine of rights" is also significant. The Court's decisions are examples of a positivistic and utilitarian jurisprudence grounded in the will of the individual. Such utilitarianism does not accord with our constitutional traditions.

The Court's use of the Ninth Amendment in *Roe* illustrates what we may refer to as new "rights" thinking. That is, since our rights are not based in God or nature, they must come from the state. The Court rejects the Blackstonian, natural law-based right to life of the unborn child inherent in the Ninth Amendment and manufactures a right to abortion for the mother that it says is contained in the Ninth Amendment. It shows no natural law basis for this right, however. What the Court actually does is to substitute its own thinking for the mandate of the natural law. It is because the Court believes itself free to do this that Robert Byrn, Robert Destro, and Charles E. Rice claim the *Roe* and *Doe*[72] decisions were an arbitrary denial by the state of the fundamental rights of an entire class of persons.[73]

Means's and the Supreme Court's understanding of the status of abortion at common law is lamentable, given the inadequate basis for asserting a common law liberty of abortion.

One final point should be made: Throughout the history of the common law, the presence of life in the unborn child was always the criterion used to determine whether abortion should be condemned. The only reason why until the 19th century quickening or some other designated point of animation was believed decisive was because it was erroneously thought no life was present until then.[74] When better knowledge was acquired in the 19th century, laws began to be enacted prohibiting abortion at every stage of pregnancy. We shall now review these laws.

III. The 19th-Century English and American Law on Abortion

In the 19th century, in both England and America, the first statutes forbidding and criminally punishing abortion were enacted. The laws were probably responding to greater biological understanding of the unborn child that began with the discovery of the ovum in 1827. Conception was then understood, and it was realized that the unborn child was a separate, distinct, and living being.

A. The English Statutes

The Court advises that the first English abortion statute, Lord Ellenborough's Act,[75] was enacted in 1803. It made the abortion of an unborn child after quickening a capital offense, and for the first time clearly made prequickening abortion a punishable act (less than a capital offense). There appears to be no record of a parliamentary debate on the bill; there is only a brief reference to Lord Ellenborough's introduction of the bill on March 28, 1803, in which the rationale for its provisions is explained. Thus, we do not know precisely what prompted the statute.

The Court mentions four other British abortion statutes that followed during the century and a half before the "liberalizing reforms" of the 1967 English abortion law.[76] Records of the parliamentary debates on these bills either do not exist or (since the abortion provisions were often part of a more comprehensive bill) do not address the subject of abortion, so we cannot gain further insights by looking at them.[77]

B. The American Statutes: Enactment and Purpose

As to 19th-century American law, the Court makes two assertions that are very important to its analysis: (1) it was "not until after the War Between the States that legislation [on abortion] began generally to replace the common law";[78] and (2) the purpose of the 19th-century statutes was solely to protect the woman.[79]

Both of these assertions are subject to question. In a footnote following the first, the Court instructs us to see Eugene Quay. Quay includes an appendix of all the statutes on abortion passed by the states and territories of the United States before 1960. We must note that in this appendix, Quay shows that a full 31 of the eventual 50 states had statutes punishing abortion *before* the Civil War. The trend of legislation seems to have accelerated noticeably after the 1827 discovery of the ovum.[80] This suggests that lawmakers were influenced to afford greater legal protection to the unborn child.

Regarding additional rationale for the statutes, the Court considers two other possible purposes for the statutes (to discourage illicit sexual conduct and to protect the unborn child), but dismisses them both. Apparently convinced of Means's position[81] on the basis of its understanding of the medical history of the time and a couple of state court cases, the Court appears convinced the statutes were solely for the protection of the woman.

Dealing first with the cases, the Court claims the following support its position: *State v. Murphy*,[82] an 1858 New Jersey case; *Smith v. State*,[83] an 1851 Maine case, and *In re Vince*,[84] a 1949 New Jersey case. The latter two are said by the Court to anchor its view because they held the woman could not be prosecuted for the abortion. It also mentions a few Texas cases (the *Roe* case was from Texas) which also held this.[85]

Let us first determine whether the Court was correct about the *Murphy* case. The following passage from it is instructive:

> *At the common law, the procuring of an abortion, or the attempt to procure an abortion, by the mother herself, or by another with her consent, was not indictable, unless the woman were quick with child. The act was purged of its criminality, as far as it affected the mother, by her consent. It was an offence only against the life of the child . . . the mischief designed to be remedied by the statute was the supposed defect in the common law . . . that the procuring of an abortion, or an attempt to procure an abortion, with the assent of the woman, was not an indictable offence, as it affected her, but only as it affected the life of the* foetus. *The design of abortions, so much as to guard the health and life of the mother against the consequences of such attempts.*[86]

The Court is indeed correct in stating that the case stands for the proposition that the statute's purpose was to protect the mother, but, contrary to the implication of the Court in saying this, it did not exclude the fact that the state was also motivated by a concern for protecting the unborn child. The passage mentions that the statute just sought to provide an additional reason for the state to punish abortion other than the one under the common law and closed a gap in the common law that prevented it from doing so. The case thus establishes two things which the Court says are not so: Abortion was a crime at common law, and the state legislature that enacted the statute did not seek to prohibit abortion *only* to protect the woman.

The *Smith* opinion states just the opposite of what the Supreme Court says it does. The Maine court quotes Coke, and holds that the woman could be guilty of a crime for causing self-abortion and then states the following:

> *In both these instances [when a woman induces her own abortion or miscarries after being beaten] the acts may be those of the mother herself and they are criminal only as they are intended to affect injuriously, and do so affect, the unborn child.*[87]

This quote comes from the very same page of the opinion which the Court referred to as establishing the opposite! What's more, the Maine court goes on to say, indirectly, that the statute did not change the woman's liability for prosecution. The statute was held to provide that "every person" who had the intent to cause the abortion of an unborn child, whether quick or not, and succeeded in the attempt, would be subject to punishment.[88]

There is nothing in the opinion that suggests that the Maine court understood its statute to exclude the protection of the unborn child. In fact, its repeated assertion that the statute required the intent to destroy the child suggests it thought quite the opposite. It also refers to the death of the woman that occurred "without [the defendant's] intending to kill; and further [that] death was not in the *execution of that unlawful design,* but was collateral or beside the same."[89] The "unlawful design," the court makes clear, is "to cause the miscarriage" of the unborn child.[90] This language suggests the statute was directed toward protecting the child. It is by performing the act of aborting the child that the law is violated.

The Court's interpretation of the *In re Vince* case is also incorrrect. The *Vince* court held that the New Jersey statute could not be interpreted to permit prosecution of the woman for conspiracy or solicitation to commit abortion because it did not specifically address this.[91] It did say, however, that the statute provided "that a woman who performs an abortion upon herself or consents to its performance upon her by others is chargeable criminally . . . if the child were quick."[92] The court said that the specific circumstances of this case would not have made the prosecution of the woman for this possible.[93] Thus, she was compelled to testify about the abortion since there was no possibility of self-incrimination. This case, along with the other, holds the opposite of what the Court in *Roe* claimed it did.

Moreover, two other decisions expressly held that the New Jersey statute did indeed have as one of its purposes the protection of the life of the unborn child. These decisions were *State v. Gedlicke*[94] in 1881 and *State v. Siciliano*[95] in 1956.

It is true that the Texas cases the Court cites do establish the position that the woman cannot be prosecuted. The explanation given by the courts in these cases that the woman is regarded as the victim in abortion, would seem to buttress the Supreme Court's point that this fact of nonprosecutibility indicated that the 19th-century statutes were indeed designed to protect the woman. The cases do not say, however, that the woman was seen as the *only* victim or that the law was not also concerned with the child. Nor did they permit a prosecution of the abortionist only when the woman was injured or killed by the operation, which would seem to be likely if she were the law's only concern. Similarly, the fact that abortion was established as a separate offense, instead of being prosecuted as an assault and battery against the woman, suggests that the unborn child must also have been the subject of concern. One thoughtful suggestion supporting the position not to prosecute the woman is to grant her immunity to testify against one performing the abortion.[96]

There were other state court decisions that expressly stated that the protection of the unborn child was at least one of the purposes of the 19th-century statutes. John D. Gorby mentions 11 such decisions.[97]

Now, let us consider the matter of the medical history. The Court stated:

> *When most criminal abortion laws were first enacted, the procedure was a hazardous one for the woman. This was particularly true prior to the development of antisepsis . . . Abortion mortality was high . . . standard modern techniques such as dilation and curettage were not nearly so safe as they are today.*[98]

In making this assertion, the Court cites only one source: C. Haagensen and

V. Lloyd's *A Hundred Years of Medicine,* published in 1943. It makes specific reference to page 19, which is in a three-page chapter entitled "18th Century Surgery and its Limitations." This page and chapter make no specific reference at all to abortion, and the entire book does not contain any references to the abortion operation, even in its chapter on obstetrics and gynecology.[99]

Two things must be pointed out. First, the chapter refers to the *18th* century. It cannot be used as a source for arguing that abortion statutes enacted in the 19th century, when medicine had progressed further, were prompted by a contemporaneous concern about the surgical hazards of abortion for the woman.[100] Second, the Court is incorrect in assuming that most abortions in the 19th century were performed by cutting or surgical procedures, as they are today. "Drugs, the human finger, and the water douche were among accepted methods of inducing abortion, and even inducing abortion by puncturing membranes was not considered dangerous to the mother, although it was risky for the child."[101]

The last phrase may seem somewhat confusing. Why should there have been a concern for the child, one might ask, when we know the purpose of abortion is to destroy the child? The answer is—and this might provide even further evidence that the 19th century statutes were not unconcerned about the unborn child—that many abortions were performed to save the life of the child at late stages in pregnancy.[102] Even professor Means was not willing to go as far as the Court in saying that "[a]bortion mortality was high."[103]

The Court's understanding of the medical dangers of abortion to the woman at the time the statutes were enacted is not well-founded. This, along with the seeming misunderstanding of the state cases, makes very doubtful the claim that the purpose of the statutes was exclusively to protect the woman. The Court seems to imply that if this was the original purpose of the statutes, *and* if medical advances have ceased making it necessary for the law to protect the woman, *and* if abortion was not a crime at common law before the statutes, then, somehow, the statutes must in 1973 be unconstitutional. This forced logic was necessary for the Court to cloak itself with the authority to declare statutes unconstitutional because they no longer fulfilled their original function.

IV. The Status of the Unborn Child in Other Areas of the Law

A. The Supreme Court's View

The Supreme Court contended that "the unborn have never been recognized in the law as persons in the whole sense."[104] An examination of the law in a number of areas demonstrates the fallacy of this assertion.

B. Tort Law

Let us consider the law of torts first. David Louisell and John T. Noonan, Jr. wrote the following about the unborn child in this area of the law:

> But perhaps the most significant cases for establishing the legal existence of a child prior to birth have been those very modern decisions which allow the parents, or survivors, to maintain such an action where the child is stillborn. Thus, the unborn child, to whom live birth never comes, is held to be a 'person' who can be the subject of an action for damages for his death.[105]

Traditionally in tort law, courts denied recovery to the unborn child. The case which perhaps began the erosion of the old rule was *Allaire v. St. Luke's Hospital*. This decision, while following the rule, produced a noteworthy dissenting opinion by Judge Boggs. According to Boggs, medical science established that, although the unborn child was within the woman's body, he was not *just* a part of it, and the law had to take this fact into account.[106] The traditional rule fell in the landmark decision of *Bonbrest v. Kotz*[107] in 1946, where a District of Columbia court rejected any lingering notion that the unborn child, at any stage of his development, was a part of his mother's body. The court added: "The law is presumed to keep pace with the sciences and medical science certainly has made progress since 1884."[108] *Bonbrest* established the new rule that recovery for the child had to be permitted *at least* at viability, and it opened the floodgates. Almost every other jurisdiction that had previously addressed the question and denied recovery reversed itself to permit it. By the time the Supreme Court first considered *Roe* and *Doe,* 29 states and the District of Columbia permitted recovery.[109] The Court was thus correct in stating that by 1973 most states permitted this, but incorrect in saying that "few courts have squarely so held this."[110] All 30 jurisdictions that by 1973 permitted recovery did so because courts "squarely held" that it was permitted.

The Supreme Court's statement in *Roe* that the unborn child could not recover damages unless "viable, or at least quick" is also not accurate. At least nine jurisdictions had rejected the viability requirement by 1973.[111] There were also 32 cases from 30 jurisdictions that permitted recovery by the unborn.[112] Only nine jurisdictions expressly required viability (by 1973, two of these no longer required it); cases in five jurisdictions expressly stated that the question of whether a nonviable child could recover was not being reached because it was not at issue in the respective case (three of these later held, prior to 1973, that viability was not required); and the remainder either did not mention whether viability was required, implied it was not, or left the matter unclear (by 1973, two of these had held it was not required).[113]

The Court stated that the legal rights of the unborn child have depended on his ultimately being born alive, the traditional rule in tort law. The Court also pointed to a trend that has gone against this when it mentions that some jurisdictions had begun to allow parents to bring wrongful death actions. Sixteen states had permitted these by the time *Roe* and *Doe* came to the Court.[114] The Court concluded, however, that these actions vindicate the parents' interest and thus demonstrate only the potentiality of the child's life. This is a misinterpretation. It is true that wrongful death actions are primarily for the benefit of the deceased's survivors or estate as compensation for the loss of the decedent's support or services.[115] As such, they *do* vindicate an interest of the parents. Nevertheless, a wrongful death action presumes that a *person* existed in the first place. Thus, the fact that the trend before 1973 was to permit these actions signifies just the *opposite* of what the Court says, and indicates instead that unborn children are indeed persons.

C. Property Law

Similarly, in the law of property, the unborn child has rights that "are as old as the common law itself."[116] Blackstone wrote the unborn is capable of having a legacy or a guardian assigned to him, to have an estate limited to his use, and to take afterwards by such limitation.[117] Starting in the late 18th century, after more of the biological facts of life before birth become known, the unborn child was held to be within the category of a devise to "children" living at the time of a life tenant's decease and "born" during a testator's lifetime.[118] The unborn child was also considered a "life in being" for the purposes of the Rule Against Perpetuities,[119] whether or not it was to benefit him.[120]

According to Louisell and Noonan, the American courts reached the same results. An unborn child could take under a will leaving property to those "living" at a testator's decease and as a tenant in common with his mother.[121] The child could begin to share in the proceeds of a trust from the date of his father's death rather than of his subsequent birth.[122]

A decision often cited to provide a summary of the state of American property law with regard to the unborn child is *In re Holthausen's Will*, decided by the New York courts in 1941. It says the following:

> *It has been the uniform and unvarying decision of all common law courts in respect of estate matters for at least the past two hundred years that a child* en ventre de sa mere *[in his mother's womb] is "born" and "alive" for all purposes for his benefit.*[123]

Another example of a "property interest" which the courts have allowed the unborn child is Social Security survivor's benefits. In 1969, the Court of Appeals for the Fifth Circuit held that a child conceived a short time before her father's death had the right to receive benefits from his earnings. The court held that the unborn child met the legal requirement of "living with" the father at the time of his death.[124]

D. Child Support Laws

Finally, there were decisions prior to *Roe* and *Doe* that held that an unborn child was entitled to support payments from his father in the same way that he would be after birth. In *Metzger v. People*,[125] the Colorado Supreme Court affirmed an order requiring a man to contribute 30 percent of his salary to the support of his unborn child.[126] In *Kyne v. Kyne*,[127] a California appeals court ruled that an unborn child has a right to have a guardian, to bring suit, to have his father's paternity declared, and to receive support from his father.[128]

We can conclude, then, that the Court's view of the status of the unborn child in other areas of the law, like its understanding of history and the purpose of the criminal abortion statutes, is inaccurate.[129]

V. The Court's Conclusions About the Status of the Unborn Child Under the Constitution and the Fourteenth Amendment

The Court states an essential question is whether the fetus is a "person" under the Fourteenth Amendment. It concluded, of course, that he is not. It also claims that the right of privacy, which it says may be found in the Fourteenth Amendment's guarantee of personal liberty, is broad enough to encompass a "woman's decision whether or not to terminate her pregnancy." We have already disputed whether there was a liberty of abortion in the Anglo-American tradition, and now we shall focus on the "personhood" question.

A. The Meaning of "Fetus" and "Person"

In the common understanding of the terms "person" and "fetus" at the time of the framing of the Constitution and the drafting of the Fourteenth Amendment, "fetus" was understood to be a "person" protected by the Constitution.[130] To put it in syllogistic terms, since a "fetus" was understood to be a "child" and a "child" is a "person," then a "fetus" would have to be judged a "person."[131]

B. The Constitutional Provisions

The Court states that the provisions in the body of the Constitution that use the term "person" could not possibly be referring to the unborn. Let us look at each of the provisions mentioned to see the difficulty the Court creates for itself in saying this. The first two references are to the Article I qualifications for holding office as United States Representatives and Senators (art. I, sec. 2, cl.2 and art. I, sec. 3, cl.3, respectively). While both of these provisions exclude an unborn child they also exclude a 20-year-old. Would the Court interpret the provisions as negating the legal personhood of a 20-year-old and permitting or requiring a state to not protect his right to life? Essentially the same point must be made about the Court's singling out the Constitution's use of the term "person" when referring to the qualifications for becoming President (art. II, sec. 1, cl.5; the Twelfth Amendment; and the Twenty-second Amendment).

If the Court's references to the emolument clause (art. I, sec. 9, cl. 8) and the electors provisions (art. II, sec. 1, cl. 2 and the superseded cl. 3) are to be taken as an indiation of who are "persons," then children after birth would likely be excluded because they are unlikely to, and in fact would probably be statutorily barred from, "holding any office of Profit or Trust"[132] under the United States. Would the Court vote to remove the protection of their right to life under the Constitution?

The extradition provisions (art. IV, sec. 2, cl. 2) also would exclude some children from being considered "persons." This is because the common law's presumption that a child below seven (the age of reason) is incapable of committing a crime would mean that he could not be "charged in any State with Treason, Felony, or other Crime," and thus could not be subject to the extradition provisions.

The Court is correct that the fugitive slave clause (art. IV, sec. 2, cl. 3) and the migration and importation provision (art. I, sec. 9, cl. 1) do not apply to the unborn. Ironically, these provisions were superseded by the Thirteenth and Fourteenth Amendments because they excluded an entire class from legal personhood: blacks descended from slaves. *Roe* has the same effect for unborn children.

As for the apportionment clause (art. I, sec. 2, cl. 3), it excludes Indians not taxed as "persons" and considers a black slave as three-fifths of a "person." Would the Court have voted to treat Indians and blacks as not "persons in the whole sense" on the basis of this provision?

It is unreasonable to construe the constitutional provisions cited by the Court as a basis for claiming that the framers excluded the unborn child from the protection of the Constitution.

C. Were the Fourteenth Amendment Protections Intended to Extend to the Unborn Child?

Now, let us consider what the possible intentions of the drafters of the Fourteenth Amendment were.

Justice Rehnquist's dissenting opinion gives a good summary focus to this inquiry. He stated that "[b]y the time of the adoption of the fourteenth amendment in 1868, there were at least 36 laws enacted by state or territorial legislatures limiting abortion."[133] He concludes from this that "the drafters did not intend to withdraw from the States the power to legislate with respect to this matter."[134] Further, only five of the states that ratified the Fourteenth Amendment did not have criminal abortion statutes on the books.[135]

There is also pertinent federal legislation on this issue. The first was the District of Columbia Divorce Act of 1860. This act provided that the offspring of a second and bigamous marriage "born or begotten before the commencement of the suit (for divorce), shall be deemed to be the legitimate issue [offspring] of the parent, who, at the time of the marriage, was capable of contracting."[136] The use of "begotten" demonstrates clearly the intent of Congress to extend legal rights to the unborn.

The second piece of legislation is the assimilative crimes provision enacted on April 5, 1866.[137] This legislation made applicable the criminal law of a state to any area that the state had ceded to and placed under the exclusive jurisdiction of the United States government where an offense specified by that state's criminal law was not prohibited under federal law. Joseph Witherspoon explains, "This provision clearly adopted as federal law state laws prohibiting abortion including those adopted or amended in the period between 1850 and 1875; most of which . . . were designed under the Storer guidelines to provide protection for the lives of unborn children."[138] This means that the Texas anti-abortion law of 1856, struck down in *Roe,* was adopted as federal law applicable to U.S. military installations located in that state.[139]

The most direct federal legislation relating to abortion in this period was enacted by Congress in 1873, five years after the Fourteenth Amendment was proposed. On March 3, 1873, it enacted "An Act for the Suppression of trade in, and Circulation of . . . Articles of Immoral Use." The purpose of this statute was to reach an area of abortion that was left uncovered by most of the state statutes. It prohibited the selling, lending, or giving away "of any article . . . for causing unlawful abortion" as defined by the criminal law of the state in which the federal enclave was located.[140]

The 1873 statute was an expression of a direct congressional condemnation of abortion for this further reason: It recognized the illegality of abortion in the District of Columbia, over whose criminal law Congress had full authority. The District came under the 1866 act because it was a territory ceded to and placed under the exclusive jurisdiction of the federal government. Congress thus adopted the criminal law of Maryland (the state that ceded the territory which became the District to the United States) in any areas of the criminal law which it had not specifically made federal offenses, including the Maryland abortion law.[141]

Professor Noonan has pointed to another fairly direct endorsement of restrictive abortion laws, and thus the principle of protecting the unborn child, by the drafters of the Fourteenth Amendment. In the 1860s the federal territories of

Arizona, Colorado, Idaho, Montana, and Nevada all made it a crime to abort "a woman then big with child." Such territorial legislation was subject to congressional approval. Many of the same congressmen and senators who voted to propose the Fourteenth Amendment voted to approve these statutes.[142]

We can conclude that the framers of the Constitution and, even more clearly, the drafters of the Fourteenth Amendment believed the law could prohibit abortion, that constitutional protection extended to unborn children.

The Court states that the state of Texas conceded in oral reargument that "no case could be cited that holds that a fetus is a person within the meaning of the fourteenth amendment."[143]

There is such a case, apparently ignored on this point by the Court. It holds as follows:

> *Rights [referring specifically to the right of privacy], the provision of which is only implied or deduced, must inevitably fall [when] in conflict with the express provisions of the Fifth and Fourteenth Amendments that no person shall be deprived of life without due process of law. The difference between this case and* Griswold[144] *is clearly apparent, for here there is an embryo or fetus incapable of protecting itself. There [in* Griswold*], the only two lives were those of two competent adults.*[145]

VI. The Court's Application of the Right of Privacy

The Court's use of the right of privacy and its discussion of the basis for that right should be critically examined. We will approach this by looking at the decisions the Court cites as precedents and the matter of whether the abortion procedure can realistically be called "private."

The *Roe* opinion makes clear that the Court relied on recent lower court abortion decisions and on some of its past privacy decisions in determining that the right to abortion was included within the right of privacy. But when we look at the decisions the Court cites as establishing a right of privacy, we can readily see that several of them pertain to matters that are in no way connected with abortions. Of the ones which are conceivably connected, only one, *Eisenstadt v. Baird*,[146] comes close to being on point. Even *Eisenstadt*, however, concerns an activity, contraception, which is qualitatively different from abortion.

Of the decisions completely unrelated to abortion, one pertained to a court-ordered medical examination in a negligence trial,[147] two to either searches or seizures, or both,[148] two to telephone taps,[149] and one to the possession of obscene materials within the confines of one's own home.[150] Of the other "related" cases, which were related only in the sense that they pertained to matters involving marriage, the family, and sex and reproduction, two concerned the right of parents to direct the education of their children;[151] one a compulsory sterilization statute directed at repeat felons;[152] another a prohibition against minors selling goods in public places even with parental consent;[153] another a statute prohibiting interracial marriage;[154] and two others, prohibiting either the use or dispensing, or both, of contraceptives.[155]

Of these, the two contraceptive decisions and the sterilization decision are the only ones that seem applicable, since they alone involve state interference with the reproductive activity of persons, as do the abortion cases. The sterilization decision is not a good precedent, however, because it pertained only to a very limited group of persons (those convicted three times of a felony), and it involved a state statute that mandated activity to interfere with individual reproduction, whereas anti-abortion statutes involved state prohibition of an individual decision regarding the reproductive activity.

Anti-contraceptive statutes are like anti-abortion statutes on this latter point. Contraception, except for those forms of it that actually constitute the termination of the new life after sperm and ovum have joined (*e.g.,* the IUD, certain types of birth control pills), is, however, a different activity by its nature than abortion. With contraception we are dealing with "preventing the creation of a new and independent life" and with abortion, "those situations wherein, voluntarily or involuntarily, the preliminaries have ended, and a new life has begun."[156]

The late Dean Joseph O'Meara gives us another reason why, at least as far as the right of privacy is concerned, abortion is different from contraception: "There is nothing private about an in-hospital abortion—a fact which Mr. Justice Blackmun seems not to understand."[157]

This is true even with an early abortion done in an outpatient clinic. Such clinics are operated as public businesses, often advertise, and must meet certain minimal state requirements. The woman must be attended to by a number of persons on the clinic's staff, and records are kept. All of those attending to the abortion are strangers, none are confidential relatives or friends. While this may all occur on a confidential basis, it is no way a solitary activity like the use of contraceptives in one's bedroom or bathroom.

Moreover, *Griswold v. Connecticut* is not a good parallel to *Roe* and *Doe* as to the right of privacy for a further reason. The Connecticut statute in question was struck down specifically because it "operate[d] directly on an intimate relation of husband and wife and their physician's role in one aspect of that relation," which "very idea is repulsive to the notions of privacy surrounding the marriage relationship."[158] *Roe* and *Doe* clearly were not premised on a notion of *marital* privacy, but of *individual* privacy, since they legalize abortion for women whether married or not. Noonan thus seems correct that *Eisenstadt,* which held anti-contraceptive statutes to be unconstitutional even if they apply only to nonmarried persons, is the only real precedent for *Roe* and *Doe*.[159] Both Justice Stewart and Justice Douglas in their concurring opinions emphasized the importance of *Eisenstadt*'s assertion of the existence of a right of individual, as opposed to marital, privacy. We know, however, from the reasons given by O'Meara and the distinctions between contraception and abortion, that even *Eisenstadt* is not a good precedent for the abortion decision.

Finally, let us consider *Union Pacific Railway Company v. Botsford,*[160] which was the first decision in which the Court expressly recognized the existence of a right of privacy under the Constitution. It is ironic that the Court cites this as a precedent in the fashioning of a woman's right that permits the destruction of an unborn child. *Botsford* concerned the question of whether a trial court could order a woman to submit to a surgical examination in the context of a case she had brought claiming injuries suffered from the defendant's negligence. In affirming the trial court's judgment that it had no legal authority to make such an order, the

Supreme Court discussed how the common law treated the question. It said that the only time such an order was permitted, allowing intrusion into the privacy of one's person, was in the case of a writ *de ventre inspiciendo*. It explained the purpose of such a writ as follows:

> . . . to ascertain whether a woman convicted of a capital crime was quick with child . . . in order to guard against the taking of the life of an unborn child for the crime of the mother.[161]

This opinion is of great significance. Even though it supports the view of a common law right to privacy, it affirms that "the common law not only acknowledged a right to life in the fetus but also recognized precedence of this right over the common law right of privacy."[162]

VII. The Status of the Unborn Child's Right to Life When in Conflict With Other Rights

Finally, let us review how the courts, before *Roe* and *Doe,* treated the right to life of the unborn child when it came into conflict with other rights. Most of these cases have involved the mother's right to refuse blood transfusions, usually on religious grounds, when she is carrying an unborn child. (Generally, the law has respected a person's right to refuse a blood transfusion for religious reasons, even if it means the person's death.) As we shall see, these cases establish that the unborn child is protected under the common law *parens patriae* doctrine.[163]

Three New Jersey decisions and one federal appeals court decision in the District of Columbia illustrate this point clearly. The first two are blood transfusion cases. In the first, *Hoener v. Bertinato* (1961),[164] the parents of an unborn child refused to allow their child to have a blood transfusion upon birth, even though physicians said he would die otherwise. The court held that the parents were neglectful of the child under the state child welfare statute and awarded temporary custody of the child, immediately after his birth, to the county welfare department to ensure that the transfusion be given. In the second, *Raleigh Fitkin-Paul Morgan Memorial Hospital v. Anderson* (1964),[165] the court ordered a blood transfusion for a pregnant woman who had refused it and who, along with her unborn child, would die without it. The court made it clear that its decision was based on a concern about protecting the child's, not the mother's, life. The federal case, *Application of the President and Directors of Georgetown College, Inc.* (1964),[166] had similar circumstances to *Anderson,* and the court came to the same conclusion. The significant point about these decisions is that they held, in effect, that the unborn child's right to life takes precedence over even one of the most fundamental rights expressly protected by our Constitution, what some have included as a "preferred right,"[167] freedom of religion.[168] It would seem that these courts indeed regarded the right to life as *the* preeminent right.

In the other case, *Gleitman v. Cosgrove* (1967),[169] the New Jersey Supreme Court faced directly the question of whether any condition of disability of the child or economic inconvenience of the parents could override the child's right to life. The parents of an infant, "on his behalf," brought suit for malpractice against a physician who failed to inform them that their child could be born with birth defects after the mother contracted rubella during pregnancy. The baby boy was born with serious sight, hearing, and speech defects. The parents claimed that if they had been so told the mother would have had an abortion. The court held that the parents were barred from recovery in these circumstances and used strong and forthright language in its opinion:

> *The right to life is inalienable in our society. A court cannot say what defects should prevent an embryo from being allowed life such that denial of the opportunity to terminate the existence of a defective child in embryo can support a cause for action . . .*
>
> . . . .
>
> *. . . The sanctity of the single human life is the decisive factor in this suit in tort . . . [and]*
>
> *We are not talking here about the breeding of prize cattle. It may have been easier for the mother and less expensive for the father to have terminated the life of their child while he was an embryo, but these alleged detriments cannot stand against the preciousness of a single human life to support a remedy in tort. . . .*
>
> *Though we sympathize with the unfortunate situation in which these parents find themselves, we firmly believe the right of their child to live is greater than and precludes their right not to endure emotional and financial injury.*[170]

VIII. Conclusion

From this review, we see how the Court in *Roe* deviated sharply from established legal history. The weight of precedent and precepts of sound legal reasoning apparently gave way to the personal political and social prejudices of the Court.

NOTES

1. 410 U.S. 113 (1973).
2. *Id*. at 129.
3. Brown expresses this relationship between infanticide and abortion. Brown, *What the Supreme Court Didn't Know: Ancient and Early Christian Views on Abortion,* in I Human Life Rev. 2 (1975). Eugene Quay also mentions this relationship. He states that as ancient Rome got away from the practice of exposing newborn infants, the number of abortions increased. Quay, *Justifiable Abortion—Medical and Legal Foundations,* (pt. 2) 49 George-town L. Rev. 395, 420 (1961).
4. A. Castiglioni, A History of Medicine (E. B. Khrumbaar trans. 2d ed. 1958).
5. Brown, *supra* note 3, at 6, and Quay, *supra* note 3, at 399.
6. Brown, *supra* note 3, at 7, and Quay, *supra* note 3, at 400.
7. Quay indicates that the code of Tiglath-Pilesar probably descended from that of Hammurabi. He informs us that the Babylonians and Assyrians were

kindred peoples and intermarried, and that there was "an unbroken tradition that carried over when the rule of the Near East passed from the South (Babylon) to the North (Assyria), *supra* note 3, at 400.

8. Brown, *supra* note 3, at 7–8.
9. Quay, *supra* note 3, at 401.
10. *Id.* at 402–03.
11. *Id.* at 401–02, citing the hymn from 2 The Cambridge Ancient History 118 (1924).
12. Quay, *supra* note 3, at 402, citing J. Needham, History of Embryology, 1st ed., 9 (1934).
13. Quay, *supra* note 3, at 403–05.
14. J. Connery, Abortion: The Development of the Roman Catholic Perspective (1977), at 11–12.
15. *Id.* at 14.
16. *Id.* at 17.
17. The Court cites both Quay, *supra* note 3, and Noonan, *An Almost Absolute Value in History,* in The Morality of Abortion: Legal and Historical Perspectives 3 (J. Noonan, ed. 1970). Both indicate that the practice was known, but only Noonan says that it was common in *both* civilizations. Noonan, *supra* at 6. Quay says that it was "common among the well to do of all classes" in Rome (at 422), but that it was infanticide, not abortion, which seems to have been more common in Greece (at 406–09). In fact, he says that Sparta did not permit abortion because they would never take the risk of losing what might be a perfect male child (at 406–07).
18. The Court gives the following as its source for this: L. Edelstein, *The Hippocratic Oath,* in Supplements to the Bulletin of the History of Medicine, no. 1, 10 (Sigerist, ed. 1943).
19. This source is A. Castiglioni, A History of Medicine, 2d ed. 227 (E. B. Krumbhaar, transl. 1958).
20. Noonan *supra* note 17 at 5, quoting Soranus, Gynecology, in 4 Corpus Medicorum Graecorum, I. 19. 60, (J. Ilberg, ed. 1927).
21. Noonan, *supra* note 17 at 7.
22. Brown, *supra* note 3, at 12, citing E. Henriot, II Moeurs juridiques et judicaires de l'ancienne Rome 173 (1865).
23. Brown, *supra* note 3, at 14 citing F. J. Dolger, *Des Lebensrecht des ungeborenen Kindes und die Fruchtabtreibury in der Bewertung der heidnischen und christlichen Antike,* in Dolger, IV Antike und Christentum (1934) (Munster: Aschendorff).
24. 410 U.S. at 131.
25. Plato, The Republic, Book V, 461C, in E. Warmington, and P. Rouse, Great Dialogues of Plato 259 (W.H.D. Rouse, transl.) Book V, 461A-B.
26. Warmington, *supra* note 25, at 259.
27. *Id.* at 258.
28. T. Pangle, *Interpretative Essay,* in The Laws of Plato 376 (T. Pangle, ed. 1980).
29. Noonan, *supra* note 17, at 5.
30. A. Bloom, *Interpretive Essay,* in The Republic of Plato 386 (A. Bloom, ed. 1968).

31. A reference is made here to Aristotle's Politics, viii, 16, 1335b, 20–27, which we shall discuss shortly.
32. Plato, Laws, Book V, 740D in The Dialogues of Plato 693 (B. Jowett, transl. 1952).
33. The Politics of Aristotle, vii 15, 1335 b 24–25, 327 (E. Barker, ed. and transl. 1972).
34. Noonan, *supra* note 17, at 5.
35. Quay, *supra* note 3, at 406–07.
36. Brown, *supra* note 3, at 11, citing Dolger, *supra* note 23, at 10, n. This information about the attitude of Lycurgus and Solon is found in a text written by Galen.
37. Castiglioni, *supra* note 19, at 227.
38. Brown, *supra* note 3, at 14.
39. Noonan, *supra* note 17, at 6.
40. Brown, *supra* note 3, at 11.
41. The source for the text of the oath is Edelstein I, *supra* note 18. Another translation of this part of the oath is found in Castiglioni, *supra* note 19, at 154: "I will give no deadly medicine to anyone if asked, nor suggest any such counsel; and in like manner I will not give to a woman a pessary to produce abortion."
42. 410 U.S. at 131–32.
43. *Id*. at 132.
44. Brown, *supra* note 3, at 13.
45. *Id*.
46. The text of this case is taken from the translation by Cyril C. Means. Means, *The Phoenix of Abortional Freedom: Is a Penumbral or Ninth-Amendment Right About to Arise From the Nineteenth-Century Legislative Ashes of a Fourteenth-Century Common-Law Liberty?* 17 N.Y.L. Forum 335, 337 (1971).
47. Destro, *Abortion and the Constitution: The Need for a Life-Protective Amendment,* 63 Cal. L. Rev. 1250, 1269–70 (1975).
48. Byrn, *An American Tragedy: The Supreme Court on Abortion,* 41 Fordham L. Rev. 807, 818 (1973).
49. The text of this case is also from the Means's translation. Means, *supra* note 46, at 339.
50. Byrn, *supra* note 48, at 818–19.
51. H. Bracton, 2 On the Laws and Customs of England 341 (S. E. Thorne, transl. and rev. 1968).
52. 2 Fleta 60–61 (Bl. I) (Selden Society ed. 1955).
53. E. Coke, Third Institute 50 (1644).
54. VI Oxford English Dictionary 523 (1961).
55. *Id*.
56. W. Blackstone, Commentaries on the Laws of England, I, 129–30 (1765). Blackstone includes a footnote in which he says the following:
    The distinction between murder and manslaughter, or felonious homicide, in the time of Bracton, was in a great degree nominal. [Recall that Bracton regarded abortion as homicide.] The punish-

ment of both was the same; for murder as well as manslaughter, by the common law, had the benefit of clergy.

57. J. F. Stephen, I A History of the Criminal Law of England 54 (1964).

58. J. Putka, The Supreme Court and Abortion: The Socio-Political Impact of Judicial Activism, 93 (1979, unpublished Ph.D. dissertation, University of Cincinnati). We have shown for the most part that abortion was rebuked at common law, even while it may not have been punished often by the criminal law for practical reasons. Destro presents another perspective on this question: When we look back at the common law to determine whether there is a constitutional right to abortion, the important question to ask is not whether it was always punished by the common law, but how the common law about it developed. The willingness by both the common law and statutory law to punish abortion grew over time, reflecting a greater ability to deal with the problems of proof as science came to understand fetal development. Destro says that to the extent that Coke may have changed the law, referring to his refusal to recognize *The Twinslayer's Case* and *The Abortionist's Case* as precedent (Coke, *supra* note 53), he did so in order to bring it "into step with the times," as was the traditional practice of the common law judge. Destro, *supra* note 47, at 1271–73.

59. The case is cited from Means, *supra* note 46, at 343.

60. *Id.*

61. Byrn, *supra* note 48, at 820.

62. *Id.*

63. Horan & Marzen, *Abortion and Midwifery: A Footnote in Legal History,* in New Perspectives on Human Abortion (T. Hilgers et al., ed. 1981), at 199.

64. Means, *The Law of New York Concerning Abortion and the Status of the Foetus, 1664–1968; A Case of Cessation of Constitutionality,* 14 N.Y.L. Forum 411, 419 (1968).

65. Horan & Marzen, *supra* note 63, at 200.

66. *Id.*

67. *Id.* at 200–01.

68. Means, *supra* note 46, at 336.

69. Kelsey, *The Ninth Amendment of the Federal Constitution,* 11 Indiana L.J. 309, 321 (1936); B. Patterson, The Forgotten Ninth Amendment 55 (1955); Rogge, *Unenumerated Rights,* 47 California L. Rev. 787, 799–804 (1959); and Redlich, *Are There 'Certain Rights . . . Retained by the People?'* 37 N.Y.U.L. Rev., 787, 795 (1962) all preceded the first recognition that the Supreme Court gave to the possibility of the right of privacy being inherent in the Ninth Amendment in Griswold v. Connecticut, 381 U.S. 479 (1965). (Justice Douglas's opinion for the Court mentioned the Ninth Amendment as one basis for the decision, but Justice Goldberg, in his concurring opinion, gave it even greater emphasis.)

70. Kelsey, *supra* note 69, at 313.

71. W. Blackstone, *supra* note 56, at I, 129–45, and cited in Kelsey, *supra* note 69, at 314. Kelsey also states that Chancellor Kent added a fourth heading which he said was the specific and characteristic contribution of American law: religious freedom.

72. Roe v. Wade, 410 U.S. 113 (1973); Doe v. Bolton, 410 U.S. 179 (1973).

73. Byrn, *supra* note 48, Destro, *supra* note 47, and Rice, *The Dred Scott Case of the Twentieth Century,* 10 Houston L. Rev. 1059 (1973).

74. Byrn, *supra* note 48, at 816.

75. 43 Geo. 3, c. 58. The provisions against abortion were actually part of a more sweeping bill that dealt with "several offences of the most criminal nature," including also assault with intent to commit murder and arson. Its proper title was Lord Ellenborough's Maiming and Wounding Bill. (36 "The Parliamentary History of England," From the Earliest Period to the Year 1803, 1245–47 (London: Hansard, 1820).

76. 410 U.S. at 136.

77. This was determined from the debates for the pertinent years in The Parliamentary Debates: Forming a Continuation of the Work Entitled The Parliamentary History of England, From the Earliest Period to the Year 1803 (2d Series, London: Hansard, 1820).

78. 410 U.S. at 139.

79. *Id.* at 151–52.

80. Quay, *supra* note 3, at 447–520 Appendix I, contains a compilation of the state statutory provisions.

81. Means, *supra* note 46, at 376–92.

82. 27 N.J.L. 112 (1858).

83. 33 Me. 48 (1851).

84. 2 N.J. 443, 67 A. 2d 141 (1949).

85. Watson v. State, 9 Tex. App. 237 (1880); Moore v. State, Tex. Cr. R. 552, 40 S.W. 287 (1897); Shaw v. State, 73 Tex. Cr. R. 337, 165 S.W. 930 (1914); Fondren v. State, 74 Tex. Cr. R. 552, 169 S.W. 411 (1914); Gray v. State, 77 Tex. Cr. R. 221, 178 S.W. 337 (1915).

86. 27 N.J.L. at 114.

87. 33 Me. at 55.

88. *Id.* at 58. The prosecutibility of the woman may have had a basis at common law, as indicated in the discussion of Fleta.

89. *Id.* at 57.

90. *Id.* at 56.

91. 2 N.J. at 451.

92. *Id.* at 450.

93. *Id.* at 451.

94. 43 N.J.L. 86 (1881).

95. 21 M.J. 249, 121 A.2d 490 (1956).

96. Byrn, *supra* note 48, at 854–55. His quote in the passage is from State v. Farnam, 82 Ore. 211, 217 (1916).

97. Gorby *The 'Right' to an Abortion, the Scope of Fourteenth Amendment 'Personhood,' and the Supreme Court's Birth Requirement,* S. Ill. U.L. Rev. 1, 16–17 (1979). The decisions, in addition to State v. Gedlicke, 43 N.J.L. 86 (1881), and State v. Siciliano, 21 N.J. 249, 121 A.2d 490 (1956), already mentioned, are the following: Trent v. State, 15 Ala. App. 485, 73 So. 834 (1916), *cert. denied,* 198 Ala. 695, 73 So. 1002 (1917); State v. Miller, 90 Kan. 230, 133 P. 878 (1913); Dougherty v. People, 1 Colo. 514 (1872); Nash v. Meyer, 54 Idaho 283, 31 P.2d 273 (1934); State v. Alcorn, 7 Idaho 599, 64 P. 1014 (1901); State v. Watson, 30 Kan. 281, P. 770 (1883); Joy v.

Brown, 173 Kan. 833, 252 P.2d 889 (1933); State v. Tippie, 89 Ohio St. 35, 105 N.E. 75 (1913); Bowlan v. Lunsford, 176 Okla. 115, 54 P.2d 666 (1936); State v. Ausplund, 86 Ore. 121, 167 P. 1019 (1917); State v. Howard, 32 Vt. 380 (1859); Anderson v. Commonwealth, 190 Va. 665, 58 S.E.2d 72 (1950); and State v. Cox, 197 Wash. 67, 84 P.2d 357 (1938). Gorby states further that the following decisions *implied* that the protection of the child was at least *one* of the purposes of the respective states' statutes: Smith v. State, 33 Me. 48 (1851); Worthington v. State, 92 Md. 222, 48 A. 355 (1901); People v. Sessions, 58 Mich. 594, 26 N.W. 291 (1886); Montgomery v. State, 80 Ind. 336 (1881); Edwards v. State, 79 Neb. 251, 112 N.W. 611 (1907); Bennet v. Hymers, 101 N.H. 483, 147 A. 2d 108 (1958); Mills v. Commonwealth, 13 Pa. St. 630 (1850); and State v. Crook, 16 Utah 212, 51 P. 1091 (1898).

 98. 410 U.S. at 149.
 99. Putka, *supra* note 58, at 109.
100. *Id.*
101. *Id.*
102. *Id.* at 106.
103. Means, *supra* note 64, at 426, quoted in Putka, *supra* note 58, at 96.
104. 410 U.S. at 162.
105. This entire passage is cited from Louisell & Noonan, *Constitutional Balance,* in The Morality of Abortion: Legal and Historical Perspectives 221, 226–28.
106. Allaire v. St. Luke's Hospital 184 Ill. 359, 56 N.E. 638 (1900). The *Boggs* opinion, part of which is quoted, is in 184 Ill. at 368.
107. 65 F. Supp. 138 (D.D.C. 1946).
108. *Id.* at 143.
109. Note, *The Law and the Unborn Child: The Legal and Logical Inconsistencies,* 46 Notre Dame Lawyer 349, 356–57.
110. Roe v. Wade 410 U.S. at 162.
111. Notre Dame *supra* note 109, at 151.
112. *Id.*
113. The lists of cases by jurisdiction holding that the unborn child may recover for injuries and that the viability requirement was rejected is found in Notre Dame, *supra* note 109, at 356–58, n. 59, 60, and 67.
114. *Id.* at 359. The list of states is contained in n. 76.
115. W. Prosser, The Law of Torts 904–06 (4th ed. 1971).
116. Notre Dame, *supra* note 109, at 351.
117. W. Blackstone, *supra* note 56, at I, 130, and cited in Notre Dame, *supra* note 109, at 351.
118. Louisell & Noonan, *supra* note 105, at 220, citing for the first example Doe dem. Clarke v. Clarke, 2 H.Bl. 399, 166 Eng. Rep. 617 (C.P. 1795) and, for the second example, Trower v. Butts, 1 Sim. & Stu. 181, 57 Eng. Rep. 72 (Ch. 1823).
119. The Rule Against Perpetuities establishes the "[p]rinciple that no interest is good unless it must vest, if at all, not later than 21 years, plus period of gestation, after some life or lives in being at time of creation of interest." Black's Law Dictionary 1195 (5th ed. 1979).

120. Louisell & Noonan, *supra* note 105, at 221, citing Thellusson v. Woodford, 4 Ves. 227, 31 Eng. Rep. 117 (ch. 1798).
121. Louisell & Noonon, *supra* note 105, at 221, citing Hall v. Hancock, 32 Mass. (15 Pick.) 255 (1834); Barnett v. Pinkston, 238 Ala. 327, 191 So. 371 (1939); Cowles v. Cowles, 56 Conn. 240, 13 A. 414 (1887); and McLain v. Howald, 120 Mich. 274, 79 N.W. 182 (1899).
122. Louisell & Noonan, *supra* note 105, at 222, citing Industrial Trust Co. v. Wilson, 61 R.I. 169, 200 A. 467 (1938).
123. 175 Misc. 1022, 1024, 26 N.Y.S.2d 140, 143 (1941), quoted from Louisell & Noonan, *supra* note 105, at 222.
124. Wagner v. Gardner, 413 F. 2d 267 (1969).
125. 98 Colo. 133, 53 P.2d 1189 (1936).
126. Cited in G. Grisez, Abortion: The Myths, The Realities, and The Arguments 226 (1972).
127. 38 Cal. App. 2d 122, 100 P.2d 806 (1940).
128. Cited in Grisez, *supra* note 125, at 374.
129. Since *Roe* and *Doe,* the trend of allowing greater opportunities for recovery by the unborn in tort law has continued. Indeed, since 1973 courts have begun to recognize causes of action for injuries suffered to children *in utero* because of *preconception* acts. Robertson, *Toward Rational Boundaries of Tort Liability for Injury to the Unborn: Prenatal Injuries, Preconception Injuries and Wrongful Life,* 1978 Duke L.J. 1401–57. Robertson criticizes this trend and suggests that recovery should be limited to infants subsequently born alive (at 1434). Regarding the property rights of the unborn child, this appears to be an area of the law long since settled, with no evidence of any trends toward change.
130. Putka, *supra* note 58, at 33.
131. J. Ash, II The New and Complete Dictionary of the English Language (London: Edward & Charles Dilly in the Poultry, 1775), cited in Putka, *supra* note 58, at 33.
132. U.S. Constitution, art. I, sec. 9, cl. 8 and art. II, sec. 1, cl. 2.
133. 410 U.S. at 174–75 (dissenting opinion).
134. *Id.* at 177 (dissenting opinion).
135. Putka, *supra* note 58, at 56. The five states were North Carolina, South Carolina, Nebraska, Tennessee, and Rhode Island.
136. The provision is from 12 Stat. 19 (1860), cited in *Testimony of J. Witherspoon Before the House Subcommittee on Civil and Constitutional Rights of the House Committee on the Judiciary,* 94th Cong., 2d Sess. (1976), cited in 5108 Cong. Rec. (March 3, 1976).
137. 14 Stat. 13 (1866).
138. Witherspoon, *supra* note 136, at 5108.
139. *Id.* at 5108.
140. *Id.*
141. *Id.*
142. J. Noonan, A Private Choice: Abortion in America in the Seventies 6 (1979).
143. 410 U.S. at 157. Texas's statement is found in 75 Landmark Briefs and Arguments of the Supreme Court of the United States: Constitutional Law 1, 819 (Kurland & Casper, eds. 1975)

144. Griswold v. Connecticut, 381 U.S. 479 (1965).
145. 321 F. Supp., 741 (1970).
146. 405 U.S. 438 (1972).
147. Union Pacific Railway Co. v. Botsford, 141 U.S. 250 (1891).
148. Boyd v. United States, 116 U.S. 616 (1886) and Terry v. Ohio, 392 U.S. 1 (1968).
149. Olmsted v. United States, 277 U.S. 438 (1928) and Katz v. United States, 389 U.S. 347 (1967).
150. Stanley v. Georgia, 394 U.S. 557 (1969).
151. Meyer v. Nebraska, 262 U.S. 390 (1923), and Pierce v. Society of Sisters, 268 U.S. 510 (1925).
152. Skinner v. Oklahoma, 316 U.S. 535 (1942).
153. Prince v. Massachusetts, 321 U.S. 158 (1944).
154. Loving v. Virginia, 388 U.S. 1 (1967).
155. Griswold v. Connecticut, 381 U.S. 479 (1965) and Eisenstadt v. Baird, 405 U.S. 438 (1972).
156. State v. Munson, 201 N.W.2d 123, 126 (S. Dak., 1972).
157. O'Meara, *Abortion: The Court Decides a Non-Case,* in I The Human Life Review, no. 4, (1975).
158. 381 U.S. at 482, 486.
159. Noonan, *supra* note 142, at 21.
160. 141 U.S. 250 (1891).
161. *Id.* at 253. The Court stated further that in civil matters such a writ was permitted at common law only for the purpose of protecting "the rightful succession to the property of a deceased person against the fraudulent claims of bastards, when a widow was suspected to feign herself with child in order to produce a supposititious heir to the estate, in which case the heir or devisee might have this writ to examine whether she was with child or not, and, if she was, to keep her under proper restraint till delivered."
162. Gorby, *supra* note 97, at 19.
163. *Parens patriae,* literally "parent of the country," refers traditionally to the role of the state as sovereign and guardian of persons under legal disability. (Black's Law Dictionary, 5th ed., at 1003, [1979])
164. 67 N.J. Supp. 517, 171 A.2d 140 (Juv. Ct., 1961).
165. 42 N.J. 421, 201 A. 2d 537, *cert. denied,* 377 U.S. 985 (1964).
166. 331 F. 2d 1000 (C.A.D.C.), *cert. denied,* 377 U.S. 978 (1964).
167. Saia v. New York, 334 U.S. 558, 562 (1945).
168. The parents in these cases refused transfusions either for the mother or the child for religious reasons.
169. 49 N.J. 22, 227 A.2d 689 (1967).
170. 227 A.2d at 693.

2 · MEDICINE

Dr. Guttmacher gives a history of his involvement with the abortion issue from the 1920s to the 1970s, and explains how his personal experiences in medicine began to shape his opinions on abortion laws. Dr. Kaiser discusses the many abortion techniques along with the dangers inherent in any medical or surgical procedure.

8 · The Genesis Of Liberalized Abortion In New York: A Personal Insight_____

Alan F. Guttmacher, M.D.
Update By Irwin H. Kaiser, M.D.

I. Prelude to Liberalized Abortion Statutes

Since my debut as an Aesculapian antedates those of other physician contributors to this volume, I thought it valuable to relate medical practices and attitudes toward induced abortion a half-century ago and to analyze the genesis, direction, and magnitude of the change in those attitudes and practices and its reflection in the legal position on abortion.

I was taught obstetrics at the Johns Hopkins Medical School by Dr. J. Whitridge Williams, one of the great medical figures of the 1920s. He was forceful, confident and didactic. To him, and therefore to us, induced abortion was either therapeutic or "criminal." He told us therapeutic abortion was performed to save the life of the pregnant woman and that the primary threats involved dysfunction by three organs: the heart, the lung, and the kidney. To these hazards he begrudgingly added toxic vomiting of pregnancy. I say "begrudgingly" because I remember full well the drastic treatment meted out to hyperemetic gravidae: isolation, submammary infusions, rectal clyses, and feeding by stomach tube. To resort to therapeutic abortion in these cases was admission of medical failure. No medical sanction was then given to abortion on socioeconomic or psychological grounds.

The experiences I encountered during by residency from 1925 to 1929 made me question the wisdom of such a restrictive medical policy. In a short period I witnessed three deaths from illegal abortions: a 16-year-old with a multiperforated

Copyright © 1986 by Leonore Guttmacher

uterus, a mother of four who died of sepsis rejecting another child, and a patient in early menopause who fatally misinterpreted amenorrhea. My skepticism of the wisdom of existing abortion laws was further reinforced by an incident involving Dr. Williams. A social worker came to me seeking abortion services for a 12-year-old black child who had been impregnated by her father. Dr. Williams was a court of one to validate abortion requests, so I sought his permission to perform the operation. He was sympathetic but reminded me that Maryland prohibited abortion except where necessary to preserve the life of the mother,[1] and he did not believe that continuation of pregnancy in this case would endanger the girl's life. When I brought up the social injustice of compelling a child to bear her father's bastard, Dr. Williams compromised, saying that if I could obtain a letter from the district attorney granting special permission to the Johns Hopkins Hospital, then I could perform the abortion.[2] I failed to get this permission and delivered the baby seven months later. At about the same time, one of the residents at a neighboring hospital showed me a child, the daughter of an army colonel, who had been hysterotomized to eliminate pregnancy conceived through "rape." Experiences such as this made me question the possibilities for social injustice and disparate treatment, ever present under a restrictive policy which gave one man the sole power to determine the validity and permissibility of abortion services.

Such a restrictive policy could only lead to reliance on those who would go outside the law to provide the desired services. Indeed, during the same period there were two competent physician-abortionists in Baltimore who practiced for many years relatively unmolested by the police. They were so well-known that an inquiry addressed to either a traffic policeman or a salesgirl would have elicited their names with equal ease. They were not partners, but close collaborators, occasionally preparing death certificates for each other. One, while attending a public national meeting in Washington, rose to defend the service provided by illegal medical abortionists who had been defamed by a speaker. He stated openly that there had been but four deaths in the 7000 abortions with which he had been associated. This was before the first use of antibiotics, "salting out," and other precautionary procedures. Finally, years later when a complaint was filed, the district attorney was compelled to take official cognizance of the existence of one of the two abortionists. At the trial, the abortionist offered to produce, in his defense, a list of 300 reputable physicians who had referred cases to him. I assume my name was among them.

On one occasion, the nestor of American gynecologists, Dr. Robert L. Dickinson, called me from New York requesting that I arrange a meeting in Baltimore with Dr. T. We lunched at a hotel, and Dr. T produced a roster of his patients, duration of pregnancy, parity, city of residence, fees, source of referral, *etc*. On another occasion Dr. T met with a few of the senior medical faculty of Johns Hopkins to disclose his technique. To minimize infection, he had invented a boilable rubber perineal shield with a rubber sleeve that fitted into the vagina and through which he worked. His technique was to pack one-inch gauze strips into the cervix and lower uterine segment the night before he was to evacuate the conceptas. After 12 hours of packing, the cervix was wide open, and he was able to empty the uterus with an ovum forceps, followed by curettage without anesthesia. In advanced pregnancies he inserted intrauterine bougies, held in place by a vaginal pack until strong contractions commenced, which not infrequently took several days.

These early medical experiences with the unavailability of abortions in reputable hospitals and the incidence of illegal abortion convinced me that permitting abortion only "to preserve the life of the mother"[3] was undesirable and unenforceable. I thus sought changes which would both curb the morbidity and mortality of illegal abortion and eliminate the ethnic and social discrimination which was inherent to all induced abortions, whether legal or illegal.

I found in my hospital contacts that obstetricians and gynecologists were the most conservative medical group in regard to abortion. Internists and psychiatrists were constantly berating us for our low incidence of legal pregnancy terminations. Indeed, there had developed a feeling of prideful accomplishment among the obs-gyn staff if one's hospital had a low therapeutic abortion rate and a feeling of disgrace if the rate was relatively high compared to similar institutions. I shared this viewpoint, no doubt swayed by the writings and addresses of obstetrical leaders such as Drs. George Kosmak and Samuel Cosgrove. My sentiment was that as long as the law was as restrictive as it was, doctors should not breach it, but work to change the law—a position which I forthrightly espoused in the classroom. Despite the fact that it was not a radical notion, this position had few adherents. Members of the medical profession were content to leave things as they were; they would frequently perform a therapeutic abortion for a favored patient because of her important social position, or at least refer her to a safe, illegal medical operator. But acceptance of generally available legal abortion was still far in the future. In the early 1930s, I was invited to present a paper on abortion reform before the New Jersey Obstetrical and Gynecological Society. One participant, Dr. Cosgrove, tore into me like a tank. I can still recall my discomfiture and frustration at the unyielding establishment.

Until 1940, the decision to permit or to deny therapeutic abortion in the individual case was made solely by the chief of the obstetrical service. The physician handling the case presented the patient's history, physical examination, and laboratory findings to the chief who, in turn, made an immediate decision. Through personal observations, I learned that it was impossible to predict how the chief would decide, for such decisions seemed to turn on his mood and on the latest article he had read on the subject.

It was in recognition of the inadequacies of such a procedure that, when I became chief of obstetrics at Baltimore's Sinai Hospital in 1942, I decided to have a staff committee of five make decisions about abortion.[4] This committee consisted of representatives from medicine, surgery, pediatrics, psychiatry, and obstetrics, with the obstetrician as chairman. As far as I knew, such a plan had never been tried, although I have since learned that it had been in force in a few other hospitals. The abortion committee system functioned well. Among other things it added medical expertise in special areas beyond obstetrics. Moreover, greater consistency was attained through adherence to guidelines adopted in cases with similar factual patterns. I do not believe that the committee system significantly affected the hospital's incidence of legal abortion, but at least all applicants were treated on an equal basis.

When I became director of obstetrics and gynecology at the Mount Sinai Hospital in New York in 1952, I learned that the department of gynecology (there had been no department of obstetrics previous to my arrival) had performed 30 abortions in the previous six months. I was told that if a private patient was denied abortion in another institution, she frequently sought abortion at Mount Sinai because of its well-known, relatively liberal policy. I recall resenting this reputation. Forthwith we introduced the committee system, the results of which have been reported in three publications.[5] The committee met each Wednesday afternoon if any case was to be heard. Forty-eight hours prior to that meeting, the staff obstetrician who wished to carry out an abortion would have provided each member a summary of the case together with recommendations from consultants, if any had examined the patient. The staff obstetrician and frequently a consultant from a medical discipline germane to the problem (for example, a cardiologist for a cardiac case or a neurologist for the mother who had borne a child with muscular dystrophy) presented their findings or views. The committee always voted in executive session, and a unanimous vote was required to authorize abortion. This requirement was not as forbidding as it sounds, for in almost every instance the other members of the committee would agree with the opinion of the member within whose discipline the problem lay.

Statistics on the number of abortions performed at Mount Sinai and at other New York hospitals over generally contemporaneous time periods are illuminating. At Mount Sinai Hospital, 207 therapeutic abortions were performed between 1953 and 1960, yielding an incidence of 5.7 abortions per 1000 live births. Partly because of my efforts to eliminate discrimination, the rate was 6.3 per 1000 live births on the private service and 4.6 per 1000 births on the ward service.[6] One commentator, in reporting figures from another large New York voluntary hospital for the years 1951 to 1954, showed an incidence of 8.1 abortions per 1000 live births on the private service and a rate of 2.4 on the ward service.[7] Statistics were also available for two New York municipal hospitals: Metropolitan Hospital (1959–61) and Kings County Hospital (1958–60). In the former, the abortion incidence was 0.077 per 1000 live births, and in the latter the incidence was 0.37 per 1000 live births.[8] Gold published a study of abortion incidence for all New York hospitals for the period 1960–62.[9] The incidence in proprietary institutions was shown to be 3.9 per 1000 live births; and in the voluntary hospitals the incidence was 2.4 on the private services and 0.7 on the ward services. Municipal hospitals showed a rate of 0.1 per 1000 live births. There was also a marked ethnic differential: the ratio of therapeutic abortions per 1000 live births was 2.6 for whites, 0.5 for Negroes, and 0.1 for Puerto Ricans.

Not only was there great disparity in the incidence rates among various hospitals but, in addition, the abortion policies and rules established by hospitals were confusingly different. Mount Sinai, for example, validated abortion for well-documented rubella (German measles), whereas Columbia-Presbyterian did not. Mount Sinai did not permit abortion for rape, whereas St. Johns in Brooklyn did. The marked differences among hospitals in regard to incidence and standards as well as patient discrimination—discrimination between ward and private patients and between ethnic groups—served to aggravate my dissatisfaction with the status quo and led to my desire for the enactment of a new law.

The question was, what should be the content of an ideal law? Because my twin brother, the late Dr. Manfred Guttmacher, a forensic psychiatrist, was a member of the American Law Institute (ALI), which was then engaged in writing a revised penal code, I was present on a Sunday afternoon in December 1959 when Mr. Herbert Wechsler (professor of law at Columbia) unveiled his model abortion statute now called the ALI bill.[10] The recommended statute provided that a doctor would be permitted to perform an abortion: (1) if continuation of pregnancy "would gravely impair the physical or mental health of the mother"; (2) if the doctor believed "that the child would be born with grave physical or mental defects"; or (3) if the pregnancy resulted from rape or incest.[11]

When Professor Wechsler had finished presenting his suggested statute, an elderly gentleman sitting at the large, felt-covered table inaudibly mumbled some comment. Mr. Wechsler said, "What did you say, Judge Hand?" The eminent federal jurist, Learned Hand said, "It is a rotten law." Mr. Wechsler asked why, and Judge Hand responded, "It's too damned conservative." How right he was. Yet most of those present, including myself, disagreed with him. The Wechsler abortion bill was passed by the institute as part of the total revised penal code revealed to the public in 1962. Many, including myself, hailed it as the answer to the legal problems surrounding abortion, which had always been the doctors' dilemma.

Even though the ALI Code had not yet been adopted by any state, its mere promulgation opened the medical profession's eyes to the preservation of health as being a justification for abortion. The most difficult health hazard to document (but equally difficult to refute) was significant trauma to the psychic stability of the pregnant individual. "Psychiatric" indications for abortion rapidly increased in importance. Tietze's figures demonstrate that in 1963 psychiatric indications accounted for 0.57 legal abortions per 1000 live births in the United States; in 1965 the rate was 0.76 per 1000, and in 1967 it was 1.50 per 1000.[12] The increasing frequency of psychiatric justifications for abortion caused concern for many. Because the psychiatric indications were so ill-defined and pliable, it was feared that they might become an upperclass ticket for legal abortion, thus increasing discrimination and doing little to lower the morbidity and mortality rates in the population at large. In 1967, Colorado, California, and North Carolina,[13] and in 1968, Maryland and Georgia,[14] all modified their respective statutes, using the ALI bill as the prototype. Between 1967 and 1968 the incidence of legal abortions in the United States increased from 2.59 to 5.19 per 1000 live births, and abortions for psychiatric indications increased from 1.50 to 3.61 per 1000 live births.[15]

In December 1968, I was appointed to Governor Rockefeller's 11-member commission which had been formed to examine the abortion statute of New York State and to make recommendations for change. When the governor convened the commission, he said, "I am not asking whether New York's abortion law should be changed, I am asking how it should be changed." The commission was made up of a minister, a priest, a rabbi, three professors of law, three physicians, a poetess, and the president of a large black woman's organization. There were four Catholics, four Protestants, and three Jews. The commission met every two weeks for more than three months. It was apparent that three members wanted no change in the old law despite the governor's charge, two wished abortion removed entirely from the criminal code, and six advocated the enactment of the ALI model with further liberalization: the majority report—approved 8–3—added legal abortion on request for any mother of four children. My proposal of adding a clause to permit abortion on request for any woman 40 years or older was voted down—this was April 1969.

The more I studied early results from the five states which had been the first to liberalize their laws, the more I began to espouse the opinion that abortion statutes should be entirely removed from the criminal code. The number of legal abortions being undertaken under the new liberalized laws, when contrasted with the figures for the previously undertaken illegal abortions, was far too low. In 1968, for example, California reported only about 5000 abortions under the new law.[16] It is true that this number has steadily increased to a present rate of over 100,000 per year, but that increase stems in large part from an increase in the number of abortions legitimized on psychiatric grounds: Over 90 percent of current abortions are performed on that ground.[17] In actuality it places the psychiatrist in the untenable situation of being an authority in socioeconomics. I examined the situation personally in Colorado and discovered that two Denver hospitals were doing vitually all of the pregnancy interruptions and these were being performed primarily on the private sector. This clearly implied that the state-imposed requirement of two psychiatric consultations was causing an effective discrimination against ward patients: private consultations were so expensive as to be available only to the wealthier patients, and psychiatric appointments in public facilities were booked solid for three months—far beyond the time limitation on obtaining an abortion. From these experiences, I reluctantly concluded that abortion on request—necessitating removal of "abortion" from the penal codes—was the only way to truly democratize legal abortion and to sufficiently increase the numbers performed so as to decrease the incidence of illegal abortions. I came to this conclusion in 1969, 47 years after abortion first came to my medical attention when I was a third-year medical student. Abortion on request, a position which I now support after having been converted by years of medical practice and observation, was soon to have its trial in New York, the state in which I reside. This gave me the opportunity to observe firsthand how effectively it would function. The three criteria to be used for evaluation were straightforward. Did abortion on request save lives? Did it minimize socioethnic discrimination? Did it reduce the incidence of illegal abortion?

UPDATE
Irvin H. Kaiser, M.D.

It is already difficult to remember the excitement and confusion that surrounded the dramatic changes in public attitude and in the law concerning abortion that descended on the unprepared medical and legal professions in 1970. Alan F. Guttmacher in his chapter in the previous edition of the present work captured this in the section which was headed "The New York Situation", the opening paragraphs of which read as follows:

> *On April 10, 1970, the New York State Legislature amended the State Penal Code, permitting licensed physicians to provide abortion services for any consenting woman less than 24 weeks pregnant. The law specifies no restrictions on place of residence, age, marital status, or consent of spouse, if married, and it makes no*

restrictions as to the type of facility where abortions might be performed. After 142 years of one of the most restrictive abortion statutes—allowing abortions only when necessary to preserve the life of the mother—New York suddenly had the most liberal abortion law in the world.

The New York State Legislature in 1969 had flatly rejected the bill produced by the Governor's Commission—basically the ALI model plus permissible abortion on request for any woman with four or more children. Those of us in favor of reform hoped in 1970 that we could somehow put through a modified ALI bill. We knew of the 'radical' bill sponsored by Constance Cook, and upstate legislator, but had no hope for passage. Much to everyone's surprise, however, it passed the House by a modest majority. When it came before the Senate there was a tie vote and an expectation that the speaker would break the tie with his negative vote since he was a strong opponent of abortion reform. However, a senator from an upstate Catholic county broke the tie by changing his negative vote to an affirmative one. The bill was to become law July 1, less than 3 months later.

The medical community was in a state of shock, not from opposition, but from total surprise. There were dire prophecies that all existing medical facilities would be dangerously overtaxed by a nationwide demand for abortion. But the New York City Department of Health began to ready the facilities of the 15 municipal hospitals, and the mayor appropriated an extra 3 million dollars to fund the new abortion service. In recognition of the financial potential, several proprietary hospitals were converted into abortoria. The voluntary hospitals agreed to do their part and some arranged to perfrom abortions on both an inpatient and an outpatient basis. Some physicians began to prepare their private offices for abortions, and others advocated free-standing clinics with built-in safety factors such as blood available for transfusion, cardiac arrest equipment, quick access to a back-up hospital, counselling before and after the operation and performance of abortion only by specialists in obstetrics and gynecology.

When July 1 arrived, the City Board of Health had not yet established its own standards for abortion services, and it did not do so until September 17. On that day the New York City Board of Health issued regulations outlawing private office abortions within New York City. They agreed that abortions could be performed in accredited hospitals and their outpatient departments. Also permitted were abortions in licensed free-standing abortion clinics which could meet certain enunciated standards regarding factors such as the size of the operating room, the availability of resuscitating equipment, and the availability of blood; furthermore, abortion of a pregnancy beyond 12 weeks could not be performed in such a free-standing clinic.

The next act in the drama took place in 1973 in the form of the Supreme Court decisions in *Roe v. Wade*[18] and *Doe v. Bolton*.[19] Based on the Supreme Court's concept of a woman's right to privacy, *Roe* established her right to terminate an unwanted pregnancy in consultation with her physician. The second case established, in view of the medical difficulties of abortion in the second trimester, that the state had a right to make regulations governing the way in which abortion would be provided at that trimester, provided that these regulations did not interfere with a woman's access to pregnancy termination. One remarkable aspect of these decisions was the extent to which the Court relied on social and medical expert advice in formulating its rules.

The opponents of abortion have been organized and extraordinarily well-financed. Soon after *Roe* they began a campaign to undo these Supreme Court decisions. In the Congress, amendments to appropriations bills have gradually withdrawn federal funds from the support of abortions, principally affecting those women dependent on welfare. The campaign also took the form of ordinances and statutes at the community and state level intended to restrict access to abortion services. In a long string of court decisions, the federal judiciary struck down one after another of these restrictive regulations until finally a group of such cases had accumulated on appeal on the docket of the Supreme Court.

In 1983, in a very firmly enunciated decision, the Supreme Court once again asserted the right of women to have access to abortion.[20] The Court declared unconstitutional a series of restrictive regulations that had been enacted in Akron, Ohio, with the explicit purpose of limiting the availability of abortion services. In addition, in related decisions announced at the same time, the Court pointed out that the greatly improved safety of techniques for abortion in the second trimester of pregnancy now made it possible to provide such abortion services on an ambulatory basis. The denial of access to this constitutes an interference with the availability of such services. The Court thereby acknowledged the evidence, accumulated over the last decade, of the safety of second-trimester pregnancy interruption by contemporary techniques.

At the present time the best estimate is that 1.5 million abortions are performed in the United States annually.[21] Approximately 91 percent of these were completed in the first trimester in 1980. The overwhelming proportion is accomplished by minimal dilatation of the cervix and suction evacuation of the products of conception, prior to the 13th week of pregnancy. The safety of this procedure, particularly if it is undertaken under local anesthesia or without anesthesia at all, is such that the best estimate of the risk of maternal death is three deaths or less per 1 million abortions.[22] The lowest rate is observed at the seventh week. Indeed, abortion of early pregnancies by this technique is so safe that Tietze has argued that the use of a barrier method of contraception such as the condom and diaphragm, in combination with abortion for the failures of these methods, results in an overall decreased risk of contraception when compared with the use of oral contraceptives or IUDs.[23] It is not necessary to accept Tietze's hypothesis entirely to recognize that interruption of pregnancy in the first trimester is an extremely safe procedure, with probably the lowest risk of any commonly undertaken surgical intervention, with the possible exception of circumcision in the newborn and cutting of the umbilical cord.[24]

The interruption of pregnancy in the second trimester results in mortality and morbidity substantially greater than that due to interruption in the first trimester, regardless of the technique employed.[25] At this duration too, however, there has been a dramatic improvement in available methods. Of the procedures commonly undertaken in the United States for abortion in the second trimester in the 1970s, almost all involved the induction of labor by the introduction into the amniotic sac of chemicals whose purpose is to kill the fetus and the placenta and thereby indirectly induce labor. In addition, some of these at the same time stimulate uterine activity. This technique results in a substantial number of complications. The earliest material used for this purpose was concentrated salt solution, which was highly efficient in inducing fetal death, but also had the hazards of salt intoxication and disseminated intravascular coagulation (DIC).[26] In some instances, labor of some violence, induced by this technique, resulted in injury to the cervix. The method therefore incurred both early and late morbidity. The replacement of concentrated saline solutions with prostaglandins and with urea, and with varying combinations of these, has markedly cut down the incidence of intoxication and DIC but has not reduced these accidents to zero. Injuries to the cervix have been minimized by the use of materials to dilate the cervix prior to or simultaneous with the intra-amniotic instillation. It is nevertheless necessary for all these patients to experience labor, and, although there are no particular limitations on the administration of drugs for pain relief, the patient's experience is nonetheless dismal.

Some special mention needs to be made of the use of ethacridine (Rivanol) for second-trimester abortion. There have been reports from the Netherlands, Sweden, Germany, and Japan of its efficacy and safety when injected by catheter in an extraamniotic position. Recently there has also been a report from the People's Republic of China (PRC).[27] A remarkably low incidence of complications is described as compared to the use of hypertonic saline and various other methods in use in the PRC. There is no comparable study of the United States experience.

Evacuation of the uterus in the second trimester by what is commonly called dilatation and evacuation (D&E) appears to be safer than these methods for the induction of labor.[28] There is no question that D&E demands a considerable degree of experience and surgical skill. It can, however, be carried out rapidly, with the use of modest amounts of analgesia and local anesthesia. Bleeding is minimal in most patients. Ideally, the patients are prepared for the evacuation, after screening by pelvic sonography, with the use of devices for dilating the cervix. These devices can be put in one, two, or even three days prior to the evacuation of the uterus, depending on the duration of pregnancy. The evacuation is therefore carried out through a prepared, dilated cervix. The evacuation itself is accomplished by forceps and suction of the fragmented fetus and the placenta. The safety of this procedure was acknowledged in the 1983 Supreme Court decisions,[29] which agreed that in properly regulated clinics, abortion in the second trimester could appropriately be performed on an ambulatory basis, provided that hospital backup was readily available.

It would be a mistake to assume that the opponents of abortion will abandon their efforts simply because the Supreme Court was most emphatic in its reiteration of the right as expressed in *Roe v. Wade*.[30] A substantial proportion of the movement consists of those who are stimulated to greater effort by the defeats they have experienced and by their basic awareness that approximately 85 percent of the adult population of the United States supports the availability of abortion. That a well-concerted effort to amend the Constitution was defeated in the United States Senate shortly after the 1983 decisions does not alter the fact that some 49 senators voted for it. This vote is looked upon as an encouraging development by some of the opponents of abortion. We can expect to have to go back to court repeatedly in actions against local legislation, enacted in the face of its obvious unconstitutionality.

II. The Outcomes of Abortion

Abortion has probably been studied in greater detail than any other surgical procedure in the history of medicine. Fortunately, in the early 1970s, the Centers for Disease Control (CDC) perceived the necessity of a careful national study of abortion services and initiated the steps to gather data prior to the 1973 Supreme Court decisions. The CDC statistics are based on reports to governmental bodies. A large number of abortions are provided in doctors' offices, and these are not necessarily reported to health departments. The Alan Guttmacher Institute (AGI) has therefore complied its own statistics, based upon reports from abortion providers in addition to those reported to the CDC. Both the CDC and the AGI have published remarkably detailed reports on abortion. The last annual summary published from the Public Health Service is that for 1978, issued in November 1980.[31] The Public Health Service has also reported a preliminary analysis of abortions in 1979 and 1980 in its Morbidity and Mortality Weekly Reports.[32] The most recent report from the AGI was published in Family Planning Perspectives for January/February, 1983 and also records data up to 1980.[33] The following statistics are based on these documents.

In 1980, some 1,553,890 abortions were performed in the United States.[34] Some 51.5 percent of these were carried out at eight weeks of gestation or less; 26.8 percent in the ninth and 10th weeks; 13 percent in the 11th and 12th weeks; and the remainder at the 13th week and beyond. Only 0.8 percent of all the abortions were carried out past the 21st week. Of these abortions, 95.6 percent were done by instrumental evacuation, which includes suction and sharp curettage in early pregnancy and dilatation and evacuation at 13 weeks' gestation and later. Only 4.3 percent were done by intrauterine instillation, prostaglandin, urea, and some combination procedures. Fortunately, only 0.1 percent of the abortions were done by hysterotomy and hysterectomy.

Nationally, approximately 30 percent of pregnancies were terminated by abortion in 1980. The highest percentage of pregnancies so terminated is found among women over the age of 40, at a rate of 51.7. However, the next highest rate is 41.7 among women up to the age of 17. For the age group 18 to 19, the percentage reaches its low point in the group 25 to 29, where the rate is 21.9.[35]

The number of deaths associated with abortion has decreased steadily since the CDC began to collect its statistics. The fewest deaths were achieved in 1980, which is the most recent year for which statistics are available.[36] In 1980, there were only eight deaths associated with legal abortion. In addition, six deaths were reported to the CDC as following spontaneous abortion, and only one death from illegally induced abortion was reported in that year. The one other abortion-related death reported in 1980 could not be classified. These figures have to be contrasted with those of 1972. In that year 88 women died of abortion-related deaths, 24 of them from legal abortion, 39 from illegally induced abortion and 25 following spontaneous abortion. The most spectacular figure, of course, is the virtual disappearance of death due to illegal abortion, there have actually been none at all in 1979.

There has now been adequate follow-up of women who have had a first-trimester suction abortion of their first pregnancy to indicate that there is no adverse effect on carrying the next pregnancy to term.[37] The incidence of mid-trimester spontaneous abortion and low-birthweight infants is not increased. However, the protective effect that a first live birth has on a subsequent birth is not observed with a prior abortion. Abortion does not appear to result in infertility. There is no clear effect of multiple abortions.

There have not been enough pregnancies studied following D&Es in the second trimester on which to base any conclusions as to later effects.

III. Techniques of Abortion in the United States

Attention has been directed over the years to developing methods of "medical" abortion, which is to say interruption of pregnancy by a nonsurgical means. Two techniques are worthy of some attention, although unfortunately both have sufficient drawbacks as that they do not adequately meet the need for a simple, noninvasive abortion method.

High-dose estrogen therapy of brief duration has been employed to prevent an unimplanted pregnancy from implanting, a therapy commonly referred to as the morning-after pill. It is not really known how frequently it prevents the successful implantation of a fertilized ovum and how frequently it simply produces sufficient hormone interference to prevent fertilization from taking place. The rate of pregnancy is nevertheless markedly reduced. There is very little question, in view of the DES experience, that estrogens are teratogenic and therefore probably not to be recommended except to patients who will certainly accept pregnancy interruption should estrogen prophylaxis fail.

Insertion of an intrauterine device is also done to prevent implantation of an unwanted pregnancy after unprotected coitus.

Considerably more attention has been directed to the use of prostaglandins for abortion, and several large study programs in this respect have been completed over the course of the last decade. The earliest hope was that the oral administration of prostaglandins could interfere with the development of the corpus luteum sufficiently to result in its degeneration and consequent abortion, because of failure of hormonal support of the early implanted pregnancy. That expectation has not been realized because luteolytic doses also result in an unacceptable incidence of side effects, particularly nausea, vomiting, and diarrhea. Administration of other prostaglandin preparations in the form of vaginal suppositories has also been attempted, but once again the success rate is not sufficiently high to justify this technique in preference to the simplicity and safety of suction evacuation. Extraamniotic instillation of prostaglandin has a substantially higher success rate than suppositories but is not a modality that can be self-administered. In sum, then, the hope of a decade ago for simple, do-it-your-self abortion techniques has not been realized.

A. Suction Curettage in the First Trimester

This technique can be employed for patients on an ambulatory basis, under local anesthesia with paracervical block, occasionally supplemented with modest doses of tranquilizers and analgesics. In patients whose cervices are prepared for the procedure either by previous vaginal delivery or by the preparatory insertion of laminaria, the procedure can be carried out without any anesthesia. Clearly it also can be accomplished under conduction or general anesthesia, but these are more than are required for the successful performance of the abortion.

In the very earliest days of pregnancy the hormonal changes have not as yet begun to soften the cervix; this is most noteworthy among patients who have never had a previous vaginal delivery. It is therefore preferable to wait to abort until approximately the seventh menstrual week of pregnancy, by which time the cervix has already begun to soften.

Laminaria is a dehydrated seaweed that can be gas sterilized and that swells up notably when moist. If on examination the cervix seems to be unusually resistant, one or more of these laminaria can be inserted into the cervix and allowed to remain for four or more hours. During this period their outer diameter enlarges as they draw water from the tissues and gradually open the cervix. Synthetic materials with similar properties are now becoming available.

The procedure is best carried out with the patient lying supine and a speculum in the vagina exposing the cervix. The cervix is stabilized with one of several grasping instruments and may or may not be cleaned off with one of a number of standard antiseptics. The operator is then obligated to test the cervix to be certain that it is sufficiently open to allow the passage of the suction curette. At present these curettes are made of transparent or translucent plastic. Some are completely rigid and others somewhat pliable. They all have blunt ends and one or two openings on either side just near the uterine end of the curette. There is a rough correlation between the diameter of the curette in millimeters and the duration of pregnancy to be interrupted, such that at the seventh menstrual week, six- or seven-millimeter curettes are sufficient, whereas at the 10th or 11th week, a 10- or 11-millimeter curette is ordinarily to be preferred. The smaller curettes will almost certainly go through the cervix of a patient who has had a previous vaginal delivery and is seven weeks pregnant, without any need for further dilatation of the cervix. With pregnancies of greater duration some dilatation is needed. This is facilitated by administration of a paracervical block with a local anesthetic agent.

Once the cervix is adequately prepared and dilated, the suction curette is inserted and then connected with a negative pressure device. The electric pumps which have become virtually standard throughout the United States generate negative pressures up to 50 to 60 centimeters of mercury. The intrauterine curette is rotated in place. Since the products of conception are less firmly attached than the endometrium itself, they come away differentially. It is possible, in view of the translucency of the curettes, to see that the abortion is being completed. It is necessary to inspect the tissue removed to identify ectopic pregnancies. With later abortions all the fetal parts should be identified.

The greater the duration of pregnancy the longer the procedure, but ordinarily the suction evacuation can be completed in a matter of a few minutes. The operator must then inspect the material that has been evacuated to see that it includes placenta. It is also possible for the operator to note immediately when the procedure has not been successful. It is standard procedure and generally required by law that this material be submitted for pathological examination.

Anatomical variations, such as the presence of uterine fibroids or double uteri, on occasion interfere mechanically with the efficient evacuation of the uterus. It is important for the operator to be aware of these possibilities.

There is not complete agreement on whether to carry out uterine sharp curettage following the evacuation of the products of conception by suction curette.

The use of antibiotic therapy prophylactically appears to reduce the incidence of infection, particularly in those patients in whom laminaria have been used. Routine use of antibiotics with suction at the seventh week is directed at a very low risk, and so its efficacy is difficult to confirm.

At the completion of the suction procedure the patient can be released to ambulatory care. The subsequent self-care differs in no particular respect from what the patient would ordinarily do at the time of a menstrual period. The evidence at the present time is that there are no immediate or late sequelae of an abortion of this sort which have any adverse impact on a patient's long-term reproductive career. There is a very low, probably less than 3 percent incidence of endometritis and, since the cervix is open and the products of conception have been efficiently cleaned out, this ordinarily responds well to antibiotic therapy and repeat curettage.

There is a curious syndrome in which clotted blood blocks the internal cervical os and additional bleeding into the uterine fundus causes severe uterine distention. This can be suspected when a patient who has had an abortion within the previous 18 hours returns for care complaining of very severe, cramping uterine pain with minimal bleeding. The syndrome can be rapidly alleviated by repeat evacuation to remove the obstructing blood clots and establish drainage.

The incidence of uterine perforation is extraordinarily low. Probably in the hands of experienced operators it should be substantially less than 1 percent. The largest proportion of perforations are the result of difficult dilatation of the cervix, which can be minimized by the laminaria techniques suggested above. Other complications are missed abortion and unidentified ectopic pregnancy.

B. Dilatation and Evacuation in the Second Trimester

There is a clear consensus that safety in the performance of D&E depends on the accurate determination of the size of the fetus by ultrasound examination. The most serious error is to undertake the abortion of a patient in the second trimester through an inadequately dilated cervix or with inadequate instrumentation. When the patient is more than 12 weeks pregnant (in this procedure the fetus must be delivered by dismemberment) the most critical single step consists of crushing the calvarium to reduce its volume. It is therefore essential to know the biparietal diameter (BPD) before initiating any procedure. Sonographic scanning of the pregnancy has therefore become an essential part of this undertaking.

At 11 to 12 weeks fetal (not menstrual) age (FA), the BPD is 20 to 26 millimeter. Therefore, dilatation to about 13 or 14 millimeters is desirable, and a

12-millimeter cannula curette is used. At 13 weeks FA, the BPD is 30 millimeters, and at 14 weeks, 36. Since some of the forceps used to deliver the fetus are as wide as 20 millimeters, dilatation to nearly that diameter is desirable.

At 14 to 15 weeks, BPDs range from 33 to 37 millimeters, and by 20 weeks has reached 50 millimeters. At the later durations difficulty in extraction can be encountered from the fetal pelvis, and special instruments are needed.

The first step in D&E is the preliminary dilatation of the cervix with gradual dilators such as laminaria. A few operators of considerable experience still use tapered metal dilators. When the pregnancy is of greater duration, the laminaria have to be left in for longer periods of time, and larger numbers of laminaria are necessary. It is entirely possible to dilate the cervix to a diameter as much as 30 millimeters by the use of multiple laminaria insertions over a span of 48 hours, increasing the number of laminaria with each successive insertion. Graduated tapered (Pratt) dilators are now available up to 89 French—or almost 30 millimeters.

As has been noted, D&E can be carried out with modest systemic sedation, making use of analgesics and tranquilizers and then employing a paracervical block to anesthetize the cervix. The procedure can also be done under general anesthesia, which allows the various maneuvers to be done more rapidly but confers no other advantage and unfortunately incurs the unavoidable risks of general anesthesia.

As with the interruptions in the first trimester, the cervix is visualized with a speculum and stabilized with a tenaculum. The adequacy of the dilatation of the cervix is then confirmed, and if necessary the cervix can be even further dilated by graduated Pratt dilators. When access to the uterine cavity is demonstrated, an appropriate suction cannula is then passed through the cervical canal into the lower uterine segment. No effort is made to introduce it to the fundus. Negative pressure is then made. With pregnancies up to 15 weeks, ordinarily the amniotic fluid is obtained and emptied out first, and then the uterus begins to contract. Some operators prefer to employ parenteral administration of 200 micrograms of Methergine at this point to enhance uterine contractility, but there is no clear consensus as to the necessity for this. Suction continues to be exerted through the curettes, which ordinarily are either 12 or 14 millimeters in diameter when the abortion to be undertaken is less than 16 weeks. Once some placenta and umbilical cord is obtained, the suction is discontinued and a grasping forceps is introduced into the fundus. The tissue that has been brought down into the lower uterine segment by the suction is then removed with the forceps until no more can be obtained. The curette is then reintroduced and negative pressure again made. By alternating from suction to removal of tissue with forceps, the products of conception can gradually be extracted. For abortion beyond 15 weeks' duration, suction is of little help except to remove amniotic fluid and thereby reduce uterine volume. The fetus must be removed with appropriate forceps.

It is essential to the procedure to be certain that the spinal column, thorax, and particularly the skull of the fetus be identified in the tissue removal, for assurance of the completeness of the evacuation. It is important after termination of the procedure to identify the long bones as well.

Bleeding during this procedure is ordinarily minimal, in all likelihood because the evacuation of the placenta takes place relatively early in the course of the procedure and uterine contraction achieves hemostasis. Extraordinary bleeding is suggestive of an inadvertent perforation or loss of normal blood coagulability rather than uterine atony, particularly if the bleeding does not respond to administration of Methergine or oxytocin.

D&E can been done as late as the 24th week of pregnancy. It would be wise to limit these late procedures to situations with urgent indication. Certainly up to the 16th week D&E appears, on the basis of several large series from careful observers, to be a feasible and a safe procedure.

The death-to-case ratio is about 7.7 per 100,000 D&Es and can be expected to fall as techniques improve. This rate, although at least an order of magnitude greater than that for suction abortion in the first trimester, is nonetheless substantially less than that for other methods of second-trimester abortion. There is agreement that prophylactic administration of tetracycline should be prescribed.

Follow-up care for D&E is essentially the same as it is for abortion in the first trimester, and the complications are essentially the same. There are occasional instances of endometritis but the incidence of this is no greater than 1 percent. On unusual occasions fragments of the fetus are left in the uterus; these ordinarily pass uneventfully in the course of the next few days. Late bleeding is unusual, and the incidence of DIC is much lower than with intraamniotic instillations. Suitable sonographic study prior to the abortion will avoid the difficulties that can occur with unrecognized multiple pregnancy, myomata, and ovarian cysts.

C. Induction of Labor in the Second Trimester

Abortion in the second trimester can be accomplished by injecting into the uterus materials that will stimulate uterine contractility and induce a premature labor. This same effect can be accomplished by the injection of corrosive materials that will kill the fetus and placenta by one of several modes of action. With the death of the placenta, labor ordinarily follows in a reasonable period of time. This period can be shortened by the administration of oxytocin and can be curtailed even further by the preliminary dilatation of the cervix with laminaria.

The first material to be used successfully in this technique was hypertonic saline solution, introduced into the amniotic cavity. This is ordinarily done after the 16th week of pregnancy. A suitable needle is inserted into the amniotic sac. Amniotic fluid may or may not be withdrawn, and a volume of 20 to 23 percent salt solution, but not more than 200 milliliters, injected into the amniotic sac. A number of techniques for doing this have been described. The essential feature of all of them is that inadvertent intravenous administration must be avoided. A patient who is conscious will ordinarily report to the operator sensations of pain and extreme thirst if the hypertonic saline is being injected into either the uterine wall or a uterine blood vessel. The procedure must be promptly terminated under such circumstances. If the saline is put into the amniotic sac, the patient ordinarily has no sensations at all. The fetal heart ceases within a half-hour of the instillation, and patients fall into labor for the most part anywhere between 12 and 36 hours later. An occasional patient experiences missed abortion.

Because of the early experience with complications of the injection of intraamniotic saline, including several deaths from hypernatremia, attention has been directed to a number of other drugs for abortion. These include the intrauterine instillation of prostaglandin F2 alpha, generally in amounts of 30 and 40 milligrams; hyperosmolar glucose, which has generally been abandoned because of problems with chorioamnionitis; urea solutions; and combinations of these. As mentioned, in some series the cervix has been prepared with laminaria and a number of regimes of additional uterine stimulation with oxytocin have also been described, to shorten induction to abortion time.

In most institutions, it is desirable that whatever is undertaken to accomplish abortion also accomplishes fetal death so that neither the patient nor the staff has the unpleasant experience of witnessing the birth of a live abortus. Indeed, one of the disadvantages of this technique of abortion is that the patient experiences labor, which in many instances is substantially more uncomfortable than normal labor at term. This has to be taken into consideration in view of the fact that a very high proportion of our patients who present for abortion in the second trimester are young adolescents with inadequate support systems.

A common complication is retained placenta, defined as failure to pass the placenta spontaneously within one hour, which may occur in as many as 50 percent of all cases. A possible exception is the use of ethacridine (Rivanol), which in the reports from the People's Republic of China has a very low incidence of placental retention when compared with prostaglandin, urea, and saline instillation. Placental retention is associated with excessive loss of blood. Therefore, a number of regimes to speed the birth of the placenta have been described, most of which involve relatively early surgical intervention, either with the use of forceps to grasp the placenta and deliver it or the employment of an intrauterine suction curette.

All of the modalities for intraamniotic instillation have resulted in episodes of disseminated intravascular coagulation, the commonest association being with saline instillation. Because of this and because of the discomforts of this form of abortion, abortion by this technique has been limited to the care of hospitalized patients. This has put a premium on abbreviating the delay from injection to abortion and the duration of the labor that ensues. A number of regimes directed toward these ends have been described. Despite this, abortion by this technique ordinarily requires a hospitalization of at least two days and, in the presence of complications, it can be substantially longer than that. Since some of the labors that ensue are rather rapid, there have resulted injuries to the cervix, producing cervico-uterine tears and subsequent cervical uterine fistulas. Uterine rupture has also been observed with extrusion of the fetus into intraperitoneal or retroperitoneal sites. The administration of intravenous oxytocin therefore has to be undertaken with care, and probably should not be done prior to the rupture of membranes.

Several techniques for induction of labor by the insertion of dilating materials in the cervix, supplemented by the instillation of oxytocic materials in an extraamniotic location, have also been described. The two preparations principally used for this purpose have been prostaglandin F2alpha and ethacridine. At the present time, it does not appear that this route of induction of abortion confers any particular advantages.

Abortion has also been induced by the intravaginal application of prostaglandin E2 and the 15 methyl form. On the average this modality results in a substantially longer delay than intraamniotic infusion and does not appear to confer any advantage except in those circumstances where intraamniotic instillation presents anatomic problems.

The advantage of these techniques for the induction of labor is that they do not require forcible dilatation of the cervix, and they do not require dismemberment of the fetus. Such follow-up studies as are available do not, however, indicate that they do not reduce the likelihood of subsequent pregnancy loss, due to injury of the cervix, as compared with D&E.

D. Abortion by Hysterotomy and Hysterectomy

As mentioned above, these major surgical procedures accounted for 0.1 percent of all abortions done in 1980. There is probably only the rarest indication for doing them, and they carry a prohibitively high morbidity and mortality rate. When a patient requests sterilization as well as abortion, risk is minimized by doing them as separate procedures. The risk of hysterectomy done solely for sterilization is excessive even in the nonpregnant state.

NOTES

1. *Cf.* Md. Ann. Code art. 43, § 137(a) (1971). The present statute is patterned after the Model Penal Code. *See* note 10 *infra* and accompanying text.
2. Presently, California follows a similar procedure in cases of incest. Cal. Health & Safety Code § 25952 (West Supp. 1971) (permitting abortion where the district attorney is satisfied that there is probable cause to believe that the pregnancy resulted from rape or incest and this validation is transmitted to the Committee of the Medical Staff).
3. *See, e.g.,* Tenn. Code Ann. § 39–301 (1955), which restricted abortions to such cases of necessity.
4. The committee method of decisions regarding abortions is prevalent and is codified in many states. Cal. Health & Safety Code § 25951 (b) (West Supp. 1971), for example, requires the consent of an approved hospital committee before an abortion can be performed. The statute requires that the committee be composed of not less than three licensed physicians and requires that the decision to permit an abortion be unanimous.
5. Guttmacher, *Therapeutic Abortion: The Doctor's Dilemma,* 21 J. Mt. Sinai Hospital 111 (1954); Guttmacher, *Therapeutic Abortion in a Large General Hospital,* 37 Surgical Clinics of North America 459 (April, 1957); Guttmacher, *The Legal and Moral Status of Therapeutic Abortion,* in Progress in Gynecology IV 279 (J. Meigs & S. Sturgis, eds. 1963).
6. Guttmacher, *The Legal and Moral Status of Therapeutic Abortion,* in Progress in Gynecology IV 289 (J. Meigs & S. Sturgis, eds. 1963).
7. C. McLane, Abortion in the United States (Calderone ed. 1958).
8. Guttmacher, *supra* note 6.
9. Gold, Erhardt, Jacobziner, & Nelson, *Therapeutic Abortions in New York City: A 20 Year Review,* 55 Am. J. of Public Health 964 (1965).
10. Model Penal Code § 230.3(2) (Proposed Official Draft, 1962).
11. *Id.*
12. Tietze, *United States: Therapeutic Abortions, 1963 to 1968,* 59 Studies in

Family Planning 5 (1970). Tietze's figures were based on hospitals reporting to The Professional Activities Survey in Ann Arbor, Michigan.

13. *See* Colo. Rev. Stat. Ann. § 40–6–101(3)(a) (1971); Cal. Health & Safety Code § 25951 (West Supp. 1971); N.C. Gen. Stat. § 14–45.1 (Supp. 1971).

14. *See* Md. Ann. Code art. 43, § 137(a) (1971); Ga. Code Ann. § 26–1202 (1971). *See also* Ga. Code Ann. § 26–9925a(a) (1971) (worded identically to section 26–1202) (a prefatory note preceding section 26–9921a indicates that there is some doubt as to which statute is in effect).

15. Tietze, *supra* note 12, at 7.

16. California's Therapeutic Abortion Act became operative November 8, 1967. During the first calendar year under the new law, legal abortions reported from the entire state were 5030. *See* Overstreet, *California's Abortion Law— A Second Look,* in Abortion and the Unwanted Child 16 (C. Reiterman ed. 1971).

17. *See* Bureau of Maternal and Child Health, 4th Annual Report on the Implementation of the California Therapeutic Abortion Act (1971).

18. 410 U.S. 113 (1973).

19. 410 U.S. 179 (1973).

20. Akron v. Akron Center for Reproductive Health, 103 S. Ct. 2481 (1983).

21. S. K. Henshaw & K. O'Reilly, *Characteristics of Abortion Patients in the United States, 1979 and 1980.* 15 Family Planning Perspectives 5 (1983).

22. Centers for Disease Control, United States Public Health Service, Abortion Surveillance 1978. (November 1980); W. Cates, Jr., *Abortion Myths and Realities: Who is Misleading Whom?* 142 Am. J. Obstet. Gynecol. 954 (1982).

23. C. J. R. Hogue, W. Cates, Jr., & C. Tietze, *Impact of Vacuum Aspiration Abortion on Future Childbearing: A Review.* 15 Fam. Plann. Perspect. 119 (1983).

24. Morbidity and Mortality Weekly Report: United States Public Health Service, February 11, 1983, 32 Abortion Surveillance: Preliminary Analysis, 1978–1980 United States 62 (1983).

25. Centers for Disease Control, *supra* note 22; Morbidity and Mortality Weekly Report, *supra* note 24.

26. S. Neubardt & H. Schulman, Techniques of Abortion, 2d ed. (1977).

27. K.-H. Tien, *Intraamniotic Injection of Ethacridine for Second Trimester Induction of Labor.* 61 Obstet. Gynecol. 733 (1983).

28. W. M. Hern, *Midtrimester Abortion.* 10 Obstet. & Gynecol. Ann. 375 (1981); W. F. Peterson, F. N. Berry, M. R. Grace, and C. L. Gulbranson, *Second Trimester Abortion by Dilatation and Evacuation: An Analysis of 11,747 Cases.* 62 Obstet. Gynecol. 185 (1983).

29. Akon v. Akron Center for Reproductive Health, 103 S. Ct. 2481 (1983).

30. 410 U.S. 113 (1973).

31. Center for Disease Control, *supra* note 22.

32. Morbidity and Mortality Weekly Report, *supra* note 24.

33. Henshaw & O'Reilly, *supra* note 21.

34. *Id.*

35. *Id.*

36. Morbidity and Mortality Weekly Report, *supra* note 24.

37. Hogue, Cates, & Tietze, *supra* note 23.

This article on abortion practices focuses on the medical indications for therapeutic abortions. Because of the discovery of new diseases, along with better treatments of older ones, the list of medical indications for abortion changes with the advancement of technology.

9 · Abortion Practices in the United States: A Medical Viewpoint_____

Kenneth R. Niswander, M.D., and
Manuel Porto, M.D.

Just 20 years ago, Alan F. Guttmacher stated, "Illegal or criminal abortion is the only great pandemic disease which remains unrecognized and untreated by modern medicine."[1] During 1965, in fact, 235 deaths, or 20 percent of all deaths related to pregnancy and childbirth, were attributed to abortion.[2] As recently as 1972, The Centers for Disease Control reported 39 maternal deaths associated with illegal abortion in the United States, this in spite of the fact that liberalized abortion legislation in many states, most notably New York and California, accounted for some 587,000 legal abortions reported nationally that year.

Since the Supreme Court decisions in 1973, the number of maternal deaths related to abortion has decreased precipitously, and in 1979 there were *no* deaths resulting from illegal or self-induced abortion procedures in the United States.[3] The overall abortion-related maternal mortality, including spontaneous (miscarriage), legal, and illegal procedures decreased from 90 women in 1972 to 16 in 1980. These figures are all the more impressive in light of the more efficient reporting mechanisms developed and the larger number of procedures performed (nearly 1.6 million in 1980).[4] Overall maternal mortality in the United States declined by 50 percent during the last decade.[5] Although contraceptive and sterilization practices have been major contributors to the overall decrease, clearly, legal abortion has also had a significant impact. As Cates so eloquently wrote, "[T]he data clearly indicate that legalization of abortion has had a definite impact on the health of American women faced with unwanted pregnancies, by providing them with a safer option than the alternative of either illegal abortion or continuing the pregnancy to term."[6]

The widespread prevalence of abortion has never been seriously questioned, nor is it a new issue. In order to fully comprehend this most controversial subject, it is important to study the historical background of abortion, the contemporary indications for therapeutic abortion, and the current legal abortion practices in the United States.

I. History

Abortion is an ancient practice. The records of almost every civilization indicate knowledge of abortifacients and abortive techniques. Among primitive peoples these were gruesome when practiced in the extreme, and remain so among certain primitive tribes today. In one tribal rite, for example, large ants were encouraged to bite the woman's body, and on occasion, the insects were taken internally.[7] Gross traumatization of the pregnant abdomen was a popular method of attempting to induce abortion, and is still used by some primitive groups. The early Hebrews knew abortive techniques, although they strongly disapproved of the practice. The Greeks, on the other hand, advocated abortion in order to control population size, and ensure good social and economic conditions. Hippocrates advised abortion in certain situations, but as a general rule condemned the practice because it so often resulted in the mother's injury or death.[8]

Christian belief in the immortality of the viable fetus' soul has largely been responsible for the Roman Catholic church's condemnation of abortion. Doctrine has placed abortion in the same category as infanticide, and the unbaptized soul of the fetus, like that of the infant, was considered in limbo. Many early canonists, however, did not feel that the soul entered the fetus at the time of conception; rather, the belief was prevalent that while the soul entered the body of a female fetus at 90 days gestation, the soul of the male fetus was present after the 40th day of gestation. Because of this belief, interruption of the pregnancy before the 40th day was punished only by a fine, whereas abortion when the soul was present was regarded as murder and was punished accordingly. In 1869, Pope Pius IX made this distinction become unimportant, since abortion before the soul entered the fetus became "anticipated homicide."[9] In spite of the church's opposition, abortion *was* practiced, and not infrequently resulted in the mother's death.

According to English common law, legal existence of the fetus was not recognized in criminal cases until quickening (the first perception of fetal motion), which usually occurs after the fourth month of pregnancy.[10] As American jurisprudence was firmly based on English common law, it is not surprising that in 1821 a Connecticut statute (followed by similar ones in 10 other states), made abortion illegal only after quickening. Indeed, abortions were quite common in early America, being performed for the most part by poorly trained practioners. It was not until 1845 that Massachusetts became the first state to make abortion, or attempted abortion, at any point in pregnancy a criminal offense. Dr. Horatio Robinson-Storer, an obstetrician-gynecologist, launched an anti-abortion crusade in 1857 with the support of the American Medical Association. By 1880, anti-abortion legislation had been adopted in 40 states and territories.[11] Into the early 1960s, abortion was prohibited throughout the United States unless the life of the pregnant woman would be endangered should the pregnancy be carried to term. Yet in the 1950s, the number of illegal abortions in the United States was conservatively estimated at 300,000 annually.[12] Kinsey noted that 22 percent of the married women he interviewed had had one or more abortions *in marriage* by the age of 45.[13] Nearly 95 percent of the premarital pregnancies in his survey were resolved by abortion.[14] Obviously, society, found a frequent need for pregnancy interruption.

The punishment for the poor Renaissance woman who induced abortion was death by crucifixion, whereas her rich sister might buy her way out of such punishment. So, too, in the United States, poor women, especially those from minority groups, were the principal victims of our restrictive abortion laws. The data clearly show that a disproportionate number of women who obtained the few therapeutic abortions done in the past were both affluent and white. A report on abortions in New York City covering a 20-year period indicated that 90 percent of the therapeutic abortions were performed on white women;[15] and the review of the abortions in two Buffalo, New York, hospitals attests to the paucity of therapeutic abortions among nonwhite patients.[16] Although the indications for abortion may have changed over the centuries, discrimination against poor and minority women, and the very real dangers of criminal abortion, remained until the early 1970s. In 1972, the second year of New York State's free-choice statute, the ratio of abortions to live births was 366 to 1000 for white women, in contrast to 736 to 1000 for nonwhite women.[17]

In 1976, some 46.5 percent of pregnancies among Medicaid-eligible women in New York State were terminated by abortion, as compared to 36 percent of pregnancies for more affluent women.[18] In California, 57 percent of the total number of induced abortions reported in 1978 were funded by Medi-Cal.[19]

Taussig, in his classic book on abortion, gives a good historical account of the medical indications for abortion and discusses some of the early authorities who referred to abortion.[20] Plato and Aristotle clearly encouraged abortion on social or economic grounds. In Rome, especially during the era of the Roman empire, abortion was approved for social indications. The influence of Christianity, although not actually diminishing the practice of abortion, did make it socially unacceptable.

Early in the Christian era, Priscianus, a physician, recommended abortion to save the life of the mother; but writings about therapeutic abortion are scarce and the ramifications of the abortion issue do not seem to have been reconsidered until 1772.[21] At that time, William Cooper suggested therapeutic abortion for cases of contracted pelvis, in order to prevent the horrors of attempted delivery through a malformed bony structure. Dewees, Velpeau, Hodge, and other prominent physicians continued to encourage abortion in cases of contracted pelvis. This suggestion was accepted by many obstetricians in Europe, and during the latter half of the 19th century "the indications, especially in Germany, were extended to include tuberculosis, heart disease, nephritis, and certain forms of psychosis."[22] These indications became more prevalent. In the years preceding liberalized abortion legislation, there was a growing tendency to abort for psychiatric or socioeconomic reasons. While these factors undoubtedly continue to exert significant influence on the decision to terminate pregnancy, there is no longer the need to label these as truly medical, or "therapeutic," abortions.

II. Contemporary Indications for Therapeutic Abortion

"The most astute medical minds could not possibly devise a predetermined list of conditions completely including each individual patient for whom a procedure is medically necessary and excluding all others. . . . The final decision as to performing the abortion must be left to the medical judgement of the pregnant woman's attending physician, in consultation with the patient. That responsibility is the physician's, both ethically and by reason of his experience."[23]

While the term "therapeutic abortion" is commonly used today to describe interruptions of early pregnancy by licensed medical personnel, the vast majority of pregnancy terminations should be classified as induced abortions. "Therapeutic abortion" is a term that should be reserved for those few instances when abortion is indicated for medical or fetal reasons. Few of these medical indications are absolute, and the decision to terminate the pregnancy frequently is based not only on the risk to the gravida's health, but also on such factors as the patient's inability to care for a child after birth. In deciding on therapeutic abortion, a couple may not wish to assume certain risks, such as those involved in pregnancy, or in the child care required thereafter. Many of the former medical and fetal indications for therapeutic abortion represented justification for abortion at the patient's request. Similarly, the vast majority of psychiatric and socioeconomic indications for therapeutic abortion have been replaced by a unilateral patient decision to terminate an unwanted gestation for personal reasons. There remain, however, numerous medical and fetal conditions for which a therapeutic abortion is warranted.

A. Medical Indications

This summary is not intended to be the definitive list of medical indications for therapeutic abortion. However, the vast majority can be included in one of the following categories of disease: cardiovascular, gastrointestinal, renal, neurologic, pulmonary, endocrine, and malignant. Each will be briefly considered. The paucity of papers in the medical literature recommending abortion for medical disease undoubtedly reflects the infrequency with which medical illnesses are currently thought to require abortion.

1. CARDIOVASCULAR DISEASE   Cardiovascular disease has long been implicated as a risk factor for maternal death during pregnancy. However, with recent advances in cardiac surgery, cardiology, and maternal-fetal medicine, the majority of pregnant cardiac patients can successfully complete a pregnancy with little risk of maternal death. Patients with unusual congenital heart disorders, such as tetralogy of Fallot, Eisenmenger's syndrome, Marfan's syndrome, and primary pulmonary hypertension, have such high maternal mortality, up to 50 percent,[24] that pregnancy termination is recommended. In patients with severe heart valvular disease, rheumatic or otherwise, and in patients with debilitating heart disease, abortion is also advisable. The unusual syndrome of peripartum cardiomyopathy, seen almost exclusively in multiparous black women, carries a poor prognosis for both mother and fetus in a subsequent pregnancy.[25]

While special precautions must be taken in pregnancy for patients with prosthetic heart valves, including anticoagulation and antibiotics to prevent valve infection, many such patients are delivered without complications. Hence, the majority of pregnant cardiac patients face the difficult decision of weighing some increased maternal and fetal risk against their desire for a new baby. Not infrequently, a major influence in the decision to interrupt the pregnancy is the appreciation of the difficult situation that could eventually face the disabled cardiac patient who must attempt to care for her newborn.

2.   GASTROINTESTINAL DISEASES   Few if any of these disorders can be considered absolute indications for therapeutic abortion. However, patients with inflammatory bowel diseases, such as Crohn's disease and ulcerative colitis, have a 50 percent risk of disease exacerbation during pregnancy.[26] These recurrences tend to be most frequent during the first trimester and the postpartum period. Ulcerative colitis seems to have little effect on pregnancy outcome.[27] While higher spontaneous abortion rates have been documented in Crohn's disease patients (up to 25 percent),[28] the fetus that is carried to term has no greater risk of malformation, stillbirth, or other pregnancy complication.

Unfortunately, a patient's previous pregnancy history provides little guidance for patient and physician in making an intelligent decision as to whether to carry or terminate a given pregnancy.[29] It appears that successive pregnancies can have varying effects on inflammatory bowel disease, and the physician cannot be certain what that effect will be.[30] Overall, as in so many other disease states, the decision to abort or continue a pregnancy in inflammatory bowel diseases must be left to the woman and her partner.

3.   RENAL DISEASE[31]   Patients in this category are likely to be victims of chronic glomerulonephritis,[32] or hypertension of renal origin.[33] While the widely available dialysis therapy for chronic renal failure is effective, it is only palliative in nature. Dialysis in pregnancy is extremely risky to both mother and fetus, and such patients are usually offered therapeutic abortion. Patients with chronic nephritis[34] (whose lives will actually be shortened by the effects of a pregnancy), women with severe chronic hypertension, and especially those with previous hypertensive exacerbations in pregnancy, are at extremely high risk for both maternal and fetal morbidity and mortality in a subsequent pregnancy.

Now that kidney transplantation has become almost commonplace, literally hundreds of women have successfully conceived after transplantation. While the vast majority of these pregnancies succeed, they are truly high-risk pregnancies, requiring close supervision and precautionary medicine.[35] Kidney transplantation prior to an attempt at pregnancy appears to be preferable to such an attempt in a patient on chronic dialysis for end stage renal failure.

Some other renal conditions which might seem to indicate therapeutic abortion, however, do not significantly affect the risk of maternal death. Often, if one kidney has been removed, there will be little increased risk for the pregnant patient as long as the remaining kidney functions well. The risk of nephrolithiasis cannot be minimized, but the instances when it might actually increase the risk of death in a pregnant patient seem remote.

4.   NEUROLOGIC DISEASE   Diseases such as multiple sclerosis,[36] myasthenia gravis,[37] post-poliomyelitis, paralysis, epilepsy, and various congenital neurologic diseases, form the bulk of the neurologic conditions for which therapeutic abortion may be contemplated. It is unusual for a patient with multiple sclerosis to be made worse by pregnancy, but the effect of pregnancy on the disease is unpredictable.[38] Several investigators have found no justifiable indication for

pregnancy interruption in patients with multiple sclerosis.[39] However, given the unpredictable course of the disease, and the likelihood of progressive deterioration of neurologic function in the mother, patients with active MS should probably be dissuaded from becoming pregnant.[40]

A patient with myasthenia gravis in pregnancy undertakes an increased risk for both herself and her offspring. According to Plauche, there is a 40 percent incidence of exacerbation of myasthenia during pregnancy and 30 percent in the postpartum period.[41] Maternal mortality is 3.4 per 100 live births, and perinatal mortality is at least five times that of uncomplicated pregnancies. While a successful outcome is likely with intensive high-risk obstetrical prenatal surveillance and treatment for myasthenic crises, it is appropriate to offer therapeutic abortion for patients suffering this condition.

Although epileptics have a twofold increase in the incidence of maternal complications during pregnancy, there appears to be no increased risk of maternal mortality. Such pregnancies are at higher risk for toxemia, labor complications, prematurity, as well as increased neonatal morbidity and mortality.[42] The major risk in pregnancies in epileptics seems to relate to the drugs used for seizure control. These will be detailed in the section dealing with drug effects on the fetus.

5. PULMONARY DISEASE   In previous years pregnancy was believed to adversely affect the tubercular patient, and in some instances, actually to increase the risk of death from tuberculosis. With the advent of drug therapy, tuberculosis has essentially disappeared as an indication for therapeutic abortion. Patients with a previous history of a documented pulmonary embolism, occurring during pregnancy, are at high risk for a potential life-threatening recurrence in a subsequent pregnancy. Patients who would prefer to avoid such risk, and the need to self-inject anticoagulants during a subsequent pregnancy, have a justifiable indication for therapeutic abortion.

6. DIABETES MELLITUS[43]   Diabetes, in varying degrees of severity, has often been an indication for therapeutic abortion. While there is no doubt that pregnancy exaggerates the metabolic defect in diabetes, there is less evidence available concerning pregnancy's effect on the complications of the disease, including arteriosclerosis, retinal disease, and renal disease. Felig and Coustan reviewed the recent literature in this regard, noting that pregnancy does not increase the risk to the mother for progression of retinal changes or visual loss.[44] They further cited a Joslin Clinic study of 144 diabetic women with preexisting nephropathy, and found that none developed renal failure following delivery.[45] They concluded that no general recommendations can be made regarding the desirability of pregnancy termination because of the presence of retinopathy or nephropathy.

With current medical and obstetrical management of diabetes, the maternal mortality rate is now essentially the same among diabetic patients as in the overall pregnant population. While fetal risk, particularly from congenital anomalies, is distinctly increased in the diabetic patient, this would seem to have little to do with the ''health'' or ''life'' of the mother. Therapeutic abortion should be offered to the brittle diabetic who has recurrent bouts of diabetic coma in pregnancy despite appropriate medical therapy. For most advanced diabetics, the decision to undertake the intensive therapy and monitoring for a successful pregnancy must be weighed individually, taking into consideration the extent of the disease, the degree of metabolic control, and of course, ultimately, the patient's desires.

7. MALIGNANCY Many physicians have long felt that pregnancy will adversely affect a patient's medical course when a prior malignancy has been treated. However, Mitchell and Capizzi in their review of neoplastic diseases in pregnancy, clearly state that pregnancy does not alter the course of a coexistent tumor.[46] Despite past suggestions to the contrary, even with a malignancy that is frequently affected by changes in female hormones, such as carcinoma of the breast, the course of the disease is unchanged by pregnancy. Patients with acute leukemia, Hodgkin's disease, and lymphomas show similar five-year survival rates in pregnant and nonpregnant groups. Majury says that "no convincing evidence has been produced which shows that subsequent pregnancy affects adversely the prognosis in extrauterine malignancy."[47] In the case of invasive carcinoma of the uterine cervix discovered in the first or second trimester, the pregnancy should be aborted immediately and therapy instituted. If detected in the third trimester, the fetus should be allowed to come almost to term, then should be delivered by cesarean section prior to initiating therapy. Similarly, ovarian carcinoma detected in the first two trimesters of pregnancy should be treated without regard to the gestation. Hence, for disease beyond stage one (disease involving more than one ovary), total abdominal hysterectomy, bilateral salpingo-oopherectomy with pregnancy in situ or preceded by therapeutic abortion, should be accomplished.

Therapeutic abortion is indicated in a select few malignant diseases where the nature of the tumor and the necessity for rapid treatment so dictate.

B. Fetal Indications

Abortion for fetal indications may be recommended in five situations: (1) where there has been an ingestion of certain harmful drugs during pregnancy; (2) where certain viral infections, especially rubella, have been contracted by the mother; (3) where the mother's abdomen has been exposed to radiation during pregnancy; (4) where there is substantial risk of fetal malformation due to genetic or congenital factors; and (5) where there is a sensitization to the Rh factor in the bloodstream.

1. DRUGS The tragedy that occurred following the ingestion of thalidomide by pregnant women, both in Europe and in the United States, is well-known to everyone. However, thalidomide is not the first drug known to cause severe fetal abnormalities. Folic acid antagonists (methotrexate and aminopterin) employed in the treatment of leukemia and other neoplasms, are proven teratogens[48] producing severe anomalies with a prevalence of about 70 percent.

Certain anticonvulsant drugs used in the treatment of seizure disorders have been clearly implicated to have teratogenic risk. Trimethodione (tridione), a drug used in the treatment of petit mal epilepsy, has a greater than 80 percent fetal risk for a spectrum of abnormalities, including abnormal facies, growth deficiency, mental retardation, skeletal malformations, cleft lip or palate, congenital heart disease, and abnormalities of the trachea and the esophagus.[49] Diphenylhydantoin (dilantin), the most commonly used drug in the treatment of grand mal epilepsy, carries a significant risk: 10 percent for serious defects, and 30 percent for one or more less serious defects. This hydantoin syndrome consists of growth deficiency, mental deficiency, abnormal facies, cleft lip or palate, cardiac defects, and abnormal genitalia.[50] Patients who have taken these drugs during the embryogenic period of the first trimester of pregnancy should be counseled and offered therapeutic abortion if desired.

The anticoagulant coumadin (warfarin, bishydroxicoumarin) has been associated with a 25 to 50 percent risk of congenital anomalies in fetuses exposed during the first trimester of pregnancy. The syndrome includes hypoplastic nose, bony abnormalities, eye problems, including optic atrophy and cataracts, as well as mental retardation.[51]

The teratogenicity of alcohol abuse during pregnancy was first reported in 1973.[52] This fetal alcohol syndrome, with microcephaly, micrognathia, microopthalmia, cardiac defects, and growth retardation has been well-documented. The risk to heavy drinkers is reportedly about 30 percent.[53]

Masculinization of female fetuses, as well as cardiac anomalies, limb reduction anomalies, and esophageal anomalies have been reported with the use of synthetic sex steroid preparations (such as those in birth control pills), in the first trimester.[54] The frequency of these abnormalities in patients exposed to sex hormones in early pregnancy is not clear; hence, patients and their physicians must make a qualified decision on the basis of the patient's desire for pregnancy at the time. Diethylstilbesterol (DES), a synthetic estrogen once believed to prevent spontaneous abortion, was later implicated as a cause for an otherwise rare vaginal cancer in female offspring.[55]

Lithium, a drug commonly used in the treatment of manic-depressive illness, has been found to produce an 11 percent incidence of birth defects, primarily serious cardiac anomalies.[56] Patients exposed to this drug during early pregnancy should be offered the possibility of therapeutic abortion.

As the rapid expansion of developmental pharmacology continues, there seems little doubt that other drugs will soon be implicated as having significant teratogenic potential. The drugs listed above comprise those with definite risk, justifying thoughtful consideration of therapeutic abortion. The risk of many other drugs remains uncertain at this time.

2. VIRAL INFECTIONS It is estimated that some 30,000 affected children were conceived during the rubella (German measles) epidemic in the United States in 1964 and 1965. Unfortunately many parents desperately sought, but failed to find, a physician who would abort these pregnancies, in spite of the relatively high likelihood that such a child would be the victim of the rubella syndrome. The most common manifestations of this syndrome include cataracts, cardiovascular abnormalities, and hearing impairment. Growth retardation is a prominent feature of the syndrome, with birthweights less than the 10th percentile being quite common. While the above abnormalities are the most frequent, virtually every organ system has been affected in some patients.

Since the introduction of rubella vaccine in the United States in 1969, the disease has had a sharp and steady decline, reaching an all-time low of approximately 2000 cases in 1981.[57] The risk of a permanently disabled infant is inversely related to the gestational age at which the disease is contracted. With maternal exposure in the first month of pregnancy, 50 percent of the infants will be permanently disabled. There remains a 6 percent risk at four and five months of gestation. Previously, gamma globulin was commonly used to reduce the risk for pregnant women exposed to rubella. However, the results were quite unsatisfactory, and gamma globulin is rarely recommended today.[58] In light of the foregoing discussion, a confirmed diagnosis of naturally acquired rubella infection in the first trimester of pregnancy is recognized as an indication for termination of the pregnancy.[59]

Cytomegalovirus (CMV), a herpes-type virus, can cause similar permanent disabilities, and is actually far more common than rubella. It is estimated that 1 percent of all newborn infants are born with some manifestation of CMV infection.[60] Unfortunately, at this writing, our understanding of the manifestations of maternal CMV infections is still quite limited. Consequently, confirmed exposure in the first and early second trimester must be dealt with individually; for it would seem that primary CMV infection in early pregnancy would warrant consideration of therapeutic abortion.

3.   RADIATION   It is generally agreed that when radiation is given in therapeutic doses to the mother in the first few months of pregnancy, malformation or death of the fetus may result.[61] According to Parlee, "[I]t appears that ionizing radiation in therapeutic doses in the early months of pregnancy are grounds for the termination of the pregnancy."[62] Doses of radiation in therapeutic quantities are usually reserved for the treatment of malignant neoplastic disease, such as carcinoma of the cervix. Fetal death and spontaneous abortion of the products of conception are the usual, but not inevitable, result of such radiation exposure.

The exposure of the human fetus to diagnostic radiation less than five rads has not been observed to cause congenital malformations or growth retardation.[63] When extensive diagnostic X-ray procedures that equal or exceed the five-rad level are used during the early weeks of pregnancy, therapeutic abortion should be offered. With modern low-dose X-ray equipment, however, such a level is rarely achieved with routine diagnostic procedures. The fact that doses of one to three rads can produce cellular effects on the fetus, and that diagnostic exposure during pregnancy has been associated with malignancy in childhood, makes appropriate patient counseling in this "gray zone" (between one and five rads), difficult for health care professionals.[64] In general, the radiation risk to the embryo or fetus should not be the predominating factor in arriving at a decision to terminate pregnancy unless exposure is in the five rad or greater range.

4.   GENETICS   Great scientific advances in the field of genetics, coupled with the safety of amniocentesis,[65] have provided an opportunity to make the firm diagnosis of nearly 200 chromosomal and congenital malformations prenatally. Indeed, genetic counseling in prenatal diagnostic centers is available nationwide, to all women over the age of 35, or with a previous history of genetic or congenital problem in the patient or her spouse. Examples of disorders that can be diagnosed by amniocentesis include Down's syndrome, other trisomies (13 and 18), Tay-Sachs disease, neural tube defects, and sickle-cell anemia. Sex-linked abnormalities such as hemophilia and muscular dystrophy (Duchenne's) either can be ruled out or the appropriate risk can be assessed.[66]

Revolutionary improvements in ultrasonic technology have recently provided the opportunity to diagnose major congenital anomalies with confidence. Such disorders, including anencephaly, spina bifida, and other neural tube defects, as well as hydrocephalus, to mention but a few, can be identified early enough in the second trimester to provide an opportunity for therapeutic abortion.

Recent work using the still experimental technique of chorionic biopsy in the first trimester may provide the opportunity for earlier diagnosis, and therefore earlier and safer first-trimester therapeutic pregnancy termination. It is this area of genetic and congenital anomalies that currently accounts for the bulk of true therapeutic abortions performed in the United States.

5.   ERYTHROBLASTOSIS FETALIS[67]   The primary hazard to the fetus affected by Rh or other antibodies produced by the maternal immune system, is anemia or lack of red blood cells. This anemia can often be corrected by intrauterine fetal transfusion at periodic intervals.[68] As a result, the baby may be born alive and maintain good health with the aid of exchange transfusion. Hence, abortion for fetal hemolytic disease, once a rather common indication for therapeutic abortion, is rarely indicated in contemporary medical practice.

The routine administration of the Rh antibody (RhoGAM) to the unsensitized gravida immediately following the delivery of an Rh positive infant prevents the formation of maternal antibodies, and thereby minimizes the risk of fetal sensitization during a subsequent pregnancy. More recently, the prophylactic administration of RhoGAM to unsensitized Rh negative women early in the third trimester reduces the risk even further.[69] Since the introduction of RhoGAM into everyday medical practice, erythroblastosis fetalis has become a most uncommon clinical entity that should become even rarer in the future.

III. Current Legal Abortion Practices in the United States

A. Changes in the Indications

In 1936, Taussig called tuberculosis "the most significant indication for therapeutic abortion in point of frequency."[70] This disease is virtually unheard of as a reason for abortion today. In the same volume, he pointed out that psychiatric indications accounted for only a small percentage of therapeutic abortions, but that such procedures were occurring more frequently. In one study, for example, psychiatric indications increased in a linear fashion from about 10 percent in 1943 to about 80 percent in 1963.[71] Perhaps at the peak of this trend, the state of California reported that during 1970 over 98 percent of the legal abortions performed in that state were indicated for reasons of mental health.[72] These "therapeutic" abortions occurred while many psychiatrists maintained that rarely is psychiatric disease an absolute indication for therapeutic abortion.[73] Until 1973, many states required a true suicidal risk to be present in the psychiatric patient legally to permit abortion. Psychiatrists were in the forefront of the fight to expand the grounds for legal pregnancy termination. There were frequently willing to find that the patient desiring abortion suffered from psychiatric disease severe enough to threaten her life. It was suggested by Rosenberg and Silver that a psychiatrist recommending therapeutic abortion was likely to be considering the socioeconomic factors at least as much as the psychiatric indications.[74] It is clear from the foregoing information that social factors had become the prime consideration in the decision to terminate pregnant long before liberalized abortion legislation took effect. Physicians performing these abortions maintained that the patient had a right to make her own decision concerning a given pregnancy.

Other interesting trends regarding the maternal age, parity, and marital status of women securing legal abortion should be noted. In one study in the 1940s, no women under 20 years of age were aborted. During the 1950s, approximately 7 percent of the patients were under 20, and from 1960 to 1964 nearly 15 percent of the patients were in this teenage group.[75] A 17 percent decline in the birthrates of New York State adolescents was experienced in the three years following legalization of abortion, in contrast to the preceding three-year period.[76] More recent data from New York reveal that more than 60 percent of unmarried teenagers terminated their pregnancy by abortion in 1978. In addition, approximately 25 percent of married pregnant teenagers also chose to terminate their pregnancy by abortion.[77] Nationally, according to the Centers for Disease Control, approximately 31 percent of women obtaining abortions in 1977 were age 19 or younger. In that same report, young teenagers were followed by women 40 years of age and above with the second highest ratio of legal abortions to live births (about 725 to 1000).[78] The proportion of nullipara[79] undergoing abortion increased from about 20 percent during the 1940s to 36 percent during the early 1960s. By 1977, a consistent inverse relationship existed between the number of living children a woman had and the percentage of abortions obtained. Fifty-two percent of abortions that year were for nulliparous women, and only 3 percent were performed for grand multiparous (five or more children) women.[80] The percentage of married patients seeking pregnancy termination has declined steadily in the last 40 years. During the 1940s, over 93 percent of abortion patients were married; this had dropped to nearly 59 percent during the 1960s.[81] By 1977, more than three of four women obtaining abortions in the United States were unmarried at the time of the procedure.[82]

It should not be surprising that since the legalization of abortion nationwide, a substantial increase in the number of repeat procedures has occurred each year. This is primarily the result of the continually increasing pool of women who have undergone their first pregnancy termination. In 1972, 14 percent of all abortions performed in New York City were repeat procedures; by 1978, 40 percent of women obtaining abortion had undergone a previous procedure.[83] Statistics from the Centers for Disease Control, however, note that only 22 percent of abortions performed in 1977 were repeat procedures.[84]

Perhaps the most encouraging trend in abortion practices in the United States since 1973 has been the steady increase in the percentage of procedures performed in the first 12 weeks of gestation. In fact, during 1977, nearly half of all reported legal abortions were performed in the first eight weeks of gestation.[85] Data from New York State indicate that more than 90 percent of abortions in 1978 were performed during the first 12 weeks of pregnancy,[86] when the procedure involves the least danger. This is in sharp contrast to the data from 1970, the first year of legalization in New York, when 30 percent of their abortions were performed beyond 12 weeks, 18 percent greater than 16 weeks.[87] This trend will be further elaborated upon in the context of the medical procedures used at various gestational ages for pregnancy termination, as well as the inherent hazard in the various types of operations performed.

B. Hazards of Induced Abortion

As we stated at the outset, the number of maternal deaths related to abortion has decreased precipitously in the last decade. This is even more impressive in light of the fact that induced abortion is the most commonly performed operation on adults in the United States.[88] Prior to the legalization of abortion, the reported experience of various investigators concerning the frequency of complications with abortion was so varied that it was difficult, if not impossible, to make any generalizations regarding the safety of induced abortion. However, as a rule of thumb, the safety of a particular procedure varies directly with the technical ease and the experience of the physician performing the operation.

One of the beneficial byproducts of the legalization of abortion has been the marked improvement in surgical expertise in the performance of the procedure. In 1971, a study of first-trimester abortions at England's Oxford University Hospital reported the complications among 812 patients undergoing vacuum aspiration (786 patients) or D&C (44 patients).[89] Seventeen percent of the patients experienced hemorrhage of at least 500 cc's of blood, 8.5 percent suffered a traumatic cervical laceration, 15 percent experienced endometritis, and nearly 2 percent suffered a perforated uterus (two patients required hysterectomies as a result of perforation). Such a report would be appalling by today's standards, as the incidence of major complications for first-trimester abortion by suction curettage is 0.4 percent or less.[90]

One reason for the dramatic improvements in abortion complications in the first trimester is the avoidance of general anesthesia in the vast majority of cases. Hemorrhage, perforation of the uterus, and cervical injury are more common with general than with local anesthesia.[91]

More common complications of first-trimester abortion include endometritis (0.75 percent), excessive bleeding, and retained products of conception (0.61 percent).[92] Antibiotic therapy and/or reaspiration will suffice in most of these cases; many times without the need for inpatient hospitalization. The risk of uterine perforation is only 0.2 percent,[93] and can often be managed by close in-hospital observation without surgery. Menstrual extraction results in failure to interrupt the pregnancy in approximately 1 percent of patients, and requires reaspiration for completion in an additional 2 percent.[94]

The effect of induced abortion on future fertility and childbearing capacity has long been a major concern. A recent study covering five years at the Boston Hospital for Women found no evidence that a single induced abortion had any effect on a woman's ability to carry a subsequent pregnancy to term. However, there was some evidence that with two or more abortions, an increased risk of miscarriage in subsequent pregnancies exists.[95] These data remain controversial.

While the complication rates for mid-trimester abortion far exceed those for first-trimester procedures, the introduction of the D&E has had a major impact on the reduction of morbidity and mortality for mid-trimester procedures, especially those less than 16 weeks. In fact, the mortality from induced abortion during the first 15 weeks of pregnancy is one-seventh the risk of dying from pregnancy and childbirth.[96] Prior to the introduction of the D&E, virtually all mid-trimester abortions were performed by the instillation techniques outlined above. These procedures are generally performed in the latter half of the mid-trimester (greater than 16 weeks) when sufficient amniotic fluid is available within the uterus.

Trauma to the cervix, including laceration and fistula formation, can occur with all mid-trimester abortion techniques. However, this problem has been markedly reduced by the widespread use of laminaria tents (sterilized dehydrated Japanese seaweed). These devices are safe, effective cervical dilators as a result of their intense higroscopic properties. A detailed account of the complications of mid-trimester abortion can be found in Drs. Guttmacher and Kaiser's chapter in this text.

IV. Conclusion

Legalized abortion on request has essentially removed criminal abortion as a major health problem in the United States. Byproducts of this legislation have included widespread availability of contraceptive, family planning, and abortion services, as well as improved medical expertise, and the consequent reduction in the morbidity and mortality of pregnancy termination. The safety of legal abortion cannot be questioned; indeed, the mortality rate for abortion is far less than that for tonsillectomy.[97] The majority of abortion procedures can be safely carried out in an outpatient or clinic setting, with a significant reduction in the cost of medical care.[98]

We must never return to the dark ages of the back-alley abortionist, a threat that seemed quite real in some states after the Hyde Amendment restricted federal funds for abortion in 1977.[99] It is most unlikely that human nature, or society as a whole, will ever completely avoid all unsafe or unwanted pregnancies. Prenatal diagnostic centers can detect nearly 200 fetal abnormalities for which abortion services must be available. While not a total solution, legalized abortion has improved the morbidity and mortality for pregnant women and has had a beneficial impact on the quality of life.

NOTES

1. Guttmacher, *Induced Abortion,* 63 N.Y.J. Med. 2334 (1963) (editorial).
2. E. C. Moore-Cavar, International Inventory of Information on Induced Abortion, New York (1974), 520, 593–95, 603–06, 642.
3. Cates, *Legal Abortion: The Public Health Record,* 215 Science 1587 (1982).
4. Henshaw et al., 14 Fam. Plann. Perspect., 5 (1982).
5. Rochat, 34 World Health Stat Q, 2 (1981).
6. Cates, *Abortion Myths and Realities: Who Is misleading whom?,* 142 Am. J. Obstet. & Gynecol., 954 (1982).
7. *See generally* Devereux, *A Typological Study of Abortion in 350 Primitive, Ancient and Pre-industrial Societies,* 97 Therapeutic Abortion, 121.
8. *See generally* F. Taussig, Abortion, Spontaneous and Induced: Medical and Social Aspects 31 (1936).
9. G. Williams, The Sanctity of Life and the Criminal Law *passim* (1957).
10. Issues in Brief, Alan Guttmacher Institute, vol. II (no. 4) 1 (January 1982).
11. *The Abortion Quandary: No Truce in Sight,* M.D. Magazine 154 (January 1982).
12. Fisher, *Criminal Abortion,* in Therapeutic Abortion: Medical, Psychiatric, Legal, Anthropological, and Religious Considerations, 3,6 (H. Rosen, ed. 1954).
13. M. Calderone, ed., Abortion in the United States 55 (1958).
14. *Id.*
15. Gold et al., *Therapeutic Abortions in New York City: A 20 Year Review,* Am. J. Pub. Health 966 (1965).

16. Niswander, Klein, & Randall, *Changing Attitudes Toward Therapeutic Abortion,* 196 J.A.M.A. 1141, 1143 (1966).
17. Abortion: Public Issue Private Decision, New York, Public Affairs Pamphlet No. 527:16 (1975).
18. Safe and Legal: 10 Years' Experience With Legal Abortion in New York State 31 (1980).
19. Induced Abortion in California: A Biennial Report to the 1980 Legislature, State of California, Office of Family Planning 7.
20. *See generally,* Taussig, *supra* note 8, at 31–45.
21. *Id.* at 277.
22. *Id.* at 278.
23. American College of Obstetricians and Gynecologists, 13671 Congr. Rec. (August 4 1977).
24. Metcalfe & Ueland, Heart Disease and Pregnancy in Cardiac Diagnosis and Treatment, 3d ed. (Fowler, ed., 1976), at 1047–48.
25. Demakis & Rahimtoola, *Peripartum Cardiomyopathy,* 44 Circulation 964 (1971).
26. Dobbins & Spiro, *Gastrointestinal Complications,* in Medical Complications During Pregnancy, 2d ed. (Burrow & Ferris, eds. 1982), at 272.
27. *Id.*
28. *Id.*
29. MacDougall, *Ulcerative Colitis in Pregnancy,* 2 Lancet 641 (1956).
30. Vender & Spiro, *Inflammatory Bowel Disease in Pregnancy: A Review of the Literature,* J. Clin. Gastroenterol (in press).
31. This is a disease pertaining to, or involving the kidneys. J. Schmidt, Attorneys' Dictionary of Medicine and Word Finder 691 (1969).
32. Chronic glomerulonephritis is a variety of kidney disease in mild form in which the tufts formed by the tiny blood vessels are inflamed. It leads to hypertension (high blood pressure) and eventually to uremia, a poisoning of the body due to failure of the kidneys to eliminate the toxic substances. Schmidt, *supra* note 31, at 365.
33. *Id.*
34. This is a prolonged and progressive form of nephritis (inflammation of the kidney or a deterioration of the tissue forming its delicate structure) which may follow an acute attack or may result from other diseases of the body, poisons, alcohol, germs, *etc.* The fine and delicate structure of the kidney becomes distorted; the fine blood vessels become thicker; the supporting tissue (the nonfunctional part) begins to overgrow the functional parts; and even the heart is affected. *Id.* at 544.
35. Lindheimer & Katz, 18 Kidney International 149 (1980).
36. Multiple sclerosis is a disease of the brain and spinal cord. In this condition, various parts of the brain and spinal cord are subjected to a type of deterioration called sclerosis. Sclerosis in this instance is a hardening of the nerve tissue and its displacement by overgrowing connective (supporting) tissue. Basically functional nerve tissue gives way to supporting, nonfunctional tissue. The disease progresses slowly but is incurable. Schmidt, *supra* note 31, at 534.101.
37. Myasthenia gravis is a syndrome of fatigue and exhaustion of the muscular

system marked by progressive paralysis of muscles without sensory disturbance or atrophy. It may affect any muscle of the body but especially those of the face, lips, tongue, throat and neck. Dorland's Medical Dictionary, 25th ed. (1974), at 1004.

38. Cohen & Kreuger, *Multiple Sclerosis and Pregnancy: Report of a Case,* 6 Obstet. & Gynecol. 144, 145 (1955).

39. Riva, Carpenter, & O'Grady, *Pregnancy Associated With Multiple Sclerosis,* 66 Am. J. Obstet. & Gynecol. 403, 407 (1953).

40. Dalessio, *Neurologic Diseases,* in Medical Complications During Pregnancy, 2d ed. (Burrow & Ferris, eds. 1982), at 458.

41. Plauche, *Myasthenia Gravis,* 26 Clin. Obstet. & Gynecol. 594 (1983).

42. Bjerkedal & Bahna, *The Course and Outcome of Pregnancy in Women With Epilepsy,* 52 Acta Obstet. Gynecol. Scand. 245 (1973).

43. Diabetes mellitus is a disease in which the metabolism (body utilization) of sugars is greatly impaired due to the faulty secretion of insulin by the pancreas. Schmidt, *supra* note 31, at 248.21.

44. Felig & Coustan, *Diabetes Mellitus,* in Medical Complications During Pregnancy, 2d ed. (Burrow & Ferris, eds. 1982), at 56–57.

45. White, *Pregnancy and Diabetes,* in Joselyn's Diabetes Mellitus, 11th ed. (Marbel, et al., eds. 1971).

46. Mitchell & Capizzi, *Neoplastic Diseases,* in Medical Complications During Pregnancy, 2d ed. (Burrow & Ferris, eds. 1982), at 510–11.

47. Majury, *Therapeutic Abortion in the Winnipeg General Hospital,* 82 Am. J. Obstet. & Gynecol. 10, 13 (1961).

48. A teratogen is an agent or factor that causes the production of physical defects in the developing embryo, Dorland's Illustrated Medical Dictionary, *supra* note 37.

49. Howard & Hill, *Drugs in Pregnancy,* 34 Obstet. & Gynecol. Survey 646, 647 (1979).

50. *Id.* at 647.

51. *Id.* at 648.

52. *Id.* at 647.

53. Ouellett, Rosett, Rosman & Weiner: *Adverse Effects on Offspring of Maternal Alcohol Abuse During Pregnancy,* 297 N.E.J. of Med., 528 (1977).

54. Janerich, Piper, & Glebatis: *Oral Contraceptives and Congenital Limb Reduction Defects,* 291 N.E.J. of Med. 697 (1974).

55. Herbst, *Diethylstilbestrol and Other Sex Hormones During Pregnancy,* 58 Obstet. & Gynecol. (supplement) 35S (1981).

56. Briggs, et al., Drugs in Pregnancy and Lactation, (1983), at 198.

57. Horstmann, *Rubella,* 25(3) Clin. Obstet. & Gynecol. 593 (1982).

58. *Id.* at 592.

59. *Id.*

60. Stagno, Pass, Dworsky, & Alford, *Maternal Cytomegalovirus Infection and Perinatal Transmission,* 25 Clin. Obstet. & Gynecol. 563 (1982).

61. Parlee, *Radiation Hazards in Obstetrics and Gynecology,* 75 Am. J. Obstet. & Gynecol. 327, 328 (1958).

62. *Id.* at 332.

63. Tabuchi, et al., *Fetal Hazards Due to X-Ray Diagnosis During Pregnancy,* 16

Hiroshima J. MEDSCI. 49 (1967); Kinlen & Acheson, *Diagnostic Irradiation, Congenital Malformations and Spontaneous Abortion,* 41 Brit. J. of Radiol. 648 (1968).

64. Brent, *The Effects of Embryonic and Fetal Exposure to X-Ray, Microwaves and Ultrasound.* 26 Clin. Obstet. & Gynecol., No. 493 (1983).

65. This involves perforating or tapping the amnion (the inner of the two bags containing the fetus) with the use of a needle. The procedure is used to remove and study part of the amniotic fluid. Schmidt, *supra* note 31, at 83.

66. Centerwall & Tennant, *Genetic Diseases,* in Manual of Obstetrics, Diagnosis and Therapy, 2d ed. (Niswander, ed. 1983), at 277–79.

67. This is a hemolytic anemia of the fetus or newborn infant, caused by the transplacental transmission of maternally formed antibodies, usually secondary to an incompatability between the blood group of the mother and that of her offspring (usually an incompatability of the Rh factor). Schmidt, *supra* note 31, at 294.701.

68. Larkin, Knochel, & Lee, *Intrauterine Transfusions: New Techniques and Results*, 25 Clin. Obstet. & Gynecol. 309 (1982).

69. Kochenour & Beeson, *The Use of Rh-Immune Globulin,* 25 Clin. Obstet. & Gynecol. 286 (1982).

70. Taussig, *supra* note 8, at 292.

71. Niswander, Klein, & Randall, *supra* note 16, at 1142.

72. Bureau of Maternal and Child Health, 4th Annual Report on the Implementation of the California Therapeutic Abortion Act, Table I (1971).

73. Sim, *Abortion and the Psychiatrist, II* Brit. Med. J. 148 (1963).

74. Rosenberg & Silver, *Suicide, Psychiatrists and Therapeutic Abortion,* 102 Cal. Med. 407, 410 (1965).

75. Niswander, Klein, & Randall, *supra* note 16, at 1141.

76. Safe and Legal, *supra* note 18, at 28.

77. *Id.*

78. Abortion Surveillance, Annual Summary (1977), Centers for Disease Control, U.S. Department of Health, Education and Welfare, 3.

79. A nullipara is a woman who has never given birth to a child. Schmidt, *supra* note 31, at 567.

80. Safe and Legal, *supra* note 18, at 4.

81. Niswander, Klein, & Randall, *supra* note 16, at 1141.

82. Safe and Legal, *supra* note 18, at 3–4.

83. *Id.* at 35.

84. *Id.* at 5.

85. *Id.* at 4.

86. *Id.* at 18.

87. *Id.*

88. Abortion Surveillance, 1979–1980, Centers for Disease Control (issued January 1983).

89. Stallworthy, Moolgaoker, & Walsh, *Legal Abortion: A Critical Assessment of Its Risks,* LANCET 1246 (1971).

90. Grimes & Cates, *Complications From Legally-Induced Abortion: A Review,* 34 (3) Obstet. & Gynecol. Survey 178 (1979).

91. Grimes, Schulz, Cates, & Tyler, *The Comparative Safety of Local vs.*

General Anesthesia for Suction Curettage Abortion. An Analysis of 54,155 Cases, Presented at the 11th Annual Meeting of the Society for Epidemiologic Research, Iowa City, Iowa (June 14, 1978).

92. Grimes & Cates, *supra* note 91, at 183.
93. *Id.* at 179.
94. Niswander, *Contraception, Abortion and Sterilization,* in Manual of Obstetrics, Diagnosis and Therapy, 2d ed. (Niswander, ed. 1983), at 21–22.
95. Issues in Brief, Alan Guttmacher Institute, vol. I, no. 9, 3 (October 1981).
96. LeBolt, Grimes & Cates, *Mortality From Abortion and Childbirth: Are the Populations Comparable?,* 248 J.A.M.A. 188 (1982).
97. National Center for Health Statistics, DHHS, Final Mortality Statistics, 1975, and Commission on Professional and Hospital Activities, (1974–75), PAS Hospital mortality data.
98. Grimes, Cates & Selik, *Abortion Facilities and the Risk of Death,* 13 Fam. Plann. Perspect. 30 (1981).
99. Gold, et al., *A Cluster of Septic Complications Associated With Illegal Induced Abortions,* 56 Obstet. & Gynecol. 311 (1980). *Harris v. McRae,* 448 U.S. 297 (1980). This confirmed the Hyde Amendment when funds could not be used for abortion unless the life of the mother is endangered if the fetus is carried to term.

Prenatal diagnosis is an area in which advanced techniques are constantly enlarging the possible knowledge of the diseases of the pregnant woman and the fetus. From radiographic pictures we have gone to ultrasound and Computerized Axial Tomography (CAT) scans; from amniotic testing we have gone to chorionic testing and fetoscopes. Professor Macintyre also brings to the fore another focus, that of counseling individuals and families affected by the various problems associated with actual or potential birth defects.

10 · The Impact of an Abnormal Fetus or Child on the Choice for Prenatal Diagnosis and Selective Abortion

M. Neil Macintyre, Ph.D.,
Llew Keltner, M.D., Ph.D.
and Dorothy A. Kovacevich, Ph.D.*

I. Introduction

Ten years ago in the last edition of this book, the introduction to this chapter by the then sole author (Macintyre) opened with this paragraph:

> In the burgeoning debate on the subject of therapeutic abortion and proposed changes in the state abortion laws, numerous situations have been proposed as valid indications for interrupting a pregnancy. Of these, the one which ordinarily has received the least attention has been the risk that the child would be born with grave physical or mental defects.

During the intervening decade, numerous significant changes have occurred. As usual, changes in the laws have resulted from changes in societal attitudes, which in turn have come about because of increased awareness and sensitivity regarding existing areas of human need or human suffering as well as the acquisition of new knowledge.

In the last decade there has been a tremendous amount of new knowledge gained concerning the principles and techniques of human genetics in general and prenatal diagnosis specifically. Much of this recent learning is of obvious importance to certain aspects of the abortion issue.

There are glimmers of change in public awareness of the nature and intensity

* We wish to express our gratitude to Leila Hocking-Keltner for her assistance in the construction and preparation of this article.

of human suffering resulting from the birth of an abnormal child. Health care professionals are showing signs of slowly learning that effective handling of such situations requires a special degree of understanding, empathy, and demonstrated caring toward the parents. Traditionally, these professionals have avoided the issue by being very clinical and appearing aloof in their presentation of data, thereby protecting themselves from becoming emotionally involved and at the same time setting up communication barriers between themselves and their patients.

II. Prenatal Diagnosis

The diagnosis of fetal disease is no longer an unusual or speculative event. Advances in medical diagnostic technology have been quickly and successfully applied to the prenatal period. A great many fetal diseases may now be detected, and the potential exists for the rapid development of diagnostic techniques for detection of many more. At present, amniocentesis and ultrasound definitely predominate in fetal diagnosis, but several other techniques either provide excellent information in specific circumstances or show great promise for future development.

A. Amniocentesis

Amniocentesis is but one of a number of techniques used in medical diagnosis for obtaining fluid from internal body cavities. Cardiocentesis consists of withdrawing fluid from around the heart, thoracentesis from the space outside the lungs, and amniocentesis from the amniotic space surrounding the growing fetus. A needle of the appropriate length and diameter is introduced into the body cavity, and fluid is withdrawn through the hollow core of the needle.

The amniocentesis needle is inserted, under sterile conditions, through the abdominal and uterine walls. Although anticipation of the procedure may produce considerable anxiety, little discomfort is involved. For example, in most cases discomfort certainly is subjectively less than in a routine pelvic examination.

The fluid in the amniotic cavity is principally fetal urine and filtered fluid from the natural bloodstream. Cells sloughed from fetal tissues populate the fluid. Current technology allows biochemical examination of the fluid for abnormalities indicating fetal disease. Also possible are isolation, growth, and examination of living fetal cells to determine both their chromosomal and their biochemical composition.

The timing of fetal amniotic fluid constituent secretion critically affects the use of amniocentesis as a diagnostic technique. A common use of amniocentesis is for determination of fetal maturity, which is accomplished by comparing the ratio of amounts of two proteins secreted by the fetal lungs. The first use of amniocentesis was for the estimation of the severity of damage to fetal red blood cells in Rh disease, requiring measurement of breakdown products from those cells. In neither of these cases are the necessary substances present in sufficient quantity in the amniotic fluid for measurement before the 24th week of pregnancy.[1]

The same is true for many substances that require the maturation of various fetal physiological systems before secretion occurs. Fetal cells are sloughed into the amniotic fluid from early in gestation. Only at the eighth week, however, is there enough fluid present for a sample to be obtained, and until about 14 weeks the number of fetal cells obtained may not be sufficient to allow successful culture.

By far the most important of the substances directly assayed from amniotic fluid is alpha-fetoprotein (AFP), a protein made by the fetal liver and a normal constituent of the fluid. The level of AFP changes very predictably with the progress of pregnancy. Abnormally high levels of AFP usually indicate leakage from fetal tissues into the fluid. Fetal diseases that allow such exposure of tissues include anencephaly (an incomplete skull with absence of much of the brain), encephalocele (herniation of the brain through the skull), spina bifida (incomplete closure of the bony spine with exposure of the spinal cord), and omphalocele (abdominal contents on the outside of the abdominal wall).[2] Intrauterine fetal death will also yield abnormally high AFP levels. Unlike many other prenatal diagnostic techniques, assessment of amniotic fluid AFP levels never can provide a specific diagnosis; an abnormally high level must always be followed with other tests—usually more expensive and time-consuming than an AFP assay—to arrive at a specific diagnosis.

Lack of certain crucial enzymes in fetal cells can lead to the buildup of metabolic products in the amniotic fluid to the point where the products can be detected. In most cases, however, the diagnoses are much more accurately made from analysis of the activity of fetal cells in culture. Direct testing of amniotic fluid for diagnosis of fetal disease in the first two trimesters of pregnancy is thus at present limited primarily to AFP assay.

The one technological breakthrough that gave the greatest stimulus to the development of prenatal diagnosis was the discovery in 1965 by Klinger and Macintyre[3] of techniques allowing fetal cells derived from amniocentesis to be cultured in the laboratory. Fetal cell cultures are used today for both chromosome and biochemical analyses.

Individuality in structure and physiological function of each person is determined to a very large extent at the cellular level. The formation of each unique chemical part of a cell is governed by one or more templates called genes. These genes are strung together end to end in microscopically visible entities, the chromosomes. The genes in each human cell are arranged on 23 matched pairs of chromosomes; one of each pair is inherited from the individual's mother, the other from the father. In males, one pair of chromosomes, the sex chromosomes, is unevenly matched. The genes inherited from the father on the Y chromosome do not match the genes inherited from the mother on the X chromosome. If a fertilized human egg contains anything other than this critical amount of genetic material, development of the fetus will be altered. Duplication or deletion of all or part of any one of the chromosomes results in birth defects of varying severity.

To assess the status of the chromosome complement of fetal cells, the cells present in the amniotic fluid sample obtained from amniocentesis are first isolated and placed in a nutrient medium. Ten to 28 days are required for the growth of sufficient numbers of fetal cells in these cultures. At maturity, the cultures are concentrated and the cells prepared for microscopic examination. The process of preparing cells has become extremely sophisticated. A combination of techniques is now routinely used that results in the production of microscope slides containing groups of chromosomes that are easily visible to the trained examiner.

The chromosomes can be individually counted and identified, and chromosomes with added or missing parts may be recognized.[4] Chromosomes from a number of cells are examined to ensure consistency of the diagnostic conclusion.

Diagnoses resulting from chromosome analysis are surprisingly specific. Most often encountered is the diagnosis of Down Syndrome, or trisomy 21, which occurs where there are three rather than two 21st chromosomes in each cell. Although each person born with Down's Syndrome is different, there are striking similarities resulting from the redundancy of specific genetic material. The facial appearance of children and adults with Down's Syndrome, which led to the unfortunate and inappropriate 'mongoloid' label, is quite consistent. Equally typical is the accompanying mental retardation. As with most syndromes resulting from chromosomal imbalance, internal organ systems are malformed in cases of Down Syndrome. With the exception of the 21st chromosome and the sex chromosomes, three copies of an entire chromosome almost invariably results in death, even though in rare instances affected fetuses may maintain respiration a short time after delivery. When only one copy of any of the chromosomes exists, again with the exception of the sex chromosomes, malformations are always fatal, with death usually occurring early in gestation.

Current techniques in cultured fetal cell preparation allow the identification of quite small missing or redundant parts of individual chromosomes as well. Several hundred specific syndromes have been described, each with very consistent presentation in the affected individual, involving particular deletions or duplications of chromosomal material.[5] Although defects in organ systems vary greatly from syndrome to syndrome, mental retardation is an alarmingly common finding when chromosomal imbalance exists.

The startling advances in biochemical technology of the last two decades have allowed analyses of many enzyme systems within cultured fetal cells. In many inheritable diseases a single gene, far too small to be visualized by the techniques of chromosome analysis, is altered. The cellular chemical coded for by that gene will then be defective, usually causing serious alterations in the function of most if not all the cells in the body. One example of such a metabolic disease is Tay-Sachs disease, which results in progressive degeneration of the nervous system and in death early in childhood. Many other serious metabolic genetic diseases have been prenatally diagnosed by simple assays of enzyme levels in amniotic fluid cell cultures.

More sophisticated techniques are also being used to directly identify altered genes. For example, specialized enzymes are used in the laboratory to break up DNA that has been isolated from cell cultures of fetuses suspected of having sickle-cell anemia. The fragments of DNA are processed and compared to similarly processed fragments of DNA from normal individuals. The existence of an altered gene for hemoglobin, the defective protein in sickle-cell anemia, can be easily demonstrated in affected fetuses.[6]

B. Ultrasound

Many areas of modern medicine have been remarkably influenced in the past decade by the advent of the noninvasive and apparently nondestructive technique of diagnostic ultrasonography. Prenatal diagnosis is certainly no exception.

To obtain an image of fetal structures, high-frequency sound waves are projected into the abdomen from a small hand-held transducer. Time differences in returning echoes reflect varying densities of internal organs, and are thus translated into a visual image.

The fetal structural defects detectable by ultrasound may be isolated defects resulting from maldevelopment of single organs. Alternatively, they may be part of syndromes occurring as a result of chromosomal anomalies, disease processes during pregnancy, exposure to teratogens (external agents causing maldevelopment), or inheritable genetic diseases. As a general rule, large defects are more easily seen than smaller ones at a given stage of fetal development. Anencephaly, encephalocele, myelomeningocele, and omphalocele are diagnosed routinely in the second trimester. Small defects such as polydactyly (more than five fingers per hand) and cardiac hypertrophy (enlarged heart) may not be visible until well into the third trimester, and detection even then is greatly dependent on the ultrasonographer's skill and on the fetal position.

Other fetal defects detectable by ultrasound examination include dwarfism, cardiac valvular defects, hydrocephaly, microcephaly, fetal tumors, and polycystic kidneys.[7] As equipment and methods become more sophisticated, more exact images of the pregnant uterus and its contents become available. Relatively small defects, like cleft lip, have been noted.[8]

Echocardiography is an offshoot of ultrasonography and has also been used in fetal diagnosis. Ultrasound equipment is used to obtain detailed information about cardiac rhythms from analysis of the movements of the fetal heart.[9] Fetal cardiac rhythm disturbances of several types have been detected using echocardiography, and cardiac structural anomalies have also been identified.[10]

C. Other Techniques

1.   DIRECT VISUALIZATION   Fiber-optic technology now allows insertion of very thin light-conducting flexible tubes through large diameter needles into the amniotic cavity. The image of the fetus or placenta obtained is used either directly in reaching diagnostic conclusions or as a guide for the placement of blood or tissue sampling devices.

Between 15 and 20 weeks of fetal development, the amniotic fluid surrounding the fetus is very transparent and the fetus is still quite small. Through a one- to two-millimeter wide fiber-optic fetoscope, an area of two to three square centimeters of the fetal surface may be seen. Positioning of the fetus is critical in determining which fetal structures may be visualized. Several otherwise difficult syndromes have been diagnosed by visualization in the fetoscope of small structural anomalies not identifiable on ultrasound.

The most important current use of the fiber-optic fetoscope is to guide the placement of tools for obtaining fetal blood samples. After 18 weeks, the fetal blood volume is great enough to tolerate the loss of one to two milliliters of blood, which is obtained from a placental vessel punctured by a sampling needle carried in a tube next to the scope. Blood samples thus obtained have been used to diagnose sickle cell anemia, thalassemia, hemophilia, immunodeficiencies, viral infections, and metabolic disorders. Culturing cells from blood samples takes only two or three days rather than the 10 to 28 days required for the culture of amniotic cells.

Fiber-optic scopes have also been used to guide instruments for obtaining biopsies of the fetal skin on scalp or flank. Skin samples have been used to diagnose several inheritable disorders which include skin changes as part of their pathology.[11] Samples of the fetal liver have also been obtained to aid in the diagnosis of metabolic disorders specific to that organ.[12]

2. BIOPSY OF CHORIONIC VILLI   One of the tissue layers surrounding the fetus is the chorion, which is also made up of cells originating from the fertilized egg. Between the eighth and twelfth weeks of gestation, it is possible to insert a small tube through the cervical opening and to aspirate a small piece of the chorion. Many cells may be obtained (allowing rapid culture) and analysis proceeds in the same manner as with cells from amniotic fluid. The chorionic villi cells are dividing very rapidly unlike amniotic fluid cells so that results of the chromosome analysis may be obtained in as short a time as 24 hours. The striking advantage of the technique is that since chorionic villi sampling can take place during the first trimester and since culture results are available much more rapidly than with amniotic cell cultures, results may be obtained as much as three months earlier in the pregnancy. The techinque is very new, however, and further study is needed to determine the associated risks and complications. Chorionic villi biopsy does have immense potential as an early prenatal diagnostic technique.[13]

3. RADIOGRAPHY   The use of X-ray fetal analysis is limited by the certain but difficult to quantify carcinogenic or other risk to the fetus. Although radiographic information could be used in the diagnosis of many conditions identifiable by ultrasound, its use is limited primarily to situations involving skeletal maldevelopment. Relatively rare syndromes like osteogenesis imperfecta (a disease involving incomplete calcification of developing bones) are difficult to diagnose with other techniques.[14] However, ultrasonography techniques are rapidly attaining a degree of sophistication which may soon eliminate the necessity for use of fetal radiography.

4. AMNIOGRAPHY   A water soluble X-ray opaque contrast material may be injected into the amniotic fluid followed by radiographic examination. The outline of the fetus is made visible by this technique, which offers diagnostic possibilities of conditions where the fetal shape has been altered, such as teratoma (a soft tissue tumor) and omphalocele.[15]

As the fetus swallows the contrast material, the fetal gastrointestinal tract can be visualized radiographically, allowing diagnosis of conditions where the course of the tract is altered. Duodenal atresia (constriction of the tract just below the stomach) and diaphragmatic hernia (protrusion of the stomach up through the diaphragm) are examples of conditions diagnosable with amniography.[16]

5. FETOGRAPHY   A variation of amniography, this technique uses an oil soluble contrast material which is absorbed by the waxy covering of the fetus. Radiography then shows the outline of the fetus, providing diagnostic information about outline altering conditions.[17]

6. MATERNAL SERUM ALPHA-FETOPROTEIN DETERMINATION   Some fetal proteins cross the placenta and enter the maternal circulation. Among these is alpha-fetoprotein (AFP). The AFP level in the maternal circulation is a reflection of the amniotic fluid AFP level, albeit at a much lower concentration. Measuring levels of AFP in the maternal serum offers increasingly accurate information about fetal status. When AFP is sufficiently elevated over successive samples, an

indication of fetal tissue exposure or distress is possible just as in amniotic fluid AFP evaluation. An association has been suggested between lower than normal AFP levels and chromosomal anomalies such as Down Syndrome.[18] The technique is as nonspecific as amniotic fluid AFP measurement, but does offer valuable initial information.[19]

D. The Future of Prenatal Diagnostic Techniques

Prenatal diagnosis is unquestionably in its infancy. The catalog of available techniques will undoubtedly increase by the addition of new methods. On the immediate horizon are enhancements of present techniques to increase the scope and accuracy of diagnostic possibility.

Chromosome analysis continues to improve steadily in terms of the resolution with which small details on a given chromosome can be seen, which allows diagnosis of additional syndromes. Improvement is likely to continue for some time, with potential breakthroughs resulting from new microscopic techniques.[20]

Recombinant DNA technology will undoubtedly allow definition of many more inheritable genetic diseases through the production of specific endonuclei. These will allow, as with sickle cell anemia at present, diagnosis of the disease from uncultured amniotic fluid.[21]

Better biochemical analysis techniques are already allowing the detection of more substances in amniotic fluid which, like AFP, are indicators of fetal disease. Some of these indicators will probably be much more specific than AFP.

Methods are under development that will allow the separation of fetal cells in the maternal circulation. In theory this technique may provide a mass screening tool for indicating the potential presence of chromosomal anomalies or metabolic disorders, but the methods remain impractical and unreliable.[22]

As ultrasound equipment becomes more sophisticated, structural defects will be more easily and thus more frequently resolved. Computer enhanced ultrasound images, perhaps similar to those provided now by computerized axial tomography (CAT scan) will very probably also be available.[23]

Nuclear magnetic reasonance scanning, a technique that can produce cross-sectional images of internal body structures similar to those produced by computerized axial tomography, is now being applied experimentally to fetal diagnosis. The technique is new, but is gaining rapid acceptance as an apparently nondamaging alternative to computerized axial tomography.[24]

Use of direct fetal biopsies via the fetoscope will probably increase. Teratogenic fetal infections and toxin levels will be measured via such biopsies, and cells obtained will more frequently be used for biochemical studies and rapid chromosome analysis. Diagnostic biopsy of internal fetal organs will become more common as the already developing techniques of fetal surgery improve. Presently available diagnostic aids, such as the electrocardiogram and electroencephalogram, will be used with direct visual guidance as fiber-optic systems improve.[25]

Although prenatal diagnostic techniques offer information now about many fetal diseases, there is great room for improvement. For example, there is not today a good technique for the prenatal diagnosis of cystic fibrosis, the most common serious inheritable disease, in spite of enormous research efforts.[26]

E. Risks of Prenatal Diagnosis

The risks involved in prenatal diagnostic techniques follow very logically from the descriptions of the methods involved. Degree of invasiveness is the most obvious factor influencing fetal risk.

Ultrasound is now so widely used largely because of its apparently benign nature. Many analyses have been made of the outcomes of pregnancies involving ultrasound diagnosis and no harmful effects have been conclusively demonstrated.[27] Deleterious fetal effects from diagnostic radiology are almost equally difficult to demonstrate, but the harmful effects of ionizing radiation are so well known that it is safe to assume the existence of a definite level of carcinogenic risk to the exposed fetus.

Introduction of sharp foreign bodies into the uterine cavity during pregnancy inherently carries the risk of damage to the fetus, the fetal blood supply, or the placenta. In one large series of amniocenteses, the rate of spontaneous abortions was found to increase by 0.16 percent following the procedure. Fetal damage not resulting in abortion was suspected in 0.3 percent of cases.[28]

The fiber-optic scope is much larger and requires more manipulation than the amniocentesis needle. It is thus not surprising that a fetal death rate of 3 percent occurred (from infection of the amniotic fluid and membranes) in one series of fetoscopic procedures. Worldwide experience shows a fetal loss of 5.6 percent following biopsy of chorionic villi.[29]

Maternal risks from prenatal diagnostic procedures are very difficult to assess. The reports of large series of amniocenteses, fetoscopies, and placental aspirations do not reveal maternal complications, but neither do the reports carefully analyze maternal sequelae.[30]

The risk of diagnostic error is particularly important in prenatal evaluation. When prenatal diagnostic techniques are applied to obtain information to be used in a decision about elective abortion, the results have obviously far-reaching consequences. False positive results from a test can lead to abortion of fetuses unaffected by the disease in question. False negative results would probably cause continuation of a pregnancy on the supposition that the fetus was normal with serious possible consequences.

Diagnostic accuracy in chromosomal analysis from cultured amniotic fluid cells has been reported from 99.53 to 99.93 percent (true positive plus true negative).[31] False positive results make up the majority of the diagnostic errors. It should be noted that follow-up is very difficult in studies of this kind, and the actual rates may be higher. Due primarily to the lower frequency of use of other fetal diagnostic methods, carefully compiled failure rates are not yet available. Methods such as ultrasound which are dependent on fetal position, maternal obesity, and other difficult to control variables are likely to have relatively high false negative rates, particularly since many anomalies are very difficult if not impossible to visualize before the time when abortion decisions must be made.

F. The Process of Prenatal Diagnosis

The course of the prenatal diagnostic process will be different for each individual pregnancy. Reasons for obtaining prenatal diagnostic services, results of tests, use of multiple tests, and response of the pregnant woman will all influence the diagnostic outcome.

1.   REASONS FOR DIAGNOSTIC TESTS   Pregnant women have procedures performed to obtain information about fetal disease either because they have a specific concern about the health of the fetus or simply to obtain general information about the pregnancy. The diagnostic process is quite different in these two situations.

When any member of a family, including very distant relatives, is known to have been born with a birth defect, to be mentally retarded, or to have been affected with a disease perceived by the family to have a heritable component, the pregnant woman or other family members normally have a need to know if the fetus is affected with the same condition. The perception of risk to the fetus may be quite different from person to person. Many factors have an impact on the level of concern in a given individual. Depth of exposure to a family member with a particular disease may have a tremendous effect on efforts to obtain prenatal diagnosis. For example, a woman who has a sibling with Down Syndrome is very likely to seek diagnosis, while a man with a second cousin born with an extra digit is much less likely to encourage his pregnant partner to do so. A greater occurrence risk of specific conditions within population groups leads to a greater demand for a diagnostic procedure as in the frequent consultations obtained by families of European Jewish descent to rule out Tay-Sachs disease.[32] Increased public awareness about risk factors for fetal disease also affects the level of concern. For example, maternal age greater than 35 years is a common reason for obtaining amniocentesis due to the well known and publicized increased chromosomal defects risk with increasing maternal age.[33]

In rare cases, one of the parents will know that their cells contain a chromosome consisting of two normal chromosomes fused together end to end—a chromosome translocation—and that any fetus is at high risk for serious disease. About 5 percent of Down Syndrome cases are the result of translocations, and parents who know they carry such a translocation usually seek amniocentesis for fetal chromosome analysis.

Information about fetal disease is very often obtained incidentally. Ultrasound is routinely used to determine fetal size and thus stage of pregnancy, and fetal defects are sometimes clearly visualized or suspected. Since maternal serum AFP is a relatively inexpensive, easily done, and virtually harmless test, it is being performed more and more often even when there are no specific indications.[34] Both ultrasound and maternal serum AFP testing are thus beginning to be used as general fetal health screening tools for the population.

Maternal conditions that have potentially harmful fetal effects are often detected by screening methods. Routine health histories may reveal maternal alcohol abuse, toxin or radiation exposure, or diabetes, all yielding increased risks of birth defects. Testing of maternal blood may reveal increased levels of antibodies to rubella and other viruses, indicating recent exposure and possible consequent fetal damage. Glucose tolerance tests are used to determine the existence of gestational diabetes.

2.   RESULTS OF TESTS   The unique characteristics of a diagnostic technique, and thus the nature of the diagnostic outcome, determine to a great extent the progression of the diagnostic process. Since ultrasound provides only a rough visualization of the fetus, an ultrasound done early in the pregnancy to determine fetal size that shows no specific structural defects is not at all definitive in ruling

out fetal disease. On the other hand, an amniocentesis providing a negative chromosome analysis for Down Syndrome is very conclusive and may be a result sufficient to terminate the diagnostic process.

Positive results are usually less equivocal, and either provide a diagnosis or suggest further study. Amniocentesis demonstrating a chromosomal defect provides very specific information about the probable fetal condition. Elevated alpha-fetoprotein—either in maternal serum or in amniotic fluid—usually requires repeat testing with continued positive results followed by chromosome analysis, ultrasound, or other diagnostic techniques to locate the specific defect present.

3.   USE OF MULTIPLE TESTS   As noted above, few of the techniques available for fetal diagnosis are used in isolation. With the increasing use of screening techniques such as ultrasound and maternal serum AFP determination, less expensive and less invasive techniques are followed by more elaborate procedures if positive results are obtained. The number and type of diagnostic techniques used are determined primarily by the degree of specificity at the time of referral for diagnosis. Suspected chromosomal abnormalities may require only amniocentesis for definitive diagnosis, while a chance finding of elevated maternal serum AFP may require follow-up with ultrasound and amniocentesis. The very elaborate techniques such as fetoscopy and fetal blood sampling are suggested only when earlier tests create very high suspicion of diseases amenable to diagnosis by the more complex methods.

4.   RESPONSE OF THE PREGNANT WOMAN   As in any diagnostic process, the most important element is the response of the patient to the information provided by the techniques used. Because of the great emotional overlay involved in the production of new human life, the process of fetal diagnosis is subject completely to the pregnant woman's interpretation and use of diagnostic information. Termination of the diagnostic process at the first sign of positive test results is a common occurrence. Successful diagnosis of fetal disease requires that an emotional environment be provided that allows for the complex of attitudes and feelings brought to the diagnostic practitioner by the client. Careful and thoughtful planning and explanation of the diagnostic process is of great benefit to the pregnant woman and to her family.

5.   EXPLAINING THE DIAGNOSTIC PROCESS   This explanation might also be labeled "information counseling" because it can and should be more than a giving of information. In fact, explaining this procedure is often done by listing the steps in writing and then using the face-to-face time to clarify, explain, and answer questions about the procedures. Professionals usually have little difficulty doing this.

It is also necessary to explain the possible hazards and risks in a realistic manner. This is not so easy. The line between frightening, cold, hard facts about the risks and the reassurance needed to undergo the relatively safe procedure is not clear. It is possible to err in either direction. One must bear in mind that the woman is frightened to begin with or she would not be seeking prenatal diagnosis. Because of age, family history or a variety of other reasons, she fears that her child may be abnormal. What she desires most is the assurance that the fetus is normal. When confronted with the possibility that the procedure may harm the baby, which in the vast majority of cases will prove to be normal, the anxiety may be overwhelming. At this point some women choose not to undergo the procedures.

For those who do undergo the procedures, particularly amniocentesis, which requires a relatively long period of suspenseful waiting before results are available, some reassurance or means of support is necessary. This could be something as simple as a phone number to call to see how the tests are coming along or to get reassurance that the process is progressing according to schedule.

During the initial visit, the patient should be made aware of all the services available in the area if advice, assistance, or counseling is needed. In that way, if the results of the tests indicate problems, the parents have had time to consider or investigate possible resources and to consider the possibility of using such services.

Some people need counseling, support, and assistance whether the results are positive or negative because they frequently have other problems that brought them in the first place. For example, having a normal child the second time does not automatically resolve the problems of having an abnormal sibling at home or in the family.

If the available resources have been mentioned in the first meeting, it will be easier to refer back to them when the diagnostic results are presented to the parents. If the fetus is found to be abnormal, the need for further counseling or referral seems more obvious to the physician even though it is not always pursued. What must not be overlooked is the need that may underlie the fear that brought them initially. No one expects the physician to do the counseling, but it is important to develop an awareness of the possible needs and to be familiar with the resources that are available in the community. Parent groups, agencies, schools, and individual counselors are becoming increasingly available, and often the families are not aware of their existence. Becoming an informed member of the developing network of resources is a duty incumbent upon every professional who works with these families.

III. Emotional Effects of the Birth of an Abnormal Child on the Parents

With the development of human cytogenetics (chromosome analysis) techniques beginning in the late 1950s, the need for effective counseling for the prospective parents became evident. At that time, genetic counseling consisted essentially of providing factual information relative to the genetics of the problem and an explanation of the techniques to be used in gathering additional data. Little attention was paid to the emotional effects that may accompany the fear of producing an abnormal child or the experience of actually giving birth to such a child.

In time it became clear that the approach used in genetic counseling was actually preventing the communication that the parents needed most, namely, an opportunity to discuss their fears and other distressing feelings. Once these parents were given the opportunity and the freedom to speak openly and honestly, in marked contrast to the limited interchange they had experienced with most health professionals, they literally overflowed with information. These parents represent a population of deeply distressed individuals who are very misunderstood and hence are inadequately ministered to.

Gradually we began to provide extended counseling for some of these families where the need appeared critical. Counseling sessions were audiotaped with the knowledge and permission of the individuals involved. These tapes contain thousands of hours of statements made by emotionally affected individuals in an environment that has allowed them free and trusting disclosure.

Both the counseling and the subsequent study of the tapes has brought out some vitally important basic information. Obviously, no two individuals react exactly the same to stressful situations, and no two of the cases are identical in all respects. However, there are certain patterns that recur so often from case to case that they are predictable. Some were also unexpected. For example, despite differences in intensity of the impact and ways in which the pain is handled, the loss of an expected child results in the same basic reaction patterns when the actual child is abnormal, whether or not the child: (1) is wanted and planned for; (2) is lost through miscarriage or after birth; (3) dies early or lives for an extended period; or (4) has relatively minor or severe structural or mental abnormalities.

Five different individuals worked in developing categories and listing recurrent patterns in the tapes. There was such a high degree of correlation among the separate evaluations of the most critical reactions that the validity of the conclusions appears certain, and those conclusions are the basis on which the following descriptions of reaction patterns have been formulated.

Most individuals never have the opportunity to gain an insight into the true nature and complexity of the emotional pain suffered by parents who produce an abnormal child. Regardless of personally held attitudes about such an emotionally charged issue as abortion, the intelligent and honest person will want to judge the behavior of those who are trapped in such a tragic situation on the basis of informed insight rather than on uninformed emotional bias or condemnation.

A. The Impact on the Individual Parent

1. INITIAL SHOCK, DENIAL, REALITY, AND ANGER   For most couples during pregnancy, certain changes in feelings and awareness ordinarily occur, whether or not they are all consciously recognized at the time. These changes include a maturing sense of responsibility, increased appreciation for each other, awe, excitement at the marvel of creating a new life, and above all, a sense of personal pride and feeling "special." There are few if any more ego-involving phenomena than being part of producing a child. Furthermore, the need for some sense of immortality seems inherent in human existence. Producing an offspring, literally a part of yourself, to continue your existence beyond your corporal lifetime probably represents the most palpable essence of immortality available. The expected child becomes a representation of the best in you and your spouse, to be eventually presented to the world with ultimate pride, and it is natural to feel that there is no way that the child will be anything but perfect and beautiful. With these feelings to buoy them up, a couple reaches a special emotional high. If the expected child is lost to death or is born with abnormalities, the plunge to an emotional low is immediate and devastating.

The initial reaction is a state of shock so overwhelming and confusing that the individual appears to be living in a nightmare, a dream world, out of touch with reality. Reality is often too painful to bear, and the reaction is one of denial as a protection from the pain, a feeling that when the nightmare is over everything will somehow be all right. Some individuals avoid recognizing the full truth of reality by viewing the tragic event as a complete blessing, thereby prolonging the avoidance of reality. The majority of individuals soon find that they cannot avoid facing the reality of the shattering event that has so upset their lives, and at that point the predominant reactions tend to be a vacillating mixture of depression, anger, and mistrust. "Why me?" "Why us?" "What have I done to deserve this?" are the big questions. The utter unfairness of the situation gives rise to overwhelming anger, anger at everything and everyone connected with the unfortunate event; in effect, anger at the world. Religious faith tends to crumble under the impact of the question: "What kind of a God would do this to me?"

From a legal standpoint, the intensity of the parental anger reaction is important to understand because even individuals who would not be likely to bring suit against physicians, staff, and the hospital involved may and do sue when they produce an abnormal child. Often such suits are based on the parents' belief that they were not adequately informed of their risk or of the availability of certain prenatal diagnostic tests, or anything else that seems plausible in their situation.

2.   THE DAMAGED SELF-IMAGE   When the anticipation of a wished-for child with all its ego-boosting effects terminates in reproductive failure, a severe blow to an individual's self-image is inevitable. There is an unavoidable feeling of failure and inadequacy leading to periods of despair and depression.

In our society, in which such great emphasis is placed on being a winner, to be a loser in such a vital and personal event as producing a child has a particularly threatening effect on a parent's self-esteem and raises the common question: "What will people think?" The answer to the question is usually clear and negative in a society that generally views a birth-defective child as a fearsome object and tends to shun it, stigmatizing both the child and parents, thereby adding to the feelings of isolation, despair, and personal worthlessness.

One might assume that this feeling of being rejected by society would bring the parents closer together in an effort to achieve mutual support, and ideally this could be; but in most cases, because husband and wife tend to react very differently in handling their emotional pain, they withdraw from each other. This phenomenon will be discussed in greater detail later in this chapter.

3.   GUILT AND THE DEATH-WISH FOR THE CHILD   We live in a culture in which the predominant method of raising children for generations has been through the use of conditional love or conditional acceptance by parents or parent figures, such as church and school. The message has been clear: Your parents won't love you if you don't do things exactly their way; God won't love you and will punish you if you deviate from the laws of the Church; the teacher will give you bad grades if you don't conform and pay strict attention, etc.

With that kind of a background so prevalent in our culture, it is inevitable that guilt becomes a significant and destructive part of the picture when a couple produces an imperfect offspring. There is generalized guilt for being a part of a major failure, disappointing not only one's own expectations but those of one's parents and family and, in effect, of society as a whole.

In addition to the generalized guilt reaction described above, specific sources of self-directed guilt result from the parent's own thinking or behavior. The most frequently occurring and probably the most frightening of these is the death-wish for the child: "I am glad the child died" or "I wish the child would die." In counseling, over 90 percent of parents admit that they are plagued with the recurring thought of wanting their child to die, and when they learn that such a thought is entirely normal under the circumstances, the depth of their relief is obvious. The death-wish for the child is so powerful that many parents have mentally considered methods of causing the child's death; some have caught themselves in the process of acting it out, and a few have probably gone further. No one recommends or condones such behavior as the appropriate solution, but it must be recognized, understood, and accepted as part of the tragic evidence of the potentially destructive effect of producing a defective child.

Guilt plays such an important part in the individual parent's loss of self-esteem that before anything else of real substance can be accomplished toward rehabilitating the individual and the couple, the self-esteem of each person must be helped to improve at least enough for him or her to be able to face other issues with some confidence and clear thinking.

One of the most harmful and cruel things that anyone, professional or otherwise, can do is to criticize or condemn the hurting and confused parent, either directly or by implication. Genuine acceptance and support are the essentials for assisting the parent.

4. MOURNING THE LOSS OF THE WISHED-FOR CHILD   When an abnormal child is born, the expected and wished-for normal child dies in that it ceases to exist as a viable possibility, and one component of the resulting mourning process is equivalent to that following the death of an apparently normal child.

Mourning the loss of a loved one at any age results in sadness and some diminution of one's normal level of effectiveness. The process is usually least painful and protracted if the beloved individual is elderly and has had a chance to live a full life. If a child dies, the sadness lasts much longer and is far more intense, partly due to the prevention of the parental desire and expectation to savor the child's growth and development and to be an essential part of it. When an abnormal child is born, the entire reaction pattern of parents is so much more complex that it is virtually impossible for them to cope with it in a truly rational fashion. Not only are they faced with the intensely saddening "death" of the wished-for normal child, but they are simultaneously smitten with the additional and more destructive emotions described earlier. In a very real sense, such parents are faced with the almost intolerable task of going through two mourning processes, different in some respects, yet overlapping and intertwined.

Mourning at best is a difficult, confusing, and often lengthy process. The amount of time required to complete the process successfully varies with the nature of the initial event, the total personality structure of the principal individual or individuals involved, and, to a significant extent, the behavior of people with whom the grieving individual is in contact. If a person is denied understanding, support, and the time required to complete the grieving process, it may continue unresolved throughout an entire lifetime.

Cultural attitudes are usually not helpful in our dealing with grieving parents. In our efforts to protect ourselves from accepting the personal discomfort that goes with watching another person mourn, we urge them to be strong, to know that in a very short time everything will be fine, *etc.,* at a time when it is impossible for the parent actually to be strong or in any way to feel optimistic. We often add to their feeling of inadequacy and worthlessness, forcing them to deny the full reality of their child's abnormality and of their own sadness. We virtually demand that they prove their worthiness by coping well. In short, we fail to provide the environment that would allow completion of the grieving process. The result is that such parents are forced to pretend that they are coping well when it is highly unlikely that they are able to do so. What passes as coping often is the equivalent of lying convincingly, and many parents become so adept at it that they fool not only those around them but themselves as well. They share their pain with no one, bearing it as it lies festering as an ongoing source of anger, despair, and deep chronic sadness.

B. Religion as a Source of Spiritual Strength or Destructive Guilt

One of the most predominant initial parental reactions to the knowledge that their child is abnormal is questioning the nature or even the existence of God. At this point members of the clergy are in a crucial position either to significantly aid or to severely impair the parents' rehabilitation process.

There is no question about the potential value of religious faith in the emotional healing process if faith can survive the severe questioning period, and if religious concepts are carefully interpreted and presented by sensitive and understanding individuals. Unfortunately, members of the clergy often suffer from the same lack of accurate information, the same lack of awareness, as health care professionals concerning the true feelings of the parents. As a result, they often inadvertently deepen the guilt and anger.

In the population we have studied and from which we have learned so much, the cases in which contact with the clergy has been harmful, particularly in the early stages of grieving, greatly outnumber those in which it has been proven to be genuinely supportive. The obvious miscarriage of what is generally considered an important source of uplifting support and spiritual strength needs to be changed.

Increased guilt is the predominant result of the misuse or inappropriate use of certain traditional and dogmatic religious statements. The classic statement that "It's God's will" almost invariably gives rise in the grieving parent to the question: "If it's God's will, what kind of a God would will this much pain on anybody?" The resulting anger at God gives rise to further guilt in an already guilt-ridden person. Our culture tells us we are not supposed to question God, much less be angry at God. Even more potently destructive is the guilt generated in the parent by being told by a religious authority that the abnormal child is in fact a beautiful gift from God at a time when the parent is desperately wrestling with the conflicting emotions of wanting to love the child and not being able to love it, or, worse, wanting it to die.

Our data indicate that there is a correlation between the degree to which a religion is fundamentalist, authoritarian, rigid, and dogmatic and its likelihood of producing guilt, anger, and a feeling of worthlessness in the grieving parent.

The type of approach required to reverse this tragic situation was clearly stated a couple of years ago at a program entitled "Mourning the Loss of the Wished-for Child." One of the speakers was a gentle, soft-spoken and courageous priest who is a chaplain at one of our hospitals. His opening remark was: "When I became a hospital chaplain, I quickly learned that in order to be effective I had to kill my God and find another one." There was an absolute hush in the audience in response to this seemingly blasphemous statement. Then that remarkable and perceptive man went on to explain that much of what had been drilled into him in seminary in the classic fashion resulted in turning most frightened and hurting hospital patients away from him. "It was at that point," he continued, "that I realized that rather than preaching to them as I had been taught to, and telling them what they ought to be feeling and thinking when they were in no condition to do so, I needed to learn to listen, to learn where they were coming from, to accept their feelings without direct or implied condemnation, and to move carefully and supportingly from there,"

In a society that espouses religions that proclaim the importance of faith, trust, forgiveness, the joy of giving, and, above all, the nature and importance of genuine love as the keystone of all religion, it is saddening to recognize a dearth of these qualities expressed in actual behavior, even among the official dispensers of the faith. Religion, mishandled, can cause guilt feelings instead of spiritual growth, and it can cause permanent harm.

True spiritual belief can be of inestimable value in working with grieving parents. True understanding, acceptance, compassion, and love, and the development of genuine trust, can pave the way for proper guidance, effective and permanent emotional healing and spiritual growth. The awesome power of genuine love in operation can be witnessed, but it is not easily explained.

What does all this have to do with abortion? Consider, if you will, the impact of all the pain and turmoil suffered by the parents of an abnormal child as described earlier, and identify with it if you can. Then consider the absolute horror of going through it again. Now recognize the shattering fact of being faced with a choice between two virtually intolerable courses of action. Consider the couple under such horrendous pressure who might choose to terminate a pregnancy as being the least destructive course for them. How would you react to them? Would you join that segment of society which would willfully heap rejection, condemnation, insults, and accusation on two such vulnerable and devastated souls, or would you be supportive?

C. The Impact on the Couple's Marital Relationship

As a part of a routine review of the records of children enrolled in two large county facilities for the mentally retarded in Northeastern Ohio in 1976, one of the authors was struck by the fact that so many of the older children (age 18 through 21) had parents who were divorced or separated.[35] The actual percentage was approximately 75 percent. A further investigation of the records indicated that the figures were lower for the parents of younger children but increased steadily as the ages of the children increased. As the first author has traveled and lectured to other professionals in the field, quoting the 75 percent figure, comments from members of the audiences have indicated a widespread acceptance of the data. This figure is about twice the national average of separation and divorce for all reasons. Since the national average includes the couples studied, the significance of the abnormal child is, if anything, understated by the quoted statistic.

In our population of couples, a large number have reached the state of seriously considering divorce before reaching out for professional help; yet less than 5 percent have ended up in separation or divorce, and most have found that by working through the effects of the tragedy with proper guidance and support and by better understanding themselves individually and collectively as a couple, they have ended with a stronger relationship than they had before the unhappy event of their abnormal child's birth.

Several things are clear: (1) parents who suffer from the effects of producing a defective child need a great deal of help; (2) most couples either do not seek help or receive inappropriate and ineffective advice; and (3) the marital relationship suffers to the point of dissolution in most cases in which the right kind of help is not forthcoming from professionals and from society in general.

There are multiple reasons for the breakup of marriage in these cases, but the study of our tapes indicates that the following three categories encompass most of them.

1. BREAKDOWN OF COMMUNICATION   In an increasingly mistrustful society, psychologists, sociologists, and specialists in related fields have long recognized that the degree of openness and honesty in communication is directly related to the level of trust existing between the individuals involved. In an increasingly untrusting and complicated world, then, it is no wonder that in terms of open communication and genuine sharing, the average marriage, even without the impact of major tragedies, is far less rewarding than it could be. Furthermore, trust and open communication are essential ingredients in the establishment of genuine love, as differentiated from purely romantic love. This is not to say that genuine love cannot be romantic but rather to point out that "falling in love," that fantastic but unrealistic state of emotional confusion, is far different from genuine, growing and lasting love. The difference is well described by Peck.[36]

To repeat two well-established truisms: You cannot trust others if you do not trust yourself, and you cannot love others if you do not first love yourself. Loving oneself in this sense translates to self-respect and feeling good about oneself— having a good self-image. Thus the steps in breakdown of communication are the development of a damaged self-image, leading to a loss of trust and love, followed by a retreat from open communication.

Communication takes many forms, from nonverbal awareness of body language, to verbalization, to tactile reaching out, to the joy of physical closeness, to the potential fulfillment of genuine and total sexual sharing. All are impaired as a result of producing a defective child.

The effects on a couple's sexual relationship is of special significance and should be dealt with at least briefly. In our culture it is extremely difficult for most individuals to reach the point of totally accepting their sexuality as a vital, powerful, and positive force which is truly a part of them, uncontaminated by guilt, ugliness, and fear. In less than a century we experienced everything from the straitlaced denial of mid-Victorianism and the guilt-producing impact of unloving religious condemnations to a rebellious and equally unfulfilling attitude of so-called sexual liberation, which in most cases has meant sex without love. Ignored has been the uniquely human capacity to accept and rejoice in sexuality and sexual sharing as the ultimate in intimate communication between two genuinely loving individuals.

Considering this kind of an insecure base, it is not difficult to understand why the sexual relationship between a husband and wife so often ceases to exist as a potential means of intimate and effective communication under the impact of all the other pain and confusion produced when a defective child is born to them. Not infrequently sexual union entirely ceases to occur or is undertaken only rarely, and then only as an outlet for purely physical need or even anger.

2.   PROJECTION OF GUILT AND ANGER   Guilt and anger have been discussed in some detail and are inevitable problems for the individual parents of an abnormal child and also a threat to the marital relationship. As already noted, both parents suffer the effects of guilt and anger, but there are significant differences between the initial reactions of the husband and wife.

For a woman, the entire pregnancy and childbirth experience is far more personal than for a man, both physically and emotionally for many reasons, some obvious, some more subtle. Guilt in the woman is likely to be self-directed initially in the form of searching for what she has done wrong with respect to nutrition, medication, activities, *etc.,* which might have caused damage to the child. Historically, our culture has directed blame and condemnation toward the woman as being responsible for all reproductive problems, from sterility to the birth of an abnormal child, and women have been expected to carry the burden of guilt. Therefore, the woman is less likely to think of blaming her spouse initially.

The husband, being less personally involved in the reproductive process, and with traditional thinking firmly on his side, is in a position to move more directly to including his wife among those whom he seeks to blame for his disappointment and pain and resulting anger. The attack on the wife may be subtle, by innuendo or the withdrawing of demonstrated affection, or it can be outspoken and more patently cruel. It is not unusual for a confused, angry, and irrational husband openly to blame his wife for infidelity, claiming that the child is not his, thereby avoiding the stigma associated with the child's being abnormal. The wife, of course, has no such avenue of escape. Regardless of the wife's greater willingness to accept the reality of personal involvement in the problem, ultimately, as communication breaks down and support for her is withdrawn in favor of blame and stigmatization, the utter unfairness of the situation generates her frustration and anger.

Guilt is a difficult burden to carry, even for normally rational people. Rather than facing up to the fact of one's shortcomings or hurtful errors in judgment and action and taking steps to correct the errors, the typical behavior, one learned early in life, is to deny the guilt of hurtful behavior and, if that is not possible, to blame some other individual or situation, reinforcing the action by anger expressed toward the target of the projected blame. For the parents we are considering, the target most readily available is the spouse, and as guilt is projected as blame and anger, neither parent is likely to recognize that the anger actually is at themselves for their own inability to handle their guilt rationally.

3.   DIFFERENCES BETWEEN HUSBAND AND WIFE IN HOW EMOTIONAL PAIN IS HANDLED   Of all the personality patterns we have recognized and studied in our patient population, the one that emerges as the greatest threat to the marital relationship, as well as to the individual parent, is based on the difference in what our culture approves of in males as compared with females in the expression of the basic emotions of pain, tenderness, warmth, affection, and genuine love.

From the first day of our birth we begin to receive the imprint of what society envisions we should become as a boy or a girl, as a man or a woman. Just listen to the manner in which nurses in a newborn nursery speak to infants they hold, and recognize that there are marked differences depending on whether the infant comes from a bassinet with a pink card or a blue card on it. When the child is presented to doting parents and relatives, it is as a bouncing, vigorous baby boy or as a beautiful, sweet, little girl.

Later, the male youngster will receive the dictate "little boys don't cry," probably even before he is out of diapers, and the attitude will continue, despite the fact that little boys, and men as well, have every bit as much need to cry as females. On the other hand, little girls are allowed to cry because it is accepted as female behavior in our society. If a man cries, it is a source of extreme uneasiness to those around him, whereas tears in a female are part of society's expectations. We overlook the well-documented fact that tears, whether they be of pain, joy or other feelings, are a biologically natural and normal response to emotion, and that the continued repression of natural emotions is hazardous to one's mental health.

Up to the age of about five years or so, the average child of either sex is comfortable in the embrace of its parents, but the little boy then begins to learn to shake his daddy's hand instead of hugging him, and even resists the embraces and kisses of his mother because such things are only for "little girls." He, by watching his role models, is on his way to becoming a man. Tenderness and uninhibited demonstration of affection and love will brand him as a sissy among his peers.

To sociologists, psychologists, and others who study the evolution of male versus female behavior in our culture, it has become increasingly clear that a major deterrent to genuinely happy and fulfilling marriages is the fact that our culture inhibits in the male the development of freedom to express emotion openly, while fostering that freedom in females. Anger is perhaps the one emotion in which the reverse tends to be true. It has also become clear that the same basic need to express emotions exists equally in both sexes. Both need to be able not only to express tenderness, affection, and love, but also to receive it. Therefore, both men and women are plagued by an underlying sense of unfulfillment and frustration, often without recognizing the basis for it.

In the last few years there has been encouraging movement toward societal acceptance of the open expression of emotions such as affection, warmth, tenderness, grief, etc. by males; however, it is our belief that there is still a great deal of room for improvement.

When a couple faces the overwhelming emotions associated with the birth of an abnormal child, the disparity between a husband's and a wife's ability to express emotions openly becomes a critical issue. Characteristically, the husband, raised to feel that he should be capable of being strong and not show evidence of deep hurt, confusion, or despair, tries to hide his pain, fearful that if he lets himself go he will fall apart emotionally. He attempts to solve his dilemma by showing anger, by not wanting to talk about the child, and as much as possible by physically avoiding contact with the situation—staying longer hours at the office or getting involved with other time-consuming activities away from home.

The wife recognizes her need to talk about her feelings, but finds access to her husband blocked. His behavior causes her to feel that she is weak and inadequate. Above all, she desperately needs to be reassured that she is still loved and wanted despite what she feels she has done in producing the abnormal child, and her husband's actions seem to indicate to her that she is neither loved nor wanted.

Furthermore, his increased time away from home makes her feel abandoned, and her anger at him mounts.

A couple in this difficult situation needs help, both as individuals and for the sake of the marriage; yet they are in no position to help each other. The husband, in his continuing attempt to solve his problems by denying them, pretends that there is little or nothing seriously wrong with him or the relationship and implies that everything would improve if his wife would only show some strength of character. She, on the other hand, is far more realistic about the fact that both she and the marital relationship are in trouble. Our data show that in almost all cases it is the wife who makes the first contact asking for professional help. The admission of needing help, particularly in the area of emotional problems, seems to be too threatening to the male ego.

Professional help is needed and is of great value providing it is of the right sort, but we have not yet trained enough professional counselors who specialize in the area of helping parents of an abnormal child. Beyond the need for professional help, and every bit as important to the rehabilitation process for the parents we have discussed, is the need for greater knowledge, awareness, acceptance, and compassion on the part of society in general. In this area, we have an even greater distance to go.

D. Siblings and Other Family Members

We have focused on parents of a birth-defective child for the purpose of this book because the decision to terminate a pregnancy when the unborn child is proven to be abnormal is primarily a parental decision. However, our efforts to help our readers take a realistic look at a complex and heartrending facet of human existence would be incomplete if we failed to point out that the event of an abnormal child's birth has an impact that extends considerably beyond the parents to those with whom they are associated, particularly the immediate family and relatives.

When an abnormal child is born, a question arises in the minds of any blood related individual as to the possibility of some heretofore hidden hereditary trait that might be present in them, and at least some of the effects that we have discussed in foregoing statements are bound to come into play. The child's grandparents are literally parents in a genetic sense and unwillingly feel a responsibility for the problem. For them, as for the child's immediate parents, the tendency is to try to get off the hook of responsibility, and the easiest and most obvious way is to focus the blame on the son-in-law or daughter-in-law. The classic remark that "nothing like that ever happened in our family" is a very likely one.

For the parents of the abnormal child, their own parents and parents-in-law can be an extremely important source of understanding and support, but, unfortunately, they become an additional problem more often than not. The same can be said for the distressed parents' siblings, aunts, and uncles of the problem child.

The siblings of a child born with an abnormality, particularly that of mental retardation, face very special problems. They suffer in an insidiously destructive way from the feeling that something must be wrong with them also. Beyond that, they are forced in many ways into a life-style that is so different from that of their peers that they often develop a pervasive feeling of resentment and anger which, in many cases, they are required to hide. The effects are likely to be lifelong in duration. In many ways, the normal siblings of an abnormal child suffer more than anyone in the long run, particularly if that child continues to live in the household.

Approximately 7 percent of all children born suffer from some problem severe enough to warrant medical intervention, thereby triggering some if not all of the effects we have discussed. If we assume as a very conservative figure for the number of living relatives that the child will have one sibling, two parents, four grandparents, two uncles or aunts, and four cousins, we recognize that at least 13 individuals are immediately and directly involved to a greater or lesser degree. Based on 1980 census figures of more than 3.2 million children under one year of age, and using the 7 percent figure for abnormal births, each such birth having an emotional impact on at least 13 people, the number of individuals just beginning to experience the effects of each abnormal birth is in excess of 3 million every year. The total number of persons suffering some emotional ill effects from this cause at any time in this country alone is inestimable.

We are faced with a very significant medical, psychological, and sociological problem in severe human suffering which has for the most part been ignored, partly through lack of information and partly through unwillingness to face the reality of the problem honestly.

NOTES

1. D. P. Cruikshank, *Amniocentesis for Determination of Fetal Maturity*, 25 Clin. Obstet. & Gynecol. 773 (1982).
2. W. F. Rayburn, *Surveillance Techniques Other Than Ultrasonography for Detecting Fetal Malformations*, 27 J. Repro. Med. 565 (1982).
3. Personal Communication.
4. A. Daniel et al., *Prenatal Diagnosis in 2000 Women for Chromosome, X-Linked, and Metabolic Disorders*, 11 Am. J. Med. Genetics. 61 (1982).
5. S. R. Stephenson & D. D. Weaver, *Prenatal Diagnosis—A Compilation of Diagnosed Conditions*, 141 Am. J. Obstet. Gynecol. 319 (1981).
6. M. S. Golbus, *Prenatal Diagnosis*, 19 Birth Defects: Orig. Art Series. 121 (1983).
7. P. A. Smith, P. Chudleigh & S. Campbell, *Prenatal Diagnosis: Ultrasound*, 6 Br. J. Hosp. Med. 421 (1984).
8. R. A. Bowerman, *Using Ultrasonography to Diagnose Fetal Malformations*, 27 J. Repro. Med. 560 (1982).
9. C. S. Kleinman et al., *Fetal Echocardiography for Evaluation of In Utero Congestive Heart Failure*, 306 N.E.S. Med. 568 (1982).
10. K. L. Reed, *Fetal Echocardiography: New Horizons in Ultrasound*, 6 Br. J. Hosp. Med. 600 (1984).
11. M. J. Mahoney & J. C. Hobbins, *Fetoscopy and Fetal Blood Sampling*, in Genetic Disorders and the Fetus. 501 (A. Milunsky, ed. 1980).
12. K. Nicolaides & C. H. Rodeck, *Prenatal Diagnosis: Fetoscopy*, 6 B. J. Hosp. Med. 396 (1984).

13. V. Cowart, *NIH Considers Large-scale Study to Evaluate Chorionic Villi Sampling,* 252 J.A.M.A. 11 (1984).
14. Stephenson & Weaver, *supra* note 5.
15. S. Semchyshyn, et al., *Fetal Tumor: Antenatal Diagnosis and Its Implications,* 27 J. Repro. Med. 231 (1982).
16. Rayburn, *supra* note 2; Stephenson & Weaver, *supra* note 5.
17. Id.
18. A. Tabor, et al., *Low Maternal Serum AFP and Down Syndrome,* 2 Lancet. 161 (1984).
19. Rayburn, *supra* note 2.
20. Daniel et al., *supra* note 4.
21. Golbus, *supra* note 6.
22. Daniel et al., *supra* note 4.
23. J. C. Hobbins et al., *Stage II Ultrasound Examination for the Diagnosis of Fetal Abnormalities With an Elevated Amniotic Fluid Alpha-Fetoprotein Concentration,* 142 Am. J. Obstet. Gynecol. 1026 (1982).
24. S. McCarthy et al., *Obstetrical Magnetic Resonance Imaging: Fetal Anatomy,* 154 Radiology. 427 (1985).
25. Mahoney & Hobbins, *supra* note 11.
26. H. Travers, M. Shwartzman & P. J. Benke, *False Positive Prenatal Diagnosis of Cystic Fibrosis by Protease Activity,* 146 Am. J. Obstet. Gynecol. 338 (1983).
27. Bowerman, *supra* note 8.
28. Daniel et al., *supra* note 4.
29. Cowart, *supra* note 13.
30. Daniel et al., *supra* note 4; Mahoney & Hobbins, *supra* note 11.
31. Daniel et al., *supra* note 4.
32. J. R. Rucquoi, *Genetic Counseling and Prenatal Genetic Evaluation,* 36 Med. North. Am. 3359 (1983).
33. S. P. Rubin, J. Malin & J. Maidman, *Genetic Counseling Before Prenatal Diagnosis for Advanced Maternal Age: An Important Medical Safeguard,* 62 Obstet. Gynecol. 155 (1983).
34. C. Marwick, *Controversy Surrounds Use of Test for Open Spina Bifida,* 250 J.A.M.A. 575 (1983).
35. Personal Communication
36. S. M. Peck, *The Road Less Traveled,* in Love (1978).

This article by Christopher Tietze is based, in part, on data from the Population Council. Even though a specific time period of 1973–80 is given, it is known that the earlier experience of New York State prior to 1973 was recognized by Dr. Tietze. Because of the importance and impact of medical statistics, this is one of two articles presented in this volume.

11 · Demographic and Public Health Experience With Legal Abortion: 1973–80

Christopher Tietze, M.D.

The liberalization of abortions laws in the United States started in 1967 and accelerated in 1970 with the passage in the state of New York of a statute that did not specify on what grounds a pregnancy could be terminated and did not limit access to abortion to residents of the state; it culminated in the landmark decisions by the Supreme Court of January 22, 1973,[1] reaffirmed on June 15, 1983.[2] These changes in the legal landscape and the resulting changes in medical practice have generated a vast amount of new information on the demographic and public health aspects of induced abortion performed in medical settings.

I. Sources of Data

Two organizations, one governmental and one private, have provided nationwide data in this area: the Centers for Disease Control (CDC) in Atlanta, an arm of the United States Public Health Service, and the Alan Guttmacher Institute (AGI) in New York City, a nonprofit corporation for research, policy analysis, and public education.

As abortion became legal throughout the nation, most states enacted laws mandating the reporting of all such procedures to the appropriate health authorities. By 1980, laws were on the books in 46 states and the District of Columbia, with substantial variation as to subject matter to be reported and level of compliance. Based on pretabulated data submitted by the states, the CDC began in 1970 to compile and publish comprehensive abortion statistics, including information on selected characteristics of the woman and of the abortion, such as residence (in state, out of state), age, race, marital status, prior births, prior induced abortions, weeks of gestation, and type of procedure. The most recent available data are those for 1980.[3]

In addition, the CDC have put in place a program of surveillance of all deaths associated with all types of abortion: legally induced, illegally induced, and spontaneous. During the period 1972–80, a total of 164 deaths directly or indirectly associated with legal abortion were identified, about three times the number of deaths attributed to that cause on death certificates. The completeness of abortion surveillance by the CDC has been carefully evaluated and was estimated to have reached 94 percent in 1972–75.[4]

The AGI conducted annual surveys of providers of abortion services from 1973 through 1978, changing to a biennial pattern in 1970–80.[5] These surveys have obtained information on the numbers of legal abortions performed in each metropolitan area and in the nonmetropolitan portion of each state, by type of service (hospital, nonhospital clinic, physician's office), but not on any characteristics of the woman or the procedure.

The number of legal abortions identified by the AGI has always been substantially greater than the number reported by the CDC. The reason for this discrepancy is that the CDC obtain most of their data from state health departments rather than by active outreach to providers as does the AGI. After the decisions by the Supreme Court, abortion services became available in areas where they had not existed before. Many states, however, did not establish reporting systems until late 1973 or even later (and a few have not yet done so), thus causing a shortfall of about 17 percent in the CDC statistics for 1973, which continued at approximately the same level during 1974–80. In order to provide an internally consistent set of abortion statistics for the United States, the AGI has prepared annual estimates based on the AGI totals and the distributions by characteristics published by the CDC. All nationwide statistics on characteristics presented in this chapter are based on these estimates, which are adjusted for changes from year to year in the number of states reporting to the CDC.[6] Some of the time series in this chapter differ slightly from those published elsewhere owing to changes in estimating procedures or use of revised denominators. No number, percentage, or rate should be interpreted as providing valid information beyond the first two digits.

In addition to the CDC and the AGI, the National Center for Health Statistics (NCHS) has tried to establish an abortion registration area by obtaining from the states records concerning individual abortions (without identification of the woman) that can be centrally tabulated. This system would have obvious advantages compared with the compilation of pretabulated data by the CDC. So far, only 13 states have joined the program, which has resulted in reports for 1977–79.[7]

II. Incidence of Legal Abortion

The total number of legal abortions in the United States increased from an estimated 50,000 in 1969 to around 200,000 in 1970, with most of the increment in the second half of that year, when New York State (mainly New York City) and several other areas made legal abortion available to nonresidents. From then onward, the number continued to increase from year to year, albeit at a decreasing

Table 1. Legal Abortions Reported to Alan Guttmacher Institute: United States, 1973–80

	1973	1974	1975	1976	1977	1978	1979	1980
Number (1000s)	745	899	1034	1179	1317	1410	1498	1554
Percent increase from prior year	na[1]	20.7	15.1	14.0	11.7	7.1	6.2	3.8
Rate per 1000 women aged 15–44 years	16.3	19.3	21.7	24.2	26.4	27.7	28.8	29.3
Percent of known pregnancies[2]	19.3	22.0	24.9	26.5	28.6	29.2	29.7	30.0

1. Not applicable.
2. Legal abortions plus live births six months later.

rate, passing the 1 million mark in 1975 and approaching 1.6 million in 1980, according to the latest AGI survey, including about 4000 residents of Canada, about 3000 residents of Mexico, and about 1000 women from other areas, mainly the Caribbean islands.[8] Because the number of women of reproductive age also increased during the period, the abortion rate per 1000 women aged 15–44 years rose somewhat less rapidly than the number of abortions, by only three-fourths from 1973 to 1979, compared with a doubling of the numbers, and by only 1.7 percent from 1979 to 1980, compared with 3.8 percent (Table 1).

A different way of looking at these statistics is to relate the number of abortions to the number of pregnancies with intended outcome, approximated by the number of known pregnancies, *i.e.*, legal abortions plus live births six months later. In 1980, three out of 10 known pregnancies were terminated by legal abortion, compared with less than one in five in 1973. Since probably not more than 2.1 million of the 3.3 million births conceived in 1978 were intended at the time of conception, it would appear that about one-half of the unwanted or mistimed pregnancies were aborted in that year, and a similar fraction in 1980.[9]

It cannot be emphasized too strongly that the rapidly increasing numbers of legal abortions in the United States do *not* reflect an equally rapid increase of the total number of induced abortions, legal plus illegal. Many legal abortions have replaced unwanted births, but large numbers of legal abortions—estimated as somewhere between a half million and a million—have replaced illegal abortions. Other factors involved have been increasing proportion of unmarried women, increasing sexual activity among teenagers, and—in some age groups of women— repeated "pill scares" resulting in changing patterns of contraception.

III. Availability of Abortion Services

It is difficult to assess the impact of the restrictions on public funding for abortion, resulting from the Hyde Amendment,[10] on the number of abortions performed. Estimates are available for the fiscal year 1978. About 250,000, or roughly 85 percent, of all Medicaid-eligible women obtaining abortions in FY77 lived in states continuing to pay for these services, while 45,000 lived in states where public funding became unavailable in FY78. However, the number of abortions funded by Medicaid also declined to about 194,000 in those states where state funds were

Table 2. Legal Abortions by Type of Services: United States 1973–80

Type of Service	1973	1974	1975	1976	1977	1978	1979	1980
Number (1000s)[1]								
Hospitals	386	418	413	417	391	351	348	341
Clinics	343	455	585	721	872	999	1087	1145
MD's offices[2]	15	25	35	41	54	60	63	68
Percent of total[3]								
Hospitals	51.8	46.5	40.0	35.3	29.7	24.9	23.2	21.9
Clinics	46.1	50.7	56.6	61.2	66.2	70.8	72.6	73.7
MD's offices[2]	2.1	2.8	3.4	3.5	4.1	4.3	4.2	4.4

1. Because of rounding, numbers in this and subsequent tables may not add up to totals in Table 1.
2. Physicians' offices reporting 400 or more abortions a year are classified as clinics.
3. Percentages in this and subsequent tables are forced to add up to 100.

still available, probably because of widespread confusion among pregnant women and among providers of abortion services concerning the availability of Medicaid funding. Based on the experience of three states, it has been estimated that nationwide some 84,000 among 300,000 Medicaid-eligible women in FY78 could not obtain Medicaid-funded abortions but were able to obtain legal abortions in the private sector, that 14,000 gave birth, and that fewer than 3000 obtained abortions from illegal (nonmedical) practitioners, mostly in states where public funding had been curtailed.[11] Comparable estimates for more recent years have not been published.

Around two-fifths of all legal abortions obtained in the United States in 1972 were performed outside the state of the woman's permanent residence. By 1980 the share of out-of-state abortions had declined to about 6 percent.[12] However, many women obtaining abortions had to travel, often considerable distances, to other communities within their state of residence. This handicap applied particularly to women living in smaller cities and towns or in rural areas. In each year from 1973 through 1980, at least 95 percent of all abortions was performed in metropolitan areas.[13]

As shown in Table 2, about 52 percent of all legal abortions in the United States in 1973 took place in hospitals, 46 percent in nonhospital clinics, and 2 percent in doctors' offices. By 1980, only 22 percent of all abortions were reported from hospitals, 74 percent from clinics, and 4 percent from doctors' offices. In addition, about one-half of all abortions in hospitals were performed on outpatients. In absolute terms, the number of abortions in hospitals remained in the vicinity of 400,000 during 1973–77 and then dropped to about 350,000 in 1978–80. In 1980, only 27 percent of all non-Catholic general hospitals and 17 percent of public hospitals provided *any* abortion services. If hospitals reporting fewer than two abortions per week are excluded, these percentages are reduced by about one-third. In 17 states, more than 50 percent of all women aged 15–44 lived in counties without abortion facilities, while in only nine states did more than 90 percent live in counties where such services were available.

An important characteristic of abortion facilities in the United States is their high degree of concentration. In 1980, a mere 80 hospitals and 379 clinics, representing 17 percent of all providers of abortion services, with 1000 or more abortions per year and an average of about 50 abortions per week per provider, accounted for 76 percent of all legal abortions.[14] This concentration probably increases the experience and competence of the professionals involved and the quality of the services. On the other hand, follow-up care is fragmented, with possible unfavorable effects on the patient.

IV. The Demographic Profile: Age, Marital Status, Parity, and Race

The demographic profile of abortion-seeking women in the United States did not change dramatically from 1973 to 1980. A majority were young (64–66 percent under 25 years), unmarried (71–79 percent), childless (55–58 percent), and white (67–74 percent). However, some trends can be discerned. The proportions of teenagers and of women in their late thirties and early forties declined, while the share of women in their twenties rose from about 50 percent to 55 percent, reflecting changes in the age distribution of the female population. Unmarried women, including single, separated, divorced, and widowed women, increased from 71 percent of the total in 1973 to 79 percent in 1980; women with no prior live births, from 55 percent to 58 percent. Both trends probably reflect changes in the sexual activity of unmarried women as well as rising ages at marriage and first birth. Conversely, abortions to women with three or more prior births dropped from 15 percent to 7 percent, probably a result of the growing acceptance of surgical sterilization by women and men. The share of nonwhite women rose from 26 percent in 1973 to a peak of 33 percent in 1976, then dropped to less than 30 percent in 1979–80, which may reflect variations in access to publicly funded abortion services.[15]

It is instructive to compare the age patterns of abortion rates per 1000 women and of the percentages of known pregnancies terminated by abortion (Table 3). In 1980, for instance, the abortion rate increased from 4.3 for women under 15 years of age (computed per 1000 women aged 13–14 years) to the very high level of 61 per 1000 at 18–19 years of age, followed by a steady decline to 3.5 for women over 40 years of age (computed per 1000 women aged 40–44 years). The proportion of known pregnancies terminated by abortion, on the other hand, was 42 percent among women under 18 years of age, dropped to 22 percent at 25–29 years when most women would be building their families, followed by a rise to 52 percent among the relatively few pregnancies to women in their forties.

Abortion rates per 1000 women aged 15–44 years and proportions of known pregnancies terminated by abortions were 4.4 and 6.6 times higher, respectively, in 1980 for unmarried women than for married women (Table 4). Abortions and births used in the computation are defined in terms of the woman's status at the time of the event. If it were possible to classify abortions and births by marital status at conception, the percentage of known pregnancies terminated by abortion would be increased for the married and substantially reduced for the unmarried.

In regard to parity, as shown in Table 5, the highest proportion of known pregnancies terminated by abortion has been consistently reported during recent years among women with no prior birth (37 percent in 1980). Many of these pregnancies were conceived out of wedlock. Among women with one prior birth, the share of abortions dropped to its lowest value (21 percent), rose again to a

Table 3. Legal Abortions by Age of Women: United States, 1973–80

Age (years)	1973	1974	1975	1976	1977	1978	1979	1980
Number (1000s)[1]								
14 or less[2]				16	16	15	16	15
15–17	244	292	340	153	166	169	179	183
18–19				210	231	250	266	261
20–24	241	287	332	392	450	489	526	549
25–29	130	163	189	220	247	266	284	304
30–34	73	90	100	110	124	134	142	153
35–39	41	49	53	57	62	65	65	67
40 or more[2]	17	19	21	21	22	21	20	21
Percent of total[1]								
14 or less[2]				1.3	1.2	1.1	1.1	1.0
15–17	32.8	32.5	32.9	13.0	12.6	12.0	11.9	11.8
18–19				17.8	17.5	17.7	17.8	16.8
20–24	32.3	31.9	32.1	33.3	34.2	34.7	35.1	35.4
25–29	17.4	18.1	18.2	18.7	18.7	18.9	19.0	19.6
30–34	9.7	10.0	9.7	9.3	9.4	9.5	9.5	9.8
35–39	5.5	5.4	5.1	4.8	4.7	4.6	4.3	4.3
40 or more[2]	2.3	2.1	2.0	1.8	1.7	1.5	1.3	1.3
Rate per 1000 women[1]								
14 or less[2]				3.9	3.9	3.8	4.3	4.3
15–17	23.9	28.2	32.5	24.2	26.2	26.9	28.8	30.2
18–19				49.3	54.1	58.4	61.9	61.0
20–24	26.2	30.4	34.3	39.6	44.3	47.2	49.9	51.4
25–29	16.9	19.6	21.8	24.1	26.9	28.4	29.6	30.8
30–34	10.9	13.0	14.0	15.0	15.7	16.4	16.5	17.1
35–39	7.1	8.4	8.9	9.3	9.8	9.8	9.4	9.3
40 or more[2]	2.9	3.3	3.6	3.7	3.9	3.6	3.4	3.5
Percent of known pregnancies[3]								
14 or less[2]					41.1	40.9	43.0	42.7
15–17	25.6	29.0	33.4	35.8	38.7	39.7	41.3	42.4
18–19					37.9	39.3	40.1	40.1
20–24	17.6	20.0	22.8	25.0	27.6	28.7	29.4	30.1
25–29	13.2	15.4	17.2	18.6	20.2	20.8	21.1	21.8
30–34	18.7	21.7	23.5	23.1	23.7	23.5	23.0	23.3
35–39	28.3	32.8	35.4	36.6	38.5	38.6	37.3	37.2
40 or more[2]	39.7	44.4	48.6	50.2	52.5	51.6	50.4	51.7

1. By reported age at abortion.
2. Rates computed per 1000 women aged 13–14 and 40–44 years, respectively. Rates for women aged 19 years or less in 1973–75, are computed per 1000 women aged 15–19 years.
3. By estimated age at conception.

higher level at parity 2 and 3, followed by a marked decline to 23 percent among women with five or more prior births because women who avoid abortion for religious or other reasons are overrepresented among women of high parity. Owing to the high correlation of parity and age, this pattern was entirely obliterated in the parity-specific abortion rates per 1000 women, aged 15–44 years, which declined from a high among the nulliparous women to a low among those with five or more prior births.

Table 4. Legal Abortions by Marital Status: United States, 1973–1980

Marital status[1]	1973	1974	1975	1976	1977	1978	1979	1980
Number (1000s)								
Married	216	248	272	290	300	331	322	320
Unmarried[2]	528	650	762	889	1017	1079	1175	1234
Percent of total								
Married	29.0	27.6	26.3	24.6	22.8	23.5	21.5	20.6
Unmarried[2]	71.0	72.4	73.7	75.4	77.2	76.5	78.5	79.4
Rate per 1000 women aged 15–44 years								
Married	8.0	9.2	10.0	10.6	10.9	12.0	11.6	11.3
Unmarried[2]	28.4	33.4	37.5	41.7	45.8	46.1	48.7	49.7
UM/M ratio[3]	3.5	3.6	3.8	3.9	4.2	3.8	4.2	4.4
Percent of known pregnancies								
Married	7.0	8.3	9.6	9.4	9.8	10.0	9.9	9.8
Unmarried[2]	57.0	59.9	62.3	64.2	66.0	65.4	66.0	64.9
UM/M ratio[3]	8.1	7.2	6.5	6.8	6.7	6.3	6.7	6.6

1. At abortion or birth.
2. Never married, separated, divorced, and widowed women.
3. Unmarried/married ratio.

Table 5. Legal Abortions by Prior Live Births: United States, 1973–80

Prior live births	1973	1974	1975	1976	1977	1978	1979	1980
Number (1000s)								
None	411	483	542	629	742	798	868	900
One	115	155	194	229	249	271	287	305
Two	104	130	156	176	186	198	207	216
Three	61	70	78	81	80	83	82	83
Four	29	32	34	34	33	33	30	29
Five or more	26	28	30	30	25	26	23	22
Percent of total								
None	55.2	53.7	52.4	53.4	56.4	56.7	58.0	57.9
One	15.4	17.3	18.8	19.4	18.9	19.2	19.2	19.6
Two	13.9	14.5	15.1	14.9	14.2	14.0	13.8	13.9
Three	8.1	7.8	7.5	6.9	6.1	5.9	5.5	5.4
Four	3.9	3.6	3.3	2.9	2.5	2.4	2.0	1.8
Five or more	3.5	3.1	2.9	2.5	1.9	1.8	1.5	1.4
Rate per 1000 women aged 15–44 years								
None	21.8	24.7	26.3	29.4	33.6	35.2	37.3	37.7
One	16.3	21.3	25.9	29.4	31.3	33.0	33.7	34.7
Two	13.0	15.8	18.5	20.2	20.5	21.0	21.1	21.2
Three	11.1	12.9	14.5	15.2	14.8	15.2	14.8	14.8
Four	9.4	10.8	11.8	12.0	12.0	12.3	11.4	11.1
Five or more	8.0	9.0	10.5	11.0	10.1	10.8	10.5	10.8
Percent of known pregnancies								
None	24.0	26.4	29.0	31.3	34.7	35.5	36.2	36.6
One	10.6	13.4	16.3	17.8	19.0	19.8	20.1	20.8
Two	19.1	22.5	25.7	26.7	27.4	27.8	27.8	28.3
Three	23.5	26.9	29.7	30.1	29.6	29.9	28.9	28.7
Four	23.6	27.2	29.6	29.7	29.7	29.9	27.5	26.1
Five or more	18.4	21.4	24.9	25.7	24.5	25.5	23.9	22.6

Table 6. Legal Abortions by Woman's Race: United States 1973–80

Woman's race	1973	1974	1975	1976	1977	1978	1979	1980
Number (1000s)								
White	549	629	701	785	889	969	1062	1094
Other	196	269	333	394	428	440	435	460
Percent of total								
White	73.7	70.0	67.8	66.6	67.5	68.8	70.9	70.4
Other	26.3	30.0	32.2	33.4	32.5	31.2	29.1	29.6
Rate per 1000 women aged 15–44 years								
White	14.0	15.7	17.2	18.8	20.9	22.3	24.0	24.3
Other	31.2	41.4	49.3	56.3	59.0	58.7	56.2	56.8
O/W ratio[1]	2.2	2.6	2.9	3.0	2.8	2.6	2.3	2.3
Percent of known pregnancies								
White	17.4	19.6	21.5	23.0	25.0	26.1	27.1	27.4
Other	25.9	31.6	35.9	38.9	40.4	39.6	38.2	39.2
O/W ratio[1]	1.5	1.6	1.7	1.7	1.6	1.5	1.4	1.4

1. Other/white ratio.

While white women represented a substantial majority of women obtaining legal abortions in the United States during 1973–80, both the abortion rate per 1000 women aged 15–44 years and the percentage of known pregnancies terminated by abortion were consistently higher among blacks and other minorities (Table 6). This differential reflects primarily a higher proportion of unintended pregnancies, rather than a greater acceptance of abortion as a means to resolve such pregnancies.[16]

V. Repeat Abortions

The issue of repeat abortion is a matter of concern, especially for those who feel that abortion is unacceptable as a primary method of fertility regulation and should be used only as a backup measure when contraception has failed. Others fear that even minor adverse effects on the health of the woman or on the outcome of later pregnancies would be cumulated by multiple abortion experiences.

Table 7 presents data on repeat abortions in the United States. The information on prior induced abortions was obtained from women seeking a subsequent termination and are, therefore, subject to response error and, in some cases, deliberate denial or understatement. It is believed, however, that few women report abortions obtained in illegal settings. Moreover, the importance of this source of underreporting declines as the number of years since legalization increases.

Numbers and percent of repeat abortions increased rapidly in the United States from 1974 to 1980. Their share among all abortions was even higher in such places as New York City where legal abortion on request became available earlier and where the abortion rate (among residents) has been much higher than in the country as a whole. The upward trend does not reflect a progressive change from

Table 7. Legal Abortions by Prior Induced Abortions: United States, 1974–80

Prior induced abortions	1974	1975	1976	1977	1978	1979	1980
Number (1000s)							
None	762	822	911	973	996	1025	1043
One	113	170	213	272	317	352	372
Two	17	30	40	54	70	86	97
Three or more	7	11	14	19	26	34	41
Percent of total							
None	84.8	79.5	77.3	73.9	70.7	68.4	67.1
One	12.5	16.5	18.1	20.6	22.5	23.5	24.0
Two	1.9	2.9	3.4	4.1	5.0	5.8	6.3
Three or more	0.8	1.1	1.2	1.4	1.8	2.3	2.6

contraception to abortion as the primary method of fertility regulation but, to a large degree, the fact that growing numbers of women who have had a first legal abortion are now at risk of having a repeat. As shown in Figure 1, the number of women at risk in 1980 was 3.5 times higher than in 1974, an increase almost equal to the increase of repeat abortions (3.7 times).

VI. Period of Gestation and Method of Termination

One of the most important factors in the evaluation of adverse effects associated with abortion is the period of gestation at which the pregnancy is terminated. The traditional division has been between abortions in the first trimester and those in the second trimester, that is, between those performed at 12 weeks from the onset of the last menstrual period (LMP) or earlier and those at 13 weeks or later. However, accumulating experience has made it clear that this dichotomy is not sufficient, because the frequency of adverse effects increases with the progress of gestation within each trimester.

In the United States, the period 1973–80 has seen a trend toward earlier performance of legal abortions, especially from 1973 to 1977 (Table 8). In 1980, more than one-half of all terminations were performed at eight weeks from LMP or earlier, more than nine-tenths at 12 weeks or earlier, and more than 99 percent

Figure 1. Repeat Abortions and Women at Risk of Repeat Abortion: United States, 1974–1980

Year	Repeat Abortions	Women at risk
1974	136,500	2,216,000
1975	212,100	3,094,000
1976	268,000	3,857,000
1977	344,200	4,780,000
1978	413,100	5,740,000
1979	472,300	6,934,000
1980	510,900	7,705,000

Table 8. Legal Abortions by Weeks of Gestation: United States, 1973–80

Weeks of Gestation	1973	1974	1975	1976	1977	1978	1979	1980
Number (1000s)								
8 or less	284	399	481	560	658	708	749	800
9–10	222	257	290	334	361	388	413	416
11–12	131	135	151	171	180	188	204	202
13–15	44	44	46	49	52	63	70	73
16–20	53	54	56	55	54	51	49	50
21 or more	10	10	10	10	12	12	13	13
Percent of total								
8 or less	38.2	44.5	46.5	47.4	50.0	50.2	50.0	51.5
9–10	29.7	28.5	28.1	28.3	27.4	27.6	27.6	26.8
11–12	17.5	15.0	14.6	14.5	13.6	13.3	13.6	13.0
13–15	6.0	4.9	4.4	4.2	4.0	4.5	4.7	4.7
16–20	7.2	6.0	5.4	4.7	4.1	3.6	3.3	3.2
21 or more	1.4	1.1	1.0	0.9	0.9	0.8	0.8	0.8

at 20 weeks or earlier. Mid-trimester abortions represent a smaller proportion of all legal abortions in the United States than in other countries where termination is permitted up to the point of viability of the fetus.[17]

The trend toward earlier abortion reflects not only a recognition by women and physicians that it is less stressful and safer (and also less expensive) than termination later in pregnancy, but also easier access to abortion services. This is illustrated by the statistics for New York State. In 1973, about 16 percent of all abortions obtained by residents were performed at 13 weeks or later, dropping to 11 percent in 1980. The corresponding fraction for nonresidents rose from 25 to 34 percent. Apparently, women in other states were increasingly able to obtain first-trimester abortions, generally available in clinics, but not second-trimester procedures which in many places were restricted, by law or medical tradition, to hospitals.

Late abortions occur most frequently among the youngest women (Table 9). In 1980, only one-third of women under 15 years of age obtained abortions at eight weeks or earlier, while 3 percent obtained them at 21 or more weeks of gestation. The corresponding fractions for women in their early thirties were 64 percent and 0.5 percent. Conversely, almost one-half of all abortions at 21 or more weeks' gestation and 44 percent of all second-trimester procedures involved teenagers, compared with less than one-fourth of all abortions at eight weeks or earlier.

The strong inverse association of period of gestation and woman's age reflects the inexperience of the young in recognizing the symptoms of pregnancy, their unwillingness to accept the reality of their situation, their ignorance about where to seek advice and help, and their hesitation to confide in adults. Economic considerations and laws or regulations prohibiting surgery on minors without parental consent also contributed to delays.

The slight decline in the proportions of abortions performed at eight weeks or earlier among older women reflects primarily the association of high-order pregnancies with economic and cultural deprivation. Abortions on medical

Table 9. Legal Abortions by Age of Woman and Weeks of Gestation: United States, 1980

Woman's age (years)	Weeks of Gestation					
	8 or less	9–10	11–12	13–15	16–20	21 or more
Number (1000s)[1]						
14 or less	5.2	4.1	2.6	1.5	1.4	0.5
15–17	67.6	54.3	33.6	13.8	10.9	3.1
18–19	113.4	78.1	41.7	15.0	10.6	2.7
20–24	282.4	151.0	71.1	25.1	15.8	4.0
25–29	180.0	74.2	31.3	10.7	6.1	1.4
30–34	97.3	34.8	13.2	4.4	2.7	0.7
35–39	41.2	15.3	6.2	2.0	1.5	0.3
40 or more	12.9	4.8	2.0	0.6	0.5	0.1
Percent by weeks of gestation, within woman's age						
14 or less	33.9	26.5	17.2	10.0	9.3	3.1
15–17	36.9	29.6	18.3	7.5	6.0	1.7
18–19	43.4	29.9	15.9	5.7	4.1	1.0
20–24	51.4	27.5	12.9	4.6	2.9	0.7
25–29	59.3	24.4	10.3	3.5	2.0	0.5
30–34	63.6	22.7	8.6	2.9	1.7	0.5
35–39	61.8	23.0	9.4	3.1	2.2	0.5
40 or more	61.9	23.0	9.4	3.0	2.2	0.5
Percent by woman's age, within weeks of gestation						
14 or less	0.7	1.0	1.3	2.1	2.9	3.7
15–17	8.4	13.0	16.7	18.9	22.0	24.1
18–19	14.2	18.8	20.7	20.4	21.4	20.9
20–24	35.3	36.2	35.2	34.3	31.9	31.1
25–29	22.5	17.8	15.5	14.6	12.4	11.3
30–34	12.2	8.3	6.5	6.0	5.4	5.6
35–39	5.1	3.7	3.1	2.8	3.0	2.5
40 or more	1.6	1.2	1.0	0.9	1.0	0.8

1. Distribution estimated by iterative adjustment of data for 13 states in 1979 to marginal totals for 1980.

grounds are also more common among older women, and some women in their forties may misinterpret the amenorrhea of pregnancy as the onset of menopause.

One category of late second-trimester abortions deserves special mention: selective termination of pregnancy to prevent the birth of an infant with major physical or mental defects.[18] In many cases, the presence of such a condition can now be determined *in utero* with certainty or near certainty, most often by amniocentesis and cell culture, but also by such other methods as biochemical analysis of the amniotic fluid, ultrasonography, and even direct visual inspection of the fetus (fetoscopy) and fetal blood sampling. Conditions that can be detected *in utero* include Down's syndrome (mongoloid idiocy), Tay-Sachs disease (amaurotic familial idiocy), sickle-cell anemia, neural tube defects (NTDs, primarily anencephaly and open spina bifida), and many others. In addition, it is possible to identify the sex of the fetus, permitting the selective abortion of male fetuses, one-half of which would be affected by sex-linked disorders, such as hemophilia, if the pregnant woman is known to be a carrier.

Because all procedures for the prenatal detection of fetal abnormalities require highly trained health personnel and some may result in injury to the pregnant woman or to a normal fetus, they are practically useful only if high-risk pregnancies can be identified. For many rare conditions, the only clues presently available are the prior birth of a defective child or such clinical signs as hydramnios, which is often associated with fetal malformation. However, pregnancies at risk for some conditions can be identified by screening tests. Tay-Sachs disease occurs most frequently among Jews of eastern European origin, one person in 30 being heterozygous for the condition and, therefore, a carrier of the disorder. Carrier matings have been successfully identified by community-sponsored blood tests.[19] In the case of sickle-cell anemia, about one-tenth of all blacks in the United States are carriers and readily identifiable, but the methods used for the diagnosis of homozygous and, therefore, affected fetuses are still experimental and not yet ready for routine use. Because the incidence of Down's syndrome increases steeply with maternal age, it has been recommended that amniocentesis be offered to all pregnant women over the age of 35 years.

Prenatal diagnosis is rarely possible prior to 16 weeks of gestation, and in some cases a definitive determination may not be available before 22–24 weeks of gestation, at the borderline of fetal viability. The importance of such procedures lies in the fact that findings are negative in more than 95 percent of cases. Although it is never possible to guarantee a perfect baby, the prospective parents can at least be reassured that their child will not suffer from the disorder that had been suspected or feared. Prenatal diagnosis backed up by selective abortion thus make procreation possible for couples who might otherwise avoid childbearing, perhaps by aborting all pregnancies.

At present, the number of abortions performed on the basis of prenatal diagnosis is quite small. Because the procedures have been in use only since 1968, most prospective parents and even some physicians are not aware of them, and comparatively few centers exist where they can be carried out. In the United States, about 125 prenatal diagnosis programs were active in 1978, but only 10 to 15 laboratories were adequately staffed and equipped for the diagnosis of Tay-Sachs disease or NTDs. The number of diagnostic amniocenteses performed in that year was on the order of 15,000, compared with 150,000 to 200,000 pregnancies at risk under currently accepted criteria. By 1982, the number of programs had risen to at least 155 and the number of amniocentesis procedures, to at least 30,000. The number of abortions then performed on the basis of prenatal diagnosis was on the order of 1500, or one-tenth of 1 percent of all legal abortions in the United States. However, each of these abortions has averted a major catastrophe for a family.

Table 10 shows the methods used for the termination of pregnancy in the United States. The overwhelming majority of legal abortions during 1973–80 and virtually all first-trimester abortions were accomplished by instrumental evacuation, including suction curettage (also called vacuum aspiration or VA), surgical curettage (D&C), and dilatation and evacuation (D&E), designating procedures at 13 or more weeks' gestation. Suction curettage is by far the most widely used

Table 10. Legal Abortions by Method of Termination: United States, 1973–80

	1973	1974	1975	1976	1977	1978	1979	1980
Number (1000s)								
Instrumental evacuation[1]	668	805	949	1101	1236	1334	1422	1487
Medical induction[2]	7.3	89	82	75	78	74	75	66
Uterine surgery[3]	4.1	5.0	3.6	2.7	2.3	1.6	1.1	1.2
Percent of total								
Instrumental evacuation	89.7	89.5	91.7	93.4	93.9	94.6	94.9	95.6
Medical induction	9.7	9.9	8.0	6.4	5.9	5.3	5.0	4.3
Uterine surgery	0.6	0.6	0.3	0.2	0.2	0.1	0.1	0.1

1. Includes vacuum curettage, surgical curettage, and dilatation and evacuation (D&E) at 13 weeks' gestation or later.
2. Hypertonic saline, prostaglandin, urea, and combinations. Also includes a small number of terminations by "other methods."
3. Hysterotomy and hysterectomy.

technique. Medical induction includes instillation of hypertonic saline, prostaglandin (PG), urea, or combinations of these into the amniotic cavity as well as a small number of PG abortions by other routes, such as vaginal suppositories. The decline of this category of abortion from 9.7 percent in 1973 to 4.3 percent in 1980 reflects in part the trend toward earlier termination, but also a shift from medical induction to instrumental evacuation, especially during the early part of the second trimester, *i.e.,* at 13–15 weeks' gestation. A substantial proportion (more than two-thirds in 1972–78) of these procedures are performed in nonhospital clinics.[20] Major surgical procedures (hysterotomy and hysterectomy) have never been used extensively in the United States as methods of abortion during the period under consideration; by 1978, their share had dropped to less than one-tenth of 1 percent of all legal abortions.

VII. Adverse Effects of Legal Abortion

With the exception of the remote possibility of prolonged survival of the woman in a "vegetable" state, resulting from cerebral anoxia, the most serious adverse effect of abortion is the death of the woman.

In the United States, as elsewhere, high levels of mortality from legal abortion prevailed during the period of restrictive legislation, when a significant proportion of the women undergoing therapeutic abortion suffered from preexisting complications that made them poor risks for any type of surgery. By 1972–75, with elective abortion more easily available to most women, mortality had declined to about three per 100,000 legal terminations, followed by a further drop to about one per 100,000 in 1976–80 (Table 11).

The total number of deaths during the entire period of CDC surveillance, 1972–80, was 164. Major causes of death, as identified by the CDC, were pelvic infection (38 cases), documented and suspected pulmonary embolism (37), hemorrhage (33 cases, including seven instances of disseminated intravascular coagulopathy), and complications of general (20) and local (7) anesthesia.[21] At

Table 11. Legal Abortions, Associated Deaths, and Mortality per 100,000 Abortions: United States, 1972–80

	Number of abortions	Number of deaths[1]	Deaths per 100,000 abortions
Total 1972–80	10,221,000	164	1.6
1972	586,800[2]	24	4.1
1973	744,600[3]	25	3.4
1974	898,600	25	2.8
1975	1,034,200	29	2.8
1976	1,179,300	11	0.9
1977	1,316,300	17	1.3
1978	1,409,600	7	0.5
1979	1,497,700	18	1.2
1980	1,553,900	8	0.5
Gestation			
8 weeks or less	4,853,000	19	0.4
9–10 weeks	2,864,000	31	1.1
11–12 weeks	1,458,000	25	1.7
13–15 weeks	481,000	20	4.2
16–20 weeks	466,000	55	11.8
21 weeks or more	99,000	14	14.1
Procedure[4]			
Instrumental evacuation:			
12 weeks or less	9,062,000	71	0.8
13 weeks or more	470,000	21	4.5
Medical induction	664,000	62[5]	9.3
Uterine surgery	25,000	10	40.0
Type of facility, 1974–77[6]			
All cases[7]			
Hospital	1,229,000	19	1.5
Other[8]	2,730,000	17	0.6
Excluding women with preexisting complications and/or concurrent sterilization			
Hospital	1,007,000	7	0.7
Other	2,296,000	15	0.7

1. Deaths identified by CDC
2. Abortions reported to CDC
3. 1973–80: abortions reported to AGI
4. See footnotes to Table 10
5. Includes six deaths associated with "other methods"
6. Grimes et al. 1981
7. At or before 12 weeks' gestation
8. Includes nonhospital clinics (95%) and doctors' offices (5%)

least one-third of the deaths during 1972–78 involved women with major preexisting medical conditions. The risk to life was 40 times greater for these women than for women without such complications.[22]

One of the main factors determining the level of mortality following legal abortion is the period of gestation at which pregnancies are terminated. In the United States during 1972–80, mortality ranged from 0.4 per 100,000 legal abortions at eight weeks or earlier to 14 per 100,000 for abortions at 21 weeks or later. The risk to life associated with instrumental evacuation was more than five times greater at 13 or more weeks' gestation than at 12 weeks or earlier, it was twice as high for medical induction as for mid-trimester instrumental evacuation, and four times higher for uterine surgery than for medical induction.

During 1974–77, mortality was higher for first-trimester abortions performed in hospitals than for abortions in nonhospital facilities. The difference disappears when women with preexisting complications and/or concurrent sterilization are excluded from the hospital experience.[23]

A subsequent paper revealed a higher mortality rate for mid-trimester abortions by instrumental evacuation (D&E) performed in hospitals, compared with those performed in clinics.[24] It is not possible in that study to exclude women with preexisting complications and/or concurrent sterilization.

Abortion-related mortality may be compared appropriately with the risk to life associated with carrying a pregnancy to term. In the United States, maternal mortality attributed to complications of pregnancy, childbirth, and the puerperium, *excluding* abortion and ectopic gestation, declined from 15.2 deaths per 100,000 live births in 1972 to 7.5 per 100,000 in 1980, for an average of 10.4 over the entire period. Weighting of the average by the numbers of abortions in successive years reduces it to 9.8 per 100,000 live births.

These rates do *not* include deaths from other causes, such as diseases of the circulatory system, occurring among pregnant women, during labor, or shortly after delivery, and presumably aggravated by the stresses of pregnancy and/or childbirth. The number of such deaths is at least one-third of that identified in the published mortality statistics by cause of death.[25] Addition of these cases raises the rate of birth-related deaths to about 13 per 100,000. Mortality is now significantly lower after first-trimester abortion and even after early mid-trimester abortion than following childbirth. During 1972–78, mortality associated with childbirth, standardized for age and race, was at least seven times higher than mortality due to legal abortion, combining all gestations.[26] Recently it has been argued that, compared with legal abortion, "natural pregnancy was found to be safer in both the first and second 20 weeks of pregnancy."[27] This may be true, but is irrelevant, since a "natural pregnancy" continues at risk until delivery, while a pregnancy aborted before 20 weeks is no longer at risk.[28]

Abortion-related deaths are of course only the proverbial tip of the iceberg. Nationwide information on the incidence of nonfatal complications of legal abortions, including major complications requiring inpatient care, is far less complete than information on abortion-related mortality. This is so because there is no agreement among investigators as to what constitutes a major complication, and no system of surveillance is in place. Available data suggest that such early adverse effects as pelvic infection with three or more days of fever, hemorrhage requiring blood transfusion, or unanticipated major surgery for the treatment of complications, have been reduced to about 0.3 percent of all abortions.[29]

Research in the United States and elsewhere has failed to demonstrate adverse effects of the termination of a first pregnancy by suction curettage on the outcome of a subsequent pregnancy. Readers seeking additional information on this and related subjects are referred to the recent article by Hogue and others.[30]

Comparative risks to life associated with fertility and fertility control, including legal abortion, have been most recently evaluated by Ory.[31]

In conclusion, legal abortion in the United States has given women a safe alternative to carrying a fetus to term. As medical technology progresses, the risk of abortion will be reduced much more than it was from 1973–1980.

NOTES

1. Roe v. Wade, 410 U.S. 113 (1973); Doe v. Bolton, 410 U.S. 179 (1973).
2. Akron v. Akron Center for Reproductive Health, 462 U.S. 416–75 (1983).
3. Centers for Disease Control, Abortion Surveillance 1979–1980 (Atlanta 1983).
4. W. Cates, Jr., et al. *Assessment of Surveillance and Vital Statistics Data for Monitoring Abortion Mortality, United States, 1972–1975.* 108 Am. J. of Epidemiology 200 (September 1978).
5. S. K. Henshaw (ed.), Abortion Services in the United States, Each State & Metropolitan Area: 1979–1980 (1983).
6. S. K. Henshaw et al. *Abortion Services in the United States, 1979 and 1980,* 14 Fam. Plann. Perspect. 5 (January/February 1982); S. K. Henshaw & K. O'Reilly, *Characteristics of Abortion Patients in the United States, 1979 and 1980,* 15 Fam. Plann. Perspect. 5–16 (January/February 1983).
7. National Center for Health Statistics, *Induced Terminations of Pregnancy: Reporting States, 1979,* 31 Monthly Vital Statistics Report, no. 7, supplement 1–35 (October 25, 1982).
8. Henshaw & O'Reilly, *supra* note 6.
9. Henshaw et al., *supra* note 6.
10. The Hyde Amendment was adapted in various forms from 1976–1980.
11. W. Cates, Jr., *The Hyde Amendment in Action,* 246 J.A.M.A. 1109 (September 4, 1981).
12. Henshaw & O'Reilly, *supra* note 6.
13. Henshaw et al., *supra* note 6.
14. *Id.*
15. Henshaw & O'Reilly, *supra* note 6.
16. *Id.*
17. C. Tietze, Induced Abortion: A World Review, 1983, (5th ed. 1983).
18. National Institute of Child Health and Human Development, *Predictors of Hereditary Disease or Congenital Defects,* in Antenatal Diagnosis (Department of Health, Education, and Welfare, 1979).
19. M. M. Kaback et al., *Tay-Sachs Disease: Heterozygote Screening and Prenatal Diagnosis,* In Tay-Sachs Disease: Screening and Prevention 13 (Kaback, M. M. ed. 1977).
20. W. Cates, Jr., & D. A. Grimes, *Deaths From Second-Trimester Abortion by Dilatation and Evacuation: Causes, Prevention, Facilities,* 58 Obstet. & Gynecol. 401 (October 1981).
21. W. Cates, Jr., & D. A. Grimes, *Morbidity and Mortality of Abortion in the United States,* in Abortion and Sterilization: Medical and Social Aspects 155 (J. E. Hodgson, ed. 1981); D. A. Grimes, personal communication, January 27, 1983.

22. S. A. LeBolt et al. *Mortality From Abortion and Childbirth: Are the Populations Comparable?* 248 J.A.M.A. 188 (July 9, 1982).
23. D. A. Grimes et al., *Abortion Facilities and the Risk of Death*, 13 Fam. Plann. Perspect. 30 (January/February 1981).
24. Cates & Grimes, *supra* note 20.
25. W. Cates, Jr., et al., *Mortality From Abortion and Childbirth: Are the Statistics Biased?* 248 J.A.M.A. 192 (July 9, 1982).
26. LeBolt et al., *supra* note 22.
27. T. W. Hilgers & D. O'Hare, *Abortion-Related Maternal Mortality: An In-Depth Analysis*, in New Perspectives on Human Abortion 69 (T. W. Hilgers et al., eds. 1981).
28. W. Cates, Jr. *Abortion Myths and Realities: Who Is Misleading Whom?* 142 Am. J. of Obstet. & Gynecol. 954 (April 15, 1982).
29. H. W. Ory et al., Making Choices: Evaluating the Health Risks and Benefits of Birth Control Methods (1983).
30. C. J. R. Hogue et al., *Impact of First-Trimester Abortion by Vacuum Aspiration on Future Childbearing: A Review*, 15 Fam. Plann. Perspect. 119 (May/June 1983).
31. H. W. Ory, *Mortality Associated With Fertility and Fertility Control: 1983*, 15 Fam. Plann. Perspect. 57 (March/April 1983).

This second article on statistics is presented by Willard Cates from research gathered by the U.S. Department of Health and Human Services. He concludes that legal abortion has had a profound impact on women's health during the 1970s.

12 · The First Decade of Legal Abortion in the United States: Effects on Maternal Health_____

Willard Cates, Jr., M.D., M.P.H.

I. Introduction

Induced abortion—whether it will be lawfully permitted and on what grounds—is a premier public policy issue that has been directly influenced by the four institutions—mass media, legislatures, regulatory agencies, and the judiciary.[1] First, the media repeatedly ascribe an importance to abortion topics that surpasses its priority among either politicians or the electorate.[2] Second, legislators have supported laws to restrict legal abortion services.[3] Third, executive agencies monitor the public funding and "quality" of clinical practice in abortion facilities.[4] However, it is the fourth tier—the judiciary—that has influenced the practice of abortion most profoundly.[5]

The Supreme Court decisions in *Roe v. Wade*[6] and *Doe v. Bolton*[7] on January 22, 1973, declared restrictive state abortion laws unconstitutional. These rulings by nine men produced a dramatic public health effect for women of childbearing age throughout the remainder of the 1970s. As the availability of safe, legal abortion diffused across the country, deaths and complications from illegal abortion declined rapidly.[8] As more nonhospital ambulatory abortion facilities sprang up, women could conveniently and inexpensively terminate their pregnancies earlier in gestation, further reducing the risks of morbidity and mortality.[9] Finally, as clinicians openly exchanged information on their experiences with the different abortion procedures, operative techniques became even safer.[10]

In this chapter, I will elaborate on the public health impact of the 1973 decisions during the ensuing decade.

II. Effects in the 1970s

The availability of abortion services in the United States has progressed through three phases: widespread lack of availability, regional availability, and national availability. Until mid-1970, when the liberalized New York State law[11] went into effect, legal abortion was generally not available—except under rather strict medical conditions. From mid-1970 to early 1973, it was available only on a regional basis—primarily on the east and west coasts, in newly legalized facilities in New York City and California. During this time, the number of legally induced abortions underwent a rapid increase (Figure 1), rising over 25-fold between 1969 and 1972.[12] The 1973 Supreme Court decisions catapulted legal abortion into the third phase—national availability—and the public health dividends were remarkable.

Before 1969, the best estimate of the annual range of induced abortions in the United States was between 200,000 and 1.2 million.[13] Nearly all these abortions were illegal, which caused sizable numbers of deaths and complications among United States women of reproductive age. For example, in 1965, some 235 deaths, or 20 percent of all deaths related to pregnancy and childbirth, were attributable to abortion, including induced and spontaneous abortions.[14] At that time, up to half of all beds in some gynecologic units of large public hospitals were occupied by women suffering complications from illegal abortions.[15]

Through the decade of the 1970s, the number of legal abortions increased to almost 1.6 million in 1980 and then stabilized through 1982.[16] Initially, the increase in legal abortions was accompanied by a progressive decline in the estimated number of illegal abortions (Figure 1). Thus, most of the initial increase in legal abortions was due to a corresponding decrease in illegal abortions.[17]

This shift from illegal to legal abortions had a dramatic impact on abortion mortality.[18] In 1965, even before the availability of legal abortion, total abortion mortality began to decline more rapidly than other causes of mortality related to pregnancy and childbirth (Figure 2). In 1970, when legal abortion was first available regionally, the decline in abortion mortality rapidly accelerated and generally continued this pace through 1976.

The Centers for Disease Control's categorization of all abortion-related deaths into one of three categories—legally induced, illegally induced, or spontaneous—permits an even clearer view of these trends (Table 1). In 1972, there were 90 abortion-related deaths, whereas in 1981 there were 11.[19] Through 1976, nearly all of this decline occurred in the illegal category, where the number of deaths decreased from 39 in 1972 to two in 1976. The reduction in illegal abortion mortality had a distinct temporal association with the increasing availability of legal abortion.

After 1976, mortality from legally induced abortion declined markedly. During the earlier years, the number of deaths after legal abortion increased slightly, consistent with the increasing number of women obtaining these procedures. In 1976, however, the number of deaths from legal abortion decreased precipitously and has remained at a low level through 1981, despite the continuing increase in the number of procedures performed. Thus, the risk of death from legal abortions has declined (Figure 3).

Morbidity trends for abortion in recent years parallel mortality trends.

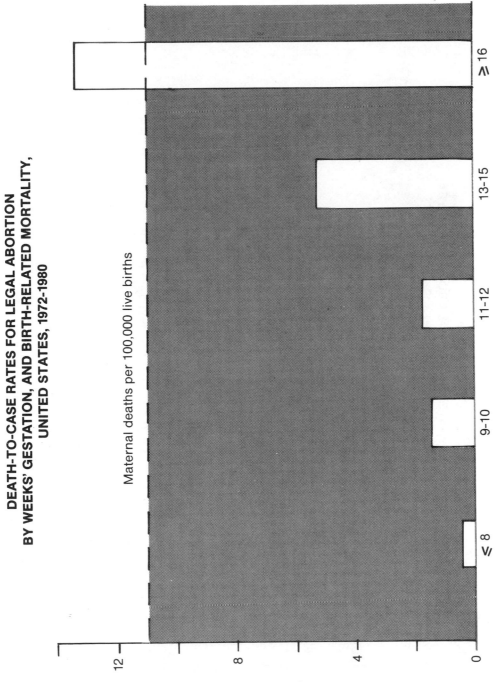

DEATH-TO-CASE RATES FOR LEGAL ABORTION
BY WEEKS' GESTATION, AND BIRTH-RELATED MORTALITY,
UNITED STATES, 1972-1980

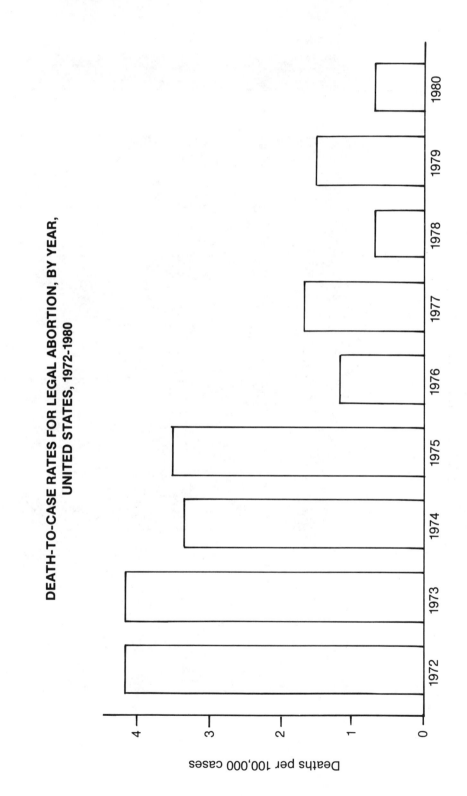

DEATH-TO-CASE RATES FOR LEGAL ABORTION, BY YEAR,
UNITED STATES, 1972–1980

Table 1. Deaths Related to Legal, Illegal, and Spontaneous Abortions in the United States, 1972–80

Year	Abortion Category			
	Legal	Illegal	Spontaneous	Unknown
1972	24	39	25	2
1973	25	19	10	3
1974	25	6	21	1
1975	29	4	14	0
1976	11	2	13	1
1977	17	4	16	0
1978	7	7	9	0
1979	18	0	8	0
1980	8	1	6	1
1981	7	1	3	0

Studies performed at national, state, and local levels show that hospitalization of women with complications resulting from abortion has decreased. Between 1970 and 1977, hospital discharges for women with complications related to other than legal abortion showed a general decline;[20] the greatest part of this decline occurred in 1973. In addition, individual hospitals on both the east and west coasts have shown similar declines.[21]

These improvements in mortality and morbidity have occurred primarily because legal abortion is safer than other alternatives available to pregnant women. Once pregnant, a woman is at increased risk of death as the pregnancy progresses, no matter what her choice of outcomes. The risks associated with pregnancy and childbirth are usually acceptable to a woman if her pregnancy is wanted; however, they are less acceptable if the pregnancy is unwanted.

Besides legal abortion, the other two options for pregnant women are illegal abortion or carrying the pregnancy to delivery. Compared to illegally induced procedures, legal abortion is markedly safer. Compared with continuing the pregnancy to delivery, terminating a pregnancy at 15 weeks' gestation or earlier is associated with lower morbidity[22] and mortality.[23] In 1980, for example, 15 percent of births were by cesarean delivery,[24] whereas only 0.07 percent of suction curettage procedures result in intraabdominal operations.[25] Therefore, the risk of having to undergo major surgery for a complication of a suction abortion is 200 times smaller than that of carrying a pregnancy to delivery. Regarding mortality, the risk of dying from induced abortion prior to 15 weeks' gestation is seven times smaller than the risk of dying from pregnancy and childbirth (Figure 4). A similar difference exists even after standardizing the population groups for differences in year, age, and race.[26]

Turning to the development of abortion techniques and expertise, the increased availability of legal abortion in the United States since 1970 has influenced both the safety of abortion methods and the skill of the physicians performing abortions. The sixfold increase in the number of abortion procedures over a relatively short interval has led to rapid improvements in technology.[27] One clinical improvement was the widespread adoption of suction curettage[28] to

**MATERNAL MORTALITY RATIOS (EXCLUDING ABORTION DEATHS)[1,2]
AND ABORTION MORTALITY RATIOS,[2] UNITED STATES, 1940-1979[3]**

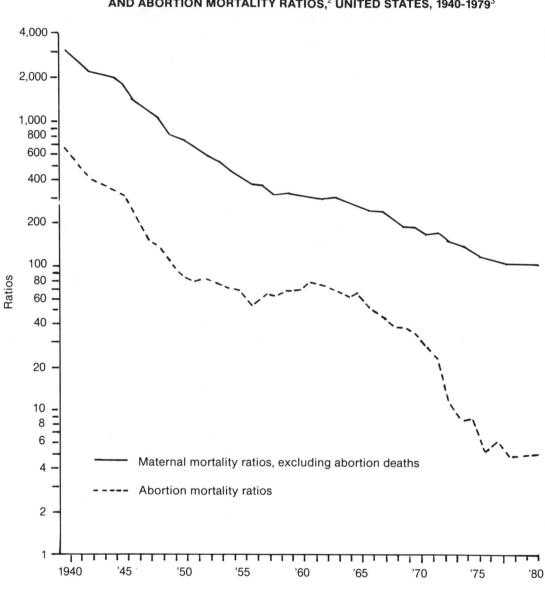

[1]Maternal mortality ratio (excluding abortion deaths) equals total maternal deaths minus abortion deaths

[2]Deaths per 1,000,000 live births

[3]Source: U.S. vital statistics, National Center for Health Statistics

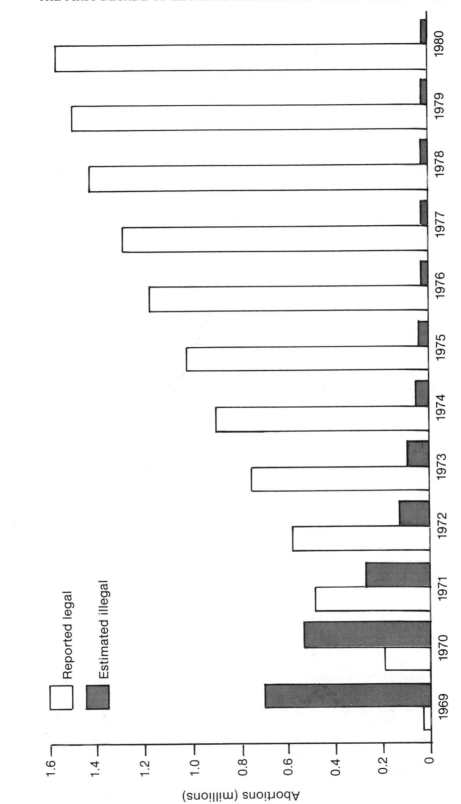

LEGAL AND ILLEGAL ABORTIONS IN THE UNITED STATES,
1969 to 1980

Reported legal

Estimated illegal

Abortions (millions)

Table 2. Percentage of Mid-trimester Procedures Performed by Dilatation and Evacuation: United States, 1974–80

Year	Percentage
1974	31%
1975	36%
1976	43%
1977	47%
1978	51%
1979	55%
1980	67%

replace sharp curettage—the classic D&C method—as the primary means of abortion. In 1970, the distribution of procedures performed by suction and sharp curettage was similar—54 percent were performed by suction and 46 percent by sharp.[29] Over the decade, the percentage of suction curettage procedures gradually increased. By 1981, suction curettage accounted for 90 percent of all curettage procedures. Of those curettage methods used at 12 weeks or earlier, 98 percent were performed by suction.[30]

Another major improvement was the recognition that dilatation and evacuation (D&E) can terminate pregnancies at 13 weeks' gestation or later more safely than instillation methods.[31] After 1973, comparative studies were undertaken to determine the safest methods of abortion after 12 weeks. Through these studies, we learned that surgical evacuation techniques, especially through 16 weeks' gestation, are safer than instillation procedures. As a result, the percentage of D&E procedures used to terminate second-trimester pregnancies has increased over recent years[32] (Table 2). In addition to improving the safety of abortion, D&E has lowered costs, minimized inconvenience, and reduced the emotional trauma of second-trimester abortions for pregnant women.

Physician skill has probably improved as well. Before the availability of legal abortion, abortion methods were not routinely taught in obstetric and gynecologic training programs.[33] The only experience with uterine evacuation for residents usually came either when performing sharp curettage on a nonpregnant uterus for diagnostic purposes or when removing retained tissue after a spontaneous abortion. These procedures differ from those involved in abortion. The legalization of abortion allowed physicians the opportunity both to learn different surgical techniques and to manage the complications associated with these techniques.

The increase in physician training and experience may be one factor that contributed to the decrease in deaths related to legal abortion after 1975. Improvements in anesthesia technique, use of more appropriate methods of dilatation, less reliance on major operations for abortion, greater willingness to reevacuate a uterus in cases of suspected retained tissue, and expertise in managing abortion complications all may have played a role.

The increasing availability of and requests for abortions have also led to two changes in when and where they are provided: first, women obtaining legally induced abortions did so at progressively earlier gestational ages;[34] and, second, most abortions are now being performed in nonhospital facilities, the so-called free-standing clinics.[35] These two factors concurrently influence the safety, convenience, and cost of abortion procedures.

In 1970, nearly one of every four abortions was performed at gestations of 13 weeks or later. By 1981, fewer than one in 10 abortions was performed this late in pregnancy.[36] Moreover, even within the first 12 weeks, abortions shifted to earlier intervals. In 1981, over half of all women having abortions terminated their pregnancies before eight weeks' gestation.[37] Because gestational age influences the risk of complications after legal abortion,[38] the trend toward obtaining abortions earlier in gestation has contributed to reducing the number of deaths and complications from this procedure.

Before the legalization of abortion, the term "in-hospital" was used almost generically to describe legal abortion procedures.[39] In 1970, women were frequently hospitalized for at least two days in order to have a legally induced abortion. The first night was for preoperative evaluation, while the second night was for postoperative recovery.[40] Even in 1973, over 60 percent of all abortions were performed in hospitals. By 1982, most abortion services were delivered by freestanding clinics;[41] in the first quarter of 1982, over 80 percent of all abortions were performed in such clinics. Also, two-thirds of the abortions performed in hospitals were on an outpatient basis. Obtaining an abortion now usually takes less than half a day, minimizing the inconvenience and cost to the woman.[42]

Legalization of abortion led to the rapid emergence of a new health care delivery system: free-standing clinics. Experience gained in the delivery of abortion services at free-standing clinics has led to an expansion of other services at these facilities. Many clinics are now providing infertility investigations, male and female sterilization procedures, family planning and contraceptive counseling, and routine outpatient gynecologic care, in addition to abortions.[43] These clinics have clearly demonstrated that ambulatory "surgi-centers" can perform minor surgical procedures safely and economically.

III. Challenges in the 1980s

Despite these clinical gains in the 1970s, substantial problems with the rigid medical foundations engrafted into the Constitution in 1973 eventually began to appear. The same Supreme Court rulings that initially allowed national dissemination of legal abortion later were used by opponents of abortion to limit its availability. For example, in 1973 the Court did not deal with the subject of abortion funding. In addition, the *Doe v. Bolton*[44] decision allowed regulation of the conditions under which the abortion could be performed. During the latter half of the 1970s, political attempts to restrict legal abortion services primarily used these two approaches—limiting public funds and dictating clinical practices.

A. Abortion Funding

The Hyde Amendment,[45] which restricted *federal* funds for abortion, was passed by Congress in 1976 and went into effect in 1977. The year before its implementation, approximately 300,000 abortions in the United States were obtained by low-income women through Medicaid.[46] During the next two years, the number of federally funded abortions averaged only 3000 per year, or just 1

Table 3. Summary of Effects of the Hyde Amendment: United States, 1977–80

Effect	National	States Continuing Funding	States Restricting Funding
Medicaid-eligible women at risk	100%	85%	14%
Legal abortion with state funds	65%	65%	0%
Legal abortion with other funds	27%	15%	12%
Pregnancies continued to term	7%	4%	3%
Illegal abortions	1%	0%	1%

percent of the previous number. The amendment, therefore, effectively stopped federally funded abortions.[47]

However, many states continued to finance abortions using state revenues,[48] thus blunting the intended impact. Approximately 85 percent of the low-income women likely to seek abortion were still covered by state funds. For the nation as a whole, over 90 percent of these women obtained a legal abortion despite the Hyde Amendment (Table 3). Seven out of 10 of these abortions were financed by state revenues, the rest by other sources of funds, including personal finances, reduced provider fees, and private contributions. About 7 percent of the low-income women continued their pregnancies to delivery, while less than 1 percent resorted to illegal abortion.[49]

A real difference in health outcome existed between states that funded abortions versus those that did not.[50] In the states that did fund abortions, 98 percent of the women at risk obtained them; only 2 percent carried their pregnancies to delivery (Table 3). In states *restricting* funds, 20 percent carried their pregnancies to term. It appears that if a *total* funding cutoff were to occur, it would cause approximately one in five women to carry a pregnancy to delivery which might otherwise have been aborted.

B. Abortion Regulations

Legislation has been introduced in the United States at local, state, and federal levels to regulate abortion services.[51] This legislation is intended to provide more comprehensive information for women considering pregnancy termination and, in the wording of the Supreme Court, to guard the health of women who choose abortion by providing safer conditions for the procedure. The prototype regulations originated in Akron, Ohio, and contain five provisions affecting delivery of abortion services: (1) the content of information provided in the preoperative counseling session; (2) a waiting period between obtaining informed consent and performing the abortion; (3) parental notification if the pregnant woman is under 18 years of age and unmarried; (4) a proscription of the use of instillation agents, such as hypertonic saline, with adverse effects on the fetus; and (5) a requirement that all second-trimester abortions be performed in hospitals.[52]

The existing information raises questions whether the regulations will achieve their stated goals.[53] For example, laws that require a woman to be informed only about the risks of pregnancy termination, without consideration of the competing risks of pregnancy continuation, do not provide fully "informed consent."[54] Moreover, mandatory waiting periods have been shown to increase the risks[55] and costs[56] of the abortion procedure, without substantially deterring the woman from abortion.

The effect of parental notification requirements has not been investigated. Parents are usually an important influence on the decision a pregnant adolescent makes.[57] Based on responses to a national survey of abortion providers, over half of teenagers younger than age 18 who obtained abortions told their parents before the procedure.[58] The younger the woman, the more likely her parents were to know—and even to have suggested the abortion initially. Yet, one-quarter of teenagers obtaining legal abortion stated they would not do so if parental notification were required,[59] preferring either to have an illegal abortion or to continue the pregnancy to delivery. As indicated earlier, this would increase the risks to the teenager. Likewise, forbidding certain abortion methods such as hypertonic saline instillation or requiring that all second-trimester abortions be performed in hospitals cannot be supported from the viewpoint of protecting the woman's health.[60]

IV. What If?

While neither restricting funds nor mandating regulations has to date greatly affected the number of procedures performed, both have made legal abortion more difficult to obtain. However, current efforts in Congress to restrict completely legal abortion services would have an altogether different impact: Legal abortion as we know it today would no longer be available. What might happen if, after the decade of the 1970s, legal abortion were proscribed in the 1980s? This question can be examined from the perspectives of both the consumer and the provider.

From the consumer's viewpoint, both the numbers and values of American women underwent major changes in the 1970s. The baby boom generation came of reproductive age,[61] more career options became available,[62] and reproductive choices were openly discussed.[63] An increasing percentage of American women experienced sexual intercourse earlier in their lives;[64] concurrently, an increasing percentage also used contraception to prevent unplanned pregnancies.[65]

Nevertheless, unplanned pregnancies still occurred, and during the era of legal abortion in the 1970s, women in the United States came increasingly to rely on this option when confronted with an unplanned pregnancy. Many women regard abortion as a standard medical service, and thus a large consumer demand for abortion services would remain, even if abortion became illegal.

From the provider's standpoint, as mentioned earlier, free-standing abortion clinics became a major source of reproductive health care in the 1970s.[66] A generation of American physicians learned to perform abortions safely, inexpensively, and quickly. Many other paraprofessionals participated in a range of services related to abortion—counseling, assisting in the procedure, and providing follow-up care.[67] The technology of abortion—laminaria and vacuum aspirators—became widely distributed in the medical community. In the 1980s, this relatively large supply of both abortion providers and abortion equipment would be in place, even if the procedure itself became illegal. Thus, clandestine procedures might be relatively easily obtainable.

So . . . what if . . . ? In one view, the consumer demand and provider supply would combine to create a high volume of illegal abortions if access to legal abortion were restricted. In pure numbers, at least as many illegal abortions might be performed in the 1980s as were performed in the 1960s—perhaps 1.5 million illegal abortions per year. However, because of advances in skill and equipment, these procedures would be performed much more safely than in the "bad old days" of the 1960s.[68] Thus, restricting legal abortion altogether, while having measurable public health impact, would not return the United States to levels of maternal morbidity and mortality of the 1960s. Rather, illegal abortions would be much safer than before.

V. Conclusion

The availability of legal abortion has had a profound impact on women's health in the decade of the 1970s. It has allowed pregnant women to make safer choices, physicians to develop better surgical techniques, and free-standing clinics to emerge as important health care providers. However, challenges in the form of restrictive public funding and abortion regulations have, in part, limited the practice of legal abortion. If a constitutional amendment completely restricted the availability of legal abortion, complications and deaths to women of childbearing age would increase—although probably not to the level in the era before the 1970s.

NOTES

1. W. Cates, Jr., *Legal Abortion: The Public Health Record,* 215 Science 1586 (1982).
2. M. W. Traugott & M. A. Vinovskis, *Abortion and the 1978 Congressional Elections,* 12 Fam. Plann. Perspect. 238 (1980).
3. H. S. Meyer, *Science and the "Human Life Bill,"* 246 J.A.M.A. 837 (1981).
4. P. Weiler et al., *The Implementation of Model Standards in Local Health Departments,* 72 Am. J. Pub. Health 1230 (1982).
5. B. Woodward & S. Armstrong, The Brethren (1979).
6. 410 U.S. 113 (1973).
7. 410 U.S. 179 (1973).
8. W. Cates, Jr. & R. W. Rochat, *Illegal Abortion in the United States, 1972–1974,* 8 Fam. Plann. Perspect. 86 (1976).
9. S. K. Henshaw, *Freestanding Abortion Clinics: Services, Structure, Fees,* 14 Fam. Plann. Perspect. 248 (1982); W. Cates, Jr. et al., *The Effect of Delay and Choice of Method on the Risk of Abortion Morbidity,* 9 Fam. Plann. Perspect. 266 (1977).
10. D. A. Grimes & W. Cates, Jr., *Abortion: Methods and Complications,* in Human Reproduction: Conception and Contraception, 2d ed, 796 (E.S.E. Hafez, 1980).
11. New York penal law, section 125.05, subsection 3, amended 1970.
12. Centers for Disease Control, *Abortion Surveillance: Preliminary analysis— United States, 1981,* 33 Morbid. Mortal. Weekly Rep. 373 (1984).
13. M. S. Calderone, Abortion in the United States (1958); J. R. Abernathy, B. G.

Greenberg, & D. G. Horvitz, *Estimates of Induced Abortion in Urban North Carolina,* 7 Demography 19 (1970).

14. National Center for Health Statistics, Final Mortality Statistics–1965 (1968).
15. E. C. Moore-Cavar, International Inventory of Information on Induced Abortion 593 (1974).
16. Centers for Disease Control, *supra* note 12; S. K. Henshaw, J. D. Forrest, & E. Blaine, *Abortion Services in the United States, 1981 and 1982,* 16 Fam. Plann. Perspect. 119 (1984).
17. C. Tietze, *Two Years' Experience With a Liberal Abortion Law: Its Impact on Fertility Trends in New York City,* 5 Fam. Plann. Perspect. 36 (1973); C. Tietze & J. Bongaarts, *The Demographic Effect of Induced Abortion,* 31 Obstet. Gynecol Surv. 699 (1976).
18. Cates & Rochat, *supra* note 8; W. Cates Jr. et al., *Legalized Abortion: Effect on National Trends of Maternal and Abortion-Related Mortality (1940–1976),* 132 Am. J. Obstet. Gynecol. 211 (1978).
19. Centers for Disease Control, *supra* note 12.
20. M. B. Bracken, D. Freeman Jr., & K. Hellenbrand, *Hospitalization for Medical-Legal and Other Abortions in the United States 1970–1977,* 72 Am. J. Pub. Health 30 (1982).
21. P. Goldstein & G. Stewart, *Trends in Therapeutic Abortion in San Francisco,* 62 Am. J. Pub. Health 695 (1972); J. T. Landman, S. G. Kohl, & J. H. Bedel, *Changes in Pregnancy Outcome After Liberalization of the New York State Abortion Law,* 118 Am. J. Obstet. Gynecol. 485 (1974); R. S. Kahan, L. D. Baker & M. G. Freeman, *The Effect of Legalized Abortion on Morbidity Resulting From Criminal Abortion,* 121 Am. J. Obstet. Gynecol. 114 (1975); G. K. Stewart & P. J. Goldstein, *Therapeutic Abortion in California: Effects on Septic Abortion and Maternal Mortality,* 37 Obstet. Gynecol. 510 (1971); P. N. Seward, C. A. Ballard, & A. L. Ulene, *The Effect of Legal Abortion on the Rate of Septic Abortion at a Large County Hospital,* 115 Am. J. Obstet. Gynecol. 335 (1973); Alan Guttmacher Institute, Safe and Legal: 10 Years' Experience With Legal Abortion in New York State (1980), 23:17.
22. V. H. Laukaran & B. J. Van Den Berg, *The Relationship of Maternal Attitude to Pregnancy Outcomes and Obstetric Complications,* 136 Am. J. Obstet. Gynecol. 374 (1980); P. J. Placek, Underlying Medical Conditions, Complications of Pregnancy, and Complications of Labor to Mothers of Legitimate Live Hospital Births in the United States. Presented at Population Association of America, Atlanta, Georgia (April 13, 1978).
23. Centers for Disease Control, *supra* note 12; S. A. LeBolt, D. A. Grimes, & W. Cates, Jr., *Mortality From Abortion and Childbirth: Are the Populations Comparable?* 248 J.A.M.A. 188 (1982).
24. P. J. Placek & S. M. Taffel, *Trends in Cesarean Section Rates for the United States, 1970–78,* 95 Pub. Health Rep. 540 (1980).
25. W. Cates, Jr, et al., *Short-Term Complications of Uterine Evacuation Techniques for Abortion at 12 Weeks' Gestation or Earlier,* in Pregnancy Termination: Procedures, Safety and New Developments. 127 (G. I. Zatuchni, J. J. Sciarra, & J. J. Speidel, eds. 1979).
26. LeBolt, Grimes, & Cates, *supra* note 23; W. Cates, Jr., & C. Tietze,

Standardized Mortality Rates Associated With Legal Abortion: United States, 1972–1975, 10 Fam. Plann. Perspect. 109 (1978).

27. P. G. Stubblefield, *Current Technology for Abortion*, 2 Curr. Prob. in Obstet. & Gynecol. 3 (1978).
28. C. Kerslake & D. Casey, *Abortion Induced by Means of the Uterine Aspirator*, 30 Obstet. Gynecol. 35 (1967).
29. Cates et al., *supra* note 25.
30. Centers for Disease Control, *supra* note 12.
31. D. A. Grimes et al., *Midtrimester Abortion by Dilatation and Evacuation: A Safe and Practical Alternative*, 296 N. E. J. Med. 1141 (1977).
32. D. A. Grimes & W. Cates, Jr., *Dilatation and evacuation*, in Second Trimester Abortion: Perspectives After a Decade of Experience. 119 (G. S. Berger, W. E. Brenner & L. Keith eds. 1981).
33. R. T. Burkman et al., *University Abortion Programs: One Year Later*, 119 Am. J. Obstet. Gynecol. 131 (1974).
34. Centers for Disease Control, *supra* note 12.
35. Henshaw, Forrest, & Blaine, *supra* note 16.
36. Centers for Disease Control, *supra* note 12.
37. *Id.*
38. Grimes & Cates, *supra* note 10.
39. C. L. Erhardt, C. Tietze, & F. G., Nelson, *United States: Therapeutic Abortions in New York City*, 51 Stud. Fam. Plann. 8 (1950).
40. B. L. Lindheim, *Services, Policies and Costs in U.S. Abortion Facilities*, 11 Fam. Plann. Perspect. 283 (1979).
41. Henshaw, Forrest, & Blaine, *supra* note 16.
42. Henshaw, *supra* note 9.
43. *Id.*
44. 410 U.S. 179 (1973).
45. The Hyde Amendment was adapted in various forms from 1976–1980 where the Court upheld it.
46. R. B. Gold, *After the Hyde Amendment: Public Funding for Abortion in FY 1978*, 12 Fam. Plann. Perspect. 131 (1980).
47. W. Cates, Jr., *The Hyde Amendment in Action: How Did the Restriction of Federal Funds for Abortion Affect Low-Income Women?* 246 J.A.M.A. 1109 (1981).
48. Gold, *supra* note 46.
49. Cates, *supra* note 47.
50. W. Cates, Jr., *Effect of the Hyde Amendment*, 247 J.A.M.A. 1128 (1982).
51. W. Cates, Jr., J. Gold, & R. M. Selik, *Regulation of Abortion Services: For Better or Worse?* 301 N. E. J. Med. 720 (1979).
52. Akron v. Akron Center Jr. Repoductive Health, 462 U.S. 416 (1983), 103 S. Ct. 2485 (1983).
53. Cates, Gold, & Selik, *supra* note 51.
54. L. J. Miller, *Informed consent: I*, 244 J.A.M.A. 2100 (1980).
55. Cates et al., *supra* note 9.
56. M. Lupfer & B. G. Silber, *How Patients View Mandatory Waiting Periods for Abortion*, 13 Fam. Plann. Perspect. 75 (1981).

57. M. B. Bracken, M. Hachamovitch, & G. Grossman, *The Decision to Abort and Psychological Sequelae,* 158 J. Nerv. Ment. Dis. 154 (1974).
58. A. Torres, J. D. Forrest, & S. Eisman, *Telling Parents: Clinic Policies and Adolescents' Use of Family Planning and Abortion Services,* 12 Fam. Plann. Perspect. 284 (1980).
59. *Id.*
60. D. A. Grimes, W. Cates, Jr., & C. W. Tyler Jr., *Comparative Risk of Death From Legally Induced Abortion in Hospitals and Nonhospital Facilities,* 51 Obstet. Gynecol. 323 (1978); D. A. Grimes, W. Cates, Jr., & R. M. Selik, *Abortion Facilities and the Risk of Death,* 13 Fam. Plann. Perspect. 30 (1981).
61. L. Y. Jones, Great Expectations: America and the Baby-Boom Generation (1980).
62. E. F. Jones, *The Impact of Women's Employment on Marital Fertility in the U.S., 1970–75,* 35 Pop. Stud. 161 (1981).
63. M. Zelnik, *Sex Education and Knowledge of Pregnancy Risk Among U.S. Women,* 11 Fam. Plann. Perspect. 355 (1979).
64. M. Zelnik & J. F. Kantner, *Sexual Activity, Contraceptive Use and Pregnancy Among Metropolitan-Area Teenagers: 1971–1979,* 12 Fam. Plann. Perspect. 230 (1980).
65. M. A. Koenig & M. Zelnik, *The Risk of Premarital First Pregnancy Among Metropolitan-Area Teenagers: 1976 and 1979,* 14 Fam. Plann. Perspect. 239 (1982).
66. Henshaw, *supra* note 9.
67. *Id.*
68. S. Polgar & E. S. Fried, *The Bad Old Days: Clandestine Abortions Among the Poor in New York City Before Liberalization of the Abortion Law,* 8 Fam. Plann. Perspect. 125 (1976).

This article on psychiatry by Richard A. Schwartz reveals the close relationship between psychiatry, abortion, and the law. Initially, it was the psychiatrist who had to prove the pregnant woman's life in danger if an abortion request were denied. Later, the psychiatrist had to substantiate the mental trauma (or lack of mental trauma) to the pregnant woman if the abortion request were granted. As more efforts are made to restrict legal abortions to cases of rape and incest or cases in which the life of the pregnant woman is endangered, the role of the psychiatrist takes on the importance it had before 1973.

13 · Abortion on Request: The Psychiatric Implications_____

Richard A. Schwartz, M.D.

I. Introduction

Before 1960, psychiatric textbooks and journals paid very little attention to abortion. The few psychiatric writings on the subject treated abortion as an experience that almost always has a harmful effect on a woman. Abortions were viewed as interfering with the primary biological instincts of womanhood, causing profound guilt, conscious or unconscious, and predisposing women to serious psychiatric disorders that often become manifest only many years later. The following excerpts are representative of the writings of this era:

> *If and when a so-called adult woman, a responsible female, seeks an abortion, unless the warrant for it is overwhelming—as say in the case of rape or incest—we are in effect confronted with a sick person and sick situation. Furthermore, and I would strongly underscore the point, neither the given person nor the given situation is likely to be remedied by the abortion,* qua abortion. *It is of course true that both the person and the situation may be relieved and somewhat ameliorated by the abortion . . . but I would like to go on record that in numerous instances both the individual and the situation are actually aggravated rather than remedied by the abortion. Bad as the situation was initially, it not infrequently becomes worse after the abortion has taken place . . . Drawing upon my experience, I would summate the major psychological effects in three terms: frustration, hostility, and guilt.*[1]

> *Despite protests to the contrary, we know that women's main role here on Earth is to conceive, deliver and raise children . . . [W]hen this function is interfered with, we see all sorts of emotional disorders and certainly the climax of these disorders is reached at the menopause when women recognize that they no longer can reproduce their kind and interpret the menopause as the end of life, rather than the change of life . . . The author has never seen a patient who has not had guilt feelings about a previous therapeutic abortion or illegal abortion.*[2]

> *I don't think there is any doubt that having an abortion is, by and large, an extremely deleterious experience in the continuity of the life of a woman.*[3]

> *Many mothers who during the first weeks felt terrified at the thought of having a child, later blessed the doctor who refused to allow them to proceed with their plans for abortion. It is also true that the woman who experiences an abortion, whether therapeutic or criminal, is traumatized by the act to such a degree that the memory becomes a potent factor in her future behavior pattern.*[4]

During the 1960s, when the taboos against abortion began to break down, abortion became the subject of widespread research and discussion within the psychiatric profession, and a major shift in psychiatric opinion took place. Whereas in 1967 only 24 percent of members of the American Psychiatric Association responding to a poll favored abortion on request, 72 percent were in favor by 1969.[5] By the end of the decade, two of the most influential organizations within the profession had published official statements favoring legalization of abortion. The first of these, published in 1969 by the prestigious Group for the Advancement of Psychiatry concluded: "We recommend that abortion, when performed by a licensed physician, be entirely removed from the domain of criminal law. We believe that a woman should have the right to abort or not, just as she has the right to marry or not."[6] The American Psychiatric Association, also in 1969, approved the following position statement:

> *A decision to perform an abortion should be regarded as strictly a medical decision and a medical responsibility. It should be removed entirely from the jurisdiction of criminal law. Criminal penalties should be reserved for persons who perform abortions without medical license or qualification to do so. A medical decision to perform an abortion is based on the careful and informed judgments of the physician and the patient. Among other factors to be considered in arriving at the decision is the motivation of the patient. Often psychiatric consultation can help clarify motivational problems and thereby contribute to the patient's welfare.*[7]

To some extent, the shift in psychiatric opinion reflected the shift that occurred in public opinion during the decade of the 1960s. The majority of psychiatrists, along with a majority of the general public, came to believe that the right of a woman to decide whether to bear a child outweighed any rights a fetus might be thought to possess. In addition to the basic issue of human rights, however, there were five additional considerations of a more specifically psychiatric nature that contributed to the profession's decision to support the freedom of choice position:

1. Dissatisfaction with the role of decisionmaker that society had forced upon the psychiatrist.
2. Concern for the plight of the woman with an unwanted pregnancy.
3. Research evidence that abortions did not have the harmful emotional sequelae previously reported.
4. A belief that family planning measures, including abortion, increase the proportion of children who receive a high quality of care during the formative years, resulting in an improvement in the mental health of the population as a whole.
5. A perception that, whereas many who oppose abortion do so on grounds of morality and see themselves as "pro-family," the policy of forcing women to bear unwanted children may be much more destructive of moral values and family stability than abortion is.

In this chapter, these five issues will be examined in further detail.

II. Dissatisfaction With the Role of Decisionmaker

Prior to the Supreme Court decision of 1973 upholding a woman's right to abortion,[8] most states had restrictive laws forbidding abortion unless necessary to save the life of the woman. When public sentiment toward abortion began to shift in a more permissive direction, increasing numbers of women from the middle and upper classes began to put pressure on their private physicians to provide abortions under safe conditions in order to avoid the dangers of illegal abortion from criminal abortionists. These women received considerable support from the medical profession, which was becoming increasingly frustrated with the abortion laws—laws that many physicians regarded as outmoded, as interfering with the doctor-patient relationship, and as preventing physicians from providing proper care to their patients. In order to accommodate the patients, physicians increasingly turned to the psychiatric profession to take advantage of the only loophole that the law provided. Because medical science has now made it possible for all but the most severely medically ill women to give birth safely, the only way that any substantial number of abortions could be construed as "necessary to save the woman's life" was if the woman could be certified as being in danger of committing suicide if an abortion were not performed. Many hospitals set up a rule that if a woman could provide a letter from a psychiatrist (sometimes two psychiatrists) stating that the abortion was necessary to prevent suicide, the abortion would be permitted. In the 1960s, therapeutic abortion on psychiatric grounds became a common practice throughout the country. From 1963 through 1965, for example, there were an estimated 8000 therapeutic abortions performed each year, one abortion for every 500 live births.[9]

The practice of therapeutic abortion on psychiatric grounds generated considerable controversy both inside and outside the psychiatric profession. It proved to be impossible to agree upon any criteria for how suicidal the patient had to be before an abortion could be permitted. The great majority of the women seeking abortion who were referred for psychiatric consultation had no previous history of suicidal tendencies, depression, or any other psychiatric problem. Yet they were in a situation in which they had been given an overwhelming incentive to threaten suicide. What should the psychiatrist do when confronted with a woman seeking abortion and threatening suicide if she couldn't have one?

Psychiatrists' responses could be divided into four categories:

1. One group of psychiatrists believed that abortions are the taking of human life and morally wrong, and that no psychiatric illness, however severe, can justify abortion. In cases of women genuinely threatening suicide, these psychiatrists typically recommended commitment to a psychiatric hosptial, and administration of antidepressant drugs or electroshock treatment. This group of psychiatrists made their views well known to their medical colleagues and, of course, received few, if any referrals for psychiatric consultation in abortion cases.[10]

2. A second group of psychiatrists, while personally not opposed to abortion, were opposed to "psychiatric" abortions on principle. These psychiatrists believed that it is hypocritical to have laws against abortion, and then to allow a few relatively affluent women to have abortions merely bcause they threaten suicide, while at the same time denying abortion to women who are too poor to afford private physicians and psychiatric consultation fees, or who refuse to threaten suicide even though they are upset and unhappy. Many of these psychiatrists also believed that the practice of psychiatric abortions has a harmful social effect because it abates pressures that might lead to liberalization of the abortion laws: By enabling the most influential segment of the population to arrange for psychiatric abortions, psychiatrists remove whatever incentive this group may have to support reform of the laws. Other psychiatrists in this group were concerned that the image of the psychiatric profession was becoming tarnished by the practice of providing "excuses" for rich women to evade the laws.[11]

3. A third group of psychiatrists, while agreeing that psychiatric abortions are hypocritical and unfair, believed that it would be unethical to refuse to consult with women who are emotionally upset and who request help. Although they were reluctant and unenthusiastic, these psychiatrists participated in abortion evaluations and conscientiously tried to determine if the suicide risk was substantial.

4. The fourth group of psychiatrists strongly believed that most women who wanted abortions would benefit from them and should be permitted to obtain them. Moreover they interpreted their highest obligation as physicians, above all other considerations, to be the protection of their patients' health and well-being. In order to help women obtain abortions, these psychiatrists were willing to authorize abortions in cases where they believed the risk of suicide to be minimal, in order to protect these women

from being forced to risk their lives at the hands of the criminal abortionists or to bear an unwanted child. This group of psychiatrists acknowledged that their policies might help to perpetuate unjust laws, but thought it more likely that encouraging the widespread practice of therapeutic abortions would help shift public opinion in the direction of accepting abortion as a routine part of medical practice.

Whether or not a patient was provided with an opportunity for a therapeutic abortion, therefore, depended not only on her pocketbook and on whether she was living in an area where private psychiatrists were available, but also on the philosophical point of view of the psychiatrist whom she happened to consult. If she saw one from the first or second group she would have been refused permission for a legal abortion. If she consulted one from the third group, she had a fair chance of obtaining the requisite approval. If she were lucky enough to happen upon one from the fourth group, she was virtually assured a safe hospital abortion.

Although each of the four groups of psychiatrists responded differently to the requests for abortion from individual women, all were opposed to the psychiatrist being routinely involved as a decisionmaker. There were only two ways that removal of the psychiatrist from the decisionmaking process could be accomplished: by making the laws more strict, forbidding all abortions without exception, or by outright legalization, making abortion a private matter between the woman and her physician.

III. The Plight of the Woman With an Unwanted Pregnancy

During the years when therapeutic abortions on psychiatric grounds were commonplace, the psychiatric profession gained considerable familiarity with circumstances that impelled women to seek abortions. One of the most widespread myths of American life is that pregnancy is or should be a beautiful and fulfilling event in the life of a woman. In reality, as psychiatrists who were involved in abortion consultation learned, there are many circumstances in which an unintended pregnancy can be harmful for the woman and her entire family as well. Some of these circumstances will be discussed below.

For single women or teenage girls, the birth of an illegitimate child can lead to loss of educational opportunity, diminished chances for a successful marriage, ostracism by family and friends, and welfare dependency.

In many instances, pregnancy in an unmarried woman may lead to a hastily arranged and often forced marriage. A study by the National Center for Health Statistics found that 19 percent of legitimate firstborn children during the period 1964–66 were conceived out of wedlock and that 42 percent of the married women under the age of 20 had been married less than eight months prior to the birth of their first child.[12]

These premature marriages have been shown to have a higher rate of divorce than marriages in which the bride was not pregnant at the altar. In one study, 4.9 percent of all sampled marriages ended in divorce, as compared with a divorce rate of 13 percent among couples who had had their first child within nine months of marriage and 17 percent among couples whose first child was born within six months of marriage.[13]

It can be assumed that even when divorce does not occur, forced marriages between unwilling and incompatible partners are less likely to be mutually satisfying than those marriages where couples made their decision freely. The awareness that one originally married because of love helps to sustain a couple through the difficult times that occur in virtually all marriages. By contrast, it is hard for two people to build a relationship of loyalty and commitment when they feel they were forced into marriage in the beginning.

Some people naively believe that most of the problems associated with unwanted pregnancy among the unmarried can be adequately solved by arranging for the women to give up their babies for adoption. Although it is certainly true that there are many unfortunate infertile couples who would welcome the opportunity to adopt a child, giving up a baby after experiencing the full nine months of pregnancy and the process of childbirth is far more repugnant to many women than undergoing an abortion in early pregnancy. The typical impluse for a woman is to want to keep her baby rather than give it away to a complete stranger. Despite pressure from families and social workers, many women will refuse to place their babies for adoption, regardless of the problems that will inevitably occur in trying to provide adequate care for the child.

Many women who suffer from serious illness lack the energy and strength to care properly for a baby. In some instances, these women already have more children than they can cope with. A woman with severe multiple sclerosis or rheumatoid arthritis, for example, undergoes a severe hardship if she bears an unwanted child merely because she has accidentally become pregnant. And with some diseases, such as cancer, the patient's prognosis may show a life expectancy of only a few months or years. Prior to 1973, the abortion laws in most states would not allow a woman even in one of these situations to abort an accidental pregnancy.

Serious mental illness, including alcoholism and drug addiction, is characterized by extremely low tolerance for frustration and stress. When mental patients are exposed to more stress than they can handle, their symptoms—anxiety, depression, psychotic behavior, excessive use of drugs or alcohol, *etc.*—increase in severity. An unwanted pregnancy can be a major stress even for a "normal" woman, but for a mental patient an unwanted pregnancy can be overwhelming and can lead to exacerbation of her symptoms, suicidal tendencies, or a complete psychotic breakdown.

Many women, although basically "normal" with respect to their emotional and mental stability, are burdened by personal problems or pressures that generate considerable nervous tension. The birth of an unwanted child in these circumstances can increase these pressures to an intolerable degree. Such situations would include women whose husbands are alcoholics or are physically ill, women who are unhappily married or in the process of divorce, and women who already have more children than they can adequately manage.

In many families, the size of the breadwinner's paycheck is inadequate to provide for the needs of a large family. If these couples can limit their number of children to one or two, the family can remain solvent. Limiting the family size can also help the family's financial situation by providing sufficient free time for the mother to hold a part-time or full-time job. In poor families several unwanted children can create severe economic hardship and can increase strains within the family to the breaking point. The family's income, which might have been adequate for a small family, must now attempt to meet the housing, nutritional, clothing, and recreational needs of several more people. With a large number of children to care for, the mother is less likely to find time for gainful employment; and if she does take a job, but is not able to afford satisfactory child care services, her children may be deprived of adequate parental care, guidance and discipline during their formative years. In circumstances such as these, it is quite common for the husband to desert the family. And women who have been deserted by their husbands and who are forced to try to raise a large family on welfare frequently sink into a chronic state of apathy or depression or turn to drugs or alcohol for escape.

Many accidental pregnancies occur in women in their forties who are entering menopause and who already have adult children. Having already devoted 20 or so years to raising their families, these women are often incapable of making the considerable emotional and psychological adjustment that would be required for them to initiate a second career of motherhood, devoting an additional 20 years to the care of children.

Rape is a common crime and one which is occurring with increasing frequency. A woman who has been raped could prevent pregnancy from occurring by immediately reporting to a physician or emergency room and arranging to have a surgical procedure, a dilatation and curettage of the uterus. However, since rape is a terrifying and humilating experience, most women are inclined to suppress the incident rather than to seek prompt medical attention. As a result, rape may result in pregnancy. Prior to 1973, the laws of most states would not allow abortion even in cases of women made pregnant by rape.

The exact incidence of incest is not known, but psychiatrists are aware from their practices that incest is not extremely rare. Prior to 1973, the laws of most states would not allow an abortion even in cases of a 12- or 13-year old girl made pregnant by her father.

Many women, both single and married, prefer careers to motherhood; still others may wish to delay motherhood until later in life in order to first pursue educational or career goals. Such women justifiably regard it as an extreme hardship to be forced, because of an unwanted pregnancy, to postpone goals for which they have worked or planned throughout their lives.

In summary, there are many situations and circumstances in which a woman may be unable or unwilling to assume adequately the burdens and responsibilities of motherhood. In the absence of foolproof methods of contraception, easy access to abortion is the only way that many thousands of women can be protected from bearing an unwanted child. Forcing these thousands of women to bear unwanted children would impose severe strain on the mental and physical health and well-being of the women and the members of their families as well.

IV. Research on the Emotional After-Effects of Abortion.

As indicated earlier in this chapter, it used to be believed that serious problems of guilt and depression commonly resulted from abortion. During the past 25 years, however, a considerable body of research has been carried out on the after-effects of abortion. One review article reported that there are in excess of 1000 articles on the psychological and social effects of abortion in the English language alone.[14] By and large, this research has failed to substantiate these earlier beliefs.

In my review of the literature, I was able to find 32 systematic and carefully designed studies on the psychological and psychiatric sequelae of abortion.[15] The numbers of women studied in these research projects varied from as few as 21 to as many as 1773, with a number of projects studying in excess of 100 women each. The length of follow-up in these studies ranged from a few hours to 16 years.

Psychiatric problems resulting from abortion were found to be rare, occurring in 1 or 2 percent of cases in most of the studies. The highest reported incidence of psychiatric problems was in two Swedish studies in which 10 and 12 percent of women respectively were found to have severe guilt and associated psychiatric symptoms, but it was not clear in these studies if the symptoms were the result of the abortion or represented preexisting psychiatric pathology.[16]

Serious psychiatric reactions occurred for the most part in two groups of patients: those who were pressured into abortion against their own judgment or against their religious or moral beliefs, and those who were mentally disturbed prior to the abortion. In this latter group, it is difficult to tell whether the psychiatric symptoms following the abortion were in fact caused by the abortion. There are serious methodological problems involved in any type of outcome research in psychiatry. Determining the presence or severity of psychiatric symptoms is subjective and depends on the full cooperation of the person being interviewed. It is difficult to be sure if the patient is giving a truthful report, whether in a psychiatric interview, filling out a questionnaire, or completing a standardized psychological test. Experimenter bias is another problem. Most people have strong views on abortion, and scientists are no exception. We cannot be certain that these investigators were completely objective in their studies and did not unconsciously overlook evidence of more serious post-abortion problems that they reported. Furthermore, it is difficult to be sure that the investigators were entirely objective in judging whether symptoms were the result of the abortion or other factors. Even if a woman with no history of psychiatric problems develops clear-cut depression after an abortion, it does not follow that the abortion per se was the cause of the symptoms. The woman may have been reacting to any number of related factors. She may have been having marital problems, or if single, she may have been encountering rejection from her family for having become pregnant out of wedlock, or reacting to abandonment by a boyfriend. In cases of women having abortions for medical reasons, the woman usually is unhappy because her medical condition won't permit her to have a wanted child, not because of the abortion itself.

If the abortion is performed in an unsupportive environment, emotional distress may result. For example, many hospitals used to house their abortion patients on the obstetrical wards, where they were treated as second-class citizens by the nursing staff. In countries such as Sweden, where motherhood is strongly encouraged by the government, and where abortion is performed only where serious health or social problems exist, a woman must go through a long humiliating series of consultations and convince a panel of doctors that there is something physically or mentally wrong with her in order to secure permission for abortion. This experience can be degrading and dehumanizing and can contribute to depression even more than the abortion itself. All the studies reviewed concerned women who obtained legal abortions. It must be remembered that legal abortions were a small percentage of the total abortions at the time of these studies. In the United States, for example, prior to 1973, it had been estimated that approximately 1 million women each year obtained illegal abortions.[17] The Institute for Sex Research studies found that between one-quarter and one-fifth of married women had obtained an abortion by the time they had reached age 45.[18] If abortions, especially the more traumatic illegal ones, were associated with a significant incidence of psychiatric illness, one would expect that abortion-related problems would be seen quite commonly in psychiatric practice. But, in fact, such problems were seen only rarely, which tends to support the findings of the follow-up studies. Kummer, in the early 1960s, surveyed 32 practicing psychiatrists in California and found that 75 percent had never encountered any moderate or severe post-abortion sequelae among their patients.[19] Twenty-five percent encountered such sequelae only rarely, with the highest incidence being six cases in 15 years of practice. Furthermore, the low risk of serious psychiatric problems following *abortion* must be contrasted with the relatively high frequency of psychosis following *childbirth*. There are some 4000 documented cases of postpartum psychosis requiring hospitalization in the United States each year, slightly less than two per 1000 deliveries.[20]

A study by Brewer in Great Britain compared the incidence of post-abortion psychosis with that of postpartum psychosis. This was a prospective study of a population of 1,333,000 people over a 15-month period. Only one case of post-abortion psychosis was found, a woman with a history of two previous episodes of postpartum psychosis. The incidence of post-abortion psychosis in this study was calculated at 0.3 per 1000 legal abortions compared to an incidence of 1.7 postpartum psychosis per 1000 deliveries.[21]

To summarize: By the early 1970s, the weight of psychiatric evidence strongly suggested that serious psychologic harm resulting from abortion is relatively rare if the woman herself desires the abortion and is not submitting to pressure from others to undergo the abortion. In those cases where there is preexisting psychiatric pathology, an unwanted pregnancy may create problems regardless of whether the pregnancy is aborted or carried to term. The previous undocumented theories about the emotional harmfulness of abortion gradually have been abandoned by the psychiatric profession.

V. The Unwanted Child

The quality of parental care received by a child has a great deal to do with his or her subsequent mental health and adjustment to life. A child who is made to feel wanted and loved and is given sufficient attention and guidance will tend to grow up as an emotionally stable and well-adjusted adult. On the other hand, a child who is rejected, belittled, abused, or neglected has a far greater likelihood of developing mental illness or serious personality and behavioral disorders, such as alcoholism and criminality. These common-sense generalizations would be disputed by very few experienced professionals in the fields of mental health, substance abuse, education, or criminology and, in addition, have been supported by countless research studies.[22] Family planning measures, including abortion, have long been recognized by many thoughtful psychiatrists as one of the few effective ways to improve the quality of child care and thus reduce the incidence of mental illness and related disorders. Sigmund Freud, the founder of modern psychiatry, said:

> [I]t would be one of the greatest triumphs of mankind, one of the most tangible liberations from the bondage of nature to which we are subject, were it possible to raise the responsible act of procreation to the level of a voluntary and intentional act, and to free it from its entanglement with an indispensable satisfaction of a natural desire.[23]

The following is a quotation from another famous psychiatrist, Karl Menninger:

> The reason that contraceptive knowledge and counsel seem to the psychiatrist to be essential is based not upon considerations of the welfare of the adult, but on the considerations of the welfare of the child. Nothing is more tragic, more fateful in its ultimate consequences, than the realization by a child that he was unwanted. . . . [P]lanned parenthood is an essential element in any program for increased mental health and for human peace and happiness. The unwanted child becomes the undesirable citizen, the willing cannon-fodder for wars of hate and prejudice.[24]

It is extremely difficult to intervene effectively in cases where children are being neglected or mistreated in the home. The problem families first have to be identified, but identification is difficult except in cases of extreme physical abuse. In order to detect those families in which children are being continuously exposed to psychologically harmful neglect or mistreatment, a system of surveillance would have to be established that would entirely counter our traditional notions of freedom and privacy. Even if problem families could be identified, getting the parents to change their behavior would be extraordinarily difficult. Many parents, lacking insight, would deny that they were doing anything wrong and would refuse to cooperate with the authorities.

Even parents who recognize that their behavior and attitudes may be harmful to their child often find it hard to change, even with skilled professional help. It often turns out that their maladaptive patterns of behavior were learned in their formative years and are deeply ingrained. This is not to say that every effort shouldn't be made to help troubled parents do a better job raising their children, but such measures are not likely to produce significant results in more than a handful of cases, not enough to make a dent in the overall social problem of child neglect, abuse, and mistreatment. For this reason, many psychiatrists believe it to be of the utmost importance to help people avoid having unwanted children, and were therefore opposed to the restrictive abortion laws that existed prior to 1973 which in effect compelled women to bear unwanted children. How can society expect parents to care properly for their children if it does not permit parents every opportunity to choose the number and spacing of their children?

Although the Supreme Court has eliminated the legal barrier to abortion, our society has maintained a financial barrier that, even today, makes it next to impossible for an indigent woman to have the opportunity for a safe legal abortion.

There have been two elaborate follow-up studies performed on children born of women who had been refused abortion. Forssman and Thuwe in Sweden studied 120 such children, following them to age 21 and comparing them to an appropriate control group.[25] The investigators found that, compared with the control group, the unwanted children had a higher incidence of many kinds of behavior maladjustments, required more psychiatric care, were arrested more often for antisocial and criminal behavior and drunkenness, received welfare assistance more frequently, and failed to achieve as high a level of schooling. In a Czech study, Matejcek and associates examined 220 children, 110 boys and 110 girls, born to women who had twice been refused an abortion.[26] The children were compared with a control group and followed for nine years. This study also demonstrated that the children born of unwanted pregnancies were more likely than the control group to have deficiencies in psychosocial development and educational achievement.

Some people, while agreeing with the principle of family planning, argue that the emphasis should be on contraception rather than on abortion. This viewpoint overlooks some of the serious drawbacks of all known methods of contraception. Other than total abstinence from sexual intercourse, there is only one contraceptive method that is 100 percent effective, the pill. However, many women refuse to use the pill for a variety of reasons. Others forget to take it daily.

The next most reliable method is the intrauterine device, which has a failure rate of approximately 2 to 3 percent per year (*i.e.*, for every 100 users, two or three will become pregnant each year). This may seem like a high rate of reliability, but as Hardin has pointed out, with 25 million fertile American women, there would be 250,000 accidental pregnancies annually even if every women used a 99 percent effective method.[27] Thus, a social policy of relying upon contraception alone to attain the goal of reducing the incidence of unwanted births to the lowest possible level is insufficient. It is necessary, in addition, to make abortion available as a backstop method of contraception when conventional methods fail.

The successful practice of contraception requires a degree of foresight and self-discipline that many women simply don't possess. The women least likely to do a good job as mothers—the mentally retarded, mentally ill and impulsive—are the very ones least likely to practice successful family planning. Since abortion requires no foresight or self-discipline, a social policy of readily available abortion would make it possible even for the most immature, emotionally unstable, and mentally retarded segments of the population to have far greater control over their reproduction than would be possible were they relying on contraception alone. The opportunity to have an abortion may give a woman who is accidentally pregnant under unfavorable circumstances a chance to give birth to subsequent children under much more favorable circumstances. For example, a teenage girl accidentally pregnant in high school may end up in an unhappy forced marriage or as a welfare single parent, and may be a very ineffective parent. The same girl, following an abortion, may go on to complete her education, become happily married, eventually have several wanted children and become an excellent parent.

The present government policy of not allowing Medicaid health insurance to be used to pay for abortions can be viewed as an extreme case of "penny wise, pound foolish." Whereas an abortion costs $200 or $300, the cost of maintaining a child on welfare for 18 years costs tens of thousands of dollars. Since childrearing practices in the poverty class are often inadequate, and because rates of mental illness and behavior disorders are high among the poor, the policy of forcing the poor to bear large numbers of unwanted children imposes huge additional expenses on the taxpayer in the form of public mental health facilities, courts, police, and prisons.

VI. Abortion, Morality and the Family

The oppoents of abortion often view themselves as upholding traditional moral standards and as being pro-family. They see legalization of abortion as destructive to traditional moral values and to the traditional family structure. Making abortion available, in this view, removes an important deterrent to sexual promiscuity and to irresponsible sexuality in general. The ready availability of abortion is seen as making it more difficult for parents to teach a young daughter to say no because she no longer has to fear a disgraceful illegitimate pregnancy. Instead she can quietly get an abortion and no one will have to know. Traditional moralists also fear that too many abortions may contribute to an erosion of respect for life and to a general increase in callousness and insensitivity to the sanctity of human life. Some even go so far as to blame the rising rate of child abuse and other forms of violence on the legalization of abortion.[28]

Psychiatrists are not inclined to dismiss these views lightly, but psychiatrists also believe that the viewpoint of the traditional moralists fails to take into account a complete understanding of how moral values are developed and transmitted within the family structure. Children develop a sense of morality, of respect for the well-being of others, largely from the example set for them by their parents. If the parents treat one another and the child with kindness and respect, the child is likely to grow up respecting self and other people. On the other hand, if the parents are self-centered or abusive to each other and to the child, the child is apt to develop an immature sense of morality in which life is viewed as a jungle with everyone out for himself or herself, and in which it is considered okay to exploit others if you can get away with it.

In this developmental view, morality is thought to be influenced much more by the cumulative effect of family interactions during the formative years than by a system of harsh penalties enacted into law. From this point of view, a social policy of allowing families to choose the number and spacing of their children is considered to help produce a more moral and family-centered society. On the other hand, a social policy of forcing large numbers of people to bear unwanted children, who then may be raised under conditions of neglect and abuse, may contribute to a breakdown of the moral order and a disintegration of the family structure.

NOTES

1. I. Goldston, *Other Aspects of the Abortion Problem,* in Abortion in the United States (M. S. Calderone, ed. 1958).
2. S. Bolter, *The Psychiatrist's Role in Therapeutic Abortion: The Unwitting Accomplice,* 119 Am. J. of Psychiat. 312 (1962).

3. T. Lidz, *Other Aspects of the Abortion Problem,* in Abortion in the United States (M. S. Calderone, ed. 1958).

4. D. C. Wilson, *The Abortion Problem in the General Hospital,* in Therapeutic Abortion (H. Rosen, ed. 1954).

5. E. Pfeiffer, *Psychiatric Indications or Psychiatric Justification of Therapeutic Abortion,* 23 Arch. of Gen. Psychiat. 402 (1970).

6. Group for the Advancement of Psychiatry, The Right to Abortion: A Psychiatric View, VII, report no. 75 (1969).

7. American Psychiatric Association, *Position Statement on Abortion,* 126 Am. J. of Psych. 1554 (1970).

8. Roe v. Wade, 410 U.S. 113 (1973); Doe v. Bolton, 410 U.S. 179 (1973).

9. C. Tietze & S. Lewit, *Abortion,* 220 Scientific Am. 21 (1969).

10. Wilson, *supra* note 4; F. J. Ayd, *Abortion: The Catholic Viewpoint,* 2 Seminars in Psychiat. 258 (1970).

11. S. L. Halleck, *Excuse-Makers to the Elite—Psychiatrists as Accidental Social Movers,* 7 Med. Opin. 48 (1971).

12. National Center for Health Statistics, U.S. Department of Health, Education, and Welfare, 18 Monthly Vital Statistics Rep. 1 (1970).

13. H. T. Christensen, *Child Spacing Analysis Via Record Linkage: New Data Plus a Summing Up From Earlier Reports,* 25 Marr. & Fam. Living 272 (1963).

14. B. K. Doane & B. G. Quigley, *Psychiatric Aspects of Therapeutic Abortion,* 125 Can. Med. Assoc. 427 (1981).

15. P. Kolstad, *Therapeutic Abortion,* 36 Acta Obstetricia et Gynecologica Scandinavica, supplement 6 (1957); B. Brekke, *Other Aspects of the Abortion Problem,* in Abortion in the United States (M. S. Calderone, ed. 1958); M. Ekblad, *Induced Abortion on Psychiatric Grounds,* 30 Acta Psychiatrica et Neurologica Scandinavica, supplement no. 99 (1955); N. Simon, A. Senturia, & D. Rothman, *Psychiatric Illness Following Therapeutic Abortion,* 124 Am. J. of Psychiat. 59 (1967); A. Peck & H. Marcus, *Psychiatric Sequelae of Therapeutic Interruption of Pregnancy,* 143 J. of Nerv. & Mental Disease 417 (1966); S. Patt, R. Rappaport, & P. Banglow, *Follow Up of Therapeutic Abortion,* 20 Arch. of Gen. Psychiat. 408 (1969); H. I. Levene, & F. J. Rigney, *Law, Preventive Psychiatry, and Therapeutic Abortion,* 151 J. of Nerv. & Mental Disease 51 (1970); B. Jansson, *Mental Disorders After Abortion,* 41 Acta Psychiatrica Scandanavica 87 (1965); M. Clark, et al., *Sequels of Unwanted Pregnancy,* 2 Lancet 501 (1968); K. H. Mehlan, Abstract in Yearbook of Obstetrics and Gynecology, Chicago, Yearbook Medical Publishers (1957–58); C. V. Ford, P. Castelnuovo-Tedesco, & K. D. Long, *Abortion. Is It a Therapeutic Procedure in Psychiatry?* 218 J.A.M.A. 1173 (1971); A. B. Barnes, et al., *Therapeutic Abortion: Medical and Social Sequels,* 75 Ann. of Internal Med. 881 (1971); R. M. Kretzschmar, & A. S. Norris, *Psychiatric Implications of Therapeutic Abortion,* 98 Am. J. of Obstet. & Gynecol. 368 (1967); A. Gillis, *A Follow-Up of 72 Cases Referred for Abortion,* 2 Mental Health Soc. 212 (1975); J. D. Osofsky & H. J. Osofsky, *The Psychological Reaction of Patients to Legalized Abortion,* 42 Am. J. of Orthopsychiat. 48 (1972); K. Malmfors, *Problem of Women Seeking Abortion,* in Abortion in the United States 133 (M. S. Calderone, ed. 1958); P. Aren, *On Legal Abortion in Sweden: Tentative Evaluation of Justification of*

Frequency During Last Decade, 37 Acta Obstetricia et Gynecologica Scandanavica, supplement no. 1 (1958); J. S. Wallerstein, P. Kurtz, & M. Bar-Din, *Psychosocial Sequelae of Therapeutic Abortion in Young Unmarried Women,* 27 Arch. of Gen. Psychiat. 828 (1972); H. S. Greer, et al., *Psychosocial Consequences of Therapeutic Abortion: King's Termination Study III,* 128 Brit. J. of Psychiat. 74 (1976); E. M. Belsey et al., *Predictive Factors in Emotional Response to Abortion: King's Termination Study IV,* 2 Soc. Sci. & Med. 71 (1977); K. R. Niswander, J. Singer, & M. Singer, *Psychological Reaction to Therapeutic Abortion. II. Objective response,* 114 Am. J. of Obstet. & Gynecol. 29 (1972); L. R. Shusterman, *Predicting the Psychological Consequences of Abortion,* 13A Soc. Sci. & Med. 683 (1979); R. Schmidt & R. G. Priest, *The Effects of Termination of Pregnancy: A Follow-Up Study of Psychiatric Referrals,* 54 Brit. J. of Med. Psychol. 267 (1981); C. Brewer, *Incidence of Post-Abortion Psychosis: A Prospective Study,* 1 Brit. Med. J. 476 (1977); J. A. Ewing & B. A. Rouse, *Therapeutic Abortion and a Prior Psychiatric History,* 130 Am. J. of Psychiat. 37 (1973); B. Lask, *Short-Term Psychiatric Sequelae to Therapeutic Termination of Pregnancy,* 126 Brit. J. of Psychiat. 173 (1975); W. F. Tsoi et al., *Psychological Effects of Abortion,* 17 Singapore Med. J. 68 (1976); D. Jacobs et al., *A Prospective Study on the Psychological Effects of Therapeutic Abortion,* 15 Comprehensive Psychiat. 423 (1974); E. C. Payne et al., *Outcome Following Therapeutic Abortion,* 33 Arch. of Gen. Psychiat. 725 (1976); E. R. Greenglass, *Therapeutic Abortion and Psychiatric Disturbance in Canadian Women,* 21 Can. Psychiat. Assoc. J. 453 (1976); J. R. Ashton, *The Psychosocial Outcome of Induced Abortion,* 87 Brit. J. of Obstet. & Gynecol. 1115 (1980); M. B. Bracken, M. Hachamovitch, & G. Grossman, *The Decision to Abort and Psychological Sequelae,* 158 J. of Nerv. & Mental Disease 154 (1974).

16. Malmfours, *supra* note 15; Aren, *supra* note 15.
17. Tietze & Lewit, *supra* note 9.
18. P. Gebbard et al., Pregnancy, Birth and Abortion (1958).
19. J. Kummer, *Post-Abortion Psychiatric Illness—A Myth?* 119 Am. J. of Psychiat. 980 (1963).
20. H. P. David, *Abortion in Psychological Perspective* 42 Am. J. of Orthopsychiat. 61 (1972).
21. Brewer, *Supra* Note 15.
22. J. Bowlby, Child Care and the Growth of Love (1965); I. Chien & D. Wilner, The Road to H: Narcotics, Delinquency and Social Policy (1964); S. Glueck & E. Glueck, Unravelling Juvenile Deliquency (1950); L. Saul & S. Wenar, *Early Influences on Development and Disorders of Personality,* 34 Psychoanal. Q. 327 (1965).
23. S. Freud, Sexuality and Aetiology of the Neuroses, Collected Papers, vol. I 238 (1959).
24. K. Menninger, *Psychiatric Aspects of Contraception,* in Therapeutic Abortion 250–51 (H. Rosen, ed. 1954).
25. H. Forssman & I. Thuwe, *One Hundred and Twenty Children Born After Application for Therapeutic Abortion Refused: Their Mental Health, Social*

Adjustment and Educational Level Up to the Age of 21, 42 Acta Psychiatrica Scandanavica 71 (1966).

26. Z. Matejcek, Z. Dytrych & V. Schuller, *Children From Unwanted Pregnancies,* 57 Acta Psychiatrica Scandanavica 67 (1978).
27. G. Hardin, *The History and Future of Birth Control,* 10 Perspect. in Biol. & Med. 1 (1966).
28. P. Ney, *Relationship Between Abortion and Child Abuse,* 24 Cana. J. of Psychiat. 610 (1979).

3 · ETHICS

This article by Daniel Callahan was originally written in 1973, but it focuses clearly on the abortion issue of the 1980s. Special note should be taken of section D, which discusses the question of when human life begins. The author mentions that collateral issues—such as when life requires protection or respect—are just as important as when life begins. Clearly, Daniel Callahan anticipated the difficulty Congress would have with the Human Life Bill, namely, reaching moral conclusions from scientific facts. To further appreciate his present article, one should also read Callahan's prepared testimony in Appendix 2.

14 · Abortion: Some Ethical Issues _____

Daniel Callahan

I. Introduction

Abortion is a peculiarly passionate topic, largely because many people invest their positions with a symbolic weight that transcends immediate social and legal issues. The most obvious examples of this tendency can be found in some segments of the women's liberation movement, on the one hand, and in some factions of those opposed to abortion, on the other. For each the way society solves the abortion problem will be taken to show just what its deepest values are. And those values have implications that extend far beyond abortion.

The women's liberation movement sees abortion as the most significant liberation of all, from the body and from male domination. The most effective solution to unwanted pregnancy, it removes the final block to full control of reproduction. Unless reproduction can be fully controlled, women will remain in bondage not only to their sexuality but, even more, to those legions of male chauvinists who use female sexuality to their own domineering ends.

By contrast, many of those opposed to abortion see the issue as indicating the kind of respect society will show the most defenseless beings in our midst. If the life of a defenseless fetus is not respected, then there is good reason to believe that the most fundamental of all human rights—the right to life—will have been subverted at its core. The test of the humane society is not the respect it pays to the strongest and most articulate, but that which it accords to the weakest and least articulate.

Of course, these arguments and the symbolic weight they carry simply bypass one another. The opposition seems so fundamental, and the starting premises so different, that any meaningful debate—the kind that leads to give-and-take, concession and adaptation—is ruled out from the start. Moreover, the very charges each side hurls at the other are of a psychologically intolerable nature. No vigorous proponents of abortion are likely to admit, either privately or publicly, that they sanction "murder"; nor are opponents of abortion likely to admit that they sanction the suppression of women. I am using the word "admit" here in a serious sense which implies that one is willing to ponder seriously the possibility that the worst things said about oneself are true. Given that possibility, there remain only two choices: change one's views and confess the errors of one's old ways or violently and aggressively deny the charges.

There is, of course, a third possibility: Concede that there may be a grain of truth in what one's opponent says and then undertake the development of a position that tries to meet and integrate the objection in some new position. But this may be the most distasteful solution of all for most people, since it entails a long, drawn-out wrestling with oneself. Abortion is a painful issue, and for just that reason people seem impelled to proceed in all haste to the comfort of "Here I stand," which ends the self-wrestling.

My comments here are not drawn from any hard evidence. They are meant only as reflections on years of trying to discuss abortion in a reasonably calm, rational way, both in public and private. My own professional training is in philosophy, a discipline which (to the despair of many nonphilosophers) places a heavy premium on precision of argument, careful distinctions, developed justifications of ethical positions, methodological elegance, and a cool, temperate mode of discourse. These traits have, to be sure, led to more than one accusation that philosophers are prone to fiddle while the city is burning; and there is probably some truth in this. Nonetheless, I think these traits are still somewhat useful, especially when discussing a topic like abortion, which many take as an invitation to express their unbridled feelings and convictions. Worse still, the politics of abortion seems to pay handsome dividends for such a stance. It can, and has, pushed many an abortion reform bill through reluctant legislatures, just as it has, in different hands, killed many a bill. When argument fails, what better tactic is there than to bring out the fetus-in-a-bottle ("See what you are doing to innocent life!") or the raped mongoloid mother of 10 with the drunken husband ("See what you are doing to her!")?

In discussing the quality and weight of ethical arguments here, I hope to achieve the most minimal kind of goal—simply to make plausible the radical notion that there remain some unresolved questions, some hazy areas, and some further points to be thought about. Before proceeding, let me state something for the record about my "position." (Experience has taught me the painful lesson that abortion politicians of either persuasion usually care not at all about one's arguments, but only about one's final "position.") My position is that abortion should be legally available on request up to the 12th week of pregnancy; that abortion is morally justifiable under a variety of circumstances, but should always be undertaken reluctantly and with a strong sense of tragedy; and that the humane society would be one in which women were neither coerced to go through with pregnancies they do not want nor coerced by social, economic, or psychological circumstances into abortion. I cannot accept the position of those who would deny all respect to the fetus. Nor can I accept the position of those who hold that the right to life of the fetus is sufficient in all cases to override the right of women to choose an abortion. On the contrary, I accord the right of women to control their procreation a high status, as a crucial ingredient of the sanctity or dignity of life.

I will not try to defend or fully explain this position here. My intent is, resolutely, to talk about what seem to me good and bad arguments. But I want to note, no less resolutely, that it is perfectly possible for those with bad arguments to come nevertheless to good conclusions. This happens all the time, even if it is a process which does some violence to logic. (Or, as is more likely the case, people begin with good intuitions and then defend them with bad reasons.) Let me begin by laying out what seem to me bad or at least incomplete arguments. For convenience, I shall set them out as propositions, most of which should be readily recognizable to anyone even faintly acquainted with the abortion literature.

II. Nine Inadequate Arguments

A. Abortion is a religious or philosophical issue, best left to the private conscience rather than to public legislation

This argument rarely makes much sense. If it means that for some churches and some religious believers their positions are the direct result of religious teachings, this hardly entails the conclusion that the issue is thus intrinsically religious. One might as well say that the Vietnamese war was a religious issue, not subject to legislation because there are some churches which declare that war immoral on religious grounds. Religious groups have taken religious stands on many social issues, including war, race, poverty, population, and ecology, without exempting those problems from public legislation or turning them into "theology."

Nor is it enough to argue "sociologically" that religion plays a large role in what people feel and think about abortion, and that, somehow, this shows the religious issue to be paramount. If that were the case (and the sociological facts are, in any event, more complicated), then everyone, regardless of position, is implicated; for virtually everyone can be identified (if only culturally) with one or another religious heritage. Why is it, however, that the person who comes out of a religious heritage (e.g., Roman Catholicism) that condemns abortion is said to be acting on "religious" grounds, while a person from a heritage which does not condemn abortion is not (particularly when the latter tradition has *theological* reasons for not condemning abortion, as with some branches of Judaism and Protestantism)?

The claim that abortion is not a religious but a "philosophical" issue is surely true. But, then, every serious social question is philosophical. What is justice? What is freedom? Those questions arise all the time, and they are philosophical (and legal) in nature. The answers to them shape legislation in a very decisive way. It is inconsistent to argue that the right of the fetus is exclusively a philosophical problem, to be left to individual conscience, while the right of women is a matter to be protected or implemented legislatively. If it is legitimate to legislate on the latter (which it is), then it should be equally legitimate to legislate on the former.

B. To remove restrictive abortion laws from the books passes no judgment on the substantive ethical issues; it merely allows individuals to make up their own minds

That an absence of legislation allows freedom of individual choice is undoubtedly true. But it would be highly surprising if a social decision to remove restrictive laws did not reflect a significant shift in public moral thinking about the issue at hand. Civil libertarians, for instance, would be outraged if it were proposed to repeal all legislation designed to protect the civil rights of blacks on the ground that this would maximize individual freedom of choice: they would accurately discern any such trend as both moral and constitutional regression.

In the instance of abortion, a public decision to leave the question up to individuals reflects at least three premises of a highly philosophical sort: (1) that private abortion decisions have few if any social implications or consequences; (2) that there are no normative standards whatever for determining the rights of fetuses, except the standard that individuals are free to use or create any standard they see fit; and (3) that changes in law have no effect one way or another on individual moral judgments. My point here is not to judge these premises (though obviously much could be said about them), but only to point out that each involves a philosophical judgment and has philosophical implications. A decision to remove abortion laws from the books is no more ethically neutral than a decision to put such laws on the books or keep them there.

C. Any liberalization of abortion laws, or a repeal of such laws, will lead in the long run to a disrespect for all human life

This is a fundamental premise of those opposed to abortion. There is no evidence to support such a judgment, however, and evidence rather than speculation is what is required.

In the first place, it is exceedingly difficult to correlate abortion attitudes throughout the world with any trend toward disrespect for nonfetal life. On the contrary, insofar as liberal abortion laws are designed to promote free choice for women, there is a prima facie case that their intent is to enhance respect for the lives of women.

Secondly, there is no evidence to support a "domino theory" of the kind that predicts a quick move from liberalization of abortion laws to the killing of the defective, the elderly, and the undesirable. This has certainly not happened in Japan or the eastern European countries, which have had liberal abortion laws for a number of years.

Finally, since most of those who support liberal abortion laws either do not believe that fetal life is human life or do not believe that it is life which has reached a stage requiring social protection, it is unfair to accuse them of harboring attitudes which inevitably lead to atrocities against all forms of human life. This kind of judgment reflects more the moral logic of the group leveling such charges than the moral principles of those at whom the charge is leveled.

D. Scientific evidence, particularly modern genetics, has shown beyond a shadow of a doubt that human life begins at conception, or at least at the time of implantation

Scientific evidence does not, as such, tell us when human life begins. The concept "human" is essentially philosophical, requiring both a philosophical and an ethical judgment. Even if it could be shown that human life begins at conception, that finding would not entail the further moral judgment that life at that stage ethically merits full protection. When human life begins and when human life, once begun, merits or requires full respect are two different questions.

It is, I think, reasonable to contend that human life begins at conception. But this is as much a philosophical and ethical position as it is scientific. At the same time, however, it is capricious to ignore all scientific evidence. As any elementary textbook in genetics shows, the fusion of sperm and egg marks a decisive first step in the life of any individual. It is only in abortion arguments that one hears vague protestations that life is just one great continuum, with no decisive, significant changes from one stage or condition to another. But if it is bad science to talk that way, it is equally bad science to say that science dictates in some normative manner when human life begins.

E. The fetus is nothing more than "tissue" or a "blob of protoplasm" or a "blueprint"

Definitions of this kind can only be called self-serving. This is not the way a fetus is defined in any dictionary or any embryological text. All life is tissue and protoplasm; that fact alone tells us nothing whatever. Would it be acceptable for a student in a college biology course to define "fetus" with a one-word term "tissue" or "protoplasm"?

It is no less unscientific to call an embryo or a fetus a mere "blueprint." Blueprints of buildings are not ordinarily mixed into the mortar; they remain in the hands of the architects. Moreover, once a building has been constructed, the blueprint can be thrown away, and the building will continue to stand. The genetic blueprint operates in an entirely different way: it exerts a directly causal action in morphological development; as an intrinsic part of the physiological structure, it can at no point be thrown away or taken out.

F. All abortions are selfish, ego-centered actions

This reflects a strain of thought which runs very deep among those violently opposed to abortion. But the argument manages to ignore the decisions of those who choose abortion out of a sense of responsibility to their living children. It also manages to beg the question of whether individuals have some rights to determine what is in their own welfare, and to choose in favor of themselves some of the time.

Most broadly, this contention typifies the widespread tendency on all sides of the abortion debate to indulge in amateur psychologizing and *ad hominem* argumentation. Those opposed to abortion are adept at reducing all pro-abortion arguments to their psychological ingredients: homicidal impulses, selfishness, the baneful effects of a decadent culture, genocidal aspirations, a hatred of children, and the like. Those favorable to abortion are no mean masters of the art themselves: since it is well-known that all opposed to abortion are dogma-ridden, male chauvinists (or females brainwashed by male chauvinists), insensitive to the quality of life, sadists, and/or fascists. In short, don't listen to anyone's arguments; it is more profitable to hunt out hidden pathologies. And don't credit anyone with a mistake in reasoning, too small and human a flaw for propaganda purposes, when it is far more emotively effective to convict them of general crimes against humanity.

G. Abortions are "therapeutic," and abortion decisions are "medical" decisions

Abortion is not notably therapeutic for the fetus—an observation I presume will elicit little disagreement. Even in the instance of a fetus with a grave defect, abortion is not therapeutic. It may be merciful and it may be wise, but, unless I am mistaken, the medical profession does not classify procedures with a 100 percent mortality rate as therapeutic.

Perhaps, then, abortion is therapeutic for the woman who receives it. That it is beneficial to her in some ways seems undeniable; she is relieved of an unwanted social, economic, or psychological burden. But is it proper to employ language which has a very concrete meaning in medicine—the correction or amelioration of a physical or psychological defect—in a case where there is usually no physical pathology at all? Except in the now-rare instances of a direct threat to a woman's life, an abortion cures no known disease and relieves no medically classifiable illness.

Thomas Szasz has been an especially eloquent spokesman for two positions. The first is that abortion should be available on request in the name of individual freedom. The second is that essentially nonmedical decisions should not be dressed in the mantle of "medical" language simply because they require medical technology for their execution. "To be sure," he has written, "the procedure is surgical; but this makes abortion no more a medical problem than the use of the electric chair makes capital punishment a problem of electrical engineering."[1]

Szasz's point seems undeniable, yet it is still common to hear abortion spoken of as a medical problem, which should be worked out between the woman and her physician. Even if that is the proper way to handle abortion, that does not make it a medical solution. The reason for this obfuscation is not far to be sought, and Szasz has stressed it as a constant theme in a number of his writings: the predilection in our society to translate value judgments into medical terms, giving them the aura of settled "scientific" judgments and the socially impregnable status of medical legitimation.

H. In a just society there would be no abortion problem, since there the social and economic pressures that drive women to abortion would not exist

This proposition is usually part of a broader political argument which sees abortion as no more than a symptom of unjust, repressive societies. To concentrate on abortion as a response to poverty, poor housing, puritanical attitudes toward illegitimacy, and racism is a cheap and evasive solution. It achieves no more than reinforcement of unjust political and social structures and institutions.

Up to a point there is some merit in this kind of argument, and that is why I believe that (as in the Scandinavian and eastern European countries) abortion should be handled in a context of full maternal and child care welfare programs. A woman who wishes to have a child but is not socially and economically free to do so is not a free woman. Her freedom is only superficially enhanced by allowing her, in that kind of repressive context, to choose abortion as a way out. She is not even being given half the loaf of freedom, which requires the existence of a full range of viable options.

At the same time, however, there are some serious limitations to the notion that abortion is nothing but a symptom of an unjust society. It utterly ignores the fact, common enough in affluent countries, that large numbers of women choose abortion because they have decided they want no children at all, or at least no more children than they already have. They are acting not out of social or economic coercion but out of a positive desire to shape and live a life of their own choosing, not dominated by unexpected pregnancies and unwanted children. In addition, it neglects the reality of contraceptive failure, which can and does occur independently of economic and social conditions (though it may of course be influenced by them). Short of the perfect contraceptive perfectly used, some portion of women, against their intentions, will become pregnant.

I. Abortion is exclusively a women's issue to be decided by women

The underpinning of this argument seems to consist of three assumptions. First, that there is no role for male judgment, intervention, or interference because it is women who get pregnant and who have to live with the pregnancies. Second, that abortion laws are repressive because they have been established by male legislators. And, third, that the fetus is a part of a woman's body and is thus exclusively subject to her judgments and desires.

While I am fully prepared to agree that approval of a male, whether husband and/or father, should not be a legal condition for a woman to receive an abortion, this should not be construed to mean that nothing is owed, in justice, to the male. Even ignoring the well-known fact that women do not get pregnant by themselves, a few other considerations remain. At the least, there is an injustice in giving males no rights prior to birth but then imposing upon them a full range of obligations after birth. If the obligations toward a child are mutual after birth, why should there not be a corresponding parity of rights prior to birth? I have not seen a satisfactory answer to that question. Moreover, if—to accept the feminist premise—women have been forced to carry through unwanted pregnancies because of male domination, the sexist shoe is put on the other foot if all the rights involved in having a child are ceded exclusively to women. One injustice is corrected at the expense of creating another, and sexism is still triumphant.

That legislatures are dominated by males is an obvious fact. That the history of abortion legislation would have been different had there been legislative equality or even a female majority, however, has not been demonstrated. Indeed, it has been a consistent survey finding that women are less willing than men to approve permissive abortion laws. There have of course been attempts to explain these rather awkward findings, since they are inconsistent on their face with claims that resistance to abortion is a male phenomenon. These efforts usually take the form of speculations designed to show that the resistant women were culturally brainwashed into adopting repressive male attitudes. This is a plausible theory, but one for which there unfortunately is no evidence whatever. And, apart from these speculations, there is no evidence that the thinking of women on abortion must, of biological and experiential necessity, be utterly different from that of men. But that is exactly the premise necessary if the contention is to be sustained that an exclusively female domination of abortion legislation would produce a different result from either a male domination or legislative equality.

In this context, it should be mentioned that childbearing and childrearing have consequences for everyone in a society, both men and women. To imply that women alone should have all the rights, even though the consequences involve the lives of both sexes, is an unfair conclusion. Or are we to overthrow, as the price of abortion reform, the long-honored principle that all of those who will have to bear the consequences of decisions have a right to be consulted? I find that price too high. Yet, since I agree that abortion decisions should not legally require the consent of husband and/or father—for I see no way to include such a requirement in the law without opening the way for a further abuse of women—I am left with the (perhaps pious) hope that there will be some recognition that problems of justice toward the male are real (however new!) and that an ethical resolution will be found.

Finally, a quick word about the contention that a fetus is "part" of a woman's body. That a fetus is *in* a woman's body is an evident biological datum. That it is thereby a *part* of her body, in much the same way that her heart, arm, liver, or leg is part of her body, is biologically false. The separate genetic constitution of the fetus, its rate of growth and development, and its separate organ system clearly distinguish the body of the fetus from the body of the mother.

Some clarity would be brought to the language of the abortion debate if this distinction were admitted. It could still be argued that, because the fetus is in the mother's body, she should have full rights in determining its fate. But that argument is different from likening the fetus to any other part of a woman's body and then transposing the rules concerning the exercise of rights over one's body. Here is a clear instance where, in order to find a constitutional precedent for women's right to control procreation, violence is often done to some elementary facts of biology.

III. Some Valid Conclusions

I have tried to show, using nine different propositions, that some bad, or at least incompletely developed, arguments are too much in currency to be allowed to go by default. Would the abortion debate be significantly altered if these arguments were no longer used by the contending sides? This is a moot question, as there seems to be little likelihood that they will cease being employed. They are too powerful to be set aside, for both good and bad reasons—the good being that they are able to elicit responses which build upon some pervasive feelings about abortion, feelings which are decisive in shaping thought and behavior, even if they are poorly articulated.

The great strength of the general movement for abortion on request (apart from the questionable validity of particular arguments brought to bear in support of it) is that it perceives and seeks to correct two elementary realities, one social and the other biological. The social reality is that women have not had the freedom to make their own choice in a matter critical to their development as persons. Society, through the medium of male domination, has forced its choice upon them. The biological reality is that it is women who become pregnant and bear children; nature gave them no choice. Unless they are given a means to control the biological facts—and abortion is one very effective means—they will be dominated by them.

Without such control, which must be total if it is to have any decisive meaning, women are fated to accept Freud's principle that "anatomy is destiny." That kind of rigid biological determinism is increasingly unacceptable, not only to women in the case of procreation, but to most human beings confronted with the involuntary rigidities of nature. The deepest philosophical issue beneath the abortion question is the extent to which, in the name of freely chosen ends, biological realities can be manipulated, controlled, and set aside. This is a very old problem, and the trend toward abortion on request reflects the most recent tendency in modern thought—namely, the attempt to subordinate biology to reason, to bring it under control, to master it. It remains to be seen whether procreation can be so easily mastered. That question may take centuries to resolve.

The great strength of the movement against abortion is that it seeks to protect one defenseless category of human or potentially human life; furthermore, it strives to resist the introduction into society of forms of value judgments that would discriminate among the worth of individual lives. In almost any other civil rights context, the cogency of this line of reasoning would be quickly respected. Indeed, it has been at the heart of efforts to correct racial injustices, to improve health care, to eradicate poverty, and to provide better care for the aged. The history of mankind has shown too many instances of systematic efforts to exclude certain races or classes of persons from the human community to allow us to view with equanimity the declaration that fetuses are "not human." Historically, the proposition that all human beings are equal, however "inchoate" they may be, is not conservative but radical. It is constantly threatened in theory and subverted in practice.

Although the contending sides in the abortion debate commonly ignore, or systematically deride, the essentially positive impulses lying behind their opponents' positions, the conflict is nonetheless best seen as the pitting of essentially valuable impulses against one another. The possibility of a society which did allow women the right and the freedom to control their own lives is a lofty goal. No less lofty is that of a society which, with no exceptions, treated all forms of human life as equally valuable. In the best of all possible worlds, it might be possible to reconcile these goals. In the real world, however, the first goal requires the right of abortion, and the second goal excludes that right. This, I believe, is a genuine and deep dilemma. That so few are willing to recognize the dilemma, or even to admit that any choice must be less than perfect, is the most disturbing element in the whole debate.

The bad reason why the arguments I have analyzed will endure is that they readily lend themselves to legal use. Nothing in our society has so muddied the ethical issues as its tendency to turn ethical problems into legal matters. The great prize, sought by all sides, is a favorable court decision. Toward that end, the best tactic is to find a way of bringing one's own ethical case under one or more constitutional protections or exclusions. If one can succeed in convincing the courts that abortion is a religious issue (which it is not), then there is a good chance that they will favor private choice and rule against legislation. The same tactic is evident in efforts to show that abortion decisions come under the constitutional protections afforded to "privacy" (which begs the question of the rights of the fetus), or, on the other side, to show that abortion violates the equal protection and due process requirements of the Constitution (which also begs the question of the rights of the fetus). Since the possibility of a legal victory is an irresistible goal, there seems to be no limit to the bad arguments which will be brought to bear to gain it.

NOTE

1. Szasz, *The Ethics of Abortion,* Humanist (September-October 1966) at 148.

President Ronald Reagan presents a bold position on the abortion issue which sets the tone for the executive branch from 1981–88. It is most interesting what impact this will have on the legislative and judicial branches during the 1980's and beyond. The Human Life Bill as mentioned by the President is presented in the appendix, as well as other pertinent legislation.

15 · Abortion and the Conscience of the Nation_____

Ronald Reagan

The 10th anniversary of the Supreme Court decision in *Roe v. Wade* is a good time for us to pause and reflect. Our nationwide policy of abortion on demand through all nine months of pregnancy was neither voted for by our people nor enacted by our legislators—not a single state had such unrestricted abortion before the Supreme Court decreed it to be national policy in 1973. But the consequences of this judicial decision are now obvious: since 1973, more than 15 million unborn children have had their lives snuffed out by legalized abortions. That is over 10 times the number of Americans lost in all our nation's wars.

Make no mistake, abortion on demand is not a right granted by the Constitution. No serious scholar, including one disposed to agree with the Court's result, has argued that the framers of the Constitution intended to create such a right. Shortly after the *Roe v. Wade* decision, Professor John Hart Ely, now dean of Stanford Law School, wrote that the opinion "is not constitutional law and gives almost no sense of an obligation to try to be." Nowhere do the plain words of the Constitution even hint at a "right" so sweeping as to permit abortion up to the time the child is ready to be born. Yet that is what the Court ruled.

As an act of "raw judicial power" (to use Justice White's biting phrase), the decision by the seven-man majority in *Roe v. Wade* has so far been made to stick. But the Court's decision has by no means settled the debate. Instead, *Roe v. Wade* has become a continuing prod to the conscience of the nation.

Ronald Reagan is the 40th president of the United States.
Reprinted by permission of Thomas Nelson Publishers. From the article "Abortion and the Conscience of the Nation." Copyright 1984 by Human Life Foundation, Inc.

Abortion concerns not just the unborn child, it concerns every one of us. The English poet John Donne wrote: ". . . any man's death diminishes me, because I am involved in mankind; and therefore never send to know for whom the bell tolls; it tolls for thee."

We cannot diminish the value of one category of human life—the unborn—without diminishing the value of all human life. We saw tragic proof of this truism last year when the Indiana courts allowed the starvation death of "Baby Doe" in Bloomington because the child had Down's syndrome.

Many of our fellow citizens grieve over the loss of life that has followed *Roe v. Wade*. Margaret Heckler, soon after being nominated to head the largest department of our government, Health and Human Services (HHS), told an audience that she believed abortion to be the greatest moral crisis facing our country today. And the revered Mother Teresa, who works in the streets of Calcutta ministering to dying people in her world-famous mission of mercy, has said that "the greatest misery of our time is the generalized abortion of children."

Over the first two years of my administration I have closely followed and assisted efforts in Congress to reverse the tide of abortion—efforts of congressmen, senators, and citizens responding to an urgent moral crisis. Regrettably, I have also seen the massive efforts of those who, under the banner of "freedom of choice," have so far blocked every effort to reverse nationwide abortion on demand.

Despite the formidable obstacles before us, we must not lose heart. This is not the first time our country has been divided by a Supreme Court decision that denied the value of certain human lives. The *Dred Scott* decision of 1857 was not overturned in a day, or a year, or even a decade. At first, only a minority of Americans recognized and deplored the moral crisis brought about by denying the full humanity of our black brothers and sisters; but that minority persisted in their vision and finally prevailed. They did it by appealing to the hearts and minds of their countrymen, to the truth of human dignity under God. From their example, we know that respect for the sacred value of human life is too deeply ingrained in the hearts of our people to remain forever suppressed. But the great majority of the American people have not yet made their voices heard, and we cannot expect them to—anymore than the public voice arose against slavery—*until* the issue is clearly framed and presented.

What, then, is the real issue? I have often said that when we talk about abortion, we are talking about two lives—the life of the mother and the life of the unborn child. Why else do we call a pregnant woman a mother? I have also said that anyone who doesn't feel sure whether we are talking about a second human life should clearly give life the benefit of the doubt. If you don't know whether a body is alive or dead, you would never bury it. I think this consideration itself should be enough for all of us to insist on protecting the unborn.

The case against abortion does not rest here, however, for medical practice confirms at every step the correctness of these moral sensibilities. Modern medicine treats the unborn child as a patient. Medical pioneers have made great breakthroughs in treating the unborn—for genetic problems, vitamin deficiencies, irregular heart rhythms, and other medical conditions. Who can forget George Will's moving account of the little boy who underwent brain surgery six times during the nine weeks before he was born? Who is the *patient* if not that tiny unborn human being who can feel pain when he or she is approached by doctors who come to kill rather than to cure?

The real question today is not when human life begins, but, *What is the value of human life?* The abortionist who reassembles the arms and legs of a tiny baby to make sure all its parts have been torn from its mother's body can hardly doubt whether it is a human being. The real question for him and for all of us is whether that tiny human life has a God-given right to be protected by the law—the same right we have.

What more dramatic confirmation could we have of the real issue than the Baby Doe case in Bloomington, Indiana? The death of that tiny infant tore at the hearts of all Americans because the child was undeniably a live human being—one lying helpless before the eyes of the doctors and the eyes of the nation. The real issue for the courts was *not* whether Baby Doe was a human being. The real issue was whether to protect the life of a human being who had Down's syndrome, who would probably be mentally handicapped, but who needed a routine surgical procedure to unblock his esophagus and allow him to eat. A doctor testified to the presiding judge that, even with his physical problem corrected, Baby Doe would have a "nonexistent" possibility for "a minimally adequate quality of life"—in other words, that retardation was the equivalent of a crime deserving the death penalty. The judge let Baby Doe starve and die, and the Indiana Supreme Court sanctioned his decision.

Federal law does not allow federally assisted hospitals to decide that Down's syndrome infants are not worth treating, much less to decide to starve them to death. Accordingly, I have directed the Departments of Justice and HHS to apply civil rights regulations to protect handicapped newborns. All hospitals receiving federal funds must post notices which will clearly state that failure to feed handicapped babies is prohibited by federal law. The basic issue is whether to value and protect the lives of the handicapped, whether to recognize the sanctity of human life. This is the same basic issue that underlies the question of abortion.

The 1981 Senate hearings on the beginning of human life brought out the basic issue more clearly than ever before. The many medical and scientific witnesses who testified disagreed on many things, but not on the *scientific* evidence that the unborn child is alive, is a distinct individual, or is a member of the human species. They did disagree over the *value* question, whether to give value to a human life at its early and most vulnerable stages of existence.

Regrettably, we live at a time when some persons do *not* value all human life. They want to pick and choose which individuals have value. Some have said that only those individuals with "consciousness of self" are human beings. One such writer has followed this deadly logic and concluded that "shocking as it may seem, a newly born infant is not a human being."

A Nobel Prize–winning scientist has suggested that if a handicapped child "were not declared fully human until three days after birth, then all parents could be allowed the choice." In other words, "quality control" to see if newly born human beings are up to snuff.

Obviously, some influential people want to deny that every human life has intrinsic, sacred worth. They insist that a member of the human race must have certain qualities before they accord him or her status as a "human being."

Events have borne out the editorial in a California medical journal which explained three years before *Roe v. Wade* that the social acceptance of abortion is a "defiance of the long-held Western ethic of intrinsic and equal value for every human life regardless of its stage, condition, or status."

Every legislator, every doctor, and every citizen needs to recognize that the real issue is whether to affirm and protect the sanctity of all human life, or to embrace a social ethic where some human lives are valued and others are not. As a nation, we must choose between the sanctity of life ethic and the "quality of life" ethic.

I have no trouble identifying the answer our nation has always given to this basic question, and the answer that I hope and pray it will give in the future. America was founded by men and women who shared a vision of the value of each and every individual. They stated this vision clearly from the very start in the Declaration of Independence, using words that every schoolboy and schoolgirl can recite:

> *We hold these truths to be self-evident, that all men are created equal, that they are endowed by their Creator with certain unalienable rights, that among these are life, liberty, and the pursuit of happiness.*

We fought a terrible war to guarantee that one category of mankind—black people in America—could not be denied the unalienable rights with which their Creator endowed them. The great champion of the sanctity of all human life in that day, Abraham Lincoln, gave us his assessment of the Declaration's purpose. Speaking of the framers of that noble document, he said:

> *This was their majestic interpretation of the economy of the Universe. This was their lofty, and wise, and noble understanding of the justice of the Creator to His creatures. Yes, gentlemen, to all His creatures, to the whole great family of man. In their enlightened belief, nothing stamped with the divine image and likeness was sent into the world to be trodden on . . . They grasped not only the whole race of man then living, but they reached forward and seized upon the farthest posterity. They erected a beacon to guide their children and their children's children, and the countless myriads who should inhabit the earth in other ages.*

He warned also of the danger we would face if we closed our eyes to the value of life in any category of human beings:

> *I should like to know if taking this old Declaration of Independence, which declares that all men are equal upon principle and making exceptions to it where will it stop. If one man says it does not mean a Negro, why not another say it does not mean some other man?*

When Congressman John A. Bingham of Ohio drafted the Fourteenth Amendment to guarantee the rights of life, liberty, and property to all human beings, he explained that *all* are "entitled to the protection of American law, because its divine spirit of equality declares that all men are created equal.'' He said the rights guaranteed by the amendment would therefore apply to ''any human being.'' Justice William Brennan, writing in another case decided only the year before *Roe v. Wade,* referred to our society as one that ''strongly affirms the sanctity of life.''

Another William Brennan—not the justice—has reminded us of the terrible consequences that can follow when a nation rejects the sanctity of life ethic:

> *The cultural environment for a human holocaust is present when-ever any society can be misled into defining individuals as less than human and therefore devoid of value and respect.*

As a nation today, we have *not* rejected the sanctity of human life. The American people have not had an opportunity to express their view on the sanctity of human life in the unborn. I am convinced that Americans do not want to play God with the value of human life. It is not for us to decide who is worthy to live and who is not. Even the Supreme Court's opinion in *Roe v. Wade* did not explicitly reject the traditional American idea of intrinsic worth and value in all human life; it simply dodged this issue.

The Congress has before it several measures that would enable our people to reaffirm the sanctity of human life, even the smallest and the youngest and the most defenseless. The Human Life Bill expressly recognizes the unborn as human beings and accordingly protects them as persons under our Constitution. This bill, first introduced by Senator Jesse Helms, provided the vehicle for the Senate hearings in 1981 which contributed so much to our understanding of the real issue of abortion.

The Respect Human Life Act, just introduced in the 98th Congress, states in its first section that the policy of the United States is ''to protect innocent life, both before and after birth.'' This bill, sponsored by Congressman Henry Hyde and Senator Roger Jepsen, prohibits the federal government from performing abortions or assisting those who do so, except to save the life of the mother. It also addresses the pressing issue of infanticide which, as we have seen, flows inevitably from permissive abortion as another step in the denial of the inviola-bility of innocent human life.

I have endorsed each of these measures, as well as the more difficult route of constitutional amendment, and I will give these initiatives my full support. Each of them, in different ways, attempts to reverse the tragic policy of abortion on demand imposed by the Supreme Court 10 years ago. Each of them is a decisive way to affirm the sanctity of human life.

We must all educate ourselves to the reality of the horrors taking place. Doctors today know that unborn children can feel a touch within the womb and that they respond to pain. But how many Americans are aware that abortion techniques are allowed today, in all 50 states, that burn the skin of a baby with a salt solution, in an agonizing death that can last for hours?

Another example: Two years ago, the *Philadelphia Inquirer* ran a Sunday special supplement on ''The Dreaded Complication.'' The ''dreaded complica-tion'' referred to in the article—the complication feared by doctors who perform abortions—is the *survival* of the child despite all the painful attacks during the abortion procedure. Some unborn children *do* survive the late-term abortions the

Supreme Court has made legal. Is there any question that these victims of abortion deserve our attention and protection? Is there any question that those who *don't* survive were living human beings before they were killed?

Late-term abortions, especially when the baby survives, but is then killed by starvation, neglect, or suffocation, show once again the link between abortion and infanticide. The time to stop both is now. As my administration acts to stop infanticide, we will be fully aware of the real issue that underlies the death of babies before and soon after birth.

Our society has, fortunately, become sensitive to the rights and special needs of the handicapped, but I am shocked that physical or mental handicaps of newborns are still used to justify their extinction. This administration has a surgeon general, Dr. C. Everett Koop, who has done perhaps more than any other American for handicapped children, by pioneering surgical techniques to help them, by speaking out on the value of their lives, and by working with them in the context of loving families. You will not find his former patients advocating the so-called quality of life ethic.

I know that when the true issue of infanticide is placed before the American people, with all the facts openly aired, we will have no trouble deciding that a mentally or physically handicapped baby has the same intrinsic worth and right to life as the rest of us. As the New Jersey Supreme Court said two decades ago, in a decision upholding the sanctity of human life, "a child need not be perfect to have a worthwhile life."

Whether we are talking about pain suffered by unborn children, or about late-term abortions, or about infanticide, we inevitably focus on the humanity of the unborn child. Each of these issues is a potential rallying point for the sanctity of life ethic. Once we as a nation rally around any one of these issues to affirm the sanctity of life, we will see the importance of affirming this principle across the board.

Malcolm Muggeridge, the English writer, goes right to the heart of the matter: "Either life is always and in all circumstances sacred, or intrinsically of no account; it is inconceivable that it should be in some cases the one, and in some the other." The sanctity of innocent human life is a principle that Congress should proclaim at every opportunity.

It is possible that the Supreme Court itself may overturn its abortion rulings. We need only recall that in *Brown v. Board of Education* the court reversed its own earlier "separate-but-equal" decision. I believe if the Supreme Court took another look at *Roe v. Wade,* and considered the real issue between the sanctity of life ethic and the quality of life ethic, it would change its mind once again.

As we continue to work to overturn *Roe v. Wade,* we must also continue to lay the groundwork for a society in which abortion is not the accepted answer to unwanted pregnancy. Pro-life people have already taken heroic steps, often at great personal sacrifice, to provide for unwed mothers. I recently spoke about a young pregnant woman named Victoria, who said, "In this society we save whales, we save timber wolves and bald eagles and Coke bottles. Yet, everyone wanted me to throw away my baby." She has been helped by Sav-a-Life, a group in Dallas, which provides a way for unwed mothers to preserve the human life within them when they might otherwise be tempted to resort to abortion. I think also of House of His Creation in Coatesville, Pennsylvania, where a loving couple has taken in almost 200 young women in the past 10 years. They have seen, as a fact of life, that the girls are not better off having abortions than saving their babies. I am also reminded of the remarkable Rossow family of Ellington, Connecticut, who have opened their hearts and their home to nine handicapped adopted and foster children.

The Adolescent Family Life Program, adopted by Congress at the request of Senator Jeremiah Denton, has opened new opportunities for unwed mothers to give their children life. We should not rest until our entire society echoes the tone of John Powell in the dedication of his book, *Abortion: The Silent Holocaust,* a dedication to every woman carrying an unwanted child: "Please believe that you are not alone. There are many of us that truly love you, who want to stand at your side, and help in any way we can." And we can echo the always practical woman of faith, Mother Teresa, when she says, "If you don't want the little child, that unborn child, give him to me." We have so many families in America seeking to adopt children that the slogan "every child a wanted child" is now the emptiest of all reasons to tolerate abortion.

I have often said we need to join in prayer to bring protection to the unborn. Prayer and action are needed to uphold the sanctity of human life. I believe it will not be possible to acomplish our work, the work of saving lives, "without being a soul of prayer." The famous British member of Parliament, William Wilberforce, prayed with his small group of influential friends, the "Clapham Sect," for *decades* to see an end to slavery in the British empire. Wilberforce led that struggle in Parliament, unflaggingly, because he believed in the sanctity of human life. He saw the fulfillment of his impossible dream when Parliament outlawed slavery just before his death.

Let his faith and perseverance be our guide. We will never recognize the true value of our own lives until we affirm the value in the life of others, a value of which Malcolm Muggeridge says, "[H]owever low it flickers or fiercely burns, it is still a Divine flame which no man dare presume to put out, be his motives ever so humane and enlightened."

Abraham Lincoln recognized that we could not survive as a free land when some men could decide that others were not fit to be free and should therefore be slaves. Likewise, we cannot survive as a free nation when some men decide that others are not fit to live and should be abandoned to abortion or infanticide. My administration is dedicated to the preservation of America as a free land, and there is no cause more important for preserving that freedom than affirming the transcendent right to life of all human beings, the right without which no other rights have any meaning.

This article by John T. Noonan, Jr. has been widely read and certainly has shown its impact on the abortion issue. The subject of fetal pain has been debated in Congress and has been focused in recent ultrasonic movies of abortions. Further writings of Professor Noonan are presented in the appendix.

16 · The Experience of Pain by the Unborn _____

John T. Noonan, Jr.*

One aspect of the abortion question which has not been adequately investigated is the pain experienced by the object of an abortion. The subject has clearly little attraction for the pro-abortion party, whose interest lies in persuading the public that the unborn are not human and even in propagating the view that they are not alive. Indeed, in a remarkable judicial opinion, Judge Clement Haynsworth has written, "The Supreme Court declared the fetus in the womb is not alive . . ."[1] Judge Haynsworth's statement is merely a resolution of the oxymoron "potential life," which is the term chosen by the Supreme Court of the United States to characterize the unborn in the last two months of pregnancy.[2] Before that point, the unborn are referred to by the Court as alive only according to one "theory of life";[3] and as the phrase "potential life" appears to deny the actuality of life, Judge Haynsworth does not exaggerate in finding that, by definition of our highest court, the unborn are not alive. From this perspective, it is folly to explore the pain experienced. Does a stone feel pain? If you know as a matter of definition that the being who is aborted is not alive, you have in effect successfully bypassed any question of its suffering.

It is more difficult to say why the investigation has not been pursued in depth by those opposed to abortion. The basic reason, I believe, is the sense that the

* John T. Noonan, Jr., is a professor of law at the University of California (Berkeley); this article first appeared in the book *New Perspectives on Human Abortion,* published by Aletheia Books (University Publications of America, Inc., Frederick, Maryland © 1981 by John T. Noonan, Jr.). Copyright 1981, by the Human Life Foundation, 150 East 35th Street, New York, New York 10016. Reprinted with permission from the *Human Life Review.*

pain inflicted by an abortion is of secondary importance to the intolerable taking of life. The right to life, which is fundamental to the enjoyment of every other human right, has been the focus. That suffering may be experienced by those who are losing their lives has been taken for granted, but it has not been the subject of special inquiry or outrage. The assumption has been that if the killing is stopped, the pain attendant on it will stop too, and it has not seemed necessary to consider the question of pain by itself. In this respect, those opposed to abortion have been, like most medical researchers, concentrating on a cure not for the pain but for the disease.

There are good reasons, however, for looking at the question of pain by itself. We live in a society of highly developed humanitarian feeling, a society likely to respond to an appeal to empathy. To those concerned with the defense of life, it makes no difference whether the life taken is that of a person who is unconscious or drugged or drunk or in full possession of his senses; a life has been destroyed. But there are those who either will not respond to arguments about killing because they regard the unborn as a kind of abstraction, or who will not look at actual photographs of the aborted because they find the fact of death too strong to contemplate, but who nonetheless might respond to evidence of pain suffered in the process of abortion. In medical research it has proved useful to isolate pain as a phenomenon distinct from disease, so it may be useful here.[4]

I. The Analogy of Animals

The best indication that attention to the pain of the unborn may have social consequences is afforded by the example of humanitarian activity on behalf of animals. Let me offer three cases where substantial reform was effected by concentrating on the pain the animals experienced. In each case it was accepted that animals would die, whatever reform was enacted; an appeal on their behalf could not be based on an aversion to putting animals to death. The only forceful argument was that the way in which the animals were killed was cruel because it was painful to the animals.

The first case is that of trapping animals by gins—traps that spring shut on the animal, wound it, and hold it to die over a probably protracted period. A campaign was launched in England against this method of trapping in 1928, and after 30 years Parliament responded by banning such trapping.[5] A second case is the butchering of cattle for meat. The way in which this was for centuries carried out was painful to the animal being slaughtered. A typical modern statute is the law in California which became effective only in 1968—all cattle are to be rendered insensible by any means that is "rapid and effective" before being "cut, shackled, hoisted, thrown or cast." Or, if the animals are being slaughtered for kosher use, their consciousness must be destroyed by "the simultaneous and instantaneous severance of the carotid arteries with a sharp instrument."[6] A third case: A 1972 California statute regulates in detail the methods by which impounded dogs or cats may be killed. If carbon monoxide is used, the gas chamber must be lighted so that the animal's collapse can be monitored. A newborn dog or cat may not be killed other than by drugs, chloroform, or a decompression chamber. The use of nitrogen gas to kill an older dog or cat is regulated in terms of an oxygen reduction to be reached within 60 seconds.[7] Each of these laws has a single goal: to assure that the animal not suffer as it dies.

It may seem paradoxical, if not perverse, to defend the unborn by considering what has been done for animals. But the animal analogies are instructive on three counts: They show what can be done if empathy with suffering is awakened. They make possible an *a fortiori* case—if you will do this for an animal, why not for a child? And they exhibit a successful response to the most difficult question when the pain of a being without language is addressed—how do we know what is being experienced?

II. The Inference of Pain

Our normal way of knowing whether someone is in pain is for the person to use language affirming that he or she is suffering.[8] This behavior is taken as a sign, not necessarily infallible but usually accurate, that the person is in pain. By it we can not only detect the presence of pain but begin to measure its threshold, its intensity, and its tolerability. Infants, the unborn, and animals have no conceptual language in which to express their suffering and its degree.

Human infants and all animals brought up by parents will cry and scream.[9] Every human parent becomes adept at discriminating between a baby's cry of pain and a baby's cry of fatigue or of anxiety. How do we distinguish? By knowing that babies are human, by empathizing, by interpreting the context of the cry. We also proceed by trial and error: This cry will end if a pain is removed, this cry will end if the baby falls asleep. But animals, we know, are not human and are, in many significant ways, not like us. How do we interpret their cries or their wriggling as pain reactions if they are silent?

What we do with animals to be able to say that they are in pain is precisely what we do with the newborn and the infant: We empathize. We suppose for this purpose that animals are, in fact, "like us," and we interpret the context of the cry. We also proceed by trial and error, determining what stimuli need to be removed to end the animal's reaction.[10] We are not concerned with whether the animal's higher consciousness, its memory, and its ability to understand cause and to forecast results are different from our own, even though we know that for us the development of our consciousness, our memory, our understanding, and our sense of anticipation all may affect our experience of pain. With animals, we respond when we hear or see the physical sign we interpret as a symptom of distress.

Once we have made the leap that permits us to identify with animals, we do not need to dwell on the overt signs of physical distress. All we need is knowledge that an injury has been inflicted to understand that the animal will be in pain. Consider, by way of illustration, this passage on the cruelties of whaling: "A lacerated wound is inflicted with an explosive charge, and the whale, a highly sensitive mammal, then tows a 300-ton boat for a long time, a substantial fraction of an hour, by means of a harpoon pulling in the wound."[11] The author does not particularize any behavior of the wounded whale beyond its labor tugging the whaleboat, nor does he need to. We perceive the situation and the whale's agony. In a similar way the cruelty involved in hunting seals is shown by pointing to their being shot and left to die on the ice.[12] The pain of the dying seal is left to imaginative empathy.

We are, in our arguments about animal suffering and in our social response to them, willing to generalize from our own experience of pain and our knowledge of what causes pain to us. We know that pain requires a force inflicting bodily injury and that, for the ordinary sentient being who is not drugged or hypnotized, the presence of such a force will occasion pain. When we see such a force wounding any animal we are willing to say that the animal feels pain.

III. The Nature of Pain

If we pursue the question more deeply, however, we meet a question of a mixed philosophical-psychological character. What is pain? Pain has in the past been identified with "an unpleasant quality in the sense of touch." Pain has also been identified with "unpleasantness," understood as "the awareness of harm."[13] In the analysis of Thomas Aquinas, *dolor* requires the deprivation of a good together with perception of the deprivation. *Dolor* is categorized as interior *dolor,* which is consequent on something being apprehended by the imagination or by reason, and exterior *dolor,* which is consequent on something being apprehended by the senses and especially by the sense of touch.[14] The Thomistic definition of exterior *dolor,* while general, is not incongruent with a modern understanding of pain, which requires both harmful action on the body and perception of the action. It has been observed that pain also has a motivational component: Part of the pain response is avoidance of the cause of the pain.[15] In the words of Ronald Melzack, a modern pioneer in work on pain, "The complex sequences of behavior that characterize pain are determined by sensory, motivational, and cognitive processes that act on motor mechanisms."[16]

Pain, then, while it may be given a general definition, turns out upon investigation to consist of a series of specific responses involving different levels and kinds of activity in the human organism. Melzack has put forward a "gating theory" of pain, in which the key to these responses is the interaction between stimuli and inhibitory controls in the spinal column and in the brain which modulate the intensity and reception of the stimuli.[17] Melzack's theory requires the postulation of control centers, and it is not free from controversy.[18] Yet in main outline it persuasively explains a large number of pain phenomena in terms of stimuli and inhibitors.

To take one illustration at the level of common experience, if someone picks up a cup of hot liquid, his or her response may vary depending on whether the cup is paper or porcelain. The paper cup may be dropped to the ground; an equally hot porcelain cup may be jerkily set back on the table. What is often looked at as a simple reflex response to heat is modified by cognition.[19] To take a more gruesome experience, a number of soldiers severely wounded on the beach at Anzio told physicians in the field hospital that they felt no pain; they were overwhelmingly glad to be alive and off the beach. The same wounds inflicted on civilians would have been experienced as agonizing.[20] For a third example, childbirth without anesthesia is experienced as more or less painful depending on the cultural conditioning which surrounds it.[21]

As all of these examples suggest, both the culture and specific experiences play a part in the perception of pain. Memory, anticipation, and understanding of the cause all affect the perception. It is inferable that that brain is able to control and inhibit the pain response. In Melzack's hypothesis, the gating mechanism controlling the sensory inputs which are perceived as painful operates "at successive synapses at any level of the central nervous system in the course of filtering of the sensory input."[22] In this fundamental account, "[T]he presence or absence of pain is determined by the balance between the sensory and the central inputs to the gate control system."[23]

What is the nature of the sensory inputs? There are a larger number of sensory fibers which are receptors and transmitters, receiving and transmitting information about pressure, temperature, and chemical changes at the skin. These transmissions have both temporal and spatial patterns. It is these patterns which will be perceived as painful at certain levels of intensity and duration when the impulses are uninhibited by any modulation from the spinal column or brain.[24]

IV. The Experience of the Unborn

For the unborn to experience pain there must be sense receptors capable of receiving information about pressure, temperature, and cutaneous chemical change; the sense receptors must also be capable of transmitting that information to cells able to apprehend it and respond to it.

By what point do such receptors exist? To answer this question, the observation of physical development must be combined with the observation of physical behavior. As early as the 56th day of gestation, the child has been observed to move in the womb.[25] In Liley's hypothesis, "[T]he development of structure and the development of function go hand in hand. Fetal comfort determines fetal position, and fetal movement is necessary for a proper development of fetal bones and joints."[26] If fetal bones and joints are beginning to develop this early, movement is necessary to the structural growth; and if Liley is correct, the occasion of movement is discomfort or pain. Hence, there would be some pain receptors present before the end of the second month. A physiologist places about the same point—day 59 or 60—the observation of "spinal reflexes" in the child. Tactile stimulation of the mouth produces a reflex action, and sensory receptors are present in the simple nerve endings of the mouth.[27] Somewhere between day 60 and day 77 sensitivity to touch develops in the genital and anal areas.[28] In the same period, the child begins to swallow. The rate of swallowing will vary with the sweetness of the injection.[29] By day 77 both the palms of the hands and the soles of the feet will also respond to touch; by the same day, eyelids have been observed to squint to close out light.[30]

A standard treatise on human physiological development puts between day 90 and day 120 the beginning of differentiation of "the general sense organs," described as "free nerve terminations (responding to pain, temperature, and common chemicals), lamellated corpuscles (responding to deep pressure), tactile corpuscles, neuromuscular spindles, and neurotendinous end organs (responding to light and deep pressure)."[31] But as responses to touch, pressure, and light precede this period, visible differentiation must be preceded by a period in which these "general sense organs" are functioning.

The cerebral cortex is not developed at this early stage; even at 12 to 16 weeks it is only 30 percent to 40 percent developed.[32] It is consequently a fair conclusion that the cognitive input into any pain reaction will be low in these early months. Neither memory nor anticipation of results can be expected to affect what is experienced. The unborn at this stage will be like certain Scotch terriers, raised in isolation for experimental purposes, who had no motivational pain responses when their noses encountered lighted matches; they were unaware of noxious signals in their environment.[33] But if both sensory receptors and spinal column are involved, may one say with assurance that the reception of strong sense impressions causes no pain? It would seem clear that the reactions of the unborn to stimuli like light and pressure are the motivational responses we associate with pain. We say that a sense receptor is there because there is a response to touch and a taste receptor because there is a response to taste. By the same token we are able to say that pain receptors are present when evasive action follows the intrusion of pressure or light, or when injection of a disagreeable fluid lowers the rate of swallowing. Liley is categorical in affirming that the unborn feel pain.[34] His conclusion has recently been confirmed by an American researcher, Mortimer Rosen, who believes the unborn respond to touch, taste, and pain.[35]

While the likelihood of weak participation by the cerebral cortex will work against the magnification of the pain, there will also be an absence of the inhibitory input from the brain which modulates and balances the sensory input in more developed beings. Consequently, the possibility exists of smaller and weaker sensory inputs having the same effect which later is achieved only by larger and stronger sensations.

As the sensory apparatus continues to grow, so does the cerebral cortex: Light stimuli can evoke electrical response in the cerebral cortex between the sixth and seventh months.[36] By this time there will be a substantial cerebral participation in pain perception, together with the likelihood of greater brain control of the sensory input. If a child is delivered from the womb at this date, he or she may shed tears. He or she will cry.[37] As we do with other newborns, we interpret these signs in terms of their context and may find them to be signs of pain. What we conclude about the delivered child can with equal force be concluded about the child still in the womb in months six through nine: That unborn child has developed capacity for pain.

In summary, beginning with the presence of sense receptors and spinal responses, there is as much reason to believe that the unborn are capable of pain as that they are capable of sensation. The ability to feel pain grows together with the development of inhibitors capable of modulating the pain. By the sixth month, the child in the womb has a capacity for feeling and expressing pain comparable to the capacity of the same child delivered from the womb. The observation sometimes made that we don't remember prenatal pains applies with equal force to the pains of being born or the pain of early infancy. Memory, it must be supposed, suppresses much more than it recalls. If we remember nothing about life before birth or life before three or four, it may even be that some recollections are painful enough to invoke the suppressive function of our memory; life in the womb is not entirely comfortable.

V. The Experience of Pain in an Abortion

The principle modern means of abortion are these. In early pregnancy sharp curettage is practiced: A knife is used to kill the unborn child.[38] Alternatively, suction curettage is employed: a vacuum pump sucks up the unborn child by bits and pieces, and a knife detaches the remaining parts.[39] In the second trimester of pregnancy and later, a hypertonic saline solution is injected into the amniotic fluid surrounding the fetus. The salt appears to act as a poison;[40] the skin of the affected child appears, on delivery, to have been soaked in acid.[41] Alternatively, prostaglandins are given to the mother; in sufficient dosage they will constrict the circulation and impair the cardiac functioning of the fetus.[42] The child may be delivered dead or die after delivery.[43]

Are these experiences painful? The application of a sharp knife to the skin and the destruction of vital tissue cannot but be a painful experience for any sentient creature. It lasts for about 10 minutes.[44] Being subjected to a vacuum is painful, as is dismemberment by suction. The time from the creation of the vacuum to the chief destruction of the child again is about 10 minutes.[45] Hypertonic saline solution causes what is described as "exquisite and severe pain" if, by accident during an abortion, it enters subcutaneously the body of the woman having the abortion.[46] It is inferable that the unborn would have an analogous experience lasting some two hours, as the saline solution takes about this long to work before the fetal heart stops.[47] The impact of prostaglandins constricting the circulation of the blood or impairing the heart must be analogous to that when these phenomena occur in born children: They are not pleasant. If, as has been known to happen, a child survives saline or prostaglandin poisoning and is born alive, the child will be functioning with diminished capacity in such vital functions as breathing and cardiac action.[48] Such impaired functioning is ordinarily experienced as painful.

Do the anesthetics the mother has received lessen the pain of the child? It is entirely possible that some drugs will cross the placenta and enter the child's system, causing drowsiness. Anesthesia, however, is not administered to the gravida with the welfare of her child in mind, nor do the anesthetics ordinarily used prevent the mother from serious pain if she is accidentally affected by the saline solution. It may be inferred the child is not protected either. Is it possible that the abortifacient agent destroys the pain receptors and the capability of a pain response earlier than it ends the life of the unborn, so that there is a period of unconsciousness in which pain is not experienced? This is possible in curettage by knife or suction, but it would seem to occur haphazardly, since stunning the child is not the conscious aim of the physician performing the abortion. In saline or prostaglandin poisoning it seems unlikely that the pain apparatus is quickly destroyed. An observation of Melzack is of particular pertinence: The local injection of hypertonic saline opens the spinal gate, he has remarked, and evokes severe pain. At the same time, it raises the level of the inhibitors and closes the gate to subsequent injections.[49] From this it may be inferred that an unborn child subjected to repeated attempts at abortion by saline solution—the baby in the *Edelin* case was such a child[50]—suffers a good deal the first time and much less on the second and third efforts. The general observation of Melzack on the mechanism of pain is also worth recalling: Any lesion which impairs the tonic inhibitory influence from the brain opens the gate, with a consequent increase in pain.[51] Any method of abortion which results first in damage to the cortex may have the initial effect of increasing the pain sensations.

From the review of the methods used, we may conclude that as soon as a pain mechanism is present in the fetus—possibly as early as day 56—the methods used will cause pain. The pain is more substantial and lasts longer the later the abortion is. It is most severe and lasts the longest when the method is saline poisoning.

Whatever the method used, the unborn are experiencing the greatest of bodily evils, the ending of their lives.[52] They are undergoing the death agony. However inarticulate, however slight their cognitive powers, however rudimentary their sensations, they are sentient creatures undergoing the disintegration of their being and the termination of their vital capabilities. That experience is painful in itself. That is why an observer like Magda Denes, looking at the body of an aborted child, can remark that the face of the child has "the agonized tautness of one forced to die too soon."[53] The agony is universal.

VI. Conclusion

There are no laws which regulate the suffering of the aborted like those sparing pain to dying animals. There is nothing like the requirement that consciousness must be destroyed by "rapid and effective" methods as it is for cattle; nothing regulating the use of the vacuum pump the way the decompression chamber for dogs is regulated; nothing like the safeguard extended even to newborn kittens that only a humane mode of death may be employed. So absolute has been the liberty given the gravida by the Supreme Court that even the prohibition of the saline method by a state has been held to violate the Constitution.[54] The Supreme Court has acted as though it believed that its own fiat could alter reality and as if the human fetus is not alive.

Can human beings who understand what may be done for animals and what cannot be done for unborn humans want this inequality of treatment to continue? We are not bound to animals to the same degree as we are bound to human beings because we lack a common destiny, but we are bound to animals as fellow creatures, and as God loves them out of charity, so must we who are called to imitate God.[55] It is a sign not of error or weakness but of Christlike compassion to love animals. Can those who feel for the harpooned whale not be touched by the situation of the saltsoaked baby? We should not despair of urging further the consciences of those who have curtailed their convenience to spare suffering to other sentient creatures.

With keener sensibilities and more developed inhibitors than animals, we are able to empathize with their pain. By the same token, we are able to empathize with the aborted. We can comprehend what they must undergo. All of our knowledge of pain is by empathy: we do not feel another's pain directly. That is why the pain of others is so tolerable for us. But if we begin to empathize, we may begin to feel what is intolerable.

We are bound to the beings in the human womb by the common experience of pain we have also known in the womb. We are bound to them as well by a common destiny, to share eternal life. As fellow wayfarers, we are bound to try to save them from a premature departure. We can begin to save them by communicating our knowledge of the suffering they must experience.

NOTES

1. Floyd v. Anders, 440 F. Supp. 535, 539 (D.S.C. 1977).
2. Roe v. Wade, 410 U.S. 113, 162 (1973).
3. *Id.* at 163.
4. On the usefulness of looking at pain as a separate phenomenon, *see* R. Melzack, The Puzzle of Pain, (1973), at 9–10.
5. C. W. Hume, Man and Beast (1962), at 214.
6. Cal. Agric. Code § 19 (1967).
7. Cal. Penal Code §§ 597 v. and w. (1978).
8. J. S. Liebeskind & L. A. Paul, *Psychological and Physiological Mechanisms of Pain,* 28 American Review of Psychology 42 (1977).
9. As to parentally cared-for animals, *see* Hume, *supra* note 5, at 45.
10. *Id.* at 94–95.
11. *Id.* at 215.
12. *Id.* at 215–216.
13. E. Boring, Pain Sensations and Reactions (1952), at v–vi.
14. Thomas Aquinas, Summa Theologica, I-II, q. 35, art. 7.
15. Melzack, *supra* note 4, at 163.
16. *Id.* at 165.
17. *Id.* at 158–66.
18. *See* Liebeskind & Paul, *supra* note 8, at 47.
19. *Cf.* Melzack, 29–31.
20. *Id.* at 29–30.
21. *Id.* at 22.
22. *Id.* at 166.
23. *Id.* at 171.
24. *Id.* at 158.
25. A. W. Liley, *The Foetus as Personality,* 6 Australia & New Zealand J. of Psychiat. 99 (1972).
26. A. W. Liley, *Experiments With Uterine and Fetal Instrumentation,* in Intrauterine Fetal Visualization, 75 (M. Kuback & C. Valenti, eds. 1976).
27. P. S. Timiras, Developmental Physiology and Aging (1972), at 153.
28. *Id.*
29. Liley, *supra* note 25, at 102.
30. T. Humphrey, *The Development of Human Fetal Activity and Its Relation to Postnatal Behavior,* in Advances in Child Development and Behavior, (H. W. Reese & L. P. Lipsitt, eds. 1973), at 12, 19.
31. Timiras, *supra* note 27, at 137.
32. G. S. Dawes, Fetal and Neonatal Physiology (1968), at 126.
33. Melzack, *supra* note 4, at 28.
34. Liley, *supra* note 26.
35. M. Rosen, *The Secret Brain: Learning Before Birth,* Harper's, 46 (April 1978).
36. Timiras *supra* note 27, at 149.
37. P. Mussen, J. Congar, & J. Kagan, Child Development and Personality (2nd ed. 1963), at 65.

38. L. M. Hellman & J. A. Pritchard, eds., Williams Obstetrics (14th ed. 1971), at 1089.
39. S. Neubardt & H. Schwelman, Techniques of Abortion (1972), at 46–47.
40. *Id*. at 68.
41. M. Denes, In Necessity and Sorrow: Life and Death in an Abortion Hospital (1976), at 27.
42. Sultan M. M. Karim, Prostaglandins and Reproduction (1975), at 107.
43. *See* Floyd v. Anders, 440 F. supp. 535 (D.S.C. 1977), for a case where the child died after delivery.
44. A. Hellegers, director of the Joseph and Rose Kennedy Institute, to the author, oral communication.
45. Id.
46. Neubardt & Schwelman, *supra* note 39, at 68.
47. Karim, *supra* note 42, at 107.
48. *See* A. I. Csapo et al. *Termination of Pregnancy With Double Prostaglandin Input,* 124 Am. J. of Obstet. & Gynecol. 1 (1976).
49. Melzack, *supra* note 4, at 181–182.
50. Commonwealth v. Edelin, 359 (N.E.2d) 4 (1976).
51. Melzack, *supra* note 4, at 171.
52. Thomas Aquinas, Summa contra Gentiles 4, 52.
53. Denes, *supra* note 41, at 60.
54. Planned Parenthood of Central Missouri v. Danforth, 428 U.S. 52 (1976).
55. Thomas Aquinas, Summa Theologica, II-II, q. 25, art. 3, reply to objection 3.

APPENDICES

It has been more than a decade since the Supreme Court heard the Wade case, yet the controversy surrounding the decision remains. Some say that the decision was wrong while others say the decision may be correct, but the Court's reasoning was in error. It should not be forgotten that many support both the result (legalized abortion) and the reasoning (right to privacy). The *Roe* case and its companion *Doe* case are presented here because of the omnipresent litigation challenging or clarifying these 1973 decisions.

Appendix 1

DECISIONS OF THE UNITED STATES SUPREME COURT IN JANUARY 1973 WITH RESPECT TO THE TEXAS AND GEORGIA ABORTION STATUTES

On January 22, 1973, the United States Supreme Court handed down its long-awaited rulings with respect to the constitutionality of the criminal abortion laws in Texas and Georgia. As a result of these two landmark decisions, not only the Texas and Georgia abortion statutes but those of several dozen additional states were overturned, and some form of revision of the abortion laws was mandated in almost every other state. The Court's decision in each case was 7–2, with Justice Blackmun (joined by Justices Burger, Douglas, Brennan, Stewart, Marshall, and Powell) delivering the opinion of the Court and Justices White and Rehnquist dissenting. The following is a transcript of the Supreme Court's rulings in the Texas and Georgia cases.

No. 70–18

Jane Roe et al., Appellants, *v.* Henry Wade.	}	On Appeal from the United States District Court for the Northern District of Texas.

[January 22, 1973]

SYLLABUS

A PREGNANT SINGLE WOMAN (Roe) brought a class action challenging the constitutionality of the Texas criminal abortion laws, which proscribe procuring or attempting an abortion except on medical advice for the purpose of saving the mother's life. A licensed physician (Hallford), who had two state abortion prosecutions pending against him, was permitted to intervene. A childless married couple (the Does), the wife not being pregnant, separately attacked the laws, basing alleged injury on the future possibilities of contraceptive failure, pregnancy, unpreparedness for parenthood, and impairment of the wife's health. A three-judge District Court, which consolidated the actions, held that Roe and Hallford, and members of their classes, had standing to sue and presented justiciable controversies. Ruling that declaratory, though not injunctive, relief was warranted, the court declared the abortion statutes void as vague and overbroadly infringing those plaintiffs' Ninth and Fourteenth Amendment rights. The court ruled the Does' complaint not justiciable. Appellants directly appealed to this Court on the injunctive rulings, and appellee cross-appealed from the District Court's grant of declaratory relief to Roe and Hallford. *Held:*

1. While 28 U.S.C. § 1253 authorizes no direct appeal to this Court from the grant or denial of declaratory relief alone, review is not foreclosed when the case is properly before the Court on appeal from specific denial of injunctive relief and the arguments as to both injunctive and declaratory relief are necessarily identical.

2. Roe has standing to sue; the Does and Hallford do not.

(a) Contrary to appellee's contention, the natural termination of Roe's pregnancy did not moot her suit. Litigation involving pregnancy, which is "capable of repetition, yet evading review," is an exception to the usual federal rule that an actual controversy must exist at review stages and not simply when the action is initiated.

(b) The District Court correctly refused injunctive, but erred in granting declaratory, relief to Hallford, who alleged no federally protected right not assertable as a defense against the good-faith state prosecutions pending against him. *Samuels v. Mackell*, 401 U.S. 66.

(c) The Does' complaint, based as it is on contingencies, any one or more of which may not occur, is too speculative to present an actual case or controversy.

3. State criminal abortion laws, like those involved here, that except from criminality only a life-saving procedure on the mother's behalf without regard to the stage of her pregnancy and other interests involved violate the Due Process Clause of the Fourteenth Amendment, which protects against state action the right to privacy, including a woman's qualified right to terminate her pregnancy. Though the State cannot override that right, it has legitimate interests in protecting both the pregnant woman's health and the potentiality of human life, each of which interests grows and reaches a "compelling" point at various stages of the woman's approach to term.

(a) For the stage prior to approximately the end of the first trimester, the abortion decision and its effectuation must be left to the medical judgment of the pregnant woman's attending physician.

(b) For the stage subsequent to approximately the end of the first trimester, the State, in promoting its interest in the health of the mother, may, if it chooses, regulate the abortion procedure in ways that are reasonably related to maternal health.

(c) For the stage subsequent to viability the State, in promoting its interest in the potentiality of human life, may, if it chooses, regulate, and even proscribe, abortion except where necessary, in appropriate medical judgment, for the preservation of the life or health of the mother.

4. The State may define the term "physician" to mean only a physician currently licensed by the State, and may proscribe any abortion by a person who is not a physician as so defined.

5. It is unnecessary to decide the injunctive relief issue since the Texas authorities will doubtless fully recognize the Court's ruling that the Texas criminal abortion statutes are unconstitutional. 314 F. Supp. 1217, affirmed in part and reversed in part.

BLACKMUN, J., delivered the opinion of the Court, in which BURGER, C. J., and DOUGLAS, BRENNAN, STEWART, MARSHALL, and POWELL, JJ., joined. BURGER, C. J., and DOUGLAS and STEWART, JJ., filed concurring opinions. WHITE, J., filed a dissenting opinion, in which REHNQUIST, J., joined. REHNQUIST, J., filed a dissenting opinion.

MR. JUSTICE BLACKMUN delivered the opinion of the Court.

This Texas federal appeal and its Georgia companion, *Doe v. Bolton, post* ——, present constitutional challenges to state criminal abortion legislation. The Texas statutes under attack here are typical of those that have been in effect in many States for approximately a century. The Georgia statutes, in contrast, have a modern cast and are a legislative product that, to an extent at least, obviously reflects the influences of recent attitudinal change, of advancing medical knowledge and techniques, and of new thinking about an old issue.

We forthwith acknowledge our awareness of the sensitive and emotional nature of the abortion controversy, of the vigorous opposing views, even among physicians, and of the deep and seemingly absolute convictions that the subject inspires. One's philosophy, one's experiences, one's exposure to the raw edges of human existence, one's religious training, one's attitudes toward life and family and their values, and the moral standards one establishes and seeks to observe, are all likely to influence and to color one's thinking and conclusions about abortion.

In addition, population growth, pollution, poverty, and racial overtones tend to complicate and not to simplify the problem.

Our task, of course, is to resolve the issue by constitutional measurement free of emotion and of predilection. We seek earnestly to do this, and, because we do, we have inquired into, and in this opinion place some emphasis upon, medical and medical-legal history and what that history reveals about man's attitudes toward the abortive procedure over the centuries. We bear in mind, too, Mr. Justice Holmes' admonition in his now vindicated dissent in *Lochner v. New York*, 198 U.S. 45, 76 (1905):

> *It [the Constitution] is made for people of fundamentally differing views, and the accident of our finding certain opinions natural and familiar or novel and even shocking ought not to conclude our judgment upon the question whether statutes embodying them conflict with the Constitution of the United States.*

I

The Texas statutes that concern us here are Arts. 1191-1194 and 1196 of the State's Penal Code.[1] These make it a crime to "procure an abortion," as therein defined, or to attempt one, except with respect to "an abortion procured or attempted by medical advice for the purpose of saving the life of the mother." Similar statutes are in existence in a majority of the States.[2]

[1] "Article 1191. Abortion

"If any person shall designedly administer to a pregnant woman or knowingly procure to be administered with her consent any drug or medicine, or shall use towards her any violence or means whatever externally or internally applied, and thereby procure an abortion, he shall be confined to the penitentiary not less than two nor more than five years; if it be done without her consent, the punishment shall be doubled. By 'abortion' is meant that the life of the fetus or embryo shall be destroyed in the woman's womb or that a premature birth thereof be caused.

"Art. 192. Furnishing the means

"Whoever furnishes the means for procuring an abortion knowing the purpose intended is guilty as an accomplice.

"Art. 1193. Attempt at abortion

"If the means used shall fail to produce an abortion, the offender is nevertheless guilty of an attempt to produce abortion, provided it be shown that such means were calculated to produce that result, and shall be fined not less than one hundred nor more than one thousand dollars.

"Art. 1194. Murder in producing abortion

"If the death of the mother is occasioned by an abortion so produced or by an attempt to effect the same it is murder.

"Art. 1196. By medical advice

"Nothing in this chapter applies to an abortion procured or attempted by medical advice for the purpose of saving the life of the mother."

The foregoing Articles, together with Art. 1195, comprise Chapter 9 of Title 15 of the Penal Code. Article 1195, not attacked here, reads:

"Art. 1195. Destroying unborn child

"Whoever shall during parturition of the mother destroy the vitality or life in a child in a state of being born and before actual birth, which child would otherwise have been alive, shall be confined in the penitentiary for life or for not less than five years."

[2] Ariz. Rev. Stat. Ann. § 13-211 (1971); Conn. Pub. Act. No. 1 (May 1972 special session) (in 4 Conn. Leg. Serv. 677 (1972)), and Conn. Gen. Stat. Rev. §§ 53-29, 53-30 (1968) (or unborn child); Idaho Code § 18-1505 (App. to Supp. 1971); Ill. Rev. Stats. c. 38, § 23-1 (1971); Ind. Code § 35-1-58-1 (1971); Iowa Code § 701.1 (1971); Ky. Rev. Stat. § 436.020 (1963); La. Rev. Stat. § 37:1285 (6) (1964) (loss of medical license) (but see § 14-87 (1972 Supp.) containing no exception for the life of the mother under the criminal statute); Me. Rev. Stat. Ann. Tit. 17, § 51 (1964); Mass. Gen. Laws Ann. c. 272, § 19 (1970) (using the term "unlawfully," construed to exclude an abortion to save the mother's life, *Kudish v. Bd. of Registration*, 356 Mass. 98, 248 N. E. 2d 264 (1969)); Mich. Comp. Laws § 750.14 (1948); Minn. Stat. § 617.18 (1971); Mo. Rev. Stat. § 559.100 (1969); Mont. Rev. Codes Ann. § 94-401 (1961); Neb. Rev. Stat. § 28-405 (1964); Nev. Rev. Stat. § 200:220 (1967); N. H. Rev. Stat. Ann. § 585.13 (1955); N. J. Stat. Ann. § 2A:87-1 (1969) ("without lawful justification"); N. D. Cent. Code §§ 12-25-02 (1960); Ohio Rev. code § 2901.16 (1953); Okla. Stat. Ann., Tit. 21, § 861 (1972-1973 Supp.); Pa. Stat. Ann., Tit. 18, §§ 4718, 4719 (1963) ("unlawful"); R. I. Gen. Laws Ann. § 11-3-1 (1969); S. D. Compiled Laws § 22-17-1 (1967); Tenn. Code Ann. §§ 39-301, 39-302 (1956); Utah Code Ann. §§ 76-2-1, 76-2-2 (1953); Vt. Stat. Ann., Tit. 13, § 101 (1958); W. Va. Code Ann. § 61-2-8 (1966); Wis. Stat. § 940.04 (1969); Wyo. Stat. Ann. §§ 6-77, 6-78 (1957).

Texas first enacted a criminal abortion statute in 1854. Texas Laws 1854, c. 49, § 1, set forth in 3 Gammel, Laws of Texas, 1502 (1898). This was soon modified into language that has remained substantially unchanged to the present time. See Texas Penal Code of 1857, Arts. 531-536; Paschal's Laws of Texas, Arts. 2192-2197 (1866); Texas Rev. Stat., Arts. 536-541 (1879); Texas Rev. Crim. Stat., Arts. 1071-1076 (1911). The final article in each of these compilations provided the same exception, as does the present Article 1196, for an abortion by "medical advice for the purpose of saving the life of the mother."[3]

II

Jane Roe,[4] a single woman who was residing in Dallas County, Texas, instituted this federal action in March 1970 against the District Attorney of the county. She sought a declaratory judgment that the Texas criminal abortion statutes were unconstitutional on their face, and an injunction restraining the defendant from enforcing the statutes.

Roe alleged that she was unmarried and pregnant; that she wished to terminate her pregnancy by an abortion "performed by a competent, licensed physician, under safe, clinical conditions"; that she was unable to get a "legal" abortion in Texas because her life did not appear to be threatened by the continuation of her pregnancy; and that she could not afford to travel to another jurisdiction in order to secure a legal abortion under safe conditions. She claimed that the Texas statutes were unconstitutionally vague and that they abridged her right of personal privacy, protected by the First, Fourth, Fifth, Ninth, and Fourteenth Amendments. By an amendment to her complaint Roe purported to sue "on behalf of herself and all other women" similarly situated.

James Hubert Hallford, a licensed physician, sought and was granted leave to intervene in Roe's action. In his complaint he alleged that he had been arrested previously for violations of the Texas abortion statutes and that two such prosecutions were pending against him. He described conditions of patients who

---

[3] Long ago a suggestion was made that the Texas statutes were unconstitutionally vague because of definitional deficiencies. The Texas Court of Criminal Appeals disposed of that suggestion peremptorily, saying only,

"It is also insisted in the motion in arrest of judgment that the statute is unconstitutional and void in that it does not sufficiently define or describe the offense of abortion. We do not concur in respect to this question." *Jackson* v. *State*, 55 Tex. Crim. R. 79, 89, 115 S. W. 262, 268 (1908).

The same court recently has held again that the State's abortion statutes are not unconstitutionally vague or overbroad. *Thompson* v. *State*, ―――― Tex. Crim. App. ――――, ―――― S. W. 2d ―――― (1971), appeal pending. The court held that "the State of Texas has a compelling interest to protect fetal life"; that Art. 1191 "is designed to protect fetal life"; that the Texas homicide statutes, particularly Art. 1205 of the Penal Code, are intended to protect a person "in existence by actual birth" and thereby implicitly recognize other human life that is not "in existence by actual birth"; that the definition of human life is for the legislature and not the courts; that Art. 1196 "is more definite than the District of Columbia statute upheld in [*United States* v.] *Vuitch*" (402 U. S. 62); and that the Texas statute is not vague and indefinite or overbroad." A physician's abortion conviction was affirmed.

In n. 2, ―――― Tex. Crim. App., at ――――, ―――― S. W. 2d at ――――, the court observed that any issue as to the burden of proof under the exemption of Art. 1196 "is not before us." But see *Veevers* v. *State*, 172 Tex. Crim. App. 162, 168-169, 354 S. W. 2d 161 (1962). Cf. *United States* v. *Vuitch*, 402 U. S. 62, 69-71 (1971).

[4] The name is a pseudonym.

came to him seeking abortions, and he claimed that for many cases he, as a physician, was unable to determine whether they fell within or outside the exception recognized by Article 1196. He alleged that, as a consequence, the statutes were vague and uncertain, in violation of the Fourteenth Amendment, and that they violated his own and his patients' rights to privacy in the doctor-patient relationship and his own right to practice medicine, rights he claimed were guaranteed by the First, Fourth, Fifth, Ninth, and Fourteenth Amendments.

John and Mary Doe,[5] a married couple, filed a companion complaint to that of Roe. They also named the District Attorney as defendant, claimed like constitutional deprivations, and sought declaratory and injunctive relief. The Does alleged that they were a childless couple; that Mrs. Doe was suffering from a "neuralchemical" disorder; that her physician had "advised her to avoid pregnancy until such time as her condition has materially improved" (although a pregnancy at the present time would not present "a serious risk" to her life); that, pursuant to medical advice, she had discontinued use of birth control pills; and that if she should become pregnant, she would want to terminate the pregnancy by an abortion performed by a competent, licensed physician under safe, clinical conditions. By an amendment to their complaint, the Does purported to sue "on behalf of themselves and all couples similarly situated."

The two actions were consolidated and heard together by a duly convened three-judge district court. The suits thus presented the situations of the pregnant single woman, the childless couple, with the wife not pregnant, and the licensed practicing physician, all joining in the attack on the Texas criminal abortion statutes. Upon the filing of affidavits, motions were made to dismiss and for summary judgment. The court held that Roe and Dr. Hallford, and members of their respective classes, had standing to sue, and presented justiciable controversies, but that the Does had failed to allege facts sufficient to state a present controversy and did not have standing. It concluded that, with respect to the requests for a declaratory judgment, abstention was not warranted. On the merits, the District Court held that the "fundamental right of single women and married persons to choose whether to have children is protected by the Ninth Amendment, through the Fourteenth Amendment," and that the Texas criminal abortion statutes were void on their face because they were both unconstitutionally vague and constituted an overbroad infringement of the plaintiffs' Ninth Amendment rights. The court then held that abstention was warranted with respect to the requests for an injunction. It therefore dismissed the Doe complaint, declared the abortion statutes void, and dismissed the application for injunctive relief. 314 F. Supp. 1217 (ND Tex. 1970).

The plaintiffs Roe and Doe and the intervenor Hallford, pursuant to 28 U.S.C. § 1253, have appealed to this Court from that part of the District Court's judgment denying the injunction. The defendant District Attorney has purported to cross appeal, pursuant to the same statute, from the court's grant of declaratory relief to Roe and Hallford. Both sides also have taken protective appeals to the United States Court of Appeals for the Fifth Circuit. That court ordered the

---

[5] These names are pseudonyms.

appeals held in abeyance pending decision here. We postponed decision on jurisdiction to the hearing on the merits. 402 U.S. 941 (1971).

III

It might have been preferable if the defendant, pursuant to our Rule 20, had presented to us a petition for certiorari before judgment in the Court of Appeals with respect to the granting of the plaintiffs' prayer for declaratory relief. Our decisions in *Mitchell v. Donovan*, 398 U.S. 427 (1970), and *Gunn v. University Committee*, 399 U.S. 383 (1970), are to the effect that § 1253 does not authorize an appeal to this Court from the grant or denial of declaratory relief alone. We conclude, nevertheless, that those decisions do not foreclose our review of both the injunctive and the declaratory aspects of a case of this kind when it is properly here, as this one is, on appeal under § 1253 from specific denial of injunctive relief, and the arguments as to both aspects are necessarily identical. See *Carter v. Jury Commission*, 396 U.S. 320 (1970); *Florida Lime and Avocado Growers, Inc. v. Jacobsen*, 362 U.S. 73, 80-81 (1960). It would be destructive of time and energy for all concerned were we to rule otherwise. Cf. *Doe v. Bolton, post,* ———.

IV

We are next confronted with issues of justiciability, standing, and abstention. Have Roe and the Does established that "personal stake in the outcome of the controversy," *Baker v. Carr*, 369 U.S. 186, 204 (1962), that insures that "the dispute sought to be adjudicated will be presented in an adversary context and in a form historically viewed as capable of judicial resolution," *Flast v. Cohen*, 392 U.S. 83, 101 (1968), and *Sierra Club v. Morton*, 405 U.S. 727, 732 (1972)? And what effect did the pendency of criminal abortion charges against Dr. Hallford in state court have upon the propriety of the federal court's granting relief to him as a plaintiff-intervenor?

A. *Jane Roe.* Despite the use of the pseudonym, no suggestion is made that Roe is a fictitious person. For purposes of her case, we accept as true, and as established, her existence; her pregnant state, as of the inception of her suit in March 1970 and as late as May 21 of that year when she filed an alias affidavit with the District Court; and her inability to obtain a legal abortion in Texas.

Viewing Roe's case as of the time of its filing and thereafter until as late as May, there can be little dispute that it then presented a case or controversy and that, wholly apart from the class aspects, she, as a pregnant single woman thwarted by the Texas criminal abortion laws, had standing to challenge those statutes. *Abele v. Markle*, 452 F. 2d 1121, 1125 (CA2 1971); *Crossen v. Breckenridge*, 446 F. 2d 833, 838-839 (CA6 1971); *Poe v. Menghini*, 339 F. Supp. 986, 990-991 (Kans. 1972). See *Truax v. Raich*, 239 U.S. 33 (1915). Indeed, we do not read the appellee's brief as really asserting anything to the contrary. The "logical nexus between the status asserted and the claim sought to be adjudicated," *Flast v. Cohen*, 392 U.S., at 102, and the necessary degree of contentiousness, *Golden v. Zwickler*, 394 U.S. 103 (1969), are both present.

The appellee notes, however, that the record does not disclose that Roe was pregnant at the time of the District Court hearing on May 22, 1970,[6] or on the following June 17 when the court's opinion and judgment were filed. And he suggests that Roe's case must now be moot because she and all other members of her class are no longer subject to any 1970 pregnancy.

The usual rule in federal cases is that an actual controversy must exist at stages of appellate or certiorari review, and not simply at the date the action is initiated. *United States v. Munsingwear, Inc.*, 340 U.S. 36 (1950); *Golden v. Zwickler, supra*; *SEC v. Medical Committee for Human Rights*, 404 U.S. 403 (1972).

But when, as here, pregnancy is a significant fact in the litigation, the normal 266-day human gestation period is so short that the pregnancy will come to term before the usual appellate process is complete. If that termination makes a case moot, pregnancy litigation seldom will survive much beyond the trial stage, and appellate review will be effectively denied. Our law should not be that rigid. Pregnancy often comes more than once to the same woman, and in the general population, if man is to survive, it will always be with us. Pregnancy provides a classic justification for a conclusion of nonmootness. It truly could be "capable of repetition, yet evading review." *Southern Pacific Terminal Co. v. ICC*, 219 U.S. 498, 515 (1911). See *Moore v. Ogilvie*, 394 U.S. 814, 816 (1969); *Carroll v. President and Commissioners*, 393 U.S. 175, 178-179 (1968); *United States v. W. T. Grant Co.*, 345 U.S. 629, 632-633 (1953).

We therefore agree with the District Court that Jane Roe had standing to undertake this litigation, that she presented a justiciable controversy, and that the termination of her 1970 pregnancy has not rendered her case moot.

B. *Dr. Hallford*. The doctor's position is different. He entered Roe's litigation as a plaintiff-intervenor alleging in his complaint that he:

> *In the past has been arrested for violating Texas Abortion Laws and at the present time stands charged by indictment with violating said laws in the Criminal District Court of Dallas County, Texas to-wit: (1) The State of Texas vs. James H. Hallford, No. C-69-5307-IH, and (2) The State of Texas vs. James H. Hallford, No. C-69-2524-H. In both cases the defendant is charged with abortion. . . .*

In his application for leave to intervene the doctor made like representations as to the abortion charges pending in the state court. These representations were also repeated in the affidavit he executed and filed in support of his motion for summary judgment.

Dr. Hallford is therefore in the position of seeking, in a federal court, declaratory and injunctive relief with respect to the same statutes under which he stands charged in criminal prosecutions simultaneously pending in state court. Although he stated that he has been arrested in the past for violating the State's abortion laws, he makes no allegation of any substantial and immediate threat to

---

[6] The appellee twice states in his brief that the hearing before the District Court was held on July 22, 1970. Appellee's Brief 13. The docket entries, Appendix, at 2, and the transcript, Appendix, at 76, reveal this to be an error. The July date appears to be the time of the reporter's transcription. See Appendix, at 77.

any federally protected right that cannot be asserted in his defense against the state prosecutions. Neither is there any allegation of harassment or bad faith prosecution. In order to escape the rule, articulated in the cases cited in the next paragraph of this opinion, that, absent harassment and bad faith, a defendant in a pending state criminal case cannot affirmatively challenge in federal court the statutes under which the State is prosecuting him, Dr. Hallford seeks to distinguish his status as a present state defendant from his status as a "potential future defendant" and to assert only the latter for standing purposes here.

We see no merit in that distinction. Our decision in *Samuels v. Mackell*, 401 U.S. 66 (1971), compels the conclusion that the District Court erred when it granted declaratory relief to Dr. Hallford instead of refraining from so doing. The court, of course, was correct in refusing to grant injunctive relief to the doctor. The reasons supportive of that action, however, are those expressed in *Samuels v. Mackell, supra*, and in *Younger v. Harris*, 401 U.S. 37 (1971); *Boyle v. Landry*, 401 U.S. 77 (1971); *Perez v. Ledesma*, 401 U.S. 82 (1971); and *Byrne v. Karalexis*, 401 U.S. 216 (1971). See also *Dombrowski v. Pfister*, 380 U.S. 479 (1965). We note, in passing, that *Younger* and its companion cases were decided after the three-judge District Court decision in this case.

Dr. Hallford's complaint in intervention, therefore, is to be dismissed.[7] He is remitted to his defenses in the state criminal proceedings against him. We reverse the judgment of the District Court insofar as it granted Dr. Hallford relief and failed to dismiss his complaint in intervention.

C. *The Does.* In view of our ruling as to Roe's standing in her case, the issue of the Does' standing in their case has little significance. The claims they assert are essentially the same as those of Roe, and they attack the same statutes. Nevertheless, we briefly note the Does' posture.

Their pleadings present them as a childless married couple, the woman not being pregnant, who have no desire to have children at this time because of their having received medical advice that Mrs. Doe should avoid pregnancy, and for "other highly personal reasons." But they "fear . . . they may face the prospect of becoming parents." And if pregnancy ensues, they "would want to terminate" it by an abortion. They assert an inability to obtain an abortion legally in Texas and, consequently, the prospect of obtaining an illegal abortion there or of going outside Texas to some place where the procedure could be obtained legally and competently.

We thus have as plaintiffs a married couple who have, as their asserted immediate and present injury, only an alleged "detrimental effect upon [their] marital happiness" because they are forced to "the choice of refraining from normal sexual relations or of endangering Mary Doe's health through a possible pregnancy." Their claim is that sometime, in the future, Mrs. Doe might become

---

[7] We need not consider what different result, if any, would follow if Dr. Hallford's intervention were on behalf of a class. His complaint in intervention does not purport to assert a class suit and makes no reference to any class apart from an allegation that he "and others similarly situated" must necessarily guess at the meaning of Art. 1196. His application for leave to intervene goes somewhat further for it asserts that plaintiff Roe does not adequately protect the interest of the doctor "and the class of people who are physicians . . . and the class of people who are . . . patients. . . ." The leave application, however, is not the complaint. Despite the District Court's statement to the contrary, 314 F. Supp., at 1225, we fail to perceive the essentials of a class suit in the Hallford complaint.

pregnant because of possible failure of contraceptive measures, and at that time in the future, she might want an abortion that might then be illegal under the Texas statutes.

This very phrasing of the Does' position reveals its speculative character. Their alleged injury rests on possible future contraceptive failure, possible future pregnancy, possible future unpreparedness for parenthood, and possible future impairment of health. Any one or more of these several possibilities may not take place and all may not combine. In the Does' estimation, these possibilities might have some real or imagined impact upon their marital happiness. But we are not prepared to say that the bare allegation of so indirect an injury is sufficient to present an actual case or controversy. *Younger v. Harris*, 401 U.S., at 41-42; *Golden v. Zwickler*, 394 U.S., at 109-110 (1969); *Abele v. Markle*, 452 F. 2d, at 1124-1125; *Crossen v. Breckenridge*, 446 F. 2d, at 839. The Does' claim falls far short of those resolved otherwise in the cases that the Does urge upon us, namely, *Investment Co. Institute v. Camp*. 401 U.S. 617 (1971); *Data Processing Service v. Camp*, 397 U.S. 150 (1970); and *Epperson v. Arkansas*, 393 U.S. 97 (1968). See also *Truax v. Raich, supra*.

The Does therefore are not appropriate plaintiffs in this litigation. Their complaint was properly dismissed by the District Court, and we affirm that dismissal.

V

The principal thrust of appellant's attack on the Texas statutes is that they improperly invade a right, said to be possessed by the pregnant woman, to choose to terminate her pregnancy. Appellant would discover this right in the concept of personal "liberty" embodied in the Fourteenth Amendment's Due Process Clause; or in personal, marital, familial, and sexual privacy said to be protected by the Bill of Rights or its penumbras, see *Griswold v. Connecticut*, 381 U.S. 479 (1965); *Eisenstadt v. Baird*, 405 U.S. 438 (1972); *id.*, at 460 (WHITE, J., concurring); or among those rights reserved to the people by the Ninth Amendment, *Griswold v. Connecticut*, 381 U.S. at 486 (Goldberg, J., concurring). Before addressing this claim, we feel it desirable briefly to survey, in several aspects, the history of abortion, for such insight as that history may afford us, and then to examine the state purposes and interests behind the criminal abortion laws.

VI

It perhaps is not generally appreciated that the restrictive criminal abortion laws in effect in a majority of States today are of relatively recent vintage. Those laws, generally proscribing abortion or its attempt at any time during pregnancy except when necessary to preserve the pregnant woman's life, are not of ancient or even of common law origin. Instead, they derive from statutory changes effected, for the most part, in the latter half of the 19th century.

1. *Ancient attitudes*. These are not capable of precise determination. We are told that at the time of the Persian Empire abortifacients were known and that

criminal abortions were severely punished.[8] We are also told, however, that abortion was practiced in Greek times as well as in the Roman Era,[9] and that "it was resorted to without scruple."[10] The Ephesian, Soranos, often described as the greatest of the ancient gynecologists, appears to have been generally opposed to Rome's prevailing free-abortion practices. He found it necessary to think first of the life of the mother, and he resorted to abortion when, upon this standard, he felt the procedure advisable.[11] Greek and Roman law afforded little protection to the unborn. If abortion was prosecuted in some places, it seems to have been based on a concept of a violation of the father's right to his offspring. Ancient religion did not bar abortion.[12]

2. *The Hippocratic Oath*. What then of the famous Oath that has stood so long as the ethical guide of the medical profession and that bears the name of the great Greek (460(?)-377(?) B.C.), who has been described as the Father of Medicine, the "wisest and the greatest practitioner of his art," and the "most important and most complete medical personality of antiquity" who dominated the medical schools of his time, and who typified the sum of the medical knowledge of the past?[13] The Oath varies somewhat according to the particular translation, but in any translation the content is clear: "I will give no deadly medicine to anyone if asked, nor suggest any such counsel; and in like manner I will not give to a woman a pessary to produce abortion,"[14] or "I will neither give a deadly drug to anybody if asked for it, nor will I make a suggestion to this effect. Similarly, I will not give to a woman an abortive remedy."[15]

Although the Oath is not mentioned in any of the principal briefs in this case or in *Doe v. Bolton, post*, it represents the apex of the development of strict ethical concepts in medicine, and its influence endures to this day. Why did not the authority of Hippocrates dissuade abortion practice in his time and that of Rome? The late Dr. Edelstein provides us with a theory.[16] The Oath was not uncontested even in Hippocrates' day; only the Pythagorean school of philosophers frowned upon the related act of suicide. Most Greek thinkers, on the other hand, commended abortion, at least prior to viability. See Plato, *Republic*, V, 461; Aristotle, *Politics*, VII, 1335 b 25. For the Pythagoreans, however, it was a matter of dogma. For them the embryo was animate from the moment of conception, and abortion meant destruction of a living being. The abortion clause of the Oath,

---

[8] A. Castiglioni, A History of Medicine 84 (2d ed. 1947), E. Krumbhaar, translator and editor (hereinafter "Castiglioni").

[9] J. Ricci, The Genealogy of Gynaecology 52, 84, 113, 149 (2d ed. 1950) (hereinafter "Ricci"); L. Lader, Abortion 75-77 (1966) (hereinafter "Lader"); K. Niswander, Medical Abortion Practices in the United States, in Abortion and the Law 27, 38-40 (D. Smith, editor, 1967); G. Williams, The Sanctity of Life 148 (1957) (hereinafter "Williams"); J. Noonan, An Almost Absolute Value in History, in The Morality of Abortion 1, 3-7 (J. Noonan ed. 1970) (hereinafter "Noonan"); E. Quay, Justifiable Abortion—Medical and Legal Foundations, II, 49 Geo. L. J. 395, 406-422 (1961) (hereinafter "Quay").

[10] L. Edelstein, The Hippocratic Oath 10 (1943) (hereinafter "Edelstein"). But see Castiglioni 227.

[11] Edelstein 12; Ricci 113-114, 118-119; Noonan 5.

[12] Edelstein 13-14.

[13] Castiglioni 148.

[14] *Id.*, at 154.

[15] Edelstein 3.

[16] *Id.*, at 12, 15-18.

therefore, "echoes Pythagorean doctrines," and "[i]n no other stratum of Greek opinion were such views held or proposed in the same spirit of uncompromising austerity."[17]

Edelstein then concludes that the Oath originated in a group representing only a small segment of Greek opinion and that it certainly was not accepted by all ancient physicians. He points out that medical writings down to Galen (130-200 A.D.) "give evidence of the violation of almost every one of its injunctions."[18] But with the end of antiquity a decided change took place. Resistance against suicide and against abortion became common. The Oath came to be popular. The emerging teachings of Christianity were in agreement with the Pythagorean ethic. The oath "became the nucleus of all medical ethics" and "was applauded as the embodiment of truth." Thus, suggests Dr. Edelstein, it is "a Pythagorean manifesto and not the expression of an absolute standard of medical conduct."[19]

This, it seems to us, is a satisfactory and acceptable explanation of the Hippocratic Oath's apparent rigidity. It enables us to understand, in historical context, a long accepted and revered statement of medical ethics.

3. *The Common Law.* It is undisputed that at the common law, abortion performed *before* "quickening"—the first recognizable movement of the fetus *in utero*, appearing usually from the 16th to the 18th week of pregnancy[20]—was not an indictable offense.[21] The absence of a common law crime for pre-quickening abortion appears to have developed from a confluence of earlier philosophical, theological, and civil and canon law concepts of when life begins. These disciplines variously approached the question in terms of the point at which the embryo or fetus became "formed" or recognizably human, or in terms of when a "person" came into being, that is, infused with a "soul" or "animated." A loose consensus evolved in early English law that these events occurred at some point between conception and live birth.[22] This was "mediate animation." Although

[17] *Id.*, at 18; Lader 76.

[18] Edelstein 63.

[19] *Id.*, at 64.

[20] Dorland's Illustrated Medical Dictionary 1261 (24th ed. 1965).

[21] E. Coke, Institutes III *50 (1948); 1 W. Hawkins, Pleas of the Crown c. 31, § 16 (1762); 1 Blackstone, Commentaries *129-130 (1765); M. Hale, Pleas of the Crown 433 (1778). For discussions of the role of the quickening concept in English common law, see Lader 78; Noonan 223-226; C. Means, The Law of New York Concerning Abortion and the Status of the Foetus, 1664-1968: A Case of Cessation of Constitutionality, 14 N. Y. L. Forum 411, 418-428 (1968) (hereinafter "Means I"); L. Stern, Abortion: Reform and the Law, 59 J. Crim. L. C. & P. S. 84 (1968) (hereinafter "Stern"); Quay 430-432; Williams 152.

[22] Early philosophers believed that the embryo or fetus did not become formed and begin to live until at least 40 days after conception for a male, and 80 to 90 days for a female. See, for example, Aristotle, Hist. Anim. 7.3.583b; Gen. Anim. 2.3.736, 2.5.741; Hippocrates, Lib. de Nat. Puer., No. 10. Aristotle's thinking derived from his three-stage theory of life: vegetable, animal, rational. The vegetable stage was reached at conception, the animal at "animation," and the rational soon after live birth. This theory, together with the 40/80 day view, came to be accepted by early Christian thinkers.

The theological debate was reflected in the writings of St. Augustine, who made a distinction between *embryo inanimatus*, not yet endowed with a soul, and *embryo animatus*. He may have drawn upon Exodus xxi, 22. At one point, however, he expresses the view that human powers cannot determine the point during fetal development at which the critical change occurs. See Augustine, De Origine Animae 4.4 (Pub. Law 44.527). See also Reany, The Creation of the Human Soul, c. 2 and 83-86 (1932); Huser, The Crime of Abortion in Common Law 15 (Catholic Univ. of America, Canon Law Studies No. 162, Washington, D. C. 1942).

Christian theology and the canon law came to fix the point of animation at 40 days for a male and 80 days for a female, a view that persisted until the 19th century, there was otherwise little agreement about the precise time of formation or animation. There was agreement, however, that prior to this point the fetus was to be regarded as part of the mother and its destruction, therefore, was not homicide. Due to continued uncertainty about the precise time when animation occurred, to the lack of any empirical basis for the 40-80 day view, and perhaps to Aquinas' definition of movement as one of the two first principles of life, Bracton focused upon quickening as the critical point. The significance of quickening was echoed by later common law scholars and found its way into the received common law in this country.

Whether abortion of a *quick* fetus was a felony at common law, or even a lesser crime, is still disputed. Bracton, writing early in the 13th century, thought it homicide.[23] But the later and predominant view, following the great common law scholars, has been that it was at most a lesser offense. In a frequently cited passage, Coke took the position that abortion of a woman "quick with childe" is "a great misprision and no murder."[24] Blackstone followed, saying that while abortion after quickening had once been considered manslaughter (though not murder), "modern law" took a less severe view.[25] A recent review of the common law precedents argues, however, that those precedents contradict Coke and that even post-quickening abortion was never established as a common law crime.[26] This is of some importance because while most American courts ruled, in holding or dictum, that abortion of an unquickened fetus was not criminal under their

---

Galen, in three treatises related to embryology, accepted the thinking of Aristotle and his followers. Quay 426-427. Later, Augustine on abortion was incorporated by Gratian into the Decretum, published about 1140. Decretum Magistri Gratiani 2.32.2.7 to 2.32.2.10, in 1 Corpus Juris Canonici 1122, 1123 (2d ed. Friedberg ed. 1879). Gratian, together with the decretals that followed, were recognized as the definitive body of canon law until the new Code of 1917.

For discussions of the canon law treatment, see Means I, at 411-412; Noonan, 20-26; Quay 426-430; see also Noonan, Contraception: A History of Its Treatment by the Catholic Theologians and Canonists 18-29 (1965).

[23] Bracton took the position that abortion by blow or poison was homicide "if the foetus be already formed and animated, and particularly if it be animated." 2 H. Bracton, De Legibus et Consuetudinibus Angliae 279 (Twiss ed. 1879), or, as a later translation puts it, "if the foetus is already formed or quickened, especially if it is quickened," II Bracton, On the Laws and Customs of England 341 (Thorne ed. 1968). See Quay 431; see also 2 Fleta 60-61 (Book 1, c. 23) (Selden Society ed. 1955).

[24] E. Coke, Institutes III *50 (1648).

[25] 1 Blackstone, Commentaries *129-130 (1765).

[26] C. Means, The Phoenix of Abortional Freedom: Is a Penumbral or Ninth-Amendment Right About to Arise from the Nineteenth-Century Legislative Ashes of a Fourteenth-Century Common-Law Liberty?, 17 N. Y. L. Forum 335 (1971) (hereinafter "Means II"). The author examines the two principal precedents cited marginally by Coke, both contrary to his dictum, and traces the treatment of these and other cases by earlier commentators. He concludes that Coke, who himself participated as an advocate in an abortion case in 1601, may have intentionally misstated the law. The author even suggests a reason: Coke's strong feelings about abortion, coupled with his reluctance to acknowledge common law (secular) jurisdiction to assess penalties for an offence that traditionally had been an exclusively ecclesiastical or canon law crime. See also Lader 78-79, who notes that some scholars doubt the common law ever was applied to abortion; that the English ecclesiastical courts seem to have lost interest in the problem after 1527; and that the preamble to the English legislation of 1803, 43 Geo. 3, c. 58, § 1, at 203, referred to in the text, *infra*, states "no adequate means have been hitherto provided for the prevention and punishment of such offenses."

received common law,[27] others followed Coke in stating that abortion of a quick fetus was a "misprision," a term they translated to mean "misdemeanor."[28] That their reliance on Coke on this aspect of the law was uncritical and, apparently in all the reported cases, dictum (due probably to the paucity of common law prosecutions for post-quickening abortion), makes it now appear doubtful that abortion was ever firmly established as a comon law crime even with respect to the destruction of a quick fetus.

4. *The English statutory law.* England's first criminal abortion statute, Lord Ellenborough's Act, 43 Geo. 3, c. 58, came in 1803. It made abortion of a quick fetus, § 1, a capital crime, but in § 2 it provided lesser penalties for the felony of abortion before quickening, and thus preserved the quickening distinction. This contrast was continued in the general revision of 1828, 9 Geo. 4, c. 31, § 13, at 104. It disappeared, however, together with the death penalty, in 1837, 7 Will. 4 & 1 Vic., c. 85, § 6, at 360, and did not reappear in the Offenses Against the Person Act of 1861, 24 & 25 Vic., c. 100, § 59, at 438, that formed the core of English anti-abortion law until the liberalizing reforms of 1967. In 1929 the Infant Life (Preservation) Act, 19 & 20 Geo. 5, c. 34, came into being. Its emphasis was upon the destruction of "the life of a child capable of being born alive." It made a willful act performed with the necessary intent a felony. It contained a proviso that one was not to be found guilty of the offense "unless it is proved that the act which caused the death of the child was not done in good faith for the purpose only of preserving the life of the mother."

A seemingly notable development in the English law was the case of *Rex v. Bourne*, [1939] 1 K. B. 687. This case was apparently answered in the affirmative the question whether an abortion necessary to preserve the life of the pregnant woman was excepted from the criminal penalties of the 1861 Act. In his instructions to the jury Judge Macnaghten referred to the 1929 Act, and observed, p. 691, that that Act related to "the case where a child is killed by a willful act at the time when it is being delivered in the ordinary course of nature." *Id.*, at 91. He concluded that the 1861 Act's use of the word "unlawfully" imported the same meaning expressed by the specific proviso in the 1929 Act even though there was no mention of preserving the mother's life in the 1861 Act. He then construed the phrase "preserving the life of the mother" broadly, that is, "in a reasonable sense," to include a serious and permanent threat to the mother's *health*, and instructed the jury to acquit Dr. Bourne if it found he had acted in a good faith belief that the abortion was necessary for this purpose. *Id.*, at 693-694. The jury did acquit.

Recently Parliament enacted a new abortion law. This is the Abortion Act of

---

[27] *Commonwealth v. Bangs*, 9 Mass. 387, 388 (1812); *Commonwealth v. Parker*, 50 Mass. (9 Met.) 263, 265-266 (1845); *State v. Cooper*, 22 N. J. L. 52, 58 (1849); *Abrams v. Foshee*, 3 Iowa 274, 278-280 (1856); *Smith v. Gaffard*, 31 Ala. 45, 51 (1857); *Mitchell v. Commonwealth*, 78 Ky. 204, 210 (1879); *Eggart v. State*, 40 Fla. 527, 532, 25 So. 144, 145 (1898); *State v. Alcorn*, 7 Idaho 599, 606, 64 P. 1014, 1016 (1901); *Edwards v. State*, 79 Neb. 251, 252, 112 N. W. 611, 612 (1907); *Gray v. State*, 77 Tex. Crim. R. 221, 224, 178 S. W. 337, 338 (1915); *Miller v. Bennett*, 190 Va. 162, 169, 56 S. E. 2d 217, 221 (1949). Contra, *Mills v. Commonwealth*, 13 Pa. 631, 633 (1850); *State v. Slagle*, 83 N. C. 630, 632 (1880).

[28] See *Smith v. State*, 33 Me. 48, 55 (1851); *Evans v. People*, 49 N. Y. 86, 88 (1872); *Lamb v. State*, 67 Md. 524, 533, 10 A. 208 (1887).

1967, 15 & 16 Eliz., 2, c. 87. The Act permits a licensed physician to perform an abortion where two other licensed physicians agree (a) "that the continuance of the pregnancy would involve risk to the life of the pregnant woman, or of injury to the physical or mental health of the pregnant woman or any existing children of her family, greater than if the pregnancy were terminated," or (b) "that there is a substantial risk that if the child were born it would suffer from such physical or mental abnormalities as to be seriously handicapped." The Act also provides that, in making this determination, "account may be taken of the pregnant woman's actual or reasonably foreseeable environment." It also permits a physician, without the concurrence of others, to terminate a pregnancy where he is of the good faith opinion that the abortion "is immediately necessary to save the life or to prevent grave permanent injury to the physical or mental health of the pregnant woman."

5. *The American law.* In this country the law in effect in all but a few States until mid-19th century was the pre-existing English common law. Connecticut, the first State to enact abortion legislation, adopted in 1821 that part of Lord Ellenborough's Act that related to a woman "quick with child."[29] The death penalty was not imposed. Abortion before quickening was made a crime in that State only in 1860.[30] In 1828 New York enacted legislation[31] that, in two respects, was to serve as a model for early anti-abortion statutes. First, while barring destruction of an unquickened fetus as well as a quick fetus, it made the former only a misdemeanor, but the latter second-degree manslaughter. Second, it incorporated a concept of therapeutic abortion by providing that an abortion was excused if it "shall have been necessary to preserve the life of such mother, or shall have been advised by two physicians to be necessary for such purpose." By 1840, when Texas had received the common law,[32] only eight American States had statutes dealing with abortion.[33] It was not until after the War Between the States that legislation began generally to replace the common law. Most of these initial statutes dealt severely with abortion after quickening but were lenient with it before quickening. Most punished attempts equally with completed abortions. While many statutes included the exception for an abortion thought by one or more physicians to be necessary to save the mother's life, that provision soon disappeared and the typical law required that the procedure actually be necessary for that purpose.

Gradually, in the middle and late 19th century the quickening distinction disappeared from the statutory law of most States and the degree of the offense and the penalties were increased. By the end of the 1950s, a large majority of the States banned abortion, however and whenever performed, unless done to save or preserve the life of the mother.[34] The exceptions, Alabama and the District of

[29] Conn. Stat., Tit. 20, § 14 (1821).

[30] Conn. Pub. Acts, c. 71, § 1 (1860).

[31] N. Y. Rev. Stat., pt. IV, c. I, Tit. II, Art. 1, § 9, at Tit. VI, § 21, at 694 (1829).

[32] Act of January 20, 1840, § 1, set forth in 2 Gammel, Laws of Texas 177-178 (1898); see *Grigsby v. Reib*, 105 Tex. 597, 600, 153 S. W. 1124, 1125 (1913).

[33] The early statutes are discussed in Quay 435-438. See also Lader 85-88; Stern 85-86; and Means II 375-376.

[34] Criminal abortion statutes in effect in the States as of 1961, together with historical statutory development and important judicial interpretations of the state statutes, are cited and quoted in Quay

Columbia, permitted abortion to preserve the mother's health.[35] Three other States permitted abortions that were not "unlawfully" performed or that were not "without lawful justification," leaving interpretation of those standards to the courts.[36] In the past several years, however, a trend toward liberalization of abortion statutes has resulted in adoption, by about one-third of the States, of less stringent laws, most of them patterned after the ALI Model Penal Code, § 230.3,[37] set forth as Appendix B to the opinion in *Doe v. Bolton, post* ———.

It is thus apparent that at common law, at the time of the adoption of our Constitution, and throughout the major portion of the 19th century, abortion was viewed with less disfavor than under most American statutes currently in effect. Phrasing it another way, a woman enjoyed a substantially broader right to terminate a pregnancy than she does in most States today. At least with respect to the early stage of pregnancy, and very possibly without such a limitation, the opportunity to make this choice was present in this country well into the 19th century. Even later, the law continued for some time to treat less punitively an abortion procured in early pregnancy.

6. *The position of the American Medical Association.* The anti-abortion mood prevalent in this country in the late 19th century was shared by the medical profession. Indeed, the attitude of the profession may have played a significant role in the enactment of stringent criminal abortion legislation during that period.

An AMA Committee on Criminal Abortion was appointed in May 1857. It presented its report, 12 Trans. of the Am. Med. Assn. 73-77 (1859), to the Twelfth Annual Meeting. That report observed that the Committee had been appointed to investigate criminal abortion "with a view to its general suppression." It deplored abortion and its frequency and it listed three causes "of this general demoralization":

447-520. See Note, A Survey of the Present Statutory and Case Law on Abortion: The Contradictions and the Problems, 1972 Ill. L. Forum 177, 179, classifying the abortion statutes and listing 25 States as permitting abortion only if necessary to save or preserve the mother's life.

[35] Ala. Code, Tit. 14, § 9 (1958); D. C. Code Ann. § 22-201 (1967).

[36] Mass. Gen. Laws Ann., c. 272, § 19 (1970); N. J. Rev. Stat. Ann. 2A:87-1 (1969); Pa. Stat. Ann., Tit. 18, §§ 4718, 4719 (1963).

[37] Fourteen States have adopted some form of the ALI statute. See Ark. Stat. Ann. §§ 41-303 to 41-310 (Supp. 1971); Calif. Health and Safety Code §§ 25950-25955.5 (West Supp. 1972); Colo. Rev. Stats. Ann. §§ 40-2-50 to 40-2-53 (Perm. Cum. Supp. 1967); Del. Code Ann., Tit. 24, §§ 1790-1793 (Supp. 1972); Florida Law of Apr. 13, 1972, c. 72-196, 1972 Fla. Sess. Law Serv., at 380-382; Ga. Code §§ 26-1201 to 26-1203 (1972); Kan. Stat. Ann. § 21-3407 (Supp. 1971); Md. Ann. Code, Art. 43, §§ 137-139 (Repl. 1971); Miss. Code Ann. § 2223 (Supp. 1972); N. M. Stat. Ann. §§ 40A-5-1 to 40A-5-3 (Repl. 1972); N. C. Gen. Stat. § 14.45.1 (Supp. 1971); Ore. Rev. Stat. §§ 435.405 at 435.495 (1971); S. C. Code Ann. §§ 16-82 to 16-89 (Supp. 1971); Va. Code Ann. §§ 18.1-62 to 18.1-62.3 (Supp. 1972). Mr. Justice Clark described some of these States as having "led the way." Religion, Morality and Abortion: A Constitutional Appraisal, 2 Loyola U. (L. A.) L. Rev. 1, 11 (1969).

By the end of 1970, four other States had repealed criminal penalties for abortions performed in early pregnancy by a licensed physician, subject to stated procedural and health requirements. Alaska Stat. § 11.15.060 (1970); Haw. Rev. Stat § 453-16 (Supp. 1971); N. Y. Penal Code § 125.05 (McKinney Supp. 1972-1973); Wash. Rev. Code §§ 9.02.060 to 9.02.080 (Supp. 1972). The precise status of criminal abortion laws in some States is made unclear by recent decisions in state and federal courts striking down existing state laws, in whole or in part.

The first of these causes is a wide-spread popular ignorance of the true character of the crime—a belief, even among mothers themselves, that the foetus is not alive till after the period of quickening.

The second of the agents alluded to is the fact that the profession themselves are frequently supposed careless of foetal life. . . .

The third reason of the frightful extent of this crime is found in the grave defects of our laws, both common and statute, as regards the independent and actual existence of the child before birth, as a living being. These errors, which are sufficient in most instances to prevent conviction, are based, and only based, upon mistaken and exploded medical dogmas. With strange inconsistency, the law fully acknowledges the foetus in utero and its inherent rights, for civil purposes; while personally and as criminally affected, it fails to recognize it, and to its life as yet denies all protection. Id., at 75-76.

The Committee then offered, and the Association adopted, resolutions protesting "against such unwarrantable destruction of human life," calling upon state legislatures to revise their abortion laws, and requesting the cooperation of state medical societies "in pressing the subject." *Id.*, at 28, 78.

In 1871 a long and vivid report was submitted by the Committee on Criminal Abortion. It ended with the observation, "We had to deal with human life. In a matter of less importance we could entertain no compromise. An honest judge on the bench would call things by their proper names. We could do no less." 22 Trans. of the Am. Med. Assn. 258 (1871). It proffered resolutions, adopted by the Association, *id.*, at 38-39, recommending, among other things, that it "be unlawful and unprofessional for any physician to induce abortion or premature labor, without the concurrent opinion of at least one respectable consulting physician, and then always with a view to the safety of the child—if that be possible," and calling "the attention of the clergy of all denominations to the perverted views of morality entertained by a large class of females—aye, and men also, on this important question."

Except for periodic condemnation of the criminal abortionist, no further formal AMA action took place until 1967. In that year the Committee on Human Reproduction urged the adoption of a stated policy of opposition to induced abortion except when there is "documented medical evidence" of a threat to the health or life of the mother, or that the child "may be born with incapacitating physical deformity or mental deficiency," or that a pregnancy "resulting from legally established statutory or forcible rape or incest may constitute a threat to the mental or physical health of the patient," and two other physicians "chosen because of their recognized professional competence have examined the patient and have concurred in writing," and the procedure "is performed in a hospital accredited by the Joint Commission on Accreditation of Hospitals." The providing of medical information by physicians to state legislatures in their consideration of legislation regarding therapeutic abortion was "to be considered consistent with the principles of ethics of the American Medical Association." This recommendation was adopted by the House of Delegates. Proceedings of the AMA House of Delegates, 40-51 (June 1967).

In 1970, after the introduction of a variety of proposed resolutions, and of a report from its Board of Trustees, a reference committee noted "polarization of the medical profession on this controversial issue"; division among those who had testified; a difference of opinion among AMA councils and committees; "the remarkable shift in testimony" in six months, felt to be influenced "by the rapid changes in state laws and by the judicial decisions which tend to make abortion more freely available;" and a feeling "that this trend will continue." On June 25, 1970, the House of Delegates adopted preambles and most of the resolutions proposed by the reference committee. The preambles emphasized "the best interests of the patient," "sound clinical judgment," and "informed patient consent," in contrast to "mere acquiescence to the patient's demand." The resolutions asserted that abortion is a medical procedure that should be performed by a licensed physician in an accredited hospital only after consultation with two other physicians and in conformity with state law, and that no party to the procedure should be required to violate personally held moral principles.[38] Proceedings of the AMA House of Delegates 221 (June 1970). The AMA Judicial Council rendered a complementary opinion.[39]

7. *The position of the American Public Health Association.* In October 1970, the Executive Board of the APHA adopted Standards for Abortion Services. These were five in number:

> a. *Rapid and simple abortion referral must be readily available through state and local public health departments, medical societies, or other non-profit organizations.*
>
> b. *An important function of counseling should be to simplify and expedite the provision of abortion services; it should not delay the obtaining of these services.*
>
> c. *Psychiatric consultation should not be mandatory. As in the case of other specialized medical services, psychiatric consultation*

---

[38] "Whereas, Abortion, like any other medical procedure, should not be performed when contrary to the best interests of the patient since good medical practice requires due consideration for the patient's welfare and not mere acquiescence to the patient's demand; and

"Whereas, The standards of sound clinical judgment, which, together with informed patient consent should be determinative according to the merits of each individual case; therefore be it

"*RESOLVED*, That abortion is a medical procedure and should be performed only by a duly licensed physician and surgeon in an accredited hospital acting only after consultation with two other physicians chosen because of their professional competency and in conformance with standards of good medical practice and the Medical Practice Act of his State; and be it further

"*RESOLVED*, That no physician or other professional personnel shall be compelled to perform any act which violates his good medical judgment. Neither physician, hospital, nor hospital personnel shall be required to perform any act violative of personally-held moral principles. In these circumstances good medical practice requires only that the physician or other professional personnel withdraw from the case so long as the withdrawal is consistent with good medical practice." Proceedings of the AMA House of Delegates 221 (June 1970).

[39] "The Principles of Medical Ethics of the AMA do not prohibit a physician from performing an abortion that is performed in accordance with good medical practice and under circumstances that do not violate the laws of the community in which he practices.

"In the matter of abortions, as of any other medical procedure, the Judicial Council becomes involved whenever there is alleged violation of the Principles of Medical Ethics as established by the House of Delegates."

should be sought for definite indications and not on a routine basis.

    d. A wide range of individuals from appropriately trained, sympathetic volunteers to highly skilled physicians may qualify as abortion counselors.

    e. Contraception and/or sterilization should be discussed with each abortion patient. Recommended Standards for Abortion Services, 61 Am. J. Pub. Health 396 (1971).

Among factors pertinent to life and health risks associated with abortion were three that "are recognized as important":

    a. the skill of the physician,
    b. the environment in which the abortion is performed, and above all
    c. the duration of pregnancy, as determined by uterine size and confirmed by menstrual history. Id., at 397.

    It was said that "a well-equipped hospital" offers more protection "to cope with unforeseen difficulties than an office or clinic without such resources. . . . The factor of gestational age is of overriding importance." Thus it was recommended that abortions in the second trimester and early abortions in the presence of existing medical complications be performed in hospitals as inpatient procedures. For pregnancies in the first trimester, abortion in the hospital with or without overnight stay "is probably the safest practice." An abortion in an extramural facility, however, is an acceptable alternative "provided arrangements exist in advance to admit patients promptly if unforeseen complications develop." Standards for an abortion facility were listed. It was said that at present abortions should be performed by physicians or osteopaths who are licensed to practice and who have "adequate training." *Id.*, at 398.

    8. *The position of the American Bar Association.* At its meeting in February 1972 the ABA House of Delegates approved, with 17 opposing votes, the Uniform Abortion Act that had been drafted and approved the preceding August by the Conference of Commissioners on Uniform State Laws. 58 A. B. A. J. 380 (1972). We set forth the Act in full in the margin.[40] The conference has appended an

---

[40]   "UNIFORM ABORTION ACT

"SECTION 1. [*Abortion Defined; When Authorized.*]

    "(a) 'Abortion' means the termination of human pregnancy with an intention other than to produce a live birth or to remove a dead fetus.

    "(b) An abortion may be performed in this state only if it is performed:

    "(1) by a physician licensed to practice medicine [or osteopathy] in this state or by a physician practicing medicine [or osteopathy] in the employ of the government of the United States or of this state, [and the abortion is performed [in the physician's office or in a medical clinic, or] in a hospital approved by the [Department of Health] or operated by the United States, this state, or any department, agency, or political subdivision of either;] or by a female upon herself upon the advice of the physician; and

    "(2) within [20] weeks after the commencement of the pregnancy [or after [20] weeks only if the physician has reasonable cause to believe (i) there is a substantial risk that continuance of the pregnancy would endanger the life of the mother or would gravely impair the physical or mental health

enlightening Prefatory Note.[41]

VII

Three reasons have been advanced to explain historically the enactment of criminal abortion laws in the 19th century and to justify their continued existence.

It has been argued occasionally that these laws were the product of a Victorian social concern to discourage illicit sexual conduct. Texas, however, does not advance this justification in the present case, and it appears that no court or commentator has taken the argument seriously.[42] The appellants and *amici* contend, moreover, that this is not a proper state purpose at all and suggest that, if it were, the Texas statutes are overbroad in protecting it since the law fails to distinguish between married and unwed mothers.

A second reason is concerned with abortion as a medical procedure. When most criminal abortion laws were first enacted, the procedure was a hazardous

---

of the mother, (ii) that the child would be born with grave physical or mental defect, or (iii) that the pregnancy resulted from rape or incest, or illicit intercourse with a girl under the age of 16 years of age].

"SECTION 2. [*Penalty.*] Any person who performs or procures an abortion other than authorized by this Act is guilty of a [felony] and, upon conviction thereof, may be sentenced to pay a fine not exceeding [$1,000] or to imprisonment [in the state penitentiary] not exceeding [5 years], or both.

"SECTION 3. [*Uniformity of Interpretation.*] This Act shall be construed to effectuate its general purpose to make uniform the law with respect to the subject of this Act among those states which enact it.

"SECTION 4. [*Short Title.*] This Act may be cited as the Uniform Abortion Act.

"SECTION 5. [*Severability.*] If any provision of this Act or the application thereof to any person or circumstance is held invalid, the invalidity does not affect other provisions or applications of this Act which can be given effect without the invalid provision or application, and to this end the provisions of this Act are severable.

"SECTION 6. [*Repeal.*] The following acts and parts of acts are repealed:

"(1)

"(2)

"(3)

"SECTION 7. [*Times of Taking Effect.*] This Act shall take effect ——————.''

[41] "This Act is based largely upon the New York abortion act following a review of the more recent laws on abortion in several states and upon recognition of a more liberal trend in laws on this subject. Recognition was given also to the several decisions in state and federal courts which show a further trend toward liberalization of abortion laws, especially during the first trimester of pregnancy.

"Recognizing that a number of problems appeared in New York, a shorter time period for 'unlimited' abortions was advisable. The time period was bracketed to permit the various states to insert a figure more in keeping with the different conditions that might exist among the states. Likewise, the language limiting the place or places in which abortions may be performed was also bracketed to account for different conditions among the states. In addition, limitations on abortions after the initial 'unlimited' period were placed in brackets so that individual states may adopt all or any of these reasons, or place further restrictions upon abortions after the initial period.

"This Act does not contain any provision relating to medical review committees or prohibitions against sanctions imposed upon medical personnel refusing to participate in abortions because of religious or other similar reasons, or the like. Such provisions, while related, do not directly pertain to when, where, or by whom abortions may be performed; however, the Act is not drafted to exclude such a provision by a state wishing to enact the same."

[42] See, for example, *YWCA v. Kugler*, 342 F. Supp. 1048, 1074 (N. J. 1972); *Abele v. Markle*, 342 F. Supp. 800, 805-806 (Conn. 1972) (Newman, J., concurring), appeal pending; *Washington v. Florida*, 250 So. 2d 857, 863 (Ervin, J., concurring) (Fla. Supp. 1972); *State v. Gedicke*, 43 N. J. L. 86, 80 (Sup. St. 1881); Means II, at 381-382.

one for the woman.[43] This was particularly true prior to the development of antisepsis. Antiseptic techniques, of course, were based on discoveries by Lister, Pasteur, and others first announced in 1867, but were not generally accepted and employed until about the turn of the century. Abortion mortality was high. Even after 1900, and perhaps until as late as the development of antibiotics in the 1940's, standard modern techniques such as dilation and curettage were not nearly so safe as they are today. Thus it has been argued that a State's real concern in enacting a criminal abortion law was to protect the pregnant woman, that is, to restrain her from submitting to a procedure that placed her life in serious jeopardy.

Modern medical techniques have altered this situation. Appellants and various *amici* refer to medical data indicating that abortion in early pregnancy, that is, prior to the end of first trimester, although not without its risk, is now relatively safe. Mortality rates for women undergoing early abortions, where the procedure is legal, appear to be as low as or lower than the rates for normal childbirth.[44] Consequently, any interest of the State in protecting the woman from an inherently hazardous procedure, except when it would be equally dangerous for her to forgo it, has largely disappeared. Of course, important state interests in the area of health and medical standards do remain. The State has a legitimate interest in seeing to it that abortion, like any other medical procedure, is performed under circumstances that insure maximum safety for the patient. This interest obviously extends at least to the performing physician and his staff, to the facilities involved, to the availability of after-care, and to adequate provision for any complication or emergency that might arise. The prevalence of high mortality rates at illegal "abortion mills" strengthens, rather than weakens, the State's interest in regulating the conditions under which abortions are performed. Moreover, the risk to the woman increases as her pregnancy continues. Thus the State retains a definite interest in protecting the woman's own health and safety when an abortion is proposed at a late stage of pregnancy.

The third reason is the State's interest—some phrase it in terms of duty—in protecting prenatal life. Some of the argument for this justification rests on the theory that a new human life is present from the moment of conception.[45] The State's interest and general obligation to protect life then extends, it is argued, to prenatal life. Only when the life of the pregnant mother herself is at stake, balanced against the life she carries within her, should the interest of the embryo or fetus not prevail. Logically, of course, a legitimate state interest in this area need not stand or fall on acceptance of the belief that life begins at conception or

[43] See C. Haagensen & W. Lloyd, A Hundred Years of Medicine 19 (1943).

[44] Potts, Postconception Control of Fertility, 8 Int'l J. of G. & O. 957, 967 (1970) (England and Wales); Abortion Mortality, 20 Morbidity and Morality, 208, 209 (July 12, 1971) (U. S. Dept. of HEW, Public Health Service) (New York City); Tietze, United States: Therapeutic Abortions, 1963-1968, 59 Studies in Family Planning 5, 7 (1970); Tietze, Mortality with Contraception and Induced Abortion, 45 Studies in Family Planning 6 (1969) (Japan, Czechoslovakia, Hungary); Tietze & Lehfeldt, Legal Abortion in Eastern Europe, 175 J. A. M. A. 1149, 1152 (April 1961). Other sources are discussed in Lader 17-23.

[45] See Brief of Amicus National Right to Life Foundation; R. Drinan, The Inviolability of the Right to Be Born, in Abortion and the Law 107 (D. Smith, editor, 1967); Louisell, Abortion, The Practice of Medicine, and the Due Process of Law, 16 UCLA L. Rev. 233 (1969); Noonan 1.

at some other point prior to live birth. In assessing the State's interest, recognition may be given to the less rigid claim that as long as at least *potential* life is involved, the State may assert interests beyond the protection of the pregnant woman alone.

Parties challenging state abortion laws have sharply disputed in some courts the contention that a purpose of these laws, when enacted was to protect prenatal life.[46] Pointing to the absence of legislative history to support the contention, they claim that most state laws were designed solely to protect the woman. Because medical advances have lessened this concern, at least with respect to abortion in early pregnancy, they argue that with respect to such abortions the laws can no longer be justified by any state interest. There is some scholarly support for this view of original purpose.[47] The few state courts called upon to interpret their laws in the late 19th and early 20th centuries did focus on the State's interest in protecting the woman's health rather than in preserving the embryo and fetus.[48] Proponents of this view point out that in many States, including Texas,[49] by statute or judicial interpretation, the pregnant woman herself could not be prosecuted for self-abortion or for cooperating in an abortion performed upon her by another.[50] They claim that adoption of the "quickening" distinction through received common law and state statutes tacitly recognizes the greater health hazards inherent in late abortion and impliedly repudiates the theory that life begins at conception.

It is with these interests, and the weight to be attached to them, that this case is concerned.

VIII

The Constitution does not explicitly mention any right of privacy. In a line of decisions, however, going back perhaps as far as *Union Pacific R. Co. v. Botsford*, 141 U.S. 250, 251 (1891), the Court has recognized that a right of personal privacy, or a guarantee of certain areas or zones of privacy, does exist under the Constitution. In varying contexts the Court or individual Justices have indeed found at least the roots of that right in the First Amendment, *Stanley v. Georgia*, 394 U.S. 557, 564 (1969); in the Fourth and Fifth Amendments, *Terry v. Ohio*, 392 U.S. 1, 8-9 (1968), *Katz v. United States*, 389 U.S. 347, 350 (1967), *Boyd v. United States*, 116 U.S. 616 (1886), see *Olmstead v. United States*, 277 U.S. 438, 478 (1928) (Brandeis, J. dissenting); in the penumbras of the Bill of Rights, *Griswold v. Connecticut*, 381 U.S. 479, 484-485 (1965); in the Ninth Amendment,

---

[46] See, *e.g., Abele v. Markle*, 342 F. Supp. 800 (Conn. 1972), appeal pending.

[47] See discussions in Means I and Means II.

[48] See, *e.g., State v. Murphy*, 27 N. J. L. 112, 114 (1858).

[49] *WAtson v. State*, 9 Tex. App. 237, 244-245 (1880); *Moore v. State*, 37 Tex. Crim. R. 552, 561, 40 S. W. 287, 290 (1897); *Shaw v. State*, 73 Tex. Crim. R. 337, 339, 165 S. W. 930, 931 (1914); *Fondren v. State*, 74 Tex. Crim. R. 552, 557, 169 S. W. 411, 414 (1914); *Gray v. State*, 77 Tex. Crim. R. 221, 229, 178 S. W. 337, 341 (1915). There is no immunity in Texas for the father who is not married to the mother. *Hammett v. State*, 84 Tex. Crim. R. 635, 209 S. W. 661 (1919); *Thompson v. State*, —— Tex. Crim. R. —— (1971), appeal pending.

[50] See *Smith v. State*, 33 Me. 48, 55 (1851); *In re Vince*, 2 N. J. 443, 450, 67 A.2d 141, 144 (1949). A short discussion of the modern law on this issue is contained in the Comment to the ALI's Model Penal Code § 207.11, at 158 and nn. 35-37 (Tent. Draft No. 9, 1959).

id., at 486 (Goldberg, J., concurring); or in the concept of liberty guaranteed by the first section of the Fourteenth Amendment, see *Meyer v. Nebraska*, 262 U.S. 390, 399 (1923). These decisions make it clear that only personal rights that can be deemed "fundamental" or "implicit in the concept of ordered liberty," *Palko v. Connecticut*, 302 U.S. 319, 325 (1937), are included in this guarantee of personal privacy. They also make it clear that the right has some extension to activities relating to marriage, *Loving v. Virginia*, 388 U.S. 1, 12 (1967), procreation, *Skinner v. Oklahoma*, 316 U.S. 535, 541-542 (1942), contraception, *Eisenstadt v. Baird*, 405 U.S. 438, 453-454 (1972); *id.*, at 460, 463-465 (WHITE, J., concurring), family relationships, *Prince v. Massachusetts*, 321 U.S. 158, 166 (1944), and child rearing and education, *Pierce v. Society of Sisters*, 268 U.S. 510, 535 (1925), *Meyer v. Nebraska, supra.*

This right of privacy, whether it be founded in the Fourteenth Amendment's concept of personal liberty and restrictions upon state action, as we feel it is, or, as the District Court determined, in the Ninth Amendment's reservation of rights to the people, is broad enough to encompass a woman's decision whether or not to terminate her pregnancy. The detriment that the State would impose upon the pregnant woman by denying this choice altogether is apparent. Specific and direct harm medically diagnosable even in early pregnancy may be involved. Maternity, or additional offspring, may force upon the woman a distressful life and future. Psychological harm may be imminent. Mental and physical health may be taxed by child care. There is also the distress, for all concerned, associated with the unwanted child, and there is the problem of bringing a child into a family already unable, psychologically and otherwise, to care for it. In other cases, as in this one, the additional difficulties and continuing stigma of unwed motherhood may be involved. All these are factors the woman and her responsible physician necessarily will consider in consultation.

On the basis of elements such as these, appellants and some *amici* argue that the woman's right is absolute and that she is entitled to terminate her pregnancy at whatever time, in whatever way, and for whatever reason she alone chooses. With this we do not agree. Appellants' arguments that Texas either has no valid interest at all in regulating the abortion decision, or no interest strong enough to support any limitation upon the woman's sole determination, is unpersuasive. The Court's decisions recognizing a right of privacy also acknowledge that some state regulation in areas protected by that right is appropriate. As noted above, a state may properly assert important interests in safeguarding health, in maintaining medical standards, and in protecting potential life. At some point in pregnancy, these respective interests become sufficiently compelling to sustain regulation of the factors that govern the abortion decision. The privacy right involved, therefore, cannot be said to be absolute. In fact, it is not clear to us that the claim asserted by some *amici* that one has an unlimited right to do with one's body as one pleases bears a close relationship to the right of privacy previously articulated in the Court's decisions. The Court has refused to recognize an unlimited right of this kind in the past. *Jacobson v. Massachusetts*, 197 U.S. 11 (1905) (vaccination); *Buck v. Bell*, 274 U.S. 200 (1927) (sterilization).

We therefore conclude that the right of personal privacy includes the abortion decision, but that this right is not unqualified and must be considered against important state interests in regulation.

We note that those federal and state courts that have recently considered abortion law challenges have reached the same conclusion. A majority, in addition to the District Court in the present case, have held state laws unconstitutional, at least in part, because of vagueness or because of overbreadth and abridgement of rights. *Abele v. Markle*, 342 F. Supp. 800 (Conn. 1972), appeal pending; *Abele v. Markle*, ——— F. Supp. ——— (Conn. Sept. 20, 1972) appeal pending; *Doe v. Bolton*, 319 F. Supp. 1048 (ND Ga. 1970), appeal decided today, *post* ———; *Doe v. Scott*, 321 F. Supp. 1385 (ND Ill. 1971), appeal pending; *Poe v. Menghini*, 339 F. Supp. 986 (Kan. 1972); *YWCA v. Kugler*, 342 F. Supp. 1048 (NJ 1972); *Babbitz v. McCann*, 310 F. Supp. 293 (ED Wis. 1970), appeal dismissed, 400 U.S. 1 (1970); *People v. Belous*, 71 Cal. 2d 954, 458 P.2d 194 (1969), cert. denied, 397 U.S. 915 (1970); *State v. Barquet*, 262 S. 2d 431 (Fla. 1972).

Others have sustained state statutes. *Crossen v. Attorney General*, 344 F. Supp. 587 (ED Ky. 1972), appeal pending; *Rosen v. Louisiana State Board of Medical Examiners*, 318 F. Supp. 1217 (ED La. 1970), appeal pending; *Corkey v. Edwards*, 322 F. Supp. 1248 (WDNC 1971), appeal pending; *Steinberg v. Brown*, 321 F. Supp. 741 (ND Ohio 1970); *Doe v. Rampton*, ——— F. Supp. ——— (Utah 1971), appeal pending; *Cheaney v. Indiana*, ——— Ind. ———, 285 N. E. 2d 265 (1972); *Spears v. State*, 257 So. 2d 876 (Miss. 1972); *State v. Munson*, ——— S. D. ———, 201 N. W. 2d 123 (1972), appeal pending.

Although the results are divided, most of these courts have agreed that the right of privacy, however based, is broad enough to cover the abortion decision; that the right, nonetheless, is not absolute and is subject to some limitations; and that at some point the state interests as to protection of health, medical standards, and prenatal life, become dominant. We agree with this approach.

Where certain "fundamental rights" are involved, the Court has held that regulation limiting these rights may be justified only by a "compelling state interest," *Kramer v. Union Free School District*, 395 U.S. 621, 627 (1969); *Shapiro v. Thompson*, 394 U.S. 618, 634 (1969), *Sherbert v. Verner*, 374 U.S. 398, 406 (1963), and that legislative enactments must be narrowly drawn to express only the legitimate state interests at stake. *Griswold v. Connecticut*, 381 U.S. 479, 485 (1965); *Aptheker v. Secretary of State*, 378 U.S. 500, 508 (1964); *Cantwell v. Connecticut*, 310 U.S 296, 307-308 (1940); see *Eisenstadt v. Baird*, 405 U.S. 438, 460, 463-464 (1972) (WHITE, J., concurring).

In the recent abortion cases, cited above, courts have recognized these principles. Those striking down state laws have generally scrutinized the State's interest in protecting health and potential life and have concluded that neither interest justified broad limitations on the reasons for which a physician and his pregnant patient might decide that she should have an abortion in the early stages of pregnancy. Courts sustaining state laws have held that the State's determinations to protect health or prenatal life are dominant and constitutionally justifiable.

IX

The District Court held that the appellee failed to meet his burden of demonstrating that the Texas statute's infringement upon Roe's rights was necessary to support a compelling state interest, and that, although the defendant presented "several compelling justifications for state presence in the area of abortions," the statutes outstripped these justifications and swept "far beyond any areas of compelling state interest." 314 F. Supp., at 1222-1223. Appellant and appellee both contest that holding. Appellant, as has been indicated, claims an absolute right that bars any state imposition of criminal penalties in the area. Appellee argues that the State's determination to recognize and protect prenatal life from and after conception constitutes a compelling state interest. As noted above, we do not agree fully with either formulation.

A. The appellee and certain *amici* argue that the fetus is a "person" within the language and meaning of the Fourteenth Amendment. In support of this they outline at length and in detail the well-known facts of fetal development. If this suggestion of personhood is established, the appellant's case, of course, collapses, for the fetus' right to life is then guaranteed specifically by the Amendment. The appellant conceded as much on reargument.[51] On the other hand, the appellee conceded on reargument[52] that no case could be cited that holds that a fetus is a person within the meaning of the Fourteenth Amendment.

The Constitution does not define "person" in so many words. Section 1 of the Fourteenth Amendment contains three references to "person." The first, in defining "citizens," speaks of "persons born or naturalized in the United States." The word also appears both in the Due Process Clause and in the Equal Protection Clause. "Person" is used in other places in the Constitution: in the listing of qualifications for representatives and senators, Art. I, § 2, cl. 2, and § 3, cl. 3; in the Apportionment Clause, Art. I, § 2, cl. 3;[53] in the Migration and Importation provision, Art. I, § 9, cl. 1; in the Emolument Clause, Art. I, § 9, cl. 8; in the Electors provisions, Art. II, § 1, cl. 2, and the superseded cl. 3; in the provision outlining qualifications for the office of President, Art. II, § 1, cl. 5; in the Extradition provisions, Art. IV, § 2, cl. 2, and the superseded Fugitive Slave cl. 3; and in the Fifth, Twelfth, and Twenty-second Amendments as well as in §§ 2 and 3 of the Fourteenth Amendment. But in nearly all these instances, the use of the word is such that it has application only postnatally. None indicates, with any assurance, that it has any possible pre-natal application.[54]

All this, together with our observation, *supra*, that throughout the major portion of the 19th century prevailing legal abortion practices were far freer than

---

[51] Tr. of Rearg. 20-21.

[52] Tr. of Rearg. 24.

[53] We are not aware that in the taking of any census under this clause, a fetus has ever been counted.

[54] When Texas urges that a fetus is entitled to Fourteenth Amendment protection as a person, it faces a dilemma. Neither in Texas nor in any other State are all abortions prohibited. Despite broad proscription, an exception always exists. The exception contained in Art. 1196, for an abortion procured or attempted by medical advice for the purpose of saving the life of the mother, is typical. But if the fetus is a person who is not to be deprived of life without due process of law, and if the mother's condition is the sole determinant, does not the Texas exception appear to be out of line with the Amendment's command?

There are other inconsistencies between Fourteenth Amendment status and the typical abortion statute. It has already been pointed out, n. 49, *supra*, that in Texas the woman is not a principal or an accomplice with respect to an abortion upon her. If the fetus is a person, why is the woman not a principal or an accomplice? Further, the penalty for criminal abortion specified by Art. 1195 is significantly less than the maximum penalty for murder prescribed by Art. 1257 of the Texas Penal Code. If the fetus is a person, may the penalties be different?

they are today, persuades us that the word "person," as used in the Fourteenth Amendment, does not include the unborn.[55] This is in accord with the results reached in those few cases where the issue has been squarely presented. *McGarvey v. Magee-Women's Hospital*, 340 F. Supp. 751 (WD Pa. 1972); *Byrn v. New York City Health & Hospitals Corp.*, 31 N.Y. 2d 194, 286 N.E. 2d 887 (1972), appeal pending; *Abele v. Markle*, ——— F. Supp. ——— (Conn. Sept. 20, 1972), appeal pending. Compare *Cheaney v. Indiana*, ——— Ind. ———, 285 N.E. 265, 270 (1972); *Montana v. Rogers*, 278 F. 2d 68, 72 (CA7 1960), aff'd *sub nom. Montana v. Kennedy*, 366 U.S. 308 (1961); *Keeler v. Superior Court*, ——— Cal. ———, 470 P. 2d 617 (1970); *State v. Dickinson*, 23 Ohio App. 2d 259, 275 N.E. 2d 599 (1970). Indeed, our decision in *United States v. Vuitch*, 402 U.S. 62 (1971), inferentially is to the same effect, for we there would not have indulged in statutory interpretation favorable to abortion in specified circumstances if the necessary consequence was the termination of life entitled to Fourteenth Amendment protection.

This conclusion, however, does not of itself fully answer the contentions raised by Texas, and we pass on to other considerations.

B. The pregnant woman cannot be isolated in her privacy. She carries an embryo and, later, a fetus, if one accepts the medical definitions of the developing young in the human uterus. See Dorland's Illustrated Medical Dictionary, 478-479, 547 (24th ed. 1965). The situation therefore is inherently different from marital intimacy, or bedroom possession of obscene material, or marriage, or procreation, or education, with which *Eisenstadt, Griswold, Stanley, Loving, Skinner, Pierce,* and *Meyer* were respectively concerned. As we have intimated above, it is reasonable and appropriate for a State to decide that at some point in time another interest, that of health of the mother or that of potential human life, becomes significantly involved. The woman's privacy is no longer sole and any right of privacy she possesses must be measured accordingly.

Texas urges that, apart from the Fourteenth Amendment, life begins at conception and is present throughout pregnancy, and that, therefore, the State has a compelling interest in protecting that life from and after conception. We need not resolve the difficult question of when life begins. When those trained in the respective disciplines of medicine, philosophy, and theology are unable to arrive at any consensus, the judiciary, at this point in the development of man's knowledge, is not in a position to speculate as to the answer.

It should be sufficient to note briefly the wide divergence of thinking on this most sensitive and difficult question. There has always been strong support for the view that life does not begin until live birth. This was the belief of the Stoics.[56] It appears to be the predominant, though not the unanimous, attitude of the Jewish faith.[57] It may be taken to represent also the position of a large segment of the Protestant community, insofar as that can be ascertained; organized groups that

---

[55] Cf. the Wisconsin abortion statute, defining "unborn child" to mean "a human being from the time of conception until it is born alive," Wis. Stat. § 940.04(6) (1969), and the new Connecticut statute, Public Act No. 1, May 1972 Special Session, declaring it to be the public policy of the State and the legislative intent "to protect and preserve human life from the moment of conception."

[56] Edelstein 16.

[57] Lader 97-99; D. Feldman, Birth Control in Jewish Law 251-294 (1968). For a stricter view, see I. Jakobovits, Jewish Views on Abortion, in Abortion and the Law 124 (D. Smith ed. 1967).

have taken a formal position on the abortion issue have generally regarded abortion as a matter for the conscience of the individual and her family.[58] As we have noted the common law found greater significance in quickening. Physicians and their scientific colleagues have regarded that event with less interest and have tended to focus either upon conception or upon live birth or upon the interim point at which the fetus becomes "viable," that is, potentially able to live outside the mother's womb, albeit with artificial aid.[59] Viability is usually placed at about seven months (28 weeks) but may occur earlier, even at 24 weeks.[60] The Aristotelian theory of "mediate animation" that held sway throughout the Middle Ages and the Renaissance in Europe, continued to be official Roman Catholic dogma until the 19th century, despite opposition to this "ensoulment" theory from those in the Church who would recognize the existence of life from the moment of conception.[61] The latter is now, of course, the official belief of the Catholic Church. As one of the briefs *amicus* discloses, this is a view strongly held by many non-Catholics as well, and by many physicians. Substantial problems for precise definition of this view are posed, however, by new embryological data that purport to indicate that conception is a "process" over time, rather than an event, and by new medical techniques such as menstrual extraction, the "morning-after" pill, implantation of embryos, artificial insemination, and even artificial wombs.[62]

In areas other than criminal abortion the law has been reluctant to endorse any theory that life, as we recognize it, begins before live birth or to accord legal rights to the unborn except in narrowly defined situations and except when the rights are contingent upon live birth. For example, the traditional rule of tort law had denied recovery for prenatal injuries even though the child was born alive.[63] That rule has been changed in almost every jurisdiction. In most States recovery is said to be permitted only if the fetus was viable, or at least quick, when the injuries were sustained, though few courts have squarely so held.[64] In a recent development, generally opposed by the commentators, some States permit the parents of a stillborn child to maintain an action for wrongful death because of prenatal injuries.[65] Such an action, however, would appear to be one to vindicate

[58] Amicus Brief for the American Ethical Union et al. For the position of the National Council of Churches and of other denominations, see Lader 99-101.

[59] L. Hellman & J. Pritchard, Williams Obstetrics 493 (14th ed. 1971); Dorland's Illustrated Medical Dictionary 1689 (24th ed. 1965).

[60] Hellman & Pritchard, *supra*, n. 58, at 493.

[61] For discussions of the development of the Roman Catholic position, see D. Callahan, Abortion: Law, Choice and Morality 409-447 (1970); Noonan 1.

[62] See D. Brodie, The New Biology and the Prenatal Child, 9 J. Fam. L. 391, 397 (1970); R. Gorney, The New Biology and the Future of Man, 15 UCLA L. Rev. 273 (1968); Note, Criminal Law—Abortion—the "Morning-After" Pill and Other Pre-Implantation Birth-Control Methods and the Law, 46 Ore. L. Rev. 211 (1967); G. Taylor, The Biological Time Bomb 32 (1968); A. Rosenfeld, The Second Genesis 138-139 (1969); G. Smith, Through a Test Tube Darkly: Artificial Insemination and the Law, 67 Mich. L. Rev. 127 (1968); Note, Artificial Insemination and the Law, U. Ill. L. F. 203 (1968).

[63] Prosser, Handbook of the Law of Torts 335-338 (1971); 2 Harper & James, The Law of Torts 1028-1031 (1956); Note, 63 Harv. L. Rev. 173 (1949).

[64] See cases cited in Prosser, *supra*, n. 62, at 336-338; Annotation, Action for Death of Unborn Child, 15 A. L. R. 3d 992 (1967).

[65] Prosser, *supra*, n. 62, at 338; Note, The Law and the Unborn Child, 46 Notre Dame Law. 349, 354-360 (1971).

the parents' interest and is thus consistent with the view that the fetus, at most, represents only the potentiality of life. Similarly, unborn children have been recognized as acquiring rights or interests by way of inheritance or other devolution of property, and have been represented by guardians *ad litem*.[66] Perfection of the interests involved, again, has generally been contingent upon live birth. In short, the unborn have never been recognized in the law as persons in the whole sense.

X

In view of all this, we do not agree that, by adopting one theory of life, Texas may override the rights of the pregnant woman that are at stake. We repeat, however, that the State does have an important and legitimate interest in preserving and protecting the health of the pregnant woman, whether she be a resident of the State or a nonresident who seeks medical consultation and treatment there, and that it has still *another* important and legitimate interest in protecting the potentiality of human life. These interests are separate and distinct. Each grows in substantiality as the woman approaches term and, at a point during pregnancy, each becomes "compelling."

With respect to the State's important and legitimate interest in the health of the mother, the "compelling" point, in the light of present medical knowledge, is at approximately the end of the first trimester. This is so because of the now established medical fact, referred to above at p. 34, that until the end of the first trimester mortality in abortion is less than mortality in normal childbirth. It follows that, from and after this point, a State may regulate the abortion procedure to the extent that the regulation reasonably relates to the preservation and protection of maternal health. Examples of permissible state regulation in this area are requirements as to the qualifications of the person who is to perform the abortion; as to the licensure of that person; as to the facility in which the procedure is to be performed, that is, whether it must be a hospital or may be a clinic or some other place of less-than-hospital status; as to the licensing of the facility; and the like.

This means, on the other hand, that, for the period of pregnancy prior to this "compelling" point, the attending physician, in consultation with his patient, is free to determine, without regulation by the State, that in his medical judgment the patient's pregnancy should be terminated. If that decision is reached, the judgment may be effectuated by an abortion free of interference by the State.

With respect to the State's important and legitimate interest in potential life, the "compelling" point is at viability. This is so because the fetus then presumably has the capability of meaningful life outside the mother's womb. State regulation protective of fetal life after viability thus has both logical and biological justifications. If the State is interested in protecting fetal life after viability, it may go so far as to proscribe abortion during that period except when it is necessary to preserve the life or health of the mother.

Measured against these standards, Art. 1196 of the Texas Penal Code, in

---

[66] D. Louisell, Abortion, The Practice of Medicine, and the Due Process of Law, 16 UCLA L. Rev. 233, 235-238 (1969); Note, 56 Iowa L. Rev. 994, 999-1000 (1971); Note, The Law and the Unborn Child, 46 Notre Dame Law, 349, 351-354 (1971).

restricting legal abortions to those "procured or attempted by medical advice for the purpose of saving the life of the mother," sweeps too broadly. The statute makes no distinction between abortions performed early in pregnancy and those performed later and it limits to a single reason, "saving" the mother's life, the legal justification for the procedure. The statute, therefore, cannot survive the constitutional attack made upon it here.

This conclusion makes it unnecessary for us to consider the additional challenge to the Texas statute asserted on grounds of vagueness. See *United States v. Vuitch*, 402 U.S. 62, 67-72 (1971).

XI

To summarize and to repeat:

1. A state criminal abortion statute of the current Texas type, that excepts from criminality only a *life saving* procedure on behalf of the mother, without regard to pregnancy stage and without recognition of the other interests involved, is violative of the Due Process Clause of the Fourteenth Amendment.

(a) For the stage prior to approximately the end of the first trimester, the abortion decision and its effectuation must be left to the medical judgment of the pregnant woman's attending physician.

(b) For the stage subsequent to approximately the end of the first trimester, the State, in promoting its interest in the health of the mother, may, if it chooses, regulate the abortion procedure in ways that are reasonably related to maternal health.

(c) For the stage subsequent to viability the State, in promoting its interest in the potentiality of human life, may, if it chooses, regulate, and even proscribe, abortion except where it is necessary, in appropriate medical judgment, for the preservation of the life or health of the mother.

2. The State may define the term "physician," as it has been employed in the preceding numbered paragraphs of this Part XI of this opinion, to mean only a physician currently licensed by the State, and may proscribe any abortion by a person who is not a physician as so defined.

In *Doe v. Bolton, post*, procedural requirements contained in one of the modern abortion statutes are considered. That opinion and this one, of course, are to be read together.[67]

This holding, we feel, is consistent with the relative weights of the respective interests involved, with the lessons and example of medical and legal history, with the lenity of the common law, and with the demands of the profound problems of the present day. The decision leaves the State free to place increasing restrictions on abortion as the period of pregnancy lengthens, so long as those restrictions are

[67] Neither in this opinion nor in *Doe v. Bolton, post*, do we discuss the father's rights, if any exist in the constitutional context, in the abortion decision. No paternal right has been asserted in either of the cases, and the Texas and the Georgia statutes on their face take no cognizance of the father. We are aware that some statutes recognize the father under certain circumstances. North Carolina, for example, 1B N. C. Gen. Stat. § 14-45.1 (Supp. 1971), requires written permission for the abortion from the husband when the woman is a married minor, that is, when she is less than 18 years of age, 41 N. C. A. G. 489 (1971); if the woman is an unmarried minor, written permission from the parents is required. We need not now decide whether provisions of this kind are constitutional.

tailored to the recognized state interests. The decision vindicates the right of the physician to administer medical treatment according to his professional judgment up to the points where important state interests provide compelling justifications for intervention. Up to those points the abortion decision in all its aspects is inherently, and primarily, a medical decision, and basic responsibility for it must rest with the physician. If an individual practitioner abuses the privilege of exercising proper medical judgment, the usual remedies, judicial and intra-professional, are available.

XII

Our conclusion that Art. 1196 is unconstitutional means, of course, that the Texas abortion statutes, as a unit, must fall. The exception of Art. 1196 cannot be stricken separately, for then the State is left with a statute proscribing all abortion procedures no matter how medically urgent the case.

Although the District Court granted plaintiff Roe declaratory relief, it stopped short of issuing an injunction against enforcement of the Texas statutes. The Court has recognized that different considerations enter into a federal court's decision as to declaratory relief, on the one hand, and injunctive relief, on the other. *Zwickler v. Koota*, 389 U.S. 241, 252-255 (1967); *Dombrowski v. Pfister*, 380 U.S. 479 (1965). We are not dealing with a statute that, on its face, appears to abridge free expression, an area of particular concern under *Dombrowski* and refined in *Younger v. Harris*, 401 U.S., at 50.

We find it unnecessary to decide whether the District Court erred in withholding injunctive relief, for we assume the Texas prosecutorial authorities will give full credence to this decision that the present criminal abortion statutes of that State are unconstitutional.

The judgment of the District Court as to intervenor Hallford is reversed, and Dr. Hallford's complaint in intervention is dismissed. In all other respects the judgment of the District Court is affirmed. Costs are allowed to the appellee.

It is so ordered.

MR. JUSTICE STEWART, concurring

In 1963, this Court, in *Ferguson v. Skrupa*, 372 U.S. 726, purported to sound the death knell for the doctrine of substantive due process, a doctrine under which many state laws had in the past been held to violate the Fourteenth Amendment. As Mr. Justice Black's opinion for the Court in *Skrupa* put it: "We have returned to the original constitutional proposition that courts do not substitute their social and economic beliefs for the judgment of legislative bodies, who are elected to pass laws." *Id.*, at 730.[1]

Barely two years later, in *Griswold v. Connecticut*, 381 U.S. 479, the Court held a Connecticut birth control law unconstitutional. In view of what had been so recently said in *Skrupa*, the Court's opinion in *Griswold* understandably did its best to avoid reliance on the Due Process Clause of the Fourteenth Amendment

[1] Only Mr. Justice Harlan failed to join the Court's opinion, 372 U.S. at 733.

as the ground for decision. Yet, the Connecticut law did not violate any provision of the Bill of Rights, nor any other specific provision of the Constitution.[2] So it was clear to me then, and it is equally clear to me now, that the *Griswold* decision can be rationally understood only as a holding that the Connecticut statute substantively invaded the "liberty" that is protected by the Due Process Clause of the Fourteenth Amendment.[3] As so understood, *Griswold* stands as one in a long line of pre-*Skrupa* cases decided under the doctrine of substantive due process, and I now accept it as such.

"In a Constitution for a free people, there can be no doubt that the meaning of 'liberty' must be broad indeed." *Board of Regents v. Roth*, 408 U.S. 564, 572. The Constitution nowhere mentions a specific right of personal choice in matters of marriage and family life, but the "liberty" protected by the Due Process Clause of the Fourteenth Amendment covers more than those freedoms explicitly named in the Bill of Rights. See *Schware v. Board of Bar Examiners*, 353 U.S. 232, 238-239; *Pierce v. Society of Sisters*, 268 U.S. 510, 534-535; *Meyer v. Nebraska*, 262 U.S. 390, 399-400. Cf. *Shapiro v. Thompson*, 394 U.S. 618, 629-630; *United States v. Guest*, 383 U.S. 745, 757-758; *Carrington v. Rash*, 380 U.S. 89, 96; *Aptheker v. Secretary of State*, 378 U.S. 500, 505; *Kent v. Dulles*, 357 U.S. 116, 127; *Bolling v. Sharpe*, 347 U.S. 497, 499-500; *Truax v. Raich*, 239 U.S. 33, 41.

As Mr. Justice Harlan once wrote: "[T]he full scope of the liberty guaranteed by the Due Process Clause cannot be found in or limited by the precise terms of the specific guarantees elsewhere provided in the Constitution. This 'liberty' is not a series of isolated points pricked out in terms of the taking of property; the freedom of speech, press, and religion; the right to keep and bear arms; the freedom from unreasonable searches and seizures; and so on. It is a rational continuum which, broadly speaking, includes a freedom from all substantial arbitrary impositions and purposeless restraints, . . . and which also recognizes, what a reasonable and sensitive judgment must, that certain interests require particularly careful scrutiny of the state needs asserted to justify their abridgement." *Poe v. Ullman*, 367 U.S. 497, 543 (opinion dissenting from dismissal of appeal) (citations omitted). In the words of Mr. Justice Frankfurter, "Great concepts like . . . 'liberty' . . . were purposely left to gather meaning from experience. For they relate to the whole domain of social and economic fact, and the statesmen who founded this Nation knew too well that only a stagnant society remains unchanged." *National Mutual Ins. Co. v. Tidewater Transfer Co., Inc.*, 337 U.S. 582, 646 (dissenting opinion).

Several decisions of this Court make clear that freedom of personal choice in

[2] There is no constitutional right of privacy, as such. "[The Fourth] Amendment protects individual privacy against certain kinds of governmental intrusion, but its protections go further, and often have nothing to do with privacy at all. Other provisions of the Constitution protect personal privacy from other forms of governmental invasion. But the protection of a person's *general* right to privacy—his right to be let alone by other people—is, like the protection of his property and of his very life, left largely to the law of the individual States." *Katz v. United States*, 389 U.S. 347, 350-351 (footnotes omitted).

[3] This was also clear to Mr. Justice Black, 381 U.S., at 507 (dissenting opinion); to Mr. Justice Harlan, 381 U.S., at 499 (opinion concurring in the judgment); and to MR. JUSTICE WHITE, 381 U.S., at 502 (opinion concurring in the judgment). See also Mr. Justice Harlan's thorough and thoughtful opinion dissenting from dismissal of the appeal in *Poe v. Ullman*, 367 U.S. 497, 522.

matters of marriage and family life is one of the liberties protected by the Due Process Clause of the Fourteenth Amendment. *Loving v. Virginia*, 388 U.S. 1, 12; *Griswold v. Connecticut, supra*; *Pierce v. Society of Sisters, supra*; *Meyer v. Nebraska, supra*. See also *Prince v. Massachusetts*, 321 U.S. 158, 166; *Skinner v. Oklahoma*, 316 U.S. 535, 541. As recently as last Term, in *Eisenstadt v. Baird*, 405 U.S. 438, 453, we recognized "the right of the *individual*, married or single, to be free from unwarranted governmental intrusion into matters so fundamentally affecting a person as the decision whether to bear or beget a child." That right necessarily includes the right of a woman to decide whether or not to terminate her pregnancy. "Certainly the interests of a woman in giving of her physical and emotional self during pregnancy and the interests that will be affected throughout her life by the birth and raising of a child are of a far greater degree of significance and personal intimacy than the right to send a child to private school protected in *Pierce v. Society of Sisters*, 268 U.S. 510 (1925), or the right to teach a foreign language protected in *Meyer v. Nebraska*, 262 U.S. 390 (1923)." *Abele v. Markle*, ——— F. Supp. ———, ——— (Conn. 1972).

Clearly, therefore, the Court today is correct in holding that the right asserted by Jane Roe is embraced within the personal liberty protected by the Due Process Clause of the Fourteenth Amendment.

It is evident that the Texas abortion statute infringes that right directly. Indeed, it is difficult to imagine a more complete abridgment of a constitutional freedom than that worked by the inflexible criminal statute now in force in Texas. The question then becomes whether the state interests advanced to justify this abridgment can survive the "particularly careful scrutiny" that the Fourteenth Amendment here requires.

The asserted state interests are protection of the health and safety of the pregnant woman, and protection of the potential future human life within her. These are legitimate objectives, amply sufficient to permit a State to regulate abortions as it does other surgical procedures, and perhaps sufficient to permit a State to regulate abortions more stringently or even to prohibit them in the late stages of pregnancy. But such legislation is not before us, and I think the Court today has thoroughly demonstrated that these state interests cannot constitutionally support the broad abridgment of personal liberty worked by the existing Texas law. Accordingly, I join the Court's opinion holding that that law is invalid under the Due Process Clause of the Fourteenth Amendment.

MR. JUSTICE REHNQUIST, dissenting

The Court's opinion brings to the decision of this troubling question both extensive historical fact and a wealth of legal scholarship. While its opinion thus commands my respect, I find myself nonetheless in fundamental disagreement with those parts of it which invalidate the Texas statute in question, and therefore dissent.

I

The Court's opinion decides that a State may impose virtually no restriction on the performance of abortions during the first trimester of pregnancy. Our previous decisions indicate that a necessary predicate for such an opinion is a plaintiff who was in her first trimester of pregnancy at some time during the pendency of her law suit. While a party may vindicate his own constitutional rights, he may not seek vindication for the rights of others. *Moose Lodge v. Irvis*, 407 U.S. 163 (1972); *Sierra Club v. Morton*, 405 U.S. 727 (1972). The Court's statement of facts in this case makes clear, however, that the record in no way indicates the presence of such a plaintiff. We know only that plaintiff Roe at the time of filing her complaint was a pregnant woman; for aught that appears in this record, she may have been in her *last* trimester of pregnancy as of the date the complaint was filed.

Nothing in the Court's opinion indicates that Texas might not constitutionally apply its proscription of abortion as written to a woman in that stage of pregnancy. Nonetheless, the Court uses her complaint against the Texas statute as a fulcrum for deciding that States may impose virtually no restrictions on medical abortions performed during the *first* trimester of pregnancy. In deciding such a hypothetical lawsuit the Court departs from the longstanding admonition that it should never "formulate a rule of constitutional law broader than is required by the precise facts to which it is to be applied." *Liverpool, New York and Philadelphia Steamship Co. v. Commissioners of Emigration*, 113 U.S. 33, 39 (1885). See also *Ashwander v. TVA*, 297 U.S. 288, 345 (1936) (Brandeis, concurring).

II

Even if there were a plaintiff in this case capable of litigating the issue which the Court decides, I would reach a conclusion opposite to that reached by the Court. I have difficulty in concluding, as the Court does, that the right of "privacy" is involved in this case. Texas by the statute here challenged bars the performance of a medical abortion by a licensed physician on a plaintiff such as Roe. A transaction resulting in an operation such as this is not "private" in the ordinary usage of the word. Nor is the "privacy" which the Court finds here even a distant relative of the freedom from searches and seizures protected by the Fourth Amendment to the Constitution which the Court has referred to as embodying a right to privacy. *Katz v. United States*, 389 U.S. 347 (1967).

If the Court means by the term "privacy" no more than that the claim of a person to be free from unwanted state regulation of consensual transactions may be a form of "liberty" protected by the Fourteenth Amendment, there is no doubt that similar claims have been upheld in our earlier decisions on the basis of that liberty. I agree with the statement of MR. JUSTICE STEWART in his concurring opinion that the "liberty," against deprivation of which without due process the Fourteenth Amendment protects, embraces more than the rights found in the Bill of Rights. But that liberty is not guaranteed absolutely against deprivation, but only against deprivation without due process of law. The test traditionally applied in the area of social and economic legislation is whether or not a law such as that challenged has a rational relation to a valid state objective. *Williamson v. Lee Optical Co.*, 348 U.S. 483, 491 (1955). The Due Process Clause of the Fourteenth Amendment undoubtedly does place a limit on legislative power to enact laws such as this, albeit a broad one. If the Texas statute were to prohibit an abortion even where the mother's life is in jeopardy, I have little doubt that such a statute would lack a rational relation to a valid state objective under the test stated in *Williamson, supra*. But the Court's sweeping invalidation of any restrictions on abortion during the first trimester is impossible to justify under that standard, and the conscious weighing of competing factors which the Court's opinion apparently substitutes for the established test is far more appropriate to a legislative judgment than to a judicial one.

The Court eschews the history of the Fourteenth Amendment in its reliance on the "compelling state interest" test. See *Weber v. Aetna Casualty & Surety Co.*, 406 U.S. 164, 179 (1972) (dissenting opinion). But the Court adds a new wrinkle to this test by transposing it from the legal considerations associated with the Equal Protection Clause of the Fourteenth Amendment to this case arising under the Due Process Clause of the Fourteenth Amendment. Unless I misapprehend the consequences of this transplanting of the "compelling state interest test," the Court's opinion will accomplish the seemingly impossible feat of leaving this area of the law more confused than it found it.

While the Court's opinion quotes from the dissent of Mr. Justice Holmes in *Lochner v. New York*, 198 U.S. 45 (1905), the result it reaches is more closely attuned to the majority opinion of Mr. Justice Peckham in that case. As in *Lochner* and similar cases applying substantive due process standards to economic and social welfare legislation, the adoption of the compelling state interest standard will inevitably require this Court to examine the legislative policies and pass on the wisdom of these policies in the very process of deciding whether a particular state interest put forward may or may not be "compelling." The decision here to break the term of pregnancy into three distinct terms and to outline the permissible restrictions the State may impose in each one, for example, partakes more of judicial legislation than it does of a determination of the intent of the drafters of the Fourteenth Amendment.

The fact that a majority of the States, reflecting after all the majority sentiment in those States, have had restrictions on abortions for at least a century seems to me as strong an indication there is that the asserted right to an abortion is not "so rooted in the traditions and conscience of our people as to be ranked as fundamental," *Snyder v. Massachusetts*, 291 U.S. 97, 105 (1934). Even today, when society's views on abortion are changing, the very existence of the debate is evidence that the "right" to an abortion is not so universally accepted as the appellants would have us believe.

To reach its result the Court necessarily has had to find within the scope of the Fourteenth Amendment a right that was apparently completely unknown to the drafters of the Amendment. As early as 1821, the first state law dealing directly with abortion was enacted by the Connecticut legislature. Conn. Stat. Tit. 22, §§ 14, 16 (1821). By the time of the adoption of the Fourteenth Amendment in 1868 there were at least 36 laws enacted by state or territorial legislatures limiting abortion.[1] While many States have amended or updated their laws, 21 of the laws

---

[1] States having enacted abortion laws prior to the adoption of the Fourteenth Amendment in 1868:
    1. Alabama—Ala. Acts. c. 6, § 2 (1840-1841).
    2. Arizona—Howell Code, c. 10, § 45 (1865).
    3. Arkansas—Ark. Rev. Stat., c. 44, div. III, Art. II, § 6 (1838).
    4. California—Cal. Sess. Stats., c. 99, § 45, at 233 (1849-1850).
    5. Colorado (Terr.)—Colo. Gen. Laws of Terr. of Colo., 1st Sess., § 42, at 296-297 (1861).

on the books in 1868 remain in effect today.[2] Indeed, the Texas statute struck down today was, as the majority notes, first enacted in 1857 and "has remained substantially unchanged to the present time." *Ante*, at ———.

---

6. Connecticut—Conn. Stat. Tit. 22, §§ 14, 16, at 152, 153 (1821). By 1868 this statute had been replaced by another abortion law. Conn. Pub. Acts, c. LXXI, §§ 1, 2, at 65 (1860).

7. Florida—Fla. Acts 1st Sess., c. 1637, III, § 10, § 11, VIII, § 9, § 10, § 11, as amended now in Fla. Stat. Ann. §§ 782.09, 782.10, 797.01, 797.02, 782.16 (1944).

8. Georgia—Ga. Pen. Code §§ 56, 57, 58, 67, 68, 69 (1833).

9. Kingdom of Hawaii—Hawaii Pen. Code §§ 1, 2, 3 (1850).

10. Idaho (Terr.)—Idaho (Terr.) Laws §§ 33, 34, 42, at 435 (1863).

11. Illinois—Ill. Rev. Code §§ 40, 41, 46, at 130, 131 (1827). By 1868 this statute had been replaced by a subsequent enactment. Ill. Pub. Laws §§ 1, 2, 3, at 89 (1867).

12. Indiana—Ind. Rev. Stat. §§ 1, 3, at 224 (1838). By 1868 this statute had been superseded by a subsequent enactment. Ind. Laws c. LXXXI, § 2 (1859).

13. Iowa (Terr.)—Iowa (Terr.) Stat. 1st Legis., 1st Sess., § 18, at 145 (1838). By 1868 this statute had been superseded by a subsequent enactment. Iowa (Terr.) Rev. Stat. §§ 10, 13, (1843).

14. Kansas (Terr.)—Kan. (Terr.) Stat. c. 48, §§ 9, 10, 39 (1855). By 1968 this statute had been superseded by a subsequent enactment. Kan. Gen. Laws c. 28, §§ 9, 10 (1859).

15. Louisiana—La. Rev. Stat. § 24, at 138 (1856).

16. Maine—Me. Rev. Stat. c. 160, §§ 11, 12, 13, 14 (1840).

17. Maryland—Md. Laws c. 179, § 2, at 318 (1868).

18. Massachusetts—Mass. Acts & Resolves c. 27 (1845).

19. Michigan—Mich. Rev. Stat. c. 153, §§ 32, 33, 34, at 662 (1846).

20. Minn. (Terr.)—Minn. (Terr.) Rev. Stat. c. 100, §§ 10, 11, at 493 (1851).

21. Mississippi—Miss. Code §§ 8, 9, at 958 (1848).

22. Missouri—Mo. Rev. Stat. Art. II, §§ 9, 10, 36, at 184 (1864).

23. Montana (Terr.)—Mont. (Terr.) Laws § 41, at 184 (1864).

24. Nevada (Terr.)—Nev. (Terr.) Laws c. 28, § 42, at 63 (1861).

25. New Hampshire—N. H. Laws c. 743, § 1, at 708 (1848).

26. New Jersey—N. J. Laws, at 266 (1849).

27. New York—N. Y. Rev. Stat. pt. IV, c. I, Tit. II, §§ 8, 9, at 550 (1828). By 1868 this statute had been superseded by subsequent enactments. N. Y. Laws c. 260, §§ 1, 2, 3, 4, 5, 6, at 285 (1845); N. Y. Laws c. 22, § 1, at 19 (1846).

28. Ohio—Ohio Gen. Stat. §§ 111 (1), 112 (2), at 252 (1841).

29. Oregon—Ore. Gen. Laws. Crim. Code, c. 43, § 509, at 528 (1845-1864).

30. Pennsylvania—Pa. Laws No. 374, §§ 87, 88, 89 (1860).

31. Texas—Tex. Gen. Stat. Dig. c. VII, Arts. 531-536, at 524 (Oldham & White 1859).

32. Vermont—Vt. Acts No. 33, § 1 (1846). By 1868 this statute had been amended by a subsequent enactment. Vt. Acts No. 57, §§ 1, 3 (1867).

33. Virginia—Va. Acts Tit. II, c. 3, § 9, at 96 (1848).

34. Washington (Terr.)—Wash. (Terr.) Stats. c. II, §§ 37, 38, at 81 (1854).

35. West Virginia—Va. Acts. Tit. II, c. 3, § 9, at 96 (1848).

36. Wisconsin—Wis. Rev. Stat. c. 133, §§ 10, 11 (1849). By 1868 this statute had been superseded by a subsequent enactment. Wis. Rev. Stat. c. 164, §§ 10, 11; c. 169, §§ 58, 59 (1858).

[2] Abortion laws in effect in 1868 and still applicable as of August 1970:

1. Arizona (1865).
2. Connecticut (1860).
3. Florida (1868).
4. Idaho (1863).
5. Indiana (1838).
6. Iowa (1843).
7. Maine (1840).
8. Massachusetts (1845).
9. Michigan (1846).

There apparently was no question concerning the validity of this provision or of any of the other state statutes when the Fourteenth Amendment was adopted. The only conclusion possible from this history is that the drafters did not intend to have the Fourteenth Amendment withdraw from the States the power to legislate with respect to this matter.

III

Even if one were to agree that the case which the Court decides were here, and that the enunciation of the substantive constitutional law in the Court's opinion were proper, the actual disposition of the case by the Court is still difficult to justify. The Texas statute is struck down *in toto*, even though the Court apparently concedes that at later periods of pregnancy Texas might impose these self-same statutory limitations on abortion. My understanding of past practice is that a statute found to be invalid as applied to a particular plaintiff, but not unconstitutional as a whole, is not simply "struck down" but is instead declared unconstitutional as applied to the fact situation before the Court. *Yick Wo v. Hopkins*, 118 U.S. 356 (1886); *Street v. New York*, 394 U.S. 576 (1969).

For all of the foregoing reasons, I respectfully dissent.

No. 70–40

Mary Doe et al., Appellants, *v.* Arthur K. Bolton, as Attorney General of the State of Georgia, et al.	On Appeal from the United States District Court for the Northern District of Georgia.

[January 22, 1973]

SYLLABUS

Georgia law proscribes an abortion except as performed by a duly licensed Georgia physician when necessary in "his best clinical judgment" because continued pregnancy would endanger a pregnant woman's life or injure her health;

---

10. Minnesota (1851).
11. Missouri (1835).
12. Montana (1864).
13. Nevada (1861).
14. New Hampshire (1848).
15. New Jersey (1849).
16. Ohio (1841).
17. Pennsylvania (1860).
18. Texas (1859).
19. Vermont (1867).
20. West Virginia (1848).
21. Wisconsin (1858).

the fetus would likely be born with serious defects; or the pregnancy resulted from rape. § 26-1202(a) of Ga. Criminal Code. In addition to a requirement that the patient be a Georgia resident and certain other requirements, the statutory scheme poses three procedural conditions in § 26-1202(b): (1) that the abortion be performed in a hospital accredited by the Joint Committee on Accreditation of Hospitals (JCAH); (2) that the procedure be approved by the hospital staff abortion committee; and (3) that the performing physician's judgment be confirmed by independent examinations of the patient by two other licensed physicians. Appellant Doe, an indigent married Georgia citizen, who was denied an abortion after eight weeks of pregnancy for failure to meet any of the § 26-1202(a) conditions, sought declaratory and injunctive relief, contending that the Georgia laws were unconstitutional. Others joining in the complaint included Georgia-licensed physicians (who claimed that the Georgia statutes "chilled and deferred" their practices), registered nurses, clergymen, and social workers. Though holding that all the plaintiffs had standing, the District Court ruled that only Doe presented a justiciable controversy. In Doe's case the court gave declaratory, but not injunctive, relief, invalidating as an infringement of privacy and personal liberty the limitation to the three situations specified in § 26-1202(a) and certain other provisions but holding that the State's interest in health protection and the existence of a "*potential* of independent human existence" justified regulation through § 26-1202(b) of the "manner of performance as well as the quality of the final decision to abort." The appellants, claiming entitlement to broader relief, directly appealed to this Court. *Held*:

1. Doe's case presents a live, justiciable controversy and she has standing to sue, *Roe v. Wade, ante*, p. ———, as do the physician-appellants (who, unlike the physician in *Wade*, were not charged with abortion violations), and it is therefore unnecessary to resolve the issue of the other appellants' standing.

2. A woman's constitutional right to an abortion is not absolute. *Roe v. Wade, supra*.

3. The requirement that a physician's decision to perform an abortion must rest upon "his best clinical judgment" of its necessity is not unconstitutionally vague, since that judgment may be made in the light of *all* the attendant circumstances. *United States v. Vuitch*, 402 U.S. 62, 71-72.

4. The three procedural conditions in § 26-1202(b) violate the Fourteenth Amendment.

(a) The JCAH accreditation requirement is invalid, since the State has not shown that only hospitals (let alone those with JCAH accreditation) meet its interest in fully protecting the patient; and a hospital requirement failing to exclude the first trimester of pregnancy would be invalid on that ground alone, see *Roe v. Wade, supra*.

(b) The interposition of a hospital committee on abortion, a procedure not applicable as a matter of state criminal law to other surgical situations, is unduly restrictive of the patient's rights, which are already safeguarded by her personal physician.

(c) Required acquiescence by two co-practitioners also has no rational connection with a patient's needs and unduly infringes on her physician's right to practice.

5. The Georgia residence requirement violates the Privileges and Immunities

Clause by denying protection to persons who enter Georgia for medical services there.

6. Appellants' equal protection argument centering on the three procedural conditions in § 26-1202(b), invalidated on other grounds, is without merit.

7. No ruling is made on the question of injunctive relief. Cf. *Roe v. Wade, supra.*

319 F. Supp. 1048, modified and affirmed.

BLACKMUN, J., delivered the opinion of the Court, in which BURGER, C. J., and DOUGLAS, BRENNAN, STEWART, MARSHALL, and POWELL, J. J., joined. BURGER, C. J., and DOUGLAS and STEWART, J. J., filed concurring opinions. WHITE, J., filed a dissenting opinion, in which REHNQUIST, J., joined. REHNQUIST, J., filed a dissenting opinion.

MR. JUSTICE BLACKMUN delivered the opinion of the Court.

In this appeal the criminal abortion statutes recently enacted in Georgia are challenged on constitutional grounds. The statutes are §§ 26-1201 through 26-1203 of the State's Criminal Code, formulated by Georgia Laws, 1968 Session, 1249, 1277-1280. In *Roe v. Wade, ante* ——, we today have struck down, as constitutionally defective, the Texas criminal abortion statutes that are representative of provisions long in effect in a majority of our States. The Georgia legislation, however, is different and merits separate consideration.

I

The statutes in question are reproduced as Appendix A, *post* ——.[1] As the appellants acknowledge,[2] the 1968 statutes are patterned upon the American Law Institute's Model Penal Code, § 230.3 (Proposed Official Draft, 1962), reproduced as Appendix B, *post* ——. The ALI proposal has served as the model for recent legislation in approximately one-fourth of our States.[3] The new Georgia provisions replaced statutory law that had been in effect for more than 90 years. Georgia Laws 1876, No. 130, § 2, at 113.[4] The predecessor statute paralleled the

---

[1] The portions italicized in Appendix A are those held unconstitutional by the District Court.

[2] Appellants' Brief 25 n. 5; Tr. of Oral Arg. 9.

[3] See *Roe v. Wade, ante* —— n. 37.

[4] The active provisions of the 1876 statute were:

"Section I. *Be it enacted, etc.*, That from and after the passage of this Act, the wilful killing of an unborn child, so far developed as to be ordinarily called 'quick,' by any injury to the mother of such child, which would be murder if it resulted in the death of such mother, shall be guilty of a felony, and punishable by death or imprisonment for life, as the jury trying the case may recommend.

"Sec. II. *Be it further enacted*, That every person who shall administer to any woman pregnant with a child, any medicine, drug, or substance whatever, or shall use or employ any instrument or other means, with intent thereby to destroy such child, unless the same shall have been necessary to preserve the life of such mother, or shall have been advised by two physicians to be necessary for such purpose, shall, in case the death of such child or mother be thereby produced, be declared guilty of an assault with intent to murder.

"Sec. III. *Be it further enacted*, That any person who shall wilfully administer to any pregnant woman any medicine, drug or substance, or anything whatever, or shall employ any instrument or means whatever, with intent thereby to produce the miscarriage or abortion of any such woman, unless the same shall have been necessary to preserve the life of such woman, or shall have been

Texas legislation considered in *Roe v. Wade, ante*, and made all abortions criminal except those necessary "to preserve the life" of the pregnant woman. The new statutes have not been tested on constitutional grounds in the Georgia state courts.

Section 26-1201, with a referenced exception, makes abortion a crime, and § 26-1203 provides that a person convicted of that crime shall be punished by imprisonment for not less than one nor more than 10 years. Section 26-1202(a) states the exception and removes from § 1201's definition of criminal abortion, and thus makes noncriminal, an abortion "performed by a physician duly licensed" in Georgia when, "based upon his best clinical judgment . . . an abortion is necessary because

> "*(1) A continuation of the pregnancy would endanger the life of the pregnant woman or would seriously and permanently injure her health, or*
> "*(2) The fetus would very likely be born with a grave, permanent, and irremediable mental or physical defect, or*
> "*(3) The pregnancy resulted from forcible or statutory rape.*"[5]

Section 26-1202 also requires, by numbered subdivisions of its subsection (b), that, for an abortion to be authorized as performed as a noncriminal procedure, additional conditions must be fulfilled. These are (1) and (2) residence of the woman in Georgia; (3) reduction to writing of the performing physician's medical judgment that an abortion is justified for one or more of the reasons specified by § 26-1202(a), with written concurrence in that judgment by at least two other Georgia-licensed physicians, based upon their separate personal medical examinations of the woman; (4) performance of the abortion in a hospital licensed by the State Board of Health and also accredited by the Joint Commission on Accreditation of Hospitals; (5) advance approval by an abortion committee of not less than three members of the hospital's staff; (6) certifications in a rape situation; and (7), (8), and (9) maintenance and confidentiality of records. There is a provision (subsection (c)) for judicial determination of the legality of a proposed abortion on petition of the judicial circuit law officer or of a close relative, as therein defined, of the unborn child, and for expeditious hearing of that petition. There is also a provision (subsection (e)) giving a hospital the right not to admit an abortion patient and giving any physician and any hospital employee or staff member the right, on moral or religious grounds, not to participate in the procedure.

---

advised by two physicians to be necessary for that purpose, shall, upon conviction, be punished as prescribed in section 4310 of the Revised Code of Georgia."

It should be noted that the second section, in contrast to the first, makes no specific reference to quickening. The section was construed, however, to possess this line of demarcation. *Taylor v. State*, 105 Ga. 846, 33 S. E. 190 (1899).

[5] In contrast with the ALI model, the Georgia statute makes no specific reference to pregnancy resulting from incest. We were assured by the State at reargument that this was because the statute's reference to "rape" was intended to include incest. Tr. of Rearg. 32.

II

On April 16, 1970, Mary Doe,[6] 23 other individuals (nine described as Georgia-licensed physicians, seven as nurses registered in the State, five as clergymen, and two as social workers), and two nonprofit Georgia corporations that advocate abortion reform, instituted this federal action in the Northern District of Georgia against the State's attorney general, the district attorney of Fulton County, and the chief of police of the city of Atlanta. The plaintiffs sought a declaratory judgment that the Georgia abortion statutes were unconstitutional in their entirety. They also sought injunctive relief restraining the defendants and their successors from enforcing the statutes.

Mary Doe alleged:

> *(1) She was a 22-year-old Georgia citizen, married, and nine weeks pregnant. She had three living children. The two older ones had been placed in a foster home because of Doe's poverty and inability to care for them. The youngest, born July 19, 1969, had been placed for adoption. Her husband had recently abandoned her and she was forced to live with her indigent parents and their eight children. She and her husband, however, had become reconciled. He was a construction worker employed only sporadically. She had been a mental patient at the State Hospital. She had been advised that an abortion could be performed on her with less danger to her health than if she gave birth to the child she was carrying. She would be unable to care for or support the new child.*
>
> *(2) On March 25, 1970, she applied to the Abortion Committee of Grady Memorial Hospital, Atlanta, for a therapeutic abortion under § 26-1202. Her application was denied 16 days later, on April 10, when she was eight weeks pregnant, on the ground that her situation was not one described in § 26-1202(a).[7]*
>
> *(3) Because her application was denied, she was forced either to relinquish 'her right to decide when and how many children she will bear' or to seek an abortion that was illegal under the Georgia statutes. This invaded her rights of privacy and liberty in matters related to family, marriage, and sex, and deprived her of the right to choose whether to bear children. This was a violation of rights guaranteed her by the First, Fourth, Fifth, Ninth, and Fourteenth Amendments. The statutes also denied her equal protection and procedural due process and, because they were unconstitutionally vague, deterred hospitals and doctors from performing abortions. She sued 'on her own behalf and on behalf of all others similarly situated.'*

The other plaintiffs alleged that the Georgia statutes "chilled and deterred"

---

[6] Appellants by their complaint, Appendix 7, allege that the name is a pseudonym.

[7] In answers to interrogatories Doe stated that her application for an abortion was approved at Georgia Baptist Hospital on May 5, 1970, but that she was not approved as a charity patient there and had no money to pay for an abortion. Appendix 64.

them from practicing their respective professions and deprived them of rights guaranteed by the First, Fourth, and Fourteenth Amendments. These plaintiffs also purported to sue on their own behalf and on behalf of others similarly situated.

A three-judge district court was convened. An offer of proof as to Doe's identity was made, but the court deemed it unnecessary to receive that proof. The case was then tried on the pleadings and interrogatories.

The District Court, *per curiam*, 319 F. Supp. 1048 (ND Ga. 1970), held that all the plaintiffs had standing but that only Doe presented a justiciable controversy. On the merits, the court concluded that the limitation in the Georgia statute of the "number of reasons for which an abortion may be sought," *id.*, at 1056, improperly restricted Doe's rights of privacy articulated in *Griswold v. Connecticut*, 381 U.S. 479 (1965), and of "personal liberty," both of which it thought "broad enough to include the decision to abort a pregnancy," *id.*, at 1055. As a consequence, the court held invalid those portions of §§ 26-1202(a) and (b) (3) limiting legal abortions to the three situations specified; § 26-1202(b) (6) relating to certifications in a rape situation; and § 26-1202(c) authorizing a court test. Declaratory relief was granted accordingly. The court, however, held that Georgia's interest in protection of health, and the existence of a "*potential* of independent human existence" (emphasis in original), *id.*, at 1055, justified state regulation of "the manner of performance as well as the quality of the final decision to abort," *id.*, at 1056, and it refused to strike down the other provisions of the statutes. It denied the request for an injunction, *id.*, at 1057.

Claiming that they were entitled to an injunction and to broader relief, the plaintiffs took a direct appeal pursuant to 28 U.S.C. § 1253. We postponed decision on jurisdiction to the hearing on the merits. 402 U.S. 941 (1971). The defendants also purported to appeal, pursuant to § 1253, but their appeal was dismissed for want of jurisdiction. 402 U.S. 936 (1971). We are advised by the defendant-appellees, Brief 42, that an alternative appeal on their part is pending in the United States Court of Appeals for the Fifth Circuit. The extent, therefore, to which the District Court decision was adverse to the defendants, that is, the extent to which portions of the Georgia statutes were held to be unconstitutional, technically is not now before us.[8] *Swarb v. Lennox*, 405 U.S. 191, 201 (1972).

III

Our decision in *Roe v. Wade, ante* ———, establishes (1) that, despite her pseudonym, we may accept as true, for this case, Mary Doe's existence and her pregnant state on April 16, 1970; (2) that the constitutional issue is substantial; (3) that the interim termination of Doe's and all other Georgia pregnancies in existence in 1970 has not rendered the case moot; and (4) that Doe presents a justiciable controversy and has standing to maintain the action.

Inasmuch as Doe and her class are recognized, the question whether the other appellants—physicians, nurses, clergymen, social workers, and corporations—present a justiciable controversy and having standing is perhaps a matter of

---

[8] What we decide today obviously has implications for the issues raised in the defendants' appeal pending in the Fifth Circuit.

no great consequence. We conclude, however, that the physician-appellants, who are Georgia-licensed doctors consulted by pregnant women, also present a justiciable controversy and do have standing despite the fact that the record does not disclose that any one of them has been prosecuted, or threatened with prosecution, for violation of the State's abortion statutes. The physician is the one against whom these criminal statutes directly operate in the event he procures an abortion that does not meet the statutory exceptions and conditions. The physician-appellants, therefore, assert a sufficiently direct threat of personal detriment. They should not be required to await and undergo the criminal prosecution as the sole means of seeking relief. *Crossen v. Breckenridge*, 446 F. 2d 833, 839–840 (CA6 1971); *Poe v. Menghini*, 339 F. Supp. 986, 990-991 (Kans. 1972).

In holding that the physicians, while theoretically possessed of standing, did not present a justiciable controversy, the District Court seems to have relied primarily on *Poe v. Ullman*, 367 U.S. 497 (1961). There a sharply divided Court dismissed an appeal from a state court on the ground that it presented no real controversy justifying the adjudication of a constitutional issue. But the challenged Connecticut statute, deemed to prohibit the giving of medical advice on the use of contraceptives, had been enacted in 1879, and, apparently with a single exception, no one had ever been prosecuted under it. Georgia's statute, in contrast, is recent and not moribund. Furthermore, it is the successor to another Georgia abortion statute under which, we are told,[9] physicians were prosecuted. The present case, therefore, is closer to *Epperson v. Arkansas*, 393 U.S. 97 (1968), where the Court recognized the right of a school teacher, though not yet charged criminally, to challenge her State's anti-evolution statute. See also *Griswold v. Connecticut*, 381 U.S., at 481.

The parallel claims of the nurse, clergy, social worker, and corporation-appellants are another step removed and as to them, the Georgia statutes operate less directly. Not being licensed physicians, the nurses and the others are in no position to render medical advice. They would be reached by the abortion statutes only in their capacity as accessories or as counselor-conspirators. We conclude that we need not pass upon the status of these additional appellants in this suit, for the issues are sufficiently and adequately presented by Doe and the physician-appellants, and nothing is gained or lost by the presence or absence of the nurses, the clergymen, the social workers, and the corporations. See *Roe v. Wade, ante*, at ———.

IV

The appellants attack on several grounds those portions of the Georgia abortion statutes that remain after the District Court decision: undue restriction of a right to personal and marital privacy; vagueness; deprivation of substantive and procedural due process; improper restriction to Georgia residents; and denial of equal protection.

A. *Roe v. Wade, ante*, sets forth our conclusion that a pregnant woman does

[9] Tr. of Oral Arg. 21–22.

not have an absolute constitutional right to an abortion on her demand. What is said there is applicable here and need not be repeated.

B. The appellants go on to argue, however, that the present Georgia statutes must be viewed historically, that is, from the fact that prior to the 1968 Act an abortion in Georgia was not criminal if performed to "preserve the life" of the mother. It is suggested that the present statute, as well, has this emphasis on the mother's rights, not on those of the fetus. Appellants contend that it is thus clear that Georgia has given little, and certainly not first, consideration to the unborn child. Yet it is the unborn child's rights that Georgia asserts in justification of the statute. Appellants assert that this justification cannot be advanced at this late date.

Appellants then argue that the statutes do not adequately protect the woman's right. This is so because it would be physically and emotionally damaging to Doe to bring a child into her poor "fatherless"[10] family, and because advances in medicine and medical techniques have made it safer for a woman to have a medically induced abortion than for her to bear a child. Thus, "a statute which requires a woman to carry an unwanted pregnancy to term infringes not only on a fundamental right of privacy but on the right to life itself." Brief 27.

The appellants recognize that a century ago medical knowledge was not so advanced as it is today, that the techniques of antisepsis were not known, and that any abortion procedure was dangerous for the woman. To restrict the legality of the abortion to the situation where it was deemed necessary, in medical judgment, for the preservation of the woman's life was only a natural conclusion in the exercise of the legislative judgment of that time. A State is not to be reproached, however, for a past judgmental determination made in the light of then-existing medical knowledge. It is perhaps unfair to argue, as the appellants do, that because the early focus was on the preservation of the woman's life, the State's present professed interest in the protection of embryonic and fetal life is to be downgraded. That argument denies the State the right to readjust its views and emphases in the light of the advanced knowledge and techniques of the day.

C. Appellants argue that § 26-1202(a) of the Georgia statute, as it has been left by the District Court's decision, is unconstitutionally vague. This argument centers in the proposition that, with the District Court's having stricken the statutorily specified reasons, it still remains a crime for a physician to perform an abortion except when, as § 26-1202(a) reads, it is "based upon his best clinical judgment that an abortion is necessary." The appellants contend that the word "necessary" does not warn the physician of what conduct is proscribed; that the statute is wholly without objective standards and is subject to diverse interpretation; and that doctors will choose to err on the side of caution and will be arbitrary.

The net result of the District Court's decision is that the abortion determination, so far as the physician is concerned, is made in the exercise of his professional, that is, his "best clinical" judgment in the light of *all* the attendant circumstances. He is not now restricted to the three situations originally specified. Instead, he may range farther afield wherever his medical judgment, properly and professionally exercised, so dictates and directs him.

[10] Appellants' Brief 25.

The vagueness argument is set at rest by the decision in *United States v. Vuitch*, 402 U.S. 62, 71-72 (1971), where the issue was raised with respect to a District of Columbia statute making abortions criminal "unless the same were done as necessary for the preservation of the mother's life or health and under the direction of a competent licensed practitioner of medicine." That statute has been construed to bear upon psychological as well as physical well-being. This being so, the Court concluded that the term "health" presented no problem of vagueness. "Indeed, whether a particular operation is necessary for a patient's physical or mental health is a judgment that physicians are obviously called upon to make routinely whenever surgery is considered." 402 U.S., at 72. This conclusion is equally applicable here. Whether, in the words of the Georgia statute, "an abortion is necessary," is a professional judgment that the Georgia physician will be called upon to make routinely.

We agree with the District Court, 319 F. Supp., at 1058, that the medical judgment may be exercised in the light of all factors—physical, emotional, psychological, familial, and the woman's age—relevant to the well-being of the patient. All these factors may relate to health. This allows the attending physician the room he needs to make his best medical judgment. And it is room that operates for the benefit, not the disadvantage, of the pregnant woman.

D. The appellants next argue that the District Court should have declared unconstitutional three procedural demands of the Georgia statute: (1) that the abortion be performed in a hospital accredited by the Joint Commission on Accreditation of Hospitals:[11] (2) that the procedure be approved by the hospital staff abortion committee; and (3) that the performing physician's judgment be confirmed by the independent examinations of the patient by two other licensed physicians. The appellants attack these provisions not only on the ground that they unduly restrict the woman's right of privacy, but also on procedural due process and equal protection grounds. The physician-appellants also argue that, by subjecting a doctor's individual medical judgment to committee approval and to confirming consultations, the statute impermissibly restricts the physician's right to practice his profession and deprives him of due process.

1. *JCAH Accreditation.* The Joint Commission on Accreditation of Hospitals is an organization without governmental sponsorship or overtones. No question whatever is raised concerning the integrity of the organization or the high purpose of the accreditation process.[12] That process, however, has to do with

[11] We were advised at reargument, Tr. of Rearg. 10, that only 54 of Georgia's 159 counties have a JCAH accredited hospital.

[12] Since its founding, JCAH has pursued the "elusive goal" of defining the "optimal setting" for "quality of service in hospitals." JCAH, Accreditation Manual for Hospitals, Foreword (Dec. 1970). The Manual's Introduction states the organization's purpose to establish standards and conduct accreditation programs that will afford quality medical care "to give patients the optimal benefits that medical science has to offer." This ambitious and admirable goal is illustrated by JCAH's decision in 1966 "to raise and strengthen the standards from their present level to minimum essential to the level of optimum achievable. . . ." Some of these "optimum achievable" standards required are: disclosure of hospital ownership and control; a dietetic service and written dietetic policies; a written disaster plan for mass emergencies; a nuclear medical services program; facilities for hematology, chemistry, microbiology, clinical microscopy, and sero-immunology; a professional library and document delivery service; a radiology program; a social services plan administered by a qualified social worker; and a special care unit.

hospital standards generally and has no present particularized concern with abortion as a medical or surgical procedure.[13] In Georgia there is no restriction of the performance of non-abortion surgery in a hospital not yet accredited by the JCAH so long as other requirements imposed by the State, such as licensing of the hospital and of the operating surgeon, are met. See Georgia Code §§ 88-1901(a) and 88-1905 (1971) and 84-907 (Supp. 1971). Furthermore, accreditation by the Commission is not granted until a hospital has been in operation at least one year. The Model Penal Code, § 230.3, Appendix B hereto, contains no requirement for JCAH accreditation. And the Uniform Abortion Act (Final Draft, August 1971),[14] approved by the American Bar Association in February 1972, contains no JCAH accredited hospital specifications.[15] Some courts have held that a JCAH accreditation requirement is an overbroad infringement of fundamental rights because it does not relate to the particular medical problems and dangers of the abortion operation. *Poe v. Menghini*, 339 F. Supp. 986, 993-994 (Kan. 1972); *People v. Barksdale*, 96 Cal. Rptr. 265, 273-274 (Cal. App. 1971).

We hold that the JCAH accreditation requirement does not withstand constitutional scrutiny in the present context. It is a requirement that simply is not "based on differences that are reasonably related to the purposes of the Act in which it is found." *Morey v. Doud*, 354 U.S. 457, 465 (1957).

This is not to say that Georgia may not or should not, from and after the end of the first trimester, adopt standards for licensing all facilities where abortions may be performed so long as those standards are legitimately related to the objective the State seeks to accomplish. The appellants contend that such a relationship would be lacking even in a lesser requirement that an abortion be performed in a licensed hospital, as opposed to a facility, such as a clinic, that may be required by the State to possess all the staffing and services necessary to perform an abortion safely (including those adequate to handle serious complications or other emergency, or arrangements with a nearby hospital to provide such services). Appellants and various *amici* have presented us with a mass of data purporting to demonstrate that some facilities other than hospitals are entirely adequate to perform abortions if they possess these qualifications. The State, on the other hand, has not presented persuasive data to show that only hospitals meet its acknowledged interest in insuring the quality of the operation and the full protection of the patient. We feel compelled to agree with appellants that the State

[13] "The Joint Commission neither advocates nor opposes any particular position with respect to elective abortions." Letter dated July 9, 1971, from John L. Brewer, M. D. Commissioner, JCAH, to the Rockefeller Foundation. Brief for *amici*, American College of Obstetricians and Gynecologists, et al., p. A-3.

[14] See *Roe v. Wade, ante*————, n. 49.

[15] Some state statutes do not have the JCAH accrditation requirements. Alaska Stat. § 11.15.060 (1970); Hawaii Rev. Stat. § 453.16 (Supp. 1971); N. Y. Penal Code § 125.05.3 (McKinney Supp. 1972-1973). Washington has the requirement but couples it with the alternative of "a medical facility approved . . . by the state board of health." Wash. Rev. Code § 9.02.070 (Supp. 1972). Florida's new statute has a similar provision. Law of Apr. 13, 1972, c. 72-196, § 1 (2). Other contain the specification. Ark. Stat. Ann. §§ 41-303 to 41-310 (Supp. 1971); Cal. Health and Safety Code §§ 25950-25955.5 (West Supp. 1972); Colo. Rev. Stats. Ann. §§ 40-2-50 to 40-2-53 (Perm. Cum. Supp. 1967); Kan. Stat. Ann § 21-3047 (Supp. 1971); Md. Ann Code Art. 43, §§ 137-139 (Repl. 1971). Cf. Del. Code Ann. § 1790-1793 (Supp. 1970) specifying "a nationally recognized medical or hospital accreditation authority," § 1790 (a).

must show more than it has in order to prove that only the full resources of a licensed hospital, rather than those of some other appropriately licensed institution, satisfy these health interests. We hold that the hospital requirement of the Georgia law, because it fails to exclude the first trimester of pregnancy, see *Roe v. Wade, ante*, p. ———, is also invalid. In so holding we naturally express no opinion on the medical judgment involved in any particular case, that is, whether the patient's situation is such that an abortion should be performed in a hospital rather than in some other facility.

2. *Committee Approval*. The second aspect of the appellants' procedural attack relates to the hospital abortion committee and to the pregnant woman's asserted lack of access to that committee. Relying primarily on *Goldberg v. Kelly*, 397 U.S. 254 (1970), concerning the termination of welfare benefits, and *Wisconsin v. Constantineau*, 400 U.S. 433 (1971), concerning the posting of an alcoholic's name, Doe first argues that she was denied due process because she could not make a presentation to the committee. It is not clear from the record, however, whether Doe's own consulting physician was or was not a member of the committee or did or did not present her case, or, indeed, whether she herself was or was not there. We see nothing in the Georgia statute that explicitly denies access to the committee by or on behalf of the woman. If the access point alone were involved, we would not be persuaded to strike down the committee provision on the unsupported assumption that access is not provided.

Appellants attack the discretion the statute leaves to the committee. The most concrete argument they advance is their suggestion that it is still a badge of infamy "in many minds" to bear an illegitimate child, and that the Georgia system enables the committee members' personal views as to extramarital sex relations, and punishment therefor, to govern their decisions. This approach obviously is one founded on suspicion and one that discloses a lack of confidence in the integrity of physicians. To say that physicians will be guided in their hospital committee decisions by their predilections on extramarital sex unduly narrows the issue to pregnancy outside marriage. (Doe's own situation did not involve extramarital sex and its product.) The appellants' suggestion is necessarily somewhat degrading to the conscientious physician, particularly the obstetrician, whose professional activity is concerned with the physical and mental welfare, the woes, the emotions, and the concern of his female patients. He, perhaps more than anyone else, is knowledgeable in this area of patient care, and he is aware of human frailty, so-called "error," and needs. The good physician—despite the presence of rascals in the medical profession, as in all others, we trust that most physicians are "good"—will have a sympathy and an understanding for the pregnant patient that probably is not exceeded by those who participate in other areas of professional counseling.

It is perhaps worth noting that the abortion committee has a function of its own. It is a committee of the hospital and it is composed of members of the institution's medical staff. The membership usually is a changing one. In this way its work burden is shared and is more readily accepted. The committee's function is protective. It enables the hospital appropriately to be advised that its posture and activities are in accord with legal requirements. It is to be remembered that the hospital is an entity and that it, too, has legal rights and legal obligations.

Saying all this, however, does not settle the issue of the constitutional propriety of the committee requirement. Viewing the Georgia statute as a whole, we see no constitutionally justifiable pertinence in the structure for the advance approval by the abortion committee. With regard to the protection of potential life, the medical judgment is already completed prior to the committee stage, and review by a committee once removed from diagnosis is basically redundant. We are not cited to any other surgical procedure made subject to committee approval as a matter of state criminal law. The woman's right to receive medical care in accordance with her licensed physician's best judgment and the physician's right to administer it are substantially limited by this statutorily imposed overview. And the hospital itself is otherwise fully protected. Under § 26-1202(e) the hospital is free not to admit a patient for an abortion. It is even free not to have an abortion committee. Further, a physician or any other employee has the right to refrain, for moral or religious reasons, from participating in the abortion procedure. These provisions obviously are in the statute in order to afford appropriate protection to the individual and to the denominational hospital. Section 26-1202(e) affords adequate protection to the hospital and little more is provided by the committee prescribed by § 26-1202(b)(5).

We conclude that the interposition of the hospital abortion committee is unduly restrictive of the patient's rights and needs that, at this point, have already been medically delineated and substantiated by her personal physician. To ask more serves neither the hospital nor the State.

3. *Two-Doctor Concurrence.* The third aspects of the appellants' attack centers on the "time and availability of adequate medical facilities and personnel." It is said that the system imposes substantial and irrational roadblocks and "is patently unsuited" to prompt determination of the abortion decision. Time, of course, is critical in abortion. Risks during the first trimester of pregnancy are admittedly lower than during later months.

The appellants purport to show by a local study[16] of Grady Memorial Hospital (serving indigent residents in Fulton and DeKalb Counties) that the "mechanics of the system itself forced . . . discontinuation of the abortion process" because the median time for the workup was 15 days. The same study shows, however, that 27% of the candidates for abortion were already 13 or more weeks pregnant at the time of application, that is, they were at the end of or beyond the first trimester when they made their applications. It is too much to say, as appellants do, that these particular persons "were victims of [a] system over which they [had] no control." If higher risk was incurred because of abortions in the second rather than the first trimester, much of that risk was due to delay in application, and not to the alleged cumbersomeness of the system. We note, in passing, that appellant Doe had no delay problem herself; the decision in her case was made well within the first trimester.

It should be manifest that our rejection of the accredited hospital requirement and, more important, of the abortion committee's advance approval eliminates the major grounds of the attack based on the system's delay and the lack of facilities. There remains, however, the required confirmation by two Georgia-licensed physicians in addition to the recommendation of the pregnant woman's own

---

[16] L. Baker & M. Freeman, Abortion Surveillance at Grady Memorial Hospital Center for Disease Control (June and July 1971) (U. S. Dept. of HEW, PHS).

consultant (making under the statute, a total of six physicians involved, including the three on the hospital's abortion committee). We conclude that this provision, too, must fall.

The statute's emphasis, as has been repetitively noted, is on the attending physician's "best clinical judgment that an abortion is necessary." That should be sufficient. The reasons for the presence of the confirmation step in the statute are perhaps apparent, but they are insufficient to withstand constitutional challenge. Again, no other voluntary medical or surgical procedure for which Georgia requires confirmation by two other physicians has been cited to us. If a physician is licensed by the State, he is recognized by the State as capable of exercising acceptable clinical judgment. If he fails in this, professional censure or deprivation of his license are available remedies. Required acquiescence by co-practitioners has no rational connection with a patient's needs and unduly infringes on the physician's right to practice. The attending physician will know when a consultation is advisable—the doubtful situation, the need for assurance when the medical decision is a delicate one, and the like. Physicians have followed this routine historically and know its usefulness and benefit for all concerned. It is still true today that "[r]eliance must be placed upon the assurance given by his license, issued by an authority competent to judge in that respect, that he [the physician] possesses the requisite qualifications." *Dent v. West Virginia*, 129 U.S. 114, 122-123 (1889). See *United States v. Vuitch*, 402 U.S., at 71.

E. The appellants attack the residency requirement of the Georgia law, §§ 26-1202(b)(1) and (b)(2), as violative of the right to travel stressed in *Shapiro v. Thompson*, 394 U.S. 618, 629-631 (1969), and other cases. A requirement of this kind, of course, could be deemed to have some relationship to the availability of post-procedure medical care for the aborted patient.

Nevertheless, we do not uphold the constitutionality of the residence requirement. It is not based on any policy of preserving state-supported facilities for Georgia residents, for the bar also applies to private hospitals and to privately retained physicians. There is no intimation, either, that Georgia facilities are utilized to capacity in caring for Georgia residents. Just as the Privileges and Immunities Clause, Const. Art. IV, § 2, protects persons who enter other States to ply their trade, *Ward v. Maryland*, 79 U.S. (12 Wall.) 418, 430 (1870); *Blake v. McClung*, 172 U.S. 239, 248-256 (1898), so must it protect persons who enter Georgia seeking the medical services that are available there. See *Toomer v. Witsell*, 334 U.S. 385, 396-397 (1948). A contrary holding would mean that a State could limit to its own residents the general medical care available within its borders. This we could not approve.

F. The last argument on this phase of the case is one that often is made, namely, that the Georgia system is violative of equal protection because it discriminates against the poor. The appellants do not urge that abortions should be performed by persons other than licensed physicians, so we have no argument that because the wealthy can better afford physicians, the poor should have non-physicians made available to them. The appellants acknowledged that the procedures are "nondiscriminatory in . . . express terms" but they suggest that they have produced invidious discriminations. The District Court rejected this approach out of hand. 319 F. Supp., at 1056. It rests primarily on the accreditation and approval and confirmation requirements, discussed above, and on the assertion that most of Georgia's counties have no accredited hospital. We have set aside the accreditation, approval, and confirmation requirements, however, and with that, the discrimination argument collapses in all significant aspects.

V

The appellants complain, finally, of the District Court's denial of injunctive relief. A like claim was made in *Roe v. Wade, ante.* We declined decision there insofar as injunctive relief was concerned, and we decline it here. We assume that Georgia's prosecutorial authorities will give full recognition to the judgment of this Court.

In summary, we hold that the JCAH accredited hospital provision and the requirements as to approval by the hospital abortion committee, as to confirmation by two independent physicians, and as to residence in Georgia are all violative of the Fourteenth Amendment. Specifically, the following portions of § 26-1202(b), remaining after the District Court's judgment, are invalid:

(1) Subsections (1) and (2).

(2) That portion of Subsection (3) following the words "such physician's judgment is reduced to writing."

(3) Subsections (4) and (5).

The judgment of the District Court is modified accordingly and, as so modified, is affirmed. Costs are allowed to the appellants.

APPENDIX A

Criminal Code of Georgia

(The italicized portions are those held unconstitutional by the District Court)

CHAPTER 26–12. ABORTION.

26-1201. Criminal Abortion. Except as otherwise provided in section 26-1202, a person commits criminal abortion when he administers any medicine, drug or other substance whatever to any woman or when he uses any instrument or other means whatever upon any woman with intent to produce a miscarriage or abortion.

26-1202. Exception. (a) Section 26-1201 shall not apply to an abortion performed by a physician duly licensed to practice medicine and surgery pursuant to Chapter 84-9 or 84-12 of the Code of Georgia of 1933, as amended, based upon his best clinical judgment that an abortion is necessary *because*:

(1) *A continuation of the pregnancy would endanger the life of the pregnant woman or would seriously and permanently injure her health; or*

(2) *The fetus would very likely be born with a grave, permanent, and irremediable mental or physical defect; or*

(3) *The pregnancy resulted from forcible or statutory rape.*

(b) No abortion is authorized or shall be performed under this section unless each of the following conditions is met;

(1) The pregnant woman requesting the abortion certifies in writing under oath and subject to the penalties of false swearing to the physician who proposes to perform the abortion that she is a bona fide legal resident of the State of Georgia.

(2) The physician certifies that he believes the woman is a bona fide resident of this State and that he has no information which should lead him to believe otherwise.

(3) Such physician's judgment is reduced to writing and concurred in by at least two other physicians duly licensed to practice medicine and surgery pursuant to Chapter 84-9 of the Code of Georgia of 1933, as amended, who certify in writing that based upon their separate personal medical examinations of the pregnant woman, the abortion is, in their judgment, necessary *because of one or more of the reasons enumerated above.*

(4) Such abortion is performed in a hospital licensed by the State Board of Health and accredited by the Joint Commission on Accreditation of Hospitals.

(5) The performance of the abortion has been approved in advance by a committee of the medical staff of the hospital in which the operation is to be performed. This committee must be one established and maintained in accordance with the standards promulgated by the Joint Commission on the Accreditation of Hospitals, and its approval must be by a majority vote of a membership of not less than three members of the hospital's staff; the physician proposing to perform the operation may not be counted as a member of the committee for this purpose.

(6) *If the proposed abortion is considered necessary because the woman has been raped, the woman makes a written statement under oath, and subject to the penalties of false swearing, of the date, time and place of the rape and the name of the rapist, if known. There must be attached to this statement a certified copy of any report of the rape made by any law enforcement officer or agency and a statement by the solicitor general of the judicial circuit where the rape occurred or allegedly occurred that, according to his best information, there is probable cause to believe that the rape did occur.*

(7) Such written opinions, statements, certificates, and concurrences are maintained in the permanent files of such hospital and are available at all reasonable times to the solicitor general of the judicial circuit in which the hospital is located.

(8) A copy of such written opinions, statements, certificates, and concurrences is filed with the Director of the State Department of Public Health within ten (10) days after such operation is performed.

(9) All written opinions, statements, certificates, and concurrences filed and maintained pursuant to paragraphs (7) and (8) of this subsection shall be confidential records and shall not be made available for public inspection at any time.

(c) *Any solicitor general of the judicial circuit in which an abortion is to be performed under this section, or any person who would be a relative of the child within the second degree of consanguinity, may petition the superior court of the county in which the abortion is to be performed for a declaratory judgment whether the performance of such abortion would violate any constitutional or other legal rights of the fetus. Such solicitor general may also petition such court for the purpose of taking issue with compliance with the requirements of this section. The physician who proposes to perform the abortion and the pregnant woman shall be respondents. The petition shall be heard expeditiously and if the court adjudges that such abortion would violate the constitutional or other legal rights of the fetus, the court shall so declare and shall restrain the physician from performing the abortion.*

(d) If an abortion is performed in compliance with this section, the death of the fetus shall not give rise to any claim for wrongful death.

(e) Nothing in this section shall require a hospital to admit any patient under the provisions hereof for the purpose of performing an abortion, nor shall any hospital be required to appoint a committee such as contemplated under subsection (b)(5). A physician, or any other person who is a member of or associated with the staff of a hospital, or any employee of a hospital in which an abortion has been authorized, who shall state in writing an objection to such abortion on moral or religious grounds shall not be required to participate in the medical procedures which will result in the abortion, and the refusal of any such person to participate therein shall not form the basis of any claim for damages on account of such refusal or for any disciplinary or recriminatory action against such person.

26-1203. Punishment. A person convicted of criminal abortion shall be punished by imprisonment for not less than one nor more than 10 years.

APPENDIX B

American Law Institute

MODEL PENAL CODE

Section 230.3. Abortion.

(1) *Unjustified Abortion.* A person who purposely and unjustifiably terminates the pregnancy of another otherwise than by a live birth commits a felony of the third degree or, where the pregnancy has continued beyond the twenty-sixth week, a felony of the second degree.

✗ (2) *Justifiable Abortion.* A licensed physician is justified in terminating a pregnancy if he believes there is substantial risk that continuance of the pregnancy would gravely impair the physical or mental health of the mother or that the child would be born with grave physical or mental defect, or that the pregnancy resulted from rape, incest, or other felonious intercourse. All illicit intercourse with a girl below the age of 16 shall be deemed felonious for purposes of this subsection. Justifiable abortions shall be performed only in a licensed hospital except in case of emergency when hospital facilities are unavailable. [Additional exceptions from the requirement of hospitalization may be incorporated here to take account of situations in sparsely settled areas where hospitals are not generally accessible.]

(3) *Physicians' Certificates; Presumption from Non-Compliance.* No abor-

tion shall be performed unless two physicians, one of whom may be the person performing the abortion, shall have certified in writing the circumstances which they believe to justify the abortion. Such certificate shall be submitted before the abortion to the hospital where it is to be performed and, in the case of abortion following felonious intercourse, to the prosecuting attorney or the police. Failure to comply with any of the requirements of this Subsection gives rise to a presumption that the abortion was unjustified.

(4) *Self-Abortion.* A woman whose pregnancy has continued beyond the twenty-sixth week commits a felony of the third degree if she purposely terminates her own pregnancy otherwise than by a live birth, or if she uses instruments, drugs or violence upon herself for that purpose. Except as justified under Subsection (2), a person who induces or knowingly aids a woman to use instruments, drugs or violence upon herself for the purpose of terminating her pregnancy otherwise than by a live birth commits a felony of the third degree whether or not the pregnancy has continued beyond the twenty-sixth week.

(5) *Pretended Abortion.* A person commits a felony of the third degree if, representing that it is his purpose to perform an abortion, he does an act adapted to cause abortion in a pregnant woman although the woman is in fact not pregnant, or the actor does not believe she is. A person charged with unjustified abortion under Subsection (1) or an attempt to commit that offense may be convicted thereof upon proof of conduct prohibited by this Subsection.

(6) *Distribution of Abortifacients.* A person who sells, offers to sell, possesses with intent to sell, advertises, or displays for sale anything specially designed to terminate a pregnancy, or held out by the actor as useful for that purpose, commits a misdemeanor, unless:

(a) the sale, offer or display is to a physician or druggist or to an intermediary in a chain of distribution to physicians or druggists; or

(b) the sale is made upon prescription or order of a physician; or

(c) the possession is with intent to sell as authorized in paragraphs (a) and (b); or

(d) the advertising is addressed to persons named in paragraph (a) and confined to trade or professional channels not likely to reach the general public.

(7) *Section Inapplicable to Prevention of Pregnancy.* Nothing in this Section shall be deemed applicable to the prescription, administration or distribution of drugs or other substances for avoiding pregnancy, whether by preventing implantation of a fertilized ovum or by any other method that operates before, at or immediately after fertilization.

Nos. 70-18 and 70-40

MR. CHIEF JUSTICE BURGER, concurring.

I agree that, under the Fourteenth Amendment to the Constitution, the abortion statutes of Georgia and Texas impermissibly limit the performance of abortions necessary to protect the health of pregnant women, using the term health in its broadest medical context. See *Vuitch v. United States*, 402 U.S. 62, 71-72 (1971). I am somewhat troubled that the Court has taken notice of various scientific and medical data in reaching its conclusion; however, I do not believe that the Court has exceeded the scope of judicial notice accepted in other contexts.

In oral argument, counsel for the State of Texas informed the Court that early abortive procedures were routinely permitted in certain exceptional cases, such as nonconsensual pregnancies resulting from rape and incest. In the face of a rigid and narrow statute, such as that of Texas, no one in these circumstances should be placed in a posture of dependence on a prosecutorial policy or prosecutorial discretion. Of course, States must have broad power, within the limits indicated in the opinions, to regulate the subject of abortions, but where the consequences of state intervention are so severe, uncertainty must be avoided as much as possible. For my part, I would be inclined to allow a State to require the certification of two physicians to support an abortion, but the Court holds otherwise. I do not believe that such a procedure is unduly burdensome, as are the complex steps of the Georgia statute, which require as many as six doctors and the use of a hospital certified by the JCAH.

I do not read the Court's holding today as having the sweeping consequences attributed to it by the dissenting Justices; the dissenting views discount the reality that the vast majority of physicians observe the standards of their profession, and act only on the basis of carefully deliberated medical judgments relating to life and health. Plainly, the Court today rejects any claim that the Constitution requires abortion on demand.

MR. JUSTICE DOUGLAS, concurring.

While I join the opinion of the Court,[1] I add a few words.

The questions presented in the present cases go far beyond the issues of vagueness, which we considered in *United States v. Vuitch*, 402 U.S. 62. They involve the right of privacy, one aspect of which we considered in *Griswold v. Connecticut*, 381 U.S. 479, 484, when we held that various guarantees in the Bill of Rights create zones of privacy.[2]

[1] I disagree with the dismissal of Dr. Hallford's complaint in intervention in *Roe v. Wade*, because my disagreement with *Younger v. Harris*, 401 U.S. 37, revealed in my dissent in that case, still persists and extends to the progeny of that case.

[2] There is no mention of privacy in our Bill of Rights but our decisions have recognized it as one of the fundamental values those amendments were designed to protect. The fountainhead case is *Boyd v. United States*, 116 U.S. 616, holding that a federal statute which authorized a court in sex cases to require a taxpayer to produce his records or to concede the Government's allegations offended the Fourth and Fifth Amendments. Justice Bradley, for the Court, found that the measure unduly intruded into the "sanctity of a man's home and the privacies of life." *Id.*, 630. Prior to *Boyd*, in *Kilbourn v. Thompson*, 103 U.S. 168, 195, Mr. Justice Miller held for the Court that neither House of Congress "possesses the general power of making inquiry into the private affairs of the citizen." Of *Kilbourn* Mr. Justice Field later said, "This case will stand for all time as a bulwark against the invasion of the right of the citizen to protection in his private affairs against the unlimited scrutiny of investigation by a congressional committee." *In re Pacific Ry. Comm'n*, 32 F. 231, 253 (cited with approval in *Sinclair v. United States*, 279 U.S. 263, 293). Mr. Justice Harlan, also speaking for the Court, in *Interstate Commerce Comm'n v. Brimson*, 154 U.S. 447, 478, thought the same was true of administrative inquiries, saying the Constitution did not permit a "general power of making inquiry into the private affairs of the citizen." In a similar vein were *Harriman v. Interstate Commerce Comm'n*, 211 U.S. 407; *United States v. Louisville & Nashville R. R.*, 236 U.S. 318, 335; and *Federal Trade Comm'n v. American Tobacco Co.*, 264 U.S. 298.

The *Griswold* case involved a law forbidding the use of contraceptives. We held that law as applied to married people unconstitutional:

> *We deal with a right of privacy older than the Bill of Rights—older than our political parties, older than our school system. Marriage is a coming together for better or worse, hopefully enduring, and intimate to the degree of being sacred. Id., 486.*

The District Court in *Doe* held that *Griswold* and related cases "establish a constitutional right to privacy broad enough to encompass the right of a woman to terminate an unwanted pregnancy in its early stages, by obtaining an abortion." 319 F. Supp., at 1054.

The Supreme Court of California expressed the same view in *People v. Belous*,[3] 71 Cal. 2d 954, 963.

The Ninth Amendment obviously does not create federally enforceable rights. It merely says, "The enumeration in the Constitution of certain rights shall not be construed to deny or disparage others retained by the people." But a catalogue of these rights includes customary, traditional, and time-honored rights, amenities, privileges, and immunities that come within the sweep of "the Blessings of Liberty" mentioned in the preamble to the Constitution. Many of them in my view come within the meaning of the term "liberty" as used in the Fourteenth Amendment.

First is the autonomous control over the development and expression on one's intellect, interests, tastes, and personality.

These are rights protected by the First Amendment and in my view they are absolute, permitting of no exceptions. See *Terminiello v. Chicago*, 337 U.S. 77; *Roth v. United States*, 354 U.S. 476, 508 (dissent); *Kingsley Pictures Corp. v. Regents*, 360 U.S. 684, 697 (concurring); *New York Times Co. v. Sullivan*, 376 U.S. 254, 293 (Black, J., concurring in which I joined). The Free Exercise Clause of the First Amendment is one facet of this constitutional right. The right to remain silent as respects one's own beliefs, *Watkins v. United States*, 354 U.S. 178, 196–199, is protected by the First and the Fifth. The First Amendment grants the privacy of first-class mail, *United States v. Van Leeuwen*, 397 U.S. 249, 253. All of these aspects of the right of privacy are "rights retained by the people" in the meaning of the Ninth Amendment.

Second is freedom of choice in the basic decisions of one's life respecting marriage, divorce, procreation, contraception, and the education and upbringing of children.

These rights, unlike those protected by the First Amendment, are subject to some control by the police-power. Thus the Fourth Amendment speaks only of "unreasonable searches and seizures" and of "probable cause." These rights are "fundamental" and we have held that in order to support legislative action the statute must be narrowly and precisely drawn and that a compelling state interest" must be shown in support of the limitation. *E.g., Kramer v. Union Free School Dist.*, 395 U.S. 621 (1969); *Shapiro v. Thompson*, 394 U.S. 618 (1969);

---

[3] The California abortion statute, held unconstitutional in the *Belous* case, made it a crime to perform or help perform an abortion "unless the same is necessary to preserve [the mother's] life." 71 Cal. 2d, at 959.

Carrington v. Rash, 380 U.S. 89 (1965); *Sherbert v. Verner*, 374 U.S. 398 (1963); *NAACP v. Alabama ex rel. Patterson.*

The liberty to marry a person of one's own choosing, *Loving v. Virginia*, 388 U.S. 1; the right of procreation, *Skinner v. Oklahoma*, 316 U.S. 535; the liberty to direct the education of one's children, *Pierce v. Society of Sisters*, 268 U.S. 510, and the privacy of the marital relation, *Griswold v. Connecticut, supra*, are in this category.[4] Only last Term in *Eisenstadt v. Baird*, 405 U.S. 438, another contraceptive case, we expanded the concept of *Griswold* by saying:

> *It is true that in Griswold the right of privacy in question inhered in the marital relationship. Yet the marital couple is not an independent entity with a mind and heart of its own, but an association of two individuals each with a separate intellectual and emotional makeup. If the right of privacy means anything, it is the right of the individual, married or single, to be free from unwarranted government intrusion into matters so fundamentally affecting a person as the decision whether to bear or beget a child.*

This right of privacy was called by Mr. Justice Brandeis the right "to be let alone." *Olmstead v. United States*, 277 U.S. 438, 478. That right includes the privilege of an individual to plan his own affairs, for, "outside of areas of plainly harmful conduct, every American is left to shape his own life as he thinks best, do what he pleases, go where he pleases." *Kent v. Dulles*, 357 U.S. 116, 126.

Third is the freedom to care for one's health and person, freedom from bodily restraint or compulsion, freedom to walk, stroll, or loaf.

These rights, though fundamental, are likewise subject to regulation on a showing of "compelling state interest." We stated in *Papachristou v. City of Jacksonville*, 405 U.S. 156, 164, that walking, strolling, and wandering "are historically part of the amenities of life as we have known them." As stated in *Jacobson v. Massachusetts*, 197 U.S. 11, 29:

[4] My Brother STEWART, writing in the present cases, says that our decision in *Griswold* reintroduced substantive due process that had been rejected in *Ferguson v. Skrupa*, 372 U.S. 726. *Skrupa* involved legislation governing a business enterprise; and the Court in that case, as had Mr. Justice Holmes on earlier occasions, rejected the idea that "liberty" within the meaning of the Due Process Clause of the Fourteenth Amendment was a vessel to be filled with one's personal choices of values, whether drawn from the *laissez faire* school, from the socialistic school, or from the technocrats. *Griswold* involved legislation touching on the marital relation and involving the conviction of a licensed physician for giving married people information concerning contraception. There is nothing specific in the Bill of Rights that covers that item. Nor is there anything in the Bill of Rights that in terms protects the right of association or the privacy in one's association. Yet we found those rights in the periphery of the First Amendment. *NAACP v. Alabama*, 357 U. S. 449, 462. Other peripheral rights are the right to educate one's children as one chooses, *Pierce v. Society of Sisters*, 268 U. S. 510, and the right to study the German language, *Meyer v. Nebraska*, 262 U. S. 390. These decisions, with all respect, have nothing to do with substantive due process. One may think they are not peripheral rights to other rights that are expressed in the Bill of Rights. But that is not enough to bring into play the protection of substantive due process.

There are of course those who have believed that the reach of due process in the Fourteenth Amendment included all of the Bill of Rights but went further. Such was the view of Mr. Justice Murphy and Mr. Justice Rutledge. See *Adamson v. California*, 332 U. S. 46, 123, 124 (dissenting). Perhaps they were right; but it is a bridge that neither I nor those who joined the Court opinion in *Griswold* crossed.

There is, of course, a sphere within which the individual may assert the supremacy of his own will and rightfully dispute the authority of any human government, especially of any free government existing under a written constitution, to interfere with the exercise of that will.

In *Union Pac. Ry. Co. v. Botsford*, 141 U.S. 250, 252, the Court said,

The inviolability of the person is as much invaded by a compulsory stripping and exposure as by a blow.

In *Terry v. Ohio*, 392 U.S. 1, 8-9, the Court in speaking of the Fourth Amendment stated:

This inestimable right of personal security belongs as much to the citizen on the streets of our cities as to the Governor closeted in his study to dispose of his secret affairs.

Katz v. United States, 389 U.S. 347, 350, emphasizes that the Fourth Amendment

"protects individual privacy against certain kinds of governmental intrusion."

In *Meyer v. Nebraska*, 262 U.S. 390, 399, the Court said:

Without doubt, it [liberty] denotes not merely freedom from bodily restraint but also the right of the individual to contract, to engage in any of the common occupations of life, to acquire useful knowledge, to marry, establish a home and bring up children, to worship God according to the dictates of his own conscience, and generally to enjoy those privileges long recognized at common law as essential to the orderly pursuit of happiness by free men.

The Georgia statute is at war with the clear messge of these cases—that a woman is free to make the basic decision whether to bear an unwanted child. Elaborate argument is hardly necessary to demonstrate that childbirth may deprive a woman of her preferred life style and force upon her a radically different and undesired future. For example, rejected applicants under the Georgia statute are required to endure the discomforts of pregnancy; to incur the pain, higher mortality rate, and aftereffects of childbirth; to abandon educational plans; to sustain loss of income; to forego the satisfactions of careers; to tax further mental and physical health in providing childcare; and, in some cases, to bear the lifelong stigma of unwed motherhood, a badge which may haunt, if not deter, later legitimate family relationships.

Such a holding is, however, only the beginning of the problem. The State has interests to protect. Vaccinations to prevent epidemics are one example, as *Jacobson* holds. The Court held that compulsory sterilization of imbeciles afflicted with hereditary forms of insanity or imbecility is another. *Buck v. Bell*, 274 U.S. 200. Abortion affects another. While childbirth endangers the lives of some women, voluntary abortion at any time and place regardless of medical standards would impinge on a rightful concern of society. The woman's health is part of that concern; as is the life of the fetus after quickening. These concerns justify the State in treating the procedure as a medical one.

One difficulty is that this statute as construed and applied apparently does not give full sweep to the "psychological as well as physical well-being" of women patients which saved the concept "health" from being void for vagueness in *United States v. Vuitch, supra*, at 72. But apart from that, Georgia's enactment has a constitutional infirmity because, as stated by the District Court, it "limits the number of reasons for which an abortion may be sought." I agree with the holding of the District Court, "This the State may not do, because such action unduly restricts a decision sheltered by the Constitutional right to privacy." 319 F. Supp., at 1056.

The vicissitudes of life produce pregnancies which may be unwanted, or which may impair "health" in the broad *Vuitch* sense of the term, or which may imperil the life of the mother, or which in the full setting of the case may create such suffering, dislocations, misery, or tragedy as to make an early abortion the only civilized step to take. These hardships may be properly embraced in the "health" factor of the mother as appraised by a person of insight. Or they may be part of a broader medical judgment based on what is "appropriate" in a given case, though perhaps not "necessary" in a strict sense.

The "liberty" of the mother, though rooted as it is in the Constitution, may be qualified by the State for the reasons we have stated. But where fundamental personal rights and liberties are involved, the corrective legislation must be "narrowly drawn to prevent the supposed evil," *Cantwell v. Connecticut*, 310 U.S. 296, 307, and not be dealt with in an "unlimited and indiscriminate" manner. *Shelton v. Tucker*, 364 U.S. 479, 490. And see *Talley v. California*, 362 U.S. 60. Unless regulatory measures are so confined and are addressed to the specific areas of compelling legislative concern, the police power would become the great leveller of constitutional rights and liberties.

There is no doubt that the State may require abortions to be performed by qualified medical personnel. The legitimate objective of preserving the mother's health clearly supports such laws. Their impact upon the woman's privacy is minimal. But the Georgia statute outlaws virtually all such operations—even in the earliest stages of pregnancy. In light of modern medical evidence suggesting that an early abortion is safer healthwise than childbirth itself,[5] it cannot be seriously urged that so comprehensive a ban is aimed at protecting the woman's

---

[5] Many studies show that it is safer for a woman to have a medically induced abortion than to bear a child. In the first 11 months of operations of the New York abortion law, the mortality rate associated with such operations was six per 100,000 operations. Abortion Mortality, 20 Morbidity and Mortality 208, 209 (1971) (U. S. Department of Health, Education, and Welfare, Public Health Service). On the other hand, the maternal mortality rate associated with childbirths other than abortions was 18 per 100,000 live births. Tietze, Mortality with Contraception and Induced Abortion, 45 Studies in Family Planning 6 (1969). See also C. Tietze & H. Lehfeldt, Legal Abortion in Eastern Europe 175 J. A. M. A. 1149, 1152 (1961); V. Kolblova, Legal Abortion in Czechoslovakia, 196; J. A. M. A. 371 (1966); Mehland, Combating Illegal Abortion in the Socialist Countries of Europe, 13 World Med. J. 84 (1966).

health. Rather, this expansive proscription of all abortions along the temporal spectrum can rest only on a public goal of preserving both embryonic and fetal life.

The present statute has struck the balance between the woman and the State's interests wholly in favor of the latter. I am not prepared to hold that a State may equate, as Georgia has done, all phases of maturation preceding birth. We held in *Griswold* that the States may not preclude spouses from attempting to avoid the joinder of sperm and egg. If this is true, it is difficult to perceive any overriding public necessity which might attach precisely at the moment of conception. As Mr. Justice Clark has said:[6]

> To say that life is present at conception is to give recognition to the potential, rather than the actual. The unfertilized egg has life, and if fertilized, it takes on human proportions. But the law deals in reality, not obscurity—the known rather than the unknown. When sperm meets egg, life may eventually form, but quite often it does not. The law does not deal in speculation. The phenomenon of life takes time to develop, and until it is actually present, it cannot be destroyed. Its interruption prior to formation would hardly be homicide, and as we have seen, society does not regard it as such. The rites of Baptism are not performed and death certificates are not required when a miscarriage occurs. No prosecutor has ever returned a murder indictment charging the taking of the life of a fetus.[7] This would not be the case if the fetus constituted human life.

In summary, the enactment is overbroad. It is not closely correlated to the aim of preserving pre-natal life. In fact, it permits its destruction in several cases, including pregnancies resulting from sex acts in which unmarried females are below the statutory age of consent. At the same time, however, the measure broadly proscribes aborting other pregnancies which may cause severe mental disorders. Additionally, the statute is overbroad because it equates the value of embryonic life immediately after conception with the worth of life immediately before birth.

III

Under the Georgia Act the mother's physician is not the sole judge as to whether the abortion should be performed. Two other licensed physicians must concur in his judgment.[8] Moreover, the abortion must be performed in a licensed hospital;[9]

[6] Religion, Morality and Abortion: A Constitutional Appraisal, 2 Loy. U. (L. A.) L. Rev. 1, 10 (1969).

[7] In *Keeler v. Superior Court*, 2 Cal. 3d 619, 470 P. 2d 617, the California Supreme Court held in 1970 that the California murder statute did not cover the killing of an unborn fetus, even though the fetus be "viable" and that it was beyond judicial power to extend the statute to the killing of an unborn. It held that the child must be 'born alive before a charge of homicide can be sustained." 2 Cal. 3d, at 639.

[8] See § 26-1202 (b) (3).

[9] See § 26-1202 (b) (4).

and the abortion must be approved in advance by a committee of the medical staff of that hospital.[10]

Physicians, who speak to us in *Doe* through an *amicus* brief, complain of the Georgia Act's interference with their practice of their profession.

The right of privacy has no more conspicuous place than in the physician-patient relationship, unless it be in the priest-penitent relation.

It is one thing for a patient to agree that her physician may consult with another physician about her case. It is quite a different matter for the State compulsorily to impose on that physician-patient relationship another layer or, as in this case, still a third layer of physicians. The right of privacy—the right to care for one's health and person and to seek out a physician of one's own choice protected by the Fourteenth Amendment—becomes only a matter of theory not a reality, when a multiple physician approval system is mandated by the State.

The State licenses a physician. If he is derelict or faithless, the procedures available to punish him or to deprive him of his license are well known. He is entitled to procedural due process before professional disciplinary sanctions may be imposed. See *In re Ruffalo*, 390 U.S. 544. Crucial here, however, is state-imposed control over the medical decision whether pregnancy should be interrupted. The good-faith decision of the patient's chosen physician is overridden and the final decision passed on to others in whose selection the patient has no part. This is a total destruction of the right of privacy between physician and patient and the intimacy of relation which that entails.

The right to seek advice on one's health and the right to place his reliance on the physician of his choice are basic to Fourteenth Amendment values. We deal with fundamental rights and liberties, which, as already noted, can be contained or controlled only by discretely drawn legislation that preserves the "liberty" and regulates only those phases of the problem of compelling legislative concern. The imposition by the State of group controls over the physician-patient relation is not made on any medical procedure apart from abortion, no matter how dangerous the medical step may be. The oversight imposed on the physician and patient in abortion cases denies them their "liberty," *viz.*, their right to privacy, without any compelling, discernible state interest.

Georgia has constitutional warrant in treating abortion as a medical problem. To protect the woman's right of privacy, however, the control must be through the physician of her choice and the standards set for his performance.

The protection of the fetus when it has acquired life is a legitimate concern of the State. Georgia's law makes no rational, discernible decision on that score.[11] For under the Act the develomental stage of the fetus is irrelevant when pregnancy is the result of rape or when the fetus will very likely be born with a permanent defect or when a continuation of the pregnancy will endanger the life of the mother or permanently injure her health. When life is present is a question we do not try to resolve. While basically a question for medical experts, as stated

[10] Section 26-1202 (b) (5).
[11] See Rochat, Tyler, and Schoenbucher, An Epidemiological Analysis of Abortion in Georgia, 61 Am. J. of Public Health 541 (1971).

by Mr. Justice Clark,[12] it is, of course, caught up in matters of religion and morality.

In short, I agree with the Court that endangering the life of the woman or seriously and permanently injuring her health are standards too narrow for the right of privacy that are at stake.

I also agree that the superstructure of medical supervision which Georgia has erected violates the patient's right of privacy inherent in her choice of her own physician.

MR. JUSTICE WHITE, with whom
MR. JUSTICE REHNQUIST joins, dissenting.

At the heart of the controversy in these cases are those recurring pregnancies that pose no danger whatsoever to the life or health of the mother but are nevertheless unwanted for any one or more of a variety of reasons—convenience, family planning, economics, dislike of children, the embarrassment of illegitimacy, etc. The common claim before us is that for any one of such reasons, or for no reason at all, and without asserting or claiming any threat to life or health, any woman is entitled to an abortion at her request if she is able to find a medical advisor willing to undertake the procedure.

The Court for the most part sustains this position: During the period prior to the time the fetus becomes viable, the Constitution of the United States values the convenience, whim or caprice of the putative mother more than the life or potential life of the fetus; the Constitution, therefore, guarantees the right to an abortion as against any state law or policy seeking to protect the fetus from an abortion not prompted by more compelling reasons of the mother.

With all due respect, I dissent. I find nothing in the language or history of the Constitution to support the Court's judgment. The Court simply fashions and announces a new constitutional right for pregnant mothers and, with scarcely any reason or authority for its action, invests that right with sufficient substance to override most existing state abortion statutes. The upshot is that the people and the legislatures of the 50 States are constitutionally disentitled to weigh the relative importance of the continued existence and development of the fetus on the one hand against a spectrum of possible impacts on the mother on the other hand. As an exercise of raw judicial power, the Court perhaps has authority to do what it does today; but in my view its judgment is an improvident and extravagant exercise of the power of judicial review which the Constitution extends to this Court.

The Court apparently values the convenience of the pregnant mother more than the continued existence and development of the life or potential life which she carries. Whether or not I might agree with that marshalling of values, I can in no event join the Court's judgment because I find no constitutional warrant for imposing such an order of priorities on the people and legislatures of the States. In a sensitive area such as this, involving as it does issues over which reasonable men may easily and heatedly differ, I cannot accept the Court's exercise of its

---

[12] Religion, Morality and Abortion: A Constitutional Appraisal, 2 Loy. U. (L. A.) L. Rev. 1, 10 (1969).

clear power of choice by interposing a constitutional barrier to state efforts to protect human life and by investing mothers and doctors with the constitutionally protected right to exterminate it. This issue, for the most part, should be left with the people and to the political processes the people have devised to govern their affairs.

It is my view, therefore, that the Texas statute is not constitutionally infirm because it denies abortions to those who seek to serve only their convenience rather than to protect their life or health. Nor is this plaintiff, who claims no threat to her mental or physical health, entitled to assert the possible rights of those women whose pregnancy assertedly implicates their health. This, together with *United States v. Vuitch*, 402 U.S. 62 (1971), dictates reversal of the judgment of the District Court.

Likewise, because Georgia may constitutionally forbid abortions to putative mothers who, like the plaintiff in this case, do not fall within the reach of § 26-1202(a) of its criminal code, I have no occasion, and the District Court had none, to consider the constitutionality of the procedural requirements of the Georgia statute as applied to those pregnancies posing substantial hazards to either life or health. I would reverse the judgment of the District Court in the Georgia case.

No. 70-40

MR. JUSTICE REHNQUIST, dissenting.

The holding in *Roe v. Wade, ante,* that state abortion laws can withstand constitutional scrutiny only if the States can demonstrate a compelling state interest apparently compels the Court's close scrutiny of the various provisions in Georgia's abortion statute. Since, as indicated by my dissent in *Wade*, I view the compelling state interest standard as an inappropriate measure of the constitutionality of state abortion laws, I respectfully dissent from the majority's holding.

The Human Life Bill—S. 158—was originally presented before the Subcommittee on Separation of Powers in 1981. Although several years have passed since the original publications, there are many important reasons why these hearings are relevant or interesting today.

First, the issues discussed during that time will be reexamined many years from now. "When life begins" was certainly not resolved from the statements of the many experts who testified and is still disputed today. Also, new scientific evidence always disinters any final opinion on life's beginning, making any opinion a temporal one at best. Whether a fetus is a human being and a person within the meaning of the Fourteenth Amendment can still be argued repeatedly both historically and legally. Any historical judgment is subject to more exhaustive research that may alter prevalent views. Legal judgments are subject to new cases and laws that can completely reverse prior opinions. However, the basic elements presented in 1981 will provide a foundation for future discussions of the abortion issue that will most certainly occur.

Second, there is no question that the Human Life Bill was debated by some of the most renowned scholars, statesmen, scientists, lawyers, clergymen, and interested persons who have ever appeared before a subcommittee of Congress. The quality of the prepared statements was often superb.

Finally, there are still strong movements to reverse the *Roe* decision, amend the Constitution to limit abortions, change state statutes on abortion, and generally limit the availability of legal abortions. These alterations in the present status of legal abortion can only be attained by carefully reviewing what occurred during the 1981 debate of the Human Life Bill.

Appendix 2

THE HUMAN LIFE BILL—Testimony Before The United States Senate

Prepared Statement of Norman Dorsen
Statement of Charles Rice
Prepared Statement of Charles Rice

Discussion:
Senator East
Mr. Dorsen
Mr. Rice
Senator Baucus
Mr. Eisenberg
Senator Heflin

HISTORICAL SECTION
A discussion of the congressional intent of the Fourteenth Amendment and whether the unborn were within its protection.

Statement of Dr. Carl Degler
Statement of James Mohr
Prepared Statement of James Mohr
Statement of William Marshner
Prepared Statement of William Marshner
Statement of Victor Rosenblum
Prepared Statement of Victor Rosenblum

POLITICAL SECTION
Prepared Statement of Sarah Weddington
Statement of Senator Bob Packwood
Statement of Senator Daniel Moynihan
Prepared Statement of Senator Daniel Moynihan
Additional Views of Senator Orrin G. Hatch
Minority Views of Senator Max Baucus

SPEAKERS AND AFFILIATIONS
Avery, Dr. Mary Ellen, Thomas Morgan Rotch Professor of Pediatrics and Physician-in-Chief, Children's Hospital Medical Center, Boston, Mass.
Baucus, Senator Max, Montana
Bongiovanni, Dr. Alfred M., Professor, University of Pennsylvania Medical Faculty, Pa.
Bork, Robert, Professor, Yale Law School, New Haven, Conn.
Callahan, Dr. Daniel, Director, Hastings Center, Hastings-on-Hudson, N.Y.
Cox, Archibald, Professor, Harvard University Law School, Cambridge, Mass.
Davis, Dr. Jessica G., Director, Child Development Center, Chief, Division of Genetics, North Shore University Hospital, Manhasset, N.Y.
Degler, Dr. Carl, Margaret Byrne Professor of American History, Stanford University, Stanford, Calif.
Dorsen, Norman, Professor, New York University School of Law, New York, N.Y.
East, Senator John P., North Carolina
Eisenberg, Theodore, Professor, UCLA School of Law, Los Angeles, Calif.

Galebach, Stephen H., Attorney, Covington and Burling, Washington, D.C.
Grobstein, Dr. Clifford, Professor of Biological Science and Public Policy, University of California, San Diego, Calif.
Hatch, Senator Orrin G., Utah
Heflin, Senator Howell, Alabama
Jefferson, Dr. Mildred F., Assistant Clinical Professor of Surgery, Boston University School of Medicine, Boston, Mass.
Marshner, William, Professor, Christendom College, Front Royal, Va.
Mohr, James, Professor, University of Maryland, Baltimore County, Md.
Moynihan, Senator Daniel, New York
Nagel, Robert, Professor, Cornell University Law School, Ithaca, N.Y.
Neel, Dr. James, Chairman, Department of Human Genetics, University of Michigan Medical School, Ann Arbor, Mich.
Noonan, John T., Professor, California School of Law, Berkeley, Calif.
Packwood, Senator Bob, Oregon
Rice, Charles, Professor, Notre Dame University, Notre Dame, Ind.
Rosenberg, Dr. Leon, Professor and Chairman, Department of Human Genetics, Yale University Medical School, New Haven, Conn.
Rosenblum, Victor, Professor, Northwestern University, Chicago, Ill.
Ryan, Dr. George M., Jr. Professor of Obstetrics and Gynecology and Community Medicine, University of Tennessee Center for the Health Sciences, Memphis, Tenn.
Tribe, Laurence H., Professor of Law, Harvard University, Cambridge, Mass.
Tyler, Dr. Carl, Assistant Director for Science, Center for Health Promotion and Education, Centers for Disease Control, Atlanta, Ga.
Uddo, Basile, Professor, Loyola University Law School, New Orleans, La.
Van Alstyne, William, Professor, Duke University School of Law, Durham, N.C.
Wardle, Lynn, Professor, Brigham Young University School of Law, Provo, Utah
Weddington, Sarah, Washington, D.C.
Williams, Dr. Jasper, Williams Clinic, Chicago, Ill.

Statement of the Bill (Original Form)

Be it enacted by the Senate and House of Representatives of the United States of America in Congress assembled, That title 42 of the United States Code shall be amended at the end thereof by adding the following new chapter:

CHAPTER 101

SECTION 1. The Congress finds that present day scientific evidence indicates a significant likelihood that actual human life exists from conception.

The Congress further finds that the fourteenth amendment to the Constitution of the United States was intended to protect all human beings.

Upon the basis of these findings, and in the exercise of the powers of the Congress, including its power under section 5 of the fourteenth amendment to the Constitution of the United States, the Congress hereby declares that for the purpose of enforcing the obligation of the States under the fourteenth amendment not to deprive persons of life without due process of law, human life shall be deemed to exist from conception, without regard to race, sex, age, health, defect, or condition of dependency; and for this purpose "person" shall include all human life as defined herein.

Sec. 2. Notwithstanding any other provision of law, no inferior Federal court ordained and established by Congress under article III of the Constitution of the United States shall have jurisdiction to issue any restraining order, temporary or permanent injunction, or declaratory judgment in any case involving or arising from any State law or municipal ordinance that (1) protects the rights of human persons between conception and birth, or (2) prohibits, limits, or regulates (a) the performance of abortions or (b) the provision of public expense of funds, facilities, personnel, or other assistance for the performance of abortions.

Sec. 3. If any provision of this Act or the application thereof to any person or circumstance is judicially determined to be invalid, the validity of the remainder of the Act and the application of such provision to other persons and circumstances shall not be affected by such determination.

Presentation by Senator John P. East

Senator EAST. I would like to attempt to summarize what, in my estimation, the purpose of this act is. I will happily stand corrected if testimony, either of a medical or legal constitutional nature, would cause us to reach another conclusion. Again, I speak only for myself. I am only summarizing for myself as chairman of this subcommittee, and my views here are not to be imputed to anyone else present here this morning or likely to be gathered with us in the future.

As I understand this bill, we would attempt to define this question of life and whether it begins at the time of conception. If the determination would be that, yes, life does commence at the time of conception, then the effect of this bill would mean that the unborn child—the fetus—is protected as a person within the meaning of the due process clause of the 14th amendment, as are all other persons under the U.S. Constitution. That is the first basic thrust of this proposed legislation.

What would I think the practical effect of it would be? I would presume it would be this: The *Roe v. Wade* decision of 1973 would be vitiated—negated—because in the majority opinion of that case it was indicated that if person included the unborn, that their decision would no longer be operative, and hence, if person is so defined, by the view of the Court in its own majority opinion, *Roe v. Wade* would be vitiated.

The issue would revert to the States. The States would then have the power to deal with the issue of abortion, as they had the power to do prior to *Roe v. Wade*.

In dealing with the issue of abortion, they of course would be constrained by the requirements of the 14th amendment in terms of treating any persons—in this case, the unborn, or the fetus.

I do not wish to imply or to suggest that the answers are easy here, either of a medical nature or of a legal or constitutional nature, but it did occur to me that there is an obligation—a mandate—on the part of the chairman of the subcommittee at least to try to give some conception of where he thinks it is that we are going.

In my judgment, at this point, without having heard all the evidence, that would be my assessment of where we are headed.

Let me comment, if I might, please, as chairman, on the nature of the hearings that we will be conducting. The hearings today and tomorrow will deal with the medical question—the scientific question—as to when life commences. Does it commence with conception? If so, what is the nature of that life? And so forth.

Again, our testimony today and tomorrow will be on the medical and scientific question, and I would like, as chairman, to make sure that our comments, either by the witnesses or by those interrogating, might be reasonably related to that issue.

We will subsequently have hearings on the legal and constitutional implications, at which time we would like to then keep our focus on those matters, and they are fundamental and important.

We shall also want to consider the possibility of additional hearings if we need them. I want to assure each and every person here, either on this panel or in this audience or in the country as a whole, that I am fully aware of the infinite importance of this issue. It is a prime issue in terms of the implications of this legislation and what it would do or what it would not do.

I intend to honor my responsibility, as chairman of this subcommittee, to see that the issues are examined thoroughly and exhaustively, and that when we have completed this process every person can say, whatever side they came down on on this issue, the hearings were fair, extensive, and exhaustive, be it on the question of the medical or scientific question, or be it on the issue of the constitutional or statutory implications, or other matters that might be germane or pertinent and worthy of our consideration.

I would like, then, as we turn to this first session this morning on the question of the scientific and medical dimensions of the problem, that we focus upon that issue. I would like to encourage the witnesses, please, to make their remarks as concise and as brief and to the point as they can, consistent with making their point. We are not trying to gloss it over. We are simply trying to make sure that we operate on a premise of conciseness, and brevity, and germaneness.

I will try to adhere to my own rule. I would like to implore my colleagues on the panel to adhere to that rule.

Again, this is not to be understood as any effort to limit the scope or the extent of debate over time. I am only asking that in a given session we hold to the time frame, that it not run away from us, that finally we become so exhausted and deadened we do not even know what others are saying, let alone care what they are saying.

I have been in the college teaching profession, and I have found 50 minutes is enough to wear somebody out, and I find in the Senate it is not uncommon to go 2, 3, and 4 hours. I submit, nobody—nobody—can follow a serious discussion in that kind of time frame.

So, what I would like to do is to keep these hearings on track and keep them germane, but I assure everyone that we will do in this subcommittee whatever is necessary over a period of time to assure that the issue is thoroughly and exhaustively considered.

Senator Hatch, I welcome you this morning; Senator Dole; Senator Nickles.

Senator Hatch, I would like to yield to you so that you may make a statement.

Statement of Senator Orrin G. Hatch

Senator HATCH. Thank you, Senator East.

I think there have been some misconceptions and misunderstandings about my attitude toward these hearings.

The Constitution Subcommittee recently discontinued its joint participation in these hearings, not because of any personal difficulties between the chairman, Senator East, and me, but because of the inherent difficulties in joint congressional hearings.

There are differing perspectives between our subcommittees on a number of matters, including (a) the scope of these hearings—that is, limitation to medical testimony—and (b) specific witness lists. These are the types of difficulties that are inherent in this process.

Senator East, in my opinion, has exercised his soundest judgment, and I have come to respect that judgment. I have chosen to allow him to develop these hearings—at least from my perspective—in the full discretion of that judgment.

Frankly, I am not yet entirely comfortable with the measures being considered here, particularly with respect to their constitutionality.

I am second to no one in my opposition to abortion, but I am equally committed to sound constitutional principles, and although I disbelieve in indiscriminate abortion in this country, I believe that the Constitution is the most important political document in the world.

I saw too many of my colleagues throw aside what both they and I know are sometimes sound constitutional principles in supporting some other matters through the years here. I want to make sure that these constitutional principles are considered and not ignored.

Thus, I will keep an open mind on these measures as well as the possibility of hearings later in my own subcommittee.

I want to compliment Senator East for his comments here today—that, in addition to the testimony given here today, he intends to hold broad and embracing hearings with regard to these issues that are of monumental importance, where both sides really do need to be heard. And he is starting today with some very interesting witnesses whom I wish we could all sit and listen to.

I have two other committee problems this morning, both of which are also equally impelling to me.

One of the things that I have difficulties with is, of course, the conflict that this type of a bill creates. S. 158 would make the congressional finding that human life shall be deemed to exist from the point of conception without regard to race, age, health, defect, or condition of dependency. It would make the further finding that person for purposes of the due guarantees of the 14th amendment would include all human life.

Does Congress have this authority under the 14th amendment? That is one of the major questions.

I emphasize that I believe in an extremely narrow conception of congressional authority under the 14th amendment. If I believed, however, in a more expansive interpretation of that authority, I would easily rely on such cases as *Katzenbach v. Morgan, South Carolina v. Katzenbach, Jones v. Mayer*, and *Fullilove v. Klutznick*. I choose not to do so because I believe that these cases were far too broad in their definition of congressional authority.

The majority of these cases argued that Congress, so long as it had a "slight rational" basis for doing so, could legislate with respect to the 14th amendment.

In *Katzenbach*, the Court allowed Congress to outlaw literacy tests in New York under the 14th amendment's authority, despite an earlier decision by the Court that literacy tests were not necessarily violative of the amendment.

The better reasoned dissent in *Katzenbach* by Harlan, in my opinion, even though it interpreted Congress 14th amendment authority much more narrowly, nevertheless concluded that the judicial branch must make its constitutional interpretations under the 14th amendment with appropriate deference for Congress legislative findings.

It requires a far more rigorous standard than the majority's "slight rational basis" standard because the findings must actually influence the Court to alter its decision, but it nevertheless requires that the Court pay them substantial heed.

Thus, under either view of the enforcement authority—and we choose, or at least I choose, the narrower view—Congress has a role in amplifying upon the terms of the 14th amendment.

Congress itself is not subject to the same kind of institutional limitations in defining when life begins as in the Court. This is the kind of decision that it routinely makes as part of the legislative process.

Congress may, in this instance—if a case can be made—be simply providing legislative factors to the Court to better enable it to make its constitutional decision.

Some of us find it ironic that some of the liberals—who so applauded decisions like *Katzenbach* and *Fullilove* when they were handed down because they granted such extensive powers to Congress—now that they see that these decisions could cut both ways, are up in arms about the quote constitutionality unquote of Congress powers to enforce the 14th amendment.

At least I am trying to be consistent. I opposed *Katzenbach* and *Fullilove* when they were decided and will refuse to rely on them, although I could, since they are the law of the land, as a basis for S. 158 or anything else.

So, what it comes down to is this. This is one of the major issues in our country today. It is an important issue. I am reserving judgment on it because I believe that we must keep the Constitution viable and we must keep the Constitution working in the best possible way.

But, on the other hand, we have broadened the 14th amendment in many ways pleasing to a number of people in our society, and perhaps there should be no lack of justification for broadening the 14th amendment in this way.

I have not made up my mind. I am very interested in these hearings, Mr. Chairman. You have some distinguished witnesses. They deserve to be listened to. Again, I am very pleased that you are going to hold extensive hearings on this matter, where we can listen to witnesses with alternative viewpoints as well, and I think that stands well for you, for this committee, and for all of us, and I am very grateful to you for that.

Statement of Dr. Leon Rosenberg

Dr. ROSENBERG. Mr. Chairman, I am pleased to have the opportunity to testify before you concerning bill S. 158.

I am a professor of human genetics, of pediatrics, and of internal medicine and chairman of the department of human genetics at the Yale University School of Medicine. Nearly 25 years ago I completed my formal education as a physician at the University of Wisconsin, after which I undertook residency training in internal medicine at Columbia University and at Yale. My research training was obtained subsequently at the National Institutes of Health. For the past 20 years I have worked as a researcher and clinician and teacher.

I have been elected to membership in such professional societies as the Association of American Physicians, the American Pediatric Society, the American Society of Biological Chemists, and the American Academy of Arts and Sciences. I am a past president of the American Society of Human Genetics and have served the National Institutes of Health, first as a member of the metabolism study section and currently as a member of the advisory council of the National Institute of Arthritis, Diabetes and Digestive and Kidney Diseases.

Today, however, I represent none of these institutions or organizations. Rather, I speak as a concerned scientist, husband, and father of three children, who, by the great good fortune of living in this free country, has been provided the opportunity to devote my career to the care of the sick, the pursuit of scientific truth, and the dissemination of knowledge.

The crux—or, if you will, the heart—of the bill before you is the statement in section 1 which states "that present-day scientific evidence indicates a significant likelihood that actual human life exists from conception."

I must respectfully but firmly disagree with this statement for two reasons: First, because I know of no scientific evidence which bears on the question of when actual human life exists; second, because I believe that the notion embodied in the phrase "actual human life" is not a scientific one, but rather a philosophic and religious one.

No Scientific Evidence Regarding Actual Human Life

I base my opposition to this bill on a third reason as well; namely, that I am convinced that the clinical implications of this bill are fundamentally counter to the best interest of the people of the United States.

With your permission, I would like to examine each of these conclusions in turn. There is no reason to debate or to doubt the scientific evidence indicating that conception is a critical event in human reproduction. When the egg is fertilized by the sperm, a new cell is formed that contains all of the genetic information needed to develop ultimately into a human being. This cell, like all living cells, has several fundamental properties: It is organized and complex; it can take energy from its environment; it can grow and develop, and it can divide.

The presence of these properties proves incontrovertibly that the fertilized human egg is a living cell with the potential for human life. But, in my view, there is an enormous difference between the potential for human life and, to repeat the critical phrase in section 1 of this bill, "actual human life."

To fulfill this potential, the fertilized egg must travel to the uterus, be implanted in the uterine wall, and undergo millions and millions of cell divisions leading to the development of its head, skeletal system, limbs, and vital organs. To be sure, this sequence of events depends on the genetic program present in each cell of the developing embryo and fetus. As surely, however, the sequence depends on the environment offered by the mother. Without the genetic blueprint of the fetal cells, human development cannot be initiated; without the protection and nutrition provided by the mother's tissues, the genetic blueprint cannot be followed to completion. This absolute dependence of fetus on mother lasts normally for 9 months, after which the birth process abruptly separates mother from child.

When does this potential for human life become actual? As a scientist I must answer I do not know. Moreover, I have not been able to find a single piece of scientific evidence which helps me with that question.

Not surprisingly, a great deal has been spoken and written on the subject. Some people argue, as you have heard, that life begins at conception; but others say that life begins when brain function appears, or when the heart beats, or when a recognizable human form exists in miniature, or when the fetus can survive outside the uterus, or when natural birth occurs.

In 1967, Dr. Joshua Lederberg, a Nobel laureate in genetics, wrote the following:

> Modern man knows too much to pretend that life is merely the beating of the heart or the tide of breathing. Nevertheless, he would like to ask biology to draw an absolute line that might relieve his confusion. The plea is in vain. There is no single, simple answer to "When does life begin?" . . . In contemporary experience, life in fact never begins—it is a continuum from generation to generation.

I have no quarrel with anyone's ideas on this matter so long as it is clearly understood that they are personal beliefs based on personal judgments and not scientific truths.

Actual Human Life is Philosophic—Not Scientific—Matter

If such beliefs are not scientific, you might ask, just why can't they be made scientific? My answer is that science, per se, doesn't deal with the complex quality called humanness any more than it does with such equally complex concepts as love, faith, or trust.

The scientific method depends on two essential things—a thesis or idea and a means of testing that idea. Scientists have been able to determine, for instance, that the Earth is round or that genes are composed of DNA because, and only because, experiments could be performed to test these ideas. Without experiments there is no science, no way to prove or disprove any idea. I maintain that concepts such as humanness are beyond the purview of science because no idea about them can be tested experimentally.

In discussing this matter with a number of scientific colleagues, I found similar views. Let me quote from two distinguished people.

Dr. Lewis Thomas, a leading medical scientist, philosopher, and author, observed that:

> *Whether the very first single cell that comes into existence after fertilization of an ovum represents, in itself, a human life, is not in any real sense a scientific question and cannot be answered by scientists. Whatever the answer, it can neither be verified nor proven false using today's scientific knowledge. It is therefore in the domain of metaphysics; it can be argued by philosophers and theologians, but it lies beyond the reach of science.*

Dr. Frederick Robbins, pediatrician, virologist, and Nobel laureate in medicine, responded as follows:

> *The question of when life begins is not, in essence, a scientific matter. Rather, it is one that evolves complicated ethical and value judgments. In fact, I doubt whether the health sciences can shed much light on such moral questions.*

Even Professor LeJeune, whom you heard from yesterday, in his Allen Award address in 1969 allowed that "scientific arguments are of little help in ethical issues."

If I am correct in asserting that the question of when actual life begins is not a scientific matter, then, you may ask, why have so many scientists come here to say that it is? My answer is that scientists, like all other people, have deeply held religious feelings to which they are surely entitled. In their remarks at these hearings, however, I believe that those who have preceded me have failed to distinguish between their moral or religious positions and their professional scientific judgments.

Adverse Clinical Implications

Some minutes ago I said I had three reasons for opposing this bill. Thus far I have discussed only those dealing with scientific evidence and the scientific method. My third reason is based on my clinical experience and judgment.

I believe that this bill has implications both far reaching and counter to the health interests of our people. This bill, if enacted into law, will prohibit the use of such commonly employed contraceptives as certain birth control pills and intrauterine devices because these forms of birth control prevent implantation into the uterus of the fertilized ovum that has, by legal decree, been made a person.

Moreover, this bill will protect the conceptus that has no possibility of realizing its human potential. Occasionally, a fertilized ovum degenerates into something called a hydatid mole, a grape-like cluster of potentially malignant cells which must be removed surgically before it becomes invasive. But such surgery would likely be prohibited by this law because the mole begins as a fertilized human ovum.

Finally, this bill would almost certainly stop all amniocentesis used for prenatal diagnosis of a growing list of genetic disorders, such as anencephaly or Tay-Sachs disease for which no successful treatment is at hand. Although amniocentesis for prenatal diagnosis has been available only for the past decade, more than 100,000 American women who realized they faced a heightened chance of bearing a child with a severe birth defect have requested and used this diagnostic procedure. More than 40,000 such genetic amniocenteses were performed in 1980 alone.

These statistics reveal the magnitude of the anxiety and fear that many American couples feel about having a child with a severe, often fatal congenital disorder. In common with all of us, these couples pray that any future child added to their family will be normal and healthy. Amniocentesis has made this prayer a reality for almost all couples who have used this procedure. It has given them the courage to undertake and complete a pregnancy despite increased risks.

Since amniocentesis carries a small, but finite, risk of causing a miscarriage, however, physicians would not be willing to carry out such a procedure under the terms of bill S. 158 and risk in turn being charged with manslaughter or murder.

Concluding Remarks

Senator East, let me conclude my remarks by divesting myself of all scientific or clinical credentials and speak to you simply as an American.

I believe we all know that this bill is about abortion, and about nothing but abortion. If this matter is so compelling that our society cannot continue to accept a pluralistic view which makes women and couples responsible for their own reproductive decisions, then I say pass a constitutional amendment that bans abortion and overturns the Supreme Court decision in *Roe v. Wade*. But, don't ask science and medicine to help justify that course because they cannot. Ask your conscience, your minister, your priest, your rabbi, or even your God, because it is in their domain that this matter resides.

Thank you. [Applause from audience.]

Discussion

Senator EAST. I would like to note that the standing rules of hearings prohibit applause. I did not want to interrupt it, but I am sure you can appreciate that both sides can do that. At some point we lose the decorum that we need to continue this discussion over the long run. Therefore, with all due respect to everyone and their various points of view on this, I would appreciate your leaving the cheering and the applause until you leave the hearing room and then congratulating the witnesses of your choice. Again, I think it will enable us to proceed more appropriately and expeditiously.

Gentlemen, I wish to thank the three of you. I would like to suggest in beginning our dialog here, perhaps as we did yesterday with the panelists, if any one of you three would like to comment upon what the other has said, lest I have unduly restrained you as far as your particular statement went, you may do so. I am not forcing you to do that, but I am simply saying if you would be so disposed, we might proceed in that manner.

Dr. Bongiovanni, would you care to add a thought? We will again move from you over to Dr. Williams and then to Dr. Rosenberg.

Dr. BONGIOVANNI. I agree with Dr. Rosenberg's comments about the scientific method and our inability to apply it in precisely defining human life. On the other hand, I submit that the practice of medicine is not pure science. We like to think it is.

I, too, have worked in the laboratory most of my life. I have been a consultant to the National Institutes of Health. I am rather proud of some of my scientific accomplishments, but I must say I am a physician in the traditional sense of the word, and we cannot match the pure scientist. We do not come anywhere near the physicist and the exact sciences.

Medicine is not an exact science. Therefore, I must concern myself with the humanities in addressing my own life to the problems of man. It is along those lines that I arrived at my own personal conclusions which I have presented to you.

They stem from my teachings and my inclinations as a practitioner of medicine, albeit I have done a lot of work in the laboratory. They are not narrowly based on religious views.

Thank you Senator.

Senator EAST. Thank you.

Dr. Williams, would you care to make an additional statement?

Dr. WILLIAMS. I do not know if a little obstetrician from Chicago has the right to debate a distinguished scientist from Yale, but I take grave issue with most of the things that Dr. Rosenberg said.

I think he assumes a role of unbelievable pessimism when he says that although we can put men on the moon, although we can transplant hearts and do a lot of other things, that we cannot define when human life begins and cannot determine when a human being begins. I think he makes the grave mistake in the very beginning of presuming that the two are synonymous.

He admits that he knows to a certain extent when human life begins. Yet, he concludes by saying that it is not a beginning but a continuing. Yet, he described a situation in which the sperm and the ovum meet and a new organism is begun, according to his genetic background.

I could debate him and it would take me perhaps an hour to go point by point and refute the things he has said because of the way he puts things together. He puts it all in a confusing posture rather than remaining strictly scientific.

Someone said once, "I came not to praise Caesar but to bury him" or "I came not to bury Caesar but to praise him"—I have forgotten how it went. This is his technique. He very subtly and cleverly all the way through says that we Americans are not able to handle a simple problem which relates to science.

He accuses me of being biased, all of us of being biased, by saying we cannot talk science, that we have to talk religion. I give him credit for being a bigger man than that.

Potential human life was one of the statements he made. He says that you cannot tell when this potential starts. I wish that he could separate in his mind that a human being is different from human life. A human being may be possessed of the quality which is human life, but that is a characteristic. As I tried to define in my paper, life is a quality which may be possessed by human life itself, by anything, that is cells—trees, animals—or a human being may possess human life. However, you may be a human being and be dead and yet you are still human. He has to separate these two things: Human life and the human being.

He says he does not know when this group of cells becomes a human being, so he is a little bit on the right track. If he will just follow that down a little bit, I think he will find out when, with a little help from some other people.

I don't know. I cannot answer that question. I know when human life begins, but I do not know when that group of cells becomes a human being, whether it is alive or not.

He attaches a great deal of importance to amniocentesis as if this is an infallible procedure which has saved a whole lot of people a whole lot of grief. I know if he has ever done one or looked at them that he knows that they make many mistakes. As many of them as have been performed, if they saved 100,000 people some grief, at least 100,000 mistakes have been made. Many times people have aborted normal children because of errors in interpretation of the amniocentesis. They ought to tell the people that when they are performing them, not have them believing that this is a great gift of man to solve all the problems of mental incompetence, et cetera.

Many people have lesser intelligence than others. Many people are born with deformities. Yet, they function well. If you ask them should they have been aborted, they will say no.

I know several who were born blind. One of them works in the hospital where I work. He works in the darkroom. He develops film every day. He gets up and down the hall and rides back and forth to work. He is a fine man making a real contribution to society.

Most of the defects that children are born with our present-day knowledge is able to correct. Anencephaly, which he mentioned, is a rare thing. I have delivered three in the 27 years I have been practicing. Only one of those went to term, and that was less than 2 or 3 weeks ago. That one would not have been diagnosed if I had thought of amniocentesis. I did not because it was a young woman, 21 years of age, and there were no problems. There was no illness, nothing. If we are going to do amnios on everybody, then we might pick it up, but we don't. I think that amniocentesis has been markedly overplayed as to its value.

With reference to birth control, he says this law would stop you from using the pill and contraceptives, that it would stop everything; you would just have to stop sex. Surely none of us would want that to happen.

I disagree. I am not on morals. I am not a theologian. I am not a priest. I do not know a lot about theology, but I know this: There is a theory that is called unwanted aggressor or something like that. If someone enters your house, you have a right to shoot them if you want to do so if they have no business in there.

If the act of conception has occurred but if no direct attack is made upon that ovum, but the mother decides "I don't want that in my uterus," and she has placed in her uterus a contraceptive device or she has taken some pills that make the endometrium nonreceptive, I don't know but it just seems to me that is not a direct attack upon the ovum and that it would be acceptable and could be used, no matter if the person is a Catholic, atheist or a Jew or a Methodist.

The reason is that in spite of this contraceptive device being there, the patient may still deliver. I deliver at least five babies a year with the contraceptive devices coming out behind them. They help, I guess, keep people from getting pregnant, but they do not stop people from getting pregnant and they do not make them abort.

I would disagree with his gloomy picture of what is going to happen to moonlight rendezvous if you pass this bill.

He made another comment saying when life begins is not scientific, but Dr. Bongiovanni already disagreed with that. The evidence I presented is clear scientific evidence. It has nothing to do with sociology, psychology, or anything else.

He quoted someone by saying, "Modern knowledge"—I do not write too well when I am trying to write in a hurry, but it looks like I have written— "Modern knowledge is too much to think that life is only a beating heart or a respiration."

I alluded to that earlier when I said that it is very difficult to define death. But, it is not difficult to define life.

I wish I had time to take his paper and to sit down and go step by step through it because the last three pages of it are zero.

Thank you.

Senator EAST. Thank you, Dr. Williams.

Dr. Rosenberg, would you like to comment?

Dr. ROSENBERG. I am sorry that Dr. Williams found me so pessimistic about life and about this country. I do not believe that people who know me would consider me a pessimist about anything—about advances in science or about advances in clinical medicine or about the way this country works. I am not pessimistic; I am, in fact, an incurable optimist. I believe that no matter how complicated and how disturbing this matter of abortion is, that this country can find its way to a resolution which will allow Americans to live with themselves.

I am not a pessimist, Dr. Williams, not about politics and not about medicine or science.

Some of the things you said about my testimony where you indicate that I felt that life was merely a continuum, those were quotes from Joshua Lederberg, a very well-known scientist and currently the president of Rockefeller University. I did not write those words; I used them to indicate the wide array of opinions that scientists have used to talk about the matter of when human life begins. To me it seems like the extreme example of how difficult it is to precisely define the moment.

Dr. Williams talked about amniocentesis and said that if there have been 100,000 amniocenteses performed for prenatal diagnosis, there have been perhaps an equal number of mistakes made. I am sorry, but I must disagree with that statement. I believe that there are statistics on this matter which have been published in reputable obstetrical and genetic journals. They indicate the frequency with which errors are made in amniocentesis and they perhaps number less than 1 percent. There is nothing like the frequency of errors which Dr. Williams just stated.

Surely there are errors because the people who carry out amniocentesis, just like anyone else, are frail and human and subject to error. That does not mean that the procedure itself has been discounted in terms of its value to the people who seek it.

I have no quarrel with Dr. Williams about his statements concerning the quality of life. I understand that there is an enormous range of opinion about the quality of life. I in no way am sitting here advocating abortion of anyone. I am simply here to say that these are the most personal matters that I believe exist.

I have counseled hundreds of families in my career. I think that the decision of a woman, of a couple, to terminate a pregnancy is one of the most painful, disturbing responses that I have ever witnessed. I do not believe people undertake this decision lightly. It is not a trivial matter. It is the most intensely personal matter I know.

Senator EAST. Thank you Doctor.

I would like to pick up on several themes here and would appreciate getting your responses to them.

First, on a very narrow point, I would like to clarify something. As I understand the two of you, Dr. Bongiovanni and Dr. Williams, as regards the narrow question of section 1 of S. 158, and that is all I am focusing upon—and, gentlemen, correct me if I am wrong because I do not mean to put words in your mouth—the two of you are saying that you find section 1, "that Congress finds that present-day scientific evidence indicates a significant likelihood that actual human life exists from conception," at least from your scientific, medical perspective, to be a meaningful and understandable concept. It is not a figment of some lawyer's imagination or someone who lacks expertise in your area. That is a meaningful, workable concept?

Dr. WILLIAMS. I do.

Senator EAST. As we were noting yesterday extensively, at the time the sperm penetrates the ovum a cell is created. That cell at that point has the capacity to develop into mature human life as we know it and understand it. Hence, in determining at what point human life begins, as you see it from your scientific, medical point of view, that is the point at which to begin the evaluation.

I appreciate it does not mean it dictates what the answer will be in all of this complex and difficult area of abortion policy. However, at least on that narrow point of section 1 of S. 158, the two of you find that a meaningful concept?

Dr. BONGIOVANNI. I do.

Dr. WILLIAMS. I do.

Senator EAST. Dr. Rosenberg, correct me if I am in error. You feel that section 1, as you see it as a medical man and as a man of science, is really not a workable, meaningful concept? The idea of human life is infinitely more complex and elusive than the simple point of conception, ovum and sperm coming together? You are very uncomfortable with it, and perhaps beyond that you think it is somewhat meaningless. It is like speculating on things to which one can never determine the answer. Hence, one might as well concede it and look for other ways to justify what you are doing, be it moral, ethical, philosophical, sociological, economic, or whatever.

I gather as a scientist you are very troubled that your profession and the expertise that it has given to human civilization is being employed here in this way.

Dr. ROSENBERG. Yes, Senator East; that is entirely correct. I tried, as clearly as I could, to distinguish the difference between a living cell and a human life. There is no question in my mind that the fertilized ovum is a living cell, but the concept of human life is not a scientific one.

Therefore, if you would like to revise section 1 to read, "The Congress finds a significant likelihood that actual human life exists from conception," of course I certainly am not in any position to tell you not to do so. However, I do not believe that there is scientific evidence on the point. The word "actual" is in my mind the critical word in addition to the words "scientific evidence."

Senator EAST. All right. Thank you.

Dr. Rosenberg, as a layman on these matters of medicine and science, let me pursue this point. I would appreciate your candid response to it.

As a layman and as a legislator confronted with a real problem in the real world of policy and politics, I do not as a Senator have the luxury simply to say the matter is complex, intricate, difficult, and, hence, we will absolve ourselves of making a decision here.

The problem that a person participating in the legal process faces is that we do have ultimately to acknowledge, do we not, that there is such a thing as human life? That is a meaningful, workable concept, at least at the broadest level of theorization. Human life is something that is. That is point No. 1.

Point No. 2 is that we have historically in the Anglo-American, Western, and indeed worldwide tradition, developed law to protect human life in the broadest sense of the word. The law has never been able to say in the Anglo-American tradition that the concept of human life is so impossible of really defining and is so complex and elusive that we could not develop laws to protect it. Hence, we would not have laws against perhaps murder, or any kind of law, and we would tend to opt out for the idea that it was elusive and vague.

It strikes me as a layman, not an expert in the field of science, that I am on sound ground in saying there is such a thing as human life. I do have a problem as a legislator of determining when it begins simply for the purpose of protecting it, inasmuch as we are all agreed the law at some point must protect it and will protect it.

I appreciate the great complexity of this problem of determining when that point is reached that the law ought to protect it. Let me ask you a rather personal question. I do not mean to put you on the spot. At what point would you protect it?

I am not going to let you off the hook by your saying, "That is complex, Senator, and I don't know," because at some point I presume you will protect it, be it at the time of birth or maybe puberty or sometime prior to the end of the continuum, which is death. At some point the law will insert itself. Convenience, rights to privacy, and other factors will not be allowed to intervene and supersede in a value sense, in a moral sense the right to life.

I agree with you that ultimately we are into the moral and ethical dimension of this, but the right to life ultimately, it strikes me as a lawyer and as a political scientist and as a former teacher of political philosophy, may very well be argued in a hierarchy of value to be the highest one. The law and the legislative body are bound at some point to have to protect it.

I am simply asking you as an individual a very difficult question, but then we have to answer it. At what point do you consider it being worthy of protection or would you allow the state to intervene in some way or other to protect it?

Dr. ROSENBERG. I am not surprised, Senator East, that you would ask me the question. I have asked myself the question ever since I was invited to testify. I will not beg the question or duck it. As long as you understand that I am giving you my personal opinion and that I am not speaking in the name of science, I will be happy to respond.

I would protect at the point of viability. I would protect at the point that the human being can exist on its own outside of the uterus.

Senator EAST. Again, I respond as a layman. It is a good point that you raise.

Is viability any more capable of precise scientific definition than, let us say, conception? It strikes me, again as a layman—and correct me if I am in error—it would be more elusive, more difficult of precise determination than the point of conception.

My agony as a legislator is that the law has to have a degree of certainty in it. Sometimes I agree that in order to have a degree of certitude in the law, we may have to be a bit more precise than we would allow, or our knowledge would allow us, to understand where the point ought to be. You say viability is that point.

Viability is elusive, isn't it? Wouldn't it be so? Just at the moment concentrating upon the unborn from the time of conception to birth, would there be unanimous agreement among gynecologists and others where viability lies?

Dr. ROSENBERG. I am sure there would not be consensus as to the precise point at which viability lies, but I think there is some greater consensus about what we mean by the word "viability." It means that the fetus, the newborn, is able to exist outside of the uterus and to grow and develop as a more independent individual.

However, I cannot help you, Senator East, with the clarity. You are asking me for something that I do not have.

Senator EAST. I am trying to find in my groping here a point of reference in protecting human life at this end of the spectrum, at the beginning, that would be more useful to us as legislators than would the idea of conception. You mentioned viability, but concede it may be even a less precise term than would be conception.

Let me just finish my thought on this matter of viability. It strikes me, again as a layman—and you have made a very telling point in your original commentary—maybe ultimately we are going to find in these hearings that science can help us in a very limited way and ultimately we get into a moral and ethical judgment here.

However, I am a little troubled about viability being the criterion by which you determine the right to life. Actually, once born, there is not viability if by viability one means the capacity to exist independently.

Viability, for example, does not exist then. The child is totally dependent upon mother and parents and family. Why, indeed, if we want to expand into a philosophical understanding, no man or woman stands or lives alone. No one is viable in the ultimate moral and ethical sense that we live freely and totally autonomously.

Then I think ultimately at the other end of the continuum of the old, the senile, the aged, the infirm, the disabled, the afflicted. If I let loose the concept into the world that viability is the ultimate criterion by which you determine the right to life, I am profoundly troubled with that as a matter of moral and ethical implication, and as a policy position I would have to disassociate myself from it. It would produce all kinds of perverse results, wouldn't it?

Why don't you respond to that, Dr. Rosenberg, and then we will hear from Dr. Williams.

Dr. ROSENBERG. Senator East, I do not think I have anything more that I can say on the matter.

What you are saying to me is that you have great problems with this area. What I am saying to you is that as a scientist I have great problems with this area as well. What I am asking you is whether this bill will help the American people resolve those great problems.

Senator EAST. I find you have been extremely helpful, although I obviously disagree with you on some points here. You have been extremely helpful in terms of suggesting there are other points of view on it and that fair-minded, reasonable people can disagree over this issue; there is no question about that.

Not to distract us, but what I find is valuable in this, and what I missed in *Roe v. Wade*, is the public dialog on the issue. We are here as a part of the legislative process—and you are making a vital contribution to it—where we can air these differences and begin to probe public feeling and sentiment on it.

I would hope this is the great virtue of the legislative deliberative process. We are better equipped to do it than the judiciary, in my opinion. We might try to see if we could build some sort of public consensus. Perhaps we never will, but I like to feel, because of the quality of your testimony and the others here, too, that you are making a very excellent contribution to the public discussion on the matter.

I would like to think in the long run, whatever happens to S. 158 or whatever happens to the constitutional amendment or whatever else is down the road, that at least we have been allowed now to begin a public discussion on a very vital, critical, important matter or moral, ethical, sociological, and economic consequence.

That little sermonette was unwarranted, but the quality of your testimony prompted me to say it.

Dr. Williams, you wanted to make a comment?

Dr. WILLIAMS. I was going to comment, but the chairman made most of the comments I was going to make.

I have great reservations about his use of the term "viability" as a time for deciding when to protect human life. Certainly when I started in medical school they talked about viability at 28 weeks. Then when I finished my residency they had backed it down to 20 weeks. Then when Edwards came out with this test tube baby, it proves that viabilty exists from the moment of conception. We have the tools and we can do it. It costs a lot of money, but we can do it.

All of this prenatal time is obviously a viable time. Then when you go on the other side of the question and look at the hundreds and thousands of babies and young folks who die on my south side of Chicago every year, I agree with the Senator that even when you get out of the uterus you may not be viable on your own. In many instances you are not.

Senator EAST. Fine. Thank you.

Dr. ROSENBERG. Senator East, I wonder if I might make just one additional comment.

Senator EAST. Yes. Please go ahead.

Dr. ROSENBERG. In these hearings I think I am correct that you have heard perhaps seven scientists and medical people say that they can accept section 1 of S. 158 and I am the only one who has appeared before you to say that I do not believe that they can. I hope that you and the rest of the subcommittee would not take that ratio of 7 to 1 to reflect the scientific opinion of the American scholar. If you wish to know more about how American scientists feel on this issue, I would hope that you will continue to seek additional opinion.

Either I am talking only to one particular group of people or else there is a very considerable fraction—I would think a great majority of the American clinicians and scientists in this country would support my side of this argument despite my distinct minority before you in the past 2 days.

Senator EAST. Doctor, you certainly make a valid point. I feel impelled to make it again and again as we go through these hearings. We would all do a disservice to our own cause to judge, for example, on 1 day's testimony or one person's testimony or the precise ratio or proportion at that time. You make a valid point. Obviously my being here this morning ought not to be interpreted as unanimity on this subcommittee or on the Judiciary Committee, let alone the U.S. Senate, on this point of view. I think your point is well taken and I appreciate your bringing that out.

Dr. Bongiovanni, you wanted to add an additional thought?

Dr. BONGIOVANNI. Thank you, Senator East. I would like to make two brief points.

I brought data with me supporting Dr. Williams' statement that the definition of viability changes every 3 or 4 years. The definition of viability in practical terms in the arenas in which all of us work is important. Do you take this fetus and put it in the nursery? You must define it. Our well-respected institutions do that. You know you are confronted with it. Babies of a certain size and a determined viability are not put in the trashcan. I know Yale would not do it and we would not do it.

We are in a spot where we have to define it. Whether we say we can or we cannot, there has to be a definition on the wall.

Your institution has one of the most heroic technological setups for keeping alive tiny little infants. I know the people in there. If you give them a 400-gram baby, they are going to do the best they can at that level but they are going to try.

This troubles me a little bit also about viability. Viability is going to change. We have to define it. Our institutions have to have something. Senator East needs something for a different set of reasons.

I also want to mention that, as in other areas of our culture today, technology has jumped ahead of us. We cannot deal with it. We see there are arguments in atomic energy. We have the same problems here.

I have great respect for Dr. Rosenberg; I want to make that clear.

I have spent my life with a disease which in biochemical terms is rather trivial and easily correctable. Now Dr. Williams is probably wrong that there are 100,000 mistakes for 100,000 correct ones, but I am with Dr. Williams because I must stand by and watch the prenatal diagnosis of a trivial disease end up in abortion.

I know what to do about this disease. It is easier to manage than diabetes. I come toward the end of my career having to face a situation in which a problem has been solved by a very simple medical means that is not heroic. Prenatal diagnosis is brought into the picture. It is regarded as justifiable cause in many places.

Thank you.

Dr. ROSENBERG. May I respond, Senator East?

Senator EAST. Yes.

Dr. ROSENBERG. I did not mean to suggest that the word "viability" was a passive word in any sense. I agree with Dr. Bongiovanni entirely that heroic attempts should be made to save the life of any premature infant, no matter how small. I am not talking about the trashcan. I am talking about viability in the sense of the result of every possible effort to save that life.

With regard to his second point, I agree with him absolutely that amniocentesis should not be used to diagnosis prenatally every condition that it might be able to diagnose. If I had the ability to diagnose the disease for which Dr. Bongiovanni has made major contributions, I would feel exactly as he does, that to diagnose that disease with the aim of aborting that fetus was an inappropriate use of medical technology. We have no argument on that matter.

Senator EAST. Fine. Thank you, Doctor.

Dr. WILLIAMS. I want to correct an impression which apparently I made. Apparently both these gentlemen think that I said that there would be 100,000 amniocentesis mistakes with 100,000 amniocenteses. I did not intend to say that.

What I was saying is if you do 100,000 amniocenteses—Dr. Rosenberg referred to that number and stated that these had helped that many people or so many people—that 100,000 would not be 100,000 mistakes. I had no intention of saying that. I said that the procedure has been given such a build up and it has been used almost indiscriminately, particularly in our teaching hospitals. Therefore, offsetting the advantage that may be gained by those 100,000 well-intended, carefully done with the percentage of error that is inherent in the procedure, there were 100,000 useless, error-making, damaging amniocenteses done last year in the United States, perhaps even more.

Senator EAST. Gentlemen, I wish to thank you. Your testimony has been valuable and useful.

I would hope that we have learned this morning a little better insight at least into how science and medicine can help us on this matter. Certainly, Dr. Rosenberg, you very well point out the great limitations of science in this area, that at some point we go beyond the matter of science and medicine and we are into the area of value judgment preference, and the philosophical, moral, and ethical. At the proper time in these proceedings we certainly want to get into those matters extensively.

You also raised good points, upon which I will forego commenting because I would like to take them up when we get to the legal and constitutional implications of this legislation.

I would like to offer that I hope that yesterday and today we have at least begun the discussion by getting into this question of when life begins within the meaning of S. 158. If conception is not a good point of making that determination, is viability? Or maybe in due course some other concept will emerge. At least we can test whether it is an improvement over what is provided for here in section 1 of S. 158.

I had indicated earlier there is a movie to be shown on this matter of conception, again simply to make graphically the point that has been made extensively on this matter of when life begins. I do not wish to suggest in the showing of this we are trying to say that dictates the total answer in the whole abortion area. We are simply saying it does clarify what our testimony has indicated—that there is a very profound event that takes place, conception; and there are those who think otherwise, as Dr. Rosenberg has very eloquently indicated. However, there are those who feel that is a workable and definitive point at which to begin consideration of this matter of protecting human life.

STATEMENT OF DR. CLIFFORD GROBSTEIN

Dr. GROBSTEIN. Mr. Chairman, I am Clifford Grobstein, professor of biological science and public policy at the University of California, San Diego. That title sugg' 'ts that my academic activity deals with the relationship between biomedical science and public policy in an effort to assist and illuminate public policy issues by reference to what we understand scientifically and technically about the issue in question. That includes the subject before us today.

I also served as dean of the school of medicine and vice chancellor for health sciences at the University of California, San Diego, for some 6 years. Earlier as a laboratory scientist I was an embryologist, one of the subdivisions of developmental biology. In that capacity I served as president of the American Society of Zoologists and the Society for Developmental Biology.

I will not read the statement which I have submitted. I would like to try to highlight some points made.

First, I suggest that scientific knowledge, particularly that relating to the process of development, has applicability to the issue before this subcommittee even though clearly other considerations are also relevant.

The matter cannot be settled by science, but it is also not a matter that can be settled without examining carefully what we know scientifically about the process of development. What we know scientifically is part of our objective knowledge, and objective knowledge has advantage because it is potentially accessible and common to all parties to a dispute. Therefore, it deserves attention in controversies of this kind.

Second, I emphasize that life in general does not begin in each generation, but rather is continuous through generations. So far as we know there is no origin of life on the contemporary Earth; all life is descended from preceding life and through continuing processes.

I also emphasize that this statement applies to human life. Eggs and sperm are alive and human, and so, too, is the cell that results from their fusion and all of its products. Fertilization is not when life begins; it is an important stage in the continuity of life from generation to generation.

A New Generation

Fertilization does initiate a new generation. It does so in two ways. It initiates development of the egg and it provides a new genetic constitution, which, speaking generally, is unique to the individual in question.

We know scientifically that at the moment of fertilization a new individual in the sense of singleness does not arise. This is known not from experiments on humans, but on nonhuman species. Those indicate that twinning can occur at stages well beyond the time of fertilization. Also, fusion of early stage embryos can be performed yielding a single individual. Therefore, in the early stages of development beyond fertilization an individual has not yet been firmly and stably established. The early embryo is in fact an aggregate of cells which have not yet formed a distinct collective in the sense of an individual organism.

At 2 weeks after implantation twinning is still possible, suggesting that even at that point a new individual has yet not been stably constituted. Two weeks is beyond implantation.

At still later stages our knowledge indicates that there is continuing transition and emergence of properties normally associated with self or personhood over a considerable period of time, just as there is with all morphological or functional characteristics of the developing individual.

There is certainly question as to what characteristics should be regarded as particularly significant with respect to defining a person, and there is question as to exactly at what time these arise. Therefore, it is not at the present time possible to make a precise statement. Definition depends on what our purposes are, and the purpose is not the business of science to decide but the business of the body politic. Therefore, science has to back off from providing any precise statement as to exactly when personhood arises.

Involvement of Central Nervous System

It is, however, clear that with respect to such characteristics as sentience or selfness or consciousness, correlation with the development of the central nervous system is very close. We know that it is not until 4 weeks that the first recognizable rudiment of a nervous system appears, and that at that time there are no identifiable nerve cells, no identifiable synaptic connections among them, and no identifiable neurotransmitters.

Through the gradual maturation of the spinal cord, and particularly of the brain, the underpinning for properties such as sentience presumably appear. It is not until 8 to 10 weeks that there are spontaneous movements in the human fetus, quickening of course not occurring until about 18 weeks. It is not known whether these early movements represent something that should be interpreted as sentience or selfness, or whether they are more in the nature of what would be called unconscious reflex activity.

Therefore, because of inadequacy of our information to date, it is not possible scientifically to specify exactly at what point selfness appears.

To conclude these comments, I have attempted to show that existing scientific knowledge is importantly relevant to discussion of the time of origin of human life; that such knowledge cannot settle all issues but it can set limits to the area of controversy; and that it is desirable that any formulated policy with respect to the matter should neither disregard nor conflict with existing scientific knowledge.

It is especially to be emphasized that with so complex and value laden a phenomenon as human development, purposes must be carefully and fully specified since suitable definitions must conform to particular purposes. To impose an arbitrary definition to satisfy one purpose may do violence to other equally or more important purposes.

A humane society cannot avoid finding this a troubling process. It is a price we pay for maintaining the right of self-decision on profoundly important personal matters that also have a public impact.

Thank you, Mr. Chairman.

Senator EAST. Thank you, Dr. Grobstein.

Our next speaker, Dr. James Neel, received his Ph.D., M.D., and doctor of science degree from the University of Rochester. He is presently chairman of the department of genetics and professor of internal medicine at the University of Michigan Medical School. He is a member of the Institute of Medicine, the National Academy of Sciences, and the American Academy of Arts and Sciences. Dr. Neel is also the president-elect of the Sixth International Congress of Human Genetics.

Dr. Neel, we welcome you.

Statement of Dr. James Neel

Dr. NEEL. Thank you.

Mr. Chairman and other distinguished members of this subcommittee, in view of the introduction, I do not think I need to repeat my credentials. Let me proceed directly to my statement. Inasmuch as it is a very brief and condensed statement to begin with, I ask permission simply to read it.

I find it impossible to address myself to the issue of when, following conception, actual human life begins without some reference to the concepts of evolution. Along with a large body of scientific thought, I subscribe to the thesis that step by step we have evolved from much simpler living creatures. We still have much to learn concerning the wonder of human evolution, but the evidence that it occurred seems sound. However, I would have great difficulty in saying at what point in that long process we passed over the threshold that separates human beings from the rest of the living world.

One of the bases for a belief in human evolution is the events of early human development. At about 30 days after conception, the developing embryo has a series of parallel ridges and grooves in its neck which are interpreted as corresponding to the gill slits and gill arches of fish. At that same time, it has a caudal appendage which is quite simply labeled "tail" in many textbooks of human embryology. Traces of this phase of our development can even be found in the adult.

The early embryo appears to pass through some of the stages in the evolutionary history of our species. The scientific dictum is: "Ontogeny recapitulates phylogeny," which translates into: during embryological development we repeat in abbreviated form many aspects of our evolutionary past. In this setting I can rephrase this as follows: the potentiality for becoming a human being is clearly present from the moment of conception, but to judge by external appearances, that potentiality is not immediately realized.

Given these facts, I find it most difficult to state, as a scientist, just when in early fetal development human personhood begins, just as I would find it impossible to say exactly when in evolution we passed over the threshold that divides us from the other living creatures. At some point as the amazing chain of events that results in a fertilized egg becoming a human being unfolds, we acquire the basis for those attributes that make us humans, but precisely when I cannot say. In other words, I can find no biological basis for saying at exactly what stage in development human personhood begins. The definition of that moment is a matter of religious conviction, philosophical inclination, or legal necessity.

Thank you.

Statement of Dr. Mary Ellen Avery

Dr. AVERY. Thank you, Senator East and Senator Baucus. I am honored to be able to speak to you today from a somewhat different perspective than my three colleagues, but I agree completely with their wise words.

I come to you as one who has specialized in the care of prematurely born infants and who has had many years of close association with their parents and their advisers on many of the complex questions that are raised in the setting of neonatal intensive care. Inasmuch as many of these issues pertain to the legislation under consideration, I would like to speak to them. I think my views are widely shared by my pediatric colleagues.

We take pride in the dramatic reduction in serious morbidity and mortality in the perinatal period that have resulted from both scientific understanding and social programs that foster care for pregnant mothers and their infants.

This remarkable lowering of mortality now permits a woman to feel reasonably confident that a given pregnancy will come to successful completion. No longer is she compelled to undertake multiple pregnancies to produce a surviving child.

I have also witnessed the extraordinary advances in the ability of physicians to detect birth defects in the first months of pregnancy and have been engaged in fostering prenatal diagnosis and genetic counseling to prevent reoccurrence of some inherited diseases. Some of the most serious, disabling, and often fatal disorders of new-born infants, such as Tay-Sachs disease, have been dramatically reduced through programs that alert potential parents to their carrier status and offer prenatal diagnosis in the first trimester. I view these advances as among the great scientific and social achievements of our age.

For many couples in whom the risk of recurrence of a major illness in the infant may be as high as 1 in 4 or sometimes even 1 in 2, prenatal diagnosis offers the options of having a normal child. Without it, some parents would have elected to have no more children.

As a pediatrician I participate with parents and their counselors in many of the very painful decisions that they may confront with respect to the birth of a very immature infant or an infant with major disabilities that cannot be treated medically or surgically. I can assure you that the kinds of decisions we must make involve a wide range of complex issues, such as ascertaining the likelihood of survival in the event of very premature birth. Troubled parents and their physicians, sometimes the clergy and members of the judiciary, find they have to struggle to come to a conclusion in a given instance even when they have all available facts at hand.

Can one conceive of any piece of legislation that could be written that would be appropriate under all of these circumstances?

Rights of Mothers and Children

Speaking now as a child advocate, I believe every child has the right to be born healthy, or at least with reasonable probability of restoration of health, to be wanted and nurtured by parents, to enter a society with the appropriate social support mechanisms and educational opportunities to support growth and development.

Women should have the option of knowing the risk of abnormalities in the fetus they bear and they should also have the right to choose whether they wish to continue that particular pregnancy. The consequences of pregnancy in the young teenager and the woman over 40 carry hazards that may adversely affect both mother and infant.

We urge health education in the prevention of unwanted pregnancy and applaud efforts of many agencies to achieve that. To deprive teenagers and others of the option for abortion is to foster the specter of illegal abortion, the associated mental and physical anguish, to set the child at risk of abuse or an otherwise less than optimally supportive environment. To prohibit termination of pregnancy in the face of knowledge of some major future problems is to inflict on parents and society an unwanted burden, often of many years' duration. Society has a profound obligation then to support that handicapped child.

Because of what I have just said, and speaking now as a woman and a pediatrician who cares deeply about fostering the best interest of children, I hope we live in a society that still allows women freedom of choice with respect to pregnancy based on the best information available in the safest possible environment. I also hope that when women choose to have children they will find themselves in a society that will make it the mother's right to have prenatal care and safe delivery and the child's right to receive appropriate support during that period of dependency, the first years of life.

Once again, I thank you for this opportunity to present my views.

Senator EAST. Thank you very much, Dr. Avery.

Statement of Dr. Daniel Callahan

Dr. CALLAHAN. Thank you, Senator.

I would like to make a variety of points on the issue of the beginning of life, particularly that issue as it relates to the pending bill. I think the bill rests on three faulty premises.

The first faulty premise is that the issue can be decided scientifically; namely, the issue of when human life begins. If one wants to define human life in the narrowest genetic terms, one might say, yes, it is true life begins then. However, I think for the purposes of a bill whose ultimate implication is to deal with abortion, one has to make a distinction between genetic human life and personhood. The bills seems to want to make a very rapid move from human life to the concept of personhood to the concept of protecting that personhood. That seems to me too rapid a leap in the bill.

I do not believe in the first place that the issue is scientific. In any event, I do not think one can move that rapidly from the notion of the scientific beginning of human life to that of personhood.

A second faulty premise, and a more subtle one, is that from scientific evidence moral conclusions can be drawn. There is an old principle in philosophy, which is my field, that one cannot derive an "ought" from an "is." In this case the argument is somehow that if we can get scientific evidence about human life, we can, therefore, morally conclude how we ought to value that life and how we ought to behave toward it. It seems to me that issue is a quite severable issue; namely, what do we do with the scientific evidence once we have it for moral purposes?

I might simply give an analogy. Science, for instance, might well argue that there is a significant likelihood that nuclear power plants are dangerous. It would not necessarily follow from that factual evidence that we ought not to build such plants, for our moral values might conclude that despite the dangers we ought to have them anyway.

I would also note that the general arguments concerning the relationship between scientific evidence and human personhood have taken a number of different directions. Some would argue strictly from genetic knowledge to the conclusion that life ought to be protected from conception. Still another school of thought would argue that it is important that there be some development, that some potentiality be realized before that protection ought to be accorded.

Others would argue that only social consequences count. They are in effect saying "draw the line anywhere you want, but only draw it on the basis of what you would take to be the most fruitful social consequences."

Still others—I suppose the most radical position—would argue that person-hood is achieved only when there is full self-consciousness, rationality, and a conscious desire to live. Obviously if somebody drew a line of that sort, infanticide would be possible and probably fairly late infanticide.

I think there is a third faulty premise behind the bill also; namely, that an issue of this kind can be decided by a legislative vote. If the issue is, indeed, a scientific issue, I would only point out that matters in the scientific community are not decided by vote.

Beyond that, one ends up with a very paradoxical situation; namely, the bill defines the issue as essentially scientific and then leaves a matter defined as scientific up to a vote by lay people—that is to say, by legislators who are not scientists. This at least is a paradox of that bill.

Now I would like to add one other consideration. If one thinks that this is a matter to be decided by legislation—namely, that the question of when human life begins can be decided by a vote—I would point out logically that another legislature in another era might very well decide that the scientific evidence has now changed, that life begins at 1 year after birth and that, therefore, we can take a vote on that and thus change the law.

It seems to me one is on a very slippery slope to decide an issue of this kind in a legislative manner and that the results could be very dangerous in quite a different setting.

I would like to stop at that point, but I would simply add one final thought. I, myself, support *Roe v. Wade*. I think the issue ought to be left up to the individual woman to decide, simply because I think the moral and philosophical issue is sufficiently in doubt to make that the only reasonable conclusion.

The real choice and the real question ought to be what ought women to think about when they go about making that choice, when they exercise their judgment.

What moral standards ought to be brought to bear in deciding to have an abortion? At that point the question of when human life begins becomes a critically important one and needs to be taken very seriously in order to come to a responsible, moral judgment.

Thank you.

Senator EAST. Thank you, Dr. Callahan.

Statement of Dr. Carl Tyler

Dr. TYLER. Thank you very much.

In addition to my present post which is given in the written statement you have before you, I have served for more than a decade as the Director of the Family Planning Evaluation Division at CDC, and I am a board-certified obstetrician/gynecologist. Those are the really more relevant reasons for my being before you.

My testimony is intended to bring you up to date on factual information with regard to the public health practice of legal abortion and how it has been related to the health of American women.

In 1969, the Centers for Disease Control (CDC) recognized that illness and death associated with abortion constituted an important public health problem and, because of the inadequacy of national statistics, CDC initiated epidemiologic surveillance of abortion. Since then, CDC has been compiling, analyzing, and disseminating data on abortion in the United States. The objectives of this activity have been twofold: First, to document the number and characteristics of women obtaining abortions and, second, to identify and eliminate preventable mortality and morbidity related to that procedure.

In 1978, the latest year for which we have data, the 50 States and the District of Columbia reported 1.2 million legally induced abortions. That was a 7-percent increase over the preceding year. The national abortion ratio also increased from 325 to 347 legal abortions per 1,000 live births.

As in previous years, women who obtained these procedures were most often young, white, unmarried, and of low parity. Two-thirds were less than 25 years of age; two-thirds were white; one-third was black and other races. Roughly three quarters of all women obtaining abortions were unmarried at the time of the procedure, and more than one-half had no previous live births.

Curettage continued to be the most widely used procedure for reported legal abortions, accounting for 95 percent of those performed in 1978. Compared with 1977, the percentage of saline instillation procedures used after 15 weeks' gestation decreased, dilatation and evacuation procedures increased, and instillation of prostaglandin and other agents remained unchanged.

Women continued to seek abortions at earlier gestational ages; over half of all abortions were performed on women who were less than 9 weeks pregnant. Ninety percent were performed within the first 12 weeks of pregnancy.

In 1978, 27 women died from abortion. That was eight fewer than in the preceding year. Four of the 11 legal abortion deaths were associated with ectopic pregnancies that were diagnosed after attempted legal abortion. There were seven deaths after illegally induced abortion and nine deaths after spontaneous abortion. The death-to-case rate for legally induced abortions decreased from 1.4 in 1977 to 0.6 per 100,000 procedures in 1978.

In August 1977, Federal funds for financing abortions of medicaid-eligible women were restricted. In order to study the health impact of this restriction, CDC reviewed medical records of women with abortion complications in three cities for 1 year before and 1 year during the restriction. A similar analysis was done for three cities where public funding for legal abortions had not been restricted.

Assuming that the number of complications reflects the number of abortions, we found that the restriction of public funding for legal abortions had not increased the number of illegal abortions, but that it had reduced the number of legal abortions obtained by poor women.

An estimated 30 to 55 million abortions are performed worldwide each year, making this one of the most prevalent means of fertility control. The majority of the world's population lives in countries where abortion is permitted either on request or for social reasons. The United States was sixth of the 18 countries reporting abortion rates and eighth of the 16 countries reporting abortion ratios. In 1978 the United States reported one of the lowest percentages of abortions to women over age 40 and to women with four or more children and one of the highest percentages to never married or previously married women and to women with no living children.

That is the end of my testimony. I will be pleased to accept questions at any time.

Senator EAST. Thank you, Dr. Tyler.

Statement of Dr. Jessica G. Davis

Dr. DAVIS. Thank you, Senator East. Thank you, Senator Baucus.

My areas of expertise not only include medical genetics and embryology, but also pediatrics with a special emphasis on the acquired and genetic problems of the developmentally disabled.

The major issue under consideration today is the validity of the statement in section 1 of your bill, S. 158, which states, ". . . present-day scientific evidence indicates a significant likelihood that actual human life exists from conception." I cannot affirm the validity of the proposition.

Let me begin by concurring with Dr. Leon Rosenberg's statements made at your last hearings before this committee. You will not hear a clearer or more humane expression of present day scientific thought.

With all due respect to the powers of Congress, I believe it is trying to do something beyond its temporal authority. It is trying to establish that mystical, ineffable instant when human life starts. From the perspective of a scientist I believe this question is not a scientific one. There is no scientific evidence that can tell us when life begins. For me, it is a theological, religious, philosophical, ethical, cultural, and moral question. It is a subject for debate and analysis perhaps, but hardly resolvable by legislative fiat.

In the interest of time, I shall not review again with this committee the generally accepted scientific facts concerning the earliest stages of development. I believe that these were magnificently reviewed last time by Dr. Rosenberg and more recently today by this morning's speakers. However, these are recorded in my testimony.

The scientific facts that we accept do not support either side of the proposition with S. 158 seeks to affirm. I believe these facts are neutral on the issue and that the question "Does human life exist from conception?" can only be answered by bringing in ideological concepts from nonscientific disciplines. The fact that scientists may be swayed by nonscientific ideology merely demonstrates that scientists, too, are human.

Other lawmakers and many philosophers have debated when life begins. Their answers vary, as you have heard, from conception to other arbitrary time periods, to quickening, to brain functioning, to the existence of the soul. Again in the interest of time, I shall not read all my examples, but I would like to cite one.

In Ecclesiastes, chapter 11, No. 5, it is said:

> As you do not know how the spirit comes to the bones in the womb of a woman with child, so you do not know the work of God who makes everything.

While an embryologist can tell you when bones develop in the womb, she cannot tell you when the spirit comes.

Now I should like to state my thoughts on the practical effects of this bill and the debate on the bill. If this bill becomes law, it will adversely affect current medical genetic practice. Three million living children are born in the United States each year. Of these, 3 to 5 percent have a significant chromosomal abnormality, such as trisomy #21 or Down Syndrome; a congenital malformation, such as a defect in the formation of the brain or spinal cord; or a genetically determined biochemical disorder, such as Tay-Sachs disease.

One-fifth of all infant deaths in our country are due to genetic problems or congenital defects. Recent studies indicate that a major portion of those pregnancies which are miscarried spontaneously after implantation do have underlying genetic problems. Genetic disorders also account for significant life-long morbidity.

During the past decade the development of new technologies, such as ultrasonography and amniocentesis, has aided physicians in diagnosing certain hereditary disorders and congenital defects in early pregnancy. The use of these optional techniques in conjunction with genetic counseling enables many couples at risk to have healthy children. Previously these couples refrained from becoming pregnant because of concern about their known recurrence risks.

Powledge and Fletcher in a 1979 report in the New England Journal of Medicine on "Guidelines for the Ethical, Social and Legal Issue in Prenatal Diagnosis" state, "The desired and intended results of prenatal diagnosis is information about the presence or absence of a possible disease or defect in the fetus."

To date, approximately 40,000 amniocenteses for antenatal genetic diagnosis have been performed in the United States. It must be emphasized that in the vast majority of cases—96 percent—the outcome results are favorable and indicate that the fetus is not affected with the condition for which the test was performed. This underscores the fact for me that amniocentesis can and does provide reassurance for the majority of individuals at risk undergoing this procedure.

According to a report of a Consensus Development Conference sponsored by the National Institute of Child Health and Human Development, "* * * should the fetus prove to be affected with the 'at risk' disorder * * *" families can now decide if they wish to avail themselves of selective abortion and subsequently have offspring "not affected with the condition for which they are at risk * * *".

Other individuals and families when faced with the intrauterine diagnosis of a fetal anomaly can use this information to become more fully informed about the nature of the defect. Parents-to-be can then maintain a pregnancy with anticipation and they can plan for any special provisions which the birth of the abnormal child may require. At the present, the responsible use of antenatal diagnostic methods permits reproductive decisions to be made on a more informed basis.

Antenatal diagnostic techniques are also essential in the development of therapeutic strategies in order to treat and cure genetic disorders. At the present time, amniocentesis enables the diagnosis and treatment of two serious biochemical disorders in the fetus: Methylmalonic acidemia and biotin dependent carboxylase deficiency. Investigators in our field hope to expand the therapeutic capability of these techniques in order to treat more metabolic conditions in utero.

If S. 158 becomes a law, antenatal diagnostic techniques may be abandoned. There is a small risk associated with amniocentesis and it does include the possibility of inducing a miscarriage. Under this proposed bill physicians may fear criminal prosecution and refrain from performing the procedure.

Furthermore, S. 158 specifically states that it would be illegal to terminate a pregnancy because of an adverse genetic diagnosis. Couples at risk for genetic disorders that can be diagnosed in utero would then be denied the possibility of having a healthy child. Our ability to diagnose, treat, and cure numerous diseases will be stopped cold; the illegal abortion will flourish and take its toll of life. Thus, the net result of this bill predictably will be to take life, to deny life, and to prevent cures of horrendous birth defects.

I would like to end by saying that Margaret Sanger said that there were three great battles for liberty in the United States: First, the American Revolution to secure political liberty. Second, the struggle to exercise freedom of religious opinion by eliminating the blasphemy laws. Third, the fight to prevent the obscenity laws from applying to birth control information.

I suggest we are in the midst of a fourth struggle: the fight to permit women safely and legally to choose when they wish to bring life on this planet without the backward authoritarianism symbolized by S. 158.

I have great faith in the institution of Congress, but I have no respect for this bill or its unstated goal of suppressing alternatives medically safe to women who elect them.

Perhaps, on reflection, this august body will concede that in our country there are many faiths and many opinions, many of which cannot be reconciled with each other on the great moral issues. Would not wisdom suggest that rather than legislate philosophical truth Congress should allow the citizens of this country to exercise their pluralistic beliefs?

It is for this reason that I urge the committee to seek the withdrawal of this bill.

Senator EAST. Thank you, Dr. Davis.

I am sorry to say that Senator Baucus and I are going to have to take a temporary recess in order to go to the floor to vote. That long bell you just heard meant a vote is coming up. Therefore, we will recess for a few minutes while we go over and do our public duty, if you would like to look upon it that way. We shall promptly return so that we can conclude these hearings by 1 o'clock. If you will be patient, we will be back soon.

Thank you.

Prepared Statement of Dr. Daniel Callahan

My name is Daniel Callahan, and I am the Director of the Hastings Center, Hastings-on-Hudson, N.Y. I was trained as a philosopher and, traditionally, philosophy is understood to be the pursuit of wisdom. For a number of years I have tried to ask myself, and others, just what constitutes "wisdom" in the nasty and controverted realm of abortion. I cannot say that I have ever achieved any final wisdom on the subject. For me at least, it remains a difficult and deeply troubling issue. I can only look with wonderment on those confident enough to take part in marches, to vociferously assail and impugn the motives of their opponents, and to be prepared to offer instant advice to courts, legislatures, and individuals.

The question of the beginning of human life is a severe test for anyone who seeks wisdom and the truth. That scientists and physicians are divided on the point is evident. That those who have not had the benefit of a scientific or medical training are no less divided is equally evident.

Why are there such differences of opinion and conviction? One reason may be that the different evaluations of the beginning of life reflect mere self-interest on the part of those doing the defining. Clearly, a definition of human life that would locate "the beginning" at conception serves the interests of the "pro-life" group. No less clearly, it serves the interests of the "pro-choice" group to see the issue as one that is inherently undecidable, and thus to be left to individual choice.

Unfortunately, this mode of analysis does not take us very far. The "pro-life" group wants to speak to the interests of the fetus and the protection of human life. That is surely not a debased or trivial interest. The "pro-choice" group wants to speak to the interests of the right of women to make their own decision concerning their procreative freedom, and that is not an unworthy or debased interest either. Each side, moreover, is prepared to proclaim that it is not insensitive to the concerns of the other side: the more responsible of those on the "pro-choice" side do not see themselves as hostile to childbearing, much less see themselves as "baby killers." The "pro-life" group, since it consists of a large number of women, hardly thinks of itself as anti-female. In sum, an examination of the motives of the opposing forces is not ultimately illuminating. Moreover, there is on both sides the usual human quota of hypocrisy, but that seems to me only to prove that human beings are not always in practice as admirable as their ideals, not a particularly original observation.

If the issue is to be decided at all, then, it must be decided on the basis of sound argument, on our conception of how we as human beings ought to live together, and how we believe difficult political and social issues ought to be decided in our society.

I cannot support the Human Life Bill, S. 158. I believe it rests on a number of faulty premises. The first faulty premise is the assumption that the issue is scientific, that science can give us a decisive answer to the question of when human life begins. The second is the assumption that one can draw obvious moral conclusions from scientific information. The third faulty premise is that matters of profound philosophical and religious depth can be decided upon by a political vote. I would like to examine each of those premises.

The first faulty premise is contained in the phrase from the bill that says "present day scientific evidence indicates a significant likelihood that actual human life exists from conception." If one wants to define "human life" as simply genetic individuality, then it is scientifically supportable to argue that "human life exists from conception." However, since genetic individuality is a necessary but not sufficient reason to characterize an entity as fully "human life," it is by no means evident that one can make the logical leap that the bill would like to make— from "human life" to "person," and from "person" to the endowment of full moral standing on the newly fertilized egg. It is both possible and useful to distinguish between "human life" and "person," which the bill lumps together. A being with a flat EEG reading whose heart and lung activity is kept going by artificial respirator is surely, genetically speaking, "human life." But just as surely that life is not a "person."

The distinction is important, since abortion is not merely a scientific issue, but, instead a moral issue with a scientific component. For moral purposes, scientific evidence is not and cannot be decisive; scientific facts do not carry their own moral meaning with them, nor do they provide any guide to behavior. They are simply meaningless raw data, in need of interpretation and evaluation. Only scientific facts in conjunction with a moral point of view and philosophical definitions can help us to determine a proper and moral course of behavior.

That point leads directly to the faultiness of the second premise. For the assumption is that from scientific evidence a clear moral conclusion can be drawn. That simply does not follow in this case. It is perfectly possible to argue, for instance, that "human life exists from conception" but to conclude that, in some circumstances, the right of a woman to take that life is the morally superior course of action. A simple analogy will make my point. Consider the following proposition: "Science indicates a significant likelihood that nuclear power plants are dangerous." It does not, however, follow from such a proposition that nuclear power plants ought not to be built. On the contrary, we may judge that the danger is worth running because of the benefits that such power plants may produce. An analogous point can be made in the case of the beginning of human life. It does not follow that a scientific definition of the beginning of human life automatically entails how that life ought to be valued, or who ought to make decisions concerning that life.

There are, in fact, at least four different schools of thought on the kinds of moral conclusions that could or might be drawn from the scientific data. The first I will call the "genetic school." It holds that genetic individuality is crucial, and that once the genetic pattern is in place the full potential for human personhood exists. That school would then want to argue that the potentiality is morally decisive, and that abortion should be prohibited from the moment of conception. The second school, which I will call the "developmental school," holds that while genetic individuality is present from conception, potentiality must be realized to some significant degree before it is appropriate to say that the right to life of the fetus ought to outweigh the right on the part of a woman to choose an abortion. The third school, which I will call the "social consequences" school, holds that it is entirely a matter of human choice where we draw the line concerning the beginning of human personhood, and that it is the social consequences of those choices that ought to be morally decisive in the making of decisions. That school would argue that the consequences of denying abortion to a woman are grave enough that we ought, therefore, draw the line on personhood comparatively late in pregnancy, or possibly up to the very end of pregnancy. The fourth school, which I will call the "full personhood" school, argues that a person does not exist until self-consciousness, rationality, and a conscious desire to live exist. In principle, this school would admit the possibility of infanticide, since the conditions for full personhood are not normally realized until some years after birth.

I personally do not find the arguments for the "social consequences" or "full personhood" schools of thought at all persuasive. In fact, they seem to me socially and morally very dangerous. The real choice, I believe, is between the "genetic" and the "developmental" schools, and I think the developmental school has the better of the argument. In essence, I believe it reasonable to contend that personhood develops gradually, and that full moral standing ought to be accorded fetuses no earlier than the twelfth week, and possibly as late as viability. I would not want to argue that this position is totally without problems. In fact, it has some significant difficulties, but I believe, on balance, that it is an approach that makes more sense than its serious competitors.

The third faulty premise behind the bill is that a matter of this kind ought to be decided by a legislative vote. If the issue is one of scientific evidence, as the bill asserts, it should be pointed out that matters of scientific truth are not, in the scientific arena, decided by a vote. Moreover, and much more importantly, a vote would prove nothing whatever concerning the beginning of human life at a scientific matter, but only be an expression of the opinion of those voting. The paradox of that situation is compounded when one recognizes that—the issue having been defined as a scientific one in the bill—it is then voted upon by non-scientists, i.e., legislators who are lay people.

There is still another consideration. If it is believed that the question of the beginning of human life can be decided by a vote, in this case a vote on conception as the beginning of life, it is by the same logic open to another legislature, in another era, to vote that human life does not begin until birth, or until three years after birth. One can, thus, just as easily vote infanticide in as vote abortion out.

At this point some further question may occur. The moral problem of abortion cannot decisively be decided by scientific evidence. And if the truth of the matter cannot be determined by a legislative vote either, then what kind of an issue is it, and what are the appropriate means of reaching decisions? It has been argued by many that the question is essentially "religious," and should thus be left to individual conscience. I consider that a wrong position. It is at least as much a philosophical as a religious issue and, in any case, there are many other issues in our society, no less religious, which we feel can be made subject to public policy.

Ultimately, I believe, the question is a philosophical one. Scientific evidence can be relevant but not decisive. In the nature of the case, it would be inappropriate and question-begging to have it decided by a legislative vote. For that reason, I believe the Supreme Court, in *Roe v. Wade*, was correct in leaving the decision up to the individual woman. That seems to me the only sensible public policy on the issue. Yet I would hate to see the matter left at that. If it is assumed by those women who avail themselves of the right to an abortion that one answer about the beginning of human life is just as good as any other—that there is no possibility of any approximation of truth in this area—then I think that a false conclusion also. That there is disagreement does not disprove that some modes of thinking about the problem are more reasonable than others, and some answers better than others.

To date in the abortion debate, the "pro-life" group has taken the lead in adding the serious question: when does human life begin, and what are the moral implications of our answer to that question? I hope that the "pro-choice" group will in the future be no less vigorous in its willingness to ask and confront that question, a trait that has not noticeably been present in the past. I support the right of women to make their own moral choice on abortion. But that is not the end of the matter. A no less fundamental moral problem is how that right might morally to be used. That is the real debate we should be having, not a debate about a bill full of philosophical fallacies.

Prepared Statement of Dr. Jessica G. Davis

Mr. Chairman and members of the Subcommittee on the Separation of Powers, I am here today to give testimony on several aspects of Bill S. 158.

I am an Associate Professor of Clinical Pediatrics in the Department of Pediatrics at Cornell University College of Medicine. At the present time, I serve as the Director of the Child Development Center and Chief of the Genetics Unit at North Shore University Hospital, a teaching affiliate of Cornell University College of Medicine. My areas of expertise include medical genetics, embryology and pediatrics with a special emphasis on the acquired and genetic problems of the developmentally disabled.

My past training includes a bachelor's degree from Wellesley College and a medical degree from the College of Physicians and Surgeons, Columbia University. Following training in pediatrics at St. Luke's Hospital-Columbia University, I completed a three-year NIH sponsored postdoctoral fellowship in medical genetics and cytogenetics at the Albert Einstein College of Medicine, Yeshiva University. I then held a two-year postdoctoral fellowship in the care and rehabilitation of the handicapped child at the Rose F. Kennedy Center at Albert Einstein College of Medicine.

During the past 16 years, I have served as a teacher and clinician and engaged in clinical research in academic medical settings. My related professional activities include membership in a number of organizations including the American Society of Human Genetics. I now serve as a member of the Society's Social Issues Committee. I am the Program Chairperson of the New York State Genetic Disease Program and President-elect of the New York State Genetic Task Force. Though I speak today as an individual I would be surprised if many of my colleagues would be in significant disagreement with my views.

The major issue under consideration today is the validity of the statement in

Section 1 of Bill S. 158 which states: ". . . present day scientific evidence indicates a significant likelihood that actual human life exists from conception."

I find the word "actual" to be a peculiar one. What is the difference between "actual human life" and merely "human life"? I don't know and therefore cannot affirm the validity of the proposition.

But let us drop the word "actual" (as the bill seems to do). The proposition on which the bill rests still cannot be affirmed. I should like to explain to this Committee why this is so.

Let me begin by concurring with Dr. Leon Rosenberg's statements made to this Committee. You will not hear a clearer or more humane expression of present day scientific thought.

With all due respect to the powers of Congress, it is trying to do something beyond its temporal authority: it is trying to establish the mystical, ineffable instant when human life starts. From the perspective of a scientist I believe this question is not a scientific one, but rather a theological, religious, philosophical, ethical, cultural or moral question. A subject for debate and exegesis perhaps, but hardly resolvable by legislative fiat.

I will try to tell this Committee what the generally accepted scientific facts are concerning human development.

What do we know about the onset of human development at the present time? We know that at conception the egg is fertilized by a sperm. The union of these two specialized cells results in a fertilized egg which contains all the genetic information necessary for the eventual development of a new being or new member of our species. Like other living cells the fertilized egg is a highly complex metabolically active cell that undergoes cell division. Again like other living cells the genetic material within the fertilized egg serves as a template so that a copy of this genetic material is incorporated into each ensuing cell.

Under normal circumstances the earliest cell divisions lead to the formation of a small cell mass which in turn is mechanically propelled to the uterine wall. After embedding in the uterine wall the as yet undifferentiated amorphous cell mass must undergo millions of cell divisions before it assumes at best a primitive humanoid form. The process takes weeks and its outcome is influenced by the complex interaction between the genetic make-up of the embryonic and fetal cells and the myriad of factors provided by and through the nourishing maternal intrauterine environment. This symbiotic relationship continues until birth.

The scientific facts which I have recited do not lend support to either side of the proposition which S. 158 seeks to affirm. I believe these facts are neutral on the issue and that the question "Does human life exist from conception?" can only be answered by bringing in ideological concepts from non-scientific disciplines. The fact that scientists may be swayed by non-scientific ideology merely demonstrates that scientists, too, are human.

Other lawmakers and numerous philosophers have debated when life begins. Their answers vary, from conception, to other arbitrary time periods, to quickening, to brain functioning, to the existence of the soul. Glenville Williams, a distinguished British professor of law, in his *The Sanctity of Life and the Criminal Law*, said:

Although we may cling to the religious belief in the existence of a soul, we have given up asking when this soul begins, because the question has become insoluble. Clearly the billions of sperm cells that go for naught in a single act of reproduction cannot be conceded to possess souls, and similarly it is impossible to find souls in unfertilized ova.

And in Ecclesiastes 11 (5) it is said:

As you do not know how the spirit comes to the bones in the womb of a woman with child, so you do not know the work of God who makes everything.

While an embryologist can tell you when bones develop in the womb she cannot tell you when the spirit comes.

Now I should like to state my thoughts on the practical effects of this bill and the debate on the bill. If this bill becomes law, it will adversely affect current medical genetic practice. Three million living children are born in the United States each year. Of these, 3-5% have a significant chromosomal abnormality (*eg.*, trisomy #21 or Down Syndrome); a congenital malformation (*eg.*, defect in the formation of the brain or spinal cord) or a genetically determined biochemical disorder (*eg.*, Tay Sachs disease). One-fifth of all infant deaths in our country are due to genetic problems or congenital defects. Recent studies indicate a major portion of those pregnancies which are miscarried spontaneously have underlying genetic problems. Genetic disorders also account for significant lifelong morbidity.

During the past decade, the development of new technologies such as ultrasonography and amniocentesis has aided physicians in diagnosing certain hereditary disorders and congenital defects in early pregnancy. The use of these optional techniques in conjunction with genetic counseling enables many couples at risk to have healthy children. Previously these couples refrained from becoming pregnant because of concern about their known recurrence risks.

Powledge and Fletcher in a 1979 report in the *New England Journal of Medicine* on "Guidelines for the ethical, social and legal issues in prenatal diagnosis" state "the desired and intended result of prenatal diagnosis is information about the presence or absence of a possible disease or defect in the fetus". To date, approximately 40,000 amniocenteses have been performed in the United States. It must be emphasized that in the vast majority of cases (96%) the results are favorable and indicate that the fetus is not affected with the condition for which the test was performed. This underscores the fact that amniocentesis can and does provide reassurance for the majority of individuals at risk undergoing the procedure.

According to a Report of a Consensus Development Conference sponsored by the National Institute of Child Health and Human Development ". . . should the fetus prove to be affected with the 'at risk' disorder . . ." families can now decide if they wish to avail themselves of selective abortion and subsequently have offspring "not affected with the condition for which they are at risk . . .". Other individuals and families when faced with the intrauterine diagnosis of a fetal anomaly can use this information to become more fully informed about the nature of the defect. Parents-to-be can then anticipate and plan for any special provisions which the birth of the abnormal child may require. At the present, the responsible use of antenatal diagnostic methods permits reproductive decisions to be made on a more informed basis.

Antenatal diagnostic techniques are also essential in the development of therapeutic strategies in order to treat and cure genetic disorders. At the present time, amniocentesis enables the diagnosis and treatment of two biochemical disorders in the fetus: methylmalonic acidemia and biotin dependent carboxylase deficiency. Investigators hope to expand the therapeutic capabilities of these techniques in order to treat more metabolic conditions *in utero*.

If Bill S. 158 becomes law, antenatal diagnostic techniques may be abandoned. The small risk associated with amniocentesis includes the possibility of inducing a miscarriage. Under this proposed bill physicians may fear criminal prosecution and refrain from performing the procedure. Furthermore, Bill S. 158 specifically states that it would be illegal to terminate a pregnancy because of an adverse genetic diagnosis. Couples at risk for genetic disorders that can be diagnosed *in utero* would then be denied the possibility of having a healthy child. Our ability to diagnose, treat and cure numerous diseases will be stopped cold; the illegal abortion will flourish and take its toll of life. Thus, the net result of this bill predictably will be to take life and prevent cures of horrendous birth defects.

Margaret Sanger said there were three great battles for liberty in the United States. First, the American Revolution to secure political liberty. Second, the struggle to exercise freedom of religious opinion by eliminating the blasphemy laws. Third, the fight to prevent the obscenity laws from applying to birth control information. I suggest we are in the midst of a fourth struggle: the fight to permit women safely and legally to choose when they wish to bring life on this planet, without the backward authoritarianism symbolized by S. 158.

I have faith in the institution of Congress but I have no respect for this bill or its unstated goal of suppressing alternatives medically safe to women who elect them.

Perhaps, on reflection, this august body will concede that in our country there are many faiths, some of which cannot be reconciled with each other on the great moral issues. Would not wisdom suggest that rather than legislate philosophical "truth" Congress should allow the citizens of this country to exercise their pluralistic beliefs?

For the reasons I have stated I urge this Committee to withdraw Bill S. 158.

Prepared Statement of George M. Ryan, Jr.

Mr. Chairman, and members of the Subcommittee, I am George M. Ryan, Jr., Professor of Obstetrics and Gynecology and Community Medicine at the University of Tennessee Center for the Health Sciences in Memphis, Tennessee. I am also currently the President of the American College of Obstetricians and Gynecologists, a medical speciality society, the membership of which includes more than 23,000 physicians who specialize in the provision of health care to women in America.

I appear before you today as an individual physician but prepared to share with you the official policies and current position of the ACOG with regard to the legislation before this Subcommittee. In either role—as a physician with nearly thirty years' experience in obstetrics and gynecology and related fields of concern, or as the President and spokesperson for the largest professional association concerned strictly with women's health—I solicit your consideration of the few points that I feel must be made here today and I invite your questions and comments.

The legislation now before the Subcommittee has been introduced in the Congress in various forms—as a proposed Amendment to the United States Constitution; as a proposed revision or addition to the United States Code; and in both forms it has been proposed with and without exceptions, explanations, and other variables. The common element in all of this legislation, however, is the goal of making the provision of abortions illegal in this country. The bill under consideration (S. 158) would permit states to end legal abortion services by means of defining human life to include that period of time during which the fetus may develop following conception. I do not wish to engage in a debate of the relative "rightness" or "wrongness" of abortion. My position and that of the American College of Obstetricians and Gynecologists is in support of the Supreme Court decision in *Roe v. Wade*. My purpose in being here is to provide expert testimony which I, as well as many of my colleagues, feel is absolutely necessary to assure that Congress has information on the broad health ramifications of this bill rather than viewing it only as a measure that simply addresses the abortion issue.

The proposed legislation reads in part:

> . . . *human life shall be deemed to exist from conception, without regard to race, sex, age, health, defect, or condition of dependency; and for this purpose "person" shall include all human life as defined herein.*

You have heard in earlier testimony before this Subcommittee, in testimony presented by reputable and qualified physicians and scientists, that "life begins at conception." I am not here to discuss this issue which many feel is not a question subject to a purely scientific answer. At conception there is cellular life, in biological terms. However the proposed legislation attempts to integrate the presence of such cellular life with a legal definition of "personhood" with all the attendant rights of citizenry which are protected by the Fourteenth Amendment to the Constitution. The concern which you must hear, from me and from my colleagues of the American College of Obstetricians and Gynecologists, is that when Congress equates cellular life to personhood it is taking a substantial leap beyond the current views of the medical and scientific community that will have a major and lasting effect upon the health care of women in this country, the practice of medicine in this country, and the personal health practices of a large portion of our population.

The legislation before you defines personhood as beginning at the moment of conception. The product of this conception, by definition of the legislation, would be entitled to Fourteenth Amendment protection as a person regardless of "health, defect, or condition of dependency." It is essential that you, as the duly elected representatives of your states and the citizens of this country, must be fully aware of the impact which can be realistically expected to result from

Congressional passage of this proposed legislation. You must know that granting the conceptus the Constitutional protections of personhood disregarding the relative and critical factors of health, defect, and condition of dependency, will have an immediate and enduring effect on women's health care.

To declare rights for the conceptus equal to those of the woman will create competition for medical care since the health interest of the fetus is not always consistent with the health interests of the pregnant woman. In fact, the physician potentially could be required to make medical decisions not in the best interest of either woman or fetus and possibly to the detriment of both.

The majority of pregnancies in this country occur in circumstances where the woman is understandably concerned with maintaining her own health and producing the healthiest child possible. We, as physicians, offer care and advice to enhance the health and quality of life of the woman, both as an individual and as the bearer of children. In this role, the physician is committed to the best interests of the woman, who entrusts herself to his or her care. This proposed legislation would create unsolvable problems for us in meeting this commitment.

Some of the major advances in obstetrics over the past twenty years relate to our ability to evaluate the intrauterine status of the fetus and perform early delivery of the fetus when indicated. Many of these premature births relate to maternal disease. Toxemia is a disease of pregnant women characterized by high blood pressure, possible convulsions, coma, and even death. Prevention of the more severe effects of this disease involves early delivery, with concomitant risk to the baby. Failure to act in this situation for fear of abridging the rights of the fetus could result in death of mother and fetus. This bill, then, would create impossible dilemmas for the practicing physician trying to meet his or her ethical responsibilities to act in the best interest of the pregnant woman. Many diseases of pregnant women require procedures or medicines which pose a risk to the fetus. Examples include appendicitis and other abdominal surgery in the pregnant woman. Medications such as dilantin for the treatment of epilepsy and cortisone-like drugs for other conditions are necessary in the interest of the pregnant woman and pose an increased risk of fetal abnormalities. These are clear-cut instances in which the physician has traditionally acted in the best interest of the pregnant woman. The proposed legislation would restrict this freedom.

Previously, I referred not only to the concern pregnant women have for their health but also their desire to have healthy children. Inherent in this is the desire of many women not to have a defective or severely handicapped child. Fortunately, we now have the capability of identifying a number of these defects in early pregnancy and offering a pregnant woman a chance to make the critical decision as to whether or not she will bear a defective child. Such a situation is seen in Tay-Sachs disease. A child born with Tay-Sachs disease is doomed to die in early childhood. Are we to deny the woman the option to avoid this tragic chain of circumstances for her and the rest of her living family?

Women in today's society constitute an increasing part of our work force. As a result many are postponing childbearing and are still completing families after age 35. At this age, they are at increased risk that their pregnancy will have a genetic abnormality, Down's Syndrome, and current practice mandates that we offer them the opportunity for screening these unfortunate occurrences. The proposed legislation would essentially nullify our current efforts at genetic screening programs.

Thus far I have spoken only to the impact of this legislation upon the pregnant woman. The woman who is *not* pregnant also has a vital and justified interest in the maintenance of good health which will be impacted by this legislation. For over 10 million women in this country, the exercise of self-determination includes management of their reproductive functions by means of the intrauterine device and the birth control pill. If the legislation as proposed were to pass, any known contraceptive which interferes with the development of the conceptus would be suspect. Consequently, I believe that it is realistic to assume that the IUD and the low dose oral contraceptive pills could be considered as abortifacients and therefore declared illegal. In fact, this objective was stated in testimony before the House Subcommittee on Health and the Environment just last month by proponents of this legislation. This Subcommittee, the Senate as a whole, and the people of this country must be made aware of the impact that removal of these popular and effective birth control methods would have. If this legislation is passed and if a state views the intrauterine device as an abortifacient, what will I as a physician do when a pelvic examination reveals that my patient has an IUD in place? Do I remove it? Do I request that she have it removed? What if she refuses? Do I report her to a law enforcement agency? Or am I indeed a party to a criminal act if I do not report her?

Mr. Chairman, these are just the highlights of our concerns about the problems which would be created by passage of this legislation. There are also complicated medical issues which would arise immediately, regardless of what approach the state legislatures might take. If the federal statute defines as human life any conceptus, regardless of health, defect or condition of dependency, we must consider how the medical profession will deal with the relatively frequent incidence of ectopic pregnancy, where the conceptus develops outside the uterus, or the hydatidiform mole, which is a "product of conception" that cannot survive, or the spontaneous abortion.

Great progress has been made in improving the quality and manner of delivery of health care for women in this country. Maternal mortality and infant mortality are the lowest in the history of this nation. To introduce into this improved environment of health care a factor as threatening as that involved in a new definition of personhood is to push backward that history of progress.

I encourage you to consider not only the primary goal of this legislation, but also its impact; in fact, I believe that you will find, as we have found in the American College of Obstetricians and Gynecologists, that regardless of the issue of abortion, this legislation presents a range and depth of problems so complicated and so far-reaching as to obscure the basic intent of the legislation. State governments would be enabled to intrude into the most personal and private decisions of pregnant and non-pregnant women. As a physician, as a citizen, and as the President of the American College of Obstetricians and Gynecologists, I ask that you acknowledge and assess the fundamental medical changes and critical side effects inherent in this legislation.

It is heartening to be invited to testify. The emotions generated by the underlying debate have made it difficult to focus attention on the many other ramifications of this bill. This has indeed been an opportunity to expose the

Subcommittee to the full measure and import of the issues surrounding this legislation in order that your votes will be assured to be informed votes.

Prepared Statement of Dr. Mildred F. Jefferson

Mr. Chairman and other honorable members of the Subcommittee: I think it does not matter a great deal that I am a general surgeon on the staff of Boston University Medical Center and Assistant Clinical Professor of Surgery on the faculty of Boston University School of Medicine. Mentioning that my earned degrees include a Master of Science Degree from Tufts University and a medical degree from Harvard Medical School might require adding that 23 institutions of higher learning across the country have awarded me honorary degrees in order to establish that I do not find the academic world a foreign land. My experience includes practice, research and teaching. I am a Diplomate of the American Board of Surgery, a member of the Boston Surgical Society, the Massachusetts Medical Society and the American Medical Association among other things. From the beginning of my medical education, I have been concerned with the complex problems that develop at the law-medicine interface.

For the past 10 years, I have been deeply involved in all aspects of the public policy debate on the life issues of abortion, infanticide and euthanasia. It has been my honor and priviledge to be one of that dedicated band of men and women who have created the focus and direction of the right-to-life movement in the United States.

The central conflict in our public policy crisis is over the proposition that some lives are less valuable than others and that lives of less value can be sacrificed for the good of other concerned individuals or the society. When the U.S. Supreme Court gave the matter of getting rid of a baby to the private decision of a woman and doctor, the High Court stepped out of its responsibility to interpret the Constitution and acted as a super-legislature to create a new body of social law. As the final decision on abortion was left up to the doctor's medical judgment, the High Court gave to my profession an almost unlimited license to kill. In assuring the execution of the privilege, the High Court separated the biological and legal meanings of personhood and denied the protection of the Constitution to the member of the human family who needed it most—the unborn child. The mischievous effect of this social law has been to induce scientists to abandon scientific method to become social mechanics and to seduce doctors to forsake usual standards of professional practice to become social technicians. With the obstetrician and mother becoming the worst enemy of the child, and the pediatrician becoming the assassin for the family, the state must be enabled to protect the life of the child, born and unborn. The Human Life Bill will make this possible.

As our nation could not exist in the last century half-slave and half-free, our nation cannot survive long into the next century destroying its own young and denying the humanity of its own. The protection of life must be the absolute priority of our society, not ever made secondary to the elitist notions that would assign a sliding scale of value to human lives.

LEGAL SECTION

Statement of Stephen H. Galebach

Mr. GALEBACH. Mr. Chairman, Senator Baucus, I appreciate the opportunity to appear before you to testify about the constitutional questions presented by the human life bill.

I have submitted for the record of this hearing a copy of the law review article that I wrote concerning the constitutionality of a congressional declaration that human life begins at conception and that all human beings are persons within the meaning of the 14th amendment.

I have also submitted a written statement concerning the constitutionality of a withdrawal of the jurisdiction of lower Federal courts to issue declaratory judgments and injunctions in certain types of abortion cases. In order to avoid repetition, I will not recite what is set forth in those documents. My law review article, however, provides much of the legal support for the testimony I will give today.

The controversy over abortions is constitutionally difficult because it involves conflicting rights of the utmost importance. On the one hand, there is the woman's privacy right, as defined by the Supreme Court, to decide whether or not to bear a child. On the other hand, once a child has been conceived, the woman's right to privacy cannot be considered in isolation from the right to life of every human being and the right and duty of Government to protect human life.

The conflict between these rights cannot be finally and fully resolved under the Constitution without first deciding whether unborn children are human beings.

In its 1973 abortion decision, the Supreme Court declared that it was unable to determine whether unborn children were human beings. The Court also held that unborn children were not persons within the meaning of the 14th amendment and that a woman's right to privacy took precedence over the State's right to protect potential life until a fetus had become viable.

The Supreme Court thus left unresolved the fundamental question of whether unborn children are human beings. The answer to this question necessarily influences the proper resolution of the abortion issue. However, if the Supreme Court is unable to decide when human life begins, who can make that decision? I submit that under the Constitution, Congress can make that decision.

The 5th and 14th amendments to the Constitution provide that no person may be deprived of life without due process of law. The 14th amendment expressly authorizes Congress to enforce its protections by appropriate legislation.

If Congress examines the question the Supreme Court was unable to answer and concludes that unborn children are human beings, then the Court's conclusion that they are not persons would be subject to change, and Congress would have the power to enforce the 14th amendment by declaring that unborn children are persons within the meaning of that amendment.

In my law review, I explained the constitutional justification of the human life bill in terms of two leading theories advanced by Supreme Court Justices concerning the power of Congress to enforce 14th amendment rights.

The first theory is found in Justice Brennan's majority opinion in the landmark case of *Katzenbach* v. *Morgan*. Under this theory, Congress has broad power to define the scope and meaning of the 14th amendment rights so long as it acts to expand those rights.

The second theory is found in Justice Harlan's dissenting opinion in *Katzenbach* v. *Morgan*. Justice Harlan took a narrower view of Congress power, allowing Congress to make legislative findings that influence constitutional determinations, but reserving to the Court the authority to make the ultimate constitutional decision.

The majority opinion in *Katzenbach* v. *Morgan* is controversial because it confers on Congress such broad power to redefine the 14th amendment rights and to force its view on the Supreme Court. There is serious question whether the Court would or should reaffirm such a broad precedent today.

However, the constitutionality of the human life bill does not depend on the validity of such a broad theory of Congress power. The narrow enforcement power described by Justice Harlan is sufficient to justify the human life bill.

For that reason, I would like to focus today on the applicability of Justice Harlan's theory to the human life bill. The key sentence in Justice Harlan's opinion in *Katzenbach* v. *Morgan* is as follows:

> To the extent "legislative facts" are relevant to a judicial determination, Congress is well equipped to investigate them, and such determinations are of course entitled to due respect.

According to this theory, congressional findings influence the Supreme Court, but do not necessarily control the Court's decisions. For example, in the 1965 and 1970 Voting Rights Acts, Congress influenced the Supreme Court to conclude that literacy tests for voting were racially discriminatory, even though in 1959 the Court held them not to be discriminatory. The Supreme Court was not persuaded, on the other hand, by Congress finding that equal protection requires the extension of voting rights to 18-year-olds in State elections.

Former Solicitor General Robert H. Bork has recognized the power of Congress, within narrow limits, to influence constitutional decisionmaking. In reference to the President's 1972 legislative proposals for busing, Professor Bork wrote that:

> The justices may be persuaded to a different view of a subject by the informed opinion of the legislature. At the very least, a deliberate judgment by Congress on constitutional matters is a powerful brief laid before the Court. A constitutional role of even such limited dimensions is not to be despised.

It is only rarely that Congress can contribute findings that will have such persuasive value as to change a constitutional determination. However, the issue of abortion presents what may well be the most appropriate issue for Congress to influence a constitutional interpretation by means of legislative findings.

The unique aspect of the abortion issue is that the Supreme Court has declared itself unable to decide the basic question of whether unborn children are human beings. Congress is well equipped, in Justice Harlan's words, to investigate and decide the issue.

If Congress finds that a live human being exists from conception, that finding will be entitled to due respect from the Supreme Court. The persuasive value of such a finding will depend on what value should be given to human life under the 14th amendment.

If all human lives are of equal value under the 14th amendment, then Congress finding that unborn children are human beings will necessarily mean that their lives are equally protected with other human lives.

The congressional finding will lack persuasive value only if the 14th amendment does not protect all human lives equally; that is, only if some human beings can be nonpersons under the amendment.

The Supreme Court has never decided whether all human beings are equally entitled to the protection of the 14th amendment's right to life. However, the legislative history of the 14th amendment speaks to this issue.

The proponents of slavery who framed that amendment repeatedly expressed their view that all human beings should be protected under the Constitution. The author of the 14th amendment, Congressman Jonathan Bingham of Ohio, spoke of the rights guaranteed by the amendment as applying to every human being. Senator Jacob M. Howard of Michigan, who sponsored the amendment on the floor of the Senate, spoke of its provisions as protecting the rights of common humanity.

In expressing these views, the framers were echoing the words of the Declaration of Independence that all men are created equal, and that all are endowed by their Creator with certain inalienable rights, among which is the right to life. In other words, any human life which has been created shares equally in the inalienable right to life.

Respect for the sanctity of all human life is thus a basic principle affirmed both at the founding of our Nation and at the framing of the 14th amendment. This basic principle underlying the 14th amendment leaves no room for an argument that some human beings are nonpersons under that amendment.

In fact, the framers of the amendment were reacting specifically against the Supreme Court's decision in the *Dred Scott* case, which held that black people were nonpersons under the law. The 14th amendment was framed after the Civil War for the purpose of insuring that never again in the United States would a class of human beings be treated as nonpersons under the Constitution.

In light of the overall purpose and specific statements of the framers of the 14th amendment, a congressional finding that unborn children are human beings will have strong persuasive value to show that they must be persons entitled to the 14th amendment's protection of life. At the very least, the Supreme Court will have to reexamine the question of personhood in light of Congress' findings on the beginnings of human life.

Of course, the Supreme Court has also said that the Constitution protects a woman's right to privacy. The human life bill does not address this right or deny its existence.

However, the Supreme Court will have to reevaluate the proper balance between the privacy right and the right to life of unborn children. The Supreme Court will still have the final say. The human life bill does not dictate what the result must be. All the bill does is ask the Court to look at the issue again in light of Congress' answer to the question that the Court said it could not resolve, namely, when does human life begin.

The Court's role as the final interpreter of the Constitution is not threatened by this approach. Congress is merely exercising its prerogative to inform the Court of its views in accordance with Justice Harlan's understanding of the appropriate role of Congress and the Court.

In order to avoid the force of this argument, critics of the human life bill have argued that the biological beginning of human life is an irrelevant question, and that the important and difficult question is what value should be given to human life and at what stage of development should value be given to an unborn human life.

These are two separate questions, and both are vitally important. The first question of when human life begins is the question that the Supreme Court said it was unable to answer. Congress can decide this question by legislative fact-finding in the exercise of its power to enforce the 14th amendment.

The second question, concerning the proper value to be given to human life, restates the important issue I have already discussed: whether all human lives are to be valued equally under the 14th amendment, or whether some lives are less deserving of protection than others.

This question also was not answered by the Supreme Court in its 1973 abortion decision. The Court did not know whether unborn children were human lives. Therefore, it did not have to decide the value of their lives.

If Congress now informs the Court that unborn children are human beings, then the Court will have to address the question of how to value their lives. In answering this question, the justices will of course be guided by the legislative history of the 14th amendment and by our Nation's historic respect for the sanctity of all human life. The Court will also have before it Congress' finding in the human life bill that the 14th amendment is intended to protect all human beings.

In light of these factors, it is very difficult to see how the Court could avoid the conclusion that what is biologically a human being is also a life that should be protected under the 14th amendment. The only alternative to this conclusion is either to deny Congress' power to answer the question the Court left open as to the beginning of human life, or to hold that some human beings, namely the unborn, are nonpersons under the law.

Congress has a uniquely compelling justification to state its views on when human life begins, because the Supreme Court has declared itself unable to answer this question, and the question is fundamental to the proper resolution of the abortion issue. Since the Supreme Court rarely disqualifies itself from answering a question necessary to a proper interpretation of the Constitution, the human life bill need not set a broad precedent.

Some branch of government must be able to decide when life begins if the constitutional guarantees of life are to be given effect. When the Supreme Court declares that neither it nor State legislatures can decide when life begins, then Congress must see if it can fulfill that essential role as coenforcer of the 14th amendment. The Supreme Court has never denied that Congress can fulfill this role, and there is no reason to assume it will.

The ability of Government to identify and protect human life is important not only for unborn children but also for people already born. The dispute over the existence of actual or meaningful human life is not limited to unborn children.

Serious scholars have argued that certain individuals are less than fully human, and that as a result, they have no right to life. Such cases include children born with severe mental or physical handicaps and people with terminal illnesses or disabilities.

An article in a prominent medical journal has advocated that we revise our traditional notions of the sanctity of human life so as to allow euthanasia for babies born with severe mental or physical handicaps.

A State judge in New York has declared that the Government has a lesser interest in the life of a terminally ill comatose patient than in the life of a fetus.

My point for purposes of these hearings is not to argue that these views are wrong, but merely to show that some branch of Government must be able to decide, first, whether such unfortunate individuals are human beings, and, second, whether their lives are equally worthy of the protection of the law.

It would make little sense for a category of human beings to go unprotected simply because no branch of government could decide whether they were human beings. Government cannot responsibly take the position that issues of life and death are too intensely personal to be resolved by the State.

If these decisions are left to the private consciences of individuals, if individuals are free to choose whether someone else shall live or die, then life ultimately has no protection.

However, our Constitution does not take such an irresponsible path. The Constitution protects life, and gives Congress power to enforce that protection. That is why the human life bill is in no sense a circumvention of the Constitution, but rather a fulfillment of it.

Thank you.

Senator EAST. Thank you, Mr. Galebach.

[The submissions of Mr. Galebach follow:]

Prepared Statement of Stephen H. Galebach

The Constitutionality of Withdrawal of Lower Federal
Court Jurisdiction In the Human Life Bill

The Human Life Bill withdraws lower federal court jurisdiction to grant declaratory or injunctive relief in certain types of abortion cases.[1] The jurisdiction of the Supreme Court is expressly left intact. The effect will be to make state courts the original forum for injunction and declaratory judgment cases concerning abortion, and to ensure that the Supreme Court will have the benefit of the views of the state courts when it exercises its ultimate power of appellate review over decisions of the highest state courts involving questions of federal law.

This allocation of jurisdiction between state and federal courts in abortion cases will serve important interests in our federal system. Before 1973 the states had power to determine, at least in the first instance, what protection should be extended to unborn children. By recognizing unborn children as persons, the Human Life Bill will give states a constitutional justification for protecting unborn children once again. State action to protect unborn children is likely to be controversial, however, and will almost certainly be challenged in the courts. It makes sense to allow state courts to have the initial opportunity to resolve these challenges without interference from lower federal court injunctions or declaratory judgments. State courts are best suited to interpret state statutes in a way that carries out the will of the legislature while conforming to the requirements of the Constitution. Federal courts have less flexibility in this area because their interpretation of the requirements of state statutes cannot be authoritative. Congress has recognized this problem in other contexts and has enacted legislation prohibiting lower federal courts from interfering in areas where important state interests are concerned. *See* 28 U.S.C. §§ 1341-42 (prohibiting lower federal court injunctions against state taxes and administrative rate orders). Even in the absence of such a statute, the Supreme Court has recognized that there are occasions when lower federal courts should defer to state court proceedings so as to avoid unnecessary federal-state conflict. *See, e.g., Younger* v. *Harris*, 401 U.S. 37 (1971) (requiring lower federal courts to abstain from issuing an injunction against a state criminal prosecution challenged on First Amendment grounds); *and Railroad Commission* v. *Pullman Co.*, 312 U.S. 496 (1941) (requiring lower federal courts to abstain from passing on a constitutional challenge to state administrative action so that state courts would have the initial opportunity to decide the issues presented by the challenge).

The lower federal courts have no monopoly of the wisdom required to interpret the Constitution. This is particularly so when the controversy concerns criminal laws protecting human life and family laws concerning the relationship between a woman, her unborn child, and perhaps the father or guardian of the unborn child. Matters of this kind have traditionally been resolved by the states, not by the federal government. Reserving such matters to state courts in the first instance will not jeopardize constitutional rights, because, under Article VI of the Constitution (the Supremacy Clause), state courts are bound by the Constitution

---

[1] The jurisdiction of the federal courts to grant other types of relief would not be affected.

just like federal courts.[2] The Supreme Court, moreover, will retain its power of appellate review over questions of constitutional interpretation. Its deliberations may well benefit from the opportunity to consider the views of state courts on matters traditionally resolved under state law.

The constitutionality of this measure cannot be seriously challenged under existing precedent. The power of Congress to limit the jurisdiction of lower federal courts has been sustained in every Supreme Court decision in which the issue was presented; and the Court has endorsed this power in the broadest terms. *See, e.g., Palmore* v. *United States*, 411 U.S. 389, 401 (1973) (Congress has the sole power of creating inferior federal courts and of "withholding jurisdiction from them in the exact degrees and character which to Congress may seem proper and to the public good"); *and Sheldon* v. *Sill*, 8 How. (40 U.S.) 440 (1850) ("Congress may withhold from any court of its creation any of the enumerated controversies").

There is clear precedent for Congressional legislation to remove a particular class of controversies from the federal courts. The Norris-La Guardia Act, for example, withdrew jurisdiction from the federal courts to issue injunctions in labor disputes. The Supreme Court sustained the constitutionality of the Act in *Lauf* v. *E. G. Shinner & Co.*, 303 U.S. 323, 330 (1938).

Some distinguished judges and commentators have argued that there are limits to the power of Congress to define the jurisdiction of the lower federal courts. None of these theories has ever been endorsed by the Supreme Court. Nevertheless, it is worth noting that the Human Life Bill is consistent with most of the theories concerning possible limits to the scope of Congress' power to withdraw lower federal court jurisdiction.

In *Martin* v. *Hunter's Lessee*, 1 Wheat (14 U.S.) 304 (1816), Justice Story suggested that Congress must vest jurisdiction over every federal claim in some federal court—either in a court of original or of appellate jurisdiction. The Supreme Court has consistently rejected this view. *See Palmore* v. *United States*, 411 U.S. 389, 401 n.9 (1973). But Justice Story's test is satisfied here in any event because the Human Life Bill maintains the Supreme Court's appellate jurisdiction over federal claims arising in abortion controversies.

Hart and Wechsler have argued that Congress may constitutionally remove lower federal court jurisdiction only when a state forum is available and there is an ultimate right of Supreme Court review. *See* Hart & Wechsler, *The Federal Courts and the Federal System* 309-65 (2d ed. 1973). This theory has merit as a policy matter, since it ensures an ultimate possibility of Supreme Court review for all federal claims; but the theory once again is not supported by existing Supreme Court precedent. *Cf. Ex parte McCardle*, 7 Wall (74 U.S.) 506 (1869) (broadly sustaining the constitutionality of legislation limiting the appellate jurisdiction of

---

[2] This analysis assumes that state court systems can provide speedy adjudication of suits for injunctive and declaratory relief, with speedy review by means of interlocutory appeals if necessary. Speedy adjudication is of particular concern in the context of abortions, since an abortion delayed is an abortion denied, and an abortion performed is a human life irrevocably ended. If any states fail to provide such speedy review, it might be held under the reasoning of Battaglia v. General Motors Corp., 169 F. 2d 254 (2d Cir.), *cert. denied*, 335 U.S. 187 (1948) (see discussion below), that lower federal court jurisdiction was constitutionally required with respect to that particular state. As to other states the jurisdictional limitation would still be valid.

the Supreme Court). The Human Life Bill satisfies the Hart and Wechsler theory because state forums are available for abortion controversies and the Supreme Court retains the power of appellate review.[3]

The United States Court of Appeals for the Second Circuit has suggested that Congress may not withdraw jurisdiction in a manner that deprives any person of life, liberty, or property without due process of law. *See Battaglia* v. *General Motors Corp.*, 169 F.2d 254, 257 (2d Cir), *cert. denied*, 335 U.S. 887 (1948). The suggestion was made in the context of a case arising from the Portal to Portal Act, which prohibited judicial review by all courts, whether state or federal. The *Battaglia* standard is satisfied by the Human Life Bill because state courts, subject to the Supreme Court's ultimate power of appellate review, provide an adequate guarantee that all due process rights will be protected.

Rotunda has argued that Congress may by withdrawing jurisdiction "restrict substantive rights that it could not directly affect." *See* Rotunda, *Congressional Power to Restrict the Jurisdiction of the Lower Federal Courts and the Problem of School Busing*, 64 Geo.L.J. 839, 842 (1976). While this argument is not without some force, it has no express Supreme Court support. For example, few would argue that the Norris-La Guardia Act did not have a major effect on substantive rights relating to labor disputes. Nonetheless, the Rotunda test is satisfied by the Human Life Bill. Requiring initial resort to state courts in abortion controversies directly affects only the procedures for resolving abortion controversies. The goal is to improve the ultimate decision on the merits by taking advantage of state court expertise in construing state laws and in evaluating difficult questions of criminal and family law. The Human Life Bill does not attempt to use power over jurisdiction as a means of coercing a particular decision on the merits. *Cf. United States* v. *Klein*, 13 Wall (80 U.S.) 128 (1872) (Congress cannot use a jurisdictional statute to compel a court to decide a case in a manner that violates the Constitution).

Finally, Eisenberg has argued that changed circumstances have now made it imperative that Congress vest lower federal courts with complete jurisdiction over all federal questions. *See* Eisenberg, *Congressional Authority to Restrict Lower Federal Court Jurisdiction*, 83 Yale L.J.498 (1974). This extreme argument finds no support in the Constitution or in Supreme Court precedent, and it goes far beyond the limits urged by other scholars. To adopt this view, the Supreme Court would have to reverse over 150 years of precedent.

To be sure, Congress has not often exercised its power to remove a particular class of controversies from the jurisdiction of the lower federal courts. This

---

[3] If state courts refused to resolve an abortion controversy, they could be ordered to do so by the Supreme Court. *See, e.g.*, Testa v. Katt, 330 U.S. 387 (1947); *and* General Oil Co. v. Crain, 209 U.S. 211 (1908). A problem might arise, however, if an abortion case was brought against a federal official to enforce federal rights. State courts lack jurisdiction over such disputes. *See* Tarble's Case, 13 Wall. (80 U.S.) 397 (1871). Since the Human Life Bill withdraws jurisdiction only in cases arising out of state action—enforcement of state laws and municipal ordinances—the Bill will not deprive lower federal courts of jurisdiction over cases challenging actions of federal officers. *Cf.* Redish & Woods, Congressional Power to Control the Jurisdiction of Lower Federal Courts; A Critical Review and a New Synthesis, 124 U.Pa.L.Rev. 45 (1975) (arguing that Congress may withdraw jurisdiction from lower federal courts except for cases involving actions of federal officers over which state courts do not have jurisdiction).

restraint can probably be attributed to the great respect Congress properly has for the important role that the lower federal courts play in guaranteeing and enforcing constitutional rights. Widespread use of Congress' jurisdictional powers might impair that role. But when special considerations justify the use of state courts as the initial forum, Congress is not restrained by the Constitution or by Supreme Court precedent from restricting the jurisdiction of lower federal courts.

As pointed out above, Congress has strong reasons to provide that state courts should be the initial forum for cases involving abortions. There is no reason to distrust the good faith and judgment of state courts to resolve the issues that will arise when states enact and enforce anti-abortion legislation. Nor is there reason for Congress to believe that the Supreme Court's power of appellate review will not provide adequate protection for constitutional rights. State courts are fully capable of compiling an adequate factual record for Supreme Court review. Any final decision on the merits by the Supreme Court will guide the state courts in their adjudication of abortion cases. State courts have not attempted to evade federal abortion decrees in the past. There is no reason to believe they will do so in the future.

The limitations in the Human Life Bill on the jurisdiction of lower federal courts are therefore well within the constitutional powers of Congress.

Statement of Laurence H. Tribe

Mr. TRIBE. Thank you very much, Senator.

Mr. Chairman, Senator Baucus, I appreciate the opportunity to be here today. I do want to abide by your suggestion that we not read our statement. Let me simply submit it for the record and highlight what I think are several fundamental propositions and several extraordinary misunderstandings in the view we have heard ably summarized by Mr. Galebach.

Respect for Constitutional Process Unites Diverse Foes of S. 158

I might begin by raising essentially a rhetorical question, although I think it is ultimately a genuine one. We have heard how divisive, complex, difficult, and troublesome the issue of abortion is. Surely it is not the kind of issue that generates consensus.

Yet, in the face of that, does it not seem remarkable that this is the one issue in this century that has generated consensus among six former Attorneys General of the United States, and among a dozen of the leading constitutional scholars in the United States, groups whose members hold the most diverse and varied views on the subject of abortion, but all of whose members have told this subcommittee that they are convinced that, however well-intended, S. 158 is clearly unconstitutional?

If one wonders why it is that an issue so divisive would generate such consensus, it seems to me one is likely to conclude that there is a deep reason. The reason is respect for the constitutional process, a respect that transcends conflicting views about the abortion issue.

Status of Fetus Under Roe *v.* Wade a Question of Law Not Fact

With that as a preface, it seems to me useful to begin with the suggestion of the Chair that this is after all a modest approach. I would agree in general that it is intelligent and reasonable not simply to leap to a constitutional amendment the moment one is in distress about a decision of the Supreme Court. If there is a modest, reasonable legislative solution, by all means try it.

The question here is: Is there a reasonable, modest legislative solution? I am convinced that there is not. I am convinced that there is not because of the Supreme Court's decision in *Roe* v. *Wade*, which, right or wrong, has been fundamentally mischaracterized before this subcommittee.

The Court, it is true, expressed its inability to give a definitive answer to what it took to be an unanswerable question: When does human life begin?

Mr. Galebach says that some branch of Government must be able to decide this intimate moral question; but I have thought if we have learned anything in the modern era, it is that sometimes Government does not have an answer and cannot have an answer.

The fact that a question is profound and important does not mean that Government must tell us how to answer it. The whole point of the Supreme Court's decision in 1973 was not simply one of judicial incapacity, for right after the Court said that it was unable to answer the question of when human life begins, the Court explained that what it really meant was that no State, by adopting its own answer to that question—choosing one theory of life rather than another—could be permitted to override the fundamental right of the pregnant woman to give an answer for herself.

One may disagree with that view. One may disagree with the view that this fundamental question must be left to the woman. However, if one disagrees with that view, one is not disagreeing on a question of fact—What is the fetus? What is a human being?—but on a basic proposition of constitutional law.

The only way to undo a proposition of constitutional law announced by the Court is by constitutional amendment, not by legislative redefinition of constitutional language and not by waving the magic wand of section 5 of the 14th amendment and saying, "We will now inform the Court as to what the fertilized ovum is."

The Court was not in a deep, dark mystery on that question. It is not as though the Court labored under the misapprehensions of an Aristotle, believing that until some late point in pregnancy the fetus was inert, not alive. There was confusion about that.

I think it is instructive, in this connection, that the National Academy of Sciences at its 118th annual meeting adopted an extraordinary resolution, a resolution which stated that the bill now before this subcommittee purports to derive its conclusions from science, but it deals with a question to which science can provide no answer.

The question of when human life begins is a shorthand for a profound, tragic moral puzzle, one which the Supreme Court said was not for Government to decide.

Congress No Freer than the States to Override Woman's Right to Choose

Even if it were true somehow that under section 5 of the 14th amendment Congress had the power to give an answer which would then elicit due respect from the Supreme Court, what one has to remember is that Congress' answer would itself be no better than an answer a State legislature can give.

I find it extraordinary that in a period when so many are struggling to find new ways of restoring power and autonomy and responsibility to the States the thesis should be propounded in defense of S. 158 that the fundamental power of the States to preserve and protect human life and all persons is somehow inferior to the power of Congress under section 5 of the 14th amendment.

On the contrary, the Court has repeatedly held that, whatever the affirmative source of the authority, the Congress of the United States comes before the bar of justice with no greater claim over matters of life and liberty than does any one of the 50 sovereign States of the Union.

Thus the same standard that led the Supreme Court to say that it was a deprivation of a woman's liberty without due process of law for a State to impose its theory of life on a woman would surely lead the Court to say that it is an identical deprivation of such liberty for the Congress of the United States to impose upon a woman its own answer to the question of when life begins.

It seems to me that as mysterious and puzzling as the moral issues are, the legal issue is extraordinarily clear. It is for that reason that there is such an extraordinary convergence of otherwise disputatious and divergent scholars and chief law enforcement officers of this country in coming to a single view on the matter.

Invalidity of S. 158's Attempt to Block Federal
Judicial Enforcement of Roe *v*. Wade

Let me say a word or two about section 2 of S. 158 because that provision, I think, is also a concern to this subcommittee.

Section 2 would attempt to prevent lower Federal courts from issuing declaratory or injunctive relief to protect the rights that women were declared to have under *Roe* v. *Wade* under section 2 of the bill. Women seeking abortions could not obtain declaratory or injunctive relief to prevent the enforcement of a restrictive abortion law.

That provision, it seems to me, is as unconstitutional as section 1, redefining "person" under the 14th amendment. The purpose of section 2 is transparent. It is not simply to channel cases dealing with abortion to the State courts. In the words of Chairman East in a question and answer memorandum that I understand was released on April 23, the purpose, quite transparently and, I think, candidly stated, is to assure continued enforcement of a State law outlawing abortion until the Supreme Court itself has ruled on the constitutionality of S. 158. That is its purpose.

Its structure is completely asymmetrical. It does not take abortion questions out of the Federal courts. Rather, it enlists the Federal courts in an antiabortion crusade.

However well-meaning, however ultimately right, perhaps, morally, that is what it does. It does so because, for example, as Senator Baucus pointed out in his questions to Congressman Dougherty, S. 158 would define all fetuses as human beings, as persons from the moment of conception, and if it were to be upheld, it would obviously mean that the State cannot pay for terminating their lives, cannot subsidize abortion of any kind.

A guardian of a fetus or a father could go into Federal court and obtain an injunction to prevent the expenditure of public moneys on abortion. If, for example, a State were to pass various restrictions on abortion but provide a public abortion subsidy, the guardian or the father could go to Federal court to prevent the expenditure of public money on abortion, while the woman could not get similar relief from that Federal court. The deck would thus be completely stacked against her.

It seems to me quite clear that section 2 of the bill is not a housekeeping jurisdictional provision as such. It is essentially a provision designed to assure that until and unless the U.S. Supreme Court strikes this law down, the rights that women were deemed to have had under *Roe* v. *Wade* could not be protected injunctively or through declaratory relief.

Congress Should Not Pass S. 158 if it Expects Supreme Court to Invalidate the Legislation

It is no answer to say that, of course, if it is unconstitutional, as all those experts seem to say and as the six ex-Attorneys General seem to say, then quickly, by an expedited means, the Supreme Court will tell us so.

That kind of buckpassing, if I may say so, is not really worthy of this Congress. If it is the best judgment of Congress that this measure is not constitutional, as the Court has thus far construed the Constitution, then the only responsible path is constitutional amendment, not sending up a constitutional trial balloon that pro- and anti-*Roe* v. *Wade* scholars alike agree is certain to be shot down.

S. 158 Would Not Restore State Autonomy in Abortion Context

Let me close with a concern that I have that would persist even if this law were to be upheld, even if it were deemed to be constitutional.

I believe that S. 158 is inherently and unavoidably defective as measured by its own aims. I think the chairman stated the reasonable aims in a way that I found almost compelling when he said that we are simply trying to return to the States a matter that perhaps ought never to have been taken over by the Federal Government in the first place. If these matters are divisive, if they are unclear, why try to resolve them nationally? Why not decentralize?

However, observe that that is not, despite its intentions, what this law does. To begin with, on the matter of State and local funding for abortions, the law leaves States no choice. In Massachusetts and in California, the State constitutions require public funds to be expended without discrimination against abortion. Under this law, spending on abortion would be forbidden because that would, if this law were upheld, amount to State action which destroys the lives of persons.

To that degree at least, the matter is suddenly nationalized and not restored to its condition as it was in 1973.

Even more fundamentally, if I may just read from the bill for a moment, it says:

> *For the purpose of enforcing the obligation of the States under the 14th amendment not to deprive persons of life without due process, human life shall be deemed to exist from conception.*

This talks about the obligation of the States. I have heard it said repeatedly in support of S. 158 that it would be up to the State legislatures. If the State legislatures chose not to do anything about the destruction of fetuses—which this statute declares to be human persons from the moment of conception—that would be just fine, proponents of S. 158 assert.

I submit that this is not a responsible reading of the bill's language. If the Constitution says, as Mr. Galeback reminds us that "persons," once we have agreed that beings are "persons," may not simply be abandoned by the State to wanton slaughter, it would surely follow once we declared that the fetus was a "person" from the moment of conception without regard to "condition of dependency," that for the State to declare open season on fetuses, and to say we are not going to prosecute those who kill them, would be a deprivation of life without due process of law.

Moreover, there is nothing I can find in this bill, despite the stated intention of its supporters not to interfere with use of the IUD and the morning-after pill, to sustain a distinction between "persons," as fetuses would become if this bill were upheld—persons in the first week after the fertilization of the ovum, even before implantation in the uterine wall.

If a State were to say we just do not care about very early abortion and will not do anything about it, I submit that, if this law were upheld, it would be a snap, a trivial matter, to go into a Federal court and get an injunction to declare unconstitutional the discriminatory policy of nonprotection of the fetus immediately after the fertilization of the ovum.

It will be said that this is not the bill's purpose, but, as the Supreme Court of the United States reminded Congress not long ago in the snail darter case, *TVA* v. *Hill*, when the language of the statute is clear, the fact that Congress may not have intended that it go quite that far will not necessarily save it.

I make this point not because I am trying to pick the statute apart as a law professor. My point is that this and the other problems I have described as to the mismatch between S. 158's purposes and its likely effects all trace to the fact that Congress knows that it cannot simply say, "*Roe* v. *Wade* is hereby overruled."

So what does Congress do? The only way, short of an amendment, for Congress to achieve the result it seeks is by giving the status of personhood to the fertilized ovum. However, when it does that, it is caught in a hopeless dilemma.

On the other hand, Congress puts all the States in a straitjacket and requires them to treat even the use of a morning-after pill as the destruction of a human being—that is, homicide—or it invites the States to pick and choose among persons, that is, to decide that some persons are not worthy of protection.

I submit that is the kind of precedent that this Congress does not want—in effect to say it is OK for States to leave some persons utterly unprotected. There is a dilemma: Either, having declared fetuses to be persons without regard to dependency, the Congress places the States in a straitjacket far more severe even than that of *Roe* v. *Wade*; or Congress creates a draconian, nightmarish precedent of saying, "Now we recognize that personhood has been broadened, but we will allow States, if they wish, to leave some persons utterly unprotected."

Conclusion

It seems to me this measure is clearly unconstitutional. That it would be so held by the Supreme Court is not a matter of guesswork. It is not a responsible thing, however well-intentioned, for this Congress to do. I would regard it as a very sad day were this very serious, difficult issue to become the occasion for futile confrontation between the Congress and the Supreme Court, with a predictable outcome—one that would not enhance respect for either body, and one that would not advance the cause either of women or of unborn life.

Thank you.

Senator EAST. Thank you, Professor Tribe.

[The prepared statement of Professor Tribe follows:]

Prepared Statement of Laurence H. Tribe

Introduction

I am a professor of constitutional law at Harvard University and am the author of the treatise, *American Constitutional Law* (Foundation Press, 1978). I am honored to have been invited by the Subcommittee to testify on the constitutionality of S. 158, a bill

> *[t]o provide that human life shall be deemed to exist from conception.*

My conclusion will come as no surprise to the Subcommittee inasmuch as I was among the twelve scholars[1] who signed a letter that was sent to Senators East and Baucus, Chairman and Ranking Minority Member of the Subcommittee, on April 21, 1981, stating:

> *Our views about the correctness of the Supreme Court's 1973 abortion decision vary widely, but all of us are agreed that Congress has no constitutional authority either to overturn that decision by enacting a statute redefining such terms as 'person' or 'human life,' or selectively to restrict the jurisdiction of federal courts so as to prevent them from enforcing that decision fully. We thus regard S. 158 and H.R. 900 as an attempt to exercise unconstitutional power and a dangerous circumvention of the avenues that the Constitution itself provides for reversing Supreme Court interpretations of the Constitution.[2]*

I should like to explain here why I hold these views, and then to answer any questions members of the Subcommittee may have about the matter.

The Constitutionality of Section 1

In section 1 of S. 158, Congress

> *finds that present-day scientific evidence indicates a significant likelihood that actual human life exists from conception,*

and that

> *the fourteenth amendment to the Constitution of the United States was intended to protect all human beings.*

---

[1] The other eleven were Paul Brest, John Hart Ely, Paul A. Freund, Erwin N. Griswold, Louis Henkin, Philip B. Kurland, Louis B. Schwartz, Telford Taylor, William Van Alstyne, Harry H. Wellington, and Charles Alan Wright.

[2] On May 1, 1981, a letter signed by six former United States Attorneys General was sent to Senators East and Baucus joining this statement. They are Herbert Brownell, Jr. (Atty. Gen., 1953–57); Nicholas Katzenbach (Atty. Gen., 1965–66); Ramsey Clark (Atty. Gen., 1967–68); Elliot L. Richardson (Atty. Gen., 1973); William B. Saxbe (Atty. Gen., 1973–74); Benjamin R. Civiletti (Atty. Gen., 1979–81).

Congress then

> *declares that for the purpose of enforcing the obligation of the States under the fourteenth amendment not to deprive persons of life without due process of law, human life should be deemed to exist from conception, without regard to race, sex, age, health, defect, or condition of dependency; and for this purpose 'person' shall include all human life as defined herein.*

In substance, Section 1 attempts to enshrine a congressional "theory of life" so as to "override the rights of the pregnant woman" under *Roe* v. *Wade*, 410 U.S. 113, 162 (1973)—precisely what the Supreme Court in *Roe* held a *state* powerless to do.[3]

The fact that Section 1 might operate merely as an authorization for the *states* to restrict the rights of pregnant women rather than as a direct restriction mandated by Congress itself is immaterial, since the Due Process Clause of the Fifth Amendment forbids Congress *either* to do by itself what the Fourteenth Amendment would prohibit states from doing *or* to license the states to do what, absent congressional permission, they would be prohibited by the Fourteenth Amendment from doing.[4]

The only possible argument supporting the constitutionality of S.158, Section 1, is that *Katzenbach* v. *Morgan, supra*, somehow empowered Congress to restrict the rights of women, or to authorize states to do so, in circumstances where states would otherwise be constitutionally forbidden to take such action. Even if *Morgan* had not been considerably restricted by *Oregon* v. *Mitchell*, 400 U.S. 112 (1970); *id.* at 295–96 (Stewart, J., joined by Burger, C.J., and Blackmun, J., concurring in part and dissenting in part), that decision obviously would *not* endow Congress with blank-check authority to restrict one set of judicially-declared rights upon Congress' decision, by majority vote, to proclaim another set of "rights" into existence.

This is so for three reasons. *First*, however expansive may be Congress' power, under Section 5 of the Fourteenth Amendment, to make empirical determinations that might have eluded the courts or to create remedial structures that the courts may have been unprepared to require on their own, no corresponding power exists simply to reject, as a legislative matter, a legal conclusion reached by the Supreme Court as to the proper interpretation of constitutional language:

> *It is emphatically the province and duty of the judicial department to say what the law is,*

Marbury v. *Madison*, 5 U.S. (1 Cranch) 137, 177 (1803), a duty in which "the

---

[3] *See also Doe* v. *Israel*, 482 F. 2d 156 (1st Cir. 1973) (a state clearly acts unconstitutionally when it attempts to enforce abortion restrictions equivalent to those invalidated by *Roe* by enacting a measure declaring that "human life commences at the instant of conception"), *cert. den.*, 416 U.S. 933 (1974).

[4] See *Weinberger* v. *Wiesenfeld*, 420 U.S. 636, 638 n.2 (1975); *Shapiro* v. *Thompson*, 394 U.S. 618, 641–42 (1968); *Katzenbach* v. *Morgan*, 384 U.S. 641, 651 n.10 (1966).

federal judiciary is supreme," *Cooper* v. *Aaron*, 358 U.S. 1, 18 (1958), *see also United States* v. *Nixon*, 418 U.S. 683, 704–05 (1974), not least because:

> *Congress is subject to none of the institutional restraints imposed on judicial decisionmaking; it is controlled only by the political process. In Article V, the Framers expressed the view that the political restraints on Congress alone were an insufficient control over the process of constitution making. The concurrence of two-thirds of each House and of three-fourths of the States was needed for the political check to be adequate. To allow a simple majority of Congress to have final say on matters of constitutional interpretation is therefore fundamentally out of keeping with the constitutional structure.*

Oregon v. *Mitchell*, *supra*, 400 U.S. at 205 (Harlan, J., concurring in part and dissenting in part).

Second, the premise of S.158, Section 1, viewed as a purported exercise of Section 5 power, is the extraordinary proposition that the identification of human life or personhood, as a basis for justifying restraints upon the freedom, equality, and bodily integrity of a pregnant woman, is an empirical matter—one which "present-day scientific evidence" might somehow resolve. Suffice it to say, however, that such questions as when "human life" exists, or what is a "person," call at bottom for normative judgments no less profound than those involved in defining "liberty" or "equality." In this context, therefore, one cannot escape the conclusion that identifying "human life" and defining "person" entail "question[s] to which science can provide no answer," as the National Academy of Sciences itself acknowledged in a Resolution passed on April 28, 1981, during its 118th Annual Meeting.[5] Congress cannot transform an issue of religion, morality, and law into one of fact by waving the magic wand of Section 5. The section empowering Congress "to enforce, by appropriate legislation, the provisions of" the Fourteenth Amendment no more authorizes Congress to transmute a matter of values into a matter or scientific observation than it authorizes Congress to announce a mathematical formula for human freedom.

Third, even if S.158, Section 1, were deemed to fall within the ambit of Congress' affirmative authority—under Section 5 of the Fourteenth Amendment or otherwise—it would still be subject to judicial invalidation as a clear violation of the Liberty Clause of the Fifth Amendment, a clause that restricts Congress in precisely the same manner that, and to precisely the same degree as, its counterpart clause in the Fourteenth Amendment restricts the states.[6] Any other approach would simultaneously denigrate the place of each state as

[5] "It is the view of the National Academy of Sciences that the statement in Chapter 101, Section 1, of U. S. Senate Bill S. 158, 1981, cannot stand up to the scrutiny of science. This section reads 'The Congress finds that present day scientific evidence indicates a significant likelihood that actual human life exists from conception.' This statement purports to derive its conclusions from science, but it deals with a question to which science can provide no answer. The proposal in S. 158 that the term 'person' shall include 'all human life' has no basis within our scientific understanding. Defining the time at which the developing embryo becomes a 'person' must remain a matter of moral or religious values."

[6] *See, e.g., United States Dept. of Agriculture* v. *Moreno*, 413 U.S. 528, 534–35 & n.7 (1973); *id.* at 538–45 (Douglas, J., concurring); *Aptheker* v. *Secretary of State*, 378 U.S. 500, 505–09, 514 (1964).

a coordinate element in the system established by the Framers for governing our Federal Union,

National League of Cities v. *Usery,* 426 U.S. 833, 849 (1976), and jeopardize the personal rights and liberties whose fate the Framers wisely declined to leave entirely to a Congress unchecked by judicial review. *See* A. Hamilton, The Federalist No. 78; 12 The Papers of Thomas Jefferson 438, 440 (J. Boyd ed. 1958); 14 *id.* 659.

Nor could the delegation of judicially unchecked power to Congress over such rights and liberties be confined to cases in which the judiciary has candidly confessed, as it did in *Roe* v. *Wade, supra,* 410 U.S. at 159, its inability to give determinate meaning to constitutional terms like "life." For when Congress acts to override, or to invite states to override, the "liberty" of pregnant women, it does not merely "inform the judiciary," in the words of Senator Hatch (Cong. Rec., April 10, 1981, p. S3913), of its legislative findings and views. Congress is empowered only to *make laws,* not to lobby or advise the courts. And if a law made by Congress can redefine terms in this one area so as to entrust to majority vote or other governmental determination a matter that the Supreme Court has held individual women entitled to resolve for themselves, then Congress has equal power to effectuate such a divestment of personal rights in other areas as well— regardless of the Supreme Court's degree of confidence or perplexity.

The only way to avoid that radical and profoundly threatening conclusion is to insist that *any* Act of Congress, even if that Act constitutes otherwise "appropriate legislation," be subject to judicial review for its consistency with the liberties secured by the Bill of Rights, under criteria no less demanding than those under which state legislation of similar effect would be scruntinized.

For these reasons, Section 1 seems to me clearly unconstitutional.

The Constitutionality of Section 2

In Section 2—which S. 158, Section 3, expressly makes severable from Section 1 but the intent of which is, of course, illuminated in part by its juxtaposition with the latter—Congress decrees that

> *[n]otwithstanding any other provision of law, no inferior Federal court ordained and established by Congress under article III of the Constitution of the United States shall have jurisdiction to issue any restraining order, temporary or permanent injunction, or declaratory judgment in any case involving or arising from any State law or municipal ordinance that (1) protects the rights of human persons between conception and birth, or (2) prohibits, limits, or regulates (a) the performance of abortions, or (b) the provision at public expense of funds, facilities, personnel, or other assistance for the performance of abortions.*

This portion of S. 158, too, seems to me unconstitutional—despite Congress' sweeping authority, under Article I, Section 8, and Article III, Section 1, to regulate the jurisdiction of the inferior federal courts. Neither Congress' power over such jurisdiction, nor its equally "plenary power over bankruptcy," *United*

States v. *Kras*, 409 U.S. 434, 441 (1973), prevented the Supreme Court from there scrutinizing the substantive validity, under the Due Process Clause of the Fifth Amendment, of an Act of Congress making a federal judicial discharge in voluntary bankruptcy unavailable to a litigant unable to pay the filing fee.[7]

The plain infirmity of Section 2 of S. 158, as a matter of Fifth Amendment due process, is that it unmistakably disadvantages a particular group—pregnant women seeking to exercise federal rights recognized by *Roe* v. *Wade, supra*—by imposing on that group a more onerous and time-consuming path to the anticipatory vindication of its federal rights (i.e., a path exclusively through the state courts, with federal judicial review available, if at all, only in the Supreme Court) than the path S. 158 leaves open to groups on the other side of the same issue—such as fathers or guardians of fetuses seeking to prevent impending abortions allegedly supported by state funds or encouraged by a policy of non-enforcement of the murder laws in abortion cases. *Cf. Linda R.S.* v. *Richard D.*, 410 U.S. 614, 618 (1973). These latter groups are left entirely free by Section 2 of S. 158 to seek and obtain timely anticipatory relief, declaratory and/or injunctive, from the very federal courts whose doors Section 2 closes to women invoking *Roe* v. *Wade*, and in the very cases in which those doors are closed to such women.

To tip the scales of legal redress in this way is to disadvantage a protected group in violation of the constitutional norm of equal treatment under law.[8] Moreover, to do so in a manner that in effect penalizes the exercise of a federal constitutional right itself violates that right.[9] And, finally, embedding such substantive discriminations and penalties in a jurisdiction regulation violates the separation-of-powers principle that Congress may not employ its jurisdiction-controlling authority as a mere "pretext," *McCulloch* v. *Maryland*, 17 U.S. (4 Wheat.) 316, 423 (1819), for substituting its legal views for those of the federal judiciary.[10]

---

[7] That a narrowly divided Court in *Kras* upheld the filing fee requirement as reasonable, in part because intimate marital and reproductive rights were not at issue, 409 U.S. at 444–45, is immaterial to the fact that all nine Justices recognized the need to review the judicial door-closing rule enacted by Congress—by applying established criteria of Fifth Amendment due process and equal protection.

[8] See *Hunter* v. *Erickson*, 393 U.S. 385, 390–91 (1969) (unconstitutional to

> *"disadvantage[] those who would benefit from laws barring racial, religious, or ancestral discriminations as against those who would bar other discriminations or who would otherwise regulate the real estate market in their favor,"*

even where

> *"the law on its face treats Negro and White, Jew and gentile in an identical manner").*

[9] See *Shapiro* v. *Thompson, supra*, 394 U.S. at 631 (penalty on right to travel); *United States* v. *Jackson* 390 U.S. 570, 83 (1968) (penalty on right to plead innocent and demand trial by jury); *Griffin* v. *California*, 380 U.S. 609, 614 (1965) (penalty on right to remain silent at trial).

[10] See *United States* v. *Klein*, 80 U.S. (13 Wall.) 128, 145 (1872) (Congress' power to regulate Supreme Court jurisdiction is deployed unconstitutionally where

> *"the language of the proviso shows that it does not intend to withhold appellate jurisdiction except as a means to an end"*

there,

> *"to deny pardons granted by the President the effect which this court had adjudged them to have").*

For all of these reasons, I am persuaded that S. 158 Section 2, would, like Section 1, be an unconstitutional exercise of Congress' power—an effort to circumvent the carefully guarded and deliberately resistant mechanism provided by Article V of the Constitution for amending the text so as to overcome those Supreme Court interpretations, and only those, with which a large majority of the Nation is unprepared to live.

Conclusion

The Subcommittee may well wonder why, despite the enormous diversity of views held by ranking constitutional experts and leading law enforcement officials on the uniquely divisive subject of abortion, the issues posed by S. 158 should have called forth such an unprecedented unison of voices—not only among professors of constitutional law who are otherwise prone to disagree deeply on such matters but also among an extraordinarily distinguished and varied group of former Attorneys General of the United States, serving under Presidents as diverse as Eisenhower, Johnson, Nixon, Ford, and Carter. Why should S. 158 be the first proposed Act of Congress in this century to inspire so unique an expression of agreement on a topic hardly known for its tendency to produce harmony and consensus?

The most likely reason, I submit, is that virtually all careful students of the Constitution—those who write and teach about it, as well as those sworn to enforce it—are likely to concur, whatever their many differences, on the overarching value of taking the document seriously—on the overriding danger and illegitimacy of toying with it, of using it as an end-run ploy, even in the noblest and most humane of causes.

I do not doubt that persons of good will, fully sharing the fidelity to the Constitution that I and those who share my views on S. 158 think fundamental, might nonetheless come to a different conclusion about this bill. But whether any *truly reasonable basis* exists for such a conclusion—or whether, as I believe, the constitutional invalidity of S. 158 is *the only plausible verdict* to which a considered analysis can lead—is another matter. Rarely can one say, with the conviction that the convergence of such disparate perspectives makes possible here, that a measure is too palpably unconstitutional to permit reasonable persons plausibly to argue the contrary. Believing this to be one of those rare cases, and believing that every member of this Subcommittee respects the integrity and importance of adherence to constitutional means of implementing whatever values we might hold, I am confident that S. 158, however well-intentioned the measure may at the outset have been, will, in the end, be rejected by this body— rejected as an unacceptable assault upon the Constitution itself.

Senator EAST. Professor Noonan?

Statement of John T. Noonan

Mr. NOONAN. Mr. Chairman, Senator Baucus, I will submit my written statement and simply highlight portions of it.

However, your sticking to the original order perhaps gives us a little more of the flavor of a dialog or debate among professors. I must say, as I heard my distinguished colleague, I was reminded of hearing him 5 years ago before Senator

Bayh's Subcommittee on Constitutional Amendments where every amendment proposed has something wrong with it. Not one of them could do the job of protecting unborn life. Senator East and Senator Baucus, Professor Tribe, in his great concern for human life, had to advise that subcommittee that whatever they tried had a fatal flaw.

I will not bother to say much on his interpretation of the statute, except to say that his returning to the notion that it mandates a homicide provision, repeating the tack taken by Senator Packwood, is just so much nonsense. We have for centuries distinguished between types of killing of human beings. We know very well there is one type of killing that we call murder. There is another type of killing which because of the circumstances we call manslaughter. There is a third type of killing which was always in the old textbooks under crimes against the person which was called abortion.

Of course, Senator Packwood or his staff slipped rather badly in saying that the common law did not ban abortion. Since the time there was a written common law set down, you can find that abortion was a serious crime.

So much on the interpretation of the law. Professor Tribe offered a few words on the jurisdictional status created by the bill. I will only offer a few words because that is all it is worth.

There is not a single case where the courts and the Supreme Court have not recognized the power of the Congress to determine the jurisdiction of inferior Federal courts. The court did so fairly recently in the *Palmore* case. It is an acknowledged plenary power of Congress.

All the imaginings, all the subtleties that may be brought in to suggest that there is some limit on congressional power, I think, are the imaginings of law professors appropriate for examination in classrooms, but not for congressional consideration.

The serious question is whether this jurisdictional provision is warranted by experience. Here we have to look at the experience of the last 8 years.

For the last 8 years, the judges of the inferior Federal courts have behaved in a partisan and prejudiced fashion in championing the abortion liberty far beyond the requirements of the Supreme Court decision.

Professor Uddo has collected those cases in 53 Tulane Law Review in an article entitled "A Wink from the Bench," which refers to a famous episode boasted of by the plaintiff's counsel in *Roe* v. *Wade*, where a Federal judge actually winked from the bench to indicate to the plaintiff in *Roe* v. *Wade* that she was going to win her case.

Along the same lines, a case that would particularly interest this subcommittee is the *Hyde* case in New York where a single Federal district judge, in cavalier disregard of article 1 of the Constitution, in effect appropriated millions of dollars to be spent on abortions contrary to the express determination of this Congress.

If that sort of thing goes on, it is time for Congress to step in. We have the precedent of the Norris-LaGuardia Act where similar outrages were documented by Felix Frankfurter in regard to the Federal Courts' use of the labor injunction. That is a perfectly good precedent for action here in restricting the power and jurisdiction of the lower Federal courts.

I want to go on to the main provisions of the act. The source of the congressional power is a portion of the U.S. Constitution, the 14th amendment, section 5, that gives Congress the power to enforce by appropriate legislation the provisions of the 14th amendment.

It can be said of section 5 what Chief Justice Marshall said of the necessary and proper clause of article 1. First, the clause is placed among the powers of Congress, not among the limitations on those powers. Second, its terms purport to enlarge, not to diminish the powers vested in the Government.

As early as 1879, in *Ex parte Virginia*, the Supreme Court interpreted that kind of power as an enlargement not of judicial power but of congressional power. As recently as last year in *Fullilove* v. *Klutznick*, the Federal funds to minority contractors case, Chief Justice Burger said that section 5 had been taken by the Court and equated with the broad powers expressed in the necessary and proper clause.

Here we have an express acknowledgment by the Supreme Court itself that you, the Congress, have been given a grant of power to enforce the provisions of the 14th amendment.

Now, that being the foundation for your action, is there any conflict with the other classic statement of the separation of powers in *Marbury* v. *Madison*?

You have heard from Senator Moynihan in particular, and again from Professor Tribe, that there is a direct attack upon the Constitution and our governmental processes in adopting this legislation. You would never believe from those statements that this method has been tried again, and again, and again, and that it is an old way of offering the judgment of the legislature to the Supreme Court.

Let me take three examples. One is a classic doctrine of the Supreme Court that States did not have power to regulate commerce between the States. The States, lacking that power, could not, as the Court put it, be regranted or reconvey the power by Congress, exactly what Professor Tribe says that Congress cannot do here. Congress could do nothing for the States which they could not do by themselves.

That was good in law in 1850, in *Cooley* v. *Wardens of Philadelphia*, and it was good in law for almost a century. Then in the teeth of that doctrine of the Court as to the power under the commerce clause, the Congress adopted the McCarran Act permitting the States to regulate insurance. In *Prudential Insurance Company* v. *Benjamin*, the Supreme Court followed the lead of Congress, reversed itself, and said that Congress could delegate this kind of power to the States.

A second example: I suppose one of the most fundamental questions is the nature of the courts. In the *Bakelite* case in the 1920's, a unanimous Supreme Court said that Congress could not determine what courts were article 3 courts and what courts were not constitutional courts. That was a constitutional judgment on which jurisdiction depended, which the Supreme Court alone was competent to decide.

Then some 30 years later in *Glidden* v. *Zdanok*, the Court looked to what Congress called an article 3 court and what it called not an article 3 court and followed the congressional determination as to what was a constitutional court and what was not. The very fundamental question of the nature of judicial power was determined by the Court looking at what Congress had done.

Finally, there are the series of cases that Mr. Galebach particularly relied on, the section 5 cases, where the Supreme Court, in *Lassiter* v. *Northampton Election Board*, had said that it was a reserved power of the States, reserved under article 1 of the Constitution, that they determine the qualifications of their electors, including of course literacy.

Here was an express holding by the Supreme Court that it was within the power of the States alone to determine literacy requirements. Congress went right ahead, passed a law affecting literacy tests in a number of states, and 7 years after *Lassiter*, the Supreme Court, in *Katzenbach* v. *Morgan* deferred to the congressional determination.

That is less time than you are acting on this law. Seven years later an expressly contrary determination was made. A little after that, in *Oregon* v. *Mitchell*, although the Justices divided on every other issue, they upheld the general congressional suspension of literacy test.

As Archibald Cox has written, the case on the literacy test provides a vast expansion of congressional power in the area of upholding human rights.

It cannot be a question of reconciling what the Court itself does with *Marbury* v. *Madison*. The only question is the context. Is this an appropriate context in which Congress should act?

You have heard the context as to the doubt expressed by the Court itself. The Court could not speculate as to when life begins. There is a second doubt the Court expressed. In the beginning of its opinion, the Court expressed a doubt as to whether the power it was referring to to invalidate the abortion statutes lay in the 14th amendment or the 9th amendment. It left those as alternatives.

If the power lies in the 9th amendment, reserving unexpressed powers to the people, it is peculiarly appropriate, Senators, for the representatives of the people to exercise their experience and knowledge and judgment as to where those powers lie.

There is a third reason why this is an appropriate context. That is the Court's reasoning as to person. The entire burden of the Court's reasoning as to the meaning of person is that an unborn child cannot be an elector, and yet person is used as to elector in the Constitution; and an unborn child cannot be a Senator or a Representative, and yet person is used in that clause; nor can an unborn child be a fugitive slave, yet persons are talked about in that clause.

The Court said, in effect, it is ridiculous to take unborn children as persons because they cannot be persons in these contexts.

However, what the Court did not advert to was that each one of these clauses would be equally effective for showing that a corporation is not a person within the 14th amendment. Yet ever since *Santa Clara County* v. *Union Pacific Railway*, a very old case, the Court has consistently treated corporations as persons within the meaning of the 14th amendment.

It really is surprising, if this is the basis of the Court's finding the unborn are not persons, that the Court has not gone on to reverse itself on corporations. Yet I doubt very much that it will do that.

The Court's reasoning shows doubt. It shows weakness. It was an unprecedently radical decision. It invalidated the statutes of every State in the Union. It gave us the most radical abortion law in the civilized world, a law that, in effect, makes abortion legal for the 9 months of pregnancy.

Also, it was an unprincipled decision, unprincipled in the sense that not even

Professor Tribe or his colleagues have found a good principle on which to explain what the Court did. It has been criticized by critics of every persuasion.

When Professor Tribe refers to these people who signed his letter, he said they stand both ways. They do not stand both ways on abortion. As far as I know, all of the people whom he has cited have done nothing for the prolife cause, but they are critics of *Roe* v. *Wade* because of its lack of constitutional principle.

Finally, it was a most destructive decision. At the highest estimates of the proabortion lobby, the greatest number of unborn lives being taken in this country before *Roe* v. *Wade* was close to 1 million. Now, by Government report, we know the number of lives being taken every year is 1.5 million, a 50-percent increase of 500,000 live entities.

You are being asked now not to make a permanent solution. This cannot be permanent. You will need an amendment. You may need more than one amendment. However, you are being asked to do something to stop this slaughter.

Thank you.

Senator EAST. Thank you, Professor Noonan.

[The prepared statement of Professor Noonan follows:]

Prepared Statement of John T. Noonan

The Constitutionality and Wisdom of the Act to Provide that Human Life Shall Be Deemed to Exist from Conception

I. The Jurisdictional Provisions of the Act.

There can be no doubt that under Article III, section 1 of the Constitution, the judicial power of the United States is vested in the Supreme Court and "in such inferior Courts as the Congress may from time to time ordain and establish." As Justice White wrote in *Palmore v. United States*, 411 U.S. 389 at 400–401 (1973), in an opinion joined by Chief Justice Burger and Justices Brennan, Stewart, Marshall, Blackmun, Powell, and Rehnquist, "The decision with respect to inferior federal courts, as well as the task of defining their jurisdiction, was left to the discretion of Congress." Congress, he went on to say, was not constitutionally required to create Article III courts nor, if they were created, "required to invest them with all the jurisdiction it was authorized to bestow." Until 1875 "the state courts provided the only forum for vindicating many important federal claims." It needs no further argument to show that the restriction on the jurisdiction of the inferior federal courts—leaving unaffected the jurisdiction of the United States Supreme Court and the state courts—is constitutional.

The only question that can appropriately be raised is whether the restriction is wise. Here the experience of the last eight years must be referred to. The judges of the inferior federal courts have shown themselves in many instances to be zealous, partisan, and prejudiced champions of those seeking and those providing abortions. They have shown a marked insensitivity to values at stake besides the abortion liberty and a marked disregard for the constitutional restraints on judicial action in this area.

To give a few examples: A judge of the First Circuit Court of Appeals has compared the termination of childbearing capacity to "excision of benign tumors which would cause subsequent neurological problems."[1] A judge of the Second Circuit Court of Appeals has interpreted *Roe v. Wade* to mean that "abortion and childbirth, when stripped of the sensitive moral arguments surrounding the abortion controversy, are simply two alternative methods of dealing with pregnancy"; and this judge proceeded to divest abortion of the moral arguments and to treat it simply as an alternative to childbirth.[2] A judge of the Eighth Circuit Court of Appeals imposed payment of the plaintiff's legal fees on the Mayor of St. Louis, because his refusal to allow elective abortion in St. Louis municipal hospitals was "a wanton disregard for the constitutional rights of the plaintiff." In this case, as the Supreme Court later decided, it was the Mayor who had the correct constitutional position.[3] A federal district judge in Brooklyn mandated the federal funding of abortions in cavalier disregard of Article I of the Constitution reserving to Congress alone the power to draw money from the Treasury.[4] A judge

---

[1] *Hathaway v. Worcester City Hospital* 475 F.2d 701 (1st Cir. 1973) at 705 (per Frank Coffin, J.).

[2] *Roe v. Norton* 408 F. Supp. 660 (D. Conn. 1975) at 663, n.5 (per Jon O. Newman, J.).

[3] *Doe v. Poelker* 515 F.2d 541 (8th Cir. 1975) at 547–548 (per Donald Ross, J.), *reversed, Poelker v. Doe* 432 U.S. 519 (1977).

[4] See *Harris v. McRae* 100 S.Ct. 2671 (1980) reversing the judgment of Dooling, J.

of the Fourth Circuit Court of Appeals interpreted *Roe v. Wade* to mean that the unborn child in the womb was not alive, even though the particular child in question had been born and lived and his death, due to wounds inflicted before his birth, was the subject of criminal investigation by the state of South Carolina.[5]

The pattern of abusive, indeed outrageous partisanship has been amply documented by Professor Uddo in his article, "A Wink From the Bench: the Federal Courts and Abortion," *Tulane Law Review* 53 (1978) 398. His title refers to a famous incident, boasted of by Sarah Weddington, counsel for the plaintiff in *Roe v. Wade*, that when she was arguing the case before a three judge panel a member of the court "winked at me as if to say, 'It's going to be all right.' " The winks from the federal bench in abortion cases parallel the partisanship the federal judges showed in labor injunction cases before the enactment of the Norris-LaGuardia Act; and just as that Act justifiably took from the federal judges the injunction power they had abused, so the proposed statute removes a jurisdiction which has been exploited in favor of one side in a two-sided controversy.[6]

II. The Fact-finding and Definitional Provisions of the Act.

The Act does four things. It finds "a significant likelihood that actual human life exists from conception." It finds that the Fourteenth Amendment was "intended to protect all human beings." It declares that for the purpose of enforcing the obligation of the States "not to deprive persons of life without due process of law," human life "shall be deemed to exist from conception." For the same purpose it declares that "person" shall include all human life as so defined. Are these findings and declarations within the power of Congress?

1. THE SOURCE OF CONGRESSIONAL POWER. The Fourteenth Amendment, section 5 declares, "The Congress shall have power to enforce, by appropriate legislation, the provisions of this article." The key terms of this constitutional grant of power are "appropriate legislation" and "enforce." In general, there must be said of this part of the Constitution what Chief Justice Marshall said in *McCulloch v. Maryland* of congressional power under the "Necessary and Proper Clause" of Article I: "1*st*. The clause is placed among the powers of Congress, not among the limitations on those powers. 2*nd*. Its terms purport to enlarge, not to diminish the powers vested in the government. It purports to be an additional power, not a restriction on those already granted."[7]

The parallel in interpretation of Congress' power under section 5 and Congress' power under Article I has very recently been affirmed by Chief Justice Warren Burger in *Fullilove v. Klutznick*. The Court, he declared, had "equated the scope of this authority with the broad powers expressed in the Necessary and Proper Clause, U. S. Const., Act. 1, sec. 18, cl. 8."[8] In the light of this interpretation, Congress has the power under section 5 to find facts, to adopt remedies, and to enact legislation it finds appropriate to secure the rights guaranteed by the Fourteenth Amendment.

It should be added that the enforcement of the Fourteenth Amendment by

---

[5] *Floyd v. Anders* 440 F. Supp. 535 (D. So. Car. 1977) at 539 (per Clement Haynsworth, J.).
[6] Cf. Frankfurter and Greene, *The Labor Injunction* (1930).
[7] 4 Wheat. 316 (1819) at 418.
[8] 100 S. Ct. 2758 (1980) at 2774.

congressional action has solid historical roots. As the Supreme Court said unanimously in 1879 in *Ex parte Virginia*, the Thirteenth, Fourteenth, and Fifteenth Amendments "derive much of their force" from the sections conferring power on Congress. "It is not said that the *judicial power* of the government shall extend to enforcing the prohibitions and to protecting the rights and immunities guaranteed . . . It is the power of Congress which has been enlarged."[9] Even if today the judicial branch has taken to itself a more active part in enforcing the Amendments, surely its more assertive role cannot deprive Congress of the power which the framers of the Amendment intended to confer, as the 1879 Court acknowledged, and which the Court in 1980 has recognized to be as broad as Article I's fundamental grant of power to make "all laws which shall be necessary and proper for carrying into Execution the foregoing Powers."[10]

2. THE POWER OF CONGRESS WHERE THE SUPREME COURT IS IN DOUBT. In *Roe* v. *Wade* the Supreme Court declared, "We need not resolve the difficult question of where life begins. When those trained in the respective disciplines of medicine, philosophy, and theology are unable to arrive at any consensus, the judiciary at this point in the development of man's knowledge, is not in a position to speculate as to the answer."[11] The Court went on to note the varying treatment of the unborn in the law of torts and property and concluded, "In view of all this, we do not agree that by adopting one theory of life, Texas may override the rights of the pregnant woman that are at stake."[12] In short, the judiciary was in no position to answer, common and statutory law gave various answers, and a state did not have power to define life.

Congress, as a coordinate branch of the national government, is of course in a position very different from any State vis-a-vis the Supreme Court. In this area it is acting within the terms of power expressly conferred by the Fourteenth Amendment and expressly recognized by the Court itself. It is acting with better sources of information than the Court—for the Court took no biological evidence and no historical evidence. It is acting with a better ability than the Court to balance competing value considerations that go to the assessment of the facts. Further, Congress is performing an essential function in the enforcement of the Fourteenth Amendment; for if the judiciary is not "in a position to speculate" when life begins, the Fourteenth Amendment must fail, in a significant way, to be implemented, unless Congress draws on its power to supply an answer.

3. THE POWER OF CONGRESS WHEN THE SUPREME COURT HAS MADE A CONTRARY DETERMINATION. The objection will be raised, however, that the Supreme Court has done more than acknowledge its incompetence to decide when life begins. The Court in *Roe v. Wade* has formally held that "the word 'person' as used in the Fourteenth Amendment, does not include the unborn."[13] Does not the proposed statute squarely conflict with this holding of the Court and, if it does so, is not the statute void?

It is clear the Congress will reach, if the proposed statute is enacted, a

---

[9] 100 U.S. 339 (1879) at 345.
[10] U.S. Constitution, Article 1, sec. 18, cl. 8.
[11] *Roe v. Wade* 410 U.S. 113 (1973) at 159.
[12] *Ibid*. at 162.
[13] Ibid. at 158.

conclusion different from the Court's in *Roe v. Wade* on the meaning of person in the Fourteenth Amendment. It does not follow that the statute is void. It follows, rather, that the Court may, and should, change its mind, give deference to the congressional findings and declarations, and overrule *Roe v. Wade*.

In the area of the Fourteenth Amendment the Court has already provided just such an example of retreating from its own announced understanding of the Constitution in deference to congressional action taken after, and contrary to, the Court's announcement of what it found the Constitution to mean. In *Lassiter* v. *Northampton Election Board* 360 U.S. 45 (1959) the plaintiff complained that a literacy test for voting was unconstitutional. The Supreme Court, unanimously, held that Article 1, section 2 of the Constitution expressly reserves to the States the power to determine the qualifications of electors. Seven years later in *Katzenbach v. Morgan* 384 U.S. 641 (1966), the Court considered an Act of Congress eliminating literacy in English as a condition for voting. If the Court followed *Lassiter*, this Act of Congress was a clear infringement on a power constitutionally reserved to the States; and the Act was clearly contrary to the holding of the Court in *Lassiter*.

The Court, however, found *Lassiter* "inapposite." Speaking through Justice Brennan and quoting *Ex parte Virginia* of 1879, the Court held the congressional action a proper exercise of congressional power under section 5 of the Fourteenth Amendment. The act was "plainly adapted" to furthering the aims of the Equal Protection Clause by securing for Puerto Ricans in New York not only the right to vote but, indirectly, nondiscriminatory treatment in public schools, public housing, and law enforcement. The action of Congress, directly contrary to the interpretation of the Constitution by a unanimous Supreme Court, was upheld by the Court. In *Oregon v. Mitchell* 400 U.S.112 (1970), while splitting on other issues, the Court unanimously upheld Congress' total elimination of literacy tests. Justice Black's opinion specifically deferred to the "substantial, if not overwhelming, evidence" on which Congress acted and to the exercise of Congressional power under section 5.[14]

4. CONGRESSIONAL ACTION AFFECTING PERSONAL LIBERTIES.   In *Shapiro v. Thompson*, a case involving the welfare residency requirement of California, it was said by way of dictum that even if Congress had consented to the residency requirement—which the Court held it had not—the requirement was invalid, because "Congress may not authorize the States to violate the Equal Protection Clause."[15] Similarly in a footnote to *Katzenbach v. Morgan*, Justice Brennan declared that section 5 "grants Congress no power to restrict, abrogate or dilute" the guarantees of the Fourteenth Amendment.[16] In a footnote to his dissent in *Oregon v. Mitchell*, Justice Brennan repeated this view, and added apropos of state statutes found to be based on unreasonable legislative findings, "Unless Congress were to unearth new evidence in its investigation, its identical findings on the same issue would be no more reasonable than those of the state legislature."[17] The question is thus presented whether the proposed Act autho-

---

[14] 400 U.S. 112 at 134.
[15] 394 U.S. 618 (1969) at 641.
[16] 384 U.S. 641 at 651–652 n. 10.
[17] 400 U.S. 112 at 249 n. 31.

rizes states to violate the Equal Protection Clause, dilutes or abrogates Four-teenth Amendment guarantees, or is based on the same evidence on which state legislatures acted unreasonably.

In recognizing the unborn as persons, so far as protection of their lives is concerned, the proposed Act treats no one unequally but gives equal protection to one class of humanity now unequally treated. It does not dilute a Fourteenth Amendment guarantee, but expands the rights of a whole class. It is based not on evidence before the state legislatures—what that evidence was we do not know—but on evidence freshly taken from leading geneticists and physicians.

Yet the question will be pressed, "Does not the Act dilute or abrogate the right to an abortion?" Necessarily, the expression of the rights of one class of human beings has an impact on the rights of others. The elimination of literacy tests in this way "diluted" the voting rights of the literate. It is inescapable that congressional expression of the right to life will have an impact on the abortion right; but in the eyes of Congress, if it enacts this law, there will be a net gain for Fourteenth Amendment rights by the expansion and the attendant diminution.

Further, it must be noted that the correctness of Justice Brennan's footnotes has been questioned by a careful scholar of Constitutional law, Professor Archibald Cox. Professor Cox suggests that Congress is free to act where "the Court has formulated some corollary to a constitutional command upon a different view of contemporaneous conditions than the legislatures" and where "the problems of application quite genuinely involved investigation and evaluation of facts." There are, Cox adds, "areas in which Congress has at least some claims to superior competence while the Court has none." In these areas, Justice Brennan's footnotes "run against the demands of logical consistency." They run also, Cox observes, against evenhandedness.[18] If Congress has been given power under the Constitution, that power is to be exercised as Congress finds "appro-priate" to the furtherance of the guarantees of the Fourteenth Amendment.

A number of Justices have, indeed, signalled their disagreement with Justice Brennan's "dilution" test. Chief Justice Burger has proposed federal legislation to modify the Court-created role excluding tainted evidence. The constitutional basis for this legislation would be section 5.[19] Such legislation would unquestionably dilute the rights of criminal defendants while it expanded the rights of government prosecutors and the victimized public.

Justices White, Blackmun, and Powell, concurring in *Trafficante v. Metro-politan Life Insurance Co.* 409 U.S. 205 at 212 (1972), admitted that they had great difficulty in seeing that the plaintiffs, tenants in nonintegrated housing, had a "case or controversy" with their landlord for his action in excluding others. But they were persuaded that Congress had the power to enact the statute giving them the right to sue, and the Justices invoked *Katzenbach v. Morgan* to explain their position. Here, in other words, was a fundamental requirement of federal jurisdiction which these judges permitted to be changed by evoking Congress' section 5 power. The power was used to expand the rights of the tenants and at the

---

[18] Cox, "The Role of Congress in Constitutional Determinations", 40 *U. Cincinnati Law Rev.* 199 (1971) at 253, 255.

[19] *Bivens v. Six Unknown Named Agents* 403 U.S. 388 (1971) at 421–424. Cf. Gunther, *Constitutional Law: Cases and Materials* (1975 ed.), 531.

same time to dilute the rights of the landlord. Justices White, Blackmun and
Powell accepted the balance struck by Congress.

In *Welsh v. United States* Justice White, in a dissent joined by Chief Justice
Burger and Justice Stewart, took the position that Congress could provide
statutory exemptions from the draft to religious objectors but not to others, thus
striking a balance between its power to raise armies and the Free Exercise of
Religion Clause. By analogy, these justices involved *Katzenbach v. Morgan*
"where we accepted the judgment of Congress as to what legislation was
appropriate."[20] In other words, in their view, a statute which balanced rights,
giving them to some and not to others, was entirely analogous to the kind of
legislative balance struck by Congress and sustained by the Court in *Katzenbach*.

5. SECTION 5 AND MARBURY V. MADISON.   The cornerstone of the judicial
power, Chief Justice Marshall's opinion in *Marbury v. Madison*, announces that
the Constitution "controls any legislative act repugnant to it" and imposes on the
judges the duty to determine this repugnancy.[21] Does the proposed Act defy or
subvert these fundamental principles?

Not in the least. Congress is not ousting the Court of jurisdiction, "overruling" the Court, or declaring its will superior to Constitution or Court. On the basis
of hearings and fresh evidence, Congress is taking a position which in one
important particular disagrees with the Court's interpretation of the Constitution
in *Roe v. Wade*. Under the principles of *Marbury v. Madison*, it will be for the
Court to decide whether, following such precedents as *Katzenbach v. Morgan*, it
should now defer to Congress' interpretation.

To suppose that the statute proposed is a challenge to judicial review assumes
a radical—I am inclined to say willful—misunderstanding of the functions of Court
and Congress. A decision of the Supreme Court interpreting the Constitution is
neither infallible nor eternal nor unchangeable. The Court has often been wrong.
The Court has often corrected itself.[22] There is nothing in our constitutional
theory that says the Court must remain forever in a mistaken position, and much
contrary example to its so doing. The proposed Act is an invitation to the Court
to correct its error itself.

The example of the Court correcting itself due to a section 5 exercise of
power of Congress has been given. There are other examples of similar interaction
between Congress and Court. Here are two. In *Ex parte Bakelite Corp.* 179 U.S.
438 (1929), the Supreme Court unanimously held that the Court of Customs
Appeals was not a court within the meaning of Article III of the Constitution. The
Court declared it to be a mistake to say that the character of the court depended
on the intention of Congress and reserved to itself the right to say what power
Congress had exercised. In *Glidden Co. v. Zdanok* 370 U.S. 530 (1962), the Court,
7-2, abandoned this approach and declared that "we may not disregard Congress'
declaration that they [the courts in question] were created under Article III."
Stressing that this deference to congressional findings did not "compromise the
authority or responsibility of this Court as the expositor of the Constitution,"

[20] 398 U.S. 333 (1970) at 371.
[21] 1 Cranch 137 (1803).
[22] Justice Brandeis provided a classic list of such corrections in *Burnet v. Coronado Oil and Gas
Co.* 285 U.S. 393 (1932) at 407–409.

Justice Harlan for the Court in fact followed the congressional lead to correct the old error.[23]

It was once settled constitutional doctrine that if the States could not regulate interstate commerce, Congress could not give them power to do so. The classic case on this point, *Cooley v. Wardens of Philadelphia* 12 How. 299 (1851), was one of the great unshakable landmarks of constitutional interpretation by the Supreme Court. It declared in ringing terms, "If the Constitution excluded the States from making any law regulating commerce, certainly Congress cannot re-grant or in any way reconvey to the States that power."[24] But in 1945, in the teeth of the *Cooley* doctrine, Congress enacted the McCarran Act, conferring on the States the power to regulate insurance. The Court in *Prudential Insurance Co. v. Benjamin* 328 U.S. 408 (1946) unanimously sustained the delegation, the opinion for the Court recognizing in Congress a "plenary and supreme authority" over interstate commerce. What had once been the Court's interpretation of the Constitution had yielded to the congressional teaching.

The story is an old one, frequently retold. The Supreme Court is not immune to reason and to instruction. It reverses itself. It listens to Congress. Those who want an institution immovable and beyond the reach of popular instruction must look elsewhere.

6. FURTHER REASONS FOR CONGRESS TO EXERCISE ITS SECTION 5 POWER HERE.   "The *Morgan* case," Archibald Cox has written, "is soundly rooted in constitutional legislation promoting human rights."[25] This expansion, as Cox observes, can be achieved by any law which "may be viewed" as having a relation to an end specified by the Fourteenth Amendment.[26] In the present context, the Fourteenth Amendment guarantees life to persons. But no one can enjoy adult life unless he or she is born. To protect the life guaranteed by the Amendment, Congress has the power under section 5 to protect the path to that life. The proposed legislation is readily seen as a way of protecting the means necessary to have life after birth.

Further, it is sometimes forgotten that the Court in *Roe v. Wade*, acknowledging that "the Constitution does not explicitly mention any right of privacy," finally located that right with some uncertainty in the Fourteenth Amendment "or, as the District Court determined, in the Ninth Amendment's reservation of rights to the people."[27] To this point in this presentation, focus has been upon the Fourteenth Amendment. But if Justice Blackmun's other basis be accepted, Congress is better suited than the Court to make the determination as to the balance struck between the rights of the States and reserved Ninth Amendment rights. Such a determination requires political discretion. As Archibald Cox has written generally of why the Court should defer to Congress in its exercise of section 5 power, such judicial following of a congressional lead "rests upon application of the fact that the fundamental basis for legislative action is the knowledge, experience, and judgment of the people's representatives, only a

[23] 279 U.S. 438 (1929) at 459.

[24] 12 How. 299 (1851) at 317.

[25] Cox, "Foreword: Constitutional Adjudication and the Promotion of Human Rights," 80 *Harv. L. Rev.* 91 (1966) at 107.

[26] *Ibid*. at 104.

[27] *Roe v. Wade* 410 U.S. 113 at 153.

small part, or even none of which may come from the hearings and reports of committees or debates upon the floor."[28] As Ninth Amendment rights are reserved to the people, the people through its elected representatives can determine, better than a nonelected elite, where the line limiting governmental power should be drawn.

7. THE "DIZZYING IMPLICATIONS" OF THE PROPOSED ACT.   Two professors of law at Harvard Law School, Messrs. Tribe and Ely, have undertaken to instruct the general public, in the *New York Times* of March 17, 1981, on "the dizzying implications" of the proposed legislation. It must be assumed that they have said nothing in a newspaper of mass circulation that they could not say to this committee even if, given the popular medium being used, they have employed language that would seem careless in another context. They speak, for example, of the proposed Act "overruling" *Roe v. Wade* when all lawyers know that only a court overrules. Still, such carelessness does leave the unfortunate impression that the proposed Act is a direct challenge to *Marbury v. Madison*, a polemical and utterly unwarranted implication.

There is a second unfortunate implication in this article due again, no doubt, to its popular audience. The unmistakable impression is given that resort to congressional power under section 5 is the brand new invention of two conservative leaders. Who would suspect from reading Tribe-Ely that Gerald Gunther, one of the senior constitutional law professors in the country, in his leading casebook on Constitutional Law had twice raised the question of whether *Katzenbach v. Morgan* gave Congress power to affect the result in *Roe v. Wade*?[29] Who would suppose that three other leading constitutional law professors, William Lockhart, Yale Kamisar and Jesse Choper, had asked, "Apart from 'specific' constitutional prohibitions, under *Morgan*, what are the limits of congressional power?"[30] Who could imagine that, as far back as 1966, Archibald Cox in the Harvard Law Review greeted *Katzenbach* as the discovery of "a vast untapped reservoir of federal legislative power to define and promote the constitutional rights of individuals in relation to state government."[31] Who would believe that Professor Tribe himself had reconciled *Katzenbach* with *Marbury v. Madison* and written, "Judicial review does not require that the Constitution be equated with the Supreme Court's view of it."[32] It would have had to have been a very intuitive reader of the *Times* to have guessed that Professor Tribe himself saw no incongruity in Congress providing criteria for constitutional decisions to the Court. Professor Tribe and Ely's fears were justified only if an assumption were made—an assumption which Professor Ely professed to repudiate—that the abortion liberty was part of the Bill of Rights.

The heart of the Tribe-Ely critique is that the proposed Act abandons "the old-fashioned" way of amending the Constitution. Surely these professors of constitutional law cannot be unaware that the correction of constitutional error has been going on for a long time. A method of correcting judicial error in

---

28   Cox, "Foreword" at 105.
29   Gunther, *Constitutional Law: Cases and Materials* (1975 ed.) at 656, 1037.
30   Lockhart, Kamisar, and Choper, *Constitutional Law* (4th ed. 1975) 1616.
31   Cox, "Foreword" at 99.
32   Tribe, *American Constitutional Law* (1978) 271.

interpretation of the Constitution that has changed the meaning of the Commerce Power, of Article III courts, of voting tests under the Fourteenth Amendment cannot be fairly described as the new invention of Senator Helms and Congressman Hyde. It is a method of "amending the Constitution," to use Tribe-Ely's misleading phrase, as traditional as the Court's "amending the Constitution" by interpretation.

Nonetheless, Professors Tribe and Ely see "dizzying implications" in the method proposed. They suggest it could be used to amend the law on libel, giving a right to libel to a defamed public official; that it could be used to authorize racially restrictive covenants; that it could authorize coerced confessions. In an impatient rhetorical burst they ask why Congress does not simply redefine "due process" to include "any law Congress or a state legislature approves." The method, they say, reduces "the Constitution to whatever those in power want it to mean."

This astounding statement proceeds as if the basis for the proposed statute had not been laid by the Court itself as far back as *Katzenbach* and as recently as *Fullilove*. The Court has not invited Congress to rewrite the Constitution at will, nor has Congress responded by arbitrary assaults on civil liberty. The trick of the kind of rhetoric Tribe and Ely engage in is to suppose that all the bad things are done by the group one disapproves of, while all the good things are done by your side. It is rhetoric persuasive only to one's own side.

There are many experts on constitutional law who have said explicitly or in effect that the Supreme Court's creation of the abortion liberty was simply the work of "those in power" making the Constitution mean "what they want."[33] An exercise of "raw judicial power" was how Justice White described the decision.[34] Oddly enough, Professor Ely was one of those who found that this was the kind of decision the Court had fashioned. Ely could find no principle or standard which had guided the Court.[35] Now when a very limited and precise means is taken, in a traditional way, to correct the exercise of raw power, the curious objection is offered that this modest measure will lead to excess of the very sort being corrected.

8. CONTEXT AND CONSTITUTIONAL INTERPRETATIONS. The parade of horribles in the Tribe-Ely piece is a truly dizzying instance of constitutional interpretation offered without context. Sound constitutional interpretation requires a look at the context in which Congress is acting and in which the Court will be responding. That context is formed by the following facts.

(1) *Roe v. Wade* was one of the most radical decisions ever made by the Supreme Court. At one stroke it set out criteria by which the abortion statutes enacted by Congress and by the fifty States became invalid. It gave the United States the most radical abortion law in the civilized world. In effect, it made abortion on demand a liberty under the Constitution.[36]

(2) The reasoning of this decision, so far as "person" is concerned, is

---

[33] See Noonan, *A Private Choice: Abortion in America in the Seventies* (1979) 29–32.

[34] *Doe v. Bolton* 410 U.S. 179 (1973) at 272.

[35] Ely, "The Wages of Crying Wolf: A Comment on *Roe v. Wade*," *Yale L. J.* 82 (1973) 920 at 946–947.

[36] Noonan, *A Private Choice*, 10–12.

remarkable in that it concentrates on showing that other uses of "person" in the Constitution—in the Fugitive Slave Clause, in the qualification for Representatives and Senators, in the disqualification of Electors, etc.—are such that they could not possibly apply to any being before birth.[37] But by the same token, a corporation could not qualify as a person under the Fourteenth Amendment. A corporation could not have been a fugitive slave, a corporation could not be a Representative or a Senator, a corporation could not be a presidential elector. If Justice Blackmun's reasoning on person is correct, the *Santa Clara County v. Southern Pacific RR* 118 U.S. 394 (1886) and all its progeny were wrongly decided, and corporations should be held unprotected by the due process clause.

Indeed it would be interesting, if the Court had in fact, adopted the reasoning of Justice Blackmun to exclude corporations from the protection of the Fourteenth Amendment, to see if the conservative critics of *Katzenbach v. Morgan* would have denied the Congress power to suggest to the Court by statute that corporations could be considered persons too. Here we deal not with a hypothesis requiring the artificial extension of the meaning of "person" but with real creatures of flesh and blood, whose brains are working, whose hearts are pumping, whose legs are kicking, but which the Court has found not to be persons because they could not vote, be a Senator or Congressman, or become a runaway slave.

(3) *Roe v. Wade* has been vigorously criticized by leading authorities on law, among them Alexander Bickel of Yale, Robert Byrn of Fordham, Archibald Cox of Harvard, Richard Epstein of Chicago, John Hart Ely of Harvard, Joseph O'Meara Jr. of Notre Dame, Harry Wellington of Yale, and Joseph Witherspoon of Texas. A professionally satisfying defense of it has not been found.[38]

(4) As a result of *Roe v. Wade* one million five hundred thousand lives per year are being taken by abortions. Even accepting the highest guesses as to the number of abortions prior to the decision, this figure represents an enormous increase—at least 50%, at least 500,000—is the number of deaths occasioned by the decision.

It is in the context of this kind of radical attack on state power, this kind of fallacious reasoning, this kind of criticism, this kind of slaughter that Congress is asked to take remedial action.

9. FURTHER STEPS.   Enactment of the proposed Act will not be the end of abortion. Legislation is not assured of being permanent. Its effect across the United States will not be uniform. No one who has observed the play of ideology in the Supreme Court can guarantee that a law, constitutional according to the principles the Court has enunciated, will actually be sustained by the Court.

Accordingly, Congress should regard passage of this Act as the first of three steps. The second step will be to pass a constitutional amendment annulling *Roe v. Wade*. That annulment can be accomplished simply by words such as, "Nothing in this Constitution or the Constitution of any State shall be construed to confer on any person the right to an abortion"; or by words couched in terms of restoring the power the Court has taken away: "The Congress and the several States shall have power to protect life, including the unborn at every stage of

---

[37] *Roe v. Wade* 410 U.S. 113 at 157.
[38] Noonan, *A Private Choice* 20–32.

biological development, irrespective of age, health, or condition of dependency.'' Either one of such Amendments would restore the status quo ante *Roe v. Wade*, and return to the States their traditional power to protect life.

A final step would be the enactment of an Amendment actually mandating the protection of human life from conception. Such an Amendment would complete the great education process of which the Act before you is the first and necessary step.

Senator EAST. Professor Van Alstyne?

Statement of William Van Alstyne

Mr. VAN ALSTYNE. This committee has sat this afternoon, Mr. Chairman, to such an extent that I am going to deal only with one point to spare the journalists, you, and the public from being redundant.

I have no doubt that the legislation is at best a complete exercise in futility, and at worst, merely a gratuitous effort to contribute to the animation that may propel a proposed amendment, by means of which, of course, super majorities in the country may change the outcome of *Roe v. Wade*.

The Reason for Profesional Consensus

I quite agree with Professor Tribe that the letter you have received, signed by a highly diverse number of constitutional experts, is significant for purposes of this committee. It is remarkable really that such ideologically very divided persons, including some of the most constitutionally conservative members of the academy, are overwhelmingly of one opinion.

I suggest to you that there is at least an issue which glues and cements them altogether. It goes to the non sequitur that if something can be rationally deemed "a human life" from some not irrational perspective, which it surely can—a zygote may, a blastula may, a very young embryo may, a developed fetus may, even a gamete may by some, then it may also be defined by Congress as a "person" as that word appears in the 14th amendment. All of this effort is mounted on the supposition that if there is some intelligent consensus that one or more of these forms of biological existence may also be subject to the descriptive term "human life," they at once, therefore, can also be described in a way which will bind the Supreme Court as within the word "person" as that word appears in the 14th amendment. I assure you that is a flat non sequitur.

This Congress may review exactly the kind of problem Professor Noonan used for colorful contrast, the treatment by the Supreme Court of corporate enterprises, fictitious entities, as "persons." It may hold elaborate hearings and have very amusing debate that they cannot find a "person" in the fictitious entity of the corporation and, therefore, reach its solemn legislative conclusion that corporations are not persons.

That is all very well for all of your purposes. It cannot, however, affect the Supreme Court's decision to the contrary. Their decision to the contrary simply goes to an adjudicated construction of a word in the document, which construction Congress cannot alter by simple statute.

Nothing in *Roe v. Wade* says that rational people may not for their own private purposes regard zygotes, blastulas, embryos, or fetuses as human beings. Nothing. They are not presuming to do so, construing a word as it appears in a document.

The Supreme Court's interpretation, on the other hand, is simply that as of 1866 when the 14th amendment was drafted and that word was selected, it was not meant to, and did not, extend to zygotes, blastulas, embryos, and fetuses. They are not within its coverage.

Corporations, since the stockholders ultimately are adult human beings, can be treated fictively as a single entity, a surrogate representing those adult persons in the form of the entity.

The seeming bizarreness of having a word like "person," that to a lay person might describe an animate biological being, may have some coherence if you attend to the kind of problem that you are dealing with, with corporate litigation arising under the 14th amendment.

These arguments that you have heard from my adverse colleagues on my right have all been made before. Their definition as to what the Reconstruction Congress might have meant by way of defining the word "person" in 1866 has been briefed before. It has been adjudicated before. It is explicit in the decision of *Roe v. Wade* that it is not acceptable.

Identically, when the case of *Dred Scott* was argued before the Supreme Court, the issue was not, I assure you, whether Dred Scott, being black, was "a human being." It is preposterous to suppose that the outcome of the case rested on a Supreme Court view that Dred Scott, being a slave, is not a human being.

The Supreme Court judges are in the professional business of trying to assign a definitive meaning to a given word in a given clause in the Constitution. In that particular instance, the clause was not in the 14th amendment. It was in article 3. The word was "citizen." They do not demean Dred Scott. They may report, as a matter of fact, a sad chapter of specific American constitutional history, that certain human beings were not meant to be benefited as citizens for the purpose of article 3.

The decision in *Roe v. Wade* is equally emphatic with regard to the meaning of the word "person" as it appears in the 14th amendment. The Reconstruction Congress did not have in mind and did not intend to include among the beneficiaries of section 1, zygotes, blastulas, embryos, or fetuses.

You may regret that, Mr. Chairman. You may appropriately seek recourse, as has been done not less than five times, by taking a disagreeable definition imputed by the Court to language in the Constitution and appropriately have it overruled by amendment.

Indeed, virtually every amendment we have had is an amendment which stands exactly upon a super majoritarian disagreement with the Court's construction of a word that appears in some clause in the Constitution.

Senator Moynihan was exactly correct in offering you as an example the very divisive decision by the Supreme Court in the first effort by the country to put together a graduated income tax for the country as a form of raising revenue which Congress thought was more equitable than flat sales taxes, for instance.

Among the things that were taxed was rental income derived from real estate. The Constitution requires that a thing called a direct tax has to be apportioned among the States according to their population. It is an unusable formula such that if this tax were described by the Supreme Court as a direct tax, then it would fall. And it fell.

Congress thought that when a tax is not directly on land and is only indirectly on land and rather on income from land, then it ought not be defined as a direct tax. That was their view. They acted upon it. The enacted legislation appropriate to their view of the definition of the word. They were held to be in error. The Supreme Court had the last word on the meaning of the word direct.

This controversy was litigated with respect to the meaning of the word "person" in *Roe v. Wade*. There is no member of the Court who dissented with regard to that feature of the case.

This is as futile an exercise as in the poetry of Omar Khayyam: "The moving finger writes and having writ moves on. Nor all your piety, nor wit can call it back or cancel out half a line."

If then you wish to reconstruct the language of the Constitution to fit what in your view, respectfully, would be a better understanding of that language, you may have your way. You may have it according to the conventional process which has been used exactly in this kind of encounter with the Supreme Court not less than five times, the first being as fresh in the country's history as 1793, to overrule the definition of the word by substituting an amendment which then gives the congressional view, and the country's view, quite a different tenor.

For that reason, all of these other matters aside, respectfully, I have a private sense of profound impatience because I do agree with one of the Senators who testified before you. That is, I do not think that this legislation, among those who have been attentive to the rudimentary difficulties of what is involved here, is seriously intended. I think rather it is frankly a stalking horse, more to dramatize the depth of private feeling that attended the decision in *Roe v. Wade*.

It is not inappropriate for Members of Congress to use the newsworthiness of proposed but futile, and in my opinion, frankly fatuous, legislation for such advertising purposes. We are not subject to the Federal Trade Commission and may not be enjoined here for deceptive trade practice.

However, this bill cannot possibly be secured on the foundation for which it is advanced. Indeed, if the theory were sound, then by a like process, it would obviously be within the capacity of this Congress to venture its preferred definition of any other term in the same document, and by having ventured that preference then, presume to bind the court to the outcome of its own definition.

It has never been that way. It never can. We are among a very few countries in the world, as our public does not know, in which the Supreme Court, indeed, for purposes of adjudication is given the last word on the adjudicated meaning of each term in the U.S. Constitution.

Most countries do not have supreme courts with that power. Indeed, most written constitutions are enforceable only by their parliaments and their supreme court cannot enforce them.

It is the legacy of our Constitution, it is its brilliance, and it is its correctness as *Marbury* v. *Madison* itself that you may not alter the meaning of that language short of an amendment itself. The rest, in my opinion, respectfully, is all just futility, and to a great extent, some posturing as well.

Thank you, Mr. Chairman.

Senator EAST. Thank you, Professor Van Alstyne.

[Three letters submitted by Prof. Van Alstyne follow:]

Letters of William Van Alstyne
March 31, 1981

The Honorable Don Edwards
Chairman, Subcommittee on Civil and Constitutional Rights
The United States House of Representatives
Washington, D. C. 20515

Dear Mr. Edwards:

H. R. 900 is both unconstitutional and wholly unworthy of Congress. Its presuppositions respecting the power of Congress to impose its own definitions upon words in the Constitution are naive and incorrect. Its additional presumptuousness in attempting to revive criminal statutes already adjudicated by the Supreme Court as violative of fundamental personal rights is unprecedented and unsound. I shall elaborate briefly on both these points. I shall be pleased to provide any additional assistance to you in your further consideration of this foolish bill.

The abortion decisions of 1973 do not mark the first occasion when a constitutional adjudication by the Supreme Court has met with very great resistance. As early as 1793, an interpretation of Article III subjected states to law suits in federal courts contrary to what many widely believed could not be done without the consent of such states. The case was *Chisholm* v. *Georgia*, 2 U.S. 519, and it was subsequently overturned by the provisions of the Eleventh Amendment in 1794. A little more than a half-century later, the Supreme Court interpreted the word "citizen" in Article III to exclude a number of persons whom many (including a minority on the Supreme Court itself) believed to be capable of acquiring that status. The case was *Dred Scott* v. *Sanford*, 60 U.S. 393 (1857), and it was subsequently overturned by the provisions of the Fourteenth Amendment in 1868. Thirty years later, the Supreme Court interpreted the phrase "direct taxes" in Article I to include a tax on income derived from the rental of real estate, contrary to the different interpretation of the same phrase by Congress (and by a minority of the Court itself). The case was *Pollock* v. *Farmer's Loan & Trust Co.*, 157 U.S. 429 (1895). It was subsequently overturned by the Sixteenth Amendment in 1913, which permitted the unapportioned taxation of such income. And as recently as 1970, contrary to Congress's own interpretation of "equal protection," a majority of the Supreme Court held that the disfranchisement of citizens over eighteen years of age (but less than twenty-one years of age) in all state and local elections was not within any corrective power of Congress pursuant to Section 5 of the Fourteenth Amendment. That outcome, too, was also overturned—by ratification of the Twenty-Sixth Amendment in 1971.

In each of these (and many other) instances, final adjudications by the Supreme Court have involved interpretations of words or phrases in the Constitution different than the interpretation imputed to the same words by state legislatures or by Congress. In the vast majority of instances, the adjudicated interpretation by the Supreme Court continued to be controlling, despite dissatisfaction by others who believed that interpretation to be unsound. That observation correctly characterizes even the single most famous (and important) decision in our entire constitutional history, the case of *Marbury* v. *Madison*, 5

U.S. (1 Cranch) 137 (1803). In part, that famous case involved the issue whether Congress could enlarge the original jurisdiction of the Supreme Court by adding into its original jurisdiction some cases that might otherwise reach the Court only on appeal. The language of Article III itself is wholly inconclusive, and an eminently reasonable argument could be made that while Congress might not have power to limit or to reduce the original jurisdiction of the Court, it could most certainly enlarge that jurisdiction by adding such cases as were otherwise within the judicial power: cases that Congress believed to be sufficiently important that they, too, should also commence in the Supreme Court itself. Chief Justice Marshall held otherwise, however, and—there being no amendment ever made to the Constitution to change that result—that remains the case even now.

Marbury v. Madison, and Martin v. Hunter's Lessee, concretely established two propositions which are themselves the essence of the American constitutional system. The first is that in the adjudication of all cases and controversies arising under the Constitution, it is the judiciary's interpretation of the Constitution, rather than that of Congress, which is final. The second is that in the adjudication of all cases and controversies arising under the Constitution, it is the judiciary's interpretation of the Constitution, rather than that of state legislatures or state courts, which is final.

In keeping with these bedrock principles, it is perfectly well understood that the finality of those Supreme Court interpretations are reversible by two means only. The first is the capacity of the Court to overrule itself. The second, as illustrated by the Eleventh, the Fourteenth, the Sixteenth, and the Twenty-Sixth Amendments, is to "overrule" the Court by amending the Constitution.

The technique of H. R. 900 is not to propose an amendment. It betrays a complete lack of confidence that the constitutional demands for two-thirds majorities in both houses, and ratification by three-fourths of the states, could be obtained to that end. Thus, in repudiation of the provisions of Article V that nothing less than these extraordinary majorities may suffice authoritatively to displace a final adjudication by the Supreme Court respecting the adjudicatory significance of a part of the Constitution, it presumes instead to instruct the Court on the "right" meaning of a particular word. This attempt is as futile (and improper) as though Congress, following the decision in Marbury v. Madison, had presumed to adopt a law in which Congress "finds" that Article III "was intended to" permit some cases to be added to the Court's original jurisdiction which cases might otherwise come only within its appellate jurisdiction. It is as futile as though Congress, following the decision in Chisholm v. Georgia, had passed a law in which it "found" that Article III did not intend to permit states to be sued in federal courts without their consent. It is exactly the same as though Congress, after the decision in Pollock v. Farmer's Loan & Trust, had adopted a statute in which "Congress finds that the phrase 'direct taxes' in Article I was not intended to include a tax on income derived merely from the rental of real estate." Indeed, if this technique were available to Congress, in no instance would amendments to the Constitution be required authoritatively to alter the Supreme Court's interpretations of the Constitution. As you (and every member of Congress) are well aware, however, our system of constitutional government, unlike that of many other nations, is not one of parliamentary supremacy. It is not the case that we are under a Constitution, but the Constitution is what Congress says it is. A

Constitution so construed cannot act as a positive law restraint upon Congress or upon the States. Rather, a Constitution so construed would permit Congress not merely to control the scope of the Fourteenth Amendment, but to define its own powers, to override all reserved state powers, and to demolish the separation of powers as well—all by the breathtaking expedient of having Congress bind the courts by presuming to "find" what every part of the Constitution was "intended" to do.

We come, then, to H. R. 900. In *Roe* v. *Wade*, the Supreme Court held that the word "person" as it appears in the Fourteenth Amendment is exclusive of gestating fetuses prior to the time of fetal viability. H. R. 900 presumes to "find" that the word "person" in the Fourteenth Amendment, to the contrary, includes not merely viable but unborn fetuses but, indeed, embryos, blastulas, and zygotes as well. Presumably, it means to "find" that the instant there is sufficient contact between a sperm and an egg as to produce any preliminary reaction whatever, and certainly at least telophase (the last step in mitosis in simple cell division), the chemical reaction at the least discernible preliminary step dates a "person" for all Fourteenth Amendment purposes.

Having discovered in the Fourteenth Amendment (?) a definition of "person" contradictory of the Supreme Court's interpretation, Congress then proposes to use that finding to validate state laws already held to be violative of another person's fundamental right as previously determined by the Supreme Court. It is, of course, the holding of *Roe* v. *Wade* that no state may criminalize a woman's decision to terminate an unwanted pregnancy within six months of conception, assuming only that she secures the assistance of a competent physician who, in assisting her, complies with reasonable medical procedures. That freedom is described by the Court as "fundamental." Nothing, in any of the subsequent decisions of the Court, reneges on that description. The ambition of H. R. 900 is not to support that freedom, or even to assist such women carrying fatally malformed fetuses, or women for whom pregnancy may be threatening to their health. To the contrary, in prior versions of the "Hyde Amendment," Congress has already set a cruel determination against such women by restricting any such assistance and by rendering, for them, even first-term, medically-indicated abortions subject to private charity and to the commercial market alone. The Supreme Court has found no adequate constitutional basis to forbid this selective vindictiveness. But I see no evidence at all that it will be impressed by Congress's cellophane effort to do indirectly (by defining words in the Constitution) what it cannot do directly (to reverse substantive constitutional decisions by the Supreme Court).

If Members in Congress frankly desire to compel the birth of every fertilized ovum, or if Members in Congress think it wise that each state be allowed to criminalize whatever abortions, in whatever circumstances they wish to criminalize, they may do so. For even freedom of speech may be ended in this country by amending the Constitution itself (to permit the criminalizing of free speech), and so, too, may any other fundamental freedom we have. But the very purpose of Article V is to disallow such changes without the sobering check that the amendment process itself imposes. And it behooves Congress to respect that process in this instance, at least as much as it did in the establishment of an income tax.

I have not devoted any time in this brief letter to an "analysis" of *Katzenbach* v. *Morgan*, and the various (even conflicting) impressions which that case has generated. I will say briefly, however, that I know of no reasonable manner in which the sound foundation of that case can be adjusted to sustain what is being proposed in H. R. 900. The basic thesis of *Katzenbach* v. *Morgan* is not complicated. That thesis is that Section One of the Fourteenth Amendment committed to the judiciary the obligation to hold invalid such state statutes as were clearly, in the Court's own view, forbidden by the Fourteenth Amendment. These, in brief, were all laws forbidden by Section One in its self-executing effect, laws so clearly (in the Court's view) in derogation of privileges and immunities, life, liberty, and property, or in derogation of equal protection, that they are invalid whether or not Congress has seen fit to say so. It is Section One, in its self-executing effect, which is the foundation of *Roe* v. *Wade*.

Section One was drafted to provide this minimum self-executing effect, moreover, partly because it was agreed in the 39th Congress (which proposed the Fourteenth Amendment) that it was unwise to leave the determination of invalid state laws merely to Congress. The original version of the Fourteenth Amendment did just that, providing only what Congress might do in respect to certain kinds of state laws, but not providing any security against state laws that Congress might not see fit to forbid. It was significantly to provide security against a remissness in Congress that the Fourteenth Amendment was redrafted (in its present form), so to make certain a self-executing effect, a minimum level of *judicially-*enforceable protection, *irrespective* of Congress's sentiment about such protection. Consistent with this understanding (which is consistent both with *Roe* v. *Wade* and with *Katzenbach* v. *Morgan*), it was also anticipated that Congress might (under Section five) reach some state laws that were not so clearly in violation of Section one as to require the courts to hold them invalid. And that, of course, is what happened in *Katzenbach* v. *Morgan* itself.

Ironically, a correct application of *Katzenbach* v. *Morgan* would be useful to sustain an Act of Congress very different from H. R. 900. For instance, although the Supreme Court has held that the due process clause does forbid any state from criminalizing medically safe abortions within the first two trimesters (a fundamental right that neither Congress nor the States may now attempt to override), it has not held that states are also constitutionally obliged to provide economically disadvantaged women an assistance for that purpose even if, without such assistance, their practical capacity to exercise their fundamental right is seriously prejudiced. Even the omission of medically-indicated abortions from a state medic-aid program *otherwise* assisting economically disadvantaged persons for medically-indicated services, has not been held by the Court as to be so utterly arbitrary as to be a *per se* violation of the Fourteenth Amendment. On the other hand, were Congress to regard such a differential treatment of women seeking medically-indicated abortions as plainly arbitrary when the state otherwise has undertaken to extend assistance to economically disadvantaged persons, then I think *Katzenbach* v. *Morgan* would come into play. The unequal treatment of economically-disadvantaged women otherwise unable to secure medically-indicated abortions might plausibly be regarded by Congress as so discriminatory and unfair under the circumstances that Congress might, on that basis, forbid the states so to discriminate against women. In this respect, exactly as in *Katzenbach*,

Congress would be acting to enhance a fundamental right, rather than to restrict or to annihilate it. *Katzenbach* does not contemplate this latter power. Neither does Section One of the Fourteenth Amendment. Rather, Section One establishes a *judicially*-ascertained, *minimum* floor of *self-executing* constitutional protection which neither Congress nor the states may violate. It was that "floor" that was held to be violated in *Roe* v. *Wade*. H. R. 900 is wholly in conflict with this proper understanding of the Fourteenth Amendment and is, accordingly, both unauthorized and invalid.

I realize that nonetheless the tendency in Congress to vote for bills such as this is very great. It may appease particular constituencies and divert all blame to the courts. But you have not been a Member of Congress to have looked at matters in this cynical fashion, and I am confident you will not do so on this occasion, either.

Sincerely,

William Van Alstyne
William R. Perkins Professor of Law

May 5, 1981

Senator Orrin B. Hatch
United States Senate
Washington, D.C. 20510

Dear Senator Hatch:
I understand you have had some reluctance to support legislation to overcome the Supreme Court's decision in *Roe* v. *Wade*, despite your belief that the decision was unsound and that states should be free to prohibit abortions. I understand that while you are prepared to introduce and to support an amendment to the Constitution, re-establishing in state legislatures the discretion to regulate abortion according to each state's own determination, you are doubtful of the constitutional power of Congress to do so by simple statute—and concerned that the theory of such a statute may seriously disserve conservative interests.

Judging the matter from the particular proposed statute I have had occasion to examine, I entirely agree with *both* of your concerns. The bill I have examined was originally sent to me from the House of Representatives (H.R. 900) and I do not have at hand the corresponding number of the Senate bill which, however, I understand to be identical. The Bill I have provides:

> *Section 1.* The Congress finds that present-day scientific evidence indicates a significant likelihood that actual human life exists from conception.

The Congress further finds that the fourteenth amendment to the Constitution of the United States was intended to protect all human beings.

Upon the basis of these findings, and in the exercise of the powers of the Congress, including its power under section 5 of the fourteenth amendment to the Constitution of the United States, the Congress hereby declares that for the purpose of enforcing the obligation of the States under the fourteenth amendment not to deprive persons of life without due process of law, human life shall be deemed to exist from conception, without regard to race, sex, age, health, defect, or condition of dependency; and for this purpose "person" shall include all human life as defined herein.

Section 2. Notwithstanding any other provision of law, no inferior Federal court ordained and established by Congress under article III of the Constitution of the United States shall have jurisdiction to issue any restraining order, temporary or permanent injunction, or declaratory judgment in any case involving or arising from any State law or municipal ordinance that (1) protects the rights of human persons between conception and birth, or (2) prohibits, limits or regulates (a) the performance of abortions, or (b) the provision at public expense of funds, facilities, personnel, or other assistance for the performance of abortions.

Section 3. If any provision of this Act or the application thereof to any person or circumstance is judicially determined to be invalid, the validity of the remainder of the Act and the application of such provision to other persons and circumstances shall not be affected by such determination.

Section 3, the severability clause, is unexceptionable and I have no comment to make. Similarly, that portion of Section 2 addressed as a restriction on inferior federal court power to issue restraining orders I shall not comment on—partly because I understand that it may now have been dropped from the bill and more substantially because I know the general subject of congressional power of federal court jurisdiction will be the subject of lengthy and separate hearings, later this month. While I have serious reservations about this portion of the bill, I think it inappropriate to deal with them here in light of these considerations.

With respect to the entire bill (including the restriction on federal court jurisdiction), I know you have received brief statements from more than a dozen very well established academic experts on constitutional law, uniformly concluding that the bill is plainly unconstitutional and clearly beyond the authorized constitutional authority of Congress. The uniform consensus of those signing these statements is professionally and politically remarkable. I do not personally know of *any* other proposed Act of Congress within the past two decades that has drawn such a response from ranking professors of constitutional law who are otherwise given to an immense range of disagreement both politically and professionally. Among them, many did not at the time (and do not now) think the Supreme Court's decision in *Roe* v. *Wade* to be correct. Among them also, several regard the powers of Congress to be extremely broad, especially in respect to the particular power relied upon in this bill, namely, Section five of the fourteenth amendment. Among them are individuals who are personally highly conservative on matters of economic policy, utterly unimpressed with "liberal" interpretations of women's rights, and severely critical of expansionist trends commonly associated with the Supreme Court. Ordinarily, House or Senate Committee holding hearings on this bill could readily expect to hear much more conflicting testimony than anything else. Erwin Griswold, Charles Alan Wright, and Phillip Kurland, for instance, are not "suspect" scholars; they are, rather, the eminent conservatives of constitutional law. The information you already have from them stating exactly the same conclusion shared with Gerald Gunther and John Ely, as well as Tribe, Brest, and myself, should in fact be *prima facie* convincing that the bill under consideration is regarded as extremely ill-advised—and that it is not simply disliked or feared by constitutional liberals.

As a legislative "precedent," it is not difficult to see why very conservative constitutionalists would be opposed to this bill. Under the fourteenth amendment, states are forbidden to "deprive" persons of certain things. They are not, on the other hand, obliged to guarantee them, to provide them, or to protect them from interference by private parties. The Supreme Court has resisted efforts to persuade it, for instance, that states must guarantee a "right" to treatment, a "right" to a certain level of education, or a "right" to a certain level of economic subsistence. A portion of *this* bill, in contrast, speaks of "the obligation" of States not to deprive "persons" of life in the additional (and strained) sense of an affirmative duty to enact criminal statutes for the particular protection of such "persons." If the theory is sound, there is nothing to forestall Congress from similarly speaking of a *constitutional obligation* of each state "not to deprive" persons of meaningful lives by failing to appropriate tax funds for their health care, their educational "needs," adequate (public) employment opportunities, or any number of things which, in the view of Congress, are important to make life, liberty, and property valuable. Upon such presuppositious determinations by *Congress*, each state may be forced to allocate resources as Congress thinks best. Linked to the power of Congress granted by Section five of the 14th amendment (power to "enforce" this article by appropriate legislation), it is exceedingly plain where this leads. If Congress can (a) determine authoritatively what *affirmative* obligations each state has in respect to the life, liberty, and property of each person, and if Congress can (b) legislate to "enforce" such affirmative obligations as determined by Congress, then indeed the rudiments of federalism are dead, the 10th amendment is meaningless, and each state becomes but the instrument of a uniform, congressional determined policy of social welfare. Some few *dicta* (and some larger number of writers) have urged this view in recent decades—but I was unaware of any conservative Member of Congress who believed it to be desirable or sound. If, moreover, Congress now moves to embrace this view in its own legislation, surely the Supreme Court will feel itself to be encouraged likewise to "declare" what the "affirmative obligations" of states to be—and correspondingly authorized to develop still additional judicial remedies to enforce them.

The bill is extraordinary in several additional respects. It employs a technique that would render unnecessary *any* amendment to the Constitution *whenever* Congress were dissatisifed with the integrity of a Supreme Court interpretation of that Constitution, by the simple (?) device of substituting a congressional definition for the Court's adjudicated definition of the same word. In this instance, the word is "person." In *Roe*, as I know you will recall, the Court held (rightly or wrongly) that the word "person" does *not* extend to pre-viable fetuses insofar as a state might presume such a definition to state a reason for criminalizing a women's decision to terminate an early pregnancy with competent medical assistance. Here, Congress presumes to instruct the Court differently on the meaning of constitutional text, for the explicit purpose of securing a different adjudicative outcome. If the theory of congressional supremacy respecting the *adjudicatory* meaning of words in the Constitution were sound, there would never be any need for amending the Constitution as a necessary means of setting aside a final constitutional adjudication by the Supreme Court. Five amendments to the Constitution have been put into place as specific reactions to Supreme Court devisions: the 11th, the 14th, the 16th, and 19th, and the 26th amendments. Each amendment was introduced, and carried through the burden of ratification, to nullify the Court's interpretation of constitutional text. It is remarkable to suppose that the amendment process itself is made quite difficult (with two-thirds majorities in both Houses, and three-fourths of the states), if it is not even necessary to amend the Constitution at all.

For example, in the original income tax case, the Supreme Court held that a tax on income derived from the rental of real estate was a "direct" tax which, because it was a "direct" tax, would have to be apportioned among the several states by population, as required by Article I. Many in Congress, and many academic commentators, believed the Court's interpretation of the word "direct" to be incorrect. By way of public reaction, the 16th amendment was proposed and, once ratified, freed Congress from having to apportion this kind of income tax. But if the approach taken in this bill is sound, all that was necessary was for Congress to have "found" that Article I was not intended to include a tax on income from real estate as though it were a tax "directly" on real estate—and to have instructed the Court (?) accordingly. No one seriously believes such a power to reside in Congress. The amendment process, and the fact of multiple amendments that "corrected" Supreme Court decisions, stand against the very notion. More importantly, *if* the technique were sound, of course it is a two-edged sword that will cut against federal and conservative interests much more frequently than it will cut in the opposite way.

But a very few years ago, the Supreme Court held that state and local employees could not be placed under the federal minimum wage law because the attempt by Congress to do so (under the commerce clause) cut too deeply into state rights, *i.e.*, to determine by *state* law the proper balance between the level of *state* and local employee wages and competing state and local needs to be met. The Court has also recently protected contractual rights of state bondholders from being ruined by state legislatures which sought to renege upon those commitments. But a very "liberal" Congress might not like either of these "conservative" decisions and might, if the theory of this bill were sound, simply presume to define the very text of the Constitution more "liberally" than the Supreme Court—and presume to revive these invalid laws. Conservatives in Congress have resisted these kinds of efforts in the past. It is scarcely safe, consistent, or prudent all of a sudden to be seen to embrace them or to appear to give them legitimacy.

Put more bluntly, the theory of this bill is inconsistent with *Marbury* v. *Madison* itself, but is even more presumptuous than that. It does not even content itself by withdrawing jurisdiction from the Court to decide certain kinds of cases; rather, it leaves them to be decided there, while "advising" the Court on the "proper" meaning of the words in the Constitution according to which the Court is to judge the case at hand.

Finally, this bill is not an application of the theory of the Court's own very controversial decision in *Katzenbach* v. *Morgan*. In that case, the Court held by a majority (and as an "alternative" holding) that a state law not deemed so arbitrary by the Court itself as to be unconstitutional might nonetheless be held by Congress to be so arbitrary that it ought not be enforced. Here, however, a reversal of that technique is employed: a state law found by the Court to be *in*valid is sought to be revived under a congressional view that such a state law is, in fact, not violative of an individual's constitutional rights. Even the *Katzenbach* view of congressional power emphatically and explicitly took care to discredit this possibility and surely it is not be expected that the more conservative members of the Court, unpersuaded in *Katzenbach* itself, would find it acceptable. It is surprising to think that equally conservative Members of Congress would rush to embrace these possibilities.

In closing, I need only add my professional regard for your different approach. As a personal matter, I know we are not in agreement on the general issue of abortion. But insofar as such matters are always open, regard for the separation of powers, for consistency in public office, and for turning "square corners," clearly compliment your own respect for *constitutional* processes. I would not endorse an amendment to the Constitution to return every woman's pregnancy to the fate of whatever criminal statutes each state might prefer. If it is to be done, however, surely it should be done in the manner contemplated by the Constitution itself—by amendment.

Sincerely,

William Van Alstyne

Statement of Senator John P. East

Senator EAST. Our hour grows late. I would like to proceed with my 10 minutes and then turn it over to Senator Baucus. I would like to assure the panelists and all the audience that we are fully aware of the pressures of time.

I am sure you, coming from the academic community, feel enormously frustrated that such momentous things are jammed into such a limited period of time. For what consolation there is, I can assure you your statements are a part of the record. I can also assure you that these matters will be explored in great depth.

What this does give us is an opportunity to form a public record and begin a public dialog.

I know all of you each have many, many things you would like to raise. I do, too, and I know Senator Baucus does. Again, we are back to this problem of I have 10 minutes and what does one say in 10 minutes before a panel of such distinguished gentlemen as the four of you, particularly when there are such deep differences of opinion.

If I might, let me direct my remarks to Professors Tribe and Van Alstyne. The others may listen if they want to.

Let me try to give you my perspective on this as a man trained in law and then in political science.

However, not because of your very fine testimony, but as I see lawyers get into this question of *Roe* v. *Wade* and its implications, I am somewhat reminded of the old statement that the law sharpens the mind by narrowing. There is a tendency, it seems to me, in discussing the narrow legal constitutional questions, which, mind you now, become very important, to lose sight of the broader political context in which this matter has to be dealt with.

Here is the frustration the legislative body has, which is the distinct political arm of the Government, concerning the power of judicial review, *Marbury* v. *Madison*, the *Federalist Number 78*.

Marbury v. *Madison* is predicated on *Federalist 78* in which you may recall Hamilton set out a very narrow conception of the power of judicial review. He said it would only be used where actions had been taken by legislative bodies contrary to the manifest tenor of the Constitution, the express provisions. For example, he noted bills of attainder and ex post facto laws. But he went on to caution that the court ought not to improve their will for a legislative judgment. He was very explicit on that. It was a very narrow conception of the power of judicial review.

Marbury v. *Madison* is in keeping with that. You four distinguished gentlemen do not need this Senator to lecture you on the meaning of *Marbury* v. *Madison*, but you may recall what it said was that in that case the Congress by the Judiciary Act of 1789 had tried to expand the power of judicial review beyond those expressly provided for in article three, namely by adding the writ of mandamus.

Therefore, it was an action of Congress contrary to the express provision of the Constitution, and, hence, an appropriate case for the power of judicial review.

I am saying it is a long, long road from *Marbury* v. *Madison* to *Roe* v. *Wade*. Many critics across the spectrum are saying this was an incredible assumption of judicial power. I remember in the dissent that Justice White and Rehnquist said that it is an improvident and extravagant use of the power of judicial review. Justice Rehnquist said it was judicial activism.

Here is the frustration Congress has: How do you respond to that? How do you deal with it?

What we are trying to do—I resist the argument, Professor Van Alstyne, that this is a trivial venture—is to find a practical, modest, appropriate approach.

If you are really saying to us, gentlemen, whenever the Supreme Court with its extravagant use of the power of judicial review intervenes into the political process, you are going to have to turn around and use the constitutional amendment process, do you know what that does to the legislative process of the Congress in terms of major substantive policy questions? We are simply debilitated. It means that we and the States together must constantly be amending the Constitution.

With such an overly active Court, we were hoping we could do something short of that kind of dramatic response where we keep adding amendments to the Constitution. Hence, this idea. Some may say it is rather novel. Maybe because of its novelty lawyers are shocked by it, they who are so embedded with tradition as they understand it in their profession.

However, what we are tyring to do is see if there might not be practical alternatives other than constitutional amendments. In *Roe* v. *Wade*, as Mr. Galebach and Mr. Noonan have pointed out, there seems to be an invitation here of sorts, an implied one. The Court said the judiciary was not equipped to define when life began, the implication being certainly some other entity of Government might be able to, perhaps the legislative branch.

We are best equipped to deal with these profound and deep and sensitive policy questions. So we are entering into that water. All we are trying to do, as Mr. Galebach has said, is to try to find some sort of definition. The Court seemed to suggest that might solve the problem.

You may be right. The bill may be enacted into law. It may return the matter to the States. The question may go directly to the Supreme Court. All we want to do is to get it to the Supreme Court. If they hold the statute unconstitutional, then those who still have this concern can move to the constitutional amendment route. However, we look upon this bill as the practical, prudent, reasonable first step.

I wanted to clarify from the standpoint of someone serving in the legislative chamber, in the political arm, that I see this on the campaign trail. There are so many things the public wants to know. Why cannot Congress do something about this major policy question, or that major policy question?

The point is the Supreme Court has short circuited the legislative process. We cannot deal with busing. No, they handle that one. Prayer in the classroom, they handle that one, too. Abortion? No, that is theirs, too.

Increasingly, as you go down the litany, you will find so many major policy questions that the Congress is no longer able to deal with. Many Members of Congress in both chambers and other parties have now reached the point where we are going to begi. to assert our policymaking role because certainly under a reasonable conception of the separation of powers, we have that prerogative. It is in that spirit which we undertake this effort.

As I say, *Roe* v. *Wade* certainly could not be justified by *Marbury* v. *Madison* or the *Federalist 78* because the Georgia and the Texas statutes were not contrary to the manifest tenor of the Constitution. The Constitution said absolutely nothing about abortion.

In short, as I was saying, in so many matters the Court has not been prudent. It has tended to frustrate the political process in this country. That is exactly why this issue is here, in my judgment.

Perhaps if we had had deliberation on this issue, if the Congress, for example, had come to the same conclusion that the Court came to in *Roe* v. *Wade*, the same policy result, that would probably have ended it. There would not be much else you could do except to try to continue to urge through political movements that Congress change that policy but the Court circumvents and frustrates the deliberative process, the political process. Then we are forced to come back and try to find some way out of this constitutional crisis. We are groping here, as I was saying, for what we think is a relatively modest solution to it. We are not trying to overreact to the problem.

However, in so doing, then of course we are chastised for perhaps being trivial and not appreciating that the Court has ruled and the only way you overcome Court rulings is through constitutional amendments.

We are then invited to go to the very heavy constitutional artillery. I just question whether in the long run if the Court continues its current practices of being so heavily involved in political decisions they leave us with no alternative but to start the amending process. That greatly distorts the nature of the American system, the federal system, and the separation of powers, which are the broader themes of the subcommittee.

Having perhaps made my point ad nauseum there, I would be interested in you two gentlemen responding.

Mr. TRIBE. Mr. Chairman, anything but ad nauseum. I understand the feeling and I think there is a great deal in it, but let me just suggest a couple of points.

First of all, I think it is easy always to imagine a kind of golden age. *Marbury* v. *Madison* one thinks of as a modest and strictly interpretivist decision. In point of fact, as my colleague, Professor Van Alstyne has shown more ably, I think, than most, *Marbury* v. *Madison* was itself a remarkable decision not clearly dictated, and probably not dictated in any serious sense by the language of article III of the Constitution.

If one goes point by point through the landmark decisions of the U.S. Supreme Court, one does not at all get the feeling that there is a sudden period of activism in the Warren Court or the Burger Court. It has really been a fairly smooth landscape throughout.

Throughout that period, Congress has not been without important devices for making its will felt and known through amending the Constitution, and not merely so frequently as might be supposed if you thought of the Court doing some terribly apocalyptic thing every other day. The decisions that are of genuine deep concern, of the kind that you would describe as leading to crisis, do not happen all that frequently.

However, apart from constitutional amendment, there are other measures. I understand that the Senate just today passed a funding cutoff in the abortion field of the sort that the Supreme Court quite clearly would uphold and which, whatever I might think about it or others might think about its wisdom or humanity, certainly expresses a powerful political sense of this body.

There are a great many things that can be done legislatively, not the least of which is effectuated through the power of advice and consent in the Senate when appointments are made to the U.S. Supreme Court.

It is not as though there is somehow a one-way dialog, with the Court handing down Olympian edicts and the Congress of the United Sates being helpless to respond by anything short of an excessive number of radical amendments.

On the contrary, I think it would be a fearsome development if, whenever the Supreme Court had spoken on a matter and there were significant disagreement, but not quite enough to amend the Constitution, a routine response became legislative redefinition of a constitutional term that has been defined by the

Supreme Court. It would be an understatement to say that such responses would be unlikely to offer productive direction for political dialog.

I think the national dialog over the human life amendment in its many incarnations, is itself, an important, valuable enterprise. I think you are certainly right, Mr. Chairman, as far as I can tell, that if the Court had gone the other way in *Roe* v. *Wade*, as the supreme court in West Germany did in holding that life was entitled to protection from the moment of conception, that, too, would have generated a serious political move in the other direction.

I do not think that is to be described as a crisis. I think that is the direction through which our system is meant to evolve. The national debate which will either produce a human life amendment or will not produce one is a healthy thing for this country.

The question then becomes whether it is a valuable thing to try to speed that process along by passing something this is quite likely to be struck down, or whether that is a diversion that in the end will make everyone look worse and accomplish very little.

I appreciate the underlying impetus behind this. I think it is not a good idea to amend the Constitution too lightly, but when we are talking about a decision of this moment, I do not think it symptomatic of an unduly casual attitude toward the Constitution to say this is the sort of thing on which only an amendment would be the appropriate response if one did not agree.

Senator EAST. Thank you.

Professor Van Alstyne.

Mr. VAN ALSTYNE. I agree with most of that, Senator East.

At the last ditch, it is one of those "cannot helps," that is to say, it is not possible to have the Supreme Court of the kind we have and expect always to be unsurprised by a particular decision.

Professor Tribe is surely correct. The Marshall Court in a variety of areas, if not *Marbury*, which I think was an activist decision, many of its other decisions, astonished the country and drew a lot of anger from a lot of people. Many of those decisions were looked at as profoundly subversive of States' rights from the very beginning. *Fletcher* v. *Peck* and a great variety of other decisions were of that kind.

I do not at all mean to make sport of the gravity of your question merely by beginning with the observation that there is no uniqueness, no novelty by the sense of the public consternation here.

There is no way ultimately to dissolve the likelihood of recurrent consternation from time to time short of fundamentally changing the nature of the accord. That, too, can be done, as I have said. I do not pass that off lightly with some smug expectation that it would never occur to anybody to do it.

Most countries of the world operate under different systems. It has only really been since World War II that the American model of a Supreme Court has picked up much enthusiasm.

The country from which we trace our immediate origins, the English, never had such a court, had no written constitution, and there is no power of judicial review, which you know very well.

The other cousins we have from the English Commonwealth have nothing like it. The New Zealand Supreme Court has no such power. Australia's has none. There is a great commotion in Canada, as you know, on exactly this.

Ultimately, I mean only to say that one needs to put it in some perspective.

I agree that there are other marginal devices. There is no question in my mind that in a variety of areas of American constitutional law, the keenness of Congress to side with Mr. Nixon's restaffing of the Court in the early 1970's did, after suitable lag time, show up in a pattern of decisions, not in this area, but in some other areas on procedural due process, on the availability of habeas corpus. There has been a shift in the pattern of those decisions.

It is not illicit of Congress to make its displeasure felt incidental of the appointment process. Hearings were held this morning on an entirely different approach. I am not enthusiastic about it, but it is a device open to Congress in selected areas, probably including this one, a device not to try to seek by redefinition the reversal of Supreme Court decisions, but really to manifest such profound displeasure with the quality of decisions by the Court, to remove from its capacity to decide certain cases at all.

Now, most of us are terribly reluctant to urge that because once you make an exception of certain kinds of cases, it may generate a public expectation that whenever there is profound dissatisfaction with a certain series or kind of decision, then, indeed, Congress will be expected equally to make an exception there and so on.

Those are risky enterprises.

I agree with Professor Tribe, too, that it is not unproductive, and I do not want to be misunderstood as being disrespectful of the profound national debate that your own efforts and others have contributed to with regard to the meaningfulness and the beginning of life.

That may work itself out. If it works itself out in an amendment, which currently I would not support as a private citizen, so be it, but I think that is perfectly proper. We have done it before. Doubtless, it shall happen again.

In the meantime, while I have the floor, I want to observe that my own view is that some of the Justices of the Supreme Court have, themselves, been very conservative in their subsequent interpretation of their own original decision in *Roe* v. *Wade*.

Mr. Tribe refers to the most current version of the Hyde amendment. We have had a series of those. Surely, Senator, an awfully large number of persons, including those not pleased with *Roe* v. *Wade*, had forecast that those limiting acts of Congress on funding and then acts of Congress freeing the States to desist from funding and devices of that kind, many of those had been predicted would necessarily also be held unconstitutional.

You know as well as I that they have all been upheld so far. There is to that extent, therefore, a certain chastening within the Court.

The constancy of this apparent incessant and frustrating dialog is not without its therapeutic ramifications. It may very well be that what ultimately best comes out is simply the shared recognition that the country is not without its resources, and the Court from time to time tends to veer in the pattern of decisions in some acknowledgement that that is so.

Mr. TRIBE. Senator East, might I add just one word?

Senator EAST. Yes, certainly.

Mr. TRIBE. I fear that the notion of an activist Court giving rise to legislative reaction of this kind might yield a kind of negative feedback of the sort that the Congress does not truly want. That is, the message, the signal that I believe the U.S. Supreme Court would get from a statute of this kind would not be the kind of chastening signal that my colleague describes in other contests.

Instead, I think it would come to the view that the Congress was willing to pass laws, engage in the solemn activity of lawmaking, almost as a kind of ersatz petition for rehearing, in effect daring the Court to say again what it had already said before.

If that were to happen, I think the Court would give less weight than it ought to give in general to decisions by Congress that a measure ought to be passed. We really ought to cultivate a climate where the Court defers more to Congress than it would if it sees Congress as simply petitioning for rehearing.

Senator EAST. It is a fascinating point, but it seems to me then, Professor Tribe, that you are suggesting we ought to be more confrontational. What I would rather do is be less so and hope, as Professor Van Alstyne is saying, that we would chasten them first of all through the very kinds of hearings that we are having.

They would be sensitive to the very profound political policy impact they have on the American system of government. It is causing enormous reverberations throughout the body politic. We are feeling it in here. Maybe they cannot quite sense it over there in the Supreme Court building, but those of us out in public life, running for public office, involved, hear this all the time.

I would hope that we could have a more modest approach. I do not think that the three branches ought to be flailing one another over the head with their heavy artillery all the time.

I would prefer to let them understand our concerns and perhaps ultimately the greatest cure would be if they would simply show restraint and get the message that they have gone further than they ought to in the policymaking area.

That would be the single greatest thing in the long run that would come out of that. However, since that message does not seem to have been fully communicated, rather than go to extreme measures, we would rather gently nudge them and say there is a problem here, if you will, in the broader sense of sound government, politics, political science. Are you hearing this?

We take a modest response. You make the argument well, but you are saying that in being too modest, they may not get the message. Therefore, you are suggesting that we go to the constitutional amendment.

However, I fear if that were done first, prior to the bill, then as Professor Noonan has already indicated, we will find those who have said you cannot do it by a statute saying. "Yes, you are going the right way, but that is a bad amendment, and that is a bad one, that is a bad one." Sooner or later, I suspect, we would be getting a lot of rhetoric from the same quarter saying really there is nothing you can do.

I come to the conclusion as a political scientist more so than a lawyer that the critical point may well be that they like the policy result of *Roe* v. *Wade*. By saying you cannot cure it by statute, you cannot cure it by constitutional amendment, what they are doing, and it is a very good political ploy—I do not mean that in a calculating Machiavellian way—a very astute way of defending your turf, the status quo, by saying there is not any way you can actually change this, although we certainly respect your right to want to change it and we understand your anxiety over the policy question involved. However, frankly, there is not any practical way to do it.

Congress works a little more unevenly than the judicial branch. We ebb and flow. These distinctions are increasingly looked upon by so many people, in fact increasingly by Congressmen and Senators, as not really sincere. I am not questioning the motives of the people, but they are really sincere constitutional objections. They are really ways and instruments of defending their political turf because they like the policy result of *Roe* v. *Wade*.

Mr. TRIBE. That is what makes it so important to recognize that among the group of scholars who signed that letter there are strong advocates of a human life amendment. There are strong opponents of *Roe* v. *Wade*. There are people who believe *Roe* v. *Wade* was the worst decision in the history of the U.S. Supreme Court.

However, they are united in the view that what you describe as a modest nudge would be seen by the Court as an unmerited kick, and would yield a recoil phenomenon that would not be productive of useful dialog.

Mr. VAN ALSTYNE. Let me add a point, if I may, on that, Senator.

As a professional matter, it is strange for me to be identified with Mr. Tribe because for about the last four or five inquiries before the Senate, I have been on the other side. My view is, for instance, that the States may convene a constitutional convention with far greater ease than many of my more liberal colleagues think.

Indeed, I was before Senator Hatch's committee 3 weeks ago urging the proposition that it would be in the national interest if Congress were to enact a statue which forbade sex and race discrimination across the board. That meant across the board, including no use of race to favor a person, which would inevitably disfavor others.

I take a far more generous view, quite frankly, of the power of Congress to keep from the Federal courts the capacity to decide cases than a good number of my colleagues in the fraternity. But I assure that my professional views do not merely follow the convenience of my preferences as a private citizen. As a private citizen, I would probably also speak resolutely against an amendment that you might propose, but I should certainly not misrepresent the authority of Congress to propose it however it might want to.

One other thing because of the question raised with me by Senator Hatch: In one sense, because the ambition of the bill is merely to restore discretion to each State to deal with this problem rather than to impose a congressional solution, from that perspective, I quite agree that the nature of the proposal that you put before us is a modest one.

In terms of the theory of the device, however, it is really very radical in terms of a role for Congress. I am very serious in speaking that way. If it is constitutional in this case for Congress to tell a State that it has an obligation of a certain kind which it must fulfill under these circumstances, by a mere parity of reason, and with no effort or desire to be sophistic about it, a more radically oriented Congress may easily as well say to each State that we believe you have an obligation to make the quality of life equally well protected for those who possess very little. Therefore, we are mandating by Federal statute that you do the following kinds of

things for the un-well-to-do, that you must provide a certain minimum complement of health care at public expense, that you must provide at State taxpayer's
expense regardless of your other needs not less than so much education for each
person, irrespective of their condition, as it were.

The theory of this, that Congress may describe the obligation of States and,
through its section 5 power, then impose upon the States Affirmative duties to
vindicate these obligations as defined by Congress, has in past years, of course,
been used by the most activist Members of Congress, the least sensitive to the
quality of States rights, to make their own fiscal decisions according to their
discretion.

The theory of the bill, therefore, as distinct from the operative proposal on its
face is one of radical congressional power in the overriding of State autonomy to
allocate the scarcity of resources according to its own best discretion in the
apportionment of those resources.

I think it is one reason on political grounds that some conservative colleagues
of yours who otherwise associate themselves intimately with your concern on the
abortion issue as such may be a little bit diffident about the approach taken in the
bill itself.

Senator EAST. Gentlemen, I appreciate your comments. Since the hour
moves on, I am going to turn over the questioning to my distinguished colleague,
Senator Baucus.

Senator BAUCUS. Thank you, Mr. Chairman.

Mr. Galebach, I would like to clear up, if we could, your understanding of
how this bill would affect State action. My understanding is that the bill, if it is
enacted without any additional State or Federal legislation, would prohibit States
from funding abortions. Is that your understanding, too?

Mr. GALEBACH. In general, except where States had a justification as
compelling as say to prevent the death of a mother.

Senator BAUCUS. In those cases, too, would the bill also prohibit States from
funding clinics that distribute IUD's and morning-after pills in your view?

Mr. GALEBACH. It could very well.

Senator BAUCUS. That is, without additional legislation, this bill, if it passes,
would have the effect of prohibiting States from funding clinics that distribute
IUD's and morning-after pills?

Mr. GALEBACH. There might be some tough legal questions that would come
up as to whether the State could fund other operations of the clinic, but the State
could not fund any device that would terminate a human life after conception.

Senator BAUCUS. Because that would be State action prohibited under the
bill?

Mr. GALEBACH. Yes.

Senator BAUCUS. Would the bill permit a State to ban all abortions?

Mr. GALEBACH. Yes; it would.

Senator BAUCUS. Would it permit a State to ban the use of IUD's and
morning-after pills?

Mr. GALEBACH. It would. As a practical matter, that would take a separate
decision by a State. That is, if a State enacted an antiabortion statute of the type
that were generally in effect before 1973, preventing the destruction of a human
life and making that a crime, it would be impossible to prosecute someone for the

use of an IUD, because you would never know if a life existed and if that life had been terminated.

However, a State could make a separate decision to ban, say, manufacture or production.

Senator BAUCUS. What I am trying to determine is if this bill passes. Whether its effect is to send the status of this question to what it was prior to *Roe* v. *Wade*. My understanding is that the effect of this bill is to place more restrictions on the States than those placed on them prior to *Roe* v. *Wade*. The bill would prohibit States from funding abortions and prohibit States from funding any device which would interfere with development of the fertilized egg.

Mr. GALEBACH. In that sense, but it is important to keep in mind—

Senator BAUCUS. That is the effect, is it not?

Mr. GALEBACH. That is correct, except it is not an infringement of a constitutional right.

Senator BAUCUS. I am not arguing whether it is an infringement of a right or not.

Mr. GALEBACH. OK.

Senator BAUCUS. The point is that the effect of this bill does not reinstate the law prior to *Roe* v. *Wade*. It goes much further.

Mr. GALEBACH. Insofar as it would outlaw State action that terminates a life after conception, it would be different from before *Roe* v. *Wade*.

Senator BAUCUS. Would you agree with that general assessment, too, Mr. Noonan?

Mr. NOONAN. To the extent I have gone into IUD's as a method of preventing pregancy or birth, I have never completely satisfied myself that there is adequate evidence as to how they operate. The problem basically is it is very hard to have clinical tests on human beings. Most of the evidence has come from animals. Animals are always somewhat different from human beings.

I think there is a basic argument as to how these operate.

Senator BAUCUS. If the medical community is unanimous in its belief that the effect of IUD's is to abort or terminate the living organism after conception, then would you agree that the effect of this bill would be to prevent States from funding any actions which would have that effect?

Mr. NOONAN. I am responding to what I think is a hypothetical contrary to what has been established. In the present state of medical knowledge, under present law, I would not answer that affirmatively.

Senator BAUCUS. You were stating earlier that most constitutional scholars say that the Congress has the power to limit inferior court jurisdiction.

Mr. NOONAN. I was saying the courts say that, not scholars.

Senator BAUCUS. Is it true that in some cases the courts have not so held where the effect of the limitation is to preclude someone from gaining a forum to determine a right or address a right?

Mr. NOONAN. I do not know of any Supreme Court precedent that limits the right of Congress.

Senator BAUCUS. In any way?

Mr. NOONAN. To limit an inferior Federal court as to its jurisdiction.

Senator BAUCUS. Would either you, Professor Van Alstyne, or Professor Tribe, have a different view on that point?

Mr. TRIBE. I certainly would. It depends, as is often the case on these matters, on definition, but to suggest that the Supreme Court has somehow granted Congress carte blanche in this area is very misleading, I think.

In one example that I described in my prepared statement, where the Court said that Congress has plenary power over bankruptcy in addition to its supposedly plenary power over lower Federal court jurisdiction, it was a closely divided Court that concluded, only because reproductive rights and family rights were not involved, that Congress did have the power in that case to make a Federal forum unavailable for bankruptcy discharges.

In an early case after the Civil War, the Supreme Court struck down an attempt to exclude certain former members of the Confederacy from practice in the Federal courts despite the fact that one could easily say that Congress, plenary power over the lower Federal courts and those who may appear there certainly includes the power to control and govern who may practice there.

Senator BAUCUS. I would like to read two different professors' views on this. I think professors are like lawyers. Each probably has a different view, but let me read a portion of a letter on this point from former Solicitor General Erwin Griswold pertaining to section 2 of this bill.

He writes in his letter to us as follows:

> Section 2 of S. 158 undertakes to restrict the jurisdiction of inferior Federal courts established under Article III of the Constitution. Although it is not wholly clear, I am inclined to think that this would be held to be unconstitutional in light of all the circumstances under general principles of the separation of powers. On the whole, it could be concluded that this is not really an effort to regulate the jurisdiction of the lower courts, but is rather a congressional effort to overturn a constitutional decision of the Supreme Court of the United States, making it virtually impossible for the issue to come before the Supreme Court by stifling access to the lower courts.

The other letter is from Prof. Charles Alan Wright, who states with respect to this section in this bill:

> I think Congress has very sweeping powers over the jurisdiction of the inferior courts. At the same time, I feel certain that Congress must exercise its power over Federal jurisdiction, as it must its other powers, in a fashion consistent with constitutional limitations. Under such cases as *Hunter* v. *Erickson* and *U.S.* v. *Klein*, I do not think Congress has authority to close the Federal court door in suits arising under laws that prohibit, limit, or regulate abortions, while allowing access to Federal courts to challenges to statutes that permit, facilitate, or aid in the financing of abortions.

Everyone has their own view, but at least those are the views of two professors.

Mr. NOONAN. If I may comment, there certainly has been a lot of professorial speculation—very result oriented, as the chairman has pointed out—not only as to abortion but as to busing. People who do not like Congress entering a field very easily tease out precedents as you heard Professor Tribe tease one out to show that there might be some restriction.

However, the fact is there are not any cases, and the power does not come from a grant of the Supreme Court as Professor Tribe characteristically phrased it, but it comes from the Constitution. The Constitution says that you have the power to establish inferior Federal courts. You have the power to establish them and you have the power to diminish them.

The leading case is still the *Norris-LaGuardia Act* case which is precisely the same kinds of response to abuse of power.

Senator BAUCUS. I was struck earlier with a point that Mr. Van Alstyne made about the role of the Supreme Court in American constitutional law and American Government compared with some countries where there tends to be more instability because the supreme court is not the final arbiter over terms of the constitution.

I think it is a very good point. In fact, it is my understanding that in the last couple of decades, some parliamentary countries are beginning to establish supreme courts as final arbiters of constitutional terms so that there will be more stability in interpretation that had previously occurred in those countries.

Is that accurate? I see a couple of heads nodding.

Mr. TRIBE. Senator Baucus, might I say something in rehabilitation of Charles Alan Wright and Erwin Griswold, although they hardly need it.

Those comments from both of those gentlemen were anything but result oriented. Both of them thought *Roe* v. *Wade* was wrong. Both are quite encouraging of congressional action in this area I believe, but they both reluctantly conclude that this is not the kind of measure that could be sustained.

The fact that there are no precedents precisely in point itself neatly demonstrates what I should have thought our history would otherwise have made quite clear. That is, that on the whole, and I include the Norris-LaGuardia Act precedent, Congress has refrained from manipulating the jurisdiction of the Federal courts in order lopsidely to undo substantive rights of a Constitution kind.

The fact that Congress has not done it helps to explain why the Court has not had to strike it down.

Mr. GALEBACH. Senator Baucus, I wonder if I could read just one sentence from the most recent Supreme Court decision that I have been able to find on this point. I think it is directly on point.

It is a 1973 decision in which Justice White, writing for seven other Justices as well, said that Congress has the sole power of creating inferior Federal courts and of "withholding jurisdiction from them in the exact degrees and character which to Congress may seem proper for the public good."

That is pretty strong language.

As to Dean Griswold's letter, I have the greatest respect also for his legal scholarship, but as a matter of fact, this withdrawal of jurisdiction will not prevent cases from coming to the Supreme Court. They will go up through the State court system. There will be many cases coming up from any State that enacts an antiabortion law.

The whole point of this bill is not to keep the Supreme Court from reviewing those sort of cases. The point is to get those cases up to the Court as soon as possible so that the Court can make a new decision informed by Congress on when human life begins.

Senator BAUCUS. I guess one other question that troubles me is when should Congress try to overrule the Court by statute?

To take an extreme case, in following Senator Moynihan's analogy, what if the Court were to hold the electronic media were protected under the first amendment? Let us assume that we in the Senate do not like radio and TV commentators, but we do like what the New York Times has to say.

Why should Congress not enact a statute that restricts the electronic media if it feels that way?

Mr. GALEBACH. I would like very much to speak to that. I think that is one of the most important questions before us today.

I think as pertains to the human life statute—

Senator BAUCUS. We could arguably pass a statute which has that effect.

Mr. GALEBACH. Yes; the one time when it is most clear to me that Congress can act is when the Supreme Court has declared itself unable for some reason to decide a fundamental question that goes to the constitutional issue. That does not happen very often. It has happened here.

As for Senator Moynihan's examples, the Supreme Court did not leave open any question there. What might be analogous is if the Supreme Court looked at the medium of television and said they did not see any indication that the framers of the first amendment intended to protect television and cannot tell for sure whether television is a news medium and held it unprotected.

I think Congress could then come in and say they do believe television is a news medium, and that changes the first amendment constitutional issue.

That is a rough analogy and there are always problems with analogies, but that is a much closer analogy to the human life bill than the sort of example Senator Moynihan was raising.

Senator BAUCUS. You are saying the Court did not decide when human life begins, and, therefore, asked Congress to make that determination. Is that what you are saying?

Mr. GALEBACH. They did not expressly do so.

Senator BAUCUS. I know they did not.

Mr. GALEBACH. They did declare themselves unable to do it.

Senator BAUCUS. They did not invite Congress to either.

Mr. GALEBACH. The real question is whether a definition of human life is relevant to the question of personhood. The only way we are going to know that for sure is by the Supreme Court reviewing the human life bill.

In *Roe* v. *Wade*, they did not say that it was irrelevant whether unborn children were human beings. They did not say they did not care. They just said they could not decide.

Mr. TRIBE. May I speak to that, Senator Baucus?

Senator BAUCUS. Yes.

Mr. TRIBE. I must say I have heard Mr. Galebach make this argument over and over again. It strikes me as increasingly implausible every time I hear it.

The Supreme Court had the candor and the good grace not to be arrogant about the matter and to say that human life is something we cannot define and something that no government can try to impose.

They had no doubt whatever about the meaning of "person" under the Constitution. They left no opening there. To encourage the Court to conceal its profound doubts about moral and theological matters by saying we will jump into the breach only when they are candid enough to scratch their heads in public seems to be to be an incredibly perverse political and philosophical doctrine. It is a trick. It has nothing to do with what the Court was really holding in *Roe* v. *Wade*.

What the Court was holding was that the State cannot impose its answer. No one has ever suggested that Congress has more power to impose an answer just by virtue of section 5 of the 14th amendment than the States do because Congress is no less limited by the due-process clause just as the States are.

I think that what you are hearing now is just really beside the point.

Mr. GALEBACH. This is a very interesting personal debate because I have heard Professor Tribe say time after time that the Supreme Court held in *Roe* v. *Wade* that Government cannot decide when life begins. The Court did not hold that.

Mr. TRIBE. I did not say that. I said the States.

Mr. GALEBACH. OK, then we agree. They said the judiciary is not in a position to speculate and the States may not decide.

The limitations on the judiciary do not apply necessarily to Congress. There are many questions Congress can decide that the judiciary simply are not in a position to decide. Whether to declare war is the sort of question you will never get a judge to decide, but Congress can decide it.

Senator BAUCUS. Is it not true though that in most cases where the Court did not decide, the Court says or implies directly that this is a question for Congress to decide?

I can think of many cases where the Court stated that this is not a matter for the Court to decide and stated or implied that it is a matter for Congress to decide.

One can read this *Roe* v. *Wade* decision in various ways, I am not trying to argue that it should necessarily be read one way or the other. However, I am not sure whether the Court said that it did not decide this issue because it could not or because it would not.

The English language is not as precise as it could be. Perhaps if we had the Supreme Court sitting here, we could delve more deeply into the recesses of their minds and their reasoning and we could be better able to determine what they meant, if they knew what they meant.

However, I suspect that they said not that they could not but that they would not. I suspect, too, that in their judgment, as a matter of public policy, it would be improper for this decision to be made basically for the reasons that Professor Tribe and others have indicated, I think they felt that the issues involved were so personally anguishing and complex that it would not be right to force a uniform or near uniform solution on the country.

I do not know if that is correct but that is the feeling I get from reading that decision and listening to the debate over it.

Mr. GALEBACH. I agree the Supreme Court did not make it explicit. If they had, we would not have anything to debate here. Therefore, it is left up to us to draw the inferences, but those inferences can be drawn either way. There are good constitutional arguments in favor of saying that the Supreme Court was unable to. The Supreme Court did not say whether or not Congress was able to. It just did not address that issue.

The Supreme Court did not say whether all human life is of equal value, or whether, as Professor Van Alstyne said, blastulas, zygotes, and embryos do not have the same value. All of those questions are open and we are only going to find out the answer to them when the Supreme Court reviews the human life bill.

Senator BAUCUS. I suspect, too, that the law on this subject is going to change the more than medical science advances with respect to the fetus.

Mr. VAN ALSTYNE. I think not, Senator. I know that is a widely held view, but it is arguable. Medical science can already create and bring to term an adult mammal from a single cell. A single cell has all the potential, for a replicated mammal.

I suggest to you it has no bearing on the constitutionality of a State criminal statute which might make it a misdemeanor to dispose of an unfertilized ovum. Nothing other than a mere embarrassment of temporary impedence to medical technology precludes us from taking an ovum under a process of cloning and bringing to term a full-grown adult. The phenomenon of asexual reproduction has already been done with amphibians. It has been done with manageable mammals. It does not make a bit of difference.

If a State wants to try to make a misdemeanor of disposing of an unfertilized ovum, it will not get anywhere insofar as the Constitution is concerned. The fact that medical technology may develop nutrient baths and make it possible to take a 5-week-old embryo and by nurturing it in the extraordinary amniotic chemical fluid of that nurturing bath to bring up a full-grown adult should not make any difference to the outcome of *Roe* v. *Wade* in my opinion.

Senator BAUCUS. Why?

Mr. VAN ALSTYNE Because despite presentations here to the contrary notwithstanding, I just utterly disagree as to the mischaracterization of the holding of the case. The fundamental characterization is that the State has no sufficient interest in this degree of life to compel a woman to go forward with it. Without saying it is not a form or stage of human life, it has no sufficient interest in that life to overbear the prerogative of the woman in respect to her decision not to carry it to term.

Insofar as by way of counterargument to that position, an argument was then made in the case that this degree of life is a "person" under the 14th amendment, then surely the State is able to protect it.

At that stage, the Court simply held that the word "person" in the 14th amendment is not inclusive of such immature forms as an historical and textual matter of 14th amendment interpretation.

Senator BAUCUS. My point is I am wondering if as medical science advances to the point that you are describing, that is if it can take a 5-week-old fetus and place it in an amniotic bath then maybe moralists, ethicists, philosophers, religious leaders might tend to reach some kind of consensus on this issue. At that point, perhaps the Supreme Court will address it. I do not know.

Mr. TRIBE. I think it is instructive that you have disagreement now between the two of us. I agree with you, Senator Baucus. It was, in a way, the genius of the Court's flexible definition of viabilty that left that very possibility open.

The Court was saying that a woman cannot be forced to remain pregnant.

Viability is a variable line. As technology advances to the point where the developing blastula may be preserved and nourished to maturity without imposing an obligation on the woman that she remain pregnant against her will, then viability will have occurred at a much earlier point, and then the Court's decision, without a change of a single word, would mean that the State from that point forward could prevent the destruction of the fetus, not perhaps its removal but its destruction.

It seems to me that in a sense the Court's decision, whatever else might be said about it, anticipated the possible advance of technology that you are describing.

Senator BAUCUS. Mr. Noonan?

Mr. NOONAN. I just wanted to have a chance to reply to your question which I understood was addressed to Mr. Galebach and me as to when Congress should enter in.

I wanted to really address the what seemed to me was the assumption of the question, that you were doing something precedent-breaking and new.

There has been no response at all from my colleagues to my contention that this is a relatively familiar process. Whether it is something that involved Congress acting contrary to a century-old precedent on insurance or a 30-year-old precedent on Federal courts or a 7-year-old precedent on voting rights, Congress has done it.

In this particular area, you have express authorization from the Constitution to do it. Clearly you should not do it all the time. However, on the one hand you have Professor Van Alstyne saying it is a trivial ploy. On the other hand, Professor Tribe is telling you this is an enormously important issue.

It seems to me that, obviously, this is an issue of great importance to many Americans. It is not something where the people are willing to wait for medical science to protect these unborn lives.

The parade of horribles that you got from Senator Moynihan are singularly unpersuasive. He speculates about what might happen if Congress ran wild in a way that is very hard to imagine. You are dealing with a Supreme Court which did run wild, which did overrun the rights of a multitude of human beings.

We are trying to create a means of coping with a real situation.

Mr. TRIBE. I think Professor Noonan owes this body a little more candor when he says: "No one answered." We were talking during the break and I was trying to explain to him why every one of those supposed precedents was radically irrelevant to the matter before us.

I do not want to bore the two of you with it, but I am surprised that he does not share those observations with you.

As to the rest, we cannot conduct this discussion, can we, on the premise that *Roe* v. *Wade* was an abomination and clearly wrong? We have a constitutional process for resolving those things. If anyone thinks that we can bootstrap ourselves into the right answer to these deep questions by simply assuming that the Court went wild and that, of course, then it is OK for this body to do anything, I do not think we can really advance the inquiry that way.

Senator BAUCUS. Mr. Galebach, you do not think, do you, that Congress should simply pass statutes for the sake of issuing advisory opinions to the

Supreme Court? I mean we should be serious about our business here and take our business very responsibly.

Mr. GALEBACH. Absolutely. I think there is one case that Professor Noonan mentioned that is a perfect instructive example. It is certainly not entirely off point. It is the case of literacy tests.

The Supreme Court said that literacy and illiteracy are neutral as to race, creed, and color. That is what the Supreme Court said in 1959. In 1970, Congress said literacy tests are discriminatory and were to be outlawed.

That is contrary to what the Supreme Court had said. Why did the Supreme Court go along with Congress? Why was their mind changed? The reason was that Congress provided findings that showed that given the educational patterns in this country, literacy tests were likely to be discriminatory against black persons.

There is something from the committee report which I would like to read just very briefly which shows the sort of finding that Congress provided to the Court which changed their mind on that constitutional question.

This was a report of the Senate Judiciary Committee on the Voting Rights Act:

> The educational differences between whites and negroes in the areas to be covered by the prohibitions, differences which are reflected in the record before the committee, would mean that equal application of the literacy tests would abridge 15th amendment rights.

That was the finding of Congress. That changed the Supreme Court's mind as to whether literacy tests were discriminatory.

In the human life bill, we have a very similar situation with Congress making findings as to whether unborn children are human beings in the expectation that that will change the Supreme Court's mind in much the same way.

We cannot be absolutely sure it will change the Supreme Court's mind, but there is certainly a good chance based on all the evidence and the legislative history of the 14th amendment.

Mr. VAN ALSTYNE. Senator Baucus, that is flatly wrong. Since I have been passive, I want to assert that. The case comparison is exactly upside down as a matter of fact.

The more appropriate comparison would be if in *Roe* v. *Wade* the woman's case having been heard and the Supreme Court having been more diffident than it was, it might then have concluded that this is a very close case, but we are not prepared to say that the woman's fundamental right has been violated. The grounds are close, but they are not clear enough.

Therefore, we hold against her claim of right, after which, in comparison with the exact case my colleague has presented to you, Congress were to say we have looked at this problem and we have concluded that State laws which so invade the woman's prerogative to decide are, indeed, arbitrary. The Court might then have sustained the act of Congress insofar as it would invalidate State statutes.

The comparison cannot run the other way. If in the first case the Court says this State law is so intrusive that even by the merely modest judicial standard we find the State has itself already violated the 14th amendment, then my colleague's suggestion is Congress can suddenly convert that.

The Congress may not rehabilitate State statutes which in the Court's view are, per se, so arbitrary that they are unconstitutional, although it is true that Congress may sometimes sweep aside State statutes which in the Court's view are not so very arbitrary that section 1 deals with them alone.

His is an inverted use of the *Katzenbach* v. *Morgan* case and there is absolutely no precedent for it. Indeed, in three different cases, the Supreme Court has said that Congress may not rehabilitate State statutes which violate judicial standards of 14th amendment tests. There is not a case to the contrary in the record.

Mr. GALEBACH. I am trying to figure out how Professor Van Alstyne can say that my example is flatly wrong. I assume it is because he is assuming Congress can expand the voting rights of persons, it can expand the privacy rights of women, but it cannot expand the right to life of human beings. I do not see why not.

Moreover, there is nothing in Supreme Court precedents to justify that assumption. The Supreme Court has said Congress can expand 14th amendment rights, but cannot contract them. The human life bill expands the rights of human beings to life.

Mr. VAN ALSTYNE. And contracts those of the woman.

Mr. GALEBACH. That is the question the Supreme Court did not address in *Katzenbach* v. *Morgan*. It did not say what happens when Congress expands one right which has the incidental effect of restricting another right. Maybe it will go one way. Maybe it will go the other. However, to say it is flatly wrong is just going too far.

Mr. VAN ALSTYNE. It is not, but let me help my colleague by quoting from a fragment of the Congressional Globe when the 14th amendment was under consideration. The first draft of the 14th amendment would have left it to Congress to define in both directions the content of protected personal rights under the 14th amendment.

Indeed, in its original form, it did not say anything about "no State shall deprive any person of life, liberty, or property." It said rather that "Congress shall have power to make laws necessary and proper" to secure these rights. That is how it was originally presented in 1866.

There were two kinds of objections that were made to that proposal in 1866. One was that it went too far by giving Congress too much power. The other was that it went too far in leaving it to Congress to determine what personal rights were, after the 14th amendment should be ratified.

When this proposal was recommitted, it was recommitted after a Congressman, as Mr. Hotchkiss among others, said:

> *This amendment proposes to leave it to the caprice of Congress, but I want them secured by constitutional amendment that legislation cannot override. Then, if gentlemen wish to go further and provide by laws of Congress for the enforcement of these rights, I will go with him.*

Respectfully then, under section 1, the language is: "No state shall deprive any person of liberty without due process." The court has said that means a State may not criminalize a woman's prerogative to receive a medically secure abortion within the first two trimesters. That is the minimum floor provided by the language as judicially enforced by the Supreme Court. That is why it is phrased that way: No state shall do that to a woman.

If then Congress wants to protect a woman's rights with regard to abortion even more than that, as by supplying money to assist her or making sure that the needy women are as readily able to secure an abortion as a well-to-do woman, Congress may go further and vindicate that right to an abortion. That is the way the amendment works.

There is a judicially provided minimum floor protection for women according to *Roe* v. *Wade*. If Congress wants to befriend women more than the Court did, Congress may do so, but it may not go below the floor. That is the theory of it. That is the answer to my colleague's strange sense of dilemma here.

Senator EAST. Gentlemen, this was very interesting.

In concluding, I cannot resist bringing to Professor Tribe's attention that Mr. Galebach is, of course, an alumnus of his very distinguished institution and faculty. To some degree, we have to hold you accountable for this young man.

Mr. GALEBACH. Professor Tribe did not have the chance to instruct me.

Mr. TRIBE. I ascertained that he was not in my constitutional law class.

Senator EAST. To some extent we are holding you and your very distinguished institution responsible here. We thought you were doing very well.

Again, we wish to thank all of you for coming. We regret that time closes in on us. It has been very fruitful and productive. We know that you will be available to members of the committee or the staff for additional questions that we might want to submit to you in writing or otherwise. We would look upon your continued counsel as valuable to our ongoing process here.

Again, thank you for coming. If there is no further point to be made, we shall stand adjourned.

[The subcommittee was adjourned at 6:26 p.m.]

Statement of Robert Bork

Mr. BORK. Thank you, Senator.

S. 158 would provide that human life would be deemed to exist from conception. The intended result is to bring 14th amendment protections of human life to bear upon upborn fetuses. The object, as I understand it, is to return to the States the power to regulate abortions that was denied by the Supreme Court in Roe against Wade.

The bill further attempts to remove jurisdiction over abortion cases from the lower Federal courts, if not from the Supreme Court, thus insuring that litigation concerning abortion laws would reach the Supreme Court through the State courts.

It seems to me, in brief, that the bill is constitutional insofar as it deprives the lower Federal courts of jurisdiction but unconstitutional insofar as it attempts to prescribe a rule of decision for the courts under the 14th amendment.

Before coming to the question of constitutionality, I should say that if this bill were enacted and accepted as constitutional it is not at all clear what the results would ultimately be.

States might choose to allow many types of abortions simply by not banning them. Under the premises of S. 158, that would be equivalent to not having a law against some kinds of homicides.

There is at least one Supreme Court decision that suggests that that might be denial of equal protection of the law, but it is highly uncertain whether or not such an attack would succeed today if the State chose not to prohibit some kinds of abortions.

It has been said that the passage of S. 158 would not interfere with private abortions, which seems to me correct since, in such cases, there is no State action.

But it has also been said that the passage of the law would preclude Federal or State funding of abortions. That seems to me not entirely clear. The State courts and ultimately the Supreme Court would have before them under this statute a case involving the clash of two constitutional rights—that of the woman and that of the fetus.

Given the clash of two constitutional rights, it is impossible to say how the Supreme Court would adjust them, and it is entirely possible that the adjustment would produce a constitutional law of abortions very much like the law of *Roe* v. *Wade*.

I mention these matters merely to suggest that S. 158 may not be a cure-all. We do not know what it would become in the hands of the courts even if they accepted it, at least nominally, as constitutional.

I turn now to my doubts that S. 158 is constitutional. Here, I am forced to defend the Supreme Court's ultimate authority to say what the Constitution means against recent decisions of the Supreme Court.

The supporters of S. 158 argue for its constitutionality from a line of cases that seem to cede to Congress a major role in defining the substantive content of the Constitution. There is no doubt that these decisions exist—you have heard about them, and I will mention them only briefly.

In the *Lassiter* case, of course, the Court held that States were constitutionally empowered to use a nondiscriminatory literacy test for voting. Yet, in *Katzenbach* v. *Morgan*, the Court held the Court (Congress) could eliminate literacy in English as a condition for voting by exercising the power granted in section 5 of the 14th amendment.

In *Oregon* v. *Mitchell*, the Court upheld Congress elimination of all literacy tests.

There are other decisions that declare a congressional power to define substantive rights guaranteed by the 13th, the 14th, and 15th amendments, by employing the power to enforce that those amendments have given to Congress.

I would conclude, therefore, that S. 158, which is an attempt by Congress, I think, to define a substantive right given by the Constitution, would be constitutional but for my conviction that each of these decisions represents a very bad and, indeed, pernicius constitutional law.

The power lodged in Congress to enforce constitutional guarantees is the power to provide criminal penalties, redress in civil damage suit, and the like, for violations of those constitutional guarantees, as they are defined by the courts.

The power to enforce is not a power to define the substantive content of the guarantees, themselves. I know of no indication that Congress was given any such power in the legislative history of these amendments and no precedent of the Supreme Court that would uphold any such power until the era of the modern activist Supreme Court.

In these respects, I agree entirely with the dissent of Justice Harlan, joined by Justice Stewart, in *Katzenbach* v. *Morgan* which stated:

> *When recognized State violations of Federal constitutional standards have occurred, Congress is of course empowered by section 5 of the 14th amendment to take appropriate remedial measures to redress and prevent the wrongs. But it is a judicial question whether the condition with which Congress has thus sought to deal is in truth an infringement of the Constitution, something that is the necessary prerequisite to bringing the S5 power into play at all.*

The majority position that Congress can define the substantive content of the 14th amendment works two constitutional revolutions at once. It replaces the Supreme Court with Congress as the ultimate authority concerning the meaning of crucial provisions of the Constitution, and it also replaces State legislatures with Congress for all matters now committed to State legislation.

A National Legislature empowered to define the meaning, for example, of involuntary servitude, privileges, and immunities, due process, equal protection, and the right to vote can void any State legislation on any subject and replace it with a Federal statute.

It is because, I think, S. 158 rests upon the principle of *Katzenbach* v. *Morgan* that I think it is unconstitutional. This places me in a somewhat uncomfortable position.

I am convinced, as I think most legal scholars are, that *Roe* v. *Wade* is, itself, an unconstitutional decision, a serious and wholly unjustifiable judicial usurpation of State legislative authority. I also think that *Roe* v. *Wade* is by no means the only example of such unconstitutional behavior by the Supreme Court.

The fact is that S. 158 proposes a change in our constitutional arrangements no more drastic than that which the judiciary has accomplished over the past 25 years.

I think the question to be answered in assessing S. 158 is whether it is proper to adopt unconstitutional countermeasures to redress unconstitutional action by the Court. I think it is not proper.

The deformation of the Constitution is not properly cured by further deformation. Only if we are prepared to say that the Court has become intolerable in a fundamental, democratic society, and that there is no prospect for getting it to behave properly, should we adopt a principle which contains within it the seeds of the destruction of the Court's entire constitutional role.

I do not think we are at that stage, but if others think we are, then we should be debating not the technicalities of S. 158 and cases such as *Katzenbach* v. *Morgan* but the question of whether we should retain, abandon, or modify the constitutional function of the courts as we have known it since *Marbury* v. *Madison*. That is a legitimate subject for inquiry, but we ought not to arrive at the answer in the narrow context of S. 158 without fully realizing what it is we are really discussing.

Thank you.

Seantor EAST. Thank you, Professor Bork.

[The prepared statement of Professor Bork follows:]

Prepared Statement of Robert Bork

My name is Robert H. Bork. I am the Alexander M. Bickel Professor of Public Law at Yale University. I am pleased to testify on the constitutionality of S. 158 at the Subcommittee's invitation.

S. 158 would provide that human life shall be deemed to exist from conception. The intended result of the law is to bring fourteenth amendment protections of human life to bear upon unborn fetuses. The object, as I understand it, is to return to the states the power to regulate abortions that was denied by the Supreme Court in *Roe* v. *Wade*, 410 U.S. 113 (1973). The bill further attempts to remove jurisdiction over abortion cases from the lower federal courts but not the Supreme Court, thus ensuring that litigation concerning abortion laws would reach the Supreme Court through the state courts.

At the outset I want to say that discussions of constitutionality are often embarrassed by the failure to note the differences, which are sometimes significant, between a prediction of what the Supreme Court will do in fact, what it would do if it followed its own precedents, and what it would do if it followed the Constitution. I will evaluate the bill primarily from the third viewpoint, discussing its validity if the Constitution itself were followed.

From that perspective, it seems to me that the bill is constitutional insofar as it deprives the lower federal courts of jurisdiction but unconstitutional insofar as it attempts to prescribe a rule of decision for the courts under the fourteenth amendment.

Before coming to that, it should be said that if S. 158 were enacted and held constitutional it is not at all clear what the results would be. States might choose to allow many types of abortions simply by not banning them. Under the premises of S. 158 that would be the equivalent of not having a law against some kinds of homicides. There is at least one, perhaps aberrational, Supreme Court decision that suggests the possibility of an equal protection attack on such an arrangement (*Skinner* v. *Oklahoma*, 316 U.S. 535 (1942)), thus requiring the states to outlaw abortions or abandon laws punishing homicide. It is highly uncertain whether or not such an attack would succeed today in this context.

It has been said that passage of S. 158 would not interfere with private abortions, which seems correct since there is in such cases no state action. But it has also been said that passage of the law would preclude federal or state funding of abortions. That seems less clear. The state courts, and ultimately the Supreme Court, would have before them a case involving the clash of two constitutional rights—that of the woman and that of the fetus. The fact that the constitutional right of the woman to an abortion is; the result of judicial legislation, is, in this context, irrelevant. Given the clash of two constitutional rights, it is impossible to say how the Supreme Court would adjust them. It is entirely possible that the adjustment would produce a constitutional law of abortions very much like the law of *Roe* v. *Wade*, 410 U.S. 113 (1973).

I mention these matters merely to suggest that S. 158 may not be a cure-all. We do not know what it would become in the hands of the courts, even if they accepted it, at least nominally, as constitutional.

I turn next to my own doubts that S. 158 is constitutional. Here I am forced to defend the Supreme Court's ultimate authority to say what the Constitution means against recent decisions of the Court. The supporters of S. 158 argue for its constitutionality from a line of Supreme Court decisions that cede to Congress a major role in defining the substantive content of the Constitution. There is no doubt those decisions exist. Since you have heard about them before, I will mention them only briefly.

In *Lassiter* v. *Northampton Election Board*, 360 U.S. 45 (1959), a unanimous Supreme Court held that states were constitutionally empowered to use a non-discriminatory literacy test for voting. Yet in *Katzenbach* v. *Morgan*, 384 U.S. 641 (1966), the Court held that Congress could eliminate literacy in English as a condition for voting by exercising the power granted in Section 5 of the Fourteenth Amendment. In *Oregon* v. *Mitchell*, 400 U.S. 112 (1979), a unanimous Court upheld Congress' elimination of all literacy tests. There are other decisions that declare a congressional power to define substantive rights guaranteed by the thirteenth, fourteenth and fifteenth amendments by employing the granted power to "enforce" the provisions of those amendments. These precedents all uphold the constitutionality of S. 158. I would conclude that S. 158 is constitutional but for my conviction that each of these decisions represents very bad, indeed pernicious, constitutional law.

The power lodged in Congress to "enforce" constitutional guarantees is the power to provide criminal penalties, redress in civil damage suits, and the like, for violations of those constitutional guarantees as they are defined by the courts. It is not a power to define the substantive content of the guarantees themselves. I know of no indication that Congress was given any such power in the legislative history of these amendments, and no precedent of the Supreme Court that would uphold any such power—until the era of the modern, activist, liberal Supreme Court. In testimony here, you have heard cited the 1879 case of *Ex parte Virginia*, 100 U.S. 339 (1879), but that decision does not contemplate any such congressional power to define substance. It held that Congress could make it a federal crime to disqualify persons from jury service on account of race because the fourteenth amendment, as interpreted by the Supreme Court, prohibited such action.

In these respects, I agree entirely with the dissent of Justice Harlan, joined by Justice Stewart, in *Katzenbach* v. *Morgan*, which stated:

> *When recognized state violations of federal constitutional standards have occurred, Congress is of course empowered by S5 to take appropriate remedial measures to redress and prevent the wrongs. (citation omitted)* But it is a judicial question whether the condition with which Congress has thus sought to deal is in truth an infringement of the Constitution, something that is the necessary prerequisite to bringing the S5 power into play at all. *(384 U.S. at 666)*

The majority position in *Katzenbach* v. *Morgan* works two constitutional revolutions at once. It replaces the Supreme Court with Congress as the ultimate authority concerning the meaning of crucial provisions of the Constitution. The majority position also replaces state legislatures with Congress for all matters now committed to state legislation. A national legislature empowered to define the meaning of involuntary servitude, privileges and immunities, due process, equal protection, and the right to vote, which includes all qualification of electors, can void any state legislation on any subject and replace it with a federal statute.

It is because I think S. 158 rests upon the principle of *Katzenbach* v. *Morgan* that I think it unconstitutional.

This places me in a somewhat uncomfortable position. I am convinced, as I think almost all constitutional scholars are, that *Roe* v. *Wade* is an unconstitutional decision, a serious and wholly unjustifiable judicial usurpation of state legislative authority. I also think that *Roe* v. *Wade* is by no means the only example of such unconstitutional behavior by the Supreme Court.

The fact is that S. 158 proposes a change in our constitutional arrangements no more drastic than that which the judiciary has accomplished over twenty-five years. Without any warrant in the Constitution, the courts have required so many basic and unsettling changes in Amrican life and government that a political response was inevitable. Though I do not think it desirable that the political response should succeed in the form this bill takes, the fact of expressed political outrage at such judicial usurpation is in many ways a healthy development in our constitutional democracy.

The judiciary have a right, indeed a duty, to require basic and unsettling changes, and to do so, despite any political clamor, when the Constitution, fairly interpreted, demands it. The trouble is that nobody believes the Constitution allows, much less demands, the decision in *Roe* v. *Wade* or in dozens of other cases of recent years. Not even those most in sympathy with the results believe that, as demonstrated by a growing body of literature attempting to justify the courts' performance on grounds of moral philosophy rather than of legal interpretation. Such justifications will not wash. The judiciary's legitimate power to set aside the decisions and actions of elected representatives and politically responsible officials comes from the Constitution alone and is limited to a fair interpretation of the Constitution.

The question to be answered in assessing S. 158 is whether it is proper to adopt unconstitutional countermeasures to redress unconstitutional action by the Court. I think it is not proper. The deformation of the Constitution is not properly cured by further deformations. Only if we are prepared to say that the Court has become intolerable in a fundamentally democratic society and that there is no prospect whatever for getting it to behave properly, should we adopt a principle which contains within it the seeds of the destruction of the Court's entire constitutional role. I do not think we are at that stage. But if others think we are, then we should be debating not the technicalities of S. 158 and cases such as *Katzenbach* v. *Morgan*, but the question of whether we should retain, abandon, or modify the constitutional function of the courts as we have known it since *Marbury* v. *Madison*, 1 Cranch 137 (1803). That is a legitimate subject for inquiry, but we ought not arrive at the answer in the narrow context of S. 158 without fully realizing what we are really discussing.

Seantor EAST. Professor Nagel?

Statement of Robert Nagel

Mr. NAGEL. Mr. Chairman, I wish to address this question: Does section 1 of the human life bill exceed congressional authority on the grounds that it would reverse Supreme Court decisions that interpret the Constitution? Or, to use Professor Bork's phrase, is this bill an "unconstitutional countermeasure."

My conclusion is that, although there are sound reasons to vote against the bill, a fear that it is inconsistent with the role of the Supreme Court in our constitutional system is not one of them.

In deeming the fetus to be a person for certain purposes under the 14th amendment, the bill might appear to conflict with the Supreme Court's opinion in *Roe* v. *Wade* because that case held that a fetus is not a person within the meaning of the 14th amendment.

However, in *Roe* the Court did not hold that it is beyond the power of Congress to extend some of the protections of the due process clause to fetuses. The issue that the Court decided was whether the clause, as a self-executing provision, protects fetuses. These are two distinct legal issues.

The Court, quite properly, said nothing in *Roe* about congressional enforcement authority because that issue was not relevant to anything in the case. However, a number of Supreme Court decisions do make it clear that Congress is authorized by section 5 of the 14th amendment to extend protection beyond what the clauses, as self-executing provisions, would require. The proper exercise of this power amounts to the enforcement of the Constitution, not its amendment.

As you know, Supreme Court decisions defining the outer limits of what is proper under section 5 are complicated and there is much academic debate on the matter.

I read the cases to suggest that you would be acting responsibly and even cautiously if you respect two principles: Congress must act appropriately to expand rather than constrict established 14th amendment protections, and Congress may not expand protection in a way that conflicts with other constitutional rights and values. I will discuss each of these two principles.

Expansion of Constitutional Protection

There can be no doubt that the 14th amendment protects persons against the deprivation of life by the State without due process of law. The human life bill appears to expand this protection because it protects persons, who would have been born but for State-aided abortions, from the deprivation of their lives before birth.

It also might be thought to expand the protection by guarding against a gradual erosion of the moral inhibition against destroying human life or by guarding against the possibility that at least some aborted fetuses might be human lives.

Whatever I might personally think of these rationales, it seems to me clear that the bill expands, it certainly does not constrict, the protection of life afforded by the due process clause.

It is certainly possible that the Supreme Court would hold that there is no reasonable or appropriate relationship between protecting the existence of something that might be a human life but which is not a person within the meaning of the 14th amendment and protecting the lives of such persons.

The Court might, for example, find fears about a possible connection between State-supported abortions and an increased willingness of officials to take the lives of persons to be too conjectural. But this is simply a possibility, and no prior decision of the Court requires this conclusion.

In fact, the Court in the past has afforded wide deference to congressional determinations about the appropriate degree of prophylactic protection that should be provided 14th amendment rights.

Moreover, in *Roe* v. *Wade* the Court limited the States' authority to prohibit abortions, not because of any finding that such prohibitions would not in fact protect potential lives, but because at some stages of pregnancy this interest was thought to be outweighed by the woman's right to privacy.

I do not deny that the mood and the tone and the emphasis of the Court's opinion in *Roe* might support a prediction that it would be inclined to reject possible empirical and judgmental bases of this bill. Nor do I deny that the decisions on Congress section 5 power would leave substantial room for such a rejection.

But if you are convinced that the protection of fetuses is appropriately related to the goal of protecting the lives of persons, then I believe it is within your constitutional authority to enact the legislation notwithstanding conjectures about the Court's possible response.

To vote against the bill merely because of the possibility that the Supreme court might disagree with your judgment would be to shift your own constitutional responsibilities on to the shoulders of the Justices. It would elevate, not the Court's constitutional interpretations, but its presumed inclinations to the status of dogma, binding the thinking and the judgment of members of a coequal branch of Government who have their own constitutional responsibilities to perform.

Moreoever, it would be to deprive the Court of the benefit of your empirical findings and your moral judgments, both of which the court has repeatedly said are useful to it in the performance of its duties.

Consistency with Other Constitutional Values

Even if it appropriately expands a 14th amendment protection, Congress authority under section 5 may not, as I said, be used in a way that conflicts with some other constitutional value.

This bill might be thought to conflict with the right of a woman to decide to obtain an abortion as enunciated in *Roe* v. *Wade*. However, operationally this bill, on its own, would only prevent States from aiding or promoting abortions and thus would leave women free to obtain abortions privately.

I know of no Supreme Court decision that establishes a constitutional right to receive State aid or support in obtaining abortions.

Nevertheless, it might be thought that the bill is unconstitutional because its objective is to authorize States to restrict the private abortion decision and thus diminish a constitutional right.

I believe that it is very likely—almost certain—that such restrictive abortion laws enacted by States in response to this bill would be struck down by the Court as violative of the right to privacy. I think this because the Court has already demonstrated how it balances the interest in privacy and the State's interest that are served by prohibiting abortion, including the interests in protecting potential life.

The new interests that a State might assert after passage of this bill are sufficiently close to the interest in protecting potential life that I doubt that the Court's calculus would change. But the probable unconstitutionality of such State statutes would not make the human life bill itself unconstitutional.

The bill would have the consequences of restricting the right to privacy only if the State should act to restrict that right, and then only if the Supreme Court were to decide to approve such restrictions. In that case, the legal right would not have been restricted but would have been redefined by the Supreme Court.

Such redefinition, while unlikely, is possible because of the nature of the Court's decision in *Roe*. That decision specifically held that the right to abortion is not absolute and may be restricted by the States, depending upon the balance between the severity of the restriction and the importance of the State's interest.

The Court, then, would not directly violate the rationale underlying *Roe* if it were to reassess its balance of those rights and interests when new information is received about their relative weights or when they are characterized or evaluated differently.

State reliance on congressional determinations about when human life begins or about the importance of protecting fetuses would not, then, be an affront to judicial review. It would enable the Court to engage in the kind of assessment process that, in *Roe*, it declared to be constitutionally relevant.

The new assessment of interests might be thought redundant and easy since the Court would already have made a closely related but not identical assessment. Or, on the contrary, it might be thought exasperating and difficult since the Court might feel impelled to explain more fully the bases of its assessments in *Roe*.

But unless the Court has to be protected from the frustrations of the task of judicial review, I cannot see how such factors could make the congressional objective improper.

Propriety of Disagreement with the Court

It might be charged, however, that the congressional objective is not only to precipitate an opportunity for judicial reassessment but also specifically to induce a reversal of *Roe* v. *Wade*. But this is merely to say that the bill might have been prompted by disagreement with the Court. The constitutional system depends upon disagreement.

We know that Supreme Court reasoning is not too precious nor too perfect to be reconsidered because the Court does so frequently.

When this reconsideration might appropriately be affected by a differing congressional evaluation of related issues, the Court ought not to be deprived of that information simply because the congressional evaluation is accompanied by a larger disagreement with the Court.

It is precisely when others think that it is wrong that the Supreme Court might be wrong, and it is then that it, like the other branches of Government, needs to know and to face up to that disagreement.

Unless the Court's direction and emphasis in its decisions amounts to a kind of civil religion, disagreement manifested in a statute that is otherwise within congressional power is not heretical. It is helpful in a system that assumes human fallibility and guards against it with institutional checks.

Seantor EAST. Thank you, Professor Nagel.

[The prepared statement of Professor Nagel follows:]

Prepared Statement of Robert Nagel

I wish to address this question: Does section 1 of the Human Life Bill exceed congressional authority on the grounds that it would reverse Supreme Court decisions that interpret the Constitution? My conclusion is that, although there are sound reasons to vote against the Bill[1] a fear that it is inconsistent with the role of the Supreme Court in our Constitutional system is not one of them.

In deeming the fetus to be a person for certain purposes under the 14th amendment, this Bill might appear to conflict with the Supreme Court's opinion in *Roe* v. *Wade* because that case held that a fetus is not a person within the meaning of the 14th amendment. However, in *Roe* the Court did not hold that it is beyond the power of Congress to extend some of the protections of the due process clause to fetuses. The issue that the Court decided was whether the clause, as a self-executing provision, protects fetuses. These are two distinct legal issues. For example, factors such as the intent of the framers of the 14th amendment or the place of social fact-finding might bear differently on congressional authority to enforce the clause than on judicial authority to interpret the words of the clause. The Court quite properly said nothing in *Roe* about congressional enforcement authority because that issue was not relevant to anything in that case.

However, a number of Supreme Court decisions do make it clear that Congress is authorized by section 5 of the 14th amendment to extend protection beyond what the clauses, as self-executing provisions, would require.[2] The proper exercise of this power amounts to the enforcement of the Constitution, not its amendment. As you know, Supreme Court decisions defining the outer limits of what is "proper" under section 5 are complicated, and there is much academic debate on the matter. I read the cases to suggest that you would be acting responsibly and cautiously if you respect two principles: (1) Congress must act appropriately to expand, not constrict, established 14th amendment protections; and (2) Congress may not expand protection in a way that conflicts with other constitutional rights and values. I will discuss each of these principles in turn:

(1) There can be no doubt that the 14th amendment protects persons against the deprivation of life by the state without due process of law. The Human Life Bill appears to expand this protection because it protects persons, who would have been born but for state-aided abortions, from the deprivation of their lives before birth. It also might be thought to expand the protection by guarding against a gradual erosion of the moral inhibition against destroying human life or by guarding against the possibility that at least some aborted fetuses might be "human lives". Whatever I might personally think of these rationales, it seems to

---

[1] First, the Bill would nationalize the issue of state support of abortion, a matter that in our federal system is more appropriately left to the states. Second, the Bill is easily subject to misunderstanding at the local level and might be interpreted as an attack on the Supreme Court or as an invitation to adopt irresponsible restrictions on abortion. For example, health regulations or parental notification rules might be rescinded on the ground that states ought not impliedly endorse the destruction of "persons" by permissive regulation. Third, with the issues so volatile, the Bill might provoke the Supreme Court to unduly limit the section 5 authority of Congress in an effort to protect its own institutional authority and prestige.

[2] Katzenbach v. Morgan, 384 U.S. 641 (1966); Rome v. United States 100 S.Ct. 548 (1980); Fullilove v. Klutznick, 100 S.Ct. 275 (1980).

me clear that the Bill expands, certainly does not constrict, the protection of life afforded by the due process clause.

Now it is certainly possible that the Supreme Court would hold that there is no reasonable or appropriate relationship between protecting the existence of something that might be a human life (but which is not a "person" within the meaning of the 14th amendment) and protecting the lives of "persons". The Court might for example, find fears about a possible connection between state-supported abortions and an increased willingness of officials to take the lives of "persons" to be too conjectural. But this is simply a possibility, and no prior decision of the Court requires this conclusion. In fact, the Court in the past has afforded wide deference to congressional determinations about the degree of prophylactic protection that should be provided 14th amendment rights. Moreover, in *Roe* v. *Wade* the Court limited the state's authority to prohibit abortions, not because of any finding that such prohibitions would not in fact protect potential lives, but because at some stages of pregnancy this interest is outweighed by the women's right to privacy.

I do not deny that the mood and tone and emphasis of the Court's opinion in *Roe* might support a prediction that it would be inclined to reject possible empirical and judgmental bases of this Bill, nor do I deny that decisions on Congress's section 5 power leave substantial room for such a rejection. But if you are convinced that the protection of fetuses is appropriately related to the goal of protecting the lives of persons, then I believe it is within your constitutional authority to enact the legislation notwithstanding conjecture about the Court's possible response. To vote against the Bill merely because of the possibility that the Supreme Court might disagree with your judgment would be to shift your own constitutional responsibilities onto the shoulders of the Justices. It would elevate, not the Court's constitutional interpretation, but its presumed inclinations to the status of dogma, binding the thinking and judgment of members of a co-equal branch of government who have their own constitutional responsibilities to perform. Moreover, it would be to deprive the Court of the benefit of your empirical findings and your moral judgments, both of which the Court has repeatedly said are useful to it in the performance of its duties.

(2) Even if it appropriately expands a 14th amendment protection, Congress's authority under section 5 may not be employed in a way that conflicts with some other constitutional value. This Bill might be thought to conflict with the right of a woman to decide to obtain an abortion as enunciated in *Roe* v. *Wade*. However, operationally this Bill on its own would only prevent states from aiding or promoting abortions and thus would leave women free to obtain abortions privately. I know of no Supreme Court decision that establishes a constitutional right to receive state aid or support in obtaining abortions.

Of course, it is possible to think of arguments to support an extension of the right to privacy to include some types of state support. Such a development would make this Bill unconstitutional but I do not know of any case that requires this development and there are some that suggest it is unlikely.[3] So the most that can be said is that the Bill might conflict with the right to privacy if the decisional law changes in significant ways.

---

[3] Maher v. Roe, 432 U.S. 464 (1977); Harris v. McRae, 100 S.Ct. 2671 (1980).

Nevertheless, it might be thought that the Bill is unconstitutional because its objective is to authorize states to restrict the private abortion decision and thus diminish a constitutional right. I believe that it is very likely, almost certain, that such restrictive abortion laws enacted by states in response to this Bill would be struck down by the Court as violative of the right to privacy. I think this because the Court has already demonstrated how it balances the interest in privacy and the states' interests that are served by prohibiting abortion, including the interest in protecting potential life. The new interests that a state might assert after passage of this Bill are sufficiently close to the interest in protecting potential life that I doubt that the Court's calculus would change.

But the probable unconstitutionality of such state statutes would not make the Human Life Bill itself unconstitutional. The Bill would have the consequence of "restricting" the right to privacy only if the states should act to restrict that right and then only if the Supreme Court were to decide to approve such restrictions. In that case, the legal right would not have been restricted but would have been re-defined by the Supreme Court. Such re-definition, while unlikely, is possible because of the nature of the Court's decision in *Roe*. That decision specifically held that the right to abortion is not absolute and may be restricted by the states depending upon the balance between the severity of the restriction and the importance of the state's interests. The Court, then, would not directly violate the rationale underlying *Roe* if it were to re-assess its balance of those rights and interests when new information is received about their relative weights or when they are characterized or evaluated differently. State reliance on congressional determinations about when human life begins or about the importance of protecting fetuses would not, then, be an affront to judicial review. It would enable the Court to engage in the kind of assessment process that in *Roe* it declared constitutionally relevant. The new assessment of interests might be thought redundant and easy, since the Court would already have made a closely related, but not identical, assessment. Or—on the contrary—it might be thought exasperating and difficult, since the Court might feel impelled to explain more fully the bases of its assessments in *Roe*. But unless the Court has to be protected from the frustrations of the task of judicial review, I cannot see how such factors could make the congressional objective improper.

It might be charged, however, that the congressional objective is not only to precipitate an opportunity for a judicial reassessment but also specifically to induce a reversal of *Roe* v. *Wade*. But this is merely to say that the Bill might have been prompted by disagreement with the Court. The constitutional system depends on disagreement. We know that Supreme Court reasoning is not too precious nor too perfect to be reconsidered, because the Court does so frequently. When this reconsideration might appropriately be affected by a differing congressional evaluation of related issues, the Court ought not be deprived of that information simply because the congressional evaluation is accompanied by a larger disagreement with the Court. It is precisely when others think it is wrong that the Supreme Court might be wrong. And it is then that it, like the other branches of government, needs to know and to face up to that disagreement. Unless the Court's direction and emphasis in its decisions amounts to a kind of civil religion, disagreement manifested in a statute that is otherwise within congressional power is not heretical. It is helpful in a system that assumes human fallibility and guards against it with institutional checks.

In summary, let me put my conclusion in context. I believe that you are considering this Bill against a backdrop of increasing and unhealthy over-emphasis throughout our system on the role of the Supreme Court. Many of the framers of our Constitution and some of our most distinguished leaders have believed that constitutional decision-making should be shared among the branches of the government.[4] Many scholars have warned that the crucial importance of the courts in our system should not be exaggerated so that the judiciary becomes the exclusive source of constitutional meaning.[5] Yet there is an increasingly wide-spread tendency in the public and among some members of Congress and even on the Supreme Court to regard the Court as the only legitimate source of constitutional meaning.[6] I think that fears about this Bill's incompatibility with judicial review extend even this inflated view of the Court's role and would necessarily elevate its statements from law to orthodoxy.

As Professor Jaffe observed,

> *There will be and there should be popular response to the Supreme Court . . .; not just the "informed" criticism of law professors but the deep-felt, emotion-laden. . . reaction of the laity. This is so because more than any court in the modern world the Supreme Court "makes policy" and is at the same time so little subject to formal democratic control . . .*[7]

The Supreme Court is an important arbitor of Constitutional meaning and is due great respect. But this Bill would not be incompatible with its function.

Senator EAST. Professor Cox?

Statement of Archibald Cox

Mr. Cox. Mr. Chairman and Senator Baucus, may I first thank the subcommittee and say that I appreciate this opportunity to appear and state my views?

I wish to submit three points to the subcommittee:

First, the enactment of section 1 of S. 158 which, if I understand it correctly, attempts to overrule the Supreme Court decision in *Roe* v. *Wade* by a simple legislative majority in both Houses would be an unconstitutional nullity.

Second, in my judgment, section 2, which would deprive the inferior Federal courts of power to interfere by injunction or declaratory judgment with the operation of State antiabortion laws, is of questionable constitutionality. I cannot

[4] See G. Gunther, Constitutional Law Cases and Materials, 25–34 (10th ed.); D. Morgan, Congress and the Constitution, 45–89 (1966).

[5] E.g., Gunther, "Judicial Hegemony and Legislative Autonomy: The *Nixon* Case and the Impeachment Process," 22 U.C.L.A. L. Rev. 30 (1974); Sandalow, "Comments on Powell v. McCormack," 17 U.C.L.A. L. Rev. 1 (1969); Wechsler, "The Courts and the Constitution," 65 Colum. L. Rev. 1001 (1965); Tr   American Constitutional Law, 27–33, 271–272.

[6] See D. Morgan, Congress and the Constitution, 335–337 (1966). See also Cooper v. Aaron, 358 U.S. 1 (1958); Powell v. McCormack, 395 U.S. 486 (1969); United States v. Nixon, 418 U.S. 683 (1974).

[7] Jaffe, "Impromptu Remarks," 76 Harv. L. Rev. 1111 (1963).

say categorically that it is unconstitutional, but I do not think one can responsibly say categorically that it is constitutional.

Third, and most important, even if S. 158 is technically within the power of Congress to enact, both sections should be rejected as radical and dangerously unprincipled attacks upon what I see as the very foundations of our constitutionalism.

The first point is elaborated on at length in my statement, and I would like simply to make one point orally. That is that the decisions in *Katzenbach* v. *Morgan* and other cases under section 5 of the 14th amendment, in my judgment, give no support whatever to an attempt to change the meaning of the Constitution, to redefine the words used in the Constitution, by simple legislative majority.

Because some of my writings about those cases have been quoted a good deal by the supporters of S. 158, I would like to quote a passage written 10 years ago before *Roe* v. *Wade* was decided and long before this controversy came up.

> *Nothing in* Morgan *suggested that the Court should defer to Congress in the process of deriving the applicable legal standard from the document and other sources of law; the opinion seemed to require Congress to apply the same standard as the Court, merely leaving it free to apply the standard differently when the application turned upon "questions of fact."*

S. 158 does not apply the same legal standard as the Court established in *Roe* v. *Wade*. S. 158 would reject the Court's standard by enacting that "persons" shall include all human life, as defined therein, which meant from the moment of conception, thereby including the unborn.

Again, in *Roe* v. *Wade*, the Court held that the woman's freedom to choose during the first two trimesters of pregnancy whether she wished to carry an unborn child until birth is constitutionally superior to any interest in or of the fetus up to the time of viability, regardless of when life may begin.

S. 158 seems to me to reject the legal standard also. It adopts one view of when life begins and then declares, contrary to the existing law, that its view of when life begins shall be controlling under the 14th amendment.

I would also wish to emphasize a little bit my third point: to wit, that the bill, even if technically within the power of Congress, should be rejected as an unprincipled—I think it can properly be called a radical—attack upon the foundations of our Constitution.

We ought to remember that the ultimate bulwarks of liberty in the United States are the Bill of Rights and the 14th amendment, as interpreted and applied by an independent judiciary, headed by the Supreme Court of the United States.

Over the years, a large number of decisions have provoked strong, shortrun political or popular opposition. Sometimes this has produced clamor for legislation.

Over the years, a few decisions have proved clearly wrongheaded, and perhaps *Roe* v. *Wade* is such a case. I, myself, wrote critically of *Roe* v. *Wade* a little while after the decision came down.

Wrongheaded decisions can be changed by time and debate or by constitutional amendment. But the very function of the Constitution and Court is to put

LEGAL SECTION 555

individual liberties beyond the reach of both congressional majorities and popular clamor.

Any principle which permits Congress, with the approval of the President, to nullify one constitutional right protected by the Constitution, as interpreted by the Court—that principle would sanction the nullification of other. That is why I say that the principle of S. 158 is exceedingly dangerous, and I can only call it radical.

I say this because, as I explained a moment ago, S. 158 simply seeks to substitute definitions of constitutional terms adopted by legislative majorities, with the approval of the President, for the terms in the Constitution.

Even if the proabortion decisions are wrong, it would be worse to accept the principle that bare majorities in the House and Senate, with the approval of the President, can change the Constitution. Indeed, it is worth taking just a minute to recall how long a struggle it was to come by that principle.

Our forefathers, in the latter part of the 18th century, came to the view that there should be some individual liberties that were beyond the power of any government, not just beyond the power of kings, not just beyond the power of elected executives, but most particularly beyond the power of legislative majorities.

At first, they did not know how to secure this, and I have quoted in my written statement some of their rather plaintive recitals, but then they did come to the view that you could do three things: (1) write down those basic liberties, (2) treat what was written down as law administered by the judiciary like other law, and, (3) maintain the independence of the judiciary.

James Madison, when the Bill of Rights was recommended to the States by the Congress, wrote: "Independent tribunals of justice will consider themselves in a peculiar manner the guardians of those rights. They will be an impenetrable bulwark against every assumption of power"—improper power—"in the Legislature as well as the Executive."

It is also worth remembering that throughout our history there have been attacks on this principle. The first came from the Jeffersonian Virginians when they sought to impeach, first, Samuel Chase and then John Marshall.

In the 1820's, the proponents of State sovereignty sought to take away the power of the Supreme Court to review State court decisions.

After the Civil War, the radical Republicans toyed with the notion of depriving the Supreme Court of jurisdiction.

There was more talk of that kind later. In 1937, President Franklin Roosevelt proposed to pack the Supreme Court with new Justices. The McCarthyites of the 1950's unsuccessfully sought to presuade Congress to limit Supreme Court jurisdiction over various programs aimed at subversives. And in 1964 some Senators and Representatives sought to deprive the courts of jurisdiction to enforce the one-man, one-vote rule.

But always in the past, despite their discontent with a particular decision, the American people and the Congress have rejected those attacks as dangerously unprincipled, in the sense that if the principle were supported by such a precedent, they would endanger a bulwark of liberty.

So I urge the subcommittee now, and then later the full committee, to reject S. 158.

Senator EAST. Thank you, Professor Cox.

[The prepared statement of Professor Cox follows:]

Prepared Statement of Archibald Cox

I appreciate the opportunity to present my views on S. 158, the bill to provide that human life shall be deemed to exist from conception. I wish to develop three points.

First, enactment of Section 1 of S. 158, which attempts to overrule the constitutional decision of the Supreme Court of the United States in *Roe* v. *Wade*, 410 U.S. 113 (1973) by a simple legislative majority would be an unconstitutional nullity.

Second, Section 2, which would deprive the inferior federal courts of power to interfere by injunction or declaratory judgement with the operation of State anti-abortion laws is of questionable constitutionality.

Third, even if S. 158 is technically within the power of Congress to enact, both sections should be rejected as radical and dangerously unprincipled attacks upon the foundations of our constitutionalism.

It may be appropriate to add that I hold no brief for the Supreme Court's decision in *Roe* v. *Wade*. My published comments have been critical. Cox, *The Role of the Supreme Court in American Government*, 51–55, 112–114.

I. Section 1. of S. 158 is Unconstitutional

S. 158, Section 1 is—in both form and function—an entirely novel effort to change the meaning of the Constitution by an Act of Congress enacted by simple majorities. If S. 158, Section 1 became law, the resulting statute would not itself create any legal rights or impose any legal duties; it would not itself require anyone to do anything, nor would it forbid anyone to do anything. Apparently, the theory is that the Fourteenth Amendment as newly interpreted by Congress would be the operative legal mandate. Because no previous Congress ever enacted a similar measure, it is exceedingly difficult either to discern the purposes or to predict the consequences. They seem to fall under three heads.

First, S. 158, Section 1—if constitutional—would apparently have the effect of modifying the Fourteenth Amendment so as to make the Fourteenth Amendment prohibit any form of State information, counselling or other assistance to any person to be used to interfere with the development of the human fetus and the birth of a child. The Fourteenth Amendment, Section 1, provides:

> *nor shall any State deprive any person of life, liberty or property without due process of law.*

S. 158 defines "person" to include any unborn person from the moment of conception; it says that "life" shall "be deemed" to commence at the moment of conception. Reading these definitions into the Fourteenth Amendment, the Amendment would then provide that no State shall deprive an unborn person of "life" without due process of law. Under familiar authority the State would be sufficiently involved in such a deprivation of life to violate the Amendment if it furnished any facilities or financial assistance for abortion, or if any State official or employee took part in an abortion. *Cf. Burton* v. *Wilmington Parking Authority*, 365 U.S. 715 (1961); *McGlotten* v. *Connally*, 338 F. Supp. 448 (D.D.C. 1972).

Conceivably, some justifications for abortion might be regarded as "due process of law," but I would suppose that any honest application of S. 158, Section 1—if constitutional—would allow a State to justify taking the life of the "unborn" only under the rare circumstances justifying taking the life of a person who has been born.

In response, one might argue that Congress could not possibly be so foolish as to think that it has power simply to redefine the words used in the Constitution and, therefore, must be supposed to have intended S. 158, Section 1, to have some independent operative effect imposing statutory restrictions upon State action. Even if a court were to reach that result in the absence of any words declaring operative rights or duties, the effect would be the same. S. 158, Section 1 would then put the States under a statutory obligation not to provide facilities or financial assistance or other aid to abortion.

Second, S. 158, Section 1—if enacted and constitutionally operative—may have the effect of requiring every State to enact and enforce against private individuals and organizations the most rigidly absolute of anti-abortion laws. The argument might take two forms.

One branch would assert that a State's failure to provide for unborn persons the legal protection customarily available for all others is itself a form of "deprivation."

The second branch would rest upon the Equal Protection Clause:

> *nor (shall any State) deny to any person within its jurisdiction the equal protection of the laws.*

Under S. 158, Section 1 an unborn fetus is a "person." The argument would therefore be that to deny to those persons the same police and legal protection against destruction of life which is available to other persons is to deny the unborn the equal protection of the laws.

One possible answer to the second branch of the argument is that S. 158 seeks to declare that "life" exists from the moment of conception and that the unborn are persons only for the purposes of the Due Process Clause and not for the purposes of the Equal Protection Clause. This is a curious view of "life"—for some purposes it exists from the moment of conception but for other purposes life begins only upon birth—and an equally curious view of the meaning of person—sometimes the unborn but other times only the already born. But perhaps those are the views of the draftsmen and should be given effect in predicting the legal consequences of S. 158.

Third, S. 158, Section 1 seeks to provide State and lower federal courts with grounds for refusing to follow *Roe* v. *Wade*, and if possible, to induce the Supreme Court of the United States to reach a contrary decision.

The only imaginable source of congressional authority to enact such legislation is Section 5 of the Fourteenth Amendment, which provides:

> *The Congress shall have power to enforce this article by appropriate legislation.*

The two decisions putting the broadest interpretation upon the "power to enforce. . . by appropriate legislation" are *South Carolina* v. *Katzenbach*, 383 U. S.301 (1964) and *Katzenbach* v. *Morgan*, 384 U.S. 641 (1966). But those decisions, even when read as broadly as I have suggested,[1] do not sustain the constitutionality of S. 158.

In *South Carolina* v. *Katzenbach* the Court upheld the power of Congress to outlaw the use of a literacy test for voting in State elections. Literacy tests themselves had been held not to violate the Fourteenth Amendment where the test was fair on its face and there had been no judicial finding of racial discrimination. *Lassiter* v. *Northampton*, 360 U.S. 45 (1959). South Carolina's chief argument was that the "power to enforce" under Section 2 of the Fifteenth Amendment is confined to preventing or redressing illegal conduct and cannot be used as a source of authority to enact prophylactic measures. The United States replied that since Section 2 gives Congress the same broad discretion in enacting measures reasonably adapted to preventing abridgement of the right to vote by reason of race or color as the "necessary and proper" clause confers upon Congress in regulating local activities where appropriate for protecting interstate commerce, Congress was not confined to dealing with discrimination in voting but might regulate or prohibit any conduct which created a danger of discrimination:

> *Congress may employ means which, "although not themselves within the granted power, were nevertheless deemed appropriate aids to the accomplishment of some purpose within an admitted power of the national government." [Brief for Defendant at 75, South Carolina v. Katzenbach, 383 U.S. 301 (1966), quoting United States v. Darby, 312 U.S. 100, 121 (1941)].*

The Court accepted this broad interpretation:

> *As against the reserved powers of the States, Congress may use any rational means to effectuate the constitutional prohibition of racial discrimination in voting. (383 U.S. at 324.)*

"The basic test to be applied in a case involving S. 2 of the Fifteenth Amendment," the Chief Justice declared, "is the same as in all cases concerning the express powers of Congress in relation to the reserved powers of the States"; and he then quoted Chief Justice Marshall's classic expression:

> *Let the end be legitimate, let it be within the scope of the constitution, and all means which are appropriate, which are plainly adapted to that end, which are not prohibited, but consistent with the letter and spirit the constitution, are constitutional. (Id. at 326.)*

In effect, therefore, *South Carolina* v. *Katzenbach* upheld the power of Congress to prohibit conduct which is not unconstitutional—the use of a literacy test—under circumstances in which the conduct is likely to lead to racial

---

[1] See Cox, *Constitutional Adjudication and the Promotion of Human Rights*, 80 Harv. L. Rev. 91 (1966). Cox, The Role of the Supreme Court in American Government.

discrimination violating an established constitutional right—there, the right of citizens to vote regardless of race or color.

The decision in *South Carolina* v. *Katzenbach* gives no support to S. 158 because S. 158 does not seek to protect any established constitutional right. On the contrary, S. 158 seeks by legislative definition of "life" and "person" to create new constitutional rights. Thus, although S. 158 apparently would prohibit conduct which is not otherwise unconstitutional—State aid to any interference with the natural development of a fetus—the analogy to *South Carolina* v. *Katzenbach* breaks down because S. 158 does not and cannot impose the prohibition in aid of an established Fourteenth Amendment right. A fetus is not a "person" under the established constitutional meaning of the word. *Roe* v. *Wade* 410 U.S. 113, 158 and cases cited. Only persons within the meaning of the Constitution have Fourteenth Amendment rights.

Katzenbach v. *Morgan*, 384 U.S. 641 (1966) grew out of a constitutional challenge to Section 4(e)(2) of the Voting Rights Act of 1965 which provided that no person who had successfully completed the sixth grade in a Puerto Rican school where instruction was in Spanish should be denied the right to vote because of inability to read or write English. The provision enfranchised thousands of Spanish-speaking citizens who had moved to New York from Puerto Rico but had been barred from voting by a New York statute requiring literacy in English. Since Congress has no general power to prescribe voting qualifications, Section 4(e)(2) could be upheld only as a measure for enforcing the Fourteenth Amendment's mandate that "no State shall . . . deny to any person within its jurisdiction the equal protection of the laws."

The Court, by a vote of seven to two, upheld the statute. One branch of opinion sustains congressional removal of the State's requirement of English literacy on the ground that Congress might have viewed the removal as a measure adapted to securing the Puerto Ricans residing in New York against unconstitutional discrimination in the provision of government services, such as public schools, public housing and law enforcement. 384 U.S. at 652–53.

The first branch of *Katzenbach* v. *Morgan* gives no support to S. 158, Section 1 for the same reason that *South Carolina* v. *Katzenbach* is distinguishable. Section 4(e)(2) was upheld as a means of securing a separate and established constitutional right—the right to equal treatment in public services without regard to race or color. Enactment of S. 158 would not protect any established constitutional right. S. 158 simply attempts to create a constitutional right for the unborn, even though it is established constitutional law that the unborn are not "persons" within the meaning of the Fourteenth Amendment.

South Carolina v. *Katzenbach* and the first branch of *Katzenbach* v. *Morgan* are plainly inappropriate for a further reason. In creating a new constitutional right for the unborn, S. 158—if effective—would cut back upon the established constitutional right of a woman to decide during the first two trimesters of pregnancy whether she wishes to bear a child. Neither of the cited precedents involved an act of Congress attempting to cut back or dilute existing constitutional rights. On the contrary, the opinion in *Katzenbach* v. *Morgan* specifically notes the difference between adding and taking away protection, and goes on to state that the rationale of the opinion does not extend to legislation curtailing individual rights. (384 U.S. at 651 n. 10):

> *We emphasize that Congress' power under S.5 is limited to adopting*
> *measures to enforce the guarantees of the Amendment; S. 5 grants*
> *Congress no power to restrict, abrogate, or dilute these guarantees.*

The second branch of the opinion in *Katzenbach* v. *Morgan* is somewhat closer to the mark, but it too gives no significant support to proponents of the constitutionality of S. 158, Section 1. The New York law that Congress was seeking to supersede denied citizens literate in Spanish the same voting rights as citizens literate in English. The discrimination was under attack as a violation of the equal protection clause in another judicial proceeding, but the Court assumed that it would not be judged unconstitutional without the aid of legislation. Nevertheless, the Court went on to say in the *Morgan* case, "We perceive a basis upon which Congress might predicate a judgment that the application of New York's English literacy requirement . . . constituted an invidious discrimination in violation of the Equal Protection Clause." 384 U.S. at 670–671. For this reason, the Court held that the New York statute must yield even though Congress' decision might differ from that which the Court would have rendered.

The essential point to be observed is that the second branch of *Katzenbach* v. *Morgan* involved only *deference to congressional determinations upon what are truly questions of fact.* There was general agreement that the legislative classification resulting from the English speaking literacy test was unconstitutional only if the classification bore no rational relationship to some permissible public purpose. That was the applicable legal standard. Section 4 of the Voting Rights Act made no effort to change that standard. Whether a State law violates that standard often depends to a large extent upon the finding and appraisal of the practical importance of relevant facts. In the case of the English literacy requirement, it turned upon such considerations as the extent to which the requirement served as an incentive to learn English and ease the process of assimilation, the availability of Spanish-language newspapers and their sufficiency to enable non-English-speaking voters to exercise the franchise intelligently, the importance of the franchise, and the relative effectiveness of other inducements to learn English.

The conventional constitutional formula called for the Court to presume the existence of facts giving validity to State legislation and to defer any State legislative findings of fact unless the findings were irrational. There is also a presumption that facts exist which sustain federal legislation and a principle of deference to congressional judgement upon questions of fact. In *Morgan* the federal and State statutes appeared to rest upon inconsistent findings and legislative evaluations of the practical conditions determining whether the discrimination against citizens literate only in Spanish was permissible or invidious. The Court, forced to choose between conflicting presumptions, applied the rule of deference to the congressional findings of fact.

S. 158, Section 1 does not rest upon any "findings of fact" in the sense in which those words were used in *Katzenbach* v. *Morgan* and the ensuing professional commentary. The bill does not ask Congress to make or declare new knowledge of actual facts or to appraise the practical operation of facts. Even the proposed finding that there is "a significant likelihood that actual human life exists from conception" rests entirely upon giving a particular meaning to the word "life." What is "life" is not simply a question of fact. Over the years many sincere people have believed that life begins at the moment of conception. Everything depends upon what one means by "life." The meaning may be established by agreement upon a dictionary definition. The meaning may represent a theological, philosophical, moral, legal or other normative declaration of when a particular collection of phenomena should be given the same theological, philosophical, moral, legal or other normative consequences as the "life" we recognize in human beings after birth and before anything that might be determined to be "death." Because the meaning of "life" must first be fixed, the existence of life is not simply a question of fact.

The rest of Section 1 of S. 158 does not even purport to deal with the facts: it says that "life" shall "be deemed" to commence at the moment of conception; it defines "person" to include any unborn person from the moment of conception.

For these reasons even the second branch of *Katzenbach* v. *Morgan* gives no support to S. 158.

For similiar reasons S. 158, Section 1 presents very different constitutional questions from the 1971 amendment to the Voting Rights Act reducing the voting age in all state and federal elections from 21 years old to 18 years old. The constitutional question was whether classifying 18-21 year-old citizens as ineligible to vote while citizens over 21 years old are permitted to vote violated the Equal Protection Clause. The classification was not invidious in the sense that it rests upon hostility or prejudice; age is relevant to the permissible State objective of securing an informed, intelligent and responsible electorate. Thus, using the twenty-first birthday to draw the line was permissible if, but only if, the knowledge, experience, maturity, and appreciation of one's stake in the community necessary for an intelligent and responsible vote of those over 21 is sufficiently greater than that of those between 18 and 21 to justify excluding the younger group from participation in self-government. These are questions of fact in the first instance, of characterization or degree after the raw data is assembled, and ultimately, of balance or relative importance.

Section 302 of the Voting Rights Act in nowise sought to change the constitutional principle. Among other supporters of the reduction I urged that Congress honestly could and should find *purely as matters of fact* that the spread and improvement of education, the age at which young people take jobs, pay taxes, marry and have children, the tremendous interest of young people in government and public affairs, and their increased knowledge and sophistication everywhere as a result of new forms of mass communications had made 18-21 year-old citizens as able to cast informed, intelligent and responsible votes as those over 21 years old.

S. 158 is altogether different because, as I have repeatedly pointed out, it does not find facts but simply and directly seeks to change the applicable constitutional standards.[2] The second branch of *Katzenbach* v. *Morgan* even when read most

[2] I should mention two other reasons for concluding that *Katzenbach* v. *Morgan* does not sustain the constitutionality of Section 1 of S. 158.

First, the inferences that I and some other commentators drew from the second ground of decision in the *Morgan* case were repudiated by five Justices in *Oregon* v. *Mitchell*, 400 U.S. 112 (1970). *Oregon* v. *Mitchell* represents the present law.

Second, Katzenbach v. *Morgan* sustained the power of Congress under Section 5 to give greater

broadly, gives no support whatever to an attempt to change the meaning of the Constitution, to redefine the words used in the Constitution, by simple legislative majorities. As I wrote ten years ago, "Nothing in *Morgan* suggested that the Court should defer to Congress in the process of deriving the applicable legal standard from the document and other sources of law; the opinion seemed to require Congress to *apply the same standard* as the Court, merely leaving it free to apply the standard differently where the application turned upon 'questions of fact.'" See Cox, *op. cit.* at 234. S. 158 does not apply the same legal standard as the Court established in *Roe* v. *Wade*. S. 158 rejects the Court's standard. In *Roe* v. *Wade* the Court held that "the word 'person,' as used in the Fourteenth Amendment, does *not* include the unborn." 410 U.S. at 158. S. 158 would reject this standard by enacting that "'person' shall include all human life as defined herein (*i.e.* from the moment of conception)," thereby including the unborn. In *Roe* v. *Wade* the Court held that the woman's freedom to choose during the first two trimesters of pregnancy whether to carry an unborn child until birth is constitutionally superior to any interest in or of the fetus up to the time of viability, regardless of when "life" may begin. S. 158 rejects that legal standard also; it adopts one view of when life begins and then declares, contrary to the existing rule of law, that its view of when life begins shall be controlling under the Fourteenth Amendment.

Thus, my present view that S. 158, Section 1 is patently unconstitutional is completely consistent with what I wrote of the power of Congress under Section 5 of the Fourteenth Amendment in 1971 (Cox, *op. cit.* at 254):

> *[The argument] affects only the latitude available to Congress in applying general rules of law to what it finds to be actual social conditions, always within the legal framework supplied by the Constitution and the principles developed by the Court. No one suggests that the Congress can read into the Constitution new general rules of law that have been rejected by the Court, regardless of whether they expand or dilute constitutional rights.*

---

statutory protection to individual rights than Section 1 of the Fourteenth Amendment provides unaided except by judicial decision. Section 1 of S. 158 does not simply extend the protection available to individual rights. On the contrary, it attempts to cut back on the rights of the individual woman by denying her an aspect of liberty secured by the Fourteenth Amendment. The opinion in *Katzenbach* v. *Morgan* specifically notes the difference between adding and taking away protection, and goes on to state that the rationale of the opinion does not extend to legislation curtailing individual rights. (384 U.S. at 651 n. 10):

> *We emphasize that Congress' power under §5 is limited to adopting measures to enforce the guarantees of the Amendment; §5 grants Congress no power to restrict, abrogate, or dilute these guarantees.*

I expressed doubt concerning the validity of this distinction in *The Role of Congress in Constitutional Determinations*, 40 U. of Cinnci. L. Rev. 199, 247–259 (1971), arguing that the Court should defer to congressional findings of fact whether the legislation enlarged or cut back on individual rights. Whatever the force of my argument in 1971, later decisions make plain that the Court's present practice is to make its own findings where the party challenging legislation is asserting a "preferred" or "fundamental" constitutional right requiring strict scrutiny of legislation. *See, e.g. First National Bank of Boston* v. *Bellotti*, 435 U.S. 765 (1978).

Consequently, my criticism rested upon a defective premise.

II. Jurisdiction

Section 2 of S. 158 would deprive lower federal courts of jurisdiction to hear cases challenging the constitutionality of state anti-abortion laws. While I strongly disagree with this limitation on federal court jurisdiction as a matter of public policy, a position that is developed in detail later in my testimony, I also have serious reservations as to the constitutionality of this kind of jurisdictional restriction.

It is well known that the Constitution gives to the Congress the power to establish such inferior federal courts as it deems appropriate. This broad power to establish lower federal courts has been interpreted to include the power for Congress to limit the kinds of cases that can be brought in those courts. Thus, there are numerous precedents that allow Congress to limit the jurisdiction of the inferior federal courts so long as the right of an aggrieved party to ultimately bring his constitutional claim to the Supreme Court is preserved.

The power of Congress to limit lower federal court jurisdiction is not, however, without bounds. This congressional power, like all others, is constrained by the other provisions of the Constitution, and must be exercised in conformance with other constitutional protections. Thus, Congress may limit federal court jurisdiction only if it does so consistent with, for instance, Fifth Amendment Due Process guarantees.

The jurisdictional limitation in S. 158 raises grave questions on this basis. The bill proposes that Congress deny to the lower federal courts the power to hear cases asserting particular federal constitutional rights. In singling out one set of constitutional rights for disfavored treatment, the bill burdens the exercise of those rights. The Supreme Court has often held that Congress may not discriminate against particular constitutional rights by burdening their exercise. See *Shapiro* v. *Thompson*, 394 U.S. 618 (1969); *Sherbert* v. *Verner*, 374 U.S. 398 (1963). To do so violates both the equal protection and due process guarantees of the Fifth Amendment. I thus believe that the jurisdictional limitation in S. 158 is of dubious constitutionality, even though I cannot categorically say it would be held unconstitutional.

III. Even if S. 158 is Technically Within the Power of Congress to Enact, it Should be Rejected as a Radical and Dangerously Unprincipled Attack Upon the Foundations of our Constitutionalism.

EFFECTS OF S. 158.   The ultimate bulwarks of individual liberty in the United States are the Bill of Rights and the Fourteenth Amendment interpreted and applied by an independent judiciary, headed by the Supreme Court of the United States. Over the years a few decisions have proved wrong-headed. The short-run unpopularity of other decisions has occasionally provoked clamor for legislation. A larger number of decisions have provoked strong, short-run political or popular opposition. From time to time political figures trading on the clamor have sought unsuccessfully to negate particular constitutional rulings by the action of congressional majorities impeaching Justices, packing the Court or curtailing jurisdiction.

S. 158 is such an attack upon our final guardian of constitutionalism. I have written critically of the abortion decision, Cox, *The Role of the Supreme Court in American Government* 51–55, 112–114, but S. 158 should be opposed by all believers in our constitutionalism, regardless of whether they agree or disagree with particular rulings. Wrong-headed decisions can be changed by time and debate, or by constitutional amendment. The very function of Constitution and Court is to put individual liberties beyond the reach of both congressional majorities and popular clamor. Any principle that permits Congress, with the approval of the president, to nullify one constitutional right protected by the Constitution, as interpreted by the Court, sanctions the nullification of others. Enactment of S. 158—if effective—would undermine the basic balance of c ⁻ institutions.

The underlying vice of Section 2 of S. 158 is simply stated. A right is only as good as the remedy. A constitutional right is at the mercy of legislative majorities unless supported by a judicial remedy. To deprive federal courts of jurisdiction granted by the federal constitution would result in a hodge-podge of inconsistent State interpretations, not all of which could be expected to rise above local selfishness or passion. This would be the practical result even if jurisdiction was left with the Supreme Court.

Section 1 of S. 158, as I have explained above, seeks to substitute legislative for judicial definitions of the words used in the Constitution in order to overturn Supreme Court decisions holding that a State may not punish abortion in the early stages of pregnancy because the prohibition deprives the woman of liberty without due process of law. S. 158 declares that "life" shall be deemed to exist from the moment of conception; it seems to define the fetus as a "person" for the purposes of the Fourteenth Amendment, and thus to give the fetus superior constitutional rights.

The vice of Section 1 of the Helms bill is the underlying premise. Even if the pro-abortion decisions are wrong, it would be worse to accept the principle that bare majorities in the Senate and House of Representatives, with the approval of the president, can change the Constitution by simple legislative definitions. If Congress can supply a binding definition of "life" or "person," it can equally declare that the provision of "separate but equal" facilities to persons of different color *is* "equal protection of the law"; or that State aid to parochial schools is not an "establishment of religion"; or that the "probable cause" necessary to validate a search or seizure means simply the good faith belief of any police officer that the arrest or search will be helpful to law enforcement.

HISTORICAL PERSPECTIVE   The balance among legislative, executive and judicial branches that these measures would disturb is the very bedrock of our constitutionalism.

In the latter part of the 18th century men came to believe that there are fundamental human rights that should be beyond the reach of any government—not just a king, not just an elected executive, but *any* government, including even a majority of the representative Congress or Legislature. They were confident of the rights, but they were at a loss to devise a method of protection. The Virginia Act of 1786 for establishing religious freedom rather plaintively declared:

> We all know that this Assembly. . . have no power to restrain the
> Acts of succeeding Assemblies. . . and . . . therefore to declare the
> Act to be irrevocable would be of no effect in law. . . [But] we are
> free to declare, and do declare, that the rights asserted are of the
> natural rights of mankind, and that if any Act hereafter be passed to

repeat the present. . . such Act will be an infringement of our natural rights.

Gradually, they discovered an answer.

First, let the fundamental human rights to be put beyond the reach of government be written down in a constitution.

Second, treat the Constitution as law to be interpreted and applied by courts in the same fashion as any other law, but also make it supreme so that in case of conflict between the Constitution and any other law, the Constitution will prevail.

Third, make the Judiciary impartial and independent.

James Madison put it in a nutshell when he said in proposing the Bill of Rights—

> *. . . independent tribunals of justice will consider themselves in a peculiar manner the guardians of those rights; they will be an impenetrable bulwark against every assumption of power in the Legislative or Executive.*

Throughout our history there have been legislative attacks upon the power of the Judicial Branch to protect constitutional rights. The Jeffersonian Democrats proposed to use impeachment as a vehicle for removing justices whose constitutional views were distasteful to the dominant party in Congress. In the 1920's, the proponents of State sovereignty sought to take away the power of the Supreme Court to review decisions by State courts on constitutional questions. After the Civil War, the radical Republicans, fearful that the Supreme Court would find the Reconstruction Acts unconstitutional, revoked the Court's authority to hear a Mississippi newspaper editor's appeal of the denial of his habeas corpus petition, and considered other methods of barring judicial review.

In 1937, President Franklin D. Roosevelt proposed legislation to pack the Supreme Court with new justices who agreed with his constitutional philosophy. The Court packing plan was defeated. The McCarthyites of the 1950's unsuccessfully sought to persuade Congress to limit Supreme Court jurisdiction over unconstitutional federal and state programs aimed at alleged subversives: In 1964, some Senators and Representatives attempted to eliminate federal court jurisdiction over reapportionment.

In the past, despite their discontent with particular decisions, the American people and the Congress have rejected these attacks upon the Court as dangerously unprincipled.

I urge this Subcommittee and later the full Committee to reach that wise result today.

Senator EAST. Professor Uddo?

Statement of Basile Uddo

Mr. UDDO. Thank you, Mr. Chairman and Senator Baucus.

It is my pleasure to have been invited before the subcommittee today to testify. I am only going to spend a very few moments on the jurisdictional limitation provision, but I am afraid I am going to start by acting irresponsibly, as

Professor Cox characterized it, because I am going to say that the jurisdictional limitation provision of the bill is, in my mind, beyond debate, constitutional.

I have addressed that question in an extensive article entitled: "A Wink From the Bench: The Federal Courts and Abortion," which appears in the Tulane Law Review and which I have submitted for the permanent record.

That article examines what I think is the clear authority and precedent for congressional control of Federal court jurisdiction, particularly when, as in this case, the jurisdiction of the Supreme Court and the State courts is left untouched.

Most of Professor Cox's references were to instances where Supreme Court jurisdiction was being attacked, and he did not mention the Norris-LaGuardia Act which, I think, is the exact paradigm for what S. 158 tries to do. You are all familiar with the Norris-LaGuardia Act and that it deprived the lower Federal courts of jurisdiction in labor injunction cases, which some people have characterized as perhaps saving the entire union movement in this country.

Objections to S. 158

Because this subcommittee is familiar with the very sound arguments supporting Congress power to enact the human life bill and because my written testimony thoroughly analyzes Congress power in this area, I will not spend much time discussing those issues. Instead, I would like to focus upon some of the objections that have been raised to S. 158 and why I think most of those are ill conceived.

One objection is that, even though Congress may have superior factfinding ability, Justice Brennan in *Roe* v. *Wade* said that Texas could not adopt one theory of life, and, the argument goes, consequently, neither may Congress. I think this objection is without merit.

Initially, it is clear that no State has ever attempted the extensive factfinding on the question of human life that this subcommittee is now undertaking. While the Texas data may have been impressive, I think these hearings are certainly more thorough and more up to date, and unprecedented.

Moreoever, it is clear to me that Congress, unlike Texas or any other State, is a coordinate, coequal branch of the American Government. Consequently, congressional determinations are owed particular respect by the Court.

Professor Cox himself has commented on this very point in explaining why a congressional determination of voter qualifications should, as the Supreme Court held, be superior to that of the State. And I quote Professor Cox:

> *Congressional supremacy over the Judiciary in the areas of legislative fact-finding and evaluation and over the State legislatures under the supremacy clause in any area within Federal power would seem to be a wiser touchstone.*

And he elaborates in the context of his article. Consequently, I think, we should say that Congress deserves deference where a State may not.

Another objection that has been raised against S. 158 is that it goes beyond factfinding in determining when life begins by also concluding that, for purposes of the due process clause, the unborn, from conception, are persons protected by the 14th amendment.

Further, the argument runs, this conflicts with the determination in *Roe* v. *Wade* that the unborn were not persons under amendment. Therefore, they conclude, on the point of personhood, the Supreme Court is not in doubt and Congress may not act.

Admittedly, S. 158—the congressional determination in S. 158 on this point— would conflict with the Court, but I do not think this would render the bill unconstitutional. The Court has, in the past, allowed Congress to differ with it on determinations relevant to the 14th amendment by deferring to the congressional view.

That, I think, is the area that this subcommitte has become very familiar with, because I am sure that you gentlemen are familiar with the voting rights cases— with *Lassiter* and *Morgan*, which have been mentioned here already today.

Your are also familiar with the more recent discussions of those section 5 powers in *Fullilove* and *City of Rome*. And, too, I think you are familiar with the Court's view that it will defer to congressional judgments that conflict with its view of the Constitution. And you also know that the Justices have always admitted that they can learn from the dialog with the Court.

S. 158 as Dialog and Teaching

So, the human life bill offers nothing so dramatic as a threat to *Marbury* v. *Madison*. It offers teaching and dialog, and the process of dialog and teaching between the Court and Congress, I would suggest, is as old and as venerable as our Constitution itself.

The bill is merely a continuation of this process on two very important points of a very important issue: When does life begin, and who is a person for purposes of protecting life.

The question might be raised: Is this congressional teaching necessary? Is it wise? Is it something Congress should do? I think that, quite clearly, it is.

The 14th amendment protection of life is meaningless if no decision can be made about life or not life. For the unborn in 1981, it is clearly meaningless. If some others get their way, the very young and very old may lose their protection under the amendment, so too the defective.

Who could doubt that the day will come when we might hear arguments that science cannot decide if infants are human life or the invalid, old, or the severely handicapped? These, it will be said, are questions of philosophy or religion, of value or opinion.

If that is the case, then no one's life is really protected because we will have decided that we cannot decide, and protection will be a matter of power, not right. Only the powerful will be able to demand protection.

Consequently, Congress considered judgment on the question of when life begins is indispensable to understanding what the 14th amendment means when it says we protect life.

Without Congress judgment, and in light of the Court's self-professed incompetence on the question, a great void exists, a void which could easily be filled by a most compromising view of whose life should be protected.

Congressional teaching on the meaning of "personhood," I think, is similarly indispensable in trying to persuade the Court that they were incorrect in writing the unborn out of the Constitution.

There is probably no more weakly reasoned part of *Roe* v. *Wade* than Justice Blackmun's approach to defining "personhood" under the 14th amendment. Rather than look to common sense, common law, medical data, or tradition, he chose to see how else the word "person" was used in the Constitution. He found that it was always used postnatally, in the fugitive slave clause, in the qualifications for Representatives and Senators, in disqualifications of electors, et cetera.

But, if course, virtually the entire Constitution was written about adult activities and would have had scant occasion to use the word "person" in any other sense.

Carried to its conclusion, Justice Blackmun's technique for defining "person" would include only adult white males, since that is who was contemplated by most of the other references to "person" in the body of the Constitution.

So, too, Justice Blackmun's approach would suggest that *Santa Clara* v. *Southern Pacific Railroad*, decided in 1886, was wrongly decided in that it held corporations to be persons under the 14th amendment. But, of course, I would suggest that the framers would have envisioned good sense as the guide to such decisions and not word games.

The Congress, I think, is on extremely solid footing in pointing out the Court's error on the question of personhood. It seems quite clear that those most familiar with the 14th amendment—its drafters—saw it as protecting all human beings.

Congressman Jonathan Bingham of Ohio, author of the 14th amendment, said it applied to every human being. Senator Jacob M. Howard of Michigan, who sponsored the amendment on the Senate floor, said it protected the rights of common humanity.

Faced with the biological, scientific, and medical data that this subcommittee has before it, is it conceivable that these men—the authors of the 14th amendment—would have said no, these humans are not to be protected? I think not.

Their concern for common humanity, for the sanctity, not the quality, of life—for the inalienable right to life—would certainly have caused them to resoundingly reject any notion that only certain lives are protected in the Constitution. The human life bill is an attempt to recapture, I think, that original intent.

S. 158 and Ratchet Theories

It is abundantly clear then, to me at least, that the human life bill is a perfectly acceptable, most likely constitutional, not very unusual bit of legislation. It employs techniques hailed by Professor Cox as, I quote, "a vast, untapped reservoir of Federal legislative power to define and promote the constitutional rights of individuals in relation to State government."

Further, Professor Cox has said: "It is a happy innovation, relieving pressures upon the Court that follows logically from familiar principles of constitutional adjudication."

Yet, some would suggest that an apparent afterthought footnote in *Katzenbach* v. *Morgan* holds the seed of this bill's unconstitutionality. In that footnote, Justice Brennan declared that section 5 "grants Congress no power to restrict, abrogate, or dilute the guarantees of the 14th amendment."

This theory of a one-way use of section 5 has come to be known as a ratchet theory. To date, it has never been used by the Supreme Court.

There are several reasons why this theory poses no problem for the human life bill. Professor Nagel elaborated on some of those.

Justice Brennan's footnote, taken at face value, would preclude congressional abrogation of rights, which presumes that such an abrogation would be the purpose of the exercise of power in the first place. Brennan's own example illustrates this: "Thus, an enactment authorizing the States to establish racially segregated systems of education would not be a measure to enforce 14th amendment rights."

Clearly, such an act would have no purpose other than the abrogation of rights. There would be no arguable expansion of 14th amendment rights explainable in nonracial terms.

On the other hand, it is quite easy to imagine an act clearly attempting to enforce or expand rights that incidentally affected other rights. *Katzenbach* v. *Morgan* is an example of this.

So it is with the human life bill. The bill, on its face, does not demonstrate an animus against a woman's right to privacy, nor is its purpose the dilution of such right. It is, instead, a dramatic reexpansion and enforcement of the rights of the unborn.

The admitted effect upon the right to an abortion is incidental and inescapable in pursuit of higher 14th amendment values.

Most important, however, I think the validity of the ratchet theory itself must be questioned. Its only explicit Court support is the two footnote references of Justice Brennan, one of which was in dissent. Beyond that, he has never elaborated on this theory or its constitutional basis.

Justice Black seems to be the only Justice to personally agree with it. In fact, the Chief Justice seems to reject it in that he has proposed Federal legislation to modify Court-created rights concerning exclusion of evidence in criminal prosecutions. Such legislation would be based upon section 5 and would certainly dilute the rights of criminal defendants, and yet it is suggested by the Chief Justice himself.

Furthermore, no case, as I said, has ever used the ratchet theory to invalidate a section 5 statute. Perhaps this paucity of use and support for the theory emanates from the weakness of the theory itself. The most careful criticism of it came, again, from Professor Cox.

His initial response was:

> It is hard to see how the Court can consistently give weight to the congressional judgment in expanding the definitions of equal protection in the area of human rights but refuse to give it weight in narrowing the definition where the definition depends upon appraisal of the facts.

A poignant criticism, I would say.

On the Rhetoric of the "Other Side"

In concluding, let me comment upon one unfortunate specter that I think has arisen during the debates upon S. 158, and that is the nature of the opposition.

Until today, most of the opposition was not presented in substantive fashion. Today, fortunately, this subcommittee has substantive comments upon which it can make some decisions.

Prior to this, a few law professors have taken to a technique, I think, unbefitting the importance or the dignity of these proceedings. Their opposition has depended largely upon misstatement, innuendo, implication, and even sarcasm. They have taken to instructing this subcommittee and the public through means that I would characterize as less than scholarly.

The most forceful argument upon which they have depended is that x number of scholars have ordained that this bill is unconstitutional. Principled reasons for this view have been notably absent.

Professor Tribe, for example, has tried to impress this subcommittee with a so-called unison of voices among virtually all careful students of the Constitution.

I would submit that the only way one can accept that such a unison of careful scholars exists is if one believes that the entire universe of careful constitutional scholars is coterminous with those who teach at certain institutions and hold certain political and legal views. As self-serving as it might be, I am not prepared to accept that definition.

Even if one were to believe that there was such a unison, one would still require more than personal assurances that the instant legislation is unconstitutional. One would expect relevant and scholarly dialog.

It is interesting to note that, had the scholars who support the constitutionality of the human life bill acted similarly, they would have been denounced as reckless incompetents.

But those who support the human life bill, I think, have offered a thorough assessment of why they believe the Constitution would allow S. 158. They believe that their scholarship is careful. They believe that they have asked this subcommittee, rather than to trust their conclusions, to evaluate the data.

Consequently, I am confident that when you men reflect upon what has been presented to you and undertake your serious responsibility of passing on this bill you will find that the weight of authority rests with its constitutionality and argues for its passage, and I think that is all that can be asked of you.

Thank you.

Senator EAST. Thank you, Professor Uddo.

Gentlemen, I wish to thank you all for your valuable testimony. As I have indicated, your written statements will be made a part of our permanent record.

As I have indicated, time always in this sort of thing becomes very precious. I would anticipate we need to wind up this phase of the discussion around 11:30 so that we can devote an hour and a half to our second panel.

Senator Baucus and I will rotate our time. I shall take about 10 minutes, which will take us to 5 after the hour, and then we will let Senator Baucus have his swing at this. So, gentleman, you are now fair game, if you will, for our questions.

A point I would like to clear up—and I suppose I am directing this comment particularly at Professors Bork and Cox—is this. I sense in both of you—certainly very strongly in Professor Bork, and I will just state my position and let you respond to it, if you will, please—a general unhappiness with *Roe* v. *Wade*, not maybe so much with the policy result, but that it is not good constitutional law. Certainly with Professor Bork there is no desire to defend the way in which the Court has proceeded to involve itself in this issue.

I sense also with you, Professor Cox, certainly not a great deal of glee in having to defend their intervention in this particular matter and that it does become an example, it would seem, of inappropriate exercise of judicial power.

I am reminded, of course, that in the dissent in *Roe* v. *Wade*, William Rehnquist and Byron White, two members of the Court, both described this as an improvident and extravagant use of the power of judicial review, both of those distinguished gentlemen suggesting that something was very much amiss in what was going on.

Many Americans—and I will include myself in that category, it is probably no great secret—share that concern.

What we are trying to do is to find some sort of reasonable, prudent, modest way out of it.

We have various kinds of alternatives in dealing with this sort of thing. You can make sure that future Court appointees think properly, but then that is always fraught with difficulty lest you try to skew it too much to your own political predilections.

You can withdraw Court jurisdiction. Obviously, Professor Cox has deep reservations about that as a remedy. We have, of course, the route of constitutional amendment, which the two of you do not rule out as a possibility here. Though I would argue, on a hierarchy of remedies, that is a pretty severe kind of thing, where you reach a point that you acknowledge the Court has done a very radical and, if you will, unprincipled thing by intervening in this way. We are trying to find some sort of reasonable, prudent way out of it.

Constitutional amendments up the ante very high. First of all, there is the difficulty of achieving it, which is not necessarily a bad thing; but, second, it would, interestingly, invert *Roe* v. *Wade* and give you a national policy wholly different in scope.

It seems to me that the human life bill has a couple of advantages. One, it is a relatively modest remedy. All we are really doing, I would argue as a defender of the bill, is inviting the Court to reconsider what it had done. It had indicated in the majority opinion that it could not define "life," and the implication is very strong—overwhelming—that if they had known when life begins they would have come to a different result. We look upon that—at least I do and many others—as, if you will, a tacit invitation that perhaps we might begin to exercise our prerogative. It certainly would be an appropriate, or certainly not an inappropriate, legislative function to look into this matter, to determine, if in fact we can determine, when life begins.

If we say we can, we are not overruling the Court. They will have another shot at it. We have not taken away their appellate jurisdiction. We are simply suggesting, well, let us try it. This is a gentle prodding of the Court to reconsider.

They can reconsider on due process grounds. Who knows? They might even, in reconsideration, get into equal protection questions.

It seems to me all four gentlemen are suggesting that we start with not a very good decision. And we start with a legitimate desire on the part of many—even the opponents here—to do something about it.

A statute that invites the Court to reconsider I would consider, Professor Cox, a very modest remedy, as opposed to the alternatives. All we are doing here is trying to enlist them in a little dialog on this very profound public issue and get them to look at it again.

They could ultimately hold the bill unconstitutional. Perhaps they would. We do not eliminate that option. Then the alternative would be, for those who feel strongly about it, to go for a constitutional amendment—a right to life amendment. But that is stronger medicine that this.

I am very sensitive—indeed, totally resistant—to the notion that what we are doing here is"radical and unprincipled." I would say it is very prudent, very modest, and merely a testing of the constitutional waters to see if the Court might not reconsider what we all seem to be agreed upon was a very poor decision in terms of the whole concept of the power of judicial review, going back to *Marbury* v. *Madison*, going back to The Federalist, No. 78.

Now, I have said my piece. Perhaps, Professor Cox, since I spoke a little bit more critically of your analysis, you might respond to that. Where do you think that I go awry on this thing?

Mr. Cox. I think—without intending to be impolite at all, Senator, and with respect—that you go awry at just about every step of your statement.

First, a constitutional amendment may be difficult to achieve, but it is a modest way of correcting a Supreme Court error, and it is one that has a good many instances of precedent in our history.

The 11th amendment resulted that way, and the income tax amendment resulted that way—certainly, those two; whether there are others, I do not recall at the moment.

An amendment could easily be phrased in a way which would provide that nothing in the 14th amendment should be deemed to deprive the States of power to enact and administer laws prohibiting abortion, if that is the purpose of S. 158. Such an amendment would not attack any basic constitutional principle.

Second, here the language is hardly phrased in terms of, "Please reconsider." It is phrased in terms of, "Life shall be deemed"—not even of factfinding—"to begin at the moment of conception." And the term "person" is defined for the Court, instead of leaving the definition of constitutional terms to the Court, which I think is where it belongs if the Constitution is to have any meaning.

Now, when I called it unprincipled, I am sure you understood, Senator—and I want to make it clear to everybody else—I am not using the word in the sense that charges anybody with lacking moral principle. I call in unprincipled because I do not think that you or anyone else would be willing to generalize the principle on which the bill necessarily rests; that is, that Congress can define the terms in the Constitution.

Think about what that means. That would mean that the Congress, by simply majority, could declare that separate education shall be deemed equal education; or that probable cause to arrest a person or search their houses, papers, or effects, "shall be deemed to be the opinion of a police officer that the search or seizure will advance the administration of justice;" or that aid to secretarian schools shall not be deemed an establishment of religion.

Once one gets into this business—it seems to me, with all respect—it is the most radical thing in the world, and any generalization of your approach would undermine our whole constitutional system.

Senator EAST. I guess the quarrel I have with you, Professor Cox, with all due respect to you, is this: The words "radical and unprincipled" I do not consider appropriate to this kind of dialog, because I would not use those words to describe your position, nor have I used them to describe *Roe* v. *Wade* really, and if they fit anywhere, they probably fit there. "Radical and unprincipled" suggest something totally unwarranted and wholly indefensible.

Now, on any major constitutional policy question, fair-minded reasonable minds can differ. I am a little in agreement with Professor Uddo that sometimes the opposition engages in some rhetorical overkill with this, with ridicule on top of it, which I find unbecoming to people skilled in the academic community.

What we are trying to do is not to label one another or to ridicule one another but to engage in a genuine, academic, intellectual—I would hope—dialog on what it is we are doing.

I do not think your position is extremist, and I do not think my position is extremist. I think what we are doing is working within the framework of the U.S. Constitution and trying to figure out where we might go. To inflame it with excess rhetoric I am not quite sure contributes to the dialog.

I do not wish to overstate my case, but I want to get on the record with it— that extreme labels and the use of ridicule in this very important debate, I find, obscure and make more difficult good discussion. It reduces it then to name-calling and to ridicule, which I have never found in my own teaching experience a good tool of instruction.

Mr. Cox. Let me emphasize again, Senator, as I tried to say a moment ago, I did not mean to use those words in any way that implied any personal—

Senator EAST. Well, they were there, and I heard them.

Mr. Cox. No, no—I used them, but I am sure you also heard me say that they did not imply any personal lack of respect for you or any question about your behaving as a man of principle.

Senator EAST. Of course, in response, you can say that, when you describe the opposition position as being of that character—I see you are now wishing to withdraw that and to deny it, and I respect that and accept it, but—

Mr. Cox. No, sir, I did not withdraw it.

Senator EAST. I do not quite know where you are with it, then. You are saying it does not apply to me personally. I presume that it applies to others—

Mr. Cox. I said that by "unprincipled" I meant a proposal resting on a principle which I thought not even the sponsors would be willing to generalize. "Lacking in principle" might have been better words, but I thought they were equivalent.

By "radical," I mean that it seems to me that the proposal goes outside the established framework of the Constitution—that it would undermine the established constitutional framework. Thus, that seems to me the most apt word I can think of for describing something that does not stay within the framework of our institutions.

Mr. UDDO. Mr. Chairman, might I just try to respond to something Professor Cox said?

First of all, I think the examples he gives of the "slippery slope" that this might put us on are a bit overdone. I think most of the examples, if not all of the examples, he uses are instances where the factfinding would be irrational and the Court would not have to defer to the factfinding. Clearly, "separate but equal" could not be equal, and that would be an irrational factfinding.

On defining terms in the Constitution, in 1971 in the Cincinnati Law Review, Professor Cox proposed, under section 5—proposed, I presume rhetorically—the Speedy Trial Act of 1971 where the sixth amendment guarantee of a speedy trial could be defined by Congress as to what would constitute a speedy trial, and suggested even that it may differ with the Court's view of what a speedy trial would be. I suspect that if this proposal is radical, so was that one.

Senator EAST. Professor Bork, I will let you respond, and then I will turn it over to Senator Baucus.

Mr. BORK. I think you are quite right about my attitude toward *Roe* v. *Wade*, which I think is in the running for perhaps the worst example of constitutional reasoning I have ever read. I would not say it is the worst, but it is certainly in the running.

In one sense, I certainly do not think this proposal is radical and unprincipled because I think Congress has done it before, and I think the Court has accepted it before.

I think it is a mistake; I think it should not have been done then, and I think it should not be done now. But I do think it is healthy to have a political response to a Court that is trenching upon the proper preserve of democratic government and is doing it repeatedly, and it has done it in this case egregiously.

So I think this kind of debate and this kind of proposal is entirely proper, even though I hope the form this response takes does not become law.

You have referred to the statute, S. 158, as an invitation to reconsider. If it were a sense-of-the-Congress resolution which expressed Congress strong feeling the *Roe* v. *Wade* is wrong, I would think that was entirely proper.

You said the Court could declare S. 158 unconstitutional. My fear is that they might declare it constitutional and thus ratify what they have done in the past, which is to give Congress control over the meaning of the terms of the Constitution, which I think is quite bad.

The problem, of course, is more widespread with the Court than simply the abortion decision, and I think I would shift the emphasis that Professor Cox has given to this problem somewhat. He has spoken of the Court as a bulwark of our liberties, which indeed it is, but the Court can also be a threat to democratic government, as it has been in this case, and then we have a real problem about what to do with the Court. It is very hard to cope with that problem.

Senator EAST. Thank you.

Senator Baucus?

Senator BAUCUS. Thank you, Mr. Chairman.

Mr. Nagel and Mr. Uddo, in your statements where you invite Congress to engage in a dialog with the Court, neither one of you ever mention the amendment process. Isn't that the process that our constitutional framers provided for overruling or overriding constitutional decisions of the Court?

Mr. NAGEL. Mr. Baucus, in my statement I did say that the proper exercise of Congress enforcement power under section 5 of the 14th amendment is not amending the Constitution. It is enforcing the Constitution. I think that is a sufficient answer to your question.

Of course, Congress can go by way of the amendment process if it wishes, but it is not required to do that as long as it is operating properly within its power under section 5, which is a part of the Constitution.

Mr. Bork just said—and I agree with him—that given the current Supreme Court caselaw on Congress authority under section 5, Congress can proceed here without any fear of amending the Constitution.

Senator BAUCUS. With all respect, I do not think you answered the question. The question is: Why is not the amendment process generally a more appropriate route for the Congress and the States to follow in trying to override the constitutional decisions of the Court?

Mr. UDDO. Could I take a shot at that?

Senator BAUCUS. Surely.

Mr. UDDO. I think the answer to that is the unique way the *Roe* v. *Wade* was decided. Justice Blackmun's opinion categorically admitted that judiciary was incapable of making the factual determination of when life begins.

I would point out two things: He said that the judiciary was incapable of making that determination. He did not say everyone was, and he did not say Congress was incapable of it. In addition, he said, "at this time in the development of man's knowledge."

It seems to me that Justice Blackmun was saying that we do not know all we might ought to know about this. Unfortunately they went on and decided the case anyway. But I think that left open a very critical factual determination which invites the exact kind of exercise of section 5 power that S. 158 represents.

Had the case said that life does not begin until such-and-such a point, it may have been a different problem, but it seems to me it left wide open a factual question which Congress is uniquely equipped to answer.

Senator BAUCUS. Let me tread on some sensitive ground—the dialog between Professor Cox and the chairman about the use of the word "unprincipled."

I would like to determine the principles that you would apply in helping us determine when the Congress should attempt to amend the Constitution, by means other than the amendment process or the judicial nomination process.

Mr. UDDO. I would endorse most of what Professor Cox has written on that subject; that is, in those areas where Congress, as a coenforcer of the 14th amendment, can amass legislative facts and make determinations on those facts, to help make decisions about 14th amendment rights, I think that it is perfectly appropriate.

Senator BAUCUS. As I understand you then, the general principle embodied in *Marbury* v. *Madison* applies to most constitutional protections except the protections of the 14th amendment?

Mr. UDDO. No, I think *Marbury* v. *Madison* applies to all protections.

Senator BAUCUS. Does section 5 give Congress more power to override the Court in the 14th amendment area than the Congress has with respect to other constitutional rights?

Mr. UDDO. I would be careful about using the word "override." I am not so sure that that is what this bill does. What I would say is that, clearly, section 5, being part of the 14th amendment, explicitly recognizes a different role for Congress in enforcing that amendment—the debates of the 14th amendment and the contemporary commentary make it clear that Congress was to be coenforcer.

In fact, some of the commentary suggests that it was more to expand Congress power than the Court's because there was a general distrust of the Court at the time.

So my answer would be that those situations which are uniquely fitted for the kind of things that Congress can do such as fact-finding carves out a role for congressional determinations.

Senator BAUCUS. It seems to me that if you agree that *Marbury* v. *Madison* is an overriding principle that should also apply to the 14th amendment rights then the basic question is: What does the term "enforce" mean? When does enforcement become an act of overruling the Court, and when is enforcing the act enforcing of rights that have been prescribed by the Court?

Mr. UDDO. I think, in 158, the distinction I would make is that the first part defining "life" is very clearly within the enforcement provision. I think the determination on "personhood"—

Senator BAUCUS. Excuse me. At that point, why is that enforcement?

Mr. UDDO. It is defining rights. It is defining and expanding the area of rights for the unborn.

On the question of defining "personhood," I think that is a clear instance where Congress determination would come into conflict with what the Court said in *Roe* v. *Wade*, and there I think I would very freely admit that *Marbury* v. *Madison* will prevail.

If 158 is passed and it gets before the Supreme Court—which certainly it will—and the Court decides that Congress information about personhood is incorrect, it seems quite clear to me that *Marbury* v. *Madison* will prevail.

Senator BAUCUS. I find one point intriguing. Your view seems to be that constitutional rights should be defined more by Congress, the legislative branch, than is currently the case.

If, for example, this bill becomes a law, and if, as Professor Bork worries, the Supreme Court might uphold it, would you be in here arguing just as strenuously for a bill which would undo—say, the opposite of this bill—that is, under the 14th amendment, this Congress now finds that at some future date—1984 or 1985—that the rights of the unborn do not go this far?

Mr. UDDO. Would I be arguing in favor of that bill?

Senator BAUCUS. Yes. Would you argue that that would be a constitutionally permissible exercise of power?

Mr. UDDO. Of course. I would have to.

Senator BAUCUS. Does that not bother you a little bit? You have a very strong personal concern for the rights of the unborn. That comes through in your statement.

Mr. UDDO. Yes.

Senator BAUCUS. Do you want a process where, by a 51-percent majority, Congress could so easily undo protected constitutional rights?

Mr. UDDO. We could have done that with the public accommodations provision of the Civil Rights Act and most of the civil rights legislation. I do not think that that is a good thing—that it can be undone by a majority vote—but it is a fact of life. That is the way legislation is.

Senator BAUCUS. But you do favor a more transitory constitutional right, then?

Mr. UDDO. No, I did not say that.

Senator BAUCUS. Or one that is more illusory, because you feel Congress should take a more aggressive role in defining constitutional rights?

Mr. UDDO. I did not say I favor it. I am here to speak about S. 158, not what I think is the ultimate solution to the abortion question or the best way to solve it.

Senator BAUCUS. What I am trying to drive at is what your principle is.

Mr. UDDO. My principle is that the cases that I have read that interpret section 5 would strongly suggest that S. 158 is constitutional.

Senator BAUCUS. Would the panel generally agree that if this bill becomes law States would be prohibited from funding abortions?

Mr. BORK. I think so.

Mr. NAGEL. I agree.

Mr. COX. I think probably so.

Senator BAUCUS. And they would also probably be prohibited from providing funds to medical clinics which distribute IUD's?

Mr. BORK. Yes.

Mr. COX. I would think probably so—yes.

Senator BAUCUS. So the effect of this bill, if it becomes law, is quite different than what the law was prior to *Roe* v. *Wade*—is that right?—insofar as prior to *Roe* v. *Wade* there was no constitutional prohibition against States conducting in such conduct.

Mr. BORK. Prior to *Roe* v. *Wade*, there was no constitutional law about abortion in any direction.

Senator BAUCUS. So the answer is yes?

Mr. BORK. *Roe* v. *Wade* created one direction, and this bill would take it in the other direction, but it would not return it to the pre–*Roe* v. *Wade* situation.

Senator BAUCUS. I am just trying to establish that, if this bill becomes law, it does not place the state of the law as it was prior to *Roe* v. *Wade*—that it goes further insofar as it prohibits State action.

Mr. COX. Indeed. I do not want to put words in his mouth, but as I read Professor Nagel's testimony, he said that the bill does not affect *Roe* v. *Wade*, the only thing it does is prevent States from funding or otherwise giving aid to those who wish to have abortions.

Mr. NAGEL. That is right.

Mr. COX. That is what you said?

Mr. NAGEL. Yes.

Mr. COX. So his position is that it is quite the reverse of simply going back to before *Roe* v. *Wade*—that it does not carry us back to before *Roe* v. *Wade* but does prevent the States from funding abortions.

Again, I really do not want to put words in your mouth, but I thought was a dramatic—

Mr. NAGEL. I should add that, although I do not think the bill by its own force, reverses *Roe* v. *Wade*—and that is why I think a lot of the reaction describing the bill as a radical departure is extreme, and over-reacting in my judgment, but I do think it might bear on the Court's reassessment of that decision in light of the different legal issue before it.

So I am not saying that the Court might not come to a different judgment about some similar issues as were decided in *Roe* v. *Wade* if this bill were passed. I am just saying the bill on its own would not reverse *Roe* v. *Wade*.

Senator BAUCUS. Another point I would make here, too, is this: Insofar as this bill would prohibit States from funding abortions and the distribution of IUD's, in a sense it is not returning the determination to the States but is establishing a national policy which prevents States from engaging in certain conduct. The effect of this bill is not to throw the question of abortion back to the States but rather it sets a national policy that would prevent States from funding abortions. That is correct, is it not?

Mr. NAGEL. In my view, that is an unfortunate aspect of the bill.

Senator BAUCUS. It is an unfortunate aspect? Why is that?

Mr. NAGEL. Because I think it ought to be a matter of States in their own judgment to decide on.

Senator BAUCUS. Thank you, Mr. Chairman. I have no more questions.

Senator EAST. Thank you, Senator Baucus.

Senator Heflin, we certainly welcome you here.

We are having two panels here this morning. We were trying to finish this one up roughly around 11:30 or thereabouts, if we could, and then move on to a second one that would take us roughly to 1 o'clock.

We certainly welcome you and would be happy to hear any statement or questions you might have.

Senator HEFLIN. I am sorry I have not been able to attend other meetings of these hearings. I have been tied up on some other matters. I am interested very much in this.

I would like to perhaps, from what I understand has been addressed, ask this panel to address the issue of the 10th amendment in relationship to this bill.

As I see this, it is a Federal approach toward solving a social ill, if you classify it as a social ill. In regard to this matter, if we are dealing in a Federal approach, will it set a precedent on the Federal preemption of all matters dealing with life which basically have been reserved to the States? I would like to have some discussion of that aspect of it.

Mr. COX. If I may, Senator, I would think that the answer was that this interpretation of section 5 of the 14th amendment reads section 5 as modifying 10th amendment in some respects.

I remember Senator Ervin was strongly convinced of that, too, and I debated the point, arguing that it did. He argued that it did not and that legislation should not be adopted of that kind.

I would think that, despite some limiting language in the bill, it is very probably that if it were valid its definition of "life" and of "person" would become controlling for the purposes of the equal protection clause and that thenceforth the States would be required to treat the unborn persons the same way they treated born persons for most purposes under the equal protection clause.

And, second, I certainly see no reason why Congress, even if it did not have that effect to begin with, should not follow up with additional legislation regulating the way State law shall deal with these questions of who is a person or what is life.

But I do want to make it plain that I have been somewhat categorical about some things this morning. I do not want to seem categorical on that one because I feel a good deal of uncertainty.

Mr. UDDO. Senator Heflin, I would just say that it is a question that we had not discussed before. I do not see that it is a precedent for federalizing questions dealing with life because I think the bill very clearly attempts to overcome some of the problems that *Roe* v. *Wade* created by taking that away from the States.

It seems to me that this is a fairly modest proposal for returning that to the States. It could be a much more expansive bill and one that involved a great deal more Federal regulation, but I do not think that that is what this bill intends to do.

I doubt seriously that anyone could say today that that would never happen, but, of course, I think that the good judgment of the Congress would see that that is not what this bill is moving toward.

Mr. BORK. Senator Heflin, if I may—I think the version of section 5 of the 14th amendment that is being propounded here in support of this bill not only federalizes the question of life but, indeed, federalizes State police powers.

Under the equal protection clause and the due process clause together, those are turned over to Congress, and there is no State legislation on any topic that I can think of that cannot be federalized if Congress so chooses.

Mr. NAGEL. I would agree with Professor Bork if he were talking about not this bill but other legislation that might follow this bill if Congress were to pass it. But if you are speaking only of this bill, I do not think this bill has those sorts of dramatic effects. I would echo what Professor Uddo said—it would not have those effects as long as Congress exercised some sensitive judgment to the needs of federalism in our system.

Senator HEFLIN. If this bill is passed and declared constitutional, it is then, in effect, a foot in the door as to all aspects of human life probably for police power. It has that potential invoved. I am just interested in that aspect of it. Most of it has been directed strictly at the 14th amendment.

Mr. UDDO. Senator Heflin, as I understood what Professor Bork said, it was that not this bill but the section 5 precedent that is already in existence.

Mr. BORK. No, I meant that, but I also meant that the version of section 5 that many supporters of this bill advance—

Mr. UDDO. The second rationale of *Morgan*?

Mr. BORK. [continuing]. Would indeed federalize every subject.

Mr. UDDO. But depending on a case that has already been decided?

Mr. BORK. If this bill were declared constitutional on those grounds.

Mr. UDDO. OK.

Senator HEFLIN. Thank you.

Seantor EAST. Senator Baucus?

Senator BAUCUS. Mr. Bork, I would like to establish the degree to which constitutional scholars are united or not united on the unconstitutionality of this bill. As you know, 12 constitutional law scholars have signed a letter and 6 former U.S. Attorneys General have signed a letter declaring this bill to be unconstitutional.

In view of Mr. Uddo's statement that perhaps there is not agreement on this question, I am just curious as to whether you think that this is a close question. Would the majority of experts be of the view that this is unconstitutional?

Mr. BORK. I do not know what the universe of experts is, Senator Baucus.

Senator BAUCUS. Say law professors and former Attorneys General—that is a good category—since we cannot ask the Court.

Mr. BORK. I really do not know. I think there is quite a division of opinion, and the discussion is confused or embarrassed by the fact that we fail to note the differences, which are sometimes significant, between a prediction of what the Supreme Court will do in fact, what the Supreme Court has held in the past, and what the Supreme Court would do it if were following the Constitution. Those are not always the same thing.

Senator BAUCUS. Taking all those views together is there any way to generalize?

Mr. BORK. I think the spread of views here today is probably indicative of the spread of views in the law teaching profession generally. I do not think there is unanimity.

Senator BAUCUS. Thank you very much. I know there is not unanimity. I am just curious as to whether—

Mr. BORK. Well, I do not think there is anything resembling an overwhelming sentiment.

Senator BAUCUS. Would it be 50–50?

Mr. BORK. That I do not know, sir.

Mr. UDDO. Senator Baucus, why not just say that those 12 people who signed that letter feel that way? Why assume that they can speak for the whole universe of constitutional scholars?

Senator BAUCUS. Obviously, that is why I asked the question.

Mr. UDDO. How will we ever determine whether it is 50–50 or 75–25? Those 12 scholars feel that way. I suggest that of the hundreds who teach constitutional law in this country there is quite a bit of divison.

Senator BAUCUS. I hope we are not at the point where constitutional law professors are so different that there is a division of opinion on whether there are 24 hours in a day.

Mr. UDDO. We will not disagree on that.

Senator BAUCUS. All right, thank you.

Statement of Norman Dorsen

Mr. DORSEN. Thank you, Senator East.

If I may, I would like to supplement very briefly the kind introduction you made of me. I would just add two points.

One, I want to say that I also was a law clerk in the Supreme Court for a great conservative justice, John Marshall Harlan, which I am very proud of as part of my background.

Second, while it is true that I am, and have been since 1976, the president of the American Civil Liberties Union, I am not testifying today on behalf of the ACLU, even though my personal views and the views of the organization are similar.

In this connection, I would like to introduce into the record a memorandum on the power of Congress to curtail the authority of the Federal courts, dated June 9, 1981 which was prepared for the ACLU by the distinguished law firm of Wilmer, Cutler & Pickering of Washington, D.C. I have been asked to do that and I hope it will be acceptable to you and your colleagues.

Seantor EAST. Fine, thank you.

Mr. DORSEN. I shall try to comply scrupulously with your very reasonable request to be as brief as possible, although I did not realize I was going to have to be extemporaneous. I am going to have to do a little selective reading.

The essential point which I shall try to make is that section 2 of S. 158, which would withdraw the jurisdiction of the Federal courts to issue injunctions or declaratory judgments relating to State laws that circumscribe the right of women to exercise their constitutional right of privacy established in *Roe* v. *Wade*, is in my judgment, beyond the power of Congress to enact since it would impermissibly curtail the power of the Federal courts to exercise its article three authority on constitutional issues, and, second, because the purpose of S. 158, from the objective record—without psychoanalyzing any individual Member of Congress—is constitutionally improper.

S. 158, One of Many Limiting Bills

Members of the Senate, including the Members of the Senate here, recognize that S. 158 must be viewed in the context of many other bills that have been introduced to restrict the jurisdiction of the Federal courts, including the Supreme Court. These bills vary significantly in approach, but it is clear to me that the enactment of any one of them would do severe damage to the judiciary and weaken the separation of powers that is the very foundation of our Constitution.

Some of these bills do not address jurisdiction directly, but rather they seek to limit the remedies available to Federal courts when they find violations of constitutional rights.

For example, some of the bills would not interfere with Federal jurisdiction over school desegregation cases but would deal with certain remedies. On its face, S. 158 also appears to address remedy that than jurisdiction, but, in my judgment, this is a distinction that does not entail a real difference because it is obvious in the abortion context that the denial of a remedy is equivalent to denial of subject matter jurisdiction.

For that reason, I think the bill, and section 2 in particular, have to be viewed as if it involved a denial of jurisdiction.

Turning to one of the two main points in my testimony, while it is true and well understood by scholars and judges that Congress has broad authority over the Federal courts, it is also true, as the Supreme Court has said on many occasions, that Congress cannot limit this jurisdiction or make exceptions to the Supreme Court's appellate jurisdiction in ways that violate other constitutional provisions.

To take an obvious example, Congress plainly could not define the jurisdiction of the Federal courts to provide that no Roman Catholic or no Jew or no Methodist could sue in Federal court. That would obviously be a violation of equal protection. Similarly, Congress cannot restrict jurisdiction in a way that infringes on a constitutional right.

One case that is widely cited, the *Battaglia* case which was written by Judge Learned Hand, made this point very clear more than a generation ago.

S. 158 would, I think, have this precise infirmity. It would eliminate the Federal courts as the principal forum for vindicating certain constitutional rights, specifically the right of women to choose to have an abortion.

To be sure, the State courts would often be available for those with claims of constitutional wrongs, although it is not clear to me that they would always be available. I have not adequately studied—I am not sure anyone has adequately studied—the precise jurisdictional situation in every State of the United States.

In any case, it is obvious that relegating a constitutional claim to State remedies, even with potential for Supreme Court review, would not grant redress to every woman who claimed a violation of constitutional right. Many cases never reach the Supreme Court at all. Its workload prevents it from hearing any but a small fraction of the cases brought before it.

Chief Justice Burger, among many other people, has argued very strenuously that the Supreme Court does not have the time or the resources to deal with all the important cases that the Court is asked to review.

If that is true, and I think it is true, then it is obvious that abortion cases coming from State courts would be among those that would not be heard by the Supreme Court.

In some constitutional cases, furthermore, State remedies are constitutionally inadequate. In the well-known *Dombrowski* case, the Supreme Court refused to make plaintiff resort to State court proceedings for protection of first amendment rights.

Similarly, in the later case of *Younger* v. *Harris* and the earlier one of *Fenner* v. *Boykin*, the Court explicitly assumed that individuals' constitutional rights in some cases could not be adequately protected except by recourse to the lower Federal courts.

Statutes enacted by Congress, such as the Norris-La Guardia Act and the Tax Injunction Act of 1937, which deprive the lower Federal courts of the power to enter certain injunctions, limit the judicial power only insofar as there are other means by which individuals can have their constitutional rights fully protected.

S. 158 is an example of a statute which goes too far. In at least some cases, denying litigants access to the lower Federal courts for redress of their constitutional grievances is tantamount to denying the litigants their constitutional rights, for State court alternatives simply are not always available and not always adequate.

This is not intended to be a criticism of the State courts, which have bulging dockets even greater than the dockets of the Federal courts. The point is that the device of curtailing the remedies of injunction and declaratory judgment amount to the very same thing as a restriction on jurisdiction because these are the typical Federal court remedies for defeating unconstitutional measures. If they are unavailable, particularly in the area of abortion where the gestation period is limited to 9 months, it is the equivalent of erasing Federal court jurisdiction altogether.

Finally on this point, S. 158 singles out claims relating to a specific subject, abortion, and separates those claims from other constitutional claims. This singling out, which of course is discrimination, runs contrary to the theory of equal treatment embodied in the 14th amendment, a basic idea of constitutional structure.

My second point is a different one. That is: While S. 158 is in form a limitation on Federal court remedies, the purpose and effect of section 2 is substantive, that is, to make it more difficult than previously for individuals to secure constitutional rights. That is the plain purpose of the bill. It is obvious that S. 158 would never have been drafted if the Supreme Court had not interpreted the Constitution to protect women's constitutional rights to abortions. I do not think anyone can deny it. That purpose, with great respect, is not constitutionally proper.

It is true that the Supreme Court has frequently applied the rule that the constitutionality of a statute must be determined on its face and without inquiry into motives and purposes. I cite a number of cases in my prepared statement.

Just as those cases are well known, so are the well-known exceptions to this principle. Perhaps the most important one involves the equal protection clause.

For many years, the Supreme Court has declared that the unequal impact of a statute is not enough to establish a violation of equal protection. There must be a governmental purpose to discriminate. In all the cases I cite, the Supreme Court, doing the very best it can in the admittedly difficult purpose analysis in those situations, has examined congressional purposes as part of the Supreme Court's duty and responsibility. The Court has held that a statute which does not on its face articulate an unlawful purpose may, because of its language and the context in which it is enacted, disclose an unlawful purpose and an inevitable unlawful effect.

Plainly, S. 158 is intended to prevent, if possible, or at least to obstruct, fulfillment of the rights recognized in *Roe* v. *Wade*. Indeed, the sponsors of this and similar bills have been frank in acknowledging that purpose.

However, it is unnecessary to rely exclusively on such statements by the bills' sponsors. My conclusion that section 2 is unconstitutional is based on the text of the bill itself. It is impossible to conceive of any jurisdictional considerations to which the bill is relevant.

To be sure, there are cases involving the performance of abortions in the Federal courts, but they constitute only an infinitesimal part of the total volume of Federal court litigation. Thus, the bill cannot be reasonably regarded as intended to reduce the burdens on the Federal courts.

Cases involving constitutionality of State law are numerous in both State and Federal courts. It could be argued that since State laws are involved, their validity should be first passed upon in the State courts. That would throw in the Supreme Court of the United States the entire burden of insuring uniformity among the States of the standards of constitutional validity. I do not think such a course would be wise as a matter of legislative policy, and it cannot reasonably be contended, I suggest, that so singular a change—involving only abortion rights— is reasonably related to a general jurisdictional purpose.

The conclusion is clear on the face of the bill that its only purpose and its inevitable effect is to obstruct the judicial protection of the constitutional rights recognized in *Roe* v. *Wade*. Such purpose and effect, in the absence of a compelling State interest, are unconstitutional.

Quoting from several Supreme Court cases:

> *It is well settled that, quite apart from the guarantee of equal*
> *protection, if a law "impinges upon a fundamental right secured by*
> *the Constitution, [it] is presumptively unconstitutional."*

Abortion is such a right. The Supreme Court so held in 1973 with, I believe, only one member of the Supreme Court dissenting from that judgment. Congress should leave decisions of these cases to the Federal courts where they belong.

Thank you very much, Mr. Chairman.

Senator EAST. Thank you, Professor Dorsen. We appreciate that.

[The prepared statement and memorandum submitted by Professor Dorsen follow:]

Prepared Statement of Norman Dorsen

My name is Norman Dorsen. I am a lawyer, admitted to practice in New York State, the District of Columbia, and other federal courts including the Supreme Court of the United States. Before entering the private practice of law, I served as law clerk to Chief Judge Calvert Magruder of the U.S. Court of Appeals for the First Circuit and for Justice John Marshall Harlan of the U.S. Supreme Court. Beginning in 1962 I have appeared as counsel in numerous constitutional cases in the Supreme Court and other federal and state courts. Since 1961 I have been a member of the faculty of New York University Law School, where I am now Stokes Professor of Law. I have been a visiting professor and have lectured at many other law schools, including Harvard, Texas, Michigan, and the University of California at Berkeley. I was President of the Society of American Law Teachers from 1973–75.

Finally, I am and have been since 1976 the President of the American Civil Liberties Union. While I am not testifying on behalf of the ACLU today, my views and its are similar on the issues before this Subcommittee. In this connection, I would like to introduce into the record a Memorandum on the Power of Congress to Curtail the Authority of the Federal Courts, dated June 9, 1981, which was prepared for the ACLU by Wilmer, Cutler & Pickering of Washington, D.C.

Section 2 of S. 158 would withdraw the jurisdiction of the federal courts to issue injunctions or declaratory judgments relating to state laws that purported to circumscribe the right of women to exercise the constitutional right of privacy established by the Supreme Court in the case of *Roe* v. *Wade*, 410 U.S. 179 (1973), and reaffirmed in numerous decisions over the past decade. In my judgment, for the reasons to follow, this provision is beyond the power of Congress to enact since it impermissibly would curtail the power of the federal courts to exercise its Article III authority on constitutional issues and, secondly, because the purpose of S. 158 is constitutionally impermissible.

Section 2 must be viewed in the context of the many other bills that have been introduced to restrict the jurisdiction of the federal courts, including the Supreme Court. These bills vary significantly in approach, but it is clear that the enactment of any one of them would do severe damage to the judiciary and weaken the separation of powers that is the very foundation of our Constitution. This is so because all of the bills would significantly limit the power of the lower federal courts to hear or grant relief in cases where constitutional rights are at stake— whether involving prayer in public schools or other public buildings, abortion, school desegregation, and sex discrimination in the armed forces. Most of the bills also would curtail the appellate jurisdiction of the United States Supreme Court over particular issues. One bill even attempts to withdraw *state* court jurisdiction over pupil assignment to schools.

Some bills do not address jurisdiction directly, but rather seek to limit the remedies available to federal courts when they find violations of constitutional rights. For example, a number of bills do not on their face interfere with federal jurisdiction over school desegregation cases, but would prohibit federal courts from requiring the assignment of students to particular schools. S. 158 also appears on its face to address remedy rather than jurisdiction—it would prohibit lower federal courts from issuing injunctions or temporary restraining orders against the enforcement of statutes and regulations governing abortion. But this is a distinction that does not entail a real difference because it is obvious that in the abortion context a denial of a remedy is equivalent to the denial of subject matter jurisdiction. Regardless of the form that Section 2 takes, the bill is designed to and would in fact frustrate the exercise of constitutional rights, and for that reason is unconstitutional.

Constitutional scholars and judges have long debated the scope of congressional power over lower federal courts under Article III. Most commentators have concluded that the "ordain and establish" language of Article III indicates that lower federal courts are creatures of Congress and not, as in the case of the Supreme Court, of the Constitution itself. Article III, therefore, has been construed to grant Congress broad discretion to establish, alter, or eliminate the jurisdiction of lower federal courts. *See*, e.g., *Lockerty v. Phillips*, 319 U.S. 182, 187 (1943) *quoting Cary v. Curtis*, 44 U.S. (3 How.) 236, 245 (1845).

But Congress' power over the federal courts under Article III is not absolute. As always, the Constitution itself restricts Congress' enumerated powers:

> *"[T]he Constitution is filled with provisions that grant Congress or the States specific power to legislate in certain areas; these granted powers are always subject to the limitation that they may not be exercised in a way that violates other specific provisions of the Constitution."*

William v. Rhodes, 393 U.S. 23, 29 (1968). Having created the lower federal courts and conferred on them jurisdiction over cases arising under the Constitution, Congress can neither limit this jurisdiction nor make exceptions to the Supreme Court's appellate jurisdiction in ways that violate other constitutional provisions. To take an obvious example, Congress plainly could not define the jurisdiction of the federal courts to provide that no Roman Catholic could sue in federal court; such a provision would violate Equal Protection. Similarly, in *Battaglia v. General Motors Corp.*, 169 F.2d 254, 257 (2d Cir.), *cert. denied*, 335 U.S. 887 (1948), it was suggested that a congressional enactment that purported to remove certain constitutional cases from the lower federal courts would be invalid as a violation of the Due Process Clause.

S. 158 would have the same infirmity. It would eliminate the federal courts as the principal forum for vindicating certain constitutional rights. That in turn would have in some cases the effect of denying certain women the right to choose to have an abortion, a right to which they are constitutionally entitled. To the extent that an Act of Congress in effect renders nugatory established constitutional rights, the Constitution will not permit it to stand. *See Eisentrager v. Forrestal*, 174 F.2d 961, 964 (D.C. Cir. 1949), *reversed on other grounds sub nom, Johnson v. Eisentrager*, 339 U.S. 763 (1950) ("no Government action which is void under the Constitution is exempt from judicial power.").

To be sure, the state courts often are available for those with claims of constitutional wrongs. But in some cases, relegating a constitutional claimant to state remedies, even with the potential for Supreme Court review, is the equivalent of denying any redress whatever. Many cases, in fact, never reach the Supreme Court at all—its workload prevents it from hearing any but a small fraction of the cases brought before it. Thus, even if Supreme Court review theoretically would remain available, elimination of access to lower federal courts would mean in fact that most people never would have an opportunity for any federal forum to consider their federal constitutional claims.

In some constitutional cases, furthermore, it is plain that state remedies are constitutionally inadequate. In *Dombrowski v. Pfister*, 380 U.S. 479 (1965), the Supreme Court refused to make a plaintiff resort to state court proceedings for protection of his First Amendment rights, finding that threats of state court criminal action could deprive the litigant of his constitutional rights and that state court proceedings would not "assure adequate vindication of constitutional rights." Similarly, in *Fenner v. Boykin*, 271 U.S. 240 (1926), and in *Younger v. Harris*, 401 U.S. 37 (1971), the Court explicitly assumed that individuals' constitutional rights in some cases could not be adequately protected except by recourse to the lower federal courts. Even statutes such as the Norris-La Guardia Act and the Tax Injunction Act of 1937, which deprive the lower federal courts of the power to enter injunctions in certain cases, limit the judicial power only insofar as there are other means by which individuals can have their constitutional rights fully protected. Such statutes confirm the unconstitutionality of S. 158 for they reinforce what the Supreme Court already has ruled: In at least some cases, denying litigants access to the lower federal courts for redress of their constitutional grievances is tantamount to denying the litigants their constitutional rights, for state court alternatives simply are not always available and adequate. The device of curtailing the remedies of injunction and declaratory judgment amount to the same thing because these are the typical federal court remedies for defeating unconstitutional measures. If they are unavailable, it is the equivalent of erasing federal court jurisdiction altogether.

Moreover, S. 158 singles out claims relating to a specific subject and separates those claims from other constitutional claims. That singling out—or discrimination—runs contrary to the political theory underlying our entire constitutional structure. There can be little doubt that S. 158 never would have been drafted if the Court had not interpreted the Constitution to protect women's rights to abortions. The bill is simply an attempt by Congress to review, and reverse, a specific Supreme Court decision that Congress finds objectionable, as well as an attempt to amend the Constitution without going through the procedures required by Article V.

Section 2 of S. 158 is in form a limitation on federal court remedies. But the purpose and effect of Section 2 of S. 158 is substantive—i.e., to make it more difficult than theretofore for individuals to secure their constitutional rights recognized in *Roe v. Wade*. This purpose is not constitutionally permissible.

The Supreme Court has applied the rule that the constitutionality of a statute must be determined on its face, and without inquiry into motives or purposes that underlie the enactment. *See, e.g., McCray v. United States*, 195 U.S. 27, 56 (1904), *United States v. Darby*, 312 U.S. 100, 113–14 (1941); *Flemming v. Nestor*, 363 U.S. 603, 617 (1960); *United States v. O'Brien*, 391 U.S. 362, 382–86 (1968). But there are well-recognized exceptions to that principle. *United States v.*

O'Brien, supra at 383 note 30; Ely, *Legislative and Administrative Motivation in Constitutional Law*, 70 Yale L.J. 1205 (1970). Perhaps the most important one involves the equal protection clause of the Fourteenth Amendment. For many years the Supreme Court has declared that the unequal impact of a statute is not enough to establish a violation of the equal protection clause; there must be a governmental purpose to discriminate. *Snowden v. Hughes*, 321 U.S. 1 (1944); *Washington v. Davis*, 426 U.S. 229 (1976); *Arlington Heights v. Metropolitan Housing Corp.*, 429 U.S. 252 (1977); *Mobile v. Bolden*, 446 U.S. 55 (1980). And it is equally well settled that, in equal protection cases, the courts are not limited to an examination of the statute on its face. *Loving v. Virginia*, 388 U.S. 1 (1967); *Green v. County School Board*, 398 U.S. 430 (1968); *Columbus Board of Education v. Penick*, 443 U.S. 229 (1979). Most important for present purposes, the Court has held that a statute which does not on its face articulate an unlawful purpose, may, because of its language and the context in which it is enacted, disclose on its face an unlawful purpose and an inevitable unlawful effect. *Grosjean v. American Press Co.*, 297 U.S. 233 (1936); *Gomillion v. Lightfoot*, 364 U.S. 339 (1960).

Plainly S. 158, including Section 2, is intended to prevent, if possible, at least to obstruct, fulfillment of the rights recognized in *Roe v. Wade*. Indeed, the sponsors of this and similar bills have been frank in acknowledging that purpose. But it is unnecessary to rely on such statements by the bill's sponsors, and my conclusion that Section 2 is unconstitutional is based on the text of the bill itself. For it is impossible to conceive of any jurisdictional considerations to which the bill is relevant. There are, to be sure, a number of litigations involving the performance of abortions pending in the federal courts, but they constitute only an infinitesimal part of the total volume of federal court litigation. Thus the bill cannot reasonably be regarded as intended to reduce the burdens on the federal courts.

Cases involving the federal constitutionality of state laws are, of course, numerous in both state and federal courts. It could be argued that since state laws are involved, their validity should be first passed upon in the state courts. That would throw on the Supreme Court the entire burden of ensuring uniformity among the states of the standards of constitutional validity, and I do not think such a course would be wise as a matter of legislative policy. But recognizing that such a decision is within the power of Congress, S. 158 accomplishes this only with respect to injunction and declaratory judgment actions involving the particular rights recognized in *Roe v. Wade*. It cannot reasonably be contended that so singular a change is reasonably related to a general jurisdictional purpose.

The conclusion is clear, on the face of the bill, that its only purpose and its inevitable effect are to obstruct the judicial protection of the constitutional rights recognized in *Roe v. Wade*. Such purpose and effect, in the absence of a compelling state interest, are unconstitutional: "It is well settled that, quite apart from the guarantee of equal protection, if a law 'impinges upon a fundamental right secured by the Constitution [it] is presumptively unconstitutional.' " *Harris v. McRae*,—U.S.—, 65 L.Ed. 2d 784, 801 (1980); *San Antonio School District v. Rodriguez*, 411 U.S. 1, 17, 31 (1973); *Shapiro v. Thompson*, 394 U.S. 618, 634 (1969).

Memorandum on the Power of Congress To Curtail the Authority of the Federal Courts

I. The Current Bills Seeking To Limit Federal Court Authority Go Much Further Than Past Limitations Enacted Into Law   A. *Current Proposals To Limit Federal Court Authority*   Numerous bills have been introduced in this session of Congress to limit the jurisdiction of federal courts or to restrict the power of federal courts to grant certain types of relief. The bills are focused on substantive issues that are controversial at this moment in our nation's history: prayer in public schools and other public buildings, methods of achieving school desegregation, abortion, and sex discrimination in the armed forces.

All of the bills would place restrictions on the lower federal courts, and most would affect the appellate jurisdiction of the Supreme Court. Some of the bills seek completely to remove federal court jurisdiction of particular subjects, while others only purport to limit the remedies available once violations are found. Of the bills that on their face deal only with remedy, some are so broad that they would effectively preclude all federal court review of the substantive areas involved.

The bills that attempt to limit federal court rulings on questions of prayer in public schools and buildings are all virtually alike.[1] They all provide that neither the Supreme Court nor the District Courts would have jurisdiction to hear any case arising out of a state law or regulation, or arising out of any Act interpreting, applying, or enforcing a state law or regulation, relating to voluntary prayer in public schools or buildings. Each bill contains the proviso that it would not apply to any case pending at the time of enactment.[2] Together, they are the broadest of all the bills under discussion, since they would completely withdraw jurisdiction of a particular subject matter, and would do so with respect to the Supreme Court as well as the lower federal courts.

The narrowest group of bills, in terms of their approach to limiting the power of the federal courts, are those that pertain to assignment of students to schools. They purport only to limit the remedies available to federal courts, rather than totally remove school desegregation cases from the courts. Some of these bills would simply prohibit any federal court from requiring attendance of students at particular schools.[3] Others, however, would sweep more widely by precluding any federal court judgment or order that has the "effect of" or "relates to" requiring the attendance of any public school student at a particular school,[4] and such broad prohibitions are more akin to denials of jurisdiction than to prohibitions on remedy. One bill in each House would permit pupil assignment only if such assignment does not run afoul of very specific guidelines as to travel time, travel distance, and school location.[5]

---

[1] H.R. 72 (Ashbrook), H.R. 326 (Holt), H.R. 408 (Quillen), H.R. 865 (Crane), H.R. 989 (McDonald), H.R. 1335 (Nichols), S. 481 (Helms).

[2] Senator Helms' bill contains the recitation that it is designed "to promote the separation of powers." S. 481. That bill also defines "voluntary prayer" so as *not* to include any prayer composed by an official or employee of a state or local government.

[3] H.R. 1079 (Hinson), H.R. 1180 (Ashbrook), H.R. 3332 (Gaydos), S. 1005 (Helms), S. 1147 (Gorton).

[4] H.R. 340 (Holt), H.R. 761 (McDonald), H.R. 869, (Crane).

[5] H.R. 2047 (Moore), S. 528 (Johnston).

Some of the bills relating to school desegregation contain other important provisions. Several invoke the authority of Congress to ensure equal protection under the Fourteenth Amendment.[6] Two of the bills, in addition to placing restrictions on federal courts, would prohibit federal *agencies* from withdrawing or threatening to withdraw federal funds from school systems as a means of pressuring school districts to change student assignments.[7] And four of the bills would explicitly authorize suits in federal court to enforce their provisions.[8]

Most of the bills that relate to abortion are somewhat analogous to the broader school assignment bills. They purport to limit remedies rather than jurisdiction, but do so in a way that arguably would preclude review of the subject by the affected courts. One bill expressly does withdraw jurisdiction from both the Supreme Court and the District Courts over any case arising out of a state law, or arising out of any Act interpreting, applying, or enforcing a state law, relating to abortion.[9] But all of the other bills only apply to lower federal courts and are phrased in terms of remedy, prohibiting those courts from issuing injunctions, restraining orders, or declaratory judgments with respect to laws regulating abortions or regulating expenditure of funds for abortions.[10] Because much if not all modern constitutional litigation in the federal courts involves declaratory or injunctive relief, or both, and because such relief would offer the only meaningful opportunity for a woman to challenge the constitutionality of state bans on abortions, these bills in practical effect would leave little room for a court to review the constitutionality of an abortion statute at all. Hence, the restrictions in these abortion bills more closely resemble the absolute jurisdictional limitations contained in the school prayer bills than the limitations on remedy contained in the narrower school assignment bills.

Some of the abortion bills have other noteworthy provisions. One bill in each House would curtail review of federal abortion laws as well as state laws.[11] And three bills—those that would declare that human life exists from conception— invoke the power given Congress by the Fourteenth Amendment to prevent deprivation of life without due process of law.[12]

The bills that concern claims of sex discrimination in the draft and in the armed forces would limit the jurisdiction of the federal courts over purely federal matters.[13] They would bar the Supreme Court and the District Courts from exercising jurisdiction to rule on the constitutionality of statutes or regulations that authorize different treatment in the armed forces on the basis of sex with respect to induction, composition of units and assignments. One of these bills states that it is designed to exercise Congress' power under Article I, Section 8 of

[6] H.R. 761 (McDonald), H.R. 2047 (Moore), S. 528 (Johnston), S. 1147 (Gorton).

[7] H.R. (Holt), S. 1005 (Helms).

[8] S. 1005 (Helms) (authorizing suits by students, parents, school boards and faculty); H.R. 2047 (Moore) and S. 528 (Johnston) (authorizing suits by the Attorney General on behalf of students or parents unable effectively to institute suits themselves); S. 1147 (Gorton) (authorizing suits by aggrieved persons or by the Attorney General to enforce provisions).

[9] H.R. 867 (Crane). The language is like Mr. Crane's H.R. 865 on school prayer and H.R. 869 on assignment of pupils.

[10] H.R. 73 (Ashbrook), H.R. 900 (Hyde), H.R. 3225 (Mazzoli), S. 158 (Helms), S. 583 (Hatch).

[11] H.R. 73 (Ashbrook), S. 583 (Hatch).

[12] H.R. 900 (Hyde), H.R. 3225 (Mazzoli), S. 158 (Helms).

[13] H.R. 2365 (Evans), H.R. 2791 (Evans).

the Constitution "to raise and support armies . . . to provide and maintain a navy . . . to make rules for the government and regulation of the land and naval forces."[14]

Finally, one bill would withdraw jurisdiction from all lower federal courts "to modify, directly or indirectly, any order of a court of a State if such order is, will be, or was, subject to review by the highest court of such State."[15] It is difficult to determine precisely what types of cases would be removed from lower federal courts by this bill.

B. Previous Laws Curtailing Federal Court Authority   Limitations on federal court authority have been enacted in the past, but not one has even come close to doing what the present group of bills seeks to accomplish. No legislative enactment upheld by the courts has ever completely removed the authority either of the lower federal courts or of the Supreme Court to hear and decide matters of constitutional dimension or to grant necessary relief in cases of constitutional violation.

The statute perhaps cited most often in support of the argument that Congress does have power to withdraw particular subjects from the Federal courts is the Norris-LaGuardia Act of 1932. 29 U.S.C. §§ 101 *et seq.* Section 7 of that Act, which has been upheld by the Supreme Court,[16] bars any federal court from issuing an injunction in any case involving a labor dispute *unless* a hearing is held and certain findings are made. 29 U.S.C. § 107. Neither that limitation nor the limitations contained in other sections of the Act[17] attempt to withdraw the authority of federal courts to enforce existing constitutional rights.

The Tax Injunction Act, 26 U.S.C. § 7421(a),[18] which provides that "no suit for the purpose of restraining the assessment or collection of any tax shall be maintained in any court," is also cited as authority by some of the proponents of these bills. But that Act, which has been sustained by the courts,[19] does not deprive any court of its authority to enforce constitutional rights. The federal courts retain full jurisdiction to hear any constitutional challenge in a suit to recover the amount of tax after collection.[20]

The statute upheld by the Supreme Court in the case of *Ex parte McCardle*,[21] relied on by some to support the notion of plenary congressional power to curtail federal court authority, bears little resemblance to the proposed bills; it did not attempt completely to remove federal court consideration of a constitutional issue. 15 Stat. 44 (1868). The statute merely removed Supreme Court jurisdiction over a narrow class of habeas corpus cases, which jurisdiction had been conferred by Congress scarcely a year earlier.[22]

[14] H.R. 2791 (Evans).
[15] H.R. 114 (Bennett).
[16] *Lauf v. E. G. Shinner & Co.*, 303 U.S. 323, 329–30 (1938).
[17] *See* particularly 29 U.S.C. §§ 103–105.
[18] This statute was first enacted as part of the Internal Revenue Act of March 2, 1867, 14 Stat. 475 (1867).
[19] *E.g., Snyder v. Marks*, 109 U.S. 189 (1883).
[20] The difference between requiring a taxpayer to pay a tax before suing to challenge it and requiring a pregnant woman to deliver her child before challenging the abortion laws seems obvious. *See* discussion at pp. 63–68 *infra*.
[21] 74 U.S. (7 Wall.) 506 (1869).
[22] *See Ex parte Yerger*, 75 U.S. (8 Wall.) 85 (1869).

Congress has enacted other limitations on federal court authority, but none has precluded federal courts from hearing, deciding or providing effective relief in constitutional cases. Thus, the Emergency Price Control Act, 56 Stat. 23 (1942), gave exclusive jurisdiction to the Emergency Court of Appeals to enjoin enforcement of price orders, subject to review by the Supreme Court. Congress thus maintained in an inferior federal court the power to grant injunctive relief,[23] and claims of constitutional right were left reviewable by federal courts.[24] The same is true of the Voting Rights Act of 1965, 46 U.S.C. § 1973b, which provides that suits by states seeking to be relieved of coverage under the Act must be brought in the District Court for the District of Columbia. This once again leaves jurisdiction in a lower federal court, with review by the Supreme Court available.[25] The statutory anti-injunction provision of 28 U.S.C. § 2283, that federal courts not issue injunctions to stay state court proceedings, has been held inapplicable where a "uniquely federal right or remedy" is involved.[26] And Section 2 of the Portal-to-Portal Act, 29 U.S.C. § 252, which precludes federal courts from enforcing certain claims for retroactive wages under the Fair Labor Standards Act, was sustained only because no constitutional right was ultimately held to be at issue.[27] Finally, it is noteworthy that in the single instance in which Congress did attempt to exercise its control over federal court jurisdiction as a means of circumventing a substantive judicial interpretation of the Constitution, the Supreme Court held that Congress had exceeded its authority.[28]

C. Failed Attempts To Enact Similar Types of Limitations   The previous subsection dealt with bills that were actually enacted. Many other bills similar to the proposals now being considered have been introduced from time to time because of dissatisfaction with one court decision or another. Those attempts to "overrule" decisions of the Supreme Court and other courts have routinely failed. This subsection will review several of them and the burials they received.

In 1958, Senator Jenner introduced a bill designed to counteract the Supreme Court's decisions in *Konigsberg v. State Bar of California*, 353 U.S. 252 (1957), and *Schware v. Board of Bar Examiners of New Mexico*, 353 U.S. 232 (1957). Those cases held that California and New Mexico had unconstitutionally denied applications for admission to their state bars, in that former Communist Party membership, use of aliases and refusal to answer questions did not amount to a rational basis for a finding of bad moral character.

The Jenner bill, as reported by the Senate Judiciary Committee, sought to withdraw Supreme Court appellate jurisdiction of any question pertaining to state

---

[23]   *See Lockerty v. Phillips*, 319 U.S. 182, 187 (1943).

[24]   *See Yakus v. United States*, 321 U.S. 414, 434 (1944).

[25]   *See South Carolina v. Katzenbach*, 383 U.S. 301, 331–32 (1966). Indeed, Congress has acted many times to specify that a certain kind of case must be brought only in a specified court. *E.g.*, 28 U.S.C. §§ 1491, 1346(a) (giving Court of Claims exclusive original jurisdiction over certain claims against the United States); 47 U.S.C. § 402(b) (providing that appeals from certain decisions of the Federal Communications Commission are to be brought in the U.S. Court of Appeals for the District of Columbia Circuit). Such limitations are obviously much narrower than the kind proposed by the current bills.

[26]   *Mitchum v. Foster*, 407 U.S. 225, 237 (1972).

[27]   *Battaglia v. General Motors Corp.*, 169 F.2d 254 (2d Cir.), *cert. denied*, 335 U.S. 887 (1948).

[28]   *United States v. Klein*, 80 U.S. (13 Wall.) 128, 147–48 (1871).

bar admissions.[29] In debate on the floor of the Senate, Senator Jenner expressed confidence that this limitation "provides a complete remedy for the evil results flowing from the Supreme Court's decisions in the Schware and Konigsberg cases."[30] So that there could be no mistake about the bill's purpose, Senator Jenner explained:

> *The evil we are seeking to correct here is assumption by the Supreme Court of control over State bar admissions and the use of this assumed control to force individual States to accept Communists as officers of their Courts. By removing such cases from the appellate jurisdiction of the Supreme Court, this assumption of power is negatived, and its exercise for the future is prevented.*[31]

The bill was reported favorably by a divided Judiciary Committee despite written opposition from the American Bar Association[32] and President Eisenhower's Justice Department.[33] The statement of the Committee members who opposed reporting the bill noted that it would be "dangerous precedent" for Congress "to whittle away at the Federal judiciary whenever the majority disagreed with a decision of the Supreme Court," and concluded that such a practice would probably result in "the complete destruction of the Federal judiciary."[34] Senator Wiley, the ranking Republican on the Committee, added: "If we begin taking jurisdiction from the Court whenever its decisions are unpopular, our property and civil rights would soon be in jeopardy."[35] Another Republican, Senator Langer, took the position that the jurisdictional limitation in the bill "will encourage other legislation which will weaken the jurisdiction of the Supreme Court to which the people look as the guardian of our constitutional guaranties."[36]

---

[29] S. Rep. 1586, 85th Cong., 2d Sess. 4–5, 9–10 (1958). The reported bill contained other substantive provisions not affecting court jurisdiction. As originally introduced in Committee, the bill would have eliminated the appellate jurisdiction of the Supreme Court in five areas: (1) any practice, jurisdiction or contempt proceeding of any congressional committee; (2) administration by the executive branch of its employee-security program; (3) any state statute or regulation to control subversive activities; (4) rules of educational governing bodies concerning subversive activities among teachers; and (5) admission to practice law in state courts. *See* 104 Cong. Rec. 18635–37 (remarks of Sen. Jenner), 18648–49 (remarks of Sen. Butler) (1958). Following amendments in Committee by Senator Butler, only the last of these remained in the bill.

[30] 104 Cong. Rec. 18643 (1958).

[31] *Id.*

[32] S. Rep. 1586, *supra* note 29, at 37–38. Additionally, the American Bar Association's Special Committee on Individual Rights as Affected by National Security protested: "It is difficult to conceive of an independent judiciary if it must decide cases with constant apprehension that if a decision is unpopular with a temporary majority in Congress, the Court's judicial review may be withdrawn." *Id.* at 38.

[33] In a letter to Senator Wiley, who was the senior minority member of the Committee, Deputy Attorney General Walsh wrote: "Aside from possible questions of constitutionality which may be raised by a provision withdrawing jurisdiction over a narrowly limited class of cases, this Department doubts the wisdom of dealing, at this time, with specific Supreme Court rulings by amendments to the Court's jurisdictional statute." *Id.* at 37.

[34] *Id.* at 16.

[35] *Id.* at 24.

[36] *Id.* at 26.

Later, during debate in the Senate,[37] Senator Wiley said that the proposed restriction on Supreme Court jurisdiction "may very well be historically the most ruinous legislation to come out of the Senate—and the Congress—in half a century."[38] After discussing in detail the vital role of the Supreme Court in our tripartite system of government, Senator Wiley summed up:

> *This legislation violently tampers with the basic law of the land as established by the Founding Fathers. It goes to the heart of our most cherished liberties. Its consequences will undoubtedly be frighteningly unwise and can be fatal to the inherent structure of American Government.*[39]

The bill was tabled by a vote of 49–41.[40]

Another attempt to overturn a Supreme Court decision by withdrawal of jurisdiction came in 1964 in response to the ruling in *Reynolds v. Sims*, 377 U.S. 533 (1964), which required apportionment of each house of state legislatures solely on the basis of population. Senator Dirksen and Senator Mansfield, respectively the minority and majority leaders of the Senate at that time, offered a nongermane amendment to the then-pending foreign aid bill to require that any court order directing state legislative reapportionment be stayed, absent unusual circumstances, until such time as state legislatures were re-elected under previously established apportionment rules and were able to offer their own reapportionment proposals.[41] Following a lengthy filibuster, a much milder substitute was eventually passed.[42]

As a substitute to the Dirksen-Mansfield amendment, Senator Thurmond introduced the so-called Tuck amendment, named for Representative Tuck who had successfully offered it in the House. That amendment sought to remove jurisdiction from the Supreme Court and the District Courts over reapportionment of any state legislature.[43] That extreme proposal was defeated by a vote of 56–21.[44] In opposing the Tuck amendment, Senator Hart argued that the only provision for changing the Constitution is by way of a constitutional amendment, and that Congress had no more business telling the courts that they could not rule in constitutional areas than the courts would have in telling Congress that it could not legislate in those areas.[45] He concluded:

> *[W]e are not the reviewing authority of the Supreme Court, and we are not supposed to put the Supreme Court out of business. The day*

[37]   104 Cong. Rec. 18681–83 (remarks of Sen. Wiley) (1958).

[38]   *Id.* at 18683.

[39]   *Id.* Senator Hennings, the leader of the opposition to the Jenner bill, warned that passage of the bill "could be the first swing of the ax in chipping away the whole foundation of our independent federal judiciary." *Id.* at 18686.

[40]   *Id.* at 18687.

[41]   110 Cong. Rec. 19449 (1964).

[42]   *Id.* at 22564, 22758.

[43]   *Id.* at 22095.

[44]   *Id.* at 22104.

[45]   *Id.* at 22102.

we do that, history will mark as the day when this Republic began to disintegrate.[46]

And Senator Morse labeled both the Tuck amendment and the Dirksen-Mansfield amendment "attempts on the part of Congress to supersede the U.S. Supreme Court and to change our Government from one of three coordinate, coequal branches of government into a government of legislative supremacy."[47]

Even though it did not purport to withdraw jurisdiction over reapportionment completely, the Dirksen-Mansfield amendment came under attack for the same reasons as the Tuck amendment did. Senator Kuchel complained that any restrictions on the Supreme Court's authority to construe the Constitution would mean that the

> *Constitution would be interpreted by 50 State supreme courts into a political jungle of conflicting rights and responsibilities, with the Federal Government not knowing where to turn or what route to follow, and with individual citizens in a perpetual quandary.*[48]

Senator Church stated his support for a constitutional amendment that would leave apportionment of state legislatures in the hands of the states, but opposed the Dirksen-Mansfield amendment as a grave threat to "the independence of our judiciary to give force and effect to the Constitution.[49] Senator Javits stated his belief that Congress could only direct the Court to stay out of state legislative apportionment by constitutional amendment,[50] and he pleaded that it is "the function of governance to avoid dreadful confrontations."[51]

A series of votes on sections of the Omnibus Crime Control and Safe Streets Act of 1968, which ultimately became law,[52] demonstrates the way in which Congress has always separated its substantive views on Supreme Court decisions from its views on jurisdictional limitations. Title II of the bill reported by the Senate Judiciary Committee[53] was designed to circumvent the Supreme Court's decisions in *Miranda v. Arizona*, 384 U.S. 436 (1966), *United States v. Wade*, 388 U.S. 218 (1967), and *Mallory v. United States*, 354 U.S. 449 (1957). *Miranda*, of course, established guidelines for determining whether confessions are voluntary under the Fifth Amendment.*Wade* invalidated eyewitness identifications of suspects who were not given the opportunity to have counsel present during identification procedures. And *Mallory* held inadmissible statements made by a suspect who had not been promptly arraigned.

Title II dealt with both jurisdiction and substance. One substantive provision, that a confession in a federal case would be admissible if a trial judge determined

[46] *Id.*
[47] *Id.* at 22101.
[48] *Id.* at 21792.
[49] *Id.* at 21886.
[50] *Id.* at 22093.
[51] *Id.* at 22092.
[52] P.L. 90–351, 82 Stat. 197 (1968). *See* especially the portions of the Act now codified at 18 U.S.C. §§ 3501 and 3502.
[53] S. Rep. No. 1097, 90th Cong., 2d Sess., *reprinted in* [1968] *U.S. Code Cong. and Admin. News*, 2112, 2123–53, 2176.

by weighing a variety of factors that it was voluntarily given, passed 55–29.[54] Another substantive part of the bill, providing that a confession in a federal case would not be inadmissible solely because of delay in arraignment, was adopted 58–26.[55] A third substantive provision required the admissibility in federal court of eyewitness testimony identifying a suspect as having committed a crime; that also was adopted, by a vote of 63–21.[56]

Other provisions would have removed federal court jurisdiction over the admissibility of confessions and eyewitness identifications, however, and those were not adopted. By a vote of 52–32, the Senate struck from the bill the prohibition on all federal courts to review a state court ruling admitting a confession as voluntarily made if that ruling was upheld by the highest state court.[57] Similarly, the Senate removed by a vote of 51–30 the portion of the bill that would have withdrawn all federal appellate court jurisdiction over any decision by either a federal or state trial court to admit an eyewitness identification of the accused.[58] In the debate, Senator Griffin, who approved of the substantive provision making eyewitness identifications admissible, opposed the limitation on jurisdiction over that area and cautioned against upsetting "the delicate balance which exists between the legislature [sic] and judicial branches of the Federal Government."[59]

More recently, a 1972 proposed amendment to the Higher Education Act would have removed all federal court authority to make any decision that would have the effect of requiring transportation of pupils to or from school. This amendment was similar to some of the bills now pending.[60] Then-Senator Mondale opposed the amendment, stating:

> *If statutory efforts to alter constitutional rights and remedies could be made successful merely by reciting the word "jurisdiction"*

---

[54] 114 Cong. Rec. 14172 (1968).

[55] *Id.* at 14174–75.

[56] *Id.* at 14180.

[57] *Id.* at 14177.

[58] *Id.* at 14181. The Senate also struck 54–27 a section of the bill which essentially would have removed all federal habeas corpus review of state court judgments and would have left Supreme Court review of state court decisions by appeal or certiorari as the only available means of federal court review. *Id.* at 14183–84.

[59] *Id.* at 14181. The views expressed by the Judiciary Committee minority in opposition to Title II of the Committee report made the following additional arguments: (1) that Congress cannot act by statute, but only by constitutional amendment, if it wishes to change the Constitution or Supreme Court decisions interpreting the Constitution; (2) that the exercise by Congress of its power under Article III, Section 2 of the Constitution to make "exceptions" to the Supreme Court's appellate jurisdiction "must be consistent with the fundamental role of the Supreme Court in our Federal system," and that interpreting that power otherwise would "nullify[ ] the supremacy clause"; (3) that the limitations "would cause the sort of basic confrontation between court and legislature that should be avoided at all costs if possible"; and (4) that the Constitution would be reduced "to a hodgepodge of inconsistent decisions." S. Rep. No. 1097, 90th Cong., 2d Sess., *reprinted in* [1968] *U.S. Code Cong. and Admin. News, supra* note 53, at 2209, 2218–20. Senator Fong, who concurred in the statement of minority views, added in a separate statement: "I had thought it settled within our federal system that what is mandated by the Constitution may not be dismissed by legislative fiat." *Id.* at 2240–41.

[60] *See* note 4 *supra*.

the Congress could overrule any court decision, and the Constitu-
tion would be just a piece of paper.[61]

Senator Cooper later expressed the same doubt "that we can by statute limit the constitutional authority of the courts."[62] And Senator Javits pointed out the difference, in terms of congressional authority, between statutes such as the Norris-LaGuardia Act, which do not involve constitutional rights, and proposals such as the 1972 amendment, which do.[63] The amendment was defeated 50–47.[64]

President Franklin Roosevelt's "Court-packing" plan of 1937, of course, was also unsuccessful as an attempt to tamper with the federal courts because of controversial decisions.[65] Following decisions by the Supreme Court holding unconstitutional certain key aspects of his New Deal reform package, President Roosevelt had a bill introduced that would have authorized the appointment of as many as six additional Justices to the Supreme Court—one for every Justice who reached age 70 after having been a federal judge for 10 years and who did not resign or retire within six months thereafter. At the time of that proposal, six of the nine Supreme Court Justices had attained age 70. The plan, of course, was never enacted.

The Senate Judiciary Committee reported the bill adversely by a unanimous vote,[66] addressing the proposal with scathing language. A list of six primary reasons for rejecting the plan included the following two reasons applicable to the current proposals:

> *It applies force to the judiciary and in its, initial and ultimate*
> *effect would undermine the independence of the courts.*
> *The theory of the bill is in direct violation of the spirit of the*
> *American Constitution and its employment would permit alteration*
> *of the Constitution without the people's consent or approval; it*
> *undermines the protection our constitutional system gives to minor-*
> *ities and is subversive of the rights of individuals.*[67]

The Committee noted that the framers of the Constitution "created a judicial branch of government consisting of courts not conditionally but absolutely independent," and that the effect of the Court-packing proposal was "to take from the Justices affected a free exercise of their independent judgment."[68] The Committee warned:

> *If we yield to temptation now to lay the lash upon the Court, we are*

[61] 118 Cong. Rec. 5681 (1972).

[62] *Id.* at 5981.

[63] *Id.* at 5962.

[64] *Id.* at 5979.

[65] Several of the past attempts to limit federal court authority have been likened to the Court-packing plan. With respect to the Jenner Bill, *see* 104 Cong. Rec. 18682 (1958) (remarks of Sen. Wiley). With respect to the Omnibus Crime Control Bill of 1968, *see* S. Rep. No. 1097, 90th Cong., 2d Sess., *reprinted in* [1968] *U.S. Code Cong. and Admin. News, supra* note 53, at 2219–20 (minority views); 114 Cong. Rec. 14181 (1968) (remarks of Sen. Griffin).

[66] S. Rep. No. 711, 75th Cong., 1st Sess. (1937).

[67] *Id.* at 3.

[68] *Id.* at 9.

> *only teaching others how to apply it to ourselves and to the people
> when the occasion seems to warrant. Manifestly, if we may force the
> hand of the Court to secure our interpretation of the Constitution,
> then some succeeding Congress may repeat the process to secure
> another and a different interpretation and one which may not sound
> so pleasant in our ears as that for which we now contend.*[69]

The Committee thus concluded:

> *It is a measure which should be so emphatically rejected that its
> parallel will never again be presented to the free representatives of
> the free people of America.*[70]

II. Congress' Article III Power to Curtail Supreme Court Jurisdiction Is Limited   A. *Supreme Court's Essential Role*

The source of congressional power over the federal judiciary is Article III of the Constitution. Congress' Article III powers are broad, but they are not plenary; they are limited, in the first instance, by Article III itself. Article III created the Supreme Court as the head of a separate and co-equal branch of the Federal Government. Section I of Article III provides that the "judicial Power of the United States, *shall be vested* in one supreme Court, and in such inferior Courts as the Congress may from time to time ordain and establish." (Emphasis added.) Section 2 of Article III defines "the Judicial Power" to include a part "all Cases, in Law and Equity, arising under this Constitution." Thus, the Constitution itself establishes the Supreme Court,[71] and establishes its powers, while the decision whether to establish lower federal courts and what jurisdiction to give them was left to the Congress.[72]

Article III establishes both original and appellate jurisdiction in the Supreme Court. The Court's original jurisdiction extends to "all Cases affecting Ambassadors, other public Ministers and Consuls, and those in which a State shall be Party."[73] The Court's appellate jurisdiction, on the other hand, extends to both "Law and Fact, with such Exceptions, and under such Regulations as the

[69] *Id.* at 10.

[70] *Id.* at 23.

[71] In contrast to the lower federal courts about which there was disagreement, there was virtually unanimous agreement on the need for a federal supreme court. *See* 1 M. Farrand, *Records of the Federal Convention of 1787* at 21, 95, 104–05, 244, 292 (1974) [hereinafter cited as "Farrand"]; 2 Farrand at 37; 3 Farrand at 600. *See* Ratner, *Congressional Power Over the Appellate Jurisdiction of the Supreme Court*, 109 U. Pa. L. Rev. 157, 161 (1960).

[72] The decision to give Congress the option of creating lower federal courts was formulated by James Madison and James Wilson. This "Madisonian Compromise" represented a middle ground between those states that wished to mandate the establishment of lower federal courts and those that opposed any such courts. 1 Farrand at 124–25. Redish & Woods, *Congressional Power to Control the Jurisdiction of Lower Federal Courts: A Critical Review and A New Synthesis*, 124 U. Pa. L. Rev. 45, 52–54 (1975).

[73] Congress may grant to other federal courts concurrent jurisdiction over classes of cases that lie within the Supreme Court's original jurisdiction. *Plaquemines Tropical Fruit Co. v. Henderson*, 170 U.S. 511 (1898); *Börs v. Preston*, 111 U.S. 252 (1884). However, Congress cannot restrict the constitutional grant of original jurisdiction. *Marbury v. Madison*, 5 U.S. (1 Cranch) 137, 174–75 (1803).

Congress shall make." The "exceptions and regulations" clause is the source of whatever power Congress has to limit the Supreme Court's appellate jurisdiction.

The language of Article III itself limits that power and provides a basis for its proper exercise.[74] The use of the words "exceptions" and "regulations" in defining congressional power is significant. The common meaning of these words, both now and at the time of the Constitutional Convention, suggests that Congress' Article III power to fashion "exceptions" and make "regulations" with respect to the appellate jurisdiction of the Supreme Court is not plenary.[75] As Professor Hart asked rhetorically in his famous article on federal jurisdiction: "You would treat the Constitution, then, as authorizing exceptions which engulf the rule, even to the point of eliminating the appellate jurisdiction altogether? How preposterous!"[76] The Judiciary Act of 1789 did not vest jurisdiction in the Supreme Court but only created exceptions to the jurisdiction that had already been established by the Constitution. Chief Justice Marshall stated:

> *Had the judicial act created the supreme court, without defining or limiting its jurisdiction, it must have been considered as possessing all the jurisdiction which the constitution assigns to it. The legislature would have exercised the power it possessed of creating a supreme court, as ordained by the constitution; and in omitting to exercise the right of excepting from its constitutional powers, would have necessarily left those powers undiminished. The appellate powers of this court are not given by the judicial act. They are given by the constitution. But they are limited and regulated by the judicial act, and by such other acts as have been passed on the subject.*[77]

[74] The history of the Constitutional Convention, however, suggests that the framers may have intended to limit congressional power to regulate the Supreme Court's appellate jurisdiction even more than suggested by the literal language of Article III itself. Prof. Merry of Purdue, for instance, has argued that the "exceptions" clause was directed at matters of fact and not of law. Merry, *Scope of the Supreme Court's Appellate Jurisdiction: Historical Basis.* 47 Minn. L. Rev. 53 (1962). Prof. Berger has also suggested this interpretation. As Prof. Berger describes it, the "difficulty, in a nutshell, was the greatly varied practice in the States respecting review of facts, not alone injury trials but in admiralty and equity as well." R. Berger, *Congress v. the Supreme Court* Ch. 9, 287 (1969). The members of the Constitutional Convention could not agree on a uniform method for review of such factual findings by lower courts. In a spirit of compromise, they decided to leave the issue to the federal legislature. The exceptions clause of Article III simply was intended to make clear that the Congress had that power.

[75] The *Webster's New Collegiate Dictionary* defines "exception" as "one that is excepted; [especially]: a case to which a rule does not apply." The meaning has not changed since the time of the Constitutional Convention. Ash's *Dictory of the English Language* (1775) defined "exception" as "an exclusion from a general rule or law." Dyche's *New General English Dictionary* (1781) defined the term as "something taken out of a number of other things, and differing in some particular. . . . " The word "regulation" similarly implies a somewhat limited authority. The modern definition of the word is "an authoritative rule dealing with details or procedure" while "regulate" is defined as "to make regulations for or concerning" or "to bring order, method, or uniformity to." This meaning has changed little since the time of the Constitutional Convention. Perry's *English Dictionary* (1805) defined the word as "[t]o adjust by rule or method, to methodise, to dispose in order, to direct."

[76] Hart, *The Power of Congress to Limit the Jurisdiction of Federal Courts: An Exercise in Dialectic*, 66 Harv. L. Rev. 1362, 1364 (1953).

[77] *Durousseau v. United States*, 10 U.S. (6 Cranch) 307, 313–14 (1810).

The limitations on Congress' power found by the language of Article III are corroborated by consideration of the Supreme Court's central role in the constitutional scheme. The Court provides an ultimate and independent forum for the interpretation of constitutional law and the resolution of conflicts between federal and state laws. As Justice Marshall wrote in *Marbury v. Madison*, 5 U.S. (1 Cranch) 137, 177 (1803): "It is emphatically the province and duty of the judicial department to say what the law is."[78] Those bills that would eliminate the Court's appellate jurisdiction over particular constitutional rights would remove the Court from part of its province and prevent the Court from performing its duty.

Early in the Constitutional Convention, it was recognized that some part of the national government necessarily must possess the power to strike down or veto state laws in conflict with national policies. Initially, however, the delegates were not in agreement as to the appropriate repository of that power. Some proposed that Congress be given the power to veto state legislation.[79] The Madisonian position, however, that "[t]he jurisdiction of the supreme Court must be the source of redress," carried the day.[80]

Significantly, the determination of the Supreme Court's appellate jurisdiction was considered concurrently with the Supremacy Clause. Draft language for a supremacy clause was offered as a substitute for the defeated proposal for congressional review of state legislation.[81] As Professor Ratner has observed, "taken together, these resolutions evidence the Convention's purpose to make the Supreme Court the principal instrumentality for implementing the supremacy clause."[82]

---

[78] The Court expressly reaffirmed this principle of *Marbury v. Madison* in rejecting President Nixon's assertion of executive privilege to prevent the release of the Watergate tapes to the Congress. *United States v. Nixon*, 418 U.S. 683, 705 (1974).

[79] The dispute, however, centered not on whether the Supreme Court would have jurisdiction to review state laws but on whether such review, if limited to the Supreme Court, would be sufficient. Wilson of Pennsylvania suggested that judicial review was insufficient, arguing that "[t]he firmness of Judges is not of itself sufficient. Something further is requisite—It will be better to prevent the passage of an improper law, than to declare it void when passed." 2 Farrand at 391.

[80] 2 Farrand at 589.

[81] 2 Farrand at 22, 2839. *See* Ratner, *supra* note 71, at 165. The draft of the Supremacy Clause states: "The Acts of the Legislature of the United States made in pursuance of this Constitution, and all treaties made under the authority of the United States shall be the supreme law of the several States, and of their citizens and inhabitants. . . . " 2 Farrand at 183.

[82] Ratner, *supra* note 71 at 165 (footnote omitted). Persuasive support for this proposition was voiced by Alexander Hamilton in *The Federalist*, No. 22, at 197:

> *A circumstance which crowns the defects of the Confederation remains yet to be mentioned,—the want of a judiciary power. Laws are a dead letter without courts to expound and define their true meaning and operaton. The treaties of the United States, to have any force at all, must be considered as part of the law of the land. Their true import, as far as respects individuals, must, like all other laws, be ascertained by judicial determinations. To produce uniformity in these determinations, they ought to be submitted, in the last resort, to one SUPREME TRIBUNAL. And this tribunal ought to be instituted under the same authority which forms the treaties themselves. These ingredients are both indispensable. If there is in each State a court of final jurisdiction, there may be as many different final determinations on the same point as there are courts. There are endless diversities in the opinions of men. We often see not only different courts but the judges of the same court differing from each other. To avoid the confusion which would unavoidably result from the*

The role of the Supreme Court as ultimate interpreter of federal law and in ensuring uniform application of that law has been recognized from the time of the earliest Supreme Court decisions. In *Martin v. Hunter's Lessee*, 14 U.S. (1 Wheat.) 304, 347–48 (1816), Justice Story wrote:

> *A motive of another kind, perfectly compatible with the most sincere respect for state tribunals, might reduce the grant of appellate power over their decisions. That motive is the importance and even necessity of* uniformity *of decisions throughout the whole United States, upon all subjects within the purview of the constitution. Judges of equal learning and integrity, in different states, might differently interpret a statute, or a treaty of the United States, or even the constitution itself: If there were no revising authority to control these jarring and discordant judgments, and harmonize them into uniformity, the laws, the treaties, and the constitution of the United States would be different in different states, and might, perhaps, never have precisely the same construction, obligation, or efficacy, in any two states. The public mischiefs that would attend such a state of things would be truly deplorable; and it cannot be believed that they could have escaped the enlightened convention which formed the constitution. What, indeed, might then have been only prophecy, has now become fact; and the appellate jurisdiction must continue to be the only adequate remedy for such evils.*

Chief Justice John Marshall articulated the same principle in *Cohens v. Virginia*, 19 U.S. (6 Wheat.) 264, 416–18 (1821):

> *[T]he necessity of uniformity, as well as correctness in expounding the constitution and laws of the United States, would itself suggest the propriety of vesting in some single tribunal the power of deciding, in the last resort, all cases in which they are involved. . . .*
>
> *. . . [The framers of the Constitution] declare, that in such cases, the Supreme Court shall exercise appellate jurisdiction. Nothing*

> *contradictory decisions of a number of independent judicatories, all nations have found it necessary to establish one court paramount to the rest, possessing a general superintendence, and authorized to settle and declare in the last resort a uniform rule of civil justice.*

A recognition of the Court's role in providing a uniform interpretation and application of federal law is evidence throughout *The Federalist*. In *The Federalist*, No. 81 at 505, Hamilton wrote: "That there ought to be one court of supreme and final jurisdiction, is a proposition not likely to be contested." He further stated, in No. 80 at 500: "If there are such things as political axioms, the propriety of the judicial power of a government being coextensive with its legislative may be ranked among the number. The mere necessity of uniformity in the interpretation of the national laws, decides the question. Thirteen independent courts of final jurisdiction over the same causes, arising upon the same laws, is a hydra in government from which nothing but contradiction and confusion can proceed." Madison wrote in No. 39 at 285, that it "is true that in controversies relating to the boundary between the two jurisdictions, the tribunal which is ultimately to decide, is to be established under the general government. . . . Some such tribunal is clearly essential to prevent an appeal to the sword and a dissolution of the compact. . . . "

seems to be given which would justify the withdrawal of a judgment rendered in a State Court, on the constitution, laws, or treaties of the United States, from this appellate jurisdiction.[83]

The circumstances of contemporary society have, if anything, only increased the Supreme Court's role in ensuring uniform application of constitutional principles. In *Cooper v. Aaron*, 358 U.S. 1 (1958), the Court considered a claim that state officials had no duty to comply with the Court's earlier holding in *Brown v. Board of Education*, 347 U.S. 483 (1954). In an opinion signed by each of the justices, the Court reaffirmed its central role in interpreting the Constitution. The Court's statement merits repeating here:

Article VI of the Constitution makes the Constitution the "supreme Law of the Land." . . . [Marbury v. Madison] *declared the basic principle that the federal judiciary is supreme in the exposition of the law of the Constitution, and that principle has ever since been respected by this Court and the Country as a permanent and indispensable feature of our constitutional system. It follows*

---

[83] *Id.* at 416–18. Justice Taney, writing in *Ableman v. Booth*, 62 U.S. (21 How.) 506, 517–18 (1859) stated:

> *But the supremacy thus conferred on this Government [by the Supremacy Clause] could not peacefully be maintained, unless it was clothed with judicial power, equally paramount in authority to carry it into execution; for if left to the courts of justice of the several States, conflicting decisions would unavoidably take place* . . . *[a]nd the Constitution and laws and treaties of the United States, and the powers granted to the Federal Government, would soon receive different interpretations in different States, and the Government of the United States would soon become one thing in one State and another thing in another. It was essential, therefore, to its very existence as a Government, that* . . . *a tribunal should be established in which all cases which might arise under the Constitution and laws and treaties of the United States, whether in a State court or a court of the United States, should be finally and conclusively decided.* . . . *And it is manifest that this ultimate appellate power in a tribunal created by the Constitution itself was deemed essential to secure the independence and supremacy of the General Government in the sphere of action assigned to it; [and] to make the Constitution and laws of the United States uniform, and the same in every State.* . . .

Equally strong language can be found in other Supreme Court decisions. For instance, in *Dodge v. Woolsey*, 59 U.S. (18 How.) 331 (1856) the Court stated:

> *[O]ur national union would be incomplete and altogether insufficient for the great ends contemplated, unless a constitutional arbiter was provided to give certainty and uniformity, in all of the States, to the interpretation of the constitution and the legislation of congress.* . . . *[T]he framers of the constitution, and the conventions which ratified it, were fully aware of the necessity for* . . . *a department* . . . *to which was to be confided the final decision judicially of the powers of that instrument, the conformity of laws with it, which either congress or the legislatures of the States may enact, and to review the judgments of the state courts, in which a right is decided against, which has been claimed in virtue of the constitution or the laws of congress.* . . . *Without the supreme court, as it has been constitutionally and legislatively constituted, neither the constitution nor the laws of congress passed in pursuance of it, nor treaties, would be in practice or in fact the supreme law of the land.* . . .

*that the interpretation of the Fourteenth Amendment enunciated by
this Court in the* Brown *case is the supreme law of the land, and Art.
VI of the Constitution makes it of binding effect on the States "any
Thing in the Constitution or Laws of any State to the Contrary
notwithstanding."*[84]

Enactment of those bills which seek to eliminate the Supreme Court's
appellate jurisdiction over particular constitutional claims would disable the Court
from performing its central role of ensuring uniform national application of
constitutional principles. Unlike the minimal congressional regulation of federal
court jurisdiction upheld in *Ex parte McCardle* and *Yakus*,[85] some of the present
bills would appear to extinguish the federal judicial power altogether, insofar as it
extends to cases arising under certain constitutional provisions. Without the
ability to review the decisions of state and lower federal courts, there would be
varying interpretations of the same Constitution, with no opportunity for resolution. Constitutional rights would vary from state to state and the Supremacy
Clause would be reduced to a nullity.

B. Separation of Powers   For the Supreme Court to be "supreme," of
course, it must be independent. The Article III provisions providing life tenure for
judges and prohibiting diminution in their compensation while they are on the
bench are designed to ensure that the federal judiciary remains an independent
and co-equal branch of the Federal Government, immune from the day-to-day
influence of the political branches. Alexander Hamilton wrote:

*The complete independence of the courts of justice is peculiarly
essential in a limited Constitution. By a limited Constitution, I
understand one which contains certain specified exceptions to the
legislative authority; such, for instance, as that it shall pass no bills
of attainer, no* ex-post-facto *laws, and the like. Limitations of this
kind can be preserved in practice no other way than through the
medium of courts of justice, whose duty it must be to declare all acts
contrary to the manifest tenor of the Constitution void. Without this,
all the reservations of particular rights or privileges would amount
to nothing.*[86]

The independence of the Supreme Court (as well as the lower federal courts)
would be fatally compromised if Congress could grant or remove jurisdiction
depending on whether it approved of a decision, or review decisions within the

---

[84] *Cooper v. Aaron*, 358 U.S. 1, 18 (1958).

[85] *See* pp. 8–9 *supra.*

[86] *The Federalist*, No. 78 at 491. In No. 78, Hamilton also wrote:

*This independence of the judges is equally requisite to guard the Constitution
and the rights of individuals from the effects of those ill humors, which the arts of
designing men, or the influence of partaicular conjunctures, sometimes disseminate
among the people themselves, and which, though they speedily give place to better
information, and more deliberate reflection, have a tendency, in the meantime, to
occasion dangerous innovations in the government, and serous oppressions of the
minor party in the community.*

Court's jurisdiction before permitting those decisions to become effective, or require the Court to decide such cases in congressionally specified ways. In the late Eighteenth Century, Congress enacted a statute empowering federal and state courts to determine the pensions to be awarded disabled veterans from the Revolutionary War, subject to review by the Secretary of War. The Ciruit Court for the District of Pennsylvania refused to entertain a suit brought under the statute, and the Attorney General sought review in the Supreme Court. Before the Supreme Court could decide the case, Congress amended the legislation. *Hayburn's Case*, 2 U.S. (2 Dall.) 409 (1792). In dismissing the case as moot, however, the Court incorporated in the margin of its opinion several authoritative views concerning the separation between the legislative and judicial branches of government. Thus, the Circuit Court for the District of New York, consisting of Chief Justice Jay, Justice Cushing and a district judge, had unanimously held:

> *[B]y the Constitution, neither the Secretary of War, nor any other Executive officer, nor even the Legislature, are authorized to sit as a court of errors on the judicial acts or opinions of this court.*[87]

Similarly, the Circuit Court for the District of Pennsylvania (consisting of two Supreme Court Justices and a district judge) had jointly written the President in 1792 protesting the Pension Act:

> *It is a principle important to freedom, that in government, the* judicial *should be distinct from, and independent of, the legislative department. To this important principle the people of the United States, in forming their Constitution, have manifested the highest regard.*

> *They have placed their* judicial *power, not in Congress, but in* "courts." *They have ordained that the "Judges of those courts shall hold their offices during good behavior" and that "during their continuance in office, their salaries shall not be diminished."*

* * *

> *. . . Such revision and control [of judicial decision by a Legislature] we deemed radically inconsistent with the independence of that judicial power which is vested in the courts; and, consequently, with that important principle which is so strictly observed by the Constitution of the United States.*[88]

A year after *Hayburn's Case*, in 1793, the separation of powers doctrine was further clarified in an exchange of correspondence familiar to every law student. Thomas Jefferson, then Secretary of State, asked the Supreme Court for a legal

---

[87] 2 U.S. (2 Dall.) at 410 n.(a).

[88] *Id.* at 411–12 n.(a) (emphasis in original). The decisions reported in the margin of *Hayburn's Case* have been approved and relied on as a correct interpretation of the Constitution in subsequent cases, including, *e.g.*, *Muskrat v. United States*, 219 U.S. 346, 352–53 (1911), and *United States v. Ferreira*, 54 U.S. (13 How.) 40 (1852) (Taney, J.).

opinion on the effect of certain treaties. The court refused, explaining to President Washington in a letter dated August 1793, that the Supreme Court may not constitutionally give advisory opinions.[89]

The importance of the Supreme Court's independence was affirmed in *United States v. Klein*, 80 U.S. (13 Wall.) 128 (1871). There, the Court refused to follow congressional legislation designed in effect to direct the outcome of a particular case. The legislation provided that possession of a pardon should be treated as conclusive proof of disloyalty and that the case seeking return of property should be dismissed for lack of jurisdiction. The Court, however, rejected the limitation. The Court stated:

> *Congress has already provided that the Supreme Court shall have jurisdiction of the judgment of the Court of Claims on appeal. Can it prescribe a rule in conformity with which this Court must deny to itself the jurisdiction thus conferred, because and only because its decision, in accordance with settled law, must be adverse to the government and favorable to the suitor? This question seems to us to answer itself.*[90]

By impermissibly encroaching upon the independence of the Supreme Court, these bills would upset the constitutional scheme of checks and balances and cripple the federal judiciary in its role, as the third branch of the national government. As Justice Jackson wrote in his concurring opinion in *Youngstown Sheet & Tube Co. v. Sawyer*, 343 U.S. 579, 635 (1952):

> *While the Constitution diffuses power the better to secure liberty, it also contemplates that practice will integrate the dispersed powers into a workable government. It enjoins upon its branches separateness but interdependence, autonomy but reciprocity.*

It is thus not exaggeration to say that passage of the proposed bills restricting Supreme Court jurisdiction would supplant the Court as the ultimate arbiter of the

---

[89] *See* 3 Johnston, *Correspondence and Public Papers of John Jay*, 486–89 (1891). *Accord*, *Gordon v. United States*, 117 U.S. 697 (1864).

[90] *Id.* at 147. As the Court stated in *Gordon v. United States*, 117 U.S. 697, 699–701 (1864):

> *The Supreme Court does not owe its existence or its powers to the Legislative Department of the government. . . .*
>
> *The existence of this Court is . . . as essential to the organization of the government established by the Constitution as the election of a president or members of Congress. . . . [T]here was . . . an absolute necessity, in order to preserve internal tranquility, that there should be some tribunal to decide between the Government of the United States and the government of a State whenever any controversy should arise as to the relative and respective powers in the common territory. The Supreme Court was created for that purpose, and to insure its impartiality it was absolutely necessary to make it independent of the legislative power, and the influence direct or indirect of Congress and the Executive. Hence, the care with which its jurisdiction, powers, and duties are defined in the Constitution, and its independence of the legislative branch of the government secured.*

Constitution. Claimants receiving an unfavorable decision in the judicial branch would, in effect, appeal to Congress seeking passage of a bill removing jurisdiction over the particular issue. Constitutional rights thereby would be subject to the whims of ever-changing political majorities, precisely the opposite of what the framers intended. As Justice Marshall wrote in *Marbury v. Madison*,

> *[T]here is no middle ground. The constitution is either a superior, paramount law, unchangeable by ordinary means or it is on a level with ordinary legislative acts, and like other acts, is alterable when the legislature shall please to alter it.*
>
> *If the former part of the alternative be true, then a legislative act contrary to the constitution is not law: if the latter part be true, then written constitutions are absurd attempts, on the part of the people, to limit a power, in its own nature illimitable.*[91]

These bills would violate separation of power principles not only by encroaching upon the constitutional prerogatives of the judiciary but also by intruding into the constitutional role of the states as co-participants in the amendatory process. Insofar as these bills would have the effect of altering the interpretation and application of the underlying constitutional right, they would effectively bypass the formal amendment process, to the exclusion of the states. Under the provisions of Article V of the Constitution, Congress may propose constitutional amendments by two-thirds vote of both Houses. Amendments are ratified by the vote of the legislatures of three-fourths of the states.[92]

The bills which seek to restrict Supreme Court jurisdiction not only would impermissibly exclude the states from the amendment process but would expand Congress' role in that process beyond that set forth in the Constitution. Although Congress was ultimately given a role in the amendatory process, early drafters of what came to be Article V excluded Congress from the amending process: "that provision ought to be made for amending the system now to be established, without requiring the assent of the National Legislature."[93] Further constraints on congressional power in the amendatory process are provided by the need to obtain state consent and by the provision authorizing state conventions to propose amendments.[94]

III. CONGRESSIONAL POWER TO CURTAIL FEDERAL COURT JURISDICTION IS LIMITED BY OTHER PROVISIONS OF THE CONSTITUTION   All of the bills, whether they purport to affect the jurisdiction of the entire federal judiciary or only that of the lower federal courts, would in some manner impair the exercise of rights guaranteed to individuals by constitutional provisions outside of Article III. To the extent that they do so, the bills would be unconstitutional.

A. *Relationship Between Article III and Other Constitutional Provisions*
Section 1 of Article III provides that the "judicial Power of the United States,

---

[91] *Marbury v. Madison*, 5 U.S. (1 Cranch) 137, 177 (1803).

[92] Constitutional amendments may be proposed and ratified by state conventions as well. U.S. Const. Art. V.

[93] 1 Farrand at 121 (emphasis omitted).

[94] Kauper, *The Alternative Amendment Process: Some Observations*, 66 Mich. L. Rev. 903 (1968).

shall be vested in one supreme Court, and in such inferior Courts as the Congress may from time to time ordain and establish." Congress proceeded to "ordain and establish" a system of lower federal courts as one of its first acts after ratification of the Constitution in 1789.[95] By successive legislative enactments, the federal court system evolved to its present form and has remained essentially unchanged since 1911.[96] Congress conferred on the District Courts original jurisdiction of cases arising under the Constitution, laws, or treaties of the United States in 1875 (now codified in 28 U.S.C. § 1331), and original jurisdiction over civil rights in 1871 (now codified in 28 U.S.C. § 1343(3)).

Constitutional scholars and judges have long debated the scope of congressional power over lower federal courts under Article III.[97] Most commentators have concluded that the "ordain and establish" language of Article III indicates that lower federal courts are creatures of Congress and not, as in the case of the Supreme Court, of the Constitution itself.[98] Article III, therefore, has been construed to grant Congress broad discretion to establish, alter, or eliminate the jurisdiction of lower federal courts.[99]

Just as Congress does not have plenary power to change the jurisdiction of the Supreme Court,[100] however, so, too, its power over the lower federal courts under Article III is not absolute. As always, the Constitution itself restricts Congress' enumerated powers:

> *[T]he Constitution is filled with provisions that grant Congress or the States specific power to legislate in certain areas; these granted*

[95] *See* An Act to establish the Judicial Courts of the United States, 1 Stat. 73 (1789).

[96] *See generally* P. Bator, P. Mishkin, D. Shapiro, H. Wechsler, *Hart and Wechsler's The Federal Courts and the Federal System* 32–49 (2d ed. 1973).

[97] Justice Story believed that the Constitution mandated the creation of lower federal courts so that federal rights and claims could be vindicated. *Martin v. Hunter's Lessee*, 14 U.S. (1 Wheat.) 304, 330–33 (1816). Justice Story erroneously assumed that state courts could not exercise jurisdiction over federal causes of action. *Id.* at 334, 337–38. One commentator has posited that, whatever its historical antecedents, Article III now prohibits Congress from abolishing lower federal courts. He argues that because of changed circumstance, including the inability of the Supreme Court to review all cases arising under federal law, lower federal courts have become anintegral part of the constitutional structure of government. Eisenberg, *Congressional Authority to Restrict Lower Federal Court Jurisdiction*, 83 Yale L. J. 498 (1971).

[98] *See, e.g.,* R. Bork, *Constitutionality of the President's Busing Proposals* (American Enterprise Institute 1972); Harzenski, *Jurisdictional Limitations and Suspicious Motives: Why Congress Cannot Forbid Court-Ordered Busing*, 50 Temple L.Q. 14, 25–26 (1976); Hart, *The Power of Congress to Limit the Jurisdiction of Lower Federal Courts: An Exercise in Dialectic*, 66 Harv. L. Rev. 1362 (1953); Redish & Woods, *Congressional Power to Control the Jurisdiction of Lower Federal Courts: A Critical Review and a New Synthesis*, 124 U. Pa. L. Rev. 45 (1975); Comment, *Congressional Power Over State and Federal Court Jurisdiction: The Hill-Burton and Trans-Alaska Pipeline Examples*, 49 N.Y.U. L. Rev. 131 (1974).

[99] *See, e.g., Lockerty v. Phillips*, 319 U.S. 182, 187 (1943), *quoting Cary v. Curtis*, 44 U.S. (3 How.) 236, 245 (1845):

> The Congressional power to ordain and establish inferior courts includes the power 'of investing them with jurisdiction either limited, concurrent, or exclusive, and of withholding jurisdiction from them in the exact degrees and character which to Congress may seem proper for the public good.'

See also Kline v. Burke Constr. Co., 260 U.S. 226, 234 (1922).

[100] *See* pp. 24–43 *supra.*

> *powers are always subject to the limitation that they may not be*
> *exercised in a way that violates other specific provisions of the*
> *Constitution.*

Williams v. Rhodes, 393 U.S. 23, 29 (1968). Having created federal courts and conferred upon them jurisdiction over cases arising under the Constitution, Congress may not curtail this jurisdiction in violation of other parts of the Constitution.[101]

The line of federal court of appeals cases following the enactment of the Portal-to-Portal Act[102] by Congress in 1947 illustrates this limitation on Congress' power. The Supreme Court had previously construed the Fair Labor Standards Act of 1938 to require that employers compensate their employees for necessary time spent on the work premises before and after performing the primary functions of their jobs.[103] For example, the Court's decisions mandated payment for time spent changing into and out of work clothes and obtaining and returning tools and equipment. These unanticipated rulings created immense liability for both private and governmental employers. In response, Congress passed the Portal-to-Portal Act, which provided that wage claims under federal law would be governed solely by express contractual terms or by custom and practice. In addition, the statute eliminated the jurisdiction of courts over pending and future federal wage actions where the alleged liability of the employer was not based on a claim compensable under the substantive provisions of the Act. The Act was clearly intended to preclude claims based on the earlier Supreme Court rulings.[104]

When the Portal-to-Portal Act was enacted, employees had already filed several suits in various federal courts to recover wages on the basis of the Supreme Court precedent. Significantly, most courts ignored the Act's jurisdictional prohibition and reached the merits of the cases, ultimately holding that Congress could retroactively alter the statutory definition of compensable work within the bounds of the Constitution.[105] One court of appeals merely concluded that it need not consider the validity of the jurisdictional limitation because the substantive provisions of the Act were constitutional.[106] *Battaglia v. General Motors Corp.*, 169 F.2d 254 (2d Cir.), *cert. denied*, 335 U.S. 887 (1948), however, directly addressed the constitutionality of the jurisdictional preclusion, and the court observed:

---

[101] *See also Glidden Co. v. Zdanok*, 370 U.S. 530, 568 (1962); Van Alstyne, *A Critical Guide to Ex Parte McCardle*, 15 Ariz. L. Rev. 229, 263–69 (1973); Rotunda, *Congressional Power to Restrict the Jurisdiction of the Lower Federal Courts and the Problem of School Busing*, 64 Geo. L. J. 839, 851–54 (1976).

[102] Portal-to-Portal Act, 61 Stat. 84 (1947), *as amended*, 29 U.S.C. §§ 216, 251–62. *See* p. 10 *supra.*

[103] *See Anderson v. Mt. Clemens Pottery Co.*, 328 U.S. 680 (1946); *Jewell Ridge Coal Corp. v. UMW Local 6167*, 325 U.S. 161 (1945); *Tennessee Coal, Iron & Railroad Co. v. Muscoda Local 123*, 321 U.S. 590 (1944).

[104] *See Battaglia v. General Motors Corp.*, 169 F.2d 254, 259–60 (2d Cir.), *cert. denied*, 335 U.S. 887 (1948).

[105] *See Thomas v. Carnegie-Illinois Steel Corp.*, 174 F.2d 711 (3d Cir. 1949); *McDaniel v. Brown & Root, Inc.*, 172 F.2d 466 (10th Cir. 1949); *Lee v. Hercules Powder Co.*, 171 F.2d 950 (7th Cir. 1949); *Potter v. Kaiser Co.*, 171 F.2d 705 (9th Cir. 1949).

[106] *Seese v. Bethlehem Steel Co.*, 168 F.2d 58, 65 (4th Cir. 1948).

> *[W]hile Congress has the undoubted power to give, withhold, and restrict the jurisdiction of courts other than the Supreme Court, it must not so exercise that power as to deprive any person of life, liberty, or property without due process of law or to take private property without just compensation.*[107]

The Portal-to-Portal cases culminating in *Battaglia v. General Motors Corp.* stand for the proposition that Congress cannot, through regulation of federal court jurisdiction, effect what it could not otherwise achieve through substantive legislation directly altering constitutional rights. Even where legislation purports to address only jurisdiction, its validity will rest on the constitutionality of its substantive result, and the two "will stand or fall together."[108] If Congress withdraws judicial power to hear and decide claims of unconstitutional infringement of rights, it has withdrawn the right itself, and its act must be tested against that result. And, of course, the courts retain jurisdiction to determine whether such withdrawal was permissible.[109] As one court observed:

> *A basic and inherent function of the judicial branch of a government built upon a constitution is to set aside void action by government officials. . . . In our jurisprudence, no Government action which is void under the Constitution is exempt from judicial power.*[110]

Professor Berger has asserted that, whatever the scope of Congress' powers over federal and state courts, "these powers cannot be so employed as to defeat one 'of the most important and avowed purposes of the proposed government'—judicial protection of constitutional rights."[111]

Congress could not constitutionally enact legislation that directly outlaws abortions[112] or requires prayer in public schools.[113] It is equally clear that for Congress to assist the states to enforce or administer similar laws would be unconstitutional.[114] It follows that, to the extent the bills now before Congress

---

[107] 169 F.2d at 257. (footnote omitted).

[108] *Id.* The First Circuit described *Battaglia v. General Motors Corp.* as holding that "the constitutional infirmity, if any such existed, could not be circumvented by the . . . jurisdictional provision. . . . " *Manosky v. Bethlehem-Hingham Shipyard*, 177 F.2d 529, 532 (1st Cir. 1949).

[109] *See* P. Bator, P. Mishkin, D. Shapiro & H. Wechsler, *Hart and Wechsler's The Federal Courts and the Federal System* 348 (2d ed. 1973): "If the court finds that what is being done [by the government] is invalid, its duty is simply to declare the jurisdictional limitation invalid also, and then proceed under the general grant of jurisdiction." Thus, so long as federal courts have federal question jurisdiction, they always have the power to decide the constitutionality of any congressional jurisdictional limitation.

[110] *Eisentrager v. Forrestal*, 174 F.2d 961, 964 (D.C. Cir. 1949) (citations omitted), *rev'd on other grounds sub nom. Johnson v. Eisentrager*, 339 U.S. 763 (1950).

[111] R. Berger, *Congress v. Supreme Court*, 282 (1969), *quoting The Federalist* No. 82 at 517 (A. Hamilton).

[112] *See Roe v. Wade*, 410 U.S. 113 (1973).

[113] *See School District v. Schempp*, 374 U.S. 203 (1963); *Engel v. Vitale*, 370 U.S. 421 (1962).

[114] For example, Congress could not require a state to prohibit abortions as a condition of receiving federal funds, nor could Congress provide funding to states for the purpose of compensating clergymen to lead prayer in public schools. *Cf. Hunter v. Erickson*, 393 U.S. 385 (1969) (city charter amendment which provided that fair housing laws had to be approved by referendum invalidated);

would eliminate the federal judiciary as the only available or effective forum for the vindication of certain constitutional rights, the jurisdictional bills would operate in violation of substantive provisions of the Constitution and would themselves accordingly be unconstitutional.[115] Insofar as the bills would have the effect of denying certain women the right to choose to have an abortion, of forcing children to attend public prayer in violation of their constitutional rights, or of depriving minority school children of the racially integrated school environment that the Constitution mandates, they would, in essence, render some constitutional rights unenforceable and nugatory—which the Constitution will not permit.[116]

Commonly cited judicial precedents upholding congressional curtailment of judicial power are not to the contrary. The Norris-La Guardia Act[117] limits federal court jurisdiction to issue injunctions or restraining orders in labor disputes, but it affects only remedies for private controversies. It does not in any way alter judicial power over unconstitutional government action. In reviewing that statute, the Supreme Court therefore had no basis for considering whether the jurisdictional bar deprived parties seeking an injunction of their constitutional rights. *Lauf v. E.G. Shinner & Co.*, 303 U.S. 323, 330 (1938).[118]

Indeed, the cases upholding restrictions on court challenges to government action have assumed that the federal courts would always be available for the vindication of constitutional rights. For example, while the Supreme Court upheld as a valid exercise of Congress' jurisdictional and war powers[119] the Emergency Price Control Act of 1942,[120] which permitted judicial review only by an

---

Reitman v. Mulkey, 387 U.S. 369 (1967) (state constitutional provision prohibiting the state or any political subdivision or agency thereof from interfering with decisions to sell or lease or not sell or lease real property invalidated).

[115] *See* Eisenberg, *Congressional Authority to Restrict Lower Federal Court Jurisdiction*, 83 Yale L.J. 498, 511 (1974).

[116] Justice Harlan, in his concurring opinion in *Oestereich v. Selective Service Board*, 393 U.S. 233 (1968), observed that an interpretation of a congressional statute to preclude challenges to federal action "would raise serious constitutional problems." 393 U.S. at 243 (Harlan, J., concurring). Justice Harlan's statement is especially significant because the case involved an area where courts have traditionally deferred to Congress—the military draft. *See also Johnson v. Robison*, 415 U.S. 361, 366–67 (1974), where Justice Brennan noted that a construction of a military benefits statute as "bar[ring] federal courts from deciding the constitutionality of veterans' benefit legislation . . . would, of course, raise serious questions concerning the constitutionality of [the statute]"

Some commentators have asserted that preclusion or substantial curtailment of judicial review of unconstitutional governmental action violates the Due Process Clause. *See, e.g.*, Comment, *Congressional Power Over State and Federal Court Jurisdiction: The Hill-Burton and Trans-Alaska Pipeline Examples*, 49 N.Y.U.L. Rev. 131, 141–42 (1974); Redish & Woods, *Congressional Power to Control the Jurisdiction of Lower Federal Courts: A Critical Review and a New Synthesis*, 124 U. of Pa. L. Rev. 45, 76–81 (1975). The substance of the deprivation, whether classified as a violation of due process or of a substantive constitutional right is the same: the inability to vindicate constitutional rights.

[117] 29 U.S.C. §§ 101–15. *See* p. 7 *supra.*

[118] Indeed, the Norris-La Guardia Act has been cited as promoting constitutional rights—the First Amendment right to peaceful picketing. *See* Rotunda, *Congressional Power to Restrict the Jurisdiction of the Lower Federal Courts and the Problems of School Busing*, 64 Geo. L.J. 839, 852 n.72 (1976), *citing Thornhill v. Alabama*, 310 U.S. 88 (1940).

[119] *Yakus v. United States*, 321 U.S. 414 (1944); *Lockerty v. Phillips*, 319 U.S. 182 (1943).

[120] 56 Stat. 23 (1942). *See* p. 9 *supra.*

Emergency Court of Appeals and the Supreme Court, by writ of certiorari to that special court, it assumed that the statutory procedures for constitutional challenges would adequately safeguard claimants' rights.[121] The Court made clear that the Constitution requires a judicial remedy for constitutional wrongs: "A construction of the statute which would deny all opportunity for judicial determination of an asserted constitutional right is not to be favored."[122] And there is some reason to believe that even this minimal structuring of federal court jurisdiction was upheld only because Congress confronted a national economic emergency during a time of war.[123]

Similarly, the cases upholding the anti-injunction provision of the Internal Revenue Code, 26 U.S.C. § 7421(a),[124] recognize that federal courts retain the power to review the constitutionality of a tax. Section 7421(a) affects only the timing of the relief and applies in cases only where remedies other than injunctions are adequate.[125] In one such case, Justice Brandeis reasoned that "[w]here only property rights are involved, mere postponement of the judicial enquiry is not a denial of due process, if the opportunity given for the ultimate judicial determination . . . is adequate." *Phillips v. Commissioner*, 283 U.S. 589, 596–97 (1931). Even so, the Supreme Court has held that the anti-injunction provision "is inapplicable in exceptional cases where there is no plain, adequate, and complete remedy at law,"[126] *i.e.*, where the tax is demonstrably unconstitutional or otherwise unlawful. *See e.g.*, *Miller v. Standard Nut Margarine Co.*, 284 U.S. 498 (1932); *Hill v. Wallace*, 259 U.S. 44 (1922).[127]

B. Inadequacy of State Court Alternatives   To be sure, the state courts often are available for those with claims of constitutional right. But in some cases, relegating a constitutional claimant to state remedies, even with the potential for Supreme Court review, is the equivalent of denying any redress whatever. This is most clearly the case in those suits that involve claims against federal officers, because a state court may be constitutionally prohibited from granting an effective remedy. *See Tarble's Case*, 80 U.S. (13 Wall.) 397 (1871) (state court may not issue a writ of *habeas corpus* to release petitioner from federal custody); *McClung v. Silliman*, 19 U.S. (6 Wheat.) 598 (1821) (state court may not issue a writ of mandamus to compel performance of a duty by a federal officer); *Pennsylvania Turnpike Commission v. McGinnes*, 179 F. Supp. 578 (E.D. Pa.), *aff'd per curiam*, 278 F.2d 330 (3d Cir.), *cert. denied*, 361 U.S. 829 (1959) (state court may not

---

[121] *Yakus v. United States*, 321 U.S. at 437:

> No reason is advanced why petitioners could not, throughout the statutory proceeding, raise and preserve any due process objection to the statute, the regulations, or the procedure, and secure its full judicial review by the emergency Court of Appeals and this Court.

[122] *Lockerty v. Phillips*, 319 U.S. at 188. *See also Yakus v. United States*, 321 U.S. at 444.

[123] *See Adamo Wrecking Co. v. United States*, 434 U.S. 275, 290 (1978) (Powell, J., concurring).

[124] *See p. 8 supra*.

[125] *See, e.g., Bob Jones University v. Simon*, 416 U.S. 725 (1978); *Phillips v. Commissioner*, 283 U.S. 589 (1931).

[126] *Allen v. Regents*, 304 U.S. 439, 449 (1938).

[127] *See Enochs v. Williams Packing & Navigator Co.*, 370 U.S. 1 (1962) where the Court reversed an order enjoining the collection of a tax because there was no showing that the United States could not ultimately prevail on the merits of the case.

enjoin a federal officer). In other kinds of cases, although there is always a theoretical possibility of Supreme Court review of state court judgments, many cases, in fact, never reach the Supreme Court at all—its workload prevents it from hearing any but a small fraction of the cases brought before it. Thus, even if Supreme Court review theoretically would remain available under some of these bills, elimination of access to lower federal courts effectively would mean that most people never would have an opportunity for any federal forum to consider their federal constitutional claims.

In some cases, furthermore, state remedies may simply be inadequate in constitutional cases. In *Dombrowski v. Pfister*, 380 U.S. 479 (1965), the Supreme Court refused to make a plaintiff resort to state court proceedings for protection of his First Amendment rights, finding that threats of state court criminal action could deprive the litigant of his constitutional rights and that state court proceedings would not "assure adequate vindication of constitutional rights." Similarly, in *Fenner v. Boykin*, 271 U.S. 240 (1926), and in *Younger v. Harris*, 401 U.S. 37 (1971), the Court explicitly assumed that individuals' constitutional rights in some cases could not be adequately protected except by recourse to the lower federal courts. The bills now under consideration totally eliminate access to lower federal courts for litigants with certain constitutional claims. In those cases when state court alternatives are not available or adequate, these bills are tantamount to denying litigants their constitutional rights and thus are unconstitutional.

C. Equal Protection   The bills also require the most careful constitutional scrutiny because they accord some constitutional claimants preferred status over other constitutional claimants, allowing some the choice of a federal or state forum, while relegating others to state courts alone. Such discrimination could violate the constitutional guarantee of equal protection which is inherent in the Due Process Clause of the Fifth Amendment,[128] if it amounts to treating people differently on the basis of which constitutional rights they choose to exercise.[129]

In *Lindsey v. Normet*, 405 U.S. 56 (1972), the Supreme Court struck down a state statute which differentiated among persons on the basis of their legal claims. The statute required most civil claimants to post a single bond to appeal adverse trial court judgments but required that claimants appealing judgments under a forcible entry and wrongful detainer statute post (and risk forfeiting) a double bond with two sureties. Finding no reasonable justification for burdening the apeals of one class of claimants but not another, the Court invalidated the double bond requirement. It reasoned that "[w]hen an appeal is afforded, . . . it cannot be granted to some litigants and capriciously or arbitrarily denied to others without violating the Equal Protection Clause." *Id.* at 77.

A variant of the Supreme Court's rationale in *Lindsey v. Normet* has been applied to cases involving criminal appellate proceedings. In *Griffin v. Illinois*, 351 U.S. 12 (1956) and *Douglas V. California*, 372 U.S. 353 (1963), the Court ruled that where states provide appellate review as an integral component of their criminal justice systems, they may not, without offending the Equal Protection

---

[128] *See Bolling v. Sharpe*, 347 U.S. 497 (1954).
[129] *See, e.g., Police Dep't v. Mosley*, 408 U.S. 92 (1972); *Skinner v. Oklahoma*, 316 U.S. 535 (1942).

Clause, deprive some defendants of access.[130] Relying on these and other cases, Professor Tribe has suggested that there may be a "fundamental right to equal litigation opportunity" protected by the Equal Protection Clause.[131] According to Tribe, like the right to an equal vote,[132] the right to litigate carries within it "a core structural idea that the right at stake is really one to equal participation in governmental and societal decision-making."[133] That right may have special significance where constitutional rights (such as the right to privacy and the guarantee of the First Amendment) are in jeopardy.[134] In that context more than in purely private controversies[135] citizens have an active role to play in affecting their government by making it conform to the dictates of the law.

The concept of equal litigation opportunity is thus comparable to the principles articulated in cases involving the interface of the First Amendment and the Equal Protection Clause, where political participation is also at issue. *Police Department v. Mosley*, 408 U.S. 92 (1972), for example, reviewed an ordinance prohibiting all picketing near a school, with the exception of labor picketing directed at the school. In holding that such discrimination violated the Equal Protection Clause, the Supreme Court stated:

> under the Equal Protection Clause, . . . government may not grant
> the use of a forum to people whose views it finds acceptable, but
> deny use to those wishing to express less favored or more contro-
> versial views.[136]

so, too, Congress may not constitutionally deny access to established lower federal courts by claimants seeking to vindicate rights that are politically disapproved at the moment.

D. *Separation of Powers* The discrimination inherent in these bills runs contrary to the political theory and spirit of our entire constitutional structure. As Chief Justice Stone observed in the famous footnote four of his opinion in *United States v. Carolene Products Co.*, 304 U.S. 144 (1938), the political process can be trusted to weed out "undesirable legislation" that affects a broad cross-section of the populace. The same is not true, however, of legislation aimed at what Chief Justice Stone called "discrete and insular minorities." This is why the Bill of

[130] Both *Griffin v. Illinois* and *Douglas v. California* involved wealth classifications. The Supreme Court held unconstitutional the refusal of states to provide for free trial transcripts and free counsel for indigent defendants on first appeal.

[131] L. Tribe, *American Constitutional Law* 1008–10 (1978), Professor Tribe also cited *Boddie v. Connecticut*, 401 U.S. 371 (1971) and *NAACP v. Button*, 371 U.S. 415 (1963) as cases "support[ing] a theory of equal protection based on an ideal that binding decision mechanisms not be structured so as to exclude any identifiable group, no matter what claims the group seeks to advance." *Id.* at 1009–10.

[132] *See, e.g., Harper v. Virginia Bd. of Elections*, 383 U.S. 663 (1966); *Reynolds v. Sims*, 377 U.S. 533 (1964).

[133] L. Tribe, *American Constitutional Law* 1006–07 (1978).

[134] *See Skinner v. Oklahoma*, 316 U.S. 535, 541 (1942); *Police Dept. v. Mosley*, 408 U.S. 92 (1972).

[135] Professor Michelman, however, asserts that there is a due process right of access to courts in all civil actions. *See* Michelman, *The Supreme Court and Litigation Access Fees: The Right to Protect One's Rights - Part 2*, 1974 Duke L.J. 527 (1974).

[136] 408 U.S. at 96.

Rights removes from majoritarian politics decisions directly and explicitly affecting such minorities. In the place of the normal majority rule, Article V establishes a constitutional amendment process that requires a two-thirds vote of both Houses of Congress and the concurrence of three-fourths of the states. The proponents of the bills pending before Congress would seek to circumvent this constitutional process by legislating explicitly against those "discrete and insular minorities" and against those rights which the Supreme Court has held protected by the Constitution.

Congress' singling out for insulation from federal court review of several specific areas where Congress disagrees with the judiciary's interpretation would be especially pernicious. Whatever the courts' reluctance to delve into questions of legislative intent to violate constitutional norms, the Supreme Court has not hesitated to strike down legislation whose only purpose and effect plainly is to curtail or discourage the exercise of constitutional rights.[137] There can be little doubt that the present bills would never have been introduced if the Supreme Court had not construed the Constitution to protect women's rights to choose abortions (in some circumstances), and children's rights to be free from prayer or segregation in public schools. Thus, even if Congress may regulate federal court jurisdiction in a neutral manner,[138] these bills raise significant constitutional problems because they are aimed at curtailing constitutional rights identified and protected by the federal judiciary.[139]

The Supreme Court in the past has found that *post hoc* congressional attempts to interfere with its decision-making violate Article III. In *United States v. Klein*, 80 U.S. (13 Wall.) 128 (1871), the Court invalidated a jurisdictional regulation, in part, because the statute

> *shows plainly that it does not intend to withhold appellate jurisdiction except as a means to an end. Its great and controlling purpose is to deny pardons granted by the President the [constitutional] effect which the court has adjudged them to have.*[140]

The pending bills are similar attempts by their proponents to review and reverse specific Supreme Court decisions that have been deemed objectionable, and they might very well be struck down on that ground alone.

IV. THE PROPOSED LIMITATIONS ON EQUITABLE RELIEF WOULD VIOLATE THE SEPARATION OF POWERS AND INDIVIDUALS' CONSTITUTIONAL RIGHTS UNDER THE FOURTEENTH AMENDMENT   Several of the bills now pending in Congress would directly prohibit federal courts from entering busing orders in

---

[137] *See Shapiro v. Thompson*, 394 U.S. 618, 631 (1968); *United States v. Jackson*, 390 U.S. 570, 581 (1968).

[138] *See* Eisenberg, *Congressional Authority to Restrict Lower Court Jurisdiction*, 83 Yale L.J. 498, 514–30 (1974).

[139] An invidious legislative motive has been held to have constitutional significance. *See Arlington Heights v. Metropolitan Hous. Dev. Corp.*, 429 U.S. 252 (1977); *Washington v. Davis*, 426 U.S. 229 (1976). An impermissible objective may be demonstrated where, as here, there is a clear legislative pattern that cannot be explained by any other rationale. *See Arlington Heights v. Metroplitan Hous. Dev. Corp.*, 429 U.S. at 266; *Gomillion v. Lightfoot*, 364 U.S. 339 (1960); *Yick Wo v. Hopkins*, 118 U.S. 356 (1886).

[140] 80 U.S. (13 Wall.) at 145.

school desegregation cases or from granting equitable relief in cases challenging abortion statutes. Busing, of course, is a remedy the federal courts have employed in order to correct past constitutional discrimination in schooling; it is not a constitutional right in itself. The busing jurisdiction bills, therefore, differ from the other bills curtailing federal court jurisdiction in that they purport to limit only the relief that federal courts could give for certain constitutional violations—not the court's ability to decide whether there was such a violation. Certain of the abortion jurisdiction bills on their face also would appear to restrict only the relief given and not the underlying constitutional right to choose an abortion. Nevertheless, the jurisdictional bills with respect to equitable relief raise substantial constitutional problems with respect to both the separation of powers and equal protection under the law.

In a school desegregation case over which a federal district court has jurisdiction and in which the court has found deprivation of a constitutional right, the court may in the exercise of its equity power enter an order requiring some busing in order to fashion an effective remedy. Similarly, federal courts having jurisdiction over challenges to abortion statutes have the power to enter injunctions and temporary restraining orders in order to give effective relief to constitutional claimants. Because the federal jurisdictional bills now pending in Congress would render such orders nugatory, they would interfere with the constitutional separation of powers. *See* the discussion at pp. 35–39 *supra. See also Schneiderman v. United States*, 320 U.S. 118, 168–69 (1943), where Justice Rutledge stated, concurring, that Congress may not make:

> . . . . *an adjudication under Article III merely an advisory opinion or prima facie evidence of the fact or all the facts determined. Congress has, with limited exceptions, plenary power over the jurisdiction of the federal courts.* But to confer the jurisdiction and at the same time nullify entirely the effects of its exercise are not matters heretofore thought, when squarely faced, within its authority.

[Footnotes omitted; emphasis added.] *Cf. Sterling v. Constantin*, 287 U.S. 378, 403 (1932) (Hughes, C.J.).

On equal protection grounds, the bills now pending in Congress that would prevent federal courts from giving certain forms of equitable relief are subject to the same attack outlined under section III of this memorandum, *supra*, namely, that the result of such regulation of remedy would be to interfere with individuals' constitutional rights with respect to school desegregation and abortion. Courts order school desegregation where they have found that the segregated conditions are due, at least in part, to intentional official conduct in violation of the Fourteenth Amendment.[141] Once a court has found a constitutional violation,

---

[141] *Swann v. Charlotte-Mecklenburg Bd. of Educ.*, 402 U.S. 1, 16 (1971); *Deal v. Cincinnati Bd. of Educ.*, 369 F.2d 55, 62 (6th Cir. 1966); *Bell v. School City of Gary, Indiana*, 324 F.2d 209 (7th Cir. 1963), *cert. denied*, 377 U.S. 924 (1964); *U.S. v. School District 151*, 286 F. Supp. 786, 797 (N.D. Ill. 1968), *aff'd*, 404 F.2d 1125 (1968); *Taylor v. Bd. of Educ.*, 191 F. Supp. 181, 182–83 (S.D.N.Y.), *aff'd*, 294 F.2d 36 (2d Cir.), *cert. denied*, 368 U.S. 940 (1961).

however, the Fourteenth Amendment requires the discriminating agency to "effectuate a transition to a racially nondiscriminatory school system," *Brown v. Board of Education*, 349 U.S. 294, 301 (1955) (hereinafter cited as "*Brown II*") and to "take whatever steps might be necessary to convert to a unitary system in which racial discrimination would be eliminated root and branch." *Green v. County School Board*, 391 U.S. 430, 437–38 (1968). The authority of the federal courts to issue orders requiring such affirmative action is inherent in their equity power. *Brown II, supra.* The validity of court orders is not affected by the fact that they may be difficult or burdensome:

> *All things being equal, with no history of discrimination, it might well be desirable to assign pupils to schools nearest their homes. But all things are not equal in a system that has been deliberately constructed and maintained to enforce racial segregation. The remedy for such segregation may be administratively awkward, inconvenient, and even bizarre in some situations and may impose burdens on some; but all awkwardness and inconvenience cannot be avoided in the interim period when remedial adjustments are being made to eliminate the dual school systems.*

Swann v. Charlotte-Mecklenburg Board of Education, 402 U.S. 1, 28 (1971).

As Chief Justice Burger observed in *Swann, supra,* at 30, busing is one "remedial technique[ ] . . . within [the] court's power to provide equitable relief . . ." in a case of constitutional injury to school children.

> *[W]e find no basis for holding that the local school authorities may not be required to employ bus transportation as one tool of school desegregation. Desegregation plans cannot be limited to the walk-in school.*

Id. Other techniques include teacher transfers, majority-minority "free" student transfers, rezoning (gerrymandered or "satellite" or both), pairing, and new school construction. Courts order busing in combination with other techniques.

> *The scope of permissible transportation of students as an* implement of a remedial decree *has never been defined by this Court and by the very nature of the problem it cannot be defined with precision. No rigid guidelines as to student transportation can be given for application to the infinite variety of problems presented in thousands of situations.*

Id. at 29 (emphasis added). The Supreme Court has ruled that, as a practical matter, busing is the *only* remedy that will correct certain violations of the Fourteenth Amendment. *See Swann v. Charlotte-Mecklenburg Board of Education*, 402 U.S. 1, 28 (1971). Thus, frustration or denial of court-ordered remedies for school desegregation cannot be distinguished from frustration or denial of the underlying Fourteenth Amendment right. *See Griffin v. School Board*, 377 U.S. 218, 232 (1964); *Cooper v. Aaron*, 358 U.S. 1, 17 (1958).

Indeed, in *North Carolina State Board of Education v. Swann*, 402 U.S. 143 (1971), the Supreme Court struck down a state statute imposing an absolute prohibition on involuntary busing of any student on grounds of race or to bring about racial balance. The court said that this ban would inescapably operate to obstruct the remedies granted in the *Charlotte-Mecklenburg* case, and noted that because

> *[B]us transportation has long been an integral part of all public educational systems . . . it is unlikely that a truly effective remedy could be devised without continued reliance upon it.*

402 U.S. at 46.

If a state anti-busing statute violates the Fourteenth Amendment "when it operates to hinder vindication of federal constitutional guarantees," it is difficult to conclude that a congressional statute achieving the same result could possibly be constitutional.

The need for equitable relief in cases challenging abortion statutes is even more plain. The very nature of the constitutional right being asserted requires that effective relief be given quickly. If a woman's constitutional right to choose what to do with her own body is to mean anything of substance, therefore, courts must have the power to restrain officials from irreversibly changing the status quo under statutes that are unconstitutional. To deny such power is to deny the right itself.

V. CONCLUSION   The bills to curtail federal court jurisdiction now pending in Congress are without precedent in the history of our Republic. Their effect would be to modify basic political relationships as set forth in the Constitution—relationships between the Congress and the federal judiciary, between federal and state governments, and between individual citizens and their governments. As a result, the bills are inconsistent with various constitutional provisions and guarantees. Those bills curtailing the jurisdiction of the Supreme Court are at odds with the Article III guarantee of an independent Supreme Court as ultimate arbiter of the Constitution. The bills eliminating lower federal court power to hear and decide cases involving specific constitutional rights would deprive various individuals of those rights and would discriminate against certain litigants in ways that would violate the Equal Protection guarantee of the Constitution. And even the bills that appear on the surface to deal only with remedies, in practical effect would directly curtail the underlying right, for the remedies they would eliminate are in many cases the only effective redress for violation of constitutional rights.

Senator EAST. Professor Rice?

Statement of Charles Rice

Mr. RICE. Thank you, Senator.

I am pleased to be here for a number of reasons, one of which is that Professor Dorsen and I are old friends from New York University. It is a great pleasure to meet him here. I wish that some day we would have the opportunity to testify on the same side of an issue.

In any event, I sympathize with Professor Dorsen and Professor Eisenberg because they obviously are opposed to this bill. They think it is unwise. But we sometimes run the risk of translating objections as to the wisdom of legislation into conclusions as to the power of Congress.

The issue here in this hearing is not the wisdom of the legislation. The issue is whether this legislation is within the power of Congress to enact.

As far as the lower Federal courts are concerned, the Constitution did not create them. It left the issue of their creation or not entirely up to Congress.

I do not want to read long passages into the record. However, I do want to take a few sentences from the extensive and very descriptive dictum by the Supreme Court in the *Palmore* case in which the Court described this question of article 3 power over the lower Federal courts.

The Supreme Court said that Congress:

> . . . *was not constitutionally required to create inferior Art III courts to hear and decide cases within the judicial power of the United States, including those criminal cases arising under the laws of the United States. . . . Nor, if inferior federal courts were created, was it required to invest them with all the jurisdiction it was authorized to bestow under Art III. "[T]he judicial power of the United States . . . is (except in enumerated instances, applicable exclusively to this court) dependent for its distribution and organization, and for the modes of its exercise, entirely upon the action of Congress, who possess the sole power of creating the tribunals (inferior to the Supreme Court) . . . and of investing them with jurisdiction either limited, concurrent, or exclusive, and of withholding jurisdiction from them in the exact degrees and character which to Congress may seem proper for the public good." Congress plainly understood this, for until 1875 Congress refrained from providing the lower Federal courts with general Federal-question jurisdiction. Until that time the State courts provided the only forum for vindicating many important Federal claims. Even then, with exceptions, the State courts remained the sole forum for trial of Federal cases not involving the required jurisdictional amount, and for the most part retained concurrent jurisdiction of Federal claims properly within the jurisdiction of the lower Federal courts.*

We have several technical problems that do come up in this respect in terms of what a statute can do. The question is: Are there absolutely no limits on the power of Congress? In a sense, yes, but in another sense, no.

I agree with Professor Dorsen that a statute could not provide, for example, that Catholics or blacks may not sue in a U.S. district court. Why would this be so? It would be so because it would collide with another prohibition of the Constitution, not because Catholics or blacks have a constitutional right to appear in Federal court but rather because they have a right to be treated without discrimination with respect to their religion or race.

A criterion saying that a Catholic or a black could not sue in a Federal court would be a criterion having nothing to do with the character of the case. That is why it would be unconstitutional.

However, Congress can surely take jurisdiction away over a class of cases.

Some of those litigants will be Catholic. Some of those litigants will be black, but they are not discriminated against because of their religion or their race.

The question then becomes can Congress do this where it has an impact on the substantive issues involved. Clearly this is not merely an economy measure. Clearly this bill is prompted by the abortion rulings. If it is enacted, it will be actuated by opposition to those rulings, but there is no limitation on article 3 such that Congress cannot take a substantive class of cases away from the Federal courts. There is absolutely no limitation which says that they cannot do it on the grounds that they disagree with those limitations. Of course they can.

There is a very basic principle that the courts should not inquire into the motive of the legislature. It is true that there has been development in racial discrimination cases, particularly where the Supreme Court has required purposeful discrimination. The reason why that has been a notable development is because it is an exception to the very healthful rule which has been retained since the early years of the Republic.

There is another limitation which we have to be careful about. The Human Life bill, or section 2 of S. 158, I believe clearly can take jurisdiction away from the U.S. district courts, as it does, but it would be improper for Congress to require the courts to decide a case in a particular way.

For example, it would be improper for the act to take away jurisdiction only to issue an injunction on one side instead of on the other side, in favor instead of against the abortion law. This, I think, is a limitation which is not violated by the language of section 2. Section 2 is evenhanded. It simply says they cannot issue an injunction either way or any way in such a case.

As far as the wisdom of the legislation is concerned, I would like to offer a remark on that because I really believe that the opposition of my distinguished colleagues is primarily based upon the fact that they disagree with the wisdom of the legislation. I respect their constitutional arguments, but they are without foundation. It comes down to a question of wisdom.

There is wisdom in section 2. It is a prudent piece of legislation because it puts the initial decision in the State courts. This is prudent because one of the valid objections to *Roe* v. *Wade*, even apart from what one thinks on the substantive issue of abortion, is that *Roe* v. *Wade* was an undue interference with the prerogatives of the states.

This is not a legal argument, but it is a prudential argument. In my opinion, it is a quite wise course for Congress to say we want to get the fullest possible ventilation of this issue in the State courts without having those courts short circuited right at the outset by interdiction from the Federal courts.

Those remarks go to the wisdom of the legislation, but there is just absolutely no question that Congress has the power to do this. It is not subject to any of the possible limitations on article 3 power over the lower courts, as I have discussed, and I just do not think there is even a ballgame about it. I think it is just so clear that it is period, paragraph, next case.

Thank you, Senator.

Senator EAST. Thank you, Professor Rice.

[The prepared statement of Professor Rice follows:]

Prepared Statement of Charles Rice

This testimony is limited to the constitutionality of Section 2 of the Human Life Bill (S. 158), which provides:

> *"Sec. 2. Notwithstanding any other provision of law, no inferior Federal court ordained and established by Congress under article III of the Constitution of the United States shall have jurisdiction to issue any restraining order, temporary or permanent injunction, or declaratory judgment in any case involving or arising from any State law or municipal ordinance that (1) protects the rights of human persons between conception and birth, or (2) prohibits, limits, or regulates (a) the performance of abortions or (b) the provision at public expense of funds, facilities, personnel, or other assistance for the performance of abortions."*

The Constitution [Art III, Sec. 1] provides, "The judicial power of the United States, shall be vested in one supreme court, and in such inferior courts as the Congress may from time to time ordain and establish." The Constitution itself did not create the lower federal courts. Instead it left to Congress the decision whether to create such courts and, if Congress chose to create them, how much of the jurisdiction encompassed within the federal judicial power it ought to confer upon them. Congress need not have created such courts at all. Having created them, it need not vest in them jurisdiction to decide the full range of cases within the federal judicial power. For instance, until 1875, the lower federal courts had no general jurisdiction in cases arising under the Constitution or laws of the United States. [See Hart and Wechsler, The Federal Courts and the Federal System (1953), 727–33] Today, the jurisdiction of the lower federal courts is limited in some respects by the requirement of jurisdictional amount and in other respects as to the classes of cases in which they are empowered to exercise jurisdiction. The Norris-La Guardia Act, for example, withdrew from the lower federal courts jurisdiction to issue injunctions in labor disputes. The constitutionality of the Norris-La Guardia Act was sustained by the Supreme Court in *Lauf v. E. G. Shinner and Co.* [303 U.S. 323, 330 (1938)]

More recently, in an extensive dictum in *Palmore v. U.S.* [411 US 389, 400–402] the Supreme Court summarized the status of the lower federal courts under Article III:

> *Article III describes the judicial power as extending to all cases, among others, arising under the laws of the United States; but, aside from this Court, the power is vested "in such inferior Courts as the Congress may from time to time ordain and establish." The decision with respect to inferior federal courts, as well as the task of defining their jurisdiction, was left to the discretion of Congress. That body was not constitutionally required to create inferior Art III courts to hear and decide cases within the judicial power of the United States, including those criminal cases arising under the laws of the United States. Nor, if inferior federal courts*

were created, was it required to invest them with all the jurisdiction it was authorized to bestow under Art III. "[T]he judicial power of the United States . . . is (except in enumerated instances, applicable exclusively to this court) dependent for its distribution and organization, and for the modes of its exercise, entirely upon the action of Congress, who possess the sole power of creating the tribunals (inferior to the Supreme Court) . . . and of investing them with jurisdiction either limited, concurrent, or exclusive, and of withholding jurisdiction from them in the exact degrees and character which to Congress may seem proper for the public good." Cary v. Curtis, 3 How 236, 245, 11 L Ed 576 (1845).[9] Congress plainly understood this, for until 1875 Congress refrained from providing the lower federal courts with general federal-question jurisdiction. Until that time, the state courts provided the only forum for vindicating many important federal claims. Even then, with exceptions, the state courts remained the sole forum for the trial of federal cases not involving the required jurisdictional amount, and for the most part retained concurrent jurisdiction of federal claims properly within the jurisdiction of the lower federal courts.

9. [This was the view of the Court prior to Martin v. Hunter's Lessee, 1 Wheat 304, 4 L Ed 97 (1816). Turner v. Bank of North America, 4 Dall 8, 1 L Ed 718 (1799); United States v. Hudson, 7 Cranch 32, 3 L Ed 259 (1812). And the contrary statements in Hunter's Lessee, supra, at 327–339, 4 L Ed 97, did not survive later cases. See for example, in addition to Cary v. Curtis, 3 How 236, 11 L Ed 576 (1845), quoted in the text, Rhode Island v. Massachusetts, 12 Pet 657, 721–722, 9 L Ed 1233 (1838); Sheldon v. Sill, 8 How 441, 12 L Ed 1147 (1850); Case of the Sewing Machine Companies, 18 Wall 553, 577–578, 21 L Ed 914 (1874); Kline v. Burke Construction Co., 260 US 226, 233–234, 67 L Ed 226, 43 S Ct 79, 24 ALR 1077 (1922).

While various theories have been advanced to argue for restrictions on Congress' power over the jurisdiction of the lower federal courts, none of them is supported by the Supreme Court. Not only does the greater discretion to create, or not, the federal courts themselves include the lesser power to define their jurisdiction, the evident intent of the framers was to vest in the Congress the capacity to make the prudential judgment as to which courts, state or federal, should decide constitutional cases on the lower and intermediate levels.

The jurisdictional provision of Section 2 of the Human Life Bill are clearly within the power of congress under Article III.

Senator EAST. We deeply appreciate the comments of all three of you. As I have indicated, we will remind people of our time factor. We expect to adjourn at 1 o'clock. We would hope then to finish up this panel at 11:30, which would give us about 35 minutes.

If it is agreeable with my distinguished colleagues here, I will ask questions for about 10 minutes, and then we will turn it to Senators Baucus and Heflin. We will see if we cannot wind up our interrogations somewhere around 11:30.

It would be helpful to the three of us who hope to learn from the three of you if you would be as concise as you can consistent with making your point as far as our inquiries go. It will give the three of us the opportunity to probe further. If we want to follow up and get more from you, certainly each Senator would have the right and prerogative to do that.

For the uninitiated who may be with us for the first time this morning, we are discussing that section of S. 158 which deals with the question of whether the lower Federal courts would have jurisdiction to hear matters involving S. 158 and the issues that it raises.

We are focusing upon a facet of this bill dealing with court jurisdiction. That is what these gentlemen are here to testify about. We are trying to take it a step at a time.

Professor Dorsen, I would like to address my remarks to you. First, I would like to correct you in that there were two dissenters in *Roe* v. *Wade*, Byron White and William Rehnquist. They both said that this was an improvident and extravagant use of the power of judicial review. They both joined in that terminology to describe *Roe* v. *Wade*.

Then in a separate dissent, Justice Rehnquist called it judicial legislation. Both made it clear that in their judgment the Court had gone way beyond reasonable conceptions of the power of judicial review as envisioned in *Marbury* v. *Madison* or the *Federalist Number 78*.

I did want to correct the record there in that we did have two dissenting opinions. It is of interest when the Court itself, its own membership, has profound reservations about what it is doing and describes it so pointedly as improvident and extravagant. That is strong language to describe that institution's decision in this area.

Let me just put it in perspective. I would appreciate your response to this. I will put it in a little broader policy context.

What you are really seeing here—let us be candid about it—is a response of the legislative body—it is very much a problem of separation of powers—to what is perceived by many, although agreed not all, as a very serious intrusion of the Federal judiciary into a legitimate legislative policymaking function.

There is little or no constitutional justification as these people see it, including Byron White and William Rehnquist, for what has been done here, and Congress is attempting to find some remedy, some way of response.

Let me put it this way: If *Roe* v. *Wade* had held that the unborn are protected from the time of conception and had defined that as a constitutional right as opposed to the right of privacy of the woman, there would be a strong movement in this country to try to change that result. I mean, it is inherent in the democratic process. There are deep poles on this question.

As Professor Rice is suggesting, and I will say candidly that I agree with him, it strikes me—I do not fault them because we all do this from time to time, perhaps consciously or unconsciously—that people are defending their political turf here.

Some people like the policy result of *Roe* v. *Wade*. They might have preferred that Congress had done it, or perhaps that all the States had done it individually, but they like it. They like it as a policy decision. Hence, when they perceive any threat to that either through legislative action by Congress or whatever, they are immediately quick to man the barricades and say this cannot be done and that cannot be done.

What we are doing here is simply accepting, as the defenders of the bill are saying, a tacit invitation by the Court to define when life begins. We have already been through that.

The second part is a matter of jurisdiction. With all due respect to both of you, and you state your arguments extremely well and I follow your line of reasoning, article 3 is rather categorical and has historically been so considered. It gets back to separation of powers, check and balance, and that there is the power of the Congress to create the Federal courts. We have the powers to abolish the lower Federal courts tomorrow. That would be generally conceded, would it not? We could abolish the courts of appeals and the district courts.

The only court that is required under article 3 is the Supreme Court. We could not abolish that one. We could take away all its appellate jurisdiction. We could leave it high and dry with its original jurisdiction.

However, great power is given by the Constitution to the Congress. It is first among equals. As a matter of political theory, I would argue that is very appropriate in a country predicated upon the idea of representative government, self government, where the major policy decisions are made by the legislative body, which is Congress.

Many people feel that over recent years there has been a gross intrusion here. I would hope the Court would take note of it. Maybe the dialog itself would cause them to put on the brakes. That right there would make the hearings useful.

To my point, is not what we are doing here a fairly modest thing? One, we are simply accepting an invitation to determine when life begins. Two, we are regulating jurisdiction, a power we have under article 3. Interestingly, we are only regulating the lower Federal courts, leaving the Supreme Court the option to get in on the act and to determine if what we are doing here is appropriate. If they found it inappropriate, I suppose for those who wished to change *Roe* v. *Wade*, one would have to go the road of the constitutional amendment, but first things first.

I am suggesting it is a very modest approach, nothing particularly radical or dramatic or overbearing about it. It is just the little old Congress trying to assert its policymaking function and just putting its little feet in the water and seeing how it is going. A lot of folks, it seems to me, are trying to frighten us away by saying whoever heard of such a thing?

The framers heard of it. They put it in article three. It is part of the checks and balances. Congress has enormous power here over the Federal courts. We are not saying we ought to exercise it in every case. We are not saying we should exercise it casually or cavalierly or precipitously, but certainly we have that power.

When the Congress feels it has gone too far, why can it not intervene? What is the great constitutional crisis that we are creating? I would argue the constitutional crisis has been created by the Supreme Court. They put us in this box. Now we are trying to find some way out of it.

I do not know what Congress will eventually do with it. I hope it stays steady on course and begins to reassert its policymaking function in a whole host of areas. This is just one.

Whatever result we end up with, whether it is in abortion or busing or any of a variety of things—we may ultimately have to face the draft issue since we do not know what the court is going to do when it hands down that decision—sooner or later Congress is going to have enough will power to say we are the principal policymakers and we are going to get involved. That is what this effort is right here.

On the modest question of article three, can I not get you to back off just a little bit and argue that what we are doing is very consistent with our constitutional prerogative?

Mr. DORSEN. I will interpret that as a question that you are directing to me.

First of all, I do want to thank you for correcting my error about the number of dissenters. I appreciate that very much. I had forgotten that Byron White had also dissented.

Let me comment on your various points. First of all, dissenters always say that the Supreme Court has usurped power. Seven justices disagreed with those two, including Mr. Justice Blackmun, a conservative justice from Minnesota, and the Chief Justice of the United States, who I have never yet heard accused of being a radical. They thought about this issue. They thought about it hard. They came out differently from Mr. Justice Rehnquist and Mr. Justice White.

Article 3 does speak in categorical terms. There are no exceptions in article 3 about the power of Congress. If that is true, why does my good and old friend Professor Rice say that a violation of the equal protection clause would occur if Congress attempted to exercise its power to cut back the jurisdiction of the Federal courts to hear cases by blacks or Roman Catholics or Jews or anybody else?

These three categories are not the only rights protected by the Constitution. There are also fundamental rights protected by the Constitution. One of those fundamental rights is the right of privacy and autonomy that seven justices of the Supreme Court, including not only the two conservatives I mentioned but also Mr. Justice Powell and Mr. Justice Stewart, again deep thinkers about the proper allocation of power in this country, upheld.

You stated very forcefully and helpfully your view of the dialog of the constitutional system. You stated that the key to our constitutional system is majority rule.

With respect, I think that is just one of the two great keys to our system. One is democracy and majority rule and I stand second to none in supporting that in situations where it is applicable.

However, there is another great key. That is the protection of minorities and the protection of dissenters and the protection of people who do not have their constitutional rights protected by the majority. We would not need the Supreme Court and we would not need the Federal courts to protect the majority, whose rights are secure in any event.

In that connection, I should note that I have testified before committees of Congress for many years on behalf of congressional power. I testified on behalf of congressional power in the war powers area and on behalf of congressional power in the executive privilege area when it was not altogether popular to do so, when many people were saying that the President has to run the country. I came before

Members of Congress and said, "No. Congress must assert its authority. It must assert its authority on behalf of the people."

However, the second part of congressional responsibility and, if Congress does not exercise it, the responsibility of courts, is to protect individual rights. We could relitigate *Roe* v. *Wade* and try to come to a decision that would satisfy all of us. I doubt if we could have unanimity in a matter of that complexity and controversy, but suffice it to say that conservative justices of the Supreme Court concluded differently from the position you are taking, sir.

I want to say one final thing. I agree with Professor Rice and with you that the issue here is not wisdom at the moment. It is constitutionality. The dicta of the cases that Mr Rice undoubtedly has quoted about the plenary power of Congress were stated in contexts bearing no remote relationship to the issue we have before us.

What we have here whether we like it or not, and some will like it and some will not, are seven justices of the Supreme Court saying there was a constitutional right. The question is not democracy. The question is whether Congress is going to undercut that constitutional right.

With respect, I do not think Congress has that power, although I would be willing to grant it vast powers in its appropriate domain.

Senator EAST. Thank you, Professor.

Let me just follow up with one question and then I will turn to Senator Baucus.

It strikes me that you and Professor Eisenberg are assuming the very thing we are setting out to decide. You are assuming the result or the conclusion. The right to privacy is what the court spun out of the Constitution. The critics will say it was out of wholly new cloth in order to reach their result, but be that as it may, they did do it. That is true.

However, what we are looking at here is the other side. Getting this back into the policy arena, there are very strong movements in this country, groups and individuals, who feel that the right to life is more critical than the right to privacy. That is a major and fundamental policy judgment. They are not content with the idea that the Supreme Court alone, uninhibited and unchallenged, can make that determination any more than in *Dred Scott* where the Court might hold that the black is a piece of property and that that would have settled the issue.

All I am saying is of course you can say that they determined the right to privacy is there, but this whole challenge is on the point that the right to life is a greater right. How do we bring that into the public arena for legitimate consideration?

Mr. DORSEN. I have an answer to that. The answer is the exact case you gave: Amend the Constitution. That is what they did after *Dred Scott*. That is what the people who oppose the Supreme Court have authority to do under our system, but not to do it through the back door in this way.

Senator EAST. I have one final comment on why we have done it this way and then to Senator Baucus.

Roe v. *Wade* is unique, so contend the supporters of S. 158, because of the contention that if they had known when life began, they would have come to a totally different conclusion. In short, the right to privacy self-destructs if you can determine when life begins. If the findings are that life begins at the time of conception, the right to privacy, under their own terms of the majority of *Roe* v.

Wade, is overshadowed. That is the very unique situation that justifies the rationale for S. 158.

Mr. RICE. Senator, could I interrupt?

Senator EAST. In deference to my good colleagues, I would not like to preempt them any further. I am going to turn it over to my distinguished colleague here lest I impose any further.

Senator BAUCUS. Thank you, Mr. Chairman.

Mr. Rice, as I hear you, you make several points. No. 1, you say that Mr. Dorsen and Mr. Eisenberg are letting their feelings about this bill interfere with their analysis of the precise issue before us. You say they find the bill unwise.

Do you find this bill wise?

Mr. RICE. Yes, sir, I do. As I explained, with respect to section 2, which is the only part we are talking about today, I think it is wise because it leaves these decisions for the time being in the State courts initially. I think that is a healthful corrective for that aspect of *Roe* v. *Wade* which is subject to much legitimate criticism, that is that it interfered with the due prerogatives of the State courts.

Senator BAUCUS. You also state that you feel that those cases where Congress might attempt to limit the rights of Jews or Catholics to sue, Congress could not limit those persons and those categories of cases because it would violate the 14th amendment and equal protection guarantees. Is that correct?

Mr. RICE. I am glad you asked that because that is one of the things I wanted to address.

Senator BAUCUS. Why is that an exception to the very clear unequivocal phrasing of article 3?

Mr. RICE. It is not an exception to the power of Congress under article 3 at all. What it is is an overlay of another constitutional prohibition which comes into effect because there is a world of difference between what section 2 of S. 158 does and a bill that provided that no black could sue in a U.S. district court.

In the latter case, what you are doing is imposing a discrimination upon that person by means of a criterion having nothing whatever to do with the case.

Senator BAUCUS. The point I am trying to make is that there are exceptions to the unequivocal—

Mr. RICE. No, not at all.

Senator BAUCUS. Let me state it different.

Article 3 is not unequivocal?

Mr. RICE. Article 3 has to do with jurisdiction and even the very existence of those Federal courts.

Now of course—

Senator BAUCUS. However, you are giving examples where Congress could not limit inferior court jurisdiction.

Mr. RICE. When you look at the Constitution, you have to look at various prohibitions. We are talking about the fifth amendment here, the fifth amendment due process clause which incorporates in it an equal protection factor. This is something that governs all congressional legislation.

You can say Congress has the power to regulate commerce. Yes, of course, but Congress cannot provide that no black or no Catholic may open a store. You do not say that that means that Congress power over interstate commerce does not really exist. That is not so. It means that there is another specific prohibition. That is what is happening here.

Senator BAUCUS. In what other classes of cases could Congress not limit lower Federal court jurisdiction?

Mr. RICE. I think this sort of case would be the only type of case. Incidentally, if I may suggest, these points were covered at some length by Prof. Paul Bator of Harvard Law School in his recent testimony before the Subcommittee on the Constitution.

Senator BAUCUS. What about first amendment freedoms? Could Congress state that lower Federal courts could not have jurisdiction over first amendment cases?

Mr. RICE. Of course, certainly. For example, Congress has taken away jurisdiction in the Norris-La Guardia Act to issue certain injunctions.

Senator BAUCUS. Could Congress pass a statute saying in all first amendment cases, free speech, freedom of religion cases, there shall be no lower Federal courts jurisdiction?

Mr. RICE. Yes, sir.

Senator BAUCUS. In every case?

Mr. RICE. Yes, sir. They have not done that.

Senator BAUCUS. Let me ask Mr. Dorsen or Mr. Eisenberg if they agree that Congress could constitutionally take away all first amendment cases from lower Federal court jurisdiction?

Mr. EISENBERG. I find it very difficult to discriminate among different classes of constitutional rights. My view is that litigants must have realistic access to lower Federal courts for all constitutional rights. Included in that category would be first amendment rights.

However, I would also have to say that I would include rights to abortions in that category. Congress could no more eliminate abortion rights than it could eliminate first amendment rights.

Senator BAUCUS. You would disagree that the only class of rights that Congress could not remove from jurisdiction would be equal protection rights.

Mr. EISENBERG. I do not think anybody really believes that the only class of rights are equal protection rights.

Senator BAUCUS. Mr. Rice does.

Mr. EISENBERG. Mr. Rice did say that. He also said Congress could not confer jurisdiction in a way that ordered courts to reach a particular result. I do not find that anywhere in article 3. Apparently there are some unwritten exceptions in article 3 that have not been revealed to the rest of us.

I should also add that there is not a word in article 3 about jurisdiction over lower Federal courts. It talks about Congress power to ordain and establish them. It does not mention jurisdiction.

Senator BAUCUS. Mr. Rice, are there any public policy reasons why Congress should not limit lower Federal court jurisdiction in certain Federal cases?

Mr. RICE. I think you could advance prudential arguments on both sides of the question.

Senator BAUCUS. I am asking you what public policy reasons would there be against limiting Federal court jurisdiction?

Mr. RICE. I think the public policy reason would be that you would want to have a dual track in every instance so you would have a choice of enforcing your rights in either the State or Federal courts because State courts have jurisdiction to entertain these constitutional claims as well.

When you get into these so-called exceptions, they vanish. They are really not exceptions. For example—

Senator BAUCUS. Excuse me. Let us assume that this bill becomes law. Let us further assume that the legislation is the subject of litigation in most of the States. After a period of time it becomes obvious that only a very small percentage of the cases litigated in the State courts reach the U.S. Supreme Court. During that period of time, there is a wide variety of State court interpretations? Does it have any bearing whatsoever on whether or not individuals are denied remedies or effectively denied their constitutional rights if they have a difficult time reaching the U.S. Supreme Court?

I am painting a hypothetical picture, but say there is mass confusion among States and very few cases litigated in the State courts reach the Supreme Court. Does that in any way affect your feeling about the propriety, let alone the constitutionality, of this particular section of the bill?

Mr. RICE. I think it would be a consideration to keep in mind. However, you must remember that this is a very modest bill in that it preserves the appellate jurisdiction of the Supreme Court intact so that the Supreme Court would very quickly have an opportunity to decide this case. That would be a precedent for other State jurisdictions.

Senator BAUCUS. You are arguing with my facts. My facts are that because of the caseload of the Supreme Court, it just cannot decide very many of these cases.

Mr. RICE. Senator, all you would need is one case in order to decide the constitutionality of this statute.

Senator BAUCUS. That is not my question. My question concerns the interpretation of different State statutes and whether the States are acting correctly or not. Different States could enact different statutes and each could present different circumstances.

Mr. RICE. Right.

Senator BAUCUS. One case alone could not handle all of these cases.

Mr. RICE. You have the first question which is the constitutionality of S. 158, assuming it passes. Is it constitutional for Congress to define the unborn child as a person and so forth? That is wide open for review as quickly as possible by the Supreme Court of the United States. There is no problem.

The State of New Jersey may enact a statute which may differ from the statute enacted by the State of Illinois. This is no different from questions which come up in other matters. You do not really add anything to the prudential wisdom of the thing by interjecting at the lower level U.S. district courts which under the circumstances would simply compound the confusion.

Senator BAUCUS. Let me ask another question. What is your view on how staticly or how rigidly the Constitution should be interpreted? The chairman raises the point that the framers intended that Congress should have the right to establish lower Federal courts and lower Federal court jurisdiction and that those are the plain words of the Constitution.

Mr. Dorsen and Mr. Eisenberg, particularly Mr. Eisenberg, outlined how at the time there were not many Federal cases that needed to reach the U.S. Supreme Court and so the circumstances when the Constitution was written were much different that they are today. The substantial increase in our population and in the Court's caseload have altered the Supreme Court's ability to hear the cases that the framers expected them to hear.

The question is how rigidly should one interpret those words in the Constitution given the circumstances and times when those words were written? Let us look for a moment at the first amendment. The first amendment says that Congress shall pass no laws abridging the freedom of speech and freedom of press. At that time there was no radio or television. The first amendment does not say anything about radio or television because there was no radio or television.

I think it is arguable, and not only arguable but probable that if the framers were to write the Constitution today, they might not use the word "press". They might use the word "media." Today they would phrase it in a way that would take radio and television into consideration.

Therefore, do you not think that when Congress passes laws and tries to determine what the Constitution means, that we must pay at least some attention to present circumstances?

Mr. RICE. I think your point argues strongly in favor of this provision in section 2.

Senator BAUCUS. How is that?

Mr. RICE. Section 2 is based on article 3, which according to the intent of the framers clearly gave to Congress the authority and responsibility of making continuing policy judgments. The framers were wise enough to envision that there would be changed circumstances.

The first amendment is flexible enough to include radio and television, as the commerce clause can include airplanes. This is an argument very strongly against freezing this thing and saying that Congress may not tamper with lower Federal court jurisdiction because circumstances may change.

The point here is if S. 158 passes, it will be because in the judgment of Congress circumstances have changed.

Senator BAUCUS. However, have circumstances not also changed with respect to an individual's ability to vindicate his or her constitutional rights? Haven't population and caseload affected access to the Federal courts?

Mr. RICE. That is a question for the judgment of Congress. One of the difficulties here arises from the Supreme Court's extravagant interpretation of the 14th amendment so as to apply the provisions of the Bill of Rights literally and strictly to the States contrary to the salutary rule of the *Twining* and *Palko* cases as articulated by Justices Cardozo, Frankfurter, and Harlan. The Supreme Court has reached out to take jurisdictions for itself and responsibilities for itself that have proven not to be wise.

Senator BAUCUS. Thank you very much.

Seantor EAST. Thank you, Senator.

Senator Heflin?

Senator HEFLIN. Professor Rice, in your response to Senator Baucus you raised an issue that interested me and started me thinking on some things. That is, you indicated that the U.S. Supreme Court would quickly or rapidly rule on this bill if it were passed. You said something to that effect, which I assume is correct.

I think this would be an issue that both sides would want to expeditiously know what the outcome would be.

If it is held unconstitutional, the prolife people would say, "Well, we wasted 2 or 3 years—as we say when hunting in the South—chasing rabbits. We went off on a detour, were led astray, and delayed the situation for 2 or 3 years during which time many abortions occurred."

On the other hand, if it is declared constitutional, then the prochoice people are going to be in a situation where I would anticipate from the feeling on this issue that a movement will be started for a constitutional amendment to reverse this bill.

Really, as I look at this, and I would like to get your thoughts, is this section 2 necessary in regard to anything pertaining to the constitutionality, or is it strictly procedural?

Mr. RICE. I do not think it affects the constitutionality of section 1. I think it is an independent judgment by Congress that it is a good thing or would be a good thing to let the State courts, unhindered from interference from lower Federal courts, come to grips with this thing subject to review by the Supreme Court. I think you have to look at these sections independently.

Senator HEFLIN. Is it really a delaying provision?

Mr. RICE. No, I do not believe so. I really believe, Senator, that one of the major objections to *Roe* v. *Wade*, apart from the merits of abortion, is that it is an undue intrusion on the power of the States.

Here you have a device which would contribute to a rectification of that by saying, "State courts, we want you to consider this. We want you to give this full consideration without some U.S. district judge coming in and hurling a thunderbolt to stop your consideration." Then let us get an orderly review of this by the Supreme Court. That is federalism in operation. It seems to me to be a very salutary thing.

Senator HEFLIN. Is this an issue on which State court or lower court rationale and writing will affect the way the U.S. Supreme Court rules on it?

Mr. RICE. It very well may. I would not speculate about that.

Senator HEFLIN. It is not like school prayer and not like a lot of other issues. It is the issue of whether or not *Roe* v. *Wade* has ruled on the subject and whether it is the law of the land. That is debatable. In my judgment, you can read it both ways depending on how you want to read it.

However, is it not almost a single thrust issue that regardless of whether you go through the State courts or whether you go through the Federal courts, it is going to come up to a rather clear decision one way or the other?

Mr. RICE. I suggest there is another factor. That is that we have suffered for some years from judicial imperialism by lower Federal courts in various areas, the school desegregation area being a rather striking example. I think people are sick of that. I think the Congress has the responsibility to say we are going to treat the State courts as if they really are courts and as if they really can handle these things. There is no constitutional presumption that a U.S. district judge is any more capable than a State judge.

Here, I think, it is important in terms of the wisdom of this legislation for Congress to say, "Let us respose the initial decision in those State courts subject to the Supreme Court." That is what this does.

Senator HEFLIN. You are taking a States rights issue in that aspect, but, on the other hand, it has to be looked at as a Federal intervention issue in regard to the substantive thing of whether it is life, as opposed to whether the State legislature should declare that, or opposed to whether or not the Federal Government should.

I mean you are arguing States rights on the viewpoint of let them handle it. Yet at the same time, are we not involved in a Federal intervention to attempt to say one thing or to cure a social ill? Therefore, you are involved in a form of violation or deprivation of States rights.

Mr. RICE. No, sir, I do not believe so because the 14th amendment, section 5, is at issue when we are talking about the point you just raised. That is not the subject of what we are talking about here today.

I would argue that it is within the power of Congress for reasons that I am submitting separately to the committee. However, the federalism concept is something which goes throughout the Constitution and the 14th amendment is part of the Constitution and so is section 5 of the 14th amendment, as is article 3.

Article 3 is not subject to exceptions. For example, in the question that I raised saying that the Congress could not tell the courts how to decide a case, I am relying there on the *Klein* case in 1872, which involved the appellate jurisdiction of the Supreme Court, but I think it is a sound principle. Congress cannot tell the courts how to decide a case, but they can take jurisdiction.

Senator HEFLIN. Regardless of the federalism issue, is the State court route one from which you can expect more delay than would be under the Federal court route?

Mr. RICE. Not necessarily. I do not think you could generalize about that, Senator. In any event, that is a matter for prudential judgment on the part of Congress. It has nothing to do with the constitutionality of the legislation.

Senator HEFLIN. Mr. Dorsen?

Mr. DORSEN. I would like to add a word about this. It is an important question you raised, Senator, and goes beyond the immediate issue in a way.

It seems to me striking that what is being proposed here is really not a modest proposal, although I understand why the chairman put it that way in the context of his earlier remarks, but it is dealing with the structure, tinkering with the structure of the Federal courts vis-a-vis the American people's rights and vis-a-vis the Supreme Court.

In the 1950's, as I am sure we all know, many proposals were made to reverse decisions by the U.S. Supreme Court by playing around with the jurisdiction of the Supreme Court and in some cases the lower courts. Senators and Representatives who proposed those very sincerely believed that it was in the best interests of the country to cut out Supreme Court jurisdiction or lower court jurisdiction because they did not like a particular result, just the way some people do not like the result in *Roe* v. *Wade*.

The Senate of the United States considered many, many such bills. They were very powerfully argued by men of great ability and dedication. Not one of those bills passed. They did not pass for the simple reason that wisdom finally came through, not because people agreed with the Supreme Court decisions but because the Members of the Senate of the United States said they would not play around with the basic structure of the system.

Senator HEFLIN. I do not think that is in answer to my question. You really testified about that previously. I am looking at the issue from a viewpoint of some resolution. If this passes and you then go toward a decision, it seems to me that as soon as the decision is made, the whole country would be better off one way or the other.

Mr. DORSEN. You mean a decision on section 1?

Senator HEFLIN. On section 1 if it is decided.

The feasibility or the wisdom of section 2 under this set of circumstances to me is highly questionable. It is also questionable in the event of a postaffirmance that this act is declared constitutional. Then I can foresee that under this section you could have State courts in certain States where they are very liberal that may respectfully dissent, but dissent in the same way and attempt to fashion decisions to prevent the full application of it. You would then be placed in a situation as after the *Brown* v. *Board of Education*, with which we are all familiar, when many, many crafty, intelligent jurists that disagreed with it attempted to fashion methods by which it would not have its full import.

Under this situation, it would be a long and delaying procedure postapproval to prevent those State court systems which disagreed from fashioning methods to try to disagree with it.

Mr. DORSEN. I agree with that analysis completely. I think it is absolutely correct.

Senator HEFLIN. You have a situation here where everybody says if this passes, then you need as expeditious a decision by the Supreme Court as possible. I raise the issue as to whether or not this will not really result in a delaying process by having to go through the State courts. Most State courts have their trial courts, then there is a court of criminal appeals, then a State supreme court, and then it would have to come up on that route there.

Mr. RICE. If I may, I would like to offer a very brief comment. We must remember that this is a statute that we are talking about. If at any time it proves to be inconvenient or burdensome or not working, you can change it right away.

It also must be remembered that the primary reliance of the framers of this Constitution for the enforcement of Federal constitutional rights in the initial stage, that is the initial enforcement of those rights, was on the State courts.

I think of course there is a possibility of diverse interpretations, but that is part of the Federal system, too. In any event, Congress retains the power since it is a statute to change it very quickly. We are not talking about changing the Constitution here.

Senator HEFLIN. I have no further questions.

Senator EAST. Thank you, Senator Heflin.

I would like to remind all participants that it is now 25 minutes to 12. We are already 5 minutes behind. Questions can certainly be submitted by all members of the subcommittee to you, that is written questions or subsequent reply.

As I understand it, Senator Baucus has one final question he would like to ask.

Senator BAUCUS. Thank you, Mr. Chairman.

Mr. Rice, I am still confused as to just what the purpose of section 2 is. Why is section 2 in this bill?

Mr. RICE. I think section 2 is in this bill for reasons of prudent federalism.

Senator BAUCUS. What do you mean by that?

Mr. RICE. As I was saying before. I think we have suffered greatly in this country in recent years from the autocratic actions of Federal judges who are unelected and appointed for life. If I were in Congress, I would vote for section 2 on the theory that it is about time for us to repose responsibility in the State courts and it is about time for us to realize that there is no inherent superiority of Federal judges over State court judges.

Senator BAUCUS. Responsibility for what? What responsibility?

Mr. RICE. For making initial constitutional determinations.

Senator BAUCUS. You are saying that lower Federal courts should not ever make constitutional determinations?

Mr. RICE. Oh, no, I would not generalize in that respect.

Senator BAUCUS. What is it about this case? Why limit lower court jurisdiction in this area?

Mr. RICE. Because this obviously is a response to *Roe* v. *Wade*. It is a response which is based on the fact that not only is *Roe* v. *Wade* an exercise in bootstrap jurisprudence through the application of this right of reproductive privacy, which is of the Supreme Court's own invention, but beyond that, *Roe* v. *Wade* is an intrusion on the prerogatives of the State. It is entirely prudent to correct it in that respect.

Senator BAUCUS. I am just trying to understand your principle here. Your principle is that Congress should limit lower Federal court jurisdiction in those cases where the Supreme Court creates a new constitutional right?

Mr. RICE. I would not generalize beyond the particular bounds of this case, Senator. What I am saying is that with respect to this statute, it seems to me to be a prudent exercise of sound governance.

Senator BAUCUS. Is that because you disagree with the Supreme Court decision?

Mr. RICE. I think I would probably take the same position if I did not because there are many who agree with abortion, for example, who think that the Supreme Court decision was an abomination in terms of federalism.

Senator BAUCUS. Then in what cases other than equal protection cases would you think Congress should not limit the jurisdiction of the lower Federal courts?

Mr. RICE. Should not limit?

Senator BAUCUS. Yes.

Mr. RICE. I think the question should be phrased the other way: In which cases should Congress limit?

Senator BAUCUS. I am asking the questions. Other than equal protection cases, in what cases should Congress not limit the jurisdiction of the lower Federal court?

Mr. RICE. It should not interfere with the existing jurisdiction of lower Federal courts in cases other than those where there was been a grave problem created by judicial excess of the Federal courts, school busing for example.

Senator BAUCUS. When you disagree with what the Supreme Court has done, then you think Congress should limit lower Federal court jurisdiction?

Mr. RICE. I would put it more strongly than that. I would say not merely disagree with it but regard it as a grave problem of judicial excess. School busing is an example. Abortion is another example.

Senator BAUCUS. What other examples do you have in mind?

Mr. RICE. I think the three that come up in contemporary terms are abortion, school desegregation, and school prayer. I am primarily concerned about the first two. I think those are particularly significant in this respect.

Senator BAUCUS. Where you think the Supreme Court has indulged in some excess or has gone too far, then Congress should limit lower Federal court jurisdiction?

Mr. RICE. I think it is not simply going too far. We must remember that the right of reproductive privacy was discovered by the Supreme Court itself in 1965, somehow in the penumbras formed by the emanations from the Bill of Rights, whatever that means. This is a judicial creation out of the whole cloth. I think it is unrealistic to regard it, since it is such, as if it was written on tablets of stone on Mount Sinai.

Senator BAUCUS. When Members of Congress think the Court has gone too far on fourth amendment cases, search and seizure cases, do you think that then Congress should limit lower Federal court jurisdiction over fourth amendment cases?

Mr. RICE. I think it is something that might be considered. I would not offer an opinion without studying the particular thing.

Senator BAUCUS. You think it is arguable that in fourth amendment cases, too, Congress should limit the jurisdiction of the lower Federal courts?

Mr. RICE. I think you have the power in Congress to do this in every case.

Senator BAUCUS. Other than 14th amendment cases.

Mr. RICE. No, including 14th amendment cases. You have the power in Congress to do this in every case.

Senator BAUCUS. It is constitutionally permissible in every case?

Mr. RICE. Yes, sir.

Senator BAUCUS. Even in equal protection cases?

Mr. RICE. Of course.

Senator BAUCUS. So that we understand each other, in the hypothetical case that Mr. Dorsen presented earlier where Congress attempt to limit lower Federal court jurisdiction to Jews or Catholics, you think that is constitutional?

Mr. RICE. You are not talking there about jurisdiction over a class of cases. You are talking there about a supervening constitutional prohibition against discrimination based on a criterion having nothing to do with the case, a criterion of race or religion.

Senator BAUCUS. I am trying to understand where you are. You say in those cases Congress could not constitutionally limit the lower Federal courts?

Mr. RICE. I think that is a fair conclusion. If that were ever done, which is very difficult to imagine, I think it is a fair conclusion that the fifth amendment due process clause would prevent Congress from saying that blacks may not sue in a U.S. district court or that Catholics may not sue in a U.S. district court, not because the power of article 3 is limited but because there is another supervening constitutional prohibition.

Senator BAUCUS. However, you think in search and seizure cases, Congress could say no lower Federal court jurisdiction?

Mr. RICE. I have no doubt about that whatsoever, yes, sir.

Senator BAUCUS. Thank you.

Senator EAST. Gentlemen, we thank you for coming.

HISTORICAL SECTION

Statement of Dr. Carl Degler

Dr. DEGLER. Thank you, Senator.

First of all, I would like to say how much I welcome, not only personally the opportunity to be here, but to recognize that a historian's testimony is being taken into consideration in these hearings, because I do think history has something to say about public policy.

There are two issues which I would like to address this morning. The first is the question of whether or not the legislative history of the 14th amendment provides support for the contention that Congress intended to include the unborn within the amendment's protections against State action. The second is whether or not the general intent of the bill is in line with American traditions.

Until a few months ago, if anyone had asked me if there was any reason for believing that the 14th amendment was intended to protect the life of the fetus, I would have said I did not believe there was.

A primary reason for my response is that I knew of no such assertion in any of the historical literature on the 14th amendment that I had read, although I have just heard this morning Professor Uddo suggest he had.

Recently, however, I have also learned that the argument had been made by Prof. Joseph B. Witherspoon after a close study of the congressional debates during the passage of the 14th amendment, and his paper had been printed in the Congressional Record in 1976.

Since Witherspoon's case is presumably the best one that can be made, I would like to examine it as a way of setting forth my own view on this historical issue.

Over the past 50 years or so, there have been several controversies among historians as to the intent of Congress in regard to the 14th amendment, such as whether the primary aim was to protect the rights of newly freed blacks or whether it was to protect the rights of corporations as legal persons.

Today, I think it is accurate to say that most historians believe that protection of the rights of former slaves was the primary purpose of the amendment. As already noted, no historian, to my knowledge, has even raised the argument, much less sought to defend the proposition, that a fetus was intended to be protected by any clause of the 14th amendment or that any construction of that amendment could be used to prohibit a State from permitting abortions, as I think S. 158 intends.

I do not think the argument and evidence advanced by Professor Witherspoon in his paper alter in any way the soundness of the traditional interpretation of the 14th amendment in regard to the unborn.

It is true, as Professor Witherspoon points out, that in the 1860's Congress was much concerned with the question of protecting the life and freedom of the newly freed slaves, but at no time did a Congressman explicitly say or even imply that the protections for the former slaves ought to be extended to the unborn.

Professor Witherspoon quotes Representative John Bingham on the sanctity of the family and the responsibility parents have for their children. "The wife," Bingham said, "owes obedience to the husband, and the husband protection to the wife, and both owe protection and care to their children." But it is clear "children" in this context, meant those already born.

Professor Witherspoon then links this discussion of the amendment's concern with the protection of life to the laws then being passed in a number of States to limit abortions.

He professes to see in these State laws an extension of the concern for the freedom of the former slaves, yet there is no mention in the discussion in Congress of these laws, nor is there any reference to abortion or to the unborn in the course of the debate on the 14th amendment.

Professor Witherspoon goes on to say that, since the 14th amendment was ratified contemporaneously with the passage in the State of antiabortion laws, that coincidence—to quote him—"constitutes a contemporaneous legislative construction by States of the meaning of the amendments they ratified."

That argument falls to the ground, I believe, when it is recognized that the State laws against abortion almost always specify that an abortion could be performed if a physician said that such a medical procedure was necessary to save the mother's life.

So far as I know, no one has suggested that the 14th amendment made or intended any distinction be made between one person and another to the extent that the life of one person could be sacrificed for another, yet that is what we would have if we followed Professor Witherspoon's argument that the construction of the 14th amendment was shaped by the antiabortion statutes of the ratifying States.

Professor Witherspoon then moves on to show from specific actions in the 1860's that Congress intended to place the life of the unborn under the protections of the 14th amendment. The amount of evidence for this eccentric interpretation, I think, is very limited.

For a period of some 15 years, between 1860 and 1875, Witherspoon is able to supply us with only five specific references in which Congress dealt with the question of abortion in any way whatsoever. All five of these actions, as I would like to show, fail to support his argument that Congress intended to treat the unborn as equal to the born.

The first is the District of Columbia Divorce Act of 1860, in which Congress said that the offspring of a second or bigamous marriage, "born or begotten" before the commencement of the suit for divorce, will be deemed the legitimate offspring of the parent who, at the time of the marriage, was capable of making such a marriage.

Professor Witherspoon sees this as an instance in which, as he puts it, "Congress legislated to protect the unborn from the time of its being begotten or conceived in the womb."

He then goes on to say that it shows that Congress, in 1860, considered "the unborn child to be a person from the time of its conception."

Yet, even as the matter is described by Professor Witherspoon himself, it is not at all clear that Congress is talking about the moment of conception. The phrase "born or begotten" is a formulation that does no more than make a distinction between being outside the womb or inside the womb for any length of time, including a period perhaps as short as 1 day prior to birth.

Moreover, the whole purpose of the law was to determine parental responsibility and the legal status of the offspring, providing the offspring was born. If an abortion had ended the pregnancy, this law would not have brought any intervention by the Government. The law offered no protection for the fetus as such.

A second piece of evidence Professor Witherspoon mentions to show that Congress intended to include the unborn within the meaning of the protection of the 14th amendment is the assimilative crimes provision, passed April 5, 1866.

This was a statute that acknowledged Congress acceptance of a State crime committed on its territories or properties within a State's boundaries when Federal law did not deal with the crime.

It is Professor Witherspoon's view that this act constituted acceptance by Congress of the antiabortion laws of the States. I think the professor was probably correct here, but that acceptance in no way committed Congress to equating the life of the unborn with the life of born individuals since not even the State statutes did that. They always permitted an abortion if a doctor certified that the fetus endangered the mother's life.

His third example of an act of Congress that allegedly recognized unborn children as persons under the 14th amendment is a law in which Congress accepted on naval bases in Connecticut, in 1866, the authority of that State's antiabortion law of 1860.

Again, the argument is that Congress was recognizing the equality of the unborn with the born, but there is no other evidence for that assumption.

He also cites the passage of the Comstock laws of March 3, 1973, as a sign of Congress protection of the unborn because that law barred abortafacients from the mails. But that still does not offer us any new evidence as to whether or not Congress was viewing the unborn and born as equal persons under the Constitution.

The Comstock laws also barred contraceptives from the mails, but I do not know that anyone has argued therefrom that Congress sought to include the human egg or human sperm prior to union as a person with the meaning of the 14th amendment.

A similar effort to expand the evidence to cover cases it was not intended to cover appears in a final instance advanced by Professor Witherspoon. In 1864, Congress provided for the establishment in the District of Columbia of a "home for friendless women and children."

Although Professor Witherspoon refers to this act as another instance of the special concern for the unborn child, he has to admit that the purpose of the home was to assist pregnant women in giving birth to illegitimate children and to help in the adoption of such children.

Again, there is no direct mention of the unborn, merely an assertion that a concern for a potential child was equal to the concern for a child already born.

I submit that this evidence—and it is presumably the best and fullest that anyone could find, since that was Witherspoon's intention—is not an adequate basis for overturning the accepted understanding of the intent of Congress in passing the 14th amendment.

Congress clearly meant to protect the life, liberty, and property of all persons, but there has not been any reason, and there is still no reason today, to suppose that Congress intended fetuses to be treated as persons within the meaning of the 14th amendment.

Let me turn now to my second reason for believing this bill is based upon bad history. In determining that all the rights of persons protected by the 14th amendment apply to fetuses, S. 158 would change significantly the way Americans have viewed abortion over the last two centuries at least.

It is now well recognized that the laws of the States did not concern themselves with the question of abortion until 1821 when the first antiabortion law was enacted in Connecticut. Then, in the course of the next 60 years or so, almost all the States passed laws limiting abortions.

It is worth noting that these legal objections to abortion did not spring out of an impatient or eager moral conscience. It took half a century or more for these laws to be enacted, refined, and established in the States. The length of time was not a sign of opposition but a measure of the small popular concern with the issue.

The primary force behind the enactment of the antiabortion statutes seems to have been physicians who believed abortions were wrong and ought to be regulated.

But even the physicians who pushed for these laws did not believe that abortion ought to be prohibited absolutely, as I think S. 158 would do. For, as I have already noted, in virtually every State an abortion to save the mother's life was permitted.

As Prof. John T. Noonan, Jr., a modern opponent of abortion himself, pointed out some years ago, "Under American law"—meaning prior to 1975—"an abortion has never been illegal." That is but another way of saying that in the United States the protection of the fetus has generally been relative rather than absolute, and never has the fetus been placed on a par with legal persons.

Moreover, the law during the 19th century also noticed a difference between the killing of a fetus illegally and homicide. Punishment of the first was almost invariably less than that of the second.

In the late 19th century, some physicians contended that feticide, as they called abortion, and homicide were identical and should be punished alike. But, importantly, no significant body of law or professional opinion followed that suggestion, and neither did the law.

I have dwelled on the attitudes and values expressed in the laws because historians put a great deal of weight on statute law as measures of public values and opinions. Legislatures, after all, are assumed to be representative of the general public. But historians also look beyond the legislative chambers in seeking to recapture past attitudes.

If, in this case, one looks beyond the legislatures, it is possible to show that although there was little vocal opposition to the antiabortion statutes when they were enacted the laws were far from accepted, and that resistance, I think, was sufficiently broad that we ought not to ignore it if we are trying to ascertain what Americans 100 years or so ago thought about abortion.

The evidence to which I refer is the large number of abortions that were performed after the procedure was declared illegal.

Obviously, we have no sure figures on this illegal activity, but studies suggest that about one out of four pregnancies during the 1920's were being aborted, and throughout the last third of the 19th century physicians thought large numbers of women were still seeking abortions and often much more casually, if the doctors are to be believed, than many women do today.

Here is a physician writing in a popular medical advice book in 1870:

> *Mine is but the common story of every physician.*

he began.

> *A woman unknown to the doctor walks into the office inquiring for the physician. She then says, "I want you to produce an abortion for me," as coolly as if ordering a piece of beef for dinner,*

the doctor noted.

Another physician about the same time wrote:

> *Astonishing as it may seem, many of the women who seek abortions are otherwise quite intelligent and refined, with a keen sense of their moral and religious obligations to themselves and to others, but deem it nothing amiss to destroy the embryo during the first months of its growth.*

These two quotations are from the early 1870's, just at the time when the new antiabortion statutes were being enacted.

Yet, 20 years later, after a generation of assertions by doctors of the evils of abortions without a physician's approval and the passage of several dozen antiabortion statutes, one physician was still complaining that many women saw nothing wrong with an abortion early in pregnancy. And these women, he pointedly noted, were neither criminals nor degenerates.

> *Many otherwise good and exemplary women,*

he observed,

> *would rather part with their right hands or let their tongues cleave to the roof of the mouth than to commit a crime, yet they seem to believe that prior to quickening it is no more harm to cause the evacuation of the contents of their wombs than it is that of their bladders or their bowels.*

This kind of testimony from physicians of the time probably exaggerated women's casual attitudes. Nevertheless, it seems to me it makes clear that an absolutist prohibition on abortion, such as S. 158 would place upon the States, is hardly within past American attitudes and practice.

S. 158 would introduce a novel and—if I may use this word, Mr. Chairman—even a radical, if you will, conception of the value of a fetus. For the first time, it would compel the States to place the fetus on the same level as the mother and presumably encourage, if not compel, the States to treat the killing of a fetus as equivalent to homicide.

As a historian, I am rather surprised to learn that proponents of this bill are often described as conservatives. By the usual historical definition, a conservative is someone who seeks to continue tradition, to enhance it, because to conservatives the past is a guide to the present. It is radicals who usually seek to overturn the past or to escape it and its wisdom.

Let no one mistake it. This bill is not a conservative measure. It does not conserve, it innovates. Rather than recognizing complexities in human affairs, as conservatives do, it asserts simplicities. Rather than drawing upon our past experience as a people and strengthening the connection between past and present, as conservatives do, it breaks, I think, with our national history. Conservatives, I think, ought to oppose it as a deeply radical measure.

Thank you, sir.

Senator EAST. Thank you, Professor Degler.

Professor Mohr, if you would, please give us your comments. And, again, I would like to encourage you, as much as you can, to state your position extemporaneously and as concisely as you can. Thank you.

Statement of James Mohr

Dr. MOHR. Thank you, Senator.

I, too, wish to express my appreciation for a chance to speak to this question; and I, too, feel that historical perspective is one of the ways we can, hopefully, at least reconsider some of the difficult issues that we face in current times.

My own view is that one of the best ways to come to grips with some of the problems we face is to try to understand how we got into the situation in the first place.

In this context, I was asked my professional opinion of section 1 of S. 158, the section which asserts that the 14th amendment to the Constitution of the United States was intended to protect all human beings.

As an historian who has written both on the Radical Republican Reconstruction era from which the 14th amendment evolved and on abortion policy in the 19th century, I must say I am uncomfortable with that statement.

I am troubled, for example by the word "intended." An historical scholarship for the last quarter-century has repeatedly demonstrated, the chief intent of the framers and ratifiers of the 14th amendment was to resolve constitutionally what they considered to be the most important problems brought about by the recently concluded Civil War.

Foremost among those problems was the future status of emancipated slaves, particularly since most of those people resided in States which, at that time, were showing little inclination to afford them the rights that accrued to American citizens.

In a sense, the former Confederates were justified in their refusal to grant civil rights to blacks in 1865 because the Supreme Court of the United States had apparently ruled in 1857 in the well-known *Dred Scott* case, prior to the war and prior to the emancipation, that blacks were not and could not be citizens of the United States or the States in which they resided.

The key first section of the 14th amendment was therefore intended in 1866 to alter that situation by eliminating constitutional ambiguities over the legal status of former slaves and by forcing the separate States to grant civil rights to all persons with their jurisdictions—black or white.

The word "person," which appears in that section, was introduced primarily in order that aliens as well as citizens would be protected under the amendment's provisions.

To argue that the framers of the 14th amendment had other intentions, or hidden agendas, or clever conspiracies, or unstated assumptions is, in my view, unwarranted.

I might add that this view of the origins of the 14th amendment has been supported by every historian of the Reconstruction period whom I was able to consult in the past few weeks regardless of where they stood on the modern debate over personhood. It is also, I think, sustained in all of the standard historical discussions of the 14th amendment and its origins.

I am also troubled by the phrase "all human beings" because the 14th amendment does not, in fact, refer to human beings. It refers to "citizens" and to "persons." I know of no direct evidence that the framers of the 14th amendment ever intended that either of those words should apply to the preborn.

None of the leading historians of the Reconstruction era whom I was able to contact, including many who have done painstaking, detailed research in the Congressional Record, in the debates, on the campaigns for reelection mounted by the framers and at the State level among the legislatures that ratified the amendment—none of these people knows of any direct evidence.

I would submit that the rights of the preborn were simply not at issue at the time of the framing and ratification of the 14th amendment.

There is, I think, evidence to indicate that they were never intended to be at issue. If I might, I would like to go quickly through some of that evidence.

First, the 14th amendment was framed and ratified by policymakers who had come to maturity in a Nation where abortion prior to quickening—quickening is the first perception of fetal movement, which generally occurs about the midpoint of gestation—had been a perfectly legal and openly tolerated practice.

That position had been inherited from British common law at the time the republic was founded, and it had been retained as legal policy in the United States long after the English themselves had moved to a new and more restrictive position.

By the middle of the 19th century, abortion prior to quickening was a surprisingly common, widespread, and commercialized practice in most of the States that ratified the 14th amendment, and there is no evidence that the legislators considered that an inconsistency when they ratified the amendment.

Second, most 19th century Americans probably considered abortion prior to quickening much closer to contraception than to manslaughter or homicide. Antebellum legislation at the State level, which typically linked those two practices together—that is, abortion and contraception—reflect, I think, that prevailing attitude.

There is strong evidence that abortion played a large role in what is called the demographic transition from high birth rates and high death rates to low birth rates and low death rates that many emerging nations go through, as ours did in the middle of the 19th century.

There is also strong evidence that antebellum State legislatures were far more concerned about that transition in birth rates and about maternal health—female safety—than they were about the legal status of the preborn.

In short, I think there were no compelling precedents either in statutes or in court decisions indicating that the word "person" in the 14th amendment at the time of its framing and ratification might apply to the preborn.

Third, a group of physicians who were interested in upgrading and modernizing their profession had, for variety of complex reasons, launched a crusade against the practice of abortion in America just prior to the Civil War. Significantly, they continued their efforts unabated after the war, notwithstanding the enactment of the 14th amendment, and, if anything, they intensified their efforts after that amendment was passed.

If apparently never occurred to them—even these people who had a strong interest in changing the Nation's abortion-related policies—that the 14th amendment had either advertently or inadvertently guaranteed due process and equal protection to the preborn.

While physicians were successful in their efforts to persuade policymakers to move away from common law tolerance toward a more restrictive official policy by the end of the 19th century, they never claimed that the adoption of the 14th amendment had any bearing on their crusade one way or the other.

Fourth, if legislatures really meant to insure rights for the preborn by ratifying the 14th amendment, they would not have felt compelled to enact the many subsequent pieces of antiabortion legislation that they did. Or, at the very least, they would have grounded that legislation in the first or fifth sections of the amendment itself. They never did that.

Fifth, there is no evidence that the Federal Government ever moved under the 14th amendment of enforce the rights of the preborn, though there is clearly a great deal of evidence that it did move to try to protect the rights of black Americans, who were the objects of their concern.

Nor is there any evidence that any State made such efforts under the 14th amendment. Indeed, the physicians who led the fight to criminalize abortion in the United States constantly complained to one another in their professional journals during the 19th century about the widespread willingness of Americans to continue to tolerate abortion as a form of fertility control even after it had been declared illegal. The reluctance of State authorities to enforce their new antiabortion statutes further dismayed the opponents of abortion, as did the difficulty of convicting anyone under them, especially when jury trials were involved.

Finally, and to my mind conclusively, the framers of the 14th amendment began their first key sentence on citizenship with the words: "All persons born * * *"

To 19th century policymakers, at least in my opinion, the concept—the basic concept—of legal personhood was tied up with the process of birth. I do not think this phraseology was accidental.

The careful constitutional lawyers who framed, debated, and ratified the 14th amendment understood the biological processes involved in gestation, they had used the word "begotten" in previous legislation, and they understood the difference between that word and the word "born."

They could have begun the 14th amendment with the words: "All persons begotten," but they did not. In my opinion, the 14th amendment was never intended to apply to the preborn, and to allege otherwise is historically unjustifiable.

I would like to conclude by pointing out an historical paradox in the situation that confronts us today as we discuss this issue in a subcommittee on the separation of powers.

It seems to me that Republican policymakers in the 1860's realized that the only sure method of reversing a constitutional finding of the Supreme Court was to amend the Constitution. This was true no matter how much they opposed that finding, and it is certainly obvious that the Republican Party of the 1860's and 1870's loathed the *Dred Scott* decision.

But President Lincoln, with his usual political sagacity, recognized the point explicitly, and he cited it publicly as one of the reasons why he elected to pocket-veto the Wade-Davis bill in 1864.

One section of that bill would have enacted emancipation by statute, but the President insisted instead upon a constitutional revision to unwrite the *Dred Scott* case.

His party went on to adopt the 13th, 14th, and 15th amendments, notwithstanding the intervention of a civil war, to insure what they considered to be the most important results of the conflict that they had just been through.

I find it, therefore, ironic that the proposers of S. 158 would cite one of those amendments at this time to justify a tactic that its framers considered insufficient and unacceptable a century ago.

If a majority of the American people wishes to endow the preborn with full civil rights from the instant of conception, a constitutional amendment to that effect should be passed, and that policy should be honored as the law of the land.

But if that is not the case, then it seems to me that the present ruling of the Supreme Court must, and historically should, remain in effect.

Thank you.

Senator EAST. Thank you, Professor Mohr.

[The prepared statement of Professor Mohr follows:]

Prepared Statement of James Mohr

My name is James Mohr. I am currently professor of history at the University of Maryland Baltimore County.

I was trained as a historian of the United States at Yale University, where I received my B.A. degree, and at Stanford University, where I received my Ph.D.

I have published two books on the Reconstruction period as well as a study entitled *Abortion in America: Origins and Evolution of National Policy, 1800-1900* (Oxford, 1978).

Section 1 of S. 158 asserts that "the Fourteenth Amendment to the Constitution of the United States was intended to protect all human beings." (page 2, lines 1, 2, and 3)

As a professional historian who has written both on the Reconstruction era (from which the Fourteenth Amendment emerged) and on the origins and evolution of abortion policy in 19th Century America, I am extremely uncomfortable with some of the historical implications of that assertion.

I am troubled, for example, by the word "intended." Historical scholarship for the last quarter century has repeatedly demonstrated that the chief intent of the framers and ratifiers of the Fourteenth Amendment was to resolve constitutionally what they considered to be the most important problems brought about by the recently concluded Civil War.

Foremost among those problems was the future status of emancipated slaves, particularly since the vast majority of those recently freed persons resided in states which then showed little inclination to afford them the rights accruing to American citizens. In a sense, the former Confederates were justified in their refusal to grant civil rights to blacks in 1865, because the Supreme Court had apparently ruled in 1857, prior to the war and the emancipation, that blacks were not and could not be citizens either of the United States or of the states in which they resided.

The key first section of the Fourteenth Amendment (another part of which is also quoted in S. 158, page 2, lines 9 and 10) was therefore intended in 1866 to alter that situation by eliminating any Constitutional ambiguity over the legal status of the former slaves (they would now be citizens of the nation and of the states where they lived) and by forcing the separate states to grant civil rights to all persons within their jurisdictions, black or white.

The word "person" was introduced in order to protect aliens as well as citizens. To argue that the framers of the Fourteenth Amendment had other intentions, or hidden agendas, or clever conspiracies, or unstated assumptions is, in my view, unwarranted.

I might add that this view of the origins of the Fourteenth Amendment has been supported by every historian of the Reconstruction period whom I have been able to consult in the past few weeks, regardless of where they stood on the modern debate over personhood, and it has been sustained in all of the standard historical discussions of the Fourteenth Amendment published during the last quarter century.

I am also troubled by the phrase "all human beings." The Fourteenth Amendment does not, in fact, refer to human beings, but rather to "citizens" and "persons." I know of no direct evidence that the framers of the Fourteenth Amendment ever intended that either of these words should apply to the preborn.

None of the leading historians of the Reconstruction era whom I was able to contact, including several who have done painstaking research both on the drafting and on the ratification of the Fourteenth Amendment, knows of any.

The rights of the preborn were simply not at issue. Moreover, there is compelling evidence that they were never intended to be. Let me briefly outline some of that evidence.

First, the Fourteenth Amendment was framed and ratified by policymakers who had come to maturity in a nation where abortion prior to quickening (which is the first perception of fetal movement and usually occurs near the midpoint of gestation) was a perfectly legal and openly tolerated practice.

That position had been inherited from British common law when the Republic was founded, and had been retained as legal policy in the United States long after the English themselves moved to a more restrictive position.

By the middle of the 19th Century, abortion prior to quickening was a surprisingly common, widespread and commercialized practice in most of the states that ratified the Fourteenth Amendment, and there is no evidence that legislators considered that an inconsistency.

Second, most mid-19th Century Americans probably considered abortion prior to quickening much closer to contraception than to manslaughter or homicide. Antebellum legislation at the state level, which had typically linked abortion and contraception together, reflected that prevailing attitude.

There is strong evidence that abortion played an important role in the historic shift in the United States from high birth rates and high death rates to low birth rates and low death rates; the so-called demographic transition that many developing nations experience as they move from pre-industrial social structures to industrial social structures.

There is also strong evidence that antebellum state legislators, to the extent they were concerned about abortion at all, were far more concerned about those shifting birth rates and about female health than they were about the legal status of the preborn.

In short, there were no compelling precedents either in statutes or in court decisions indicating that the word "person" might apply to the preborn.

Third, a group of physicians who were interested in upgrading and modernizing their profession had, for a variety of complex reasons, launched a crusade against the practice of abortion in America just before the Civil War.

They continued their efforts unabated after the war, notwithstanding the enactment of the Fourteenth Amendment, and if anything, intensified their crusade after 1856-67. It apparently never occurred, even to them, that policy makers had advertently or inadvertently guaranteed due process and equal protection to the preborn by ratifying the Fourteenth Amendment.

While the physicians were successful in their efforts to persuade policy makers to move away from common law tolerance toward a more restrictive official policy by the end of the 19th Century, they never claimed that the adoption of the Fourteenth Amendment had any bearing on their crusade one way or the other.

Fourth, if legislators really meant to insure rights for the preborn by ratifying the Fourteenth Amendment, they would not have felt compelled to enact the many subsequent pieces of anti-abortion legislation that they did, or, at the very least, they would have grounded their subsequent policies upon the first or fifth sections of the Amendment itself. None of this was done.

Fifth, there is no evidence that the federal government ever moved under the Fourteenth Amendment to enforce the rights of the preborn, though it took many actions to try to protect the rights of black Americans.

Nor is there any evidence that any state made such efforts under the Fourteenth Amendment. Indeed, the physicians who led the fight to criminalize abortion in the United States constantly complained to one another about the widespread willingness of Americans to continue to tolerate abortion as a form of fertility control even after it had been declared illegal.

The reluctance of state authorities to enforce their new anti-abortion statutes further dismayed the opponents of abortion, as did the difficulty of convicting anyone under them, especially where juries were concerned.

Finally, and to my mind conclusively, the framers of the Fourteenth Amendment began their first key sentence on citizenship with the words, "all persons *born*." (My emphasis)

To 19th Century policy makers the concept of legal personhood was tied up with the process of birth. Nor was this phraseology accidental. The careful constitutional lawyers who framed, debated and ratified the Fourteenth Amendment understood the biological processes involved in gestation, at least in a general sense.

They had used the word "begotten" in previous legislation (District of Columbia Divorce Act of 1860), and they understood the difference between that word and the word born. They could have begun the Fourteenth Amendment with the words, all persons begotten. But they did not. In my opinion, the Fourteenth Amendment was never intended to apply to the preborn, and to allege otherwise is historically unjustifiable. Consequently, in my view, the underlying premise of proposed S. 158 cannot be substantiated.

I would like to conclude by pointing out a historical paradox in the situation that confronts us today as we discuss these issues in a Subcommittee on the Separation of Powers. Republican policy makers of the 1860s realized that the only legitimate method of reversing a constitutional finding of their Supreme Court—however much they loathed that finding—was to amend the Constitution itself.

President Lincoln, with his usual political sagacity, recognized this point explicitly. He cited it publicly as one of the reasons why he elected to pocket veto the Wade-Davis bill in 1864; one section of that bill would have enacted emancipation by statute, but the President insisted instead upon constitutional revision.

His party went on to adopt the Thirteenth, Fourteenth and Fifteenth Amendments, notwithstanding the unprecedented upheavals of the Civil War, to reverse the antebellum findings of the Supreme Court and to insure what they considered to be the most important results of the conflict they had just been through.

I find it ironical that the proposers of S. 158 would cite one of those Amendments now to justify a tactic that its framers considered insufficient and unacceptable a century ago. If a majority of the American people wishes to endow the preborn with full civil rights from the instant of conception, a constitutional amendment to that effect should be passed and that policy should be honored as the Law of the Land. Otherwise, the present ruling of the Supreme Court should, and historically must, remain in effect.

Thank you.

Senator EAST. Professor Marshner.

Statement of William Marshner

Mr. MARSHNER. Mr. Chairman, I will try to summarize as much of my remarks as I can.

I think that I have far less stringent conditions than Professors Degler and Mohr for the historical appropriateness—that is to say, the appropriateness to history—of the human life bill, S. 158.

After all, historical interpretation differs in nature from legal interpretation. Whereas historical interpretation establishes only what was explicitly considered in a statute's past, legal interpretation must ponder a statute's relevance to new and unforeseen contingencies. Therefore history cannot settle the scope of the 14th amendment in advance; it can only establish certain parameters of appropriateness.

I think that S. 158 will be historically appropriate legislation if only three claims can be established:

One, that scientific evidence indicating a significant likelihood that actual human life exists from conception was known to physicians and State legislators from the middle decades of the 19th century forward.

Two, that the passage of antiabortion statutes by those legislators in those decades was significantly influenced and motivated by such evidence.

Three, that the medical, moral, and legal climate in which the 14th amendment was ratified was therefore a climate in which it was a settled conviction that the unborn human fetus at every stage of gestation was a human being entitled to protection of life and, hence, a climate in which absolutely no conflicting right having the character of a privacy right of a woman to abort was conceded to exist by any court or any legislature, State or Federal, in this country or in any Western nation.

I think it well known that these three claims are fully supported by at least one version of the history of antiabortion legislation. It is the version of history which I call the standard history.

The standard history begins with the origins of our civilization in the Judeo-Christian moral tradition, recognizes commitment to protection of fetal life and condemnation of abortion as distinguishing characteristics of that tradition. It notes the passage of these moral attitudes into canon law and into the civil laws of medieval Christendom.

Standard history observes that the extent of the civil protection of fetal life was limited by evidentiary problems stemming from ignorance of reproductive biology.

The rather elastic and subjective test of quickening had to serve both as the indicator of pregnancy and as the indicator of human life in the child. Hence the great project of Western man to protect unborn life through the criminal prosecution of abortion, though never abandoned in principle, was doomed to be thwarted often in practice until better science could equip the law with better arms. That was in the impasse in English common law which the early decades of our own country's history inherited.

Standard history then explores the several medical advances which began in the last decades of the 17th century, which undermined the importance of the quickening test and which eventually established the existence of a distinct being from conception through such discoveries as that of the ovum in 1827.

Standard history continues that as the new knowledge disseminated among American physicians and through them to the general public, the legislatures of the several States were galvanized to pass tougher antiabortion laws.

No less than 30 States and territories passed such laws in the years between 1854 and 1876. The general characteristic of those laws was to drop the quickening distinction.

In other words, the same States which ratified the 14th amendment were busy passing antiabortion bills explicitly designed to protect human beings in their fetal right to life.

The congressional sponsors of the 14th amendment explicitly stated that it applied to "any human being" and to every member of the human race. Therefore, to hold or to deem that the unborn at every stage of gestation are among those protected by the 14th amendment from State action depriving them of life without due process of law is at least plausible on the historical grounds appropriate to legal interpretation.

Whereas, to hold with the Blackmun court, that the 14th amendment not only must not include the unborn but even creates a privacy right to abort them in the teeth of all State statutes contemporary with that amendment, is historically absurd.

Thus far, the standard history. I believe that if the standard history holds up, the three claims necessary and sufficient to establish the historical appropriateness of S. 158 also hold up.

What we need to do, however, is to evaluate a challenge to that standard history, and the challenge takes the form of a revisionist history.

The revisionist picture largely ignores moral and canonical traditions. It holds that certain 14th century precedents in English common law established in fact a woman's liberty to abort at least in the early months of pregnancy.

American women inherited and enjoyed this common law right until it was taken away from them in the last third of the 19th century by some anomalous set of circumstances. What the anomalous circumstances were differs from revisionist to revisionist.

According to some, what triggered the end of the liberty was a rising incidence of abortion-related maternal deaths. So the original and controlling motivation for antiabortion legislation was State concern to protect women's health.

According to another school of revisionism, the antiabortion statutes of the 1860's to 1880's arose out of a combination of nativist depopulation scare with the AMA's struggle to consolidate its power over American medical practice.

Both forms of revisionism challenge the standard history in two ways: first, by replacing the protection of unborn life with other, more transient, motives for the rise of American abortion statutes; and, second, by positing a primordial common law liberty of abortion, which the Supreme Court could plausibly reinvigorate when the transient motives lost their point.

I shall now argue that the revisionist challenge, although it offers some interesting sidelights, fails to dislodge the standard history.

I begin with the contention that State concern to protect maternal health rather than to protect unborn life was the original and controlling motive for antiabortion statutes. The contention is based primarily on a section of the New York revised statutes of 1829 and on an 1858 New Jersey decision, *State v. Murphy*.

As a matter of fact, apart from those two, the contention has no basis whatsoever. Even in those, it has no basis.

New York law of 1829 had two antiabortion sections. The first concerned abortion attempted on any woman pregnant with a "quick" child and provided that such action was second degree manslaughter in case either the child or the mother died. The intent to protect fetal life was already clear.

It becomes clearer in the light of the nature of the exception clause. It said that: "unless the same shall have been necessary to preserve the life of such a mother or shall have been advised by two physicians to be necessary for such a purpose." That is a stringent clause. Not appearance of necessity, not advice of physicians for some other purpose, not appearance of necessity for life, the only exception was for objective necessity to avoid the death of the mother.

Had maternal health been the primary issue, the exception would surely have been made for some reasonable appearance or supposition of necessity.

The second antiabortion section in this 1829 law of New York provided a jail term and fine for all other abortional acts—that is, those before quickening—whether successful or not. It is this section on which revisionists primarily seize because it is thought to resemble a kind of poison control law.

But this section also carries an exception clause, and it is the same kind of stringent exception clause as found in the previous section. If, despite the fact that the fetus was unquickened and therefore allegedly had no common law standing, his offering an appearance of danger to this mother's life was not deemed sufficient grounds for an exception under this act, then the section as a whole can hardly be interpreted to have maternal health as its primary concern.

I will skip my discussion of *New Jersey State* v. *Murphy*. I will also skip the discussion of State statutes and State court decisions which bear on their face evidence of intention to protect unborn life in these mid-19th century abortion statutes.

I want to pass the contention that the AMA promoted antiabortion legislation on its own professional interest as a means of eliminating its competition.

The public reasons published all over the country from the 1840's to the 1870's for which the AMA advocated abortion legislation where clearly centered on the moral duty to stop the slaughter of unborn children. These reasons are frankly noted even in *Roe* v. *Wade*.

So the medical self-interest contention is merely a complement to the standard history, not a challenge to it, unless the revisionists wish to contend that the AMA's publicized reasons were hypocritical. This last contention is not, in fact, made.

So we have, at most, a situation in which sincere scientific and moral conviction coincided with self-interest, which is hardly a rare situation in any epoch.

But even this harmless coincidence cannot really be sustained by the historical record, given the logic of the AMA's alleged situation.

The regular physicians sought to consolidate power in the medical market, we are told, through the legislatures. Why? Well, because they were losing position and losing patients to the quacks, we are told. Why were they losing patients to the quack? Because they would not compete with them for the abortion business, we are told. But why could they not compete? To this question, there is no revisionist answer.

The only answer is the standard historical answer—that they could not compete because they believed it would be scientifically unwarranted and morally bankrupt to do so. At the bottom of the so-called self-interest of the AMA lay nothing but the very same moral principle which lay on the top of its public rhetoric.

Finally, I turn to the contention that a common law right to early abortion had existed some centuries prior to the recent era of abortion prescription.

The contention is quickly disposed of. It is based on mishandling by the revisionists of two 14th century cases, later cited by Coke. Both cases involved indictment of a man for causing an abortion. The first case is extremely confused. The outcome in the second case is clear—the indictment was dismissed: One, because of a defect in pleading; two, because it was impossible to prove that the man had actually killed the child. The case dates, I think, to 1348.

Revisionists conclude from this that abortion was not a crime in 14th century England, but the cases prove the contrary on their face. The second case was not dismissed on the ground that abortion was not a crime in common law but for other reasons. If abortion had not been a crime in common law, there would have been no indictment in the first place.

The distinction between the thing not being a crime and its being a crime for which hardly anyone is ever convicted is neither fine nor fuzzy. The difficulty, the rarity, indeed, the virtual nonexistence of successful prosecution for what is nevertheless a recognized crime does not create a liberty or a right to child and spouse abuse.

Revisionist talk of a common law right to abortion is therefore, historically untenable and conceptually disingenuous.

I will pass over other criticisms which I have of this attempt to project back into time something like what we now would speak of as a right to abortion. I conclude simply that the revisionist history of the rise of antiabortion legislation in the United States fails to refute or displace the standard history and that that history speaks loudly in favor of S. 158.

Thank you.

Senator EAST. Thank you, Professor Marshner.

[The prepared statement of Professor Marshner follows:]

Prepared Statement of William Marshner

Historical interpretation differs in nature from legal interpretation. Whereas historical interpretation establishes only what was explicitly considered in the minds of those drafting and passing a statute, legal interpretation must ponder a statute's relevance to new and unforeseen contingencies. Therefore history cannot settle the scope of the Fourteenth Amendment in advance; it can only establish certain parameters of appropriateness in that Amendment's legal interpretation. The Human Life Bill involves a legal interpretation of the Fourteenth Amendment; the relevance of history, therefore, is not to pronounce whether the content of the Bill corresponds to some explicit thought of the Amendment's framers, but only whether the Bill's content represents an appropriate application of the Amendment, given what was historically thought in its framing.

In that light, I submit the following thesis.

The Human Life Bill (S. 158) will be historically appropriate legislation if three claims can be established: (1) that scientific evidence indicating a significant likelihood that actual human life exists from conception was known to physicians and state legislators from the middle decades of the 19th century forward; (2) that the passage of anti-abortion statutes by those legislators in those decades was significantly influenced and motivated by such evidence; and (3) that the medico-moral and legal climate in which the 14th amendment was ratified was therefore a climate in which it was a settled conviction that the unborn human foetus, at every stage of gestation, was a human being entitled to protection of life, and hence, a climate in which absolutely no conflicting right having the character of a privacy right of a woman to abort was conceded to exist by any court or any legislature, state or federal, in this country or in any Western nation.

As is well known, these three claims are fully supported by what I shall call the "standard history" of anti-abortion legislation.[1] The standard history begins with the origins of our civilization in the Judaeo-Christian moral tradition. It recognizes a commitment to the protection of foetal life and a condemnation of abortion as distinguishing characteristics of that tradition, in deliberate and studied contrast to ancient pagan practices.[2] It notes the passage of these moral attitudes into canon law[3] and into the civil laws of medieval Christendom.[4] The

---

[1] Extended presentations of the standard history include Robert M. Byrn, "An American Tragedy: The Supreme Court on Abortion," *Fordham Law Review* 41 (1973) 807–849; Germain Grisez, *Abortion: The Myths, the Realities, and the Arguments* (New York: Corpus, 1970) chapters 4 and 5; John T. Noonan, Jr., *Contraception* (Harvard, 1965) and "An Almost Absolute Value in History," in John T. Noonan, ed., *The Morality of Abortion* (Harvard, 1970) pp. 1–59; the same standard view is presented in innumerable judicial opinions cited in these works.

[2] Exodus 21:22 (LXX); Galatians 5:20; Didache 2:2; Clement of Alexandria, *Paedagogus* 2.10; Athenagoras, *Embassy for the Christians* 35; Tertullian, *Apologeticum* 1,15; Jerome, Epistle 22; Augustine, *De nuptiis et concupiscentia* 1.15.17; John Chrysostom, Homily 24 on the Epistle to the Romans; etc.

[3] Council of Ancyra, canon 21 (314 A.D.); Council of Elvira, canon 53 (305 A.D.); Gratian, *Decretum* 2.32.2.7 (The canon *Aliquando*); Pope Gregory IX, *Decretales* 5.12.5 (=the canon *Si aliquis*) and 5.12.20 (=the canon *Sicut ex*).

[4] Grisez cites provisions of the Visigothic code, Frankish law, and Anglo-Saxon law prior to the Norman conquest, *op.cit.*, p. 186; the criminality of abortion in the English common law in the high Middle Ages is reflected in the well-known comments of Bracton and Fleta; See Byrn, *op.cit.*, p. 816f.

standard history observes that the severity of punishment in both sorts of law for the abortion offense depended on a philosophical distinction between the animated and pre-animated foetus, a distinction maintained in large part on the basis of inadequate biology.[5] This history further observes that the extent of *civil* protection of foetal life was limited by evidentiary problems stemming from the same ignorance of reproductive biology.[6] The rather elastic and subjective test of quickening (sensation of the child's movement in the womb) had to serve both as the indicator of pregnancy and as the indicator of the human life of the child.[7] Hence the great project of Western man to protect unborn life through the criminal prosecution of abortion, though never abandoned in principle, was doomed to be thwarted often in practice, until better science should equip the law with better arms. Such was the impasse in the English common law, during the centuries when these colonies were formed and achieved their independence.[8] The standard history then explores the several medical advances which, beginning in the last decades of the 17th century, first undermined the importance of "quickening" in the eyes of savants and then established the existence of a distinct living being *from conception*, through the discovery of the ovum in 1827 and other aspects of the fertilization process.[9] As the new knowledge disseminated among American physicians and, through them, among the general public in the 1850s and '60s, the legislatures of the several states were galvanized to pass tougher anti-abortion laws, which protected the foetus at every stage of gestation.[10] No less than 30 states and territories passed such laws in the years between 1854 and 1876.[11] In other words, the same states which ratified the 14th amendment were busy passing anti-abortion bills explicitly designed to protect human beings in their foetal right to life. The Congressional sponsors of the 14th amendment explicitly stated that it applied to "any human being"[12] and to every member of the human race.[13] Therefore to hold, or to deem, that the unborn, at

[5] A full discussion of the Scholastic positions on animation and "formation," as well as the moral and canonical applications of these positions is found in the article, "Animation," in the *Dictionnaire de Theologie Catholique* 1,2, *s.v.*

[6] Byrn, *op.cit.*, pp. 817–827.

[7] Coke, Third Institute 50 (1644); William Blackstone, *Commentaries* 1 at *129–30, and 4 at *198; Byrn, *loc.cit.*

[8] The same impasse is reflected in an 1812 Massachusetts Supreme Court decision, *Commonwealth v. Bangs*, which remained influential until the 1850s.

[9] Fienus and Harvey had already made observations which cast doubt on the discontinuity alleged to occur at "quickening"; on the discovery of the ovum, see Byrn, *op.cit.*, p. 825. In the United States, the accumulating medical evidence against the quickening test was effectively presented by John B. Beck, "Infanticide," in T. R. Beck, ed., *Elements of Medical Jurisprudence*, 5th edition (Albany, 1835). Thirty years later, a more complete case was made in the seminal works of the Harvard medical professor, Horatio R. Storer. In 1868 Storer collaborated with F. F. Heard to produce the classic treatise, *Criminal Abortion: Its Nature, Its Evidence, and Its Law* (Boston: Little, Brown & Co.).

[10] The tighter protection was accomplished by dropping references to "quickening" and by wording the statutes in such a way that, in most cases, pregnancy did not have to be proved; attempted abortion or abortifacient action was itself the crime. As to determining what was abortifacient, the progress of the law was helped, paradoxically, by the commercial standardization of abortive pills, potions and procedures in the 1840s.

[11] A detailed survey of these statutes is given in James C. Mohr, *Abortion in America* (Oxford, 1978), chapters 5 and 8.

[12] Rep. John A. Bingham, *Cong. Globe*, 39th Congress, 1st session (1866), p. 1089.

[13] Sen. Jacob Howard, *ibid.*, p. 2766.

every stage of gestation, are among those protected by the 14th amendment from state action depriving them of life without due process of law, is eminently plausible on historical grounds.[14] And to hold, with the Blackmun Court, that the 14th amendment not only must not include the unborn but even creates a privacy right to abort them, in the teeth of all state statutes contemporary with the amendment, is historically absurd.[15] Thus far the standard history.

As I have mentioned, so long as the standard history holds up, the three claims necessary and sufficient to establish the historical appropriateness of S. 158 also hold up. The purpose of the present testimony, therefore, is to evaluate a challenge to the standard history.

The challenge takes the form of a revisionist history of anti-abortion legislation.[16] The revisionist picture largely ignores the moral and canonical traditions, concentrating instead on the criminal laws. It holds that certain 14th century precedents in English common law (subsequently misused by Coke) established in fact a woman's liberty to abort, at least in the early months of pregnancy.[17] American women inherited and enjoyed this common-law right, until it was taken away from them, in the last third of the 19th century, by an anomalous set of circumstances. Exactly what these circumstances were varies somewhat from revisionist to revisionist.

According to some, what triggered the end of the liberty was a rising incidence of abortion-related maternal deaths. The abortifacient pills and decoctions of the mid-19th century were often dangerous, especially in large doses, and the surgical procedures, innocent of antisepsis, would easily cause infection. Hence the original and controlling motivation for anti-abortion legislation was state concern to protect women's health.[18] With the emergence of safe, modern abortion techniques, this state interest collapses, of course, and along with it, the constitutionality of statutes abridging the common law right to terminate early pregnancy.

According to another school, what put an end to this right (temporarily) was a combination of two factors. First, in the 1840s abortion ceased to be a relatively uncommon thing (the resort of unmarried women desperate to preserve their reputations) and became instead a common way for middle- and upper-class Protestant housewives to control their family size.[19] This sudden upsurge in feminine demand met with an equal upsurge of medical supply, but—and here was

[14] Grisez, *op. cit.*, pp. 410–423; Byrn, *op.cit*, pp. 835–9.

[15] Byrn, *loc. cit.*

[16] The foremost revisionists are Cyril C. Means, Jr., "The Law of New York concerning Abortion and the Status of the Fetus, 1664–1968: A Case of Cessation of Constitutionality," *New York Law Forum* XIV, no. 3 (Fall, 1968) and "The Phoenix of Abortional Freedom: Is a Penumbral or Ninth-Amendment Right About to Rise from the Nineteenth Century Legislative Ashes of a Fourteenth Century Common Law Liberty?" *ibid.* XVII (1971); James C. Mohr, *Abortion in America*, cited above, note 11; and of course Chief Justice Blackmun himself, *Roe v. Wade* in *United States Reports*, vol. 410, pp. 113ff.

[17] Means, "The Phoenix," p. 335; cited with approval in *Roe v. Wade*, p. 135. Mohr seems to agree, speaking *passim* of early abortion as a "common law right." E.g., in the context of American abortion statutes before 1840, Mohr observes: "the right to attempt an abortion prior to quickening, though challenged in a few states, remained essentially intact. . ." *op.cit.*, p. 119.

[18] Thus Means, "The Law of New York," and *Roe v. Wade*, p. 151.

[19] Mohr, *op.cit.*, chapter 4.

the rub—the supply did not come from the nation's regular physicians. These men, the graduates of reputable medical schools, bound by the Hippocratic Oath and influenced by the mounting scientific evidence against quickening, refused to prescribe abortifacients as such and so were losing a steady stream of patients (not to mention a lucrative source of income) to "irregular" physicians or quacks.[20] Now enters the second factor. These "irregulars" (eclectics, botanics, homoeopaths and charlatans) could not be put out of business by licensing restrictions, because licensing did not exist in the laissez-faire medical market of mid-century America. Moreover, the high standing of the "regulars" among learned folk did not extend to the masses. In the popular mind, there was little to choose between regulars and irregulars because, frankly, until the discovery of the connexion between disease and bacteria in the 1860s, the regulars could cure little more than the quacks.[21] Therefore, in order to defend their position in society, the regular physicians espoused the anti-abortion cause as the best way of putting their competition out of business. Soon after the founding of the AMA in 1847, the regulars began in earnest to lobby the state legislatures, often using the nativist argument that abortion was depleting the ranks of the old, Anglo-Protestant stock.[22] Hence, according to this school of revisionism, the anti-abortion statutes of the 1860s to '80s arose out of a combination of nativist depopulation scare with the AMA's struggle to consolidate its power over American medical practice.[23] Today, since the AMA has won its struggle, and since the demand for abortion has risen again, everyone's interests are served by voiding the statutes, restoring the right to abort, and allowing the AMA to reap the profits.

Both forms of revisionism challenge the standard history (1) by replacing the protection of unborn life with other, more transient motives for the rise of American abortion statutes, and (2) by positing a primordial, common law liberty of abortion, which the Supreme Court could plausibly reinvigorate, when the transient motives lost their point. And since these transient motives have nothing to do with the aims of the 14th amendment, nor with the determination of when a human life begins, the revisionist history makes S. 158 appear to contain an idea new to serious legislative history, a kind of new foundation for anti-abortion policy.

I shall now argue that the revisionist challenge, although it offers a number of interesting and valuable sidelights on the 19th century struggle, fails to dislodge the standard history.

I begin with the contention that state concern to protect maternal health, rather than to protect unborn life, was the original and controlling motive for anti-abortion statutes. The contention is based primarily on a section of the New York Revised Statutes of 1829 and on an 1858 New Jersey decision, *State v. Murphy*. Indeed, apart from these two loci, the contention has no basis whatsoever.

The New York law of 1829 had two anti-abortion sections. The first (N.Y.

---

[20] *Ibid.*, chapters 3, 5, and 6.
[21] *Ibid.*, pp. 32–34.
[22] *Ibid.*, pp. 166–7.
[23] Mohr's thesis is most succinctly stated on p. 258.

Rev. Stat. (1829) pt. IV, ch. 1, tit. 2, section 9) concerned abortion attempted on "any woman pregnant with a quick child" and provided that such action was second degree manslaughter in case *either* the child *or* the mother died. The intent to protect foetal life is already clear, and it becomes clearer in the light of the exception clause: "unless the same shall have been necessary to preserve the life of such mother, or shall have been advised by two physicians to be necessary for such purpose." The clause is quite stringent, requiring objective necessity or medical judgments of objective necessity of the procedure to avoid the mother's death. A mere threat to her health created no exception at all, no matter how many physicians perceived that threat. If maternal health had been the primary issue, the exception would surely have been made for a reasonable appearance or supposition of necessity, or simply for the advice of two physicians, regardless of whether they advised abortion for life or health-saving reasons. As Robert Byrn has commented, the stringent exception clause can only mean that "The child's life was considered so precious, that in the view of the legislature, it could not be sacrificed to a lesser value than life itself."[24]

The second anti-abortion section (*ibid.* tit. 6, section 21) provided a jail term and/or a fine for all other abortional acts (i.e. before quickening), whether successful or not. It is this section on which the revisionists seize, because it is thought to resemble a poison-control law. But this section also carries an exception clause, and, astonishingly enough from the point of view of maternal health, it is the same stringent exception as in the section previously discussed. If, despite the fact that the foetus was unquickened and therefore had no common-law standing, his offering an *appearance* of danger to his mother's life was not deemed sufficient grounds for an exception, the section as a whole can hardly be interpreted to have maternal health as its primary concern.[25]

The New Jersey case, *State v. Murphy*, arose under an 1849 statute which made all attempted abortions criminal, made it a crime to offer advice or directions for performing an abortion, and provided penalties in case the woman died. Against revisionist interpretation, the point of the statute itself and of a famous comment on it in *Murphy*[26] is not primarily to address maternal health but to remedy a defect of the common law, whereby the guilt of the defendent depended wholly upon the relation of his act to the child, irrespective of the consequences to the mother. New Jersey wanted to add additional penalties in case of maternal death, so as to hang *that* around the abortionist's neck as well.

Finally, if we look at other states, or other dates, the maternal health contention is contradicted by abundant facts. In 1851, the Maine Supreme Court applauded the elimination of quickening from a statute: "There is a removal of the unsubstantial distinction, that it is no offense to procure an abortion, before the mother becomes sensible of the motion of the child, notwithstanding it is then capable of inheriting an estate; and immediately afterwards it is a great misdemeanor."[27] In 1881, the New Jersey Supreme Court wrote of the law already

[24] Byrn, *op.cit.*, p. 831.

[25] For further remarks, see Byrn, *loc. cit.*

[26] Andrew Dutcher, reporter, *Reports of Cases Argued and Determined in the Supreme Court and the Court of Errors and Appeals of the State of New Jersey* (Trention, 1859), III, p. 114. The comment is quoted in Mohr, *op. cit.*, p. 137.

[27] Smith v. State, 33 Me. 48, 57 (1851); cited in Byrn, *op. cit.* p. 829.

discussed: "This law was further extended March 26th, 1872 . . . to protect the life of the child also, and inflict the same punishment in case of its death, as if the mother should die."[28] In 1916 an Alabama court asked: "Does not the new being, from the first day of its uterine life, acquire a legal and moral status that entitles it to the same protection as that guaranteed to human beings in extrauterine life?"[29] These statements, and there are many more like them, flatly contradict the revisionist claim of *Roe v. Wade* that "the few state courts called upon to interpret their laws in the late 19th and early 20th centuries did focus on the State's interest in protecting the woman's health rather than in preserving the embryo or foetus."[30]

I now pass on to the contention that the AMA promoted anti-abortion legislation in its own, professional interest, as a means of eliminating its competition.

I note first that the public reasons, published all over the country in the 1840s to '70s, for which the AMA advocated abortion legislation, were clearly, directly and unequivocally centered on the moral duty to stop the slaughter of unborn children, from conception forward. These reasons were frankly noted even in *Roe v. Wade*.[31]

Therefore the medical self-interest contention is merely a complement to the standard history, not a challenge to it, unless the revisionists also contend that the AMA's publicized reasons were hypocritical or insincerely professed. This last contention is not in fact made, however; it has even been denied by a prominent revisionist historian.[32] Therefore we have at most a situation in which sincere scientific and moral conviction coincided with self-interest, hardly a rare state of affairs in any epoch, and hardly a challenge to the standard history.

Secondly, I note that even this harmless coincidence cannot really be sustained, given the logic of the AMA's alleged situation. The regulars sought to consolidate power in the medical market, we are told, through the legislatures. Why? Because they were losing position and losing patients to the quacks, we are told. Why were they losing patients to the quacks? Because they couldn't compete with them for the abortion business, we are told. But why couldn't they compete? To this question there is no revisionist answer; there is only a standard-historical answer. They couldn't compete because they believed it would be scientifically unwarranted and morally bankrupt to do so. At the bottom of the so-called self-interest of the AMA lay nothing but the very same moral principle which lay on the top of its public rhetoric.

I turn, finally, to the contention that a common law right to early abortion had existed for some centuries prior to the "recent era" of abortion proscription.

On one level, this contention is quickly disposed of. It is based on a mishandling by the revisionists of certain 14th century cases, later cited by Coke. Both cases involved indictment of a man for causing an abortion; the outcome of the first case, and even the nature of the surviving report of it, are confused and

[28] State v. Gedicke 43 N.J.L. 86, 90 (Sup. Ct. 1881); cited in Byrn, *op. cit.* p. 828.
[29] Trent v. State, 15 Ala. App. 485, 488, 73 So. 834, 836 (1916).
[30] *Roe v. Wade*, p. 151.
[31] *Ibid.* pp. 141–142.
[32] Mohr, *op. cit.*, pp. 164–166.

controversial; the outcome of the second case is clear: the indictment was dismissed (a) because of a defect in pleading and (b) because it was impossible to prove that the man had actually killed the child.[33] Revisionists conclude the abortion was not a crime in 14th century England. But the cases prove the contrary on their face. The second case was not dismissed on the ground that abortion was not a common law crime, but for other reasons. Transparently, if abortion had not been a common law crime, there would have been no indictment in the first place.[34] The distinction between a thing's not being a crime and its being a crime for which hardly anyone is ever convicted is neither fine nor fuzzy; it is straightforward and clear. For the difficulty, the rarity, indeed the virtual non-existence of successful prosecution for what is nevertheless a recognized crime does not create a *liberty* or a *right* to do that crime. Else there was, until almost the day before yesterday, a right to child and spouse abuse. Revisionist talk of a common law "right" to abortion is historically untenable and conceptually disingenuous.

More deeply, however, what flaws the celebration of a long-lost right is its ahistoricality, where ideas and beliefs are concerned. Talk of a pre-scientific right to abortion takes a modern term, 'abortion,' which means the *intentional* termination of pregnancy, indeed, the intentional expulsion of a living fetus, and projects the term back into a time when what was often happening was no more than the *de facto* termination of pregnancy by some intentional act, a time when women did not even know they were pregnant, when they took potions to "release stopped menses," on the advice of physicians who distinguished sharply between that therapeutic intent and the intent to abort, a time when the unborn child was not even known to be a living entity before the fifth month, so that our distinction between abortion and contraception was very imperfectly understood.

Above all, the revisionist picture leaves out of focus the genuine problem of the law in its relation to scientific progress. We now know what no farmer knew twenty years ago about the effect of DDT. Would we hail a Supreme Court decision striking down all federal and state measures banning the use of DDT? Would we hail it as a restoration of a farmer's "historic common law right" to use the pesticide of his choice?

Conclusion: the revisionist history of the rise of anti-abortion legislation in the U.S. fails to refute or displace the standard history, and *that* history speaks loudly in favor of S. 158.

Senator EAST. Professor Rosenblum?

Statement of Victor Rosenblum

Mr. ROSENBLUM. Mr. Chairman, I would like at the outset to express my appreciation for the opportunity to appear before this Subcommittee on the Separation of Powers.

Almost 25 years ago, my late mentor and colleague, Peter Odegard and I prepared materials for the Fund for Adult Education of the Separation of Powers in the American System of Government.

---

[33] Means, "The Phoenix," pp. 336–341; Byrn, *op. cit.*, pp. 816ff.
[34] Byrn, *loc. cit.*

One of the statements we made in our concluding essay remained a cornerstone of my own beliefs. We said at the time: "The strength and stability of the American Government depend upon the three powers: President, Congress, and Court, moving in concert to realize the great ends set forth in the preamble to the Constitution."

Certainly, the concert is not without its discordant notes, but the strength of the whole system may be said to depend upon the tensions arising from the potential tug of war among the constituent parts.

Thrust and counterthrust, check and balance, power versus power, ambition against ambition, and an appropriate sense of restraint on proper occasions—these are not only safeguards of liberty but sources of energy in a system that strives for more perfect union and the blessings of liberty.

The discussion today is in large part a consequence of the failure of the Supreme Court to exercise appropriate restraint in 1973. The Justices donned legislative garb in ruling that States violate the due process clause of the 14th amendment insofar as they controvert the right to privacy through State laws protecting the life of the child in the womb.

Restraint would have led Justice Blackmun who wrote for the majority to leave the crucial issue of regulation of abortion to the traditional regulating powers of each State.

Far from providing rational answers to difficult questions, the Supreme Court's legislation through the *Roe* v. *Doe* decisions of 1973 simply abolished protection for what even they had termed potential life. And, as numerous scholars have pointed out, they avoided or misinterpreted the history of protection of the unborn.

What is especially interesting to me as an occasional torts teacher is that tort law has been far more supportive of the personhood of the child in the womb than the Supreme Court's 1973 rulings on abortion.

As the late Dean Prosser pointed out in his classic treatise on torts: "Judicial decisions have changed dramatically regarding recovery by or on behalf of the child when a pregnant woman is injured and the fetus suffers injury as a consequence."

Thus, Prosser's fourth edition, which was published in 1971, summarized and reiterated the devastating criticism heaped by major legal writers on the old rule of judicial denials of recovery to the child.

Said Prosser:

> *All writers who have discussed the problem have joined in condemning the old rule as well as in maintaining that the unborn child in the path of the automobile is as much a person in the street as the mother.*

And in urging that recovery should be allowed upon proper proof.

In an important recent review of the law of tortious prenatal death, Prof. David Kader of the University of Arizona noted that in *Roe* v. *Wade* the Supreme Court discussed prenatal death recovery under State law as support for its assessment that the fetus does not warrant recognition as a person.

Professor Kader commented in this article of 1980 that:

The discussion by the Supreme Court was perfunctory and, unfortunately, largely inaccurate and should not be relied upon as the correct view of the law at the time of Roe v. Wade."

For many centuries, the predominant scientific understanding was similar to that of Aristotle who identified life with the animation of a formed fetus. Partly for this reason, by the middle of the 17th century the beginning of actual individual human life was equated with movement or quickening, when the mother first felt the unborn child move in her womb. Thus, the English common law established criminal penalties for abortion after quickening.

We now know that the child actually moves long before the mother feels quickening, but our ancestors had to judge by the best information available to them at the time.

Only in the second quarter of the 19th century did biological research advance to the extent of understanding the actual mechanism of human reproduction and of what truly comprised the onset of gestational development.

The 19th century saw a gradual but profoundly influential revolution in the scientific understanding of the beginning of individual mammalian life. It was the new research finding which persuaded doctors that the old quickening distinction embodied in the common law and some statutory law was unscientific and indefensible.

My distinguished fellow academician, Professor Mohr, has made important scholarly contributions to the history of abortion with his comprehensive study of the activity and influence of 19th century physicians in reforming the abortion laws State-by-State to extend legal protection to the unborn.

Dr. Mohr identifies the period of 1860 to 1880 as the one in which a "physician's campaign against abortion produced the most important burst of antiabortion legislation in the Nation's history."

In that era, Professor Mohr reports, 40 antiabortion statutes of various kinds were enacted by States and territories. Of these, 13 outlawed abortion for the first time, and 21 revised old antiabortion laws by making them more stringent.

Professor Mohr's work is, indeed, of recognized professional distinction. I must nonetheless respectfully dissent from at least two dimensions: one of omission, the other of commission.

Dr. Mohr related the activities and arguments of the physicians and medical societies who fought for the unborn. But he did not acknowledge the background of new biological research and discovery which convinced these doctors that early abortion takes the lives of human beings.

In fact, there was a direct cause-effect relationship between the scientific discoveries and the physicians' and legislators' responses.

Dr. Mohr's omission of this scientific motive leads to a rather strained hypothesis—that the movement was a product of medical chauvinism, a vehicle by which the so-called regular physician could drive midwives and other rivals out of business.

It is clear from Professor Mohr's book that the campaign the doctors articulated in striving to persuade State legislatures was geared to the conviction that abortion kills human life before as well as after quickening. Whatever subjective motives may be postulated for the physicians, the life-protective motive of the legislatures is clear.

The climate of opinion and the nature of State laws at this time—that is, at the time of the adoption of the 14th amendment—is significant because it was in 1866 that the 14th amendment was proposed by Congress and in 1868 that it was declared ratified. Therefore, his chapter on 1860 to 1880 is particularly significant.

The contemporaneous attitude of the State legislatures and the public is of relevance to the understanding of the framers and ratifiers of the 14th amendment with regard to whether the unborn were to be included as persons protected by it.

It is important, once again, to remember the intent of the 14th amendment. It was enacted after the Civil War so as forever to enshrine in the Constitution the principle of human equality under law.

Blacks had been excluded from equality under the domestic institution of slavery, specifically justified by the Supreme Court in the infamous *Dred Scott* decision.

The spirit of the amendment requires that members of the human species before birth be acknowledged by the law. It does not postulate the existence of a class of individual human beings who may be disposed of by other human beings at will.

Recognition of a right to cause the death of any member of the species, including the human fetus, runs contrary to the expansive conception of humanity that motivated those who sponsored the 14th amendment.

Since the 14th amendment with its broad protection of the lives of all persons was ratified by State legislatures while these very same legislatures, persuaded by newly discovered scientific and medical evidence, were extending the protection of the criminal law to encompass all the unborn from the time of conception or fertilization, it is a fair assumption that the unborn were not excluded from those persons covered by the amendment.

Some might argue that because the framers did not say explicitly that the unborn were included that therefore the framers and ratifiers of the 14th amendment could not possibly have deemed the unborn to be persons under it.

If such there still may be who make that argument, they might well compete for the Roger B. Taney Award for Documentary Interpretation for theirs is precisely the method of discredited argumentation used by Chief Justice Taney in 1857 to get around the plain language of the Declaration of Independence and conclude that it in no way required or implied citizenship for black people.

Justice Taney had said: "The language of the Declaration of Independence says: 'We hold these truths to be self-evident: that all men are created equal * * *'

"The general words above quoted would seem to embrace the whole human family, and if they were used in a similar instrument at this day, would be so understood. But," said Taney, "it is too clear for dispute, the the enslaved African race were not intended to be included, and formed no part of the people who framed and adopted this Declaration; for if the language, as understood in that day, would embrace them, the conduct of the distinguished men who framed the Declaration of Independence would have been utterly and flagrantly inconsistent with the principles they asserted; and instead of the sympathy of mankind, to which they so confidently appealed, they would have deserved and received universal rebuke and reprobation."

Justice McLean in his dissent in the case made much more sense, and that is the accredited and accepted interpretation of our time.

Justice McLean said: "I prefer the lights of Madison, Hamilton, and Jay, as a means of construing the Constitution in all its bearings, rather than to look behind that period, into a traffic which is now declared to be piracy, and punished with death by Christian nations.

"While I admit," said McLean, "the Government was not made especially for the colored race, yet many of them were citizens of the New England States and exercised the right to suffrage when the Constitution was adopted, and it was not doubted by any intelligent person that its tendencies would greatly ameliorate their condition."

Justice McLean rightly recognized that the enunciation of great principles in fundamental documents is often designed to represent aspirations rather than previous practices.

It is an affront to the framers as well as to the meaning of their language to reduce the aspirations to the level of previous practice instead of raising future practice to the level of the aspirations.

Chief Justice Taney assumed that the framers of the Nation's fundamental documents could not have hoped thereby to make tomorrow more ethical and moral than the practices of yesterday and today.

Not only did this denigrate the conscience and aspiration of those who, like Thomas Jefferson, saw slavery as evil, but it ruled as a constitutional absolute that even plain language cannot transcend the previous conduct of its author.

I believe we constitutionally can and should interpret language plainly and, as in New Year's resolutions, strive to do what we think right in the future rather than perpetuate the failings of the past.

I mentioned earlier that despite Professor Mohr's impressive scholarship and very important contribution to our understanding of the history of abortion in America I had a bone of commission as well as of omission to pick with him.

The bone of commission is this: Dr. Mohr views the abortion prohibition legislation in the 19th century as an anomaly against a background of leniency toward abortion both before and since. In this I believe he errs.

Abortion was almost universally condemned prior to the 19th century. Professor Mohr, like Professor Means before him, assumed that the criminal law was the only mechanism employed by the State to prohibit abortion.

But an essay by my friends, Dennis Horan, the past chairman of the American Bar Association's Medicine and Law Committee, and Tom Marzen, in the forthcoming book "New Perspectives on Human Abortion," demonstrates that this was not the case.

Both in Europe and in colonial America, legislatures prohibited abortion at any stage of gestation through their regulation of midwives. For example, New York City from 1716 required all midwives to take an oath not to abort those in their charge.

The significance of these laws is not too difficult to discern. Midwives attended women in pregnancy and childbirth. They performed most abortions as well. Regulations such as the 1716 law would therefore severely limit access to abortion services.

Indeed, since the 1716 law required anyone who assisted women in pregnancy and childbirth to be licensed and then to abide by the provisions forbidding abortion, it in effect proscribed abortion in a manner analogous to the statutes enacted in the next century.

For centuries, the English common law of property has recognized the unborn child as an autonomous human being. To the argument that such a child was a nonentity a leading court replied:

> *Let us see what this nonentity can do. He may be vouched in a recovery, though it is for the purpose of making him answer over in value. He may be an executor. He may take under the statute of distributions. He may take by devise. He may be entitled under a change of raising portions. He may have an injunction; and he may have a guardian.*

In short, Mr. Chairman, the physicians' crusade of the 19th century to extend the protection of the criminal law to cover the unborn from the moment of conception, which Professor Mohr so ably documents, was not, as he said, a period of interruption or deviation from the norm.

Rather, 19th century protection of the unborn was one of many chapters in human history demonstrating an ongoing and nearly universal concern for protection of unborn human life.

Above all, Mr. Chairman, I believe the evidence clearly demonstrates that the 14th amendment was intended to protect all human beings and that many of those who brought the amendment into being through ratification contemporaneously regarded the unborn, from conception, as human beings protectable by law.

Thank you.

Senator EAST. Thank you, Professor Rosenblum.

[The prepared statement, bibliography, and article submitted by Professor Rosenblum follows:]

Prepared Statement of Victor Rosenblum

My name is Victor G. Rosenblum. I have been a professor of law and political science at Northwestern University in Illinois for some 20 years. The affection I have for my school should not hold it accountable in any way for my opinions. I am here today testifying solely as a private individual. For purposes of identification I submit a brief biography. I also have a bibliography on the subject of my testimony, which I would appreciate being entered in the record, together with a 6-page article on "Abortion and Midwifery," by my colleagues in the law Dennis Horan and Tom Marzen, which I would appreciate being placed in the record in its entirety if that is possible.

I'd like at the outset to express my admiration for the concern of this Subcommittee with the nature and requirements of our system of separation of powers. Almost 25 years ago, my late mentor and colleague Peter Odegard and I prepared materials for the Fund for Adult Education which we called *The Power to Govern: An Examination of the Separation of Powers in the American System of Government*. One of the statements we made in our concluding essay remains a cornerstone of my own beliefs and provides a context for this testimony.

> *As the stability of atoms depends upon a nice balance of protons and electrons moving in their appointed orbits, so the strength and stability of the American government depends upon the three powers—President, Congress, and Court—moving in concert to realize the great ends set forth in the Preamble to the Constitution. Certainly the concert is not without its discordant notes. But the strength of the whole system may be said to depend upon the tensions arising from the potential tug of war among the constituent parts. Thrust and counterthrust, check and balance, power versus power, ambition against ambition, and an appropriate sense of restraint on proper occasions; these are not only safeguards of liberty, but sources of energy in a system that strives for 'more perfect union' and 'the blessings of liberty.'*[1]

The discussion today is in large part a consequence of the failure of the Supreme Court to exercise appropriate restraint in 1973. The Justices donned legislative garb in ruling that states violate the due process clause of the Fourteenth Amendment insofar as they controvert the right to privacy through state laws protecting the life of the child in the womb. Restraint would have led Justice Blackmun, who wrote for the majority, to leave the crucial issue of regulation of abortion to the traditional legislative powers of each state. Such restraint was especially warranted in light of the court's own proclamation that "We need not resolve the difficult question of when life begins. When those trained in the respective disciplines of medicine, philosophy, and theology are unable to arrive at any consensus, the judiciary, at this point in the development of man's knowledge, is not in a position to speculate as to the answer."[2]

If the majority of the Court thought it inappropriate to speculate on the

---

Note.—Footnotes appear at the end of prepared statement.

difficult question of when life begins, how could they morally, ethically, or constitutionally authorize what, even from their vantage point, could be the demise of life? If, as a legal matter, the majority believed that life could begin before the third trimester, how could the same justices who had properly placed the most stringent of constitutional restrictions on the death penalty for criminals place a new judicial seal of approval on the destruction of life of innocents for reasons of convenience or caprice? Far from providing rational answers to difficult questions, the Supreme Court's legislation through the *Roe* and *Doe* decisions simply abolished protection for what even they had termed "potential life," and, as numerous scholars have pointed out, avoided or misinterpreted the history of protection of the unborn.[3]

What is especially interesting to me as a teacher of torts for the past decade is that tort law has been far more supportive of the personhood of the child in the womb than the Supreme Court's rulings on abortion.

As the late Dean Prosser pointed out in his classic treatise on torts, judicial decisions have changed dramatically regarding recovery by or on behalf of the child when a pregnant woman is injured and the fetus suffers injury as a consequence. The denial of recovery to the child in cases prior to 1946, according to Prosser, was generally based on the proposition that the defendant could not be placed under a duty to a person not yet born at the time of the injury.[4]

Prosser's fourth edition, published in 1971, summarized and reiterated the devastating criticism heaped by major legal writers on judicial denials of recovery to the child. Said Prosser, "All writers who have discussed the problem have joined in condemning the old rule as well as in maintaining the unborn child in the path of the automobile is as much a person in the street as the mother and in urging that recovery should be allowed upon proper proof."[5] Invoking Herzog's textbook on *Medical Jurisprudence* written in 1931,[6] and Malloy's textbook on *Legal Anatomy and Surgery* written in 1930,[7] Prosser maintained that "Medical authority has recognized long since that the child is in existence from the moment of conception and for many purposes its existence is recognized by the law. The criminal law regards it as a separate entity, and the law of property considers it in being for all purposes which are to its benefit, such as taking by will or descent."[8]

While many jurisdictions held that the child must be born alive for an action for prenatal injury to be maintainable, Prosser noted that a slight majority of the courts, having become more concerned with compensation for the distressing wrong in the loss of the child, were allowing recovery for prenatal injuries even where the child was stillborn.[9]

I cast my lot with Dr. Seuss' children's story, *Horton Hears a Who*, which made lovingly clear the proposition that "a person is a person, no matter how small."[10] Courts in tort cases increasingly have been enhancing this conclusion by providing recovery by or on behalf of the child injured in the womb regardless of whether he or she is born alive or stillborn.

In an important recent review of the law of tortious prenatal death, Professor David Kader of the University of Arizona noted that in *Roe v. Wade* the Supreme Court discussed prenatal death recovery under state law as support for its assessment that the fetus does not warrant recognition as a person. Professor Kader commented that "the discussion [by the Supreme Court] was perfunctory, and unfortunately largely inaccurate and should not be relied upon as the correct view of the law at the time of *Roe v. Wade*".[11]

As of 1971, the publication date of Prosser's treatise, the division of case authority on the issue of whether a fetus was a person in accordance with requirements of wrongful death statutes was 14–11 *favoring* recovery for the wrongful death of a stillborn fetus. Kader added, "Had the Supreme Court done further research, it would have found that between 1971 and 1973, courts in five additional jurisdictions had considered the question, four more allowing recovery. . . ."[12]

As to the Supreme Court's holding in *Roe v. Wade* that the term "person" as used in the Fourteenth Amendment "does not include the unborn,"[13] Kader reminded us and the Court that the meaning the Justices have given to person for purposes of applying the Fourteenth Amendment "has embraced entities both within and without the human gene pool."[14]

In the words of John Noonan, condemnation of abortion has been "an almost absolute value in history."[15] That condemnation has resulted in the nearly universal protection of the unborn by the law from the point of their gestation at which the science of the day has indicated a living individual is first present.

For many centuries, the predominant scientific understanding was that of Aristotle, who identified life with the "animation" of a formed fetus.[16] For this reason, by the middle of the 17th century the beginning of actual individual human life was equated with movement or "quickening," when the mother first felt the unborn child move in her womb. Thus, the English common law established criminal penalties for abortion after quickening. This principle, first known to have been stated by the eminent commentator Lord Coke,[17] was recognized by Blackstone in 1769 in his famous *Commentaries on the Laws of England*: "Life . . . begins in contemplation of law as soon as an infant is able to stir in the mother's womb."[18]

We know now that the child actually moves long before the mother feels "quickening"—only when the child has grown large enough to crowd the uterus are his or her movements felt, and even then the relative thinness or obesity of the mother can affect when she first feels movement.[19] Quickening is thus quite irrelevant to the objective development or stage of gestation of the child, depending instead primarily on the subjective impressions of the mother. Our ancestors, however, had to judge by the best information available at the time, and so they protected unborn life under the criminal law from quickening onward—when with their best, but comparatively primitive, scientific understanding they believed individual human life actually began.

Only in the second quarter of the nineteenth century did biological research advance to the extent of understanding the actual mechanism of human reproduction and of what truly comprised the onset of gestational development. The nineteenth century saw a gradual but profoundly influential revolution in the scientific understanding of the beginning of individual mammalian life. Although sperm had been discovered in 1677, the mammalian egg was not identified until 1827. The cell was first recognized as the structural unit of organisms in 1839, and the egg and sperm were recognized as cells in the next two decades.[20] These developments were brought to the attention of the American state legislatures and public by those professionals most familiar with their unfolding import—physicians. It was the new research findings which persuaded doctors that the old "quickening" distinction embodied in the common and some statutory law was unscientific and indefensible.[21]

My distinguished fellow academician, Professor James Mohr, has made important scholarly contributions to the history both of abortion and of the medical profession in America with his comprehensive and well-documented history of the activity and influence of 19th century physicians in reforming the abortion laws, state by state, to extend legal protection of the unborn to the time of conception or fertilization.[22]

Dr. Mohr identifies the period of 1860 to 1880 as the one in which a "physicians' campaign against abortion produced the most important burst of anti-abortion legislation in the nation's history."[23] In that era, reports Mohr, 40 anti-abortion statutes of various kinds were enacted by states and territories. Of these, 13 outlawed abortion for the first time and 21 revised old anti-abortion laws by making them more stringent, generally by extending the protection of the unborn backwards from quickening to conception.[24]

States acted throughout the period to restrict abortion: 1860—Connecticut, Pennsylvania; 1861—Colorado, Nevada; 1864—Arizona, Idaho, Montana, Oregon; 1866–67—Alabama; 1867—Illinois, Ohio, Vermont; 1868—Florida, Maryland; 1869—Massachusetts, Wyoming; 1870—Louisiana; 1872—California, New Jersey; 1873—Virginia, Michigan, Minnesota, Nebraska; 1875—Arkansas; 1876—Georgia.[25]

The "physicians' campaign" chronicled by Mohr began about 1857.[26] The American Medical Association, which was founded in 1847, actively opposed abortion.[27] According to Dr. Mohr, much of the impetus for the doctors' anti-abortion activism was grounded in the medical community's antipathy towards the "quickening doctrine," upon which much of the older anti-abortion laws were based. By 1857, the year the Supreme Court rendered the infamous *Dred Scott* decision,[28] it had come to be accepted within medicine that "quickening" is a scientifically and biologically insignificant point in pregnancy. In 1867, a New York State Medical Society resolution stated that ". . . from the first moment of conception, there is a living creature in process of development to full maturity . . . and . . . any . . . interruption to this living process always results in the destruction of life . . ."[29]

Professor Mohr states that this physicians' crusade against both abortion in general and the quickening doctrine in particular was the key factor in persuading the states to pass tougher anti-abortion statutes. In almost every instance, the new laws passed in the 1860–1880 directly or effectively abolished the "quickening doctrine."[30]

Mohr's study of the doctor-led abortion abolition movement of the nineteenth century effectively discredits the earlier theory, propounded by Cyril Means[31] and accepted by the Supreme Court in legalizing abortion[32] that the statutes prohibiting abortion enacted in the nineteenth century were passed in order to protect the mother from the clinical dangers of surgery rather than from solicitude for the unborn. His work confirms the historical conclusion of Sauer, who, like Dr. Mohr, is not identified with the pro-life cause, that:

One can infer from an analysis of nineteenth-century laws that the safety of the foetus was a major concern of many State legislatures. A law which has maternal health as its sole or main consideration is not likely to be worded in such a way that the human status of the foetus is recognized, since such recognition would also require that the foetus be given human rights protected by law. In a law where the concern is with the woman's health, a woman is likely to be labelled as 'pregnant' rather than as 'being with child' or some other phrase which gives a human status to the foetus. Although a number of the initial State laws contained a distinction based on quickening which gave lower value to early foetal life, the large majority of State laws never made this distinction, and most of these laws referred to a woman as 'being with child' or some similar phrase which attributed a human status to the foetus. Furthermore, many of the States which initially had this distinction written into their law later dropped it and also referred to a woman at any period of her pregnancy as 'being with child'.[33]

Profesor Mohr's work is of recognized professional distinction. I must nonetheless respectfully dissent from at least two dimensions, one of omission, the other of commission.

Dr. Mohr related the activities and arguments, and articulated the beliefs of the physicians and medical societies who fought for the unborn. But at no point in his book did he acknowledge the background of new biological research and discovery which convinced these doctors that early abortion takes the lives of human beings. In fact, there was a direct cause-effect relationship between the scientific discoveries and the physicians' and legislators' responses.

Dr. Mohr did concede that physician opposition to the "quickening" doctrine was based on their belief in the "inherent difficulties of determining any point at which a steadily developing embryo becomes somehow more alive than it had been the moment before."[34] But he failed to note that the "quickening" doctrine was scientifically superseded only in the years immediately preceding the genesis of the abortion abolition drive.

An 1872 quotation from Dr. Hodge, one of the leaders of the abortion abolition movement, confirms the causal effect of the new scientific information. He wrote:

If. . . the profession in former times, from the imperfect state of their physiological knowledge, had, in any degree, undervalued the importance of foetal life, they have fully redeemed their error and they now call upon the legislatures of our land . . . to stay the progress of this destructive evil of criminal abortion.[35]

Dr. Mohr's failure of omission of this scientific motive leads him to a quandry in trying to explain why, historically, the abortion abolition movement arose when it did. He therefore arrives at the rather strained hypothesis that the movement was a product of medical chauvinism, a vehicle by which the so-called "regular" physicians could drive midwives and other rivals out of business.

But regardless of whatever may have been the possible motivation behind the medical profession's efforts to see that expansively protective legislation was passed in 1860–1880, it is clear from Professor Mohr's book that the campaign the doctors articulated in striving to persuade state legislatures was geared to the conviction that abortion kills human life before as well as after quickening. I believe it is appropriate, then, to say that the doctors persuaded legislators (1) that the child in the womb is a human being at all points in gestation, (2) that therefore all abortions kill human life, and (3) that therefore the quickening doctrine needed to be abolished in favor of a comprehensive abortion ban. Whatever subjective motives may be postulated for the physicians, the life-protective motive of the legislatures is clear.

In their "physicians' crusade," the abortion abolition activists encountered some apathy and a number of reports emphasizing the frequency of occurrence of the evil they sought to combat. But there was no organized opposition—no group banded together to defend a "freedom" to abort. Sauer reports that "not one statement by any nineteenth-century commentator can be found which was in any way sympathetic to women desiring abortions."[36]

The climate of opinion and the nature of state laws at this time is significant because it was in 1866 that the Fourteenth Amendment was proposed by Congress and in 1868 that it was declared ratified.[37] The contemporaneous attitude of the state legislatures and public is of relevance to the understanding of the framers and ratifiers of the Fourteenth Amendment with regard to whether the unborn were to be included as "persons" protected by it.[38] It is a fair assumption that the Members of Congress were aware of the growing anti-abortion sentiment and did nothing to repudiate it.

It is important to remember the intent of the Fourteenth Amendment. It, as well as the Thirteenth and Fifteenth Amendments, was enacted after the Civil War so as forever to enshrine in the Constitution the principle of human equality under law. Blacks had been excluded from equality under the "domestic institution" of slavery, specifically justified by the Supreme Court in (Dred) *Scott v. Sanford*.[39] Justice Douglas and Black have noted that in 1873, "Mr. Justice Miller in the *Slaughter-House Cases*, 16 Wall. 36, 71, adverted to events 'almost too recent to be called history' to show that the purpose of the Amendment was to protect human rights, primarily the rights of a race which had just won its freedom."[40] One class of individuals, biologically members of the human species, had been excluded from full membership in society. Congress and the states wanted to be sure that never happened again.

Thus, Congressman John Bingham, the House sponsor of the Fourteenth Amendment, stated that the Amendment was intended to be "universal" in its protection, and to apply to "any human being."[41] The rights bestowed by the Fourteenth Amendment were intended not only to "pertain to American citizenship but also to common humanity."[42]

The Senate sponsor of the Amendment, Senator Jacob Howard, emphasized that it applied to every member of the human race, giving "to the humblest, the poorest, the most despised of the race" the same legal rights as "the most powerful, the most wealthy, or the most haughty."[43]

The "spirit" of this Amendment demands that members of the human species before birth be acknowledged before the law; it does not postulate the existence of a class of individual human beings that may be disposed of by other human beings at will. Recognition of a right to cause the death of any member of the species, including the human fetus, runs contrary to the expansive conception of humanity that motivated those who sponsored the Amendment.

Since the Fourteenth Amendment, with its broad protection of the lives of all persons, was ratified by state legislatures while these very same legislatures, persuaded by newly discovered scientific and medical evidence, were extending the protection of the criminal law to encompass *all* the unborn from the time of conception or fertilization, it is a fair assumption that the unborn were not understood to be excluded from those "persons" covered by the Amendment.

It is true, of course, that when the Fourteenth Amendment was ratified in 1868,[44] the success of the physicians' crusade was as yet not fully complete, and that there were a number of states whose criminal law, statutory or common, protected the unborn only after quickening. The Fourteenth Amendment could not of its own force alter that situation, since it prohibited only state action, not private action, which deprived persons of their lives.[45]

But some might argue that the contemporaneous existence of such lack of protection, even though the trend was the other way, is evidence that the framers and ratifiers of the Fourteenth Amendment cannot be assumed to have deemed the unborn to be persons under it.

If such there be, they deserve the Roger B. Taney Award for Documentary Interpretation, for theirs is precisely the method of argumentation used by the late Chief Justice to get around the plain language of the Declaration of Independence and conclude that it in no way implies the equality of Blacks:

> *The language of the Declaration of Independence. . .proceeds to say: "We hold these truths to be self-evident: that all men are created equal . . . ."*
>
> *The general words above quoted would seem to embrace the whole human family, and if they were used in a similar instrument at this day, would be so understood. But it is too clear for dispute, that the enslaved African race were not intended to be included, and formed no part of the people who framed and adopted this Declaration; for if the language, as understood in that day, would embrace them, the conduct of the distinguished men who framed the Declaration of Independence would have been utterly and flagrantly inconsistent with the principles they asserted; and instead of the sympathy of mankind, to which they so confidently appealed, they would have deserved and received universal rebuke and reprobation.[46]*

To this reasoning, Justice McLean cogently replied in dissent:

> *I prefer the lights of Madison, Hamilton, and Jay, as a means of construing the Constitution in all its bearings, rather than to look behind that period, into a traffic which is now declared to be piracy, and punished with death by Christian nations. [He refers, of course, to the slave trade, whose existence at the adoption of the Declaration and Constitution Chief Justice Taney had adduced to declare that those documents did not imply Black equality.] I do not like to*

> *draw the sources of our domestic relations from so dark a ground.*
> *Our independence was a great epoch in the history of freedom; and*
> *while I admit the government was not made especially for the*
> *colored race, yet many of them were citizens of the New England*
> *States, and exercised the rights of suffrage when the Constitution*
> *was adopted, and it was not doubted by any intelligent person that*
> *its tendencies would greatly ameliorate their condition.*
>
> *Many of the States, on the adoption of the Constitution, or*
> *shortly afterward, took measures to abolish slavery within their*
> *respective jurisdictions; and it is a well-known fact that a belief was*
> *cherished by the leading men, South as well as North, that the*
> *institution of slavery would gradually decline, until it would become*
> *extinct.*[47]

Justice McLean rightly recognized that the enunciation of great principles in fundamental documents is often designed to represent the aspirations rather than previous practices of the framers, and that it is an affront to the framers, as well as to the meaning of their language, to reduce the aspirations to the level of practice instead of raising future practice to the level of the aspirations. Chief Justice Taney assumed that the drafters of a nation's fundamental documents could not have hoped thereby to make tomorrow more ethical and moral than the practice of yesterday and today. Taney maintained that the language of the Declaration of Independence, "all men are created equal," could not apply to blacks because many framers were slaveowners. Not only did this denigrate the conscience and aspiration of those who, like Thomas Jefferson, saw slavery as evil even while owning slaves, but it ruled as a constitutional absolute that even plain language cannot transcend the previous conduct of its authors as a key to their intent in writing it.

Surely, instead, we ought, as in New Year's Resolutions, to strive to do what we think right in the future rather than perpetuate the failings and inconsistencies of the past.

When the Fourteenth Amendment was adopted, the virtually undisputed trend of the age was toward the full protection of the unborn as fellow human beings, fellow people, from the time of conception, and the fact that the movement which created and fulfilled that trend did not achieve complete success until some years after its adoption must not blind us to the vision of the Amendment's ratifiers. That vision saw the protection of all humanity, and both logic and history include the unborn within that scope.

In considering whether the term, "person" as used in Section 1 of the Fourteenth Amendment, was to include the unborn, you may hear some raise a question about the use of the same term in Section 2 of the Amendment, by which the number of Members of Congress in the House of Representatives for each state is to be "apportioned among the several States according to their respective numbers, counting the whole number of persons in each State." It may be asked whether this requires, or has been regarded as requiring, that the unborn be counted in the census for the purpose of reapportionment. It is true that they have not been so counted. But as Robert Destro points out in an article in the California Law Review:

A thorough examination of the varied usages of the word [person] throughout the text of the Constitution leaves little doubt that the meaning of the word is generally derived from the context in which it is used. . . . A reading of the Constitution as a whole makes it clear that the only clauses in which context does not supply the meaning of "person" are the due process clauses of the fifth and fourteenth amendments [and the equal protection clause of the fourteenth]. . . . Thus, even if it be assumed that most constitutional usage of "person" in [other] sections does not apply to the unborn, it does not follow that the same must hold true for purposes of due process.[48]

Destro goes on to point out that corporations are not counted in the census, yet they have been held to be "persons" under Section 1 of the Fourteenth Amendment.[49] Indeed, the Supreme Court's ruling in 1886 that a corporation was a 'person' required and received immunity from the plain meaning of language. Such immunity is not necessary to recognize that personhood for purposes of protecting life precedes birth. An entirely plausible construction of Section 1 of the 14th Amendment, contrary to the position of my learned opponents at this hearing, is that it allows for the existence of personhood before birth. As Justice Black pointed out in his dissent in *Connecticut General Co. v. Johnson*, in which he decried the extension of personhood to corporations, "The history of the Amendment proves that the people were told that its purpose was to protect weak and helpless human beings. . . ."[50] Section 1 of the Fourteenth Amendment begins by declaring that certain persons are citizens. Birth or Naturalization and subjection to the jurisdiction of the U.S. are preconditions to federal and state citizenship. But whereas you must be born, and born in a particular geographic area, to acquire citizenship, the Amendment establishes no preconditions whatsoever to personhood. States are not prevented only from denying due process and equal protection to citizens; a state must not deny equal protection to "any person within its jurisdiction" and must not deny due process to "any person." In short, the Amendment recognizes that personhood is other than and prior to birth.

In the dissent from which I have quoted, Justice Black noted that, of the cases in this Court in which the Fourteenth Amendment was applied during the first fifty years after its adoption, less than one-half of one percent invoked it in protection of the negro race, and more than fifty percent asked that its benefits be expanded to corporations."[51] If it was ironic that the Court had been more solicitous of the protection of corporations than of the blacks whom it was designed to protect, it is equally ironic—and tragically so—that the modern Court has continued to expand the protection of corporations under the Fourteenth Amendment[52] while withdrawing its protection from prenatal human beings.

I mentioned earlier that, despite Professor Mohr's impressive scholarship and very important contribution to our understanding of the history of abortion in America, I had two bones to pick with him.

The bone of commission is this: Dr. Mohr views the abortion prohibition legislation in the nineteenth century as an anomaly against a background of leniency toward abortion both before and since. In this he errs; abortion was almost universally condemned prior to the nineteenth century. I have noted that following Aristotelian embryology, the theory of late animation was accepted by some philosophers. Under this theory, life come to the embryo at some time midway during its development.[53] English common law reflected this by punishing abortion after "quickening." Nonetheless, during many centuries when the distinction between civil and ecclesiastical law was slight or non-existent, both religion and society condemned abortion at any stage of embryological development.[54]

Professor Mohr, like Professor Means before him, assumed that the criminal law was the only mechanism employed by the state to prohibit abortion. But an essay by my friends Dennis Horan, Past Chairman of the American Bar Association's Medicine and Law Committee, and Thomas Marzen in the forthcoming book, *New Perspectives on Human Abortion*,[55] demonstrates that this was not the case. Both in Europe and in colonial America, legislatures prohibited abortion at any stage of gestation through their regulation of midwives.

On July 27, 1716, the Common Council of New York City enacted "A Law Regulating Mid Wives within the City of New York,"[56] which required all midwives to take a solemn oath before the mayor, the recorder, or an alderman to abide by its provisions before they might practice their profession. Defaults and failure to be so licensed were heavily fined; enforcement could be secured by the civil authorities or by private prosecution.[57] I quote:

> *ITEM You Shall not Give and Counsel or Administer any Herb Medicine or Potion, or any other thing to any Woman being with Child whereby She Should Destroy or Miscarry of that she goeth withall before her time.*[58]

This law remained in effect at least until the middle of 1776,[59] when the war between the British and the American colonies intervened. There is evidence that similar laws were enacted elsewhere in the colonies.[60] Such laws were not without precedent. Continental Europe possessed a municipal system of law regulating the practice of midwifery as early as 1452,[61] and England had enacted similar regulations by 1512.[62] In every case, such regulations forbade the midwife to perform or induce abortion.

The significance of these laws is not too difficult to discern. Midwives attended women in pregnancy and childbirth; they performed most abortions as well.[63] Regulations such as the 1716 law would therefore severely limit access to abortion services. Indeed, since the 1716 law required anyone who assisted women in pregnancy and childbirth to be licensed and then to abide by the provision forbidding abortion, it in effect proscribed abortion in a manner analogous to the statutes enacted in the next century.

This combination of common law protection of the unborn after quickening and pre-quickening protection through regulation of midwives was consistent with the approach to the unborn in other areas of the law.

I have already talked about the protection of the unborn in tort and wrongful death law.

For centuries the English common law of property has recognized the unborn child as an autonomous human being. It has thus reflected a basic psychological evaluation that in law, as in ordinary language, "child" includes the conceived but as yet unborn. In 1795 an English court interpreted the ordinary meaning of "children" in a will to include a child in the womb: "An infant *en ventre sa mere*, who by the course and order of nature is then living, comes clearly within the description of 'children living at the time of his decease.' "[64] Thereafter another court rejected the contention that this was a mere fiction of construction: "Why should not children *en ventre sa mere* be considered generally as in existence? They are entitled to all the privileges of other persons."[65] To the argument that such a child was a non-entity that court replied:

> *Let us see what this non-entity can do. He may be vouched in a recovery, though it is for the purpose of making him answer over in value. He may be an executor. He may take under the statute of distributions. He may take by devise. He may be entitled under a charge for raising portions. He may have an injunction; and he may have a guardian.*[66]

The evidence cited by Professor Mohr that there was widespread availability of abortifacient advice in many medical manuals in the early nineteenth century[67] and of advertising for abortifacients in the 1840's through 1870's[68] demonstrates only that the laws were flouted, not that they did not exist. Indeed, the resort to abortion, together with the gradual replacement of midwives with physicians as the typical attendants to pregnancy, may be seen as providing another source of the impetus for the campaign to enshrine protection of the unborn from conception in the criminal law itself.

In short, Mr. Chairman, the physicians' crusade of the nineteenth century to extend the protection of the criminal law to cover the unborn from the moment of conception, which Professor Mohr so ably documents, was not, as he says, a "period of interruption, or deviation from the norm,"[69] brought about to serve "the short-term interests of regular physicians in the face of an unprecedented crisis in the history of medical practice . . . and the shift in the socio-demographic role of abortion in America."[70] Rather, nineteenth century protection of the unborn was one of many chapters in human history demonstrating an ongoing and nearly universal protection of unborn human life.

Above all, Mr. Chairman, the historical evidence clearly demonstrates that the Fourteenth Amendment was intended to protect all human beings, and that many of the state legislatures which brought the Amendment into being through ratification contemporaneously regarded the unborn, from conception, as human beings who ought to be protected by law.

Thank you.

NOTES

[1] P. Odegard & V. Rosenblum. *The Power to Govern: An Examination of the Separation of Powers in the American System of Government* (1956).
[2] Roe v. Wade, 410 U.S. 113, 159 (1973).
[3] "Potential life": *Id.* at 163. For criticism, *see, e.g.,* A. Cox, *The Role of the*

Supreme Court in Government 113 (1976); Strong, *Bicentennial Benchmark: Two Centuries of Evolution of Constitutional Process*, 55 N. Car. L. Rev. 1, 96–104 (1976); Epstein, *Substantive Due Process By any Other Name—the Abortion Cases*, 1973 S.Ct. Rev. 159; J. Ely, *The Wages of Crying Wolf: A Comment on Roe v. Wade*, 82 Yale L. J. 920 (1973).

4 W. Prosser, *Handbook of the Law of Torts*, 335–38 (4th ed. 1971).

5 *Id.*

6 *Id.*

7 *Id.*

8 *Id.*

9 *Id.*

10 Seuss (pseud.), *Horton Hears a Who* (1954).

11 D. Kader, *The Law of Tortious Prenatal Death Since Roe v. Wade*, 45 Mo. L. Rev. 639, 652–53 (1980).

12 *Id.* at 654.

13 Roe v. Wade, 410 U.S. 113, 158 (1973).

14 Kader, *op.cit.* n. 11, at 656–57.

15 J. Noonan, Jr., *An Almost Absolute Value in History*, in *The Morality of Abortion, Legal and Historical Perspective* 1 (J. Noonan ed. 1970).

16 Aristotle, *History of Animals*, 7.3.583b.

17 Coke, *The Third Part of the Institutes of the Law of England*, ch. 7 (3d ed. 1660).

18 1 Blackstone, *Commentaries on the Laws of England* 124 (1769).

19 D. Horan et al., *The Legal Case for the Unborn Child*, in *Abortion and Social Justice* 105, 124 (Hilgers & Horan ed. 1973).

20 L. Arey, *Developmental Anatomy[:] A Textbook and Laboratory Manual of Embryology* 45 (6th ed. 1954).

21 R. Sauer, *Attitudes to Abortion in America, 1800–1973*, 28 Population Studies 53, 58–59 (1974).

22 J. Mohr, *Abortion in America [:] The Origins and Evolution of National Policy* (1978).

23 *Id.* at 200.

24 *Id.*

25 *Id.* at 200–225.

26 *Id.* at 149.

27 *Id.* at 157.

28 Scott v. Sandford, 60 U.S. 691 (19 How. 393) (1857).

29 Mohr, *op. cit.* n. 22 at 216.

30 *Id.* at 224–25.

31 C. Means, *The Law of New York Concerning Abortion and the Status of the Foetus 1644–1968: A Case of Cessation of Constitutionality*, 14 N.Y. Law Forum 411 (1968).

32 Roe v. Wade, 410 U.S. 113, 151–52 (1973).

33 R. Sauer, *op.cit.* n. 21 at 58.

34 Mohr, *op. cit.* n. 22 at 165.

35 H. Hodge, *Foeticide or Criminal Abortion* 5 (1872).

36 R. Sauer, *op. cit.* n. 21 at 56.

[37] Congressional Research Service, Library of Congress, *Constitution of the United States of America [:] Analysis and Interpretation* 31 n.6 (1973).

[38] *See* Roe v. Wade, 410 U.S. 113, 175–77 (1973) (Rehnquist, J., dissenting).

[39] Scott v. Sandford, 60 U.S. 691 (19 How. 393) (1857).

[40] Wheeling Steel Corp. v. Glander, 337 U.S. 562, 577 (1949) (Douglas, J. dissenting) (joined by Black, J.).

[41] Cong. Globe, 39th Cong., 1st Sess. 1089 (1866).

[42] Cong. Globe, 40th Cong., 1st Sess. 514 (1868).

[43] Cong. Globe, 39th Cong., 1st Sess. 2766 (1866).

[44] Congressional Research Service, *op. cit.* n. 37.

[45] Civil Rights Cases, 109 U.S. 3 (1883).

[46] Scott v. Sandford, 60 U.S. 691, 702–703 (19 How. 393) (1857).

[47] *Id.* at 755–56 (McLean, J., dissenting).

[48] R. Destro, *Abortion and the Constitution: The Need for a Life-Protective Amendment*, 2 Human Life Rev. 30, 51 (1976).

[49] Santa Clara County v. Southern Pacific Railroad Co., 118 U.S. 394, 396 (1886).

[50] Connecticut General Company v. Johnson, 303 U.S. 37, 87 (1937).

[51] *Id.* at 90.

[52] *See, e.g.,* First National Bank of Boston v. Bellotti, 435 U.S. 765 (1978) (holding corporations have a constitutionally protected right of free speech).

[53] Means, *op. cit.* n. 31, at 411.

[54] Noonan, *op. cit.* n. 15.

[55] D. Horan and T. Marzen, *Abortion and Midwifery: A Footnote in Legal History*, in *New Perspectives on Human Abortion* 199 (1981).

[56] "Minutes of the Common Council of the City of New York" 3 (1712–1729).

[57] *Id.* at 123.

[58] *Id.* at 122.

[59] *See generally* "Minutes of the Common Council of the City of New York" 3 (1712–1729).

[60] D. Wertz & R. Wertz, *Lying-In [:] A History of Childbirth in America* 7 (1977).

[61] J. Donnison, *Midwives and Medical Men: A History of Inter-Professional Rivalries and Women's Rights* 5 (1977).

[62] *Id.* at 5–6.

[63] J. Donegan, *Women and Men Midwives: Medicine, Morality and Misogyny in Early America* 22 (1978); Donnison, *op. cit.* n. 61 at 4; S. Arms, *Immaculate Deception* 17 (1975).

[64] Doe v. Clarke, 2 H.Bl. 399, 126 Eng. Rep. 671 (1795).

[65] Thelluson v. Woodford, 4 Ves. 227, 31 Eng. Rep. 117 (1798).

[66] *Id.* at 322.

[67] Mohr, *op. cit.* n. 22, at 6.

[68] *Id.* at 47.

[69] *Id.* at 250.

[70] *Id.* at 259.

Bibliography

Selected Publications

"Administrative Law and the Regulatory Process" in Contemporary Public Administration, pp. 145–173, Thomas Vocino and Jack Rabin, editors [Harcourt, Brace & Jovanovich, 1981];

The Making of a Public Profession (with Frances Kahn Zemans) American Bar Foundation, 1981;

"On Integrating Empirical Realities into Administrative Law and Vice Versa," 32 Ad.L.Rev. 1 (1980) pp. 59–68;

Co-editor (with William R. Hazard) of "Education: Progress and Prospects," special edition of American Behavioral Scientist (Nov.–Dec. 1979);

"Schoolchildren Yes, Policemen No—Some Thoughts About the Supreme Court's Priorities Concerning the Right to a Hearing in Suspension and Removal Cases," 72 Nw.U.L.Rev. 146 (1977);

"The Administrative Law Judge in the Administrative Process: Interrelations of Case Law with Statutory and Pragmatic Factors in Determining ALJ Roles," in Recent Studies Relevant to the Hearings and Appeals Crisis, Subcommittee on Social Security of the Committee on Ways and Means, U.S. House of Rep. 94th Cong., 1st Sess. (Committee Print, Dec. 20, 1975) 171–245;

"Dealing with Federal Regulatory Agencies," Ch. V in Legal Issues for Post-secondary Education, American Ass'n of Community and Junior Colleges (1976);

"Dimensions of Purpose and Priority in Federal Regulation of Utilities," 14 Proceedings of the Iowa State U. Regulatory Conf. 12 (1975);

"Handling Citizen-Initiated Complaints: An Introductory Study of Federal Agency Procedures and Practices," 26 Ad.L.Rev. 1 (1974) 1–47; Reprinted in A Formula for Liberals, pp. 131–150 (Nellen Pub. Co., 1979);

"The Continuing Role of Courts in Allocating Common Property Resources," in The Governance of Common Property Resources," edited by Edwin T. Haefele (Johns Hopkins Univ. Press, 1974) 119–143;

"Of Beneficiaries and Compliance," in The Limits of Law: NOMOS XV (Lieber-Atherton, 1974) 256–267;

Constitutional Law: Political Roles of the Supreme Court, co-edited with A. Didrick Castberg (Dorsey Press, 1973);

"Legal Dimensions of Tenure" (Ch. 4) in Faculty Tenure (Report of the Commission on Academic Tenure in Higher Education) [Jossey-Bass, 1973];

"On Davis on Confining, Structuring, and Checking Administrative Discretion," 37 Law & Contemporary Problems (Winger 1972) 49–62;

"A Place for Social Science Along the Judiciary's Constitutional Law Frontier," 65 Nw.U.L.Rev. 455 (1971);

"Justiciability and Justice: Elements of Restraint and Indifference," 15 Cath.U.L.Rev. 141 (1966);

"Low Visibility Decision-Making by Administrative agencies—The Problem of Spectrum Allocation," 18 Ad.L.Rev. 19 (1965);

"Realities of Regulation," in Krislov and Musolf, The Politics of Regulation, pp. 247–254 (1964); "Regulation in Orbit: Administrative Aspects of the Communication Satellite Act of 1962," 58 Nw.U.L.Rev. 216 (1963);

"The Federal Communications Commission and Miami's Chanel 10" in The Use of Power, pp. 174–228(A. Westin, ed.) [Harcourt, Brace 1962].

Bibliography on the History of Embryology
[To accompany testimony of Victor G. Rosenblum before Subcommittee on Separation of Powers, Senate Committee on the Judiciary, June 1, 1981.]

Arey, Developmental Anatomy [:] A Textbook and Laboratory Manual of Embryology 3–6 (1954).
Cole, Early Theories of Sexual Generation (1930).
Meyer, The Rise of Embryology (1939).
Needham, A History of Embryology (1934).
Nordenskiöld, History of Biology (1929).
Russell, The Interpretation of Development and Heredity (1930).

POLITICAL SECTION

Prepared Statement of Sarah Weddington

Mr. Chairman, Senator Baucus, and members of the Subcommittee, I want to thank you for giving me the opportunity to appear before you today. I am here specifically representing the 34 million members of 75 national organizations who care about the health and welfare of women, and who are committed to the rule of constitutional law in this country. From your work with the various right-to-life groups, Mr. Chairman, you must be aware how difficult it is for organizations to come to an agreement on any particular piece of legislation. And so my presence today is of particular significance, for although these groups I represent have widely differing purposes and goals, as well as differing natural constituencies, they have found a common agenda in opposing the bill that the committee has before it. Each of these organizations has prepared a statement for the record, and I now respectfully request that all of these statements be included in the hearing record.

It seems I often find myself in a representative capacity; when I argued Roe v. Wade before the Supreme Court in 1973, I was representing women and girls across the country who found their ability to make decisions regarding childbearing circumscribed by state laws prohibiting abortions, often to the severe detriment of their mental and physical health and the well-being of their families.

The history of events has brought us to the point where I again feel compelled to speak in their behalf, for they are very much on my mind. In the course of these hearings, on a bill whose purpose is to reverse the Supreme Court ruling which struck down those restrictive abortion laws, none of these women has been permitted to speak for herself before this committee.

You have heard from constitutional scholars as to whether or not Congress has the authority to pass this law. You have heard from academicians and clinicians as to whether scientific fact supports the premise of this bill. You have heard from theologians on the religious implications of the legislation. And you have heard from governmental officials on its implementation and enforcement.

But you have not heard from the people who will have to live under this law if it is passed. You have not heard from the family of the 11-year-old in Nebraska who became pregnant and who had an abortion last month, but who might not have had that choice if this bill were law. You have not heard from the pregnant welfare mother of three from Philadelphia, who has cancer and who might have had to forego treatment for that disease if this bill were law. You have not heard from the Virginia mother who is watching her child die an agonizing death from Tay-Sachs disease, who is pregnant again, and who, if this bill were law, would face the possibility of condemning another infant to the same torture. I am here in the place that is rightfully theirs, to speak out for the sake of the millions of women in this country who have, on the basis of a personal moral decision, chosen abortion, and those who, while they might not choose it for themselves, strongly believe the choice must remain available for others.

I do not think there is a need for further in-depth analysis of the constitutional issues raised by S. 158. The committee has received very fine and extensive testimony on those issues from Lawrence Tribe and Robert Bork who, while they disagree on abortion, are unanimous in their opposition to this bill, and I would refer you, once more, to their comments. As one of the attorneys who argued the Roe case before the Supreme Court, I feel a need to use part of my time to clarify some serious misunderstandings of Roe that apparently remain, and I find also that I must challenge some of the statements and conclusions that you, Mr. Chairman, and some of the witnesses before me have made.

That interpretation of Roe which would permit one to contend that this legislation is constitutional is incorrect it is a product of wishful thinking and deliberate misunderstanding. According to this interpretation, the following statement of the Court in Roe is an *invitation* to Congress to make a positive finding of fact: "when those trained in the respective disciplines of medicine, philosophy and theology are unable to arrive at any consensus (on when life begins), the judiciary, at this point in the development of man's knowledge, is not in a position to speculate." To conclude that the high court was assigning such a speculative task to a body of politicians, who are neither philosophers nor theologians, nor scientists, stretches the meaning of the words beyond reason.

The Court did not abdicate its role of defining constitutional terms. It said very clearly that in the Fourteenth Amendment the term person *does not*—not "should not," nor "might not," nor "pending further information not," but *does not* refer to the unborn. The Court went on to say that there was no point in its engaging in philosophic or theological speculation on the beginning of life, since there was no consensus among those who concern themselves with such things, and since the constitutional meaning of 'person' was already clear without the court assuming a function which was foreign to it.

But even if the primary rationale of this bill were correct, i.e. that the court in Roe invited Congress to make a finding of scientific fact, that finding which is necessary to justify this bill constitutionally cannot be made on the basis of the testimony you have heard.

There is no greater consensus today than there was in 1973. The court had before it a broad range of briefs and research from scientific, religious and legal authorities. There have been no significant scientific discoveries to discredit or fundamentally alter the data since that time. In fact, some of the scientists who supported the finding in S. 158 did so by quoting standard textbooks which were widely used prior to 1973, and therefore would have been available to the Supreme Court as well.

One cannot escape the monumental lack of consensus in our society on when life begins. Given the testimony which this committee received, how are you as legislators to decide? On the one hand you have the National Academy of Sciences, and American College of Obstetrics and Gynecology, the American Medical Association, 1200 scientists in Massachusetts and Connecticut and the 8 scientists of impeccable credentials who testified orally before this committee expressing opposition to the bill's definition of human life; on the other you have Drs. LeJeune, Gordon, Mathews-Roth, and the 5 others, also of impeccable credentials, who testified in support of the scientific hypothesis of the bill. What criteria do you as non-scientists use to evaluate these? Which testimony will you credit, which will you discredit?

Finally, even if one should determine on the basis of science that the beginning of human *life* is conception, it does not logically follow that one therefore can define legal *personhood* by equating it with that human life. That definition of personhood ignores all the traits and functions, obvious to everyone, that are commonly associated with persons, and reduces them to genes, chromosomes and DNA molecules. The Fourteenth Amendment considers life an attribute of persons, not identical to them. I would like to remind the subcommittee that there is at least one other attribute of persons which is protected by the Fourteenth Amendment and ranked alongside life itself—and that attribute is liberty.

The ultimate goal of proponents of S. 158, including the author and chief congressional sponsors, is to eliminate the freedom to choose abortion in this country except in the most dire circumstances, when a woman's life is at stake. For them, this bill is an interim measure which encourages states to ban abortion, pending passage of a constitutional amendment requiring them to do so. If it were ruled constitutional, I join the legal scholars in believing that S. 158, in establishing by law that the fetus is a person from the moment of conception, could have much the same impact as an amendment, through enforcement of the definition of person by the courts. I am certain, however, that at the very least, S. 158 will do far more than reverse Roe.

The champions of this bill claim that, in deciding Roe, the Court imposed upon the states a federal policy on abortion, and that S. 158 will reestablish the right of the states to determine abortion policy. Neither of these assertions is accurate. Actually, what the Court did was recognize the private nature of the abortion decision and remove it from the realm of government, state or federal. Having determined that the word "person" as used in the Fifth and Fourteenth Amendments was not intended to include the unborn, the court concluded that the state does not have a right to unduly burden the conscientious decision that a woman, whose right to privacy is protected by the Constitution, might make on abortion. Thus, rather than establishing a federal policy of abortion on demand from conception until birth as a form of birth control, the court was applying a fundamental principle of the Constitution: that a state may pass no laws which infringe on the basic civil and constitutional rights of its citizens.

Yet even though the court acknowledged constitutional claims only for the born, it recognized that individual states may have an interest in the potential life of the fetus prior to birth. It was also sensitive to the problems that are peculiar to the issue of abortion. So in articulating the concept of trimesters, the court was actually permissive in allowing individual states the authority to regulate abortions in the second and third trimesters.

For instance, Roe specifically allows states to outlaw abortion when the fetus becomes viable, except when the life or health of the mother is at risk. This most certainly is not abortion on demand as a method of birth control right up until birth. Perhaps confusion arises in the mind of the public because viability appears to be a very imprecise concept, since it is obviously impossible to predetermine a specific point at which *all* fetuses will become viable. However, in individual cases it is much more identifiable than conception, which can only be inferred from information available no earlier than two weeks after the conception actually has taken place. Medical witnesses have testified repeatedly before the courts that viability is a concept with which they have no problem using.

Viability is determined operationally rather than scientifically. The court describes it as the point in gestation at which "the fetus then presumably has the capability of meaningful life outside the mother's womb." It is not the same as independence, for all of us are dependent on one another to varying degrees. Rather, prior to viability the fetus has no hope of surviving outside the womb, with or without the best technology medical science has to offer.

Abortion on demand as a form of birth control right up until the time of birth is a myth. The question of viability becomes important in less than 1% of the time, since in over 99% of the cases, there is absolutely no question that the fetus may be viable. Over 90% of all abortions take place in the first trimester before the 12th week of pregnancy and the 10th week of fetal development. (In 1978, the most recent year for which statistics are available, 99.2% of all abortions took place prior to the 21st week of gestation, and medical doctors are agreed that prior to that time there is virtually no chance for survival outside the womb.) Nevertheless, if for any reason abortion is induced—and in late trimesters what I am referring to is actually early induced delivery—and it results in a live birth, that newborn is protected by the laws as a person.

Returning now to a state's ability to establish public policy on abortion under Roe, I would like to make one further point. States remain free under Roe to pursue positive programs which are aimed at or help in reducing the number of abortions. Thus they may, and do, provide support for family planning programs, economic assistance to families, sex education, tax breaks for contributions to charitable institutions, adoption programs, health and custodial care for the mentally retarded and physically disabled, and so on. What they *are* prohibited from doing is, *coercing women* into making a particular decision regarding a pregnancy. No matter how strong our zeal for states' rights, we must always remember that the Constitution remains the highest law in the land and stands to protect the rights of the individual over and against the action of any legislative body.

As a former member of the Texas state legislature, I have an immense respect for the role of state government, and I am very concerned with the need to preserve flexibility for the states within constitutional bounds. Furthermore, I certainly trust the wisdom and compassion of the American people. But this bill allows for neither flexibility on the part of the states nor the exercise of wisdom and compassion on the issue of abortion.

S. 158 does not return the country to the pre-1973 period when the states exercised the authority to permit or restrict abortion within their boundaries. It is something new under the sun. Never before has federal law defined a fertilized egg as a person for any purpose whatsoever. To adopt this concept would grant to fetuses rights far greater than those now granted to existing persons, for the law presently allows no person the right to touch, interfere with, or in any way use the body of another law-abiding person against his or her will, let alone the right to use the body of another in a parasitic way, as does the fetus. The National Center of Health Statistics reports that there were health complications in 54% of all pregnancies which were carried to term in 1978. In compelling all women to continue their pregnancies, this bill takes the unprecedented step of forcing them to place their own health and lives at risk. Only in the case of drafting men for war has the state ever passed a law which compels a person, regardless of his will, to place his life or personal health in jeopardy.

By requiring states to enforce the Fourteenth Amendment due process protection using that definition of person, as the author of the bill testified, S. 158 automatically prohibits the use of state funds and facilities for abortions and abortion related services. This means that in your state of North Carolina, Mr. Chairman, which has, for the past three years, chosen to fund Medicaid abortions for the poor, legislators would not be free under this bill to exercise their own wisdom and judgement. Poor women who are victims of rape or incest would be unable to obtain medical assistance to terminate a resulting pregnancy. The legislature could not choose to give assistance to a woman with heart disease whose pregnancy was not immediately life threatening but obviously dangerous to her health. State hospitals would not be able to provide amniocentesis and genetic counselling to the Jewish couple who has already had one child afflicted with Tay-Sachs disease, because of the degree of risk to the fetus associated with the test. In these instances, North Carolina and other states would have no options.

While you, Mr. Chairman, say that the bill itself does not directly require states to pass anti-abortion legislation or impose criminal penalties for abortion, it is designed to provide the states with a compelling interest in fetal life which could override the interests of the woman and ban abortion in all but the most extreme cases. Some believe the bill obliges states to protect all fertilized eggs and fetuses under existing statutes implementing due process protections. In this case, is there any state which has a statute which justifies the taking of any person's life except for the preservation of another or in cases of capital punishment? If the Chairman is correct and this bill would give states wide latitude to permit abortion in certain circumstances, then he has an obligation to make that clear in the language of the bill. He ought not to endorse or allow a bill which permits another interpretation.

Today is the last day of hearings on S. 158, and still the public has no definitive answer as to what this bill would authorize their legislatures to do or would do automatically. I am dismayed at the refusal of the subcommittee to provide any guidance to the states about the full range of options in abortion legislation opened to them by this bill. An expression of trust in state legislatures is commendable, but not helpful to them in understanding the limits of permissable action, or in informing the courts about Congress' understanding of these limits, if there are any.

Is it possible to deny that in some states abortion may be classified as murder, in others as manslaughter with criminal penalties attached? Medical treatment for pregnant women will become very problematic if the appropriate treatment for her poses a risk to the fetus. Can we be certain that the law will permit a doctor to take action in her behalf even when he or she is aware that the treatment may jeopardize the life of the fetus? Would the physician be made legally liable for any consequences to the health of that fetal person? Under any circumstances would a pregnant woman who miscarries be subject to charges of negligent homicide?

If the states felt they should protect fetal life by prohibiting pregnant women from participating in activities at work or in sports, which might jeopardize the life of the fetus, would they be permitted to do so? And certainly, any legal definition of person which encompasses the fertilized egg will necessarily have a tremendous impact on birth control practices in this country. Some of the most effective and widely used forms of contraception, the IUD and some forms of the pill, which work after fertilization to prevent the implantation of the fertilized ovum on the uterus, would not longer be available in state-funded programs. Could the states prohibit these altogether? Could state or private interests initiate court action on behalf of a fetus to protect it from potential harm? Conceivably, would the federal government be able to pass additional laws implementing fetal personhood on the basis of their authority to enforce the Fourteenth Amendment?

Section Two of S. 158 prohibits lower federal courts from issuing injunctions and declaratory judgments on anti-abortion laws passed by states and localities pursuant to S. 158—even if these laws violate fundamental constitutional rights. Doesn't this place in jeopardy an underpinning of our form of government: the principle of checks and balances? Although Section Two allows Supreme Court review of state court decisions, it is important to note that the Supreme Court cannot rule on more than a small percentage of the cases brought before it. This relegates review of anti-abortion laws to state courts which are not designed to interpret the full effect of statutes such as S. 158. What is to prevent fifty states from enacting and upholding fifty different interpretations of S. 158? Isn't it dangerous to allow basic constitutional rights to differ depending on residence? Isn't every citizen in this country entitled to certain liberties no matter where he or she lives? Isn't it a violation of the principle of equal protection when existing rights of pregnant women to seek relief in the lower federal courts are eliminated while newly created rights for fetuses permit fetal rights to be litigated in federal courts?

We submit, Mr. Chairman, that these concerns are not farfetched "horror stories," as we heard them described to this subcommittee last week, but legitimate legal questions which must be answered. We were shocked to hear that the Attorney General from the state of Utah say that there should be no worries about the possible consequences of this bill, since in his experience anti-abortion laws were seldom enforced and violators seldom prosecuted. Do the proponents of this measure really mean to propose its passage on the likelihood that its enforcement would be disregarded? If not, then a serious, thorough exposition of all of the potential effects of the legislation is mandatory.

Passing this bill without knowledge of its full ramifications has been compared to pulling the pin on a grenade, setting it down in a field and walking away from it. Mr. Chairman, you have said you are untroubled by not knowing what state laws will be passed subsequent to this bill; that you are quite willing to allow them to weigh the issue. But the people have a right to know what *could* happen so they can make their will known to their representatives.

Even if S. 158 were to effect a simple reversal of the Supreme Court in Roe, a conclusion I believe is totally unjustified, none of the organizations for whom I speak today believes that is a desirable or even an acceptable goal. Prior to 1973, nearly one million abortions were performed annually. By reversing Roe and retreating to an earlier time, you will not reduce the number of abortions, because you will not have eliminated the reasons that women feel compelled to seek abortions.

The proponents of this bill evidence a blithe disregard of the tragedies of life which have through the ages led women to choose to terminate a pregnancy. To callously describe the decision as one of "convenience" denigrates the integrity and humanity of *all* those millions of women who have throughout the ages been forced to take that course. To the girl who has been raped, abortion is not a "convenience"; to the woman who is carrying an anacephalic fetus with no brain, abortion is not a "convenience"; to the teenager who faces the loss of her home and parental support if her pregnancy is discovered, abortion is not a "convenience"; for the family who cannot feed or clothe the children they already have, abortion is not a "convenience." And for those who, before 1973, faced the very real possibility of death or maiming from a back alley procedure, rather than carry a pregnancy to term, abortion was not a "convenience."

The groups I represent today encompass a wide range of segments of the American population. As individual organizations they hold varying attitudes and interests and concerns on the issue of abortion, but they are all agreed on one fundamental principle: the abortion decision must remain, as it is now, a matter of individual decision, free from governmental interference and from the moral and religious dictates of others. This principle has the overwhelming support of the American public, as consistently shown in every single opinion survey since 1973. The most recent ABC-Washington Post poll, in fact, showed that only 10% of the population supports the anti-abortion concept embodied in this statute.

It is inconceivable to us that the Congress of the United States could seriously consider the passage of a bill which so blatantly disregards the integrity of the constitutional process, the separation of powers, the religious liberty of our citizens, the will of the people, the sound practice of medicine and the desperate needs of women facing problem pregnancies. On behalf of the organizations I represent, their individual members, and the millions of affected American women, I urge this subcommittee to vote against S. 158.

Statements From Organizations Submitted by Sarah Weddington to Senate Judiciary Subcommittee on Separation of Powers June 18, 1981
The Alan Guttmacher Institute
American Association of University Women
American Civil Liberties Union
American College of Obstetricians and Gynecologists
American Home Economics Association

American Psychological Association-Division of Psychology of Women
American Public Health Association
Americans for Democratic Action
Americans United for Separation of Church and State
B'nai B'rith Women
Catholics for a Free Choice
Center for Population Options
Coalition of Labor Union Women
Committee to Defend Reproductive Rights of Coalition for Medical Rights of Women
Episcopal Urban Caucus
Federation of Organizations for Professional Women
MS. Foundation
National Abortion Federation
National Abortion Rights Action League
National Alliance for Optional Parenthood
National Association of Commissions for Women
National Conference of Puerto Rican Women, Inc.
National Education Association
National Family Planning and Reproductive Health Association
National Federation of Temple Sisterhoods
National Women's Health Network
National Women's Political Caucus
The Physicians Forum, Inc.
Planned Parenthood Federation of America, Inc.
Preterm Reproductive Health Center, Inc.
Religious Coalition for Abortion Rights
    American Baptist Churches, National Ministries
    American Ethical Union
    American Ethical Union, National Women's Conference
    American Humanist Association
    American Jewish Congress
    American Jewish Congress, Women's Division
    B'nai B'rith Women
    Catholics for a Free Choice
    Christian Church (Disciples of Christ), Division of Homeland Ministries
    Episcopal Urban Caucus
    Episcopal Women's Caucus
    National Council of Jewish Women
    National Federation of Temple Sisterhoods
    Presbyterian Church in the U.S., Committee on Women's Concerns
    Presbyterian Church in the U.S., General Assembly Mission Board
    Union of American Hebrew Congregations
    Unitarian Universalist Association
    Unitarian Universalist Women's Federation
    United Church of Christ, Board for Homeland Ministries
    United Church of Christ, Office for Church and Society
    United Methodist Church, Board of Church and Society

United Methodist Church, Women's Division, Board of Global Ministries
United Presbyterian Church, U.S.A., The Program Agency
United Presbyterian Church, U.S.A., Council on Women and the Church
United Synagogue of America
Women's League for Conservative Judaism
Young Women's Christian Association
Sociologists for Women in Society
Southeastern Pennsylvania Task Force on Abortion Rights
ACLU of Philadelphia
Americans for Democratic Action
Clara Bell Duvall Education Fund
Choice
Christian Association
Congresso De Latinos Unidos
Democratic Socialist Organizing Committee
Elizabeth Blackwell Center
Episcopal Community Service
Family Planning Service-CCMC
Feminist Therapy Collective
Graduate Hospital
Health Law Project
Juvenile Law Center
Lutheran Settlement House
Medical College of PA
Naral of SE PA
Naral of Pennsylvania
NOW of Pennsylvania
Penn Women's Center
PA for Justice and Freedom of Choice
People's Emergency Center
Philadelphia Lawyer's Guild
Phila. Reproductive Rights Coalition
Philadelphia NOW
Planned Parenthood, Bucks County
Planned Parenthood, SE Pennsylvania
Puerto Rican Alliance
Religious Coalition for Abortion Rights
Reproductive Health and Counseling Center
Welfare Rights Organization
Women Associates
Women Organized Against Rape
Women's Health Concerns Committee
Women's International League for Peace & Freedom, Bucks County
Women's Law Project
Women's Political Caucus
Women's Project, American Friends Service Committee
Women's Resource Center
Women's Suburban Clinic

Women's Switchboard
YWCA, Central Montgomery County
Union of American Hebrew Congregations
Union Wage
United Church of Christ-Coordinating Center for Women in Church and Society
United Church of Christ-United Church Board for Homeland Ministries, Division
of Health and Welfare
United Church of Christ-Nebraska Conference
United States Women's Health Coalition
War Resisters League
Women Against Pornography
Women for Racial and Economic Equality
Women's Equity Action League
Women's League for Conservative Judaism
Women, USA
Young Women's Christian Association
Zero Population Growth

Statement of Senator Bob Packwood

Senator PACKWOOD. Mr. Chairman, Senator Baucus, I am pleased to have this opportunity to appear before your subcommittee today on the subject of abortion.

I think it is essential to make it perfectly clear from the outset of my testimony that this bill is about abortion. While the testimony on when life starts may have been intellectually invigorating, it begged the true purpose of this bill and the true motivation of its supporters.

Congressman Mazzoli, a chairman of the prolife caucus, says it very well in his testimony which will soon follow when he says: "In essence, the caucus supports the enactment of the Right to Life Act as an interim step until a Human Life Amendment is adopted."

Congressman Hyde has said essentially the same thing: S. 158 will ban abortions.

Stephen Galebach, in the pamphlet he authored entitled "A Human Life Statute," reiterates the same thing. S. 158 is a means to outlaw abortion in lieu of a constitutional amendment.

Therefore, the issue, Mr. Chairman, is not when does life start. The issue, stated clearly, is when does society deem an abortion to be a homicide?

S. 158, and these hearings, in my mind, are designed to conclude that abortion from the moment of conception is murder.

Now, having established the true purpose of these hearings, two key questions must be answered: One, should abortions be banned in this country; two, is S. 158 a legal and proper method to achieve that goal?

Let me address myself to the second issue first: Is S. 158 a proper vehicle to achieve that end, that is, to reverse the Supreme Court decision legalizing abortion?

In its decision legalizing abortion, the Supreme Court clearly said that at least during the first trimester of pregnancy, a woman has a constitutional right to decide for herself without hindrance or help from anyone, including the Government, whether or not she wants to have an abortion.

If S. 158 passes, it would allow not only the States to declare abortion from the moment of conception murder, but it would allow the Federal Government to do the same thing if we wanted to make abortion a Federal crime. The Court would then be faced with the constitutional issue of whether or not the constitutional right of a women to have an abortion can be overridden by a statute making abortion murder.

I doubt that the Supreme Court would find the statute constitutional, but I will not dwell longer on this subject.

You have seen the letter from the six former U.S. Attorneys General opposing S. 158, and another letter from 12 renowned constitutional scholars—interestingly some prochoice, some antiabortion, some of whom disagree with the Supreme Court's original decision, and some of whom agree with it—all indicating that this statute is an unconstitutional way to reverse a Supreme Court decision. The panel of constitutional scholars will address that issue much more fully than I.

Therefore, let me address myself to the other and, I think, the more fundamental question: Is it wise public policy to outlaw all abortions?

First, let us examine what has been the abortion policy of this country throughout its history. Abortion before quickening was not a crime at common law in England. We carried that common law to the United States, adopted it as ours, and when we broke from England, that law remained as ours.

When our Founding Fathers deliberated at Philadelphia and brought forth our Constitution, abortion before quickening was legal. They chose to leave it so.

In the 19th century, States chose to outlaw abortions for justifiable medical, but, in my mind, unjustifiable moral reasons. By the mid-20th century, any medical justification for prohibiting abortion had disappeared.

In the 1950's and 1960's, we began to challenge the moral underpinnings banning abortions. In the late 1960's, a few States legalized abortion. Then came the momentous Supreme Court decision legalizing abortion for all women throughout the entire country.

Today, there is admittedly a difference of opinion whether abortion should be legalized or outlawed. The difference are sharp and passionate.

Over the course of these hearings, I hope you will hear testimony from religious leaders of all faiths, which will indicate the sharp divisions, sometimes even within faiths, on the issue of abortion.

The one statement that can be made without fear of contradiction is that there is no consensus on this subject.

One thing is clear, however. The overwhelming bulk of the American people do not think abortion is murder. The American public disapproves of murder. They would not be likely to support abortion if they thought it was murder.

The American Medical Association, certainly an organization familiar with and concerned about human life, supports a woman's right to have an abortion. They would not do so if they thought it was the wanton taking of human life. Dozens of other medical organizations echo the views of the A.M.A.

The American Bar Association, certainly an organization familiar with, yet with even a reverence for the law, would not endorse the right of a woman to choose an abortion if they thought it was murder.

The dozens and dozens of religious organizations that have endorsed a woman's right to choose would not do so if they thought it was murder.

Last, I cannot believe that the woman who ultimately has to make the painful decision herself to have an abortion feels that she is committing murder.

I would suggest to you, Mr. Chairman, that it is not only unwise but unworkable to try to impose your idea of morality on this country by legislation when there is no agreement on your conclusions.

Every generation witnesses a new group of citizens who believe themselves the keepers of the faith. It is not a disease unique to America. The difference is that in America we have seen and experienced the dangers of moralists who are so convinced they are right that they choose to impose their morality on us.

There is a growing force in this country, fueled by a Cotton Mather mentality, that wishes to impose on this country a Cotton Mather morality. From the perspective of one who is a practicing politician, I hope that we will always remember that passion can obscure judgment.

We should remember that governing officials in dictatorships and democracies find it easy and convenient to bend to transitory public opinion and popular prejudices which would subjugate individual liberties.

Those of us in public office should always remember that we can never err enough on the side of protecting individual liberty and freedom. We who have been elected to a position of public trust should be willing at all costs to withstand the buffets of a temporary storm that would trammel or even extinguish our freedom for the alleged common good.

Mr. Chairman, the danger to the liberties of all Americans is most threatened by those who want to compel conformity of thought and deed. Conversely, our liberties are most secured by a decent respect for diversity, and most especially on those subjects upon which there is no consensus.

God did not speak to any one of us and say, "You are right and those who disagree with you are wrong." If any one of us thinks that God had ordained us to speak for him, we are wrong. Worse, if we are in a position of power and we believe we speak for God, we become dangerous.

For, indeed, if I am right and you are wrong, then it is just a short step to the end justifies the means. I do not need to tell you, Mr. Chairman, who has taught political science, what that philosophy means to your liberties, and mine, and all Americans.

Thank you.

Senator EAST. Thank you, Senator Packwood.

Senator Moynihan, we welcome you. We were encouraging our witnesses to summarize their remarks as concisely as they could. Their statements, of course, will be made a part of the permanent record following their oral presentation.

We are going to allow all panelists to speak. Then Mr. Baucus and I would be able to follow up with questions.

Statement of Senator Daniel Moynihan

Senator MOYNIHAN. Mr. Chairman, I thank you for the opportunity to be here. My remarks, which will not require a length of time, will address themselves to the constitutional issue of S. 158, as I understand it, both as a Senator and someone whose profession has been that of a professor of government at Harvard University and other such institutions, as you have been a professor of government, sir.

I wish to say to this distinguished panel that in my view this legislation constitutes a direct assault upon the constitutional processes and concepts of the U.S. Government.

From the beginning of our country, and most famously incorporated in the *Marbury v. Madison* decision of Chief Justice Marshall, we have held that it is for the Court to decide what the Constitution says, that the Congress can set in motion a process for amending the Constitution, but with respect to the interpretation of the words of the Constitution, the Court is the supreme branch of the Government.

Sir, this was tested. Our commitment to this idea was tested in a most dramatic and extended and prolonged way in 1894. The Supreme Court, in its wisdom, held in the *Pollock v. Farmer's Loan and Trust Company* that the income tax was, in fact, a direct tax as understood in the Constitution and therefore had to be apportioned among the States. It could not be directly applied to individuals.

This was clearly wrong. The Court had been holding otherwise for a century. It was thwarting a major political judgment of the time, which was the United States should have an income tax.

Yet a succession of Presidents, of majority leaders in the Senate, Speakers in the House, and chairmen of the Finance Committee, of which I am a member, urged to pass a bill saying the Supreme Court is wrong and we define the income tax to be a direct tax, said they would not do that. That would violate the processes of the Constitution. That would tell the Court what the words of the Constitution mean. That would open up to Congress power to change anything.

They patiently waited 20 years until the 16th amendment was adopted that said that an income tax was, in fact, constitutional.

Mr. Chairman, let me just raise for you the possibilities that we open with such a proposal as we have here.

Take the first amendment. The first amendment of the Constitution says: "Congress shall make no law respecting an establishment of religion."

If we follow the precedent of S. 158, what would be the possibility of a law being enacted in the Congress that says any State or municipality that provides tax exemption to a church building is, in fact, participating in the establishment of religion and that is unconstitutional? Defining tax exemption as the establishment of religion is perfectly logical if you can define what these words mean.

The first amendment guarantees freedom of speech. What if we were to pass a law saying that does not mean freedom to write what books you might like and only means speech when you talk? You can stand on a street corner and talk, but you may not write any book you wish or any letter you choose because we here defined speech to mean only talk involving the larynx.

The Constitution guarantees freedom of the press. What if we were to pass a law that says the press means something with a printing press? It does not mean television. It does not mean radio. It does not mean photo offset.

That is the kind of Pandora's box you open. Find any word you like in the

Constitution and change its meaning by passing a law. This legislation would tell the Court what is a person, and would commence for the first time in our history a serious invasion by the legislative branch of the judicial branch.

I cannot, as a Senator or as a student of government, support it. I hope very much that we will return to well-established and effective ways of working the will of the Congress which are well-known and not this assault on the constitutional processes.

I regret having to say that to a panel which I respect so deeply, but I feel it strongly. The issue here is the preservation of the constitutional processes of the United States.

Senator EAST. Thank you, Senator Moynihan.

[The prepared statement of Senator Moynihan follows:]

Prepared Statement of Senator Daniel Moynihan

As a legislator, I have considered at length the specific provisions of S. 158. After much deliberation, I find that I cannot support this bill which I hold to assault fundamental constitutional concepts and processes. I would like to enumerate briefly what I consider the most compelling arguments against it.

S. 158 defines a fetus as a person, and thus subject to the guarantees of the Fourteenth Amendment. Whether this is so in fact is irrelevant to the issue at question. The Supreme Court, obviously contrary to fact, held in *Santa Clara County v. Southern Pacific Railroad*, 118 U.S. 394 (1896) that a corporation falls within the constitutional category of "person" in the Fourteenth Amendment. The Supreme Court held in *Roe v. Wade*, 410 U.S. 113 (1973) and *Doe v. Bolton*, 410 U.S. 179 (1973) that a fetus is not a person for the purposes of the Fourteenth Amendment and is thus not subject to the Fourteenth Amendment's guarantee of equal protection of the laws. This leads to the central question raised by the Human Life Statute. Is it within Congress's constitutionally-prescribed power to declare that a fetus is a person after the Supreme Court has declared that it is not? In other words, can an Act of Congress overturn the Supreme Court's interpretation of the Constitution? I believe the answer is, unequivocally, that it is not.

Congress may, and often does, overturn Supreme Court decisions by changing the law. But these decisions are interpretations of statutes, not of the words of the Constitution. This distinction is crucial, for the Supreme Court has time and again declared that it is fundamentally a function of the judiciary to declare what the Constitution says and who is subject to which of its guarantees. I venture to say that most schoolchildren know this, and can cite the source of the doctrine that it is the Supreme Court that interprets the Constitution. For there may well be no more famous case in American jurisprudence than *Marbury v. Madison*, 1 Cranch 137, and few more famous dicta than Chief Justice Marshall's declaration in *Marbury* that "(i)t is emphatically the province and duty of the judicial department to say what the law is." (1 Cranch 137, 177). In our own time, the Court has elaborated this, declaring in *Cooper v. Aaron* that "the federal judiciary is supreme in the exposition of the law of the Constitution," 358 U.S. 1, 18), and in *United States v. Nixon* that the power of interpretation rests with the Supreme Court (418 U.S. 683, 705).

And the Supreme Court has found that a fetus is not a person for the purpose of the Fourteenth Amendment. Under our system of government, only changing the Constitution can change that determination. The process for altering the Constitution is explicitly spelled out by Article V of the Constitution. It may not be done by statute. It must be done by amendment.

Supporters of the Human Life Statute cite *Katzenbach v. Morgan*, 384 U.S. 641, as evidence of the bill's constitutionality. I disagree. I find compelling the arguments made by Charles Alan Wright, William B. Bates Professor of Law at the University of Texas and Thomas I. Emerson, Stirling Professor of Law, Emeritus, at Yale University. These two men are as dissimilar in political view as they are alike in professional eminence. Permit me to quote from correspondence each has had with this Subcommittee. Professor Wright states:

> *It has seemed clear to me since* Oregon v. Mitchell, *400 U.S. 112,*

that Morgan *is to be confined to the racial discrimination area from which it comes and that there is to be no extension of the rationale from that decision. 400 U.S. at 129 (opinion of Black, J.) 296 (opinion of Stewart, J.).*

In the Oregon *case Justice Harlan made a statement that seems to me wholly applicable to S. 158. 'Congress is subject to none of the institutional restraints imposed on judicial decisionmaking; it is controlled only by the political process. In Article V, the Framers expressed the view that the political restraints on Congress alone were an insufficient control over the process of constitution making. The concurrence of each House and of three-fourths of the States was needed for the political check to be adequate. To allow a simple majority of Congress to have final say on matters of constitutional interpretation is therefore fundamentally out of keeping with constitutional structure.'*

Professor Emerson takes a similar view:

. . .(T)he language of Justice Brennan in Katzenbach v. Morgan *can give no comfort to the proponents of S. 158. Justice Brennan made it entirely clear that his views of the power of Congress under Section 5 did not authorize that body to abrogate the constitutional rights of individuals under the Fourteenth Amendment as previously secured to them by Supreme Court decisions. Using a footnote, apparently on the theory that the proposition was so obvious as not to require elaboration, he said,*

'We emphasize that Congress's power under Section 5 is limited to adoption measures to enforce the guarantees of the Amendment; Section 5 grants Congress no power to restrict, abrogate, or dilute these guarantees.' 384 U.S. at 651.

The Supreme Court's interpretation of the Constitution has not always met with Congressional (or popular) approval. But this does not diminish Congressional responsibility to respect the established method of "correcting" a Supreme Court decision: amendment.

There are many instances of Congressional disagreement with a Supreme Court decision. As a member of the senate Finance Committee, the one I know best is Congressional reaction to an 1895 decision that found the federal income tax law of 1894 unconstitutional (*Pollock v. Farmers' Loan and Trust Co.*, 157 U.S. 429). Records of the period show that several Congresssmen considered legislation to overturn the Court's decision that a direct income tax violated the Constitution. Despite the strongest of feelings, Congress ultimately decided that the only responsible way—indeed, the only *permissible* way—to overturn the Court's decision was to amend the Constitution. Only with passage of the Sixteenth Amendment, some twenty years later, did an income tax become constitutional.

The amendment process is lengthy. It is cumbersome. Its outcome, as we have seen with the Equal Rights Amendment, is far from guaranteed. But it is the only one legitimately available to us. To proceed in any other way to change a Supreme Court interpretation of the Constitution is to undermine the Constitution.

This is not the view of one Senator. It is a view shared by six former Attorney Generals, who communicated their opposition to S. 158 to the Judiciary Committee. It is shared by the twelve legal scholars who wrote a joint letter to the Committee and by the eighty law professors who have written to Senator Baucus, the ranking Democrat on this Subcommittee. It is shared by the legal experts of the Congressional Research Service. It is even shared by the legal counsel of Catholic Charities. I can think of only 2 scholars who support this bill, Professors Stephen Galebach and John Noonan. Professor Galebach has written about S. 158 at length, most notably in the *Human Life Review*. I do not find his arguments persuasive, and, indeed, Professor Emerson dismisses the Galebach interpretation as "in error on all counts." As I am hardly a legal scholar, I cannot judge which of these men is, ultimately, right. But I do suggest that the near unanimity of legal opinion on this subject is not to be dismissed lightly.

I do not wish to consider whether abortion is a desirable or even defensible policy. This is a personal judgment unrelated to consideration of the Human Life Statute. But that bill raises a corollary policy question which, while also personal, is often overlooked. Even if S. 158 were constitutional, and Congress could enact it without problem, would Congress want to enact a bill that very well may make criminal the use of abortifacient birth control devices, such as the IUD and the so-called Morning-After pill? I have seen no conclusive proof that S. 158 would make the use of abortifacients illegal. But I think it does, and so does the American Life Lobby, which took this view in a letter to Congress. I do not think that Congress wants to, or even ought to, prohibit birth control devices. This, I think, is something we ought to consider carefully.

But I must return to the central issue before us: the Human Life Statute is a fundamental assault on Constitutional processes. We must not allow that to occur.

Additional Views of Senator Orrin G. Hatch

The Subcommittee on the Separation of Powers and Senator East have made an important contribution to the public debate on abortion with its consideration of S. 158, the proposed Human Life Bill.

It is with great reluctance, however, that I am forced to express serious reservations about the constitutionality of S. 158. Such reluctance comes from the fact that I fully share the frustrations of the bill's proponents with the continuing destruction of unborn human life that has resulted from the appalling Abortion Cases of 1973.

In the decisions of *Roe v. Wade* 410 U.S. 113 (1973) and *Doe v. Bolton* 410 U.S. 179 (1973) and their progeny, the Supreme Court has created a virtually limitless right of a woman to obtain an abortion, for virtually any reason, during virtually any stage of her pregnancy. In identifying a previously undetected right to abortion in the 14th Amendment and elsewhere in the Constitution, the Supreme Court has created a regime in which abortion is available on demand within this country. In the process of outlining this new "right", the Supreme

Court has overturned laws enacted by the elected representatives of the people in all fifty States of the Union.

There is no disagreement between myself and the proponents of S. 158 that the Abortion Cases must be overcome and that legal protection must be restored to unborn human life. I must conclude, however, that *Roe* and *Doe* can only be overturned by an amendment to the Constitution, not by a simple statute such as S. 158. Completely apart from my own doubts about the constitutional propriety of S. 158, I have little reason to believe that the Supreme Court as presently comprised would be likely to uphold the exercise of Congressional authority in this measure. No legislation that is not ultimately sustained by the Court will contribute anything toward saving unborn lives.

I am in basic agreement with Professor Robert Bork, formerly of the Yale Law School, and formerly Solicitor General of the United States, who has posed the issue in the following terms:

> *The question to be answered in assessing S. 158 is whether it is proper to adopt unconstitutional countermeasures to redress unconstitutional action by the Court. I think it is not proper. The deformation of the Constitution is not properly cured by further deformations.*

There is no doubt in my mind that the *Roe* and *Doe* decisions represented "deformations" of the Constitution of a magnitude exceeded only perhaps by the *Dred Scott* decision in 1857, *Scott v. Sandford* 60 U.S. 393. In each of these decisions, the Supreme Court significantly reduced the scope of constitutional protections for classes deemed un-worthy of "person"-hood. The constitutional response of this nation to the *Dred Scott* decision—the 14th Amendment—ought to be emulated in the present circumstance.

Regrettably, I, with Professor Bork, view S. 158 as a "further deformation" of the Constitution. S. 158, in my view, rests upon a principle of constitutional law, articulated in the *Katzenbach v. Morgan* case, 384 U.S. 641 (1966), that I simply cannot accept. I do not believe that the case would be decided similarly today and, even if it were to be, I cannot in good conscience support legislation that finds its authority in the *Katzenbach* principle.

In *Katzenbach*, the Supreme Court upheld legislation enacted by Congress to limit the use of literacy tests by the State of New York even though the Court itself, in an earlier decision, had determined that such tests were not necessarily violative of the "equal protection" clause of the 14th Amendment. The Court concluded that Congress possessed this authority under the 5th Section of the 14th Amendment which grants to Congress the power to "enforce" the provisions of the Amendment.

In finding this authority in Congress, the Court in effect declared a Congressional power, not merely to *enforce* those rights already identified by the courts, but the power itself to *define* substantive rights under the 14th Amendment. The implications of this doctrine are substantial and in radical violation of traditional principles of American federalism.

Quite simply, the 14th Amendment is a limitation upon the States, while section 5 of the 14th Amendment is a conferral of authority upon the Congress. To enhance that Congressional authority, but transforming it from mere authority to establish remedies for substantive constitutional violations into authority to define what constitute such violations, is to significantly erode the division of powers between the State and national governments.

If Congress can define what constitutes a "person" for purposes of the due process clause of the 14th Amendment and impose that definition upon the States, and obligate the States to abide by that definition, then Congress would equally be empowered to interpret and define other Substantive provisions of the 14th Amendment (as well as the other Reconstruction Amendments). As Professor Bork has observed:

> *A national legislature empowered to define the meaning of involuntary servitude, privileges and immunities, due process, equal protection, and the right to vote, which includes all qualifications of electors, can void any State legislation on any subject and replace it with a Federal statute.*

Professor Van Alstyne of the Duke University School of Law has also noted in this regard:

> *If Congress can (a) determine authoritatively what affirmative obligations each State has in respect to the life, liberty, and property of each person, and if Congress can (b) legislate to "enforce" such affirmative obligations as determined by Congress, then indeed the rudiments of federalism are dead, the 10th Amendment is meaningless, and each State becomes but the instrument of a uniform, congressional determined policy of social welfare.*

Even in the service of a good cause (and there is no better cause than the pro-life cause), I am not prepared to accord further legitimacy to the *Katzenbach* doctrine. I concur with Justice Harlan who observed in his dissent in that case that it could not be sustained,

> *except at the sacrifice of fundamentals in the American constitutional system—the separation between the legislative and the judicial function and the boundaries between federal and State political activity.*

What makes the case for S. 158 an even more difficult proposition than the statute involved in *Katzenbach* is that S. 158 purports to interpret the Constitution in direct contravention of a previous Supreme Court decision.

While I am in agreement with the view expressed by Professor *Charles Alan Wright of the University of Texas Law School*—and indeed of many proponents of S. 158—that the argument in support of the constitutionality of the measure "must rest . . . exclusively" on *Katzenbach*, I recognize the efforts of proponents to suggest an alternative basis for argument.

Proponents of this basis argue that even Justice Harlan's dissent in *Katzenbach* is compatible with S. 158 in its recognition of the fact that the Court

owes deference to Congressional determinations of "legislative facts". Justice
Harlan observed there that:

> *To the extent "legislative facts" are relevant to a judicial determi-*
> *nation, Congress is well equipped to investigate them and such*
> *determinations are, of course, entitled to due respect.*

I would respond to the reliance upon Justice Harlan's remarks in the
following respects:

First, I would disagree that the "legislative facts" of S. 158 are "relevant" to
any judicial determination involved in *Roe v. Wade*. I simply do not see the ray of
shining light that S. 158 proponents see in *Roe v. Wade* in respect of the Court's
supposed invitation to Congress to define when life begins. In this respect,
perhaps, I view *Roe* as a more undilutedly bad decision than even proponents of
S. 158. I do not believe that the Supreme Court was as "undecided" on this issue
as do proponents. Professor Lynn Wardle of the Brigham Young University Law
School has argued:

> *In* Roe v. Wade, *the Supreme Court specifically held that the term*
> *"person" as used in the 14th Amendment does not include the*
> *unborn. The point was made whole and complete in itself. Contrary*
> *to the implication of [proponents], that holding was* not *predicated*
> *or contingent upon a prior finding that the Court did not know when*
> *human life began. In fact, the Court did not address the question of*
> *when human life began until after it has separately analyzed and*
> *specifically concluded that the unborn are not "persons" protected*
> *by the 14th Amendment.*

In *Roe v. Wade*, the Supreme Court initially determined that the 14th
Amendment contained a "right to privacy" which was broad enough to encompass "a woman's decision whether or not to terminate her pregnancy." Finding
this to be a "fundamental" right, the Court declared that State laws infringing
upon this right could only be sustained if necessary to uphold a "compelling"
state interest. The first proposed "compelling" interest that it considered was that
the unborn were legal "persons" under the 14th Amendment. The Court
observed:

> *[Appellee] argues that the fetus is a "person" within the language*
> *and meaning of the 14th Amendment. In support of this, they outline*
> *at length in detail the well known facts of fetal development. If this*
> *suggestion of personhood is established, the appellant's case, of*
> *course, collapses for the fetus' right to life would then be guaran-*
> *teed specifically by the Constitution.*

The Court, however, expressly rejected this argument and concluded that
unborn life was not entitled to the protections of "person"-hood. This conclusion
was reached after analysis of the text of the Constitution, the history of the 14th
Amendment, and earlier Federal Court decisions.

I emphatically reject the analysis by the Court in this regard. I believe that it was poorly conceived and wrong. I do not, however, see how we can get around this analysis by suggesting that it did not, in fact, take place. As a legal analysis of the *Roe* decision by Will Caron, General Counsel of the U.S. Catholic Conference, has observed,

> *Clearly, the Court's determinations were a product of legal analysis which explicitly and repeatedly rejected the human "personhood" of the unborn as a proper measure of the rights of the mother, the unborn, or the State. . . in the Court's view, the mother's constitutional right necessarily presupposes the absence of 14th Amendment personhood for prenatal life.*

The second response to the reliance upon Justice Harlan's dissent as a rationale for S. 158 is that Congress is doing far more in this bill than simply stating Congressional findings of fact and attempting to call these to the attention of the Court. If this is its objective, Congress is always free to pass a sense of the Senate resolution or to file an amicus brief with the Court. What Congress is trying to do here is entirely different. It is attempting to enact a law. It is attempting to enact a law in the face of an absolutely contrary Supreme Court decision. This law would redefine the term "person" in the 14th Amendment; it would not simply apprise the Court of Congress' perspective on biological issues or "when human life begins". Congress is attempting to exercise its constitutional lawmaking authority on the basis of its own "legislative fact" determinations. Congress itself is purporting to act on these determinations; it is not simply raising the flag of "legislative fact" determinations to see whether or not the Court will salute. Congress is attempting to impose upon the States the provisions of S. 158 which to all extents and purposes will be the law of the land, at least until the Court is able to review (and almost certainly reject) this exercise.

Third, I do not agree with the reliance upon the Harlan language because I believe that it misreads Harlan. What is most explicit in his opinion is that Congress cannot make substantive determinations about constitutionally-guaranteed rights. The authority of Congress in this regard is absent. Justice Harlan, I believe, was clearly discussing "legislative fact finding" in the context of the traditional remedial role of Congress under the 14th Amendment. In his dissent, he stated,

> *In passing upon the remedial provisions [of the Act], we reviewed first the voluminous legislative history as well as judicial precedents supporting the basic Congressional finding that the clear commands of the 15th Amendment had been infringed by various State subterfuges. Given the existence of the evil, we held the remedial steps taken by the legislature under the enforcement clause of the 15th Amendment to be a justifiable exercise of congressional initiative. . . To the extent that legislative facts are relevant to a judicial determination, Congress is well equipped to investigate them and such determinations are, of course, entitled to due respect. In* South

> Carolina v. Katzenbach, *such legislative findings were made to show that racial discrimination in voting was actually occurring.*

The case discussed by Justice Harlan, *South Carolina v. Katzenbach*, 383 U.S. 301 (1965), involved an undisputed exercise by Congress of its remedial authority under the 15th Amendment. It sought to create no new substantive rights of authority.

Finally, I would argue that the rationale in reliance upon the Harlan dissent misconstrues the basic function of Congress. While I would be in total agreement that the Court, as illustrated in the *Roe* case, has itself lost sight of its proper constitutional role, I would repeat Professor Bork's warning that one "deformation" of the Constitution "is not properly cured by further deformations". Even if S. 158 was no more than a Congressional attempt to get the Court to take another look at its 1973 decisions, there would still be no basis for the Congress to "advise" the Supreme Court on the "proper" meaning of the Constitution. The role of the Congress is to legislate. When Congress passes legislation, there ought to be a presumption that such legislation is valid at the outset. This presumption could not obtain under the circumstances of S. 158. Passage of S. 158 would mean that there would be in existence two conflicting "laws" derived from the Constitution. These would exist simultaneously, at least until the Court was confronted with a "case or controversy" allowing the matter to be resolved (as it would certainly be in favor of the Court-interpreted law). Such a situation would be highly detrimental to our constitutional system.

Let me conclude by saying that I have given every possible presumption of constitutionality to this legislation. I have reluctantly voted it out of Subcommittee in order to sustain the debate on its provisions. I will continue to maintain an open mind on this proposal. I am favorably disposed to virtually any measure to save the lives of the unborn, even if it is not my first or second or third choice. At this point, however, I cannot state my support for this legislation.

My present views on S. 158 are, if anything, strengthened by its extremely limited scope. Even if I believed the bill to be constitutional and even were it to be sustained by the Court, all that the bill would do, arguably, is to allow individual States to bar publicly funded abortions. As this Report notes,

> *while S. 158 will prevent States from funding or performing abortions on demand, it will not prevent the performance of abortion by private means. The 14th Amendment only provides that no State shall deprive any person of life without due process of law.*

I am not even sure whether or not it is clear that States would be required to prohibit such "publicly-supported" abortions. All that S. 158 would seem to ensure, given that it is upheld, would be to ensure that there be some element of "due process" prior to an abortion. Given that the mother would retain "fundamental" right to abortion, I am not clear as to what circumstances would satisfy the "due process" requirement. Given the tendencies of the judiciary in this area, I am not much comforted by this "guarantee".

Despite my disagreement with the Chairman of the Subcommittee on the Separation of Powers, Senator John East, on some aspects of S. 158, let me express my admiration for his willingness to place the issue of abortion as the priority issue on the agenda of his subcommittee. The hearings that he has conducted on this have ensured the development of a strong record by Congress on the tragedy of abortion and they have ensured that the abortion issue continues to be a matter of highest public debate. These are no small achievements. I would strongly concur with the report of the subcommittee in virtually all particulars with the exception of the discussion on the constitutional issues relating to S. 158.

Minority Views of Senator Max Baucus

Seldom in this nation's history have the public policy questions surrounding an issue been as complex or controversial as they are with abortion. Abortion has divided Americans for decades. I fully appreciate the depth of feeling on all sides of the abortion question.

While there are many activists in favor of or opposed to S. 158, I believe there also are many more Americans who—like me—are wrestling in the deepest part of their souls with the questions raised by abortion. The issue involves highly intimate and personal decisions. As we discuss the constitutional and legal arguments we should not forget that millions of individual lives are touched by this issue.

In the final analysis, the issue presented by S. 158 is not the controversy surrounding abortion or *Roe v. Wade*. Rather, it is whether the Congress wishes to end run the constitutional amendment process and undermine the central role of the judiciary as the final arbiter for defining the terms of the Constitution. In my view, that is what is at stake—not abortion or *Roe v. Wade*.

The Constitutionality of S. 158

The abortion decision of 1973 was not the first controversial Supreme Court decision in our nation's history. The framers of the Constitution wisely provided within Article V a mechanism for Congress and the citizenry to respond to such decisions.

Several of the amendments to our Constitution have been direct responses to Supreme Court decisions. The Eleventh Amendment was a response to the Court's holding in *Chisolm v. Georgia* which subjected the states to law suits in federal courts. The Fourteenth Amendment was in response to the Court's holding in *Dred Scott v. Sanford* that the constitutional term "citizen" did not include Black Americans. The Sixteenth Amendment overturned the Court's interpretation of the constitutional term "direct taxes" in *Pollack v. Farmer's Loan and Trust Company*. And the Twenty-sixth Amendment was a response to the Court's holding in *Oregon v. Mitchell* that the Congress could not lower the voting age in state elections to 18 years of age.

Since the *Chisolm* case was decided in 1793, this country has had a long and consistent history of responding to constitutional decisions of the Supreme Court. The issue raised by S. 158 is not the correctness or wisdom of *Roe v. Wade*, but rather whether we should retain our historic tradition of utilizing Article V to amend the Constitution.

Our nation's most distinguished constitutional scholars who have analyzed S. 158 have come to the conclusion that it is an attempt to overturn a constitutional decision of the Supreme Court by simple statute. Even those who believe that *Roe v. Wade* was incorrectly decided, believe that S. 158 is an unconstitutional attempt to alter that decision.

Professor Charles Alan Wright of the University of Texas Law School, stated in a letter to the Separation of Powers Subcommittee:

> *I find* Roe *unpersuasive. Nevertheless,* Roe *exists, it has been repeatedly reaffirmed and even extended, and I do not think Congress has authority by statute to overrule a constitutional decision of the Supreme Court. Whatever the arguments might have been if the matter where one of first impression, we have long since accepted the notion that "it is emphatically the province and duty of the Judicial Department to say what the law is,"* Marbury v. Madison, *that the duty is now more specifically that of "this court,"* United States v. Nixon, *and that "the federal judiciary is supreme in the exposition of the law of the Constitution. . ."* Cooper v. Aaron.

Professor Phillip Kurland of the University of Chicago Law School wrote in his letter to the Subcommittee:

> *The question is not whether the Supreme Court decisions are sound or unsound. The question is what is the meaning of the word "person" in the due process clauses of the Fifth and Fourteenth Amendments. The Supreme Court has decided that a fetus is not a "person" within the meaning of those provisions. If that constitutional determination is to be overruled, it can be done only by the Supreme Court or by constitutional amendment.*

Former United States Solicitor General Erwin Griswold wrote the following to the Subcommittee:

> *For the Congress to undertake to interfere with that decision, even under Section V of the Fourteenth Amendment, would, in my view, be an inappropriate legislative interference with the judicial power, and thus, a violation of the separation of powers, which is one of the two major premises of the United States Constitution— the other being the appropriate division of powers between the states and the federal government.*

Former United States Solicitor General Archibald Cox told the Subcommittee:

> *Over the years, a few decisions have proved clearly wrong headed, and perhaps* Roe v. Wade *is such a case, I, myself, wrote critically of* Roe v. Wade *a little while after the decision came down.*
> *But wrong headed decisions can be changed by time and debate or by constitutional amendments. But the very function of the*

constitution and Court is to put individual liberties beyond the reach of both Congressional majorities and popular clamor. Any principle which permits Congress, with the approval of the President, to nullify one constitutional right protected by the Constitution, as interpreted by the Court—that principle would sanction the nullification of others, and that is why I say that the principle of S. 158 is exceedingly dangerous, and I can only call it radical.

And finally, former United States Solicitor General Robert Bork told the Subcommittee:

The question to be answered in assessing S. 158 is whether it is proper to adopt unconstitutional countermeasures to redress unconstitutional action by the Court. I think it is not proper. The deformation of the Constitution is not properly cured by further deformation. Only if we are prepared to say that the Court has become intolerable in a fundamentally Democratic society and that there is no prospect whatever for getting it to behave properly, should we adopt a principle which contains within it the seeds of the destruction of the Court's entire constitutional role. I do not think we are at that stage.

The views of these distinguished constitutional scholars was supported by the common view of former Attorneys General Brownell, Katzenbach, Clark, Richardson, Saxbe, and Civiletti.

The consensus position of the six former Attorneys General of the United States was communicated in a letter to the Subcommittee. They wrote:

Our views about the correctness of the Supreme Court's 1973 abortion decision vary widely, but all of us are agreed that Congress has no constitutional authority either to overturn that decision by enacting a statute redefining such terms as "person" or "human life," or selectively to restrict the jurisdiction of federal courts so as to prevent them from enforcing that decision fully.

We thus regard S. 158 and H.R. 900 as an attempt to exercise unconstitutional power and a dangerous circumvention of the avenues that the Constitution itself provides for reversing Supreme Court interpretations of the Constitution.

The proponents of S. 158 acknowledge that in most cases judicial independence and the doctrine of separation of powers would require Congress to respond to a constitutional decision of the Supreme Court by constitutional amendment. They argue that *Roe v. Wade* is a special case and an exception to this rule because the court in *Roe v. Wade* invited Congress to define when human life begins.

The passage of Justice Blackmun's opinion in *Roe v. Wade* that they rely on reads as follows:

> *We need not resolve the difficult question of when life begins.*
> *When those trained in the respective disciplines of medicine, phi-*
> *losophy, and theology are unable to arrive at any consensus, the*
> *judiciary, at this point in the development of man's knowledge, is*
> *not in a position to speculate as to the answer.*

If the hearings on S. 158 held by the Separation of Powers Subcommittee
were conclusive on any one point it is that in 1981 there remains no consensus
among scientists, philosophers and theologians on the question of when life
begins. The candid observation of the Supreme Court in 1973 is as accurate a
description of the Subcommittee's record as it was of the record before the Court
in *Roe*. The Subcommittee heard conflicting testimony from each of several
disciplines. The testimony of the scientists, physicians, philosophers and theologians who appeared before the subcommittee made it apparent that our society is
as divided on the question today as it was eight years ago, and that man's
knowledge on the subject has not appreciably increased during the eight year
period. Congress to answer the question of when life begins. The proponents of S.
158 simply feel the Court abdicated its role in not addressing the issue. But that
does not alter the status of the Court's constitutional holding in the case.
Constitutional experts who are in sharp disagreement on the correctness of *Roe v.*
Wade agree that the theory behind S. 158 is based on a misreading of *Roe*.

Sarah Weddington, who argued *Roe v. Wade* before the Supreme Court, in
her statement to the Subcommittee, clearly explained the nature of the holding in
Roe:

> *The Court did not abdicate its role of defining constitutional*
> *terms. It said very clearly that in the Fourteenth Amendment, the*
> *term person does not—not "should not," nor "might not," nor*
> *"pending further information not," but does not refer to the unborn.*
> *The Court went on to say that there was no point in its engaging in*
> *philosophic or theological speculation on the beginning of life, since*
> *there was no consensus among those who concern themselves with*
> *such things, and since the constitutional meaning of "person" was*
> *already clear without the Court assuming a function which was*
> *foreign to it.*

In support of this position, Professor Lynn D. Wardle of the Brigham Young
University Law School, who is a strong supporter of a human life amendment,
commented in his analysis of the constitutionality of S. 158:

> *Contrary to the implication of Galebach, that holding (Roe)*
> *was not predicated or contingent upon a prior finding that the Court*
> *did not know when human life began. In fact, the Court did not*
> *address the question of when human life began until after it had*
> *separately analyzed and specifically concluded that the unborn are*
> *not "persons" protected by the Fourteenth Amendment.*

And, finally on this point, the General Counsel to the U.S. Catholic

Conference, Wilfred Caron, critiqued this point in his legal memorandum on the constitutionality of S. 158:

> *In this regard, it should be noted that when the Court acknowledged the judiciary's inability to speculate as to when human life begins, it did so in the context of the state's interest in safeguarding potential life—not in the context of the question of personhood under the Fourteenth Amendment. The Court's candid admission cannot reasonably be regarded as opening the way for what is contemplated by these bills.*

The constitutional scholars who examined S. 158 in its original form generally took the position that the only possible argument supporting its constitutionality was that *Katzenbach v. Morgan* empowered Congress to "enforce" the Fourteenth Amendment by expanding the coverage of the due process clause. There is no constitutional doctrine or case law supporting the proposition that Congress has the authority to grant states a compelling interest in any activity that the Supreme Court explicitly stated the states had no interest in.

As the Supreme Court noted in the well known footnote 10 of *Katzenbach v. Morgan*:

> *Section 5 does not grant Congress power to exercise discretion in the other direction and to enact "statutes so as in effect to dilute equal protection and due process decisions of this court." We emphasize that Congress' power under Section 5 grants Congress no power to restrict, abrogate, or dilute these guarantees.*

The language of Section 3 of S. 158 cannot be supported under the authority of Congress' power to enforce the Fourteenth Amendment. There is no other Congressional power that can serve as the basis for Congress to overturn constitutional decisions of the Supreme Court.

The consequences of a decision by the Supreme Court to uphold the Congress' power to enact S. 158 would be disastrous for our system of government as we now know it. If Congress can alter the court's ruling on a constitutional term as basic as the interpretation of "person" under the Fourteenth Amendment, then there is virtually no constitutional protection that congress couldn't dilute or eliminate by simple majority vote.

Additionally, if Congress can find today by statute that life begins at conception, then a future Congress can alter or reverse that result. This approach envisions a system of government where constitutional protections are more transitory or illusory than they are today. The basic terms of the Constitution are left to be determined by the shifting majorities in Congress.

It is for these basic reasons that most of the country's leading scholars and those who have served the nation as the highest ranking legal officers have publicly announced their view that S. 158 is unconstitutional. It is highly unusual to find agreement among six former Attorneys General, three former Solicitors General, and the nation's most distinguished constitutional scholars on such a controversial issue. In my view, the consensus among them provides significant evidence that the question of the constitutionality of S. 158 is not a "close call." Rather, the theory behind the legislation runs counter to principles of judicial independence and the separation of powers that lie at the very heart of our constitutional system. I oppose the bill on that basis.

Impact of S. 158 on State Sovereignty and State Abortion and Contraceptive Policy

There is another aspect of S. 158 that should be considered carefully. That is the impact of S. 158 on the central role of our state governments as basic decision makers in our federal system.

Although S. 158 is touted as returning power to the states, its long term impact will be to set a precedent that will lead to increased federal intervention and an erosion of state authority.

As former Solicitor General Bork stated at the Subcommittee hearings in response to a question from Senator Heflin:

> *Senator Heflin, if I may—I think the version of Section V of the Fourteenth Amendment that is being propounded here in support of this bill not only federalizes the question of life, but indeed, federalizes state police powers. Under the equal protection clause and the due process clause together, those are turned over to Congress, and there is no state legislation on any topic that I can think of that cannot be federalized if Congress so chooses.*

And, in a letter to Senator Hatch, Professor William Van Alstyne of the Duke University School of Law, further expounded on this aspect of the bill by stating:

> *If Congress can (a) determine authoritatively what affirmative obligations each state has in respect to the life, liberty and property of each person, and if Congress can (b) legislate to "enforce" such affirmative obligations as determined by Congress, then indeed the rudiments of federalism are dead, the Tenth Amendment is meaningless, and each state becomes but the instrument of a uniform, Congressional determined policy of social welfare.*

More specifically, the hearings on S. 158 have brought to light the fact that with regard to state and local decision making over abortion and contraception questions, the current state latitude over these areas would be substantially restricted.

Today, states are free to make their own policy decisions about what abortions to fund or not to fund. However, the intent of S. 158 is to thwart that current authority. Supporters and opponents of S. 158 who testified before the Subcommittee agreed that without any additional legislation, S. 158 would have the effect of preventing any state from engaging in conduct that interferes with the development of the fertilized egg. In other words, states would not be free to fund abortions or fund hospitals or clinics that performed abortions.

Additionally, under S. 158, states could not fund or support any person or facility involved with the use or distribution of those contraceptives that interfere with the development of the fertilized egg (e.g., IUDs and morning-after pills). State action with regard to currently available contraceptives would be prohibited without any additional legislation.

During the Subcommittee hearings of May 21, 1981, the author of S. 158, Stephen Galebach, clarified these points in the following exchange:

> *Senator BAUCUS. Mr. Galebach, I would like to clear up, if we could, your understanding of how this bill would affect state action. My understanding is that the bill, if it is enacted without any additional state or federal legislation, would prohibit states from funding abortions. Is that your understanding too?*
>
> *Mr. GALEBACH. In general, except where states had a justification as compelling as, say, to prevent the death of a mother.*
>
> *Senator BAUCUS. In those cases, too, would the bill also prohibit states from funding abortion clinics that distribute IUDs and morning-after pills in your view?*
>
> *Mr. GALEBACH. It could very well.*
>
> *Senator BAUCUS. That is, without additional legislation, this bill, if it passes, would have the effect of prohibiting the states from funding abortion clinics engaged in the distribution of IUDs and morning-after pills?*
>
> *Mr. GALEBACH. There might be some tough legal questions that would come up as to whether the state could fund other operations of the clinic, but the state could not fund any device that would terminate a human life after conception.*
>
> *Senator BAUCUS. Because that would be state action prohibited under the bill?*
>
> *Mr. GALEBACH. Yes.*

State legislatures could no longer make basic abortion funding decisions that they are free to make today. S. 158 precludes states from funding any abortion unless they have a "compelling" state interest. Most experts on both sides of the question agree that such an interest would only exist where the life of the mother was at stake. Therefore, states could no longer fund abortions in the case of rape or incest if they determined that was appropriate public policy.

Professor Robert Nagel of Cornell, a supporter of S. 158, criticized the bill for its curtailment of state authority at the Subcommittee hearings of June 1:

> *Senator BAUCUS. Insofar as this bill would prohibit states from funding action, in a sense that is not returning the determination to the state but is establishing a national policy which prevents states from taking certain action. That is, the effect of this bill is not to throw the question of abortion back to the states—generally, it certainly is not—and it sets a national policy insofar as the bill will prevent states from funding abortions. That is correct, is it not?*
>
> *Mr. NAGEL. In my view, that is an unfortunate aspect of the bill—yes.*
>
> *Senator BAUCUS. It is an unfortunate aspect? Why is that?*

> *Mr. NAGEL. Because I think it ought to be a matter for states in their own judgment to decide on.*

Following that exchange, I wrote Professor Nagel and asked him his analysis of the degree to which state conduct would be limited by S. 158. I asked him whether states would be permitted to fund abortions in the case where the life of the mother was threatened. I also asked him whether a state would be permitted to fund abortions in the case of rape or incest or the detection of serious genetic defects.

By letter of July 2, Professor Nagel responded to my letter as follows:

> *Although you state that there seems to be agreement that states would be permitted to fund abortions where the life of the mother was threatened, I must say that I believe the matter is far from certain . . .*
>
> *In any event, it seems clear to me that even if a state does not violate due process standards when it encourages the destruction of fetuses in order to save the lives of mothers, it does not follow that a state would be permitted to perform or fund abortions in cases of rape or incest or genetic defect. In such situations, the states aid, whatever its justification, would amount to the destruction of "persons" (in the statutory sense) and thus violate the statute. There is not general doctrine that a state may encourage the destruction of persons for "compelling" reasons.*

The majority report remains silent on these important questions. The report states that the courts should decide these matters on a case-by-case basis. It is my view that it is irresponsible to pass this bill without the Senate stating its own view on whether this bill is likely to result in the substantial curtailment of state authority over abortion funding. Leaving such matters to the discretion of the courts runs counter to the spirit of those who offer this legislation as an antidote to judicial activism.

Furthermore, when legislating, it is irresponsible to leave basic questions on state authority like these unanswered:

1. Would S. 158 prohibit the states from funding clinics and hospitals that distribute drugs or devices that interfere with the development of the fertilized egg, such as IUDs and morning-after pills?
2. Would the state have a "compelling interest" in funding abortion in the case of rape that would override the fetus' protection as a person under the Fourteenth Amendment?
3. Would the state have a compelling interest in funding abortions in the case of incest?
4. Would the state have a compelling interest in funding an abortion in the case of a detectable genetic disease of the fetus?
5. Would the state have a compelling interest in funding abortion when the life of the mother was at stake?

These are serious questions. The answers to them can profoundly affect state and local decision-making over basic health and safety issues. Those who support such state authority should not take these questions lightly.

S. 158 and Removal of Lower Federal Court Jurisdiction

Section 4 of S. 158 would remove the jurisdiction of the lower federal courts over certain types of abortion cases. The reason that has been cited by advocates of S. 158 for inclusion of this provision in the bill is that a limitation of the available remedies in federal court will encourage prompt review of the statute in the Supreme Court. A report issued by Senator East's office entitled Questions and Answers on S. 158 offers the following explanation for the provision:

> *Question. Why should Congress be so concerned to prevent review of the Act by lower federal courts?*
>
> *Answer. The anti-injunction clause of the bill is designed to prevent lower federal courts from interfering with the enforcement of the Act. An example of this problem arose in Judge Dooling's injunction against the Hyde Amendment respecting federal funding of abortion. That injunction remained in effect for approximately two years before the Supreme Court reviewed the case and upheld the legislation. The anti-injunction provision of the bill assures the continued enforcement of the State law outlawing abortion until the Supreme Court has had an opportunity to interpret it.*

Section 5 of S. 158, as amended, contains a provision that directly addresses this concern for speedy review by the Supreme Court. It specifically provides for an expedited review of the legislation by the Supreme Court. This addresses the primary concern articulated by those who supported the section of S. 158 which limits lower federal court jurisdiction. In my view, it addressses those concerns in a manner that is less controversial and less threatening to our system of government.

Many questions have been raised about the constitutionality and wisdom of attempts to limit lower federal court jurisdiction. Several leading constitutional scholars have raised serious concerns about the specific provision contained in S. 158.

Professor Charles Alan Wright of the University of Texas Law School observed in his letter to the Subcommittee:

> *I think Congress has very sweeping power over the jurisdiction of the inferior courts . . . At the same time, I feel certain that Congress must exercise its power over federal jurisdiction, as it must its other powers, in a fashion consistent with constitutional limitations . . . Under such cases as* Hunter v. Erickson *and United States v. Klein, I do not think Congress has authority to close the federal court door in suits arising under laws that prohibit, limit or regulate abortions, while allowing access to federal court for challenges to statutes that permit, facilitate, or aid in the financing of abortions.*

Even if Congress has the power to remove lower federal court jurisdiction over constitutional matters, it must do so neutrally. It would have to remove lower federal court jurisdiction over all abortion cases. The provision in S. 158 effectively keeps out litigants on one side of the issue and allows in litigants from the other. Challenges to statutes that restrict or prohibit abortions would not be permitted to be brought in the lower federal courts. Attempts to enjoin abortions from occurring, or challenges to statutes that fund abortions, could be brought in the lower federal courts.

This aspect of Section 4 of S. 158 not only raises constitutional questions, but it underscores the true intent of the provision. The provision is designed to restrict the jurisdiction of the lower federal courts so as to prevent them from enforcing certain rights fully. In my view, in such an instance, the Congressional attempt to remove lower federal court jurisdiction is violative of that provision of the Constitution from which the right flows.

Additionally, we ought to consider the public policy implications of attempts to remove constitutional issues from the jurisdiction of the lower federal courts. My own view is that while the creation of the lower federal courts was initially within the discretion of Congress, the growth of our nation has significantly altered the role of the lower federal courts in our federal system. Certainly, in 1789 the Supreme Court was able to handle its role as the primary vindicator of federal rights.

But the Supreme Court case load has increased dramatically since the birth of our nation, and this has had significant consequences for the lower federal courts. For a litigant who desires to vindicate his federal constitutional rights, access to the lower federal courts is an essential element in giving those rights true meaning. It is my view that we do great damage to our structure of government if we deny the central role of the lower federal courts in modern times.

It is because of these arguments that I think we should use the Congressional power to limit the jurisdiction of the federal courts over constitutional issues quite sparingly. If it is invoked at all, and I personally do not think that it should be, it should only be utilized where no other alternative is available and where it can be shown to have results that are helpful to society.

Because of the expedited Supreme Court review provision now contained in S. 158, I believe that a large portion of the rationale in favor of a section to remove lower federal court jurisdiction has been removed. Furthermore, I believe the section itself is unconstitutional and I oppose it on that basis.

The Intent of the Fourteenth Amendment

There is an implication in the majority report that the Fourteenth Amendment was intended to protect the unborn. While it is clearly appropriate for Congress to state its opinion on whether the Fourteenth Amendment ought to apply to the unborn, that is far different from suggesting that the framers of the Fourteenth Amendment intended for the amendment to apply to the unborn.

Distinguished historians who appeared before the Subcommittee addressed this issue. It is clear from their testimony that during the long debate on the Fourteenth Amendment in the 39th Congress, and during all debates in the states on the ratification of the Fourteenth Amendment, there was never any explicit mention made of the unborn, nor any reference to the issue of abortion. This is undisputed.

In his testimony before the Subcommittee, Professor Carl Degler of Stanford University disputed the thesis propounded by Professor Witherspoon with regard to this finding. Professor Degler stated:

> *Professor Witherspoon then links this discussion of the amendments concerned with the protection of life to the laws then being passed in a number of states to limit abortion. He professes to see in these state laws an extension of the concern for the freedom of the former slaves. Yet there is no mention of the discussion in Congress of these laws, nor is there any reference to abortion or to the unborn in the course of the debate on the Fourteenth Amendment.*

In his testimony before the Subcommittee, Dr. James Mohr of the University of Maryland at Baltimore stated:

> *I am also troubled by the phrase "all human beings." The Fourteenth Amendment does not, in fact, refer to human beings, but rather to "citizens" and "persons." I know of no direct evidence that the framers of the Fourteenth Amendment ever intended that either of these words should apply to the preborn.*
>
> *None of the leading historians of the Reconstruction Era whom I was able to contact, including several who have done painstaking research both on the drafting and on the ratification of the Fourteenth Amendment, knows of any.*
>
> *The rights of the preborn were simply not at issue. Moreover, there is compelling evidence that they were never intended to be.*

Finally, the Congressional Research Service has issued a report entitled, "Examination of Congressional Intention In The Use Of The Word 'Person' In the Fourteenth Amendment: Abortion Considerations." The report concludes with this analysis:

> *A reading of the legislative history of the Fourteenth Amendment does not reveal any references to the unborn. There are no statements in the debates of the 39th Congress indicating that the framers ever considered the unborn in connection with the Amendment's protection . . .*
>
> *Beyond this examination of the legislative history, one enters the realm of speculation and theorizing concerning what the framers of the Fourteenth Amendment actually intended when they used "person" in the language of this Amendment.*

The record created by the Separation of Powers Subcommittee is very clear on this point. The majority report may express the views of the majority of the Subcommittee on the coverage of the Fourteenth Amendment, but that should be distinguished from the concrete evidence available to the Subcommittee on the intent of the framers of the Amendment.

Scientific Testimony on S. 158

The majority report implies that there was substantial agreement among scientific witnesses on the question of when an individual human life begins. The report attempts to minimize the diversity of views expressed by the scientific witnesses. I would simply suggest that the testimony of the scientific witnesses underscored the real complexity of the issues involved.

Dr. Lewis Thomas, Chancellor of the Memorial Sloan-Kettering Cancer Center and formerly Dean of Yale Medical School told the subcommittee:

> *The question as to when human life begins, and whether the very first single cell that comes into existence after fertilization of an ovum represents, in itself, a human life, is not in any real sense a scientific question and cannot be answered by scientists. Whatever the answer, it can neither be verified nor proven false using today's scientific knowledge.*
>
> *It is therefore in the domain of metaphysics: it can be argued by philosophers and theologians, but it lies beyond the reach of science.*
>
> *Such a cell does not differ, in its possession of all the genes needed for coding out a whole human being, from any of the other, somatic cells of the body, nor indeed from any of the billions of human cells now being cultured in research laboratories all around the world. The difference is that the progeny of a fertilized ovum develop systems for differentiation and embryogenesis; we do not yet understand this system. But the fact remains that all human cells contain the same full complement of human DNA.*
>
> *There are two criteria that I can think of for determining the stage of an embryo's development when the the essential characteristic of a human being begins to emerge. One is the start-up of spontaneous electrical activity in the brain; this could be interpreted as the beginning of human life just as we take the cessation of such activity to indicate the end of human life. The second is the appearance of those molecular signals (antigens) at the surfaces of the embryonic cells which are the unequivocal markers of individuality and selfness. There is, in this immunological sense, a stage in embryonic development at which the fetus becomes a specific individual.*
>
> *This is as far as I can see science making a contribution to the question of the point at which an embryo becomes a human self. It is a limited contribution at best, and tells us nothing about the "personhood" of a single cell.*

Dr. Frederick Robbins, President of the Institute of Medicine of the National Academy of Sciences, wrote the following to the Subcommittee:

> *Even the most elementary understanding of biology suggests that, from the moment of conception, the human zygote is biologically alive in that it is capable of dividing and growing. That there*

is biological "life" is not in dispute for the fertilized egg or for other cells of human origin. What is at question is at what point the growing mass of cells—that is, the product of conception—takes on the attributes of "personhood." That is, at what point in the sequence of development do we choose to say that the organism is a person, and therefore, of special value? Clearly, the answer to such questions rests not on scientific judgments, but solely on what we choose to define as the qualities and attributes of being a person. Is it the capacity to sustain life on one's own? To think or reason? To feel? Or is it some intangible quality that we cannot quite specify?

In my view, it is social, philosophical, and religious values that provide the guidelines for making such determinations, not science. Science can answer such questions as, for example, when does an embryo's nervous system develop the capacity to sense pain, but science cannot answer the question of whether that particular developmental attribute therefore makes that organism a person. Science can outline the steps of prenatal brain development, but it is the broader society that evaluates such information and chooses to label one stage of life as "personhood" and another as not.

Dr. James Ebert, President of the Carnegie Institution, stated in this letter to the Subcommittee:

I do not believe that the statement in Chapter 101, Section 1 can be supported. This Section reads "The Congress finds that present day scientific evidence indicates a significant likelihood that actual human life exists from conception." This statement embodies and expresses a dogmatic and dangerously narrow definition of "actual human life", for human life cannot properly be said to begin at any single moment fixed in time.

Indeed, human life is a continuum, proceeding generation after generation. The eggs contained in the ovary of a very young girl ripen and are shed over her reproductive lifetime. These eggs like the other cells of the woman's body are living. The sperm maturing in the human male are no less alive. The union of living egg and living sperm results in a living zygote, no less alive than its parental predecessors, but differing from both of them. But the zygote is but one fleeting morphologic and physiologic entity in the panorama that is human development. When does "personhood begin?" In my opinion, the question cannot be answered scientifically. Some might argue for the moment of conception, others for the moment at which the heart first begins to beat, or the face takes shape, or the brain begins to function. Some physiologic functions do not come into play until after birth; and as Peter Medawar has written "birth is a moveable feast in the calendar of development."

Dr. Robert Ebert, President of the Milbank Memorial Fund and former Dean of Harvard Medical School, wrote the Subcommittee as follows:

*I know of no ". . . current medical and scientific data . . ."
that supports the contention ". . . that human life in the sense of an
actual human being or legal person begins at conception." Life in
the biologic sense does not begin the moment that an ovum is
fertilized by a sperm, since both have life prior to that event.*

*In my view, the question of human personhood is neither a
medical nor a scientific question. In one sense it is a philosophical
question which can be debated endlessly and has to do with how one
defines a person and "self." But in the context of the present
legislative proposal, I believe it can best be described as a religious
question.*

Dr. Clifford Grobstein, Professor of Biological Science and Public Policy
Science and former Dean of the School of Medicine at the University of California
at San Diego listed for the Subcommittee what he considered to be the consensus
views of science and then concluded:

*The implication of these statements is that at fertilization a new
generation in a genetic sense is constituted, but that two weeks later
a new and stable biological entity or individual is not yet certainly
present. Exactly when such an entity arises is not known for certain
in the human species but it is probably not many days later. The
development of such an entity, therefore, is gradual and involves a
number of transitions and stages. No single moment nor event is
known scientifically to mark its initiation, rather it emerges steadily
out of the developmental process as an additional characteristic
beyond being alive and biologically human.*

Returning to the language of Roe v. Wade *and S. 158, it would
be scientifically more accurate to say that "human life does not
begin with fertilization (conception) but hereditary individuality
does. Individuality in the sense of singleness and wholeness, however, cannot be said to be established until more than two weeks
after fertilization."*

And finally, the National Academy of Sciences forwarded to the Subcommittee the following resolution passed by its membership at its annual meeting on
April 24, 1981 concerning the original text of S. 158:

Resolution.—*It is the view of the National Academy of Sciences
that the statement in Chapter 101, Section 1, of the U.S. Senate Bill
S. 158, 1981, cannot stand up to the scrutiny of science. This section
reads "the Congress finds that present-day scientific evidence
indicates a significant likelihood that actual human life exists from
conception." This statement purports to derive its conclusions from
science, but it deals with a question to which science can provide no
answer. The proposal in S. 158 that the term "person" shall include
"all human life" has no basis within our scientific understanding.
Defining the time at which the developing embryo becomes a
"person" must remain a matter of moral and religious value.*

Conclusion

I cannot support S. 158 because I believe it is an attempt to end run the constitutional amendment process. The legislation undermines the central role of the judiciary as it has existed in this country since *Marbury v. Madison*. The theory underlying the bill envisions a system of government where constitutional protections are illusory and where the basic protections of the Constitution can be diluted or eliminated by simple majorities of the Congress. In my view, the legislation runs counter to principles of judicial independence and the separation of powers that lie at the very heart of our constitutional system.

Additionally, I am deeply concerned that S. 158 will lead to an erosion of the central role of the states in our federal system. Not only could the theory behind the bill lead to an expanded federal role in almost every area of the law, but S. 158 eliminates a state's authority to set policy on state funding of abortions and distribution of contraceptives (e.g. IUD's and morning after pills) at state supported hospitals.

Finally, I believe the provision eliminating lower federal court jurisdiction over certain abortion cases is unconstitutional. I personally am opposed to efforts to remove federal court jurisdiction over constitutional cases. However, even if Congress has the power to remove lower federal court jurisdiction over constitutional cases, it must do so in a neutral, even-handed manner. Section 4 of S. 158 effectively closes the federal courthouse to citizens on one side of the issue, while keeping it open to citizens on the other. It, therefore, represents an unconstitutional exercise of Congress' power to control the jurisdiction of the lower federal courts.

S.J. Res. 3 was a joint resolution to amend the Constitution, and the hearings before the Subcommittee on the Constitution were held in 1983. Many who were opposed to the Human Life Bill eventually supported S.J. Res. 3, or the Human Life Amendment, but it was defeated by the Senate, ending for a time an intense congressional battle on abortion. Since 1983, the abortion issue has continued to be debated—extending to the presidential election of 1984 as well as many state and local elections. Despite the fact that the *Roe* decision has been affirmed, all three branches of government have become even more involved with abortion and probably will do so in the future.

Appendix 3

A PROPOSED AMENDMENT TO THE CONSTITUTION ON ABORTION

98th CONGRESS
1st Session

S. J. Res. 3

To amend the Constitution to establish legislative authority in Congress and the States with respect to abortion.

IN THE SENATE OF THE UNITED STATES

JANUARY 26 (legislative day, JANUARY 25), 1983

MR. HATCH (for himself, MR. NICKLES, MR. BOSCHWITZ, MR. DENTON, MR. ZORINSKY, MR. HUMPHREY, and MR. EAGLETON) introduced the following joint resolution; which was read twice and referred to the Committee on the Judiciary

JOINT RESOLUTION

To amend the Constitution to establish legislative authority in
Congress and the States with respect to abortion.

*Resolved by the Senate and House of Representatives of the United States of
America in Corgress assembled (two-thirds of each House concurring therein),*
That the following article is proposed as an amendment to the Constitution of the
United States which shall be valid to all intents and purposes as part of the
Constitution when ratified by the legislatures of three-fourths of the several States
within seven years from the date of its submission by the Congress:

2

"ARTICLE—

"SECTION. A right to abortion is not secured by this Constitution. The
Congress and the several States shall have concurrent power to restrict and
prohibit abortion: *Provided*, That a provision of a law of a State which is more
restrictive than a conflicting provision of a law of Congress shall govern."

Prepared Statement of Laurence H. Tribe

Mr. Chairman and members of the Subcommittee:

I am honored to appear at the Subcommittee's invitation to explore the issues
posed by the constitutional amendments to overturn the Supreme Court's
abortion decision, *Roe* v. *Wade*, 410 U.S. 113 (1973), by restoring state and/or
federal legislative power to restrict abortion.

1. I ask the Subcommittee to include in the record my testimony on this
same subject on October 5, 1981; and a memorandum that I sent to the full Senate
Judiciary Committee on March 3, 1982, on the Human Life Amendment as
proposed by Senator Hatch (appended hereto). Today, I would like simply to add
a few words about vhat I regard as the basic fallacies in *any* of the so-called
states'-rights compromises on the abortion issue. If I am correct, these compromises should succeed only in uniting everyone against them.

2. Under any version of the proposed compromise in which states would
have the authority only to *restrict* or *prohibit* abortion, and in which a congressional restriction would override any less restrictive posture of any state, it is
manifestly deceptive to claim that matters would be returned to their pre-*Roe* v.
Wade posture. On the contrary, the effect of any such compromise would be to
make the states and Congress indirect vehicles for bans on abortion, and *not* to
empower state and local governments to make a free choice on this subject.

3. Even permitting each state to choose for itself—to the degree such choice
would be exercised against abortion—would return government to the role of
policing the most personal of matters; would turn back the clock on the still
incomplete emergence of women as self-determining members of society; would
restore the days of illegal, back-street abortions; would do little to help the unborn
and nothing to alter the conditions that make abortion seem tragically necessary

for so many; and would once again use "states' rights" more as a hypocritical slogan than as a meaningful buffer against the flow of power toward the central government.

4.   Having recently argued in favor of greater state and local autonomy in two Supreme Court cases,[1] I think I can appreciate quite well the virtue of granting wider leeway to levels of government that are closer to the people than the National Government can plausibly hope to be. But just as a nation half-slave and half-free could not long endure, so the question of whether women must bear children against their will—and the question of whether the unborn may be relegated to the mercy of private choice—cannot, in the long run, be resolved differently in different parts of the nation. Both for the advocates of women's freedom to choose and for the defenders of unborn life, the issue must ultimately be seen as the fundamental—too constitutive of what our nation stands for—to be left to state or local majorities. This is part of what nationhood *means*; and it is especially so in light of the interstate mobility of all but the poorest and most burdened of women. As in the struggle over slavery, the crucial division would again become that between those who are trapped by economic and other circumstances and those who are trapped by economic and other circumstances and those who can somehow manage to escape the boundaries of geography and the shackles of domination. Neither side in the debate over *Roe* v. *Wade* can, with self-respect, purport to find that an acceptable prospect.

5.   The parallel to slavery—which opponents of *Roe* v. *Wade* are fond of invoking as they compare that decision, I believe wrongly, to the Supreme Court's abomination in the *Dred Scott* case—compels me to add, in light of Senator Eagleton's recent emergence as an advocate of a states'-rights "solution" to this problem, that the *last* thing we need here is a second "Missouri Compromise." This one would be unlikely to last even as many decades as the first; I believe it has no place in a Constitution written for the ages rather than for the media or for immediate constituencies.

6.   There is another parallel I cannot resist suggesting. In what must surely be the most famous compromise ever conceived, King Solomon proposed, to two women claiming motherhood of the same infant, that he would cut the child in two rather than decide for either. We all know what ensued. Solomon's idea earned him unique honor in the history of wisdom because it *uncovered* the truth by transforming reality without sacrificing *either* life *or* liberty.[2] In a genuinely sad sense, the states'-rights compromise similarly proposes to divide the unborn rather than to choose definitively between fetal life and women's freedom. But, unlike Solomon's idea, this one is surely destined for the dustbin of history—because it *obscures* the truth by leaving the underlying reality unchanged while sacrificing *both* life *and* liberty.

7.   Unending battle over the abortion issue is no happy prospect; many an able and otherwise conscientious lawmaker will be returned to private life for

---

[1] On November 1, 1982, representing Boston in *White v. MCCE*, No. 01-1003; and on January 17, 1983, representing California in *Pacific Gas & Electric Co. v. State Energy Resources and Development Commission*, No. 81-1945; both cases await decision.

[2] See M. Minow, "The Judgment of Solomon and the Experience of Justice," in R. Cover & O. Fiss, *The Structure of Procedure* (1979).

failing to take the "right" position on the matter. The appeal of almost *any* compromise that promises to make the issue recede, even temporarily, from the forefront of the public agenda is thus understandable. But if I am correct about such artificial compromises as those advocated by Senator Hatch and Senator Eagleton, then their appeal should be resisted; the respite they offer is likely to be illusory, the relief short-lived. More promising, if longer and more demanding, is the path toward a society in which every pregnancy is one both partners want, every child one both parents welcome, and no unborn life a life that anyone would willingly end.

Memorandum to the Senate Judiciary Committee on the Proposed Human Life Amendment

This memorandum analyzes what I understand to be the latest version of the proposed Human Life Amendment: "Nothing in this Constitution shall be construed to secure a right to abortion or to deny the concurrent power of Congress and the several states to protect unborn human life by restricting and prohibiting abortion."

1. The amendment would negate "a right to abortion" but, so far as appears, not the right to equal protection of the laws, the right against deprivation of liberty without due process of the law, and such other rights as those of travel, speech and press. For example, I assume the amendment is not intended to authorize Congress or any state to penalize poor or black women more severely than others when abortions are involved; to deny general welfare benefits to women who have had abortions; to criminalize abortion in language too vague to be understood by ordinary people; to ban interstate travel by people seeking lawful abortions; or to restrain the truthful advertising of abortion services that might be available in other countries. But if these assumptions are correct, then how about a law that bans the IUD or the morning-after pill? Unless the right to contraception is also being negated by this amendment, such laws would presumably remain unconstitutional. But if that is so, then a great deal of line-drawing litigation will invariably be spawned by the proposal. And, as opponents of the Equal Rights Amendment are fond of pointing out, no one can predict with confidence what the outcome of such litigation would be.

2. The amendment attempts to remove *Roe* v. *Wade*, 410 U.S. 113 (1973), and its progeny as obstacles to anti-abortion laws, state and federal, but does not appear to confer upon Congress any *affirmative power* to restrict abortion—power Congress did not have even before *Roe* v. *Wade*. The only way to escape that conclusion would be to read the first four words of the proposed amendment so broadly as to obliterate the Constitution's entire structure of limited federal powers—a structure under which Congress has no authority that is not delegated to it, expressly or impliedly, by the Constitution itself. Unless the amendment were given that radical and anti-states'-rights a reading, it would probably fail to give Congress the power that its proponents obviously want Congress to enjoy in this area.

3. Even if Congress were deemed to have affirmative authority to enact anti-abortion laws under this amendment or otherwise, the statement that "nothing in this Constitution shall be construed . . . to deny the concurrent power of . . . the several states" in this field seemingly encompasses even the

Supremacy Clause of Article VI, with the result that Congress could not override *any* aspect of whatever integrated legal scheme a given state might choose as *its* way "to protect unborn human life by restricting and prohibiting abortion" in some circumstances but not in others. Thus, if California chose to "protect unborn human life" by making abortion a misdemeanor in the third trimester while facilitating and even funding the earliest possible abortion choices prior to that point (in order to maximize cooperation with, and enforceability of, the law), while North Carolina chose to "protect unborn human life" by making *all* abortions punishable by life imprisonment, Congress would seem equally powerless to override either choice. The only escape from that conclusion would seem to be an interpretation of the amendment under which states may be *more* restrictive of abortion than Congress but not *less*. But inasmuch as the prior version of the amendment, embodying just such a principle, has evidently been abandoned as unworkable (it would have caused a veritable litigation nightmare), no such interpretation seems plausible. The result is that the amendment probably fails to meet the right-to-life objective of preventing "liberal" states from becoming safe havens for freedom of choice.

> *My conclusion is that the current draft, like its predecessors, poses at least as many questions as it answers, falls considerably short of its apparent purposes, and would contribute more to already overcrowded judicial dockets than to the cause of human life. I do not suggest that there is no possible amendment that could appropriately overrule* Roe v. Wade. *But the lesson of the current effort may be that the task is far more challenging than most people have supposed, precisely because* Roe v. Wade *reflects the convergence of constitutional principles both broader and deeper than many opponents of* Roe v. Wade *have assumed.*

Senator HATCH. Professor Wardle, of the Brigham Young University, has built a reputation as one of the Nation's leading scholars on the legal issues associated with abortion. He has authored two books and several articles on the subject. I personally have great respect for your work, Professor Wardle, and I welcome you back to the subcommittee and look forward to what you have to say on this subject today.

Statement of Lynn Wardle

Professor WARDLE. Thank you very much, Mr. Chairman.

I am honored to participate in these important hearings today, and I commend you personally, Mr. Chairman, and the members of your committee, for facing the issue of the constitutionality of abortion and abortion restrictions. I believe the record that is being made today and during these proceedings will be an historic document. The importance of the work that has already begun by the members of this committee is already recognized by many thoughtful citizens across this Nation, and I believe that in years to come, the recommendations this subcommittee makes, and the vote of the committee and of the Senate will be acknowledged to the credit or the discredit of every Member of the 98th Congress.

I think we are engaged in a very important debate, and this committee is playing a central role in moving things to a conclusion that will be recognized for a long time as an important one.

I appear before the subcommittee today to recommend that it propose and the Senate pass an amendment to the Constitution that would reverse *Roe* against *Wade*. Because of the sensitive nature of the abortion dilemma and because of the sensitive process of amending the Constitution, I would prefer not having to make this recommendation. But an appropriate respect for the complex nature of our constitutional system does not require that Congress shrink from every confrontation with the other, coequal branches of Government. Rather, proper regard for the constitutional system of checks and balances will compel Congress to respond when, as in the present circumstances, the Supreme Court unilaterally and continuously acts in such a manner that the constitutional balance of powers to deal with a matter of such significant importance is threatened.

I would like to rephrase the issue. I think the question is whether the right of the people to protect human life is to be abridged. A decade has passed since *Roe* against *Wade* was decided, a decade in which Federal courts have faced a flood of abortion litigation, in which Congress has faced a deluge of abortion proposals, and in which the number of abortions performed annually has reached in excess of 1.5 million, a total approaching 15 million since *Roe* v. *Wade*.

Moreover, as many commentators have predicted, since *Roe*, there has been a profound and appalling increase in the kinds of inhumane acts that manifest a disregard for and involve even the destruction of other forms of unwanted, defenseless human life. Not only are human beings who bear the stigma of being labeled defective because of some potential physical or mental condition being ruthlessly destroyed before birth, but since *Roe*, they have increasingly become the victims of infanticide and selective nontreatment, to use the euphemism.

Nor is it surprising to find that human beings belonging to racial minorities are being denied the opportunities of life and being destroyed in egregiously disproportionate numbers. The poor and the unwanted have always been the victims of such evenhanded rules of law as abortion on demand.

While these practical and doctrinal excesses are approaching shocking extremes, the Supreme Court has refused to reconsider *Roe* against *Wade*. Thus, at this time, 10 years after that disaster, I feel the sentiments of the English statesman and orator, Edmund Burke, who is reported to have said, "An event is happening about which it is difficult to speak, but about which it is impossible to remain silent." I believe the time has come for Congress to restore the right of the people to protect all human life.

The current source of the constitutional dilemma in *Roe* v. *Wade*, and that is where my remarks must begin. I am going to skip my prepared remarks, a final version of which I would like to submit to the committee, if I may.

Senator HATCH. Without objection, they will be placed as a complete version in the record.

Professor WARDLE. The Supreme Court in *Roe* against *Wade* effectively amended the Constitution, by holding as they did that a pregnant woman has a fundamental right to choose whether or not to terminate her pregnancy. That holding amounts to a judicially adopted amendment to the U.S. Constitution. As a direct result of that amendment, two profound changes have occurred in the delicate balance of powers, and I wish to focus on those for just a moment.

First, there has been a significant shift of responsibility and power from the States to the Federal Government, which has resulted in a substantial increase in congressional involvement with and responsibility for abortion policy. Second, there has been a significant shift in policymaking power from the legislative branch to the judicial branch, generally.

Now, I would like to focus on those briefly here, and more extensively in my prepared remarks.

Our constitutional system of government is founded upon a belief that a concentration of power in any one branch of government or at any one level of government is a dangerous thing. One of the most obvious, and perhaps the most immediate impact of the abortion decisions of the Supreme Court has been the aggrandizement of Federal judicial power. By giving the right to choose abortion the status of a fundamental right, the Supreme Court substantially restricted the authority of the legislative branches to legislate concerning the subject and substantially increased the responsibilty of the Judiciary for defining and monitoring regulation of the fundamental right. By declaring that a woman has this fundamental right, the Supreme Court gave the Judiciary a substantially greater role, and conversely, the legislatures were left with substantially less authority.

Perhaps the magnitude of the tremendous shift of responsibility to the Judiciary from the State legislatures is best evidenced by the dramatic explosion in Federal court abortion litigation. We can compare before and after. During the entire decade before *Roe* was decided, there was a total of only 18 opinions published by all Federal courts and all cases dealing with abortion or abortion regulations—only 18. That includes everything from criminal prosecutions of abortionists to challenges on abortion laws. However, in the decade since *Roe*, there have been nearly 200 published opinions—more than a tenfold increase.

I should pause and emphasize that this only counts the published opinions. There have been a tremendous number of unpublished Federal court opinions. The courts are not anxious, because of the tremendous controversy, to have their opinions in this area published, and so a great many decisions have been rendered and not been published.

Likewise, there has been a similar dramatic jump in the number of State court cases dealing with abortion since *Roe* against *Wade* was decided.

In the library at Brigham Young University Law School, there sits on a shelf in the reserve room four volumes called ''The Abortion Law Reporter'' which take up over a foot of space, reporting the different State and Federal court decisions, and I do not believe that ''Reporter'' is complete or comprehensive. There has been a tremendous deluge of litigation.

The scope of these abortion cases has likewise mushroomed to incredible proportions in the last decade. Before *Roe*, those cases dealt for the most part with questions of whether or not traditional 19th century abortion laws were constitutionally too narrow. However, since *Roe*, Federal court cases have dealt with such diverse subjects as domestic relations, zoning, advertising, religious liberty, the licensing of doctors, hospitals and clinics, burial, informed consent, the expenditure of public funds, hospital administration, and so forth.

Not only has the breadth of the issues encompassed by the abortion cases expanded dramatically, but so also has the depth and detail of the questions which the courts have been called upon to resolve. In the decade since *Roe*, the advocates of abortion have returned to the Federal courts time and time and time again to fill in the details of the broad right that the Supreme Court established. This has resulted in the development by the Federal Judiciary of a set of rules, all presented as part of the supreme constitutional law of the land, that has become increasingly intricate and technical. Can a State require second trimester abortions to be performed in hospitals if dilation and evacuation abortions can be safely performed until about the 18th or 20th week in out-patient clinics? That is an example of the detail of the questions and one of the issues before the Supreme Court right now. Can a State require a woman to be informed of the facts of fetal development before she agrees to an abortion? What about the likelihood of fetal pain? Is a 24-hour waiting period constitutional? How about a 48-hour waiting period? Can a State require parental consent before an abortion is performed on a minor? Can it require parental notification generally? What about if she is a mature minor? How is that to be defined? Can a state require pathological reports following abortion? And so on and so on—greater and greater detail.

It is now painfully apparent that the constitutionalization of abortion is a slippery slope, leading ever downward into increasingly more detailed technical questions. As the courts have become increasingly more involved in supervising the enactment and enforcement of abortion regulations, the fundamental question keeps reappearing—why should the courts, rather than State legislatures, be deciding these issues? The answer, of course, is that they should not.

The exercise of judicial power to invalidate legislation affects the relationship between the coequal branches of government. The assumption by the Judiciary of a major role in supervising abortion regulation represents a substantial shift in the delicate balance of power.

I believe that the issue of abortion is the type of issue that should appropriately be left to legislative resolution. When employed unwisely or unnecessarily, the Supreme Court's power to declare legislative acts unconstitutional constitutes a threat to the continued effectiveness of the Federal courts as well as to the stability of our democratic system. After all, there is some irony that a people who are self-governing cannot establish the laws dealing with such a fundamental question as the regulation and legality of abortion.

I think the Solicitor General of the United States put it best when he recently acknowledged that the best way to determine who is right and who is wrong in these issues concerning abortion is to permit and encourage the opposing sides to exercise their persuasive efforts in the State legislatures.

At this point, I would like to just pause to respond to a point that Professor Tribe raised. I believe that how restore the balance, how we establish in the law the fundamental value of respect for life, may be as important as what we do. Especially if we believe that there is value in our constitutional system, which has served us well for 200 years. We need to preserve the balance. This particular issue will not always be with us. However, I disagree strongly with Senator Packwood when he says another 2 years and we will be done, this issue will go away. It will not go away. It will remain with us until *Roe* is repudiated. But it is important that as we deal with this issue, before we do damage to our system of government, that we restore the balance and allow the State legislatures, as the founders and drafters of the Constitution intended, to deal with this issue.

I would like to turn to that point right now, and it is the second and final point I would like to make, that the Supreme Court's usurpation of a major legislative function of the States has not lessened the legislative burden of Congress. The Court has aggrandized its own power, and put a greater burden upon Congress. In fact, the effect of *Roe* has been to substantially increase the amount of time and resources Congress has been forced to devote to the numerous abortion issues generated by *Roe*.

Roe v. *Wade* has shifted the balance of power and responsibility for abortion away from the States and onto the Federal government. This is very simply explained. In *Roe* v. *Wade*, the Supreme Court constitutionalized the abortion issue. It had not been constitutionalized before that time. Constitutionalizing it made it a national issue, and that means that it is unavoidably a concern and a responsibility of Congress. Abortion will continue to be a major responsibility of Congress until *Roe* v. *Wade* is overturned.

The best evidence of the shift in power and responsibility for regulating abortions to the Federal Government and the Congress in particular is data concerning abortion-related legislation that has been introduced and passed by Congress. There has been a dramatic, persistent increase in the demand upon Congress to deal with abortion since *Roe*. For instance, preliminary research reveals that during the entire decade before the Supreme Court decided *Roe*, only 10 bills were introduced in Congress relating to abortion. Moreover, all 10 of those were introduced after the Federal courts began to invalidate abortion restrictions—that is, the first one was 1970, when the Federal courts had already begun to say this is a matter of Federal constitutional law. So, even the earliest Federal legislation introduced—and Senator Packwood, to my knowledge, was the first one to introduce a bill—that was not introduced until after the federalizing process had begun in the Federal courts. But there were only 10 bills.

In contrast, in the last decade since *Roe* against *Wade* was decided, more than 60 bills dealing with abortion have been introduced in Congress. I want to emphasize that that is just the result of preliminary research. The final draft of my prepared statement will be more complete, and we will, I am sure, find there are even more bills that have been introduced since *Roe* against *Wade*. My prepared statement lists 490 bills that have been introduced.

This only represents the number of primary, substantive bills that have been introduced. The number does not include any riders or amendments to bills that do not directly deal with abortion. As you know, that has been the major way that profile legislators have been able to get some protection before Congress, through amendments and riders.

It also does not include the many appropriations or budget measures, such as the Hyde amendment or the Ashbrook amendments, which have been introduced in Congress every year since 1974 and which have involved the House of Representatives and the Senate in some very draining and very heated legislative battles.

I have not yet mentioned the joint resolutions that have been introduced in Congress, proposing constitutional amendments. For instance, in calendar year 1981 alone—that is, the 97th Congress first session—there were 23 separate joint resolutions introduced, proposing constitutional amendments. In both the House and Senate, extensive hearings have been held dealing with those.

I have not yet mentioned the memorials to Congress from State legislatures, requesting Congress to propose antiabortion amendments. Since 1973, at least 23 State legislatures have sent memorials to Congress of that nature. Furthermore, 19 State legislatures have passed and sent to Congress petitions asking Congress to convene a constitutional convention for the purpose of proposing an antiabortion amendment to the Constitution.

The burden upon Congress has been profound. A tremendous number of requests and attempts, and what has come out of it—well, again, a comparison between pre-*Roe* and post-*Roe* legislation is instructive. Currently, there is in the U.S. Code four statutes or sections of the U.S. Code that deal with abortion that were enacted before 1973. However, again, all of them were enacted or amended after 1970 when this judicialization, judicial constitutionalization, began to occur.

However, since *Roe* against *Wade* was decided, at least seven additional pieces of legislation enacting or amending four other sections of the U.S. Code have been passed by Congress.

In other words, the conclusion is very apparent that there has been a tremendous increase in the burden upon Congress to deal with an issue that it did not deal with in any major respect, only in peripheral ways—that is, only incidentally—before *Roe* against *Wade*.

Now, I think that that represents a very profound shift because it deprives the States of the opportunity to do what State legislatures do best, and it gets the courts involved in doing what courts do not do well at all, and that is to legislate and determine legislative policy. It takes away from the local people what local government can do best and puts on Congress what it is very difficult for Congress to do, and that is to deal with local sentiments, local attitudes, and local values.

Finally, I recommend that Congress enact a constitutional amendment reversing *Roe* against *Wade* and restoring the constitutional balance of powers that existed before that decision. There are a number of verbal formulations that could be used to accomplish that purpose. I do not think it is essential to use any particular set of words to achieve this restoration.

However, I believe the first sentence of Senate Joint Resolution 3 would do the job nicely. That sentence provides, "A right to abortion is not secured by this Constitution." The effect of adopting this or similar language would be to achieve a restoration of the crucial constitutional allocation of powers. I can explain why this is so by contrasting what the language would do with what it would not do.

In my prepared remarks, Mr. Chairman, I have 10 points describing what this language would do and 10 points describing what it would not do. In the interest of time, I will not read those now, but let me just touch on three or four on both sides.

One, I believe that it is clear that it would repeal the rule that the Constitution protects a woman's right to abortion. It would directly repeal the Court's holding that a woman has a fundamental right to determine whether or not to terminate her pregnancy.

Another point, it would restore to the States their general police power to restrict and prohibit abortions. The States could enact legislation to the same extent they could prior to *Roe*.

It would disestablish—only disestablish—and not establish constitutional rights. It would not establish any new constitutional rights. In essence, the amendment does not attempt to say what balance between the interests of the unborn and the interests of the pregnant women is established by the Constitution, if any, but it makes clear what balance is not—namely, that there is no right to abortion.

Finally, it would restore the constitutional balance of power between the States and the Federal Government and between the legislative and judicial branches of Government. It would restore the status quo ante *Roe* insofar as the power and responsibility to resolve abortion issues is concerned.

Now, what it would not do, again there are 10 points, but let me just touch on about four of them. It would not compel or prohibit the adoption by any State legislature or by Congress of any legislation restricting abortion. Again, at this point, I must allude to a statement that Professor Tribe made about truth in labeling. He said this would only allow the enactment of laws outlawing abortion. That is true. But it would not require the enactment of such laws. This simply returns the issue to the States. His statement, I think, assumes that if the States do nothing, and if there is no law, that abortions would not be legal. Well, it would take some judicial creativity, or at least some constitutional reasoning that it does not presently exist to reach that point.

Moreover, Senate Joint Resolution 3, in its first sentence, would not preclude judicial review of abortion laws. It would not prohibit a court from holding a proabortion law unconstitutional, as inadequate, for instance, under the fourteenth amendment, nor would it prevent a court from holding some abortion restrictions unconstitutional if that restriction violated other constitutional provisions, unless to do so would effectively create a right to abortion.

What I am saying is that racially discriminatory abortion laws could be invalidated, but not ordinary abortion restrictions.

This approach, which Senator Eagleton endorsed this morning, would not give the States any new authority to regulate abortion either. Their general police powers to regulate abortion would be restored, but would not be enhanced. In short, it would not alter the constitutional allocation of power between the Federal and State governments or between the legislative and judicial branches.

Thus, an amendment that contains only the first sentence of Senate Joint Resolution 3 or similar language would be a very modest amendment. It would simply restore the constitutional balance of powers with respect to abortions. That is precisely what it should do. Congress should not now try to do more. To try to do more at this time would be to embrace the same mistake the Supreme Court committed when it decided *Roe* v. *Wade* as it did. That mistake consists of shifting the balance of powers, abandoning our faith in and losing our vision of the fundamental tenets of the Constitution. What is sorely needed today is a restoration of those principles and a reaffirmation of those ideals.

It has been said that generations come into possession of ideas about law and government as they come into possession of public buildings—they call them their own and forget who built them and for what purpose. To our generation has fallen the special challenge of maintaining the balance of powers under the Constitution. We must not forget the reasons why the founders of our government erected a system of checks and balances. It is of utmost importance that Congress restore the balance with respect to the power to establish State policies concerning and enact local regulation of abortion.

I respectfully urge the members of this subcommittee and all Members of the Senate to pass a constitutional amendment that will reverse *Roe* against *Wade*.

Thank you, Senator.

Senator HATCH. Well, thank you, Professor Wardle. May I also say that you have grasped well my intent for the first ten words of Senate Joint Resolution 3.

In your opinion, then, would this 10-word standard that Senator Eagleton discussed earlier and that is the first sentence in my amendment have any detrimental effect on other established legal doctrines, such as the right to privacy?

Professor WARDLE. No, it would not. The phrase that is used in the first 10 words is, "A right to abortion * * *," and that clearly distinguishes, focuses, and narrows the subject of the repealer; namely, a right of a woman to choose to terminate her pregnancy, only that one manifestation of the right of privacy. Family privacy cases, the contraception cases, and other privacy doctrines would not be affected at all.

Senator HATCH. I agree. How would this amendment affect statutes designed to regulate postviability statutes?

Professor WARDLE. This amendment would restore the power of the States to protect all human life. It would reinstate the right of the State legislatures to enact laws that would prohibit late-term abortions.

Senator HATCH. In your opinion, do these 10 words reverse or do away with *Roe* v. *Wade*?

Professor WARDLE. Clearly, they do.

Senator HATCH. What effect, in your opinion, would these 10 words have upon court rulings that relied upon *Roe*?

Professor WARDLE. They would be a dead letter in the law.

Senator HATCH. For instance, *Doe* v. *Bolton*, that reversed the Georgia statute requiring a physician to find an abortion necessary—what would happen to that case?

Professor WARDLE. It would become a dead letter in the law. Senator, I think that Professor Tribe and I agree on that point, that *Roe* and its progeny would clearly be repealed.

Senator HATCH. So we could just go through every one of those cases, including *Planned Parenthood* v. *Danforth*, and they would be reversed or done away with?

Professor WARDLE. Exactly. *Doe, Planned Parenthood, Collautti*, the whole kit-and-caboodle.

Senator HATCH. What authority will the Federal Government retain with respect to abortion in the event that this amendment is ratified—let us say, the 10 words that Senator Eagleton was talking about?

Professor WARDLE. Well, again, I think Senator Eagleton answered that question correctly when he said there would be a restoration of the power that existed in Congress before 1973, before *Roe* v. *Wade*. The scope of that power is limited. There is no delegation in the Constitution to Congress of the authority directly to deal with abortion, and yet there are other provisions of the Constitution, and Congress can enact necessary and appropriate legislation under the "necessary and proper" clause, under the interstate commerce clause, and so forth.

Before *Roe* against *Wade*, there were four statutes on the books, but again, they were peripheral. The power of taxation, of course, would remain. So I would say it would be an incidental power, a power to regulate incidentally, but not a power to regulate directly. Remember, Congress does not have a general police power.

Senator HATCH. It would have a residual power.

Professor WARDLE. Precisely.

Senator HATCH. So, basically, if those 10 words were adopted and ratified, this issue would really, in precise terms, go back to the States?

Professor WARDLE. Precisely. That is my belief. There would still be some residual, to use your term, Senator—I think that is correct—some residual responsibility of Congress. For instance, in funding, how Federal funds are used has to be determined by Congress. But as to police power, regulation, prohibition, the burden would shift back upon the States; the primary burden would fall to them.

Senator HATCH. Well, thank you, Professor Wardle. We are going to submit questions to you, as well, and keep the record open so that any member of this subcommittee or full Judiciary Committee can submit questions to you. We appreciate you making this effort to be here with us, and we particularly appreciate the extensive work you went to in preparing the long, but very good statement you have.

Professor WARDLE. Thank you, Senator.

Senator HATCH. So we will be pleased to print that complete written statement in all detail, including all footnotes.

We appreciate it, and thank you very much for coming.

With that, we will recess this committee until next week.

[Whereupon, at 11:45 a.m., the subcommittee was adjourned.]

[The prepared statement of Prof. Lynn D. Wardle follows:]

Prepared Statement of Lynn Wardle*

Restoring the Constitutional Balance: The Need for a Constitutional Amendment to Reverse Roe v. Wade

I am very honored to participate in these important hearings. I commend the members of this committee for facing the issue of the constitutionality of abortion and abortion restrictions. I believe that the record being made today and during the remainder of these proceedings will be an historic document. The importance of the work that has been begun by the members of this Subcommittee is recognized already by thoughtful citizens throughout the nation, and in the years to come the recommendations of this Subcommittee and the further action of the Senate Judiciary Committee and of the Senate will be acknowledged to the credit or discredit of every member of the 98th Congress.

I appear before the Subcommittee today to recommend that it propose and that the Senate pass an Amendment to the Constitution reversing *Roe v. Wade*, 410 U.S. 113 (1973). Because of the sensitive nature of the abortion dilemma, and because of the sensitive nature of amending the Constitution, I would prefer not having to make this recommendation. But an appropriate respect for our constitutional system does not require that Congress shrink from every confrontation with the other coequal branches of the federal government. Rather, a proper regard for our constitutional system of checks and balances will compel Congress to respond when, as in the present circumstances, the Supreme Court unilaterally and continuously acts in such a manner that the constitutional balance and allocation of powers is threatened.

A decade has passed since *Roe v. Wade* was decided—a decade in which the federal courts have faced a flood of abortion litigation, in which Congress has faced a deluge of abortion-related proposals and in which the number of abortions performed annually has increased to over 1.5 million (and the number of total abortions performed in the country since *Roe* is approaching 15 million). Moreover, as many commentators had predicted, since *Roe* there has been a profound and appalling increase in the incidence of inhumane acts that manifest a disregard for, and even involve the destruction of, other forms of unwanted, defenseless human life. Not only are human beings who bear the stigma of the label "defective" because of some potential mental or physical condition being ruthlessly destroyed before birth, but since *Roe* they have increasingly become the victims of infanticide through "selective nontreatment." Nor is it surprising to find that human beings belonging to racial minorities are being denied the opportunities of life in egregiously disproportionate numbers. (The poor and "unwanted" have always been the victims of such "evenhanded" rules of laws.) And while these abusive practices have reached shocking extremes, the Supreme Court has repeatedly refused to reconsider *Roe v. Wade*. I feel to echo the sentiments of the English statesman and orator, Edmund Burke, who is reported to have said: "An event is happening about which it is difficult to speak, but about which it is impossible to remain silent."[1]

Review of Roe v. Wade

The source of the current Constitutional dilemma is *Roe v. Wade*, 410 U.S. 113 (1973). So that is where my remarks must begin. In *Roe v. Wade*, the Supreme

Court of the United States declared the abortion laws of Texas to be unconstitutional. In the course of its opinion, the Supreme Court made four very important points.

First, the Supreme Court announced a new constitutional right: the right of abortion privacy. Beginning with certain precedents which recognized a constitutional right of privacy in very limited situations, the Court held that a pregnant woman has a fundamental constitutional right to decide "whether or not to terminate her pregnancy."[2] Under established standards of judicial review, laws that infringe upon fundamental constitutional rights will only be upheld if they are necessary to effectuate compelling state interests. Thus, the new right recognized by the Court was immediately established as an extraordinarily important personal right.

Second, the Court held that the people have no compelling interest to prohibit abortion generally. The Court rejected the argument that states have a compelling interest in protecting the lives of unborn persons because it found that the unborn are not persons in a constitutional sense. Likewise, it rejected the argument that states have a compelling interest in maternal health sufficient to justify even medical regulation of abortions before the end of the first trimester. It also rejected the argument that there is a compelling interest in preventing the destruction of unborn human life before viability, because philosophers, theologians, and the justices could not say with certainty when life begins.

Third, the Court concluded that states must permit abortion on demand, at least until viability. The Court defined, in regulatory detail, a trimester scheme of constitutional abortion regulation. Only after viability (approximately at the beginning of the third trimester) may states generally prohibit abortion, and then they must (the Court has never explained why) permit any abortion that is necessary to preserve the life or the health of the mother. Before viability, states may not interfere with a pregnant woman's decision to have an abortion for any reason—or for no reason at all. During the second trimester, however, health and sanitation regulations can be enforced to the extent they are necessary to ensure that abortions are safely performed. During the first trimester, virtually no regulation of abortion is constitutionally permissible.

Fourth, the Supreme Court effectively declared that all abortion laws are unconstitutional. The judgment in *Roe v. Wade* invalidated the nineteenth century abortion law which were then in effect in Texas. The judgment in the companion case, *Doe v. Bolton*, 410 U.S. 179 (1973), likewise invalidated major portions of Georgia's recently enacted abortion law, which was based upon the progressive Model Penal Code. Taken together the rulings that day effectively invalidated, totally or in part, abortion restrictions in all 50 states and the District of Columbia.[3]

Roe v. Wade, was the beginning, not the end, of a chain of revolutionary changes in American Law. Those enormous changes have been discussed in an enormous body of literature to which both Professor Tribe and I have contributed. But today I wish to focus on two particular changes or types of changes that have resulted directly from *Roe v. Wade*, and on the disastrous consequences of each.

The Supreme Court Caused the Constitutional Balance of Powers to Shift When it Decided *Roe* v. *Wade* As It Did

In my opinion, *Roe v. Wade* has caused a dangerous shift in the balance of powers and in the fundamental values upon which this government is founded. It is necessary to reverse *Roe v. Wade* to restore the constitutional balance of powers and to restore the fundamental values upon which our government and our society are founded.

As a direct result of the Supreme Court's decision in *Roe v. Wade*, two profound changes have occurred in the delicate balance of powers of government. First, there has been a significant shift of power and responsibility from the states to the federal government, which has substantially increased Congressional involvement in and responsibility for abortion policy. Second, there has been a significant shift in policy-making power from the legislative branch generally to the judicial branch.

Our constitutional system of governments is based upon the principle that a concentration of powers in any one branch of government or at any one level of government is a dangerous thing. The drafters of the Constitution were persuaded by Montesquieu who warned that "men entrusted with power tend to abuse it."[4] The Constitution was drafted and defended in light of Montesquieu's arguments for limiting the role of a central government,[5] and his warning that "[t]here can be no liberty" if the executive, legislative and judicial powers are not separated.[6] The authors of the Constitution were clearly convinced that fragmentation of governmental power was necessary to secure individual liberty.[7]

To prevent a concentration of power in any one branch or level of government, the drafters of the Constitution divided the power of government two ways. They alloted only specific and limited powers to the national government, all remaining powers being reserved to the states. And they specifically divided the powers of the national government among the legislative, executive, and judicial branches. *Roe v. Wade* has substantially affected the balance of powers in both respects.

A Loss of the Power of Self-Government   The most immediate and obvious impact of abortion decisions has been the aggrandizement of federal judicial power. By giving the right to choose abortion the status of a *fundamental* constitutional right, the Supreme Court substantially restricted the authority of the legislative branch to legislate concerning the subject, and substantially increased the responsibility of the judiciary for defining and monitoring regulation of the new fundamental right. The standard of judicial review of ordinary legislation is really quite modest. However if someone claims that a law interferes with their exercise of a "fundamental" constitutional right, then the standard of judicial review is much stricter. Thus, by declaring that a pregnant woman has a fundamental constitutional right to choose whether or not to have an abortion, the Supreme Court gave the judiciary substantially greater role and, conversely, left the legislatures with substantially less authority, to regulate abortion.

Perhaps the magnitude of the tremendous shift in responsibility is best evidenced by the dramatic explosion in federal court abortion litigation. During the entire decade before *Roe v. Wade* was decided, there was a total of only *18* opinions published by all federal courts in all cases dealing with abortion or abortion regulations.[8] However, in the decade since *Roe* there have been *nearly 200* published opinions—more than a tenfold increase.[9] And that represents only the number of federal court opinions that have been published.[10] There has been a similar dramatic jump in the number of state court cases dealing with abortion since *Roe v. Wade* was decided.[11]

The scope of these abortion cases has likewise mushroomed to incredible proportions in the last decade. The pre-*Roe* cases dealt, for the most part, with the question of whether or not traditional nineteenth century abortion laws were constitutionally too narrow. Since *Roe*, however, the federal court cases have dealt with such diverse subjects as domestic relations (the rights of parents or spouses to participate in the abortion decision), zoning, advertising, religious liberty, the licensing of doctors, hospitals, and clinics, burial, informed consent, the expenditure of public funds, hospital administration, maternal health, the definition of viability, methods of abortion, hospital record keeping, etc.[12]

As the breadth of the abortion cases has expanded, so also has the depth and detail of the questions which the courts have been called upon to resolve. *Roe* only described this new constitutional right of abortion privacy in broad terms. In the decade since *Roe* the advocates of abortion have returned to federal courts over and over again to fill in the details, resulting in the developments by the federal judiciary of a set of rules (all presented as part of the Supreme Law for the Land) that has become increasingly intricate and technical. It is now very apparent that the constitutionalization of abortion is a slippery slope leading ever downward into ever more, and ever more detailed, questions. Can a state require second trimester abortions to be performed in hospitals, if some dialation and evacuation abortions can be safely performed in outpatient clinics? Can a state require that a woman be informed of the facts of fetal development before she agrees to an abortion? What about the likelihood of fetal pain? Is a 24 hour waiting period constitutional? How about a 48 hour waiting period? Can a state require pathological reports following every abortion? Following some of them? All of these issues have been decided by federal courts in the decade since *Roe*, and some of them are presently before the Supreme Court to be decided this term.[13]

As the courts have become increasingly more involved in defining the right to abortion and reviewing abortion regulations, the fundamental question is being asked more frequently: why should the courts, rather than the state legislatures, be deciding these issues? The answer, of course, is that they should not.

Every exercise of the judicial power to invalid legislation affects the relationship between coequal branches of the government.[14] The assumption by the judiciary of a major role in supervising abortion regulation represents a substantial shift in the delicate balance of powers, and must be remedied for three reasons.

First, the judiciary is not well-suited to the task of formulating abortion policy and supervising its enforcement. Professor John Hart Ely wrote that "precisely because the claims involved [in the abortion dispute] are difficult to evaluate, I would not want to entrust to the judiciary the authority to guess about them—certainly not under the guise of enforcing the Constitution."[15] In the same vein, Justice Jackson warned that "judicial usurpation is . . . no more justifiable and no more promising of permanent good to the country than any other kind."[16] The founding fathers emphatically rejected the suggestion that the federal judiciary serve as a "Council of Revision" to pass upon the wisdom of "every act of the

National Legislature before it shall operate. . . ."[17] Nearly two centuries later, that same sentiment was echoed by Judge Learned Hand who wrote: "For myself it would be most irksome to be ruled by a bevy of Platonic Guardians, even if I knew how to choose them, which I assuredly do not."[18] And Justice Felix Frankfurter expressed his strenuous "objection to the imposition by judges of their private notions of social policy upon the . . . states."[19] He was of the opinion that the use of the veto power of the Supreme Court over social legislation was irresponsible and

> *because it so often turns on the fortuitous circumstances which determine a majority decision and shelters the fallible judgment of individual Justices, in matters of fact and opinion not peculiarly within the special competence of judges, behind the impersonable dooms of the Constitution.[20]*

Second, while the power of the Supreme Court to declare unconstitutional legislative acts is necessary, "when employed unwisely or unnecessarily it is also the ultimate threat to the continued effectiveness of the federal courts in performing that role."[21] Repeated confrontation between the life-tenured judiciary and the elected representatives of the people (like those which have been occurring for an entire decade with respect to the limits of abortion regulation) erodes the confidence of self governing people in the judiciary.[22] This problem is compounded when, as in the abortion cases, the justifications given by the Court for its decisions are so obviously political and so unpersuasive.[23] So long as *Roe* remains the rule of law, the source of a continuing constitutional confrontation between the judicial and the political branches remains. That continuing irritation inevitably will provoke a congressional challenge to the independence of the Federal judiciary.

Third, the types of questions that are posed in the abortion controversy are best answered by the legislative branch of government, not the judiciary. The Legislature has a superior ability to discern facts. Unlike the judicial branch, the legislature can take the initiative to ascertain the factual basis upon which resolutions depend. Also, legislators are the elected representatives of the people, and periodically must account to them. Thus, abortion legislation vindicates the right of the people to determine the laws by which they will be governed. Moreover, the legitimacy of the laws is ensured when controversial issues of public policy are exposed to the legislative process and resolved in the fires of the political arena. As the Solicitor General has recently written "[t]he best way to determine who is right and who is wrong on those issues [concerning abortion] is to permit and encourage the imposing sides to exercise their persuasive efforts on state legislators."[24] Justice Jackson voiced concern in these words: "Each such decision [of the Supreme Court to strike down controversial social policy legislation] takes away from our democratic federalism another of its defenses against domestic disorder and violence. The vice of judicial supremacy, as exerted for 90 years in the field of policy, has been its progressive closing of the avenues to peaceful and democratic conciliation of our social and economic conflicts."[25]

Another problem with judicial intervention to settle controversial political questions is that the people

*lose the political experience, and the moral education and stimulus
that comes from fighting the question out in the ordinary way, and
correct in their own errors. . . . The tendancy of the common and
easy resort to this great function, now lamentably too common, is to
dwarf the political capacity of the people and to deaden its sense of
moral responsibility.*[26]

As Justice Powell noted: "[w]e should be ever mindful of the predictions that
would arise if a democracy were to permit general oversight of the elected
branches of government by a nonrepresentative and in large measure insulated,
judicial branch."[27]

Increased Congressional Workload   Ironically, the Supreme Court usurpation of a major legislative function regarding abortion has not lessened the
legislative burden of Congress. In fact, it has substantially increased the amount
of legislative resources Congress has been forced to devote to the numerous
abortion issues generated by *Roe v. Wade. Roe v. Wade* shifted the balance of
power and responsibility for abortion away from the states and toward the federal
government.

In *Roe v. Wade* the Supreme Court constitutionalized the abortion controversy. That made it a national issue. And that means that it is an unavoidable
concern and responsibility of Congress. Abortion will continue to be a major
responsibility of Congress until *Roe v. Wade* is overturned.

Involvement of Congress with any particular subject that is ordinarily dealt
with by the states dramatically increases whenever the state power to regulate
that subject matter is restricted by the Supreme Court. Not only is this true when
the Supreme Court approves an expansion of federal legislative domain at the
expense of state legislative authority,[28] but even when the state legislative
authority is reduced by the Supreme Court in the name of preserving individual
liberties the impact is felt in Congress.[29] This is so for three reasons. First, when
state legislative authority is reduced, the relative size and importance of federal
legislative power is enhanced. Second, if states are powerless directly to regulate
a subject, the well-established ability of Congress to regulate indirectly subjects
that they cannot directly regulate is an irresistable invitation to federal lobbying.
Third, when the Supreme Court restricts state legislative authority in the name of
preserving individual liberties, the source of the restrictions that it is imposing is
federal law, namely the United States constitution. For these reasons, since *Roe
v. Wade*, there has been a tremendous increase in the pressure on Congress to
address abortion questions.

The best evidence of the shift in power and responsibility for regulating
abortion to the federal government, and to Congress in particular, is data
concerning abortion-related legislation that has been introduced or passed by
Congress. There has been a dramatic, persistent increase in the demand upon
Congress to deal with abortions since *Roe*.

For instance, preliminary research reveals that during the entire decade
before the Supreme Court decided *Roe v. Wade*, only ten bills were introduced in
Congress relating to abortion.[30] (Moreover, all ten of these bills were introduced
after the federal courts began to invalidate abortion restrictions. The first bill was
introduced in 1970, the same year that a federal district court in Texas held the
Texas Abortion Laws to be unconstitutional in *Roe v. Wade*, 314 F.Supp. 1217

(N.D. Tex. 1970). So even most of early federal legislative involvement with abortion was not until after the federal judiciary had begun to invalidate state abortion restrictions.)

By contrast, *in the decade since Roe v. Wade was decided, nearly 500 separately numbered bills dealing in some way with abortion have been introduced to Congress!* The congressional workload has increased by approximately 1000 percent!

During the Ninety-Third Congress (1973-1974) a total of 93 separately-numbered pieces of legislation were introduced, 90 in the House of Representatives and three in the Senate.[31] Forty-five of the measures proposed Amendments to the Constitution to overturn *Roe v. Wade* in that respect,[32] seventeen proposed various protections for the rights of conscience of those opposed to abortion,[33] fifteen proposed investigation of the impact of *Roe*,[34] eight proposed restrictions on abortion or fetal experimentation,[35] five proposed to limit the jurisdiction of the federal courts in some manner, one proposed a restriction on abortion funding,[36] another proposed a congressional definition of personhood,[37] and one pro-choice proposal was introduced. However, no abortion-related piece of legislation was enacted.

During the Ninety-Fourth Congress (1975–1976) 100 separately-numbered pieces of legislation relating to abortion were introduced, 89 in the House of Representatives and eleven in the Senate.[38] Seventy-eight of the measures introduced proposed Amendments to the Constitution to overturn *Roe v. Wade* in some respect,[39] eleven related to investigations or education regarding the impact of *Roe*,[40] four proposed to limit the jurisdiction of the federal courts,[41] another four proposed restrictions on the federal funding of abortion,[42] one proposed restrictions on abortion or fetal experimentation,[43] one related to population research or family planning,[44] and one related to protecting the rights of conscience of those opposed to abortion.[45] Two of the proposals were enacted, one restricting the expenditure of public funds for abortion,[46] and the other protecting welfare recipients against being coerced into abortion.[47]

During the Ninety-Fifth Congress (1977–1978) 125 separately numbered pieces of legislation relating to abortion were introduced, 102 in the House of Representatives and 23 in the Senate.[48] Sixty-five of the measures proposed Amendments to the Constitution to overturn *Roe v. Wade* in some respect,[49] 21 proposed restrictions on the expenditure of public funds for abortion,[50] seven proposed protection for the rights of conscientious objectors to abortion,[51] three dealt with international affairs concerning abortion,[52] two proposed investigations relating to the consequences of *Roe*,[53] two proposed limits on the jurisdiction of federal courts relating to abortion,[54] two concerned pregnancy-related benefits,[55] two dealt with alternatives to abortion,[56] two proposed to limit the authority of the (prochoice) Civil Rights Commission regarding abortion,[57] one proposed modifying the criminal code concerning abortion,[58] and one other proposed a National Day of Atonement. Additionally, eighteen of the proposals could be labeled "prochoice," including ten proposals relating to family planning and teenage pregnancy,[59] six proposals authorizing abortion counseling or services,[60] and one proposal to repeal a Legal Service Corporation restriction concerning abortion.[61] Nine of the bills containing prolife provisions became law, including five abortion funding restrictions,[62] one act protecting rights of conscience,[63] one concerning pregnancy benefits,[64] one concerning foreign assistance,[65] and one limiting the authority of the Civil Rights Commission.[66]

During the Ninety-Sixth Congress (1979–1980) a total of seventy-four separately numbered pieces of legislation relating to abortion were introduced, including sixty-six in the House of Representatives and eight in the Senate.[67] Thirty-six of them proposed Amendments to the Constitution to overturn *Roe v. Wade*,[68] twenty proposed various restrictions on the federal funding of abortions,[69] five proposed protections for rights of conscience,[70] four proposed restrictions on the jurisdiction of the federal courts,[71] four proposed parental involvement in the abortion decisions of minors or other protections for family life,[72] two concerned the creation of the Department of Education,[73] one proposed to limit certain activities of the Legal Services Corporation,[74] and two were prochoice proposals relating to family planning and teenage pregnancy.[75] Nine of the bills containing prolife provisions became law including seven abortion funding restrictions,[76] one bill protecting rights of conscience,[76A] and one pertaining to the newly created Department of Education.[77]

During the Ninety-Seventh Congress (1981–1982) eighty-three separately numbered pieces of legislation relating to abortion were introduced, fifty-eight in the House of Representatives and twenty-six in the Senate.[78] Twenty-six of the measures proposed Amendments to the Constitution to overturn *Roe v. Wade*,[79] thirty-four of the measures proposed restrictions on the funding of abortions,[80] eight proposed parental involvement or other protections for family life,[81] four proposed Human Life Bills defining personhood,[82] three others solely restricted the jurisdiction of federal courts,[83] three related to fetal research or experimentation restrictions,[84] one proposed further protections for rights of conscience,[85] one pertained to Legal Service Corporation activities,[86] and two other measures were prochoice family planning or teenage pregnancy proposals.[87] Eight of the proposals restricting the use of public funds for abortion were enacted.[88]

In the first month of the Ninety-Eighth Congress (January, 1983) fifteen separately numbered pieces of legislation relating to abortion were introduced, ten in the House of Representatives and five in the Senate.[89] Ten measures proposed Amendments to the Constitution to overturn *Roe v. Wade*,[90] three proposed permanent restrictions on the federal funding of abortion,[91] and two proposed Human Life Bills defining personhood.[92]

Additional mention must be made of the Memorials to Congress from state legislators requesting Congress to propose an anti-abortion amendment to the Constitution. Since 1923, at least 23 state legislatures have sent such memorials to Congress.[93] Additionally, 19 state legislators have passed and sent to Congress Petitions asking Congress to convene a constitutional convention for the purpose of proposing an anti-abortion Amendment to the Constitution.[94]

Thus, the evidence is clear and it yields these undeniable conclusions: *Roe v. Wade* has resulted in increased public demand for Congress to become involved in regulating abortion. *Roe v. Wade* has shifted onto Congress a major new area of legislative responsibility.

To date, Congress has not been particularly receptive to proposed prolife legislation. Nevertheless, despite its lack of enthusiasm for handling this "hot potato," Congress has repeatedly become enmeshed in considering the details of various abortion regulations. And it has enacted some substantive legislation dealing with peripheral abortion issues.

Again, a comparison between pre- and post-*Roe* activity is instructive. Presently there are four different statutes in the United States Code which were enacted before 1973 that deal with abortion.[95] (However, all were enacted or amended since 1970, which is when the federal courts began to invalidate state laws prohibiting abortion.) In the decade since *Roe v. Wade* was decided, at least twenty-eight additional pieces of legislation, containing prolife provisions have been passed by Congress.[96] Clearly, abortion has become a congressional concern.

Finally, one of the most repugnant consequences of the Supreme Court abortion decisions has been their effect to shut off the opportunity for innovation and experimentation by the states. Once a social issue like abortion has been "constitutionalized" the anemic orthodoxy of judicially mandated conformity replaces the vital pluralism of constitutional federalism.

In *Roe v. Wade* the Court acknowledged that a central question in assessing the constitutionality of abortion laws concerns when human life begins. The Court noted a "wide divergence of thinking" among philosophers, doctors, and theologians about when life begins. 410 U.S. at 160. Moreover, the Court acknowledged that it was not in a position to resolve the question either. *Id.* It seems, therefore, incredible that the Court proceeded to override the long-debated, extensively-reviewed abortion laws that had been adopted in all states. It is particularly ironic that just a few months later the same Court declared, with regard to another deeply controversial issue:

> "The ultimate wisdom as to these [issues] is not likely to be defined for all time even by the scholars who are now so earnestly debating [them]. In such circumstances, the judiciary is well advised to refrain from imposing upon the States inflexible constitutional restraints that could circumscribe or handicap the continued research and experimentation so vital to finding even partial solutions . . . and to keeping abreast of ever changing conditions.[97]

This approach is essential to the democratic process of searching for truth because whenever an issue is constitutionalized, it is removed from the refining democratic process. "Constitutionalization eliminates all but one of the competing points of view as acceptable alternatives; the issue is removed from the realm of public debate and decision making.[98] Over sixty years ago, during the hayday of another era of substitutive due process, Justice Holmes wrote:

> "There is nothing that I more depreciate than the use of the Fourteenth Amendment beyond the absolute compulsion of its words to prevent the making of social experiments that an important part of the community desires, in the insulated chambers afforded by the several States, even though the experiments may seem futile or even naucous to me and to those whose judgments I most respect."[99]

A few years later, Justice Frankfurter echoed that concern. He wrote:

"The veto power of the Supreme Court over the social-economic legislation of the States, thus exercised through the due process clause, is the most vulnerable aspect of undue centralization. It is . . . the most destructive, because judicial nullification on grounds of constitutionality stops experimentation at its source, and bars increase to the fund of social knowledge by scientific tests of trial and error. . . . The inclination of a single Justice or two, the tip of his mind or his fears, may determine the opportunity of a much needed social experiment to survive, or may frustrate for a long time intelligent attempts to deal with a social evil."[100]

These sentiments were summed up eloquently by Justice Brandeis a few years later in his famous dissenting opinion in *New States Ice Co. v. Liebmann*, 285 U.S. 262, 311 (1932) (Brandeis J. dissenting):

To stay experimentation in things social and economic is a grave responsibility. Denial of the right to experiment may be fraught with serious consequences to the Nation. It is one of the happy incidents of the federal system that a single courageous State may come if its citizens choose, serve as a laboratory, and try novel social and economic experiments without risk to the rest of the country. *This Court has the power to prevent this experiment . . . We have the power to do this, because the due process clause has been held by the Court applicable to matters of substantive law as well as to matters of procedure. By in the exercise of this high power, we must be ever on our guard, lest we erect of prejudices into legal principles."* (Emphasis added.)

There is no better evidence of the reality of the stifling, suffocating effects of substitutive process than the abortion decisions of the Supreme Court. The Supreme Court abortion decisions destroyed a healthy, democratic dialogue on abortion. During the 1960's a significant tendency to liberalize abortion laws was developing throughout the United States. In 1962 the American Law Institute published its proposed Model Penal Code recommending that the exceptions to anti-abortion laws be increased. By 1972, fourteen states had liberalized their abortion laws in a manner responsive to Model Penal Code. Four more states had gone even further and legalized abortion on demand during a certain period early in pregnancy. In fact, in less than seven years between 1966 and 1972, a total of 18 states liberalized their abortion laws and most, if not all, of the other state legislatures had considered abortion reform proposals.[101]

Roe v. Wade ended all of that. Since 1973 all states have had to conform to the same model of abortion privacy. No state legislature can restrict or regulate abortion in a way that deviates from the official rules announced by the federal courts. Abortions are obtainable as freely in Utah as in New York, with little or no room for variation to account for local conditions, circumstances, values, attitudes, or innovation.

The authors and defenders of *Roe v. Wade* would have us believe that this is necessary because democracy had failed with regard to the abortion controversy.

But the facts do not support that claim. The truth of the matter is that our constitutional system was working beautifully in the abortion controversy. Democratic processes were functioning. What went wrong is that the Supreme Court failed.

Restoring the Balance by Constitutional Amendment   I recommend that Congress enact a constitutional amendment reversing *Roe v. Wade* and restoring constitutional balance of powers that existed before that decision. There are a number of verbal formulations by which that could be accomplished. I do not think it is essential to use any particular set of words to achieve this restoration. But I believe that the first sentence of S.J.Res 3 would do the job nicely. That sentence provides: "A right to abortion is not secured by this Constitution." The effect of adopting this or similar language which would be to achieve a restoration of the crucial constitutional allocation of powers. I can explain why this is so by contrasting what this language would and would not do.

Adoption of the first sentence of S.J.Res 3 would accomplish ten things.

1. It would repeal the rule that the constitution protects a woman's rights to abortion. In *Roe*, the Court held that a woman's decision whether or not to terminate her pregnancy" is a fundamental right protected by the constitution. The first sentence of S.J.Res 3 directly repeals that.
2. It uses the phrase "a right to abortion." That phrase has been used in over 80 federal court decisions as shorthand for the constitutional right created in Roe and its progeny, i.e., the right of a woman to chose whether or not to have an abortion without undue state interference.
3. It would prevent the creation of any other right to abortion in the harbor of any other provision of the constitution. The article "a" makes the scope of the repeal broader than if the article "the" were used. "The" might be construed as limiting the repealer as to "the" particular doctrine of law that has developed in Roe and its progeny. Use of the article "a" makes it declare that no other "right to abortion" is sheltered by the Constitution.
4. It would avoid the unnecessary repudiation of the doctrine of privacy. The use of the carefully phrased "right to abortion" makes it clear that the amendment repeals only the abortion decisions. Other extensions of the right of privacy, such as in the contraception cases and the family privacy cases, would not be repealed.
5. It would mean that laws impinging upon the abortion decision would be examined under the ordinary standard of judicial review (unless they infringe other constitutional rights which do not constitute a "right to abortion"—e.g., law prohibiting only black women from obtaining abortions would still be examined under a strict scrutiny test because of the racial discrimination. Inasmuch as the Supreme Court has repeatedly acknowledged that states have a strong legitimate interest in protecting potential life throughout pregnancy, laws protecting right to life of the unborn would necessarily be upheld as rationally related to those profound interests.[102]
6. It would repudiate implicitly all of the bag and baggage of *Roe* and its progeny. The ludicrous statement that the law does not recognize the

personhood of the unborn as well as subsequent holdings such as those prohibiting parental and spousal participation in the abortion decision, and postliability abortion restrictions would become dead letters in the law.

7. It would restore to the states their general police power to restrict and prohibit abortion. The states could enact legislation to the same extent that they could prior to *Roe*. The right of the people to protect human life would be revived.

8. It would restore Congress' limited power to restrict and prohibit abortion (mostly through indirect means) as necessary and appropriate to perform its constitutional responsibilities to control interstate commerce, federal lands, federal taxation, spending, etc.

9. It would disestablish a class or type of constitutional right. It would not establish any new constitutional rights. In essence, the Amendment does not attempt to say what balance between the interests of the unborn and the interests of the pregnant woman is established by the Constitution, if any, but it makes clear what balance is not established (i.e., there is no right to abortion).

10. It would restore the constitutional balance of power between the states and the federal government and between the legislative and judicial branches of government. In sum, it would restore the *status quo ante Roe* insofar as the power and responsibility to resolve abortion issues is concerned.

It is equally important to acknowledge what the first sentence of S.J.Res 3, or similar language, would *not* do.

1. It would not establish any new constitutional right. It would only reestablish the right of the people to protect the unborn, as it existed before *Roe*.

2. It would not prohibit the Supreme Court from interpreting the Fourteenth Amendment to protect all humans, including the unborn. The only right that could not be distilled from the Constitution would be a "right to abortion."

3. It would not compel or prohibit the adoption by any state legislature or by Congress of any legislation restricting abortion.

4. It would not preclude judicial review of abortion laws. It would not prohibit a court from holding proabortion laws unconstitutional.

5. It would not prevent a court from holding some abortion restrictions unconstitutional if they violated other constitutional provisions, unless to do so would effectively create a "right to abortion." Thus, racially discriminatory abortion laws could be invalidated, but not ordinary abortion restrictions.

6. It would not affect state constitutions. It would not prohibit the citizens in any state from adoption (or, for that matter, any state supreme court from creating) a right to abortion under the state constitution.

7. It would not give Congress any power directly to restrict or prohibit abortion.

8. It would not deprive Congress of its limited constitutional authority to regulate abortion (mostly by indirect means) under its authority to regular interstate commerce, control federal lands, to tax, to spend, etc.

9. It would not give the states any new authority to regulate abortion, either. Their general police powers to regulate abortion would be restored, but would not be enhanced.

10. In short, it would restore but not alter the constitutional allocation of power between the federal and state governments, or between the legislative and judicial branches.

Some ask: Is it not possible that language such as the first sentence of S.J.Res 3 might be construed by hostile judges in such a manner as to not restore the power to restrict and prohibit abortion? The answer is yes and no.

If the question is approached as if we are playing a game and the object is to completely evade the plain meaning and clear intent of the language used, the answer, of course, must be yes. But if those are the ground rules, then the same would be true of any verbal formulation. The nature and limits of human language are such that it is utterly impossible to prevent an intelligent person from intentionally distorting the meaning of any language. So any *language* used in *any amendment* could be intentionally misconstrued by designing judges. But, of course, the drafters of the Constitution realized that the potential for mischief such as this would always exist and they included an impeachment clause in the Constitution.

More realistically, assuming the integrity of federal judges and assuming that they will be faithful to their oaths of office, and uphold the Constitution despite their personal disdain for the democratic principles embodied therein, that is an entirely different matter. Under those circumstances, the answer is no—it is not reasonably possible that the first sentence of S.J.Res 3 or similar language would not reverse *Roe v. Wade* and restore the right of the people to restrict and prohibit abortion. (Those who cannot accept these assumptions either misjudge the integrity of the men and women who sit on the federal bench, or they fail to appreciate the importance of congressional committee reports which clarify the meaning and intent of Constitutional Amendments.)

Thus, an amendment that contained only the first sentence of S.J.Res 3 would be a very modest amendment. It would simply restore the constitutional balance of powers with respect to abortion. That is precisely what it should do. Congress should not now try to do more. To try to do more would be to embrace the same mistake the Supreme Court committed when it decided *Roe v. Wade* as it did. That mistakes consists of abandoning our faith in and losing our vision of the fundamental tenets of the Constitution. What is sorely needed today is a restoration of those principles and a reaffirmation of those ideals.

It has been said that generations come into possession of ideas about law and government as they come into possession of public buildings: they call them "their own" and forget who built them, and for what purposes.[103] To our generation has fallen the special challenge of maintaining the balance and allocation of powers under the Constitution. We must not forget the reasons why the founders of government erected a system of checks and balances. It is of the utmost importance that Congress restore the balance with respect to the power to establish the law governing the practice of abortion. Thus, I respectfully urge the members of this Subcommittee and all members of the Senate to pass a constitutional amendment that will reverse *Roe v. Wade*.

Appendix A. Reported Federal Court Abortion Decision, 1963–1972

Abele v. Markle, 351 F. Supp. 224 (D. Conn. 1972), *vacated*, 410 U.S. 951 (1973) (right to decide cannot be completely abridged by emergency Connecticut statute prohibiting abortion except to save mother's life).

Grossen v. Attorney General of Commonwealth of Kentucky, 344 F. Supp. 587 (Ed. Ky 1972), *vacated*, 410 U.S. 950 (1973) (Kentucky abortion statute not vague and state has a compelling reason for statute).

Abele v. Markle, 342 F. Supp. 800 (D. Conn. 1972) *vacated*, 410 U.S. 941 (1973). (Conn. statute prohibiting all abortions except to preserve life of mother unconstitutional).

Young Women's Christian Association of Princeton, N.J. v. Kugler, 342 F. Supp. 1048, (D. N.J. 1972) *vacated and remanded*, 475 F. 2d 1398 (3rd Cir. 1973).

Poe v. Menghini, 339 F. Supp. 986 (D. Kan. 1972) (held Kansas statute requiring certification of circumstances requiring abortion violated due process and equal protection).

Mitchell Family Planning Inc. v. City of Royal Oak, 335 F. Supp. 738 (E.D. Mich. 1972) (billboard advertisement not a clear and present danger).

Corkey v. Edwards, 322 F. Supp. 1248 (W.D. NC, 1971) *vacated* 410 U.S. 950 (1973) (upheld N.C. abortion statute as not placing unconstitutional burdens or fundamental liberty).

Doe v. Scott, 321 F. Supp. 1385 (N.D. Ill. 1971) (Illinois abortion statute invalid).

Steinberg v. Brown, 321 F. Supp. 741 (N.D. Ohio 1970) (Ohio abortion statute not unconstitutionally vague and does not violate protected right of privacy, or equal protection clause, or cruel and unusual punishment prohibition).

Doe v. Bolton, 319 F. Supp. 1048 (N.D. Ga. 1970) *appeal dismissed*, 402 U.S. 936 (1971), *reversed on other grounds*, 410 U.S. 179 (1973).

Rosen v. Louisiana State Board of Medical Examiners, 318 F. Supp. 1217 (E.D. La. 1970) *vacated*, 412 U.S. 902 (1973) (held statute authorizing removal of physician's certification for aiding an abortion, constitutional).

Roe v. Wade, 314 F. Supp. 1217 (N.D. Tex. 1970) *aff'd in part, rev'd in part*, 410 U.S. 113 (1973) *reh'g denied*, 410 U.S. 959 (1973). (Texas abortion law unconstitutional because deny women their 9th Amend right to choose whether or not to have children).

Doe v. General Hospital, 313 F. Supp. 1170 (D.D.C. 1970) *motion denied*, 434 F. 2d 423 (D.C. Cir. 1970) (injunction against hospital denial of the abortions for mental health reasons).

Babbitz v. McCann, 310 F. Supp. 293 (E.D. Wis. 1970) *appeal dismissed*, 400 U.S. 1 (1970) (upheld Wisconsin statute making it a criminal offense to perform nontherapeutic abortions).

United States v. Vuitch, 305 F. Supp. 1032 (D.D.C. 1969) *reversed*, 402 U.S. 62 (1971) (D.C. abortion statute provisions held invalid for failure to give certainty essential in a criminal statute).

Doe v. General Hospital, 434 F. 2d 423 (D.C. Cir. 1970) (denies motion to find defendant in contempt, but promulgates interim rules allowing therapeutic abortions).

United States v. Vuitch, 402 U.S. 62 (1971) (D.C. abortion statute construed to permit abortions to protect mental health of pregnant women and held not to be void for vagueness).

Wayne v. United States, 318 F.2d 205 (D.C. Cir. 1963) (Evidence substantial conviction for attempted abortion).

Appendix B. Federal Court Abortion Decision Published in official Reports Since June, 1980

A. *U.S. District Court Opinions Dealing With Abortions Published Since June 1980*

Smith v. Bentley, 493 F. Supp. 916 (E.D. Ark. 1980).
Planned Parenthood League of Mass. v. Bellotti, 499 F. Supp. 215 (D. Mass. 1980)
Gary-Northwest Indiana Women's Services, Inc. v. Bowen, 496 F. Supp. 894 (N.D. Ind. 1980)
Leigh v. Olson, 497 F. Supp. 1340 (D.N.D. 1980);
Wolfe v. Stumbo, 519 F. Supp. 22 (W.D. Kent. 1980)
Birth Control Centers, Inc. v. Reizer, 508 F. Supp. 1366 (E.D. Mich. 1981)
Women's Medical Center of Providence, Inc. v. Roberts, 512 F. Supp. 316 (D. R.I. 1981)
American Federation of Government Employees v. Devine, 525 F. Supp. 250 (D.D.C. 1981)
Women's Medical Center of Providence, Inc. v. Roberts, 530 F. Supp. 1136 (D.R.I. 1982)
Planned Parenthood of Central and Northern Arizona v. Arizona, 537 F. Supp. 90 (D. A.Z. 1982)
Florida Women's Medical Clinic, Inc. v. Smith, 536 F. Supp. 1048 (S.D. Fla. 1982)
Scheinberg v. Smith, 550 F. Supp. 1112 (S.D. Fla. 1982)
Christensen v. Wisconsin Medical Board, 552 F. Supp. 565 (1982)

B. *U.S. Court on Appeals Decisions Dealing with Abortion Published Since June 1980*

Northern Virginia Women's Medical Center v. Balch, 617 F. 2d 1045 (4th Cir.) (1980)
McKenna v. Ortho Pharmaceutical Corp. 622 F.2d 657 (3rd Cir. 1980)
Charles V. Carey, 272 F. 2d 772 (7th Cir. 1980)
Women's Health Services, Inc. v. Maher, 636 F. 2d 23 (2d Cir. 1980)
Women's Services v. Thone, 636 F.2d 206 (8th Cir.)
Planned Parenthood League of Mass. v. Bellotti, 641 F.2d 1006 (1st Cir. 1981)
D——— R——— v. Mitchell, 645 F.2 852 (10th Cir.)
Akron Center for Reproductive Health, Inc. v. City of Akron, 651 F.2d 1198 (6th Cir. 1981)
Mobak v. United States, 658 F.2d 471 (1981)
Scheinberg v. Smith, 659 F.2d 476 (1981)
Valley Family Planning v. North Dakota, 661 F.2d 99 (8th Cir. 1981)
Deerfield Medical Center v. Deerfield Beach, 661 F.2d 328 (5th Cir. 1981)
Planned Parenthood of Kansas City v. Ashcroft, 664 F.2d 687 (6th Cir. 1981)
Doe v. Busbee, 684 F.2d 1375 (11th Cir. 1982)
Women's Health Center of Beaumont v. Texas Health Facilities, 685 F.2d 974 (5th Cir. 1982)

Women's Services v. Thorn, 690 F.2d 667 (8th Cir. 1982)

    C.   *U.S. Supreme Court Decisions Dealing with Abortion Published Since the end of June, 1980.*

H.L. v. Matheson, 450 U.S. 398 (1981).

Appendix C.

Preliminary List of Substantive Bills Dealing With Abortion Introduced in Congress, 1963–1972

1963	none
1964	none
1965	none
1966	none
1967	none
1968	none
1969	none
1970	S. 3746, 91st Cong. 2d Sess. (1970) (authorize abortions in the U.S.).
1971	S. 1750, 92d Cong. 1st Sess. (1971) (authorize abortions in the U.S.).

S. 1751, 92d Cong. 1st Sess. (1971) (authorize abortions in the District of Columbia).

H.R. 4144, 92d Cong. 1st Sess. (1971) (abortions in the military—perform in accordance with state law).

H.R. 4257, 92d Cong. 1st Sess. (1971) (abortions in the military—perform in accordance with state law).

H.R. 6700, 92d Cong. 1st Sess. (1971) (abortions in the military—perform in accordance with state law).

H.R. 10240, 92d Cong. 1st Sess. (1971) (abortions performed in DOD facilities).

1972   H.R. 14715, 92d Cong. 2d Sess. (1972) (to enforce constitutional right of females to terminate pregnancy).

H.R. 15143, 92d Cong. 2d Sess. (1972) (to enforce the Constitutional right of females to terminate pregnancies).

H.R. 16195, 92d Cong. 2d Sess. (1972) (to enforce the Constitutional right of females to terminate pregnancies).

Total number of substantive bills relating to abortion introduced in Congress in the decade before *Roe v. Wade* 1963–1972: *10* (all introduced after 1969). AVERAGE OF ONE PER YEAR.

Appendix D-1.

Legislative Proposals Introduced in the 93rd Congress Containing Provisions Relating to Abortion.

Proposed Amendments to the Constitution:

H.R.J.Res. 261, H.R.J.Res. 281, H.R.J.Res. 284, H.R.J.Res. 290, H.R.J.Res. 298, H.R.J.Res. 364, H.R.J.Res. 394, H.R.J.Res. 423, H.R.J.Res. 427, H.R.J.Res. 468, H.R.J.Res. 471, H.R.J.Res. 473, H.R.J.Res. 476, H.R.J.Res.

485, H.R.J.Res. 488, H.R.J.Res. 509, H.R.J.Res. 520, H.R.J.Res. 537, H.R.J.Res. 544, H.R.J.Res. 561, H.R.J.Res. 599, H.R.J.Res. 603, H.R.J.Res. 631, H.R.J.Res. 646, H.R.J.Res. 647, H.R.J.Res. 659, H.R.J.Res. 711, H.R.J.Res. 717, H.R.J.Res. 759, H.R.J.Res. 769, H.R.J.Res. 827, H.R.J.Res. 872, H.R.J.Res. 877, H.R.J.Res. 889, H.R.J.Res. 953, H.R.J.Res. 966, H.R.J.Res. 974, H.R.J.Res. 975, H.R.J.Res. 984, H.R.J.Res. 1041, H.R.J.Res. 1079, H.R.J.Res. 1096, H.R.J.Res. 1098, S.J.Res. 119, S.J.Res. 130.

Proposed Protections for Rights of Conscience:
H.R. 4797, H.R. 5708, H.R. 5709, H.R. 5811, H.R. 6219, H.R. 6445, H.R. 7227, H.R. 7235, H.R. 7340, H.R. 7478, H.R. 7542, H.R. 7601, H.R. 8242, H.R. 8681, H.R. 8852, H.R. 12375, S.J.Res. 64.

Proposed Investigations of the Impact of *Roe*:
H.R.Res. 585, H.R.Res. 683, H.R.Res. 691, H.R.Res. 697, H.R.Res. 829, H.R.Res. 1032, H.R.Res. 1037, H.R.Res. 1063, H.R.Res. 1088, H.R.Res. 1180, H.R.Res. 1220, H.R.Res. 1257, H.R.Res. 1283, H.R.Res. 1302, H.R.Res. 1388.

Proposed Restrictions on Experimentation:
H.R. 6849, H.R. 7725, H.R. 7850, H.R. 8778, H.R. 8779, H.R. 8780, H.R. 9459, H.R. 9488.

Proposed Limitations on Federal Jurisdiction:
H.R. 8682, H.R. 14337, H.R. 14760, H.R. 15636, H.R. 16118.

Proposed Restrictions on Abortion Funding:
H.R. 8683.

Proposed Definitions of Personhood:
H.R. 14801. See also H.R. 8682.

Pro-Choice Proposals:
H.R. 254.

Appendix D-2.

Legislative Proposals Introduced in the 94th Congress Containing Provisions Relating to Abortion.

Proposed Amendments to the Constitution:
S.J.Res. 6, S.J.Res. 10, S.J.Res. 11, S.J.Res. 91, S.J.Res. 140, S.J.Res. 141, S.J.Res. 143, S.J.Res. 178, H.R.J.Res. 41, H.R.J.Res. 61, H.R.J.Res. 96, H.R.J.Res. 97, H.R.J.Res. 99, H.R.J.Res. 121, H.R.J.Res. 132, H.R.J.Res. 144, H.R.J.Res. 147, H.R.J.Res. 170, H.R.J.Res. 180, H.R.J.Res. 187, H.R.J.Res. 189, H.R.J.Res. 197, H.R.J.Res. 221, H.R.J.Res. 238, H.R.J.Res. 246, H.R.J.Res. 248, H.R.J.Res. 259, H.R.J.Res. 261, H.R.J.Res. 275, H.R.J.Res. 279, H.R.J.Res. 311, H.R.J.Res. 317, H.R.J.Res. 326, H.R.J.Res. 337, H.R.J.Res. 369, H.R.J.Res. 383, H.R.J.Res. 397, H.R.J.Res. 403, H.R.J.Res. 405, H.R.J.Res. 419, H.R.J.Res. 422, H.R.J.Res. 425, H.R.J.Res. 447, H.R.J.Res. 451, H.R.J.Res. 467, H.R.J.Res. 483, H.R.J.Res. 485, H.R.J.Res. 520, H.R.J.Res. 525, H.R.J.Res. 527, H.R.J.Res. 541, H.R.J.Res. 565, H.R.J.Res. 566, H.R.J.Res. 567, H.R.J.Res. 568, H.R.J.Res. 584, H.R.J.Res. 602, H.R.J.Res. 632, H.R.J.Res. 658, H.R.J.Res. 675, H.R.J.Res. 681, H.R.J.Res. 741, H.R.J.Res. 747, H.R.J.Res. 753, H.R.J.Res. 773, H.R.J.Res. 774, H.R.J.Res. 775, H.R.J.Res. 779, H.R.J.Res. 783, H.R.J.Res. 790, H.R.J.Res. 796, H.R.J.Res. 834, H.R.J.Res. 841, H.R.J.Res. 842, H.R.J.Res. 871, H.R.J.Res. 872, H.R.J.Res. 942, H.R.J.Res. 1084.

Proposed Investigations of the Impact of *Roe:*
H.R.Res. 32, H.R.Res. 52, H.R.Res. 69, H.R.Res. 102, H.R.Res. 220, H.R.Res. 280, H.R.Res. 297, H.R.Res. 354, H.R.Res. 486, H.R.Res. 1075, S.Con.Res. 36.
Proposed Limitations on Federal Jurisdiction:
H.R. 1133, H.R. 1515, H.R. 5658, H.R. 15169.
Proposed Restrictions on Abortion Funding:
H.R. 12327, H.R. 14232, H.R. 15105, S. 318. See also S. 66.
Proposed Restrictions on Experimentation:
H.R. 326.
Proposals Concerning Population Control and Family Planning:
H.R. 5720. See also S. 66.
Proposed Protections for Rights of Conscience:
S. 66.
Proposals Enacted:
H.R. 14232, Pub. L. No. 94–439, Sept. 30, 1976 (funding restriction); S. 66, Pub. L. No. 94–63, July 29, 1975 (prohibits coercion of welfare recipients).

Appendix D-3.
Legislative Proposals Introduced in the 95th Congress Containing Provisions Related to Abortion.
Proposed Amendments to the Constitution:
H.R.J.Res. 5, H.R.J.Res. 84, H.R.J.Res. 88, H.R.J.Res. 89, H.R.J.Res. 115, H.R.J.Res. 133, H.R.J.Res. 145, H.R.J.Res. 154, H.R.J.Res. 155, H.R.J.Res. 159, H.R.J.Res. 185, H.R.J.Res. 186, H.R.J.Res. 192, H.R.J.Res. 198, H.R.J.Res. 204, H.R.J.Res. 208, H.R.J.Res. 218, H.R.J.Res. 225, H.R.J.Res. 233, H.R.J.Res. 236, H.R.J.Res. 243, H.R.J.Res. 245, H.R.J.Res. 248, H.R.J.Res. 260, H.R.J.Res. 278, H.R.J.Res. 290, H.R.J.Res. 298, H.R.J.Res. 307, H.R.J.Res. 308, H.R.J.Res. 310, H.R.J.Res. 311, H.R.J.Res. 330, H.R.J.Res. 335, H.R.J.Res. 340, H.R.J.Res. 359, H.R.J.Res. 361, H.R.J.Res. 407, H.R.J.Res. 415, H.R.J.Res. 419, H.R.J.Res. 437, H.R.J.Res. 442, H.R.J.Res. 453, H.R.J.Res. 464, H.R.J.Res. 469, H.R.J.Res. 498, H.R.J.Res. 520, H.R.J.Res. 583, H.R.J.Res. 606, H.R.J.Res. 610, H.R.J.Res. 616, H.R.J.Res. 673, H.R.J.Res. 680, H.R.J.Res. 688, H.R.J.Res. 694, H.R.J.Res. 696, H.R.J.Res. 733, H.R.J.Res. 735, H.R.J.Res. 823, H.R.J.Res. 871, H.R.J.Res. 956, S.J.Res. 6, S.J.Res. 14, S.J.Res. 15, S.J.Res. 38, S.J.Res. 84.
Proposed Restrictions on Abortion Funding:
H.R.J.Res. 662, H.R.J.Res. 1139, H.R. 7555, H.R. 7912, H.R. 7977, H.R. 10611, H.R. 10735, H.R. 12929, H.R. 12931, H.R. 13635, H.R. 1555 (H.R.A. 376), H.R. 10929 (H.R.A. 1106), H.R. 12929 (H.R.A. 1163), H.R. 12929 (H.R.A. 1164), S. 2910, H.R. 7555 (S.U. 602), H.R. 7555 (S.U. 604), H.R. 7555 (S.U. 605), S. 1437 (S.U. 1155), S. 3085 (S.U. 1463). See also H.R. 10691, H.R. 12222.
Proposed Protections for Rights of Conscience:
H.R. 4518, H.R. 6710, H.R. 9025, H.R. 9418, H.R. 12185, S. 784, S. 2159.
Proposed Restrictions on Abortion in International Affairs:
H.R. 10691, H.R. 12222, S. 2420. See also H.R. 12931.
Proposed Investigations of the Impact of *Roe*:
H.R.Res. 26, H.R.Res. 66.

Proposed Limitations on Federal Jurisdiction:
H.R. 1914, H.R. 4273.
Proposed Pregnancy-Related Benefits:
H.R. 6075, S. 995.
Proposed Abortion Alternatives:
H.R. 12400, S. 2614.
Proposed Restriction of the Civil Rights Commission:
H.R. 12432, S. 3067.
Proposed Modification of the Criminal Code:
H.R. 13959.
Proposed National Day of Atonement:
H.R.J.Res. 189.
Prochoice Proposals Concerning Family Planning and Teenage Pregnancy:
H.R. 8283, H.R. 9989, H.R. 10076, H.R. 11007, H.R. 11925, H.R. 11926, H.R. 12894, H.R. 13111, H.R. 13278, S. 2697.
Prochoice Proposals Authorizing Abortion Services:
H.R. 6894, H.R. 11879, S. 2694, S. 2694, S. 2695, S. 2696, S. 2698. See also H.R. 7555 (S.U. 602).
Prochoice Proposals to Eliminate Legal Service Corporation Restriction.
H.R. 3179.
Proposals Enacted:
H.R.J.Res. 662, Pub. L. No. 95–205 (Dec. 9, 1977) (funding restriction); H.R.J.Res. 1139, Pub. L. No. 95–482 (Oct. 18, 1978) (funding restriction); H.R. 12929, Pub. L. No. 95–480 (Oct. 18, 1978) (funding restriction); H.R. 12931, Pub. L. No. 95–481 (Oct. 18, 1978) (funding restriction); H.R. 13635, Pub. L. No. 95–457 (Oct. 13, 1978) (funding restriction); H.R. 9418, Pub. L. No. 95–215 (Dec. 19, 1977) (prohibits discrimination on basis of abortion views); S. 995, Pub. L. No. 95–555 (Oct. 31, 1978) (excludes abortions from mandatory insurance coverage); H.R. 12222, Pub. L. No. 95–424 (Oct. 6, 1978) (excludes abortions from eligibility for foreign assistance funding); S. 3067, Pub. L. No. 95–444 (Oct. 10, 1978) (denies Commission of Civil Rights authority relating to abortion).

Appendix D-4.
Legislative Proposals Introduced in the 96th Congress Containing Provisions Relating to Abortion.
Proposed Amendments to the Constitution:
H.R.J.Res. 9, H.R.J.Res. 17, H.R.J.Res. 45, H.R.J.Res. 49, H.R.J.Res. 51, H.R.J.Res. 56, H.R.J.Res. 64, H.R.J.Res. 90, H.R.J.Res. 101, H.R.J.Res. 108, H.R.J.Res. 116, H.R.J.Res. 124, H.R.J.Res. 132, H.R.J.Res. 135, H.R.J.Res. 138, H.R.J.Res. 139, H.R.J.Res. 142, H.R.J.Res. 165, H.R.J.Res. 197, H.R.J.Res. 211, H.R.J.Res. 214, H.R.J.Res. 232, H.R.J.Res. 236, H.R.J.Res. 250, H.R.J.Res. 294, H.R.J.Res. 297, H.R.J.Res. 300, H.R.J.Res. 323, H.R.J.Res. 354, H.R.J.Res. 475, H.R.J.Res. 479, H.R.J.Res. 576, H.R.J.Res. 621, H.R.J.Res. 626, S.J.Res. 12, S.J.Res. 22.
Proposed Restrictions on Abortion Funding:
H.R.J.Res. 402, H.R.J.Res. 404, H.R.J.Res. 412, H.R.J.Res. 440, H.R.J.Res. 609, H.R.J.Res. 610, H.R.J.Res. 617, H.R.J.Res. 637, H.R.J.Res. 644, H.R. 2040,

H.R. 4389, H.R. 4473, H.R. 4580, H.R. 4962, H.R. 5359, H.R. 7542, H.R. 7583, H.R. 7998, H.R. 8061, H.R. 8105.

Proposed Protections for Rights of Conscience:
H.R. 3436, H.R. 3633, H.R. 3849, S. 230, S. 664.

Proposed Limitations on Federal Jurisdiction:
H.R. 993, H.R. 5440, H.R. 7307, S. 2138.

Proposed Protections for Family Life:
H.R. 6028, H.R. 7445, H.R. 7955, S. 1808.

Proposed Creation of the Department of Education:
H.R. 2444, S. 210.

Proposed Limitations on the Activities of Legal Service Corporations:
S. 2337.

Prochoice Proposals Concerning Family Planning and Teenage Pregnancy:
H.R. 360, H.R. 361.

Proposed Restrictions on Abortion in International Affairs:
See also H.R. 4473, H.R. 7542.

Proposals Enacted:
H.R.J.Res. 412, Pub. L. No. 96–86 (Oct. 12, 1979) (funding restriction); H.R.J.Res. 440, Pub. L. No. 96–123 (Nov. 20, 1979) (funding restriction); H.R.J.Res. 610, Pub. L. No. 96–369 (Oct. 1, 1980) (funding restriction); H.R.J.Res. 644, Pub. L. No. 96–536 (Dec. 16, 1980) (funding restriction); H.R. 5359, Pub. L. No. 96–154 (Dec. 21, 1979) (funding restriction); H.R. 8061, Pub. L. No. 96–530 (Dec. 15, 1980) (funding restriction); H.R. 8105, Pub. L. No. 96–527 (Dec. 15, 1980) (funding restriction); S. 210, Pub. L. No. 96–88 (Oct. 17, 1979) (Department of Education); S. 210, Pub. L. No. 96–76 (Sept. 29, 1979) (rights of conscience).

Appendix D-5.

Legislative Proposals Introduced in the 97th Congress Containing Provisions Relating to Abortion.

Proposed Amendments to the Constitution:
H.R.J.Res. 13, H.R.J.Res. 27, H.R.J.Res. 32, H.R.J.Res. 39, H.R.J.Res. 50, H.R.J.Res. 62, H.R.J.Res. 92, H.R.J.Res. 99, H.R.J.Res. 104, H.R.J.Res. 106, H.R.J.Res. 122, H.R.J.Res. 125, H.R.J.Res. 127, H.R.J.Res. 133, H.R.J.Res. 198, H.R.J.Res. 249, H.R.J.Res. 372, H.R.J.Res. 380, H.R.J.Res. 504, H.R. 392, H.R. 900, S.J.Res. 17, S.J.Res. 18, S.J.Res. 19, S.J.Res. 110, S.J.Res. 137.

Proposed Restrictions on Abortion Funding:
H.R.J.Res. 631, H.R. 3400, H.R. 3512, H.R. 3566, H.R. 3982, H.R. 4121, H.R. 4522, H.R. 4559, H.R. 4560, H.R. 4995, H.R. 6086, H.R. 7144, H.R. 7158, H.R. 7205, H.R. 7355, H.R. 3512(H.R.A. 21), H.R. 3480(H.R.A. 54), H.R. 4121(H.R.A. 195), H.R. 3566(H.R.A. 441), H.R. 4559(H.R.A. 470), S.J.Res. 8, S. 1196, S. 1947, S. 2372, S. 2806, S. 2916, S. 2917, S. 2951, S. 3075, H.R. 3512, H.R.J.Res. 520(S.P. 3266), H.R.J.Res. 520(S.P. 3267), H.R.J.Res. 520(S.P. 3268), H.R.J.Res. 520(S.P. 3269). See also H.R. 4207, H.R. 6455.

Proposed Protections for Family Life:
H.R. 311, H.R. 2446, H.R. 2447, H.R. 3955, H.R. 4207, S. 1090, S. 1378, S. 2322. See also H.R. 3982.

Proposed Definitions of Personhood:
H.R. 3225, S. 158, S. 1741, S. 2148.
Proposed Limitations on Federal Jurisdiction:
H.R. 73, H.R. 867, S. 583. See also H.R. 3225, S. 158.
Proposed Restrictions on Experimentation:
H.R. 6457, H.R. 6457(H.R.A. 884), H.R. 6457(H.R.A. 887). See also H.R. 3566, S. 3075.
Proposed Protections for Rights of Conscience:
H.R. 6455.
Proposed Limitations on the Activities of Legal Service Corporations:
H.R. 3480.
Prochoice Proposals Concerning Family Planning and Teenage Pregnancy:
H.R. 1059, H.R. 1060.
Proposal Requiring Informed Consent:
H.R.J.Res. 356.
Proposals Enacted:
H.R.J.Res. 631, Pub. L. No. 97–631 (Dec. 21, 1982) (funding restrictions); H.R. 3512, Pub. L. No. 97–12 (June 5, 1981) (funding restrictions); H.R. 3982, Pub. L. No. 97–35 (Aug. 13, 1981) (funding restrictions); H.R. 4522, Pub. L. No. 97–91 (Dec. 4, 1981) (funding restrictions); H.R. 4559, Pub. L. No. 97–121 (Dec. 29, 1981) (funding restrictions); H.R. 4995, Pub. L. No. 97–114 (Dec. 29, 1982) (funding restrictions); H.R. 7144, Pub. L. No. 97–378 (Dec. 22, 1982) (funding restrictions); S. 1196, Pub. L. No. 97–113 (Dec. 29, 1981) (funding restrictions).

Appendix D-6.
Legislative Proposals Introduced in the 98th Congress Containing Provisions Relating to Abortion.
Proposed Amendments to the Constitution:
H.R.J.Res. 15, H.R.J.Res. 26, H.R.J.Res. 59, H.R.J.Res. 73, H.R.J.Res. 82, H.R.J.Res. 84, H.R.J.Res. 92, S.J.Res. 3, S.J.Res. 4, S.J.Res. 8.
Proposed Restrictions on Abortion Funding:
H.R. 512, H.R. 513, H.R. 618.
Proposed Definitions of Personhood:
S. 26, S. 210.
Proposed Protections for Family Life:
See also H.R. 512, H.R. 513.

NOTES

* The author is indebted to Mr. Bryan Husted for his valuable and timely research assistance.
[1] *See* J. Powell, Abortion: The Silent Holocaust 2 (1981).
[2] 410 U.S. at 153.
[3] *See* Tribe, *The Supreme Court 1972 Term, Foreword Toward a Model of Roles in the Due Process of Law,* 87 Harv. L. Rev. 1, 2 (1973); L. Wardle, The Abortion Privacy Doctrine xi n. 1 (1981).

4 Corwin, *Introduction to the 1972 Edition*, The Constitution of the United States of America: Analysis and Interpretation xxii (1973).

5 The Federalist No. 9 (A. Hamilton).

6 The Federalist No. 47 (J. Madison).

7 The Federalist No. 51 (J. Madison); *see also* R. Lee, A Lawyer Looks at the Constitution 64 (1981) (hereinafter R. Lee).

8 *See* Appendix A.

9 Most of the reported abortion decisions rendered by the federal courts between January, 1973 and June, 1980 are collected in L. Wardle, The Abortion Privacy Doctrine, at Tables A, B and C. The reported federal court abortion decisions since June of 1980 are listed in Appendix B.

10 A great number of federal court abortion decisions have not been published. *See* L. Wardle, The Abortion Privacy Doctrine, at xiii nn. 15, 16.

11 *See id.* at n. 17. Many of the state court decisions as well as the unreported federal court decisions are listed in the N.A.R.A.L./Antioch Law School, Abortion Law Reporter.

12 *See* generally, L. Wardle and M. Wood, A Lawyer Looks at Abortion (1982) (hereinafter cited as A Lawyer Looks at Abortion).

13 *See* City of Akron v. Akron Center for Reproductive Health, Inc., 651 F.2d 1198 (6 Cir. 1981), *cert. granted,* 50 U.S.L.W. 3928 (No. 81–746) and Ashcroft v. Planned Parenthood Association, 664 F.2d 687 (8 Cir. 1981), *cert. granted* 50 U.S.L.W. 3928 (No. 81–623).

14 Valley Forge Christian College v. Americans United for Separation of Church and State, 102 S. Ct. 752, 759 (1982).

15 Ely, *The Wages of Crying Wolf: A Comment on Roe v. Wade,* 82 Yale L. J. 920, 935 n. 89 (1973).

16 R. Jackson, The Supreme Court and the American System of Government 61–62 (1955), cited in Fullilove v. Klutznick 448 U.S. 448, 491 (1980).

17 M. Farrand, The Records of the Federal Convention of 1787 at 21 (1911).

18 L. Hand, The Bill of Rights 70 (1958).

19 F. Frankfurter, The Public and Its Government 49, 50 (1930).

20 *Id.* at 50, 51.

21 *Valley Forge Christian College,* 102 S. Ct. at 759.

22

23 Epstein, *Substantive Due Process by Any Other Name: The Abortion Cases,* 1973 Sup. Ct. Rev. 159, 179.

24 Brief for the United States as Amicus Curiae, City of Akron v. Akron Center for Reproductive Health, Inc. No. 746, at 12–14. I have relied on many of the sources that were cited by the Solicitor General in this brief.

25 R. Jackson, The Struggle for Judicial Supremacy 321 (1941), cited in *Fullilove,* 448 U.S. at 490, 491.

26 J.B. Thayer, John Marshall 106–107 (1901). *See also* Plyler v. Doc, 102 S. Ct. 2382, 2408 (1982) (Burger, C.J., dissenting).

27 United States v. Richardson, 418 U.S. 166, 188 (1974).

28 R. Lee, *supra* note 7, at 56–62.

29 *But see id.* at 63–64.

30 *See* Appendix C.

31 *See* Appendix D-1.

32 *Id.*
33 *Id.*
34 *Id.*
35 *Id.*
36 *Id.*
37 *Id.*
38 *See* Appendix D-2.
39 *Id.*
40 *Id.*
41 *Id.*
42 *Id.*
43 *Id.*
44 *Id.*
45 *Id.*
46 Departments of Labor and Health, Education and Labor Appropriations Act, Pub. L. No. 94–439 (Sept. 30, 1976).
47 Nurse Training Act, Pub. L. No. 94–63 (July 29, 1975).
48 *See* Appendix D–3.
49 *Id.*
50 *Id.*
51 *Id.*
52 *Id.*
53 *Id.*
54 *Id.*
55 *Id.*
56 *Id.*
57 *Id.*
58 *Id.*
59 *Id.*
60 *Id.*
61 *Id.*
62 Joint Resolution Making Further Continuing Appropriations for Fiscal Year 1978, Pub. L. No. 95–205 (Dec. 9, 1977); Resolution Making Continuing Appropriations for Fiscal Year 1979, Pub. L. No. 95–482 (Oct. 18, 1978); Department of Health, Education and Welfare Appropriation Act, Pub. L. No. 95–480 (Oct. 18, 1978); Foreign Assistance And Related Proposals Appropriations Act, Pub. L. No. 95–481 (Oct. 18, 1978); Department of Defense Appropriations Act, Pub. L. No. 95–457 (Oct. 13, 1978).
63 Amendments to the Public Health Service Act, Pub. L. No. 95–215 (Dec. 1, 1977).
64 Amendments to Title VII of the 1964 Civil Rights Act, Pub. L. No. 95–555, (Oct. 31, 1978).
65 Amendments to the Foreign Assistance Act of 1961, Pub. L. No. 95–424 (Oct. 6, 1978).
66 Civil Rights Commission Act, Pub. L. No. 95–444 (Oct. 10, 1978).
67 *See* Appendix D-4.
68 *Id.*
69 *Id.*

[70] *Id.*

[71] *Id.*

[72] *Id.*

[73] *Id.*

[74] *Id.*

[75] *Id.*

[76] Joint Resolution Making Continuing Appropriations for Fiscal Year 1980, Pub. L. No. 96–86 (Oct. 12, 1979); Joint Resolution Making Further Continuing Appropriations, Pub. L. No. 96–126 (Nov. 20, 1979); Joint Resolution Making Continuing Appropriations for Fiscal Year 1981, Pub. L. No. 96–369 (Oct. 1, 1980); Joint Resolution Making Further Continuing Appropriations for Fiscal Year 1981, Pub. L. No. 96–369 (Dec. 16, 1980); Department of Defense Appropriations Act, 1980, Pub. L. No. 96–154 (Dec. 21, 1979); District of Columbia Appropriations Act, 1981, Pub. L. No. 96–530 (Dec. 15, 1980); Department of Defense Appropriations Act, 1981, Pub. L. No. 96–527 (Dec. 15, 1980).

[76A] Nurse Training Amendments of 1979, Pub. L. No. 96–76 (Sept. 9, 1979).

[77] Department of Education Organization Act of 1979, Public L. No. 96–88 (Oct. 17, 1979).

[78] *See* Appendix D-5.

[79] *Id.*

[80] *Id.*

[81] *Id.*

[82] *Id.*

[83] *Id.*

[84] *Id.*

[85] *Id.*

[86] *Id.*

[87] *Id.*

[88] Supplemental Appropriations and Rescission Act, 1981, Pub. L. No. 97–12 (June 5, 1981); Adolescent Family Life Amendment to the Public Health Service Act, Pub. L. No. 97–35 (Oct. 13, 1981); District of Columbia Appropriations Act, 1982, Pub. L. No. 97–91 (Dec. 4, 1981); Foreign Assistance and Related Proposals Appropriations Act, Pub. L. No. 97–121 (Dec. 29, 1981); Department of Defense Appropriations Act, 1982, Pub. L. No. 97–114 (Dec. 29, 1981); International Security and Development Cooperation Act, Pub. L. No. 97–113 (Dec. 29, 1981); District of Columbia Appropriation Act, Pub. L. No. 97–378 (Dec. 22, 1982); Further Continuing Appropriations Act, 1983, Pub. L. No. 970377 (Dec. 21, 1982).

[89] *See* Appendix D-6.

[90] *Id.*

[91] *Id.*

[92] *Id.*

[93] L. Wardle & M.A. Wood, *supra* note 12, at 219–222.

[94] *Id.* at 211–216.

[95] Abortion legislation enacted before 1973:

  42 U.S.C.A. sec. 300a-6 (West 1982) (funds for voluntary family planning not to be used where abortion is a method of family planning);

18 U.S.C.A. sec. 1462 (West Supp. 1982) (importation of any drug or article to produce abortion is illegal);

18 U.S.C.A. sec. 1461 (West Supp. 1982) (articles intended for producing abortion are nonmailable);

18 U.S.C.A. sec. 552 (West 1976) (officers of the United States who aid the importation of articles designed to procure abortion to be punished).

[96] *See* Appendices D-1 through D-6.

[97] San Antonia School District v. Rodriguez, 411 U.S. 1, 42, 43 (1973).

[98] Brief for the United States, *supra* note 24, at 15, 16.

[99] Truax v. Corrigan, 257 U.S. 312, 342–344 (1921) (Holmes, J., dissenting).

[100] F. Frankfurter, *supra* note 19, at 50, 51.

[101] L. Wardle & M.A. Wood. *supra* note 12, at 42–44.

[102] *Roe,* 410 U.S. at 162–163; Maher v. Roe, 432 U.S. 464, 478 (1977).

[103] *See* S.R. Davis, The Federal Principle 1 (1978) *citing* R. Koebner & H.B. Schmidt, Imperialism xiii (1964).

Statement of the American Medical Association

The American Medical Association takes this opportunity to express opposition to Senate Joint Resolution 3 which would amend the Constitution of the United States to authorize the federal and state governments to restrict or prohibit the performance of abortions.

We understand the purpose of this proposal is to overturn the decision of the U.S. Supreme Court holding that a woman has a constitutionally protected qualified right to an abortion. If adopted, this constitutional amendment would allow the federal and state government to legislate a ban or place restrictions on the performing of abortions.

Our concern with such legislation is that women could potentially be denied a necessary medical procedure. Abortion is a recognized medical procedure. The medical indications for abortions are numerous including ectopic pregnancy, incomplete spontaneous abortion (miscarriage), malignant embryo, cardiovascular conditions of the mother, and the use of prescription drugs that are essential to the mother that may have serious adverse effects on the fetus. The consequences of not having an abortion when these indications are present can be grave, even fatal.

If Senate Joint Resolution 3 is adopted, we are gravely concerned that legislation will be enacted establishing a "national policy" that gives a fetus the legal status of a person. Such a policy could have an adverse impact on the patient and her relationship with her physician and could create endless medical, ethical and legal difficulties for the people of this nation. Women would be faced with critical personal decisions difficult to make today that would be made even more difficult if not impossible by the elevation by law of a fetus to the status of a legal person. A physician would face serious dilemmas in advising pregnant patients. The physician would be responsible for the welfare of every fetus whose legal and health interest would, in the eyes of the law, be equal to, but may be in conflict with, those of the woman. Such legislation would also improperly interfere with one of the most delicate aspects of the physician-patient relationship.

The social implications for our society of ever-tightening rules to restrict prenatal medical intervention would be substantial. A "national policy" that gives legal status as a person to a fetus could severely limit research and advancement of the art and scientific knowledge of pregnancy, fetal development, prenatal diagnosis and medical intervention.

We are also concerned with the precedent for and the possibility of improper governmental interference into medical practice by singling out a single medical procedure for banning or restriction.

It is also important to view the consequences of a ban on abortion in human terms. A woman who has determined that she cannot carry a pregnancy to term will still seek an abortion even if abortions are prohibited by law. Those who have had to deal with the consequences, both physical and mental, caused by illegal abortionists and self-help efforts cannot understand an action which would permit a return to that state of affairs.

We are concerned with Senate Joint Resolution 3 not only because of the potential authority for total prohibition, but also because of the authority to place restrictions on performing abortions such as when they can be performed, by whom, and appropriate indications for performing abortions. Any regulatory or other scheme designed to determine the legality of "allowable" abortions would improperly interfere with the confidential and personal physician-patient relationship. Any system that would be used to determine the legality of an "allowable" abortion would bring bureaucrats who administer these provisions or the courts into the position of second-guessing and potentially overruling a physician's determination as to medical necessity and the best course of medical treatment for his or her patient. Such an invasion of privacy and the limitations on good medical practice are unacceptable.

Conclusion

If Senate Joint Resolution 3 is adopted, we are gravely concerned that women may be denied necessary medical care. We are also concerned about the physical and mental consequences that may be suffered by women who resort to illegal abortions. The precedent for and the possibility of improper governmental interference into medical practice by singling out a medical procedure for prohibition or restriction is inappropriate. The interference in the relationship between a woman and her physician that may result from this amendment causes us great concern. For these reasons, we oppose Senate Joint Resolution 3.

The Breakdown of Senate Voting

SENATE'S ROLL-CALL ON ABORTION PLAN*

Washington, June 28 (AP)— Following is the roll-call vote by which the Senate today rejected a proposed constitutional amendment that would have allowed Congress and the states to ban or restrict abortions. Senator Jesse Helms, Republican of North Carolina, an abortion foe, voted "present." Passage would have required approval by a two-thirds majority, or 67 senators, since all 100 voted.

FOR AMENDMENT—49

Democrats—15

Chiles, Fla.	Heflin, Ala.	Nunn, Ga.
DeConcini, Ariz.	Huddleston, Ky.	Proxmire, Wis.
Eagleton, Mo.	Johnston, La.	Randolph, W. Va.
Exon, Neb.	Long, La.	Stennis, Miss.
Ford, Ky.	Melcher, Mont.	Zorinsky, Neb.

Republicans—34

Abdnor, S.D.	East, N.C.	Mattingly, Ga.
Andrews, N.D.	Garn, Utah	McClure, Idaho
Armstrong, Colo.	Grassley, Iowa	Murkowski, Alaska
Baker, Tenn.	Hatch, Utah	Nickles, Okla.
Boschwitz, Minn.	Hatfield, Ore.	Pressler, S.D.
Cochran, Miss.	Hawkins, Fla.	Quayle, Ind.
D'Amato, N.Y.	Hecht, Nev.	Symms, Idaho
Danforth, Mo.	Humphrey, N.H.	Thurmond, S.C.
Denton, Ala.	Joseph, Iowa	Trible, Va.
Dole, Kan.	Kasten, Wis.	Warner, Va.
Domenici, N.M.	Laxalt, Nev.	
Durenberger, Minn.	Lugar, Ind.	

* Source: *The New York Times* June 29, 1983

AGAINST AMENDMENT—50

Democrats—31

Baucus, Mont.
Bentsen, Tex.
Biden, Del.
Bingaman, N.M.
Boren, Okla.
Bradley, N.J.
Bumpers, Ark.
Burdick, N.D.
R. Byrd, W.Va.
Cranston, Calif.
Dixon, Ill.

Dodd, Conn.
Glenn, Ohio
Hart, Colo.
Inouye, Hawaii
Hollings, S.C.
Jackson, Wash.
Kennedy, Mass.
Lautenberg, N.J.
Leahy, Vt.
Levin, Mich.
Matsunaga, Hawaii

Metzenbaum, Ohio
Mitchell, Me.
Moynihan, N.Y.
Pell, R.I.
Pryor, Ark.
Riegle, Mich.
Sarbanes, Md.
Sasser, Tenn.
Tsongas, Mass.

Republicans—19

Chafee, R.I.
Cohen, Me.
Goldwater, Ariz.
Gorton, Wash.
Heinz, Pa.
Kassebaum, Ken.

Mathias, Md.
Packwood, Ore.
Percy, Ill.
Roth, Del.
Rudman, N.H.
Simpson, Wyo.
Specter, Pa.

Stafford, Vt.
Stevens, Alaska
Tower, Tex.
Wallop, Wyo.
Weicker, Conn.
Wilson, Calif.

INDEX